Future of Business and Finance

The Future of Business and Finance book series features professional works aimed at defining, analysing, and charting the future trends in these fields. The focus is mainly on strategic directions, technological advances, challenges and solutions which may affect the way we do business tomorrow, including the future of sustainability and governance practices. Mainly written by practitioners, consultants and academic thinkers, the books are intended to spark and inform further discussions and developments.

Ioannis Giannakouros

Cryptocurrencies and Tradable Crypto-Tokens

Introduction to the Sector's Economic Design

Springer

Ioannis Giannakouros
Financial and regulatory risk consultant
Zurich, Switzerland

ISSN 2662-2467 ISSN 2662-2475 (electronic)
Future of Business and Finance
ISBN 978-3-031-98422-8 ISBN 978-3-031-98423-5 (eBook)
https://doi.org/10.1007/978-3-031-98423-5

This Springer imprint is published by the registered company Springer Nature Switzerland AG
The registered company address is: Gewerbestrasse 11, 6330 Cham, Switzerland

To my family, the flower of the tree of my life

Artificial Intelligence Pledge

The author pledges his honour that all parts of this book were produced manualy and that no Artificial Intelligence software or capabilities were used in their writing or editing. All text, figures, and tables were compiled by the author directly, using standard Microsoft Office software with no invocation of any Generative AI capabilities whatsoever. In the latter part of writing this book some Internet-accessible Artificial Intelligence capabilities were used for research validation purposes, i.e. to validate some facts that had already been gleaned by the author using traditional search engines. The content of all URLs included in footnotes/endnotes was read by the author directly before deciding to include them as references.

Acknowledgment

The author gratefully acknowledges many useful information exchange discussions with Ms. Lisa J.Y. Tan, author of the excellent book "*Economics and Math of Token Engineering and DeFi: Fundamentals of Token Economics*" (self-published, 2020). It is there that the idea of having three main design "lenses" (focused on markets, mechanisms and tokens) was first proposed, to the best knowledge of this author. Out of respect for Ms. Tan's work, the current book aligns both with that idea—in terms of its logical layout, using it in effect as "base framework" for an *exegesis*—and with her use of the term "design factor". What this author explicitly set out to do was to both extend the base framework in many new directions (especially around token and bonding function designs) and—more importantly—thoroughly interpret it from a Banking and Financial Markets (including Insurance) domain perspective. In that sense, the author is indebted even more to Ms. Tan, as her original ideas started a lineage of intellectual work that could be extended to other domains.

Competing Interests The author has no competing interests to declare that are relevant to the content of this manuscript.

Introduction

May 2025

Zurich, Switzerland

Imagine that we are again in the Age of Discovery, and that a new country has just been founded, in a land previously unknown. People have settled it already as there are commodities which are commercially exploitable at a cost competitive with that of other countries. Also, a significant proportion of these settlers have skills in providing services which are in demand internationally. The settlers would like to offer these resources and services from within their new country. They have started thinking about creating institutions, such as branches of government, and are committed to staying in their land. So, all in all, the seeds of a sustainable country are in place.

So far, they have only been *bartering* goods and services among themselves, as there is as yet no national currency. Being educated people, they are familiar with the principles of economics and the value of international trade, and are convinced that their new country needs to have its own currency. They know that if the country intends to specialize in extracting and trading a particular commodity, then a foreign buyer's need to acquire this commodity will be the incentive to hold the new country's currency. If the country instead sees its competitive advantage in providing a particular service, then a buyer's need to consume this service will be the incentive to acquire the new country's currency. Such a buyer will thus need to use their own fiat currency (or another asset, which is exchangeable and transferable) to buy the new currency. How will this new currency be minted—against which collateral, or based on whose credit—and put into circulation? How and where will it be exchanged for other currencies, or for other assets? And what factors will decide its bilateral convertibility and parity rates? Furthermore, suppose that the value in the international markets of the new country's main commodity or service increases over time. Then some recurrent buyers might be willing to acquire and hold quantities in the new currency purely as a risk-hedging strategy. What should the total supply of the new currency then be? If those quantities become material, will buyers also consider the new currency as a store of value—a reserve currency, for all intents and purposes—and start including it in accounting reports submitted in their home jurisdictions? If those holdings are kept instead within the country issuing the new currency, will buyers be obliged to report them locally? Who in the new country should decide on those things?

So, there are expectations on the part of the settlers to create governance institutions, build physical infrastructure (roads, marketplaces, information exchange networks) and notional infrastructure (laws, regulations, information templates), and, finally, issue and circulate a new currency so as to enable economic life, investments, and trade. And, it goes without saying, all those new designs must stand together—in theory and in practice.

How do the above relate to blockchain-based token ecosystems?

Such ecosystems typically start as projects targeting the monetization of a particular value proposition, a specific "[business] use case" revolving around the exchange of assets and services. Central to the success of the said business use case is the notion of "token", a digital representation of value. This must capture both the essence and the fruits of cooperation on the blockchain, but, more importantly, it must be a reliable means for satisfying the individual purposes of each and every participant in the business use case. Tokens do not pre-exist, rather they are continuously introduced into circulation through ecosystem agents expending resources (time, energy, other tokens) to bring them to life. Tokens are used to pay for services within the perimeter of the ecosystem but are also swapped for other stores of value (other tokens, or even fiat-currency denominated assets represented in ecosystem transactions, serving, e.g., as collateral for token-denominated loans).

The process of initiating, organizing, and maintaining economic life within a Blockchain-based ecosystem, whose participants create and consume specific assets and services, using Tokens to transact with each other and with third parties, is akin to the process of setting up the institutions, infrastructure, laws, and currency of a new country. It is, fundamentally, an exercise in economic design.

However, this book focuses explicitly on the fact that such ecosystems stand and fall with their *tokens*. It is this interplay among economic agents (on and off the blockchain) and tokens; how the latter are created, exchanged, stored, tracked, and destroyed within and across their native ecosystems; that is here explained.

The explanation is systematic and supported throughout by a wealth of references to current crypto-market practice, in the form of links to actual token project documentation, statistics, industry publications, and other knowledge sources available in the public domain. The concepts and terminology underlying blockchain protocols, consensus mechanisms, and token ecosystems are introduced in the beginning, to provide a clearly delimited "sandbox" for the reader to use as a proving ground for the subsequent notions. Then tokens; their taxonomy (cryptocurrencies, NFTs, utility, security tokens, and others); typical modes of creation, storage, and use; associated business processes and technical mechanisms are almost "dissected" in front of the reader—as are their containing ecosystems. A **particular methodology is explained** and then applied to achieve this, based on **clearly laid-out analysis and design principles**, proved to be applicable across token projects and individual token types.

Each stage (or "pillar") of the methodology is laid out in depth, then individually fact-checked through analysis of a particular token project—chosen among the most prominent ones in the Crypto industry—used as case study. Finally, all pillars applied together are fact-checked through an "end-to-end" case study, using yet another well-known token project. Hence, the reader can see the methodology and its design principles in action.

Importantly, this book is consciously written from the point of view of a practitioner in traditional Banking and Financial Markets (BFM), or at least of a student in the same domain. Each case study (as well as many other passages) begins with a summary of an established BFM business area, and then the particular token project of focus is introduced in such a way as to make the analogy between traditional and blockchain-based artifacts (assets, money flows, property rights) clear to the reader. The economic agents, business rationale, technical mechanisms, and rules of token issuance and usage—both within and across ecosystems—are thus made transparent. The book contains more than 200 (two-hundred) original illustrations purporting to explain every concept of relevance in detail. Two chapters in the book focus on the important area of Bonding Functions, which is the basis of Decentralized Finance ("DeFi"). The book also introduces the novel concept of transactional token analysis by way of the underlying protocol's "Notional Balance Sheet".

Based on the book's proposed analysis and design methodology, all cryptocurrencies (Bitcoin, Ethereum, Solana, Central Bank Digital Currencies, etc.) and tradable crypto-tokens of all possible types can thus be explained by reference to their generating ecosystems and stated business use cases.

The principles and tools put forth in the book can be used by new token projects and their stakeholders, to better align and fine-tune their use cases, token designs, Smart Contract implementations, mechanism designs, and ultimately financial business cases. For this audience, the methodology would be used primarily as a *design-side* one.

The exact same principles and tools can be used by other financial professionals tasked with analysing existing or prospective token designs. Financial advisors seeking to understand the actual risk/return profile of particular tokens before recommending them to clients; quantitative analysts creating portfolios of disparate token types; auditors paid for due diligence on token issuance and investment cases; Venture Capital providers needing to understand the role of a particular Special-Purpose-Vehicle behind a token project Foundation; anti-financial-crime consultants mandated with forensic analysis of token transactions; regulators needing to authorize initial-token- or continuous-token-offerings; legal professionals asked to deliver opinions on token categorization (security, derivative, governance, etc.) or on the appropriateness of a "Distributed Autonomous Organization" designation in the context of a business and taxation structure can all use this book's methodology to identify the correct information needed for their purposes and then process it systematically to arrive at clear, explainable results.

This book was started as a personal quest to put order to what threatened to become an increasingly chaotic field of knowledge. It evolved as a disciplined exercise, discovering new concepts and either validating or rejecting industry practices as they were being propagated in the Crypto industry. The fact-finding was through-and-through uncompromising (there are more than 2000—two thousand—references, in the form of footnotes, and each and every one of them was read by the author; quite a few more were considered but ultimately not included). References that seemed to, at least partially, negate or wholly repudiate some point in the text were always thoroughly analysed, and—thankfully—always found to necessitate either a minor correction or a qualification, but never a total rewrite. It is the outcome of thorough, systematic, research and of objective conceptualization. Some people might even consider it to be the fruit of honest intellectual toil.

It was thus all the more gratifying in the end, in that all case studies presented (and quite a few more that were analysed as well, but ultimately considered superfluous) seemed to validate the proposed methodology. It goes without saying that some of the references in the footnotes will become deprecated sooner or later. Projects will change their documentation, while some tokens and business use cases will evolve or even disappear. The author cannot guarantee that all footnotes will keep being valid long past the time of writing. However, as mentioned in the very last chapter of the book, this is a book about principles. Principles of methodological analysis and design, originating in economics but transplanted into the context of cryptocurrencies and crypto-tokens. It is highly probable that those principles will remain the same, supported by new or updated references, irrespective of future technological or business developments. Using them to interpret the evolutionary stage which the whole field undergoes at any given time (the *high-level "cause and effect"* intent) and to understand the ramifications of new business and technical token features implemented by individual blockchain ecosystems (the *methodology and technical knowledge* intent), the reader will be able to remove blind spots and confusion—now and in the future.

Cryptocurrencies and crypto-tokens will make—and keep making—sense.

Contents

List of Figures

List of Tables

Foundations of Token Ecosystems

1

Cryptocurrencies and tradable crypto-tokens can be understood only against the background of their generating use cases. Even though they can be traded in exchanges, their primary[1] markets are the blockchain-based ecosystems where these use cases are operationalized. The tokens' features, their design attributes, are dictated by the needs of said ecosystems. Hence, it is imperative to first situate them firmly in their proper context before analysing their uses as stores of value and investable instruments across the digital-to-physical worlds divide.

This chapter will lay out the foundation of notions and terminology that are necessary to be able to understand the ideas and methodological explanations of the rest of the book.

1.1 The Blockchain

The focus of this book is not the blockchain per se. Readers interested in learning the technical and operational details of constructing and using blockchains would be much better served through other excellent publications that are already covering those aspects. That said, the blockchain concept is such a central pillar of the notions to be expounded in this and the following chapters that it is imperative to explain at least its basic terminology and the reasons for its existence.

Given the interlinkage between notions from technology and economics inherent to the subject, the explanation will follow a pedagogical approach, from simple terms to more evolved ones, making this interlinkage clear from the beginning.

Each entity (individual or corporation) conducting business activities is obliged to keep records of accounts. The most basic description of how this recording activity is to be carried out is provided by the Chart of Accounts ("CoA"). The CoA lists all

[1] I.e., where issuance (by first creation) and redemption (by destruction or retirement) of crypto-assets is guaranteed to occur by exchanging them at par value with some other assets.

I. Giannakouros, *Cryptocurrencies and Tradable Crypto-Tokens*, Future of Business and Finance, https://doi.org/10.1007/978-3-031-98423-5_1

individual accounts that need to be updated on a per-product, per-service, per-process, or per-transaction type and represents the way that the entity wants to organize its business. So, imagine that we have a corporation "A" which keeps accounts conforming to a CoA specifying that there need to be cash, inventory, payables, receivables, etc., accounts. Another corporation "B" follows a CoA specifying a cash, insurance premia, insurance claims, reserves, etc., accounts. The common theme across CoAs is the use of "Journaling", meaning that every record in every account needs to demonstrate when the record was created ("**timestamp**"), in which business context ("**context-references**") and how it relates to other records in other accounts ("**cross-account-relations**"). For example, corporation "A" records every transaction by journaling a transactions account, containing a timestamp, the context-references of the product, service, or activity this transaction relates to, and the cross-account-relations in the products, product inventory, services, service contracts, purchase orders, sales orders, clients accounts, etc. The practical way through which the cross-account-relations are recorded is by prepending some "**identifier**" or "**key**" (say, an arbitrary but *unique* number, word, or combination of digits and letters) to the record of every single account in the CoA. In the same example, every record in the clients account will have its own, unique, Client_Identifier data; every record in the product account will have its own, unique, Product_Identifier data, and similarly records in the product inventory, purchase orders, etc., accounts will have corresponding, unique, Product_Inventory_Identifier, Purchase_Order_Identifier, etc., data. Done properly, every new entry in the transactions account will contain a Transaction_Identifier and will also state the correct Product_Inventory_Identifier, Client_Identifier, Purchase_Order_Identifier creating the cross-account picture of which client, through which purchase order, is to be allocated which inventory item to honour which transaction. Proper use of journaling allows one to know precisely which business activity took place, and which other processes of the corporation need to be aware of it (e.g. a purchase and a subsequent inventory change). Importantly, journaling allows one to control when, and how to implement single-entry vs double-entry accounting postings. For example, the operating procedures of the corporation may dictate that every purchase order must be recorded at once, but inventory changes only once the corresponding amount has been paid by the customer; this involves reconciling the cash and inventory accounts against each other. In short, the CoA and journaling mechanisms allow an entity such as a corporation to literally *control* its business.

The aggregated content of a collection of related accounts forms a ledger. This is just an organizational concept, pertaining to how to control individual parts of the business, how to create accounting statements for statutory purposes, etc. For instance, when the corporation wants to have an overview of the material end-to-end information contained in all its accounts, it aggregates their records in some appropriate manner to form the General Ledger. All other ledgers, i.e. aggregated at levels below the end-to-end one, are considered to be "Sub-Ledgers" (cf. Fig. 1.1).

It goes without saying that the typical corporation considers all information recorded in its accounts and aggregated in the General Ledger to be proprietary

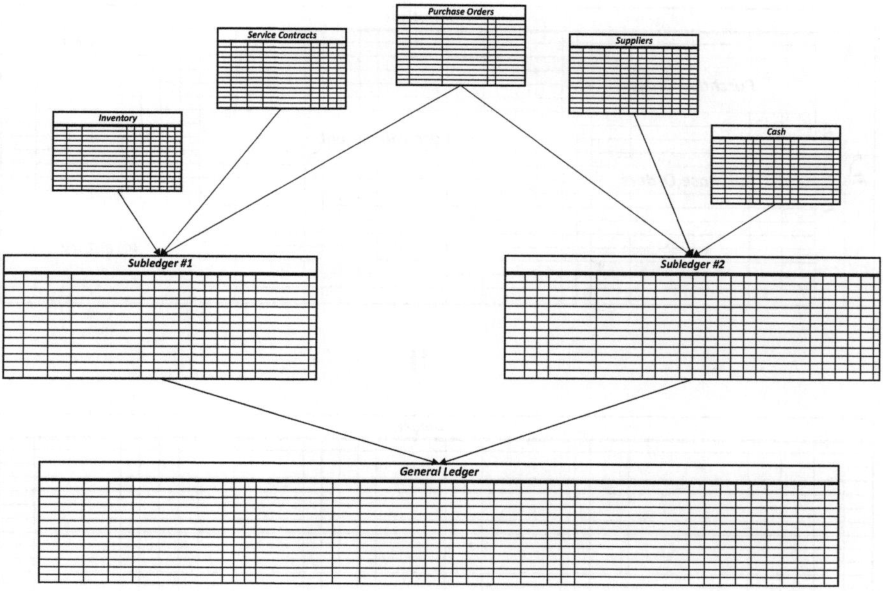

Fig. 1.1 Structure of Charts of Accounts (CoAs) and centralized ledgers

and confidential. Company law in every jurisdiction imposes general obligations on how, when, and by whom material types of business information are updated, read, and used (and even stricter obligations in the case of publicly listed companies). Hence the corporation is obliged to reserve for itself all rights and responsibilities of handling this information so that it is accurate, complete, and up to date. Centralizing said rights and responsibilities onto a single authority (the corporation itself, through its internal functions) creates a so-called "Centralized Ledger" paradigm.

For the purposes of the current discussion, please consider now a corporation with the simplest of CoAs—containing only a single account, namely "Transactions". Journaling is still carried out and the record of each transaction has many fields allowing to write in the information about client, product, service, purchase order, cash, inventory, etc., all in one go. There is still a timestamp and identifiers on the record and only those data that are relevant are written, whereas the rest can be left empty. For example, one transaction record (identifier "Tr_1") contains only data of a client and a purchase order—through their identifiers. Another (identifier "Tr_2") contains data of a purchase order, an inventory item—through their identifiers—and a cash amount. A third record (identifier "Tr_3") contains data of a client, a purchase order, and a guarantee claim—either through identifiers or through amounts. In short, the table "Transactions" now allows for very comprehensive individual records which contain disparate information within the same table structure (cf. Fig. 1.2).

Hence this corporation accepts, by choice, to have the most simplistic ledger structure, and, by repercussion, that whenever a "history" about a particular client or

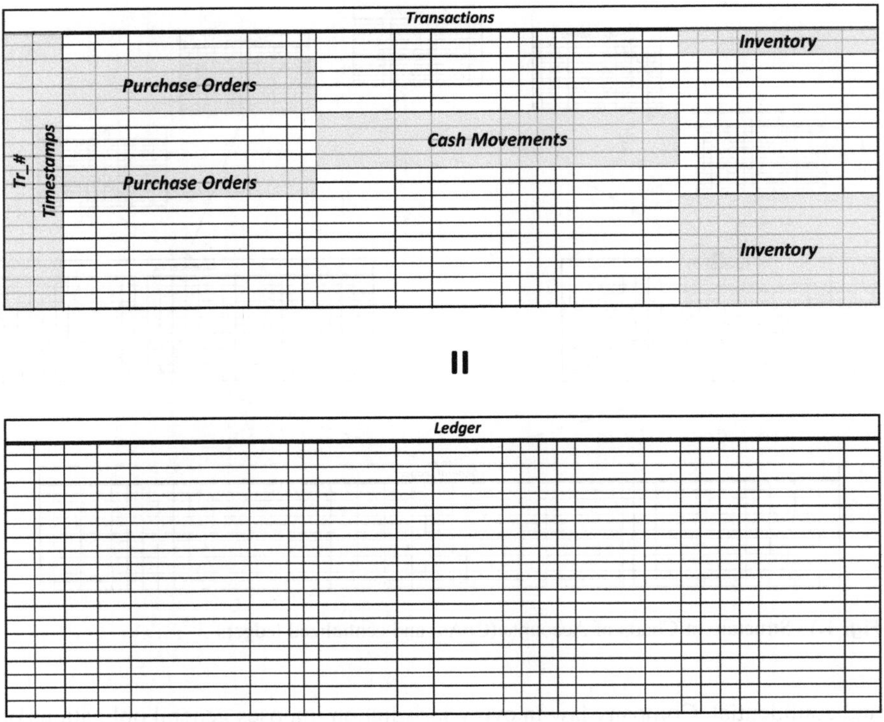

Fig. 1.2 CoA containing a single account "Transactions". The general ledger is the single account

a particular business activity needs to be reported it has to be reconstructed by "piecing together" all records that relate to said client or business activity. Please note that the account "Transactions" now contains individual records that may not always represent "transactions" in the business sense, i.e. movement of money. They can also represent movement of value, or change of position, which may or may not be monetary in nature. Only this way can *a single account* be used to represent all information that is material to the corporation.

All bookkeeping is still internal, i.e. an accountant has control of this ledger and updates, resp. reports through, it within the corporation. Nobody outside the corporation or without explicit authorization by the ledger owner can update or view the contents of the ledger. The corporation considers all information in its primary form, as recorded in the ledger, to be proprietary and confidential. It keeps complete control of how it is updated, read, and used (e.g. for statutory reporting purposes). It centralizes into its internal functions the right and responsibility of keeping this information accurate, complete, and up-to-date, truly reflecting the business activities of the corporation. In other words, this is still a "Centralized Ledger" paradigm.

Now consider the following situation: assume that many entities (individuals and corporations) have agreed to share accounts while keeping the Chart of Accounts in

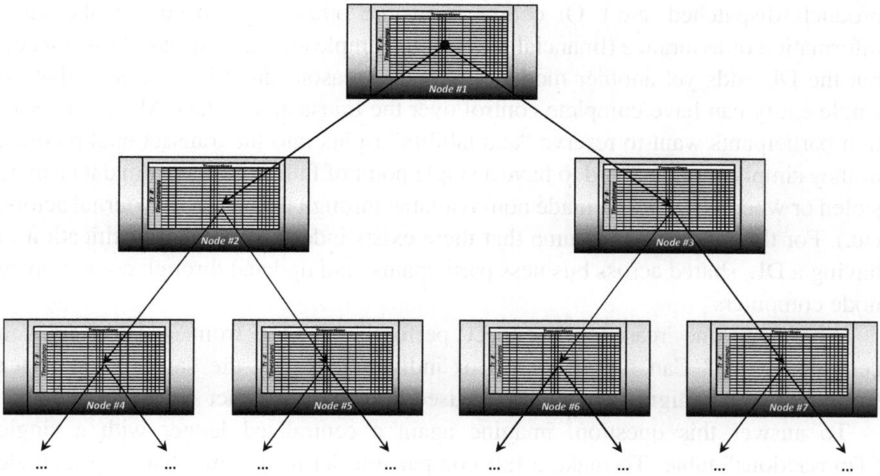

Fig. 1.3 Distributed ledger

the simplest possible form, that of a single "Transactions" table. The structure of the transactions record is still very comprehensive, allowing to register generic movements of value and changes of positions, which may also be movements of funds. Of course, they all must be careful to ensure that what is written in this table is the least common denominator from the point of view of the single individual/corporation and would not compromise the confidentiality of their business transactions even if were to be read by third parties. The practical ways to achieve this would be, for example, encryption (e.g. only encrypted names, amounts, and other information are written in the table; and the decryption keys are kept safely by the originating individual/corporation itself), partitioning between on-table and off-table information (e.g. using only identifiers in the common view, while these identifiers have business meaning only in conjunction with other information which the individual/corporation keeps off the table), restriction of the type of information allowed to be recorded (e.g. no names, no product types, no amounts), etc.

Finally, also assume that the entire "Transactions" table is physically stored in the memory not of a single computer but copied (the exact same table) onto the memory of many computers that are located across the Internet. Each participating computer keeps exactly one copy of the table. The way this can be done is, e.g. if it can be ensured that the "Transactions" table is the same across all participating computers at a given time t_0, and then than each new transaction record for time $t > t_0$ is copied sequentially across all computers. This construct is an example of a *Distributed Ledger (DL)* (cf. Fig. 1.3).

What is the reason behind such a construct? Why would any corporation, or any individual for that matter, choose to share information (even encrypted or otherwise obfuscated) with other parties?

One reason might be to unequivocally prove to the other parties, in a short amount of time, that some action has indeed taken place (some funds were indeed paid, some products dispatched, etc.). Of course, there are other ways to convey the same information or assurance (financial messaging, simple email, trust-based assurance); but the DL adds yet another modality. Another reason might be to ensure that no single entity can have complete control over the transactional data. Maybe transaction participants want to reserve "auditability" rights into the transactional records, or they simply cannot afford to have a single point of failure (wherefrom data can be stolen or where data can be made non-available through the action of external actors, etc.). For the time being, assume that there exists indeed a business justification in having a DL, shared across business participants, and updated through copy-convey node computers.

What can one reasonably expect performance-wise from a DL versus a centralized one? Can a corporation or individual expect the same performance from the two paradigms when they are used to record the exact same transactions?

To answer this question, imagine again a centralized ledger with a single "Transactions" table. To make a fair comparison, let us assume that only a single entity—a "ledger owner"—is authorized to write all records, receiving and quality-assuring data which are submitted to it by other parties while doing business. Every transaction participant would logically expect to have a record written into the table as soon as the information is submitted to the ledger owner. So, the logical course of action for the centralized ledger owner would be to: receive the content of a single record from another party; quality control the content; if content is legitimate, write immediately a corresponding record into the table.

Now imagine a DL with the same "Transactions" table. A transaction participant would now submit the information to the nearest k replicating node computers (the integer "k" is always >1). The latter performs the following sequence: receive the content of the single record; quality control the content; if content is legitimate, write immediately the record into their copy of the table; transmit the new record to the next k replicating node computers. The latter in their turn quality control the content; if content is legitimate, write immediately the record into their own copy of the table; then transmit the new record to the next k replicating node computers. The latter repeat the quality control/insert/transmit cycle, and so on until all replicating node computers (cf. Fig. 1.4) have executed the same cycle.

It is obvious that, even if the replicating node computers were to execute only the exact two process steps (content quality control and record insertion) as the centralized ledger does, they would never match the latter's transaction-writing speed. The extra two steps (node discovery/information transmission) *per node* computer would in effect multiply the time it takes for the DL to record the same transaction by approximately N, the total number of replicating node computers, times $[2 / k]$.

In all generality, for the time-to-update of the transactions table a relation of the following form[2] would hold true between the two paradigms:

[2]This is of course an over-simplification. Transmission network latency will probably skew the difference in favour of the centralized ledger further still.

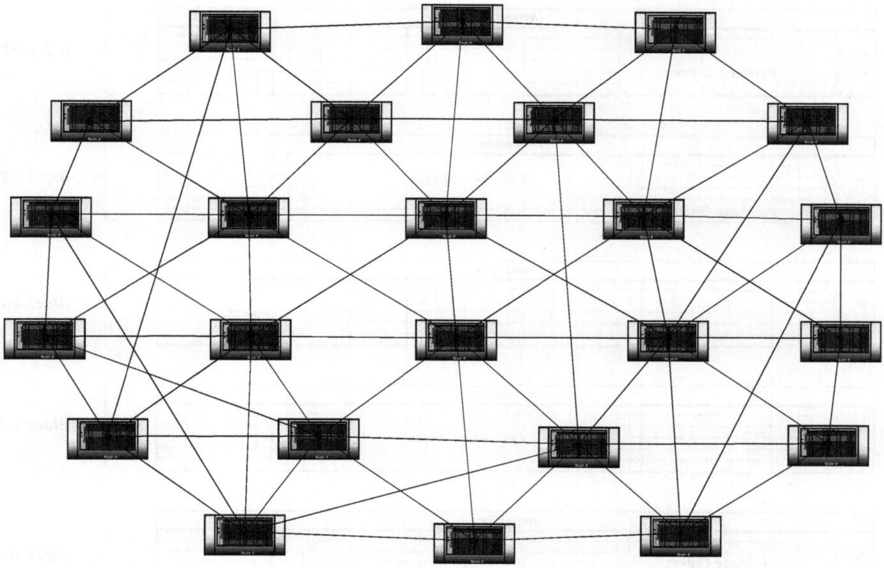

Fig. 1.4 Network of node computers replicating a DL

$$T_{\text{Distributed Ledger}} \sim T_{\text{Centralized Ledger}} \cdot \frac{2 \cdot N}{k}$$

If N were to be in the thousands and k between 2 and 10, then the time to update a single record in the DL would be literally hundreds of times longer than that for the centralized ledger. The DL would simply not be able to compete.

A way to reduce the extent of the disadvantage of the DL would be to not execute the "content quality control/ record update/ information transmission" cycle for each and every transaction, but to wait until many transactions have accumulated into one "block", and then start the cycle for the entire block of transactions as a single package. Thus, if a receiving node could accumulate *"m"* transactions (with $m \gg 1$) in time comparable to that of executing one local "cycle", then the entire across-the-network update would take time:

$$T_{\text{Distributed Ledger}} \sim T_{\text{Centralized Ledger}} \cdot \frac{2 \cdot N}{k \cdot m}$$

So, if m can be made sufficiently large (this of course depends on the limits of technology), then the average *per record* time-to-update of the DL can move closer to that of the centralized ledger. In other words, if the DL were programmed to process not individual transactions, but rather *blocks of transactions* then its performance could theoretically reduce the gap with the centralized ledger.[3]

[3] It will of course always be at a disadvantage—this is the price to pay for resting control of the ledger from the hands of a central authority.

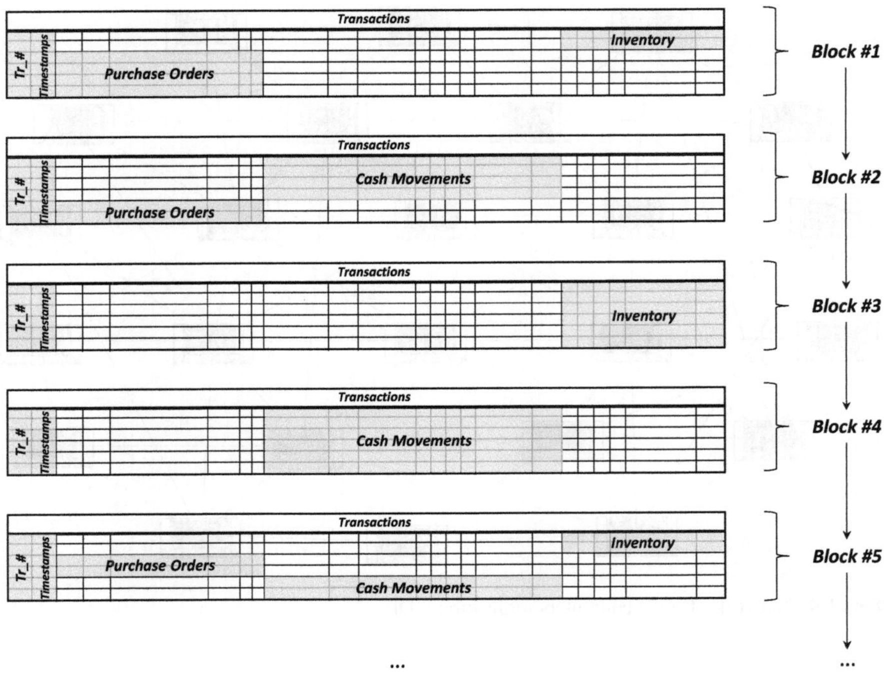

Fig. 1.5 Chain of blocks, pieced together to form the DL

The DL would be used, in effect, to "chain together" such blocks of transactions (cf. Fig. 1.5).

This is precisely the concept behind the blockchain. It presupposes an underlying DL and mandates a sequence of processing steps (content quality control/ record updates/ information transmission) to be executed not upon single transactions, but upon *blocks of transactions*; these steps are repeated across the network of replicating node computers. By "**chaining**" together such blocks of transactions (i.e. creating the certainty of what comes first, then second, then third, etc.), the sequential view of traditional databases can be replicated; that is, the data "view" of line-by-line records as in a centralized ledger.

Striving to narrow the performance gap with centralized databases, two further concepts are used:

(a) Instead of having *all* node computers execute the same three actions (content quality control/record updates/information transmission), have only a lesser ("cut-off") percentage do so and let the rest execute only two of them (i.e. record updates / information transmission). If this cut-off is above 50% of the node computers and if the omitted action is the "content quality control" one, that would mean that once a "high-enough" majority of nodes have controlled the content of a block, then the rest would just update the local copy of the ledger and simply transmit further. This is obviously intended as a compromise between algorithmic correctness and speed of completion. Most current blockchains implement such a mechanism, with the cut-off set appropriately (e.g. at 51% for Proof-of-Work or 66.7% for Proof-of-Stake ones).

(b) Instead of leaving the algorithmic definition of the "content quality control" step at the discretion of each node provider, have it standardized and ensure that all nodes execute the exact same technical algorithm. This way, each individual node provider gives unequivocal trust in the outcome of previous work (performed by some unknown node somewhere on the Internet) and in return they can be certain of unequivocal trust being given in the outcome of their own node's work. The end result is that the entire network of node computers guarantees mutual "trust" in the accuracy and consistency of what is written in the DL.

There is a fundamental problem in this process, namely, how to ensure that some group of replicating nodes are not colluding to change the content of what arrives to them into something totally different leaving from them. For example, suppose that a malicious individual acquired a number of computers, declared them as Proof-of-Work replicating nodes, and set out to redirect a proportion of funds in each transaction to accounts controlled by them. If the computers and the network were fast enough, then this individual could have their own, maliciously updated, blocks propagated to the 51% of nodes before the untampered ones did. Far from being at theoretical problem, this is a well-known "network attack" pattern in computer science, referred to as a "**Sybil attack**" [1, 2]. As the value of transactions moving through blockchains increases, there is real incentive for financial criminals to exploit such technical blind spots. In short, all blockchains must be able to withstand Sybil attacks.

To guard against this risk, one of two concepts (mutually exclusive ones) is implemented by all current blockchains:

(a) *Node permissioning*. Allow only vetted nodes ("permissioned nodes") on the blockchain and authorize specific ones (an "eponymous" subset) to quality control and update blocks in the DL. This presupposes a vetting process, which must be specified and enacted by some sort of blockchain governance. It in effect assumes that the blockchain obeys some guardianship concept, which lies in between that of the (centralized) ledger and that of the (totally decentralized) DL operation. The blockchain in this case sacrifices "pure" decentralization in return for a robust "trust" concept.

(b) *First-validation hurdle and rewards*. Make the block quality control step objectively difficult and reward the node(s) carrying out its first-in-time completion with a monetary benefit; make all subsequent quality control steps redundant. Hence nodes are incentivized to compete to execute the first-and-only block validation, the level of competition being commensurate with the size of the monetary reward. The algorithmic specification of the quality control step can be calibrated so that the requisite effort is high enough to deter tampering by malicious actors and its successful completion is directly verifiable by non-involved nodes. The higher the algorithmic difficulty, the more reliable the block validation outcome is. This design pattern entails that only the node computers participating in the first-and-only validating action execute all three block steps (content quality control/record updates/information transmission), all the rest being then expected to perform only the last two steps (record updates/ information transmission) against the DL.

As already mentioned, these two design patterns are mutually exclusive in the current generation of blockchains: a blockchain is assumed to implement either node "permissioning" or "first-validation hurdle and rewards". In the former case it is termed a "**permissioned**", in the latter a "**permissionless**" blockchain.

What are described above are in effect the different ways that current blockchain designs solve a particular problem in computer science: the "**consensus problem**" [3]. This denotes situations where a large number of processes (or agents) need to reach an agreement about what a single data value should be. Said processes have to act on the same set of inputs but are otherwise free to reach their own estimate about this value, without guarantee that any of them will act ethically or even competently. In the blockchain context, this single data value is the correctness or not of the block content.

It is important to keep this in mind because in the "permissionless" blockchain case the exact algorithmic specification of the quality control step has come to be termed as its "**Consensus Mechanism**". So, when blockchain "A" is said to implement "Proof-of-Work" (PoW [4]), blockchain "B" to implement "Proof-of-Stake" (PoS [5]), others "Proof-of-History" (PoH [6]), "Delegated-Proof-of-Stake" (DPoS [7]), etc., the expression ["*Proof-of-<#>*"] is nothing else than the type of this permissionless blockchain's "consensus mechanism". In short, a reference to how exactly (through which algorithm) the nodes of this blockchain are expected to validate the content of each block of transactions submitted to the DL in order to claim the first-validation monetary reward.

Summarizing the above, the fundamental concept underlying the blockchain paradigm is the existence of a DL, copied on computer nodes across the Internet. To compete at all with centralized ledgers performance-wise, it is imperative to write not single records but blocks of records into the DL at once; "these blocks chained together" to create a ledger is precisely the blockchain concept. All participating computer nodes must execute one or more of three sequential steps to achieve this, even though they cannot know nor trust each other. This is a "consensus problem" in computer science, and different blockchain types solve it in different ways. In the particular case of "permissionless" blockchains, there is a first-validator monetary reward, contingent on solving an intentionally difficult algorithmic problem as part of block validation. The type of this algorithmic problem is the "consensus mechanism" of permissionless blockchains.

1.2 The Prefix "Crypto-"

The prefix "crypto-", used in compound words such as "cryptography", "Cryptocurrency", "crypto-asset", etc., is the transliteration of the ancient Greek stem "*κρυπτ-*" (pronounced "*kreept-*") denoting something which is intentionally hidden, concealed.[4]

As already mentioned in Sect. 1.1, the DL in the core of the blockchain architecture is in effect a one-table Chart-of-Accounts, shared and accessible by network participants who cannot know nor trust each other. Said participants can only safeguard the confidentiality of proprietary business information in transaction records written into the ledger by submitting the least possible amount of information, and by using appropriate concealment techniques such as encryption. In effect, only encrypted names, amounts, and other data, are written in the submitted record and the decryption keys are kept safely by the originating entity (individual or corporation). Encryption as a mechanism is also used during transmission of records and blocks over the Internet, and (as will be explained in later chapters) in the definition of "public address" and "private address" pairs—the unique identifiers and the associated passwords—assigned to individual participants in blockchain ecosystems. Thus, use of encryption is central to the blockchain, both by architectural assumption and for reasons of operational robustness.

This gratuitous use of encryption at several processing steps for data stored in, and transmitted through, blockchain platforms gave the impetus for denoting practically everything related to the blockchain by prepending its usual term with the prefix "crypto". For example, "Cryptocurrencies" (meaning "hidden currencies", "concealed currencies") has come to denote "currencies" (media of exchange) that are defined, created, used, and stored exclusively on blockchain platforms.

1.3 Crypto-Tokens

The word "token" was used in the past to denote something tangible, fungible, of specific practical utility, and of face value defined by the owner of infrastructure where this utility could be consumed. Every token could be purchased and redeemed at face value at designated points-of-sale. A historical example would be telephony tokens, which were in circulation in long-forgotten times when mobile phones were to be found only in science fiction novels, and when state monopolies or corporate oligopolies completely controlled by law the supply and operation of all—fixed, of course—phones (public and private) and of the underlying—copper, of course—

[4]"I hide" in ancient Greek is "*κρύπτω*" (pr. "*kreepto*"), "hidden" is "*κρυπτόν*" (pr. "*kreepton*", intonation on the last syllable—neuter form of adjective), etc. An alternative form of the stem uses "*φ*" ("*f*" instead of "*pt*"), as in "*κρυφόν*" (pr. "*kreefon*", intonation on the last syllable—neuter form).

infrastructure. Staying in touch while on the go meant using public phones, and those were operated solely by means of said tokens. A token was like an ordinary coin, with the logo of the network operator on it, and having by design different dimensions to those of currency coins for obvious reasons. One could buy as many tokens as desired by going to a designated point-of-sale and paying their face value, and then happily insert them in the receiving slot of the nearest public phone—as many of them as the call type (local, long-distance, international) necessitated. In short, each token was fungible, had specific utility, was issued by way of privilege and its face value had nothing to do with the value of the metal used to produce it. It also was tied to a specific network infrastructure.

The blockchain world found this metaphor useful, and so it came that "token" became the industry term for any digital representation of value which is created, consumed, and destroyed exclusively through a specific blockchain platform. Token "A" being created in blockchain platform "B" can only be consumed on "B", different platforms create different tokens, tokens can be issued and redeemed against fiat currencies, and their face value is set by some market mechanism. Tokens are obviously the focus of the book at hand; thus the reader will find detailed explanations of their usage, typology, lifecycle, and design in Chaps. 3, 4, 5, and 10 respectively.

As both the industry and the general public currently use the prefix "crypto" to succinctly refer to a blockchain context, digital representations of value in said context are simply referred to as "crypto-tokens".

1.4 Why "Token Ecosystems"?

The blockchain is a technical infrastructure paradigm, upon which very generic business use cases can be implemented. For example, the very first operational blockchain (2009 - Bitcoin [8–10]) was designed around a peer-to-peer payments use case. Its native token was what is known today as the Bitcoin Cryptocurrency (BTC). Subsequent blockchain platforms showed that the paradigm lends itself to much broader uses with both economic and social significance. It is fair to say that the limits of what a blockchain can be used for are still being explored.

As will be explained in detail in subsequent chapters, the blockchain also serves as a keeper of records for interactions among economic agents which represent varied interests and concerns. These economic agents use the blockchain as the foundation of marketplaces, where goods, services, and information are exchanged and priced through tokens. As in physical marketplaces, different agents have different roles; some are sellers of goods, some of services; others are buyers of goods, or intermediaries bringing together supply and demand; others provide financing, insurance, etc. They form an "ecosystem" as it were, around a business case that has blockchain as its infrastructure and tokens as its media of exchange, stores of value and title.

The next chapters will demonstrate that tokens should be understood (analysed and designed) only in the context of the ecosystem in which they are primarily used.

They may have value outside their primary ecosystem, but once this ecosystem no longer exists, they themselves can no longer exist.

In effect "token ecosystems" is just an abbreviation, as the correct expression should rather be "blockchain-based transactional ecosystems using tokens". We propose to make use only of the abbreviation from now on, for the sake of brevity.

1.5 The Notion of Blockchain "Layers"

A final piece of terminology needed to be able to succinctly convey notions in the blockchain space is the "Layer" type. Industry publications will commonly refer to, e.g. "issues specific to Layer 1 blockchains" (or L1-blockchains), "necessity to increase throughput through Layer 2 solutions", etc. Even though this is only an abstraction indicating a roughly similar technical envelope, it is nevertheless important to understand its probable repercussions for the transactional aspects of blockchain-based ecosystems in general, and of their tokens in particular.

The blockchain as a term does not denote any specific software brand, but is simply the generic term for a digital architecture concept. In previous sections, this was explained as being based on the existence of a DL and of algorithms solving the "consensus problem" of cooperating agents through enforced validation and chaining of transaction blocks. Talking about "the blockchain" is like talking about "the office building". There exist many different designs following the blockchain concept, in the same way that there exist many different designs following the general concept of an office building. Each specific design, however, determines a particular "**blockchain platform**", i.e. a concrete set of technical components orchestrating pieces of bespoke software, operating a particular kind of DL and executing specific algorithmic logic to validate and then chain together blocks of transactions. The technical orchestration process varies across platforms, as does the DL and the validation/chaining algorithmic logic. All these platforms are "blockchains". But, when talking about a "Bitcoin" or an "Ethereum" or an "Avalanche" blockchain, then one means not the generic blockchain concept but rather a specific design (in the sense of specific orchestration logic, DL, software code, parametrization, etc.) which implements that concept in practice—i.e. a blockchain platform.

A related term which is a prerequisite to explaining the notion of "Layer" is that of the blockchain "Protocol".

- Blockchain "**Protocol**" denotes a specific combination of blockchain platform, *business* processes, implementing software, and tokens.

As an example, a project using Ethereum as blockchain platform, defining particular business processes, implementing them with own written software on top of the platform, and specifying own tokens to be created and used in said processes is said to have created an own "protocol A". Another project using again Ethereum, defining the same processes, but implementing them with different

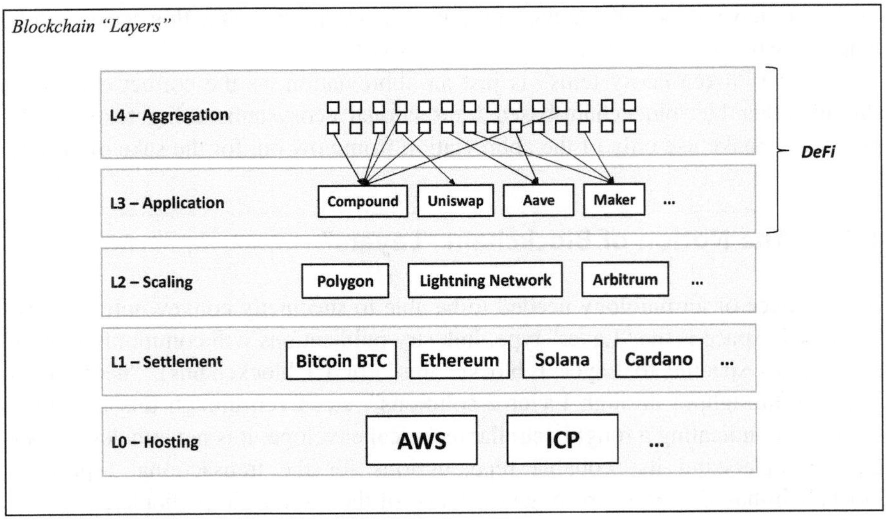

Fig. 1.6 Blockchain "Layer" terminology

software and through different tokens is said to have created a different "protocol B". Similarly, when protocol A either changes its processes, makes major changes to its software, or institutes a different constellation of tokens, it then becomes a different (named) version of "A" or a totally different "protocol C".

With the above in mind, blockchain "Layers" are defined as per Fig. 1.6.[5]

(a) *Layer-0*, or "**Hosting**" layer. This is the infrastructure on which blockchain platforms can be created. It may or may not involve blockchain itself. For example, Amazon Web Services, Microsoft Azure, or Google Cloud Platform are non-blockchain-based hosting layers. The Internet Computer blockchain network [12, 13] is a blockchain-based Layer-0.
(b) *Layer-1* or "**Settlement**" layer[6]. This is the native layer of blockchain platforms, where transaction records are assembled into blocks, and where block validation and consensus take place. Only Layer-1 protocols operate a DL. Protocols of Layers 2 and above write their transaction records in blocks validated by Layer-1 protocols.

[5] Please note that this depiction departs from a concept put forth in [11]. In that publication there was no Layer-0, the Layer-2 was defined as "Asset Layer"—not specifically pertaining to scalability—and Layer-3 was the "Protocol Layer". We believe that the currently prevailing crypto-market practice is reflected better in the terminology of Sect. 1.5 and in Fig. 1.6.

[6] Also denoted as "Consensus" layer.

(c) *Layer-2*,or "**Scaling**" layer[7]. This layer acts in effect as scalability enhancer to Layer-1. Typical architectural features of Layer-2 protocols include off-loading of transaction processing from Layer-1 and returning bulk results back to it, implementing a different consensus logic on "partitions" of the Layer-1 DL, etc. Layer-2 protocols exist only in conjunction with corresponding Layer-1 ones.

(d) *Layer-3* or "**Application**" layer[8]. This is the layer of business-focused applications, allowing protocols to create bespoke use cases, implement sophisticated end-user interfaces, create marketplaces and exchanges, and generally create digital business ecosystems around products and services. All infrastructure-level transaction processing and blockchain consensus is delegated by Layer-3 to lower-level protocols.

(e) *Layer-4* or "**Aggregation**" layer. In essence, this is a "business orchestration" layer, where protocols add value by bundling together functionalities from Layer-3 ones and then superposing a bespoke layer of functionality for specific use cases or end-user groups. Layer-4 protocols in effect "subcontract" business steps to Layer-3 and are thus dependent on the latter for end-to-end processing.

Hence, a "Layer" is an abstraction indicating a roughly similar technical envelope of features enabling blockchain applications. It is useful as a means to convey the business relevance of a protocol and the probable extent of its dependencies on other protocols. As an aside (albeit important in reference to the creation and use of crypto-tokens), Layer-3 and -4 protocols are precisely the domain of what has come to be called "Decentralized Finance" ("DeFi" for short). This term denotes their ability to implement fully autonomous processes replicating financial products and services already known from traditional finance, as well as creating new ones leveraging the power of the blockchain. The use of the word "decentralized" in DeFi denotes the absence of a centralized point-of-control, i.e. of a human-based organization tasked with business-relevant decision-making.

1.6 Summary

Cryptocurrencies and tradable crypto-tokens can be understood only against the background of their generating use cases in blockchain-based ecosystems. This chapter laid out a foundation of notions and terminology, starting from the explanation of the blockchain as technical architectural paradigm. These notions are necessary to be able to understand the process of value creation and the role of tokens in said ecosystems.

[7] Also referred to as "Scalability" layer.

[8] Also denoted as "dApps" layer, from the industry abbreviation for "Distributed Application": "dApp" or "DApp".

The next chapter will interpret blockchain-based ecosystems in general, and token ecosystems in particular, as enablers of economic outcomes in the context of a digital economy.

References

1. Sybil attack. (2024, October 21). In *Wikipedia*. Retrieved March 17, 2025, from https://en.wikipedia.org/wiki/Sybil_attack
2. Newsome, J., Shi, E., Song, D., & Perrig A. (2004). The Sybil Attack in Sensor Networks: Analysis & Defenses. In *IPSN'04, Proceedings of the 3rd international symposium on Information processing in sensor networks*, pp. 259–268. https://dl.acm.org/doi/10.1145/984622.984660 (primary source). Retrieved March 17, 2025, from https://netsec.ethz.ch/publications/papers/newsome_shi_song_perrig_sybil.pdf
3. Consensus (computer science). (2024, October 5). In *Wikipedia*. Retrieved March 17, 2025, from https://en.wikipedia.org/wiki/Consensus_(computer_science)
4. Proof of work. (2025, March 12). In *Wikipedia*. Retrieved March 17, 2025, from https://en.wikipedia.org/wiki/Proof_of_work
5. Proof of stake. (2025, March 12). In *Wikipedia*. Retrieved March 17, 2025, from https://en.wikipedia.org/wiki/Proof_of_stake
6. Blockchain Council. (2024, September 17). *What Is Proof of History and How Does It Work?* Retrieved March 17, 2025, from https://www.blockchain-council.org/blockchain/what-is-proof-of-history-and-how-does-it-work/
7. Delegated proof of stake (DPoS). (2025, March 12). In *Wikipedia*. Retrieved March 17, 2025, from https://en.wikipedia.org/wiki/Proof_of_stake#Delegated_proof_of_stake
8. Blockchain. (2025, March 7). In *Wikipedia*. Retrieved March 17, 2025, from https://en.wikipedia.org/wiki/Blockchain
9. Nakamoto, S. (2008). *Bitcoin: A Peer-to-Peer Electronic Cash System*. Retrieved March 17, 2025, from https://bitcoin.org/bitcoin.pdf
10. Tardi, C. (2024, May 8). *Genesis Block: Bitcoin Definition, Mysteries, and Secret Message*. Retrieved March 17, 2025, from https://www.investopedia.com/terms/g/genesis-block.asp
11. Schär, F. (2021). Decentralized Finance: On Blockchain- and Smart Contract-Based Financial Markets. *FRB of St. Louis Review*. Retrieved March 17, 2025, from https://doi.org/10.20955/r.103.153-74
12. The DFINITY Foundation is a major contributor to the Internet Computer blockchain. https://dfinity.org/.
13. Hanke, T., Movahedi, M., & Williams D. (2018). DFINITY Technology Overview Series Consensus System, Rev.1., *Technology Overviews*, DFINITY Stiftung. Retrieved March 17, 2025, from https://dfinity.org/pdf-viewer/pdfs/viewer?file=../library/dfinity-consensus.pdf

A New Paradigm of Economic Organization

2

As is the case with every important technological development, the blockchain has allowed existing processes to become more efficient. More importantly, it has also created the potential for totally new business processes making use of its seminal features of consensus-based fault tolerance, on-chain validation, transaction finality, and non-repudiation. Hence new products and services can be designed, offered, and sold using a blockchain as transactional ledger.

In the current chapter, we argue that the blockchain achieves much more than that. Viewed from the standpoint of a modern digital society, blockchain-based ecosystems create new potential for technology to facilitate economic outcomes. One that transcends notions of micro-, platform-, and macro-economics. Decentralized digital marketplaces run on a blockchain can follow the steps of counterparties negotiating and executing a single transaction; replicate the production and management activities of an entire firm; achieve coordination of suppliers and consumers transacting on a centralized platform; enable prearranged and ad hoc transactional pathways of entire global value chains with no central control point; and more. The exact same transactional infrastructure can scale to enable interactions of two private individuals, of all individuals in a single organization, and of all individuals and corporations taking part in global value chains.

Thus, blockchain-based ecosystems in general, and token ecosystems in particular, represent in effect a new paradigm for organizing economic life in a digital economy. The most varied economic agents and the broadest scope and scale of economic activities can all be brought under this paradigm as long as the associated data can be registered and validated on a blockchain. We explain these concepts in the sequel, departing from a reinterpretation of the notion of "factors of production" in the context of a modern digital society.

I. Giannakouros, *Cryptocurrencies and Tradable Crypto-Tokens*, Future of Business and Finance, https://doi.org/10.1007/978-3-031-98423-5_2

2.1 The Journey to Digital Ecosystems

Human organizational evolution, starting from primitive, close-knit societies of hunter-gatherers all the way to impersonal, global value chains of corporations and digitally enabled workers, is in essence the story of technical evolution and of its effects on social and economic life. Harnessing fire, creating the wheel, constructing the plough, discovering metal alloys, engineering the printing press, finding ways to transform and control energy sources, inventing the digital computer, etc., were all liberating events for human ability and productivity. With each new seminal discovery or invention, humans were gaining the potential for faster production cycles, broader interactions, better health and safety, more free time, expanded knowledge, and, ultimately, wealth as an enabler of better life quality. And with each time that "old ways of doing things" had to be abandoned, new skills learned, and new organizational paradigms introduced, there were inescapable societal changes to consider as wealth creation potential (and with it, power to influence society at large) was being reallocated from one group of humans to another. Across each one of those transitions, old norms and conventions had to be re-examined and then either reinterpreted, evolved, or rejected. Ignoring for a moment the effects of changes in the natural environment (natural catastrophes, pests, and pandemics, climate change, etc.), human organizational evolution has always been a process of economic and social readjustment responding to new discoveries and/or inventions.

The earliest major transition in human history, that from hunter-gatherer to agrarian societies, created the first understanding of the importance of having stores of goods that represented both utility and value. Subsequent transitions highlighted the importance of specialization, hence the value of exchanging goods and services among individuals as an economic optimization mechanism. The practical limitations of barter trade created the need for stores of value which had no discernible practical use other than being media of exchange. Each and every technological evolution in means of production, storage, transport, or communication responded to one of those needs. New technologies were always used to expand:

- The universe of tradable goods and of ways to extract or manufacture them.
- The universe of tradable services and of ways to create or deliver them.
- The universe of stores of value and of ways to construct, transport, and store them.
- The ways for people to organize themselves so as to optimally produce and exchange goods, services, and stores of value.
- The governance mechanisms of economic and social life, existing so that human interactions can take place in a predictable manner, in spite of all possible risks that might arise in the natural or economic environment.

The importance of the two last points cannot be overstated. What is represented through them is nothing short of the economic and social paradigms of markets, corporations, branches of government, and organized religions. Underlying them are fundamental social contracts validating the necessity of keeping (formal or informal) ledgers of accountability and trust, formalized as laws and supplemented by religious beliefs and cultural norms. Said contracts are fundamentally predicated on the acceptance of the existence of rights of ownership over property and of decision and action on the part of the individual. Furthermore, on the understanding that some of these rights need to be ceded to governance structures (deemed more powerful than the individual) for the sake of social stability and of rational management of scarce resources for the common good. Different calibrations of said paradigms have produced all the different forms of organized economic activity and forms of government that have appeared in history. Thus, it is impossible to interpret their appearance and evolution without knowing the technological means available to their members in the course of their existence. The repercussion is that to understand, and project to a potential future, our own evolutionary stage today as a society we need to acknowledge the capabilities, limitations, and potential of currently prevailing technologies—the blockchain being one of them.

Economics has traditionally sought to explain the behaviour of interacting social systems by focusing on aspects of value creation and consumption. Value creation must logically precede value consumption, hence the seminal notion of "factors of production", meaning a typology of inputs to the process that is logically at the centre of self-sustaining social systems.

Being also an empirical science, economics was historically "calibrated" (or "advised", if you will) by its surrounding social context. Thus, it is perhaps inescapable that the four traditionally accepted *basic factors of production*, as still being taught today, can be thought of as rather reflecting the realities of agrarian and industrial societies. They are taken to be [1, 2]:

1. Land
2. Labour
3. Entrepreneurship, and
4. Capital

In line with several previous attempts to bring these notions closer to more modern contexts [3, 4], we will attempt to "reinterpret" them in a way that will help better explain economic value creation in digital societies. But first, we will need to add a *fifth basic factor* that is simply missing, namely:

5. Information

Information is an exogenous input in production processes, with its own creation and transformation dynamics which are not controlled by labour, entrepreneurship, or capital. For example, weather data potentially suggesting e.g. that an entrepreneur should harvest short-term one crop rather than another, exist independently from the entrepreneur and their crops. Prices of raw materials in specific marketplaces, shipping rates among pairs of loading/unloading ports, energy network capacities per geographic area, applicable rules and regulations in a particular trade, component

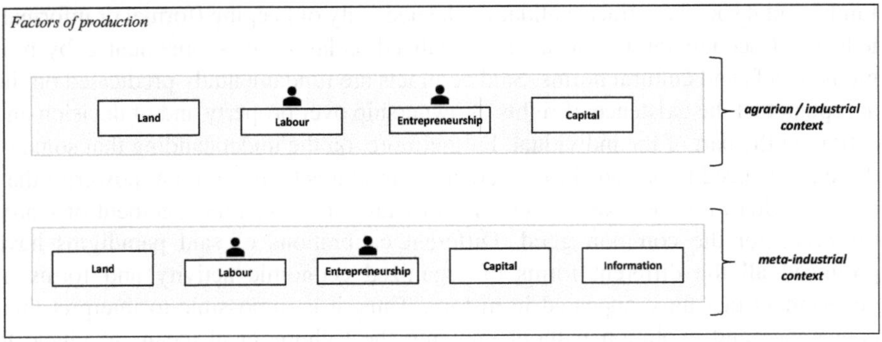

Fig. 2.1 Evolution of basic factors of production

blueprints and manuals of operation, etc., are all instances of inputs that are necessary for particular value creation processes but which have their own "existence" irrespective of whether or not they are used as such.

It can be argued that "information" is at least partially contained as an ingredient of "labour", "entrepreneurship", and "capital", in the form of know-how and intellectual property. This is indeed how we will proceed shortly. However, there are forms of information (observational data, expired patterns, etc.) that cannot be logically captured in any of the existing factor definitions. They are needed for production processes and are partially used as inputs by "labour" and "entrepreneurship", but they exist independently and in their own right. They are useful as production inputs but can be exploited only if purposely included in combination with other factors of production. They may represent the outcomes of previous production cycles, but then so does labour (as product of education and training, the latter having as inputs the factors "land"—schools and facilities—, "entrepreneurship"—school administrators, endowment managers, "labour"—educators, credentials examiners—, and of course "capital"). By the same token so does entrepreneurship (as product of training—the previous list applies—and potentially of subsidies—which are a form of "capital"—, etc.), and naturally so does capital itself. Thus, we will include "information" as a separate, basic factor of production which is especially important in the modern, meta-industrial, social context. Accepting this new basic factor is simply registering social evolution, as per the depiction in Fig. 2.1 (wherein a "bust" icon denotes a factor embodied in humans).

Departing from the five "meta-industrial" basic factors of production, we can now reinterpret them into a typology more useful for analysis in a modern context. First of all, "Land" is indisputably a representative of tangible working assets (cf. Fig. 2.2).

"Labour" in its turn can be thought of as consisting of various combinations of two distinct sub-factors, namely "services" and "know-how" (cf. Fig. 2.3).

For example, there can be production processes involving "labour" in the sense of "passive execution by unskilled humans of simple process steps coordinated by automation", in which case "know-how" is an attribute solely of the automation—a

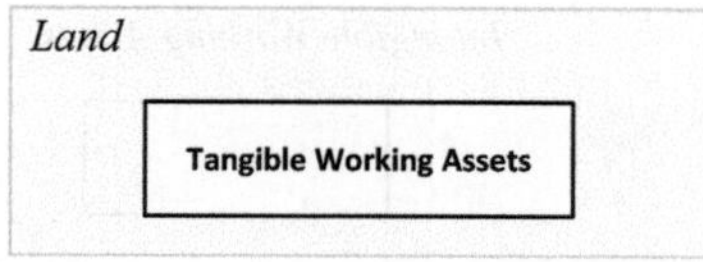

Fig. 2.2 Reinterpretation of factor "Land"

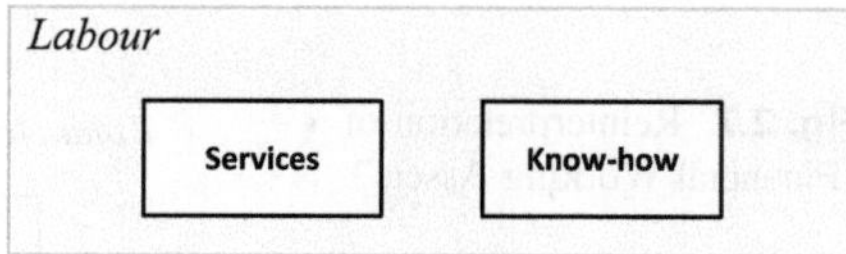

Fig. 2.3 Reinterpretation of factor "Labour"

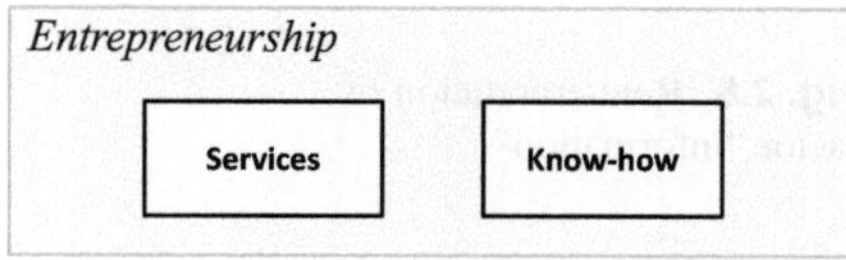

Fig. 2.4 Reinterpretation of factor "Entrepreneurship"

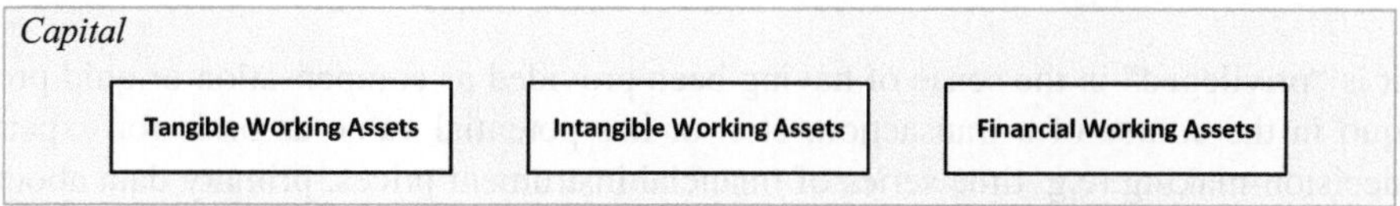

Fig. 2.5 Reinterpretation of factor "Capital"

form of intangible working asset and of capital employed (cf. below)—hence "labour" can equate to a bare "Services" sub-factor. There are other processes still where the cognitive aspect implied by "know-how" is much more pronounced. "Entrepreneurship", on the other hand, is typically taken to encompass "drive", "initiative", "active contribution to outcomes from a leading position", and "direct responsibility for the coordination of resources", which again can all be interpreted as combinations of the same two sub-factors as under "Labour" (cf. Fig. 2.4).

The activity of entrepreneurs is in effect provision of services, while the intangible aspect of whatever notionally precedes them (vision, conviction, ideas) is captured by the cognitive content of "know-how" in the sense of "knowing what is to be done". It would be tempting to include "character" or "mentality" as sub-factors of "entrepreneurship", but these are first, not inputs of production, and second, not always present in entrepreneurial endeavours. "Capital" employed in production can be similarly reinterpreted as consisting of the sub-factors depicted on Fig. 2.5.

We find again tangible working assets as under "Land". Capital employed in the form of intangible working assets can be interpreted as consisting of sub-factors as per Fig. 2.6. "Data" is proprietary information in raw, unprocessed form that either has intrinsic value *per se* (e.g. when capital was needed to glean and store it, or when

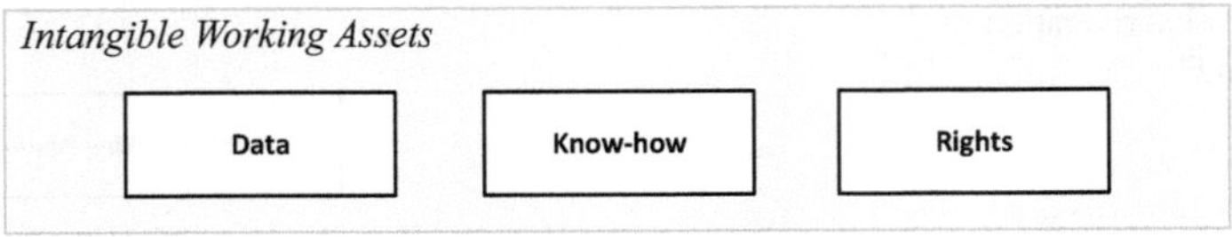

Fig. 2.6 Reinterpretation of "Intangible Working Assets"

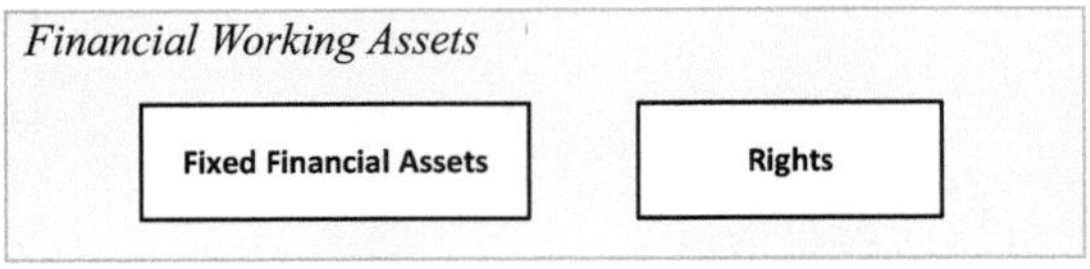

Fig. 2.7 Reinterpretation of "Financial Working Assets"

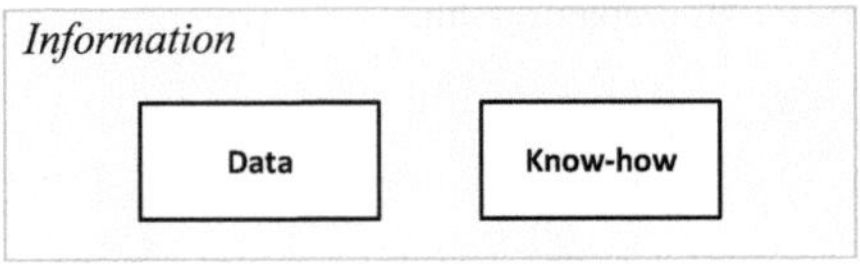

Fig. 2.8 Reinterpretation of factor "Information"

it is "privileged" in the sense of having been provided as compensation or quid pro quo in the course of a transaction, etc.) or has potential value as basis for expert decision-making (e.g. time series of financial instrument prices, primary data about real estate transactions in a particular area, chemical composition data of a particular substance, etc.). "Know-how" is proprietary information about processes that has been captured in manuals, blueprints, etc., or is contained in algorithms implemented through software or hardware. "Rights" encompasses capital in the form of patents, licences, or privileges that have been acquired for monetary value. They are "rights" in that they can in principle be used to generate value, but they may also not be required—their use for value creation is conditional on an eventual need. Their owner has the right to employ them and is contributing this right as an optionality to the production process.

Financial working assets (cf. Fig. 2.7) can be distinguished into two sub-forms. "Fixed financial assets" are either liquid funds or financial instruments with predictable cash flows that have already been purchased or financed and can be liquidated. "Rights" are financial instruments with uncertain cash flows, conditional on events, that have also already been purchased, financed, or secured. Insurance policies, banking and corporate guarantees, credit facilities, and some financial instruments (swaps, derivatives, etc.), all belong to this sub-form. They are "rights" in that they represent the right to request from counterparties to honour financial obligations entered into, conditional on events which may or may not materialize.

The two possible sub-forms of "information" (cf. Fig. 2.8) have already been explained in the context of "intangible working assets" above. If the reader will forgive the repetition for the sake of reading convenience, "data" is proprietary information in raw, unprocessed form that has either intrinsic value per se or

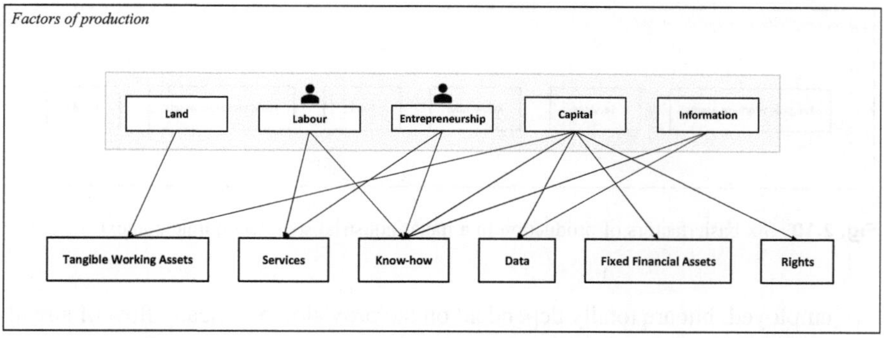

Fig. 2.9 Unearthing commonalities as new factors of production

potential value as basis for expert decision-making, whereas "know-how" is proprietary information about processes that has been captured in manuals, blueprints, etc., or is contained in algorithms implemented through software or hardware. In the present context, we will augment the notion of "know-how" to include knowledge about processes that is intrinsic to a service provider without having been captured in an archival form.

Aggregating "sub-factors" from across the five basic factors of production allows one to identify commonalities. This aggregating action is depicted schematically on Fig. 2.9.

Hence, the commonalities that appear in terms of sub-factors can be condensed in the postulation of *6 (six) basic factors of production in a meta-industrial socio-economic context*:

1. Tangible working assets
2. Services
3. Know-how
4. Data
5. Fixed financial assets, and
6. Rights

where "Rights" are simply optionalities to claim intangible and financial assets that may be only conditionally available or ultimately used.

This picture of six pervasive factors of production (cf. Fig. 2.10, outcome of our attempt at reinterpretation of the four "traditional" basic factors plus "information") is rather important for the sequel. The reasons are threefold:

(a) "**Data**" appears as a distinct factor of production, which would be difficult to justify in an agrarian/industrial context. The explosive growth in data and analytics characterizing our times would seem to validate the existence of value-producing chains that are not capital intensive in the sense of either primary ("fixed financial") or transformed ("tangible working") assets

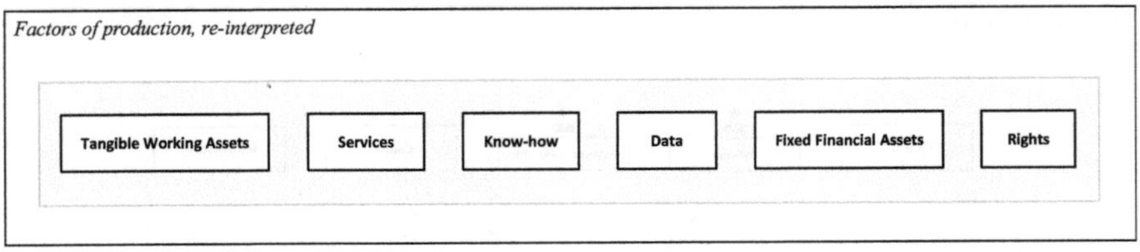

Fig. 2.10 Six basic factors of production in a meta-industrial socio-economic context

employed, but are totally dependent on the provision of a steady flow of already available (exogenous) high-quality data [5].

(b) "**Know-how**" becomes explicit as a factor of production related, but distinct, to services, data, or forms of capital. This would seem to align with the existence of "knowledge-based" value chains and can serve to differentiate among processes where the same quantities of tangible working and fixed financial assets are employed to process the same amounts of data, but the depth of knowledge underpinning the services provided is materially different. It would help justify a distinction between "commoditized" and "expert-based" services. and thus validate the importance of research and development investment levels as a predictor of economic outcomes [6].

(c) "**Services**" become disassociated from the type of providing agent. They are indeed a factor of production, but now their effects can be analysed by not necessarily presupposing the existence of human providers but by also considering automation mechanisms that are software and abstract systems (implementing data-processing algorithms) as providers. This is very useful in the examination of a prominent modern technology-enabled economic coordination paradigm, namely the "digital business ecosystem" [7, 8].

Similarly to a natural ecosystem, a *business ecosystem* is a cooperation space where disparate, non-affiliated suppliers and consumers of goods and services come together to produce economic outcomes. These outcomes may be bilateral transactions along the same value chain; execution of multiparty transactions implementing an entire, end-to-end, predefined value chain; production of customized deliverables by forming an ad hoc value chain; etc. The term "ecosystem" implies some sense of affiliation, collocation, or at least proximity, and an acceptance of a symbiotic relationship among participants. This is what differentiates an ecosystem from a marketplace, where the emphasis is more on competition than on symbiosis.

A *digital business ecosystem* (DBE) implements this symbiotic cooperation space through information technology, which vastly expands the notions of "collocation" and "proximity". Now suppliers and consumers are no longer constrained by geography but may be subject to other limitations (e.g. participation and transaction-level approvals) which are meant to frame the ecosystem boundaries. Once they become part of the ecosystem, they can execute bilateral transactions [9] and take part in end-to-end predefined value chains [10] or in ad hoc value chains [11].

There are two observations that need to be made in reference to the current state of DBEs:

(i) The prevalent digital platform efforts in the first two decades of the Internet revolution were focused on the "Business-to-Consumer" (B2C [12]) and "Business-to-Business" (B2B [13]) e-commerce value propositions. In those use cases, there were only two types of participants, suppliers and consumers. Most of the time the objects of transactions were either goods or services, less often data, seldom other information (know-how), and almost never financial assets. The less frequent transaction types were typically provided by in-house platforms of corporates (banks, investment fund providers, insurance companies, specialized consulting firms, etc.) which were strictly controlling access and monitoring usage. The next evolution state, which is currently being manifested, is the bringing together of many "economic agents" [14, 15] of disparate legal personality, field of activity, scale of resources, and role in extended value chains as part of the same ecosystem. What is more, the role of each agent is allowed to change in each new transaction facilitated in the ecosystem. One company may sell a financial instrument in one; packaged data in another; act as a credit or liquidity provider in yet another, etc. In effect, this is an **"Agent-to-Agent"** *(A2A) paradigm*, where all ecosystem participants are assumed to be defined only in the abstract as rationally acting, permissioned providers of any possible combination of the six factors of production appearing on Fig. 2.10.

(ii) The costs of designing, setting up, operationalizing, and maintaining the necessary infrastructure of a typical DBE could be quite high. This infrastructure involved investments not only in technology but also in operational (participant registration/authorization/credentialing/monitoring and supporting, transaction negotiation and execution, contractual agreements, transaction fee and commission calculation, value-added-tax calculation, exception handling, dispute resolution, information archiving, etc.) and risk management (participant due diligence, transaction monitoring and surveillance, information security, network security, etc.) processes. In cases where provision of credit to, or among, economic agents was also part of the use case, the infrastructure costs were typically high enough that only a corporate or a consortium of corporates could bear the investment risk. This risk comes from the fact that, unless binding participation agreements are already in place, DBE investment pay-off is a "chicken-and-egg" problem. The DBE will return its investment only once a critical mass of participants and transactions are served by it, but at the same time, each new participant can justify taking part only if a critical mass of other participants are already present and transacting. Reaching such a critical mass typically implies business development activities, which are an additional cost. That is why *digital business ecosystems are still typically owned and operated by large corporates or consortia.*

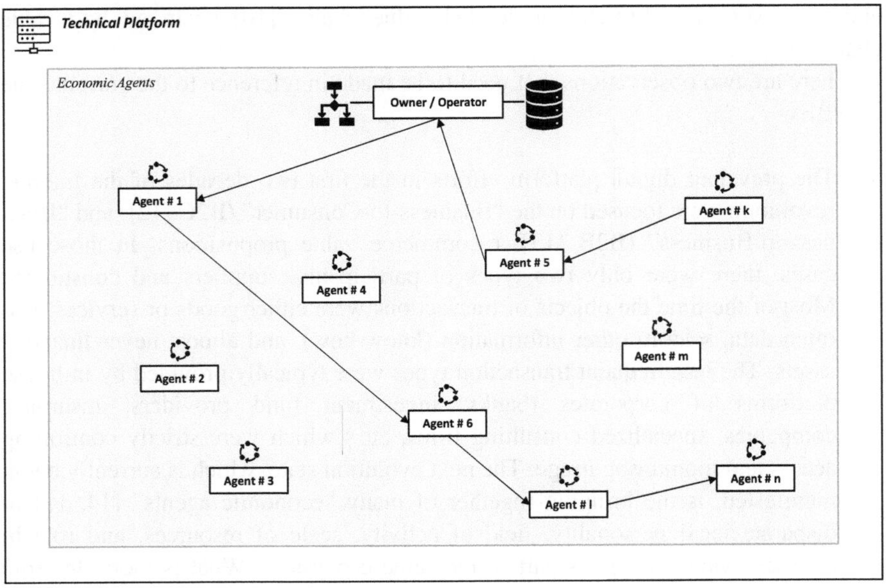

Fig. 2.11 Agent-to-Agent interactions in digital ecosystems. The ledger of transactions and state transitions is centralized

Thus, current digital business ecosystems can be conceptualized as per the depiction of Fig. 2.11.

A single transaction may be initiated by an agent #k and until the goods or services are delivered to the end-buyer (agent #n) there may be a whole chain of ecosystem participants adding value along the process. All process steps, or at least those needing ecosystem participants, are carried through the DBE technical platform.

The technical platform on which the DBE depends is owned and operated by a legal entity (single corporate or consortium) which assumes responsibility for all operational, business, and risk management activities. The business case behind the DBE typically means that the owner/operator expects a direct or indirect profit through its existence. This implies that either inter-agent transactions are facilitated for a fee or commission, or the owner/operator can also be one of the transacting agents and occupies a privileged position among them. Being in this privileged position helps unlock the indirect profit stream. For example, it can occur that the owner/operator uses the DBE as a vehicle for market expansion, increase in market share, long-term binding of existing clientele, informed product development (e.g. through the behavioural and transaction analytics gleaned on the platform), or for any other purpose fitting its business strategy.

Why does this legal entity not operate the entire value chain in-house? Why does it see a value in creating a DBE instead of creating all productive capacity under its own management and supervision?

This is precisely where the digital business environment deviates from the concept of the "firm" as an economic activity organizational paradigm [16, 17]. In all its interpretations, a firm organizes labour, acquires assets, exercises governance over resource allocation, manages its risks, and assumes responsibilities towards its shareholders, having set specific long-term goals and formulated them as strategy. At both the strategic and tactical levels, one of the important decisions that firm management is entrusted with is the "make or buy" one. Any new business opportunity or threat may necessitate specific assets and capabilities to be employed. If those assets and capabilities are not yet within its available means, then they must be acquired. Generally, this involves three possibilities: in-house creation, purchase,[1] or partnership. Each one of the three carries its own risks, which firm management must weigh carefully. Creating and operating a DBE offers a fourth possibility: neither "make", nor "buy", nor "partner", but "loosely include", in the sense of "loosely include in own value chain, in return for direct or indirect profit".

Apart from company-specific reasons, there may be strong arguments in favour of taking the DBE way when the assets and capabilities sought are intangible. That would be the case of e.g. specialized software, electronic libraries, data streams, process know-how, etc. Especially intangible assets produced and distributed digitally and containing significant know-how in the form of specialized algorithms, proprietary data models, knowledge-based libraries, or intellectual property protected by patents create a particularly high barrier to entry for competitors. Not only does producing the original version of such assets entail significant investments in research and development performed by scarce resources (by itself, enough to deter less sophisticated competitors), once they are produced, they have relatively low reproduction and distribution costs due to their digital nature. Once a piece of specialized software is tested and commercialized, any subsequent costs for its distributor are likely to be due to defect removal, standard maintenance, certification on new platforms, and licensing activities (contracts, patents, etc.). There are no physical production activities, no transport costs, no inventory, no theft insurance, and no distribution network to finance. The digital infrastructure costs for electronic storage and distribution, cyber security, and user support are orders of magnitude lower than those for physical infrastructure needed for manufactured goods. As shown on Fig. 2.12, digital asset based models exhibit a degressive total cost function and (as the marginal cost of production at any Quantity-Cost point (Q_0, C_0) is simply the derivative of the cost curve) a near-zero marginal cost of production.

In short, it makes little sense for the capability-seeking company to try to compete with specialized digital asset producers. It would have to finance the same high investments in research and development, assuming it could hire the same or equivalent amount of specialized scarce resources. From the other remaining options, partnering with the producer creates long-term commitment with no guarantee of exclusivity, and buying them outright binds financial resources at the risk

[1] Either outright or under time-based contract to an external supplier; under various financing forms, including leasing.

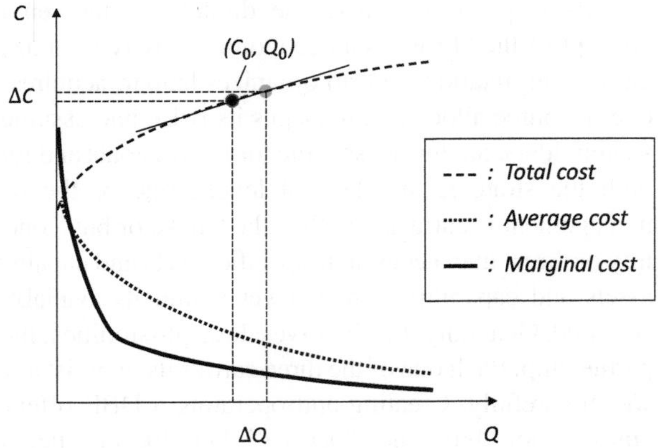

Fig. 2.12 Near-zero marginal cost of production for digital assets

that key experts may decide to leave and reproduce an improved asset version with no obligation to keep supporting the original one. Operating an own DBE and including the digital asset producer as value chain participant may well represent the optimum from a combined cost and risk perspective.

A similar situation occurs in the case of specialized digital *service* providers. Once their expertise has been used to create business processes, technical infrastructure, and the specialized software needed to tie everything together, then remote delivery through digital channels alone is possible as long as there are no legal or institutional barriers. In short, their cost structure is entirely different from that of in-person service providers. Again, binding them in an own operated DBE may be the only sensible strategy compared to trying to compete against them, buying them outright, or partnering with them in a non-exclusive setting. The digital world thus creates totally new competition realities, and this is one of the reasons for us proposing to think in terms of the six "new" basic factors of production (as per Fig. 2.10) instead of the four "traditional" ones. Only by bringing the factors "services", "know-how" and "data" explicitly to the forefront can an analyst deduce the probable behaviour of digital-age economic agents.

Competitive pressures aside, a digital business ecosystem can act as a parallel distribution channel complementing the traditional ones already used by the owner/operator. If the latter is prepared to see the entire market as consisting of the established channels plus the DBE, then (barring cannibalization effects) they may well experience a shift of their demand curve to the right (cf. Fig. 2.13), with the result that a new market equilibrium results. This transition can be reasonably expected to occur in a DBE for a simple reason: a DBE is a competition-promoting mechanism. Different economic agents offering the same or similar goods or services will have to compete for the business of the other ecosystem participants. In most DBEs it is easy to implement explicit or implicit rating mechanisms ("user satisfaction", "recommendation" ratings, etc.) and most of the time these are actually part of the "register of reputation and trust" mechanism design, as explained later in

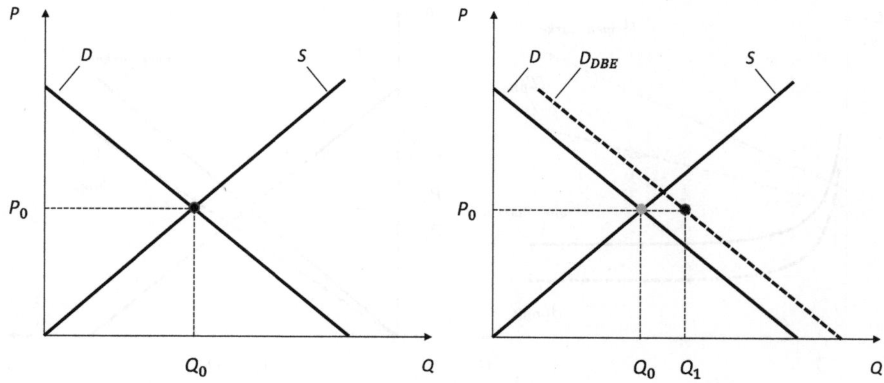

Fig. 2.13 Market equilibria, without and within a digital business ecosystem setting, for the owner/operator

the book. It is also technically easy to implement auctions for price discovery, as long as the owner/operator is prepared to safeguard their fairness through technical and organizational measures. Thus, ecosystem participants must expect to eventually come under competitive pressure in return for access to enlarged markets and to broader value chains. This competitive pressure will create either downward pressure on prices or outward pressure on offering envelopes, which will add to the value proposition of transacting on the DBE—hence to indirect increase in demand for the owner/operator's own offerings—if they are deemed indispensable or compelling enough for ecosystem transactions. In effect, should lower offering prices ensue for the average DBE participant, then the result will be manifestation of "complementarity effects" [18] as already known in platform economics. In all these cases, the end result will be a shift of the owner/operator's demand curve to the right as shown above.

Thus, the decision to assume the investment risk of a digital business ecosystem instead of keeping all operations in-house may be anchored on a competitive as well as on a market development strategy. By seemingly ceding control of parts of the value chain, a DBE owner/operator actually profits from the volume of business transacted on the entire value chain both directly and indirectly.

What is the value proposition of a DBE for the other ecosystem participants? Why do they not pursue their business entirely on the open market instead?

First of all, DBE participation is voluntary and non-exclusive. At any time it can be terminated, interrupted, and even forfeited. So, from the standpoint of the ecosystem participant, the DBE is just an additional channel. It can increase the volume of business and even help reach a new, global market. There is however also a beneficial effect in terms of cost reduction. We will explain this through the example of a particular type of ecosystem participant, namely services companies.

The cost base of service providers consists of a fixed part (infrastructure and corporate administrative investments that are relatively stable in time) and a variable one that scales almost linearly with the volume of business. This is the case when the

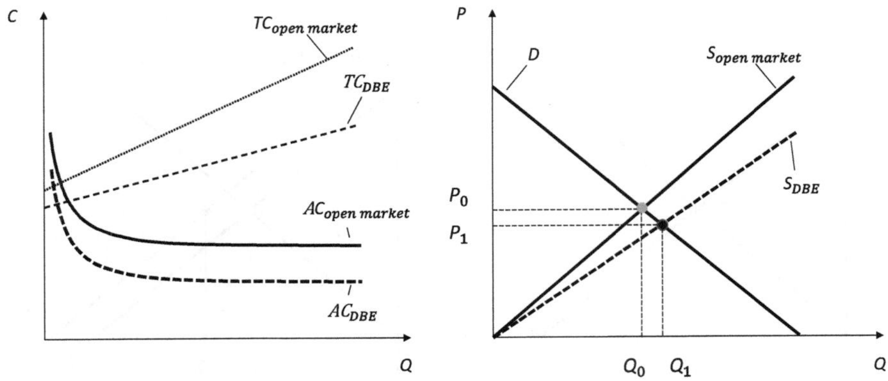

Fig. 2.14 Cost curves (TC: total, AC: average) and market equilibria, in the open market and in a DBE, for service provider

service offering is not fully digitized but necessitates significant human input in terms of content and delivery, which is the most generic type in existence today. For these economic agents, a non-negligible proportion of both the fixed and variable costs is due to business development, client origination, client onboarding, credit due diligence, supplier due diligence, cash cycle management, transaction compliance, client and portfolio analytics, etc., i.e. in effect, non-core-business related. The resources needed to execute these tasks can be reduced significantly for business pursued and executed on a DBE. For client-acquisition-related costs, for example, the DBE acts in effect as a focusing lens onto that part of the market which is prepared to share data, let be discovered, and submit to rating and scoring opinions as a way to lower its own transaction costs. For transaction execution, compliance, and reporting related tasks, in most DBEs these can be outsourced to the owner/operator or to other ecosystem participants for a fee, typically much lower than the cost of keeping them in-house (in the latter case, partially due to the aforementioned competition-promoting effect of the DBE). The combined effect is a reduction in both the fixed and the per-transaction costs of the service provider when trading in the DBE. As shown on Fig. 2.14, both the cost curves and the market equilibria of the open-market vs DBE service provider create an argument in favour of ecosystem participation.

Hence all ecosystem participants other than the owner/operator can profit from increased volumes of business, geographical market expansion, and generally reduced infrastructure and operational costs (especially non-core-business related).

Summarizing the above, whereas a hierarchical firm organizes and allocates its own or contracted resources for well-defined economic outcomes, the digital business ecosystem is a vehicle for a privileged economic agent (owner/operator) to create both a marketplace for their own offerings and a facilitation mechanism for other economic agents to self-organize into ad hoc supply chains. Viewed as marketplaces, DBEs are platforms for transaction negotiation and execution in goods, services, capital, and information. Viewed as facilitation mechanisms, they are platforms for counterparty discovery, competitive price formation, market expansion, and optimal resource allocation. By assuming the initial set-up and ongoing operating costs, the owner/operator avoids a "make, buy, or partner" investment decision, opting instead for including loosely third parties in their own value chain in return for direct or indirect profit.

A hierarchical firm exercises strict operational risk management over all its resources and transactions, whereas the DBE owner/operator can only ensure that transparency and fairness is prevalent in the ecosystem so that participating economic agents can reliably assess and manage their own operational risks. As DBE participation is voluntary and can be interrupted or forfeited at any time, the contractual aspect of this organizational paradigm becomes crucial. Binding terms and conditions for onboarding and active participation need to be clear, and adherence to them always observed in all interactions between economic agents bilaterally and among all third-party economic agents and the owner/operator in particular. This combination of contractual obligation setting and behavioural monitoring represents the baseline capability through which the DBE owner/operator can achieve governance of risks in the ecosystem. Even though transaction-level decision-making is ceded to the DBE participants, the right to define interaction workflows, protocols, and controls rests exclusively with the owner/operator. So, the latter does centralize in and of themselves (i.e. do not relinquish) the right to exercise operational risk management and control, but only for those risks that can be justified in reference to the ecosystem as a whole. The information sets that are typically retained and processed by the owner/operator to that end include:

(i) Identifying data for all participating economic agents.
(ii) Transaction-level data for all transactions concluded in the ecosystem.
(iii) State transitions at both the economic agent and transaction levels.
(iv) Ratings, scorings, opinions, and comments offered by economic agents voluntarily.

The owner/operator may decide to augment said information sets with still other data aspects (e.g. analytics, supporting documents, etc.).

What is the purpose of culling and keeping data relating to the individual points i. to iv. above?

Economic agent identifying data are kept to enable onboarding and ongoing due diligence, channelling of user-targeted information flows, and creation of searchable directories. It is the fundamental basis for approvals, monitoring, publishing, billing, reporting, and customer support processes undertaken by the DBE governance. For instance, there is no point in trying to monitor transaction flow on the DBE when the information about transaction counterparties is invisible. Transaction funding requests, credit requests, transaction controls, fraud detection, etc., are all predicated on being able to ascertain agent-level attributes, hence having reliable identifying information about agents is the absolute prerequisite.

Transaction-level data are kept to evidence what, and how, was agreed and ultimately exchanged in the interactions executed on the DBE. It is meant primarily for the protection of each transacting economic agent and for the risk management activities of the DBE owner/operator. For example, the latter needs to be aware of what purposes its ecosystem is actually being used for and whether or not these are commensurate with the terms and conditions set as a prerequisite for onboarding. Credit approvals, cash-flow management, transaction reporting, fee and commission allocation, ongoing counterparty due diligence, transaction amendments, exception handling, and dispute resolution are all predicated on the availability of this data.

"**State**" refers to all data that, either alone or in combination, describe completely the situation of their subject. An economic agent may have the state variables "activity status", "solvency status", "authorization status", "credit rating", "reputation rating", etc. In reference to a transaction, state variables may be "lifecycle stage", "execution stage", "amendment stage", "dispute resolution stage", "services performed to date", "cash flows executed to date", "amendment requests to date", "exceptions occurred to date", "objections registered to date" and similar. What exactly qualifies as ecosystem-relevant state, i.e. which data are kept by the owner/operator, is a DBE design decision which must be commensurate with the business case. What is required for purposes of ecosystem governance and risk management is the ability to register *state transitions,* and to be able to track those back to generating events ("transition events") and ultimately to actions by economic agents. For exceptional situations, it is precisely this ability that enables the link from pathologies back to root causes; and to ultimately suggest appropriate corrective action alternatives, which is the essence of governance. More importantly, by registering these state transitions across all economic agents and their transactions, the owner/operator can then define a state machine [19], i.e. prescribe what should follow in terms of process steps and controls. These are the "business rules" [20] that need to be observed across the DBE. They can be formally documented as part of the ecosystem workflows and enforced automatically through software [21, 22] embedded in the technical infrastructure. This automation constitutes an important part of the coordinating tasks reserved by the owner/operator. It is precisely that technical mechanism which enables cross-participant value chains, risk management controls, and ecosystem-wide data aggregation at scale.

Ratings, scorings, opinions, and comments register the "subjective" part of participants' experience in the ecosystem. Through them, economic agents express their perception about: other participants; their offerings; price levels in relation to quality of offering and quality of service, voice complaints and make improvement suggestions for the ecosystem as a whole. Apart from being a feedback mechanism to individual agents about their competitiveness, and a signalling mechanism for new product development, they are very useful for the owner/operator as a pointer to operating model blind spots and hidden risks.

On top of being a governance and risk management mechanism for the purposes of the DBE owner/operator, is there any value in registering this data from the point of view of the other economic agents participating? Apart from data logically needed for onboarding them onto the ecosystem, why would they cede rights to further information visibility and usage to a third party? And where would they be justified in drawing a line between what is requested and what is economically justifiable to provide?

The short answer is that by moving away from a hierarchical firm organization to orchestrating a voluntary participation of asset and capability providers submitting to own governance, the DBE owner/operator also assumes an implicit role: that of the *keeper of* precisely those *ledgers of accountability and trust* that held close-knit early human societies functioning and stable. In an impersonal, digital, world of economic agents possibly located half a planet away, where alone the communication aspects of risk-managing each and every transaction bilaterally would make ad hoc value chains impractical, it is the owner/operator that ultimately provides assurance that bilateral risks are controlled and that each individual economic agent can trust all others. Each onboarding approval, each credit check, each fall in experience ratings, each transaction dispute tracked back to fraud, incomplete information, factual misrepresentation or simply to unjustified delays in transaction execution, is de facto part of the control framework safeguarding the quality of the digital business ecosystem as a whole, preserving it as a marketplace of goods, services, capital, and information that is safe and fair for all its participants.

2.2 The Blockchain as Business Ecosystems Infrastructure

In the previous section, the digital business ecosystem (DBE) was explained as being a coordinated space, enabled through information and communication technologies, where disparate, non-affiliated suppliers and consumers of goods, services, capital, and information come together to produce economic outcomes. As the up-front investment needed to design, set-up, and operationalize a DBE infrastructure is typically high, they are usually owned and operated by large corporates or consortia. The latter assume the role of owner/operator, centralizing in themselves powers of ecosystem governance and operational control over processes and associated data. The data are kept and processed in data stores under the exclusive control of the owner/operator, whereupon the business rules of the ecosystem are enforced. The governing entity thus controls central ledgers of accountability and trust (cf. Fig. 2.11).

The arrival of the blockchain as a novel technical paradigm for the exchange and recording of transactional data has changed the economics of DBEs. This occurred in the following ways:

- The blockchain obviated the need for expensive, centralized infrastructure to record, persist, and process transactional data.
- It enabled decentralization of the ledgers of accountability and trust so that individual economic agents (no longer a single, privileged owner/operator) can implement their own state machines and business rules.
- It expanded the universe of tradable goods, services, stores of value (forms of capital), and information exchange patterns that economic agents can use to self-organize in supply chains.

- It enabled transferring the responsibility for ecosystem governance and risk management from a single, central authority to a federation of economic agents performing these tasks as a remunerated service.
- By doing so, it created the potential for distributing both the risk and the rewards (direct and indirect profits) of operating a DBE away from a central owner/operator to each and every willing economic agent in the ecosystem.
- This in effect brought into life *a new paradigm of economic organization*, whereby factors of production self-organize in controllable, prearranged or ad hoc value chains to achieve concrete economic outcomes.

There are several blockchain features that helped unlock this potential. One is its being based on the ICT architectural pattern of Distributed Ledger Technology (DLT). As already explained in the previous chapter, the notions "blockchain" and "DLT" are not synonymous; blockchain is but one way of implementing a Distributed Ledger (DL). In effect, the DLT consists in a dual concept:

1. Having copies of all records of interest replicated at trusted nodes around the Internet, and
2. Using sequential record-validating actions by trusted nodes that are totally independent of each other and, once a critical number of nodes have validated (or, once a "consensus" is reached, in industry terminology), then authorizing global replication.

The first part of the concept means that no central authority has complete and exclusive visibility on data, nor is the privilege of data processing and insight-generating analytics accorded to a single economic agent. The second part means that whatever data are submitted to the ledger are by definition to be read by a potentially large number of third parties before they are committed and replicated globally. This creates a very real data confidentiality risk, which is unacceptable in commercial transactions. Hence, operational use of DLT in a business setting has two important corollaries:

- Use of *encryption is necessary* to limit information security and privacy risks. Encryption is applied both at the level of data that are to be made part of the record and at the level of data transmission across the communications network.
- The "**consensus**" mechanism *must simply validate that the record of data* under examination is *consistent* in some technical sense, but does not need to examine the reasonableness of the data itself.

In short, what is submitted for recording into the DL is at the discretion of each individual economic agent using the DL. No central authority imposes rules on what is written (the content, an "information model") or how and when. This is another important difference to the privileges of the owner/operator in the generic DBE case.

It is important to mention that on practical grounds there exists also here an "Owner/Operator" of sorts but possessing much less power than before. The reason

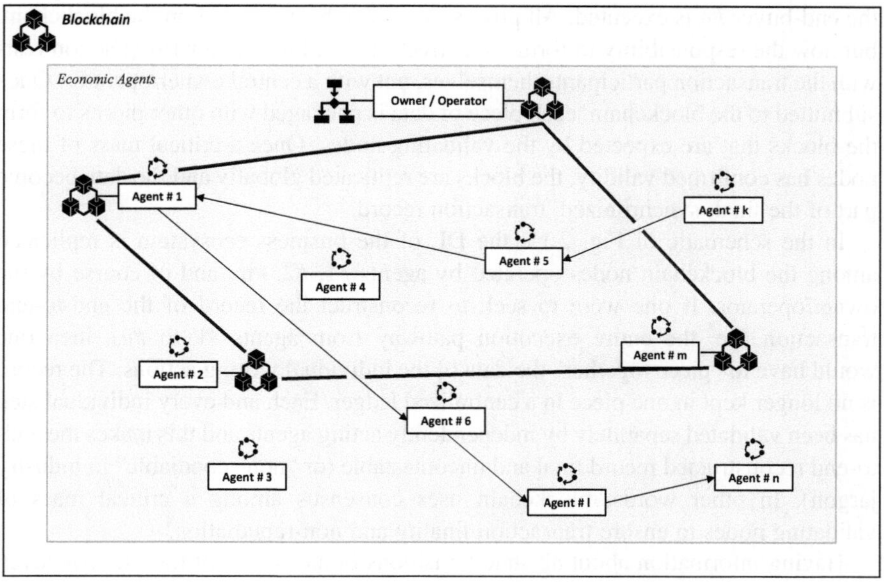

Fig. 2.15 Agent-to-Agent interactions in blockchain-based ecosystems. The ledger of transactions and state transitions is copied and synchronized among distinct nodes ("distributed")

is that, as for generic DBEs, it is inescapable that blockchain-based ecosystems come into being at the initiative of specific economic agents. The latter typically undertake the first costs of setting up the basic DLT infrastructure (which, more often than not, is open-source [23] software, i.e. free to copy and re-use within the terms of its licence) and of at least a small number of "validation nodes" keeping the first replicated instances of the DL. As an investment, this is typically a small fraction of the corresponding one (in terms of working assets) needed for the generic, centralized, DBE. The initiative-taking economic agents do also operate a copy of the DL, but otherwise have no privileges in terms of data specification and usage. They are indeed considered an "Owner/Operator" because they reasonably have a vested interest in seeing their initiative achieving its objectives in the long run, whatever those may be. Hence, they typically also assume duties of coordination and at least facilitation of governance outcomes, especially if ecosystem token(s) are to be created on the blockchain (cf. Sect. 2.3). These activities do have an opportunity cost, which the initiating "Owner/Operator" expects to recoup primarily through token circulation.

In a mature stage, the blockchain-based ecosystem will have attracted many more "validation nodes", keeping DL copies and helping to generate the intended economic outcomes. As mentioned above, each and every economic agent is free to write their own data, at a time and in cooperation with other economic agents of their own choosing. As shown on Fig. 2.15 (in juxtaposition to Fig. 2.11 for the generic DBE case), the same transaction initiated by an agent #k and involving a whole chain of ecosystem participants adding value until the goods or services are delivered to the end-buyer #n is executed. All process steps can be registered on the blockchain, but now the responsibility to form the correct data and invoke a writing action rests with the transaction participants themselves, not with a central owner/operator. Once submitted to the blockchain, each piece of data is packaged with other pieces to form the blocks that are expected by the validating nodes. Once a critical mass of these nodes has confirmed validity, the blocks are replicated globally and the data become part of the final, synchronized, transaction record.

In the schematic of Fig. 2.15, the DL of the business ecosystem is replicated among the blockchain nodes operated by agents #1, #2, #m, and of course by the owner/operator. If one were to seek to reconstruct the record of the end-to-end transaction (i.e. the entire execution pathway from agents #k to #n), then one would have to "piece together" the data of the individual writing actions. The record is no longer kept in one piece in a centralized ledger. Each and every individual step has been validated separately by independently acting agents and this makes the end-to-end reconstructed record final and uncontestable (or "non-repudiable" in industry jargon). In other words, blockchain uses consensus among a critical mass of validating nodes to ensure transaction finality and non-repudiation.

Having information about all state transitions in the course of transactions (even vetted and encrypted) available to cooperating agents enables them to implement their own business rules and data processing. They can reconcile data of other participants with their own to identify deviations, track transaction execution many steps downstream to have an estimate of their own cash conversion cycle times, subscribe to be notified of exceptional situations (e.g. credit or operational events), etc. As long as they have "keys" to unlock the information of interest behind the data stored on the DL ("keys" shared, for example, only among participants of the same value chain on a "need to know" basis), they can implement their own business processes and still stay coordinated with all their partners, suppliers, and customers in the ecosystem. As an aside, they can also choose which data to "attach" to their own blockchain entries for evidentiary purposes.

For example, a supplier may link a URL to the purchase order or to the freight forwarder's receipt for physical goods delivered in the course of a transaction, augmented with metadata such as timestamp and digital signature. This information may or may not be redundant, but in any case becomes part of the non-repudiable evidentiary record of transaction execution. The opportunity cost savings accruing to all involved supply chain participants by making this information available straightaway vs having to locate and corroborate it in exceptional situations (e.g. dispute resolution) is but a simple indication of the value proposition of the blockchain.

In short, it allows each and every economic agent to be proactive in promoting accountability and trust, thus elevating these attributes to prominent quality features of the entire ecosystem as a whole. They in turn provide the logical impetus for new economic agents to decide to join the ecosystem, setting in action a virtuous cycle of growth and trust.

The visibility of transactions on the blockchain promotes trust in the ecosystem in an indirect way as well: as proof of auditability. In the eyes of an auditor, the DL is a database of audit trails. Having permanent and non-repudiable records of which transaction step was concluded, by whom (even hidden behind an encrypted identifier), in which sequence, and with which attached information, in the course of which end-to-end collaborative process, is not simply useful. It is the necessary factual basis upon which further information requests can be justified and investigative correlations authorized on the way to corroborating pathologies and their root causes.

In short, the decentralized transaction validation and recording paradigm of the blockchain, despite the use of encryption, does not obfuscate but rather disseminate useful information. In doing so, it incentivizes good behaviour, not through the threat of reprisals but as a rational economic strategy. When mistakes occur, or when malicious actors violate expected norms of behaviour among prudent people of business, the same paradigm facilitates fact-finding for—initially—dispute resolution. In that respect, the operational time scales of the paradigm are important, as they correlate with those of information discovery. Of course, validating and synchronizing blocks on the blockchain does not happen instantly but is of the order of seconds or at most minutes. For transactions that are not time-critical below this scale (a counter-example would be high-frequency trading), the blockchain features of record finality and non-repudiability have already demonstrated its distinct advantages over more traditional paradigms. For example, in addressing three specific business problems:

(a) How to reduce the administrative costs of multi-agent, multi-transaction coordination. Such coordination would be exemplified, for instance, by asset-based securitization. The entire asset-based securities (ABS) value chain (from origination to asset ring-fencing to creation of special purpose vehicle, asset tranching, emission and allocation of securities, collateral management, asset servicing, all the way to redemption and potentially resecuritization) has been traditionally an area of administrative choreography, with no upside profit potential and lots of downside operational loss potential. The blockchain appears to be predestined to tackle the costs of such administrative tasks [24–26].

(b) How to reduce the time and cost of transferring title to stores of value among economic agents and across geographies. For instance, cross-border payments and remittances have traditionally incurred high fees [27, 28] and commissions, mostly to account for settlement risk. This is due largely to the time (of the order of days) needed to clear sequential transfers between process intermediaries while making the right bookings and foreign exchange conversions in their accounting systems. Using a blockchain avoids this risk, settling the transaction in a few transparent steps and in a matter of minutes[2] at most.

[2] The Bitcoin (BTC) Whitepaper [29] targeted, after all, a payments use case. Quoting verbatim from it: "A purely peer-to-peer version of electronic cash would allow online payments to be sent directly from one party to another without going through a financial institution.... The cost of mediation increases transaction costs, limiting the minimum practical transaction size and cutting off the possibility for small casual transactions,... What is needed is an electronic payment system ..., allowing any two willing parties to transact directly with each other without the need for a trusted third party..."

(c) How to facilitate price discovery of digital assets (resp. services) exchanged (resp. performed) only digitally. The underlying DL functions as a signalling mechanism of the prospects of specific types of transactions. Interested parties can validate that a market for some assets and services does indeed exist, estimate its descriptive statistics, and validate assumptions to assist their own product development and price discovery. In the absence of such an aggregating historical ledger, transactions in digital assets and services would be entered with at least one party ignoring actual needs and true depth of liquidity in the addressable market. In other words, the blockchain helps minimize information asymmetries [30] which have been proved to affect price discovery [31], especially when intermediaries are involved [32].

By reducing frictions in the lifecycle of assets and services, the blockchain has already helped change the cost point of transactions to such an extent that totally new digital assets and value chains became possible. New types of stores of value in the form of cryptocurrencies and tradable crypto-tokens (cf. Chap. 4) are representative of how this potential has already manifested itself.

Of course, decentralizing data keeping and decision-making not only liberates the creativity of economic agents to come up with new products, services, and value chains; it also creates a landscape of new risks that can be very difficult to control. For instance, each new set of business rules acting on a particular subset of the data visible on a blockchain creates risks of operational losses due to non-vetted data quality, algorithmic model miscalibration, errors in the code implementing the model, non-existent code documentation, etc. Similarly, each new value chain being formed creates the need for agreement on terms and conditions, due diligence on transaction participants and assets employed, verification of compliance with other process controls, mechanisms for dispute resolution and action verification, etc., to only name a few of the procedural risk controls. The absence of a central authority similar to the DBE owner/operator changes the risk profile for each and every participating agent. This is yet another area where the organizational paradigm enabled by the blockchain proves materially different from that of digital business ecosystems.[3] Thankfully, the same blockchain features (i.e. existence of an underlying DL, necessity of validating actions, and finality and non-repudiation of replicated records) that generate its business potential also help contain heightened risks.

[3]The corporate owner/operator of the generic DBE needs to be aware at all times of their sources of risk and can become liable when there are gaps in risk coverage, especially when products and services offered on the DBE are subject to consumer protection laws or to enhanced due diligence regulatory obligations. This is why introduction of new products or services, at least at corporates above SME size and cognizant of their legal and (actual or potential) regulatory obligations, typically involves internal controls. As an example, corporates offering financial services have invariably risk management frameworks mandating "New Business Approval", "New Product Approval", or "New Transaction Approval" processes before new financial instruments or services can be offered to clients.

As will be shown in subsequent chapters, blockchain-based ecosystem governance makes use of on-chain stores of value (tokens) to incentivize active participation of economic agents in risk management activities. For example, "risk management as a service" is promoted through financial rewards accruing to service-providing agents, based on governance-type utility tokens (cf. Sect 4.2.2). This service is meant to be bid for and performed competitively by otherwise disinterested parties (i.e. outside their interest in the financial reward). Ecosystem governance uses this "transactional pattern" (based on utility tokens) to maximize the breadth and effectiveness of risk management activities in the context of both idiosyncratic and ecosystem-wide ("systemic") risks.

To get a sense of the potential of the blockchain paradigm, one need actually look no further than the six meta-industrial basic factors of production as shown on Fig. 2.10. As will be demonstrated in the sequel of this book, the blockchain enables the creation and automated delivery of new fixed financial assets, digital services, data, and rights and allows to certify in a new, unambiguous, and non-repudiable manner the existence and quality attributes of tangible working assets, know-how, data and rights. It does so at time scales and cost points that would be impossible without the delegated decision-making made feasible by the concept of the decentralized ledger. In short, the blockchain allows to extend the typology of and reduce the cost point of employing, all basic factors of production.

It must not be forgotten that the blockchain is just a technological paradigm, a tool. What was explained in this section was its transformative potential when used specifically as business infrastructure. It was shown how it allows economic agents to self-organize into a digital business ecosystem where there is no privileged owner/operator, and where tasks of process governance and operational risk management are decentralized. This in effect ushers into life *a new paradigm of economic organization*, whereby factors of production can form controllable, prearranged, or ad hoc value chains with concrete economic outcomes.

2.3 Blockchain-Based Token Ecosystems

Economic agents of blockchain-based digital ecosystems take part in transactions in which assets, services, data, and rights are offered and consumed on-chain. And, even though it would be theoretically possible to keep costs down by letting agents simply barter with each other, such a marketplace strategy would be utterly counter-intuitive. The reasons are mainly the usual ones afflicting bartering systems, namely:

(a) Need for double coincidence of wants.
(b) Indivisibility of assets, data, and rights.
(c) Absence of common measures of value.
(d) Extreme difficulty to calculate and collect value-added tax.
(e) Impediments to specialization.
(f) Impediments to economies of scale.

but also additional ones, stemming from operational repercussions unique to digital ecosystems, such as:

(g) Information asymmetries due to lack of standardization.
(h) Impossibility of creating generic ratings scales to rank offerings and counterparties.
(i) Near impossibility of using domain-agnostic information models as registers of trust.
(j) Impossibility of claiming partial refunds to compensate for quality defects in deliverables.
(k) Need for double coincidence of wants *also in restitution.*
(l) No logic in returning digital services, assets, and rights *once they have been used.*

In short, the existence of a *medium of exchange* and a *unit of account* is even more critical in digital ecosystems than in physical ones. It can be argued that having a *store of value* is also very important (though not as critical for many point-in-time transactions), as the time element introduces the need for a measure of value discounting, which is indispensable for price comparisons. If the ecosystem intends to facilitate transactions in physical and financial assets as well, then all three functions are indispensable.

This is where the notion of "tokens" comes into play. Tokens (explained in more detail in Chap. 4) are digital representations of value, which are issued and/or accepted for value on blockchain-based ecosystems. They can assume the role of media of exchange *and* units of account if the rules of the ecosystem so provide.

For the purposes of the current chapter, the important information is that blockchain enables the creation of digital values in relation to which assets, services, data, and rights can be priced. These are the blockchain-ecosystem tokens. Having them solves the problems of price formation, price discovery, counterparty discovery, creation of accountability and trust metrics, and long-term storage of value. Being digital information objects, they can be part of DL entries, hence their transfer can be recorded through on-blockchain transactions among economic agents. Hence, token usage (to pay for assets, services, etc.) also inherits the attributes of transaction finality and non-repudiation.

Through the use of tokens, ecosystem "assets" can now include also on-chain representations of off-chain—i.e. physical world—tangible working assets and financial assets (both depicted on Fig. 2.16). The reason is that their imputed off-chain repercussions—in terms of, e.g. taxes, fees, charges, accounting—on transaction participants can also be accommodated by reference to tokens, assuming that a mechanism for the latter's convertibility to off-chain value (e.g. to fiat currency and back) exists.

With each transaction step recorded on the DL, data about token amounts, exchange sequences and timestamps, references to counterparties, etc., can be used to piece together all information that is needed to create (and, if needed, reconstruct) the ecosystem's ledger of accountability and trust.

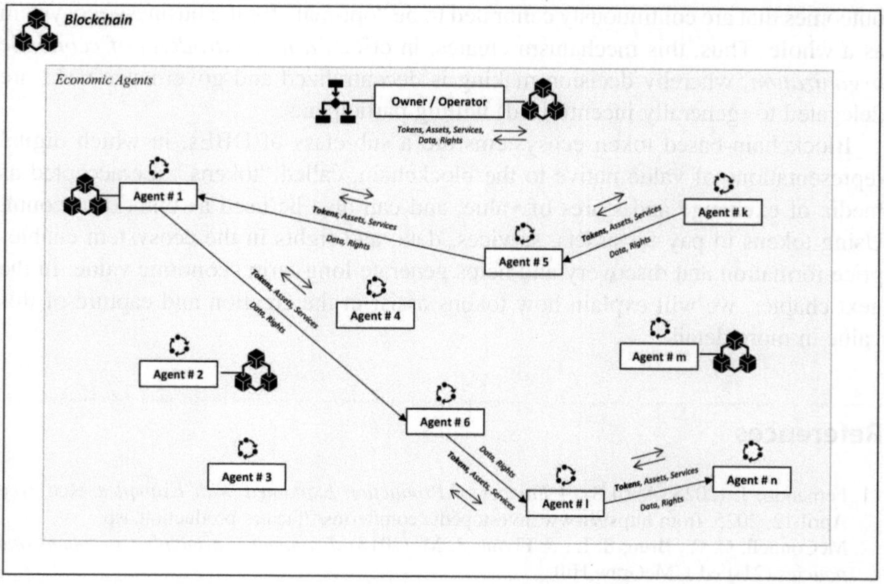

Fig. 2.16 Agent-to-Agent interactions in blockchain-based Token ecosystems. On each interaction step, tokens are potentially exchanged for assets, services, data, rights, or other tokens

We will distinguish blockchain-based token ecosystems from non-token ones (i.e. from DBEs that are blockchain-based but admit no tokens covering at least the two roles of media of exchange and stores of value). The rest of this book will concern itself only with the former and will make this fact explicit wherever needed.

2.4 Summary

In summary, the blockchain can be regarded as a specific kind of technical infrastructure used to create a digital business ecosystem (DBE). It has the concept of "Distributed Ledger" at its core, using a consensus mechanism among a critical mass of validating nodes to ensure transaction finality and non-repudiation. The resulting technical construct can act both as a system of record and as a state machine for DBEs.

Taken together, these functionalities enable technical workflows through which coordination of action among economic agents can be achieved. Decision-making, transaction execution, risk management, exception handling, governance, and information feedback are all delegated to each and every economic agent willing to take part in prearranged, or ad hoc, value chains. The DL of the blockchain becomes the business ecosystem's ledger of accountability and trust, whereupon ecosystem participants can make decisions about how to allocate their own resources, how to create and exchange assets, services, capital, and information, and how best to create and take part in complete value chains. It thus creates the potential for economic outcomes that are continuously calibrated to be "optimal" for the business ecosystem as a whole. Thus, this mechanism creates, in effect, *a new paradigm of economic organization*, whereby decision-making is decentralized and governance tasks are delegated to (generally incentivized) willing participants.

Blockchain-based token ecosystems are a sub-class of DBEs, in which digital representations of value native to the blockchain, called "tokens", are accepted as media of exchange and stores of value, and can also be used as units of account. Using tokens to pay for assets, services, data, and rights in the ecosystem enables price formation and discovery and helps generate long-term economic value. In the next chapter, we will explain how tokens assist in the creation and capture of this value in more detail.

References

1. Fernando, J. (2025, April 8). *4 Factors of Production Explained With Examples*. Retrieved April 12, 2025, from https://www.investopedia.com/terms/f/factors-production.asp
2. McConnell, C. R., Brue, S. L., & Flynn, S. M. (2018). *Economics; principles, problems and policies* (21st ed.). McGraw Hill.
3. Factors of production. (2025, February 26). In *Wikipedia*. Retrieved March 17, 2025, from https://en.wikipedia.org/wiki/Factors_of_production
4. Menegaki, A. N. (Ed.). (2018). *The economics and econometrics of the energy-growth nexus*. Academic Press.
5. [Example: YouTube] How YouTube Works. Retrieved March 17, 2025, from https://www.youtube.com/howyoutubeworks/.
6. OECD, Paris. (2015). *The Impact of R&D Investment on Economic Performance: A Review of the Econometric Evidence*. Retrieved March 17, 2025, from https://one.oecd.org/document/DSTI/EAS/STP/NESTI(2015)8/en/pdf
7. European Union. (2007). *Digital business ecosystems*. Publications office of the European Union. https://op.europa.eu/en/publication-detail/-/publication/53e45e55-4bd2-42a4-ad25-27b339b051e0/language-en
8. Dietz, M., Khan, H., & Rab, I. (2020, August 7). How do companies create value from digital ecosystems? *McKinsey Digital*. https://www.mckinsey.com/business-functions/mckinsey-digital/our-insights/how-do-companies-create-value-from-digital-ecosystems
9. [Ecosystem example: Etsy] *About Etsy*. Retrieved April 3, 2025., from https://www.etsy.com/about
10. [Ecosystem example: Amazon] Amazon FBA: Fulfillment services for your ecommerce business. Retrieved April 3, 2025, from https://sell.amazon.com/fulfillment-by-amazon.
11. [Ecosystem example: Alibaba] About Alibaba.com. Retrieved April 3, 2025, from https://activities.alibaba.com/alibaba/following-about-alibaba.php.
12. Kenton, W. (2024, June 24). *B2C: How Business-to-Consumer Sales Works, Types, and Examples*. Retrieved March 17, 2025, from https://www.investopedia.com/terms/b/btoc.asp
13. Chen, J. (2024, May 10). *Business-to-Business (B2B): What It Is and How It's Used*. Retrieved March 17, 2025, from https://www.investopedia.com/terms/b/btob.asp
14. Agent (economics). (2024, September 6). In *Wikipedia*. Retrieved March 17, 2025, from https://en.wikipedia.org/wiki/Agent_(economics)
15. *New Palgrave Dictionary of Economics* (3rd ed.). Palgrave Mcmillan (2018), p. 107, p. 114.
16. Theory of the firm. (2025, February 18). In *Wikipedia*. Retrieved April 3, 2025, from https://en.wikipedia.org/wiki/Theory_of_the_firm

17. Williamson, O. E. (2002). Theory of the firm as governance structure: From choice to contract. *Journal of Economic Perspectives, 16*(3), 171–195. Retrieved March 17, 2025, from https://www.aeaweb.org/articles?id=10.1257/089533002760278776
18. McAfee, A., & Brynjolfsson, E. (2017). *Machine, platform, crowd: Harnessing our digital future*. W.W. Norton.
19. Finite-state machine. (2024, December 9). In *Wikipedia*. Retrieved March 17, 2025, from https://en.wikipedia.org/wiki/Finite-state_machine
20. Business rule. (2023, December 11). In *Wikipedia*. Retrieved March 17, 2025, from https://en.wikipedia.org/wiki/Business_rule
21. Business rule management system. (2024, August 31). In *Wikipedia*. Retrieved March 17, 2025, from https://en.wikipedia.org/wiki/Business_rule_management_system
22. Graham, I. (2007). *Business rules management and service oriented architecture: A pattern language*. Wiley.
23. Open source. (2025, March 13). In *Wikipedia*. Retrieved March 17, 2025, from https://en.wikipedia.org/wiki/Open_source
24. (2020, March 11). *Figure Achieves Breakthrough With Completion of First Asset-Backed Securitization on Blockchain, Generating Over 100 Basis Points of Savings*. businesswire. Retrieved March 17, 2025, from https://www.businesswire.com/news/home/20200311005452/en/Figure-Achieves-Breakthrough-With-Completion-of-First-Asset-Backed-Securitization-on-Blockchain-Generating-Over-100-Basis-Points-of-Savings
25. (2019, February 22). *What Blockchain Could Mean For Structured Finance*. S&P Global. Retrieved March 17, 2025, from https://www.spglobal.com/en/research-insights/articles/what-blockchain-could-mean-for-structured-finance
26. Pan, W., & Qiu, M. (2020). Application of Blockchain in Asset-Backed Securitization. *2020 IEEE 6th Intl Conference on Big Data Security on Cloud (BigDataSecurity), IEEE Intl Conference on High Performance and Smart Computing, (HPSC) and IEEE Intl Conference on Intelligent Data and Security*, 71–76. Available at https://ieeexplore.ieee.org/document/9123058 and https://www.semanticscholar.org/paper/Application-of-Blockchain-in-Asset-Backed-Pan-Qiu/7b3325afb26700d83eec165845506a5620b67da2
27. Käärmann, K. (2021, May 5). Ending remittance hidden fees: the international community calls for action. *Worldbank*. Retrieved March 17, 2025, from https://blogs.worldbank.org/peoplemove/ending-remittance-hidden-fees-international-community-calls-action
28. Bank for International Settlements. (2018). *Cross-border retail payments*. BIS, Committee on Payments and Market Infrastructures. Retrieved March 17, 2025, from https://www.bis.org/cpmi/publ/d173.pdf
29. [Bitcoin (BTC) Whitepaper] Nakamoto, S. *Bitcoin: A Peer-to-Peer Electronic Cash System*. Retrieved March 27, 2025, from https://bitcoin.org/bitcoin.pdf
30. Leshno, J., & Pradelski, B. (2019, January 28). The Importance of Memory for Price Discovery in Decentralized Markets. Retrieved March 17, 2025, from https://doi.org/10.2139/ssrn.3057554
31. De Jong, F., Mahieu, R., Schotman, P., & Van Leeuwen, I. (1999). Price Discovery on Foreign Exchange Markets with Differentially Informed Traders. *Tinbergen Institute Discussion Papers 99-032/2*, Tinbergen Institute. Retrieved March 17, 2025, from https://ideas.repec.org/p/tin/wpaper/19990032.html. Please note: updated (2001) version available at http://faculty.georgetown.edu/evansm1/NewMicro/Schotmanetalpricediscovery.pdf
32. Osler, C. L., Menkhoff, L., & Mende, A. (2007). Price Discovery in Currency Markets. *Currency Markets, EFA 2006 Zurich Meetings*. Retrieved March 17, 2025, from SSRN: https://ssrn.com/abstract=890774

Economic Value Creation in Token Ecosystems

3

Blockchain-based token ecosystems were explained in Chap. 2 as representing a new paradigm for organizing all factors of production that are relevant in the digital age. In principle, they are multi-sided Agent-to-Agent ("A2A") marketplaces, where tokens play at least the roles of media of exchange and stores of value. The present chapter has two immediate objectives: to demonstrate how these ecosystems create economic value for their participants, above and beyond what is feasible in non-blockchain ones; and to explain the role of tokens in facilitating and ultimately capturing this added value.

Indirectly, this will also be a foundational chapter on which to base a token taxonomy (in Sect. 4.1) and to rationalize the factors of token design (in Sect. 10.5). The ultimate goal is to equip the reader with the requisite knowledge and a robust methodology to enable them to answer the important questions of token valuation, namely: Is there an intrinsic value in a particular cryptocurrency or tradable crypto-token? Where does it come from, and how can it be assessed?

3.1 Value-Creation Processes in Blockchain-Based Token Ecosystems

To explain value creation in a blockchain context it is expedient to begin with a simple explanation of what economic life in such an ecosystem consists of. As explained in the previous chapter, blockchain-based ecosystems represent an Agent-to-Agent transactional paradigm.

Economic agents must be explicitly accepted as ecosystem members as a precondition for their blockchain transactions to be valid, i.e. they must be **"onboarded"**.[1] That is, there needs to be a vetting process, whereby the new prospective participant

[1] Also in "permissionless" ecosystems, once tokens need to be transacted with, a wallet needs to be connected with a pair of valid public/private blockchain keys.

I. Giannakouros, *Cryptocurrencies and Tradable Crypto-Tokens*, Future of Business and Finance, https://doi.org/10.1007/978-3-031-98423-5_3

submits appropriate credentials, for due diligence to be performed thereupon by some designated ecosystem agent. The latter is entrusted with a duty and must thus be given the authority and resources necessary to discharge it. If not discharged properly, malicious actors may obtain access to other agents' credentials and resources; be allowed to take part in transactions which they will not honour; or engage in fraud and even in financial crime. Hence, due diligence is a serious task which must be performed thoroughly. It is a service; its provider has the right to expect to be fairly compensated for the technical infrastructure employed and for the opportunity cost of its allocated resources.

Once onboarded, each new participant needs to be *made visible through their identifying data and through their offerings*. They must have working assets, services, know-how, data, or rights that other ecosystem participants can use. If their working assets on offer are tangible (e.g. quantities of raw materials, other inventory items, semi-finished or finished goods), then they must be represented in some form on the blockchain before they can be transacted upon. If their working assets are intangible, but still originate outside the blockchain, the same need arises; whereas if they are first created on the blockchain then they need to be "joined" by a description of what their features are, the property rights that are transferred with them, and any other data or metadata needed to facilitate their discovery by prospective buyers. Services, know-how, data, or rights offerings must similarly be made blockchain-compatible, either by registering them on an ecosystem catalogue or by making blockchain-compatible description and consumption interfaces available. There need to be descriptions of what the services, know-how, etc., are; how much they cost, against which media of exchange, assets, or services; and how they are to be delivered or consumed. All these preconditions represent business tasks that must have been performed by technical means and potentially human resources before the new participant can start participating in transactions.

Bilateral transactions need to be risk-managed by both sides and possibly also by the ecosystem as a whole. Counterparty due diligence, transaction negotiation, price discovery, bilateral funding and credit controls, transaction structuring, contractual binding and documentation, transaction execution (exchange of agreed assets/services/data/rights for funds), exception handling, dispute resolution, etc., are all process steps that must be ultimately visible on the blockchain. If this is not the case, then there will be no possibility to have business rules; no audit trails; and no evidentiary records for dispute resolution. Remember, the blockchain is the technical infrastructure underlying the records; and the state machine of the ecosystem. Apart from its DL, there is to be no other common ledger shared among participating economic agents, no other mechanism to register outcomes and reconstruct past actions with. All the aforementioned steps (i.e. from due diligence to dispute resolution) can be either *simply registered*—i.e. essentially their outcomes—on the blockchain, or also *fully executed* as services on it. The latter would e.g. be the case if an economic agent were to provide "due diligence as a service" to the entire ecosystem. Interested parties would submit the identifying information about a prospective counterparty together with the "**aspects of interest**" (e.g. assets, credit history, transaction execution ratings, quality of service ratings, etc.) and receive the

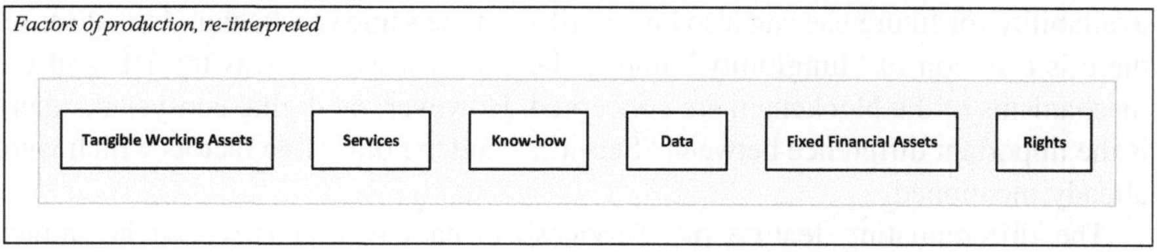

Fig. 3.1 Six basic factors of production in a meta-industrial socio-economic context

filled-in matrix of *aspect history and risk ratings* as per ecosystem records. Another economic agent might be offering a transaction insurance service, whereby applicants would submit all requested data about counterparties and transaction financials and would receive back insurance quotes and terms. The latter could be based on actuarial models (behavioural—and application-based) condensing both ecosystem, as well as off-ecosystem—e.g. provided through Oracles[2]—, transactional experience and funding costs for insurable risks. Such services, pertaining to bilateral transaction risks, must be performed through technical infrastructure and potentially human resources whose opportunity costs must be reasonably compensated.

There are many more practical points of agent-to-agent interactions on blockchain-based ecosystems, around for example supply chain formation, ad hoc participation, market making, etc. The intention is not to tire the reader with minutiae of what is obvious for any digital business ecosystem (DBE); it is rather to use the four aforementioned processes (onboarding, offering registration, transaction inception and execution) as examples of the same basic fact, namely that:

- All necessary process steps for economic agents to interact with each other can be thought of as *services* catalogued, recorded when executed, and having binding economic outcomes on the same blockchain.

Services that would usually be expected to be provided by, e.g. a centralized registry of companies, corporate credit rating agencies, insurance companies, market makers, etc. (whereupon humans exchange information, specify requests, give answers, and are available for clarifications), are now assumed to be obtainable through—otherwise disinterested—economic agents viewing and processing data on the same DL. These "new" service providers, once registered and "certified" on the blockchain, *need no longer be human*; they can be purely technology-based ("algorithmic") or at least mixed technology/human based, in the latter case humans potentially playing only a small part for decision-making—e.g. in exceptional situations. This is one of the reasons for reinterpreting the basic factors of production in a meta-industrial context as we did in the previous chapter (cf. Fig. 3.1 below, repeated for reading convenience).

Please note that the fact of having employed any one of the six factors in transactions can be recorded on the blockchain. Their specific attributes and

[2]Trusted providers of off- or of combined on–/off-chain data. This functionality is explained in Sect. 6.4.

availability for future use can also be recorded on the same blockchain. In that sense, there is a notion of "fungibility" among the six, at least as far as the DL and the mechanisms of the blockchain are concerned. However, on digital ecosystems there is the important difference between "Services" and the other five factors which were already mentioned.

The differentiating feature of "Services" is namely that they can be almost exclusively technology-based (i.e. provided with practically no human intervention outside their initial configuration), while still leaving a valid, complete, transparent, audit trail recorded on the blockchain.

Of course, services have a price, which represents their use of resources, sophistication of underlying knowledge, absence of alternatives, cost of funds, etc., depending on the case; this price can be *also* quoted on the blockchain—as a separate service. They can be accessed, consumed, validated, and rated—all on the blockchain. The fundamental attributes of the DL (consensus, transaction finality, and non-repudiation) ensure the transparency of services usage and quality-of-service attributes to all economic agents in the same blockchain ecosystem. Any interested party can thus decide for them if the price is fair, if the outcome is as expected, or, if not, if there is indeed the potential for another agent to provide the same service on better terms. Blockchain is transparency, and transparency uncovers inefficiencies. Removing inefficiencies is the essence of competition.

Importantly, when viewed as a cooperative competition paradigm, the underlying *consensus mechanism* acting on DL submissions is error correcting for the entire ecosystem; it is a quality assurance guarantor per se. On the other hand, when viewed as a blockchain-based *services enabler*, it helps address two important problems of economic organization, namely:

(a) *Agency* [1, 2]
(b) *Economic rents* [3, 4]

The agency-relating argument becomes clear by considering that blockchain-native services can be solely technology-based, with transparent execution logic, outcomes, and pricing. As long as a service can be automated, then any conflicts of interest will be discovered by analysing the algorithmic logic of the automation. Even when the service needs human calibration or intervention at critical decision nodes, the blockchain is able to register all inputs, intermediate states and outputs of the logical steps in the Service—and all of those state variables are in principle auditable. Should a service provider refuse to open their algorithmic logic to inspection, or to log calling inputs and resulting outputs for monitoring, then that is a fact that needs to be taken into account by prospective service consumers. The decentralized paradigm is by itself a strong disincentive for information hiding and biases, as on-chain services are always remunerated. In effect, having to pay for the execution and validation of a needed decentralized service, ecosystem participants are forced to act as informed consumers. Pricing data (raw or proxied) per service usage can also be registered on-chain so that any preferential treatment for particular counterparties or transactions can be exposed through analytics. Hence, services can

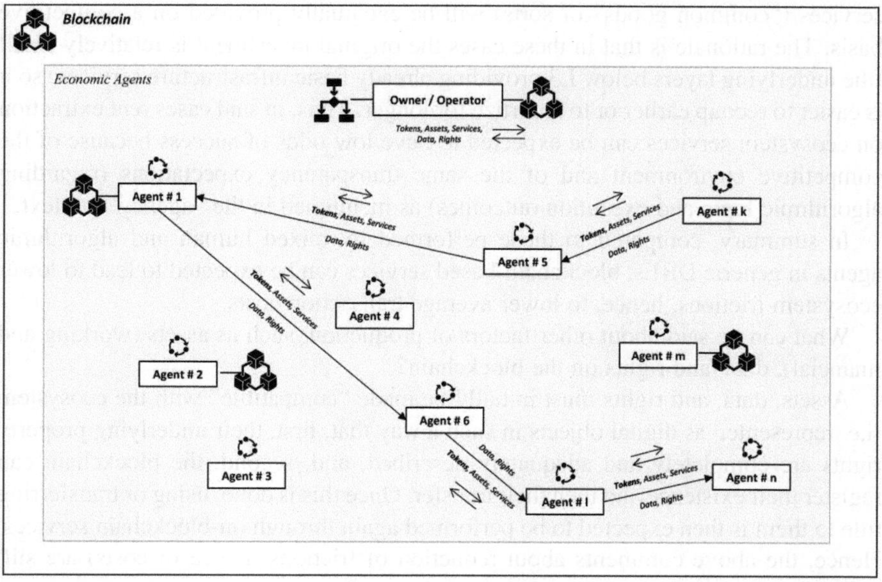

Fig. 3.2 Agent-to-Agent interactions in blockchain-based token ecosystems. On each interaction step, tokens are potentially exchanged for assets, services, data, rights, or other tokens

be expected to materially align with the intended outcomes, under the threat of third-party examination of their algorithmic logic (pre-execution) and of their operational data (post-execution), both being registered on the blockchain. In short, the agency problem of blockchain-based service provision[3] has a low probability of occurrence; and this is fundamentally because of the transparency afforded by the blockchain's DL.

The argument relating to economic rents can be justified only if there is de facto no privileged economic agent providing services on preferential terms. For example, as mentioned in the previous chapter, even in blockchain-based ecosystems there generally exists—at least in the initial implementation stages—a de facto "Owner/ Operator" (cf. Fig. 3.2, repeated here for convenience), assuming the costs of setting up the basic DLT infrastructure and thus having a vested interest in seeing this investment eventually recouped. They typically assume duties of coordination and at least facilitation of governance outcomes, but they may also choose to offer ring-fenced ecosystem services. That would be indeed a case of a privileged service provider, able to extract economic rent. However, in established ecosystems, and especially in blockchain layers L3/L4, it can be expected that even governance

[3] In reference to the "Principal-Agent" problem setup, we consciously choose not to answer here the legitimate question: "Is the Principal always clear on the Blockchain?" Services that can be thought to benefit the entire ecosystem (e.g. onboarding) are logically mandated by ecosystem governance. The features of the latter (its agents and mechanisms) are addressed in detail in Chaps. 6 and 8, wherein the above question is essentially answered.

services ("common goods" of sorts) will be eventually provided on a competitive basis. The rationale is that in these cases the original investment is relatively small (the underlying layers below L3 providing already basic infrastructure services) so it is easier to recoup earlier or to amortize for longer. Thus, in said cases rent extraction on ecosystem services can be expected to have low odds of success because of the competitive environment and of the same transparency expectations (regarding algorithmic logic and execution outcomes) as mentioned in the "agency" context.

In summary, compared to those performed by mixed human and algorithmic agents in generic DBEs, blockchain-based services can be expected to lead to lower ecosystem frictions, hence, to lower average transaction costs.

What can be said about other factors of production, such as assets (working and financial), data, and rights on the blockchain?

Assets, data, and rights must initially be made "compatible" with the ecosystem (i.e. represented as digital objects in such a way that, first, their underlying property rights are completely and adequately described, and, second, the blockchain can register their existence and then their transfer. Once this is done, using or transferring title to them is then expected to be performed again through on-blockchain services. Hence, the above comments about reduction of frictions (hence of costs) are still valid.

How do blockchain-based ecosystems influence the turnover and profit potential of their participants?

The answer is that there are some modalities of value addition that are shared among all DBEs, and others that are specific to blockchain-based ones. Also, not all business cases will have the same upside potential on the blockchain. In all generality, ecosystem participants can expect the blockchain as a platform to have distinctly positive effects on value creation through:

- Achieving network effects
- Enabling creation and price discovery of new asset classes and services
- Focusing liquidity into specific business cases
- Allowing fast creation of ad hoc value chains
- Facilitating signalling
- Remunerating the provision of platform services
- Creating direct feedback loops from the marketplace to ecosystem governance

The term "**Network effects**" refers to a pattern [5, 6], observed in several branches of engineering and economics, pursuant to which the value of participating as a node to a network of resources correlates superlinearly with the total number of interconnected nodes. The implication is that once a critical mass of participating nodes is reached then the value of network participation increases very rapidly. This creates strong incentives to become and remain connected ("stickiness" effect), locking the added value into the network. Having attained provable "network effects" is usually interpreted as an indication that the ecosystem of resources is economically self-sustainable. A particular superlinear correlation referred to in this context is "Metcalfe's law", which postulates a network value $V(n)$ scaling with the square of the number n of connected nodes:

$$V(n) \sim n^2, n \to \infty.$$

The important fact is that, apart from being theoretically expected, Metcalfe's law has also been proved empirically to hold true in blockchain-based token ecosystems [7, 8]. Of course, as the correlation holds only in the limit, there are threshold values that need to be crossed (in terms of number of nodes and rate of increase in new connections) before it can be significantly observed. What needs to be kept in mind is that this is a statistical correlation, valid only under assumptions. There are strong arguments as to why it can overstate and even understate the actual network value. For example, nodes may be once connected but then stay inactive; in which case the network value is less than predicted (that would be the case, e.g. if many service providers get onboarded but after some time stop transacting). Similarly, a node holding assets worth 1 token and another one with assets worth one million tokens are weighted equally under this correlation; in which case the network value is understated. In short, there are strong uniformity assumptions in the network model behind this equation, which may or may not hold true in actual ecosystems. Under these caveats, economic agents in blockchain-based token ecosystems can expect the value of their participation to increase strongly once network effects set in.

As the rapid evolution of ecosystems built around cryptocurrencies and asset tokens (such as non-fungible tokens—"NFT" for short[4]) can attest, the blockchain enables creation of entirely *new asset classes*. Ideas about how to package assets and income streams into value representations can have an immediate application in terms of tokens, as explained also in Sect. 3.2 below and in the following chapter). Cross-border transactions can be made cheaper and faster through new stores of value accepted as media of exchange; performing art licensing rights can be registered and their consumption tracked so that income flows directly back to the performing artists themselves; liquidity in alternative assets assumed to be illiquid in traditional finance can be freed before them vesting; new event-based payoff-risk profiles can be implemented in on-blockchain derivatives; asset servicing value chains simplified so that securitization thresholds are lowered; liquidity provision in digital marketplaces remunerated, etc., are but few examples of business needs addressed through novel blockchain-based asset classes. The underlying DL and its attributes of fast transaction finality and consensus-based acceptance have lowered the effective barriers to entry for service providers who would otherwise be constrained by geography or infrastructure costs. As blockchain-based ecosystems are multi-sided marketplaces, economic agents profit by being both suppliers and consumers of such new assets and services.

Price formation and discovery around new assets and services are also facilitated on account of the *business-case-focused* character of most token ecosystems. This means that only economic agents that are affine to a particular business use case, or at least to related value chains, are expected to transact in said assets and services. Having this affinity can be interpreted as a sign of specialized knowledge, and

[4]Please refer to Chap. 4 for detailed explanations of these terms.

indirectly as vested interest in the survival of the ecosystem. A culture of "coopetition" [9] among economic agents thus results, through which honest advice about the right features and price points of offerings is communicated through transaction ratings and direct feedback. As several token ecosystems also act as liquidity facilitators (through e.g. automated market makers allowing investors to fund specific token pools and even concentrated liquidity positions[5]) for their use cases, they act as direct "voting" mechanisms for the value proposition of tradable tokens. The combined effect of the above is the reduction of business development costs for suppliers and faster, informed fine-tuning of assets and services so as to better align to actual market needs and buyer cost expectations.

As was explained in the previous chapter, the DL underlying a blockchain plays the role of a collective ledger of accountability and trust which is constantly updated through informed consensus. Taken together with due diligence processes that are executed both at onboarding and as a result of transactional experience recorded in the ledger, there emerges a picture of up-to-date visibility on eligible counterparties afforded to blockchain-ecosystem participants. Simply put, economic agents can discover quickly which other agents offer which assets, services, know-how, and rights; also, what has been the average corresponding rating on them, hence the probable risk profile as per past experience across the ecosystem. Hence, creation of *ad hoc value chains* is possible both through bilateral steps and through a coordinating agent who is so willed. This was the basis for postulating a "new paradigm of economic organization" in the previous chapter. Blockchain-based ecosystems facilitate initiatives for collective value creation by using already existing, ecosystem-internal, information to minimize the risk of transactional frictions while responding to evolving market needs. It must be noted that for "repeat" value chains (i.e. mature value chains with participants already trusting each other from past transactional experience) the blockchain advantage may prove to be marginal relative to generic DBEs. It is rather the case of new products and services, or of bespoke requests for chaining them into a new sequence of deliverables, that pertains to the "ad hoc" value chain proposition. The more difficult to achieve a demanding end-to-end deliverable; the more unfamiliar the territory in terms of process steps and potential co-participants; the higher the contribution to the added value of each chain participant can be expected to be; then the higher the total added value available for redistribution at transaction completion will be. This is the operating point where blockchain-based ecosystems can make a distinct difference in total added value.

"**Signalling**" is a notion from economics [10–13] postulating that a party holding asymmetric information in a marketplace can facilitate a transaction if they can send "signals" indicating the existence of this information to prospective counterparties. An example would be the "dividend signalling" [14] effect, whereby the marketplace is the stock market and the signal is the increase in stock dividend announced

[5]Please refer to Sect. 12.2 for a detailed explanation of how such automated market makers function.

by a company's management. This increase can be interpreted as an indication of the management's certainty about future company earnings growth, hence about an increase in the company's share price. Hence, the signal is the dividend increase and the intended transaction is investing in the company's shares.

In the case of token ecosystems, agents can create signalling effects in several ways. One is through the provision of particular assets and services; another is through quality assurance. As an example of the former case, the more sophisticated the algorithm behind a service is, or the higher the average rating the service receives, the more incentive it generates for new prospective consumers. In the latter case, if a service provider invests e.g. in a bug-bounty program,[6] then this is a signal that their offering is expected to be of high quality. In the same vein, the creator of a new token type may opt for more robust and operationally expensive token designs (cf. Chap. 10)—for example using a supporting token model or high overcollateralization—to signal that their new token will have reduced downside price risk. Regular token audits by certified audit providers are also a way for the token project to convey the information to prospective buyers that assets or services are correctly built into their token as per its design.

Agents profit also from signalling effects generated by ecosystem governance. If the owner/operator incentivizes active cooperation in strategic and operational decision-making (through e.g. rewards to active utility tokens—cf. Sect. 4.2.2) then this is an indication of striving to create a robust ecosystem community. Well-managed fine-tunings of the end-to-end economic design of the ecosystem create trust in the sustainability of its native tokens as well. Funding technical improvements to increase transaction scalability, thus reducing latency and/or costs, lead to similar effects. In all those cases, the signal is the investment in feedback mechanisms from economic agents to the ecosystem governance and in subsequent corrective actions; the intended outcome is the proliferation of transactions in the ecosystem and the preservation of the value of its tokens.

Several operational functions in DBEs are of a quasi-administrative nature. Due diligence services, for example, are preconditions for acquisition and retaining of access to ecosystem transactions by any individual economic agent. Their performance increases the value for the entire ecosystem by either enabling it to reach network effects or by identifying and removing counterparty risks. Such functions can be thought of as "public goods" [15] which could be argued to be candidates for remuneration through some form of taxation at the ecosystem level. Blockchain ecosystems facilitate a "privatization" pattern, whereby ecosystem participants who are willing to undertake such "utility functions" can draw extra income by taking them on as "delegated subcontractors" of sorts. In this pattern, ecosystem governance is willing to *delegate and remunerate the execution of utility functions* by disinterested economic agents, as long as their costs and quality of outcomes are controllable.

[6] I.e. financially rewarding third-parties in the ecosystem to search for, and correct, defects in the source code implementing part of the service.

Taking the pattern further, even functions that would usually qualify as "government prerogatives", such as enforcement of rules, allocation of platform resources, decisions about infrastructure investments, etc., could be similarly "privatized" if a given cost/performance ratio could be ensured. Blockchain-based ecosystems have precisely those in-built mechanisms (decentralized, consensus-based validation of outcomes, finality, and non-repudiation of records on a DL) that help cross-validate work performance, quality of outcomes, and cost appropriateness. They thus can and do create potential for income stream accruing to economic agents willing to undertake "utility functions". In other words, there is the possibility for economic agents to be active on a blockchain-based ecosystem solely as providers of utility services. How they are rewarded, in reference to the value directly or indirectly created through them, is a subject introduced through Sect. 3.2 below and expanded on further in Chaps. 4 and 10.

Are there any negative effects of blockchain-based ecosystems for their participants?

As in any DBE, there are generic business and operational risks which need to be managed at the level of the individual economic agent. However, blockchain-based ecosystems may have idiosyncratic risks that also need mentioning, namely:

(a) Liquidity and investment risk
(b) Lack of transaction scalability
(c) Lock-in risk
(d) Lack of interoperability

Onboarding an ecosystem which has not yet reached network effects is a business risk, especially if the economic agent intends to act as a liquidity provider. Even if this is not the case, the necessary investments in terms of technological and process alignment should be weighed against the risk that they may never be fully recouped. Prospective participants who are incentivized in some way by the owner/operator or incumbent members (e.g. for hosting a blockchain validation node in return for rewards-participation tokens, or for undertaking specific and funded tasks along the incumbent members' value chains) may be able to net incentives against sunk costs. If the economic agent intends to simply use or invest into the ecosystem tokens, with no expectation of asset or services provision to other participants, then their risks can be managed in ways similar to those of any transaction or investment with the same tenor. There are different considerations depending on the risk aspects in focus (settlement, liquidity, investment), the asset-holding horizon, etc. However, the best precondition for *liquidity and investment risk* minimization is for the economic agent to join a mature ecosystem which has already proved the sustainability of its use case on the blockchain.

Not all blockchains sustain high throughput rates (number of transactions per second). As L-1 layer technology matures and as L-2 protocols add robust scalability solutions to accommodate Web3 needs, it can be expected that the blockchain as platform infrastructure will eventually achieve high *transaction scalability*. Until that point is reached, however, both suppliers and consumers of ecosystem assets and services must be cognizant of the fact that there may be technical barriers to achieving their expected volume of business. If their functional envelopes can be served below these barriers, then there is no risk to manage. If not, then their business case for ecosystem participation may have to be reviewed.

Being part of a successful ecosystem which has achieved network effects tends to create a tacit "barrier to exit" which may or may not be a risk depending on the case. If this ecosystem keeps attracting high-quality offerings and directs resources towards upgrading its infrastructure to align with market demand, then its participants can only profit. Otherwise, a "**lock-in risk**" situation results for economic agents who have already invested heavily in their participation. If this is their only sales channel, or if they are otherwise constrained by geography or other factors to reach a market of a similar size, then this is a risk that must be managed.

Lack of *interoperability* among blockchain platforms is a problem afflicting the first generation of token ecosystems and its solution has been identified as critical [16, 17] before large-scale systemic investments in this area can proceed. Several second-generation blockchains (such as Cosmos [18] and Polkadot [19]) have invested heavily in interoperability, and the problem for economic agents may be one of simply being aware of technical developments before investing in any specific platform. This may also not be a risk as long as ecosystem participants are prepared to focus their investment on a single token ecosystem, even though they may thus be sacrificing market expansion potential.

Summarizing the above, blockchain-based token ecosystems enable value creation in ways beyond those available in generic DBEs. They reduce frictions of economic life by alleviating the principal-agency problem and exposing economic rents, thus lowering the average cost of transactions among economic agents. They generate potential for significant added value through creation and price discovery of totally new asset classes and services, liquidity focusing, ad hoc value chains and network effects, while providing direct feedback loops from the marketplace to ecosystem governance for corrective action. As long as their distinct operational and business risks can be properly managed, they allow each and every participant to profit from network effects. These are the salient points of value creation in said ecosystems.

3.2 The Role of Tokens

Having explained the value-creation processes in blockchain-based ecosystems, it is necessary to also explain the role of their tokens. It must be made clear that the blockchain as technical infrastructure per se does not presuppose the existence of tokens. If economic agents are comfortable with using the platform only as keeper of the DL and as enforcer of process state machines, then on-chain tokens are not needed as long as it is clear to all participants how platform costs are to be funded. That said, it is a fact that the first operational blockchain (2009 - Bitcoin [20–22]) was designed to be specifically a token creation and exchange infrastructure. The largest (by either market capitalization [23] or revenue [24]) blockchain-related

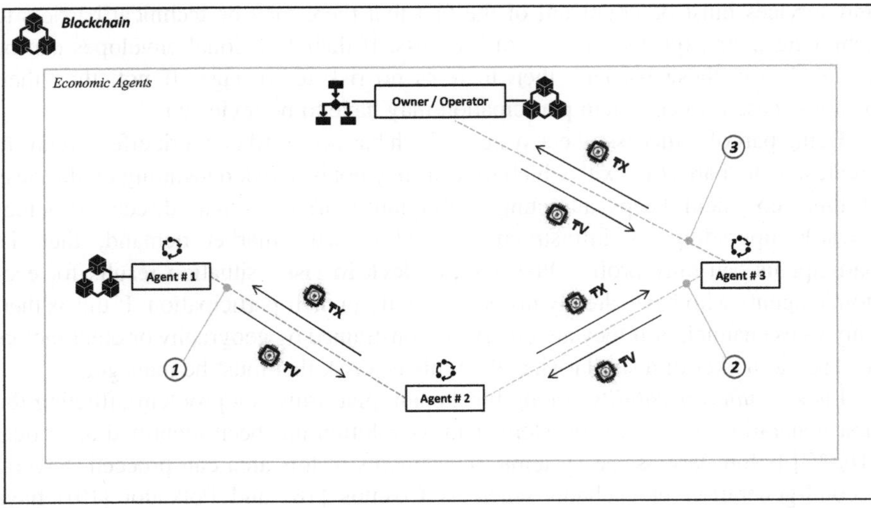

Fig. 3.3 Exchange and value tokens in transactions

DBEs are token ecosystems. Hence, it can be argued that tokens were the reason for the creation of blockchains in the first place and still the main reason for their proliferation.

The basis for the explanation will be again the model of Agent-to-Agent interactions, under the oversight of a blockchain owner/operator, as depicted on Fig. 3.2. Agents take part in bilateral transactions along multi-sided value chains, and the owner/operator can be either a simple transaction participant or the provider of infrastructure services. Value is created in the ecosystem because of new assets and services, organized value chains, and new participants (targeting network effects). Ecosystem governance, represented by the owner/operator, can delegate execution of "utility functions" to disinterested economic agents striving for compensation or benefits.

The main roles of tokens will be explained in reference to two high-level situations: one where the ecosystem governing body itself participates in asset or services transactions, and one where they use transactions to incentivize platform participation or extract platform fees.

The former is depicted schematically on Fig. 3.3. Three separate bilateral transactions are denoted by "1", "2", and "3". They are not necessarily related; they are only meant to typify representative interaction patterns. Three economic agents, #1, #2, #3, and the owner/operator are involved. Agents #1, #2, and #3 have already been onboarded, which in practical terms means that the entities (human, corporate) controlling them have been vetted, and were granted permissions to take part in particular kinds of transactions. The ecosystem identifier of each agent is their "blockchain address" (their "public key"), a string of characters and numbers that is unique on the particular blockchain. An agent transacting on the blockchain may be the digital representation of a single human or of a group of humans, or of a corporation; or it may be an automation, a piece of software. As long as their controlling entity[7] is known and has been vetted, an agent is the same as any other as far as the blockchain is concerned. The only thing that the blockchain needs to know to register transactions between agents is their ecosystem identifiers.

In transaction "1", economic agent #2 acquires an asset from agent #1. This asset has an intrinsic value and has already been represented on the blockchain through a token, registered as being owned by the identifier of #1. It may represent a working asset in whole, part of a working asset, a financial asset, a right to use a patent, an intellectual property right, etc. The value of the token comes from the value of the property right which it represents. It is understood that *transferring the token* between two agent identifiers on the blockchain *is equivalent* to *transferring ownership of the underlying asset* between their corresponding controlling entities. Hence, the token is an on-chain representation of economic substance "in being". We will call it "value token", denoted as "₸V" on the figure.

There may be more than one ₸V exchanged, but for the purposes of the example please accept that the information about quantity is secondary to that about type.

Still in "1", economic agent #2 compensates agent #1 by an amount of a different kind of tokens, "₸X", the purpose of which is to act as media of exchange in the ecosystem. I.e. when negotiating the transaction, agents #1 and #2 could exchange messages of the form "I believe that 1 ₸V is worth *K* ₸X", or "I am prepared to offer *N* ₸V for *M* ₸X", etc., knowing that ₸X are tokens that are by default accepted as media of exchange in transactions of this ecosystem. The role of these "exchange tokens" is very important, as they are the enablers of price discovery and of storage of value for later consumption. If they did not exist, only barter trade would be possible on the blockchain. Exchange tokens enable negotiation, price formation, investments, and, more fundamentally, competition. Their ownership by individual agents is registered on the blockchain by assignment to the corresponding ecosystem identifiers. *Subtracting an amount of exchange tokens* from the balance assigned to an agent identifier and *adding the same amount* to the balance *assigned to another* identifier is equivalent to *transferring ownership of this amount* between the corresponding agents.

In transaction "2", agent #2 purchases performance of a service from agent #3. The service can be provided immediately upon transaction conclusion, or at some point in the future. It can also be a "net service", in the sense of an exchange of services between the two agents with the one provided by #3 to #2 expected to have higher value than the opposite one. Examples of such services would be market making, insurance, securitization, etc. The evidence of either service performance, or of commitment for future service performance, is registered on the blockchain in the form of a token. *Transferring this token* from the identifier of agent #3 to that of #2 is understood to signify *request for completion, or commitment of future completion, of services* between the agents in the appropriate direction. Hence this token is again an

[7]In case of a group of humans or of a corporation, their authorized decision-makers; in case of software, the humans, groups of humans or corporates who own and have the right to use it.

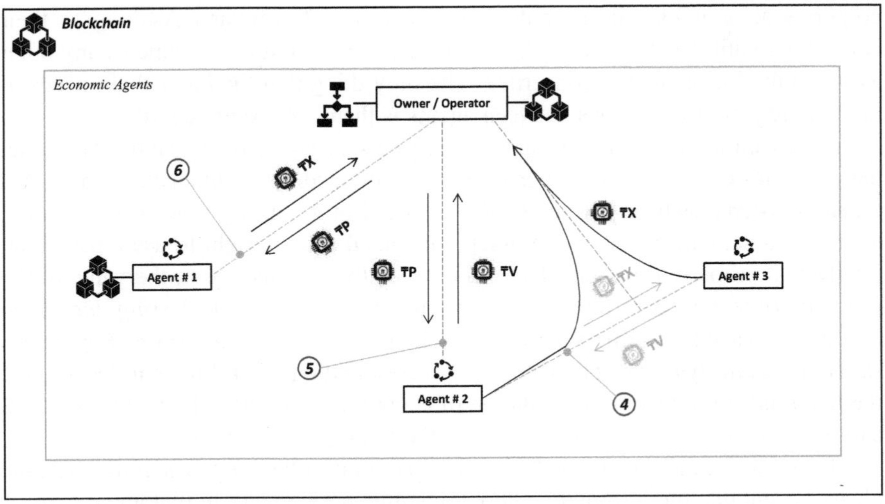

Fig. 3.4 Participation, exchange, and value tokens in transactions

on-chain representation of economic substance, but this time it is value "in action". It represents the value of services requested and performed or committed to be performed. It is also a "value token", again denoted by the same symbol "₸V" on the figure. Agent #2 compensates #3 by transferring an amount of the same exchange tokens ₸X (through the same pattern of subtracting/adding blockchain entries to the balances assigned to agent identifiers as in transaction "1"). Exchange tokens enable again price discovery (this time in the case of services) and storage of value for later consumption.

Still on Fig. 3.3, transaction "3" takes place between ecosystem governance and agent #3. The owner/operator also has an own ecosystem identifier (a "blockchain address") and in that respect is no different to other economic agents when it comes to bilateral "value-against" transactions. In this transaction, agent #3 uses an amount of exchange tokens ₸X to purchase assets or services from the governing entity. The latter are again in the form of "value tokens" "₸V". Their transfer signifies either outright transfer of underlying property rights, or request for completion, or commitment for future completion, of services performance.

Situations where ecosystem governance enters as a counterparty, but to a different kind of transactions, are depicted on Fig. 3.4. Three separate transactions are denoted by "4", "5", and "6".

Transaction "4" principally involves the swap of value tokens for exchange tokens between agents #2 and #3 (depicted through the greyed-out icons). All ecosystem transactions typically incur "platform fees", meant to compensate for the operational costs of the technical infrastructure and the administrative costs of governance tasks. Fee policy is set by ecosystem governance and typically mandates that said fee is payable in media of exchange that can be represented on the same blockchain, meaning the own exchange tokens. In all generality, both transaction counterparties owe these fees, hence the arrows starting from both agents #2 and #3 and converging towards the owner/operator. Platform fees are a steady income stream, which is aggregated into a "reserve pool" managed by the owner/operator. The growth of the reserve pool is correlated with the increase in the rate of transactions in the ecosystem, i.e. in effect with the increase in the number of active economic agents. Hence, it captures a large part of the appreciation in ecosystem value due to network effects. Indirectly (as transaction fees may be also prorated to transaction size), it also captures part of the appreciation of all assets registered in the ecosystem's DL, as well as the added value of services performed. Thus, the size of the reserve pool correlates with total ecosystem value.

In transaction "5", economic agent #2 performs, or accepts to perform, a "utility function" on behalf of ecosystem governance. The economic substance of this services value is passed to the owner/operator in the form of a value token. What agent #2 receives in return is not an exchange token, but a different kind of token which entitles the receiver to participate in the added value accruing to the platform through this service. The precise calculation to estimate this added value and the participation percentage is service specific. It is also possible that economic agents may be invited to bid to perform the service task in an auction, in which case token price ultimately depends on supply and demand. We call this a "participation token", denoted with "₸P" on the figure. The name is meant to signify participation in some form to an expected increase in value of the entire ecosystem. In this transaction, value addition is attributable to the performance of a "utility" task. An *amount of participation tokens* is *added to the balance assigned* to agent #2 on the DL. Depending on whether or not they were originally issued only for this transaction, they may or may not have to be subtracted from a balance assigned to a blockchain address of ecosystem governance.

Finally, in transaction "6", economic agent #1 in effect "buys into" the platform (as a short- or long-term investment) by swapping exchange tokens for participation tokens. This is the case, for example, when ecosystem governance chooses to enable participation in the growth of its "reserve pool" for a fee, as an incentive for agents to remain long-term in the ecosystem and to engage actively in decision-making on ecosystem direction and investments. In such a case, agent #1 sees this transaction as primarily an investment, whereas for the owner/operator, it serves two purposes: first, to increase the ecosystem's chances of reaching and retaining network effects, and second, to assure long-term feedback loops from marketplace to governance, in order for the latter to keep aligned with market needs and technological developments. In that sense, this transaction is an investment also for the governing body; namely, an investment into passive market intelligence and long-term knowledge management. For both ₸P and ₸X tokens, the *subtracting/adding entries in the DL are the same* as explained in previous transactions, with amounts appropriately assigned to the corresponding blockchain addresses.

In conclusion, tokens play three major roles in the value-creation processes of blockchain-based ecosystems: as exchange tokens, to enable price discovery, execution of transactions, and storage of value for later consumption; as value tokens, to capture the economic substance of assets represented (values "in being") and services exchanged (values "in action"); and as participation tokens, to incentivize taking part in governance tasks and to safeguard the value of network effects. These are the three pillars of the intrinsic value of blockchain-based ecosystem tokens.

Importantly, understanding these three roles is also the basis for rationalizing token valuation. The following Chap. 4 and especially the later Chap. 10 on token design will go into much more detail on the possible typologies and features of tokens, beyond the three high-level types explained here. Taken together, the previous section on value creation in blockchain-based ecosystems and the current one are meant to support one fundamental assertion, namely that:

- There is real economic life manifesting itself on blockchain-based ecosystems. Well-defined economic agents create and then exchange assets and services, data, rights, and know-how among themselves and with ecosystem governing bodies. In short, there is real economic *value* created in said ecosystems and robust ways to initiate and facilitate both its creation and growth. *Ecosystem tokens are precisely the means to create, express, and capture this economic value.*

3.3 Summary

Blockchain-based token ecosystems enable value creation in ways beyond those available in generic digital business ecosystems, through new asset classes and services, liquidity focusing, ad hoc value chains, and finally network effects. They reduce usual frictions of economic life by alleviating the principal-agency problem and by exposing economic rents, thus lowering the average cost of transactions among economic agents. They also incentivize direct feedback loops from the marketplace to ecosystem governance for corrective action towards ensuring its sustainability. As long as their distinct operational and business risks can be properly managed, they allow each and every participant to profit from net-positive network effects. The end result is preservation and growth of total ecosystem value.

Tokens play three major roles in the value-creation processes of blockchain-based ecosystems. They enable price discovery, execution of transactions, and storage of value for later consumption. They capture the economic substance of assets represented (values "in being") and services exchanged (values "in action") through the DL. They incentivize otherwise disinterested economic agents to take part in governance tasks and to safeguard the value of network effects. In short, tokens are the means to facilitate, quantify, and capture economic value creation and growth within their ecosystems.

Based on the notions explained in the present chapter, the following one will introduce a much more detailed token taxonomy.

References

1. Chen, C. (2025, April 5). *Agency Problem: Definition, Examples, and Ways To Minimize Risks*. Retrieved April 12, 2025, from https://www.investopedia.com/terms/a/agencyproblem.asp
2. (2018). *The New Palgrave Dictionary of Economics*, 3rd Ed., Palgrave Mcmillan. Referenced text to be found in p. 101.
3. Hays, A. (2023, September 1). *Economic Rent: Definition, Types, How It Works, and Example*. Retrieved March 1, 2025, from https://www.investopedia.com/terms/e/economicrent.asp
4. (2018). *The New Palgrave Dictionary of Economics*, 3rd Ed., Palgrave Mcmillan. Referenced text to be found in, p. 11522.
5. Network effect. (2025, January 22). In *Wikipedia*. Retrieved April 12, 2025, from https://en.wikipedia.org/wiki/Network_effect
6. Economides, N. (1996). The economics of networks. *International Journal of Industrial Organization, 14*, 675–699. https://doi.org/10.1016/0167-7187(96)01015-6
7. Alabi, K. (2017). Digital blockchain networks appear to be following Metcalfe's law. *Electronic Commerce Research and Applications, 24*, 23–29. https://doi.org/10.1016/j.elerap.2017.06.003
8. Alabi, K. (2020). A 2020 perspective on 'digital blockchain networks appear to be following Metcalfe's law'. *Electronic Commerce Research and Applications, 40*, 100939. https://doi.org/10.1016/j.elerap.2020.100939
9. Hays, A. (2022, March 25). *Coopetition Meaning, Benefits to Business, Example*. Retrieved March 1, 2025, from https://www.investopedia.com/terms/c/coopetition.asp
10. Signalling (economics). (2025, March 9). In *Wikipedia*. Retrieved April 3, 2025, from https://en.wikipedia.org/wiki/Signalling_(economics)
11. (2018). *The New Palgrave Dictionary of Economics*, 3rd Ed., Palgrave Mcmillan. Referenced text to be found in p. 12309.
12. Spence, M. (1973). Job Market Signaling. *Quarterly Journal of Economics, 87*(3), 355–374. https://doi.org/10.2307/1882010
13. Goldlücke, S., & Schmitz, P. W. (2014). Investments as signals of outside options. *Journal of Economic Theory, 150*, 683–708. https://doi.org/10.1016/j.jet.2013.12.001
14. Hays, A. (2022, August 29). *Dividend Signaling: Definition, Theory, Research, and Examples*. Retrieved March 1, 2025, from https://www.investopedia.com/terms/d/dividendsignaling.asp
15. Fernando, J. (2024, May 31). *What Are Public Goods? Definition, How They Work, and Example*. Retrieved March 1, 2025, from https://www.investopedia.com/terms/p/public-good.asp
16. World Economic Forum. (2021). *Defining Interoperability* [White paper]. Retrieved March 1, 2025, from https://www3.weforum.org/docs/WEF_Defining_Interoperability_2021.pdf
17. Johnson, M. (2022, January 3). Interoperability is fundamental to Blockchain's future. *International Banker*. Retrieved March 1, 2025, from https://internationalbanker.com/technology/interoperability-is-fundamental-to-blockchains-future/
18. [Cosmos Token ecosystem.] https://cosmos.network/
19. [Polkadot Token ecosystem.] https://polkadot.network/
20. Blockchain. (2025, March 7). In *Wikipedia*. Retrieved April 3, 2025, from https://en.wikipedia.org/wiki/Blockchain
21. Nakamoto, S. (2008). Bitcoin: A Peer-to-Peer Electronic Cash System. Retrieved March 1, 2025, from https://bitcoin.org/bitcoin.pdf
22. Tardi, C. (2024, May 8). *Genesis Block: Bitcoin Definition, Mysteries, and Secret Message*. Retrieved March 1, 2025, from https://www.investopedia.com/terms/g/genesis-block.asp
23. Cryptocurrency Market Data. Retrieved March 1, 2025, from https://www.slickcharts.com/currency
24. Johnston, M. *6 Biggest Blockchain Companies*. Retrieved March 1, 2025., from https://www.investopedia.com/10-biggest-blockchain-companies-5213784

Cryptocurrencies and Tradable Crypto-Tokens

4

In the previous chapters, we put forward the notion of the blockchain-based ecosystem as a new organizational paradigm of economic activity. In that context we explained tokens as having three roles: first, to enable price discovery, execution of transactions, and storage of value for later consumption; second, to capture the economic substance of assets represented (values "in being") and services exchanged (values "in action"); and third, to incentivize active participation in governance tasks so as to safeguard the value of network effects.

Those were indeed useful but rather generic fundamentals of economic design. They are not by themselves able to convey the richness and sophistication of actual working ecosystems where tokens are already demonstrating their effectiveness in carrying out their intended roles. For the purposes of introducing more detailed economic design blueprints, it is thus imperative to have an understanding of what has already been proved possible through tokens in actual business use cases. Such an understanding will then serve as the stepping stone to new token designs.

We thus propose to create an overview and glossary of the "token state of the art" by reference to individual use cases, accompanied with concrete examples and links to documentation. Apart from forming a reference for future chapters, the immediate outcome would be to justify our postulated distinction between "cryptocurrencies" and "tradable crypto-tokens".

4.1 Introduction to a Crypto-Token Typology

We begin by proposing some common terminology to be used throughout this and the remaining book chapters. Our definitions will not necessarily be the ones prevailing across the current trade literature, but it will be important to give clarity to notions while retaining logical consistency throughout.

The context of our *exposé* is that of blockchain-enabled ecosystems. So, there will exist a Distributed Ledger (DL) and a consensus mechanism assuring transaction finality (we will not distinguish between public/private, permissioned/

I. Giannakouros, *Cryptocurrencies and Tradable Crypto-Tokens*, Future of Business and Finance, https://doi.org/10.1007/978-3-031-98423-5_4

non-permissioned blockchains, nor among different consensus mechanisms ["Proof-of-<#>" [1]]). In this context, and in reference to a specific ecosystem of economic agents, we define[1] a "token" to be a blockchain-based digital representation of value, accepted in transactions within said ecosystem.

Is a token a form of money?

It can be designed as, but does not necessarily have, to be so. There are several observations to make in that regard. First, the generally accepted functions of "money" are its being a medium of exchange, a storage of value, and a unit of account. However, one can design a token in a particular ecosystem to be accessible as storage of value only but not be admissible as a medium of exchange (example: $FXS [2] in FRAX [3]). Second, "money" in which setting? If a token is "money" in one ecosystem, is it also "money" (meaning, is it admissible, convertible, or even exchangeable for goods and services transactions) in another ecosystem, which just happens to be the one which we are designing? There are tokens that are "money" in one ecosystem, and recognized as "reserve" currency, but not admissible for transactions in another (example, ETH in NexusMutual [4]). Third, a particular token type, non-fungible-token, is commonly used to represent unit rights in physical assets (works of art, etc.) or in intellectual property (music piece royalties, etc.). Could you use an NFT to pay for goods or services? Well, could you use a painting to pay a utilities bill? You probably could in the (improbable, but theoretically not impossible) event of your utilities company being a legally adventurous one, but even then you would not be using "money"—apart from the problem that keeping accounts denominated in paintings (the "unit of account" detail) would be an interesting task for any accountant.

Is a token a form of currency?

It can be designed as, but does not necessarily have, to be so. Formally speaking, a currency is a medium of exchange accepted as legal tender within a particular legal jurisdiction. It may or may not have an intrinsic value (be a commodity by itself) or be backed by a claim against this jurisdiction's official reserves of value, or simply by its credit. Drawing its value from its exchangeability with goods and services within this jurisdiction (and convertibility against media of exchange of other jurisdictions recognizing each other's legal systems), it can then be a store of value and a unit of account, i.e. money. However, the single most important characteristic is its close link (economic, legal) to a particular legal jurisdiction and, in human physical terms, a country. So, what is the legal jurisdiction of a blockchain-based ecosystem? Do its governance structures (as per market design, to be formally explained later in Chap. 6) provide for a legislative function at all? Do they provide for a dispute resolution and outcomes enforcement (judicial) function? Is the token of this ecosystem a claim against its governance structures, and, if so, in which form? This is a particularly important point from both a token-based

[1] An alternative definition (with common law contract terminology in mind) could be: "In reference to a specific ecosystem of economic agents, a 'Token' is a blockchain-based digital representation of value, accepted as consideration within said ecosystem."

ecosystem designer's and a token investor's point of view: if a token is indeed a medium of exchange within the ecosystem, it should be clearly specified:

- If it is *the single* acceptable, or only one of many possible admissible media of exchange, for all or only particular goods and services, within this ecosystem.
- If it otherwise represents a claim (in any form) against the governance body of the ecosystem or not.
- How is this claim practically enforceable within the ecosystem.

There are still other questions that need to be asked to clarify features which we tacitly expect in a "currency", even though they may not, strictly speaking, always be valid. For example, fungibility and denominations. In the physical (non-digital) world, one expects that a 1-EUR or 1-USD coin will be no different in its practical usage than any other 1-EUR or 1-USD coin in circulation. They are fungible. The same is tacitly expected from currency notes, i.e. a 100-EUR or 100-USD note should be fungible with others in circulation. However, please note the following points:

- A note has a serial number, a coin does not.
- All notes and coins must be "in circulation", i.e. not deprecated.
- Denominations in currencies exist for practical reasons and have withstood the test of time.

In principle, human jurisdictions do "mark" and "block" notes with particular serial numbers from being accepted in transactions. They can also use them to "follow" activities and owners (usually in the context of law enforcement). The transition from physical to electronic (commercial-bank account-based) money has partly obviated the need for this mechanism, however, the fact is that individual physical currency notes do have a distinct personality, which can be invoked at the discretion of their issuing jurisdiction, even though they are tacitly assumed to be fungible.

Currencies being "in-circulation" implies another prerogative of their issuing jurisdiction, that of empowering a single centrally controlled authority with managing all aspects of currency lifecycle. This authority can "introduce into", or "remove from", circulation entire generations of currencies as it sees fit. Such transitions are not always smoothly change-managed, as informed readers will surely know (citizens of some—physical—jurisdictions have found themselves sitting in long queues frantically trying to exchange "old" for "new" currency notes before a hastily imposed deadline). But what is the notion of a currency-issuing "centrally controlled authority" in a consensus-driven blockchain ecosystem?

Denominations are also tacitly assumed to be a medium of convenience (when large sums of money have to be physically transported, etc.) in a currency system. Can one expect denominations in a token? Well, what would be the purpose of denominations in a digital currency? A denomination can be both an enabling and a limiting factor. Even in the physical world, a denomination can be used to *restrict*, rather than enable, the usage of physical cash. For example, banks are perfectly entitled to *refuse* to exchange particular denominations of foreign currencies for their domestic equivalent as part of their anti-money-laundering controls. However, nothing technically precludes a token design admitting denominations.

In summary, a token can be designed, but it does not have, to be the currency of its ecosystem. Should this be the intention, token design will necessarily have to convincingly address questions of jurisdiction, enforceability, and transactionality. Many ecosystems have chosen their tokens to have the attributes of currency (and also of money), hence justifying the industry term "Cryptocurrency". Others have consciously opted for tokens that act only as representations of value but not as media of exchange. The point of departure in any token design should be an examination of its objectives so that its functions may emerge. Of course, the generic objective of all blockchain-based tokens is to incentivize the preservation and growth of their native ecosystems. However, it is the specific objectives of a particular token, viewed in the context of its business use cases, that act as drivers of function.

In some ecosystems, specific token objectives may include enabling transactions against goods and services and creating an observable parity rate against other tokens and fiat currencies. If the ecosystem is specialized in the supply chain of a particular commodity (say, a rare earth) which is otherwise scarce, then a buyer's need to invest in this supply chain is the incentive to hold the token. If the ecosystem is specialized in providing a particular service (e.g. insurance coverage of a particular risk) at a cost very competitive to that of other ecosystems, then a buyer's need to consume this service at low rates is the incentive to acquire the token.

Now suppose that the value (i.e. roughly, the product of demand and utility) of this particular service or commodity increases and is projected to increase still more. What will this mean for the native token?[2] Will its parity rate against other tokens and fiat currencies, that need to be exchanged to acquire it, increase? Will persistent buyers be willing to acquire and hold token quantities purely as a hedging tool against the risks of non-availability or appreciation? If said quantities start becoming material, will they also consider the token as a store of value and start including it in their accounting reports?

So, token objectives lead ultimately to token functions. In the aforementioned case, the specific[3] objectives to enable transactions and to represent value lead to all three functions of "money". Generalizing from the above example, the direct and indirect objectives of a "currency" token are to:

[2]The notion of "Commodity Currency" [5] is applicable in this case, and its relation to blockchain-based tokens will become apparent in Chap. 6.

[3]The general objective of ecosystem preservation and growth must not be forgotten, simply put temporarily in the background. There are known pathologies of "Commodity Currencies" [6] which can be found in token ecosystems as well.

1. Monetize the value proposition of the ecosystem (the economic purpose of providing the service or of supplying the commodity).
2. Enable all transactions (primary and ancillary) within the ecosystem.
3. Enable creation of a parity rate against other tokens and fiat currencies which will have to be exchanged in order to transact in the particular token within the ecosystem.
4. Incentivize foreign economic agents (i.e. those not yet participating in the ecosystem) to buy it, either because they need it as a medium of exchange or because they regard it as a compelling store of value.
5. Allow long-term investors to profit from appreciation in assets denominated in it.
6. Create a feedback mechanism for monitoring systemic risks (price stability, frictions, misallocation of resources, rent effects, concentration risk, treasury risk) of the ecosystem.
7. Allow comparisons with other token-based ecosystems towards recalibrating for higher competitiveness of its relative value proposition to the eyes of outside investors.

These are the objectives of issuing a generic "currency" token. There are, of course, specific ones for particular currency-token subcategories (e.g. Stablecoins and Central Bank Digital Currencies, etc.). We will expand on such taxonomies in due course, however for the time being, we respectfully suggest to the reader that the above list provides a reliable least common denominator across currency tokens.

What are the objectives of "non-currency" tokens?

The short answer is: whatever their designer wants them to be, as long as there is an economic purpose for them. There is literally no limit to what objectives a non-currency token may serve. To demonstrate the variety of possible objectives, we examine in some detail two specific token types, namely *utility token* and *non-fungible token (NFT)*.

A *utility token* gives its holder the right to either access or provide some service within the ecosystem in exchange for a benefit, an income stream, or a one-off reward. This service can be in the form of, e.g. particular functionalities, participation in a governance function (for example, the right to vote on platform strategy or operations, in which case it is a *governance token*), or simply investing in an operational function (such as rating the accuracy of a result, or the reputation level of an economic agent, or the odds of an expected outcome—the latter are precisely the use cases of *token curated registries*, and of *escrow* (or staking-based) *prediction markets*). The income stream accruing to the token holder can be in the form of either direct or indirect cash flows. For instance, it can consist of savings from standard rates; increased income from higher service availabilities; newly minted tokens (i.e. through token inflation—explained in detail in Sect. 10.5.3); a percentage of third-party transaction fees, etc. There are also many variations in terms of one-off rewards, such as in prediction markets where a mechanism may increase the value of the token—accumulating on top of its purchase price—should its predicted outcome be close to the finally observed one. The degree to which a particular economic agent type considers this income stream, or event-based payoff, to be important is the driving mechanism behind token price discovery. As utility tokens confer a privilege, i.e. represent value, to holders, they can also be used to store value.

The objective behind creation and circulation of a utility token is to establish that agent typology, respectively to incentivize that agent behaviour, which will promote the economic value of the ecosystem. For example, staking tokens in a prediction market [7] is signalling a strong opinion (based on actual knowledge, potentially also privileged information) about a particular outcome, which contributes to truth discovery, thus validating the ecosystem business case. The more successful a prediction market is, the more participants will be attracted to it, and hence will consider acquiring its utility token. Similarly, acquiring a *voting token* is the first conscious step in helping to optimize the ecosystem's operations or total business case, hence sustaining and growing it. As voting tokens can accrue fee income from platform rewards, the more successful the ecosystem, the more incentives for participating in its governance processes.

A *non-fungible token (NFT)* is intended to prove the title of ownership that its holder has on something unique, genuine, and authentic. The underlying "something" does not need to be a whole asset but can also be part of an asset—and this is where the value of NFTs comes to the fore. Usually the "whole-asset" case is found in digital assets (e.g. "skins" in online games, which are meant to signify attainment of a level of achievement, akin to a physical trophy in traditional sports), but this is not a necessary restriction. The "partial asset" case is the most generic and economically interesting one. A collection of old wines can be "tokenized" on the blockchain, each token representing ownership in a fraction of the entire collection. The painting created by a young and promising artist can be split into NFTs and auctioned on the blockchain to support them financially while they pursue their calling. In both of these cases, NFTs act as financial instruments for investment in illiquid assets through partial ownership. It must be mentioned that "fractionalization" as a paradigm is not blockchain-specific. For example, platforms such as BondbloX [8] enable fractional ownership of bonds by providing an issuance platform and marketplace [9] for transformed securities positions; however, those are not tokens. What is different in the NFT case is the ability to access illiquid assets precisely because of the tokenization ability inherent to the blockchain.

The "partial asset" NFT case is more similar to that of unit funds of illiquid assets ("alternative investment [10, 11] funds" in traditional finance), but in a form that is more transparent (as there is no fund manager involved) because of the blockchain. It is a win-win value proposition for both the original owner(s) of the asset and the investor(s). Owners can choose which proportion, or even which distinct part, of the asset to monetize, whereas investors can choose the precise asset class and investment outlay to invest into. This is especially important when it would be difficult to locate and invest directly in an asset, were it not for the global visibility created by blockchain-enabled ecosystems. An added value for the end investor is the existence of mandated due-diligence processes on assets and sellers when onboarding them onto the platform, which differentiates the NFT business case fundamentally from e.g. crowd-sourcing paradigms.

One can argue that investing into illiquid assets through NFTs has the potential to replicate the private equity and venture capital value propositions on the blockchain and make them both accessible to an expanded investor universe, potentially including retail investors. Viewed from this angle, the objective of issuing NFTs is to enable optimal economic and social outcomes not for, but through, the blockchain ecosystem. Whenever liquidity is freed before vesting of an illiquid asset, or a struggling artist can get more predictable funding to continue creating art; economic and social outcomes are now equal considerations. The token itself is simply a vehicle to capture asset appreciation for the sake of the investor and to free liquidity for the sake of the original asset owner. An example of a (digital) whole-asset protocol NFT would be Axie Infinity [12, 13] AXS [14, 15]. Examples of whole-asset NFT platforms would be OpenSea [16], Rarible [17], Pictoclub [18] (for digital), and WiV [19] (for real-world assets). Examples of partial-asset NFT (or fractional-NFT, sometimes abbreviated as "F-NFT") platforms would be Fractional [20] (for digital) and Londontradeart [21] (for real-world assets).

Summarizing the above, a "token" is a blockchain-based digital representation of value, which can *in some circumstances* be used as money, or as an alternative to money, within a digital ecosystem. There are several possible token types already in existence, evidencing a tremendous number of design modalities to serve individual business use cases. Each and every such type is essential, either for enabling the economic purpose of their ecosystem in the first place or for helping to capture its total value and driving it to growth. A token does not live in isolation but must be understood within the context of its native blockchain-enabled ecosystem, in reference to both general and specific design objectives.

4.2 Main Crypto-Token Types

The purpose of this and the next section is to establish and justify a robust crypto-token typology. As already mentioned, our focus throughout will be on logical consistency, with each piece of terminology rationalized and then linked to examples of actual tokens from live blockchain ecosystems. The intention is both to capture current industry practices through nomenclature and to prepare the reader for the token ecosystem design framework which will be presented in subsequent chapters.

As of yet there exists no globally acceptable crypto-token typology, in spite of quite a few (mainly academic) attempts [22]. This has caused a certain degree of confusion among financial market practitioners and, most importantly, regulators [23, 24]. There are probably two main reasons for this confusion: First, difficulty to recognize that there are several lenses through which to observe a single token. Second, the sheer number of combinations in terms of functional features that token types can exhibit. It may also be the case that, as different kinds of professionals (token developers, venture capital investors, investment advisors, lawyers, regulators, etc.) are interested in different aspects of token functionality; and as they try to find associations with their own trusted terminology and experience (sometimes never having worked across the traditional-finance/decentralized-

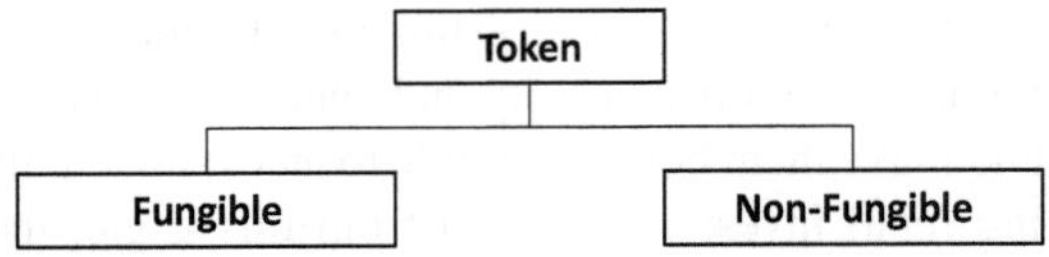

Fig. 4.1 The two fundamental token natures

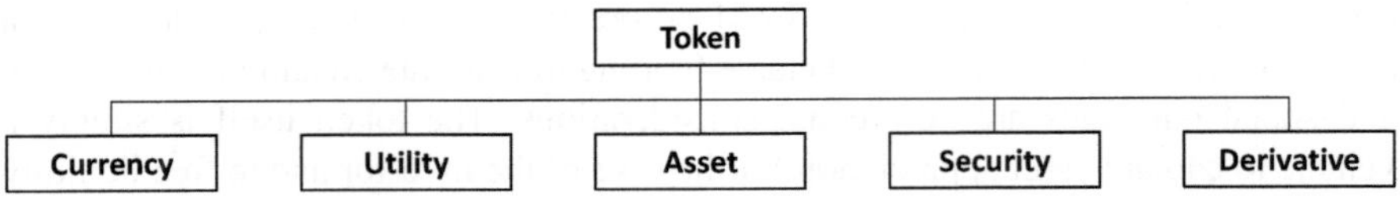

Fig. 4.2 High-level token typology

finance divide); consensus building is stumbling at terms instead of proceeding to substance.

We propose that there exists indeed an inclusive crypto-token typology, as long as one stays at the level of foundational types; and once the economic purpose of the token within its generating ecosystem is taken as the primary lens. An additional lens, also important for current and future use cases, is the fundamental token "nature" from the standpoint of its *fungibility*. It is of course inescapable that composite, hybrid token forms will also emerge. However, once foundational types are described and their salient features tabulated, then the constellation of economic purposes of even the most complex hybrid token becomes clear. One might consider foundational token types as "primitives". Knowing those primitives is useful for two different tasks: token analysis; and design. Analysis is generally the only consideration from the standpoint of token buyers, investors, advisors, and regulators. However, as there is no such thing as design without analysis, this knowledge will prove useful to cryptocurrency and crypto-token designers as well.

At the highest level of abstraction, tokens can be considered to have two distinct "natures"—fungible and non-fungible (cf. Fig. 4.1).

Then, using the economic function of a token as primary lens, the high-level types of Fig. 4.2 are currently observed across blockchain-based ecosystems:

In the rest of this chapter, we explain each of these high-level, foundational types and then list their observed *sub*types. We also provide corresponding examples of already circulating crypto-tokens in the context of their individual use cases.

4.2.1 Currency Tokens

In reference to the terminology and explanations provided in Sect. 4.1, *currency tokens* are those minted to have explicitly the combined roles of media of exchange and stores of value within a particular ecosystem. Accounting as an activity or

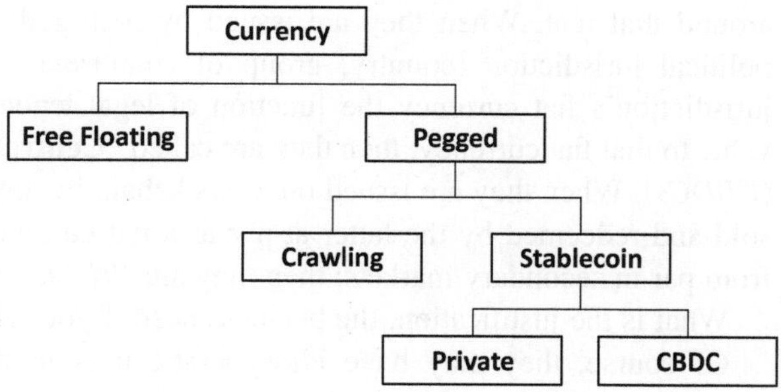

Fig. 4.3 Currency-token typology (high-level)

obligation cannot be always pre-supposed[4] (especially in decentralized ecosystems), so the "unit of account" requirement is not imposed. A high-level currency-token typology is as depicted in Fig. 4.3,[5] where "Private" means "issued and managed by non-state-affiliated bodies" (i.e. not by state governments, neither by central banks nor by state-sponsored organizations) and "CBDC" stands for "Central Bank Digital Currency".

Bitcoin (BTC) would be an example of a *free-floating token*, the price of which is dictated purely by supply and demand in the marketplace. There exist several design parameters able to influence valuation[6] of such tokens, however, their three fundamental characteristics are:

(a) The ab initio design as medium of exchange for transactions carried out on a specific blockchain.
(b) The absence of any ancillary income stream accruing to their holder (which, if present, would force them to be categorized as a security token, cf. Sect. 4.2.4 below).
(c) The absence of any feature intended to keep them aligned to a reference rate (on- or off-chain).

Pegged tokens inherit only the first two characteristics listed above. The peg is typically an observable rate, either on- or off-chain (e.g. supplied through dedicated price feeds called Oracles[7]), such as price of a specific fiat currency or a commodity, or even of another token.

Crawling tokens are meant to be following an observable reference rate, but only within *adjustable parity ranges*.

The important type of *Stablecoins* are currency tokens that are designed to be *strictly* following an observable reference rate, i.e. to vary only within a *tight range*

[4]Even though ecosystem governance may indeed necessitate taking stock of tokens in circulation or inventory for staking and rewards attribution, in which case token accounting will take place.

[5]Please note that "soft-peg" and "hard-peg" are sometimes used to denote "Crawling" tokens and Stablecoins, respectively.

[6]Cf. Sect. 10.5.4.

[7]Cf. Sect. 6.4, in particular the part on Oracles.

around that rate. When they are issued by prerogative of the Central Bank of a political jurisdiction (country, group of countries); expressly sharing with said jurisdiction's fiat currency the function of legal tender; in enforced 1:1 parity in value to that fiat currency; then they are called **"Central Bank Digital Currencies"** (*CBDC*s). When they are issued on a blockchain by any other issuing organization; sold and redeemed by the latter at par to a fiat currency, but freely tradable away from par in secondary markets; then they are *Private*[8] *Stablecoins*.

What is the justification, the business need if you wish, for Private Stablecoins?

Of course, they may have idiosyncratic uses in different ecosystems, but in general there are five main use cases that are materially facilitated on the blockchain through the existence of Stablecoins. These are:

1. Payments and remittances.
2. Liquidity reserves.
3. Liquidity positions.
4. Flight-to-safety.
5. Collateral posting.

In reference to *payments and remittances*, bilateral money transfers (in-country and international) through digital channels obviously pre-existed the blockchain era. Credit card transactions and international remittances are two such long-established business lines, actually sharing a common feature: non-negligible [25] processing fees [26–29] levied on both sides of the transaction. Private Stablecoins act to disrupt those business lines, enabling low-cost, near-real-time money transfers with minimal price risk by definition [30–32] and with zero settlement risk due to the transaction finality feature of the blockchain.

It is a fact that moving funds between the blockchain and the off-chain world (changing fiat for crypto-tokens—called "on-ramping" in the trade jargon—and the other way around—"off-ramping") may, depending on the exchange venue, incur relatively high commissions (or "exchange fees" [33, 34]). Hence, traders exiting crypto-token positions and moving their returns to "waiting liquidity reserves" have two options: either to off-ramp to a fiat currency, thus paying the high *agio;* or to remain on-chain by settling their positions into Private Stablecoins tracking the exact same fiat currency—without incurring *agio*. This is the "Private Stablecoins as [in-between-trading] **liquidity reserves**" use case.

Issuance and management of investment funds offered to the public are always subject to regulatory obligations. One of them is to have a stated investment policy, in the sense of a document declaring the investable asset classes (shares, bonds, liquid alternatives, etc.) and the percentage of funds allocated to each one. Said percentages are always expressed in range values (i.e. an investment fund

[8] I.e. not state-issued.

prospectus[9] may state: "corporate bonds 20%–25%") and, importantly, will always include an allocation to "liquidity". These *liquidity positions* serve three objectives within the fund: first, to create a "low-risk" anchor (typically allocated short-term to repos or money-market funds); second, to allow taking advantage of short-term investment opportunities and realizing their gains for reinvestment; third, to deposit position-related income streams (stock dividends, bond coupons, etc.) for reinvestment. If an investment fund invests in crypto-tokens (e.g. [37, 38]) or is itself a security token (cf. Sect. 4.2.4 below), then it should keep all its internal fund transfers on-chain for the same reason explained in the "liquidity reserves" use case. It must be mentioned that some Private Stablecoin issuers add in-situ yield-bearing features (cf. "Money Market tokens" in Sect. 4.2.4), making their equivalence to traditional money market funds quite explicit.

The "**flight-to-safety**" use case is related to the "liquidity reserves" one, but refers specifically to situations when severe market dislocations cause a flood of position liquidations (voluntary or enforced, e.g. through margin calls). Due to scalability limitations of current blockchains, those may prompt other investors to act urgently to close positions, thus precipitating "domino effects". If the latter become systemic, then they can disrupt and even threaten the existence of trading venues, e.g. in the case of centralized exchanges, by jeopardizing their ability to keep making markets. If traders instead have the certainty that they can quickly move trading positions to "on-chain" liquidity with minimal price risk *vis-à-vis* fiat currencies, then that incentivizes them to remain invested in crypto-tokens. Hence, having the option to settle positions into Private Stablecoins contributes to systemic stability [39] to the benefit of all market participants [40–43].

The "**collateral posting**" use case refers to two important business contexts. First, it reflects the business model of several protocols, with crypto-tokens being minted as "collateralized loan positions"[10] whereby the admissible on-chain collateral usually includes Private Stablecoins. Thus, as the Total Value Locked (TVL) of these protocols increases, so does the need for token investors to purchase Stablecoins. Second, it applies to crypto-derivatives transactions (cf. Sect. 4.2.5 below) wherein they form the collateral supporting what is in effect initial and variation margin in the sense of traditional finance [41].

Private Stablecoins are generally categorized in reference to their price stabilization mechanisms [43, 45] as falling into one of three classes: "**algorithmic**", "**reserve-backed**", and "**hybrid**". We provide an extensive analysis of the relevance and implications of this categorization in the context of token design (cf. Sect. 10.5.8). There are many such Stablecoins issued already [46], tracking several fiat currencies such as USD, EUR, and CHF.

[9] Also termed "Key Investor Information Document" in the context of funds aligning with the European Union "Undertakings for the Collective Investment in Transferable Securities" Directive 2009/65/EC [35, 36].

[10] E.g. FRAX [44].

"Central Bank Digital Currencies" (*CBDCs*) may or may not be issued (or exclusively issued) on the blockchain. In the former case they are termed "token-based", in the later "Account-based". They represent direct liabilities of a jurisdiction's central bank towards their holders. As per fundamental analysis and design work carried out under the auspices of the Bank for International Settlements [47, 48], they can be allocated to two broad use cases:

(i) "**Wholesale**", when used among financial institutions, and between financial institutions and their central bank, to settle high-value trades in financial markets.
(ii) "**Retail**" or "**General-purpose**", when intended for use by the general public.

There are several predicted uses of retail CBDCs, depending strictly on the intention of the individual central banks to also employ them as instruments of monetary and/or social policy. As also identified by the BIS working groups [49, 50], beneficial effects expected by the introduction of CBDCs include:

- Additional access to central bank money.
- Resilience of the payments system.
- Increased payments diversity.
- Broader financial inclusion.
- Improving cross-border payments.
- Supporting privacy of transactions.
- Facilitating fiscal transfers.
- Controlled usage of state subsidies.

However, there are also detrimental systemic effects predicted [51] at the level of the individual jurisdiction, due to the concomitant reduction of core liquidity at commercial banks and the resulting increase in borrowing rates offered to general credit takers so as to compensate for the banks' own cost of funding. As already mentioned, the extent of both beneficial and detrimental effects will depend on the "calibration" that a central bank will impose on its CBDC (in the sense of its functional and non-functional design parameters, i.e. of its token design as explained in Chap. 10 of this book).

Several CBDCs are in various stages of introduction into the global payments system [52] (e.g. Digital Yuan—"e-CNY" [53–55]). However, there exists as yet no global standard specifying their functional envelope and parametrization, nor is there any international agreement on technical implementation requirements, convertibility, and cross-border acceptance.

The two most important practical advantages of CBDCs *vis-à-vis* private Stablecoins tracking the same fiat currencies are: absence of price risk and minimized credit risk (issuer and counterparty, reflecting the creditworthiness and political risk of the respective jurisdiction). It is important to mention that CBDC is not necessarily synonymous with "state-sponsored cryptocurrency", which can also exist and have its own specific risk profile (e.g [56, 57].).

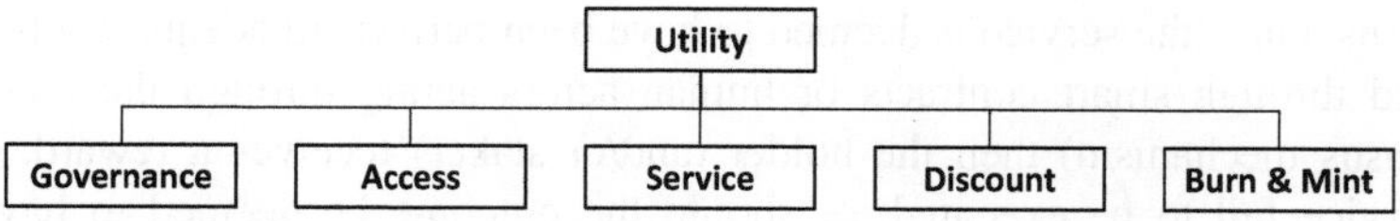

Fig. 4.4 Utility token subtypes

The current naming convention is to refer to Private Stablecoins simply as "Stablecoins" and keep only the distinction with CBDCs in reference to the issuing bodies. Having explained the rigorous typology of Fig. 4.1, we will also align with this convention in the sequel so as to avoid confusion on the part of the reader when confronted with industry news and legal/regulatory texts. Hence, for the rest of this book, pegged currency tokens will be either "crawling [-pegged]", Stablecoins, or CBDCs.

4.2.2 Utility Tokens

As already mentioned, acquiring a *utility token* gives its holder the right to either access or provide some service within the ecosystem, in exchange for a benefit, an income stream, or an one-off reward. Taking stock of the current cryptoassets universe, we can identify five major subtypes of utility tokens, as depicted in Fig. 4.4 below.

Governance tokens: These are tokens that are staked by an economic agent in exchange for the right to take part in governance functions[11] of the ecosystem. Whether or not a governance token also returns some sort of reward in addition to conferring a right is prescribed in mechanism and token designs, explained later in this book. Examples of such protocol governance tokens would be: MakerDAO [58, 59] MKR [60], Uniswap [61, 62] UNI [63, 64], and Vesper [65, 66] VSP [67, 68].

Access tokens: Acquiring (or earning/accumulating them) them offers access to resources to perform a service and reap rewards. Similar to implementing a market segmentation strategy, they are used to align service providers with different levels of access to ecosystem resources and also indirectly as "status" markers to incentivize transition to higher levels. They can also be thought of as implementing a merit-based "decentralized hierarchy" among utility providers, akin to a traditional corporate hierarchy whereby high worker performance leads to promotion, meaning access to more resources (subordinates, work equipment, facilitation network, information, mentoring) and potentially more rewards to incentivize still higher performance, etc. An example of protocol access token would be Access Protocol [69] ACS [70, 71].

Service tokens: Acquiring (and/or staking) them confers the right to have a service provided to the ecosystem of a type other than relating directly to governance

[11] Please refer to Chap. 8 for a discussion on said functions.

functions. Once the service is deemed to have been performed adequately (decision reached through smart contracts or human actors acting through the blockchain consensus mechanism) then the holder (and/or staker) receives a reward. Should the service fail to be executed, or should the outcome be deemed to have been inadequate, then the holder/staker is penalized (either the reward is annulled or a haircut is applied to the original service token amount). Examples of protocol service tokens would be: Bancor [72] BNT [73, 74], Augur [75] REP [76, 77], Keep Network [78] KEEP [79–81], and Kleros [82] PNK [83–85].

Discount tokens: Acquiring them offers discounts on transaction fees when their holder transacts within the ecosystem (i.e. they are an implicit incentive for increasing the ecosystem turnover). Currently there are two prevalent paradigms of discount token design, depending on whether or not staking is involved. In the first paradigm, the fee discount is activated only when the agent uses this particular token to pay for the transaction—an **"on-pay discount"**. In the second, the protocol specifies a discount pool available to all stakers, and the discount to a particular agent's transaction fees is calculated as a function of said agent's rights to the staking pool—an **"on-stake discount"**. Examples of "on-pay discount" protocol tokens would be Binance [86] BNB [86–88] and Bitfinex [89] LEO [90–92]. An example of "on-stake discount" token would be Sweetbridge [93] SWC [94, 95].

"Burn & Mint"[12] *tokens*: They are also used to incentivize execution of services in the ecosystem, but they differ from service tokens in two important respects: first, they are offered not to potential service providers but to service consumers; and, second, the reward accruing through them to individual providers is a function of the total volume of transactions across consumers. Service consumers submit tokens for cancellation (the "burn" leg), tagging a particular service provider, and the total amount of tokens thus cancelled across consumers is used to calculate the reward to the tagged service provider—potentially, in terms of new tokens created (the "mint" leg). The economic outcome for the service consumer is the same as if they were paying directly for the service (either transferring or burning them, they are parting with their tokens anyway), and the platform profits from moving towards a network effect. Examples of "Burn & Mint" tokens would be Accumulate [96] ACME [97–100] and Helium [101] HNT [102, 103].

As the landscape of services transacted on in blockchain-based ecosystems expands, there will probably be more utility token subtypes appearing in the future.

4.2.3 Asset Tokens

Pursuing the economic purpose of token ecosystems generally involves transactions in services *and* assets. As economic agents can have principals transacting also off-chain, it is inescapable that the digital and physical representations of the objects of their transactions will occasionally overlap. For example, there are many

[12] Or, for the sake of accuracy, "Burn & Mint Equilibrium" tokens.

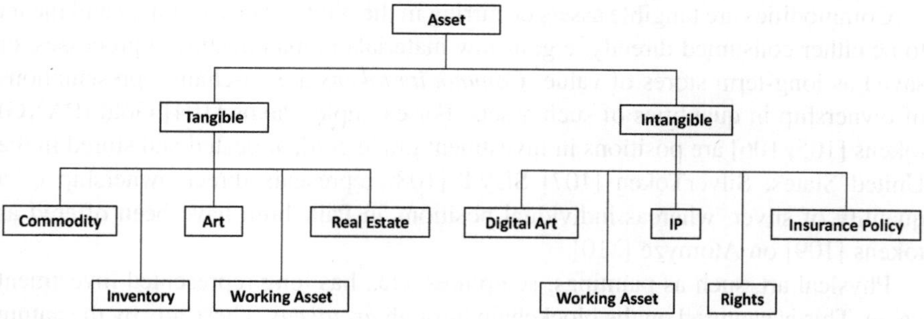

Fig. 4.5 Asset token typology (high-level)

blockchain business use cases where the digital asset that is being exchanged is a representation of value that already exists in the physical world. In such cases, the token objectifies a property right, registered on the blockchain, but existing only in reference to a corresponding off-chain property right. We define an **"asset token"** to be the blockchain representation of value of a physical-world property right, when the latter is neither a sum of money, nor a financial security nor a derivative. This token type covers all business contexts where the blockchain is intended to be used as the primary technical infrastructure for registration, verification, certification, transformation, lifecycle management, order management, and owner management of real-world assets. The use of the word "transformation" in the list is meant to cover e.g. fractionalization[13] use cases, such as when an off-chain asset which is an indivisible piece of property (e.g. a gem or a piece of art) is transformed into many non-fungible-tokens, each to be traded individually on the blockchain. "Registration" is the very important first step, particularly when the blockchain is meant to be the *only* registration venue for title to said asset. For example, when issuing company common stock solely on-chain, thus creating a business context interpolating the Central Securities Depository, Securities Settlement System, and Intermediated Securities registration paradigms.

We distinguish between the two physical-world cases of (a) *tangible* vs (b) *intangible* assets. For the sake of flexibility to also accommodate not-yet-implemented asset classes, we also provide for a catch-all "working asset token" (meaning "working asset, not yet captured by other asset classes"). With this proviso, we propose the asset token typology depicted in Fig. 4.5. It is to be considered a "high-level" one, as more granular subtypes will depend on individual project needs and may have to align with eventual industry standards (describing, e.g. "Life-Insurance" vs "Property & Casualty Insurance" policy tokens).

[13]There exist of course also "reverse Fractionalization" and several other property right transformation use cases. Importantly, several such cases were created and depend almost entirely on the blockchain as registration and transactional platform. For example, an NFT which has been created through an Ethereum ERC-721 smart contract can be transformed into many fungible "unit-fund" investments by "wrapping" through an ERC-20 one.

Commodities are tangible assets occurring in the physical environment and meant to be either consumed directly, e.g. as raw materials in manufacturing processes, or saved as long-term stores of value. *Commodity tokens* are on-chain representations of ownership in quantities of such assets. For example, Paxos [104] Gold (PAXG) tokens [105, 106] are positions in investment grade gold, allocated and stored in the United States, SilverToken [107] SLVT [108] represents direct ownership of a quantity of silver, whereas individual positions in Palladium have been offered as tokens [109] on Atomyze [110].

Physical art, such as paintings, sculptures, etc., has long represented investment value. This is captured on the blockchain through *art tokens*. These are, by the nature of the underlying asset, non-fungible and can represent either whole or partial ownership. Examples of full ownership tokenization would be works by Picasso [111, 112], whereas a work by Warhol was only partially tokenized [113].

Real Estate tokens allow investment in either full or partial ownership of both residential and commercial real estate, in a pattern complementary to that of real estate investment funds. A significant difference between them and commodity or art tokens comes from the fact that laws in several countries may prohibit, or at least make very costly, fractional ownership in land or buildings. In other jurisdictions, physical asset tokenization is not yet provided for in commercial law. The repercussion is that many such token projects choose to form a corporation, wholly owning the particular real estate, and then issue tokens representing shares in the corporation. As that is a single-asset legal entity, we choose to not categorize those as equity tokens. Examples: individual buildings in the United States [114, 115], bespoke protocols such as RealT [116] (issuing Realtokens and providing a marketplace [117, 118]), specialized issuers/marketplaces such as RedSwan [119], etc. Due to the size and transactional frictions of the global real estate market, this has the potential to become a widely used asset token type [120].

Inventory tokens are different from commodity ones because they represent title to semi-finished and finished *goods*. In difference to postings in traditional Enterprise Resource Planning (ERP) systems, which only provide visibility within the confines of a single company, such tokens can be made to represent physical assets in cross-company processes. For instance, physical goods are used as collateral in working capital transactions (such as trade finance and supply trade finance), where trading counterparties, banks, service providers, etc., all need visibility into the current state of transaction execution. For example, the XinFin network [121] was used to issue NFTs representing trade finance positions [122], while CargoX [123] used the blockchain to transfer title of Marine Bills of Lading [124–126].

On the "intangibles" side, *digital art tokens* represent works of art that have been created and digitized outside the blockchain, but then traded in a token ecosystem. An example would be digitized books and eBooks, including audiobooks. Such tokens are traded e.g. on NFT platforms such as Book Token [127], Bookchain [128], and Publica [129].

Intellectual property tokens serve adjacent use cases to the Art ones; however, they can be also associated with IP-generated income streams. These cases are quite prominent, e.g. in the music licensing business which has been a notoriously difficult one to adequately monetize in the past from the standpoint of the artists themselves. Blockchain allows to represent the licences of both the IP and the associated income stream, independently of how and where the music piece is consumed, in a single repository. An example of a music-licence token platform would be Royal [130], whereas Opulous [131] is both an issuing platform and a marketplace.[14]

Another category under "intangibles", *insurance policy tokens*, serve use cases around the on-chain representation and, more interestingly, the trading (selling, as an alternative to surrendering) of insurance policies. Depending on the insurable risk represented in the underlying policies, issuing and trading agents run the entire gamut from large corporates to private persons. Such tokens were used for example to transfer natural catastrophe [132] and marine facultative [133] risks in corporate settings. They are implemented as cover-specific NFTs in Nexus Mutual [134]. An early protocol ("fidentiaX", now apparently no longer functioning [135]) even tried to create an insurance policy trading marketplace [136, 137].

Even though it can be argued that IP tokens are by default also *rights tokens*, the latter are meant to explicitly represent rights in income streams, or any other off-chain benefit, *not* associated with intellectual property (i.e. *not* royalties). There are various usufructuary and equitable rights, for instance, that can be brought under this category. An example of such a token marketplace would be Coreledger [138], a blockchain project enabling profit participation investments (i.e. tokenizing and selling future revenue streams) in a physical-world business, instead of outright tokenizing ownership shares.

Our proposed "asset token" typology is only a high-level one and arguably non-inclusive. There are few limits to what off-chain assets can be represented through blockchain tokens and how, and most of those limits are imposed by law and regulation rather than by technology or on account of practicality. For example, collections of fine wines [139], watches, and collectibles have all been tokenized (the Swiss bank Sygnum provides both primary token issuance and secondary market platforms [140]). A particular project (pursuing active sustainability strategies) even made it possible to tokenize individual trees [141]. However, it would not be very useful to insist on a granular taxonomy including wine, watch, tree, etc., token as a result.

4.2.4 Security Tokens

To best explain the notion of security tokens it is expedient to begin by clarifying the term "securities" in the first place. Even though traditional finance is a global business, there is no globally valid legal definition of what a security is. Instead of describing general identifying attributes, major jurisdictions have opted for

[14] Including a lending platform for loans backed by real-world music assets and future royalties as collateral.

specifying lists of financial instruments qualifying as "securities" for the purposes of contract drafting and of satisfying legal and regulatory obligations.

In the United States, for example, federal law[15] postulates:

'The term "security" means any note, stock, treasury stock, security future, security-based swap, bond, debenture, evidence of indebtedness, certificate of interest or participation in any profit-sharing agreement, collateral-trust certificate, preorganization certificate or subscription, transferable share, investment contract, voting-trust certificate, certificate of deposit for a security, fractional undivided interest in oil, gas, or other mineral rights, any put, call, straddle, option, or privilege on any security, certificate of deposit, or group or index of securities (including any interest therein or based on the value thereof), or any put, call, straddle, option, or privilege entered into on a national securities exchange relating to foreign currency, or, in general, any interest or instrument commonly known as a "security", or any certificate of interest or participation in, temporary or interim certificate for, receipt for, guarantee of, or warrant or right to subscribe to or purchase, any of the foregoing.'

In the European Union, EU Law[16] defines not securities per se, but Financial Instruments, as including:

'(1) Transferable securities;
(2) Money-market instruments;
(3) Units in collective investment undertakings;
(4) Options, futures, swaps, forward rate agreements and any other derivative contracts relating to securities, currencies, interest rates or yields, or other derivatives instruments, financial indices or financial measures which may be settled physically or in cash;
(5) Options, futures, swaps, forward rate agreements and any other derivative contracts relating to commodities that must be settled in cash or may be settled in cash at the option of one of the parties (otherwise than by reason of a default or other termination event);
(6) Options, futures, swaps, and any other derivative contract relating to commodities that can be physically settled provided that they are traded on a regulated market and/or an MTF [this author's note: Multilateral Trading Facility[17,18]];
(7) Options, futures, swaps, forwards and any other derivative contracts relating to commodities, that can be physically settled not otherwise mentioned in C.6 and not being for commercial purposes, which have the characteristics of other derivative financial instruments, having regard to whether, inter alia, they are cleared and settled through recognised clearing houses or are subject to regular margin calls;
(8) Derivative instruments for the transfer of credit risk;
(9) Financial contracts for differences.
(10) Options, futures, swaps, forward rate agreements and any other derivative contracts relating to climatic variables, freight rates, emission allowances or inflation rates or other official economic statistics that must be settled in cash or may be settled in cash at the option of one of the parties (otherwise than by reason of a default or other termination event), as well as any other derivative contracts relating to assets, rights, obligations, indices and

[15] Section 2(a)(1) of the Securities Act of 1933 (15 U.S.C. 77b(a)(1)), as amended.

[16] Annex I, Section C, and Article 4(1), point 18 of Directive 2004/39/EC are referenced by all subsequent EU directives and regulations in the areas of Financial Markets and Services.

[17] Multilateral Trading Facility, ibid., Article 4(1), point 15.

[18] Article 4(1)(22) of Directive 2014/65/EU.

measures not otherwise mentioned in this Section, which have the characteristics of other derivative financial instruments, having regard to whether, inter alia, they are traded on a regulated market or an MTF, are cleared and settled through recognised clearing houses or are subject to regular margin calls.'

whereas

'18) "Transferable securities" means those classes of securities which are negotiable on the capital market, with the exception of instruments of payment, such as:
(a) shares in companies and other securities equivalent to shares in companies, partnerships or other entities, and depositary receipts in respect of shares;
(b) bonds or other forms of securitised debt, including depositary receipts in respect of such securities;
(c) any other securities giving the right to acquire or sell any such transferable securities or giving rise to a cash settlement determined by reference to transferable securities, currencies, interest rates or yields, commodities or other indices or measures;'

In the UK, the FCA Handbook [142] (codifying UK law for regulatory purposes) distinguishes between securities, defined as:

'(1) (except in LR and CONC122) (in accordance with article 3(1) of the Regulated Activities Order (Interpretation)) any of the following investments specified in that Order:
(a) share (article 76);
(b) debenture (article 77);
(ba) alternative debenture (article 77A);
(c) government and public security (article 78);
(d) warrant (article 79);
(e) certificate representing certain securities (article 80);
(f) unit (article 81);
(g) stakeholder pension scheme (article 82(1));
(ga) personal pension scheme (article 82(2));
(gab) pension scheme which provides safeguarded benefits (article 82(3)) (but only in relation to advising on conversion or transfer of pension benefits);
(gb) emission allowance (article 82B); and.
(h) rights to or interests in investments in (a) to (g) (article 89).
(2) (in LR) (in accordance with section 102A of the Act) anything which has been, or may be admitted to the official list.
(3) (in CONC) in accordance with article 60 L of the Regulated Activities Order, in relation to a credit agreement or a consumer hire agreement, a mortgage, charge, pledge, bond, debenture, indemnity, guarantee, bill, note or other right provided by the borrower or hirer or at the implied or express request of the borrower or hirer to secure the carrying out of the obligations of the borrower or hirer under the agreement.
(4) (in COLL) in addition and to the extent it does not fall within (1), an investment which would have been within the definition of "security" in the FCA Handbook immediately before IP completion day.'

and derivatives, defined as:

'(1) (other than in REC, MAR 5 and MAR 5A) a contract for differences, a future or an option (see also securitised derivative).

(2) (in REC, MAR 5 and MAR 5A) those financial instruments defined in article 2 (1)(24) (c) of MiFIR or referred to in paragraphs 4 to 10 of Part 1 of Schedule 2 to the Regulated Activities Order.

[Note: article 2(1)(29) of MiFIR].'

In Singapore, the law[19] also differentiates between securities and "securities-based derivatives contracts":

'"securities" means —
(a) shares, units in a business trust or any instrument conferring or representing a legal or beneficial ownership interest in a corporation, partnership or limited liability partnership;
(b) debentures; or
(c) any other product or class of products as may be prescribed, but does not include —
(d) any unit of a collective investment scheme;
(e) any bill of exchange;
(f) any certificate of deposit issued by a bank or finance company, whether situated in Singapore or elsewhere; or
(g) such other product or class of products as may be prescribed;
"securities-based derivatives contract" means any derivatives contract of which the underlying thing or any of the underlying things is a security or a securities index, but does not include any derivatives contract that is, or that belongs to a class of derivatives contracts that is, prescribed by regulations made under section 341;'

Please note that collective investment schemes, bills of exchange and certificates of deposit are not classified under "Securities" in Singapore law. In the same vein, US law classifies futures and options as securities, whereas both UK and Singapore laws do not. EU law mentions separately "transferable securities", money-market instruments, and units in collective investment undertakings. UK law includes "emissions allowances" explicitly under securities, whereas other jurisdictions do not.

As is evident from the above, the approach of specifying particular financial instruments qualifying as "securities" may be quite practical for enabling the lawgiver to assist economic life, but at the risk that different economic and regulatory priorities may be reflected in different terminologies in different jurisdictions. This can be reflected in different regulatory set-ups and differing court interpretations in what is essentially a global business. This is what is seen, for example, in the European Union where the European Securities and Markets Authority is responsible for regulation and oversight of both "transferable securities" and derivatives, whereas in the United States those tasks are divided between the Securities and Exchange Commission and the Commodity Futures Trading Commission. There exists yet another, rather more important, risk. Namely, that, as banking products and financial instruments evolve, statutory law and regulation can lag market practices to such an extent that existing legal frameworks may prove unable to accommodate them. If and when that happens, repercussions are felt across market participants, as differences of opinion about correct asset classification [143] can lead to confusion

[19] Interpretation, S. 2. (1), of the Securities and Futures Act 2001.

about imputed legal and regulatory obligations. Across jurisdictions, the same risk can manifest itself through regulatory arbitrage practices and potentially through financial crime.

Thankfully, there exists yet another source of law: case law, meaning outcomes of court cases that serve to clarify the correct context and applicability of statutory provisions. With reference to securities, one such landmark US court case was *SEC v. Howey* [144], in which the US Supreme Court gave guidance as to when a generic goods and services contract constitutes an investment contract, i.e. when it in effect represents a security within the meaning of US securities law. This guidance has since been implemented as a practical aid, in the form of the so-called "*Howey test*", for financial instrument classification. Importantly, it has come to be accepted by US regulators [145] as applicable also in the case of blockchain-issued digital assets.

Under the Howey test, if a contract involves:

(i) Investment of money
(ii) In a common enterprise
(iii) With a reasonable expectation of profits derived from efforts of others

then this contract represents a security within the meaning of US securities law.

The higher the correlation of features of a particular contract offering with the elements of the Howey test, the stronger the possibility that it constitutes a security in the eyes of US law. When it comes to digital marketplaces, and especially in blockchain-based ecosystems, there are several situations where each of the three elements of the test may be subject to interpretation based on analogies between the physical and the digital worlds. To that end, the use case; business context; and ecosystem design should all be taken into account. For example, as mentioned in the SEC guidance framework on digital assets, one of the determinants of a contract purchaser relying on the "efforts of others" is the existence of an "Active Participant (AP)", when:

> *'An AP creates or supports a market for,* [17] *or the price of, the digital asset. This can include, for example, an AP that: (1) controls the creation and issuance of the digital asset; or (2) takes other actions to support a market price of the digital asset, such as by limiting supply or ensuring scarcity, through, for example, buybacks, "burning," or other activities.'*

Consider a use case using an Automated Market Maker (AMM) relying on smart contracts parametrized through active governance processes. Would that algorithmic AMM constitute an "Active Participant" because governance allows recalibration after token-based voting by humans, as opposed to no longer being recalibrated at all (as in a DAO-governed project)? Questions such as this may be best answered by examining the use case against the background of the end-to-end design of the token ecosystem.

This book defines *security tokens* to be all investment products that are first issued on the blockchain in token form and that are not zero-sum games [146, 147]. Important points in this definition:

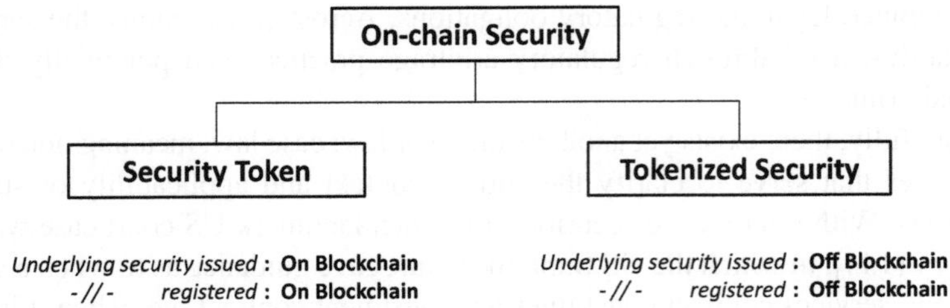

Fig. 4.6 Security tokens vs tokenized securities

Fig. 4.7 Single- vs multi-asset security tokens

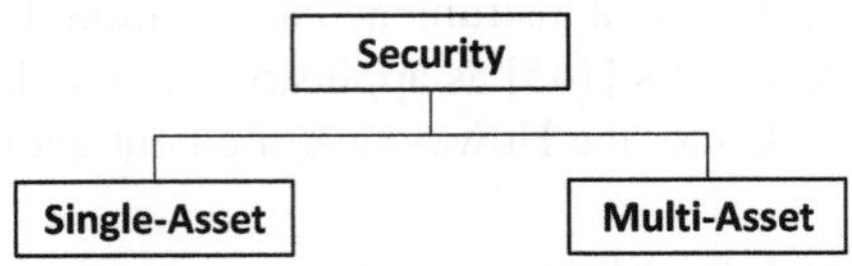

(a) Being "*in token form*" means being transferable as a single blockchain asset to a single investor, as opposed to bundling together property rights of many investors that need to be unwound before a single investor can buy or sell an allotment. The latter would be the case of a multi-party investment contract simply evidenced on the blockchain.
(b) Excluding investments that are "*zero-sum games*" is meant to differentiate between security and derivative tokens.
(c) Being "*first issued on the blockchain*" is meant to distinguish between two forms of on-chain securities, which are logically related but have quite different operational lifecycles and legal natures. Traditional financial securities, such as public company shares and corporate bonds, are either "registered" [148] or "intermediated" [149], meaning that there exists a record of their issuance (and per jurisdiction also of their individual owners) in non-blockchain-based registries, organized either at company, national, or international levels [150–153]. This, by law, registration requirement has implications for the operational processes regarding their trading and custody (including global custody). Even if those securities are proxied as blockchain tokens (cf. asset tokens category above), the fact is that they were first issued (and hence their master record exists) outside the blockchain. Hence they are called "tokenized securities" [154] to differentiate them from "security tokens" (focus of the present analysis), whose record of first issuance is the blockchain. The schematic of Fig. 4.6 serves to clarify this distinction.

There are many ways to categorize security tokens depending on analysis focus, e.g. one can choose to distinguish between tokens that represent claims to a single asset or to several (cf. Fig. 4.7).

As our intention is to create a token typology, we choose to allocate them (as was the case with asset tokens) to asset/risk classes in order to make clearer their correspondence to established notions from traditional finance. Of course, there

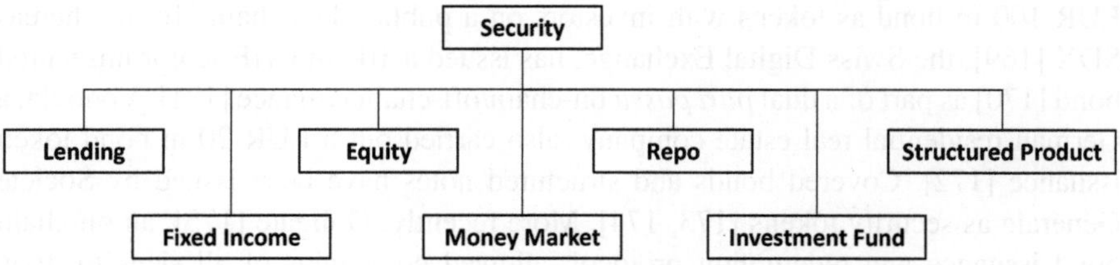

Fig. 4.8 Security token typology (high-level)

will be occasional differences between the two worlds, which will be highlighted through explanations of new terms as appropriate. Those differences are mostly due to new asset, cash flow, and value flow constellations enabled by the blockchain as operational platform, creating in effect new asset classes with no traditional parallel.

Please note that the asset/risk classes as categorized below (cf. Fig. 4.8) consciously depart from the "traditional" (common stock, preference shares, bonds, etc.) vs "alternative" (real estate, commodities, private equity, venture capital, art, etc.) classification. The reasons are, first, that the notions of public and private equity are becoming blurred when blockchain is used as the single issuance/registration platform for both; and, second, that off-chain asset classes such as commodities and art are best allocated as underlying the "asset token" type previously explained.

Lending tokens are both certificates of assets (currency tokens, Stablecoins, other tradable crypto-tokens) deposited with, and corresponding claims on both capital and realized returns against, liquidity pools lent out to borrowers on the blockchain. TrueFi [155] is one such protocol enabling uncollateralized lending [156], whereby lenders receive tradable ERC-20 tokens [157] representing their claims to principal and interest against the lending pool. Loan exposures [158] are visible at all times on the blockchain. Compound Finance [159] offers collateralized lending and borrowing token [160] issuance and a corresponding marketplace. There are also purpose-specific lending protocols, such as Liticapital [162], a crypto protocol specializing in litigation finance. Its tokens [161] represent shares in litigation outcomes funded by a capital pool, their yield realized in the form of dividends (note that a similar business case had been introduced by a no-longer functioning protocol, Ryval [163]). Aave [164], a protocol whose business case revolves around on-chain lending and borrowing[20], is currently offering lending functionality by way of on-chain swaps [165, 166] but not through lending tokens.[21]

Fixed income tokens are issued as on-chain equivalents to corporate or government bonds and to credit notes. For example, Banco Santander acted as tokenization agent for an own corporate bond [167]. The European Investment Bank has placed a

[20]Please note that the business transactions, tokens, and mechanisms of Aave are explained in detail in Chap. 14

[21]This is a distinction that will appear more prominently in the "Derivative Tokens" case, explained in Sect. 4.2.5.

EUR 100 m bond as tokens with investors on a public blockchain [168], whereas SDX [169], the Swiss Digital Exchange, has issued a 100 m CHF senior unsecured bond [170] as part of a dual *pari passu* on-chain/off-chain issuance [171]. Vonovia, a German residential real estate company, also carried out a EUR 20 m bond token issuance [172]. Covered bonds and structured notes have been issued by Société Générale as security tokens [173, 174]. More recently, Obligate [175], an on-chain bond issuance and redemption protocol, allowed companies of all sizes to draw funds through bonds and commercial paper issued as tokens [176, 177], at reduced cost to traditional venues.

Equity tokens are the equivalent of registered shares on the blockchain for both public and private companies. For example, Sygnum Bank [178], a Swiss Bank, registered all its equity shares on its in-house tokenization platform [179]. The intention was for capital increases and all primary and secondary market transactions (including the shareholder registry) to be blockchain-based. Still in Switzerland, Aktionariat [180], a blockchain platform, offers public share issuance as ERC-20 tokens and an associated marketplace. In the United States, SpaceX, a privately held space technology company, issued tradable tokens [181] representing an economic interest in its shares [182].

Money market tokens are meant to re-create tenor and risk/return profiles of traditional private and corporate cash equivalents. For example, CGS-CIMB, an Asian financial services provider, issued blockchain-registered commercial paper [183] in the form of tradable tokens [184]. The algorithmic Compound Finance [159] interest-rate protocol helped launch regulated time deposit[22] tokens for use by corporate treasuries [185].

Repo tokens replicate the repo/inverse-repo paradigm in token form and with tokenized assets as collateral. CoinFLEX Repo Market [186] was an early example of such a—exchange-traded—token marketplace. The institutional repo market has since followed [187].

Investment fund tokens are the equivalent of open-end investment funds on the blockchain, also exhibiting the variety of that traditional asset class. For example, ADDX [188], a Singapore-based asset manager, created a late-stage "Unicorn fund" [189] with shares created both on- and off-chain [190]. Yearn Finance [191] created the concept of "yVaults" [192] which are in effect quantitative investment funds underlain by several predefined investment strategies each [193] and managed by a combination of algorithmic and human managers (the latter tasked only with capital management or critical interventions). Tokens [194] ("yToken" [195]) are issued to investors in lieu of participation units.

Structured product tokens are also available on the blockchain. Antimatter [196] issued and traded a structured product ("Dual Investment" [197]) in token form. Uniswap [61] v3 concentrated liquidity positions [198] are in effect bespoke structured products [199] issued as NFTs.

[22] Also called "fixed-term deposits" or "fixed deposits".

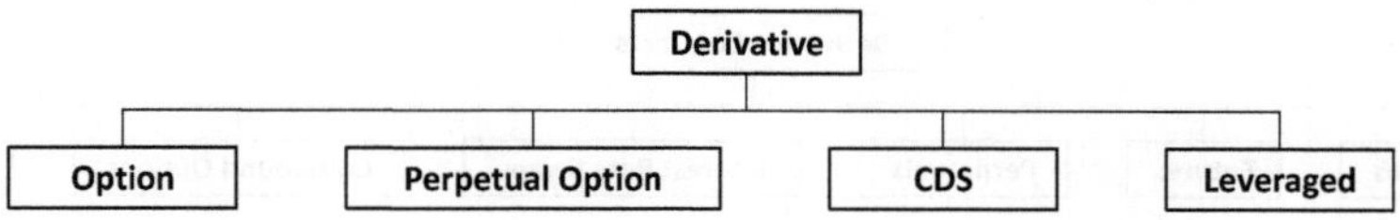

Fig. 4.9 Derivative token typology (high-level)

The above typology is meant only to indicate the variety of security tokens that are possible across business use cases. It is not exhaustive and is obviously aligned with "traditional finance" terminology in order to make the correspondence of asset classes and risk profiles between the on- and off-chain worlds clearer. The intention behind it is to show that blockchain-based use cases can in principle accommodate all traditional security classes. However, the notion of "token" is able to accommodate new income and value streams, thus creating new on-chain securities that have no equivalent in traditional finance.

4.2.5 Derivative Tokens

We define *derivative tokens* to be all investment products that are first issued on the blockchain in token form and that are zero-sum games. The meaning and importance of the wordings "first issued on the blockchain" and "*in token form*" was already explained in Sect. 4.2.4. On the former term, for instance, there are already many financial instruments marketed as "Cryptocurrency derivatives", but even though they reference prices of tokens they themselves are issued and traded outside any blockchain. They are indeed derivatives on blockchain tokens but are issued and registered in traditional financial marketplaces [200, 201], have ISIN numbers [202] or marketplace-specific identifiers, etc. The latter term ("in *token form*") has a particular significance in the case of derivative instruments, as their function can be encapsulated in two distinct forms:

- Tokens, and
- Contracts.

Both can be registered on a blockchain, but only tokens are immediately tradable with third parties, as opposed to only with the issuer. There are several protocols and exchanges (both CEX and DEX) offering on-chain derivative contracts. These are *not* derivative *tokens*. We will explain and provide examples of both tokens and contracts but will use only the former as part of the reference typology.

Derivative token types that proved resilient in time are as depicted in Fig. 4.9.

Option tokens have all the features of their counterparts from traditional finance, their only differences being in terms of allowable underlyings and denomination of premiums—underlyings now being tokens or at least blockchain-referenceable assets. For example, the protocol PsyFi [203] first issued call and put American

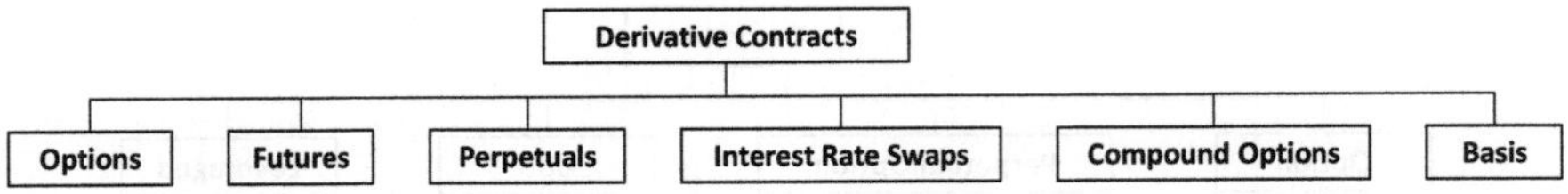

Fig. 4.10 Derivative contracts (*not* tokens) available on exchanges

option tokens [204, 205] and structured products [206]. Similarly, Opium Network [207] allows users to mint and trade call and put option tokens [208, 209].

Perpetual option tokens similarly replicate a traditional finance paradigm, which is that of an option with no expiry date [210]. As an example, Antimatter [196] issues such perpetual option tokens [211, 212].

Credit Default Swap tokens (*CDS tokens*) are meant to protect against issuer (token-issuing project) non-performance risk. The causes of non-performance can be credit events as known also from traditional finance (e.g. insolvency or bankruptcy of the project governing body), but also events specific to the crypto-token world, such as dissolution of the token-issuing project, forced delisting of the token from particular exchanges, etc. Opium Network [207] is an example of a protocol offering CDS tokens [213].

Leveraged-position tokens (*leveraged tokens*) reference other, already circulating, tokens and are priced at a fraction of the spot price of the underlyings. The inverse of this fraction is the leverage value, which can be significant (standard terminology would be "10x" which means "leveraged 10 times"). In return for this leverage, they are subject to liquidation risk if the reference token moves against the position and the posted funds no longer cover the issuance terms. In effect the purchase price represents collateral which must be posted to cover a margined position, like those in traditional finance. Leveraged tokens are issued, e.g. by Synthetix [214, 215] and Bybit [216–218].

Exchange-traded[23] derivative *contracts* on tokens on the other hand are much more varied, covering the entire gamut from futures to swaps to options on futures, as known from traditional finance, including perpetual positions. An indicative taxonomy as observed in current market practice is given on Fig. 4.10.

Many off- and on-chain (centralized and decentralized) exchanges offer such contracts [219], for example:

Options on tokens are call and put contracts [220] referencing prices of listed tokens. They are offered by several exchanges, e.g. CME [221, 222], MIAX [223], Binance [224], BitMEX [225, 226], Delta Exchange [227], Deribit [228], Hegic [229, 230].

Futures on tokens are contracts [231] referencing token prices at specific future dates and can be either deliverable or cash-settled. They are listed and traded at CME [232–234], Kraken [235], Binance [236], BitMEX [237], Deribit [238], among

[23] As opposed to Over-the-Counter (OTC), i.e. bilateral, contracts which are generally concluded among financial institutions and professional counterparties such as large corporates.

others. *Inverse futures* allow to sell such contracts at an exchange, thus taking a short position in an underlying. They are offered, e.g. by BitMEX [239].

Perpetual futures on tokens and token indices serve the same function as traditional "Contracts for Difference" [240]. They are margined positions with no expiry date [241], offered by exchanges such as Deribit [242] and BitMEX [243, 244]. *Inverse perpetual futures* are similarly non-expiring and can be used for hedging as traded at, e.g. BitMEX [245]. The term is used interchangeably with "**Perpetual Swaps**" [246] in some exchanges, such as Flipster [247].

Interest rate swaps on tokens are contracts exchanging reference yield rates on positions as specified by counterparties. They are offered by, e.g. IPOR [248, 249], BitMEX [250].

Compound options on tokens are second-order derivatives (options on options, options on futures, etc.) referencing token prices. Examples of exchanges trading such contracts: CME [251] and Eurex [252].

Basis trading [253] on tokens is also possible through contracts available at, e.g. CME [254, 255] and Opium Network [256].

In summary, there are many possible ways for token transaction participants to either hedge risks (market, counterparty credit, etc.) or to speculate, using instruments similar to traditional financial derivatives. The entire spectrum is covered through contract types traded e.g. in centralized exchanges, but relatively few are minted and traded on-chain as derivative tokens.

4.2.6 Hybrid Tokens

The above representations are necessarily high-level and non-inclusive, serving only to derive a basic token typology in this domain. For example, "deposit tokens", combining the features of Bank accounts and programmable money, have been introduced by some financial institutions [257–260]. Said tokens could be thought of as a hybrid type between asset and currency tokens. Similarly, when it comes to derivative tokens, there are already blockchain-derivatives that are difficult to categorize, but the important criterion is their function and allocation to potential use cases. As hedging and speculation needs evolve, new token types are expected to appear, either mirroring traditional financial contracts or creating hybrid, "exotic" forms. The combination of more sophisticated blockchain-based use cases and availability of off–/on-chain time series (provided e.g. through Oracles) is bound to eventually produce hybrid derivative token forms with combinations of token, physical or notional (e.g. weather [261]) underlyings, and with more complex payoff profiles.

4.2.7 A Note on NFTs

The case of *non-fungible tokens* (NFTs) deserves particular commentary. As we explained in Sect. 4.2, fungibility is a fundamental attribute, a "nature", of tokens shared across token types. It is a technical feature[24] designed to certify uniqueness built into a token, purposely reflecting the uniqueness of either the underlying asset (e.g. a work of art in the off-chain world, as in asset tokens) or of the circumstances under which it is created, or simply in order to distinguish it from other tokens.

For example, Uniswap [61] v3 concentrated liquidity positions [198] (which are in effect staked quantities of different currency tokens, bundled together to facilitate execution of the underlying automated market maker[25]) are technically implemented as NFTs [262–264]. They actually have to be, as the liquidity provider must declare the precise parity rate limits inside which they are staking token quantities, thus creating a "unique" asset. If two liquidity providers declare parity rate limits that are just decimals apart from each other's, then depending on market conditions one of the two liquidity positions may never execute.

The interplay between the two token natures and the need to avoid confusion in their use is quite obvious to financial, legal, and technical experts. For example, ignoring the underlying IP rights of the original author of copyright-protected works will create liability risk for project issuing NFTs against them and potentially for buyers[26] of those tokens as well. Similarly, robust fractional-NFT use cases rely on rigorous identification of the underlying property rights and their appropriate inclusion in the token design, so that imputed legal and regulatory obligations can be complied with. Only once those are clear can the "wrapping" of NFTs into fungible tokens proceed [265, 266]. More generally, property rights transformation through a combination of fungible and non-fungible token types is an investable business case [267, 268].

As an aside, NFTs can be used to simulate closed-end investment funds or private placements in the sense of traditional finance. Those will generally be security tokens, not asset ones.

Even though, as explained, fungibility is a token "nature", not a type, in the crypto-markets the term "NFT" has come to be mostly associated with one particular token *type*, namely asset tokens. Some underlying assets, such as tangible and intangible art (physical paintings, digital art, musical piece intellectual property, individual real estate, etc.) have indeed the de facto uniqueness attribute which NFTs can certify on the blockchain. Others, however, do not. The fact of the matter is that, in the earlier stages of crypto-token evolution, the focus was on business development and technical implementation, not on branding consistency. Developers had to quickly implement and bring their tokens to market so that their financial backers (venture capitalists, angel investors, community members, etc.) could see network effects taking hold. The most successful early implementations of the "non-fungible" concept were in digital art. Once this success had generated a critical mass of

---

[24] Implemented e.g. through smart contracts such as ERC-721 on Ethereum (cf. the comprehensive discussion in Sect. 10.5.5).

[25] Cf. Chaps. 10 and 12.

[26] Cf. Sect. 10.5.6.

news reports, and as more and more follow-on projects tried to address the same investing market, then the term "NFT" was tacitly accepted by trade publications, general publications, and by the investing public as being synonymous with "non-fungible *asset* token".

It is quite probable that non-fungible asset tokens will become increasingly important as an asset class. Emerging organizational and technical paradigms such as Web3 [269] and Metaverse [270] appear to be ideal proving grounds for blockchain-based digital ecosystems to generate novel socio-economic interactions [271] and marketplaces [272]. If that becomes true, then the notion of digital asset ownership will probably be central to their success, and non-fungible asset tokens are already a proven example of the applicability of this notion [273]. Interestingly, even trade publications appear to be using the term "NFT" interchangeably [274], even though what is really meant is only "non-fungible *asset* tokens".

Consistency in the use of terminology is very important, especially among experts. However, when it comes to markets and investors, one must accept the fact that the need for conciseness of terminology is a real, practical one. If close to, say, 90% of issued NFTs at any given time are in effect asset tokens, then it is the task of the expert (technical professional, legal counsel, industry standards organization), rather than of the non-expert, to help correctly identify the occasional 10%. Respecting this reality, we will use the term "NFT" as generally signifying "non-fungible *asset* token" in the reference token typology of the next section and will occasionally point out the technically correct usage in the rest of the book, wherever necessary.

4.3 Reference Token Typology for This Book

Summarizing the observed crypto-token universe, an overview such as that of Table 4.1 can be created.

How useful is that level of detail for economic design?

We believe that such an overview is indeed useful at several levels. A first consideration is that, in order to design, one first needs to analyse. If one is familiar with the salient features of existing token types, then one can allocate one's own specific use case requirements to "most probable" functional features, and see if other projects have already implemented them in their tokens. This way, design does not need to start from scratch but can profit from patterns and antipatterns in tokens that have already been vetted by the marketplace. In other words, familiarity with existing token typology facilitates *baseline design by association.*

Second, clarity of terms facilitates clarity of *design alternatives* to reach objectives. Ambiguity, let alone confusion, about terms employed in complex multidisciplinary projects (as typical crypto-token projects de facto are) is a major risk factor for said projects' business case, architecture, implementation, and funding. Having a glossary linking descriptions of underlying assets, cash flows, value flows, fungibility features, etc., to existing token types should help iterate the design of all those features in ones' own token. Understanding what features have

Table 4.1 Observed cryptocurrency and crypto-token typology

Token Type	Subtype—Level 1	– Level 2	– Level 3
Currency			
	Free floating		
	Pegged		
		Crawling	
		Fixed	
			Stablecoin
			CBDC
Utility			
	Governance		
	Access		
	Service		
	Discount		
	Burn and Mint		
	Mixed		
Asset (fungible/NFT)			
	Tangible		
		Commodity	
		Inventory	
		Art	
		Real estate	
		Working asset	
	Intangible		
		Digital art	
		Intellectual property	
		Rights	
		Insurance policy	
		Working asset	
Security			
	Lending		
	Fixed income		
	Equity		
	Money market		
	Repo		
	Investment fund		
	Structured product		
Derivative			
	Option		
	Perpetual option		
	CDS		
	Leveraged		
Hybrid			

previously caused an existing token to be classified as a cryptocurrency vs a security token should guide an understanding of the repercussions of adding yield income to the own token and under which optionalities (price events, market-making liquidity provision, etc.). Hence, clarity of terms greatly assists *token design.*[27]

Third, at some point in the evolution of any token-issuing project, legal and regulatory repercussions will have to be understood and risk-managed. This will invariably entail communications with experts, auditors, legal counsel, and regulators. In these interactions, it will be essential for the key project roles to be able to explain design features clearly and to help interlocutors understand why certain assumptions and assessments on their part may eventually not be correct. Knowing what the underlying property rights, income streams, and holder or staker obligations in similar cryptocurrencies or marketable crypto-tokens are will be very useful argumentation to help justify why one's own token should be classified as being of type A rather than of another type B. In short, *stakeholder interactions* can profit by a robust token typology, along which a new token can be properly placed.

There are several other points that can be made, but we believe that the value to future token projects of having a (ideally recognized industry-wide) reference token typology is already evident. Importantly, a token typology may by itself be a "statement of facts", an "examination point" if you wish, upon which to agree industry standards and guide thinking by experts and stakeholders at large.

Take for example the postulation of a commodity token (under the tangible asset token type) which is distinct from the free-floating currency token as per Table 4.1.

In Singapore, the Payment Services Act 2019 [275] defines:

'"digital payment token" means any digital representation of value (other than an excluded digital representation of value) that –

(a) *is expressed as a unit;*
(b) *is not denominated in any currency, and is not pegged by its issuer to any currency;*
(c) *is, or is intended to be, a medium of exchange accepted by the public, or a section of the public, as payment for goods or services for the discharge of a debt;*
(d) *can be transferred, stored or traded electronically; and,*
(e) *satisfies such other characteristics as the Authority may prescribe;'*

and

'"e-money" means any electronically stored monetary value that –

(a) *is denominated in any currency, or pegged by its issuer to any currency;'*

Those definitions have been interpreted by legal commentators [276] to correspond to "Free-Floating" and "Pegged" currency tokens as per Table 4.1, respectively.

[27] Cf. Sect. 10.5, where token design factors are addressed in detail.

In Switzerland, the official federal factsheet "Blockchain and cryptoassets in the financial sector" [277] mentions:

> '***Cryptoassets*** *is a collective term for digital assets that are usually recorded on a blockchain. These include not only the so-called Cryptocurrencies that are often the focus of attention and have no backing (e.g. bitcoin) or are linked to a fiat currency in order to reduce their volatility (so-called Stablecoins), but also so-called asset tokens that represent rights (e.g. shares) or physical assets (e.g. wine).*'

The legal basis for the introduction of cryptoassets into the Swiss Civil Code consists of a Federal Law and an Ordinance [278], the latter amending:

(i) The Anti-Money Laundering Ordinance of 11 November 2015 [279], to include (in Art. 4 paras. 1 and 1bis) the text.

> '1bis *Cashless means of payment include, in particular:...*
>
> (b) *virtual currencies which are actually used or intended by the organiser or issuer to be used as a means of payment for acquiring goods or services or as a means of money and value transfer.*'

(ii) The Financial Market Infrastructure Ordinance of 25 November 2015 [280], to include the text.

> '*Art. 58j Other requirements relating to services in the area of central custody, clearing or settlement*
> *(Art. 73e para. 2 of the FinMIA)*
>
> ...
>
> *For a DLT trading facility, liquidity in a currency in accordance with Article 67 paragraph 1 of the FinMIA also includes cryptobased assets, insofar as the payment obligation is to be fulfilled in the same virtual currency.*'

We believe that several crypto-issuing projects make it very clear in their whitepapers that their stated intention had been to mint and circulate currency tokens, functioning exclusively as media of exchange within their respective token ecosystems and imparting no concomitant revenue stream or other property rights to token buyers. For example, the Bitcoin (BTC) Whitepaper [281] explains their business case as being that of "*Bitcoin: A Peer-to-Peer Electronic Cash System*". Similarly, the Ethereum Whitepaper [282] states:

> '*The Ethereum network includes its own built-in currency, ether, which serves the dual purpose of providing a primary liquidity layer to allow for efficient exchange between various types of digital assets and, more importantly, of providing a mechanism for paying transaction fees.*'

Other jurisdictions (notably, as of the time of writing, the United States) have opted for declaring what are termed "currency tokens" in Sect. 4.2.1 as "commodities". We respectfully refrain from analysing the individual circumstances of token classifications for each and every involved jurisdiction[28,29], instead pointing to the feasibility of postulating a "commodity token" type (defined to be a subtype of tangible asset token) that captures tokenized physical commodities and a distinct, well-defined, "currency token" type following the path taken by the lawgiver in Singapore and in Switzerland.

This is the path that we will also follow in the rest of this book. We propose to keep both cryptocurrencies and the other tradable crypto-token types as part of the same token typology but to distinguish clearly between the two classes. By doing so, we are simply following the actual market dynamics, and at the same type creating clarity of terms for token designers, experts, and project stakeholders (including, in the broader meaning of the word, auditors and regulators).

We believe that Table 4.1 provides an essentially complete picture of actual circulating token types, but we cannot preclude that some projects will opt for creating "hybrid" or "mixed" tokens in the future, combining features of several archetypes. In effect, choosing a *candidate* token type is usually expected to happen early on in the ecosystem design process, as this will provide the basic template to thereupon refine functional features such as lifecycle events, transaction modalities, and operational parameters; then on to specifying the precise underlying asset class, the cash flows or value flows, etc. This allows to replicate on-chain the entire gamut of traditional asset classes from single securities (equities, bonds, convertible bonds, commodities, etc.) to investment funds. The added degree of freedom in reference to traditional securities is that both off-chain and on-chain assets will be possible in the mix. In short, nothing prevents mixing a tokenized off-chain security with a native on-chain asset within a token's reference assets. Therefore, we will keep open the option of "hybrid" or "mixed" token types appearing in the future. In that sense, in spite of its level of detail, Table 4.1 still only represents a non-exhaustive taxonomy.

[28] In the United States for example, it appears that the original claim of CFTC jurisdiction on cryptocurrencies was codified in its own administrative order *In the Matter of: Coinflip, Inc., d/b/a Derivabit, and Francisco Riordan, CFTC Docket No. 15–29.3,* itself based on the (pre-internet, let alone pre-blockchain) *Board of Trade of City of Chicago v. SEC,* 677 F. 2d 1137, 1142 (seventh Cir. 1982). The official CFTC brochure *An Introduction to Virtual Currency - This downloadable brochure is a quick guide to virtual currencies that covers how virtual currencies can be purchased, why they are considered commodities,...* (available through a link embedded in the text of [283]) states simply: "Virtual currencies have been determined to be commodities under the Commodity Exchange Act". The act itself [hereafter CEA] is available at e.g. https://www.law.cornell.edu/uscode/text/7/chapter-1]. It can be argued that the definition of "excluded commodity" in the same CEA ["*(19) Excluded commodity. The term "excluded commodity" means—(i) an interest rate, exchange rate, currency, security,...*"—Note: please note the absence of the word "foreign" before "currency"] would suffice to put cryptocurrencies outside the scope of the CEA.

[29] The US State of Wyoming, in its 2019 Digital Assets law ("SF0125" [284]) makes a distinction among "digital consumer asset", "digital security", and "virtual currency". The latter is defined (at Chapter 29, DIGITAL ASSETS, 34–29-101, Definitions) as "a digital asset that is: (A) Used as a medium of exchange, unit of account or store of value; and (B) Not recognized as legal tender by the United States government".

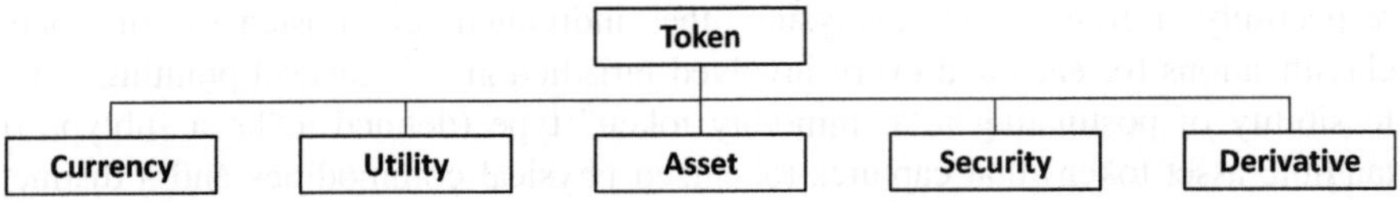

Fig. 4.11 Token typology (high-level, carried over from Fig. 4.2)

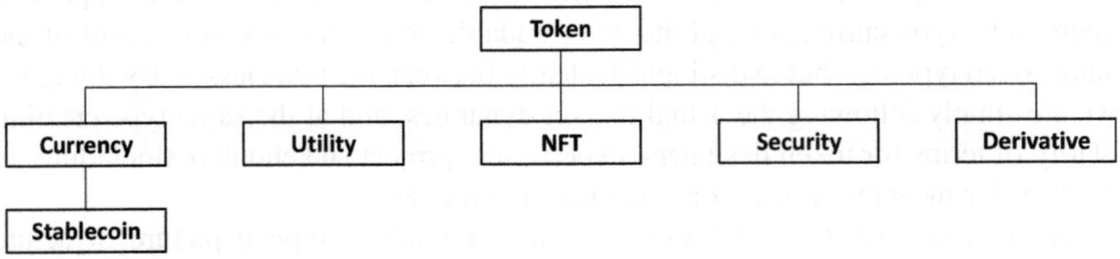

Fig. 4.12 Reference token typology (high-level)

In order to better explain the design *process* put forward in Chaps. 6, 8, and 10 (i.e. to be as specific as possible when describing stages and factors of token design), we propose to *not* "carry with us" the entire taxonomy of Table 4.1. Instead we will focus on the most material token types as observed in the crypto market, and as predicted to influence market dynamics with at least a mid-term horizon. Earlier in this chapter we had proposed a high-level token typology as per Fig. 4.11, reproduced here for convenience:

Having explained the hierarchy of corresponding subtypes, we believe that blockchain-based ecosystems will be increasingly concentrated around the value proposition of particular token types. These will be taken to form our own "reference typology" which we will follow in the rest of the book, to best explain economic token design in the context of end-to-end ecosystem design. This reference token typology will be as per Fig. 4.12.

In comparison with both Fig. 4.11 and Table 4.1, the reference typology will keep in effect only two previously declared "subtypes", namely Stablecoin and NFT, elevating the latter to the role of representative of the entire "asset token" class. As shown in the figure, the important distinction between cryptocurrencies and other tradable crypto-tokens is still preserved, while the potential to encompass new, evolving types, such as real-world asset tokens (cf. Sect. 14.5.3.9), is already captured through security tokens.

All other subtypes as per Table 4.1 will be abstracted through the salient functional features of their parent types, allowance being made for any additional features to be explained separately wherever needed.

4.4 Summary

The rapid evolution of blockchain-based token ecosystems has created a rich universe of tokens, across distinct use cases and through various constellations of underlying property rights.

In this chapter, we propose a comprehensive taxonomy that captures most of the usecase/property rights combinations currently observed. We explain the salient features of each token type, resp. subtype; and give concrete examples of each, with references to their respective ecosystem's documentation. In the process we explain fundamental legal and operational considerations that need to drive token analysis and design. The aspect of "jurisdiction" was shown to be important, both for the individual token as representation of property rights and for its usage within the intended use case. We gave arguments justifying a clear distinction between cryptocurrencies and other tradable crypto-tokens. Finally, we proposed a thinned-down "reference" token typology to use in subsequent chapters, which nevertheless captures the most material types as currently observed in the marketplace and as predicted to remain so with at least a mid-term horizon.

In the following chapter, we will introduce a methodological approach for end-to-end economic design of blockchain-based token ecosystems.

References

1. Mansa, J. (2024, June 02). *What Are Consensus Mechanisms in Blockchain and Cryptocurrency?* Retrieved March 17, 2025, from https://www.investopedia.com/terms/c/consensus-mechanism-Cryptocurrency.asp
2. CoinMarketCap FXS page. CoinMarketCap. Retrieved April 4, 2025, from https://coinmarketcap.com/currencies/frax-share/
3. [Frax ecosystem dApp]. https://app.frax.finance/
4. [NexusMutual Token ecosystem]. https://nexusmutual.io/
5. Commodity currency. (2024, November 20). In *Wikipedia*. Retrieved March 17, 2025, from https://en.wikipedia.org/wiki/Commodity_currency
6. Cashin, P., Céspedes, L., & Sahay, R. (2003, March). Commodity Currencies. *Finance and Development*, 40(1). Retrieved March 17, 2025, from https://www.imf.org/external/pubs/ft/fandd/2003/03/cash.htm
7. Peters, K. (2023, September 19). *Prediction Market: Overview, Types, Examples*. Retrieved March 17, 2025, from https://www.investopedia.com/terms/p/prediction-market.asp
8. [BondbloX, an electronic marketplace for bonds]. https://www.bondblox.com/
9. BondbloX. (2020, August 12). *The BondbloX Bond Exchange Goes Live*. Retrieved March 17, 2025, from https://bondevalue.com/news/the-bondblox-bond-exchange-goes-live/
10. Chen, J. (2024, July 4). *What Are Alternative Investments? Definition and Examples*. Retrieved March 17, 2025, from https://www.investopedia.com/terms/a/alternative_investment.asp
11. Baker, K., & Filbeck, G. (Eds.). (2013). *Alternative investments; instruments, performance, benchmarks, and strategies*. Wiley.
12. [Axie Infinity Token ecosystem]. https://axieinfinity.com
13. [Axie Infinity Whitepaper]. (2021, November). *Axie Infinity*. Retrieved March 18, 2025, from https://whitepaper.axieinfinity.com/
14. Axie Infinity Shards (AXS). Retrieved March 18, 2025, from https://axieinfinity.com/axs/

15. Newbery, E. (2021, July 20). *What Is Axie Infinity (AXS), and Should You Buy It?* Nasdaq/ The Motley Fool. Retrieved March 18, 2025, from https://www.nasdaq.com/articles/what-is-axie-infinity-axs-and-should-you-buy-it-2021-07-20, https://www.fool.com/the-ascent/Cryptocurrency/articles/what-is-axie-infinity-axs-and-should-you-buy-it/
16. [OpenSea NFT marketplace]. https://opensea.io/
17. [Rarible NFT marketplace]. https://rarible.com/
18. [Pictoclub NFT marketplace]. https://www.pictoclub.com/product-category/NFT's/?swoof=1&product_tag=nft&really_curr_tax=1326-product_cat
19. [OpenSea WiV wine collection NFT marketplace]. https://opensea.io/collection/wiv, https://www.wiv.io/nft-marketplace/
20. [Fractional NFT ecosystem]. https://fractional.art/
21. [London Trade Art shares market]. https://www.londontradeart.co.uk/en/artworks/categories/nft-art-shares
22. Freni, P., Ferro, E., & Moncada, R. (2022). Tokenomics and blockchain tokens: A design-oriented morphological framework. *Blockchain: Research and Applications, 3*(1), 1–16. Retrieved March 18, 2025, from https://www.sciencedirect.com/science/article/pii/S2096720922000094
23. Helms, K. (2021, August 4). *SEC Has No Authority Over Pure Commodities Like Crypto Assets, Says CFTC Commissioner*. Bitcoin.com News. Retrieved March 18, 2025, from https://news.bitcoin.com/sec-no-authority-over-pure-commodities-crypto-assets-cftc-commissioner/
24. Joy, J. (2021, November 24). *The Race to Regulate Crypto: CFTC vs. SEC.* Retrieved March 18, 2025, from https://www.jurist.org/commentary/2021/11/john-joy-crypto-sec/
25. Browne, R. (2022, January 17). *Amazon halts plan to stop accepting Visa credit cards in the UK.* Retrieved March 18, 2025, from https://www.cnbc.com/2022/01/17/amazon-halts-plan-to-stop-accepting-visa-credit-cards-in-the-uk.html
26. CFI Team. *Payment Processing Fees - The costs incurred by business owners when processing payments from customers*. Corporate Finance Institute (CFI). Retrieved March 18, 2025., from https://corporatefinanceinstitute.com/resources/knowledge/finance/payment-processing-fees/
27. Caporal, J. (2025, February 14). *Average Credit Card Processing Fees and Costs in 2024.* Motley Fool Money. Retrieved March 18, 2025, from https://www.fool.com/the-ascent/research/average-credit-card-processing-fees-costs-america/
28. World Bank. (2024, September). Remittance Prices Worldwide Quarterly, Issue 51, 11–32. Retrieved March 18, 2025, from https://remittanceprices.worldbank.org/sites/default/files/rpw_main_report_and_annex_q324.pdf, https://remittanceprices.worldbank.org/en/about-remittance-prices-worldwide
29. World Bank. Remittance Prices Worldwide Quarterly. https://remittanceprices.worldbank.org/en
30. PayPal stablecoin - Built for payments. *1 USD : 1 PYUSD on PayPal*. https://cointelegraph.com/news/paypal-Stablecoin-what-it-could-mean-for-payments. Retrieved March 18, 2025, from https://www.paypal.com/us/digital-wallet/manage-money/crypto/pyusd
31. Adams, J. (2022, January 11). *PayPal poses big threat to banks in race to develop stablecoins.* American Banker. Retrieved March 18, 2025, from https://www.americanbanker.com/payments/news/paypal-poses-big-threat-to-banks-in-race-to-develop-Stablecoins
32. Rajpal, A. & Marschall, P. (2021, July 13). *Op-ed: Stablecoin is the future of virtual payments. How wise regulation can foster its growth.* CNBC. Retrieved March 18, 2025, from https://www.cnbc.com/2021/07/13/op-ed-the-future-is-Stablecoin-wise-regulation-can-foster-its-growth.html
33. Redman, J. (2019, December 24). *Getting In and Out of the Cryptocurrency Economy Can Be Costly*. Bitcoin.com News. Retrieved March 18, 2025, from https://news.bitcoin.com/getting-in-and-out-of-the-Cryptocurrency-economy-can-be-costly/

34. Reiff, N. (2024, September 11). *How Much Are Cryptocurrency Exchange Fees?* Retrieved March 18, 2025, from https://www.investopedia.com/tech/how-much-does-it-cost-buy-cryptocurrency-exchanges/
35. Directive 2009/65/EC of the European Parliament and of the Council of 13 July 2009 on the coordination of laws, regulations and administrative provisions relating to undertakings for collective investment in transferable securities (UCITS) (recast). Retrieved March 18, 2025, from https://eur-lex.europa.eu/eli/dir/2009/65/oj/eng
36. European Securities and Markets Authority (ESMA). (2023, June 14). *Questions and Answers; Application of the UCITS Directive*. ESMA34–43-392. Retrieved March 18, 2025, from https://www.esma.europa.eu/sites/default/files/library/esma34_43_392_qa_on_application_of_the_ucits_directive.pdf. Section II explains details for the preparation of the Key Investor Information Document.
37. Hayes, A. (2024, December 2). *Bitcoin ETF Fee Comparison*. Retrieved March 18, 2025, from https://www.investopedia.com/bitcoin-etf-fee-comparison-8749352
38. Torpey, K. (2024, July 19). Spot Ether ETF Issuers Unveil Expenses - Here's How They Compare. Retrieved March 18, 2025, from https://www.investopedia.com/spot-ether-issuers-unveil-expenses-here-s-how-they-compare-8680055
39. Sinclair, S. (2021, September 14). Dollar-Backed Stablecoins Are Holding Their Own Amid Coronavirus Chaos. *CoinDesk*. Retrieved March 18, 2025, from https://www.coindesk.com/markets/2020/03/18/dollar-backed-Stablecoins-are-holding-their-own-amid-coronavirus-chaos/
40. Van Straten, J. (2025, January 31). *Stablecoin Market Surges Past $200B, Signaling Potential Crypto Price Upswing*. CoinDesk. Retrieved March 18, 2025, from https://www.coindesk.com/markets/2025/01/31/stablecoin-market-surges-past-usd200b-signaling-potential-crypto-price-upswing
41. Adachi, M., Born, A., Gschossmann, I. & van der Kraaij, A. (2021, November). The expanding functions and uses of Stablecoins. *Financial Stability Review*. European Central Bank. Retrieved March 18, 2025, from https://www.ecb.europa.eu/pub/financial-stability/fsr/focus/2021/html/ecb.fsrbox202111_04~45293c08fc.en.html
42. Adachi, M., Pereira Da Silva, P.B., Born, A., Cappuccio, M. Czák-Ludwig, S., Gschossmann, I., Pellicani, A., Philipps, S.-M., Plooij, M., Rossteuscher, I., & Zeoli, P. (2022, July). *Stablecoins' role in crypto and beyond: functions, risks and policy. Macroprudential Bulletin*. European Central Bank. Retrieved March 18, 2025, from https://www.ecb.europa.eu/press/financial-stability-publications/macroprudential-bulletin/html/ecb.mpbu202207_2~836f682ed7.en.html
43. Bank for International Settlements. (2019, October). *Investigating the impact of global Stablecoins*. Committee on Payments and Market Infrastructures. Retrieved March 18, 2025, from https://www.bis.org/cpmi/publ/d187.pdf
44. Curve AMO [Algorithmic Market Operation minting FRAX Stablecoins]. Frax Finance documentation pages. Retrieved March 18, 2025, from https://docs.frax.finance/frax-v3-100-cr-and-more/amos#curve-amo, https://docs.frax.finance/minting-and-redeeming
45. Arner, D., Auer, R. & Frost, J. (2020, November). *Stablecoins: risks, potential and regulation*. BIS Working Papers No 905. Monetary and Economic Department, Bank for International Settlements. Retrieved March 18, 2025, from https://www.bis.org/publ/work905.pdf
46. Top Stablecoin Tokens by Market Capitalization. CoinMarketCap. Retrieved March 18, 2025, from https://coinmarketcap.com/view/stablecoin/
47. Bank for International Settlements. (2018, March). *Central bank digital currencies*. Committee on Payments and Market Infrastructures & Markets Committee. Retrieved March 18, 2025, from https://www.bis.org/cpmi/publ/d174.pdf
48. BIS Innovation Hub work on central bank digital currency. Retrieved March 18, 2025, from https://www.bis.org/about/bisih/topics/cbdc.htm

49. Bank for International Settlements. (2021, September). *Central bank digital currencies: system design and interoperability*. Retrieved March 18, 2025, from https://www.bis.org/publ/othp42_system_design.pdf
50. Bank for International Settlements. (2021, September). *Central bank digital currencies: user needs and adoption*. Retrieved March 18, 2025, from https://www.bis.org/publ/othp42_user_needs.pdf
51. Bank for International Settlements. (2021, September). *Central bank digital currencies: financial stability implications*. Retrieved March 18, 2025, from https://www.bis.org/publ/othp42_fin_stab.pdf
52. Central Bank Digital Currency Tracker. Atlantic Council. Retrieved March 18, 2025, from https://www.atlanticcouncil.org/cbdctracker/
53. Huang, R. (2024, July 15). *A 2025 Overview Of The E-CNY, China's Digital Yuan*. Forbes. Retrieved March 18, 2025, from https://www.forbes.com/sites/digital-assets/2024/07/15/a-2024-overview-of-the-e-cny-chinas-digital-yuan/, https://www.investopedia.com/digital-yuan-and-china-crypto-plans-5215329
54. Digital renminbi. (2025, January 18). In *Wikipedia*. Retrieved March 18, 2025, from https://en.wikipedia.org/wiki/Digital_renminbi
55. Working Group on E-CNY Research and Development of the People's Bank of China. (2021, July). Progress of Research & Development of E-CNY in China. People's Bank of China (PBoC). Retrieved March 18, 2025, from http://www.pbc.gov.cn/en/3688110/3688172/4157443/4293696/2021071614584691871.pdf
56. Petro (token). (2024, November 17). In *Wikipedia*. Retrieved March 18, 2025, from https://en.wikipedia.org/wiki/Petro_(token)
57. (2022, February 26). *Petro (PTR): What it Means, Concerns, FAQs*. Retrieved March 18, 2025, from https://www.investopedia.com/terms/p/petro-cryptocurrency.asp, https://www.investopedia.com/terms/p/petro-Cryptocurrency.asp
58. [MakerDAO Token ecosystem] https://makerdao.com/en/https://makerdao.com/en/. Retrieved April 4, 2025. Please note: MakerDAO is currently a subset of the Sky Token ecosystem (https://sky.money/).
59. [MakerDAO Whitepaper – MCD version preceding migration to Sky.money] *The Maker Protocol: MakerDAO's Multi-Collateral Dai (MCD) System*. Retrieved April 5, 2025., from https://makerdao.com/whitepaper/White%20Paper%20-The%20Maker%20Protocol_%20MakerDAO%E2%80%99s%20Multi-Collateral%20Dai%20(MCD)%20System-FINAL-%20021720.pdf, linked into from https://makerdao.com/en/whitepaper
60. Use of the MKR Token in Sky Governance. Retrieved April 4, 2025, from https://makerdao.com/en/whitepaper/#use-of-the-mkr-token-in-sky-governance. Please note: MakerDAO is currently a subset of the Sky Token ecosystem (https://sky.money/)
61. [Uniswap Token ecosystem.] https://uniswap.org/
62. Adams, H., Zinsmeister, N., Salem, M., Keefer, R. & Robinson, D. (2021, March). *Uniswap v3 Core*. Retrieved April 4, 2025, from https://uniswap.org/whitepaper-v3.pdf
63. (2020, September 16). *Introducing UNI*. Uniswap blog. Retrieved March 18, 2025, from https://uniswap.org/blog/uni/
64. *Uniswap Governance Forum*. Uniswap governance pages. Retrieved March 18, 2025., from https://gov.uniswap.org/
65. [Vesper Token ecosystem]. https://vesper.finance/
66. Frequently Asked Questions. Vesper documentation pages. Retrieved March 18, 2025, from https://docs.vesper.finance/faq
67. VSP Token: Supply, Issuance, & Rewards. Vesper documentation pages. Retrieved March 18, 2025., from https://docs.vesper.finance/vsp-economics/supply-dynamics
68. Governance Principles. Vesper documenation pages. Retrieved March 18, 2025, from https://docs.vesper.finance/community-participation-and-governance/founding-principles-of-governance
69. [Access Token ecosystem]. https://www.accessprotocol.co/en

70. [Use of ACS Token]. Access documentation pages. Retrieved March 18, 2025, from https://docs.accessprotocol.co/guide#basics#deeper-explanation
71. CoinMarketCap ACS page. CoinMarketCap. Retrieved March 18, 2025, from https://coinmarketcap.com/currencies/access-protocol/
72. [Bancor Token ecosystem]. (2017, April 28). https://bancor.network/whitepaper linked into from https://bancor.network/about, please search on the Webpage for "DeFi Primitives).
73. [Bancor Whitepaper]. (2017, April 28). https://bancor.network/whitepaper, linked into from https://bancor.network/about, please search on the Webpage for "DeFi Primitives", "Constant Product". Note: there are 3 (three) links under "DeFi Primitives", each corresponding to a different generation of the ecosystem.
74. (2019, March 5). What Is Bancor Network Token? Introduction to BNT Token. CryptoBriefing. Retrieved March 18, 2025, from https://cryptobriefing.com/what-is-bancor-network-token-introduction-to-bnt-token/
75. [Augur Token infrastructure software.] https://github.com/AugurProject
76. [Augur v2 Whitepaper], Peterson, J., Krug, J., Zoltu, M., Williams, A.K. & Alexander S. (2025, March 21). *Augur: a Decentralized Oracle and Prediction Market Platform (v2.0)*. Forecast Foundation. Retrieved April 12, 2025, from https://github.com/AugurProject/whitepaper/releases/latest/download/augur-whitepaper-v2.pdf
77. Kraken Learn team. (2024, October 18). *What is Augur? (REP)*. Retrieved March 18, 2025, from https://www.kraken.com/learn/what-is-augur-rep
78. [Keep Token ecosystem]. https://keep.network/
79. [Keep Whitepaper] Luongo, M. & Pon, C. (2019, February 19). *The Keep Network: A Privacy Layer for Public Blockchains*. Retrieved March 18, 2025, from https://coinpare.io/whitepaper/keep-network.pdf
80. Kraken Learn team. (2022, January 19). *What is Keep Network? (KEEP)*. Retrieved March 18, 2025, from https://www.kraken.com/en-gb/learn/what-is-keep-network
81. About KEEP Tokens. Keep documentation pages. Retrieved March 19, 2025, from https://staking.keep.network/keep-tokens/staking-with-keep
82. [Kleros Token ecosystem]. https://kleros.io/
83. [Keep Whitepaper] Lesaege, C. Ast, F. & George, W. (2019, September). *Kleros - short Paper v.1.0.7*. Retrieved March 19, 2025, from https://kleros.io/static/whitepaper_en-8bd3a0480b45c39899787e17049ded26.pdf
84. PNK Token. Retrieved March 19, 2025, from https://kleros.io/token/
85. George, W. (2018, June 7). *Why Kleros Needs a Native Token?* Medium. Retrieved March 19, 2025, from https://medium.com/kleros/why-kleros-needs-a-native-token-5c6c6e39cdfe
86. [Binance Token ecosystem]. https://www.binance.com/en
87. BNB: Understanding its Utility on Binance. Retrieved March 19, 2025, from https://www.binance.com/en/bnb
88. CoinMarketCap BNB page. CoinMarketCap. Retrieved March 19, 2025, from https://coinmarketcap.com/currencies/bnb/
89. [Bitfinex Token ecosystem]. https://www.bitfinex.com/
90. UNUS SED LEO Token Holder Benefits. Bitfinex support pages. Retrieved March 19, 2025, from https://support.bitfinex.com/hc/en-us/articles/900000064023-UNUS-SED-LEO-Token-Holders-Benefits
91. [LEO -] A token designed to empower the Bitfinex community. Retrieved March 19, 2025, from https://leo.bitfinex.com/
92. CoinMarketCap UNUS SED LEO page. CoinMarketCap. Retrieved March 19, 2025, from https://coinmarketcap.com/currencies/unus-sed-leo/
93. [Sweetbridge Token ecosystem]. https://sweetbridge.com/
94. How SWC fits in. Retrieved March 19, 2025, from https://sweetbridge.com/how-swc-fits-in/
95. SWC transactions. Retrieved March 19, 2025, from https://etherscan.io/token/0xff32d68d8a4608fba6b51f07d1f138a63a149211
96. [Accumulate Token ecosystem]. https://accumulatenetwork.io/, https://www.factom.com/

97. [Accumulate Whitepaper] Michelson, K., Sridharan, A., Can Çabuk, U., Reesor, E., Stolman, B., Mailen D., Bunfield, D., Smith, J., & Snow, P. (2022, April 12). *Accumulate: An identity-based blockchain protocol with cross-chain support, human-readable addresses, and key management capabilities*. Retrieved March 19, 2025, from https://accumulatenetwork.io/Accumulate-Whitepaper-4-12-22.pdf
98. Powered by ACME. Retrieved March 19, 2025, from https://accumulatenetwork.io/#acme
99. ACME-related Accumulate FAQ's. Retrieved March 19, 2025, from https://accumulatenetwork.io/learn/#acme
100. LiveCoinWatch ACME page. LiveCoinWatch. Retrieved March 19, 2025, from https://www.livecoinwatch.com/price/Accumulate-ACME
101. [Helium Token ecosystem]. https://www.helium.com/
102. [Helium Whitepaper] Haleem, A., Allen, A., Thompson, A., Nijdam, M. & Garg R. (2018, November 14). *Helium; A Decentralized Wireless Network*. Retrieved March 19, 2025, from http://whitepaper.helium.com/
103. The Helium Network Token. Helium documentation pages. Retrieved March 19, 2025, from https://docs.helium.com/blockchain/helium-token
104. [Paxos Token ecosystem]. https://www.paxos.com
105. [Paxos Gold Whitepaper] Cascarilla, C. (2019, September 5). *PAX GOLD White Paper, V1.0*. Retrieved March 19, 2025, from https://www.paxos.com/pax-gold (through the link labelled "Read now" underneath "Pax Gold White Paper").
106. Paxos Gold (PAXG) Token. Retrieved March 19, 2025, from https://www.paxos.com/pax-gold
107. [Silvertoken Token ecosystem]. https://silvertoken.com/
108. *Understanding Silver Token (SLVT)*. Retrieved March 19, 2025., from https://silvertoken.com/silvertokens/ (please search in the Webpage for "SLVT").
109. (2023, December 28). *Nornickel's digitalisation firm issues tokens for platinum group metals*. Nornickel. Retrieved March 19, 2025, from https://nornickel.com/news-and-media/press-releases-and-news/nornickel-s-digitalisation-firm-issues-tokens-for-platinum-group-metals/
110. Atomyze. Retrieved March 19, 2025, from https://atomyze.us/
111. (2021, July 15). *Artemundi and Sygnum Bank present the world's first tokenization of a Picasso listed by a regulated bank*. Artemundi. Retrieved March 19, 2025, from https://artemundi.com/artemundi-and-sygnum-bank-present-the-worlds-first-tokenization-of-a-picasso-listed-by-a-regulated-bank/, https://artemundi.com/artemundi-and-sygnum-bank-present-the-worlds-first-tokenization-of-a-picasso-listed-by-a-regulated-bank/
112. Schroeder, S. (2021, June 24). *Sotheby's to auction Picasso painting together with NFT*. Mashable. Retrieved March 19, 2025, from https://mashable.com/article/picasso-nft
113. (2018, September 6). Maecenas successfully tokenises first multi-million dollar artwork on the blockchain. Maecenas. Retrieved March 19, 2025, from https://blog.maecenas.co/blockchain-art-auction-andy-warhol/
114. Fries, T. (2018, October 7). $30 Million Manhattan Property Tokenized in 'Landmark Deal'. TheTokenist. Retrieved March 19, 2025, from https://tokenist.com/30-million-manhattan-property-tokenized-in-landmark-deal/, https://tokenist.com/30-million-manhattan-property-tokenized-in-landmark-deal/
115. Fries, T. (2019, January 20). Aspencoin Transitions to Securitize After Raising $18 Million in Security Token Offering. TheTokenist. Retrieved March 19, 2025, from https://tokenist.com/aspencoin-transitions-to-securitize-after-raising-18-million-in-security-token-offering/
116. Fractional and frictionless real estate investing. RealT. Retrieved March 19, 2025, from https://realt.co/
117. (2024, December 16). What can I do with my RealTokens? How to use them as collateral? RealT FAQ pages. Retrieved March 19, 2025, from https://faq.realt.co/en/article/what-can-i-do-with-my-realtokens-how-to-use-them-as-collateral-1085fsh/, https://wiki.realt.co/far/realt-realtokens

118. (2025, January 30). Secondary Market: What is the YAM? How does the Whitelisting work? How to use them as collateral? RealT FAQ pages. Retrieved March 19, 2025, from https://faq.realt.co/en/article/secondary-market-what-is-the-yam-how-does-the-whitelisting-work-mp71wo/, https://realt.co/marketplace
119. RedSwan ("Regulated and Compliant Advisors for Tokenized Real Estate"). Retrieved March 19, 2025., from https://redswan.io/
120. Redolfi, A. (2021, October 27). The Future Of Real Estate Transactions On The Blockchain. Forbes. Retrieved March 19, 2025, from https://www.forbes.com/councils/forbesbizcouncil/2021/10/27/the-future-of-real-estate-transactions-on-the-blockchain/, https://www.forbes.com/sites/forbesbizcouncil/2021/10/27/the-future-of-real-estate-transactions-on-the-blockchain/
121. XDC Network (Decentralized Smart Contracts Platform). Retrieved March 19, 2025, from https://xinfin.org/
122. Monteiro, L. (2021, September 28). XinFin and Tradeteq launch trade finance-based NFT transaction. IBS intelligence. Retrieved March 19, 2025, from https://ibsintelligence.com/ibsi-news/xinfin-and-tradeteq-launch-trade-finance-based-nft-transaction/, https://ibsintelligence.com/ibsi-news/xinfin-and-tradeteq-launch-trade-finance-based-nft-transaction/
123. [CargoX platform for Blockchain Document Transfer (BDT)]. Retrieved March 19, 2025, from https://cargox.io/
124. (2018, August 13). CargoX Completes Trial Shipment with 1st Ever Smart Bill of Lading. Offshore-Energy. Retrieved March 19, 2025, from https://www.offshore-energy.biz/cargox-completes-trial-shipment-with-1st-ever-smart-bill-of-lading/
125. Manaadiar, H. (2018, October 3). Product Review : CargoX's Blockchain based Smart Bill of Lading. ShippingAndFreightResource. Retrieved March 19, 2025, from https://www.shippingandfreightresource.com/cargox-blockchain-based-smart-bill-of-lading/
126. [Provenance Token ecosystem.] https://www.provenance.io/
127. [Book Token ecosystem.] https://book.io/
128. [Bookchain Token ecosystem.] https://www.bookchain.ca/
129. [Publica NFT platform.] https://publica.com/
130. [Royal Token ecostystem.] https://royal.io/
131. [Opulous Token Ecosystem.] https://opulous.org/
132. (2016, June 15). *Blockchain technology successfully piloted by Allianz Risk Transfer and Nephila for catastrophe swap*. Allianz corporate communication. Retrieved March 19, 2025, from https://www.allianz.com/content/dam/onemarketing/azcom/Allianz_com/migration/media/press/document/Press_Release_ART_Blockchain_pilot_final.pdf
133. (2021, January 27). Eurapco and B3i introduce blockchain risk transfer solution. Life Insurance International. Retrieved March 19, 2025, from https://www.lifeinsuranceinternational.com/news/eurapco-b3i-introduce-blockchain-risk-transfer-solution-unity/
134. Cover [products undewritten through Nexus Mutual]. Nexus Mutual documentation pages. Retrieved March 20, 2025, from https://docs.nexusmutual.io/protocol/cover
135. [PitchBook fidentiaX page, showing company status] PitchBook. Retrieved March 20, 2025, from https://pitchbook.com/profiles/company/469789-39#overview
136. [fidentiaX Whitepaper] Xchange with Confidence. Retrieved March 20, 2025, from https://www.allcryptowhitepapers.com/wp-content/uploads/2018/05/fidentiax.pdf
137. Braun, A., Cohen, L.H. & Xu, J. (2019, May). *fidentiaX: the Tradable Insurance Marketplace on Blockchain*. Harvard Business School Case 219–116. Retrieved March 20, 2025, from https://www.hbs.edu/faculty/Pages/item.aspx?num=56189
138. [CoreLedger tokenization platform.] https://coreledger.net/
139. Sinclair, S. (2021, February 1). *Fine Wines Become First Tokenized Securities Under New Swiss Blockchain Law*. Retrieved March 20, 2025, from https://www.coindesk.com/business/2021/02/01/fine-wines-become-first-tokenized-securities-under-new-swiss-blockchain-law

140. [Sygnum Bank Tokenization services] Retrieved March 20, 2025., from https://www.sygnum.com/solutions/tokenization/
141. (2024, December 10). *Tokenizing Tree Planting*. Retrieved March 20, 2025, from https://treetherium.io/tokenizing-tree-planting/
142. [U.K.] Financial Conduct Authority (FCA). *Glossary*. FCA Handbook. Retrieved March 20, 2025, from https://www.handbook.fca.org.uk/handbook/glossary.
143. Rubin, J. (2021, September 14). *CFTC Commissioner Says SEC Lacks Authority Over Commodities, Including 'Crypto Assets'*. CoinDesk. Retrieved March 20, 2025, from https://www.coindesk.com/markets/2021/08/05/cftc-commissioner-says-sec-lacks-authority-over-commodities-including-crypto-assets
144. [The Howey case] SEC v. Howey Co., 328 U.S. 293 (1946). Judgment retrieved March 20, 2025, from https://supreme.justia.com/cases/federal/us/328/293/
145. [U.S.] Securities and Exchange Commission. (2024, July 5). *Framework for "Investment Contract" Analysis of Digital Assets*. Retrieved March 20, 2025, from https://www.sec.gov/corpfin/framework-investment-contract-analysis-digital-assets
146. The Investopedia Team. (2024, August 11). Zero-Sum Game Definition in Finance, With Example. Investopedia. Retrieved March 20, 2025, from https://www.investopedia.com/terms/z/zero-sumgame.asp
147. (2018). *The New Palgrave Dictionary of Economics*, 3rd Ed. Palgrave Mcmillan. Referenced text to be found in p. 14697.
148. Loev, D.M. & Gillies, J. (2017, April 27). *What Constitutes a Security and Requirements Relating to the Offer and Sales of Securities and Exemptions From Registration Associated Therewith*. American Bar Association. Retrieved March 20, 2025, from https://www.americanbar.org/groups/business_law/resources/business-law-today/2017-april/what-constitutes-a-security-and-requirements-relating-to-the-off/
149. Geneva Convention - UNIDROIT Convention on Substantive Rules for Intermediated Securities. International Institute for the Unification of Private Law (UNIDROIT). Retrieved March 20, 2025, from https://www.unidroit.org/instruments/capital-markets/geneva-convention/
150. Central securities depository. (2025, March 29). In *Wikipedia*. Retrieved April 12, 2025, from https://en.wikipedia.org/wiki/Central_securities_depository
151. Bindseil, U., & Pantelopoulos, G. (2023). *Introduction to payments and financial market infrastructures*. Springer. Referenced text to be found in ch. 8.
152. Binder, J.-H., & Saguato, P. (Eds.). (2021). *Financial market infrastructures: Law and regulation*. Oxford University Press. Part III.
153. Yates, M., & Montagu, G. (2013). *The law of global custody* (4th ed.). Bloomsbury Professional.
154. (2019, November). *Tokenised Securities - A Roadmap for Market Participants and Regulators*. Asia Securities Industry and Financial Markets Association (asifma). Retrieved April 3, 2025, from https://asifma.org/wp-content/uploads/2019/11/tokenised-securities-a-roadmap-for-market-participants-final.pdf
155. [TrueFi Token ecosystem]. https://truefi.io
156. Gilbert, J. (2022, October 6). *The Investor's Guide to TrueFi Capital Markets*. BlockWorks. Retrieved March 20, 2025, from https://blockworks.co/news/the-investors-guide-to-truefi-capital-markets, https://blog.trusttoken.com/introducing-truefi-the-defi-protocol-for-uncollateralized-lending-9bfd6594a48
157. TrueFi. (2022, April 1). *Introducing Repayment-Free Loans*. Medium. Retrieved March 20, 2025, from https://medium.com/trust-token/introducing-repayment-free-loans-fa430ab475c1
158. [TrueFi dApp]. https://app.truefi.io/loans
159. [Compound Token ecosystem]. https://compound.finance/
160. [Compound] cTokens; Introduction. Compound documentation pages. Retrieved March 20, 2025, from https://docs.compound.finance/v2/ctokens/

161. The LITI Token - private equity's best kept secret. LitiCapital. Retrieved March 20, 2025, from https://liticapital.com/liti-capital-tokens/
162. [LitiCapital Token ecosystem]. https://liticapital.com/
163. Chang, E. & McCarthy, S. (2022, March 16). *Litigation Finance and Crypto Tokens: How a Blockchain Startup Seeks to Create Financing Marketplaces for Disputes*. Kluwer Arbitration blog. Retrieved March 20, 2025, from https://arbitrationblog.kluwerarbitration.com/2022/03/16/litigation-finance-and-crypto-tokens-how-a-blockchain-startup-seeks-to-create-financing-marketplaces-for-disputes/
164. [Aave Token ecosystem]. https://aave.com/
165. [Aave] Borrow. Aave documentation pages. Retrieved March 20, 2025, from https://docs.aave.com/faq/borrowing
166. [Aave] Flash Loans. Aave documentation pages. Retrieved March 20, 2025, from https://aave.com/docs/concepts/flash-loans
167. (2019, September 12). *Santander launches the first end-to-end blockchain bond*. Santander Corporate Communication. Retrieved March 20, 2025, from https://www.santander.com/en/press-room/press-releases/santander-launches-the-first-end-to-end-blockchain-bond
168. (2021, April 28). *EIB issues its first ever digital bond on a public blockchain*. European Investment Bank. Retrieved March 20, 2025, from https://www.eib.org/en/press/all/2021-141-european-investment-bank-eib-issues-its-first-ever-digital-bond-on-a-public-blockchain
169. SIX Digital Exchange. Retrieved March 20, 2025, from https://www.sdx.com/
170. (2021, November 18). *SIX Launches its SIX Digital Exchange by Successfully Issuing the World's First Digital Bond in a Fully Regulated Environment*. SIX Corporate Communication. Retrieved March 20, 2025, from https://www.six-group.com/en/newsroom/media-releases/2021/20211118-six-sdx-digital-bond.html, https://www.six-group.com/en/newsroom/media-releases/2021/20211118-six-sdx-digital-bond.html
171. Digital Bonds at SDX. Swiss Digital Exchange (SDX). Retrieved March 20, 2025, from https://www.sdx.com/digital-bonds/, https://www.sdx.com/exchange/market-activity/bonds
172. Ngetich, D. (2021, January 14). *Europe's Top Real Estate Company Taps Stellar Blockchain To Issue €20 Million Bond*. Crypto.news. Retrieved March 20, 2025, from https://crypto.news/europes-top-real-estate-company-taps-stellar-blockchain-to-issue-e20-million-bond/, https://crypto.news/europes-top-real-estate-company-taps-stellar-blockchain-to-issue-e20-million-bond/
173. (2019, April 23). *Societe Generale issued the first covered bond as a security token on a public blockchain*. Societe Generale Corporate Communication. Retrieved March 20, 2025, from https://www.societegenerale.com/en/news/newsroom/societe-generale-issued-first-covered-bond-security-token-public-blockchain, https://www.societegenerale.com/sites/default/files/19038_pr_sg_first_covered_bond-security_tokens-blockchain_en_0.pdf
174. (2021, April 15). *Societe Generale issues the First Structured Product on Public Blockchain. Societe Generale Corporate Communication*. Retrieved March 20, 2025, from https://www.societegenerale.com/en/news/press-release/first-structured-product-public-blockchain, https://www.societegenerale.com/en/news/press-release/first-structured-product-public-blockchain
175. Obligate - Debt capital markets on-chain. Retrieved March 20, 2025, from https://www.obligate.com/
176. eNote [Class of debt securities structured as on-chain tokens]. Obligate Glossary pages. Retrieved March 20, 2025, from https://docs.obligate.com/obligate/glossary#enote
177. eNote legal framework. Obligate documentation pages. Retrieved March 20, 2025, from https://docs.obligate.com/legal/enote-legal-framework
178. Sygnum Bank. Retrieved March 20, 2025, from https://www.sygnum.com/
179. (2020, December 14). Sygnum Bank tokenizes its shares, and lays foundation for potential future public offering. Sygnum Bank corporate communications. Retrieved March 20, 2025, from https://www.sygnum.com/news/sygnum-bank-tokenizes-its-shares-and-lays-foundation-for-potential-future-public-offering/, https://www.insights.sygnum.com/post/sygnum-the-world-s-first-bank-to-tokenize-its-shares-lays-foundation-for-future-public-offering

180. Aktionariat [Equity tokenization platform]. Retrieved March 20, 2025, from https://www.aktionariat.com/
181. Soars, B. (2019, April 9). USPX — A Security Token backed by a derivative of SpaceX shares. Medium. Retrieved March 20, 2025, from https://medium.com/@briansoans/uspx-a-security-token-backed-by-a-derivative-of-spacex-shares-488d1045c4aa
182. (2019, April 11). You Can Now Own Tokenized Shares of SpaceX Stock. BeInCrypto. Retrieved March 20, 2025, from https://beincrypto.com/you-can-now-own-tokenized-shares-of-spacex-stock/
183. (2021, May 5). *CGS-CIMB and iSTOX Roll Out Digital Securities Issuance in S$150-million Commercial Paper Programme*. TheTokenizer. Retrieved March 20, 2025, from https://thetokenizer.io/2021/05/05/cgs-cimb-and-istox-roll-out-digital-securities-issuance-in-s150-million-commercial-paper-programme/
184. *Genesis Bond - A digitised short-term bond with attractive coupons.* ADDX corporate communications. Retrieved March 20, 2025., from https://addx.co/en/investments/genesis/index.html, https://addx.co/en/investments/cgs-cimb/
185. Goschenko, S. (2021, June 30). *Compound Launches Treasury to Introduce Institutions to Defi*. Bitcoin.com. Retrieved March 20, 2025, from https://news.bitcoin.com/compound-launches-treasury-to-introduce-institutions-to-defi/, https://news.bitcoin.com/compound-launches-treasury-to-introduce-institutions-to-defi/
186. (2020, June 29). *CoinFLEX Launches Centrally Cleared and Traded Repo Market.* BusinessWire. Retrieved March 20, 2025, from https://www.businesswire.com/news/home/20200629005543/en/CoinFLEX-Launches-Centrally-Cleared-and-Traded-Repo-Market
187. (2024, November 11). ABN AMRO embraces intraday repo, wCBDC, in ECB DLT settlement trials. LedgerInsights. Retrieved March 20, 2025, from https://www.ledgerinsights.com/abn-amro-embraces-intraday-repo-wcbdc-in-ecb-dlt-settlement-trials/
188. https://addx.co/en/
189. Unicorn Opportunity Fund. ADDX corporate communications. Retrieved March 20, 2025, from https://addx.co/en/investments/unicorn/index.html
190. How ADDX works for you. ADDX corporate communications. Retrieved March 20, 2025, from https://addx.co/en/how-addx-works/index.html
191. [Yearn Token ecosystem.] https://yearn.fi/
192. [Yearn] yVaults. Yearn documentation pages. Retrieved March 20, 2025, from https://docs.yearn.fi/getting-started/intro#yvaults
193. [Yearn] yVault Types. Yearn documentation pages. Retrieved March 20, 2025, from https://docs.yearn.fi/getting-started/products/yvaults/overview
194. [Yearn] Vault Tokens. Yearn documentation pages. Retrieved March 20, 2025, from https://docs.yearn.fi/getting-started/products/yvaults/vault-tokens
195. [Yearn] yToken [definition]. Yearn Glossary pages. Retrieved March 20, 2025, from https://docs.yearn.fi/resources/defi-glossary#ytoken
196. [Antimatter Token ecosystem.] https://invest.antimatter.finance/
197. [Antimatter] Structured Products. Retrieved March 20, 2025, from https://invest.antimatter.finance/#/dual_invest
198. [Uniswap] Concentrated Liquidity. Uniswap documentation pages. Retrieved March 20, 2025, from https://docs.uniswap.org/concepts/protocol/concentrated-liquidity
199. Lambert, G. (2021, June 23). *Uniswap V3 LP Tokens as Perpetual Put and Call Options.* Retrieved March 20, 2025, from https://lambert-guillaume.medium.com/uniswap-v3-lp-tokens-as-perpetual-put-and-call-options-5b66219db827
200. Cryptocurrency futures and options. CME Group asset class pages. Retrieved March 20, 2025, from https://www.cmegroup.com/markets/cryptocurrencies.html#overview, https://www.cmegroup.com/markets/Cryptocurrencies.html-explore-our-Cryptocurrency-products
201. The trusted path to crypto - Cryptocurrency Derivatives. Eurex product pages. Retrieved March 20, 2025, from https://www.eurex.com/ex-en/markets/crypto

202. International Securities Identification Numbers (ISIN) Organization. Retrieved March 20, 2025, from https://www.isin.org/
203. [PsyFi Decentralized Options Token ecosystem.] https://app.psyfi.io/
204. Thurman, A. (2023, May 11). *PsyOptions Raises $3.5M for Options Liquidity Mining and NFT Derivatives.* CoinDesk. Retrieved March 20, 2025, from https://www.coindesk.com/business/2021/10/19/psyoptions-raises-35m-for-options-liquidity-mining-and-nft-derivatives
205. The Oasians. (2022, January 13). *PsyOptions Analysis - The Battle of Options on Solana.* Medium. Retrieved March 20, 2025, from https://medium.com/the-oasians/psyoptions-the-battle-of-options-on-solana-bbc87a661325
206. Why use PsyFi? PsyFi documentation pages. Retrieved March 20, 2025, from https://docs.psyfi.io/
207. [Opium Token ecosystem.] https://opium.network/
208. Biosas, R. (2021, September 27). *Build a call option on Opium.* Medium. Retrieved March 20, 2025, from https://medium.com/opium-network/build-a-call-option-on-opium-432c055fcbfa
209. Opium derivatives. Opium documentation pages. Retrieved March 20, 2025, from https://docs.opium.network/complex-description/opium-derivatives, https://docs.opium.network/complex-description/opium-derivatives
210. Mitchell, C. (2022, July 25). *Perpetual Option (XPO): What it Means, How it Works, Example.* Retrieved March 20, 2025, from https://www.investopedia.com/terms/p/perpetual-option.asp
211. Antimatter Perpetual Options introduction. Antimatter documentation pages. Retrieved March 20, 2025, from https://docs.antimatter.finance/antimatter-perpetual-options/introduction, https://docs.antimatter.finance/antimatter-perpetual-options/structure
212. [Antimatter dApp] Retrieved March 20, 2025., from https://app.antimatter.finance/#/option_trading
213. (2021, May 7). *Opium Insurance.* Opium "Academy" pages. Retrieved March 20, 2025, from https://opium.finance/academy/opium-insurance/academyinsurance/
214. [Synthetix Token ecosystem]. https://www.synthetix.io/
215. [Synthetix Leveraged Tokens] The Simplest Way to Trade with Leverage. Synthetix product pages. Retrieved March 20, 2025, from https://leverage.synthetix.io/
216. [Bybit Centralized Exchange]. https://www.bybit.com/en
217. (2025, March 18). *Introduction to Bybit Leveraged Tokens.* Bybit product pages. Retrieved April 12, 2025, from https://www.bybit.com/en/help-center/article/Introduction-to-Bybit-Leveraged-TokensLeveraged_Token_UTA
218. (2024, October 30). *How to Get Started With Bybit Leveraged Tokens.* Bybit support pages. Retrieved April 12, 2025, from https://www.bybit.com/en/help-center/article/How-to-Get-Started-with-Bybit-Leveraged-TokensLeveraged_Token
219. Top Cryptocurrency Derivatives Exchanges. CoinMarketCap. Retrieved March 20, 2025, from https://coinmarketcap.com/rankings/exchanges/derivatives/
220. Downey, L. (2024, November 15). *What Is Options Trading? A Beginner's Overview.* Retrieved March 20, 2025, from https://www.investopedia.com/options-basics-tutorial-458301
221. Bitcoin Futures and Options. CME Group asset class pages. Retrieved March 20, 2025, from https://www.cmegroup.com/markets/cryptocurrencies/bitcoin/bitcoin.html
222. FAQ: options on Cryptocurrency futures. CME Group support pages. Retrieved March 20, 2025, from https://www.cmegroup.com/articles/faqs/frequently-asked-questions-options-on-cryptocurrency-futures.html
223. Trade Bitcoin Binary Options. Miax Derivatives Exchange. Retrieved March 20, 2025, from https://www.miaxdx.com/
224. FAQ [on Crypto-Options]. Binance support pages. Retrieved March 20, 2025, from https://www.binance.com/en/support/faq/c-4?navId=4#19

225. Perpetual Contracts Guide. BitMEX product pages. Retrieved March 20, 2025, from https://www.bitmex.com/app/perpetualContractsGuide
226. Futures Guide. BitMEX product pages. Retrieved March 20, 2025, from https://www.bitmex.com/app/futuresGuide
227. [Delta Exchange | Global - Crypto-Options and Futures Centralized Exchange.] https://global.delta.exchange/, https://www.delta.exchange/
228. Inverse Options [on Cryptoassets]. Deribit support pages. Retrieved April 12, 2025, from https://support.deribit.com/hc/en-us/articles/25944688327069-Inverse-Options, https://www.deribit.com/kb/options
229. [Hegic - Crypto-Options and Structured Products Decentralized Exchange]. https://www.hegic.co/
230. [Entry to Hegic product pages] Introduction. Hegic product pages. Retrieved April 12, 2025, from https://www.hegic.co/app#/learn/introduction
231. Fernando, J. (2024, April 10). What Is Futures Trading? Retrieved March 21, 2025, from https://www.investopedia.com/terms/f/futures.asp
232. Micro Cryptocurrency futures and options. CME Group product pages. Retrieved March 21, 2025, from https://www.cmegroup.com/markets/cryptocurrencies/micro-cryptocurrency-futures-and-options.html
233. Micro Bitcoin - Futures and Options. CME Group product pages. Retrieved March 21, 2025, from https://www.cmegroup.com/markets/cryptocurrencies/bitcoin/micro-bitcoin.html
234. *Micro Ether - Futures and Options*. CME Group product pages. Retrieved March 21, 2025, from https://www.cmegroup.com/markets/cryptocurrencies/ether/micro-ether.html
235. [Crypto] Futures trading. Kraken [Centralized Exchange] product pages. Retrieved March 21, 2025, from https://www.kraken.com/features/futures
236. Trade Crypto Futures. Binance (Centralized Exchange) product pages. Retrieved March 21, 2025, from https://www.binance.com/en/futures/home
237. Quanto Futures. BitMEX (Centralized Exchange) product pages. Retrieved March 21, 2025, from https://www.bitmex.com/app/quantoFuturesGuide
238. Futures (inverse). Deribit support pages. Retrieved April 03, 2025 from https://support.deribit.com/hc/en-us/articles/25944756746397-Futures-inverse
239. Inverse Futures. BitMEX product pages. Retrieved March 21, 2025, from https://www.bitmex.com/app/inverseFuturesGuide
240. Chen, J. (2024, June 7). *Contract for Difference (CFD) Definition, Uses, and Examples*. Retrieved March 21, 2025, from https://www.investopedia.com/terms/c/contractfordifferences.asp
241. (2019, July 15). What Are Perpetual Futures Contracts? Binance "Academy" pages. Retrieved March 21, 2025, from https://academy.binance.com/en/articles/what-are-perpetual-futures-contracts
242. [Deribit BTC Perpetual Future page] Retrieved March 21, 2025., from https://www.deribit.com/futures/BTC-PERPETUAL
243. Perpetual Contracts Guide. BitMEX product pages. Retrieved March 21, 2025, from https://www.bitmex.com/app/perpetualContractsGuide
244. Quanto Perpetual Contracts. BitMEX product pages. Retrieved March 21, 2025, from https://www.bitmex.com/app/quantoPerpetualsGuide
245. Inverse Perpetual Contracts. BitMEX product pages. Retrieved March 21, 2025, from https://www.bitmex.com/app/inversePerpetualsGuide
246. Sergeenkov, A. (2021, October 5). *What Is a Perpetual Swap Contract?* CoinDesk. Retrieved March 21, 2025, from https://www.coindesk.com/learn/what-is-a-perpetual-swap-contract/
247. Perpetual Swaps. Flipster (Centralized Exchange) support pages. Retrieved March 21, 2025, from https://flipster.io/en/support/guide/perpetual-swaps
248. [IPOR Token ecosystem.] https://www.ipor.io/
249. Interest Rate Derivative. IPOR documentation pages. Retrieved March 21, 2025, from https://docs.ipor.io/interest-rate-derivatives/interest-rate-derivative

250. [Interest Rate Perpetual] XBTUSD: Contract Specification. BitMEX product pages. Retrieved March 21, 2025, from https://www.bitmex.com/app/seriesGuide/app/contract/XBTUSD
251. Cryptocurrency Options on Futures. CME Group product pages. Retrieved March 21, 2025, from https://www.cmegroup.com/markets/cryptocurrencies/options.html
252. Options on FTSE Bitcoin Index Futures [EUR] (OBTE). Eurex product pages. Retrieved March 21, 2025, from https://www.eurex.com/ex-en/markets/crypto/bitcoin-ethereum/Options-on-FTSE-Bitcoin-Index-Futures-EUR%2D%2D3706920
253. Scott, G. (2025, April 11). *Basis Trading: Definition, How It Works, Example*. Retrieved March 21, 2025, from https://www.investopedia.com/terms/b/basis-trading.asp
254. Basis Trade at Index Close (BTIC) and new BTIC+. CME Group product pages. Retrieved March 21, 2025, from https://www.cmegroup.com/trading/equity-index/btic-transactions.html, https://www.cmegroup.com/trading/equity-index/btic-transactions.html-cryptocurrency
255. Basis Trade at Index Close (BTIC) on Cryptocurrency futures. CME Group product pages. Retrieved March 21, 2025, from https://www.cmegroup.com/trading/btic-on-cryptocurrency-futures.html, https://www.cmegroup.com/articles/faqs/btic-on-cryptocurrency-futures-faq.html
256. [Basis trading] Opium swaps (TMtm). Opium documentation pages. Retrieved March 21, 2025, from https://docs.opium.network/complex-description/opium-swaps-tmtm
257. Deposit Tokens - A foundation for stable digital money. Kinexys by J.P.Morgan. Retrieved March 21, 2025, from https://www.jpmorgan.com/kinexys/content-hub/deposit-tokens
258. (2023, March). *The Deposit Token - New money for digital Switzerland.* Swiss Bankers Association White Paper. Retrieved March 21, 2025, from https://www.swissbanking.ch/_Resources/Persistent/9/4/1/1/941178de59b98030206fc15ac8c99012f65df30b/SBA_The_Deposit_Token_EN_2023.pdf
259. (2024, September 18). *Swiss banks sign memorandum of understanding to explore the feasibility of a jointly issued Swiss franc deposit token.* Swiss Bankers Association corporate communication. Retrieved March 21, 2025, from https://www.swissbanking.ch/en/news-and-positions/news/schweizer-banken-unterzeichnen-absichtserklaerung-um-die-machbarkeit-eines-gemeinsam-emittierten-schweizer-franken-buchgeld-tokens-zu-pruefen
260. European Banking Authority (EBA). (2024, December 12). *The EBA assesses potential benefits and challenges of tokenised deposits*. EBA corporate communication. Retrieved March 21, 2025, from https://www.eba.europa.eu/publications-and-media/press-releases/eba-assesses-potential-benefits-and-challenges-tokenised-deposits
261. Hussain, A. (2022, May 20). *Weather Derivative: Definition, How It Works, Types & Examples*. Retrieved March 21, 2025, from https://www.investopedia.com/terms/w/weatherderivative.asp
262. Asset [definition in Uniswap]. Uniswap Glossary pages. Retrieved March 21, 2025, from https://docs.uniswap.org/protocol/concepts/V3-overview/glossary#asset
263. [Uniswap v3 Whitepaper] Adams, H., Zinsmeister, N., Salem, M., Keefer, R. & Robinson, D. (2021, March). Uniswap v3 Core. Retrieved April 4, 2025, from https://uniswap.org/whitepaper-v3.pdf. Please consult chapter 2, titled Concentrated Liquidity.
264. AARON. (2021, June 1). *Everything You Need to Know About Uniswap LP NFTs*. APY.vision. Retrieved March 21, 2025, from https://blog.apy.vision/uniswapnft/
265. McConaghy, T. (2021, June 5). *NFTs & IP 3: Combining ERC721 & ERC20. Representing base IP with ERC721 and fungible IP licenses with ERC20, to combine benefits of both.* Retrieved March 21, 2025, from https://blog.oceanprotocol.com/NFT's-ip-3-combining-erc721-erc20-b69ea659115e
266. NFT and FT with Royalty Distribution System #3601. Ethereum EIP GitHub pages. Retrieved March 21, 2025, from https://github.com/ethereum/EIPs/issues/3601
267. Hoogendoorn, R. (2020, May 8). *Niftex Allows NFT Investing Through Partial Ownership*. Medium. Retrieved March 21, 2025, from https://medium.com/play-to-earn/niftex-allows-nft-investing-through-partial-ownership-4e706ca3c9c1

268. Understanding the benefits of fractional ownership in NFTs. Coinbase. Retrieved March 21, 2025, from https://www.coinbase.com/en-de/learn/crypto-basics/understanding-the-benefits-of-fractional-ownership-in-nfts
269. Web3. (2025, April 15). In *Wikipedia*. Retrieved April 15, 2025, from https://en.wikipedia.org/wiki/Web3
270. Kaur, G. (2023, August 1). *What is metaverse in blockchain? A beginner's guide on an internet-enabled virtual world*. CoinTelegraph. Retrieved March 21, 2025, from https://cointelegraph.com/metaverse-for-beginners/what-is-metaverse-in-blockchain, https://cointelegraph.com/metaverse-for-beginners/what-is-metaverse-in-blockchain
271. Napoli, R. (2021, December 27). *The NFT Metaverse: Building A Blockchain World*. Forbes. Retrieved March 21, 2025, from https://www.forbes.com/sites/forbestechcouncil/2021/12/27/the-nft-metaverse-building-a-blockchain-world/
272. Cantú, C., Franco, C. & Frost, J. (2024, February 7). *The economic implications of services in the metaverse*. BIS Papers No 144. Bank for International Settlements (BIS). Retrieved March 21, 2025, from https://www.bis.org/publ/bppdf/bispap144.pdf
273. Choi, J. & Ha, J. (2021, July 22). *Fueling the Path toward the Metaverse*. Stanford Journal of Blockchain Law & Policy (16). Retrieved March 21, 2025, from https://stanford-jblp.pubpub.org/pub/toward-the-metaverse/release/1
274. (2021, December 8). *Why NFTs Are The Keys To Accessing The Metaverse*. Retrieved March 21, 2025, from https://www.binance.com/en/blog/nft/why-NFT's-are-the-keys-to-accessing-the-metaverse-421499824684903085
275. [Singapore] Payment Services Act 2019. Retrieved March 21, 2025, from https://sso.agc.gov.sg/Acts-Supp/2-2019/Published/20190220, https://sso.agc.gov.sg/Acts-Supp/2-2019/Published/20190220
276. Anderson, P. (2024, August 2). *In Depth: Virtual Currency Regulation - Singapore*. Lexology. Retrieved March 21, 2025, from https://www.kgplegal.com.sg/wp-content/uploads/2024/08/Lexology-In-Depth-Virtual-Currency-Regulation-Singapore.pdf
277. [Switzerland] State Secretariat for International Finance. (2023, September 20). Blockchain / DLT. Retrieved March 17, 2025, from https://www.sif.admin.ch/en/blockchain-dlt-en
278. [Switzerland] Ordinance of June 18, *2021 on the Alignment of Federal Law to Developments in the Technology of Distributed Electronic Ledgers* (primary legal source exists only in German). Retrieved March 17, 2025, from https://www.fedlex.admin.ch/eli/oc/2021/400/de, https://www.sif.admin.ch/dam/sif/en/dokumente/Blockchain/blockchain_dlt_verordnung.pdf.download.pdf/DLT Ordinance.pdf
279. [Switzerland] 955.01 - Ordinance on Combating Money Laundering and Terrorist Financing (Anti-Money Laundering Ordinance, AMLO) of 11 November 2015 [as amended]. Retrieved March 17, 2025, from https://www.fedlex.admin.ch/eli/cc/2015/791/en
280. [Switzerland] 958.11 - Ordinance on Financial Market Infrastructures and Market Conduct in Securities and Derivatives Trading (Financial Market Infrastructure Ordinance, FinMIO) of 25 November 2015 [as amended]. Retrieved March 17, 2025, from https://www.fedlex.admin.ch/eli/cc/2015/854/en
281. [Bitcoin (BTC) Whitepaper] Nakamoto, S. *Bitcoin: A Peer-to-Peer Electronic Cash System*. Retrieved March 27, 2025., from https://bitcoin.org/bitcoin.pdf
282. [Ethereum Whitepaper] (2025, February 12). *Ethereum Whitepaper*. Retrieved March 27, 2025, from https://ethereum.org/en/whitepaper/
283. Digital Assets. [U.S.] Commodity Futures Trading Commission (CFTC). Retrieved March 21, 2025., from https://www.cftc.gov/digitalassets/index.htm
284. *SF0125 - Digital Assets Act no.39 of 2019*. [U.S.] State of Wyoming. Retrieved March 21, 2025., from https://www.wyoleg.gov/Legislation/2019/sf0125

5 The Need for Token Ecosystem Design

A comprehensive token taxonomy was presented in the previous chapter, with each proposed type exemplified by concrete crypto-tokens already trading in the crypto markets. What should be apparent from that *exposé* is that, irrespective of their type, tokens are inseparable from the business use case(s) of their generating ecosystem. They are issued ("minted") only on a particular blockchain, serving the economic purposes of a particular ecosystem, through processes defined and controlled by the latter's governance. Once used in transactions, they can have economic effects both on and off the blockchain. In specific token cases (e.g. when they have de facto the attributes of securities), their issuance and usage impute legal and operational risks that need to be managed also in the off-blockchain, physical world.

It is thus important to have an understanding of the end-to-end design parameters of the business case(s) behind any particular token. Both opportunities and risks must be placed in a proper context before decisions can be reached. The current chapter will explain why this design context needs to be that of the *entire* blockchain-based ecosystem in which the token is issued and used.

5.1 Token Lifecycle and Usage

In Chap. 3 it was asserted that there is real economic value created in blockchain-based ecosystems and that tokens are the means to create, express, and capture this value.

If their role in ecosystems is that important, a number of questions can validly be raised, such as: How exactly are economic agents supposed to use them? Can there be both use and misuse of tokens? Can any agent (or outside factor for that matter) harm the ecosystem through its tokens? Can there be harmful effects outside the ecosystem because of its tokens? Is there ever a valid case for tokens to be completely withdrawn from circulation?

I. Giannakouros, *Cryptocurrencies and Tradable Crypto-Tokens*, Future of Business and Finance, https://doi.org/10.1007/978-3-031-98423-5_5

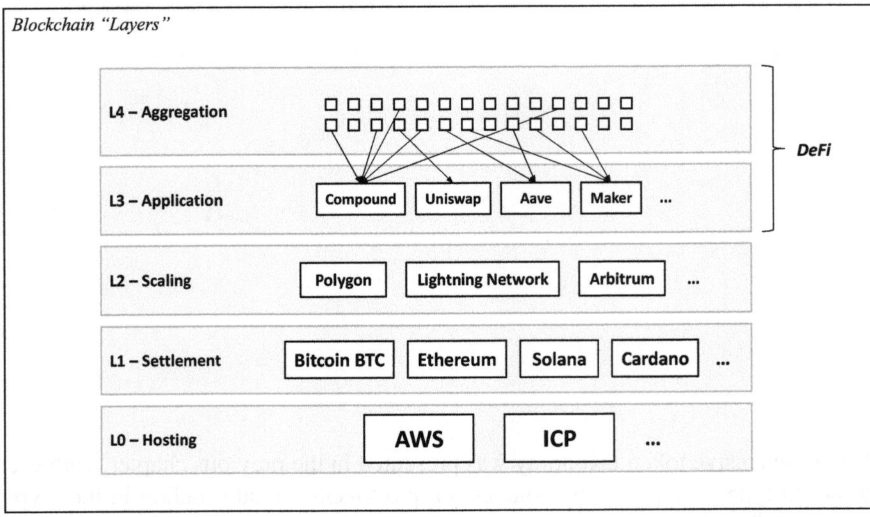

Fig. 5.1 "Platform layers" of blockchain-based ecosystems

To answer these questions, it is expedient to begin by examining the typical stages in the "life", so to speak, of tokens. In other words, by understanding how they are created, how they are used, how and when they are withdrawn—and by whom.

Token creation has come to be called "minting" in industry parlance. The term evokes notions of forging coins from metals, but in the digital space, it is only a metaphor. However, the very real concept behind the metaphor is that of something having an intrinsic "value". In short, in analogy to the tangible, commodity value of the material inside a coin, there is *always* value "inserted" into a token at its creation. There is no such thing as an ecosystem token[1] created without some value having been "inserted" into it.

There are two concepts that need to be considered in order to concretize this notion. First, the "blockchain layers"[2] on which ecosystems are created and, second, the six meta-industrial factors of production—both repeated here for convenience in Figs. 5.1 and 5.2 respectively. Tokens are minted in platform layers L1 and higher, with L3/L4 dependent on L-1/L-2 for infrastructure services which also impact their minting options.[3] In fact, tokens issued on permissionless L-1/L-2 blockchains have one more minting mode which is missing from L3 and higher ones: the "reward for validation" through consensus mechanisms [1] ["Proof-of-<#>"]). As explained in Chap. 1, updating the underlying Distributed Ledger (DL) necessitates validating the

[1] Of course, there can be "scam tokens". As always, caveat emptor. Due diligence is the right and responsibility of every serious buyer or investor. It is also the reason for the emergence of a financial services industry branch dedicated exclusively to token audit and assurance.

[2] Cf. Sect. 1.5.

[3] A comprehensive overview of minting mode variations is presented in Sect. 10.5.5.

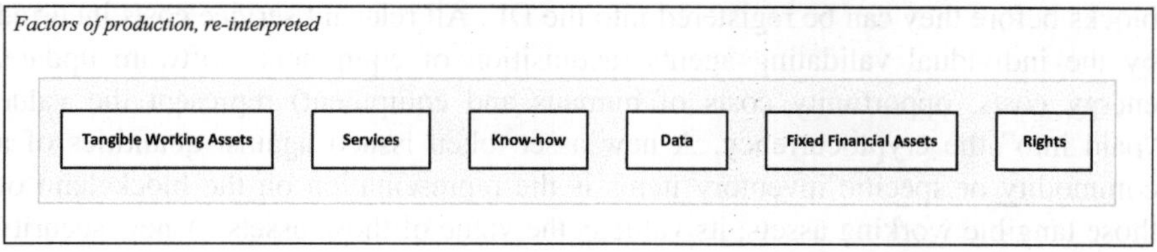

Fig. 5.2 Six basic factors of production in a meta-industrial socio-economic context

integrity and consistency of transactions contained in each new candidate block. This validating action is executed in parallel by independent agents who, once successful, are rewarded by newly issued tokens. Only upon their reaching consensus, in the sense of this parallel validating process, is the new block allowed to be "appended" to the blockchain and, concomitantly, its contained transactions to be recorded into the DL. This is the minting mechanism behind cryptocurrencies of L1 blockchains such as Bitcoin [2] (BTC [3]—issued through "Proof-of-Work" validation [4]), Ethereum [5] (ETH [6]—originally through "Proof-of-Work" [7], then transitioned into a "Proof-of-Stake" [8] paradigm), Avalanche [9] (AVAX [10]—"Proof-of-Stake" [11]), Solana [12] (SOL [13]—a hybrid between "Proof-of-Stake" and "Proof-of-History" [14]), etc. And similarly for some cryptocurrencies of L-2 blockchains, such as Polygon [15] (POL [16]—minted through a modified "Proof-of-Stake" [17] validation), etc.

Typically for ecosystems of L-3 and higher, the usual minting mode is by "Smart Contract". A smart contract ("SC" for the sake of brevity in the following) is simply a piece of code stored on the blockchain, programmed to execute once some pre-specified conditions have been met, as registered on the underlying DL. Minting is only one among the many uses of SCs (cf. detailed discussion in s. 10.5.5), while there are various alternative technical specifications to follow in their implementation, depending on the underlying blockchain and the idiosyncrasies of the target use case.

For the purposes of the current chapter, the important fact is that token minting through SCs always involves "*something of value*" that is "*backing*" the token. In other words, an SC acts as the transformation logic through which a specific value (a mix of tangible or intangible assets, financial assets, services, know-how data, rights; or even another token or a mix of tokens) is being expended, committed, or "paid-in" so that the token can be issued against it. The logic in question may be expressed in mathematical form, linking e.g. token types and amounts "paid-in" to "new token amounts" issued; in which case the committed value is said to be "bonded" to the smart contract, and the precise mathematical form is called a "bonding function"[4] in industry parlance.

Thus a newly minted cryptocurrency such as Bitcoin or Ether is akin to a payment for services rendered, the latter being the validation of the consistency of transaction

[4]"Bonding Functions" and their uses are explained in detail in Chap. 12

blocks before they can be registered into the DL. All relevant service costs incurred by the individual validating agents (acquisition of equipment, software update, energy costs, opportunity costs of humans and equipment) represent the value "paid into" the cryptocurrency. A new asset token issued against quantities of a commodity or specific inventory items is the representation on the blockchain of those tangible working assets; its value is the value of those assets. A new security token represents at least the value of the underlying financial assets; for particular subtypes (e.g. investment fund tokens) it also includes the costs of (a) assembling and hedging all securities needed to create the risk-return profile declared in the investor documentation, (b) know-how behind this service, (c) compiling the investor documentation and having it approved by the relevant regulators. Similarly, a newly minted NFT against a piece of intellectual property represents both data (original, or certified copy, of said IP) and some constellation of property rights around them. We will call this the "underlying value" of a new token. Based on the "detailed" token typology (as per Sect. 4.3, Table 4.1), it is possible to gain an overview of how each newly minted token type is linked to which factors of production creating its underlying value. This overview appears in the following Table 5.1.

It is important to add that some blockchain-based ecosystems provide for both "issuance" and "redemption" services, the latter signifying accepting own tokens and paying back a value denominated in some pre-specified assets. However, ecosystems will typically have token "issuance", but not necessarily "redemption" service points. Harking back to notions of traditional finance, a token's "Primary Market" for issuance will be its own ecosystem. However, redemption may be possible only in a "Secondary Market" where price quoting and possibly market-making in terms of token pairs (possibly even between tokens and fiat currencies) is available. Centralized exchanges ("CEX" for short) and decentralized exchanges ("DEX") are the secondary markets of the crypto-world; the former signifying a marketplace controlled and operated by a central authority with significant human decision-making, the latter one which is blockchain-specific and mostly algorithmically-driven.

If an ecosystem provides both "issuance" and "redemption" service points, it may still be technically possible for agents to "export" (resp. "import") tokens to (resp. from) outside exchanges, or even other ecosystems. In such a case, the constellation of "primary" and "secondary" markets provides a mechanism for token price discovery through arbitrage (explained below).

"Primary Market" issuance of a generic token " Ŧ " is depicted in Fig. 5.3, whereby blockchain-based ecosystem "A" is assumed to provide only an "issuance" service point. Economic agent #1 supplies the requisite value for a quantity of Ŧ's to be minted and credited to #1's blockchain address on the underlying DL. #1 can now use their Ŧ's in ecosystem transactions.

In the chain of transactions shown schematically on Fig. 5.4, "1" is the minting transaction of a cryptocurrency Ŧ. Agent #1 uses an amount of Ŧ's to pay for services provided by agent #2. The latter uses said Ŧ's to acquire assets sold by agent #3, who in turn decides to top them up with more Ŧ's and use the total to acquire an insurance

Table 5.1 Factors of production creating the value that goes into newly minted tokens, arranged by token type

Token type	Tangible working assets	Services	Know-How	Data	Fixed financial assets	Rights
Currency						
Free floating		×				
Pegged						
Crawling		×	×		×	
Fixed						
Stablecoin		×	×		×	
CBDC					×	
Utility						
Governance					×	×
Access	×	×	×		×	×
Service					×	×
Discount	×	×			×	×
Burn & Mint		×	×		×	×
Asset (fungible/NFT)						
Tangible						
Commodity	×					
Inventory	×					
Art						×
Real estate	×				×	
Working asset	×					
Intangible						
Digital art			×	×		×
IP				×		×
Rights						×
Insurance policy		×	×		×	×
Working asset		×	×	×		×
Security						
Lending					×	
Fixed income					×	
Equity					×	
Money market					×	
Repo			×		×	
Investment fund			×		×	
Structured product			×		×	×
Derivative						
Option					×	×
Perpetual option			×		×	×
CDS					×	×
Leveraged			×		×	×

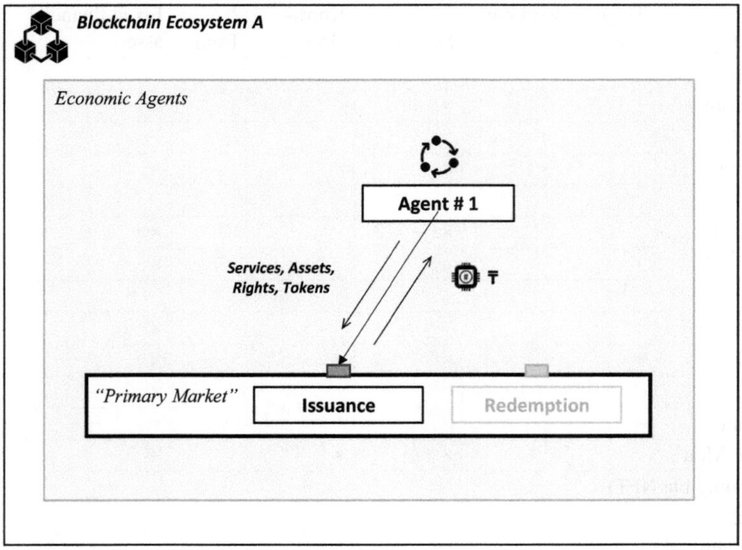

Fig. 5.3 Token issuance in its "Primary Market" (ecosystem "A")

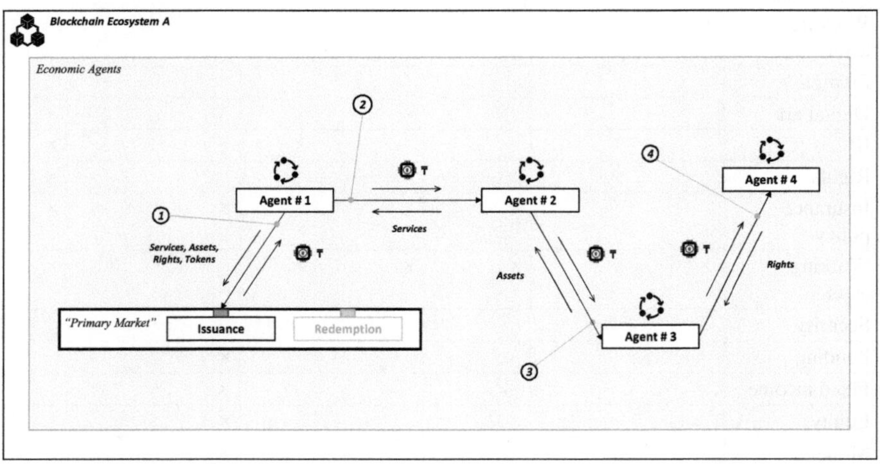

Fig. 5.4 Token issuance and use in ecosystem "A"

policy from agent #4. In each of these transactions, there occurs price negotiation, contractual agreement, transfer of Ŧ's and settlement against assets or services, etc. All these transactions are registered through the blockchain on the DL of ecosystem A. The blockchain addresses of agents #1 to #4 are credited and debited sequentially as Ŧ's are exchanged.

Ecosystem A governance may have decided to limit the circulating amount of Ŧ's, either by inducing scarcity or by controlling the issuance and redemption rates

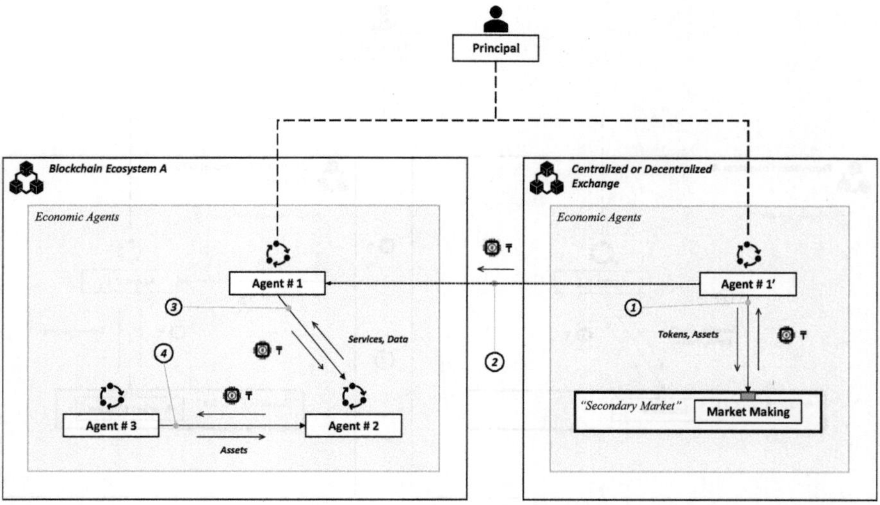

Fig. 5.5 Token purchase in secondary market and use in ecosystem "A"

("inflation"[5]). In such a case, there may occur market situations when there is a dearth of available ₸'s in A to exchange in transactions.

This is where exchanges (the "Secondary Market") step in. As depicted in Fig. 5.5, agent #1 (onboarded and participating in blockchain ecosystem A), needing but not finding ₸'s on A, is controlled in the physical world by a principal—here assumed to be a human, only for the sake of example. Said principal is also onboarded and allowed to transact in a CEX or DEX as agent " #1′ ". There they can acquire ₸ at the secondary market price (transaction "1"). Assuming interconnectivity between A and the secondary market, they then transfer the ₸'s onto A in transaction "2" (in practical terms, there will be a crediting entry against the blockchain address of agent #1 in the DL of A and a corresponding debiting one by reference to that of #1′ in the accounts of the CEX/DEX). Transactions "3" and "4" then proceed as usual.

For the sake of completeness, it must be noted that all those ecosystem transactions without exception—including the token minting one, #1 in Fig. 5.4—may incur "platform fees" (a kind of taxation to fund ecosystem governance tasks) which may also be ₸-denominated. CEX/DEX transactions on the other hand are also loaded with commissions or other charges, which may or may not be payable in ₸.

Staying with the case of ₸ being a cryptocurrency, the same principal controlling agents #1 and #1′ may discover that the quoted price for ₸ in the secondary market is

[5]The meaning of notions such as "scarcity", "inflation", etc., in the context of cryptocurrencies and other tradable crypto-tokens are explained in detail in Chap. 10

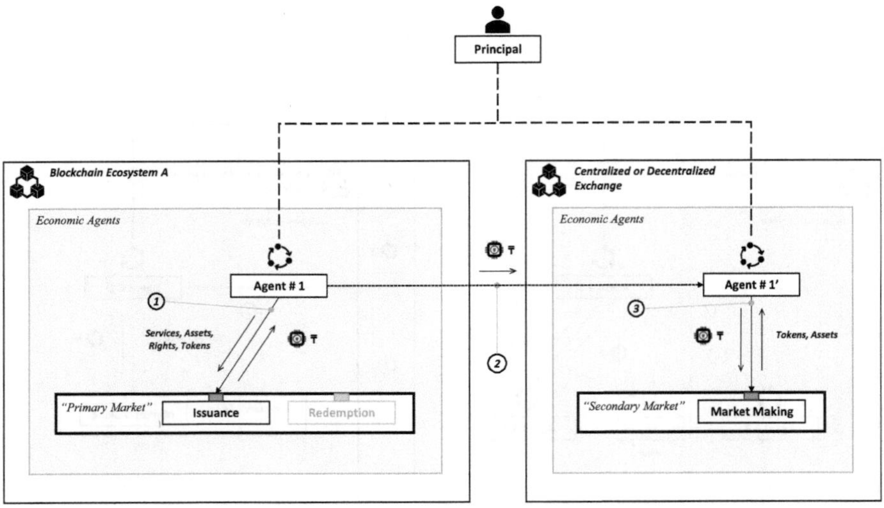

Fig. 5.6 Token issuance in the primary market and sale in the secondary market

temporarily higher than the implied one for value in the primary market (after platform fees, commissions, and charges). They may thus choose to buy Ŧ at issuance, then transfer and sell Ŧ on the exchanges. Without going into the practical details of cross-charging between blockchain addresses and accounts, the sequence of transactions is as depicted on Fig. 5.6.

Assuming that blockchain ecosystem A offers both "issuance" and "redemption" points for Ŧ, reversing the flow of transactions ordered by the principal explains the other leg of arbitrage mechanisms on the basis of continuous price discovery for circulating cryptocurrencies. The pattern is explained in Fig. 5.7, where agent #1′, acting for their principal, buys Ŧ's in transaction #4, then transfers them to agent #1 on A, who finally exchanges them for value at par in the primary market. This series of transactions is profitable as long as (after platform fees, commissions, and charges) the market price of Ŧ is lower in the secondary market than in the primary one.

In summary, the existence of both "issuance" and "redemption" points, taken together with negotiability in CEX/DEX marketplaces, serves to effect convergence between primary and secondary market opinions on the actual value of cryptocurrencies.

When several blockchain-based ecosystems use the same blockchain infrastructure (e.g. all use the Ethereum blockchain, etc.), then tokens minted in any of them can technically be used also in the others. We use the terms "native" and "foreign" to denote token provenance in this case. For example, as depicted on Fig. 5.8, a Ŧ quantity is minted for agent #1 in ecosystem "A"; A is its primary market, hence Ŧ is "native" to A. Agent #1 uses some Ŧ's to purchase services from agent #2, also a participant in A. The principal of #1 is also that of agent #1′ in a separate ecosystem "B" which uses the same blockchain infrastructure. Said principal chooses to transfer

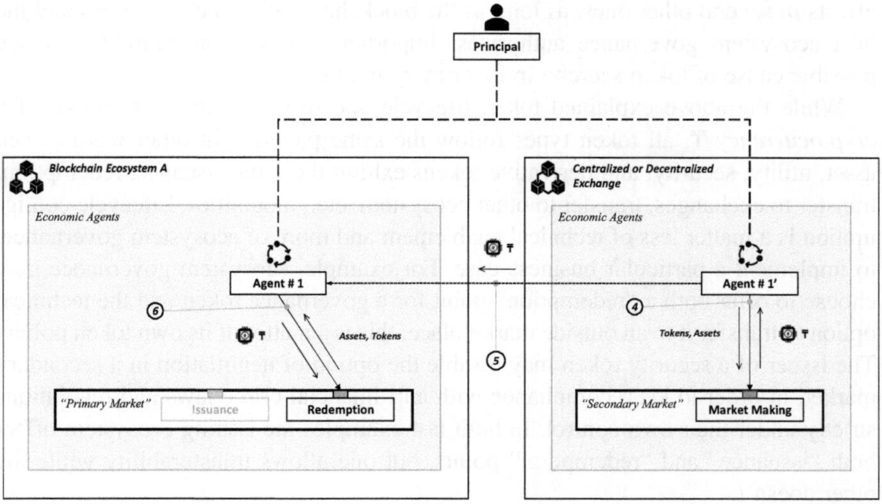

Fig. 5.7 Token purchase in the secondary market and redemption in the primary market

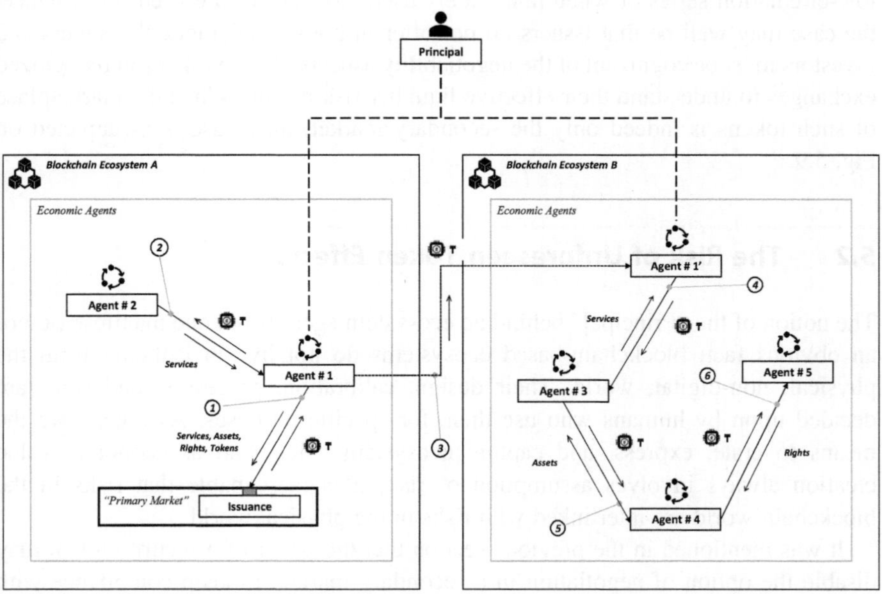

Fig. 5.8 Token issuance in ecosystem "A", and use in ecosystems "A" and "B"

a quantity of ₸'s from #1 to #1′ (transaction "3"). If authorized for usage by ecosystem B governance, ₸ can be used in transactions on B as a "foreign" token, as its recording in the underlying DL is technically the same as in A. Agent #1′ thus uses ₸'s to purchase services from #3 (transaction "4"), who then swaps them for assets with #4, etc. Hence, minting of tokens in one ecosystem can have economic effects in several other ones, as long as the blockchain infrastructure allows and the host ecosystem governance authorizes. Importantly, this "transferability" is one possible cause of token scarcity in its primary market.

While the above explained token lifecycle and use through the example of a *cryptocurrency* T̄, all token types follow the same patterns. In other words, even asset, utility, security, and derivative tokens exhibit the same issuance, redemption, transfer to exchanges, transfer to other ecosystem, etc., modalities. Lifecycle configuration is a matter less of technical enablement and more of ecosystem governance, to implement a particular business case. For example, ecosystem governance may choose to offer both a "redemption" point for a governance token and the technical option to transfer it to an outside marketplace; this is a matter of its own token policy. The issuer of a security token may disable the option of negotiation in a secondary market, in order to keep compliance with anti-financial-crime laws and regulations strictly under their own control. In both last examples the issuing ecosystem offers both "issuance" and "redemption" points, but one allows transferability while the other doesn't.

For non-fungible asset tokens in particular (which we also accepted to call simply "NFTs" in the interest of having a simplified reference typology), especially for low-circulation series or when non-widely used blockchains are used for issuance, the case may well be that issuers do not offer in-house "redemption". Buyers and investors must be cognizant of the negotiability aspects of such tokens in recognized exchanges to understand their effective liquidity risk profile. When the marketplace of such tokens is indeed only the secondary market, token use is as depicted on Fig. 5.9.

5.2 The Risk of Unforeseen Token Effects

The notion of the "Principal" behind an ecosystem agent is but one manifestation of an obvious fact: blockchain-based ecosystems do not live in isolation from the physical, non-digital, world. Their design, calibration, processes, and rules are decided upon by humans who use them for specific purposes. As tokens are the means to crate, express, and capture ecosystem value, and as economic value creation always involves assumption of risk, it is inescapable that risks in the blockchain world are interlinked with risks in the physical world.

It was mentioned in the previous section that the issuer of a security token may disable the option of negotiation in a secondary market, to keep compliance with anti-financial-crime laws and regulations strictly under their own control. This is one example of token risk interlinkage between the blockchain and the physical worlds. The governance of the issuing ecosystem cannot know how robust the agent onboarding and transaction control processes in other ecosystems or exchanges actually are. No blockchain project has the resources to execute due diligence on each and every other project using the same blockchain infrastructure, especially as this due diligence must be regularly repeated in order to be on the safe side.

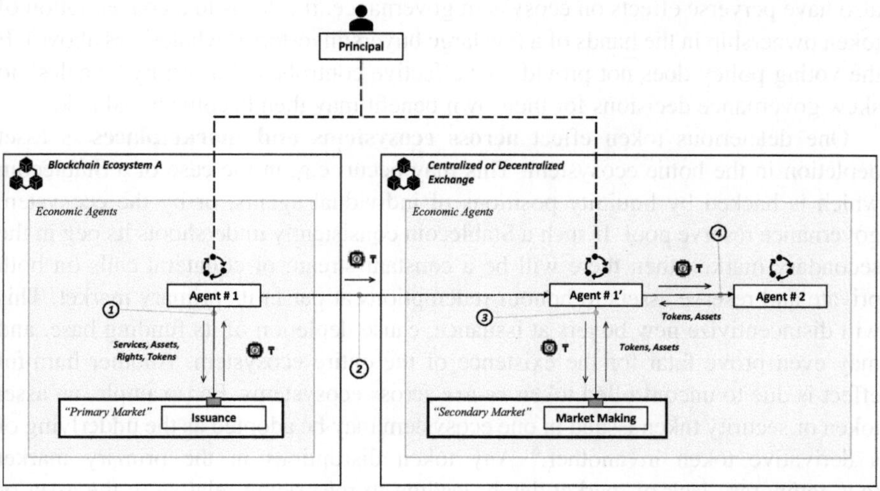

Fig. 5.9 Only token issuance in ecosystem "A", while marketplace in exchanges

What we call "unforeseen token effects" are simply the risks that must be taken into account[6] before token lifecycle and use are operationally activated. At a high level, they can be brought under three categories of effects that a token may have:

- On its own, issuing, ecosystem.
- Across ecosystems and marketplaces.
- Straddling the blockchain and physical worlds.

Indicative examples of pathologies aligning to the above points are:

The **issuing ecosystem** may experience deviation between intended token use (as per whitepaper) and actual one. For example, a cryptocurrency which is issued as medium of exchange may become increasingly a store of value. In that case, it may attract large investors ("whales" in industry jargon) who may drain the ecosystem of liquidity needed for ordinary transactions. Then, ecosystem governance may find that it has a reduced ability to remedy the situation, especially if the token has built-in scarcity.[7] The combined effect can be a loss of control by the ecosystem governance over the sustainability of its original business case. Tokens that are minted exclusively through smart contract rely on accuracy and robustness of the underlying algorithmic implementation. Should those attributes be compromised, leading to deficient smart contract logic, the immediate effects on token owners may range from erroneous balance sheet positions to complete loss of tokens through financial criminals exploiting this technical vulnerability. Legal and reputational risks for the issuing ecosystem will then ensue. Uncontrolled issuance of governance tokens may

[6] Please note that Chap. 10 is dedicated to this and many other aspects of token design.

[7] The notion of token scarcity is explained in detail in Sect. 10.5.2.

also have perverse effects on ecosystem governance, if it leads to a concentration of token ownership in the hands of a few large buyers/investors ("whales", as above). If the voting policy does not provide for effective controls, collusion by "whales" to skew governance decisions for their own benefit may then become a real risk.

One deleterious token effect **across ecosystems and marketplaces** is asset depletion in the home ecosystem. This may occur, e.g. in the case of a Stablecoin which is backed by liquidity positions of individual agents, or by the ecosystem governance reserve pool. If such a Stablecoin consistently undershoots its peg in the secondary market, then there will be a constant stream of collateral calls on both private and reserve assets to honour redemptions at par in its primary market. This will disincentivize new buyers at issuance, cause depletion of its funding base, and may even prove fatal for the existence of the entire ecosystem. Another harmful effect is due to uncontrolled token *re-use* across ecosystems. For example, an asset token or security token issued in one ecosystem may be adopted as the underlying of a derivative token in another.[8] Any token disruptions in the primary market (e.g. temporary lack of market depth, leading to mispricing relative to the asset or income stream backing the token) will then cascade immediately to the re-using ecosystem(s). Token re-use is a risk also in the opposite direction, i.e. from the re-using ecosystem to the home one. An example would be a security token issued in a foreign ecosystem which bundles the native token in its underlying portfolio. A high flow of transactions in the foreign token will drain circulation from the native ecosystem, temporarily (at least) disrupting the use of the native token in productive supply-chain transactions. Risks of the secondary market may be transmitted to the primary market of a token in ways that may be difficult to control. As the aforementioned Stablecoin example shows, the secondary market has its own dynamics. If a new exchange decides to offer a market in a tradable crypto-token, there is no guarantee that it will also adopt the risk management framework of the issuing ecosystem. For example, an exchange may implement less robust due diligence and anti-financial-crime controls, leading e.g. to criminals laundering money by purchasing the token in the secondary market. Furthermore, intentional attack vectors from the secondary to the primary market cannot be ruled out. For instance, lax exchange controls may allow large positions to be built in a tradable governance token which can then be used to influence the governance policies of its issuing ecosystem.

Severe unforeseen side effects **straddling the blockchain** and **physical** worlds can be caused by incorrect asset classification of the token. Such a situation can arise, e.g. if a token has effective attributes of a financial instrument but is not treated as such by its issuing project. As a result, legal and regulatory obligations of both the issuer/marketplace operator (instrument authorizations, pre-marketing approvals, broker-dealer licensing, etc.) and of the buyers/investors (transaction reporting, tax reporting, etc.) may be completely ignored, or at least misunderstood and miscommunicated. Probable repercussions can include significant legal costs,

[8] This "*Composability*" pattern is explained as a token design factor in Sect. 10.5.9 and as a bonding function design factor in Sect. 12.4.5.

fines, adverse publicity, etc., which may put the continuing circulation of the token in doubt and might possibly threaten the viability of the business case of its entire ecosystem. NFTs accompanied by inexact or incomplete definitions of underlying property rights (especially those issued against real estate and intellectual property) can generate significant legal risks for their buyers.[9] The latter may then seek redress from the tokens' issuing project. Finally, the risk of financial crime in marketplaces implementing insufficient counterparty and transaction controls qualifies as a deleterious effect under this category as well.

It must be stressed that the above are only indicative examples. The possible pathologies are numerous and difficult to allocate systematically into a typology, as they depend on ecosystem business case, individual token design, and jurisdictions involved. In other words, each combination of ecosystem, token type, and jurisdiction creates its own probable risks. The comprehensive token typology explained in the previous chapter is but one of the three degrees of freedom defining such combinations. This should serve as an indication of how multi-faceted the risks of unforeseen token effects can be.

5.3 The Need for End-to-End Ecosystem Design

Having an understanding of the salient points of token lifecycle and usage, and of the possible pathologies that may manifest themselves in both the blockchain and physical worlds, is important in its own right. However, it also serves a wider purpose when designing cryptocurrencies and other tradable crypto-tokens. Namely, to explain the importance of *designing* tokens not in isolation but rather as part of a *more comprehensive design* effort.

Blockchain-based ecosystem tokens are human constructs. They are created in a home ecosystem to serve its own economic purposes, while in all generality will be expected to also have economic outcomes on other ecosystems, and also across the blockchain-physical world divide. When traded on exchanges they will have legally binding effects on the financial position of buyers and sellers who may be scattered across the globe. In other words, the repercussions of introducing a crypto-token to circulation may be far-reaching in scope and scale. Anticipating and managing them will be a matter of finding appropriate answers to many, intertwined, questions such as:

(a) What assets to use to "fund" a cryptocurrency or other crypto-token? What property rights will be embedded into it, how will they be structured, and in which physical world jurisdiction?
(b) What aspects of the token lifecycle will remain within its home ecosystem and which delegated to other ecosystems and exchanges? How will

[9] Those are explained in detail in Chap. 10, which is focused on token design.

interconnectedness with said ecosystems and exchanges be technically and legally enabled, and how will it be monitored?

(c) How will the token be technically introduced? What kind of risk management framework will be built to control potential harmful side effects to its home ecosystem and to the outside world? Is there imputed liability on any persons or legal entities in the physical world if such a risk framework is not put in place?

(d) Who will implement the technical infrastructure of the token, its issuance and redemption mechanisms and its accompanying smart contracts? Which blockchain will be used and why? Where will the validating nodes of the DL be placed? How will cyber security attacks be defended against, under whose coordination?

(e) Will this technical implementation be a self-funded community effort or a long-term professional investment? In both cases, who will be entrusted with technical decisions and project management? Will there be independent oversight of these activities, on grounds of quality assurance?

(f) In which quantities will a cryptocurrency be issued? How often? Will it be redeemable in its home market or not? Will any ecosystem agent be responsible for monitoring its circulation and parity rates to other cryptocurrencies or fiat currencies?

(g) If a crypto-token qualifies as a financial instrument, who will undertake the coordination of necessary activities to respond to regulatory requests and submit legally required information? How will these activities be funded?

(h) Will there be regular audits of token design and operations? By whom will they be executed, and through which funding sources? To whom will audit issues be reported? Who will undertake corrective action? Is there imputed liability on any persons or legal entity in the physical world if such activities do not take place?

(i) How exactly will token governance function? If a cryptocurrency becomes extremely volatile, or if a Stablecoin consistently loses its peg, who is responsible for its eventual re-calibration? Through which decision-making process and using which technical means?

(j) Will it be necessary to track token ownership statistics? What happens if a few principals end up controlling a critical mass of a cryptocurrency's or a utility token's circulation? What is this critical mass? How can such undesired behaviours be guarded against?

(k) Is there a need for written policies around token lifecycle and usage? Which ecosystem agent should be entrusted with creating them? Should the same agent also have policy enforcement rights and responsibilities?

Answering those, and still more, questions will obviously necessitate coordinated analysis and design activities. Once recognizing this fact, the next step calls for answering a more fundamental question:

- What should be the **level** and **limit** of said activities?

In other words, what should be their granularity and where should they stop? Are smart contract programming guidelines in scope? Should "monetary policies" of an agent playing the role of a cryptocurrency's "Central Bank" be provided for? Is a "3-Lines-of-Defence" concept such as is typically the case for financial services companies called for? Should "taxation schedules" at the level of the individual token transaction be written? Is it expected to have ring-fenced mechanisms to fund issuance and operations for each token issued in an ecosystem? Should the legal issues of token classification be answered before, during, or after token design? Regarding the limits of design: does it make sense to prescribe token usage in transactions on probable foreign ecosystems and trading marketplaces as well? Should the design describe processes around a single cryptocurrency or tradable crypto-token on its home ecosystem only, or should it encompass all potential processes around it in all ecosystems and marketplaces using the same blockchain infrastructure?

Addressing each and every such aspect only once it is identified and shown to be relevant, but without having systematic guidance in reference to aspect granularity and scope, is not a practical value proposition. It probably could have been in the early days of cryptocurrency issuance, when only a few whitepapers were being published and "trial-and-error" operational design had the allure of exploring new, uncharted, territory. However, given the amassed business and technical experience in the current crypto-token universe; the ever-increasing sophistication of use cases; the scale of financial assets already tied up in crypto-assets; and the multitude of legal and regulatory edicts around such assets already codified in statutes and case law of several jurisdictions; a "starting from scratch", "trial-and-error", design approach is no longer tenable.

It is rather obvious that the granularity limit of design activities is a function of the scope limit. For example, if the latter is to be defined by the typology of all agents expected to use the token across ecosystems, then the requisite depth of analysis and design is different than if it is to be only by its issuing ecosystem and its secondary market. Hence the highest-level guidance should be around where to place the "design cut-off".

- We propose that **the natural "design cut-off" limit for cryptocurrencies and tradable crypto-tokens is the perimeter of their issuing ecosystem**.

Justification: First of all, it cannot be a foregone conclusion that a token will be accepted as a foreign one in cooperating ecosystems. Even if it does get accepted, the home ecosystem may prevent inclusion (directly or by reference) in third-party tokens which it cannot control. And even if it gets accepted by reference (e.g. a derivative token in ecosystem B references the rate of a token of ecosystem A, as reported through Oracles), then there are no direct feedback loops to its primary market. In any case, the primary design consideration should be identifying and calibrating **directly controllable factors**. Indirectly controllable ones should be also identified, but rather with a view to optimizing the own risk management framework.

When it comes to token market-making in exchanges, the linkage between an exchange and an issuing ecosystem is typically a loose one. There are token listing requirements that must be met as a prerequisite, contractual agreements that need to be put in place, and risk management frameworks that must continuously align for such a linkage to be mutually beneficial. In short, the linkage may be severed at any time if market conditions, or risk events, give the necessary impetus to one of the two parties. Cryptocurrencies and other crypto-tokens can be [18], and have been, delisted from exchanges in the past (also having a cascading effect on indexes and token pairs [19, 20]) and, inversely, exchanges can be, and have been, blacklisted, e.g. by regulators [21, 22].

If the token design perimeter were to be a subset of an ecosystem, e.g. a particular constellation of economic agents or specific transactions, etc., there would be two major repercussions. First, said agents would be de facto barred from using other tokens (existing or future ones), as otherwise they could transfer value in-between token types; if those other token types were associated with a different, partially overlapping group of economic agents (i.e. if agents were providers of several asset and service types at once) that would immediately defeat the purpose of restricting token use in the first place. Second, ad hoc value chains involving different kinds of transactions would have to be executed using different token types in different process steps, potentially having to continuously alternate. If platform fees were also to depend on token type, that would create the impetus for supply-chain re-configuration for cost-sensitive participants. In short, choosing to ring-fence only a subset of the ecosystem for token design would end up creating transactional frictions in the middle of the ecosystem and would be most probably circumvented anyway. It must be added that ecosystem governance typically has end-to-end powers and would not be expected to use business rules selectively. Ecosystem governance must be able to create end-to-end standards, otherwise risks cannot be managed end-to-end.

For new ecosystems that are being built specifically around a particular token use case, the design scope is obvious. For existing ecosystems considering issuing a new token type, the design scope can only be, again, the entire ecosystem. Reasons include: to fundamentally avoid cannibalization effects among tokens; ensure fairness in platform fee schedules for different transactions; avoid contagion effects (managing systemic risk onset and propagation if the new token should fail); prioritize allocation of requisite investment amounts from the reserve pool; and finally ensure that governance structures evolve to accommodate the new operational requirements, thus preserving their ability to carry out end-to-end risk oversight.

We could list much more comprehensive argumentation and even mention examples from accumulated crypto-token project experience which suggest both patterns and anti-patterns of token design, all pointing to the same direction: namely, that proper, robust token design can only be *an aspect of* a robust *end-to-end* blockchain-based *ecosystem design*. We believe however that the above points suffice to support this assertion.

5.4 Summary

This chapter explained the salient points of token lifecycle and use, relating to both cryptocurrencies and other tradable crypto-tokens. It was demonstrated that, in general, their usage straddles ecosystems. Furthermore, as principals of ecosystem agents straddle the blockchain and physical worlds, any unforeseen effects of said usage will generally have legally binding effects on the financial position of buyers and sellers who may be scattered across the globe. Unforeseen token effects are a consequence of failure to predict and manage risks already at the token design phase. Thus, in the absence of robust token design, there exist potential far-reaching repercussions for the issuing project, including liability, fines, adverse publicity, etc., which may put the continuing circulation of a token in doubt, and might possibly threaten the viability of the business case of its entire ecosystem.

It was asserted that a robust *token design* can be understood as only *one aspect* of a robust *end-to-end* issuing *ecosystem design*. This of course creates the need for guidance on how to systematically pursue blockchain-based ecosystem design. Otherwise, starting from scratch is not a practicable value proposition, in light of the complexity and interdisciplinary character of all potential design aspects.

The next chapter will introduce precisely such an end-to-end blockchain-based ecosystem design framework.

References

1. Investopedia Team. (2024, June 2). What are consensus mechanisms in Blockchain and Cryptocurrency? Retrieved March 22, 2025, from https://www.investopedia.com/terms/c/consensus-mechanism-Cryptocurrency.asp
2. [Bitcoin Token ecosystem]. https://bitcoin.org/en/
3. *CoinMarketCap Bitcoin (BTC) page*. CoinMarketCap. Retrieved March 22, 2025, from https://coinmarketcap.com/currencies/bitcoin/
4. [Bitcoin (BTC) Whitepaper] Nakamoto, S. *Bitcoin: A Peer-to-Peer Electronic Cash System*. Retrieved March 27, 2025, from https://bitcoin.org/bitcoin.pdf Bitcoin Whitepaper: https://bitcoin.org/bitcoin.pdf
5. [Ethereum Token ecosystem]. https://ethereum.org/en/
6. CoinMarketCap ETH page. CoinMarketCap. Retrieved March 22, 2025, from https://coinmarketcap.com/currencies/ethereum/
7. [Ethereum Whitepaper]. (2025, February 12). *Ethereum Whitepaper*. Retrieved March 27, 2025, from https://ethereum.org/en/whitepaper/
8. (2024, September 3). *Proof-of-stake (POS)*. Ethereum documentation pages. Retrieved March 22, 2025, from https://ethereum.org/en/developers/docs/consensus-mechanisms/pos/
9. [Avalanche Token ecosystem]. https://www.avax.network/
10. CoinMarketCap AVAX page. CoinMarketCap. Retrieved March 22, 2025, from https://coinmarketcap.com/currencies/avalanche/
11. [Avalanche Whitepaper] Buttolph, S., Moin, A., Sekniqi, K. & Gün Sirer, E. (2020, June 25). *Avalanche native token ($AVAX) dynamics*. Retrieved March 22, 2025, from https://assets.website-files.com/5d80307810123f5ffbb34d6e/6008d7bc56430d6b8792b8d1_AvalancheNativeTokenDynamics.pdf
12. [Solana Token ecosystem]. https://solana.com/

13. CoinMarketCap SOL page. CoinMarketCap. Retrieved March 22, 2025, from https://coinmarketcap.com/currencies/solana/
14. [Solana Whitepaper] Yakovenko, A. *Solana: A new architecture for a high performance blockchain v0.8.13*. Retrieved March 22, 2025, from https://solana.com/solana-whitepaper.pdf
15. [Polygon Token ecosystem]. https://polygon.technology/
16. CoinMarketCap POL page. CoinMarketCap. Retrieved March 22, 2025, from https://coinmarketcap.com/currencies/polygon-ecosystem-token/
17. [Polygon Whitepaper] Bjelic, M., Nailwal, S., Chaudhary, A. & Deng, W. POL: One token for all Polygon chains. Retrieved March 27, 2025, from https://polygon.technology/papers/pol-whitepaper
18. (2023) *Delisted token recovery on Bitfinex – Frequently Asked Questions (FAQ)*. Bitfinex support pages. Retrieved March 22, 2025, from https://support.bitfinex.com/hc/en-us/articles/900004249026-Delisted-token-recovery-on-Bitfinex-Frequently-Asked-Questions-FAQ-
19. Cohen, M. (2021, July 25). *Largest Ethereum-based decentralized exchange delisting tokens*. Yahoo!finance. Retrieved March 27, 2025, from https://finance.yahoo.com/news/largest-ethereum-based-decentralized-exchange-185831503.html
20. Young, M. (2021, July 26). Uniswap delists 100 tokens from interface, including options and indexes. CoinTelegraph. Retrieved March 27, 2025, from https://cointelegraph.com/news/uniswap-delists-100-tokens-from-interface-including-options-and-indexes
21. U.S. Department of the Treasury. (2021, September 21). *Publication of updated Ransomware advisory; cyber-related designation*. Office of Foreign assets control. Retrieved March 22, 2025, from https://home.treasury.gov/policy-issues/financial-sanctions/recent-actions/20210921
22. De, N. (2021, September 21). US sanctions enforcer blacklists a crypto exchange for first time. CoinDesk. Retrieved March 22, 2025, from https://www.coindesk.com/policy/2021/09/21/us-sanctions-enforcer-blacklists-a-crypto-exchange-for-first-time/

Market Design

6

This chapter introduces a token ecosystem design framework.[1] A fundamental analogy is postulated in the beginning, that of designing the economy of a country that just came into being. This allows to interpret all facets of token ecosystems in reference to basic concepts from sociology and economics. Design decisions then evolve naturally as transpositions to the digital world of concepts and practices from traditional human ecosystems in the physical world.

Armed with the understanding that this analogy allows, the design framework is explained as mainly consisting of three pillars: market, mechanism, and token designs. The structural design of the economic agents active in the ecosystem is the market design. The behavioural framework for said economic agents to interact amongst themselves is the mechanism design. The design of the media of exchange and stores of value is the token design.

The current chapter is focused on the first pillar, namely market design.

6.1 The "New Country" Analogy

Let us start by explaining the "new country" analogy. Imagine that a new country has just been created in a land previously unknown. People have settled it already as there are commodities (oil, gas, minerals, rare earths, or soft commodities like grains or coffee) which are commercially exploitable at a cost competitive to that of other countries. Also, a significant proportion of the settlers have some skills in a particular services-related trade, which is in demand internationally. The settlers would like to offer these services from within the country. They have started thinking also about

[1] As mentioned in the "Acknowledgement" preamble, the idea for such a framework, as well as its postulation of design pillars "markets, mechanisms, tokens", first appeared—to the best knowledge of this author—in the excellent book: Tan L.J.Y, *Economics and Math of Token Engineering and DeFi: Fundamentals of Token Economics*, (self-published), 2020. This is why we refrain from writing "our framework", instead referring to "the proposed framework" throughout this book.

I. Giannakouros, *Cryptocurrencies and Tradable Crypto-Tokens*, Future of Business and Finance, https://doi.org/10.1007/978-3-031-98423-5_6

creating branches of government and are committed to making their country succeed. So, all in all, the seeds of an economy in being are already in place.

The settlers so far have only been bartering goods and services among themselves, as there is as yet no currency. Being educated people, they are already familiar with the principles of economics and international trade and are convinced that their new country needs to have its own currency. They know that if the country intends to specialize in extracting and trading a particular commodity (say, a rare earth) which is otherwise scarce, then a buyer's need to acquire this commodity will be their incentive to hold the new country's currency. A buyer from another country will then have to use their own fiat currency (or another asset, which is exchangeable and transferable) to buy the new currency. Furthermore, if the country sees a competitive advantage in providing a particular service (say insurance of a particular risk), then a foreign buyer's need to consume this service will be their incentive to acquire the new country's currency. Again, the buyer will need to effect a foreign exchange transaction to that end. Thus, a framework for foreign exchange transactions will need to be created.

Now suppose that the value of this particular service or commodity in the international market increases over time and is then projected to increase even more. Will persistent buyers be willing to acquire and hold amounts in the new currency purely as a hedging tool? And, if said amounts become material, will buyers also consider the new currency as a store of value? Will they start using it in accounting reports in their home jurisdictions? If those new currency holdings are kept instead within the issuing country issuing, will holders also be obliged to submit accounting reports in the host jurisdiction?

Thus, settlers of the new country understand that there are governance institutions to create, physical (roads, networks, marketplaces) and notional (laws, regulations, information templates) infrastructure to build, and, last but not least, a new currency to issue and circulate, so as to enable long-term economic life, maintenance of infrastructure, and investments.

How can the above relate to blockchain-based token ecosystems?

Recall that such ecosystems typically start as investment business cases, targeting monetization of a particular value proposition which (according to the vision and conviction of key persons behind the concept) is ideally suited for on-chain implementation. In the initial stage, the purpose behind a new token-issuing project needs to be communicated to prospective project contributors and financiers. The fundamental artefact of the envisioned blockchain-based project at this stage is the "Whitepaper" [1, 2]. This is a document postulating the project's business context and economic objectives (the "use case"); the intended functioning of acceptable media of exchange and stores of value (i.e., its token(s)) in the particular business context; and the processes of how decisions that affect all economic participants in the use case are reached and implemented (its "governance").

In effect, it expresses the aforementioned vision and also gives basic organizational and technical directions for the creation of a new token-based ecosystem. The operational implementation, however, of those directions into working processes and physical artefacts (code, accounts, users) is a matter of organized execution. The latter is typically undertaken by a governing body (foundation or any other legal form), as the monetary aspect of agent interactions creates the inescapable risk of liability—hence the need for answerability. So, there is always the need for a higher authority, a privileged economic agent.

Central to the success of the business case is the notion of token. It must capture the essence of blockchain paradigms, but, more importantly, it must be a reliable means for satisfying the purposes of all participants in the business case. This token does not pre-exist. It is continuously introduced into circulation through agents expending resources (time, energy, etc.) to bring it to life. Actually, the first quantities of token produced in each project are typically pre-funded by investors. The intention is to facilitate a critical mass of circulating tokens, so that third parties can see the functioning of the end-to-end use case and be convinced of the merits of its value proposition on the blockchain. Afterwards, tokens are used to sell services within the perimeter of the ecosystem, but can be also swapped for other stores of value (e.g., for different tokens or for fiat-denominated assets) in either outright or collateralized transactions. Of course, parity rates must be maintained for such swaps to take place.

- We propose that the resulting process of organization and maintenance of token-based economic life, undertaken as a dedicated project, with a particular business objective, shared among economic agents that must be explicitly declared as participants of a delimited ecosystem, is **akin to the process of setting up the institutions, infrastructure, and currency of a new country**.

A new country's currency needs similarly to be financed in the beginning, then its circulation maintained by expending resources and against assets serving as collateral backing its supply. This currency must be declared legal tender in order that the country can grow based on optimal use of its own resources (and so that infrastructure and institutions can be financed by its own means). The currency parity rate against other media of exchange must be monitored, and possibly defended, to protect the interests of the country in international trade. It may appreciate in value, becoming attractive as a long-term investment for citizens of other countries as well, or simply fluctuate in value within a range; thus, currency risk management mechanisms may need to be put in place by, and for, its holders and investors. All those phenomena are in evidence, *without exception*, in token-based ecosystems as well.

It is the premise of this book that the blockchain paradigm in general and the token concept in particular (in the form of either cryptocurrencies or other tradable crypto-tokens—cf. Chaps. 4 and 10) do much to enable many more degrees of freedom in economic life than what is possible in traditional, physical paradigms. However, they come with their own notions of value and risk, which must be understood through both economic and technological lenses. Those are not always easy to conceptualize without deep economic and technical understanding at once, which is not a usual combination of skills. That is the reason behind introducing this "new country" analogy.

The intention is to explain some concepts *by analogy* to pre-existing, mostly similar and easily relatable, notions from traditional physical economic systems. We believe that this method will help generate at least a level of subconscious acceptance towards new ideas and methods, so that more technical explanations can find room to grow.

6.2 Introduction to Market Design

A "Market" is a venue where sellers and buyers of goods and services come together to transact with each other. "Venue" and "come together" nowadays include the modalities offered by the digital world. Markets can be either "ad hoc" or organized ones, the latter implying the existence of rules governing their participants, processes, and ways of exchanging information, goods/services, and moneys. It is tacitly assumed that "ad hoc" is synonymous with "un-coordinated", in effect higher-risk for at least one side of participants. Due to the importance of economic life for the stability of human societies, there arose a branch of economics specifically focused on the controllability of organized markets, i.e. on the ways in which specific markets can be **designed** to track particular economic and/or social objectives. The word "controllability" should be understood to imply both a priori (pre-operations, pre going-live) and a posteriori (post going-live) features.

That a market can be assumed to be created "by design" presupposes the existence of a set of actors possessing some sort of authority, either by way of their level of market knowledge or by way of their being given a mandate (a privilege and responsibility at once) to achieve such a design. On the other hand, the expectation that all participants of the market in focus should follow said design—in spite of, e.g. pressures from competition and profit maximization—implies a sense of obligation or at least wilful agreement to act in particular ways. Finally, ensuring that the market operates "as designed" entails the existence of actors tasked with monitoring and (eventually) with enforcement. All of the above entail allotment of resources (time, knowledge, working assets, etc.), resources which are thus detracted from other societal pursuits—i.e. not only relating to the direct market participants. In summary, the decision to dedicate resources to track specific economic and/or social objectives can only be taken by a set of actors having a recognized level of authority above that of the direct market participants. This automatically implies a localized societal hierarchy, which then leads inescapably to the postulation of the existence of **governance bodies** for the market in focus.

The above observations relate to the discipline of "Market design" [3–8] which is a modern and still evolving branch of economics. Said discipline focuses on the theoretical foundations, applied methodologies, and analytical tools for the systematic creation of markets that align with specific economic and societal goals. As this knowledge area is very wide, we cannot hope but present only some of its rudimentary elements, namely those that will be needed by the reader to follow its application in this book.

First of all, market design involves modelling of economic systems, i.e. creation of abstractions and approximations to their complete nature. A "model" of a real system entails necessarily a degree of simplification, either in terms of the system's components taken into account, or in terms of the allowed degrees of freedom in their behaviour. In the case of market design, such a fundamental simplification consists in the assumption that all active participants of the socioeconomic system can be allocated to only a small number of "types". These types map to distinct action patterns, i.e. templates describing which actions a particular type is allowed to undertake, to which economic or informational inputs it can react, which economic or informational outputs it can produce, and in which constellation with other types. Each such distinct type of behaviour is called an "**economic agent**" [9, 10]. Please note that economic agents do not necessarily map to single persons (humans) but can also be assumed by groups of humans, technical systems, or even combined human/technical systems.

Second, market design includes both organizational and procedural descriptions of the system. Organizational descriptions answer the question "what are its agents and environment", whereas procedural ones the question "how do its agents interact among themselves and with their environment, through which means and in which possible sequence(s)". Note that both organizational and procedural descriptions are "static", in that they are not allowed to be varying in time. During the actual operation of the system, departing from the same starting point, an agent may initiate different procedures, but all such possible procedures must have been described in market design, in lieu of "well-defined pathways" (together with possible branching points).

Third, market design may or may not specify governance bodies for the system in focus. As mentioned above, the existence of such bodies is implicit in the assumption of specific socioeconomic objectives set for, and in the expectation of controllability of, the system. Absence of a governance specification may be justified in traditional markets operating within pre-existing organized societies, as then governance bodies exist at the level of the wider societal environment; in other words, then they are external to the market in focus, and only their edicts are felt by the latter. Totally self-contained and self-organized markets should be assumed to have internal governance bodies, though.

Similarly to markets, blockchain-based ecosystems are social as much as they are economic constructs. Concepts of cooperation, competition, and trust are at play in them, which at the most basic level presuppose a common understanding about what a particular ecosystem consists of and what its purpose is.

In the "new country" analogy, this would be an understanding about what the citizen population is; what different types of skills can they offer as services; what natural resources does the country possess; what is the economic model that the country intends to pursue; what kinds of interactions will need to exist for this economic model to be feasible (i.e. for the internal market to function); how are these interactions to be organized; what will the form of government be; what are its branches and structure (i.e. for the internal market to have controllability), etc. In short, it would be a set of answers to the basic "*what*" questions about the country, when the latter is viewed as a social and economic system.

How to interpret "government" and "government structure" in the context of blockchain-based token ecosystems?

As already mentioned, the seminal "constitutive" document of the typical blockchain-based project is the "Whitepaper", which nevertheless contains only a vision—a statement of intent if, you will—and high-level organizational and technical directions. Strategic and operational implementation of those directions implies the need for a higher authority, a **privileged economic agent**, to guide resource allocation and resolve problems of coordination. Without going now into a discussion of whether or not this agent should consist only of humans or of any combination of humans and algorithms,[2] this need (and responsibility) can be interpreted as fundamentally one of *institutionalizing informed decision-making* to the utmost benefit of all economic agents. This agent will be "privileged" in three respects:

- Scope of their **powers**.
- Amount of **information** in their possession.
- Effect of their **decisions**.

Similar to the circumstances of a "new country", it can be expected that said agent—the governing body—will be called upon to exercise three functions: design and document laws, take strategic and operational decisions, and resolve disputes. We propose that this notion of functions of government (legislative, executive, and judicial) carries over unaltered to token-based ecosystems. Should there be *distinct economic agents* exercising those functions, then they will be the corresponding *branches of government*.

The exercise of governance rights and responsibilities will be addressed in the later Chap. 8 on mechanism design. For the time being, it suffices to postulate that a blockchain-based ecosystem which uses tokens as enablers of its economic purpose will be expected to have a "social structure". That is, there will be "general" economic agents and "privileged" ones (governing bodies). All of them will be able to interact in everyday economic life. They will deal with goods and services; negotiate prices, terms, and conditions; conclude contracts; exchange funds; execute transactions; coordinate actions; and have misunderstandings and disputes. Describing the "what" of the underlying *structure*, namely:

1. The **typology of governing bodies**
2. The **typology of the other (non-privileged) economic agents**, and
3. All **possible "transactional pathways"** among all economic agents

is the object of market design. In other words, market design is nothing else than the *structural design* underlying the economic life of the token-based ecosystem.

[2]Indeed, the value proposition of paradigms such as "Distributed Autonomous Organization"—cf. Sect. 9.7—and "Decentralized Finance"—cf. Chap. 15—is the benefit of ultimately removing completely human decision-making from operational governance.

6.3 Rationale of Market Design for Token-Based Ecosystems

Let us return to the "new country" analogy. Traders of goods and services have legitimate expectations of trust among transacting counterparties and of certainty of transaction execution. This is akin to saying that economic agents can draw upon a common social capital. In small communities, this social capital is informal and stems from proximity and familiarity, but after a critical population scale is reached then there is an inescapable need for institutionalization. From that point on, known personal attributes become less relevant than more abstract, impersonal ones, such as commercial creditworthiness and quality of product offering. Hence, the new country will need to find ways to maintain a "registry of commercial trust". It will also need to build trust in its new currency, as citizens need to know that it can be used reliably as both a medium of exchange and as a store of value. At first, they would expect to be informed about how this currency was/is put into circulation, what reserves shore it up, who manages them, and how. As prudent people of business, they also expect to be kept informed about trends in the general level of prices in the economy—also denominated in the new currency—so that they can plan their liquidity outlays and long-term investments. The country's government would also expect to secure financing sources in order to build and maintain basic infrastructure and to cover its own operating expenses. For instance, it would need to know that it can count on some form of tax revenue—levied as some function of recorded assets and/or incomes. This means, fundamentally, trust in the function of the new currency as unit of account.

Hence, there is a fundamental need for trust and clarity on the part of both general economic agents and of branches of government. Transactions enabled by the new currency will serve to illuminate those salient features of the economic system—its fundamental structural elements—where clarity is needed most so that the entire system can be built to be short- and long-term controllable. Market design is precisely meant to provide a basic level of clarity, answering to this need. In short:

- Market design is the **structural design** of the ecosystem.

At its core, it seeks to build a basic "economic agent's guide" through blueprints, glossaries, and typologies. That would contain answers to the most basic "what"[3] questions about economic life in the ecosystem.

For example: Which are the governing bodies and what is their legal form? Is there an explicit or implicit allocation of responsibilities among them? Is there one entity tasked with managing the ecosystem's reserves? What are the possible kinds of non-privileged economic agents? Can some of them have dual roles? What are the possible interactions among privileged and non-privileged economic agents? What are the possible interactions in general and transactions in particular among non-privileged agents? Is there a distinct governance body issuing its token(s), or

[3] As opposed to "how", which is the object of mechanism design, cf. Chap. 8.

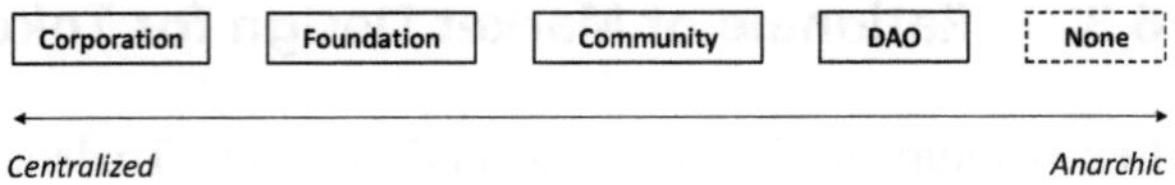

Fig. 6.1 Privileged agent typology, decision-making power and accountability

are tokens "created" as a result of transactions among agents? Is there an entity responsible for removing tokens from circulation? Are all economic agents digital proxies of humans or can some of them be algorithms—e.g. obeying some blockchain-compatible specifications ("templates"[4])? Are there any dependencies of transactions upon third-party agents (i.e. external to the ecosystem)? If so, what/who are those?

Such questions are of the type meant to be answered by market design. About the legal form of governing bodies, for instance. In that respect, a usual typology of blockchain ecosystems is as depicted schematically in Fig. 6.1, representing governance association forms observed in current crypto-market practice. Those differ in the allocation of decision-making powers among privileged agents, ranging here from "Centralized" to "Anarchic".

A corporation is governed by its directors and is answerable only to its shareholders, which may or may not be visible on the blockchain. It generally has no obligation for external consensus building if its statutes so provide. A foundation, on the other hand, does have a legal entity form empowering directors with decision-making, but it must conform to specific investment and outlay constraints. A community may be simply an association of like-minded individuals, operating de facto on a consensus paradigm. These are only a few indicative types of privileged agent, but they already convey important information.

For example, as of the time of writing this book, the token Tether (USDT, "soft-pegged" to the USD) is a Stablecoin issued and redeemed through two affiliated corporations [11] ("Tether Limited" for transactions involving US persons, and "Tether International Limited" for non-US persons). The token DAI (similarly "soft-pegged" to the USD) is also a Stablecoin issued by a protocol (MakerDAO [12]) governed by a Distributed Autonomous Organization (DAO [13, 14]), i.e. subject to ancillary governance rights [15] accorded to all holders of its (native to the ecosystem) governance token MKR [16]. So, here are two tokens of the same type, targeting the same addressable market of buyers and investors, and issued by ecosystems with totally different governance structures. They imply different allocation of decision-making powers among economic agents, different concepts of accountability, and, in the end, totally different risk profiles of their respective tokens. This is only one kind of information conveyed by market design, from the standpoint of governance alone.

Imagine that this information were hidden, or difficult to find, for token buyers and investors. Would they be reasonably expected to consider acquiring the token in order to transact in the ecosystem?

[4]The notion of "Smart Contracts" was created to represent precisely such algorithmic economic agents.

Now, assume that governance information were clear, but that the information about the possible market participants and the possible types of ecosystem transactions were hidden. What kinds of buyers and investors would then consider acquiring its token(s), and to what end? If it is not clear that buyers can acquire the products they want or the services they need, and from whom, why should they be expected to be interested in the ecosystem token(s)? Should a token be itself the object of the transaction (e.g. exchanged for fiat currency or other tokens), what are the possible ways of acquiring it? Do different acquisition modes entail potentially different price points or timescales for transaction completion?

Answering the above is only one of the reasons why market design is a fundamental pillar of the proposed token ecosystem design framework.

In short, market design is the basic blueprint answering legitimate questions about economic structure, as they pertain to the ecosystem, and as a prelude to explaining the function of its token(s). Its creation before any token(s) can circulate is necessary, as the aforementioned "critical population scale" threshold is reached much faster in digital than in human, physical, ecosystems.

It can, and should ideally be, a living design as the ecosystem evolves. For instance, if the legal form of a governing body changes in-between ecosystem generations, or if a new type of economic agent is admitted by extending its business use case, then it is the market design that will make those changes most evident, in a succinct and unambiguous manner, to prospective token buyers and investors.

6.4 Market Design for Token-Based Ecosystems in Short

Market design is a form of social and economic engineering, taking into consideration the functional and technical features of blockchain platforms. It describes the typology of economic agents, both privileged (governance) and unprivileged, that are explicitly declared as ecosystem market participants. It clarifies any third-party (i.e. external) dependencies of the ecosystem's use case(s). Importantly, it also lays out the possible "transactional pathways" among economic agents (both internal and third-party) as enabled by, or required for, token usage.

We already gave an example in the previous section about the significance of the governance body typology. Unprivileged economic agents must similarly be allocated to types in order to answer important questions. Example agent types expected in token ecosystems appear in Fig. 6.2, where human-controlled agents[5] ("human agents" for the sake of brevity) have a "bust" icon to distinguish them from algorithmic or mixed ones.

The chosen constellation will depend on how explicit the separation of roles needs to be for the design to be representative of the ecosystem. For instance, "Traders" could be also "Consumers" and "Suppliers", but they may have to be declared as a separate type if their specific function in the ecosystem is important.

[5] i.e. whose decision-making is carried out by humans.

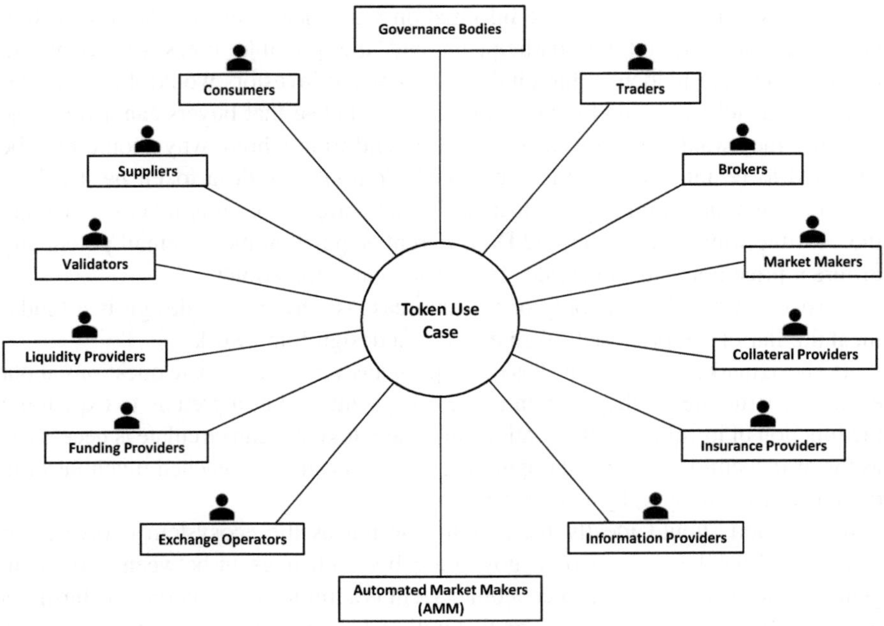

Fig. 6.2 Example economic agent typology in token ecosystems

"Valuation Providers" could be included under "Suppliers" (as suppliers of the service "Valuation"), or they may form a separate economic agent type for market design to describe in more detail the transactional pathways explicitly involving them. That would be expedient, for example, if a token use case is heavily focused on valuation. Similarly, suppliers of on-chain derivatives could also fall under "Suppliers" or "Insurance Providers", or may need to form a separate type "Derivatives Manufacturers" if a use case is focused on financial instruments. And (especially in decentralized finance) "Market Makers" may always need to form an own category, separate from "Liquidity Providers", as the latter may not always exist. Design can be at once parsimonious and descriptive, as long as the necessary information is carried through.

The typology is more important than the nomenclature as long as a glossary, other explanatory notes, or references to the whitepaper are attached to the design. For example, the "Information Providers" type should ideally be further explained as to information type and provenance (information generated within the ecosystem or sourced from the outside world, etc.). As already mentioned, market design needs to make explicit consideration of the blockchain paradigm and information provision is one of the points demonstrating this need. At the highest level of abstraction, blockchain admits two types of information provision agents (cf. Fig. 6.3), namely:

- (human) **Information Providers**, and
- **Oracles.**

Fig. 6.3 High-level information provision agent typology

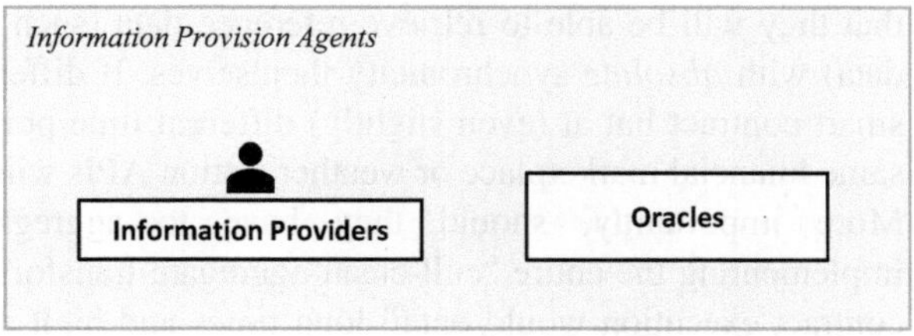

Oracles are software mechanisms that transmit specific and well-defined (both semantically and format-wise) data across blockchain boundaries. They may be ingesting this data from a single source or aggregating it from many other primary sources (which can be within a particular blockchain, straddle blockchains, or originate purely off-chain, including online). They undertake cleaning of data before making it available, as they are meant to provide "sources of truth" to enable certainty of factual basis for downstream decision-making.

An example of an Oracle would be a software mechanism that provides near-real-time market prices of financial instruments, tagged with their time stamps, to requestors of this data through an Application Programming Interface (API). Blockchain smart contracts[6] [17] can call this API, specify the particular financial instrument (e.g. through ISIN or Symbol) and timestamp of requested price snapshot, and thus retrieve the price that they need for their internal algorithms. This Oracle may reside outside any blockchain, sourcing its data directly from databases or through APIs provided by the same financial marketplaces where said financial instruments are traded. It will clean data, and possibly change their format, before making them available through its own API.

Another example of an Oracle would be software that aggregates weather-related information from websites, databases, or APIs of meteorological services, or directly from measurement stations. After data cleaning, aggregation, and reformatting, it may make those aggregated time series available through APIs to smart contracts of ecosystems where this information is needed, e.g. to price weather derivatives or assist price discovery of same derivatives through decentralized automated market makers.[7] The Oracle may reside completely outside blockchains, may itself be part of a blockchain ecosystem serving weather use cases, or may straddle several cooperating blockchains.

Oracles can have a variety of functional features [18, 19] and be made to follow different technical architectures [20, 21]. For the purposes of this discussion, their most important attribute is that they provide deterministic time-allocated information (or allocated to other well-specified independent variables).

Why are Oracles important for blockchain ecosystems?

Because, when registering transactions, blockchains obey a consensus paradigm. When different nodes execute independent block validations, it cannot be assured

[6]Cf. detailed discussion in Sect. 10.5.5.

[7]Cf. Sect. 12.2.1.

that they will be able to retrieve reference data (such as market prices or weather data) with *absolute* synchronicity themselves. If different nodes execute the same smart contract but at (even slightly) different time points, then reaching out to the same financial marketplace or weather station APIs will bring back different results. More importantly, should they have to aggregate primary data sources, implementing the entire "cull-clean-aggregate-transform" cycle as part of the smart contract execution would entail long times and high platform costs at the level of each and every validation, on each and every participating blockchain node. In short, it is an architectural anti-pattern, something that had better be avoided. Oracles provide precisely a way to avoid this.

Hence, a market design specifying the use of Oracles already provides very important information about how the business case is meant to execute on the blockchain. We already saw several examples (governance bodies, service-providing agents, and information provision agents) where the building blocks of market design provide at once abstraction and specificity, thus helping token buyers and investors understand the value proposition of their enclosing ecosystems. However, market design was defined to be "structural design". It must contain explanations of not only what the building blocks are, but also how they are put together. An example of part of such a design is provided by Fig. 6.4.

The ecosystem is schematically depicted as having a perimeter and two distinct classes of agents. There are two governance bodies and seven different types of other economic agents, six of which are to be filled in by humans. The information is already meaningful and use-case relevant. The design can be extended by also including external dependencies (cf. Fig. 6.5). A new information is the intended cooperation of the ecosystem with crypto-asset exchanges of both centralized and decentralized types (CEX and DEX, respectively). There is also an information flow among the reference ecosystem and four types of Oracles.

Market design also entails the definition of "Transactional Pathways". That means describing what kinds of interactions can occur among economic agents and how, in order for specific transactions to take place. Fig. 6.6 contains an example of such a pathway from the design of a particular type of token-enabled ecosystem. This is a two-token DEX, where traders come together to swap one kind of token for another, both being made available in the DEX's liquidity pool. There are several economic agent types (both human and algorithmic) involved in this transaction. Possible steps and corresponding token flows are also indicated. This is a "Transactional Pathway".

In summary, market design is the definition of all economic agent types (privileged or otherwise) relevant for the token ecosystem; along with a description of all material transactional pathways among them, also denoting the types of token (s) transacted on. Market design is meant to provide:

- Clarity about how the intended use cases of the token-based ecosystem are facilitated through the typology of economic agents.
- Clarity about how the intended token(s) of its protocol(s) is (are) to be used in transactions among said agents.

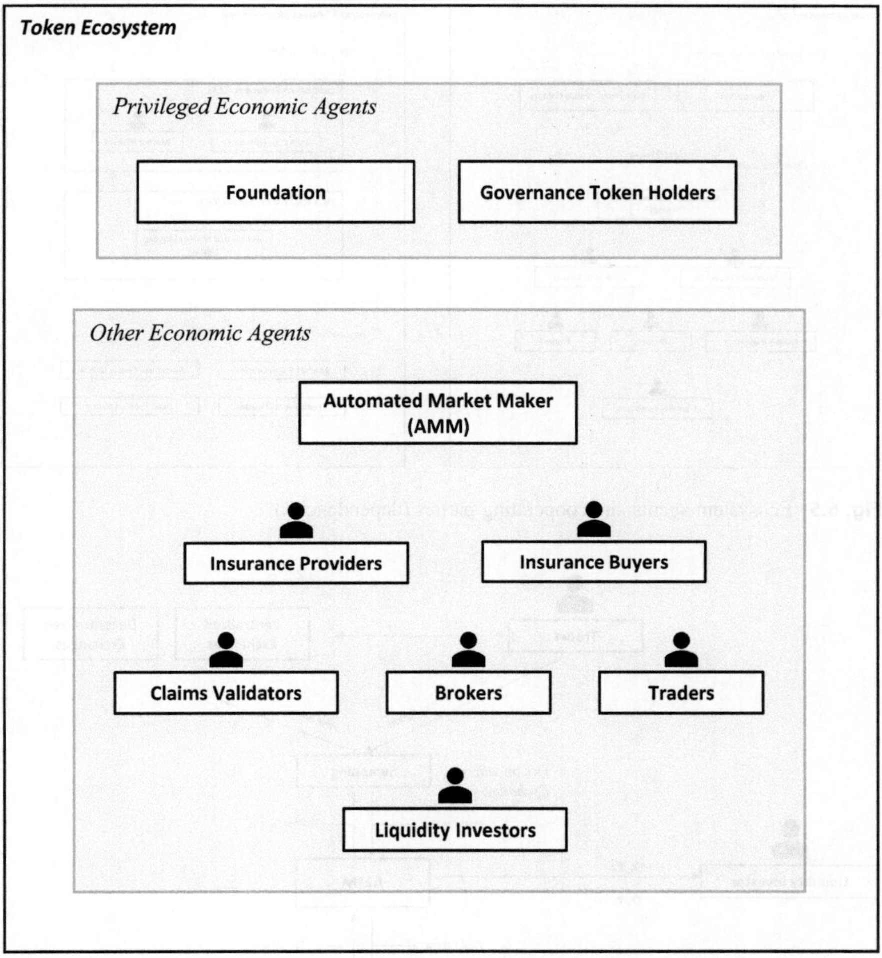

Fig. 6.4 Structure of internal economic agents in a particular token ecosystem

- A contextual basis for the other main pillars of the design framework, namely the mechanism and token designs.

Market design is the *structural* design of the *economic environment* within which participants and governance bodies will be interacting with each other. It thus entails both social and economic engineering.

6.4.1 Process and Components of Market Design

To design, we first need to analyse.

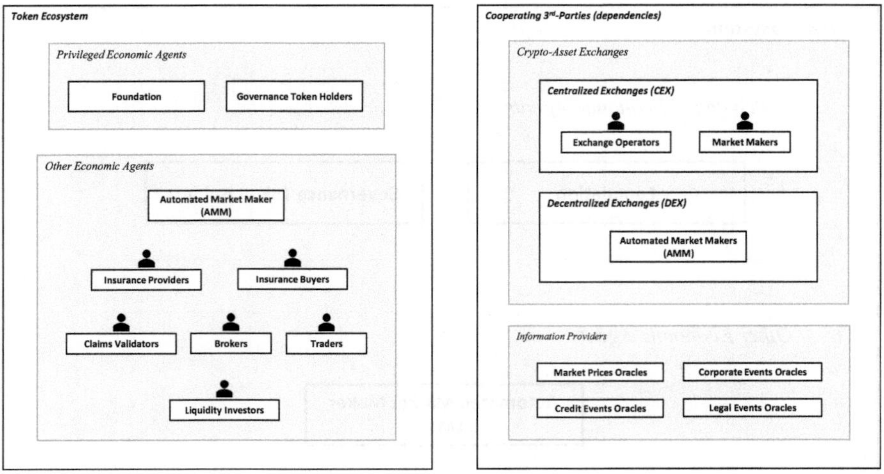

Fig. 6.5 Ecosystem agents and cooperating parties (dependencies)

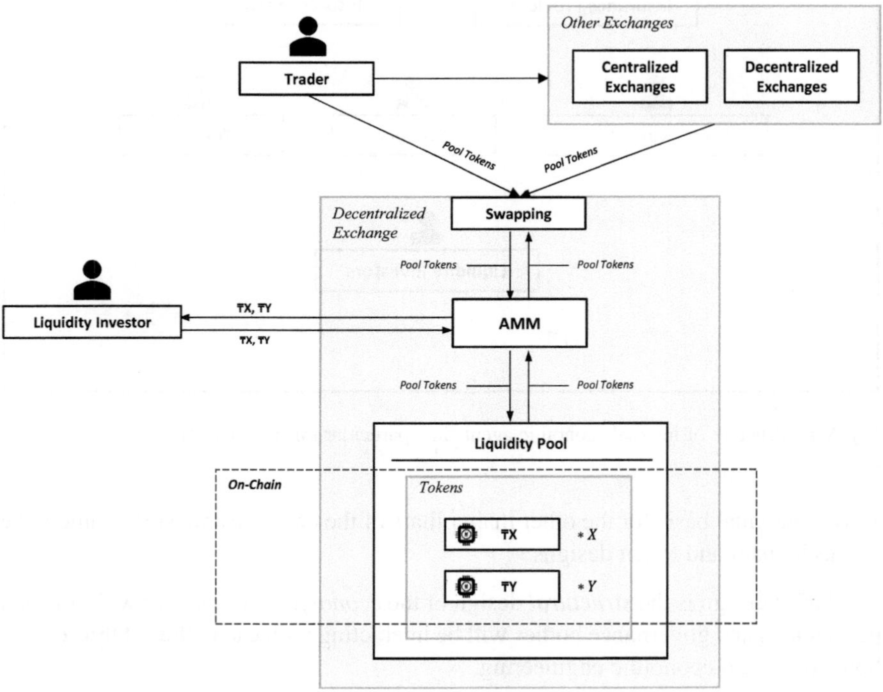

Fig. 6.6 DEX market design example—economic agents and transactional pathways

The starting point of market design will be general functional and operational directions, i.e. statements of intent[8] about:

- The project's business context and economic objectives, in terms of assets and services exchanged (the "use case").
- The blockchain platform on which it will be architected.
- The lifecycle stages and functional attributes of its token(s) within said use case.
- The project's governance arrangements, potentially also involving some token type(s).[9]

Its end point will be a description of **economic agent** types and **transactional pathways** among them:

1. A typology of all admissible economic agents (both those representing "branches of government"—"privileged"—and those that are ordinary transaction participants—"non-privileged") within the token ecosystem.
2. A typology of all third-party (cooperating) economic agents from other ecosystems, exchanges, Oracles, etc., that are needed to carry out the use case operationally.
3. For each and every admissible economic agent:
   (a) Its fundamental attributes (main functional characteristics).
   (b) Its nature along the "human" to "algorithmic" axis ("performed by humans", "performed by algorithms", "mixed", "conditional").
   (c) Its relevance to the ecosystem token(s).
4. For each and every transaction pathway with ecosystem token relevance, a clear blueprint (document, diagram, or any other artefact providing an unequivocal description) of:
   (a) The types of economic agents that take part.
   (b) The token(s) that will be exchanged in the course of each transaction, and among which economic agents.

The analysis phase will seek to identify all high-level technical and functional attributes needed to validate that the endpoint is reasonable and implementable.

In terms of necessary design tools, any **textual or diagrammatic (modelling) tool** should be used as a minimum, as conceptual consistency of the final description is critical; additional, more analytical or numerical, tools can be employed together with the main conceptual one if deemed necessary, e.g. for fact-checking of

[8]The project "Whitepaper" may or may not yet exist, depending on its intended level of detail and sophistication. Very detailed whitepapers will be finalized only at the end of the token ecosystem design process. Simple, generic "statement of intent" whitepapers may precede the first market designs.

[9]Governance (utility) token, cf. 4.2.2.

assumptions behind the design. In practical terms, conceptual consistency entails that:

- Economic agent typologies will need to be accompanied by a glossary, for the sake of clarity and completeness.
- Ecosystem tokens must be clearly identified as such within transactional pathways; they need not be described in any detail beyond their type (detailed token features will be produced by token design[10]).
- Transactional pathways should be best described through diagrams, so as to avoid logical voids and conflicting ideas, as the latter tend to be exposed quickly by visualization.

Market design is necessarily iterative, as all pillars of the token ecosystem design framework (including mechanism and token designs) are expected to be. Not only can decisions be revised within market design alone, but changing mechanism and token designs may also necessitate market redesigns.

6.5 Characteristics of a Successful Market Design

Let us refer back to the "new country" analogy. Imagine that a country has just come to exist. Its location on the map is clear, and it is known that it possesses natural resources, and that it is populated by skilled and able people. However, neither its natural nor its human capital has been catalogued. There are no government institutions, no dispute resolution venues, nor a country currency. There exist roads and basic infrastructure, but their extent is not clear, so all economic activities are local in nature. Exchanges of goods and services are always subject to bilateral negotiation. People are used to bartering goods and services, or to exchanging them for foreign currency. The only stores of value are physical assets and foreign currencies, so people hoard them for security in their future. **This is time zero.**

Imagine the same country at a later time. Government institutions now exist, and citizens have recourse to official venues for dispute resolution. Working infrastructures have been created and are mapped, so citizens know the timescales and costs of travelling. There are several distinct economic sectors operating, and country citizens are already active in them across the country. The country now has an own currency, in which goods, services, and stores of value are priced. Projected cash flows of investments can be estimated, so people now invest for their future. **At this time, a reviewer is tasked with rating the country's economic structures.**

What criteria will this reviewer use?

The reviewer in question will probably base their judgement on answers to the following questions:

[10]Cf. Chap. 10.

- Are all governance institutions of the country evident, with clear legal forms and written mandates?
- Do governance institutions have oversight over all forms of capital (natural, financial, human) in the country? Or are there some forms of capital lacking any governance oversight?
- Is it clear what kinds of infrastructure the country has? Does this infrastructure align with the needs of the citizens, corporations, and governance institutions of the country?
- Are all economic sectors employing citizens within the country transparent? Is it clear which goods and services are exchanged in them, and how?
- Which occupations do the country's citizens undertake in order to serve those sectors? Do they cover the entire spectrum needed, or are there any voids in coverage? If the latter, how else are they covered?
- How are the needs of these economic sectors served by governance institutions? Are there needed governance services that are not yet provided for?
- What are the media of exchange and stores of value admissible in the country? Are they all issued within the country? If there are specific uses per medium of exchange, what are those?

More questions can be asked as details gradually emerge. They can be themed so as to map to the desired quality attributes of market design, namely that it should:

1. Cover all structural aspects of governance, both institutionally and operationally.
2. Completely describe the typology of all economic agents of the token ecosystem's use case(s).
3. Align the granularity of economic agents with that of assets and services that will be exchanged during use case execution.
4. Completely describe the possible transactions and other material interactions among economic agents within the ecosystem.
5. Define the ecosystem token(s) in terms of high-level attributes such as nature and function (type).
6. Map the intended use of the ecosystem token(s) along each transaction and material interaction path.
7. Provide for managed change, in accordance with parallel changes in mechanism and token designs.
8. Respect the idiosyncrasies of the blockchain platform underlying the particular token ecosystem.
9. Strive to optimize use of resources—financial, human, and technological.

Points 8 and 9 are those where the technological aspect of digital ecosystems comes to the fore. Even though it could be argued that digital marketplaces are simply different channels of achieving the same results as in physical ones, the fact is that they come with their own constraints (as well as opening up additional potential) in process execution. We already mentioned in subsection 6.6.4 the occasional need for Oracles as a way to address blockchain consensus practicalities in market design, which corresponds to point 8. Use of automated market makers (smart contracts of a particular functional scope,[11] used heavily in decentralized finance) is a manifestation of point 9. There are many more, which are explained in this and subsequent chapters. The important message is that market design is not simply about listing of typologies and diagramming use of tokens. It is an analysis and design activity, advised by knowledge and experience, taking several business and technical factors into consideration.

On the business side of design, defining economic agents of the appropriate granularity means being able to identify their correct needs in terms of information, price discovery, negotiation tasks, risk management, and asset exchange sequenes along transactions. Not having the appropriate granularity ultimately leads to compromises, as only the least common denominator of functional needs is registered, with the burden then placed on exception handling (gleaned during mechanism design) to account for missing functionalities. Similarly, not providing for *actual operational needs* (gleaned through experience or advised by third-party experts) may well cause the business use case to fail. For example, traditional (non-blockchain) digital marketplaces use ratings volunteered by consumers to facilitate both functional and price discovery of new product offerings. If this rating functionality is absent from conceptual design, every new buyer would have myriad options to choose from with *no visibility on the relative merits and risks* of each. The result would be at least drastic deceleration of order flow and possibly buyer disillusionment. Vendors, on the other hand, would face the risks of excessive product returns and higher customer service costs. All in all, there would be less transaction velocity and non-optimal allocation of resources in the entire ecosystem. Desired functional features of products would be identified only by chance, and prices would not be commensurate with product utility and quality. Similar considerations would apply to the provision of services, including after-sales support and monetary transaction execution. Hence, identifying the appropriate typology and granularity of economic agents is of utmost importance for market stability and growth. If the value proposition of the new market is contingent on reaching a critical scale, then in this case the requisite scale may never be reached. Design failure will mean market failure.

Other pathologies will manifest themselves if the designed *governance* structures do not possess appropriate legal form, functional responsibilities, and operational flexibility attributes, nor show receptivity to community feedback loops, such as those needed for corrective actions. All in all, in reference to the "new country" analogy, imagine that a reviewer came to the conclusion that there are important governance functions that are missing, entire branches of government even; that the country's economic model ignored the absence of critical skills and necessary resources; that needed services were not considered essential, so that economic agents had to continuously improvise workarounds, wasting time and resources; that private persons or corporations needing specific goods and services did not

[11] Cf. Sect. 12.2.1.

know how and where to find them or had to make long journeys to discover for themselves who their providers within the country were. What would that imply for the stability of the country's economy and the long-term prospects of its currency as a store of value? Ultimately, should the country expect net immigration or emigration of skilled economic agents?

Viewed from a technology angle, blockchain-based token ecosystems are just one example of "smart market platforms". Those are a new paradigm of digital marketplaces, based on sophisticated algorithms that: optimize allocation of finite resources among transaction participants; and are driven by continuous streams of both deterministic and fuzzy variables as inputs, culled from many sources (humans, sensors, the Internet); interpret data as information in its proper business context; are able to continuously recalibrate themselves; can simulate basic human thought processes; and actively assist human decision-making. Such smart market platforms increasingly employ artificial intelligence, for both technical recalibration and human interaction purposes. Ignoring, or being agnostic about, the technical capabilities inherent in them entails that their full potential will not be used, i.e. that market design will *not be optimized.*

For example, not considering all possible design patterns enabled by smart contracts will restrict the options available to ecosystem governance to gather feedback from market participants, project developers, and governance token holders; reach and execute strategic decisions; allocate funding to infrastructure investments; and recalibrate basic operational parameters as dictated by market conditions or user experience. Similarly, using only currency and no asset tokens in automated market makers may fail to capture all possible economic value in the ecosystem. Also, not exploring all options to monitor frictions in information flows may hide the need for Oracles and thus cause token transactions to be arbitraged.

As a final remark, the value proposition of tokens in the context of their surrounding market design may be susceptible to "*winner-takes-all*" market dynamics. Academic research is not conclusive on whether this is the case for general currency tokens ([22–24]—but may be true for Stablecoins under particular market conditions [25]). However, for other token types, there are indeed anti-patterns to consider, e.g. when a token's function as a store of value hinges on the success of a particular use case[12], or even on its creating market differentiation in specific steps of a particular value[13] or supply[14] chain. What may happen is that the market design may indeed provide for the right transactional pathways but may fail to consider the need to monitor market thickness. Such situations may entail that only those token ecosystems that first manage to reach a critical scale will ultimately survive, as ecosystem liquidity and reputation will then function as effective barriers to entry.

[12]E.g. the Aave AAVE [26] and compound COMP [27] tokens used in on-chain lending use cases.

[13]E.g. the Chainlink LINK [28] token for Oracle use cases.

[14]E.g. the Filecoin FIL [29] token for decentralized storage use cases.

Hence, careful initial design and subsequent fine-tuning of functional and operational envelopes should be focused on the avoidance of said anti-patterns. All ecosystem design pillars, but especially market design, are critical success factors in that respect.

In summary, successful market designs encourage economic agents to participate in transactions, thus realizing the economic purposes of the token ecosystem and helping it to ultimately achieve network effects, making it self-sustaining. As ecosystem value growth is both facilitated and captured through its tokens, market design success is ultimately token success.

6.6 Factors of Consideration in Market Design

If the economic utility of the ecosystem's business case is realistic, market design can influence its success by taking its salient dependencies into account. Those, of course, will be contingent on the specific combination of use cases and blockchain platform; however, in our experience, there are some factors of consideration that are ever-present, while also shared with generic (i.e. not crypto-specific) ecosystems.

Thus, a robust market design must:

- Create **thickness**.
- Overcome **congestion**.
- Ensure **safety**.
- Prioritize **usability**.
- Take **social norms** into account.

We explain each point in some detail in the following sections.

6.6.1 Thickness

A market is said to exhibit adequate thickness when many economic actors are willing and able to take both sides of transactions at any given time. The importance of this concept lies in three implied outcomes: first, the optionality it frees for buyers, in terms of being able to compare among different offerings, different counterparties, and prices; second, the possibilities it gives to suppliers for price and features discovery, so that they can better calibrate cost basis for increased profitability; and third, the high amounts of liquidity that can make the market's business value proposition self-sustaining.

In the context of market design [30], the objective should be to structure governance, economic agent typologies, and transaction pathways in such a way as to facilitate increased levels of market thickness [31]. For example, if analysis indicates that scaling the token ecosystem is dependent on economies of scope, then the chosen economic agent typology should enable a broader variety of asset or service offerings, while transactional pathways should have enough commonality for suppliers to be able to collaborate. Similarly, should information provision be judged to be a definite enabler of transaction initiation, then every effort should be made to increase the amount and quality of information available, either on-chain or across blockchain boundaries, e.g. through Oracles. More generally, any gaps in needed functional coverage in terms of offerings or tokens (gaps, which analysis shows are not economically viable to close within the ecosystem) may be reduced through partnerships or implicit synergies with other token ecosystems, or through external agents. Such a case was depicted already in Fig. 6.5, where third-party cooperating agents take part in either price discovery or transaction execution.

Examples of thickness calibration can be readily found in existing token ecosystems. For instance, Aave [32] created a permissioned pool to attract institutional investors [33] so that it could augment its footprint beyond the retail market. Sushiswap [34] governance was able to increase market thickness by "air-dropping" [35, 36] a batch of native tokens to existing ecosystem participants. Yearn [37] introduced a partner program [38, 39] to facilitate synergies with third-party protocols, while itself referencing functionalities from cooperating protocols such as Curve [40, 41]. Enzyme [42] similarly provided for integration points with several other protocols [43] in its transactional pathways.

6.6.2 Congestion

"Congestion" is one of those terms that can mean different things in different contexts, in this case even in different marketplace contexts [44, 45]. We therefore find it expedient to provide an own definition, strictly in the context of digital marketplaces.

A digital marketplace will be said to be congested if there is insufficient time or information for a participant to decide to take part in a transaction. That means insufficient time or information to either evaluate or execute a potentially available transaction. Congestion can be either a temporary or a permanent situation, and as such it is ultimately an outcome of design decisions about the platform. Hence, a factor of consideration in market design.

Examples of platform features affecting congestion would be any time limits on closing a transaction, and any limits on the size of the market that a potential seller or buyer is practically able to see. An example of the first limit would be exchange-supplied token prices which are quoted as valid for only one minute, whereas prospective buyers feel that they would need to compare with other exchanges as well, the prices of which are not visible from within the same digital marketplace. Not including the other exchanges as cooperating economic agents, or not including at least their price streams through an Oracle, is a market design decision. An example of the second limit would be the absence of any information provision agent implementing rating and filtering mechanisms. Both suppliers and consumers can see the *entire* market, but they cannot isolate *that part of the market of interest to them*. What they can practically do is use the entire list of participants/offerings and then filter through it by their own means and to the best of their abilities. This is an effective visibility constraint, which reduces their chances of transacting in the best possible way; hence, it might deter them from concluding any transactions at all. Not including an information provision agent with the correct functional coverage is again a market design decision.

In the context of market design, the objective should be to structure economic agent typologies and transaction pathways in such a way as to minimize congestion. To that end, the analysis stage should consider all possible timescales influencing decisions by economic agents to enter or execute transactions. Also, the kinds and sources of information that will be generally needed by said actors before accepting to enter a transaction should be identified. At design convergence, agent typologies and transaction pathways should be calibrated towards reaching appropriate timescales and facilitating discovery and usage of information.

Market designs targeting congestion reduction are evident in existing token ecosystems. For instance, Yearn Finance uses on-chain data [46] to suggest the best investment returns as a function of interest rates offered and limits on deposited funds. It also makes some of its products visible only to whitelisted addresses [47–50] as a way of effecting client segmentation. The MakerDAO token ecosystem [12] uses both internal and external price feeds (provided through Oracles [51]) to quote token prices or to use them in smart contracts.

Please note that some level of market congestion may be a consciously accepted side effect of end-to-end ecosystem design decisions. For example, any time-limited auctions (e.g. liquidity auctions in maker [52]) or concentrated liquidity positions (as available in Uniswap [53]) are examples of platform design features *purposely increasing* market congestion. As in all design activities, achieving best results in one area may necessitate reaching compromises in another, and the last two examples demonstrate that. One purpose of us listing influencing factors for all token ecosystem design pillars is to provide designers with an understanding of what probable end-to-end consequences individual calibrations might have.

6.6.3 Safety

A marketplace is safe if its participants are protected from losses due to factors outside their control. Such factors can be fraud, theft, and other financial crimes; technical deficiencies; platform interruptions; mis-selling of products and services (which are factually, or per documented policy, non-suitable for some buyers/investors); predatory lending; undue influence; information hiding, or exploitation of information asymmetries by transaction counterparties; etc. The list of potential factors can be rather long and depend on the individual use case. However, all such loss events can be represented by transferring the definition of operational risk from the traditional banking world [54] to the context of the individual market participant in blockchain-based token ecosystems:

- These are losses resulting from inadequate or failed internal processes, people, and systems, or from external events.

Token ecosystems inherit all operational risk pathologies of traditional finance and additionally exhibit risk patterns that are specific to the blockchain paradigm. For example, what is known as "front-running" [55] in general marketplaces is also known in blockchain exchanges, but adds an additional dimension: in several blockchain platforms, on-chain automated traders ("crypto-bots") can legitimately "up-bid" in execution fees in order to have their own transactions validated before others[15] [56]. As transactions in permissionless blockchains are broadcast to the entire network of validating nodes as a matter of course, delays in their execution (if a crypto-bot pushes them down in priority) create a moral hazard situation similar to the one that led to the "High-Frequency-Trading" concerns [57] in the past. Similarly, because a basic blockchain automation paradigm is the use of smart contracts, any fault in their internal logic or in their technical implementation can be, and has repeatedly been [58], exploited by hackers to redirect the outcomes of transactions.

Market safety features are the sum of attributes (i.e. structures, mechanisms, processes) designed to protect market participants from such losses. In all generality, they are expected to be present in both market and mechanism designs. From the point of view of market design, such features can be either protective or corrective. An example of protective feature would be on-chain insurance coverage provided only through vetted insurance providers, included as part of the market design typology or through cooperating ecosystems. Similarly, token staking can included as a mandatory part of transactional pathways on the understanding that fraudulent behaviour by market participants will cause their tokens to be forfeited. Corrective measures could be e.g. governing structures managing a liquidity reserve meant to cover restoration of tokens lost to market participants due to fraud or technical errors. Tasking a governance body with quality assurance (e.g. managing token pools declared as reward for "bug-hunting bounties") is also such a measure.

Safety features are evident in market designs of most existing token ecosystems. For example, governance of Kyber Network [59] has a mandate to commission regular independent audits of its code base [60–62]. Specialized token-protocol audit firms publish the results of such audits in the public domain [63, 64]. Practically all large token-based ecosystems have "bug-hunting" initiatives [65–68] managed by their governing bodies. Smaller ecosystems can avail themselves of the services of specialized platforms, which are also token-based [69]. Furthermore, synergies among ecosystems to improve safety have also occurred, e.g. when Yearn Finance cooperated with Nexus Mutual [70] to offer loss insurance [71] to its ecosystem participants. Specialized token-insurance firms, such as Ease [72], also provide insurance coverage to individual token holders across token protocols, thus providing an additional third-party cooperating agent option to include in mechanism designs.

[15] Cf. also the discussion about "Maximum Extractable Value" in Ethereum PoS validation in Sect. 12.4.7.

Defining appropriate safety measures in market design is necessary in order to convince potential market participants to join the token ecosystem. Absent such measures, economic agents may try to manage their risks through workarounds that damage the marketplace as a whole, or otherwise exploit information asymmetries (e.g. to prevent their transaction counterparties from negotiating better offers). In worst-case scenarios, financial crime may manifest itself within the ecosystem, harming its participants and damaging its reputation. Market and mechanism designs should be aligned and updated as needed to avoid these risks.

It is important to add that, whereas market thickness and congestion are useful considerations in market design, safety, and usability (cf. also next section) factors may, under circumstances, transcend the boundary between consideration and obligation. For example, should the ecosystem token(s) qualify as financial instruments (cf. Sect. 4.2.4), or should the ecosystem use case fall within the definition of financial services activities covered under securities or banking laws of any concerned jurisdiction, then auditability, operational risk management, and governance accountability measures become legal obligations. In such cases, all pillars of the token ecosystem design framework are to be reviewed from the standpoint of accommodating legal and regulatory requirements as well.

6.6.4 Usability

Usability refers to all attributes of the ecosystem that make participation of economic agents cost-effective in terms of time and resources. As regards market design, it implies consideration of all structural features that can help minimize frictions in the ecosystem.

One possible friction involves onboarding, i.e. the task to identify and allow new economic agents as ecosystem participants. If the agent typology does not take into account different needs and permissions per type, or if transactional pathways ignore technical features of the blockchain or of the dApps built around it, then onboarding difficulties will ultimately mean loss of time and goodwill on the part of prospective token users.

Other possible frictions are: absence, reduced availability, or non-timeliness of needed information; long transaction execution times; objective difficulty to retrieve needed documentation or to request online help; non-intuitiveness of the graphical user interface; etc. Market design can help minimize such frictions from the beginning, by e.g. defining the appropriate agent typology; providing for third-party cooperating agents (e.g. Oracles, Identity/KYC ecosystems); creating governance bodies with a mandate to update documentation and operate helplines and chatbots; and similarly with a mandate for usability audits, etc.

Token-based ecosystems have found several ways to enhance the usability of their offerings. For example, interoperability is the driver behind increasing use of cross-ecosystem token wallets such as Metamask [73], whereas lower transaction timescales is the business case of Near [74]. There are also bespoke usability-focused offerings such as the Fio protocol [75]. Of course, as technology evolves, so do the usability imperatives.

As already mentioned in the previous section, usability, under circumstances, may have to be examined from the standpoint of accommodating legal and regulatory requirements (e.g. order management, client documentation) as well.

6.6.5 Social Norms

The token use case cannot of course be illegal. However, as legality and morality are two different things, there is an important consideration in market design about the need to avoid unintentionally creating a "repugnant" market.

In economics, a "repugnant" market denotes an area of economic activity that is considered by society to be outside the limits of what most people would consider moral or ethical. Sometimes the relevant goods and services can be acceptable when provided pro bono, but to exchange them for money is taboo. Such examples would be markets in:

(a) Human genes and living tissue.
(b) Human organs.
(c) Children (i.e. when adoption is offered in a market driven by pure profit).
(d) Surrogacy (i.e. where surrogate mothers are offering to carry babies as a service to willing buyers).
(e) Sex services.
(f) Mercenary services.
(g) Voting (i.e. where voters offer their votes for sale).
(h) Friendship.
(i) School admissions.
(j) Prizes of achievement (e.g. Nobel prizes).

As is evident from the list, the same market can be outright illegal in some countries, whereas in others it may be tolerated or simply considered immoral. For example, buying sex is illegal in some Scandinavian countries but not in the rest of the world. However, it can be argued that society at large does indeed consider the prostitution market as immoral. Hence, the degree of "repugnance" of a particular market (along the axis of legality) can be dependent on the cultural norms of particular societies.

One important aspect of this notion of repugnance in economic design is that it affects the ability to enter and carry out valid transactions.

In any well-functioning economic system, the ability to transact is preconditioned on the existence of written norms to guide the negotiation of contracts (counterparties, object, terms) and of mechanisms to enforce said contracts in case of problems (objective or subjective) arising during transaction execution. Those norms are codified in the Law of Contract (Common Law systems), or Law of Obligations (most Civil Law systems), of the respective jurisdiction. In both cases, law makes the validity of the ensuing contract (or obligation) predicated on the legality of the economic objective of the contracting counterparties. If the purpose of a contractual agreement is either illegal or contrary to public policy, then the contract is considered void or invalid (i.e. as if it has never been entered into).

However, it can be argued that what makes some of the aforementioned markets repugnant is not their bringing together supply and demand for a particular good or service per se, but rather the monetary aspect which generates the implicit demand for middlemen and the incentive to move the ensuing transaction outside the main economy (i.e. into the "grey economy", or indeed the "black" one). For example, imagine if there were a way to create a completely visible digital "marketplace" where people willing to adopt and people (sadly) needing to offer their own babies for adoption to well-meaning foster parents could come together. They could exchange the same material information that would be needed even if they were to meet in person and then would decide on the next steps. A couple willing to adopt could thus "screen" several offering couples or single parents, and the latter could also "screen" candidate foster couples. Then, this "marketplace" would no longer involve middlemen, nor would it involve monetary transactions. So, the absence of any monetary expectations, from either the "demand" or "supply" sides, makes this possibly repugnant market an altruistic one. This can now be implemented through a token-based paradigm with an appropriate market design.

Similarly, imagine if there were a way to enable altruistic organ donation in non-obvious situations, which can exist in the physical world but do not render themselves easily to an economic transaction-based paradigm [76]. Consider the example of a married couple where one spouse needs a kidney and the other spouse is willing to donate one of their own but is not a matching donor. Suppose there are other couples with the same problem, in the same or in different countries. Then, the willing donor of couple A can offer their kidney to the asking recipient of couple B, under the condition that the willing donor of couple B would be offering theirs to the asking recipient of couple A *and* that they would be located in the same country. Then also tri-party or even multi-party "transactions" [77] could be enabled, i.e. where several couples are involved (offering and accepting kidneys within the same country or adjacent countries) until a matching donor for the first couple in the same country is found. If this process could be implemented on the blockchain, then a platform token can be the means to finance the operational costs of the "transaction" (travel, examinations, surgery) through crowdfunding or by any other on-platform financing mechanism—which would be entirely transparent and auditable on account of the blockchain.

Generalizing from the previous examples, in the digital world, where information comes together on a global scale, some traditionally "repugnant" markets can be transformed into socially acceptable "brokerage" platforms, not necessarily involving a monetary aspect but still incorporating safety and ease-of-use elements such as the ones already mentioned in the previous sections. Ensuring information exchange (i.e. "altruistic" information sharing) while removing the constraints of traditionally "repugnant" markets is what makes the value proposition of token-based ecosystems evident in this setting. Designing such a market is the objective of token-based market design.

Hence, the degree to which an economic activity is, or can be considered, repugnant is a fundamental parameter of whether or not resulting transactions among economic agents are morally acceptable (and at least legally valid). A token-based platform has the potential to transform traditionally repugnant markets into socially acceptable and legally valid ones. Effecting this objective calls for appropriate definition of economic agents and of the possible ways in which they can interact on the platform, such that the ensuing transactions are valid ones. Hence, it is by definition part of market design.

6.7 Summary

In the beginning of this chapter, we made the analogy of designing a token-based market with designing a new country-level economy. This is always a great undertaking, ideally backed by vision and conviction. Vision is needed to have clarity about what is to be achieved (that is, which products and services to offer, to whom, how to source them, how to distribute them, how to exchange them, etc.). Conviction is needed as to why this vision facilitates or enables a societal need. Conviction will be translated in practical terms into design principles, leading to optimal outcomes.

The structural aspect of said outcomes is the object of market design. It was explained as consisting essentially of the typology of the ecosystem's economic agents, external dependencies, and transactional pathways, along with the token typology evidenced in the latter. Its salient influencing factors (thickness, congestion, safety, usability, social norms) were also explained in a token ecosystem setting.

We did not strive to give a detailed list of criteria, only guiding principles, for good market design. Said principles condense current Crypto-market experience and are meant to facilitate subsequent design decisions at the mechanism and token levels.

In the next chapter, we will give a concrete example of market design from an existing token-based ecosystem.

References

1. Hays, A. (2024, August 4). White Paper: Types, purpose, and how to write one. Retrieved March 22, 2025, from https://www.investopedia.com/terms/w/whitepaper.asp
2. Kaur, G. (2023, August 2). What is a white paper? A beginner's guide on how to write and format one. CoinTelegraph. Retrieved March 22, 2025, from https://cointelegraph.com/ico-101/what-is-a-white-paper-and-how-to-write-it%20
3. Market design. (2025, January 13). In *Wikipedia*. Retrieved March 22, 2025, from https://en.wikipedia.org/wiki/Market_design
4. (2018). *The new Palgrave dictionary of economics* (3rd ed.). Palgrave Macmillan. Referenced text to be found in p. 8481.

5. Vulkan, N., Roth, A. E., & Neeman, Z. (Eds.). (2013). *The handbook of market design*. Oxford University Press.
6. Roth, A. E. (2015). *Who gets what – And why: The new economics of matchmaking and market design*. HarperBusiness.
7. Haeringer, G. (2017). *Market design; auctions and matching*. MIT Press.
8. Echenique, F., Immorlica, N., & Vazirani, V. V. (Eds.). (2023). *Online and matching-based market design*. Cambridge University Press.
9. Agent (economics). (2024, September 6). In *Wikipedia*. Retrieved March 22, 2025, from https://en.wikipedia.org/wiki/Agent_(economics)
10. (2018). *The new Palgrave dictionary of economics* (3rd ed.). Palgrave Macmillan. Referenced text to be found in p. 107 and in p. 114.
11. *Legal* [terms and conditions of interacting with the Tether ecosystem]. Tether ecosystem webpages. Retrieved March 22, 2025, from https://tether.to/legal/
12. [MakerDAO Token ecosystem]. https://makerdao.com/en/. Retrieved April 4, 2025. Please note: MakerDAO is currently a subset of the Sky Token ecosystem (https://sky.money/).
13. Decentralized autonomous organization. (2025, April 5). In Wikipedia. Retrieved April 12, 2025, from https://en.wikipedia.org/wiki/Decentralized_autonomous_organization
14. Hertig, A. (2017, March 30). What is a DAO? A decentralized autonomous organization, or DAO, is an organization that's governed by code instead of leaders. CoinDesk. Retrieved March 22, 2025, from https://www.coindesk.com/learn/what-is-a-dao/
15. Maker Governance Voting Portal. MakerDAO governance pages. Retrieved March 22, 2025, from https://vote.makerdao.com/. Please note: MakerDAO is currently a subset of the Sky Token ecosystem (https://sky.money/).
16. *Maker Operational Manual*. MakerDao governance documentation pages. Retrieved March 22, 2025, from https://manual.makerdao.com/. Please note: MakerDAO is currently a subset of the Sky Token ecosystem (https://sky.money/).
17. Smart contract. (2025, April 14). In *Wikipedia*. Retrieved April 16, 2025, from https://en.wikipedia.org/wiki/Smart_contract
18. Collins, P. (2020, September 2). What is a Blockchain Oracle? And what's the oracle problem? Why can't blockchains themselves make API calls? Medium. Retrieved March 22, 2025, from https://medium.com/better-programming/what-is-a-blockchain-oracle-f5ccab8dbd72
19. Beniiche, A. (2020, July 14). A study of Blockhain oracles. Retrieved March 22, 2025, from https://arxiv.org/pdf/2004.07140
20. Pasdar, A., Dong, Z. & Lee, Y.C. (2021, June 17). Blockchain Oracle design patterns. Retrieved March 22, 2025, from https://arxiv.org/pdf/2106.09349
21. Müller, M., Rodriguez, G. S., & Küpper, A. (2020). COST: A consensus-based Oracle protocol for the secure trade of digital goods. In *2020 IEEE International Conference on Decentralized Applications and Infrastructures (DAPPS)* (pp. 72–81). https://doi.org/10.1109/DAPPS49028.2020.00008
22. Gandal, N., & Hałaburda, H. (2014) *Competition in the Cryptocurrency market*. Bank of Canada Working Paper No. 2014-33. Retrieved March 22, 2025, from https://www.econstor.eu/handle/10419/103022
23. Gandal, N., & Halaburda, H. (2016). Can we predict the winner in a market with network effects? Competition in cryptocurrency market. *Games, 7*, 16. https://doi.org/10.3390/g7030016
24. Noam, E. (2019, November 18). The macro-economics of crypto-currencies: Balancing entrepreneurialism and monetary policy, SIPA, Columbia University. (2018). Retrieved March 22, 2025, from https://papers.ssrn.com/sol3/papers.cfm?abstract_id=3493333
25. Anisiuba, C. A., Egbo, O. P., Alio, F. C., Ifediora, C., Igwemeka, E. C., Odidi, C. O., & Ezeaku, H. C. (2021, March 23). Analysis of cryptocurrency dynamics in the emerging market economies: Does reinforcement or substitution effect prevail? *Sage Open, 11*(1), 21582440211002516. https://doi.org/10.1177/21582440211002516

26. CoinMarketCap AAVE page. CoinMarketCap. Retrieved March 22, 2025, from https://coinmarketcap.com/currencies/aave/
27. CoinMarketCap COMP page. CoinMarketCap. Retrieved March 22, 2025, from https://coinmarketcap.com/currencies/compound/
28. CoinMarketCap LINK page. CoinMarketCap. Retrieved March 22, 2025, from https://coinmarketcap.com/currencies/chainlink/
29. CoinMarketCap FIL page. CoinMarketCap. Retrieved March 22, 2025, from https://coinmarketcap.com/currencies/filecoin/
30. Roth, A. E. (2007). The art of designing markets. *Harvard Business Review, 85*(10), 118–126. Retrieved March 22, 2025, from https://hbr.org/2007/10/the-art-of-designing-markets
31. Golde, S. (2010, March). The economics of market thickness. Ph.D. Dissertation, Stanford University. Retrieved March 22, 2025, from https://stacks.stanford.edu/file/druid:dm505cj9642/Golde_Dissertation_submission-augmented.pdf
32. [Aave Token ecosystem]. https://aave.com/
33. Redman, J. (2025, March 14). Aave labs introduces compliance-friendly DeFi platform for institutional investors. Bitcoin.com News. Retrieved March 22, 2025, from https://news.bitcoin.com/aave-labs-introduces-compliance-friendly-defi-platform-for-institutional-investors/
34. [SushiSwap Token ecosystem]. https://sushi.com/
35. Investopedia Team. (2024, May 11). Cryptocurrency airdrop: What is it and how does it work. Retrieved March 22, 2025, from https://www.investopedia.com/terms/a/airdrop-cryptocurrency.asp
36. (2022, March 18). Give me that airdrop money. Cryptonary. Retrieved March 22, 2025, from https://cryptonary.com/research/give-me-that-airdrop-money/
37. [Yearn Token ecosystem]. https://yearn.fi/
38. (2021, March 7). Yearn finance Newsletter #25. Retrieved March 22, 2025, from https://yearn.substack.com/p/yearn-finance-newsletter-25
39. [Yearn Partneship Program] *Eligibility*. Yearn documentation pages. Retrieved March 22, 2025, from https://docs.yearn.fi/partners/introduction
40. [Curve Token ecosystem]. https://curve.fi/
41. (2021, September 14) More boosts, compounding, and mojitos for you with yvBOOST. Yearn's collaborative relationship with Curve.fi is core to our infrastructure, and core to you boosting your boosts. Medium. Retrieved March 22, 2025, from https://medium.com/iearn/thats-boost-folks-7afae75db826
42. [Enzyme Token ecosystem]. https://enzyme.finance/
43. El Isa, M. (2021, February 24). Announcing Sulu; enzyme's next release & roadmap. Medium. Retrieved March 22, 2025, from https://medium.com/enzymefinance/announcing-sulu-enzymes-next-release-roadmap-5c754b8e9f42
44. Mitchell, C. (2024, September 26). Market congestion: What it means, causes, and example. Retrieved March 22, 2025, from https://www.investopedia.com/terms/c/congestion.asp
45. Farmer, R. N. (1964). The economics of congestion. *Transportation Journal, 4*(1), 28–34. (Penn State University Press). http://www.jstor.org/stable/20711927
46. *Welcome to the Vaults at Yearn*. Yearn public pages. Retrieved March 22, 2025, from https://vaults.yearn.finance/
47. [Yearn] *yVault Types*. Yearn documentation pages. Retrieved March 20, 2025, from https://docs.yearn.fi/getting-started/products/yvaults/overview
48. [Yearn] yVaults v3. Yearn documentation pages. Retrieved March 20, 2025, from https://docs.yearn.fi/getting-started/products/yvaults/v3
49. [Yearn] yVaults v2. Yearn documentation pages. Retrieved March 20, 2025, from https://docs.yearn.fi/getting-started/products/yvaults/v2
50. *Token & Contract Addresses*. Yearn documentation pages. Retrieved March 20, 2025, from https://docs.yearn.fi/developers/addresses

51. *Oracle Module – The Maker Protocol's Oracles*. MakerDAO documentation pages. Retrieved March 22, 2025, from https://docs.makerdao.com/smart-contract-modules/oracle-module. Please note: MakerDAO is currently a subset of the Sky Token ecosystem (https://sky.money/).
52. *The Auctions of the Maker Protocol*. MakerDAO documentation pages. Retrieved March 22, 2025, from https://docs.makerdao.com/smart-contract-modules/oracle-module. Please note: MakerDAO is currently a subset of the Sky Token ecosystem (https://sky.money/).
53. [Uniswap] Concentrated Liquidity. Uniswap documentation pages. Retrieved March 20, 2025, from https://docs.uniswap.org/concepts/protocol/concentrated-liquidity
54. Bank for International Settlements (BIS). (2011, June). *Principles for the sound management of operational risk*. Basel committee on banking supervision. Retrieved March 22, 2025, from https://www.bis.org/publ/bcbs195.pdf
55. Mitchell, C. (2024, September 16). *Front-running definition, example, and legality*. Retrieved March 22, 2025, from https://www.investopedia.com/terms/f/frontrunning.asp
56. DeGate Team. (2021, May 4). An analysis of Ethereum front-running and its defense solutions. Medium. Retrieved March 22, 2025, from https://medium.com/degate/an-analysis-of-ethereum-front-running-and-its-defense-solutions-34ef81ba8456
57. Conerly, B. (2016, December 28). Flash boys and high frequency trading: Trust markets, not regulators. Forbes. Retrieved March 22, 2025, from https://www.forbes.com/sites/billconerly/2016/12/28/flash-boys-and-high-frequency-trading-trust-markets-not-regulators/
58. Young, M. (2021, February 5). Yearn finance dai vault exploited for $11 million, YFI Dumps. Retrieved March 22, 2025, from https://beincrypto.com/yearn-finance-dai-vault-exploited-for-11-million-yfi-dumps/
59. [Kyber Token ecosystem]. https://kyber.network/
60. ChainSecurity. (2018, July 9). Kyber. Network audit completed. Retrieved March 22, 2025, from https://medium.com/chainsecurity/kyber-network-audit-completed-b737acb1860f
61. Nikashin, B. (2019, July 18). Kyber network smart contracts security analysis. Medium. Retrieved March 22, 2025, from https://medium.com/chainsecurity/kyber-network-audit-completed-b737acb1860f
62. ChainSecurity. (2021, April). *KyberSwap classic—Security audit*. Retrieved March 22, 2025, from https://www.chainsecurity.com/security-audit/kyberswap-classic/
63. [Hacken – Crypto Assurance company]. https://hacken.io/audits/
64. [DeFiSafety – Crypto Assurance company]. https://www.defisafety.com/
65. [Ethereum network] *Bug Bounty Program*. Ethereum.org. Retrieved March 22, 2025, from https://ethereum.org/en/bug-bounty/
66. [Uniswap Labs – Uniswap bounty program]. Retrieved March 22, 2025, from https://cantina.xyz/bounties/f9df94db-c7b1-434b-bb06-d1360abdd1be
67. (2024, November 26) *$15.5M bug bounty for uniswap v4: The largest in history*. Retrieved March 22, 2025, from https://blog.uniswap.org/v4-bug-bounty
68. (2022, March 8). How traditional and crypto bounty programs differ. Cryptopedia. Retrieved March 22, 2025, from https://www.gemini.com/cryptopedia/bounty-program-crypto-bounty-campaigns-hack-bounty
69. [Cryptocurrency bounty hunting platform]. https://bounty0x.io/
70. [Nexus Mutual Token ecosystem]. https://nexusmutual.io/
71. (2020, September 1). Yearn finance launches DeFi token insurance with nexus mutual. BeInCrypto. Retrieved March 22, 2025, from https://beincrypto.com/yearn-finance-launches-defi-token-insurance-with-nexus-mutual/
72. [Ease Token ecosystem]. https://ease.org/
73. [Web browser extension & mobile app to manage Private Keys – Virtual Wallet] https://metamask.io/
74. [Near Blockchain Protocol]. https://near.org/blockchain
75. [Fio Protocol]. https://fio.net/

76. Roth, A. E., Sönmez, T., & Ünver, M. U. (2004). Kidney exchange. *The Quarterly Journal of Economics, 119*(2), 457–488. https://doi.org/10.1162/0033553041382157
77. Ashlagi, I., & Roth, A. E. (2012). New challenges in multihospital kidney exchange. *American Economic Review, 102*(3), 354–359. Retrieved March 22, 2025 from https://dspace.mit.edu/handle/1721.1/74595 (Open Access)

Case Study in Market Design: Nexus Mutual 7

In the previous chapter we laid out theoretical foundations and notions of market design. Here we proceed with a case study of how those notions are evident in an existing blockchain-based token ecosystem. The focus of our analysis will be "Nexus Mutual" [1] which is currently among the top DeFi insurance-sector protocols by token market capitalization [2].

We begin with the closest analogues to Nexus Mutual's business cases from traditional finance in order to help the reader interpret its main transactional pathways later in the chapter.

7.1 Non-Life Insurance

The insurance business is one of the fundamental pillars of economic activity in any modern economy. For private persons for example it is a prudent choice—and, in several jurisdictions, a legally mandatory obligation—to be paying for health insurance for oneself and for one's dependents. The availability of life insurance, automobile insurance, property insurance, etc. has come to be self-evident for the average citizen. However, its implications for the society at large are felt most prominently at the corporate and macro levels. No large corporate acquisition and no infrastructure project can be financed without insurance coverage against possible risks occurring. In that sense, the availability of insurance enables new economic models, creates private workplaces and helps optimize public finances. Hence, it can be argued that the insurance business provides an important contribution to the maintenance and evolution of both the physical and the economic life in our societies.

The notion of insurance coverage itself needs no introduction. Insurance providers channel risk capital (i.e. contingent capital commitments by private and corporate liquidity providers) to contracts—"Insurance Policies"—accepted by "Policyholders" who expect to be receiving a compensation upon registering the occurrence of a covered event—"filing a Claim"—up to the amount agreed in said

I. Giannakouros, *Cryptocurrencies and Tradable Crypto-Tokens*, Future of Business and Finance, https://doi.org/10.1007/978-3-031-98423-5_7

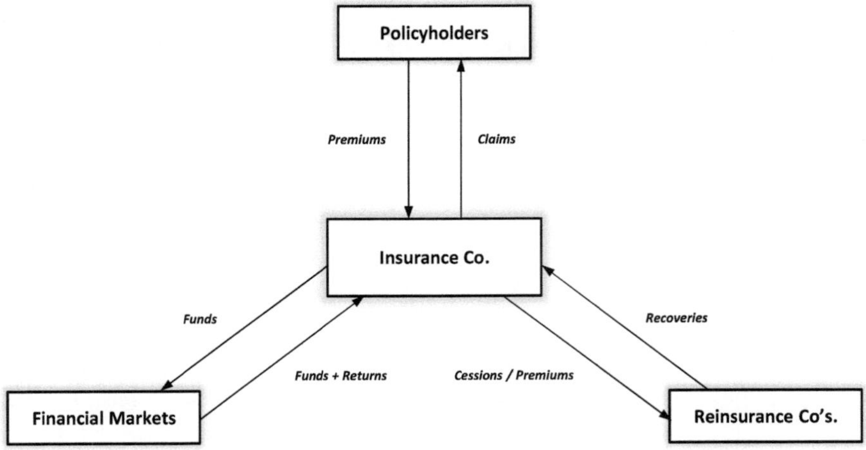

Fig. 7.1 Insurance companies' business model

contracts—"Insurance Cover Amount". Policyholders in return pay periodic sums of money—"Premiums"—to said insurance providers. Premiums reflect both the general and idiosyncratic levels of risk of the insured subject/object/activity as evidenced by statistical models—"Actuarial Models"—of financial losses attributable to the occurrence of risk events. Due to the level of technical expertise and depth of financial resources necessary to provide an effective insurance coverage, this business is strongly regulated and its providers are always legal entities, i.e. Insurance Companies.

Insurance policies are understood in reference to "Perils", which are the root causes of losses. For example, fire, hail, flood, car accident, cybercrime, are all perils. Beyond the covered perils, the actuarial model underneath the premium calculation of a specific insurance policy needs as parameters the idiosyncratic characteristics—the "Hazards"—completing the risk profile of the person/object/activity given the peril. The age of a building and its main materials of construction are, e.g., such hazards in reference to the peril "Fire". Together with the insurance cover amount, these parameters (static or behavioural) define the requisite premium against which the insurance company accepts to issue—"Underwrites"—the policy.

Across perils and policy types, the business model of the typical insurance company is as depicted schematically on fig. 7.1.

The "Insurance Co." receives regular premiums from policyholders and provides risk coverage leading to eventual payouts in the occurrence of insured events; said payouts follow policyholders' loss notifications, which become claims. The steady inflow of premiums generates a liquidity base, which is used by the insurance co. to fund investments in the financial markets. The latter are used both to generate returns on said investments and also to fund operating capital requirements, thus cumulatively "Funds + Returns" are drawn back continuously or as needed. Importantly, part of the aggregate incoming liquidity is redirected to reinsurance companies,

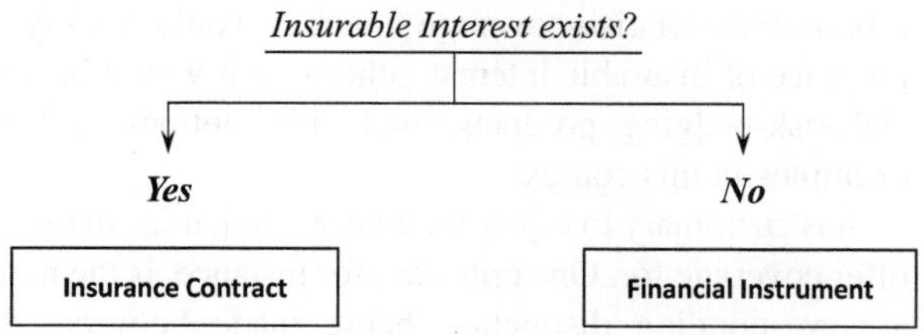

Fig. 7.2 Fundamental importance of the "Insurable Interest" requirement

which are in effect the "insurers of the insurers" (cf. Sect. 7.2 below). Against those outflows ("Cessions/Premiums" in Fig. 7.1), reinsurers accept to cover part of the claims' amounts owed to the policyholders. The industry jargon for these inflows from the reinsurers back to the insurance co. is "[Loss/Claim] Recoveries". The objective of the business model is for the insurance co. to achieve a sustained operation whereby the three inflows are, in the aggregate, consistently higher than the three outflows. This is precisely why actuarial models for the calculation of premiums vs. expected losses are crucial, as premiums are the "main fuel" of the Insurance "engine cycle" as it were. If premiums underestimate expected losses, then the "Claims" amounts will be higher, and the invested funds lower, than needed for a sustainable operation. On the other hand, if premiums severely overestimate losses then another insurance co. with better model parametrization will be able to offer more competitive insurance policies to the same policyholder target group, thus drawing premium flows to itself.

Actuarial models aside, an important requirement for the validity of an insurance contract is the existence of an "Insurable Interest" on the part of the intended policyholder. This is a legal term crystallized through legal precedent and transplanted back as requisite industry practice. In English law[1] for example, it is usually interpreted to mean that there must exist a direct and immediate relationship between the intended policyholder and the person/object/activity for which insurance coverage against the onset of a peril is sought. If this relationship is only indirect or non-immediate, then the existence of Insurable Interest may be denied by the insurance co. and no policy can be underwritten. For example, one may have one's own car insured against accidents, but not another car of the same make but belonging to a third person. Similarly, one may take out a Life Insurance policy on one own's life or that of their spouse; however, one may not take out a Life Insurance policy on an unrelated person's life. What is missing in the counterexamples is the element of a direct and immediate relationship between one's own circumstances and the loss from a peril to an insured person/object/activity. There are well founded reasons (moral hazard, etc.) for this requirement, which can be found in any book on insurance law [4].

In a financial services setting, the repercussions of the existence or not of a formal insurable interest lead to a clear categorization of any subsequent risk coverage contract entered into under the circumstances. As depicted schematically in Fig. 7.2,

[1] Cf. a consise and excellent introduction to the subject at [3].

a premiums-for-risk-coverage contract would qualify as insurance contract in the presence of insurable interest, otherwise it would be a financial instrument.[2] Financial risk-hedging products, including options and warrants, would be typical examples in this context.

It is customary to typify insurance companies in reference to the perils which they offer coverage for. One criterion, for instance, is the number of perils; hence, there is a corresponding distinction being made between "Monoline" and "Multiline" insurers: the former accept to insure only events attributable to a single peril. There can be various reasons for this focus, ranging from historical actuarial experience to geographical concentration to objective operational limitations (e.g. in terms of the number and skillset of Underwriters working for the company). Another, quite important, criterion is the type of perils insured. For example, entire companies (and operating business-lines within the same company) can be focused only on "Life & Health" [6, 7] or on "Property & Casualty" [8, 9] insurance. It is also legitimate to distinguish between "Life" and "Non-Life" Insurance, which is quite justified in light of the differences in the fundamental assumptions underlying the respective actuarial models [10, 11], and their repercussions for the management of balance sheet risk by insurers. With a view to opening the discussion to the Nexus Mutual token ecosystem later on, we will confine our current focus to the "Non-Life" Insurance business—hence the title of the current section.

Due to the pervasiveness and fundamental importance of the insurance industry to modern societies, and in view of the depth and breadth of know-how needed to robustly operate insurance as a business, it should come as no surprise that it is strongly regulated. Apart from national-level insurance laws and regulations, the interconnectedness of modern societies through international trade and cross-border private activities ultimately created the need for international insurance standards. The latter are nothing else but recognized industry best practices (spanning origination, contract formation, accounting, risk/capital management, regulatory and statutory reporting), codified through international industry bodies and then accepted as guidance by all insurance industry participants. The existence of said standards allows cross-border coverage of perils, accurate execution and accounting of cross-border insurance money flows, comparison and monitoring of financial performance of internationally active insurers, and, importantly, robust functioning of the (de facto international) reinsurance markets.

One such standard is the European Union's "Solvency II" [12] capital adequacy operating framework, the source texts of which are the Solvency II Directive (2009) [13] and Regulation (2015) [14]. Among other things, Solvency II regulates aspects of insurance (and reinsurance) accounting. For example, it imputes a particular methodology (and guides the implementation of specific operational steps) for the presentation of insurance and reinsurance balance sheets. The most important

[2]For a demonstration of such a misunderstanding, even among professionals, in the context of the 2008 Global Financial Crisis, please read the 2010 Financial Times article: "Repeat after me: CDS are not insurance" [5].

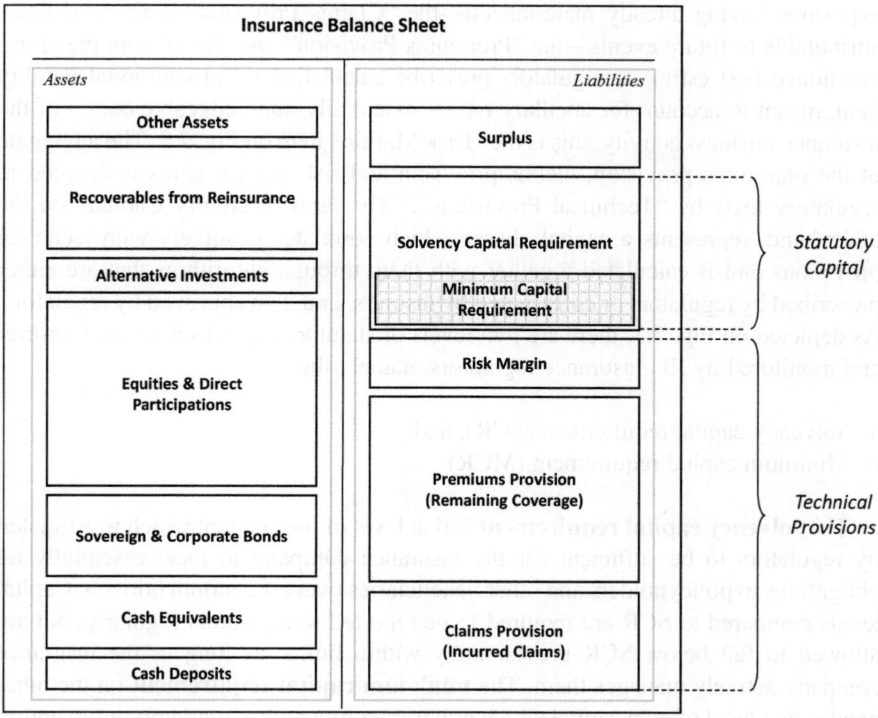

Fig. 7.3 Balance sheet of insurance company as per Solvency II

provisions concern the preparation of liability-side items [15], which must conform to a schema such as that schematically depicted on Fig. 7.3.

All liability-side terminology is formally defined in the EU legal source texts, while concise glossaries are also provided by some industry participants.[3] For the purposes of the current case study the most important terms are those corresponding to "Statutory Capital" on the figure, hence we will explain them in some detail. Insurance companies are obliged to make estimations of their future monetary outflows to their policyholders, using both descriptive statistics of past actuarial experience and reasonable assumptions for its evolution contingent on the occurrence of insurable events—both modalities drive claims models with different maturity profiles. In parallel, they are obliged to also make reasonable estimations of their monetary inflows encompassing premiums and reinsurance recoverables—again, with different maturity profiles. Both outflow and inflow profiles are then discounted to the present using interest rate curves prescribed by regulators, and the net sum represents the "best estimate" of their net liabilities on account of their core (insurance) business. At any given time (i.e. with any new presentation of a Solvency II balance sheet), regulators expect insurers to also distinguish between risk

[3]E.g. [16].

exposures having already materialized—the "Claims Provision" item—and those attributable to future events—the "Premiums Provision" one. Apart from the aforementioned best estimate, regulators prescribe calculation of an additional liability item, meant to account for ancillary risks—essentially non-hedgeable ones—of the insurance business activity; this is the "Risk Margin" item on Fig. 7.3. The aggregate of the premiums provision, claims provision and risk margin items is denoted in regulatory texts by "Technical Provisions".[4] The term "Statutory Capital" on the other hand, represents a capital charge which correlates positively with technical provisions and is calculated together with them through algorithms that are either prescribed by regulators or constructed by insurers, and then approved by regulators. As depicted on Fig. 7.3, there are two levels of statutory capital set for each insurer and monitored by EU insurance regulators, namely the:

a. Solvency capital requirement (SCR), and
b. Minimum capital requirement (MCR).

The **solvency capital requirement** is that level of own capital which is estimated by regulators to be sufficient for the insurance company to meet essentially all obligations to policyholders and other beneficiaries over a 12-month horizon. Capital levels compared to SCR are required to be reported to regulators regularly, but are allowed to fall below SCR provisionally within limits, as long as the insurance company actively manages them. The **minimum capital requirement** on the other hand is that level of own capital which will trigger immediate regulatory intervention if crossed downwards, i.e. it is meant to be a strict prudential measure. The precise methodology of SCR, resp. MCR, calculation for non-life insurers is prescribed in the Solvency II Regulation, Articles 83–90 and 114–135, resp. articles 248–250. The interested reader will be able to ascertain that the regulatory formulas for both SCR and MCR involve directly and indirectly technical provision calculations, while some formulas are recursive, e.g. those linking the Risk Margin and the SCR. In short, the preparation of an insurer's balance sheet following Solvency II entails quite sophisticated calculations, whereby actuarial and financial models (and their calibrating assumptions) interlink with each other. The robustness and sophistication built into this regulatory framework is simply an indication of the importance of the insurance business for the societal fabric of the EU. Note that Solvency II has been retained by the UK jurisdiction as basis regulatory framework even after its secession from the block.

[4]For a more detailed explanation of the basic methodology for the calculation of Technical Provisions, please consult the Solvency II Directive, Articles 77–86, and the Solvency II Regulation, Articles 22–36. The corresponding methodology for the Risk Margin is explained in the Solvency II Regulation, Article 38, S.1; however, the calculation itself necessitates a value for the SCR, cf. ibid., Articles 37 and 38, S.2.

7.2 Non-Life Reinsurance

As already depicted in Fig. 7.1, the insurance business model also relies on the existence of reinsurers, i.e. of companies prepared to underwrite part of an insurer's risk book in return for Cessions or Premiums. Insurers are said to "cede" part of their "book" (i.e. of both their cash inflows and of their policyholders' eventual claims) to the reinsurance companies. The latter (acting in effect as "Insurers of the Insurers" as per an old industry adage) usually rely on a portfolio approach to risk-taking, whereby the act of accepting lots of logically uncorrelated risks is expected to produce netting effects, such that the composite portfolio has much more predictable statistics than its component risks. Reinsurers' is a numbers game where a basic play tactic is to avoid "tail risks", i.e. to avoid risk exposures with profiles that can negate the netting effects of the portfolio. This is one reason why reinsurers may opt to accept only risk "tranches", as will be depicted below. For the time being, please accept that a fundamental difference between insurance vs. reinsurance business models is that the clients of insurers are private or corporate policyholders in any line of business, whereas those of reinsurers are only corporate insurers.

There are several ways to create a typology of the reinsurance business. One important, high-level, distinction is between "Facultative", "Treaty" and "Semi-Obligatory" Reinsurance, cf. Fig. 7.4.

"**Facultative**" refers to ceded constellations of risks that are in some sense "unique", for example construction and/or operational risks of a specific nuclear power plant, or of a specific vessel, etc. "**Treaty**", on the other hand, implies the existence of a portfolio of many similar insurance policies (i.e. covering the exact same perils, or the same combinations of perils; within the same geography or in affine—in some quantifiable sense—geographies, etc.). Said portfolio is chosen from the entire population of policies by applying some well-described selection criteria, agreed by both parties and documented as part of the reinsurance contract—i.e. of the "Treaty". For example, ceding part of all auto insurance policies underwritten by a global insurer in Germany would qualify as treaty reinsurance. Sometimes "Treaty" is also referred to as "Obligatory", the last term stemming from the fact that, once selection criterial are applied, then the ring-fenced portfolio of insurance policies is ceded as a whole and does not allow cherry-picking from either side: the ceding insurer is *obligated* to offer the entire portfolio as specified by the agreed criteria, and the reinsurer is *obligated* to accept all its risks. This also indirectly explains the previous term "Facultative" (i.e. non-obligatory) for "unique" risks; the reinsurer is *not obligated* to accept them but is free to decide on a per-case basis *if* to accept them.

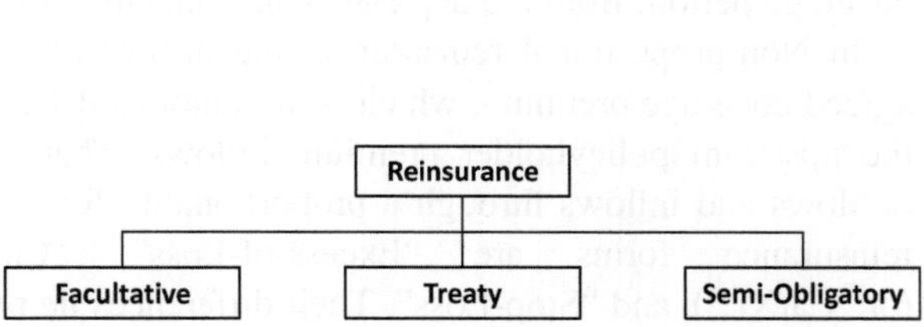

Fig. 7.4 Highest-level reinsurance typology

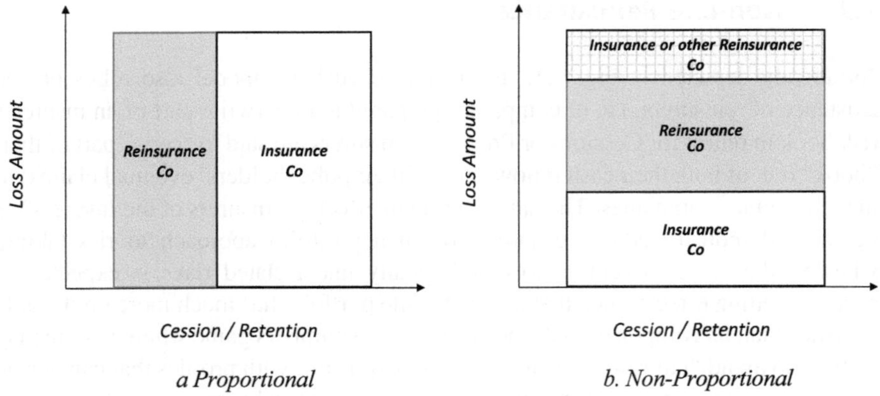

Fig. 7.5 Classes of reinsurance, high-level; risk book allocation and limits (cession/retention against loss amount)

"**Semi-Obligatory**" is a hybrid cession form, whereby one of the parties has *discretion* to act, whereas the other is *obligated* to act. For example, "Facultative-Obligatory" would mean that the insurer has the option to cede risks, but the reinsurer is then obligated to accept them. Inversely, "Obligatory-Facultative" gives the obligation to the insurer, but a right of refusal to the reinsurer. Note that in this usage the word "Facultative" no longer has necessarily the connotation of "unique" risks being ceded, but can also refer to policy portfolios.

Yet another distinction is usually made in relation to any limits in potential loss exposures accepted by the reinsurer(s), and to conditions linking cessions with corresponding premium volumes from policyholders—both parameters are referred to as "cover options". With respect to cover options, two high-level classes are "**Proportional**" and "**Non-Proportional**" reinsurance, typical forms of which are as per Fig. 7.5.

The term "Proportional" signifies that both the inflows (premiums) and the outflows (losses and expenses) are shared between insurer and reinsurer according to a *proportion* (i.e., ratio), applying within specified exposure limits. The two usual sub-forms of proportional reinsurance are "**Quota Share**"—whereby this ratio is agreed to apply from loss amount 0 (zero) upwards—and "**Surplus**"—whereby it is calculated only after some loss amount has been exceeded; in the latter case the insurer assumes 100% of losses (and thus retains all corresponding premiums) up to a retention limit, and the reinsurer assumes losses above that and up to an own reinsurance limit, with the premiums split proportion calculated at the end of the coverage period. Both are depicted schematically on Fig. 7.6.

In Non-proportional reinsurance, the insurer ("cedant") pays the reinsurer an agreed coverage premium, which is *not* automatically calculated as a proportion of the upstream policyholder premium inflows. That is, there is no split of both outflows and inflows through a proportionality formula. Typical non-proportional reinsurance forms are "Excess-of-Loss", "Catastrophe Excess-of-Loss" (or "CatXL"), and "Stop-Loss". Their differences lie primarily in the risks included in the coverage and in the way loss thresholds are calculated.

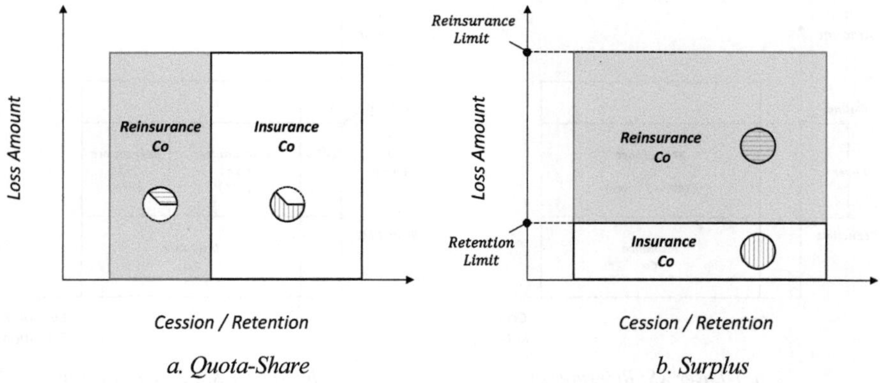

Fig. 7.6 Quota-share vs. surplus reinsurance; vertical-striped are retained, horizontal-striped recovered loss parts

Before explaining them, it is expedient to consider two relevant industry terms, namely "per Risk" and "per Event" covers. "Risk" in this context can denote any individually identifiable source of losses, in the sense of either peril or individual policy. For example, assuming treaty reinsurance, specifying a cover amount "per Risk" may mean an upper loss limit per each of, e.g., flood, fire, theft, cybercrime, etc. So, if a Treaty regulates cession of a portfolio of primary insurance policies covering lots of perils, then "per Risk" reinsurance will first recognize each Peril in the portfolio and then consider losses per peril. In effect, "per Risk" will mean "per each recognized/identified risk dimension". As already mentioned, even some policies with individual characteristics (e.g. higher hazards) may constitute a separate risk dimension for reinsurance purposes. An "Event", on the other hand, denotes the simultaneous manifestation of several separate perils at once. Imagine that an office building collapses, with the result that plumbing lines flood, exposed electrical circuits cause fires, and looters steal physical equipment. Hence, damages (and subsequent claims to the insurer) will be attributable to each of flood, fire, and theft. The collapse of the building and its repercussions for the insurer across perils constitute precisely an "Event". Thus, "per Event" reinsurance will not need to allocate cover amounts to each peril, but will consider the aggregate loss amounts summed over all covered perils.

With that in mind, "**Excess-of-Loss**" Reinsurance accepts to cover "per Risk" loss amounts which are in-between a lower ("Deductible") and an upper limit ("Ceiling"). The depiction of Fig. 7.7a. demonstrates this simple terminology. Losses below the deductible are retained by the insurer, whereas higher ones up to the ceiling are recovered by the reinsurer. The difference between ceiling and deductible is the Excess-of-Loss "Cover". In the example of Fig. 7.7a. the reinsurer participates to 100% of the losses, and of course charges a commensurate Premium to the cedant. The reinsurance terminology for this coverage is "*Cover xs Deductible*", spoken out as "Cover amount in excess of Deductible amount". Thus, a reinsurance contract reading "10 mil EUR xs 5 mil EUR" would refer to an

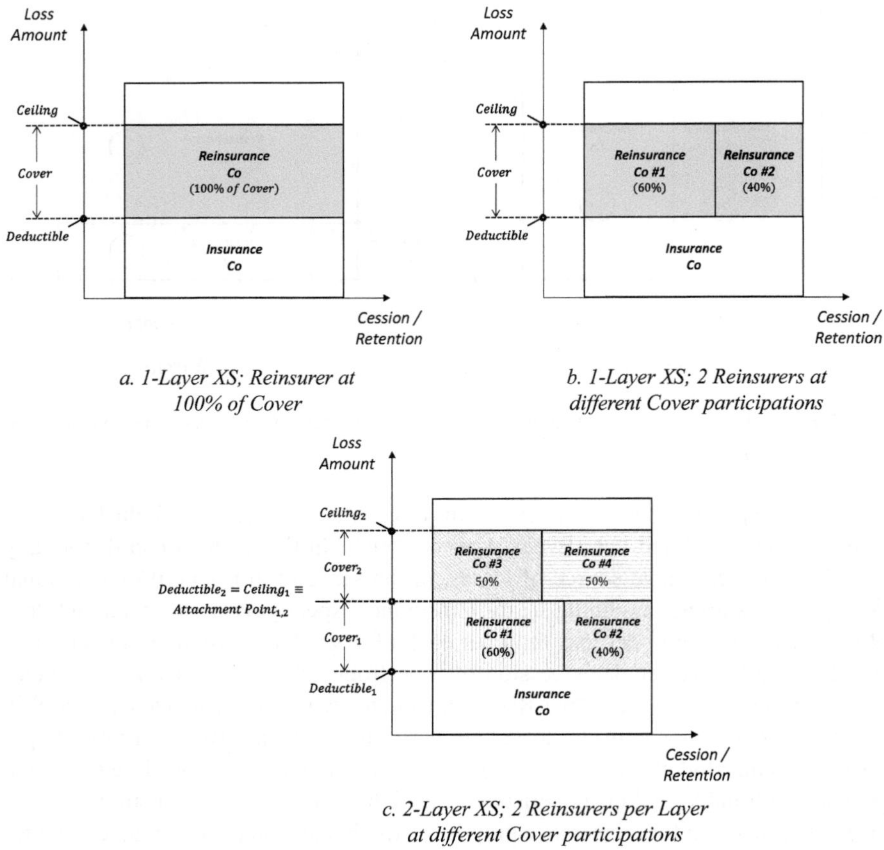

Fig. 7.7 Excess-of-loss reinsurance (Cover xs Deductible), different constellations of layers and participating reinsurers

excess-of-loss coverage with a 5 mil EUR deductible and a 10 mil EUR cover, i.e. up to a loss amount ceiling of 15 mil EUR.

Please note that very rarely would a single reinsurer accept to assume 100% of loss amount participation. The usual practice in this business is for several reinsurance companies to assume complementary parts of the same loss amount tranche (called "Layer" in industry parlance) ceded by a single insurer. The simplest example would be as per Fig. 7.7b., whereby reinsurers #1 and #2 participate in the cover by 60% and 40% respectively. Under the leadership of a leading reinsurer, or of a reinsurance broker, more layers with sequential covers can be arranged for a cedent, as depicted on Fig. 7.7c. This shows a retained layer, followed by two excess-of-loss layers, covered by four different reinsurers through different deductibles and cover participation percentages. Note that the loss amount where two consecutive layers meet (ceiling of the lower and deducible of the upper) is also called "Attachment Point" in industry jargon.

"**Catastrophe Excess-of-Loss**" (or "**CatXL**") reinsurance follows the same logic, but this time loss amounts are calculated not "per Risk", but "per Event". As the name suggests, it is meant to help the cedant recover claims from catastrophic

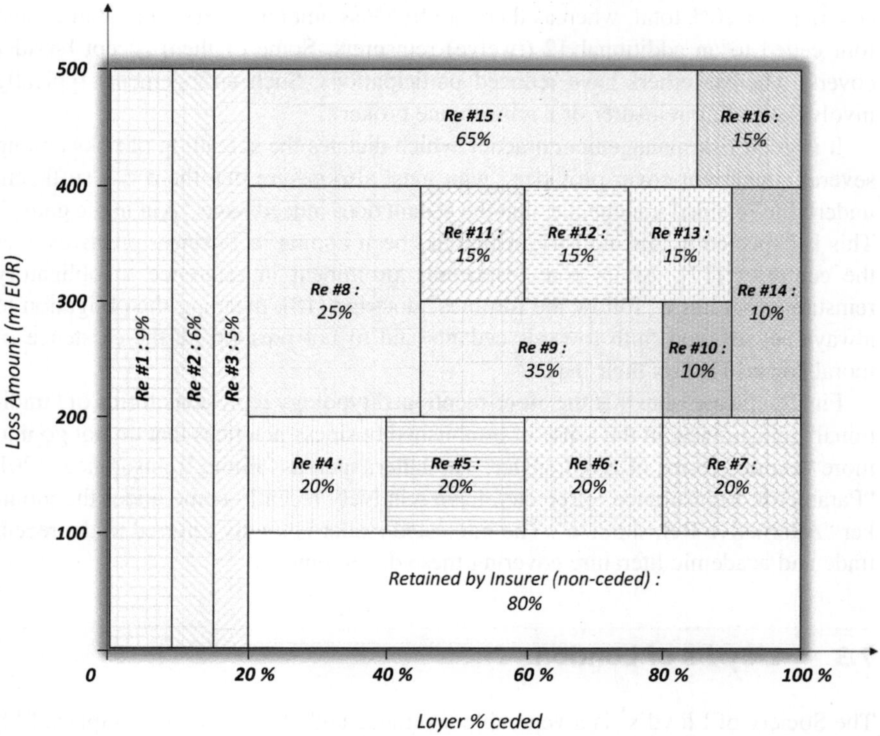

Fig. 7.8 Indicative reinsurance structure; quota share and excess-of-loss layers ceded to 16 different reinsurers

(i.e. inordinately large) loss events, whereby lots of risks manifest themselves at the same time. Its deductibles are thus much higher than those of standard "Excess-of-Loss", as it serves a different economic need.

"**Stop-Loss**" reinsurance defines again "at Risk" deductibles and ceilings, however in reference not to loss amounts but to percentages of claims over premiums. Hence, the y-axis of, e.g. Fig. 12.26a, would read not "Loss Amount", but "Loss Percentage". The nomenclature now would be "*Cover% xs Deductible%*"; for example "150% xs 100%", meaning a cover equal to 150% of the current underwriting period's policyholders' premiums volume. Even though this would seem to serve the same economic purpose as standard "Excess-of-Loss", it is actually more flexible in two respects: first, it explicitly links covers (and premiums) to the actual inflows of the cedant, and, second, it can help recover against an unusually high frequency of claims before actuarial models can be recalibrated.

As already mentioned, the reinsurance business is a team-based paradigm, a case of "Cooperative Competition" *par excellence*. No single company will assume entire ceded portfolios, and even single Layers will be shared by at least two reinsurers. For large Cessions, it is not unusual for the reinsurance map of a cedant to look like the one depicted schematically on Fig. 7.8. Three reinsurers underwrite "Quota-Share" coverage for 20% total; whereas there are five loss amount layers, one retained and four ceded to an additional 12 (twelve) reinsurers. Some of them accept broader covers, whereas others have reduced participations. Such arrangements typically involve a leading reinsurer or a reinsurance broker.

It is good risk management practice which dictates the spreading of risks among several concurrent cover providers, who must also ensure that there is a sufficient underlying retained tranche, i.e. that the cedant does indeed have "skin in the game". This is expected in this industry, which has been honing its business practices over the centuries [17]. At its core (especially prominent in reference to obligatory reinsurance) it has a "follow the fortunes" doctrine [18], meaning the obligation to always act in good faith towards cedants and to not presuppose the existence of moral hazard [19] on their part.

Finally, please note that the afore-mentioned typology represents forms of "traditional" reinsurance, in the sense of established business practices that do not go into more "exotic" forms of risk transfer. The latter, such as "Finite Reinsurance" [20], "Parametric Reinsurance" [21], etc., have relatively recently come under the moniker "Alternative Reinsurance". The interested reader is kindly referred to the recent trade and academic literature covering these developments.

7.3 Lloyd's of London

The Society of Lloyd's[5] is a venerable insurance and reinsurance marketplace [22] located in London, UK. It is neither an insurance nor a reinsurance company, but a collection of independent market participants overseen by a governance body called "The Corporation of Lloyd's" [23]. Insurance cover for particular risks [24] is provided to direct clients ("Policyholders") by underwriters, supported by brokers and authorized agents ("Coverholders"). Underwriters (risk-takers and liquidity providers) are either individuals—"Names"—or corporates, acting individually or organized in syndicates. Both names and corporate underwriters are considered to be "Lloyd's Members". Names have historically assumed unlimited liability, with sometimes rather predictable results [25]. Since the early 2000s the balance of underwriting capital has continuously shifted in favour of corporate members assuming strictly limited liability. The marketplace operates within a robust legal [26] and regulatory [27] framework, with oversight exercised by both the prudential [28] and conduct [29] financial regulators of the UK.

The Lloyd's marketplace is in effect an *ecosystem* of insurance providers, insurance clients, brokers, underwriting specialists, and other service providers. It has general rules of engagement [30], but, other than that, business processes rely on a mix of well-honed operational practices [31–34] and expert judgement. Human expertise is very important in this marketplace, both for matching insurance demand

[5] https://www.lloyds.com/, not to be confused with the Lloyds Banking Group (https://www.lloydsbankinggroup.com/) nor with Lloyds Register (https://www.lr.org/en).

with supply and for pricing risk fairly and in a way conducive to long-term business sustainability. The current constellation of economic agents in this ecosystem is:

a. Policyholders.
b. Brokers.
c. Coverholders.
d. Members (Name, corporate).
e. Underwriting syndicates.
f. Member's agents (managing or servicing).
g. InsurTech start-ups.

As already mentioned, a syndicate is formed by members grouping together to either pool risk capital or underwrite specific (specialized) risks. It is managed by a (corporate) managing agent, who has in effect director's duties. Syndicate members must explicitly opt-into the syndicate every single year. The fact that a syndicate is expected to act as a bespoke insurance company has implications for both its risk capital management and for its alignment to the annual renewals cycle.

Syndicate-level risk capital management is important for the sustainability of the entire Lloyd's marketplace, as the latter's capital structure operates on the basis of a three-tier "chain of security" [35]. According to this concept, insurance claims are paid to policyholders by drawing sequentially on:

1. The covering syndicate's funds, expected to exist in its own "Premiums Trust Fund" ("PTF").
2. Member's capital deposited at Lloyd's—"Funds at Lloyd's" ("FAL"). Finally, on
3. The Lloyd's central assets, including its "Central Fund" liquidity positions.

These are the three links of the "chain of security". Importantly, it is tacitly expected that each syndicate separately and the Corporation of Lloyd's will have arranged for reinsurance coverage of their respective exposures (1. and 3.), acting in their own discretion.

The last economic agent type above ("InsurTech start-ups") is one of the ways Lloyd's has been pursuing to better align with the speed and standardization requirements of the digital economy. Two other ways, and rather the more relevant ones for the purposes of the current discussion, have been:

- Lloyd's 40% participation [36] in the not-for-profit company "Placing Platform Limited" [37] ("PPL"), which was set up in 2016 to "*allow brokers and insurers to quote, negotiate and bind business electronically*" [38].
- The "syndicate-in-a-box" [39] concept, which is meant to streamline access to the Lloyd's marketplace for new economic agents, namely underwriting innovators willing to help expand the ecosystem's perimeter [40].

Please note that participation in the Lloyd's marketplace (i.e. for all economic agents other than type "Policyholder") entails paying access and service fees according to a schedule defined by its governance [41].

In summary, Lloyd's of London is a self-governed insurance and reinsurance marketplace, and one of the lynchpins of traditional, global finance. Corporations and individuals wishing to purchase insurance for particular risks can access its services through either human or electronic channels. Its decisions on risk coverage structure and participation have been for centuries, and still are, de facto decentralized. Its governance structures prescribe and monitor legal and regulatory compliance through strict rules and procedures, striving to ensure a sustainable business with a clear fee structure. Lloyd's is also represented in the UK commercial and specialty risk insurance industry body ("London Market Group" [42]).

7.4 Mutual Insurance Companies (UK)

The "Mutual-Ownership" business model in the UK describes an incorporated association which is "*characterized by the extent to which business members have democratic control of the business and share in its profits*" [43]. It does not impose a particular legal entity structure [44] (partnerships and limited liability partnerships, as well as limited liability companies, are all free to adopt a "mutual" business model), nor does it exclude non-profit objectives; the latter can be accommodated by simply specifying that all nominal profits will be re-distributed to members or other beneficiaries, including social ones.

In short, it generally characterizes associations that are member-owned and either not-for-profit, or for-profit with the understanding that all profits will be either re-invested within the business or re-distributed to the members in some form.

General insurance "mutuals", i.e., mutual-ownership businesses with the purpose to provide insurance coverage to their members, have been long established in the UK. The "Mutual Insurance" model is thus subject to clear laws [45] and regulations [46, 47], including arrangements relating to rights and responsibilities of regulatory oversight [48–50]. Case law [51, 52] has also contributed to clarify aspects of "mutuality", especially regarding entitlements and liabilities of members contributing to a mutual's governance. There exists a public register of UK mutual societies [53], as well as industry bodies [54] representing their interests.

In short, the notion of an incorporated association (of declared members) which:

- Exists for the sole purpose of providing insurance coverage to its members by pooling resources among them
- Accords exclusive rights of specifying governance arrangements and profit redistribution policy to its members

is a long-established concept in traditional finance with business practices founded on robust legal and regulatory frameworks in the UK (and in other jurisdictions [55–57] for that matter).

7.5 Nexus Mutual

The introducing sections of the current chapter must have seemed somewhat out of place in a book about cryptocurrencies and crypto-tokens, but they will hopefully prove useful to explain the market design of Nexus Mutual. The points of departure are the following: First of all, insurance is a well understood traditional finance field, so it should not be a surprise that blockchain-based protocols have sought to replicate its business model. Second, the "mutual insurance" business model is also well understood and accepted in the business and legal worlds. Third, insurance marketplaces where different economic agents come together to form ad-hoc value chains—i.e. insurance ecosystems—are nothing new; Lloyd's with its brokers and cover holders is the proof, as the venerable society has been making its living this way for centuries now. Fourth, legal and regulatory frameworks are able to keep up with such ecosystems very well indeed, as the UK jurisdiction has proved and as myriads of specialized insurance buyers around the world accept in the case of Lloyd's.

Thus, think of Nexus Mutual as a Lloyd's equivalent in the blockchain world. Like its traditional finance cousin, it is a mutualized insurance and reinsurance marketplace for risks that are visible on the blockchain. Its basic concept is the same as that behind Lloyd's; insurance cover seekers, insurance providers, underwriting experts, risk capital providers, etc., come together to form an ecosystem—i.e. Nexus Mutual—with clear rules of engagement. Information exchange is unhindered, as long as the end-result of transaction negotiation is registered on the Ethereum blockchain.

The second part of the protocol's name signifies its ownership structure. The protocol's founders chose originally to incorporate in the UK as a "mutual insurance company" [58], under the terms and conditions explained in 7.4 above. The "mutual" ownership model means that all onboarded ecosystem participants are considered "members" of the mutual, and this will also be reflected in the protocol's market design. Accordingly, Nexus Mutual onboarding entails a customer identification/vetting step (encompassing both "Know-Your-Customer" [59]—"KYC" and "Anti-Money-Laundering" [60]—"AML" aspects) and payment of a small membership fee in ETH [62]. Thus there results indeed a list of identifiable "members" whereby blockchain addresses are mapped to off-chain natural persons.

We propose to the reader to examine the high-level attributes of this ecosystem as if one were examining a traditional insurance marketplace. For example, in the latter case pertinent high-level questions would be: "what are the perils covered", "what forms or insurance or reinsurance are offered", "what are the terms of coverage", etc. More granular questions would be, e.g., "how is an Insurable Interest established", "what are the contractual aspects of coverage provision", "in which currency(-ies) are cover amounts and insurance premiums denominated", etc. In due course one can begin addressing more fine-granular procedural and operational questions still, e.g. those pertaining to the constellations of economic agents and the transactional steps usually expected. We will cover all of the above in the sequel.

In its current generation, Nexus Mutual helps members cover risks through the following form/peril constellations [61]:

1. Insurance against distinct operational risks of specific protocols ("Protocol Cover", "Bundled Protocol Cover", "DeFi Pass Cover", "Native Protocol Cover", "Fund Protocol Cover"; as of the time of writing).
2. Insurance against financial risks of Ethereum "Proof-of-Stake" validation ("ETH Slashing Cover").
3. Quota share reinsurance against losses accruing to crypto primary insurers ("Quota Share Cover").
4. Real Work Risk insurance and reinsurance.

Protocol Cover is offered to members who possess crypto assets committed to "Ethereum-Virtual-Machine" [63] -compatible ("EVM-compatible") blockchain protocols, i.e. those with technical artefacts compatible with the standard Ethereum runtime. There are several possible causes of operational failures in such protocols, ranging from programming defects in their code—especially smart contracts[6] [64]—to non-performance of third-parties—such as Oracles[7]—to inadequacy of their Mechanisms (cf. later Chap. 8 on mechanism design). Nexus Mutual helps arrange covers against financial losses caused by such failures, e.g. when impacted assets have been committed to a single (simply "Protocol Cover" [65]) or to several ("Bundled Protocol Cover" [66]) named protocols. Policytakers include private persons (regarding the two afore-mentioned and the "DeFi Pass Cover" [67] products); token project teams ("Native Protocol Cover" [68]); and institutional investors—e.g. Asset Managers—and Family Offices ("Fund Portfolio Cover" [69]).

The consensus mechanism of the Ethereum blockchain currently follows a "Proof-of-Stake"[8] (PoS) paradigm. The important technical actors operationalizing this paradigm are "PoS Validators" and their respective "Node Operators". Their constellation is explained in the later Sects. 9.4 and 9.6.1. The important facts relevant to the current chapter are that they can be penalized in financial terms for non-performance and that such penalization events are termed "Slashing Events" in industry jargon. Hence, **ETH Slashing Cover** is offered to members who are principals of the afore-mentioned actors and consists in partial compensation for financial losses suffered due to own Slashing Events [70].

Quota share reinsurance, on the other hand, is offered only to principals or bodies representing other crypto-insurance/-assurance protocols[9] [71]. Two existing

[6] Please consult Sect. 10.5.5 for an explanation of Ethereum ERC20 Smart Contracts.

[7] Trusted providers of off-blockchain or of combined on–/off-blockchain data. They are explained in Sect. 6.4.

[8] Cf. the discussion near the end of Sect. 1.1.

[9] To identify the most prominent ones, one can use a regularly updated insurance coin list such as [71] and then search for the protocols behind the coins.

cedants are LUNOS [72] (which insures operational risks of crypto-protocols [73]; ex-UnoRe [74]) and Sherlock [75] (which facilitates continuous monitoring and assurance assessments [76] of the same; the protocol also offers facultative smart contract insurance coverage [77], hence the reinsurance need). It is fair to ask "why does Nexus Mutual only offer Quota Share" and not other reinsurance forms as well. One answer would be obvious by revisiting the previous Fig. 7.8: there simply are not many other Crypto-insurance protocols in existence (yet), and definitely not with the same underwriting capacity as Nexus Mutual. That said, nothing would in principle preclude Nexus Mutual from participating with other Insurance protocols in layered reinsurance constructs in the future, assuming that all said protocols could also source the requisite know-how.

Nexus Mutual has been working on implementing additional form/peril constellations, and in particular **Real World Risks** [78–80], i.e. risks that would ordinarily fall in the purview of traditional insurers/reinsurers. Corresponding business and technical artefacts created on the protocol to serve this market are actively in development as of the time of writing this book [81].

Regarding insurance **cover terms**, all of the afore-mentioned insurance/reinsurance products are based on formal and publicly accessible "terms & conditions" sheets, linked into from the protocol's documentation pages. They are to be found, e.g., in the individual product pages for Protocol [82], Bundled Protocol [83], ETH Slashing [84], Quota Share (bespoke for Sherlock [85] and LUNOS (ex-UnoRe [86]) covers.

Apart from the stipulations in "terms & conditions" sheets, there is an additional process meant to ensure that an **insurable interest** is present. However, in deviation to the traditional finance insurance paradigm, this control step is carried out not at cover inception, but only once a claim has been submitted. In detail, the first step of cover payout approval is a "proof of loss" check, e.g. for protocol cover [87], mandating claim assessors to verify that:

- The blockchain address owning the affected crypto assets is indeed a Nexus Mutual member address.
- The member's cover was active when the claimed loss event occurred.
- The assets in question were indeed committed to the covered protocol when the loss event occurred.
- There was indeed a loss of assets, either in number or in value, as a result of said event.
- Said loss amount can be estimated and is indeed above the cover's deductible.

Only then can the claims process, e.g. for Protocol Cover [88] cases, continue. In effect, Nexus Mutual allows any member to buy cover, but only checks for actual insurable interest after the fact. This is a business process decision, which nevertheless has the same effect for the protocol as if the check were carried out in advance. In any case, the process may well change in future iterations of Nexus Mutual.

The "terms & conditions" sheets are only part of the salient **contractual aspects of cover provision**, another being the nature and legal capacity of the counterparties.

To explain that (and also as a precursor to the latter section on market design) it is expedient to go in some detail into the legal personality of Nexus Mutual's entities behind the protocol.

Cover provision is contingent on membership to Nexus Mutual, and this first (onboarding) step already involves the protocol as counterparty. In effect, project documentation clearly states (in the publicly accessible document "DAO Member Agreement"[10] [89]):

MEMBER AGREEMENT
of
NEXUS MUTUAL,

a Decentralized Autonomous Organization

Dated as of February 24, 2022.[11]

And later:

This Member Agreement (this "Agreement") is the official legal Agreement of Nexus Mutual, a decentralized autonomous organization (the "DAO"), made and entered into effective as of February 24, 2022 (the "Effective Date") by and among its members (each a "DAO Member").

Subsequently:

ARTICLE 2
NAME, PURPOSES AND STRUCTURE OF THE DAO
2.1 Name. The name of the DAO is Nexus Mutual.
2.2 Decentralized Autonomous Organization. The DAO is a ***"decentralized autonomous organization"— i.e., an unincorporated association of individuals, entities, associations and/or other persons or groups of persons.***
2.3 Activities and Purpose. The activities and purposes (the "Purposes") to be conducted or promoted by the DAO are:

(a). *to establish a mutual fund for the payment of claims relating to certain liabilities, losses or expenses incurred by DAO Members on a discretionary basis;*
(b). *to promote, encourage and facilitate membership of the DAO for persons who support the DAO's vision of providing a decentralized alternative to the traditional insurance industry for the purpose of its DAO Members' risk management.*
(c). *any other purpose that either directly or indirectly supports (a) or (b).*

2.4 ***Legal Personality. The DAO is not intended to, and shall not be deemed to, be a legal person or have a legal personality separate from the DAO Members.*** *Without limiting the generality of the foregoing, the DAO is not intended to be, and shall not be deemed to be, a partnership.*
2.5 Transactions and Transfers. The DAO Members shall utilize the Designated Smart Contract (a smart contract deployed to the Designated Blockchain at the Designated

[10] Passages quoted in the main text are current as of the time of writing

[11] Please note that the italic font in the above and following passages denotes text taken verbatim from the original document, however the formatting is that of this book's author.

Blockchain Address) as the exclusive method of holding, allocating among the DAO Members, and spending or otherwise distributing any Tokens that are DAO Property, of minting and issuing DAO Membership Tokens and holding and recording votes of the DAO Members. The DAO may also utilize the Designated Smart Contract to administer and facilitate certain other arrangements and transactions involving the DAO and the DAO Members.

And further on:

ARTICLE 4
BINDING EFFECT OF THE DESIGNATED SMART CONTRACT
4.1 General Binding Effect

...

(b) Smart Contract Preempts Contrary Legal Contracts. Except as set forth in Section 4.1 (a), if in connection with any DAO Matters there is any conflict or inconsistency between: (A)(1) this Agreement or (2) any other Contract between or among any DAO Members; and (B) any Contract created or implied by, or embodied in, the machine, assembly or other code, or the results of operation, of the Designated Smart Contract, then the Contract referred to in the preceding clause "(B)" shall prevail over the Contract referred to in the preceding clause "(A)".

Finally:

ARTICLE 6
DEFINITIONS

...

6.19 "Person" means any human, robot, bot, artificial intelligence, corporation, partnership, association or other individual or entity recognized as having the status of a person under the law.

(please note that bold-font highlighting is applied in this and later verbatim references by this book's author only). The governing law of the above "Member Agreement" is that of the British Virgin Islands.

Hence, this document equates Nexus Mutual membership with membership to a DAO. Setting this document aside for a moment, DAO stands for "Distributed Autonomous Organization" [90], a term the precise meaning of which is currently in a state of flux—unfortunately also in the legal domain. For some parts of the crypto-token industry [91] it *should only mean* "an organization governed purely by decisions taken by automated, non-human, agents", while others consider it to signify *at best* 'an organization run by consensus (i.e. without being directed by a central authority) among humans, who use Blockchain-based automation to reach governance decisions by voting'. We write "organization" and not "corporation" (nor "legal entity") because the legal form of a DAO is precisely one of the sources of ambiguity in the meaning of the term. Simply put, different token project teams can currently declare their Governance Body to be a DAO and still mean totally different organizational (and especially legal) setups. Some helpful jurisdictions [92, 93] have already provided for concrete legal entity forms able to achieve the same organizational goal [94, 95] while others leave the meaning as a matter of interpretation to business (and investing) agents. It is up to the individual token project, depending on their level of knowledge, access to legal advice [96–99], base of activities, etc., to design and potentially incorporate [100] a DAO form appropriate for them. It is quite possible that, as the crypto-token industry matures, the question of liability [101] associated with their decisions will become central to the eventual regulation of DAO's.

The precise nature of the rights and responsibilities exercised by the Nexus Mutual DAO will be clarified in the later Sect. 7.6.1. For the time being, it is important to mention that each of the afore-mentioned "terms & conditions" sheets mentions something beyond the DAO, namely:

> *Reimbursements*
> *8. In the event the Claim made by the Covered Member is approved and redeemed under this Protocol Cover the Covered Member agrees to:*
> *8.1. assign all rights over any recoveries or Reimbursements to Nexus Mutual DAO* ***and/or the Foundation****; and*
> *8.2. forward any recoveries or Reimbursements received by the Covered Member to Nexus Mutual DAO* ***and/or the Foundation*** *upon receipt.*
> ...
> *'****Foundation****' means Terrapin International Foundation.*

Thus, there is now a legal entity which is accorded the same level of rights as the DAO in the cover-related documents of Nexus Mutual. What is this entity and what is its connection with the ecosystem?

To answer this question it is important to give some historical context about Nexus Mutual, supported by evidence in the public domain. There are several points in the protocol's documentation where a "Foundation" is mentioned. First, the main documentation pages [102] mention:

> *The Foundation*
> *The Foundation is a community interest company (CIC) that supports the protocol and is made up of the Engineering, Business Development, and Product teams. These teams receive external funding from the Foundation.*
> *The Foundation exists to maintain the Nexus Mutual protocol and user interface; promote product development; and provide support to prospective and existing members.*

Community Interest Companies are constructs in English law, defined [103] as:

> *Details*
> *A Community Interest Company (CIC) is a limited company, with special additional features, created for the use of people who want to conduct a business or other activity for community benefit, and not purely for private advantage.*

and assigned a bespoke regulator [104]. As per NexusMutual historical Governance records [105],

> *Nexus Mutual has a "Foundation",* ***Collective Risk Services CIC (CRS),*** *which employs the core team and pays for other costs such as website, hosting, marketing, audits etc. CRS is a community interest company that operates on a non-profit basis.*

...
The Foundation.
In addition to being a non-profit with no equity, the Foundation has an asset lock that ensures assets can only be used for its core objects which are specified in detail here. The primary object is "creating and implementing community risk sharing ecosystems". The combination of clearly defined objects and an asset lock ensures there are significant legal restrictions on the use of the Foundations funds.

An entry for "Collective Risk Services CIC" does indeed exist [106] in the UK Companies' House. The company is active as of the time of writing. Importantly, there is also a "Nexus Mutual Limited" entry [58] in the same registry. It is a company which is currently dormant: In the "Filing History" section of its registry record, there appears an entry:

03 Jun 2024 Accounts for a dormant company made up to 31 August 2023

linking to a PDF [107], wherein it is mentioned:

Nexus Mutual Limited (registered number: 10917763) did not trade during the current or preceding financial year. For the financial year ending 31 August 2023 the company was entitled to exemption from audit under section 480 of the Companies Act 2006 relating to dormant companies.

Financial statements in this PDF document were signed by "H Karp", titled "Director". Hugh Karp is also a Director both of Nexus Mutual Ltd. [108] and of Collective Risk Services CIC [109]. Importantly, the same "Filing History" section for Nexus Mutual Ltd. as above contains an entry:

Resolutions
*11 Mar 2022 • Private interest foundation, **terrapin international foundation** shall be formed/ all assets of the company be transferred to the foundation, less a nominal amount withheld for winding down/ all members, except directors to resign membership in the company. All members and directors be bound by the DAO Member agreement of nexus mutual. 21/02/2022*

linking to a corresponding PDF [110] document of record. Also importantly, a US court document [111] in the public domain, titled:

In re: FTX TRADING LTD., et al.,*1 Debtors. Chap. 11.*

Case No. 22–11068 (JTD) (Jointly Administered).

TRANSFER OF CLAIM OTHER THAN FOR SECURITY", filing of a claim IN THE UNITED STATES BANKRUPTCY COURT FOR THE DISTRICT OF DELAWARE relating to the resolution of the FTX companies.

also mentions:

Name of Transferee:

Terrapin International Foundation
Name and Address where notices and payments should be sent:
Hugh Karp
Duplex No. 6 Obarrio,
Calle 61, Panama

In summary: according to the above facts, membership in Nexus Mutual DAO is taken to be tantamount to membership in the Nexus Mutual token ecosystem. Financial matters (rights and responsibilities) of members relating to the provision of insurance or reinsurance cover through the ecosystem are arranged with "Terrapin International Foundation" acting as counterparty on account of the DAO. There exists another, separate, affiliated Foundation (Collective Risk Services CIC) which was originally created to channel funding to teams undertaking technical, business development and operational tasks on behalf of the ecosystem.

The above should serve to give the general, current, context of the Nexus Mutual business case. For the sake of completeness, the project's Whitepaper (latest [112], as well as the original [113], versions) should also be consulted, together with the project's official documentation and governance pages. The following sections make explicit reference to all relevant public-domain Nexus Mutual records in archival form, in order to reconstruct both the economic agent model and the transactional pathways, including the lifecycle and flow of ecosystem tokens.

7.6 Nexus Mutual Market Design

As per Chap. 6, good Market design must prescribe all protocol **economic agent** types and **transactional pathways** among them:

1. A typology of all admissible economic agents (both "privileged" and "non-privileged") within the token ecosystem.
2. A typology of all third-party (cooperating) economic agents from other ecosystems that are needed for the use case operationally.
3. For each and every admissible economic agent:
   a. Its fundamental attributes (main functional characteristics).
   b. Its nature along the "human" to "algorithmic" axis ("performed by humans", "performed by algorithms", "mixed", "conditional").
   c. Its relevance to the ecosystem token(s).
4. For each and every transaction pathway involving ecosystem token(s), a clear blueprint (document, diagram, or any other artefact providing an unequivocal description) of:
   a. The types of economic agents taking part.
   b. The token(s) to be exchanged in the course of each transaction, and among which economic agents.

We will replicate the above for Nexus Mutual, and also demonstrate how the protocol calibrates the salient market design factors (thickness, congestion, safety, usability, social norms).

7.6.1 Economic Agent Typology

Having adopted a "mutual" ownership structure, all ecosystem participants are "members" (they have to be explicitly declared as such, and own the structure; eventual earnings are either re-invested or re-distributed to the members). However (as in the Lloyd's case), they can have different functions within the ecosystem.

As depicted on Fig. 7.9, the Nexus Mutual ecosystem admits the following non-privileged economic agent types:

a. Staking Pool Managers.
b. NXM Stakers.
c. Insurance Cover Buyers.
d. Claim Assessors.
e. Channel Integrators.

Its privileged (i.e. governance-related) economic agents are:

f. The Nexus Mutual Decentralized Autonomous Organization [114] ("DAO").
g. An Advisory Board [115].
h. All holders of the native token (NXM [116, 117]), who are thus entitled to vote for governance decisions.

A **Staking Pool Manager** is an NXM member responsible for creating and managing staking pools [118], i.e. pools of committed capital intended to underwrite specific insurance/reinsurance cover exposures. The role presupposes relevant business know-how and is rewarded with a part of the premiums stream above and beyond what usual NXM Stakers expect (in lieu of a "pool management fee" [119, 120]). It is up to the discretion of this agent type if they will keep the pool funds private or if they will open them for staking by NXM Stakers.

An **NXM Staker** is an NXM member who acts as liquidity provider to one or more staking pools [121]. They are said to "delegate" their NXM tokens to said pools, in return for a part of the premiums stream [122]. As with all staking pool participants, part of their committed NXM tokens can be burned [123] (and their funds forfeited) to cover justified claims by insurance cover buyers.

An **Insurance Cover Buyer** is an NXM member who buys any of the insurance/reinsurance products mentioned in Sect. 7.5, and in particular to cover one of three possible loss events [124] relating to EVM-compatible blockchain protocols:

1. **Protocol** related, namely loss of own funds due to operational failures in such protocols, ranging from programming defects in their code—e.g. smart

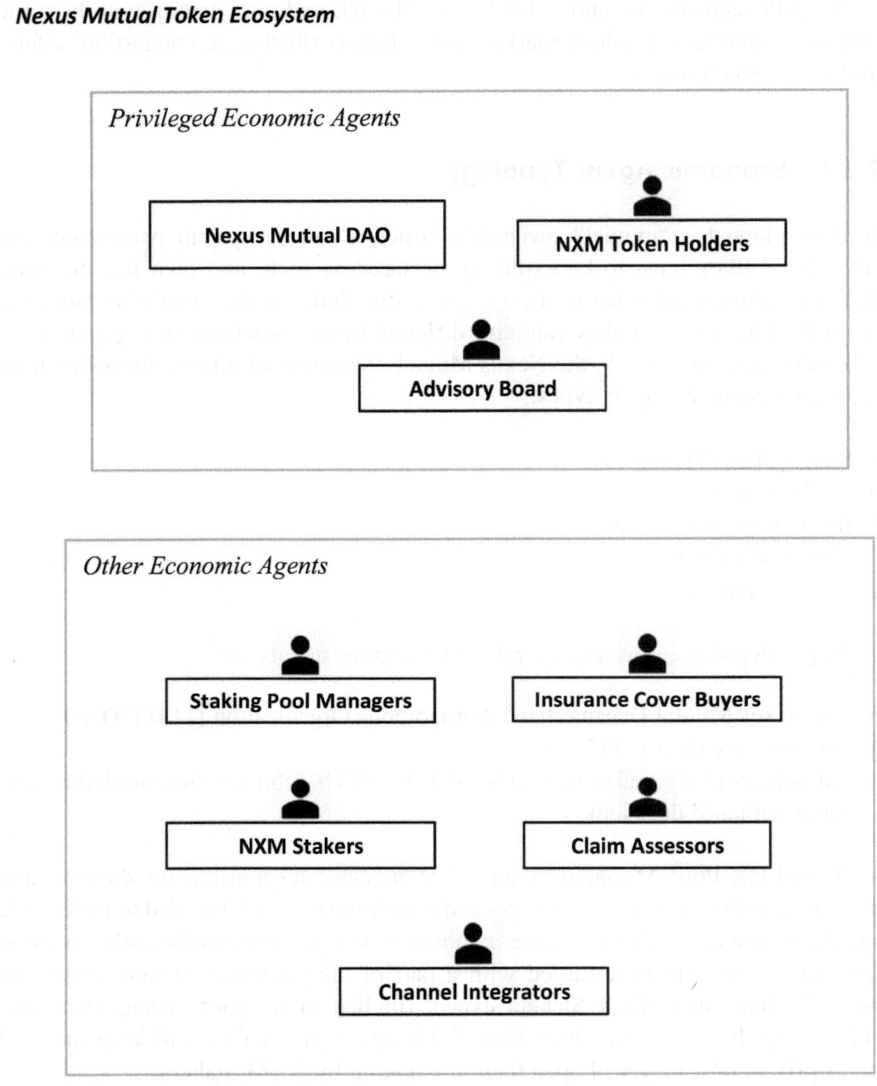

Fig. 7.9 Nexus Mutual economic agent model

contracts—; to non-performance of third parties—e.g. Oracle inadequacy or manipulation—; to failure of their Mechanisms—leading to Treasury liquidations, etc., (what are generally termed "Severe Economic Events" in protocol documentation).

2. **ETH Slashing** related, i.e. loss of staked funds due to non-performance by PoS validators (and their respective "Node Operators") of the Ethereum blockchain Proof-of-Stake consensus operational process.

3. **Insurance Loss** related, in risk portfolios underwritten by principals or bodies representing other crypto-insurance/-assurance protocols and ceded to Nexus Mutual under quota share reinsurance.

As in traditional insurance/reinsurance, Insurance Cover Buyers specify the covered peril, loss event, duration of cover, cover amounts, etc., and also accept standardized "terms & conditions" of cover, when interacting with other Nexus Mutual members through the protocol.

A **Claim Assessor** is an NXM member who is prepared to ascertain [125] that a particular claim against an insured event is correct or incorrect, in exchange for a share of the Fee Pool of the NXM platform [126] (i.e. of the aggregated surplus in traditional insurance terms). Claim assessors are responsible for their own due diligence and have to defer to a voting outcome [127] as defining the ultimate success of the claim in question.

Channel Integrators are NXM members who implement own technical mechanisms brokering between cover product suppliers and prospective Insurance Cover Buyers. They act in effect as an indirect sales channel, by integrating NXM protocol artefacts into own functionality [128], such as bespoke user interfaces in third-party portals outside the protocol. They can enable their own order management processes, or can simply redirect prospects to the Nexus Mutual dApp [129]. Channel integrators are incentivized by a commission [130] on the purchased cover price.

The **Nexus Mutual DAO** is the highest governance structure. As already mentioned, the protocol founders originally chose to incorporate in the UK, and that scheme of things implied a human-driven DAO. In April 2021, the assembly of NXM token holders initiated a proposal to transition to a purely smart-contract-driven DAO [131]. This proposal was approved on February 2022 [132], with the outcome that a fiduciary structure in Panama[12] [110] was used as an intermediate step in legal structure transition. The governance structure depicted on Fig. 7.9 is still valid, with the understanding that the DAO is progressively moving to a smart-contract-driven governance. As of the time of writing, however, only voting submissions and execution are "by smart contract only", whereas other strategic and operational protocol tasks remain essentially human-driven. Indicatively, the current governance setup delegates whole work streams to five (5) "**DAO Teams**", activities of which are funded by the DAO Treasury [133]. They are as follows:

a. Community Team [134], tasked with member/community training and interactions.
b. Marketing Team [135], tasked with business development.
c. Investment Committee [136], focused on protocol asset investment strategy and execution facilitation.

[12] cf. discussion relating to "Terrapin International Foundation" in Sect. 7.5.

d. Operations Team [137], active in providing project management and operational coordination of members/teams.
e. Research & Development Team [138], tasked with technical roadmap definition and implementation.

All **NXM token holders** have the right to vote for governance decisions, including for allocation of Nexus Mutual DAO Treasury funds. Voting is done on the Snapshot platform [139], and the voting power is linearly proportional to a member's NXM tokens [140] up to a cap,[13] after which it remains constant.

The **advisory board** consists of five (5) Nexus Mutual members elected by governance vote [115]. It is allowed to take operational decisions that are at once important and time critical; necessitating involvement of key knowledge-holders acting in close coordination; in ways that might be impossible by following the usual governance decision-making processes. These members are chosen on the basis of their concentration of technical, business and governance expertise, including a proven commitment to the viability of the protocol. Indicatively, Advisory Board members acting with a three-out-of-five quorum have powers to:

- Make protocol smart contract changes unilaterally.
- Provisionally deactivate the NXM Primary Market's Ratcheting Automated Market Maker (RAMM) smart contract, cf. Sect. 7.6.3.1.
- Set the starting price for each new cover product in staking pools, which sets the initial condition for a Dutch auction mechanism [141].
- Adjudicate on instances of suspected fraudulent voting by claim assessors [142], which may cause forfeiture of their staked funds.

Thus, the advisory board is meant to be a failsafe mechanism for the protocol. It is to act whenever strategic and important operational decisions are needed that either cannot be entrusted to rules-based technical systems; or cannot be realistically achieved within the usual time-scales of the governance voting process.

[13] Theoretically, malevolent participants could attempt to circumvent the voting cap by using different wallet addresses. However, one needs to remember that NexusMutual onboarding involves a KYC step, whereby the prospective member must submit official documentation. Hence, it is possible to glean the physical-world person (or entity) behind the wallet address voting.

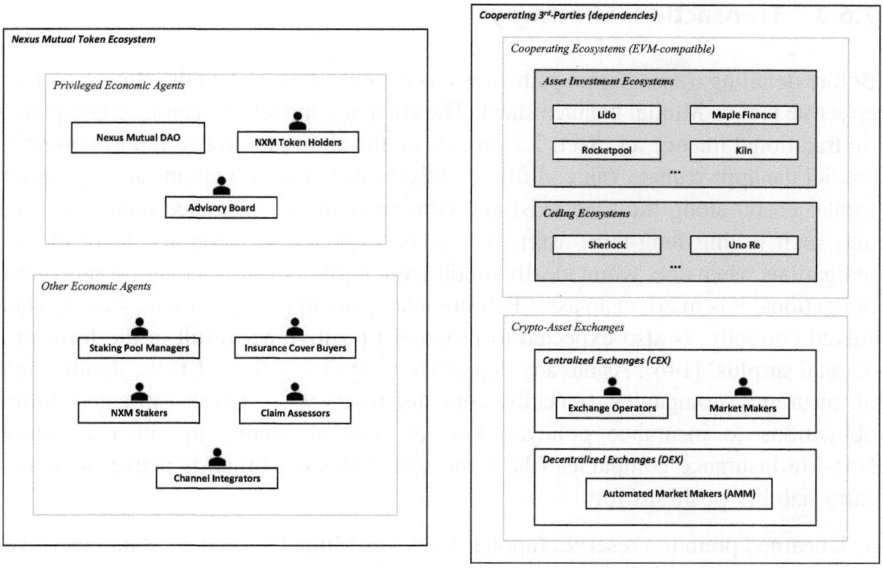

Fig. 7.10 Nexus Mutual and cooperating third parties

7.6.2 Cooperating Ecosystems

Nexus Mutual's business case entails interaction with a number of cooperating third parties (cf. Fig. 7.10), including with other blockchain-based token ecosystems. The latter can be broadly distinguished into two categories, namely:

a. Asset investment, and
b. Ceding

Ecosystems. Paralleling the traditional insurance business paradigm—cf. the example Solvency II insurance balance sheet on Fig. 7.3 of Sect. 7.1—, Nexus Mutual incentivizes investing of available (uncommitted) token funds for extra yield in third-party protocols. There are several such investments at any given time, which are declared [143] in the project's documentation pages and are also observable through a bespoke Dune dashboard [144] implemented by the afore-mentioned DAO Teams. The respective fund destination ecosystems are the ones appearing in the box titled "**Asset Investment Ecosystems**" on Fig. 7.10. Those in the box titled "**Ceding Ecosystems**", on the other hand, are nothing else than the purchasers of quota share reinsurance covers. They are "cooperating" and not simply internalized agents, as they have their own internal processes of premiums and claims allocation which ultimately need to interface with the reconciliation processes of Nexus Mutual.

Previous iterations of the protocol also availed themselves of Oracles as cooperating third parties, however this is no longer the case as of the time of writing this book.

7.6.3 Transactional Pathways

Before detailing transactional pathways it is expedient to explain the structure of the effective Nexus Mutual balance sheet. The solvency model of insurance companies (in traditional finance, cf. Sect. 7.1) hinges on the ability to do two things correctly: predict the approximate value of future obligations (insurance claims and operating/ capital costs) along the time axis; and constantly invest insurance premia inflows into such rolling long-term assets as can be expected to cover the level of said obligations when due, while ideally minimizing liquidity risk of covering short-term obligations. It is in effect an asset-liability management [145] problem, which, when solved correctly, is also expected to produce a positive net result in the form of a 'capital surplus' [146]. As already depicted on Fig. 7.3 of Sect. 7.1, the liability side of insurance companies typically contains reserves to cover estimated future obligations to insurance policyholders, as well as claims by other creditors. Non-life insurance companies (the same sector Nexus Mutual is active in) would carry liability positions for:

a. Unearned premium reserves (applies to Nexus Mutual as well, as insurance cover buyers must select duration of cover as explained in 7.6.1 above)
b. Loss and loss-adjustment reserves
c. Incurred but not reported (IBNR) reserves

Nexus Mutual has the exact same asset-liability management problem to solve [147], whereby said assets and liabilities are denominated in blockchain-based ecosystem tokens. As we are only interested in the market design of Nexus Mutual in this chapter, we will not address the conversion of cover purchases to reserves. Suffice it to say that all the above positions are present on the liability side of its effective balance sheet and that they are denominated in the native token, NXM. Also, membership in the Nexus Mutual is represented not in the form of any paid-in capital (common stock or treasury shares), but rather through holdings in terms of the same native token, NXM. As specified in protocol documentation [147], and as also evidenced through the relevant Dune dashboard [144], the asset-side of the Nexus Mutual balance sheet contains three types of positions:

i. Ethereum (ETH) tokens.
ii. DAI [148] Stablecoins (pegged to USD).
iii. ERC-20[14] tokens and yield-generating products of third-party Ethereum blockchain—and generally EVM-compatible—protocols (denoted collectively in the sequel as ₸-ETH tokens, for brevity).

[14]Please consult Sect. 10.5.5 for an explanation of Ethereum ERC-20 Smart Contracts.

On the liabilities side, there are two large blocks of positions which we will denote as "Liabilities" (in the sense of liabilities to NXM Stakers, Insurance Cover Buyers and third parties) and "Platform Rewards".

The latter block is also referred to in project documentation as "DAO Treasury". It is meant to play the same role as "free funds" of a traditional finance insurance/reinsurance company, and does indeed aggregate all net direct and indirect yield—in the sense of commissions, fees, net investment returns, etc.—generated by the protocol for the benefit of its members. We thus choose to make this latter fact explicit by naming it "Platform Rewards" for the purposes of the current case study. By examining the blockchain address of its "safe" [149, 150] one can see positions in ETH, NXM, DAI and other tokens which are also ERC-20 compatible (as of the time of writing).

The "Liabilities" block is by far the most interesting one. Without wanting to pre-empt the latter *exposé* on transactional pathways, we can still make reference to project documentation to glean this block's main positions. First of all, protocol liabilities to insurance cover buyers are represented—and returned to their crypto wallets—as non-fungible tokens [151] (NFT's, following the ERC-721 Ethereum smart contract standard[15]). Second, protocol liabilities to NXM stakers are similarly represented and returned as non-fungible tokens. Third, the largest liability position consists in an NXM liquidity pool. This contains both ring-fenced staking pools [152] (the same pools of committed NXM funds managed by Staking Pool Managers) and free, uncommitted, NXM token amounts owned by Nexus Mutual members, including those managed by its governance bodies.

Importantly, in direct analogy to the "Minimum Capital Requirement" (MCR) position to be found in Solvency II insurance balance sheets (cf. the discussion in Sect. 7.1 around Fig. 7.3), Nexus Mutual constantly calculates and ring-fences a sum of NXM tokens which it designates as MCR [153]. The protocol's MCR is defined in the project Whitepaper [112] to be:

> ***MCR$_{ETH}$*** *= The minimum amount of capital required to support existing covers, Minimum Capital Requirement, in Ether. The MCR is calibrated to a 99.5% solvency level.*

and was originally used to also calibrate the protocol's continuous token model for NXM issuance [154]. The documentation of the current iteration of the protocol mentions simply:

> *The MCR represents the minimum amount of funds the Mutual needs to be very confident it can pay all claims. It is represented by the following formula:*
>
> *MCR = f(Cover) = Total Active Cover Amount / 4.8.*[16]

[15] Please consult Sect. 10.5.5 for an explanation of the Ethereum ERC-721 NFT Smart Contract.

[16] From the point of view of Mechanism Design (introduced in the next chapter) it would be necessary to examine the adequacy of the MCR calibration. Even though this is not in-focus for the present case study, we can still point to the protocols's documentation [155] where it is

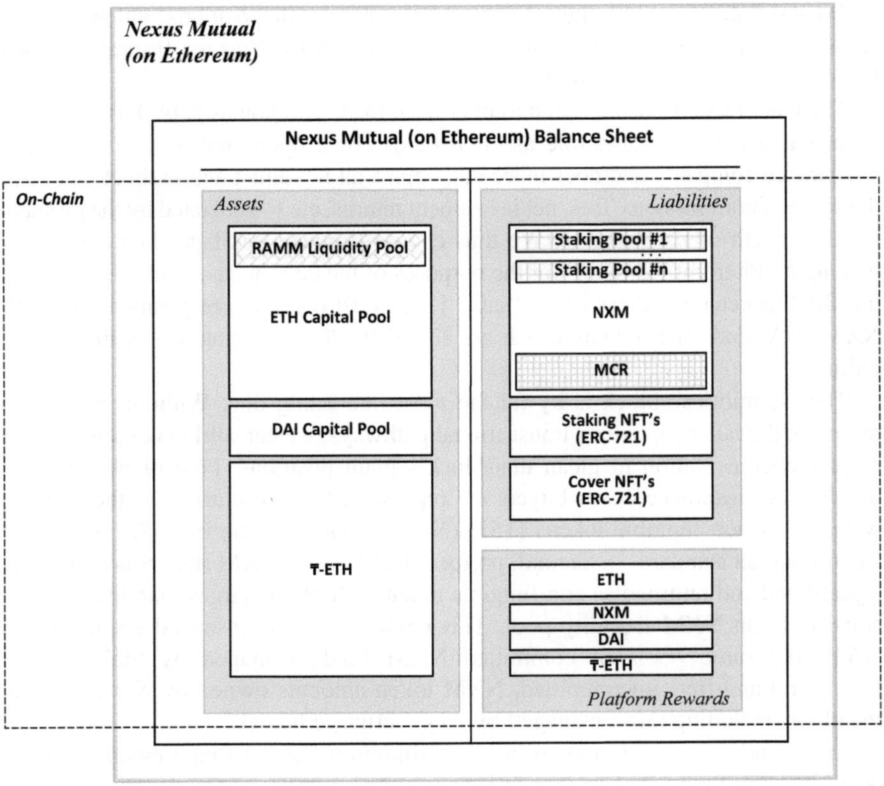

Fig. 7.11 Effective (notional) Balance Sheet of the Nexus Mutual protocol

As we have yet to examine mechanism design (which is introduced in Chap. 8), for the purposes of this case study it is sufficient to note that there indeed exists a floor of NXM funds on the "Liabilities" side, which is monitored and actively controlled through mechanisms implemented by governance. In summary, the Nexus Mutual *effective* balance sheet is as depicted schematically in Fig. 7.11.

Please note that this is a "notional balance sheet" view at the protocol level, and not an actual accounting one kept by Nexus Mutual. Depicting token-based transactional pathways against such a "notional balance sheet" view is an original technique proposed by this book's author and not—yet—an established industry practice. It is proposed, and implemented consistently here and in the later sections of this book, as providing a rather intuitive basis on which to follow transactional pathways involving ecosystem tokens.

mentioned that "*Nexus Mutual implemented the capital model by assuming a fixed gearing factor applied to the active cover in ETH terms. .... If the full capital model (which is run off-chain) starts producing results that are materially different to the current gearing factor it is anticipated that the factor will be updated* via *a governance action*". The "gearing factor" is the value "4.8".

Based on the above we can begin drawing the transactional pathways among ecosystem agents, also depicting the corresponding token flows.

7.6.3.1 NXM Token Holder Acquires NXM Tokens in the Primary Market

The prerequisite knowledge for this transaction is the fact that NXM tokens [116] can only be purchased and used within the Nexus Mutual ecosystem. They have no use outside of it, and are thus not bought/sold in exchanges, neither centralized nor decentralized ones.[17] They are created and destroyed[18] on Nexus Mutual itself, which is thus the "Primary Market" for its issuance and redemption. NXM tokens are needed in order to access the ecosystem services, to fund staking pools for rewards, and also to vote in governance. Hence, as per the reference typology of Chap. 4, they are utility tokens of combined "access", "service" and "governance" types (cf. Sect. 4.2.2).

This transactional pathway thus describes the way in which an NXM member purchases NXM tokens in the primary market, becoming an NXM token holder.

The technical artefact enabling this purchase is a smart contract implementing token-exchange ("Swapping" in industry jargon) functionality, converting between ETH and NXM tokens and returning the latter to the invoker's crypto wallet. This entails an embedded algorithm calculating a parity rate between ETH/NXM and a different one actually creating ("minting") the NXM tokens, then reconciling them to the protocol's balance sheet. The afore-mentioned smart contract is thus said to be implementing an "automated market maker"[19] ("AMM"), i.e. an automated issuance/redemption functionality allowing the primary market to function without the presence of human agents. A brief overview of the workings of this AMM is provided in the project's documentation [158], including a link to a more detailed explanation contained in a bespoke whitepaper [159]. For the purposes of this section, the important information is that this particular AMM is termed "Ratcheting AMM" ("RAMM" for short) and consists of two different algorithms implementing two distinct parity rates, one for each of the NXM buy (issuance) and sell (redemption) sides. They are conjoined at a reference parity rate NXM/ETH defined by the protocol and are meant to create a "spread" between "ask" and "bid" rates.[20]

---

[17] Strictly speaking, there exists an ERC-20 token called "Wrapped NXM" ("wNXM") which is pegged to NXM and bought/sold against the latter by third parties. This possibility and the exchange functionality are referred to in the project's documentation [156] and even linked to from the Nexus Mutual dApp [157]. However, the project takes care to issue a disclaimer that this functionality is not supported operationally by Nexus Mutual, nor does it take responsibility for it. This fact notwithstanding, wNXM is indeed traded in Exchanges and is also present in the holdings of the Nexus Mutual DAO Treasury itself (gleaned through examination of the positions in the "safe address" linked to from [149], as of the time of writing).

[18] In industry jargon "minted" and "burned" respectively, cf. later Chap. 10 on token design, especially Sect. 10.5.5.

[19] Please note that the function and calibration of "Automated Market Makers" (AMM's) is explained in detail in the later Chap. 12 on Bonding Function design.

[20] Please find an explanation of these terms in Sect. 13.1 on the mechanics of traditional Market Making.

Technically speaking, the Nexus Mutual RAMM consists of two "Constant Product Market Makers"[21] ("CPMM") with different constants but conjoined at a particular parity point. The protocol creates a "virtual pool of availability" for NXM before they are minted, which controls NXM scarcity[22] and inflation[23] in the internal market, hence also NXM parity to ETH.[24] Please note that all these notions are explained in detail in the subsequent Chaps. 10 and 12, and their use demonstrated through later case studies. The only information that is needed here is that there exists a Nexus Mutual smart contract calculating bid/ask NXM/ETH parities and swapping NXM for ETH (at NXM issuance) and ETH for NXM (at NXM redemption).

The transactional pathway in focus is depicted schematically in Fig. 7.12.

As given in the figure, the protocol's dApp [129] will first request that a user connects a crypto wallet, whereby the validation that their blockchain address matches that of a Nexus Mutual member takes place. The user will have already acquired ETH in their wallet, whereupon they are ready to exchange them for NXM tokens by the "Mint & Redeem" functionality [160] of the dApp. By declaring an ETH token amount to swap and accepting the indicated parity and estimated "slippage",[25] they can then invoke the Nexus Mutual Swapping smart contract (SC, step #1 in Fig. 7.12) which calls the RAMM to effect the transaction. The SC will deposit the ETH into the protocol's ETH Capital Pool (step #2) and will cause equivalent NXM tokens to be minted. Those are recorded on the Liabilities side, and then returned through the SC (#3) to the crypto wallet of the user (#4), who thus assume the agent type "NXM token holder". The protocol may or may not raise a commission on the transaction (depicted as step #5 on the figure, whereby an amount of ETH is shown to be directed into Platform Rewards, i.e. the DAO Treasury) depending on its actual policy. This completes the transactional pathway.

Please note that the exact same way is followed in reverse (steps #4 to #1) in the NXM redemption case. The same smart contract and the same RAMM act in the latter case as well. Whether or not the user ceases to be an NXM token holder depends of course on any remaining NXM balance in their crypto wallet.

Importantly, the smart contract imposes restrictions on both issuance and redemption transactions [161], depending on the state of the protocol's balance sheet and in particular on the estimated liquidity and solvency risks. In that respect, e.g. the depth of the available ETH Capital Pool as a source of the liquidity pools underlying the RAMM is juxtaposed with the Minimum Capital Requirement (MCR) metric and with other metrics proxying for capital pool change velocity. As we have not yet addressed mechanism design (this follows in Chap. 8), we will refrain from explaining these restrictions further.

---

[21] Cf. explanations in Sect. 10.5.7, also succinctly in Sect. 12.1 (and thereafter in Chap. 12).

[22] Cf. Sect. 10.5.2.

[23] Cf. Sect. 10.5.3.

[24] Cf. Sect. 10.5.4.

[25] in effect, the potential deviation from the indicated swapping parity due to liquidity effects of AMM's, cf. also Sect. 12.2.2 where the provenance of "slippage" is explained in detail.

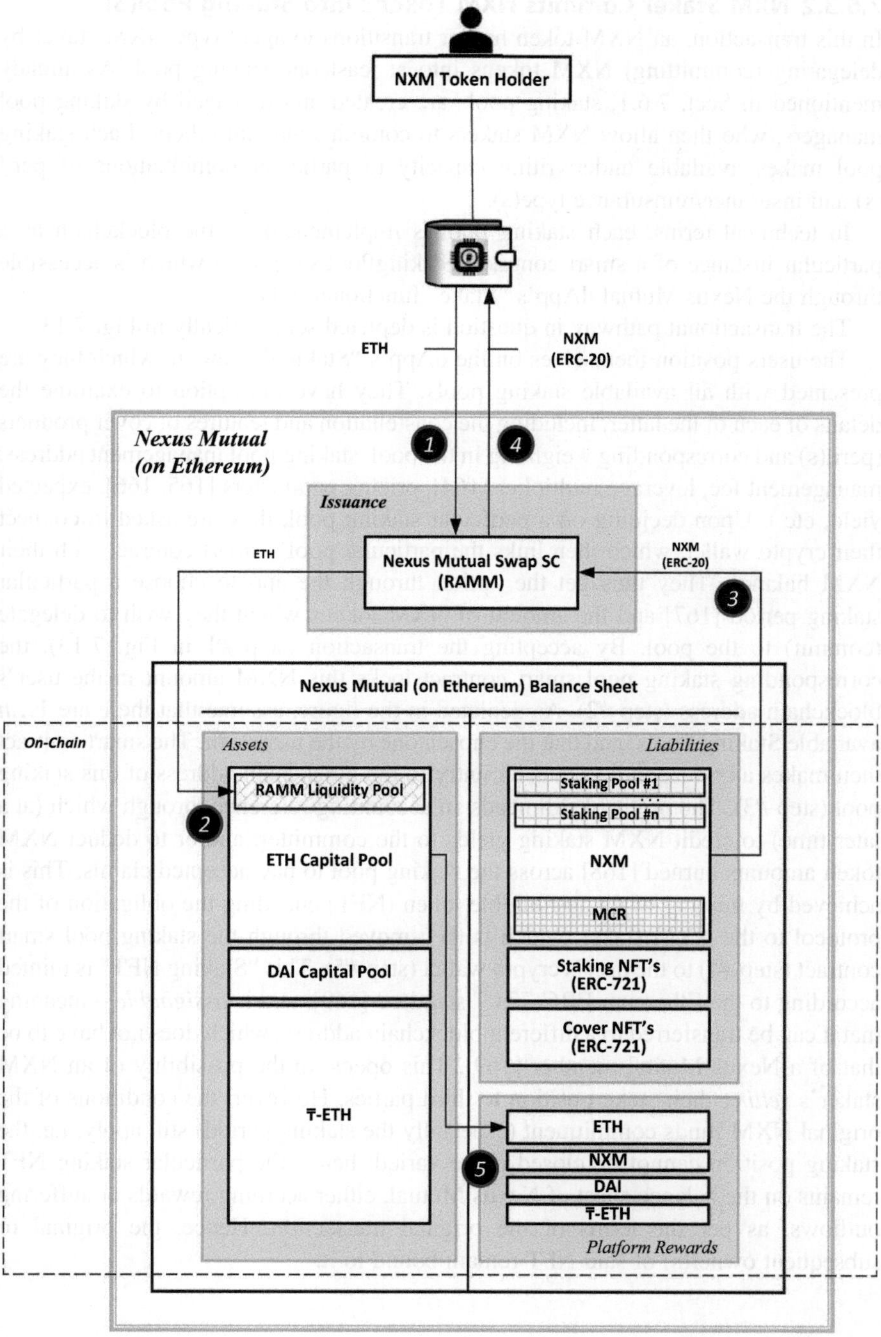

Fig. 7.12 NXM member becomes NXM token holder on the primary market; transactional pathway

7.6.3.2 NXM Staker Commits NXM Tokens into Staking Pool(S)

In this transaction, an NXM token holder transitions to agent type NXM staker by delegating (committing) NXM tokens into at least one staking pool. As already mentioned in Sect. 7.6.1, staking pools are created and managed by staking pool managers, who then allow NXM stakers to commit funds into them. Each staking pool makes available underwriting capacity to particular combinations of peril (s) and insurance/reinsurance type(s).

In technical terms, each staking pool is implemented on the blockchain as a particular instance of a smart contract (StakingPool.sol [162]) which is accessible through the Nexus Mutual dApp's "Stake" functionality [163].

The transactional pathway in question is depicted schematically in Fig. 7.13.

The users position themselves on the dApp's "Staking" view, in which they are presented with all available staking pools. They have the option to examine the details of each of the latter, including the constellation and features of cover products (peril(s) and corresponding weighting in the pool, staking pool management address, management fee, leverage multiplier [164], pricing parameters [165, 166], expected yield, etc.). Upon deciding on a particular staking pool, they are asked to connect their crypto wallet, which then links the particular pool's smart contract with their NXM balance. They thus get the option through the app to choose a particular staking period [167] and the amount of NXM tokens which they wish to delegate (commit) to the pool. By accepting the transaction (step #1 in Fig. 7.13), the corresponding staking pool smart contract locks this NXM amount in the user's blockchain address (step #2). As depicted in the figure, assume that there are $1\ldots n$ available Staking Pools, and that the chosen one by the user is *#n*. The smart contract then makes a corresponding transfer entry to the blockchain address of this staking pool (step #3). The protocol still needs an accounting reference through which (at a later time) to credit NXM staking yields to the committer, and/or to deduct NXM token amounts burned [168] across the staking pool to pay accepted claims. This is achieved by minting of a non-fungible token (NFT) encoding the obligation of the protocol to the NXM staker, which is then moved through the staking pool smart contract (step #4) to the user's crypto wallet (step #5). This "Staking NFT" is minted according to the Ethereum ERC-721[26] standard [169], and is *assignable*—meaning that it can be transferred to a different blockchain address, which does not have to be that of a Nexus Mutual member [169]. This opens up the possibility of an NXM staker's *selling* their stake position to third parties. However, the conditions of the original NXM funds commitment (especially the staking period) still apply, i.e. the staking position cannot be closed or be varied; hence the particular staking NFT remains on the balance sheet of Nexus Mutual, either accruing rewards or suffering outflows, as per the terms of the original transaction. Hence, the original or subsequent owner(s) of said NFT remain bound to it.

[26] Please consult Sect. 10.5.5 for an explanation of Ethereum ERC-721 Smart Contracts.

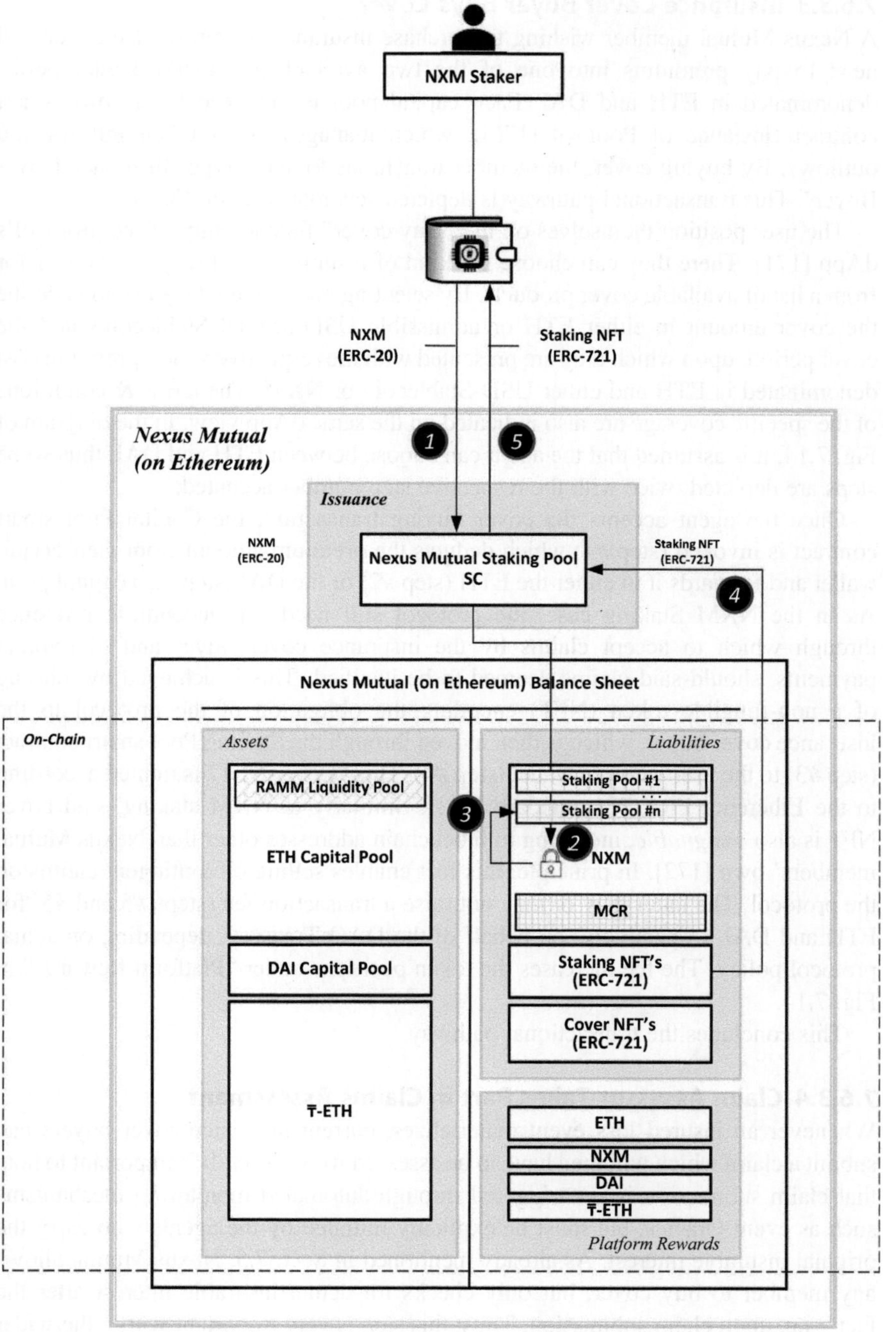

Fig. 7.13 NXM member stakes NXM tokens; transactional pathway

7.6.3.3 Insurance Cover Buyer Buys Cover

A Nexus Mutual member wishing to purchase insurance or reinsurance cover will need to pay premiums into one of the two available asset-side capital pools, denominated in ETH and DAI. Each capital pool is managed by an own smart contract (instance of Pool.sol [170]), which manages direct token inflows and outflows. By buying cover, the member transitions to agent type 'Insurance Cover Buyer'. This transactional pathway is depicted schematically on Fig. 7.14.

The user position themselves on the "Buy cover" functionality of the protocol's dApp [171]. There they can choose the kind of insurance peril they need cover for from a list of available cover products. By selecting one product they can then define the cover amount in either ETH or admissible USD-pegged Stablecoins and the cover period, upon which they are presented with the respective yearly premium cost denominated in ETH and either USD-Stablecoin or NXM. The terms & conditions of the specific coverage are also indicated on the same dApp view. In the diagram of Fig. 7.14, it is assumed that the agent can choose between ETH and DAI, thus some steps are depicted twice with the respective step number accented.

Once the agent accepts the cover buying transaction, the Capital Pool smart contract is invoked (step #1) which deducts the premium amount from their crypto wallet and forwards it to either the ETH (step #2) or the DAI (step #2′) capital pool. As in the NXM Staking case, the protocol still needs an accounting reference through which to accept claims by the insurance cover buyer and to redirect payments, should said claims deemed to be justified. This is achieved by minting of a non-fungible token (NFT) encoding the obligation of the protocol to the insurance cover buyer, which is then moved through the Staking Pool smart contract (step #3) to the user's crypto wallet (step #4). This "Cover NFT" is minted according to the Ethereum ERC-721 standard [151]. Similarly to NXM staking, said cover NFT is also *assignable*, including to blockchain addresses other than Nexus Mutual members' own [172]. In principle, this fact enables selling of contingent claims on the protocol. The latter may or may not raise a transaction fee (steps #5 and #5′ for ETH and DAI, respectively) on behalf of the DAO Treasury, depending on actual protocol policy. The fee increases the token positions under "Platform Rewards" in Fig. 7.14.

This concludes the transactional pathway.

7.6.3.4 Claim Assessor Takes Part in Claims Assessment

Whenever an insured loss event materializes, current insurance cover buyers can submit a claim which will then have to be assessed for validity. It is important to note that claim submission is *not* triggered through automated monitoring mechanisms such as event Oracles, but must be explicitly initiated by the agents who carry the original insurable interest. As already mentioned in Sect. 7.5, Nexus Mutual allows any member to buy cover, but only checks for actual insurable interest after the fact—i.e. upon claim submission. Thus, this step is very important within the wider context of the claim assessment process.

The process of claim validation also invokes staking of tokens, namely NXM tokens by the claim assessor(s) who have to be already Nexus Mutual members. The

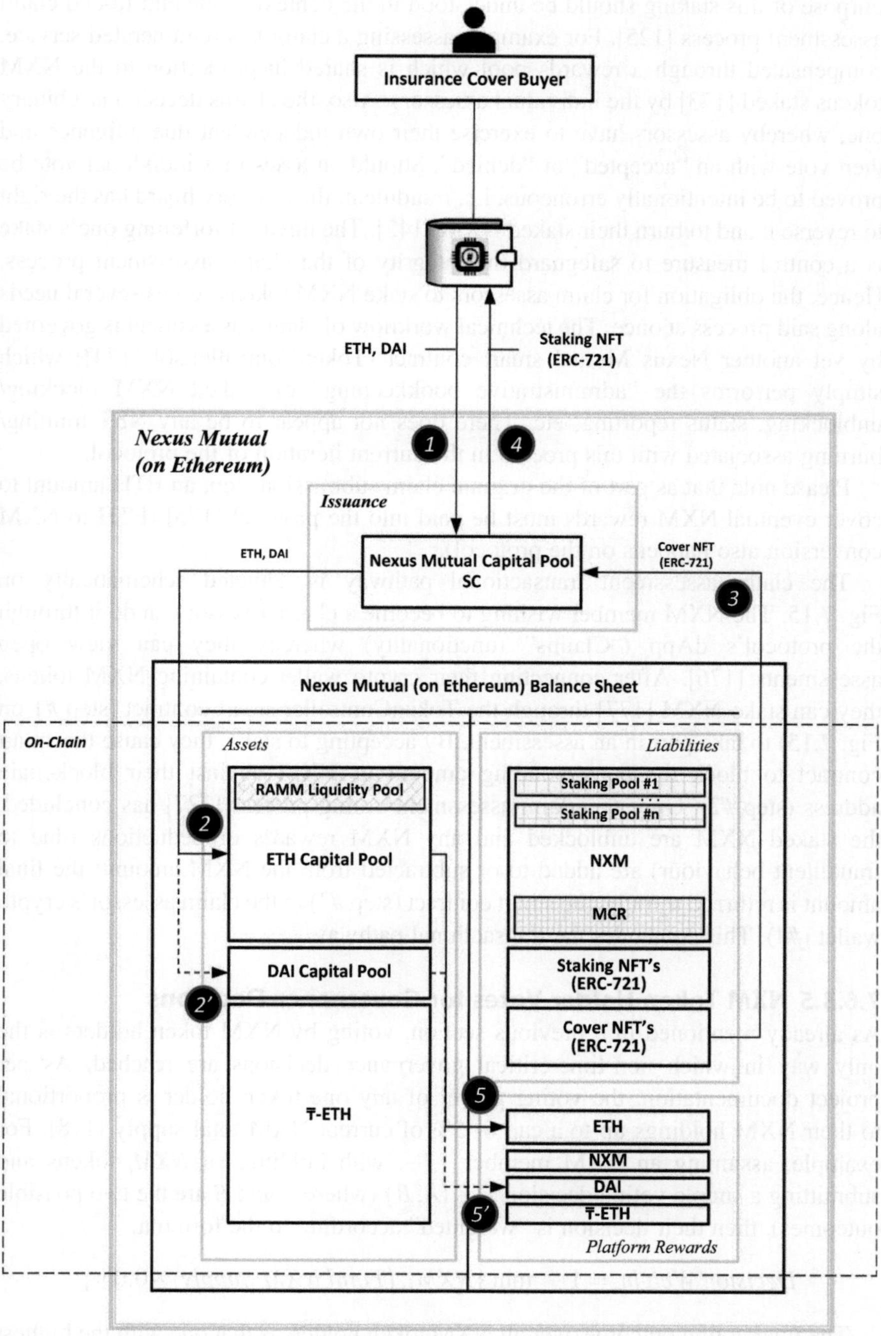

Fig. 7.14 NXM member buys insurance cover; transactional pathway

purpose of this staking should be understood in the context of the end-to-end claim assessment process [125]. For example, assessing a claim is a remunerated service, compensated through a rewards pool which is shared in proportion to the NXM tokens staked [173] by the individual assessors. Also, the claims decision is a binary one, whereby assessors have to exercise their own independent due diligence and then vote with an "accepted" or "denied". Should an assessor's individual vote be proved to be intentionally erroneous, i.e. fraudulent, the advisory board has the right to reverse it and to burn their staked NXM [142]. The threat of forfeiting one's stake is a control measure to safeguard the integrity of the claims assessment process. Hence, the obligation for claim assessors to stake NXM tokens serves several needs along said process at once. The technical workflow of claims assessment is governed by yet another Nexus Mutual smart contract (TokenController.sol [174]) which simply performs the "administrative bookkeeping" of staked NXM blocking/ unblocking, status reporting, etc. There does not appear to be any NFT minting/ burning associated with this process in the current iteration of the protocol.

Please note that as part of the original claim submission step, an ETH amount to cover eventual NXM rewards must be paid into the protocol [175] (ETH to NXM conversion also happens on the protocol).

The claim assessment transactional pathway is depicted schematically on Fig. 7.15. The NXM member wishing to become a claim assessor can do it through the protocol's dApp ("Claims" functionality) whereby they can view open assessments [176]. After connecting their crypto wallet containing NXM tokens, they can stake NXM [177] through the TokenController smart contract (step #1 on Fig. 7.15) to take part in an assessment. By accepting to stake, they cause the smart contract to block the corresponding amount of NXM against their blockchain address (step #2). Once the claim assessment voting process [127] has concluded, the staked NXM are unblocked and any NXM rewards or deductions (due to fraudulent behaviour) are added to or subtracted from the NXM amount; the final amount is returned through the smart contract (step #3) to the claim assessor's crypto wallet (#4). This concludes the transactional pathway.

7.6.3.5 NXM Token Holder Votes for Governance Decisions

As already mentioned in a previous section, voting by NXM token holders is the only way in which non-time-critical governance decisions are reached. As per project documentation, the voting power of any one token holder is proportional to their NXM holdings up to a cap of 5% of current NXM total supply [178]. For example, assuming an NXM member $-i-$, with holdings of NXM_i tokens and submitting a simple voting decision $V_i \epsilon \{A, B\}$ (where A and B are the two possible outcomes), then their decision is "weighted" according to the formula:

$$Decision\ Weight_i = 1 + \min\{NXM_i, (Total\ NXM\ Supply) \times 0.05\}$$

The final voting outcome over all NXM token holders is that one with the highest sum of decision weights.

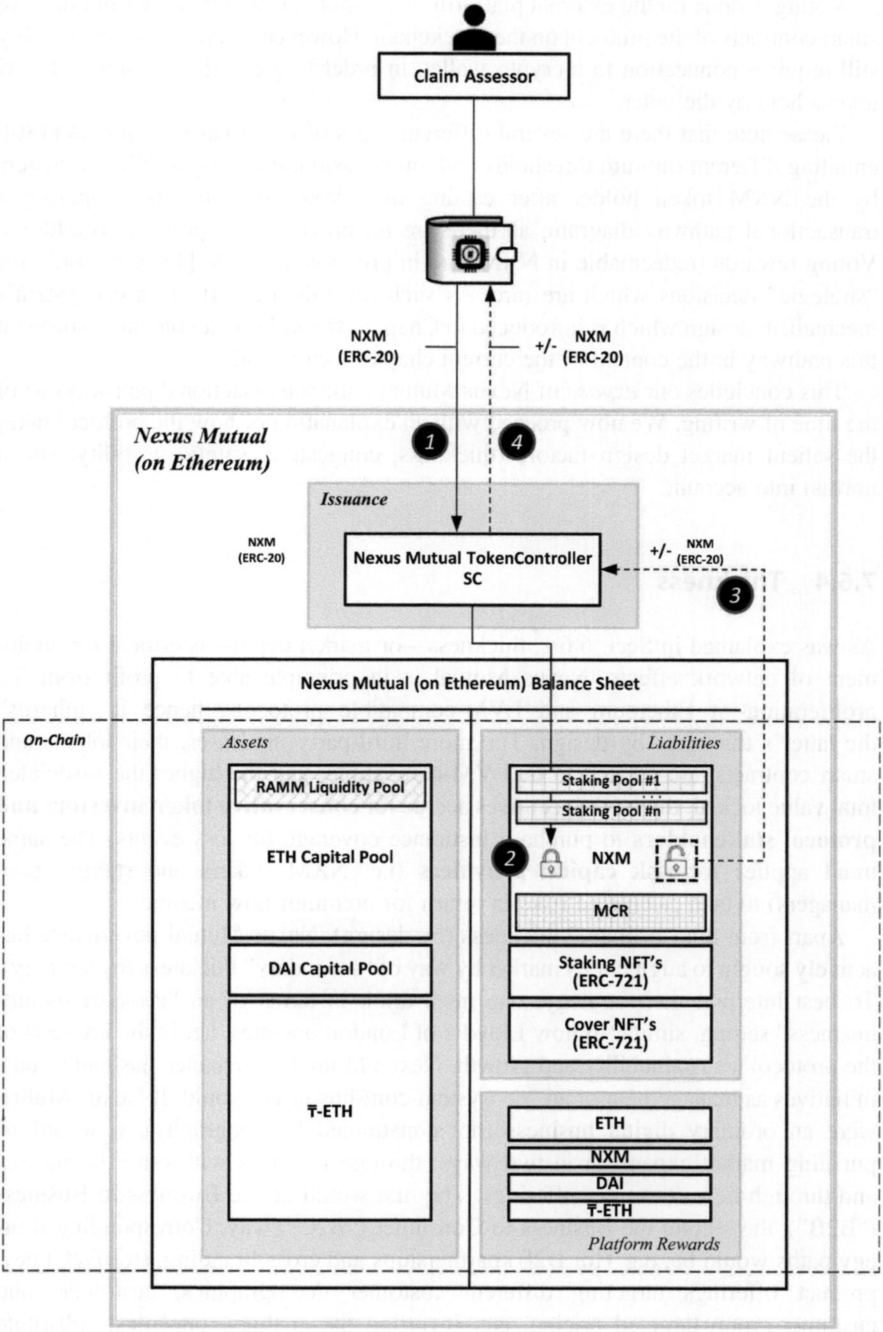

Fig. 7.15 NXM member becomes claim assessor; transactional pathway

Voting is done on the external platform "Snapshot" [179], i.e. it does not involve smart contracts of the protocol on the blockchain. However, Snapshot's functionality still requires connection to a crypto wallet, in order to glean the amount of NXM tokens held by the voter.

Please note that there are several different types of governance proposals [180], entailing different quorum thresholds and, on occasion, blocking of NXM transfers by the NXM token holder after casting their vote. We are not supplying a transactional pathway diagram, as there are no on-chain components to address. Voting rewards (redeemable in NXM) are in principle possible [181], but only for "strategic" decisions which are rare. As such rewards are part of an ecosystem's mechanism design which is introduced in Chap. 8, we will not devote more space on this pathway in the context of the current chapter's case study.

This concludes our *exposé* of Nexus Mutual's main transactional pathways as of the time of writing. We now proceed with an explanation of how the protocol takes the salient market design factors (thickness, congestion, safety, usability, social norms) into account.

7.6.4 Thickness

As was explained in Sect. 6.6.1, thickness—or market depth—is critical for attainment of network effects. Nexus Mutual is in principle able to profit from the proliferation of Ethereum and EVM-compatible protocols, hence it "inherits" the latter's thickness by design. The more third-party use cases, their tokens and smart contracts, are created to be EVM-compatible, and the higher the associated total value locked, the more incentives accrue for **conservative token investors and protocol stakeholders** to purchase insurance coverage for loss events. The same trend applies for **risk capital providers** (i.e. NXM stakers and staking pool managers) to take calculated risks in return for premium-flow income.

Apart from this "primary" thickness (by design), Nexus Mutual governance has actively sought to augment its market by way of "secondary" thickness (by strategy). To best interpret their strategy, one must think in terms of an "ecosystem-cum-business" setting, similar to how Lloyd's of London operates, i.e. in the interests of the protocol's sustainability and growth, Nexus Mutual governance has had to take initiatives as management of an "ecosystem-cum-business" would. If Nexus Mutual were an ordinary digital business (not constrained by geography), it would be pursuing market expansion in two ways: through alliances with other businesses and through new consumer offerings. The first would be the Business-to-Business ("B2B"), the second the Business-to-Consumer ("B2C") way. Corresponding strategy paths would be, e.g. (for B2B) partnerships and cross-branding, (for B2C) new product offerings targeting different customer demographics, customer- and customer-group targeted pricing, etc. Inverting the analogy, one must substitute "Ecosystem" (or "Protocol") for "Business"; i.e. in a blockchain-ecosystem setting, Business-to-Business would be re-interpreted as "Ecosystem-to-Ecosystem" (or "Protocol-to-Protocol"), Business-to-Consumer as "Ecosystem-to-Member" (or "Protocol-to-Member"), etc. Hence, *secondary* thickness calibration by Nexus Mutual appears to be pursued through:

- Ecosystem-to-Ecosystem (akin to "B2B") strategies. Nexus Mutual works with other (EVM-compatible) ecosystems to offer insurance coverage to their members. Ways this has already been pursued: **whitelabeling** and **protocol partnerships**.
- Ecosystem-to-Member (akin to "B2C") strategies. Nexus Mutual strives to extend its member demographics and to effect product differentiation. Ways this has been pursued: **new product offerings**; **new transaction types**; and **transaction-specific inducements**.

Whitelabeling: Nexus Mutual has in the past allowed its insurance offerings to be included as part of services packages sold by other protocols under the latter's own "branding". For example, in 2020 Yearn Finance [182] started using Nexus Mutual for insurance cover of new token positions [183], namely in Aave, Balancer, Compound, Curve, Synthetix, etc. Instead of token investors having to educate themselves about protocol insurance and then do their independent due diligence, Yearn Finance offered insurance coverage out-of-the-box as part of their own suggested token investment packages.

Protocol Partnerships: In difference to Whitelabeling, these are "symbiotic" partnership agreements whereby the added thickness comes not from individual offerings but from the entire foreign protocol ecosystem as a whole. Nexus Mutual and the foreign protocol in effect go to market together as equal partners strengthening each other's value proposition. Using again Yearn Finance as the example to demonstrate the difference, in 2021 they decided to offer insurance for the protocol as a whole instead of for specific token investments. The value proposition was that Nexus Mutual protocol insurance would help harden the partner protocol's technology stack, thus helping convince more risk averse investors to participate in Yearn Finance. Another example would be Bright Union [184], which is an "Insurance Aggregator" ecosystem having partnered with Nexus Mutual to complete the spectrum of its insurance products offered to token investors.

New Product Offerings: This is an obvious thickness augmentation strategy, exemplified in the past by e.g. Nexus Mutual creating a community fund to support new insurance cover types [185] (Oracle failures, insured savings accounts on Yearn Finance or Idle [186], fixed-interest protocols with built-in credit default swaps, etc.). As of the time of writing, the protocol's stakeholders actively pursue new cover types for Real World Risks [187] (RWR's), envisaged to include perils such as fire, theft, accidental damage, directors & officer's liability, errors & omissions, cyber liability, etc. The foray of Nexus Mutual into Reinsurance through its quota share cover offering (which was not present in the first iteration of the protocol) can also be interpreted as a strategic market design reconfiguration step by its Governance. Similarly, the 2022 transition of the Ethereum blockchain from a "Proof-of-Work" [188] to a "Proof-of-Stake" [189] consensus mechanism was used by Nexus Mutual Governance as an opportunity to offer a new cover type (ETH Slashing Cover) to PoS Validator Node Operators.

New Transaction Types: The correct term should rather be "new transaction pathways", created for example because the agent typology changes across protocol iterations, or in order for the transaction itself to become more agent-type specific, etc. Using "Protocol Cover" as an example, Nexus Mutual Governance used this as a base to create "Bundled Protocol Cover" offerings [190] so that a particular member demographic—i.e. members investing across several yield-farming and yield-trading protocols at once—could be served. Another recent initiative (proposal accepted by Governance in 2024) concerns the extension of the asset-side of the balance sheet to admit also USDC as capital pool token [191], the stated rationale being that this Stablecoin's market capitalization—hence, potential liquidity flow into Nexus Mutual—is several times higher than DAI's.

Transaction Inducements Through "Integrations": The protocol's "Channel Integrator" type agents (i.e. NXM members who create an indirect sales channel, by integrating NXM protocol artefacts into own functionality [128], such as bespoke user interfaces in third-party portals), are an example. Channel integrators are allowed to charge commission [130] on any cover products sold through their channel. Importantly, they are also accorded the privilege to sell cover to non-members of the protocol, by whitelisting an own—onboarded—blockchain address as proxy [192]. This suggests that they were conceived precisely as a means to achieve thickness augmentation.

7.6.5 Congestion

With reference to Sect. 6.6.2, we remind the reader that congestion denotes inherent frictions in the creation or execution of transactions. There are of course different transaction setup aspects depending on the Nexus Mutual agent type (insurance cover buyer, NXM staker, etc.). For example, NXM stakers are expected to carry out their own due diligence on available staking pools and this would be reasonably expected to need time and effort. However, the protocol per se does not impose a time scale or measure of proof for the completion of said due diligence. At the same time, staking pool managers have the discretion to apply pool capacity to many different cover products ("leverage" factor [164]) which speeds up underwriting decision-making considerably. All member types have access to a whole-market view through the protocol's dApp (through "Buy cover" [193], "Swap" [194], "Stake" [163] and "Claims" [195] views) and there are mechanisms to create several "filtered" views. There are no barriers to participation on any side of transactions, as long as member onboarding has already taken place. Technical limits for transaction execution are those of the Ethereum blockchain.

That said, there are friction points built into some transactional pathways by design (a combination of market and mechanism designs, as the intention is to elicit appropriate behaviour and avoid moral hazard situations—which is quite relevant in the insurance domain). An example would be "cooling periods", i.e. time delays imposed by Nexus Mutual in-between transactional process steps such as in claim assessments.[27] There are actually several such "cooling periods" imposed by Nexus Mutual. As their precise placement along transactional pathways (upon which event, until which event) and calibration (how many hours, etc.) changes in-between protocol generations, a complete listing of them here would run the risk of becoming non-exhaustive and quickly obsolete. It is also unavoidable that explaining them in detail would straddle the boundaries between market and mechanism designs. The interested reader is kindly referred to the relevant sections of the protocol documentation website [202], as well as to the updated link of the Nexus Mutual Whitepaper.[28]

Making the covered perils and loss events more granular is another way that Nexus Mutual uses to decrease congestion. For example, in 2021 the covered perils were extended (from smart contract failures) to include malevolent attack vectors such as Oracle attacks, governance attacks, severe economic exploits, and a variety of L-1 and L-2 blockchain exploits. Having more situation-specific insurance coverage is meant to incentivize faster decision-making from interested members, who would otherwise struggle to assemble a bespoke package fitting their needs from among the standardized protocol offerings.

7.6.6 Safety

The crucial safety feature of Nexus Mutual is the member onboarding due diligence (including written DAO membership agreement [196], KYC requirements [59] and privacy policy [197]), however this is more an aspect of mechanism than market design. The same interpolation of design pillars is evident in the "cooling periods" feature which is also a safety mechanism. From the standpoint of pure market design, the constellation of economic agents and transactional pathways enhances member safety, as:

- Available insurance coverage is based strictly on the willingness of Risk Assessors to stake NXM tokens.[29] There is no mismatch between fund commitments and risk exposures, nor any non-linear payoff profiles as in the case of derivative instruments. In that sense, moral hazard on the part of Insurance Cover Buyers acting more as speculators than legitimate risk hedgers is minimized, because the multitude of expert staking pool managers using

[27] E.g., for review of claim outcomes: https://docs.nexusmutual.io/protocol/claims-assessment#fraudulent-votes.

[28] Current Whitepaper as of the time of writing is v. 2.3.

[29] Subject to a "Minimum Capital Requirement" ("MCR", as per [196]).

thorough risk due diligence would tend to remove information asymmetries between the two agent types.

- The amount of NXM funds staked by NXM stakers on loss events is reported clearly on the protocol dApp, hence the expert consensus on the relative risks of perils and protocols is immediately advised to prospective insurance buyers. If prospective buyers do not agree with the expert consensus, they are free to not accept the insurance offer. However, it is always made clear to them how many staking pools exist, and with which staked NXM exposures.
- Claim assessors and NXM stakers have competing and mutually exclusive interests when it comes to profiting from the Platform Rewards pool. This of course does not preclude off-blockchain collusion, but the thicker the market the less the odds for such an occurrence. In any case, the design of these two agent types is targeted towards increased safety on-chain.
- The existence of a MCR, i.e. of a requisite minimum amount of NXM-denominated funds below which the protocol will cease providing coverage, acts as a safety mechanism for its members. In this case, "safety" should be interpreted as "protection of long-term financial position". The protocol's documentation [155] implies that the MCR calibration adequacy is monitored and controlled by governance.
- To avoid NXM burns it is in the interests of NXM stakers to perform thorough due diligence, or at least to be able to draw on providers of said due diligence, on insurable loss events. Staking pool managers are expected to form precisely this pool of expertise on which NXM stakers can count. However, they are not the only safety mechanism pursued by Nexus Mutual. For example, in 2021 the protocol instituted[30] [199] (in partnership with Immunefi [200]) a bug-hunting bounty matching program for insurable protocols. This is a pool of funds meant to incentivize "white-hat hackers" [201] (i.e. ethical hackers) to discover technical deficiencies that can cause loss events and then suggest solutions to remove them before they can be exploited by malevolent actors. This is a win-win value proposition for both the target protocol and for Nexus Mutual itself. On the one hand, protocols listed on Nexus Mutual close their vulnerabilities and thus avoid financial losses and reputational risk. NXM stakers get extra assurance about the eventual profitability of their staked NXM positions, hence are incentivized to remain Nexus Mutual members. This creates impetus for more members to become NXM stakers, which deepens the risk coverage pools, which in turn attracts more insurance cover buyers, etc. The virtuous circle thus created aligns the interests of both the target protocols and of Nexus Mutual to keep investing in ecosystem safety.

[30] Nexus Mutual matched third-party payouts per valid critical bug report up to USD 200 K (or 2500 NXM) as per September 2021 announcement. The target protocols at launch included Alpha Finance, Badger DAO, Bancor, Compound, Pool Together, Sushiswap, Synthetix, Vesper Finance and Yearn Finance. The partnership was renewed in April 2022, as per [198].

- Last but not least, the "mutual" ownership model which was chosen by Nexus Mutual is also a safety-promoting factor. The fact that all platform rewards have to be either re-invested or re-distributed among the members means that protocol governance has to avoid speculative investments and focus on platform sustainability, as it is ultimately accountable only to its members. Otherwise, DAO members can initiate voting to force governance alignment with the prudence expectation.

7.6.7 Usability

The Nexus Mutual dApp has a clean interface for navigation. Members have access to essential information (through "Buy cover" [193], "Swap" [194], "Stake" [163] and "Claims" [195] views) and can purchase or write insurance and offer services in a few, intuitive and standardized, steps. A traditional insurance professional would recognize immediately the business process steps, which can help lower the "mental barrier" of experimenting with crypto assets. The accompanying documentation website [202] and corresponding GitHub [203] appear to be kept updated and synchronized with the dApp.

Protocol terms and conditions, rules and access to governance are easy to locate, both through the Nexus Mutual dApp and website and also through internet search engines. Ensuring the continued quality and actuality of documentation is, of course, dependent on the resources and diligence of the token project's team. Different user types will naturally have different expectations of documentation depth (e.g. on risk control calibration), in which case access to governance will be important for a prospective member's due diligence towards the protocol.

The dApp dashboard is also useful for pre-transaction fact discovery, which helps to make members comfortable with the investment risk that they are assuming. For example, the dashboard helps users to visually understand the network status by showing the number of NXM tokens staked and the rewards that can be withdrawn. It also shows annual percentage yields, staking periods and other relevant metrics to estimate investment payoffs. All-in-all, Nexus Mutual calibrates usability with a view to, first, serving the legitimate information needs of potential investors and, second, making transaction steps as intuitive and hassle-free as possible for all ecosystem agent types.

7.6.8 Social Norms

The business use cases of Nexus Mutual violate no social norms. Regarding its operating procedures, the member onboarding process [204] is designed with a know-your-customer focus and respects legal restrictions to accessibility from specific jurisdictions. Membership conditions and obligations are well documented in writing [205]. A note is in order regarding its apparent deviation from traditional insurance practices when it comes to member voting power: as already mentioned, a member's NXM holdings weigh on decisions up to a 5% total supply cap [178]. However, mutual insurance companies are generally expected to obey the principle of "one person – one vote" [206, 207]. It is up to prospective Nexus Mutual members to decide if they are comfortable with this deviation.

7.7 Summary

Nexus Mutual, an Ethereum blockchain decentralized insurance/reinsurance protocol was used as a market design case study. This chapter explained the legal and regulatory drivers of its ownership model, its economic agent typology, and its transactional pathways involving its native tokens.

It was shown through examples how the salient influencing factors (thickness, congestion, safety, usability, social norms) expounded in the previous chapter are in evidence in the Nexus Mutual Market design.

In summary, it was demonstrated how the first pillar of the proposed token ecosystem design framework aligns with industry market practices; thus, how it can be used as both an analysis and a design tool for blockchain-based token ecosystems.

References

1. [Nexus Mutual Token ecosystem]. https://nexusmutual.io/
2. *Top Insurance Tokens by Market Capitalization*. CoinMarketCap. Retrieved March 22, 2025, from https://coinmarketcap.com/view/insurance/
3. Ganado Advocates. (2023, April 11). The principle of insurable interest. Insights [by Ganado Advocates]. Retrieved March 22, 2025, from https://ganado.com/insights/publications/the-principle-of-insurable-interest/
4. E.g.Arnold-Dwyer, F. (2020). *Insurable interest and the law* (1st ed.). Routledge.
5. Ishmael, S. -M. (2010, March 9). *Repeat after me: CDS are not insurance. Financial Times* Retrieved March 22, 2025, from https://www.ft.com/content/09aa387d-fe2d-397f-b22c-2a5387ab9a21
6. Howard, P. (2025, February 28). Life insurance*:* What it is, how it works, and how to buy a policy. Retrieved March 22, 2025, from https://www.investopedia.com/terms/l/lifeinsurance.asp
7. Kagan, J. (2024, September 20). Health insurance*:* Definition, how it works. Retrieved March 22, 2025, from https://www.investopedia.com/terms/h/healthinsurance.asp
8. Twin, A. (2024, July 18). Property insurance*:* Definition and how coverage works. Retrieved March 22, 2025, from https://www.investopedia.com/terms/p/property-insurance.asp
9. Kagan, J. (2023, August 7). Casualty insurance*:* Definition, types, and examples. Retrieved March 22, 2025, from https://www.investopedia.com/terms/c/casualtyinsurance.asp
10. Rotar, V. I. (2014). *Actuarial models: The mathematics of insurance* (2nd ed.). Chapman and Hall/CRC.
11. Tse, Y.-K. (2023). *Nonlife actuarial models: Theory, methods and evaluation* (2nd ed.). Springer.
12. European Commission. (2015, January 12). *Solvency II overview—Frequently asked questions*. Retrieved March 22, 2025, from https://ec.europa.eu/commission/presscorner/detail/fr/MEMO_15_3120

13. *Directive* 2009*/138/EC of the European Parliament and of the Council of 25 November 2009 on the taking-up and pursuit of the business of Insurance and Reinsurance (Solvency II) (recast)*. Retrieved March 22, 2025, from https://eur-lex.europa.eu/legal-content/EN/TXT/?uri=celex%3A32009L0138. Please note that "Annex I" of said Directive contains a typology of Non-Life Insurance.
14. *Commission Delegated Regulation (EU) 2015/35 of 10 October* 2014 *supplementing Directive 2009/138/EC of the European Parliament and of the Council on the taking-up and pursuit of the business of Insurance and Reinsurance (Solvency II)*. Retrieved March 22, 2025, from https://eur-lex.europa.eu/legal-content/EN/TXT/?uri=CELEX%3A02015R0035-20220802
15. Dieckhoff, L. (2015, December 10). *Understanding the Solvency II balance sheet*. European insurance and occupational pensions authority [EIOPA] presentation. Retrieved March 22, 2025, from https://register.eiopa.europa.eu/Publications/Speeches%20and%20presentations/Presentation%201%20SII%20Balance%20Sheet.pdf
16. Solvency II Glossary. Lloyd's regulatory information pages. Retrieved March 22, 2025, from https://www.lloyds.com/conducting-business/regulatory-information/solvency-ii/tools-and-resources/glossary
17. Holland, D. (2012, September 21). Reinsurance*: A brief history*. The Actuary. Retrieved March 22, 2025, from https://www.theactuary.com/archive/old-articles/part-3/2012/09/21/reinsurance-brief-history
18. (2017, August 14). *Utmost good faith: Follow the fortunes, the theory and the reality: What are the implications for cedents and for reinsurers?* FindLaw. Retrieved March 22, 2025, from https://corporate.findlaw.com/corporate-governance/utmost-good-faith-follow-the-fortunes-the-theory-and-the.html
19. Kenton, W. (2025, March 4). Moral Hazard: Meaning, examples, and how to manage. Retrieved March 22, 2205, from https://www.investopedia.com/terms/m/moralhazard.asp
20. Blessing, E. (2022, April 22). Finite reinsurance*:* What it is, how it works, pros and cons. Retrieved March 22, 2025, from https://www.investopedia.com/terms/f/finitereinsurance.asp
21. Parametric insurance. (2024, November 19). In Wikipedia. Retrieved March 22, 2025, from https://en.wikipedia.org/wiki/Parametric_insurance
22. *Our market. What is Lloyd's?* Lloyd's public pages. Retrieved March 22, 2025, from https://www.lloyds.com/about-lloyds/what-is-lloyds
23. *The Lloyd's Corporation. An independent guardian*. Lloyd's public pages. Retrieved March 23, 2025, from https://www.lloyds.com/about-lloyds/what-is-lloyds/corporation-of-lloyds
24. *What Lloyd's insures*. Lloyd's public pages. Retrieved March 23, 2025, from https://www.lloyds.com/about-lloyds/what-we-insure
25. Timeline of significant events at Lloyd's. (2025, March 20). In *Wikipedia*. Retrieved March 23, 2025, from https://en.wikipedia.org/wiki/Lloyd%27s_of_London#Timeline_of_significant_events_at_Lloyd's
26. [U.K.] Lloyd's Acts. The Lloyd's acts which are currently in force. Lloyd's public pages. Retrieved March 23, 2025, from https://www.lloyds.com/conducting-business/market-oversight/acts-and-byelaws/lloyds-acts
27. *List of U.K.Primary and Secondary Legislation (regulations) relating specifically to Lloyd's of London*. UK Parliament. Retrieved March 23, 2025, from https://www.legislation.gov.uk/primary+secondary?title=Lloyd's
28. *Prudential regulation*. Bank of England public pages. Retrieved March 23, 2025, from https://www.bankofengland.co.uk/prudential-regulation
29. *[U.K.] Financial Conduct Authority (FCA)*. FCA public pages. Retrieved March 20, 2025, from https://www.fca.org.uk/
30. *Placing risk. The diversity of our market sets Lloyd's apart*. Lloyd's public pages. Retrieved March 23, 2025, from https://www.lloyds.com/en-co/lloyds-around-the-world/how-to-place-a-risk
31. *Conducting business*. Lloyd's public pages. Retrieved March 23, 2025, from https://www.lloyds.com/conducting-business

32. *Market oversight.* Lloyd's public pages. Retrieved March 23, 2025, from https://www.lloyds.com/conducting-business/market-oversight
33. Lloyd's Byelaws. The Byelaws which are currently in force. Lloyd's public pages. Retrieved March 23, 2025, from https://www.lloyds.com/conducting-business/market-oversight/acts-and-byelaws/lloyds-byelaws
34. *Regulatory information including regulatory communications and solvency II.* Lloyd's public pages. Retrieved March 23, 2025, from https://www.lloyds.com/conducting-business/regulatory-information
35. *Capital structure.* Lloyd's public pages. Retrieved March 23, 2025, from https://www.lloyds.com/about-lloyds/investor-relations/capital-structure
36. (2020, February 26). *Lloyd's ready to deliver first phase of transformation, with major investment in PPL and first risk exchange pilot.* Retrieved March 23, 2025, from https://placingplatformlimited.com/news/lloyds-ready-to-deliver-first-phase-of-transformation-with-major-investment-in-ppl-and-first-risk-exchange-pilot/
37. *The London market reimagined for a digital future.* Placing Platform Limited. Retrieved March 23, 2025, from https://placingplatformlimited.com/
38. *About us.* Placing Platform Limited. Retrieved March 23, 2025, from https://placingplatformlimited.com/about-us/
39. *Syndicate in a box.* Lloyd's public pages. Retrieved March 23, 2025, from https://www.lloyds.com/join-lloyds-market/underwriter/syndicate-in-a-box
40. [Syndicate in a box] *Participating options.* Lloyd's public pages. Retrieved March 23, 2025, from https://www.lloyds.com/join-lloyds-market/underwriter/compare-options
41. *Lloyd's governance structure.* Lloyd's public pages. Retrieved March 23, 2025, from https://www.lloyds.com/about-lloyds/the-corporation/governance-structure
42. *London Market Group.* Retrieved March 23, 2025, from https://lmg.london/the-lmg/#overview
43. *Mutual ownership models: A guide.* U.K. Government publication pages. Retrieved March 23, 2025, from https://www.gov.uk/government/publications/mutual-ownership-models-a-guide
44. [U.K.] Department for Business Innovation & Skills. (2011, November). A guide to mutual ownership models. U.K. Government publication pages. Retrieved March 23, 2025, from https://assets.publishing.service.gov.uk/government/uploads/system/uploads/attachment_data/file/31678/11-1401-guide-mutual-ownership-models.pdf
45. [U.K.] *Friendly Societies Act 1992.* U.K. legislation pages. Retrieved March 23, 2025, from https://www.legislation.gov.uk/ukpga/1992/40/contents
46. HM Revenue & Customs. (2023, October 6). [U.K.] *HMRC internal manual – General insurance manual. GIM9000 -Mutual insurance.* U.K. Government pages. Retrieved March 23, 2025, from https://www.gov.uk/hmrc-internal-manuals/general-insurance-manual/gim9000
47. HM Revenue & Customs. (2023, October 6). [U.K.] *HMRC internal manual – General insurance manual. GIM7360 -Equalisation reserves: The tax rules: Mutuals and partial mutuals.* U.K. Government pages. Retrieved March 23, 2025, from https://www.gov.uk/hmrc-internal-manuals/general-insurance-manual/gim7360
48. [U.K. FCA] *Mutual societies.* FCA public pages. Retrieved March 23, 2025, from https://www.fca.org.uk/firms/mutual-societies
49. [U.K.] FCA. (2023, February 24). Registered mutual society rules and obligations. FCA public pages. Retrieved March 23, 2025, from https://www.fca.org.uk/firms/becoming-mutual-society/registered-mutual-society-rules-and-obligations
50. [U.K. legistlation and concomitant FCA functions and activities relating to mutual societies]. FCA Handbook. Retrieved March 23, 2025, from https://www.handbook.fca.org.uk/handbook/EG/19/2.html

51. Municipal Mutual Insurance Ltd *v Hills (Inspector of Taxes)* [1932] UKHL TC_16_430 (15 March 1932). Judgment. Retrieved March 23, 2025, from https://www.bailii.org/uk/cases/UKHL/1932/TC_16_430.pdf
52. Walter Fletcher *on his own behalf and on behalf of Trustees and Committee of Doctor's Cave Bathing Club v The Commissioner for Income Tax (Jamaica)* [1971] UKPC 30 (6 October 1971). Judgment. Retrieved March 23, 2025, from https://www.bailii.org/uk/cases/UKPC/1971/1971_30.pdf
53. [U.K.] *Mutuals Public Register*. FCA public pages. Retrieved March 23, 2025, from https://mutuals.fca.org.uk/
54. [U.K.] *Association of Financial Mutuals*. Retrieved March 23, 2025, from https://www.financialmutuals.org/
55. Kagan, J. (2023, September 26). Mutual insurance company: Definition and how they invest. Retrieved March 23, 2025, from https://www.investopedia.com/terms/m/mutual-insurance-company.asp
56. [U.S.] *12 CFR § 380.11 – Treatment of mutual insurance holding companies*. Legal Information Institute. Cornell Law School. Retrieved March 23, 2025, from https://www.law.cornell.edu/cfr/text/12/380.11
57. *Amice* [European mutual/cooperative insurance sector industry body]. Retrieved March 23, 2025, from https://amice-eu.org/
58. [Record of] *Nexus Mutual Limited – Company number 10917763*. [U.K.] Companies House pages. Retrieved March 23, 2025, from https://find-and-update.company-information.service.gov.uk/company/10917763
59. [Nexus Mutual member] *KYC requirements*. Nexus Mutual documentation pages. Retrieved March 23, 2025, from https://docs.nexusmutual.io/overview/membership#kyc-requirements
60. [Nexus Mutual] membership agreement conditions. Nexus Mutual documentation pages. Retrieved March 23, 2025, from https://docs.nexusmutual.io/overview/membership#membership-agreement
61. *Cover Products*. Nexus Mutual documentation pages. Retrieved March 23, 2025, from https://docs.nexusmutual.io/overview/cover-products/
62. [Nexus Mutual member] *Welcome* [dApp page]. Nexus Mutual documentation pages. Retrieved March 23, 2025, from https://app.nexusmutual.io/membership
63. (2025, January 20). Ethereum Virtual Machine (EVM). Ethereum.org. Retrieved March 23, 2025, from https://ethereum.org/en/developers/docs/evm/
64. Smart contract. (2025, April 14). In *Wikipedia*. Retrieved April 17, 2025, from https://en.wikipedia.org/wiki/Smart_contract
65. *Protocol Cover Wording*. Nexus Mutual documentation pages. Retrieved April 17, 2025, from https://docs.nexusmutual.io/overview/cover-products/protocol-cover#protocol-cover-wording
66. Bundled Protocol Cover Wording. Nexus Mutual documentation pages. Retrieved April 17, 2025, from https://docs.nexusmutual.io/overview/cover-products/bundled-protocol-cover#bundled-protocol-cover-wording
67. DeFi Pass Cover Wording. Nexus Mutual documentation pages. Retrieved April 17, 2025, from https://docs.nexusmutual.io/overview/cover-products/defi-pass-cover/#defi-pass-cover-wording
68. Native Protocol Cover Wording. Nexus Mutual documentation pages. Retrieved April 17, 2025, from https://docs.nexusmutual.io/overview/cover-products/native-protocol-cover/#native-protocol-cover-wording
69. Fund Portfolio Cover Wording. Nexus Mutual documentation pages. Retrieved April 17, 2025, from https://docs.nexusmutual.io/overview/cover-products/fund-portfolio-cover/#fund-portfolio-cover-wording
70. ETH Slashing Cover Wording. Nexus Mutual documentation pages. Retrieved April 17, 2025, from https://docs.nexusmutual.io/overview/cover-products/eth-slashing-cover/#eth-slashing-cover-wording

71. *Top Insurance Coins by Market Cap*. Coingecko. Retrieved March 23, 2025, from https://www.coingecko.com/en/categories/insurance
72. [LUNOS Token ecosystem]. https://lunos.xyz/
73. *Web3 Coverage* [products] – *Simplified and secure*. Retrieved March 23, 2025, from https://lunos.xyz/#coverage
74. Lunos. (2023, August 17). Uno re partners with Nexus Mutual, propelling Uno WatchDog to unprecedented levels! Medium. Retrieved March 23, 2025, from https://medium.com/@LunosDAO/uno-re-partners-with-nexus-mutual-propelling-uno-watchdog-to-unprecedented-levels-eced2326fc01
75. [Sherlock Crypto Assurance company and marketplace]. https://www.sherlock.xyz/
76. *Intro to Sherlock*. Sherlock documentation pages. Retrieved March 23, 2025, from https://docs.sherlock.xyz/
77. Protocol Teams. Sherlock documentation pages. Retrieved March 23, 2025, from https://docs.sherlock.xyz/#protocols
78. Sandor, K. (2024, May 14). RWA platform re debuts tokenized reinsurance fund on avalanche with $15M commitment from Nexus Mutual. CoinDesk. Retrieved March 23, 2025, from https://www.coindesk.com/business/2024/05/14/rwa-platform-re-debuts-tokenized-reinsurance-fund-on-avalanche-with-15m-commitment-from-nexus-mutual
79. [Ensuro, regulated Blockchain-based (Re)insurer]. https://ensuro.co/
80. (2024, November 22). *Nexus Mutual and Ensuro partner to connect onchain capital with real-world risk*. Retrieved March 23, 2025, from https://nexusmutual.io/blog/nexus-mutual-and-ensuro-partner-to-connect-onchain-capital-with-real-world-risk
81. *Real World Risk* [protocol developments]. Nexus Mutual documentation pages. Retrieved March 23, 2025, from https://docs.nexusmutual.io/overview/cover-products/real-world-risk
82. [Protocol Cover] Nexus Mutual Protocol Cover Terms and Conditions (the "Cover Terms"). Retrieved April 17, 2025, from https://api.nexusmutual.io/ipfs/QmdunFJm4A5CUW1ynM7bevsGt6UzQfw6K4ysKqvsqpjWCQ, linked to from https://docs.nexusmutual.io/overview/cover-products/protocol-cover#protocol-cover-wording
83. [Bundled Protocol Cover] Nexus Mutual Protocol Cover Terms and Conditions (the "Cover Terms"). Retrieved April 17, 2025, from https://api.nexusmutual.io/ipfs/QmWV9woyKJirjHd73MhibV59qmqzp1w1gqfMfZBQhneSL8, linked to from https://docs.nexusmutual.io/overview/cover-products/protocol-cover#bundled-protocol-cover-wording
84. [ETH Slashing Protocol Cover] Nexus Mutual Protocol Cover Terms and Conditions (the "Cover Terms"). Retrieved April 17, 2025, from https://api.nexusmutual.io/ipfs/QmWepFbtMYSzJt22ddF1CK9PwbrYgiLk9qJjryDrgpGuus, linked to from https://docs.nexusmutual.io/overview/cover-products/eth-slashing-cover#cover-wording
85. [Sherlock Quota Share Cover] Nexus Mutual Protocol Cover Terms and Conditions (the "Cover Terms"). Retrieved April 17, 2025, from https://api.nexusmutual.io/ipfs/QmbQAsbisyGK6i1to4d85SqE2f2e98PsXHAuSzrprpsYe8, linked to from https://docs.nexusmutual.io/overview/cover-products/quota-share-cover#sherlock-quota-share-cover-wording
86. UnoRe Quota Share Cover terms (the "UnoRe Quota Share Terms"). Retrieved April 17, 2025, from https://api.nexusmutual.io/ipfs/QmWXYjBYjdKoRw6kyUvp5gYKjj2ojPPVxNYKr1gDjMLssY, linked to from https://docs.nexusmutual.io/overview/cover-products/quota-share-cover#sherlock-quota-share-cover-wording
87. [Protocol Cover] *Proof of Loss*. Nexus Mutual documentation pages. Retrieved April 17, 2025, from https://docs.nexusmutual.io/overview/cover-products/protocol-cover#proof-of-loss
88. [Protocol Cover] *Claim Filing Process*. Nexus Mutual documentation pages. Retrieved April 17, 2025, from https://docs.nexusmutual.io/overview/cover-products/protocol-cover/#claim-filing-process
89. [Nexus Mutual] DAO Member Agreement. Retrieved April 17, 2025, from https://uploads-ssl.webflow.com/62d8193ce9880895261daf4a/63d0f45aacb2752b543ddcaf_Nexus-Mutual-

DAO-Member-Agreement-FIN.pdf (linked to from https://docs.nexusmutual.io/overview/membership#membership-agreement).
90. Decentralized autonomous organization. (2025, April 5). In *Wikipedia*. Retrieved April 09, 2025, from https://en.wikipedia.org/wiki/Decentralized_autonomous_organization
91. Hertig, A. (2023, January 17). What is a DAO? Coindesk. Retrieved March 23, 2025, from https://www.coindesk.com/learn/what-is-a-dao/
92. File No. SF0068. Enrolled Act No. 16, *Senate*. U.S. State of Wyoming. Retrieved March 23, 2025, from https://wyoleg.gov/2022/Enroll/SF0068.pdf
93. *Title 11: Corporations, Partnerships and Associations. Chapter 025: Limited Liability Companies. Subchapter 012: Blockchain-Based Limited Liability Companies*. [U.S. State of] Vermont statutes online. Retrieved March 23, 2025, from https://legislature.vermont.gov/statutes/section/11/025/04173
94. Kurtin PLLC (2022). Wyoming's digital assets law and how to use it. https://kurtinlaw.com/wp-content/uploads/2022/09/Wyoming-Digital-Assets-Laws-01.2022.pdf
95. *Decentralized Autonomous Organization (DAO): Frequently asked questions*. Business Division. Wyoming Secretary of State. U.S. State of Wyoming. Retrieved April 17, 2025, from https://sos.wyo.gov/Business/Docs/DAOs_FAQs.pdf
96. Mienert, B. (2021). How can a decentralized autonomous organization (DAO) be legally structured? *E-Journal for Business Law & Digitalization LRZ, 2021*, 336–367. Retrieved March 23, 2025, from https://lrz.legal/en/the-lrz/how-can-a-decentralized-autonomous-organization-dao-be-legally-structured
97. Jennings, M., & Kerr, D. (2022, June). *A legal framework for decentralized autonomous organizations*. Written for "Andreesen Worowitz" (https://a16z.com/), a venture capital firm. Retrieved March 23, 2025, from https://a16zcrypto.com/wp-content/uploads/2022/06/dao-legal-framework-part-1.pdf
98. Jennings, M., & Kerr D. (2022, June). *A legal framework for decentralized autonomous organizations; Part II: Entity selection framework*. Written for "Andreesen Worowitz" (https://a16z.com/), a venture capital firm. Retrieved March 23, 2025, from https://a16zcrypto.com/wp-content/uploads/2022/06/dao-legal-framework-part-2.pdf
99. Riva, S. (2019, October). Decentralized Autonomous Organizations (DAOs) as subjects of law; the recognition of DAOs in the Swiss legal order. Master's Thesis. Université de Neuchâtel, Switzerland. Retrieved March 23, 2025, from https://libra.unine.ch/entities/publication/ff50adfa-70b9-40ec-b1b7-72e29cc7d1ff/details
100. (2025, April 16). *The ENS Foundation*. Retrieved April 17, 2025, from https://docs.ens.domains/v/governance/the-ens-foundation
101. Andersen, D. (2023, May 16). Bancor DAO hit with class-action suit over impermanent loss protection promises. CoinTelegraph. Retrieved March 23, 2025, from https://cointelegraph.com/news/bancor-dao-hit-with-class-action-suit-over-impermanent-loss-protection-promises
102. *The Foundation*. Nexus Mutual documentation pages. Retrieved March 23, 2025, from https://docs.nexusmutual.io/overview/#the-foundation
103. Office of the [U.K.] Regulator of Community Interest Companies. (2012, September 1). *Guidance – Community interest companies: Forms and step-by-step guides*. Retrieved March 23, 2025, from https://www.gov.uk/government/publications/community-interest-companies-business-activities
104. Office of the [U.K.] Regulator of Community Interest Companies. *About us*. Retrieved March 23, 2025, from https://www.gov.uk/government/organisations/office-of-the-regulator-of-community-interest-companies/about
105. (2020, April). *Foundation Funding*. Nexus Mutual governance discussion pages. Retrieved March 23, 2025, from https://forum.nexusmutual.io/t/foundation-funding/36
106. [Record of] *Collective Risk Services CIC – Company number 11353187*. [U.K.] Companies House pages. Retrieved March 23, 2025, from https://find-and-update.company-information.service.gov.uk/company/11353187

107. *Nexus Mutual Limited (A company limited by guarantee). Unaudited Financial Statements for the financial year ended 31* August 2024. *Pages for filing with the registrar.* Retrieved March 23, 2025, from https://find-and-update.company-information.service.gov.uk/company/10917763/filing-history/MzQyNDA0Nzc5MWFkaXF6a2N4/document?format=pdf&download=0
108. [Officers of] *Nexus Mutual Limited – Company number 10917763.* [U.K.] Companies House pages. Retrieved March 23, 2025, from https://find-and-update.company-information.service.gov.uk/company/10917763/officers
109. [Officers of] *Collective Risk Services CIC – Company number 11353187.* [U.K.] Companies House pages. Retrieved March 23, 2025, from https://find-and-update.company-information.service.gov.uk/company/11353187/officers
110. *Company number 10917763. Private Company Limited by Guarantee. Special Resolution of Nexus Mutual Limited (the "Company"). February 21, 2022.* Retrieved, March 23, 2025, from https://find-and-update.company-information.service.gov.uk/company/10917763/filing-history/QUFaMVdLNUVhZGlxemtjeA/document?format=pdf&download=0
111. *In re: FTX TRADING LTD., et al., Debtors. Transfer of Claim other than for security.* U.S. Bankruptcy Court for the District of Delaware. Chapter 11 Case No. 22–11068 (JTD) (Jointly Administered). Doc 4481 (Filed 12/05/23). Retrieved May 19, 2025, from https://restructuring.ra.kroll.com/FTX/ExternalCall-DownloadPDF?id1=MjYwNTM2NQ==&id2=0&cid=0
112. [Nexus Mutual Whitepaper v.2.3] Karp, H. & Melbardis, R. Nexus Mutual. A peer-to-peer discretionary mutual on the Ethereum blockchain. Retrieved April 17, 2025, from https://uploads-ssl.webflow.com/62d8193ce9880895261daf4a/641444d29741e43db9b43394_nmx_white_paperv2_3.pdf
113. [Nexus Mutual Whitepaper, v. of 2018] Karp, H. & Melbardis, R. Nexus Mutual. A peer-to-peer discretionary mutual on the Ethereum blockchain. Retrieved April 17, 2025, from https://docs.nexusmutual.io/assets/files/nexus-mutual-whitepaper-2018-e8ff99ed739190b0309cc46dd32884a1.pdf
114. Karp, H. (2018, June 14). DAO governance: A pragmatic approach. Medium. Retrieved March 23, 2025, from https://medium.com/nexus-mutual/dao-governance-a-pragmatic-approach-27d529ad0819
115. [Governance] Advisory Board. Nexus Mutual documentation pages. Retrieved March 23, 2025, from https://docs.nexusmutual.io/governance/#advisory-board
116. NXM Token. Nexus Mutual documentation pages. Retrieved March 23, 2025, from https://docs.nexusmutual.io/protocol/nxm-token/
117. *CoinMarketCap wNXM page.* CoinMarketCap. Retrieved April 4, 2025, from https://coinmarketcap.com/currencies/wrapped-nxm/
118. *Staking pool managers.* Nexus Mutual documentation pages. Retrieved March 23, 2025, from https://docs.nexusmutual.io/protocol/staking/staking-pools#staking-pool-managers
119. [Staking pool] *Management fee.* Nexus Mutual documentation pages. Retrieved March 23, 2025, from https://docs.nexusmutual.io/protocol/staking/staking-pools#management-fee
120. [Staking pool] *rewards.* Nexus Mutual documentation pages. Retrieved March 23, 2025, from https://docs.nexusmutual.io/protocol/staking/staking-pools#rewards
121. Staking NXM. Nexus Mutual documentation pages. Retrieved March 23, 2025, from https://docs.nexusmutual.io/protocol/staking/#staking-nxm
122. [Staking] *Rewards.* Nexus Mutual documentation pages. Retrieved March 23, 2025, from https://docs.nexusmutual.io/protocol/staking/#rewards
123. *Risk of NXM burns.* Nexus Mutual documentation pages. Retrieved March 23, 2025, from https://docs.nexusmutual.io/protocol/staking/#risk-of-nxm-burns
124. *[Nexus Mutual]* Cover Products. Nexus Mutual documentation pages. Retrieved March 23, 2025, from https://docs.nexusmutual.io/overview/cover-products/
125. Claim Assessment. Nexus Mutual documentation pages. Retrieved March 23, 2025, from https://docs.nexusmutual.io/protocol/claims-assessment

126. *Claim assessment rewards*. Nexus Mutual documentation pages. Retrieved March 23, 2025, from https://docs.nexusmutual.io/protocol/claims-assessment#4-claim-assessment-rewards
127. [Claim outcome] *Voting process*. Nexus Mutual documentation pages. Retrieved March 23, 2025, from https://docs.nexusmutual.io/protocol/claims-assessment#2-voting-process
128. [Nexus Mutual] *Integrations* [into 3rd party dApps]. Nexus Mutual documentation pages. Retrieved March 23, 2025, from https://docs.nexusmutual.io/protocol/integrations
129. [Nexus Mutual dApp]. https://app.nexusmutual.io
130. [Nexus Mutual integration into 3rd party dApps] *Commission*. Nexus Mutual documentation pages. Retrieved March 23, 2025, from https://docs.nexusmutual.io/protocol/integrations#commission
131. (2021, December). *Operation Wartortle* [transition to a stateless DAO structure] *next steps: Draft execution proposal*. Nexus Mutual governance discussion pages. Retrieved March 23, 2025, from https://forum.nexusmutual.io/t/operation-wartortle-next-steps-draft-execution-proposal/746
132. [Filing history of] *Nexus Mutual Limited – Company number 10917763*. [U.K.] Companies House pages. Retrieved March 23, 2025, from https://find-and-update.company-information.service.gov.uk/company/10917763/filing-history
133. [Nexus Mutual] *DAO treasury*. Nexus Mutual documentation pages. Retrieved March 23, 2025, from https://docs.nexusmutual.io/governance/dao#dao-treasury
134. *Community team*. Nexus Mutual documentation pages. Retrieved March 23, 2025, from https://docs.nexusmutual.io/governance/dao/#community-team
135. *Marketing team*. Nexus Mutual documentation pages. Retrieved March 23, 2025, from https://docs.nexusmutual.io/governance/dao#marketing-team
136. [Protocol Assets] *Investment Committe*.Nexus Mutual documentation pages. Retrieved March 23, 2025, from https://docs.nexusmutual.io/governance/dao#investment-committee
137. *Operations team*. Nexus Mutual documentation pages. Retrieved March 23, 2025, from https://docs.nexusmutual.io/governance/dao#operations-team
138. *R&D team*. Nexus Mutual documentation pages. Retrieved March 23, 2025, from https://docs.nexusmutual.io/governance/dao#rd-team
139. Nexus Mutual DAO *Treasury* [votes on proposals]. Nexus Mutual Snapshot page. Retrieved March 23, 2025, from https://snapshot.org/#/community.nexusmutual.eth
140. DAO governance power. Nexus Mutual documentation pages. Retrieved March 23, 2025, from https://docs.nexusmutual.io/governance/#dao-governance-power
141. *Pricing* [of products in Staking pools]. Nexus Mutual documentation pages. Retrieved March 23, 2025, from https://docs.nexusmutual.io/protocol/pricing
142. *Fraudulent votes*. Nexus Mutual documentation pages. Retrieved March 23, 2025, from https://docs.nexusmutual.io/protocol/claims-assessment#fraudulent-votes
143. [Capital Pool] *Investments*. Nexus Mutual documentation pages. Retrieved March 23, 2025, from https://docs.nexusmutual.io/protocol/capital-pool/investments
144. [Nexus Mutual Capital Pool and ownership allocation]. Retrieved March 23, 2025, from https://dune.com/nexus_mutual/capital-pool-and-ownership
145. Banton, C. (2024, July 31). Asset/Liability Management: Definition, meaning, and strategies. Retrieved March 23, 2025, from https://www.investopedia.com/terms/a/asset-liabilitymanagement.asp
146. Kagan, J. (2023, September 29). Policyholder Surplus: What it is, How it Works. Retrieved March 23, 2025, from https://www.investopedia.com/terms/p/policyholder-surplus.asp
147. [Nexus Mutual DAO] Capital Pool. Nexus Mutual documentation pages. Retrieved March 23, 2025, from https://docs.nexusmutual.io/protocol/capital-pool/
148. CoinMarketCap DAI [rebranded to USDS] *page*. Retrieved March 23, 2025, from https://coinmarketcap.com/currencies/multi-collateral-dai/
149. [Nexus Mutual] DAO treasury address. Nexus Mutual documentation pages. Retrieved March 23, 2025, from https://docs.nexusmutual.io/governance/dao/#dao-treasury-address

150. [Nexus Mutual] DAO treasury asset composition. Nexus Mutual documentation pages. Retrieved March 23, 2025, from https://app.safe.global/balances?safe=eth:0x586b9b2F8010b284A0197f392156f1A7Eb5e86e9
151. [Insurance] *Cover.* Nexus Mutual documentation pages. Retrieved March 23, 2025, from https://docs.nexusmutual.io/protocol/cover
152. [Nexus Mutual] Staking pools. Nexus Mutual documentation pages. Retrieved March 23, 2025, from https://docs.nexusmutual.io/protocol/staking/staking-pools
153. [Nexus Mutual] Minimum Capital Requirement. Nexus Mutual documentation pages. Retrieved March 23, 2025, from https://docs.nexusmutual.io/protocol/capital-pool/mcr
154. *History of Capitalisation Controls* [of Nexus Mutual]. Nexus Mutual documentation pages. Retrieved March 23, 2025, from https://docs.nexusmutual.io/protocol/nxm-token/history-capitalisation-controls
155. *f (Cover Amount).* Nexus Mutual documentation pages. Retrieved March 23, 2025, from https://docs.nexusmutual.io/protocol/nxm-token/history-capitalisation-controls/#fcover-amount
156. Wrapped NXM and the NXM Wrapper. Nexus Mutual DAO pages. Retrieved March 23, 2025, from https://nexusmutualdao.io/wrapped-nxm
157. "*NXM – Unwrap WNXM to NXM, or wrap NXM to WNXM*" functionality in the Nexus Mutual dApp. Retrieved March 23, 2025, from https://app.nexusmutual.io/nxm/unwrap
158. [Nexus Mutual] Token Model. Nexus Mutual documentation pages. Retrieved March 23, 2025, from https://docs.nexusmutual.io/protocol/nxm-token/token-model
159. [Ratchetting Automated Market Maker Whitepaper] Melbardis, R., Prisacaru, A. & Milidrag, M. *The Ratchetting AMM ("RAMM") for Nexus Mutual [V1.0].* Retrieved March 23, 2025, from https://docs.nexusmutual.io/assets/files/nexus-mutual-ramm-whitepaper-v1-2023-80163504ce80b4c5342f4ee0a073656e.pdf, linked to from https://docs.nexusmutual.io/protocol/nxm-token/token-model#the-ratcheting-amm-whitepaper
160. "*NXM – Contribute ETH to mint NXM tokens, or redeem NXM tokens for ETH*" functionality in the Nexus Mutual dApp. Retrieved March 23, 2025, from https://app.nexusmutual.io/nxm
161. [NXM Tokens] *Redemption and purchase restrictions.* Nexus Mutual documentation pages. Retrieved March 23, 2025, from https://docs.nexusmutual.io/protocol/nxm-token/history-capitalisation-controls#redemption-and-purchase-restrictions
162. [Nexus Mutual Staking pool Smart Contract code] Nexus Mutual GitHub directory. Retrieved March 23, 2025, from https://github.com/NexusMutual/smart-contracts/blob/release-candidate/contracts/modules/staking/StakingPool.sol
163. [NXM Staking functionality in the Nexus Mutual dApp]. https://app.nexusmutual.io/staking
164. *Product weight* [as leverage indicator] Nexus Mutual documentation pages. Retrieved March 23, 2025, from https://docs.nexusmutual.io/protocol/staking/staking-pools#product-weight
165. *Product* [target] *pricing.* Nexus Mutual documentation pages. Retrieved March 23, 2025, from https://docs.nexusmutual.io/protocol/staking/staking-pools#product-pricing
166. [Product] *Pricing* [model] Nexus Mutual documentation pages. Retrieved March 23, 2025, from https://docs.nexusmutual.io/protocol/pricing
167. *Staking periods.* Nexus Mutual documentation pages. Retrieved March 23, 2025, from https://docs.nexusmutual.io/protocol/staking/#staking-periods
168. *Risk of NXM burns* [as a result of claim payouts]. Nexus Mutual documentation pages. Retrieved March 23, 2025, from https://docs.nexusmutual.io/protocol/staking/#risk-of-nxm-burns
169. *Tokenized staking positions.* Nexus Mutual documentation pages. Retrieved March 23, 2025, from https://docs.nexusmutual.io/protocol/staking/#tokenized-staking-positions
170. [Nexus Mutual Capital Pool Smart Contract code] Nexus Mutual GitHub directory. Retrieved March 23, 2025, from https://github.com/NexusMutual/smart-contracts/blob/release-candidate/contracts/modules/capital/Pool.sol
171. ["Buy cover" functionality in the Nexus Mutual dApp]. https://v2.nexusmutual.io/cover/buy-cover

172. [Types of] *Tokenized Cover* [sold in Nexus Mutual] Nexus Mutual documentation pages. Retrieved March 23, 2025, from https://docs.nexusmutual.io/protocol/cover#tokenized-cover
173. *Individual rewards* [for claim assessors] Nexus Mutual documentation pages. Retrieved March 23, 2025, from https://docs.nexusmutual.io/protocol/claims-assessment#individual-rewards
174. [Nexus Mutual Token Controller Smart Contract code] Nexus Mutual GitHub directory. Retrieved March 23, 2025, from https://github.com/NexusMutual/smart-contracts/blob/release-candidate/contracts/modules/token/TokenController.sol
175. *Claim submission* [process steps in Nexus Mutual] Nexus Mutual documentation pages. Retrieved March 23, 2025, from https://docs.nexusmutual.io/protocol/claims-assessment#1-claim-submission
176. [Active claim assessments overview in Nexus Mutual dApp]. https://app.nexusmutual.io/claims/assessments
177. ["NXM Staking for assessments" functionality in Nexus Mutual dApp]. https://app.nexusmutual.io/claims/stake
178. *Protocol governance power* [(weighting of individual NXM holdings for governance votings)] Nexus Mutual documentation pages. Retrieved March 23, 2025, from https://docs.nexusmutual.io/governance/#protocol-governance-power
179. [Snapshot voting management platform]. https://snapshot.org
180. *Governance proposals* [policy and processes in Nexus Mutual] Nexus Mutual documentation pages. Retrieved March 23, 2025, from https://docs.nexusmutual.io/governance/#governance-proposals
181. *Voting incentives* [for NXM holders] Nexus Mutual documentation pages. Retrieved March 23, 2025, from https://docs.nexusmutual.io/governance/#voting-incentives
182. [Yearn Token ecosystem]. https://yearn.fi
183. (2021, June). *Nexus Mutual Yearn Vaulg by Vault Coverage*. Yearn governance discussion pages. Retrieved March 23, 2025, from https://gov.yearn.fi/t/nexus-mutual-yearn-vault-by-vault-coverage/10911
184. [Bright Union Insurance Aggregator ecosystem]. https://brightunion.io/
185. Petrie, K. (2021, March 22). Our community grants is live! Medium. Retrieved March 23, 2025, from https://medium.com/nexus-mutual/our-community-grants-programme-is-live-cd4b10451405
186. Karp, H. (2021, July 9). Yield Token Cover: Nexus Mutual's DeFi protection for money Legos. Medium. Retrieved March 23, 2025, from https://medium.com/nexus-mutual/yield-token-cover-nexus-mutuals-defi-protection-for-money-legos-6a92dd8162fd
187. (2023, August 8). *Nexus mutual expands cover capacity in the UK with on-chain capital.* Retrieved March 23, 2025, from https://nexusmutual.io/blog/nexus-mutual-expands-cover-capacity-in-the-uk-with-on-chain-capital
188. (2024, March 29). *Proof-of-Work (PoW).* Ethereum.org. Retrieved March 23, 2025 from https://ethereum.org/en/developers/docs/consensus-mechanisms/pow/
189. (2024, September 3). *Proof-of-Stake (PoS).* Ethereum.org. Retrieved March 23, 2025 from https://ethereum.org/en/developers/docs/consensus-mechanisms/pos/
190. *Bundled Protocol Cover*. Nexus Mutual documentation pages. Retrieved March 23, 2025, from https://docs.nexusmutual.io/overview/cover-products/bundled-protocol-cover
191. *Governance record for proposal "223. Add USDC as an asset within the Capital Pool"*. Nexus Mutual governance discussion pages. Retrieved March 23, 2025, from https://app.nexusmutual.io/governance/view?proposalId=223
192. [Indirectly] *Selling cover to non-members* [of Nexus Mutual DAO]. Nexus Mutual documentation pages. Retrieved March 23, 2025, from https://docs.nexusmutual.io/protocol/integrations/#selling-cover-to-non-members
193. ["Buy cover" functionality in Nexus Mutual dApp]. https://app.nexusmutual.io/cover
194. ["Swap NXM" functionality in Nexus Mutual dApp]. https://app.nexusmutual.io/nxm
195. ["Claims" functionality in Nexus Mutual dApp]. https://app.nexusmutual.io/claims

196. Token Model. Nexus Mutual documentation pages. Retrieved March 23, 2025, from https://docs.nexusmutual.io/protocol/nxm-token/token-model/
197. (2022, October 7). *Nexus Mutual Privacy Policy*. Retrieved March 23, 2025, from https://nexusmutual.io/pages/Privacy-Policy.pdf
198. Immunefi. (2022, April 12). Nexus Mutual community renews bounty matching program with $600k war chest. Medium. Retrieved March 23, 2025, from https://medium.com/immunefi/nexus-mutual-community-renews-bounty-matching-program-with-600k-war-chest-1f4f4a5751d2
199. (2021, September 16). Bug bounty matching program with Immunefi. Medium. Retrieved March 23, 2025, from https://medium.com/nexus-mutual/bug-bounty-matching-program-with-immunefi-b8933d129a
200. [Immunefi page relating to] Nexus Mutual. Immunefi. Retrieved March 23, 2025, from https://immunefi.com/bug-bounty/nexusmutual/information/
201. White hat (computer security). (2025, April 16). In *Wikipedia*. Retrieved April 17, 2025, from https://en.wikipedia.org/wiki/White_hat_(computer_security)
202. *Getting Started* [with Nexus Mutual DAO] Nexus Mutual documentation pages. Retrieved March 23, 2025, from https://docs.nexusmutual.io
203. [Nexus Mutual project root directory on GitHub]. https://github.com/NexusMutual
204. [Nexus Mutual DAO] *Membership* [aspects]. Nexus Mutual documentation pages. Retrieved March 23, 2025, from https://docs.nexusmutual.io/overview/membership
205. [Nexus Mutual] *DAO Member Agreement*. Retrieved March 23, 2025, from https://nexusmutual.io/pages/Nexus-Mutual-DAO-Member-Agreement-FIN.pdf
206. International Cooperative and Mutual Insurance Federation (2020). *A practical guide to understanding mutual insurance*. Retrieved March 23, 2025, from https://www.icmif.org/wp-content/uploads/2020/07/Guide_Mutual-insurance_Icmif.pdf
207. *ISC § 4210: Election of directors of domestic mutual life insurance companies*. New York Consolidated Laws, Insurance Law. Retrieved March 23, 2025, from https://codes.findlaw.com/ny/insurance-law/isc-sect-4210/

Mechanism Design

8

We refer again to the analogy that was introduced in Chap. 6, namely of designing the economics of a token-based ecosystem being akin to designing the economics of a new country. The token-based economic design framework followed in this book consists of three main pillars: market design defines the typology of economic agents active in the country and the possible ways for said agents to interact with each other; mechanism design prescribes the rules and incentives/disincentives of economic agent interactions; and token design describes the functioning of the country's currency and stores of value.

In this chapter we will expand on notions of the second pillar: mechanism design.

8.1 Introduction to Mechanism Design

Having specified the economic agents (including governance ones) and their interaction pathways, a designer is now confronted with the fundamental question: how can the ecosystem achieve its expected economic outcomes, even in the presence of uncertainty?

Where does such uncertainty originate? First of all, from non-deterministic variations in inputs, either due to the actions of other agents or due to changes of conditions exogenous to, but influencing the workings of, the ecosystem. Second and most important, from the obvious fact that economic agents may represent human principals, each with their own interests, priorities and preferences. Hence, it can never be guaranteed that an agent's action will be as would be considered most probable (or even rational) in the circumstances of a given interaction. In short, the aggregate ecosystem response to all probable input and agent actions is, in all generality, non-deterministic. Should the ecosystem prove to be *stable*, then it can at best be expected to have *probable outcomes* within finite ranges of variability around them.

It now becomes the task for the designer to somehow "steer" the ecosystem towards *stability*, i.e. so that it stays within preferred outcome ranges, without

I. Giannakouros, *Cryptocurrencies and Tradable Crypto-Tokens*, Future of Business and Finance, https://doi.org/10.1007/978-3-031-98423-5_8

exhibiting unforeseen and uncontrollable behaviour. This task is the objective of the discipline of mechanism design [1–4].

Mechanism design generally involves carrying out both analytical and prescriptive steps. The former kind are meant to codify the phenomenology of non-deterministic variations in the state of an economic system (e.g. of information content, of agent actions, etc.). For example, mapping out behavioural responses of agents to random inputs can involve a particular mathematical methodology, namely Game Theory [5–9]. However, it can be simplified by postulating a reduced set of probable inputs, thus generating a correspondingly reduced set of deterministic outputs and in the process obviating the need for through-and-through probabilistic modelling. The latter (prescriptive) kind generally involves the creation of parametrized processes (called "Mechanisms") restricting or rewarding specific agent behaviours at specific points along their interactions. Restrictive mechanisms are "Rules", whereas rewarding ones are "Incentives". Both have the intended objective to "coax" preferred responses at the level of a single interaction, with the expectation (or having already calculated) that each one of said responses leads to a preferred economic outcome for the whole ecosystem.

Mechanism design drives the expected behaviours along agent interactions. For example, for specific constellations of economic agents it will describe which transactions are allowed among them, under which conditions, involving the exchange of which kinds of assets or services, and entailing which kinds of fees (taxes, platform fees) payable to whom (to other transaction participants, to the market itself, or to platform governance agents). Said rules can be made [10] to be valid only if also documented in human-readable form (codes of obligations, voting mechanisms, consensus specifications, etc.) or simply by being embedded in source code (e.g. in smart contracts[1]). Note that transactions with monetary outcomes are only one kind of possible interactions among economic agents. Thus, mechanism design will cover interaction pathways in general.

One differentiating factor of blockchain-based ecosystems *vis-à-vis* other economic coordination paradigms (e.g. traditional physical human ecosystems) is that, in the former, policies and procedures regulating interactions can be codified and enforced exclusively through technology. For example, a policy can be interpreted as being a workflow specification, whereby economic agents must take well-defined logical steps with expected outcomes. These logical steps can be then translated into algorithmic steps to be programmed to execute automatically on the same foundational technical infrastructure (i.e. software platform) built around the blockchain. All generations of a particular policy will thus be clear through the corresponding versioned software code and its human-readable documentation. This affords complete visibility on what exactly a policy is, how it was progressed, how it was calibrated and how it is currently implemented. In this paradigm there are no

[1]Explained in Sect. 10.5.5.

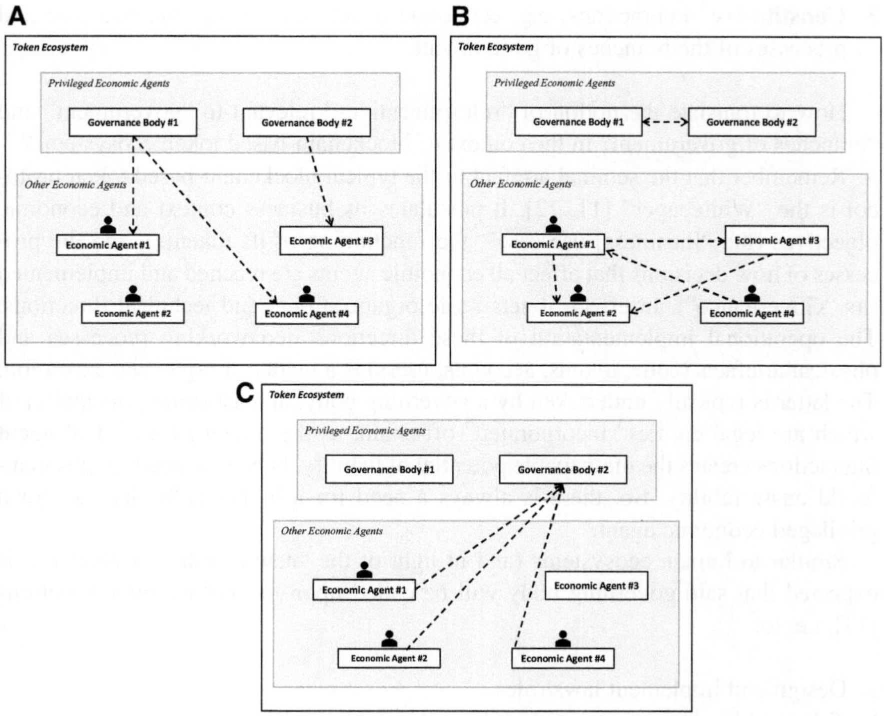

Fig. 8.1 Interaction levels in Mechanism design

unwritten rules, no hidden policies[2], no unclear calibration or lax execution (symptoms typical of physical human ecosystems, such as associations, marketplaces or even entire countries).

For the generic token-based ecosystem, there are three levels of interaction which we will need to consider, namely (cf. Fig. 8.1):

1. **Hierarchical**[3] interactions, e.g. governance bodies representing branches of ecosystem government interacting with other, non-governmental, economic agents.
2. **Horizontal** interactions, e.g. equally privileged economic agents interacting among themselves.

[2]However, due to information asymmetries in the run-up to policy formulation, there is still potential for hiding real *causes* of specific policy calibration decisions. It is up to the ecosystem governance to define appropriate mechanisms for vetting such decisions, so as to preclude exploitation by unscrupulous economic actors engaging in "policy arbitrage" for own benefit.

[3]In essence "**top-down**", denoting manifestation of a hierarchy—hence the term used.

3. **Constitutive**[4] interactions, e.g. economic agents influencing the structure and processes of the branches of government.

How to translate the notion of "rules/incentives" relevant to "government" and "branches of government" in the context of blockchain-based token ecosystems?

Remember that the seminal artefact of the typical blockchain-based token protocol is the "Whitepaper" [11, 12]. It postulates its business context and economic objectives (the "[business] use case", the functioning of its token(s), and the processes of how decisions that affect all economic agents are reached and implemented (its "Governance"). In effect, it sets basic organizational and technical directions. The operational implementation of these directions into working processes and physical artefacts (code, tokens, accounts, users) is a matter of organized execution. The latter is typically undertaken by a governing body, at least some principal(s) of which are legal entities[5] incorporated[6] off-chain, as the monetary aspect of agent interactions creates the inescapable potential of liability, hence the need for physical-world answerability. So, there is always a need for a higher authority, i.e. for a privileged economic agent.

Similar to human ecosystems (and in light of the "new country" analogy), it is expected that said governing body will be called upon to exercise three functions [13], i.e. to:

a. Design and implement laws/rules,
b. Take and implement operational decisions, and
c. Resolve disputes.

As in the chapter on market design, we propose that this notion of functions of government (legislative, executive, and judicial) carries over unaltered to the mechanism design of token ecosystems. The economic agents exercising said functions are the ecosystem's *de facto* "branches of government".

Actual examples of government functions from existing ecosystems:

- In MakerDAO [14], all MKR [15] token holders have the right to vote if the DAI [16] token savings rate [17] is to be updated, and at which new level to set it. Thus, they act collectively as a direct legislative body.
- In Bancor [18], only core developers acting on behalf of a particular non-profit organization ("Bprotocol Foundation" [19]) can update the main smart contract's parameters [20]. They single-handedly implement protocol policies [21], hence they are organs of the executive body.

[4]In essence "**bottom-up**", in order to influence the basic operating framework of Governance.

[5]To the best of this author's knowledge, there has not been any attempt to have a legal arrangement represented on-chain so far (cf. also the discussion on Trusts on the blockchain in Sect. 15.3).

[6]Typically as a Foundation, but also in any other legal form fitting the particulars of the business case as per Whitepaper.

– In Nexus Mutual [22], only NXM token stakers [23] are allowed to adjudicate on whether a particular insurance claim is valid or not [24]. Thus, they act as judiciary.

Not all ecosystems provide for all three functions of government. For example:

– Liquity [25] operates without an ongoing legislative function. The protocol hard-codes economic parameters into its smart contracts [26].
– Yearn Finance [27] does not have a judicial function. The protocol operates without a dispute resolution mechanism [28].

However, it is impossible to have token ecosystem governance without at least an **executive** function. The reason is the practical need to design, plan and execute operational tasks, such as implementing the token whitepaper into blockchain-executable code. So, in analogy with human ecosystems, it must always be present.

Robust and mature token ecosystems provide for all three of the "functions of government". This is, we believe, what should ideally be strived for—a goal of end-to-end design. Another goal is clarity about the constellation and duties of the "branches of government". Having such a clarity allows to answer for example the following questions: Are the functions of government concentrated in a single organizational entity or in several, independent ones? Is it necessary to provide for an authority that decides on governing laws, a separate one tasked with operational decisions, and still a third one tasked with dispute resolution, or not? Is it necessary to provide for distinct and independent agent constellations embodying said authorities, or not? Those will be high-level design decisions.

Lower-level, but similarly important, decisions are meant to answer questions such as: can non-privileged economic agents influence the constitution and functioning of the privileged ones (similarly to election rights of candidates into the legislative and executive bodies), or not? How can economic agents initiate a bilateral transaction and under which preconditions? When is a bilateral or multilateral transaction valid and irrevocable? Which economic agents are entitled to fees payable upon conclusion of a transaction by totally unrelated agents? When can an economic agent initiate dispute resolution and how?

The above are fundamental questions in the context of any organized economic activity. There are still many others, which in effect boil down to understanding the ideal execution, as well as possible pathologies, of all interaction pathways at each of the three levels (hierarchical, horizontal, constitutional) postulated previously. Answering those questions is the goal of mechanism design.

8.2 Rationale of Mechanism Design for Token-Based Ecosystems

In Chap. 6, we learnt that market design is about designing the structural environment for participants to interact and transact with each other through tokens. Mechanism design is about influencing agent behaviours along interactions and transactions. It is about creating clarity about what courses of action are accessible to each type of economic agent, and what is expected of them when interacting with each other through, or on account of, their tokens. It is also about manifesting the hierarchy of economic agents through rules of engagement, e.g., with governance structures. Without those there is risk of instability in the ecosystem, as the process of self-organization by principally self-interested economic agents will be a chaotic one.

Drawing from human ecosystems, acceptance of the necessity of some governance structures having a set of "privileges" towards other actors has been the outcome of societal evolution. Indeed, throughout history the struggle among ideas and interests to agree commonly accepted delineations of said privileges caused not only tremendous progress, but also tremendous suffering. Modern and stable human ecosystems rely invariably on agreed upon, clear and codified, legal frameworks.

Following the "country economy" analogy, a blockchain-based token ecosystem without clarity on rules and responsibilities of its governance would be akin to a closed country with own currency, but without any written laws and without any accepted rules of engagement among its governing bodies, ordinary citizens and legal entities. Such a country could still begin exhibiting some economic activity, as groups of humans exchange goods and services and are compensated in the country's currency. But the whole edifice of the country would be inherently unstable. Sooner or later, fundamental questions would be asked by its citizens.

For instance: What are the rules for using the basic infrastructure of the country—the roads for goods to move on, the networks for services to be delivered through? If they somehow already exist, who pays for their operation and maintenance, based on which schedule? Who controls the minting of the own currency? Which currency transfers are final and how can it be proved that payment in the country's currency has indeed taken place? Which transactions are valid and irrevocable, which transactions are considered fair? How can instances of theft or fraud be proved? What are the means of redress to the injured party, and who is responsible for their enforcement? Are governing bodies answerable to anyone, and if so, through which processes? Which decisions can a governing body take unilaterally, and which must be necessarily reached by quorum, or even by consensus building, among which critical mass of economic agents?

Mechanism design strives to answer all those questions and more. Fundamentally, by influencing behaviours of all economic agents (including privileged ones) it aims to safeguard the long-term sustainability of the token-based ecosystem. Importantly, it also seeks to account for changes of choices made by a critical mass of economic agents, by providing ways for said choices to be fed back into ecosystem design. In short, mechanism design is about three things: governance, economic stability, and change management. Of course, there is no "one size fits all" rulebook for a token-based ecosystem, as there exists no "one size fits all" legal and regulatory framework in human marketplaces—and definitely not across time.

Why is mechanism design different than market design? Once the typology and structure of economic agents is defined, and their interaction pathways clarified, why do additional rules need to be specified?

Because, even with robust governance institutions in place, markets are not perfect. Recent manifestations of this fact, where country-level governance structures have had to step in to recalibrate legal and regulatory frameworks:

1. All major financial jurisdictions had a stable regulatory setup in the run-up to the 2008 Global Financial Crisis (GFC). Practically all had instituted clear allocation of responsibilities among their Central Banks and their prudential and conduct financial regulators. The structural setup of regulation and supervision was fundamentally the same before and after the GFC. However, the *behavioural* setup (how deeply can the prudential regulator influence a Bank's capital and liquidity requirements, what are the allowable rules of engagement among Banks and their customers, what constitutes "mis-selling", what can be considered "predatory lending", what transactions are allowable per end-client segment and which not, etc.) was drastically different after the GFC than it was before [29].
2. "Laissez-faire", or "light-touch", or any other gradations of regulatory involvement, were prescribed by government policy. Thus, policy changes [30, 31] implied concomitant changes in the calibration of regulatory functions, i.e. changes in the allocation of imputed regulatory rights and responsibilities [32] among counterparties of bilateral financial transactions.

In the above examples, the currency of the countries did not change. The setup of the economic agents (governing bodies—legislative bodies, Central Banks, regulators/supervisors, courts, etc., other economic agents—borrowers, investors, Banks, insurers, service providers, etc.) did not change either. What was different before and after the GFC was the *behavioural calibration* (the rules of engagement and the accompanying laws and regulations) of the same structural setup. Mechanism design comes in to address the same calibration problem in a blockchain-based setting, i.e. to ensure that rules of engagement of all economic agents (privileged or not) are clear and aligned with the intended economic outcomes of the token ecosystem. In short:

- Mechanism design is the **behavioural design** of the ecosystem.

Mechanism design affects the long-term sustainability of decentralized token ecosystems. It acts both as an enabler of governance and as a guarantor of fairness among each and every economic agent transacting in the ecosystem's token(s).

8.3 Mechanism Design for Token-Based Ecosystems in Short

Mechanism design is a form of economic and social engineering. First of all, it entails postulating formal **rules** to govern the interactions of economic agents (including governing bodies) within the token ecosystem. In simple words, it specifies what economic agents can and cannot do, and provides incentives to guide what they should and should not do, along each individual interaction pathway in isolation. Mechanism design is also allowed to create **incentives** conducive to intended economic outcomes. Such mechanisms are fundamentally needed because economic agents are naturally non-cooperative; unless there is an obligation or incentive to cooperate, persons and corporations are usually selfish in their actions.

Rules and incentives, the fundamental concepts of mechanism design, are simply "behaviour drivers", as depicted on Fig. 8.2.

Mechanism design is meant to provide:

1. Alignment with the market design, i.e. no economic agents or possible interaction pathways should be omitted.
2. Complete set of rules of engagement for each and every possible interaction pathway and corresponding constellation of economic agents.
3. Clarity about how the intended economic outcome of the token-based ecosystem is facilitated through the designed ruleset.
4. Clarity about how the tokens(s) of the protocol is (are) to be used in principle to implement said ruleset.

As the reader by now probably suspects, the proposed end-to-end token ecosystem design framework (i.e. mainly the market, mechanism, and token designs[7]) is in principle an iterative process. For example, mechanism design scenario analysis concluding that a first-iteration rule is impossible to apply operationally may necessitate changing the market and/or token designs first, before a robust alternative is found. All design pillars will generally change across ecosystem generations, moving from one converged state to the next as new use cases are proposed and transactional pathways implemented. And, of course, any pathology discovered during technical implementation—or even during operational use—may necessitate re-calibration, or even complete redesign, of one or more of said pillars.

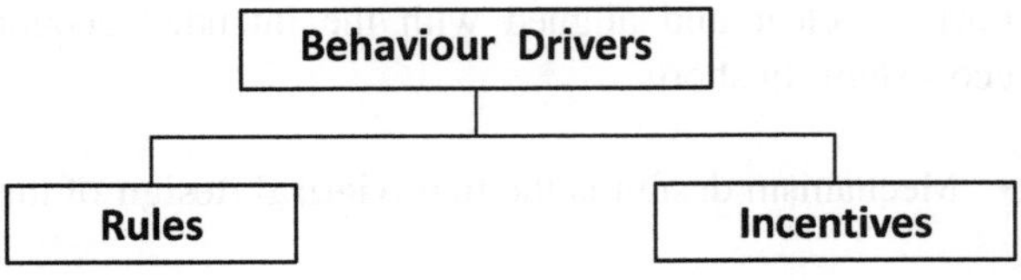

Fig. 8.2 Mechanism design fundamentals

[7] Plus the Bonding Function design (cf. Chap. 12), if such functions are needed.

8.3.1 Process and Components of Mechanism Design

To design, we first need to analyse.

The starting point of mechanism design will be the end point of market design:

- The typology and hierarchy of economic agents.
- All possible interaction pathways (including, of course, transactional pathways) among economic agents.

Its end point will be a clear map of **rules** and **incentives**:

1. For each and every interaction pathway, a clear blueprint (document, code, or any other artefact providing an unequivocal description) of:
   a. The kinds of economic agents that can initiate the interaction, and how.
   b. The kinds of messages and assets (token-denominated or other property) that will be exchanged in the course of each interaction, among which economic agents, and how.
   c. The states of the interaction signifying that a particular right was exercised or a particular obligation fulfilled, and how are those states to be documented.
   d. The possible deviations from the expected interaction pathway, what the corrective actions can be and taken by whom (exception handling, and dispute resolution).
2. For alternative interaction pathways with the same or similar outcomes, a clear calculation basis (in a text document, or other unequivocal description) of what the relative merits of pursuing one vs. the other(s) are.

The analysis phase will also involve keeping records of deliberations on how best to go from the starting to the end point.

The need for rules (1. above) is self-evident. That for incentives (2.), however, requires some explanation. The economic objective of the token ecosystem should be achieved by the combined action of all economic agents. However, there are three main aspects that must to be considered in that respect. First, economic agents are naturally non-cooperative in nature; unless there is an incentive to cooperate, both individuals and corporations are usually selfish in their actions, and this may ultimately endanger the stability of the entire ecosystem. Second, the actions of economic agents are not always rational, as the whole corpus of behavioural economics can attest to; hence, in all generality there should exist ways to risk-manage individual agent behaviour for the sake both of both the agents themselves and of the stability of the ecosystem as a whole. Third, the inherent features (the fundamental calibration) of the ecosystem may change in time. Better ways (technological, procedural, etc.) of executing interactions and transactions among agents may be either suggested by experience or necessitated by technological evolution. Similarly, a better constellation of economic agents (new governing bodies, new types of transacting agents, etc.) may be proposed over time. Hence, there may result a need to revisit the starting market design and then to *incentivize* transition to a new one (and, of course, change-manage this transition). In summary, all three of those aspects are reasons why creation of incentives is part of mechanism design.

What form can such incentives take?

There are many ways to arrive at the same outcome but at different cost. For instance, the fees levied by governance may be chosen to be different along different pathways. Similarly, the mechanisms of price discovery, negotiation and transaction execution may be made more resource-efficient in one pathway versus another. Posting of different sums of collateral, and in different asset types (tokenized or not), may be specified for different pathways. In short, there are several alternatives, and no way of knowing in advance the optimal one, for incentivizing one specific interaction mode over another in a particular design iteration: no "one-size-fits-all" algorithm. This is precisely why creation of such incentives must be the object of careful deliberations, i.e. of mechanism design.

What are practical analytical tools of use in mechanism design?

In early stages, any **conceptual, technical or algorithmic, descriptive modelling tool** will do. The objectives should be:

- Starting from a particular interaction pathway there needs to be clarity on what the interaction objective (transaction, voting, or consensus, etc.); and what the basic constellation of economic agents (direct transaction counterparties; guarantee providers; collateral providers; the platform itself; its governing bodies; etc.) are. This is the *conceptual* analysis model, to be expressed **in text or in diagrams.**
- The sequence and branching of events during interaction need to be documented next (who initiates the transaction; what are the expected phases; which are the states signifying phase completion; what is the negotiation process; are there indicative quotes expected; when are token-denominated and other assets transferred; in which form of property rights, and among which agents; are transaction cancellations possible; if so, at which sequence step and within which time interval; are there penalties to be paid for transaction cancellation; when and in which form is a record of the transaction valid; etc.). This is the *technical* part of the analysis, expected to be in **either textual or graphical form**.
- Optimal technical parameters of interaction execution (how long are indicative quotes valid for; can non-reaction mean approval or rejection; what are the maximum amounts—denominated in tokens or not—allowed; are there Oracles expected to be involved; how many such parallel transactions are allowed on the platform; is there a critical mass of transactions before the platform itself will need to be in any way re-calibrated; how high are the fees to the platform on account of which parameters; etc.) are best analysed through **algorithmic modelling tools**. This is the *algorithmic* analysis part.

In intermediate stages, individual economic outcomes and their consequences for other agents (including the platform itself) are merged using **non-cooperative game-theoretical tools**. There, as economic designers we focus on how different calibrations along each modelling step (conceptual, technical, or algorithmic) influence outcomes for both individual agents and for the ecosystem as a whole (**sensitivity analysis**). At the end of this step, the **optimal** sequence of events and corresponding calibration parameters are specified.

The important, final, stage is deciding how precisely to achieve this optimal outcome, i.e. **if it should be pursued through rules or through incentives**, or through both.

Even though we mention "stages", it goes without saying that the mechanism design process is an iterative one, as insights gained when analysing a particular interaction pathway may end up influencing others—which may have already undergone a design cycle before—thus necessitating their own *redesign*. The main outcome should be, like in any good architecture, a behavioural blueprint across all interaction pathways that is clear, consistent, effective, and ideally efficient in its implementation and operational use.

A secondary outcome of mechanism design is the understanding of why and how rules and incentives are optimal for different participating agents. The objective should then be to achieve combinations of mechanisms that can be made optimal for several agent types at once [33], to avoid—if possible—zero-sum games. Only then will the token ecosystem offer a real added value to a broad population of agents, and only then will they be inclined to purchase and use its token(s). To achieve this, it is imperative that our analysis should also seek to understand the potential *pitfalls* associated with incentives and information (about rules, assumptions, expectations) from the individual participants' point of view.

At the most basic level, mechanism design should strive to ensure that no agent type benefits at the expense of others. Fairness is a precondition of trust, and trust (in the rules, the outcomes, the functioning of the entire token ecosystem) is in turn the precondition of agents' participation.

8.4 Characteristics of a Successful Mechanism Design

Let us please remind the reader that the three main pillars of the proposed token-ecosystem design framework are the market, mechanism and token designs. They correspond to the structural, behavioural and financial/monetary enablers of economic outcomes.

In reference to the basic analogy of designing a new country-level economy, imagine that all governance bodies of a country have already been created. Imagine also that the country's currency has been minted and ready for circulation. Also, apart from its constitution, no other laws, no regulations, no administrative acts have been published. Imagine that a tax service is in place, but there is no tax code. There exists a basic technical infrastructure (networks, utilities, etc.) but no rating or billing schedules. Citizens and corporations are ready to exchange goods and services, but there are no standard contracts as there is as yet no contract law. **This is time zero.**

Fast forward to a later time. Laws, regulations, administrative acts have been published. The tax service is operating on the basis of a documented tax code. Network operators and utilities rate service offerings and bill consumers accordingly. Citizens and corporations transact among each other and with the governing bodies, exchanging goods and services, and getting paid in the country's currency. Courts are handling contractual disputes and dispensing justice. Citizens vote to fill positions in the executive and the legislative branches of government, and in referenda. Offices in the judiciary are filled in a transparent way. **At this time a reviewer is tasked with rating the functioning of the country's economic system.**

How can this reviewer decide if the rules and incentives of economic life within the country are "good"? And, if they are deemed to be good, are they "good enough", or "the best they can be"?

We believe that the reviewer in question will probably base their judgement on both theoretical principles and empirical facts:

- Are all rules and incentives documented? Are they clear and unequivocal? Is it clear how they were, and are being, created?
- How well do the rules and incentives cover the possible economic agents? Are there any interactions (incl. transactions) among particular kinds of economic agents that are not covered by any rules or incentives at all?
- How well does the economy of the country function at review time? Does the currency circulate unhindered or is there lack of liquidity for particular transactions?
- Have any particular types of economic agents been experiencing systematic capital depletion or lack of liquidity? Have any particular types of economic agents become extremely wealthy at the expense of others?
- Have the infrastructure utilities been covering their costs? Are they operating at consistent loss or consistent profitability? If the latter, is it higher than the average for all corporations in the country?
- Is a relatively high percentage of transactions disputed? What is the average time for resolving these disputes?
- Is there persistent inflation or deflation? How stable are the prices of goods and services as denominated in the country's currency?
- Have citizens or corporations been deserting the country? Have citizens and corporations been abandoning the country's currency? How has its parity rate with other currencies been evolving?

And still others. All such legitimate questions map to what we would propose are the essential features of a good mechanism design, namely that it should:

1. Be clear, documented, and auditable.
2. Be completely aligned with the market and token designs.
3. Not disadvantage particular market participants to the benefit of others (including the Governance of the platform itself).

4. Not favour particular goods or services offered by, or available to, the market participants at the expense of others.
5. Promote price stability of goods and services, as denominated in the ecosystem token(s).
6. Promote competitiveness of the ecosystem relative to others offering the same or similar goods or services.
7. Engender trust in the validity and non-repudiation of transactions carried out through the admissible token(s).
8. Engender trust in its economic outcomes.
9. Engender trust in its dispute resolution mechanisms.
10. Have feedback mechanisms built-in (performance or risk indicators observable by all, or at least by voting members, etc.).
11. Contain self-correcting institutional mechanisms (based on voting, or consensus, etc.).
12. Provide for managed change, aligning with concomitant market and token changes.
13. Promote the long-term sustainability of the token-based ecosystem.

It can be argued that the above criteria are valid for any economic system having an own currency. However, they are much more important in a decentralized (in the blockchain sense) paradigm, on account of three factors:

The **first** differentiating factor stems from the "consensus-driven" nature of economic outcomes in such a paradigm. Consensus still hinges on individual decision-making. Although people are not perfect, we generally assume that they will act rationally based on the information that they privately possess. This is a strong assumption, and indeed it may be relaxed for analysis purposes. However, for the purposes of mechanism design it is recommended to accept it as valid in the average, i.e. in the context of pursuing outcomes that facilitate total economic value creation and preservation.

The **second** differentiating factor stems from the implicit existence of a "social choice function" in a blockchain token-based context. Postulating a social choice function entails the assumption that consideration and analysis of alternatives has taken place before a collective decision was reached. This decision could be maximizing utility, minimizing costs, reducing time spent, increasing happiness, ensuring equality of individuals, etc.

Why is postulating a "social choice function" important?

Because ultimately all market participants can be reasonably expected to want the ecosystem to sustain itself and succeed. I.e., they can be expected to want to make a collective decision to achieve such a sum of all economic outcomes in the ecosystem (the "social goal") that it is beneficial for all of them (the "social choice"). Accordingly, one can judge how "good" a mechanism design is, based on the extent to which it manifestly promotes a particular social choice function. In other words, the quality of mechanism design depends on the degree to which particular social function objectives can be reasonably expected to be fulfilled in practice. Such objectives include:

a. **Pareto efficiency** [34]
b. **Strategy-proof mechanisms** [35].
c. **Fairness** [36]
d. **More general goals,** e.g. represented by a Bergson-Samuelson social welfare function [35]

Hence, another important criterion of good mechanism design (complementing the numbered list above) is that it should:

14. Enable attainment of the target social choice function, under the assumption of rational consensus building.

The **third** differentiating factor stems from the fact that in a centrally governed ecosystem (e.g. a planned economy, a corporation, etc.), a central entity can convene at will to deal with any situation that threatens the ecosystem's intended economic objectives. But, what about in a decentralized ecosystem? Who has the right to have the final say about blocking or removing your account? Who is responsible for eradicating bad behaviours, or for punishing "bad" actors? If there are indeed "bad" actors, who and how is to assure the interests of "good" actors so that they keep participating in the ecosystem?

This is essentially the **final and most important criterion** of what "good" mechanism design in a token-based ecosystem is all about. Namely the recognition that, based on the "country" analogy, this is a special kind of country. It is a country where central governing institutions are lean and, apart from the executive branch, they may not even exist. The currency may be minted and removed from circulation constantly, in amounts that cannot be pre-determined but must still be risk managed. There may be very few kinds of goods or services to spend one's wealth on. The economic actors can communicate with each other in a language with few words, so "signalling" is a necessary ingredient of economic life. Transactions are possible only in a pre-determined, and fast-paced, manner. There may be several parallel currencies in circulation, and not all of them may be admissible at once as media of exchange and stores of value inside the country. It is a matter of personal choice in which currency one's property will be saved and accounted for, as some currencies (mind you, within the same country) may be valid only as capital and others only as liquidity. Individual choice depends on personal priorities, and those may not always be rational.

In short, good mechanism design should also:

15. Completely respect the idiosyncrasies of the decentralized (blockchain) nature of the token ecosystem.

The importance of this final criterion cannot be overstated. It is also the reason why we would recommend to always settle for a "good enough", rather than "the best it can be", mechanism design. For example, decentralized decision-making typically found in (blockchain-based) token ecosystems entails the unpredictability of all possible outcomes. Risk-managing such an ecosystem means monitoring and controlling *ranges* of stochastic outcomes, not individual ones. The practically optimal output can only be the stability of ecosystem behaviour *in the aggregate*, which may be achieved in several different ways. Hence, there can be no "absolutely best result", but rather only "good enough *under the particular circumstances*".

8.5 Factors of Consideration in Mechanism Design

From an economics point of view, mechanism design can be a complex endeavour as there are potentially many factors influencing the interaction of economic agents. Depending on the idiosyncrasies of the blockchain ecosystem, of the particular business use case, and of the token(s) used, it may have to span the gamut from general equilibrium theory to non-classical paradigms. For complex token-based ecosystems (i.e. those enabling various business models at once) it can be thought of as laying the general normative foundations of economic policy.

However, as this is a book about methodology in crypto-token ecosystem design, we will follow the pedagogical approach and start by laying out some very basic concepts first. Theoretical (and practical) sophistication will follow in due course.

In that vein, a good mechanism design should:

1. Specify all aspects of **governance**.
2. Define the ecosystem's **market structure**.
3. Prescribe clear and measurable **(financial and non-financial) incentives**.

In a refined mechanism design there will be more, potentially many more, design factors to consider. However, not all of them will have the same importance, or even relevance across time, to the token ecosystem. The three afore-mentioned ones will always be important and relevant, across token use cases and across designs.

8.5.1 Governance

Ecosystems (token-based or otherwise) exist to facilitate interactions among participants. This outcome is much easier to achieve in centralized ecosystems because a central authority has the final (and sometimes the only) say in design, operational and exception-handling decisions. However, in decentralized ones the mechanics of governance become a crucial factor in outcomes facilitation.

At the highest level of abstraction, designing governance mechanisms entails specifying **how decisions are to be made and implemented**, and **how problems are to be resolved**. Encoding such specifications in a token-base setting involves several layers of procedural and technological (e.g. smart contract) blueprints, but encoding must be accompanied by parametrization and controls—which may or may not be automated. In general:

- How decisions are made is expressed through a **consensus mechanism**. This is usually non-automated.
- How decisions are implemented is the task of the ecosystem's **executive body**. This task is also usually non-automated.
- How problems are being resolved is codified in a **resolution mechanism**. This is usually (but not always) automated through smart contracts.

Fundamentally, governance mechanisms should be primarily aligned with use cases, ecosystem objectives and token usage. However, when trying to align with the more granular aspects of use cases, objectives, etc., the need for design compromises arises—and the potential for mechanism mis-calibration appears. For example, usual mechanism design pitfalls include: non-optimal balance between centralization and decentralization, inadequate or inefficient consensus mechanisms, conflicting rules, and deficient smart contracts. An example of the importance of avoiding the first pitfall is afforded by the September 2020 KuCoin incident [37, 38], when a hacker was able to steal the equivalent of $285 million in various tokens from the KuCoin Centralized Cryptocurrency Exchange (CEX) and swap them for other assets. This can happen whenever governance controls break down in any token-based ecosystem. In centralized ecosystems, the decision may be taken to fork the protocol code in order to retrieve the stolen tokens (case of the Ocean Protocol [39]); whereas in decentralized ecosystems the only feasible reaction may be to continue operating on the same code base and simply strive for better controls execution (case of the Synthetix protocol [40]). As in the KuCoin case, individual token ecosystems will have to strike the right balance of governance along the "centralized-to-decentralized" continuum, as they will have to live with the consequences.

8.5.2 Market Structure

In modern economics, the term "market structure" [41–43] denotes all aspects relating to price discovery in a market. It is meant to include both the factors influencing price formation in individual transactions and their aggregate outcome to the functioning of the entire market. For example, such factors would be the relative strength (and resulting effective concentrations) of buy- or sell-side market participants, features of offered product and services (differentiation/substitutability/perishability, etc.), the practical price negotiation modalities (usual procedures, market practices, usance, etc.), contractual formation and execution, built-in frictions, barriers to entry/exit, etc. Aggregate outcomes of such factors for the entire market would be, first, effective turnover of buy- or sell-side participants, and second, the emergence of imperfect competition pathologies, which will cause the economic system to be categorized at some point along the continuum from perfect competition to monopoly.

Hence, any design decision influencing price formation will have repercussions for the potential of the economic ecosystem to attract and retain its economic agents, i.e. for its long-term sustainability and competitiveness with other similar ones.

This is particularly true for blockchain-based ecosystems, as their digital nature makes information feedback loops much shorter in time that for non-digital ones.

Of course, there are still other considerations specific to token ecosystems. Designing token-based market structure involves specifying how on-chain token-denominated transactions will be negotiated and concluded, what would the ancillary (governance) fee structure be, and what information flows (through on-chain and off-chain channels) are expected to occur. In terms of mechanism design:

- How transacting economic agents negotiate with each other is specified in a **bargaining mechanism**. This can be either non-automated, automated through smart contracts, or hybrid.
- How the platform fee structure is applied on transactions is defined in a **taxation mechanism**. This is usually automated through smart contracts.
- How the on-chain and off-chain worlds are connected to each other for the purposes of concluding transactions is codified through an **information exchange mechanism**. This is usually automated through smart contracts.

As indication of the impact of each design point on the functioning of the entire ecosystem, let us concentrate briefly on information exchange mechanisms. Those will regulate how (on-chain to on-chain, off-chain to on-chain, or on-chain to off-chain) will market participants be allowed to exchange transaction-relevant data **aligning with the bargaining mechanism**. Said data will of course need to be observable, as in any digital ecosystem. Thus, they can be used to affect the degree to which very influential participants (aka "whales"[8]) may influence price formation.

The discerning reader will at this point already have discovered a conceptual overlap of the "Market Structure" notion with those of "Thickness" and "Congestion" in market design (cf. Sects. 6.6.1 and 6.6.2). Some of the analysis points already mentioned in the frame of designing appropriate market thickness ("what goods or services are being offered or asked?", "what is the depth of the supply?", "what is the depth of the demand?", "who offers what, at which price", etc.) appear to be the same ones considered in "Market Structure" design. Similarly, some of the points of consideration in "Congestion" design ("is there enough time and information to process the optionality?", "what are the tools available to help economic agents make a decision to transact?", etc.) are also in-scope for the information exchange mechanism design.

This is indeed true.

As mentioned in several passages already, the book at hand proposes a specific token-based economic design framework with three main pillars, all of which (market, mechanism and token designs) must align with each other at the end.

[8]Industry jargon term denoting participants with disproportionate pricing power on account of their on-chain token-denominated assets or on-/off-chain token- or Fiat-denominated liquidity.

This holistic design process can only be *iterative*, as, e.g., decisions in mechanism design can cause market redesign, etc. This case of "Market Structure" feeding back into "Thickness" and "Congestion" designs is nothing else but a manifestation of the attachment points inherent to said iterative decision-making.

Next, we observe how these concepts manifest themselves in the crypto-market. Specific examples of how particular **bargaining mechanism** options are implemented in actual token-based ecosystems are provided in Table 8.1 (entries are arranged in alphabetical order). Please note that, depending on the use case, the tokens representing the assets or services acquired may be only created ("minted") as outcomes of successful transactions, not otherwise.

Whilst "transaction fee" is a more common term than **taxation mechanism**, they both refer to the same outcome, wherein the user pays a certain amount—specified either in absolute terms or as a function of the transaction notional—to some third-party agent (usually governance) in the same ecosystem. Taxation is simply a fee on each ecosystem transaction to fund the provision of "common goods" (such as basic infrastructure operation and maintenance). The following Table 8.2 contains specific examples of taxation mechanism calibrations from already productive token-based ecosystems.

Finally, Table 8.3 provides examples of how a particular **information exchange mechanism** option (namely use of Oracles; cf. Sect. 6.4) is implemented in actual token ecosystems. The general context is of a transaction between economic agents, one of which can be the underlying platform itself. Different transaction stages entail different information discovery needs. Tokens may be involved both as objects of the transaction (the asset is a security token, or the service is embedded in a utility token, etc.) or simply as media of exchange for its monetary aspects (direct payments, assets posted as collateral, insurance premia, warranties and guarantees, etc.). At transaction inception, for example, the need is to clarify all attributes of the token-denominated asset or service, including its expected price level. This information can be subject to bilateral negotiation or can be provided unequivocally from a mutually trusted source. The table informs of latter cases, where said source is an Oracle. Entries are arranged in alphabetic order (Table 8.3).

This concludes our *exposé* on market structure as mechanism design factor.

8.5.3 Incentives (Financial and Non-Financial)

Token-based economics relies as much on incentives as it does on rules to achieve desired economic behaviours. The important difference between the two is that the action of incentives is *indirect*. The intended outcome is *not* the course of action favoured by the incentive, but rather *the result of* said course of *action*—either by a single agent, or, ideally, by many agents. The intended result may actually be multi-faceted, which makes the design of the incentive all the more important.

An example of desired behaviour is active participation in an ecosystem's governance processes. We already mentioned a particular token type (utility token, cf. Sect. 4.2.2) as embodying active incentivization of otherwise disinterested agents

Table 8.1 Bargaining mechanism calibrations in existing token ecosystems

All-pay auction	A token-denominated asset or service is auctioned, with the understanding that: • All bids are silent, i.e. no bidder is aware of the other bid price points. • The asset or service will be ceded entirely to the highest bidder. • All non-winning bidders will forfeit their bid sums.	Augur [44]
Bonding curve	A token-denominated asset or service is continuously offered through an "automated market maker", a smart contract which quotes dynamic prices based on the relative proportion of tokens in defined liquidity pools. The buyer is a pure price-taker.	Uniswap [45], Bancor [18]
Dutch auction	A fixed supply of token-denominated assets or services is offered at an initial price. After a fixed amount of time, if there are no price takers, the offered price is lowered. After a fixed amount of time, if there are no price takers at the new price level, the offered price is lowered again. The pattern repeats, until a (low) "reserve price" is reached, or until the available supply is exhausted, whichever comes first. At any time, price takers can buy the corresponding amount of the supply.	Gnosis [46], Algorand [47]
Forward auction	A token-denominated asset or service is auctioned with the understanding that: • All bids are open, i.e. bidders are aware of the other bid price points. • The asset or service will be ceded entirely to the highest bidder. • Non-winning bidders will not forfeit any sums, except for eventual participation fees. • There may be a starting (floor) bid price.	Rarible [48]
PID controller	A token-denominated asset or service is continuously offered through an "automated market maker", a smart contract which quotes dynamic prices based on a mathematical formula parametrized through a PID Controller [49]. The buyer is a pure price-taker.	FRAX [50]
Single-price auction	A fixed supply of token-denominated assets or services is auctioned, with the understanding that: • All bids are submitted until a cut-off time. • All bidders declare both their bid price and their requested amount of the supply. • The highest bidder will be allocated their requested amount of the supply at their bid price. • The next highest bidders will be allocated their requested amounts of the supply at their bid prices. • The process continues until the offered supply is entirely allocated. The bid price of the last supply tranche allocated becomes the "single price" of the entire auction. All successful bidders will be charged only this price for their already allocated supply tranches.	Hegic [51]

(continued)

Table 8.1 (continued)

Vickrey auction	A token-denominated asset or service is auctioned, with the understanding that: • All bids are open, i.e. bidders are aware of the other bid price points. • The asset or service will be ceded entirely to the highest bidder. • Non-winning bidders will not forfeit any sums, except for eventual participation fees. • The price charged to the highest bidder will be not the one bid by them, but that of the second-highest bidder.	Fairblock [52]
Vickrey-Clarke-Groves auction	A fixed supply of token-denominated assets or services is offered, with the understanding that: • All bids are silent, i.e. no bidder is aware of the details of other bids. • All bidders declare both their bid price and their requested amount of the supply. • The successful bidders will be only those whose price-amount requested combinations are socially optimal for the entire ecosystem.	Celer Network [53]

to undertake important operational governance tasks. But, who would care to undertake more strategic or even tactical—but not operational—decision-making in a decentralized setting? Of course there is expected to exist a core project team (the people behind the Whitepaper, and their sponsors), but growing an ecosystem means gauging and responding to *actual* needs, which in turn entails culling feedback on *assumed* needs by precisely those persons who will need to become principals of agents exchanging tokens to satisfy said needs. As digital ecosystems are impersonal and ideally populous, it cannot be expected that the core project team will be able to keep contact data of a critical mass of prospective principals on which to run market research. Thus, feedback—which is but one form of contribution to decision-making – needs to be somehow incentivized. Another example of agent incentivization—this time in the context of constitutive interactions, cf. Sect. 8.1 above—targets broad participation in governance voting rounds (either for agent elections to governing bodies, or for any other tactical decision taken by, in effect, a referendum). By reference to the "country" analogy, how would one achieve a wide enough participation in elections or referenda, if one does not even have a voter registry?

This is but one objective of incentives in mechanism design.

Let us stay with governance as example context of incentives design. At the highest level of abstraction, designing governance incentives is equivalent to deciding **if and how:**

(a) **Voting** on ecosystem decisions is to be encouraged, and
(b) Active participation to governance tasks—above the operational level—is to be **rewarded by allocation of existing ecosystem resources**.

Table 8.2 Taxation mechanism calibrations in existing token ecosystems

Service fee	Similar to Goods and Services Tax (VAT) in traditional economic systems, it is meant to reward the platform for enabling the added value accruing to transaction participants. For consumers, this added value comes from acquiring—or, "accessing"—a requested asset/service; for suppliers, from drawing a profit by providing them. The fee is front-loaded and can be differently weighed between consumers and suppliers depending on the use case. The schedule (fixed or variable) is at the discretion of the protocol.	Sushiswap [54] withholds 0.3% of the notional as trading fee for each transaction [55].
Performance fee	Similar to investment performance fees in traditional finance, it occurs in use cases where the platform provides services which explicitly or implicitly facilitate appreciation of assets purchased on the ecosystem. Also, whenever the platform itself acts as a supplier of discretionary investment management services. It is typically back-end loaded and can have both a fixed and a variable component.	Loop [56] has a performance fee of 2% of assets [57], payable by the seller upon execution of sale.
Management fee	Similar to investment management fees in traditional finance, it is typically imposed whenever the platform acts as both a custodian and a supplier of discretionary investment management services. It typically has only a fixed component, but its level can vary with the amount of invested funds.	Enzyme v2 [58] imposes a management fee rate of 1% of assets under management (AUM) [59].
Mixed (combined) fee structure	A combination of service (or "access"), management and performance fees. Its plausibilization and calibration depend on the particular use case.	Yearn [27] v2 yVault [60] fees are structured: 2% of AUM as management fee plus 20% of profits earned by the yVault as performance fee [61].

Correspondingly:

- How voting is enabled is expressed through a **voting mechanism**. This is usually non-automated.
- How the ecosystem allocates resources is the task of an **allocation mechanism**. This task is usually automated through smart contracts.

Table 8.3 Information exchange mechanism calibrations in existing token ecosystems

Consensus-based Oracle(s)	Information is aggregated from several (purely on-chain or mixed on-/off-chain) sources, including other Oracles, then rated for accuracy through a consensus paradigm (human expert judgement, on-chain "prediction markets", etc.) before being made available.	MojitoSwap [62] used Witnet [63] for DEX-sourced data feeds for trading.
Hardware Oracle(s)	Data are collated from off-chain physical devices (RFID sensors, Internet-of-Things devices, etc.) and aggregated into a single "source of truth". The process is repeated with set frequency, so that quality-controlled time series are continuously available. These are made available to smart contracts through software interfaces (Application Programming Interfaces – "API").	VeChain [64] used physical sensor data to track the state of supply chains [65].
Inbound Oracle(s)	Data sourced from other token ecosystems (Decentralized Exchange prices, NFT data, Decentralized Oracles, etc.) are vetted for accuracy and made available through software interfaces (Application Programming Interfaces—"API").	Centrifuge [66] Tinlake used a combination of price Oracles and NFT "Provenance Oracles" for collateral valuation [67].
Outbound Oracle(s)	The ecosystem itself publishes own state variables (financial instrument trading prices offered by Automated Market Maker, payment authorization approvals, physical events from mobile devices, etc.) as "single source of truth" data accessible from smart contracts through software interfaces (Application Programming Interfaces—"APIs"s).	AirBie [68] offers its "Smart Bike Lock" data as outbound Oracle.
Software Oracle(s)	Data are collated from off-chain sources where it officially originates (stock and commodities exchanges, weather reporting agencies, sports news aggregators, etc.), reconciled, and cleaned into a single "source of truth". The process is repeated with set frequency, so that quality-controlled time series are continuously available. These are made available to smart contracts through software interfaces (Application Programming Interfaces—"APIs").	Augur Turbo [69] used Chainlink Data Feeds [70] for sports prediction markets.

On the basis of the "country" analogy, the discerning reader will have foreseen already that incentives will generally be both financial and non-financial in nature. But the question can be asked clearly, nevertheless:

Why are both financial and non-financial incentives needed?

One reason is to take into account the different priorities of individual economic agents. Whereas financial incentives may be similarly important to all, some non-financial incentives (e.g. ability to impact the strategic direction of the entire platform through voting privileges) may well have the highest priority for some.

Another reason is to be able to react at different time scales to observed transactional behaviour on the platform, as observing this behaviour is in effect observing the outcomes of current choices, especially in the presence of information asymmetries. In short, non-financial incentives can achieve an optimal outcome for the ecosystem by eliciting a better understanding of the transactional dynamics at play (under no conflicts of interest) and by judging objectively the actual outcomes of past choices. As an example, reputation is also a noteworthy incentive reducing information asymmetry, leading participants to report their true information, and so reducing moral hazard and adverse selection in ecosystem transactions.

Still another, and quite important, reason why non-financial incentives may be needed is because of the inevitably *incomplete nature* of smart contracts. As most ecosystems evolve continuously, some exceptional transactional situations are difficult to foresee, or to adequately describe in advance. And even if they were, it would be a challenge to justify accommodating them without a pressing need into existing smart contract designs and implementations.

Incentive pitfalls are of course possible. While we want to ensure that agents' principals are incentivised to be active participants of the ecosystem, we also want to avoid inadvertently eliciting harmful behaviours. For example, in the context of voting, such behaviours include: vote buying; plutocracy; "Sybil attacks"; last-minute vote swings by voter collusion; disinterested eligible voters abstaining; uninformed voters casting random votes; etc. To that end, various principles from economics and engineering (especially complexity theory) can be used to design effective incentives. The core design principles stem from traditional and behavioural economics, which seek to understand why people behave the way they do. Complexity theory comes into play to better understand the operational aspects of decentralized systems, and to thus optimize response calibration. The two angles of attack are complementary.

As token ecosystems are by nature continuously evolving and adapting to new information, it would be futile to seek to design an "incentives steady state" where incentive mechanisms are fixed and statistics are in equilibrium. The task is rather one of constantly incentivising stable economic outcomes, while striving to interpret the observed actions of decentralized ecosystem participants and project them to possible future ecosystem states.

Particular examples of **voting mechanism** designs from actual token-based ecosystems can be found in the following Table 8.4 (entries arranged in alphabetic order). The general context is that of governance processes which, for a binding outcome, necessitate reaching a critical mass of opinions expressed by token holders

Table 8.4 Voting mechanism calibrations in existing token ecosystems

Commit-reveal	• Each individual voter openly "publishes" their vote. • All voters have the right to request validation of the eligibility of other individual voters and of the agreement between what they ultimately voted for and what they had "published".	Ethereum [71]
Conviction voting	• Voting takes place continuously for a set amount of time. • Many voting contexts are activated in parallel, and voters can allocate their votes to (i.e. stake token amounts for) several contexts. • An absolute threshold of votes is needed to approve a decision. • Once this threshold is reached within the set time, the decision is approved.	Giveth [72]
Delegated voting	Voting token owners can delegate their voting rights to other economic agents ("Delegates").	Tezos [73]
Partial-lock commit-reveal voting	• Voting takes place in two stages, "Commit" and "Reveal". • A "partial-lock" locks voting tokens upon their staking in "Commit". • All locked tokens are hidden until they are counted for the voting outcome (in "Reveal"). • Many voting contexts are activated in parallel, and voters can allocate their votes to (i.e. stake token amounts for) several contexts. • It allows voters to withdraw at any time the maximum number of tokens not currently locked. • This voting pattern is also possible operationally in Token Curated Registries.	AdChain [74]
Politeia voting	• Voting takes place continuously for a set amount of time. • Staking is explicit by buying "voting tickets" denominated in voting tokens. • A transaction fee may also be levied on each buy. • Ticket holders may upvote or downvote a proposal.	Decred [75, 76]
Private voting	• Votes are always private, enforced by encryption. • Voters cannot reveal their votes. • Voters can allocate voting token amounts in parallel contexts. • This voting pattern is also possible operationally in Token Curated Registries.	Secret Network [77, 78]
Proportional voting	• The number of voting tokens possessed by a voter, as a proportion of the total number of circulating voting tokens, is the weighting factor for their vote in the final outcome. • It can also be described as "one-token-one-vote".	Maker DAO [15]

(continued)

Table 8.4 (continued)

Quadratic voting	• Many voting contexts are activated in parallel, and voters can distribute their votes to (i.e. stake token amounts for) several contexts. • The cost of voting per context (i.e. the amount of tokens that need to be staked) increases quadratically with the number of tokens. • This voting pattern incentivizes partitioning of votes among several contexts. • It also dilutes the voting power of large token positions.	Gitcoin [80, 81]
Quorum voting	• An absolute threshold of votes is needed to approve a decision. • This threshold depends on the quorum that is present to vote.	Aave [82]

exercising voting rights. In most token ecosystems, governance tokens and utility tokens in general[9] carry such rights. Existing token owners are either by default eligible to vote or have to "stake" them (i.e. pledge token positions as surety for a set amount of time) before they are allowed to. Voting contexts run the entire gamut from tactical calibration issues (e.g. increasing a borrowing or lending rate for collateralized tokens, adjusting bonding curve parameters of a token-minting smart contract, or changing transaction fee structure and levels) to strategic investment decisions ("do you agree that x thousand tokens should be invested for this re-engineering project?") all the way to fundamental "constitutional" decisions of the platform (transferring legal ownership of the platform from a Foundation to a Decentralized Autonomous Organization—"DAO", etc.). The whole voting process may be fully automated on-chain, e.g. through a smart contract.

Are there any criteria to guide selection of one voting mechanism option over another?

The subtle problem with design and calibration of voting mechanisms is that their effectiveness will need to be assessed across several possible combinations of economic agents, and against potential pathological behaviours whose causes may be idiosyncratic. It is thus an inescapable reality that each individual token use case will probably necessitate a bespoke incentivization method. That said, experience from existing token ecosystems does indeed suggest some guiding practices which can serve to at least identify first-order approximations to more refined solutions (or indeed a combination thereof). They align with the attributes of good mechanism design as identified in 8.4 above and include:

1. **Ease of understanding/communication**. Both token purchasers and governance participants must not be dissuaded by unclear documentation and overly complex processes. **Proportional voting** can be a starting point to achieve this.

[9] Cf. Chap. 4 for an explanation of token typology.

2. **Avoidance of "double voting"**. The decentralized nature of the blockchain can facilitate moral hazard based on delayed identity validation, such as voting with the same tokens on parallel contexts (which is the problem that Web3 "Decentralized Identity" projects such as SpruceID [83] are aiming to address comprehensively). Simple solutions can start by considering **Commit-reveal**.
3. **Increased community involvement**. Influence of large token positions ("whale" addresses) on governance outcomes can under circumstances be considered "undue", bordering on Plutocracy [84], to the point that the original economic purpose of the token ecosystem is skewed. This effect can be quantified by blockchain adaptations of traditional macroeconomic tools such as Gini and Nakamoto coefficients [85]. One way to reduce this risk is designing voting mechanisms based on **Quadratic voting**.
4. **Stability of governance**. There exists a grey area straddling strategic and operational decision-making. Too frequent or too fine-granular decisions consistently delegated to the highest governance bodies may end up paralysing the ecosystem. **Quorum voting** should be considered as a design option on the road to an optimal solution.
5. **Minimizing effects of information asymmetries**. In especially large or continuously evolving token ecosystems encompassing a multitude of use cases, it is natural that oversight of all possible strategic directions and their consequences is impossible for token owners who cannot devote the same time as platform experts do.[10] Governance of such ecosystem may need to consider **Delegated voting** as a way to striking the right balance between voter participation and technocratic expertise.
6. **Scaling to large numbers of voters**. Large ecosystems will have, at some point, to enable large participation in parallel voting contexts. The **Partial-lock commit-reveal** pattern can address the base practicalities of such an enablement. Of course, analysing scalability considerations more closely may surface other concerns as well, in which case a combination of patterns may be needed.
7. **Increased decentralization of end-to-end governance**. Once token-issuing projects grow out of the "seeding phase", there may be need for increased decentralization of decision-making to incentivize community participation as a way to achieving network effects. In such cases, **Politeia voting** can be considered as a possible voting mechanism option.
8. **Revealing true preferences of the voting population**. An important signalling mechanism than can be leveraged for fine-tuning governance decisions is the ability for token holders to vote not on exclusive outcomes, but also on "best", "second-best", etc., ones. For example, if the primary decision ultimately turns out to be impractical or highly conditional on market circumstances, it helps if a "next-best action" has already been identified. **Conviction voting** should be a possible design option to enable such signalling effects.

[10] A demonstration of the intricacies of technical debt carried by the first generation (Proof-of-Work based) of the Ethereum platform can be found in [86].

Table 8.5 Allocation mechanism calibrations in existing token ecosystems

Egalitarian	• Rewards are distributed uniformly per token staked or accounted for. • Total rewards pool may depend on level of across-the-board community participation. • Rewards per token position may be allocated only upon verified participation in decision-making.	Algorand [47, 87]
Reputation-based	• Rewards are higher for token positions owned by addresses with higher "reputation" metrics. • Reputation facts can be active community participation, past investment success, aggregate of direct and indirect trust metrics, etc. • Reputation facts and weightings are protocol dependent.	TRON [88, 89]

Two examples of incentivizing decision-making by **allocation mechanisms**, as implemented in actual token-based ecosystems, appear in Table 8.5. The context is that of reaching investment decisions (either in comparatively less frequent strategic contexts, or in more frequent tactical ones) by weighing token holdings of eligible decision makers. Incentives are usually expressed in platform rewards, i.e. pay-backs in the form of same or different tokens, for demonstrably influencing decision-making.

A very succinct list of indicative criteria for identifying candidate first-order allocation designs appears in the list below.

a. **Ensuring fairness of rewards allocation**. Fairness can mean one or all of: "transparency", "taking account of individual circumstances", "cost-awareness", "risk awareness". Each token ecosystem may focus on different aspects, and also change focus depending on project phases or on its own idiosyncratic governance pathologies. The precise function of the rewards-accumulating token (governance, other utility token, etc.) can also guide the metrics [90] that will proxy for "fairness". Monitoring or simulating such metrics can then be used to calibrate **"egalitarian" logic** (e.g. through bonding functions, cf. Chap. 12) that can be implemented through **auditable smart contracts**.
b. **Reducing power of "whales"**. If large token positions have been expressly identified as a risk for the ecosystem there are several established allocation and distribution metrics to describe its magnitude [91]. Mitigating this risk often entails a "wealth re-distribution effect", i.e., "weighing" privileges (rewards, voting power, etc.) to the benefit of smaller positions, for instance by allocating rewards as a decreasing function of existing position size. This however raises questions of fairness towards long-term investors (as per point above), and, if done without proper controls, can create a back-door for several pathologies such as Sybil Attacks [92] and voter collusion.
c. **Avoiding uninterested or "random" voting**. Misuse of governance privileges can range from "vote selling" to the less benign pathologies of voter abstention and "random" (i.e. non-thought-through) voting. For small voter communities and critical governance decisions their combination can have uncontrollable side-

effects. There are several ways to minimize such misuse, some (withdrawal of existing privileges, reduction of quality of service) more drastic than others, and all must be chosen based on their merit in the context of the specific use case. For example, a way to minimize "random" voting odds is through imposition of staking as a precondition to vote casting. However, that might prevent large but actively traded token positions from being represented in the final tally.

There are still others of course. Their applicability will have to be judged on the facts of the particular token use case and in light of the existing market design. The same proviso as in voting mechanism guidance applies here as well.

8.6 Summary

In this chapter, we pursued further the analogy of designing a token-based ecosystem being akin to designing a new country-level economy. The focus here was on the second main pillar of the proposed ecosystem design framework, namely on mechanism design.

We expanded on fundamental mechanism design choices having their origins in governance philosophies, traditional and behavioural economics, and lastly, on blockchain architecture specifics. This was a rather complex *exposé*, trying to make justice to a rather complicated subject. The three most important factors of mechanism design (governance, market structure and incentives) were explained, and the most important parameters of how to calibrate each identified, complete with examples from current ecosystems. The reader must surely grasp by now the variety of choices available when configuring the behavioural design of token-based ecosystems, which is also among their most attractive characteristics—one that makes them at once robust, flexible and adaptable as a new paradigm of economic activity.

As token ecosystems are by nature continuously evolving and adapting to new information, we would recommend to always settle for a "good enough", rather than "the best it can be", mechanism design. The decentralized nature of decision-making in them entails the unpredictability of all possible outcomes. This is undoubtedly a challenge, but an intriguing one nevertheless. Mechanism design is an art as much as it is a science, just like economics itself.

In the next chapter, we will give concrete examples of how mechanism design is evident in the workings of an operational token-based ecosystem.

References

1. Mechanism design. (2025, March 19). In *Wikipedia*. Retrieved March 24, 2025, from https://en.wikipedia.org/wiki/Mechanism_design
2. (2018). *The New Palgrave Dictionary of Economics* (3rd ed.). Palgrave Mcmillan. Referenced text to be found in p. 8632.

3. Hurwicz, L., & Reiter, S. (2006). *Designing economic mechanisms*. Cambridge University Press.
4. Diamantaras, D. with Cardamone, E. I., Campbell, K. A., Deacle, S., & Delgado, L. A. (2009). *A toolbox for economic design*. Palgrave Macmillan
5. Game theory. (2025, April 16). In Wikipedia. Retrieved April 17, 2025, from https://en.wikipedia.org/wiki/Game_theory
6. (2018). *The New Palgrave Dictionary of Economics* (3rd ed.). Palgrave Mcmillan. Referenced text to be found in p. 5014
7. Osborne, M. J. (2003). *An introduction to game theory*. Oxford University Press.
8. Dutta, P. K., & Vergote, W. (2022). *Strategies and games; Theory and practice* (2nd ed.). MIT Press.
9. Roughgarden, T. (2016). *Twenty lectures on algorithmic game theory*. Cambridge University Press.
10. Mookherjee, D. (2008). The 2007 Nobel memorial prize in mechanism design theory. *Scandinavian Journal of Economics, 110*(2), 237–260. Retrieved March 24, 2025, from https://papers.ssrn.com/sol3/papers.cfm?abstract_id=1167544 (also available from https://www.jstor.org/stable/25195341)
11. Hayes, A. (2024, August 4). *White Paper: Types, Purpose, and How to Write One*. Retrieved March 24, 2025, from https://www.investopedia.com/terms/w/whitepaper.asp
12. Kaur, G. (2023, August 2). What is a white paper? A beginner's guide on how to write and format one. CoinTelegraph. Retrieved March 22, 2025, from https://cointelegraph.com/ico-101/what-is-a-white-paper-and-how-to-write-it%20 https://cointelegraph.com/ico-101/what-is-a-white-paper-and-how-to-write-it
13. *Branches of Government*. The House Explained. United States House of Representatives. Retrieved March 24, 2025, from https://www.house.gov/the-house-explained/branches-of-government
14. [MakerDAO Token ecosystem] https://makerdao.com/en/. Retrieved April 4, 2025. Please note: MakerDAO is currently a subset of the Sky Token ecosystem (https://sky.money/)
15. [MakerDAO Whitepaper – MCD version preceding migration to Sky.money] The Maker Protocol: MakerDAO's Multi-Collateral Dai (MCD) System. Retrieved April 5, 2025 from https://makerdao.com/whitepaper/White%20Paper%20-The%20Maker%20Protocol_%20MakerDAO%E2%80%99s%20Multi-Collateral%20Dai%20(MCD)%20System-FINAL-%20021720.pdf, linked into from https://makerdao.com/en/whitepaper
16. [MakerDAO Whitepaper – DAI] The Dai Stablecoin System. Retrieved April 5, 2025, from https://makerdao.com/whitepaper/DaiDec17WP.pdf, linked into from https://makerdao.com/en/whitepaper/#the-dai-stablecoin
17. The Dai Savings Rate. Retrieved April 4, 2025, from https://makerdao.com/en/whitepaper/#the-dai-savings-rate. Please note: MakerDAO is currently a subset of the Sky Token ecosystem (https://sky.money/)
18. [Bancor Token ecosystem] https://www.bancor.network/
19. [Bancor – Bprotocol page on P2PF Wiki] https://wiki.p2pfoundation.net/Bancor
20. (2022, March). *BIP15: Proposing Bancor 3*. Bancor governance discussion pages. Retrieved March 24, 2025, from https://gov.bancor.network/t/bip15-proposing-bancor-3/3445#governance-11
21. [Bancor Whitepaper]. Hertzog, E., Benartzi, Gu. & Benartzi, Ga. (2017, May 30). Bancor Protocol. Continuous Liquidity and Asynchronous Price Discovery for Tokens through their Smart Contracts; aka "Smart Tokens". Retrieved March 24, 2025, from https://www.allcryptowhitepapers.com/wp-content/uploads/2018/05/Bancor.pdf
22. [Nexus Mutual Token ecosystem] https://nexusmutual.io/
23. What is staking? Retrieved March 24, 2025, from https://www.coinbase.com/learn/crypto-basics/what-is-staking
24. *Claim Assessment*. Nexus Mutual documentation pages. Retrieved March 23, 2025, from https://docs.nexusmutual.io/protocol/claims-assessment

25. [Liquity Token ecosystem] https://www.liquity.org/
26. Official Liquity documentation. Liquity documentation pages. Retrieved March 24, 2025, from https://docs.liquity.org
27. [Yearn Token ecosystem] https://yearn.fi
28. *Yearn documentation (User, Dev, DAO).* Yearn documentation pages. Retrieved March 24, 2025, from https://docs.yearn.fi/ https://gov.yearn.finance/
29. Griffith-Jones, J. (2016, June 30). *Global regulation in the post-crisis era.* Retrieved March 24, 2025, from https://www.fca.org.uk/news/speeches/global-regulation-post-crisis-era
30. Gramm–Leach–Bliley Act. (2025, April 2). In *Wikipedia.* Retrieved April 17, 2025, from https://en.wikipedia.org/wiki/Gramm-Leach-Bliley_Act
31. Dodd–Frank Wall Street Reform and Consumer Protection Act. (2025, April 10). In *Wikipedia.* Retrieved April 17, 2025, from https://en.wikipedia.org/wiki/Dodd-Frank_Wall_Street_Reform_and_Consumer_Protection_Act
32. Bailey, A. (2019, April 23). The future of financial conduct regulation. Retrieved March 24, 2025, from https://www.fca.org.uk/news/speeches/future-financial-conduct-regulation
33. Nash equilibrium. (2025, April 12). In *Wikipedia.* Retrieved April 17, 2025, from https://en.wikipedia.org/wiki/Nash_equilibrium
34. Ross, S. A. (1973). The economic theory of agency: The principal's problem. *The American Economic Review, 63*(2), 134–139.
35. Samuelson, P. A. (1977). Reaffirming the existence of "reasonable" Bergson-Samuelson social welfare functions. *Economica, 44*(103), 81–88.
36. Kahneman, D., Knetsch, J. L., & Thaler, R. H. (1986). Fairness and the Assumptions of Economics. *The Journal of Business, 59*(4), 285–300. Accessible at http://www.jstor.org/stable/2352761
37. Hui, A. & Zhao, W. (2021, September 14). *Over $280M Drained in KuCoin Crypto Exchange Hack.* CoinDesk. Retrieved March 24, 2025, from https://www.coindesk.com/markets/2020/09/26/over-280m-drained-in-kucoin-crypto-exchange-hack/
38. (2020, November 21). *The Latest Updates About the KuCoin Security Incident - Continually Updated.* KuCoin corporate communication. Retrieved March 24, 2025, from https://www.kucoin.com/news/en-the-latest-updates-about-the-kucoin-security-incident
39. Foxley, W. (2021, September 14). *Ocean Protocol Forks to Retrieve Tokens Stolen From KuCoin Exchange.* CoinDesk. Retrieved March 24, 2025, from https://www.coindesk.com/tech/2020/09/28/ocean-protocol-forks-to-retrieve-tokens-stolen-from-kucoin-exchange/
40. Chong, N. (2020, September 29). Synthetix founder speaks on Kucoin hack of $2.5m in SNX, millions in other DeFi coins. CryptoSlate. Retrieved March 24, 2025, from https://cryptoslate.com/synthetix-founder-speaks-on-kucoin-hack-of-2-5m-in-snx-millions-in-other-defi-coins/
41. Market structure. (2025, April 4). In *Wikipedia.* Retrieved April 12, 2025, from https://en.wikipedia.org/wiki/Market_structure
42. *Market Structure - How different industries are classified and differentiated based on their degree and nature of competition for services and goods.* Corporate Finance Institute. Retrieved March 24, 2025, from https://corporatefinanceinstitute.com/resources/economics/market-structure/
43. https://www.investopedia.com/articles/stocks/11/securities-market-introduction.asp
44. [Augur Token infrastructure software] https://github.com/AugurProject
45. [Uniswap Token ecosystem] https://uniswap.org/
46. [Gnosis Token ecosystem] https://www.gnosis.io/
47. [Algorand Token ecosystem] https://www.algorand.com/
48. [Rarible NFT marketplace] https://www.rarible.com/
49. Proportional–integral–derivative controller. (2025, April 17). In *Wikipedia.* Retrieved April 18, 2025, from https://en.wikipedia.org/wiki/Proportional-integral-derivative_controller
50. [Frax Token ecosystem.] https://frax.finance/
51. [Hegic Token ecosystem] https://www.hegic.co/
52. [Fairblock Blockchain platform] https://fairblock.network/

53. [Celer Blockchain interoperability protocol] https://www.celer.network/
54. [Sushiswap Token ecosystem] https://sushi.com
55. *What is Sushi*. SushiSwap documentation pages. Retrieved March 24, 2025, from https://docs.sushi.com/what-is-sushi
56. [Loop Finance Decentralized Exchange] https://juno.loop.markets/
57. [Loop Finance] Platform Fees. Loop Finance documentation pages. Retrieved March 24, 2025, from https://docs.loop.markets/loop-finance/nft-marketplace/platform-fees
58. [Enzyme Token ecosystem] https://enzyme.finance/
59. Herger, I. (2021, March 10). Monetising your Vaults: the inner workings of fees on Enzyme. Medium. Retrieved March 24, 2025, from https://medium.com/enzymefinance/monetising-your-vaults-the-inner-workings-of-fees-on-enzyme-d5b275e7b9f5
60. [Yearn] Vault Tokens. Yearn documentation pages. Retrieved March 20, 2025, from https://docs.yearn.fi/getting-started/products/yvaults/vault-tokens
61. Olszewicz, J. (2021, January 28). Yearn Finance Price Analysis – v2 yVaults launch. Retrieved March 24, 2025, from https://bravenewcoin.com/insights/yearn-finance-price-analysis-v2-yvaults-launch
62. [MojitoSwap Token ecosystem] https://www.mojitoswap.finance/
63. [WitNet Token ecosysetm] https://witnet.io/
64. [VeChain Token ecosystem] https://www.vechain.org/
65. Investopedia Team. (2024, July 31). *VeChain: What It Is, How It Works, Examples, and History*. Retrieved March 24, 2025, from https://www.investopedia.com/terms/v/vechain.asp
66. [Centrifuge Tokenization platform and Token marketplace] https://centrifuge.io/
67. Schmitt, L. (2019, November 6). *Centrifuge Tinlake: Adding real-world assets to MCD*. Medium. Retrieved March 24, 2025, from https://medium.com/centrifuge/centrifuge-tinlake-adding-real-world-assets-to-mcd-68cbcb67e9a4
68. [AirBie bicycle fleet management software platform] https://airbie.io/en/description/
69. Licorish, E. (2021, May 24). *Decentralized Prediction Market Platform Augur Turbo Launches With Chainlink Oracles*. ChainlinkToday. Retrieved March 24, 2025, from https://chainlinktoday.com/decentralized-prediction-market-platform-augur-turbo-launches-with-chainlink-oracles/
70. [Chainlink Data Feeds] *Decentralized data feeds for smart contracts*. Chainlink product pages. Retrieved March 24, 2025, from https://chain.link/data-feeds
71. Griffith, T.A. (2018, December 14). *Commit Reveal Scheme on Ethereum. Hiding Actions and Generating Random Numbers*. Retrieved March 24, 2025, from https://medium.com/gitcoin/commit-reveal-scheme-on-ethereum-25d1d1a25428
72. (2021, October). *Conviction Voting*. Giveth governance discussion pages. Retrieved March 24, 2025, from https://forum.giveth.io/t/conviction-voting/154
73. [Tezos] *Voting Power*. Tezos documentation pages. Retrieved March 24, 2025, from https://octez.tezos.com/docs/active/voting.html#voting-power-quebec
74. AdChain. (2017, September 6). Dev Diary I: A Walkthrough of PLCR Voting in Solidity. Medium. Retrieved March 24, 2025, from https://medium.com/metax-publication/a-walkthrough-of-plcr-voting-in-solidity-92420bd5b87c
75. *What is Politeia?* Decred documentation pages. Retrieved March 24, 2025, from https://docs.decred.org/governance/politeia/overview/
76. *Introduction to Decred Governance*. Decred documentation pages. Retrieved March 24, 2025, from https://docs.decred.org/governance/overview/
77. [Secret Token ecosystem] https://scrt.network
78. Confidential Voting. *Secret documentation pages*. Retrieved March 24, 2025, from https://docs.scrt.network/secret-network-documentation/confidential-computing-layer/ibc/usecases/confidential-voting
79. Buterin, V., Hitzig, Z. & Weyl E.G. (2018). Liberal Radicalism: A Flexible Design For Philanthropic Matching Funds. Available at SSRN: https://ssrn.com/abstract=3243656 or https://doi.org/10.2139/ssrn.3243656

80. [Gitcoin Grants initative] https://www.gitcoin.co/
81. (2021, October 23). *What is Quadratic Voting/Funding? How did we improve it?* Retrieved March 24, 2025, from https://hidorahacks.medium.com/what-is-quadratic-voting-funding-how-did-we-improve-it-70989e813cf9
82. *Governance*. Aave documentation pages. Retrieved March 24, 2025, from https://aave.com/docs/primitives/governance
83. [SpruceID]https://coinquora.com/ethereum-foundation-supports-spruces-view-of-decentralized-identity-verification Identity infrastructure for the digital world. SpruceID product pages. Retrieved March 24, 2025, from https://spruceid.com/
84. Plutocracy. (2025, March 21). In *Wikipedia*. Retrieved March 25, 2025, from https://en.wikipedia.org/wiki/Plutocracy
85. Rude Jensen, J., Von Wachter, V., & Ross, O. (2021, February 2). *How Decentralized is the Governance of Blockchain-based Finance: Empirical Evidence from four Governance Token Distributions*. Retrieved March 25, 2025, from https://arxiv.org/abs/2102.10096
86. Robinson, D. & Konstantopoulos, G. (2020, August 28). *Ethereum is a Dark Forest*. Retrieved March 25, 2025, from https://www.paradigm.xyz/2020/08/ethereum-is-a-dark-forest/
87. Decentralized Algorand Governance Proposal (mentions "One Algo, one vote"). Available at https://prismic-io.s3.amazonaws.com/algorandfoundationv2/1f4bd113-3f64-4d3e-b69b-bcd988305359_ALG102-21Q2-C_Governance+Proposal_en-IE_FINAL.PDF
88. [TRON Token ecosystem] https://tron.network/
89. *Super Representatives*. TRON developer documentation pages. Retrieved March 24, 2025, from https://developers.tron.network/docs/super-representatives
90. Karakostas, D., Kiayias, A., Nasikas, C. & Zindros, D. (2019, July 4). *Cryptocurrency Egalitarianism: A Quantitative Approach*. Retrieved March 24, 2025, from https://arxiv.org/abs/1907.02434
91. (2020, June 9). *Coin Metric's State of the Network: Issue 54*. Retrieved March 24, 2025, from https://coinmetrics.substack.com/p/coin-metrics-state-of-the-network-49c
92. Sybil attack. (2024, October 21). In *Wikipedia*. Retrieved March 17, 2025, from https://en.wikipedia.org/wiki/Sybil_attack

Case Study in Mechanism Design: Lido 9

The previous chapter set theoretical foundations of mechanism design in the context of blockchain-based token ecosystems. How their practical application is evident in the workings of already operational token protocols will be now demonstrated through a case study. Its focus will be "Lido" [1], which is currently one of the top DeFi projects (by token market capitalization) in the "Liquid Staking" category [2].

As in the previous case study, we begin with the cl osest analogues to Lido's business case from traditional finance in order to help the reader interpret its main transactional pathways. A brief foray to the ecosystem's market design will be necessary in order to concretize Lido agent types and interaction pathways, as only then can mechanisms be properly identified and examined for consistency. Project documentation will be used to identify them, and its governance records to then interpret them as design choices. Finally, we will seek to trace in them the influence of the design factors (governance, market structure, financial/non-financial incentives) promulgated in the previous chapter.

9.1 Promissory Notes

What are today known as "Promissory Notes" [3] have a documented history going back to at least the twelfth century AD/CE [4] in Europe. Before the establishment of money lending institutions that introduced the paradigm of capital market intermediation [5], all lending transactions were bilateral. The practical need to somehow document the fact that such a transaction ever took place led to the creation of two simple forms of written attestation, which gradually became expected practice in commercial life:

a. The Promissory Note
b. The Bill of Exchange

I. Giannakouros, *Cryptocurrencies and Tradable Crypto-Tokens*, Future of Business and Finance, https://doi.org/10.1007/978-3-031-98423-5_9

The **promissory note** (PN) is written from the standpoint of the borrower, who thus acknowledges the principal amount and the effective annual interest due to the lender at either a definite future time or whenever the lender requests. The **bill of exchange** (BoEx) is written from the standpoint of the lender, who thus orders the borrower to return the principal amount plus the accrued interest at again either a definite time or upon request. The economic effects of the two written forms are the same, however their variations, usage modalities, and legal repercussions may be different depending on the jurisdiction. Their significance for commercial life (also for international trade) eventually became so important that their content and expected usance had to be standardized and enshrined in law—and eventually in international treaties).

In the UK for example [6–8], in order to be valid, a Promissory Note must be an "*unconditional promise in writing made by one person to another signed by the maker*", etc., and satisfying additional conditions which at a minimum include evidences of:

- When was the note issued ("**Issue Date**").
- A clear identification of who the **borrower** (also termed "**Issuer**" or "**Promisor**") and the **Lender** (also termed "**Payee**" or "**Promisee**") are.
- Declaring either a fixed ("**Payable by**") or an unspecified ("**Payable on demand**") **tenor**.
- Specifying the interest rate modality (fixed, variable) and reference rates applying, within an "**Annual Percentage Rate**" (**APR**) section.

Apart from these minimal conditions, there are several variations having to do, e.g. with the existence of two or more borrowers signing the note together (thus assuming joint and several liability for repayment of borrowed funds), the posting of collateral ("**Secured Note**"), the postulation of other legally valid and mutually accepted terms (such as late payment fees and penalties), etc. Fig. 9.1 shows schematically the simplest case of an unsecured promissory note.

The constellation depicted by this simple case is recognized in the commercial laws of practically all legal jurisdictions, both common-law and civil-law. A promissory note issued in the US [9], Singapore [10] or Hong-Kong [11], a "*Wechsel/Billet à ordre/Pagherò*" issued in Switzerland [12], a "*Billet à ordre*" in France [13], or a "*Pagaré*" in Spain [14] refer to the same lending transaction with the same

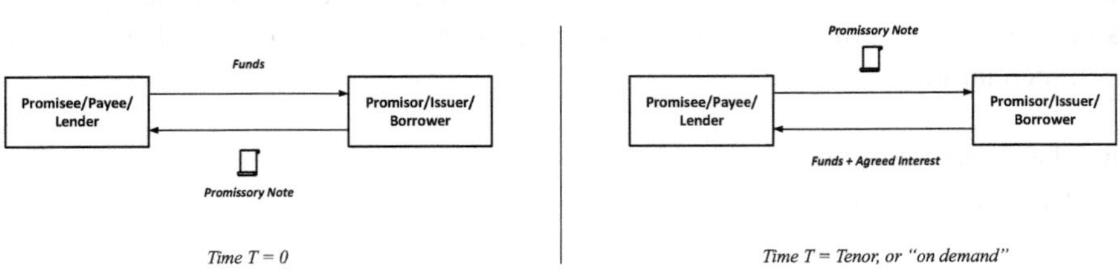

Fig. 9.1 Promissory note

usances, and based on a written attestation recording the same expected minimal terms as those of a promissory note issued in the UK.

An important feature of a promissory note is its "assignability", meaning the prerogative of the promisee to sell it (formally, to "**assign** the right to collect on the note") to a third party without having to first request permission from the promisor. This is usual practice in all major legal systems and is meant to accommodate practical needs of people of business. For example, imagine a promisee being confronted with pressing liquidity needs and having no other option than to sell illiquid assets on its balance sheet (a promissory note being one such by definition, as it represents a claim on future receivables) at a discount. A third party, after performing due diligence on the creditworthiness of the promisor and on the legality and validity of the claims represented by the promissory note, offers to buy the right to collect against the promisor, at a discount to the face value of the claim. After **negotiating** and finally agreeing on a discount acceptable to both, the promisee countersigns ("**endorses**") the physical document and surrenders it to the new owner (the new "**bearer**") receiving the agreed sum in return.

This simple assignment transaction is depicted on Fig. 9.2, where alternative terms for the main participants are also given.

Note that the new bearer may eventually sell the promissory note on to yet another fourth party, again by **negotiating** a discount and then **endorsing** the note's physical document, without having to request permission from either the promisor or the original promisee. There is no prescribed limit to the number of times that a promissory note can be assigned, as long as certain assignment formalities (which may be jurisdiction-specific) are observed. It goes without saying that a promissory note can nowadays be issued in electronic form,[1] which, again, may entail different assignment formalities to those of the physical-document form.[2]

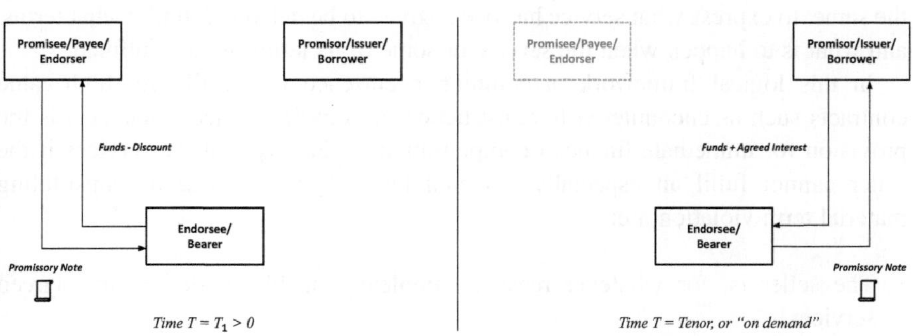

Fig. 9.2 Assignment of promissory note

[1] One of the earliest legally acceptable *electronically*-issued Promissory Notes wat the South Korean "eNote", introduced by way of [15].

[2] A list of expected procedural steps (and updated terminology) specific to the US jurisdiction can be found at [16].

Summarizing the above, a promissory note, which starts by being the simple attestation of debt owed by borrowers to lenders, is legally allowed to become a negotiable and assignable financial instrument by both common-law and civil-law jurisdictions. The face value of said financial instrument increases with time, as per the annual percentage rate calculation prescribed in its terms and conditions. In its simplest form it is a bilateral instrument, evidencing a financial obligation of one issuer towards one payee/bearer.

As a final note, in many jurisdictions there exists yet another written document form to evidence the financial obligation of a borrower towards a lender, namely through a so-called "IOU" [17] (pronouncing out the vowels reads "I owe you", there being no other meaning behind the initials). We mention it only for the sake of completeness, but must also make clear that its legal status (enforceability) is not as unassailable as that of a promissory note; there are no expected terms and conditions implying validity of its content, and furthermore it is typically non-negotiable. It is at best an informal written agreement, which may or may not become admissible as proof in a court of law.

9.2 Financial Guarantees: Surety

Whenever a service needs to be delivered in the real economy, a written or verbal contract is agreed. A contract is fundamentally an expression (documentation, if in writing) of the allocation of rights and responsibilities which is being accepted by the contracting parties. Its terms specify at a minimum what is to be delivered, up until which time, in what stages and at what price. There are still other terms meant to explain what the repercussions of non-fulfilment of some or all of the basic terms would be. There are details of the elements of a valid contract that differ among common-law and civil-law jurisdictions[3] [18], however the logical framework is the same: to express what service has been agreed to be delivered, under what terms, and what is to happen when the service or some of its terms are not fulfilled.

In this logical framework, a common occurrence (especially for high-value contracts such as encountered in construction or complex projects delivery) is the provision for immediate financial compensation of the buyer of the services if the seller cannot fulfil an especially essential term. Typical situations constituting material term violation are:

- The seller is, for whatever reason, completely unable to deliver the agreed services.
- The seller delivers services of different features than those described in the contract.

[3] A relevant concise reference would be [18].

- The quality of deliverables is demonstrably inferior to the level agreed upon in the contract.
- The seller does not deliver the agreed services within the agreed timeframe.

And still others, the direct outcome of which is that the buyer suffers financial losses or reputational damage, or any other undue deterioration to its own business prospects. Hence, to cover this risk, most services delivery contracts provide for concrete proof that a financial reserve of a specific amount is ready to be transferred to the ownership of the buyer should the risk materialize. This amount is dependent on the prior business track-record of the seller, its proven level of up-to-date expertise, the depth of its delivery resources, its creditworthiness, etc. The entire reserve constitutes in effect an insurance amount, upon which the buyer can draw as per the contract in case of material non-performance on the part of the seller. It goes without saying that, once the seller delivers a service which is accepted by the buyer as complying with the terms of the contract, then all contingent rights of the buyer to the financial reserve are withdrawn.

There are two general ways in which proof of this financial reserve is provided:

a. By posting *à priori* the entire amount in an escrow account, to which both the buyer and the seller have access.
b. By delivering a legally binding promise in writing by another party acceptable to the seller, that the prescribed amount will be made immediately available to the buyer in case of proven contractual non-performance by the seller.

The first case is termed (in traditional finance) **"providing a financial guarantee in the form of capital"**.

The second is termed **"providing a Surety Guarantee"**.[4] "Surety" [20] stems from the legal term "Suretyship" which is generally defined [21] as "a promise to answer for the duty of another".

There are various usages of this term in commercial practice, such as "being in a Suretyship position", or "having a Suretyship provision", etc. In all cases, there is an assumed basic constellation of actors (cf. Fig. 9.3):

1. The debtor or promisor may incur a liability, contingent on an event.
2. The creditor or promisee is the actor to whom said liability will be due.
3. The guarantor or surety is the actor promising to cover said liability if the debtor/promisor cannot.

Hence, the surety will deliver a written promise (a surety guarantee) to the promisee that a specified amount will be transferred to their ownership in case of proven contractual non-performance by the promisor. The promisor will "buy" this

[4] A Surety Guarantee is also a kind (subtype) of Performance Bond, cf. for example [19]

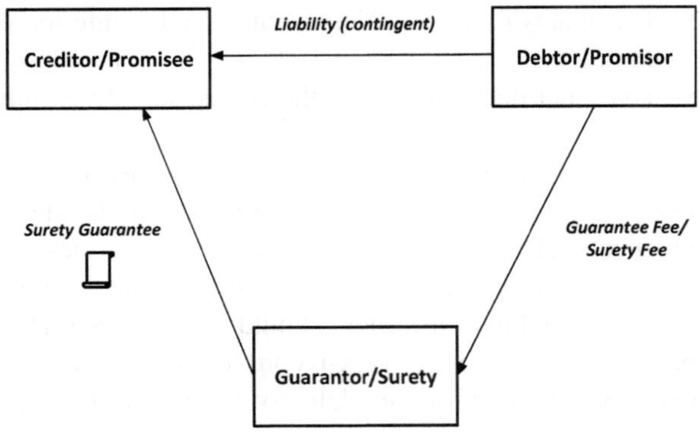

Fig. 9.3 Actors of a Suretyship transaction

written guarantee by paying immediately a fee (guarantee fee or surety fee) to the surety.

It was already mentioned that the financial reserve in question constitutes in effect an insurance amount. Hence it should come as no surprise that the main institutional sureties in traditional finance are the same types of companies that dominate the counterparty credit risk business: Banks and credit insurers. They have that expertise in the credit and actuarial space that allows them to price the surety fee, taking all relevant factors about the debtor/promisor and the contractual obligation (hence the contingent risk) in question into account. It is usual for a promisor to request guarantee quotes from several banks/insurers before deciding to "buy" a particular guarantee.

A note is in order on two points relating to the (very succinct) explanation on financial guarantees above: first, a surety guarantee is not [22, 23] a generic Bank ("Demand") guarantee; second, the decision of whether to post capital in an escrow account or to buy a surety guarantee is a matter for both of the (services) contractual counterparties to negotiate. Both options have pros and cons, and idiosyncratic circumstances (types of risk inherent to the performance contract, preference or legal requirements on the part of the buyer, solvency, rsp. creditworthiness of the seller, etc.) will ultimately dictate the one to decide on.

9.3 Alternative Investment Funds

An important part of the financial services industry revolves around the creation, distribution, marketing, and advising of financial instruments, for the purposes of wealth accumulation by private individuals, and capital appreciation by institutional investors. This is the domain of asset managers, of large Banks and of financial advisors.

Portfolio risk management, which is at the heart of this industry, is an area of financial expertise which underwent a significant paradigm change approximately from the mid-1970s until the mid-1990s. Most current concepts about investment typologies (except for the crypto-token universe) and financial risk management tools were crystalized in the period immediately after this paradigm change. The reasons for this change were varied: abandonment of fixed parities among major currencies in the mid-1970s [24], creation of the first mathematically plausible models for pricing of hedging instruments in the mid-1970s [25], financialization of major economies in the 1980s and 90s [26], new capabilities and relative affordability of novel computing systems that came of age in the early 1990s [27], and still others. All of them, taken together, created the impetus for the gradual acceptance of the notion that a more mathematical understanding of the workings (and, ultimately, controllability) of financial markets than was the case before the 1970s was indeed possible. One of the outcomes of that paradigm change was the creation of investment products based on portfolios of financial instruments that were outside the "traditional" mix typically recommended to investors: long-only positions in equities, bonds (corporate or sovereign), and cash (or cash equivalents)—typically denominated in the base currency of the investor. For example, the fact that market risk could (at least theoretically) be hedged through options led to the creation of the first generation of hedge funds—literally denoting "investment portfolios with hedged positions" at the time. However, as adventurous fund managers started offering shares in "mix-and-match" portfolios with only loose correlations among positions and still calling them "Hedge Fund Investments", compounded by the fact that hedging proved to be a bit more complicated in practice [28] than what theory suggested, the term "Hedge Fund" ultimately came to signify any managed portfolio that combined long and short positions across asset classes. In other words, any portfolio that was not long-only in equities, bonds, and cash.

As more and more investable products of a "non-traditional" mix started being created and marketed to investors, there arose the practical need (also put forth by financial regulators) for a typology—and terminology—applicable to this particular financial domain. The outcome was the term "Alternative Investments", meaning initially investments that were "non-traditional", in the sense of **not** being portfolios of long-only positions in equities, bonds, and cash. As single-class positions (e.g. equity options) were also caught under this "catch-all" meaning, the industry ultimately settled on the practical solution of listing what asset classes (and portfolios thereof) would actually qualify as "Alternatives". This "listing approach" is what still applies today in the asset management industry. Event though there is nowadays extensive literature [29] around alternative investments, and the most important Asset Management jurisdictions have established corresponding robust regulatory frameworks [30–38], there are still no clear-cut criteria [39] of what asset classes precisely fall under those regulations; hence the listing approach is by default not inclusive.

An alternative investment taxonomy that is frequently used in traditional finance includes:

1. Hedge Funds [40]
2. Private Equity [41]

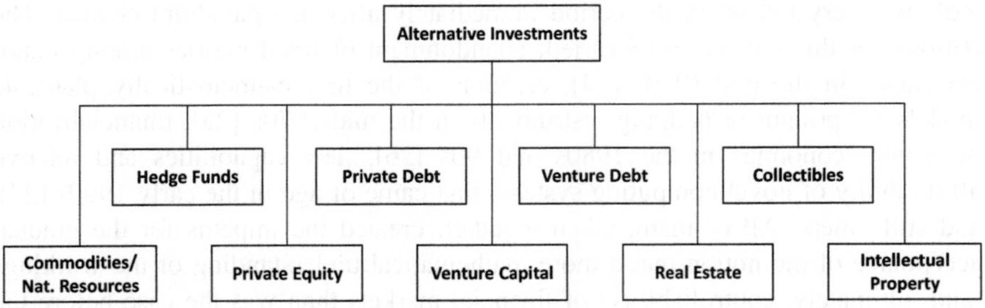

Fig. 9.4 Alternative investment asset classes in traditional finance (i.e. omitting crypto-tokens)

3. Private Debt[5]
4. Venture Capital [42]
5. Venture Debt [43]
6. Real Estate [44]
7. Commodities [45]/Natural resources [46]
8. Collectibles [47]
9. Intellectual Property [48]

as depicted on Fig. 9.4 (please note that crypto-tokens are currently sometimes included among the alternative asset classes [49] and sometimes not [50]; the current *exposé* limits itself to traditional finance).

Each of the afore-mentioned asset classes comes with sub-classifications, reflecting more fine granular criteria such as the precise asset sub-class, the economic sector and/or geography targeted, the type of the investment recipient, or even the strategy used to allocate investments. For example, a publication in the "Knowledge Series" of the Chartered Alternative Investment Analyst (CAIA [51]) Association® proposes [52] the following classification of Hedge Funds according to their underlying investment strategy:

i. Macro and managed futures
   a. Macro
   b. Managed futures
ii. Event-driven
   a. Activists
   b. Merger arbitrage
   c. Distressed
   d. Event-driven multistrategy
iii. Relative value
   a. Convertible arbitrage
   b. Volatility arbitrage

[5]Please refer to Sect. 14.3 for a concise explanation

   c. Fixed-income arbitrage
   d. Relative value multistrategy
iv. Equity
   a. Long/short
   b. Market neutral
   c. Short selling
v. Funds of hedge funds

Each of these sub-classifications comes with its own set of idiosyncrasies (e.g. there is a bespoke corpus of knowledge on Convertible arbitrage [53], and similarly for all other items in the classification list above). Hence, this traditional finance field is quite complex and constantly evolving.

Even though the original evolution of alternative investments focused on the needs of large institutional and private wealth investors, the sector eventually started packaging positions into portfolios that could be invested into through participation units. This offering replicated the traditional paradigm of mutual funds, however with some (regulator-imposed) investment thresholds, reflecting the idiosyncratic risk profile (such as illiquidity and volatility) of some alternative assets. In short, as long as prospective investors could bear the idiosyncratic risk of alternatives, alternative investment funds (or "Alternative Mutual Funds" [54]) were offered to them. Issuance and distribution of such funds is nowadays robustly regulated, along with the rest of the alternatives continuum.

An important note is in order, regarding the structure of fees charged to investment fund investors in general and to alternative investment fund investors in particular. Each investment fund has a manager (role can be assigned to a single human or to a legal entity), tasked with investment decisions and general portfolio management.[6] Depending on the review and update needs of the investment strategy chosen (especially on the frequency of portfolio rebalancing and concomitant hedging/overlay strategies) a manager may have either a mostly passive or a more active role. This has repercussions for the fees that are ultimately charged to fund investors.

The typical fee structure has two components:

a. Management
b. Performance

Management fees are charged as a percentage of the amount invested in the fund (or "Assets Under Management"), calculated at time points prescribed in the fund

[6] There are typically several other actors involved, such as Administrators, Legal Documenters, Servicers, etc. An explanation of the generic Asset Management Fund setup falls outside the scope of this section.

Prospectus[7] [55]. **Performance fees** are instead charged as a percentage of the profits achieved by the investment strategy, and calculated at the end of holding period intervals also prescribed in the prospectus. Performance fees are typically much (usually around ten times) higher than management fees, the intention being to incentivize the manager to achieve the best result possible.

Several traditional investment fund products (such as index-tracking exchange-traded funds, and others where there is no outperformance goal against an observable market benchmark) involve only fixed management fees. However, alternative investment funds typically promise active management (e.g. either taking timed directional views or dynamically hedging) of a portfolio. Hence, both management and performance fees are generally expected in this funds category. There are also some fund subtypes—especially Venture Capital (VC) funds legally incorporated as a Limited Partnership [58, 59]—where the Manager ("General Partner" in the VC funds case) can demand quite high performance fees from individual investors ("Limited Partners") in the fund.

9.4 Staking and "Liquid Staking"

In Chap. 1, Sect. 1.1, we mentioned the type of consensus mechanism as being a distinguishing characteristic of any given blockchain. One such type is the "Proof-of-Stake" (PoS) [60], which entails delegating the task of consensus verification to authorized agents, who then have to post a specific amount of admissible tokens (the "Stake") in lieu of performance guarantee.

For example, this amount in the case of the Ethereum 2 L-1 blockchain is currently set at a minimum of 32 ETH [61]. Posting this stake causes a new entity (i.e. a public address [62] on the Ethereum blockchain) to be authorized for the task, and the requisite software—"validating", "consensus" and "execution" components—to be activated for download by the corresponding node operator (i.e. the human agent(s) owning and operating the technical infrastructure on which said software will run). The agent undertaking this task ("Validator" in Ethereum parlance [63]) has to then retain a balance of at least 16 ETH posted at all times [64] in what is in effect an escrow account administered by the Ethereum governance. Each successful consensus verification action is rewarded by newly minted ETH [65], hence a regular income stream can accrue to the agent if their assigned task is carried out repeatedly and consistently.

On the other hand, if individual validators are shown to be grossly negligent in the execution of their task (i.e. whenever their non-performance threatens the integrity of the Ethereum blockchain [66] and potentially indicates malicious behaviour [67]), then their stake can be forfeited (either partially through "Penalties" [68], or entirely

[7] In some jurisdictions there are specific (similar, but more standardized) documentation forms prescribed by the Asset Management regulators, e.g. the EU "Key Investor Information Document" [56] or "Key Investor Document" [57], etc.

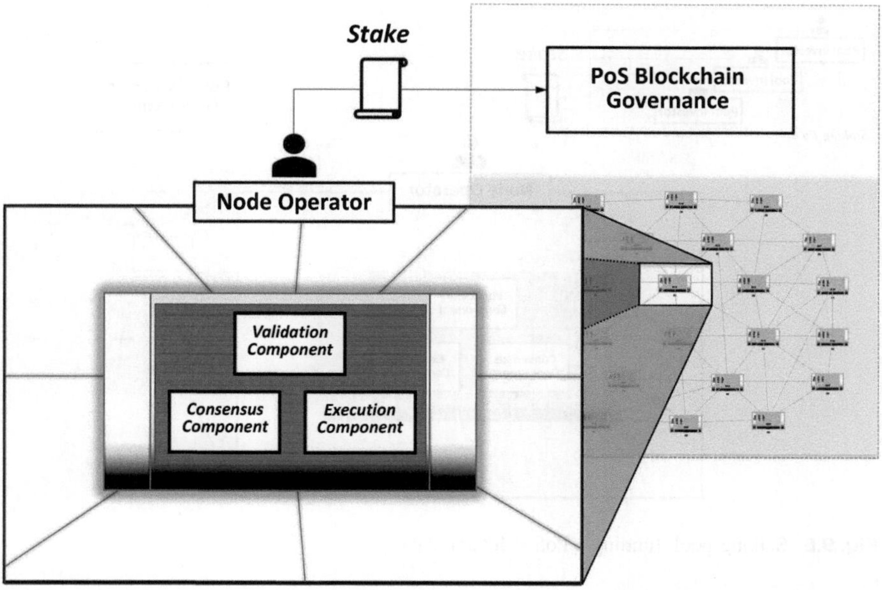

Fig. 9.5 Staking in PoS blockchains; node operator controls an authorized PoS validator (Ethereum)

through "Slashings" [69–71]). Slashings, if not rectified, can result in the eviction of an agent from the registry of validators. The Ethereum PoS setup is depicted schematically in Fig. 9.5.

In summary, becoming a PoS validator is a privilege accorded by Ethereum governance to agents that are prepared to stake at least 32 ETH as a financial guarantee, in return for a potential ETH income stream. Severe non-performance events attributable to them can cause loss of this privilege and may result in partial or total forfeiture of their guarantee. Importantly, the ETH stake, once posted, remains in the possession of (so to speak, "is locked by") the Ethereum governance for period of time, the duration of which is subject to both governance decisions[8] and practical operational constraints [72, 73].

This clearly represents a liquidity risk to the validator, compounded by the opportunity cost of not investing those 32 (minimum) ETH—a non-negligible amount [74]—elsewhere in the crypto space instead of having them locked up in the expectation of staking rewards. This liquidity risk is not unique to Ethereum validators but applies to agents supporting consensus in other PoS-based blockchains as well. This fact has led to the emergence of specialized token ecosystems, the business case of which revolves around finding ways of "liberating" liquidity from PoS staking positions. They are in fact an evolution of a previous business model (cf. Fig. 9.6), whereby several investors have been forming

[8]It was initially up to 2 years in the run-up to Ethereum 2.

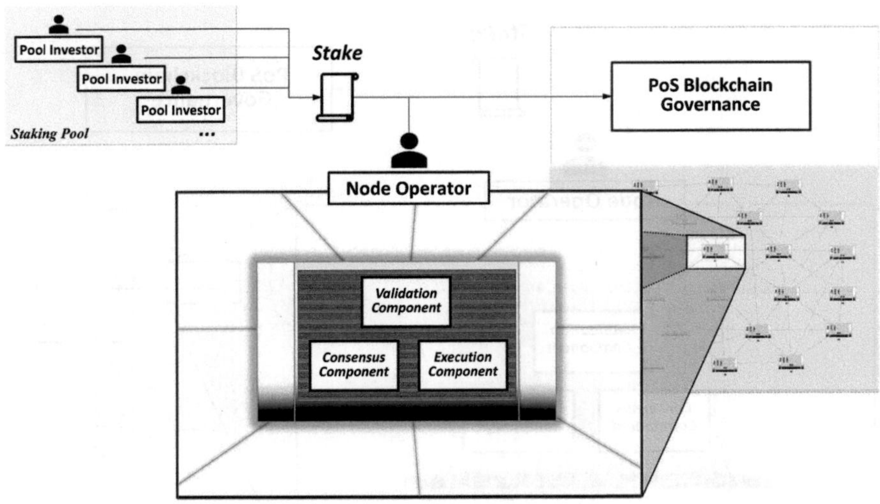

Fig. 9.6 Staking pool, funding a PoS validator stake

"Staking Pools" [75]. That meant pooling tokens together so as to reach the minimum staking amount (32 ETH in Ethereum, other minimum thresholds in other blockchains) needed to be posted as financial guarantee by a designated validator. The pool makes a loan to the validator equal to the requisite stake, in exchange for a percentage of its staking rewards.

The liquidity "liberating" business case, however, is a different one. Namely, it is still based on a "pooling" paradigm to assemble the Stake, but through the intermediate stage of minting pool-participation tokens which are then immediately returned to staking investors. If said tokens can be priced in such a way as to make them acceptable by other token ecosystems or by CEX/DEX as stores of value, then their owners can use them as liquidity for token swaps or other investments in parallel to the staking one. This is the general concept behind liquidity-liberating business cases on the basis of committed PoS staked amounts (cf. Fig. 9.7).

It goes without saying that said business cases typically entail the ecosystem charging a fee, as a percentage of the initial investment itself and/or of its yield. This fee is meant to compensate not only for the costs of setting up the requisite operational infrastructure (smart contracts[9] for minting/burning of participation tokens, accounting, treasury operations, etc.), but also—primarily—for managing the resulting business (counterparty and operational) risks. The latter come from the provision of the financial guarantee towards the target PoS blockchain, which is a risk-transfer transaction. The "liquidity-liberating" token ecosystem in effect enters into a managed risk-transfer transaction on behalf of all its investors, the aggregate funds of which function as a risk-pool. Each individual investor swaps an amount

[9]Please refer to Sect. 10.5.5 for a detailed discussion on the nature and role of Blockchain Smart Contracts.

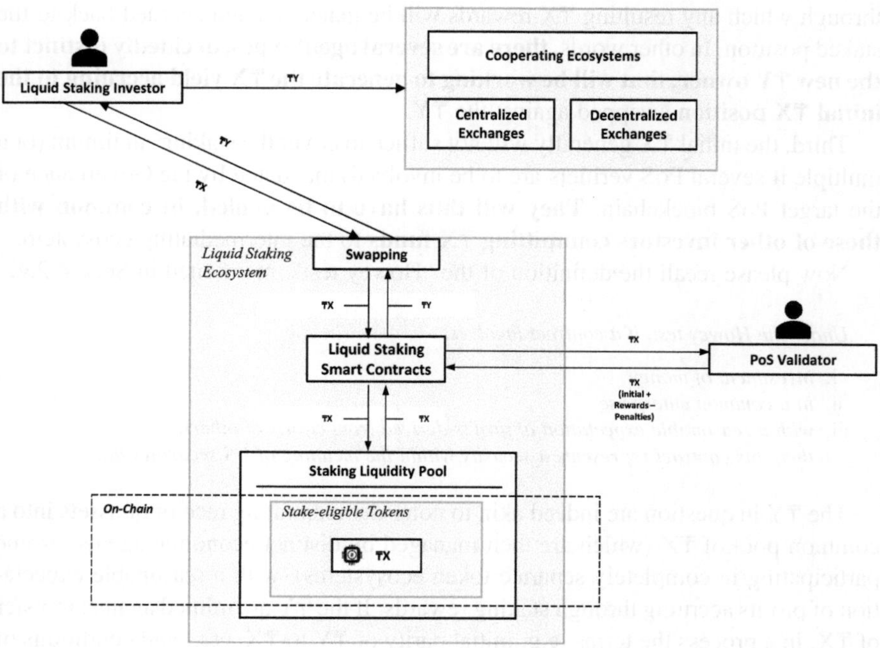

Fig. 9.7 The "Liquid Staking" business concept; ŦY are staking pool-participation tokens

denominated in tokens ŦX (say ETH—or other accepted as equivalent—if the target PoS blockchain is Ethereum) for an amount denominated in participation tokens ŦY minted by the intermediating ecosystem. The ŦX are transferred to PoS consensus verifiers ("Validators" in Ethereum) and generate yield, but are also at risk of Slashing Events; which is the risk that must also be managed as part of the contractual agreement with the investor. The ŦY are free for the investor to use and they—the same in identity or equal in number, if minted as fungible tokens—will need to be exchanged back (and burned) to recover the invested ŦX plus yield.

What is the token type (as per the token typology introduced in Chap. 4) of these ŦY?

First of all, they are minted and returned to their new owner as a "receipt" for the initial amount of ŦX plus whatever yield[10] eventually accrues to them during their holding period through the rewards of PoS validators. So, they clearly represent an **expectation of profit**.

Second, they are minted by an intermediating ecosystem, the agents of which are distinct to the ŦY owner. Said agents (human or algorithmic) are then expected to forward the initial ŦX to PoS verifiers, which are again generally not the same as the ŦY owner. Using the Ethereum PoS processes as an example, there are several agent types—not only Validators—that will cooperate in the execution of processes

[10] Again, assuming Slashing risk can be hedged.

through which any resulting ŦX rewards will be generated and accrued back to the staked position. In other words, **there are several agent types, decidedly distinct to the new ŦY owner, that will be working to generate the ŦX yield accruing to the initial ŦX position** swapped against the ŦY.

Third, the initial ŦX generally will not suffice to cover the staking minimum (or a multiple if several PoS verifiers are to be involved) mandated by the Governance of the target PoS blockchain. **They will thus have to be pooled, in common with those of other investors committing ŦX funds** to the intermediating ecosystem.

Now please recall the definition of the "Howey test", mentioned in Sect. 4.2.4:

Under the Howey test, if a contract involves:

i. *investment of money*
ii. *in a common enterprise*
iii. *with a reasonable expectation of profits derived from efforts of others,*
then this contract represents a security within the meaning of US securities law.

The ŦY in question are indeed akin to notes demonstrating receipt of assets into a common pool of ŦX (which are then managed by distinct economic agents—some participating in completely separate token ecosystems), with a reasonable expectation of profits accruing through staking rewards. If the ŦY are minted against transfer of ŦX, in a process the terms (e.g. initial parity of ŦY to ŦX, etc.) and conditions of which are:

a. described accurately through clear documentation openly available to prospective investors,
b. implemented algorithmically in a way completely conforming to said documentation,
c. having their acceptance by both parties and execution registered unambiguously, and
d. their outcomes enforceable by the governing laws of a specific off-chain jurisdiction,

said process is then perfecting a ***de facto* contractual agreement**. Hence, all prongs of the "Howey test" are satisfied and the ŦY minted by the PoS-intermediating ecosystem constitute security tokens.

Please note that: where no such ŦY minted and returned to the liquid staking investor, but their ŦX simply deposited for custody to a common pool, with no control of the custodian/pool operator on the when; how many ŦX; and from which investor; to forward to designated node operators of PoS validators, then the Howey Test might no longer be satisfied [76].

In reference to Fig. 9.7, such "liquidity-liberating" token protocols owing their business case to the existence of minimal PoS Stake requirements and nonlocking periods have come to be termed "**Liquid Staking**" [77] ones in industry parlance. The returned ŦY (as per the *exposé* above) have similarly been termed "**Liquid**

Staking Derivatives" (LSD) [78, 79]. Industry nomenclature aside, we respectfully suggest that (based on the discussion of Sect. 4.2.5), they should be properly classified as *security* tokens and *not* as derivative tokens—as they do not represent zero-sum games. We will still use the term LSD in the sequel for reasons of conformance to prevailing industry practice (paralleling the tacit acceptance of misuse of the term "NFT"), however we will ask the reader to note their proper classification as per Chap. 4.

An important detail regarding the Ethereum PoS processes is: as already mentioned, an initial Stake of 32 ETH causes a new authorized entity to be made visible in the Validators registry and the requisite software to be activated for download by the corresponding node operator. Up until the "Pectra" Ethereum blockchain upgrade,[11] a second stake of 32 ETH would mandatorily cause a second, independent, authorized validator entity to be declared in the registry—even if it were provided by the exact same agent(s) behind the initial one. That is, any add-on to the original 32 ETH that brought the stake, e.g. anywhere between 32 and 64 ETH, would make no difference to the amount of rewards accruing to the validator; those would still be calculated on the 32 ETH floor. The repercussion was that agents with enough ETH to stake could (still can) activate several validating entities in parallel by submitting chunks of 32 ETH. The "Pectra" update, however, allowed Validators to stake anywhere from 32 (minimum) to 2048 (maximum) ETH in a single validating instance [80] while accruing rewards prorated on the entire balance—i.e. no longer on only the 32 ETH floor as per pre-"Pectra" regime.

Either way, the staking business model has the preconditions to achieve economies of scale, which is precisely what allows liquid staking protocols to scale their business case to significant TVL—potentially to the tune of millions of ETH, as is the case with Lido.

9.5 Lido

Lido is a successful blockchain-based token ecosystem in the liquid staking space. Originally focusing on the Ethereum PoS value chain, it then expanded to other EVM-compatible L-1 and L-2 blockchains having the same type of consensus mechanism. However, not all of these forays proved resilient [81–83]; hence in the sequel we will focus on its established Ethereum-based business case. Lido allows economic agents to:

A. Swap ETH for native LSD tokens, accumulating rewards through the actions of third-party staking validators.
B. Transfer native LSD tokens to other protocols accepting them as collateral for token loans, such as collateralized debt positions (CDP) [84].

[11] Rolled out in March-April 2025.

C. Transfer native LSD tokens to other protocols accepting them as liquidity positions, to generate extra yield beyond the staking one.
D. Withdraw ETH liquidity by swapping yield-accrued native LSD tokens back to ETH.

Having gone through the basic notions of promissory notes, financial guarantees and alternative investment funds in previous sections, the reader is now equipped to also interpret Lido's use cases A.–D. above through a traditional finance lens. The intention is to show, first, how traditional financial instruments have their close analogues in this token ecosystem, and second, how the design of rules and incentives around said analogues' creation and use (i.e. the ecosystem's mechanism design) is calibrated by their nature as tradable crypto-tokens.

In the sequel we will examine Lido primarily through the lens of mechanism design. It is, however, inevitable that we will also have to make brief forays into the other two main design pillars (market and token designs), as it will be impossible to interpret mechanisms outside the context of economic agents' token transactions.

9.6 Lido Market Design Basics

As per methodology introduced in Sect. 6.4, blockchain ecosystem market design must prescribe all possible **economic agent** types, **transactional pathways**, and protocol **tokens** created or exchanged. Having already explained the generic "Liquid Staking" concept in Sect. 9.4, we proceed with explaining the specific calibration of this concept in Lido. The focus will be on the main transactional pathways, as those will expose the interplays of agents and tokens, and allow us to then concentrate on analysing mechanisms. Our analysis will be based on Lido's official documentation and on public domain information contained in specifications repositories and discussion/voting records of Lido governance.

The word "basics" in the title of this is intended to make clear that we do not go into Lido's market design in detail (e.g. we do not examine influencing factor calibrations), the focus of the present case study being mechanism design.

9.6.1 Economic Agent Typology

As depicted on Fig. 9.8, Lido ecosystem agent types are few in number, however one of them can have several, delegated, roles as will be explained in the sequel. Non-privileged economic agent types are:

a. Stakers
b. Node Operators

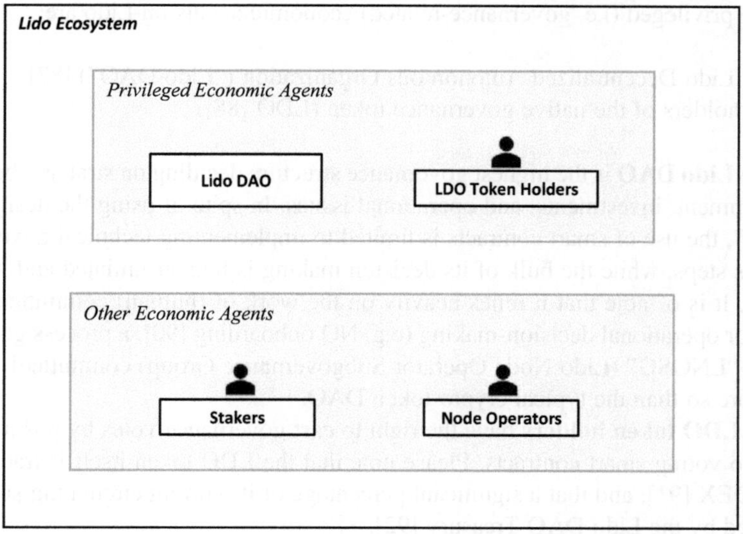

Fig. 9.8 Lido economic agent model

A **staker** is equivalent to a liquid staking investor in the generic "Liquid Staking" case. It is an entity committing ETH to Lido and expecting to profit from staking rewards. Lido will pool together ETH from different Stakers, split the total into chunks, und allocate each chunk to PoS validators.

A **node operator** is an entity controlling one of several PoS validator instances. Please recall the explanations in Sect. 9.4, as the difference between node operators and PoS validators needs to be made clear. As per Ethereum PoS terminology, a validator is defined by a pair of keys (and a withdrawal address) tied to a validator software[12] instance. A validator is also tied to a specific 32 (minimum) ETH stake. A separate stake will generally be tied to a new pair of keys and a new software instance—irrespective of whether or it will run on the same technical infrastructure—i.e. on the same or on a separate physical node.[13] Lido does not elevate the validator to the level of an economic agent, as, first, stake ownership (and the accruing rewards or penalties) has repercussions in the real world (e.g. funds provenance controls, taxation, etc.), and second, there needs to be accountability for when PoS validation essentially fails and needs to be corrected. Hence, the relevant Lido economic agent was chosen to be the Node Operator (denoted hereafter by "NO" for the sake of brevity). A NO may control several PoS validator instances and several nodes. The largest NO's will control significant amounts of computing power, thus using many stakes at once.

[12]Downloadable from code repositories cooperating with Ethereum; the Stake is needed so that said software can be activated.

[13]But, of course, in different logical software partitions, e.g. Virtual Machines [85], Containers [86], etc.

The privileged (i.e. governance-related) economic agents on Lido are:

a. The Lido Decentralized Autonomous Organization ("Lido DAO") [87]
b. All holders of the native governance token (LDO [88])

The **Lido DAO** is the highest governance structure deciding on strategy, business development, investments, and operational issues. In spite of using the designation "DAO", the use of smart contracts is limited to implementing technical governance process steps, while the bulk of its decision making is human-initiated and human-driven. It is of note that it relies heavily on the work of (human) committees [89], even for operational decision-making (e.g. NO onboarding [90], a process governed by the "LNOSG" (Lido Node Operator Subgovernance Group) committee], probably more so than the typical crypto-token DAO.

All **LDO token holders** have the right to cast governance votes by posting their LDO to voting smart contracts. Please note that the LDO token itself is tradable in CEX/DEX [91], and that a significant percentage of its current circulating supply is reserved by the Lido DAO Treasury [92].

More details about Lido governance processes will be given in the later section on mechanism design.

9.6.2 Cooperating Ecosystems

Lido's liquid staking business case is facilitated, and in some cases materially enabled, through cooperating ecosystems. Figure 9.9 depicts these linkages, whereby the box titled "*Cooperating Ecosystems (EVM-compatible)*" purposely omits L-2 protocols. As already mentioned in the first paragraph of Sect. 9.5, not all L-2 forays of Lido Governance proved successful,[14] thus the depiction confines itself to the market design of Lido on Ethereum—which will always be the core Lido ecosystem. All token ecosystems in this box are "yield-extending" ones, by admitting Lido-native tokens as equals into their own (lending, liquidity mining, investment, etc.) business cases, i.e. they serve primarily to increase market thickness for Lido.

The remaining two boxes are instead essential for Lido's core business processes to function. Starting from the bottom one ("*Crypto-Asset Exchanges*"), this embodies a fundamental dependency of Lido Governance, since it is the only post-ICO path for new voters to acquire the LDO tokens necessary to vote. It is also critically important for the Lido ecosystem's resiliency, e.g. should the Lido DAO ever need to liquidate Treasury LDO holdings to cover funding emergencies it will have to consider selling LDO on the Exchanges. The last remaining ("*Information*

[14] E.g., the Polygon L-2 Lido instance (whereby MATIC was staked in exchanged for stMATIC) was in the process of being sunset as of the time of writing. That has meant the discontinuation of Lido on Polygon as per Q1' 2025. Unstaking of MATIC tokens was scheduled to still be possible until end of Q2' 2025 through Lido, but later through third-party tools only.

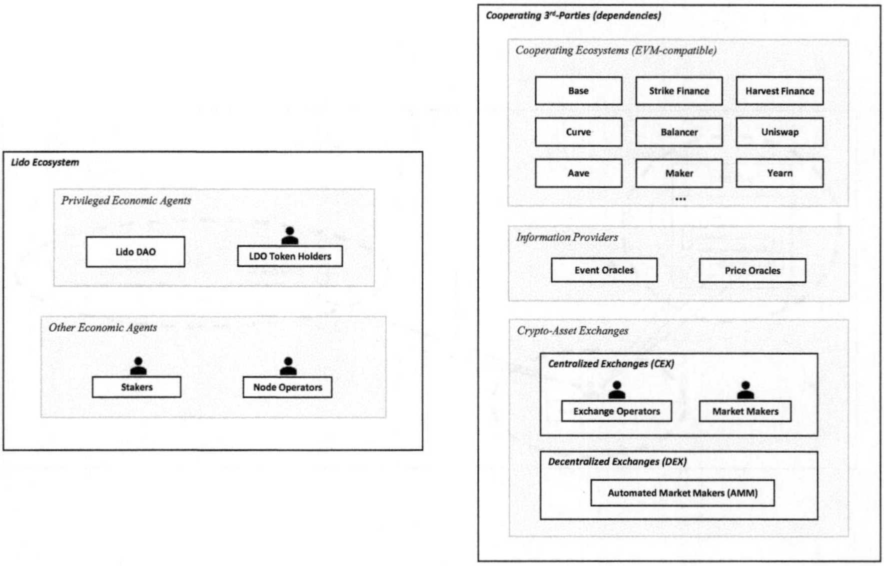

Fig. 9.9 Lido and cooperating third-parties

Providers") box represents dependencies for a multitude of **operational** Lido processes, which will be explained in detail in the mechanism design section. Some of them can still be mentioned in passing, for example pricing Oracles [93] are needed for Lido's smart contracts to calculate ETH-swapping rates for stakers, and stETH/ETH (also stETH/USD [94]) parities [95] for both internal liquidity pool calculations and token swaps. Also, an internal Lido smart contract implements an "Accounting Oracle" [96] which is needed to aggregate ETH balances across validators, state of validators themselves (hence to source information from event Oracles), etc. The calculation of total staking rewards accruing to the entire Lido staking pool and (as ecosystem fee revenue) to the Lido treasury also depends on Oracles [97], some of them aggregating data feeds also off-chain.

Crucially, selected node operators act also as information providers. This is one of their extended roles within Lido, apart from the obvious one as resource providers for PoS validator instances. As schematically depicted on Fig. 9.10, operational (day-to-day) tasks entrusted to Lido DAO committees are also predicated on the involvement of node operators. Those involved are registered and approved through well-defined Lido governance processes [98].

There are still more reasons why node operators are critical enough for Lido to consider them as first-class economic agents. Subsequent sections will explain them in more detail.

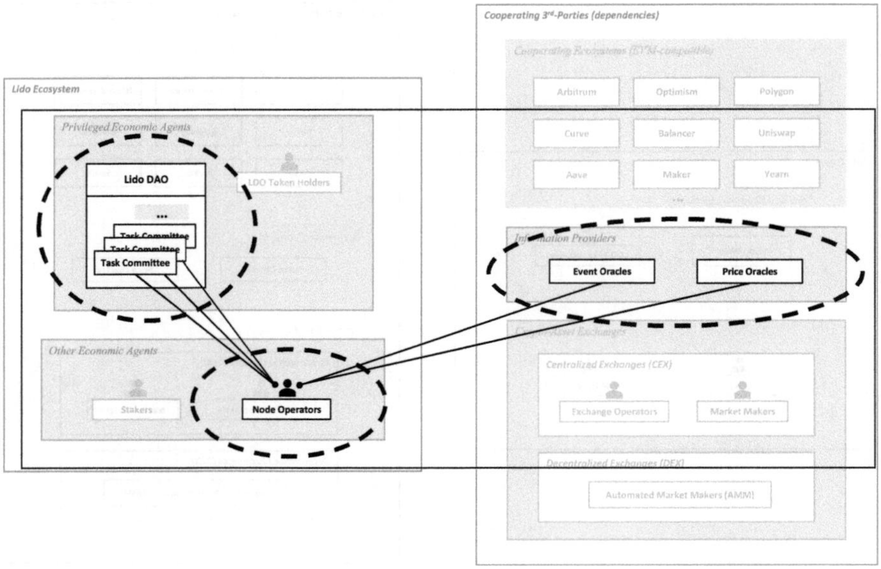

Fig. 9.10 While mainly running PoS validators, node operators may assume additional responsibilities on Lido

9.6.3 Transactional Pathways

We will explain the most salient transactions involving the afore-mentioned economic agents, namely: stakers' ETH deposits for newly minted stETH tokens, stakers' wrapping of stETH into new wstETH tokens, and LDO holders' acquisition and voting submission of LDO tokens. The following sections detail their pathways, also indicating the order of execution of each process step. There exist another two transactions (unwrapping of wstETH back into stETH tokens, and stakers' withdrawal of stETH/wstETH—i.e. unstaking of the equivalent ETH—through minting of an intermediate NFT [99]) which are simply reversing the afore-mentioned ones. Please note that Lido is a non-custodian protocol, thus all transactional pathways require connecting to the initiating agent's crypto wallet from within the Lido dApp [100–102].

We begin with the stakers' ETH deposit transaction, as it embodies the main business case of Lido.

9.6.3.1 Staker on Ethereum Stakes ETH, Acquires stETH

In this transaction a participant becomes a "Staker" by committing ETH to Lido, which then uses them to fund PoS validator stakes. The pathway (and some of its subsequent branches) is depicted schematically on Fig. 9.11. As in the previous case study in Chap. 7, please note that this is a "notional balance sheet" view (not an actual, accounting one) gleaned by the author from the protocol's documentation.

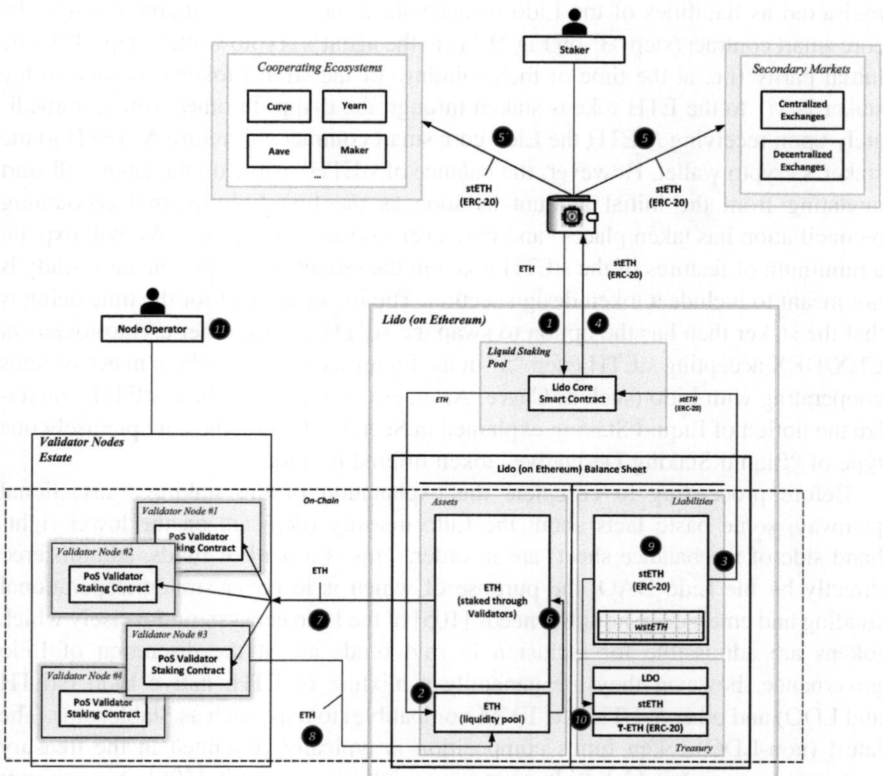

Fig. 9.11 Staker deposits ETH on Lido and acquires stETH; swaps them outside Lido, all the while accruing staking rewards

The Lido dApp [100] will request that the user first connects a crypto wallet. The staker will already have acquired ETH, which will be made visible to Lido through the connection. By requesting to stake an amount of ETH, the agent invokes the Lido Core smart contract [104] which accepts said amount (depicted by step "1" on Fig. 9.11) and forwards it to the Lido ETH liquidity pool[15] (step "2"). The asset-side of the Lido balance sheet on Ethereum contains two large ETH token positions: those already staked and those in the liquidity pool. The latter is meant to act, first, as a staging ("assemblage") account allowing Lido to gauge projected availability of funds for candidate PoS validators and, second, as a current account to cover short-term ETH withdrawal (unstaking) requests without having to recall stakes or liquidate treasury positions. Lido implements specific mechanisms to manage the relative sizes of its asset-side staked and liquidity pools.

Even while waiting to the staked, the agent's ETH tokens already cause an amount of Lido-native **stETH** ("staked ETH") ERC-20 tokens to be minted,

[15] Also referred to as "the buffer" in the Lido documentation [103].

registered as liabilities of the Lido balance sheet, and made available through the core smart contract (step "3" on Fig. 9.11) to the agent's crypto wallet (step "4"). The initial parity (i.e. at the time of their minting) of the stETH tokens credited to the staker is 1:1 to the ETH tokens staked through the dApp. In other words, immediately upon receiving *N* ETH the Lido core smart contract will return *N* stETH to the staker's crypto wallet. However, the balance of stETH visible on the latter will start deviating from the initial amount as soon as the first Lido-internal accounting reconciliation has taken place—and may even conceivably reduce. We will explain a minimum of features of the stETH token in the sequel, as the present case study is not meant to include a token design section. The important fact for the time being is that the staker then has the option to swap the stETH against other crypto-tokens in CEX/DEX accepting stETH (step "5" in the Figure), or to invest them in ecosystems cooperating with Lido (such as Curve, Aave, etc.—step "5"). These stETH concretize the notion of Liquid Staking explained in Sect. 9.4 before; they are precisely one type of "Liquid Staking Derivative" token offered by Lido.

Before proceeding to complete the explanation of the staking transactional pathway, some basic facts about the Lido treasury (depicted on the lower right-hand side of the balance sheet) are in order. This is a pool of funds, administered directly by the Lido DAO, the purpose of which is to cover strategic/operational funding and emergency liquidity needs [105] of the Lido ecosystem. Precisely which tokens are admissible for inclusion in said funds are at the discretion of Lido governance, however they are generally a mixture of ETH, native Lido (stETH and LDO) and other Ŧ-ETH (i.e. EVM-compatible) tokens, such as Stablecoins. The latest (non-LDO) token funds composition is typically contained in the treasury performance reports which Lido governance publishes monthly [106]. A significant source of new treasury funds comes from the fact that, in return for managing the pooling, allocation and performance controlling of staking funds to PoS validators, Lido extracts a commission (a service "fee") on whatever rewards are accrued by said validators. This commission is expressed as a percentage (currently 10% [107], further split between Lido and Node Operators[16]) of rewards in terms of new ETH tokens, which are booked into Lido's balance sheet as new stETH. This is the source of the stETH-denominated part of the Lido treasury, as depicted on Fig. 9.11.

Back to the staking transaction, whenever the liquidity pool has aggregated enough ETH to fund several stakes, Lido's smart contracts allocate them to node operators found in its NO Registry [108]. As explained in previous sections, a NO controls the infrastructure on which several PoS validators can be deployed, each one tied to a distinct 32 (minimum) ETH stake. Hence Lido executes a rebooking from the ETH liquidity to the staking pool (step "6"), followed by binding of each designated stake against the designated key pair of the target PoS validator (step "7").

[16] "The Node Operators' part of the fee is distributed between the active Node Operators proportionally to the number of validators that each Node Operator runs", as per [97].

As already explained in Sect. 9.4, it is not a foregone conclusion that a PoS validator will generate only staking profits. If its NO is not diligent, slashing events may reduce and even nullify the stake. However, Lido's market and mechanism designs are geared towards ongoing minimization of slashing risk. This is pursued, first, by rigorous vetting processes before NO's can be onboarded to the ecosystem and, second, by active monitoring [109] of the operational performance of PoS validators—tasks executed by Lido DAO committees aided by decision-support smart contracts (such as internal Lido Oracles [110]).

In anticipation of the subsequent mechanism design section, please assume that Lido-funded PoS validators will generally experience only staking rewards. Those will be aggregated daily through smart contract—"Accounting Oracle" [111]—and booked as ETH balances to the ETH liquidity pool (step "8"). As they represent an increase in the total assets of the ecosystem, a corresponding stETH increase will be recorded on the liabilities side (step "9"), minus the protocol fee accruing to the Lido treasury (step "10") and the split with the node operator(s) (step "11"). At the next crypto wallet connection to Lido, the staker will see a new stETH balance (step "3" repeating for the added stETH allocated to them).

The reason for this updated balance is that Lido chose to implement stETH technically as a "rebase" [112] (also called "rebasing" or "rebaseable") token. Such tokens—let us denote them by $₸_{\text{rebasing}}$—do not represent a distinct type (in the sense of the typology proposed in Chap. 4), but rather a different minting nature—such as that of NFT's. Very simply, they replicate the notion of a **unit of account**, an account that is changing in value on the blockchain. Imagine that you had invested in a traditional financial instrument, fluctuating in value, and marked-to-market at fixed time intervals. If your base currency (your accounting unit of account) were EUR, then you would have acquired a position valued initially at *A* EUR, then changing in value with every re-marking-to-market. Now, instead of in EUR, imagine that you had acquired an on-chain investment denominated in $₸_{\text{rebasing}}$. Every time your investment's total valuation changes, then you would simply have a different amount in terms of $₸_{\text{rebasing}}$. Such $₸_{\text{rebasing}}$ are not formally Stablecoins, as they respond to different business use cases and their valuations are re-adjusted much less frequently[17].

Lido's business case, creating the need for such a token in the first place, called for precisely a "unit of account token". That would be minted 1:1 to the originally staked ETH position, while still being able to transfer the updated balances of the asset-side ETH liquidity pool (through either staking rewards or slashings) to the liabilities-side stETH pools. In short, Lido needed a distinct native token that would be both ETH-pegged and useable as a denomination of liquidity positions, intended to be forwarded to a Staker's Wallet and used outside Lido itself. This was the reason behind the stETH token design; as a native token, intended as unit of account. Every time the Lido Oracles notify new rewards being booked to the ETH liquidity pool

[17] Please refer to the explanation of Stablecoin stabilization mechanisms in the subsequent Chap. 10 on token design.

(step "8" in Fig. 9.11), then an equivalent amount of new stETH tokens are minted and posted to the liabilities ("9") and to the treasury ("10"). As mentioned in the official Lido documentation [97]:

> *At any time point, the total amount of stETH tokens is equal to the total amount of ether controlled by the protocol …*

However, there are caveats on the use of stETH outside Lido which ultimately led to the creation of a secondary transactional pathway for stakers, explained in the section immediately below. Please note in passing that this "rebasing" effect is technically achieved by the token's smart contract *not* implementing fully [113] the ERC-20 specification.[18]

Before concluding this section, it is expedient to pose this question: how can this transactional pathway be interpreted from a traditional finance viewpoint, and what are the types of tokens used by Lido? To answer it, it is useful to go into some detail about what property rights are exchanged along the pathway and through the tokens.

A staker committing ETH to Lido clearly makes an investment with the expectation of profit, under terms and conditions (T&C) explained in Lido's documentation [115]. However, Lido is no bank and no asset manager, it is just (according to the Lido FAQ pages [116]) "*… a family of open-source peer-to-system software tools deployed and functioning on the Ethereum, … networks*". It is telling that the T&C documentation page does not mention any legal entity as counterparty to stakers' transactions (it is simply "the interface", presumably in the sense of the Lido dApp software). The T&C page does mention a governing law (Cayman Islands) and a seat of arbitration (London), however several terms in it would make for uncomfortable reading in the eyes of any prudent investor: (listing *verbatim* paragraph titles only from the "Binding Provisions" part of the document):

> 11.1 *Interface Maintainers Have No Business Plan and May Discontinue, Limit, Terminate, or Refuse Support for the Interface*
> …
> 11.2 *No Regulatory Supervision*
> …
> 11.3 *Regulatory Uncertainty*
> …
> *11.4 No Warranty*
> …
> *11.7 No Interface Fees; Third-Party Fees Irreversible*
> …
> *14. Non-Reliance*
> …
> *15.5 Tax Issues*
> …

[18] Restricting instead the triggering of the "Transfer()" event function [114] whenever a "rebasing" calculation occurs.

It would appear that stakers enter a bilateral agreement with a non-regulated counterparty, at their own risk. Furthermore, the stETH returned to a staker's Wallet are not even constant in amount, as they are rebasing: they may increase through rewards or reduce through slashing events.[19] In that sense, the entire stETH position simply embodies a *promise* by Lido to increase them (when valued as equivalent to ETH) *on a best effort basis* by an expected "Annual Percentage Rate" (APR) clearly stated by the protocol [118]. Lido acknowledges them indeed as an obligation owed back to the staker, and (the whole value proposition of liquid staking) they are indeed exchangeable on cooperating exchanges and token ecosystems. That is, the entire stETH position is assignable—can be sold—to follow-on owners.

Thus, stETH have all the hallmarks of a security token (as per the analysis of the previous Sect. 9.4), and the entire stETH position is akin to a promissory note in traditional finance (cf. Sect. 9.1)—with Lido being the promisor.

Would the stETH position qualify instead as a TradFi IOU, a certificate of deposit, or a loan even to Lido?

We believe not, as:

a. IOUs are practically never assignable,
b. Certificates of deposit assume a depositary (regulated entity) as counterparty, and
c. Loan terms are usually controlled by law to avoid usury or other predatory practices.

None of the above apply in the current circumstances.

On the asset-side of the balance sheet, funds sent to PoS validator's staking Contracts (step "7" on Fig. 9.11) are "used" by their respective node operators, but are still both owned[20] [119] and controlled[21] by Lido. Each (32–2048) ETH stake is clearly a financial guarantee (performance guarantee in the surety sense, cf. Sect. 9.2) provided directly by Lido as guarantor.

The price for this guarantee is the Lido-retained part of the service fee (commission on staking rewards, steps "8" and "10").

In summary, Lido accepts cryptocurrency deposits by stakers, issuing them promissory notes quoting an APR in return. The protocol pools many such deposits together and uses the aggregate sums to fund financial guarantees to third parties (node operators) that need them in order to be allowed to operate Ethereum PoS validators. Node operators fund said guarantees by committing to surrendering a large (currently 95%) percentage of their yield (staking rewards) to Lido. Lido keeps

[19] Please note that Lido Governance does indeed hedge its Staking business risk (on account of Slashing) by paying into an "insurance fund" [117]

[20] As per [120], *"Staking Router's purpose is to orchestrate deposits and, eventually, withdrawals through different modules in a way that satisfies the stake distribution desired by the DAO"* … [this author's note: WC stands for "Withdrawal Credentials"] *"All Lido deposits are submitted with the Lido-approved WC to ensure that only Lido can withdraw user funds"*.

[21] A Node Operator funded by Lido is expected to declare only withdrawal addresses defined by Lido itself [121].

5% of this surrendered yield for internal costs coverage and uses the rest to fund its liabilities to stakers (the APR on the promissory notes). A cryptocurrency pool is used as liquidity buffer in the process.

9.6.3.2 Staker on Ethereum Wraps stETH Into wstETH

As already mentioned in the previous section, stETH is a rebase token tracking ETH at a 1:1 target price. The total stETH position of a staker changes almost daily through its proportion of incoming rewards to the Lido staking pool (barring slashing events not covered by the Lido insurance). This creates an obvious problem for cooperating token ecosystems willing to accept the staker's position as exchangeable (or at least convertible) for other tokens in their own transactional pathways. Imagine an agent drawing liquidity in a lending marketplace, posting their Lido-assigned stETH position as collateral—the position equalling 100 stETH at posting, and then rebasing to 101, 102, 103, etc., stETH, i.e. continuously upwards-valuing afterwards. If the marketplace had not considered rebasing tokens when implementing its smart contracts accepting collateral (e.g. if its software relied on functions triggered by specific blockchain events, and said functions were not being triggered when rebasing tokens were involved in transactions), then its mechanisms might break as a result. For example, some risk control (e.g. loan-to-value calculation) might not be executed at all, or might be producing erroneous results, etc. Such problems, stemming from the admittance of rebase tokens, have been documented by several token ecosystems [122, 123] in the past.

Lido addresses this risk to cooperating ecosystems by enabling a secondary transactional pathway for stakers, involving the wrapping of stETH into a new type of Lido-native token: **wstETH** ("wrapped staked ETH"), which is a **non-rebasing** ERC-20 token.

The concept behind wstETH tokens is a simple one: imagine that at time t_0 a snapshot of the Lido balance sheet is taken, and all stETH owed to stakers are counted. This gives a sum of stETH—$S_{stETH,\ 0}$—which is practically equal to the same amount in ETH – $S_{ETH,\ 0}$. Now assume that at this precise moment a new, parallel, token ₮-Lido is introduced, at an initial parity of a ₮-*Lido:ETH* = *1:*P_0. So, at time t_0 the liabilities of Lido to its stakers can be equally reported as:

$$\mathcal{L}_0 = \frac{S_{stETH,0}}{P_0} \text{₮} - \text{Lido} \cong \frac{S_{ETH,0}}{P_0} \text{₮} - \text{Lido}$$

Lido then converts all outstanding stETH to ₮-Lido at the current parity. During the next epoch (until End-of-Day-0), all ETH arriving by new stakers are used to mint new ₮-Lido at this initial parity. Assume that $N_{ETH,\ 0}$ ETH have arrived, so at End-of-Day-0 the new number of ₮-Lido in existence is:

$$\mathcal{L}_{End-of-Day-0} = \frac{S_{ETH,0} + N_{ETH,0}}{P_0} \text{₮} - \text{Lido}$$

Denoting the new ETH as being a difference to the existing ones as time t_0: $N_{ETH,\,0} \equiv \Delta S_{ETH,\,0}$

$$\mathcal{L}_{End-of-Day-0} = \frac{S_{ETH,0} + \Delta S_{ETH,0}}{P_0} \text{₸} - \text{Lido} = \frac{S_{ETH,End-of-Day-0}}{P_0} \text{₸} - \text{Lido}$$

and, of course, the ratio of liabilities expressed in ETH to the same expressed in ₸-Lido equals $P_{0.}$. Now assume that no new ₸-Lido are allowed to be minted at the change of accounting time from End-of-Day-0 to Start-of-Day-1. Hence,

$$\mathcal{L}_{Start-of-Day-1} = \mathcal{L}_{End-of-Day-0}$$

Immediately after the start of Day-1, the Staking results are reported from the PoS Validators. Assume that (after Lido fees are withheld) a positive ETH amount (denote it by $R_{ETH,\,1}$) results. This is added to the Lido liquidity pool and credited to existing stakers. So, liabilities now equal:

$$\mathcal{L}_{Start-of-Day-1}{}^{+} = \mathcal{L}_{Start-of-Day-1} + R_{ETH,1}$$

Obviously, as no new ₸-Lido have been minted, then the parity of ₸-*Lido* to *ETH* has just increased, to $P_1 > P_0$.

Assume again that during the next epoch (until end-of-Day-1), all ETH arriving by new stakers are used to mint new ₸-Lido at this new parity P_1. The parity stays the same until the transition from End-of-Day-1 to Start-of-Day-2, when the arrival of new, positive, PoS validator rewards increases it further to $P_2 > P_1$. All new ETH committed by stakers in the new epoch (until End-of-Day-2) are minted to new ₸-Lido at fixed parity P_2, and the cycle repeats for all subsequent epochs. Of course, should the cumulative staking results at any given day be negative, then the parity ₸-*Lido:ETH* will momentarily *decrease*.

Now, assume that Lido stakers have the *option* to choose **if** to receive ₸-Lido **or** to stay with their existing stETH tokens. As far as Lido is concerned, the balance-sheet accounting is the same, under the obvious proviso that ₸-Lido and stETH will not be counted doubly in the liabilities calculation. That, is, Lido will have to calculate its liabilities *both ways*, as if all were stETH **and** as if all were ₸-Lido, and report ₸-Lido positions only to those stakers opting for them. Lido then would have to have a way to "cancel" stETH positions at the moment that opted-in ₸-Lido tokens are minted.

The concept explained above is precisely the logical Lido algorithm for the minting of wstETH. In short, wstETH tokens are minted and accounted for so that existing stakers accepting them do not see new balances in their crypto wallets, but only **new parities** against ETH. Of course (to help Lido avoid double-counting), by accepting wstETH they have their stETH "cancelled" in some way, explained immediately below. They still have the option to convert back to stETH, but they have to first return the corresponding wstETH tokens, which are then immediately burned.

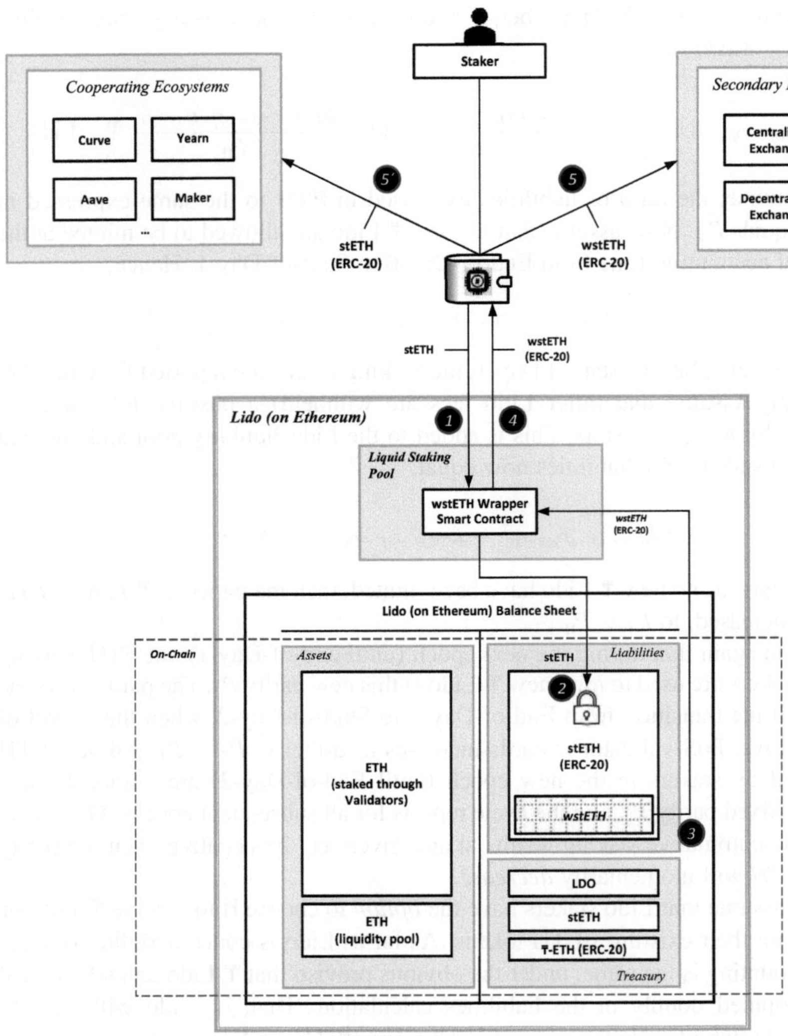

Fig. 9.12 Staker wraps stETH into wstETH; swaps them outside Lido, all the while accruing staking rewards

The wstETH-minting pathway is depicted on Fig. 9.12. The Lido dApp [124] will request that the user connects a crypto wallet showing a stETH balance. The dApp already states the current parity rate to stETH (valued 1:1 to ETH) and estimated maximum transaction costs. By selecting an amount of stETH to wrap and proceeding, the staker invokes the Lido wstETH (Wrapping) smart contract [125] which accepts said amount (step "1" in Fig. 9.12) and causes it to be "locked" on the liabilities side (step "2"). New wstETH tokens are minted at the stated parity, booked in the wstETH-specific part of the liabilities, and made available through the smart contract (step "3") to the agent's crypto wallet (step "4"). These new tokens can now

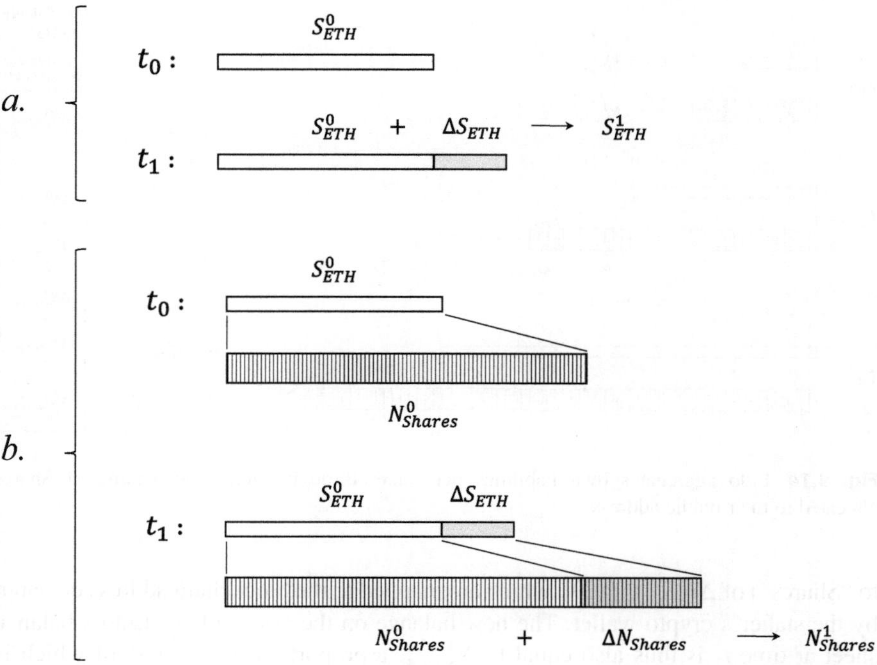

Fig. 9.13 How Lido keeps track of staker funds: a. ETH staked, b. Internal accounting through "Shares"

be used outside Lido, either swapped against other crypto-tokens in CEX/DEX accepting wstETH (step "5") or invested in cooperating ecosystems (step "5" in the figure). They still accrue staking rewards on Lido, though, which are reflected in their changing price [126, 127].

This concludes the wstETH-minting transactional pathway.

Let us pose again the question: how can this pathway be interpreted from a traditional finance point of view? What property rights have been morphed into wstETH tokens?

To answer it, let us go into some detail on how Lido *technically* creates them, under the hood so to speak. Whenever a staker commits ETH to Lido through the core smart contract, the protocol keeps track of its liabilities to this particular staker. It does so by internal bookkeeping mechanisms which are invisible to stakers. Those mechanisms are based on the postulation of an internal unit of account, called "Share" [128]. Its value is kept at a constant parity to ETH, under the control of the protocol. As depicted on Fig. 9.13—part a., denote the balance of ETH on the asset-side of Lido's balance sheet at time t_0 by S^0_{ETH}. At time t_1 a staker deposits an additional amount of ΔS_{ETH}, which is credited to the ETH liquidity pool, thus producing the new balance S^1_{ETH}. Through the internal bookkeeping, the starting balance is also calculated as equalling an amount N^0_{Shares} of shares (Fig. 9.13 – part b.). The staker's deposit at time t_1 creates a parallel entry (after conversion from ETH

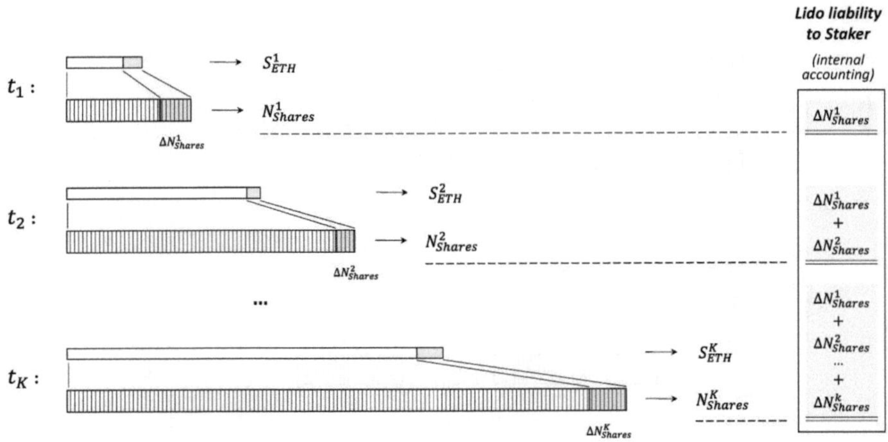

Fig. 9.14 Lido aggregates own liabilities per staker through internal accounting of Shares allocated to their public address

to "Shares") of ΔN_{Shares} [129], which are mapped to the blockchain address declared by the staker's crypto wallet. The new balance on the asset-side of Lido's balance sheet at time t_1 is thus also equal to N^1_{Shares}, a proportion $q = \frac{\Delta N_{Shares}}{N^1_{Shares}}$ of which is allocated to the staker's address.

As all ETH managed by Lido (across the asset-side staking and liquidity pools) are equally profiting from staking rewards, the proportion of said rewards allocated to the particular staker from time t_1 onwards is exactly q. The intent of this internal bookkeeping is to replicate the notion of **user accounts** in Lido.

For instance, imagine the same staker depositing ETH in several instalments to the protocol (cf. Fig. 9.14). Please follow the same bookkeeping conversions from ETH to Shares across time. At time t_1 the staker's deposit is accounted for through ΔN^1_{Shares} new shares, and their proportion to the new total shares under management by Lido $q^1 = \frac{\Delta N^1_{Shares}}{N^1_{Shares}}$ is used to prorate the new staking rewards allocated to the staker from t_1 onwards. At time t_2 the same staker deposits a second amount of ETH, which are converted internally to ΔN^2_{Shares} new shares and add to a new total for shares under management of N^2_{Shares}. The new ratio $q^2 = \frac{\Delta N^2_{Shares}}{N^2_{Shares}}$ is used to prorate staking rewards allocated to the staker from t_2 onwards. Following several deposits (and no withdrawals), the same staker deposits a new ETH amount at time t_k, which is converted internally to ΔN^k_{Shares} new shares and gives a new total for shares under management of N^k_{Shares}. The new ratio $q^k = \frac{\Delta N^k_{Shares}}{N^k_{Shares}}$ is used to prorate staking rewards allocated to the staker from t_k onwards, etc.

Whenever a staker withdraws ETH, the protocol uses the same internal conversion mechanism in reverse to calculate the current balance of ETH in their "account" and then authorize the withdrawal—afterwards destroying the corresponding amount of shares. Through this mechanism, Lido is able to track its current liabilities to a specific blockchain address, both in absolute terms and as a proportion of total ETH assets under management.

This is precisely the (intermediate) technical mechanism used for the minting and burning of wstETH tokens. Whenever a staker requests to wrap stETH to wstETH, Lido first retrieves the amount of shares that the staker is credited with (remember that stETH has the target value of 1 ETH, hence the conversion is immediate). The wrapping smart contract then locks the underlying stETH and mints wstETH tokens equal in value to the corresponding shares. Said wstETH start accruing staking rewards in exactly the proportion of these shares to the total shares managed by the protocol. Incoming ETH rewards allocated to the staker in this proportion are credited [130] as new shares which, by the reverse share-to-ETH calculation, increase the value in terms of ETH (or stETH) of their wstETH tokens—but not their amount.

Whenever a staker requests to unwrap wstETH tokens back to stETH ones, the same intermediate bookkeeping in terms of shares is used [131] to calculate the correct amount of stETH that are to be updated as liabilities. The wstETH tokens in question are, of course, burned.

Both the wstETH-wrapping [132] and the core [133] Lido smart contracts implement methods directly or indirectly handling shares.

The above explanation can now guide an interpretation of the wstETH minting transaction from a traditional finance viewpoint. wstETH tokens can be best understood as equivalent to investable units of an open-ended [134] alternative investment fund (cf. Sect. 9.3). The typical processes of setting up [135], managing [135], accounting for [136], and valuing units in such funds [137] have their analogues in how Lido sets up liquidity pools; manages stakes; accounts for net asset value; and updates valuation of wstETH tokens. Both fund units and wstETH tokens are assignable, and they both can be redeemed at their primary market. As per reference typology proposed in Chap. 4, wstETH is of course a security (*not* a Derivative) token.

In summary, wstETH is a distinct type of "Liquid Staking Derivative" token minted by Lido, replicating an open-ended alternative investment fund unit in the traditional finance sense. Positions in wstETH tokens are generated by locking existing stETH positions into a Lido smart contract. Said tokens can then be swapped/invested outside Lido, while still accruing staking rewards on the protocol. Their main difference to their underlying stETH is their non-rebasing nature, which is reflected in their changing price.

9.6.3.3 LDO Token Holder Acquires LDO and Votes

In this transaction, a Lido participant acquires LDO tokens and uses them for Lido governance voting. LDO [138] is a governance token (subtype of utility token, as per Sect. 4.2.2). There are several LDO utility use cases as per protocol documentation [139], and still others are possible [140] in the future. Its principal utility is the ability

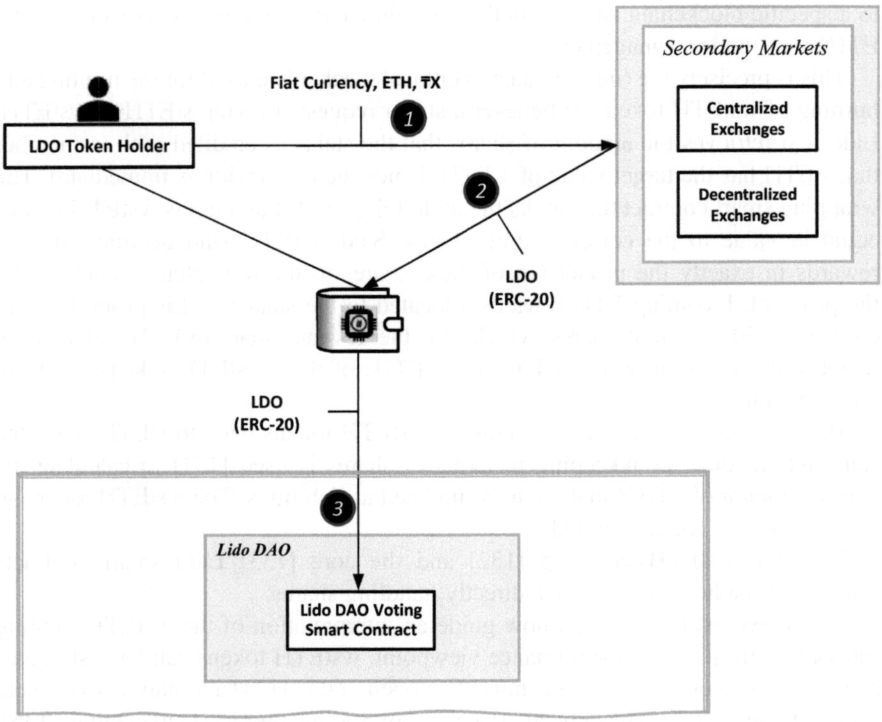

Fig. 9.15 LDO token holder acquires LDO, uses them to vote in Lido DAO

of its holder to influence the direction of the Lido protocol[22] and thus profit from network effects [146] eventually captured through the token's valuation. The latter can further increase if Lido treasury ever decides to use part of its funds [105] to burn LDO [147]. Please note that LDO has been admitted in the past in some cooperating ecosystems [148] as foreign token supplied by liquidity providers for yield. The token is available in exchanges (CEX [91] /DEX [149]). It is formally an ERC-20 token [88].

The pathway is depicted schematically on Fig. 9.15.

A new LDO holder will need to first acquire LDO tokens in the secondary market and move them to their crypto wallet (steps "1" and "2"). In order to vote, the Lido dApp [102] will first request the connection to this wallet. There are several underlying voting mechanisms, which will be explained in the subsequent mechanism design section. For the time being please assume an on-chain mode enabled

[22] Please note that Lido uses Snapshot [141] as part of its "regular" voting process [141]. This means that, as per Snapshot documentation [138, 143], voting is only allowed if the required tokens were held at the time of proposal creation and not afterwards (e.g. during the voting period, which is currently 7 days [145]).

through smart contract [150]. This simply expects the user to make their LDO tokens visible and then sign the transaction (schematically depicted as step "3" in Fig. 9.15).

This concludes the enumeration of the most salient transactional pathways of Lido, as the explicit focus of this case study is mechanism design.

9.7 Lido Mechanism Design

As per Sect. 8.3.1, token ecosystem mechanism design must prescribe rules and incentives along each **interaction (not only transactional) pathway** among privileged and non-privileged agent types.

Having explained the basics of Lido's market design in the previous section, we have both the protocol-specific terminology and its business case angle at our disposal to be able to interpret mechanisms after identifying them. Our analysis can be further systematized by considering the three salient mechanism design factors:

i. Governance
ii. Market structure
iii. Financial/non-financial incentives

as "lenses" through which to examine pathways. We proceed by identifying Lido's mechanisms through the project's documentation and relevant public domain sources.

The main governance body of the project is the Lido DAO. As already mentioned in Sect. 7.5, for some parts of the crypto-token industry [151] a "DAO" *should only mean* "an organization governed purely by decisions taken by automated, non-human, agents"; while others consider it to signify at best "an organization run by consensus (i.e. without being directed by a central authority) among humans, who use blockchain-based automation to reach governance decisions by voting". As of the time of writing, the current Lido DAO can best be described [152] as a non-incorporated business association [153–155] run essentially on consensus by humans [156, 157] who use blockchain-based automation to reach governance decisions by voting. It is important to note that, even though there is no apparent legal entity assuming liability for decisions impacting the direction and operations (including transactions, cf. Sect. 9.6.3.1) of Lido, third party legal entities can and do assume liability for own transactions referencing Lido-native tokens [158]. The Lido DAO assumes both strategic and operational tasks [159]. To carry them out it allocates distinct areas of responsibility to committees (we will call them "Task Committees"), the mandate and membership of which is decided by governance vote. Task committees currently in existence include:

a. Lido Node Operator Subgovernance Group ("LNSOG" for short)
b. reWARDS Committee ("reWARDS")—Liquidity Observation Lab
c. Resourcing and Compensation Committee ("RCC")

d. Lido Ecosystem Grants Organization ("LEGO")
e. Referral Program Committee ("RFC")
f. Deposit Security Committee ("DSC").

Each is free to define its own processes, but they all are expected to publish activity reports in the main operational governance pages (called "Research Forum" [160]).

The **Lido Node Operator Subgovernance Group** was originally created "*to represent node operators in the DAO structure and to help evaluate and onboard new operators to help secure and decentralize Lido*" [161]. It formalized and implemented processes [162] for Node Operator (NO) onboarding [90]; admittance to the Lido NO registry [108]; imputed monitoring tasks in managing the underlying PoS Validator instances [163]; validator offboarding processes [164]; and general NO community management duties [165, 166]. Note that operational risk events denoting PoS Validator non-performance are regularly reported in the research forum [167, 168].

The **reWARDS Committee** was envisaged to be "*dedicated to managing, deploying, tracking and reporting incentives for Lido assets. … Allow the committee autonomy to deploy allocated rewards budget as they see fit with monthly reporting on the decision-making process and community feedback. There will be broad categories around each of the initiatives as well such as 'maintain liquidity', 'increase usage in DeFi', 'facilitate trading volume' etc. These will come with category breakdowns*". [169]. It publishes both regular reports [170] and ad-hoc analyses [171, 172], and creates own sub-task groups, e.g. proposing [173] —and steering the implementation ([173], please search for *"Multisig Disclosure for Liquidity Observation Lab"*)—of updated liquidity risk management strategies [174] for the Lido ecosystem. Please note that it was subsequently evolved into a **Liquidity Observation Lab** [173] (still operating as a Task Committee [175]), but its core mandate remains essentially the same.

The **Resourcing and Compensation Committee** was conceived as a means "*to streamline the hiring, onboarding, remuneration and payout process for DAO contributors below the senior-most level*" [176]. Its duties were proposed to be "*dedicated to managing, executing, tracking, and reporting on hiring and contributor-related operating expenses for full time DAO members. ... Allow the committee autonomy to deploy a bi-yearly allocated resourcing budget as they see fit with quarterly reporting on the decision-making process and allowing for community feedback. Budgets will be proposed on an annual basis and may be revised during the year. Funding for each 'budget period' (6 months) will be disbursed from the Lido treasury to the RCC wallet twice a year, via DAO vote*" [176]. In accordance with its charter, its budget requests are first submitted to the Research Forum [177]. Please note the existence of a parallel "**Token Rewards Plan**" [178] ("TRP"—governed by a "TRP Committee"), meant to reward and further incentivize Lido DAO contributors [179] on an individual basis [180].

The purpose of forming the **Lido Ecosystem Grants Organization** was "*to provide valuable resources to contributors who help to improve Lido. By rewarding* *talent early with developer incentives, bounties, and infrastructure support, LEGO acts as a catalyst for growth and helps to maintain Lido as a leading and most useful liquid staking protocol in the whole space*" [181]. Since its inception it has formalized its own processes [182] and publishes their outcomes regularly [183], also producing dynamically updated reporting views [184, 185].

Please note the existence of bug bounty programs [186] actively pursued [187] by the Lido DAO as a matter of policy [188] (together with audit programs, which are also actively pursued and publicly reported [189]).

The explicit **Referral Program Committee** goals were "*to boost brand awareness and adoption of decentralised distributed ledger protocols. Moreover, the Program will encourage software developers of wallets and other DeFi protocols to promote our staking protocol among their users, and will positively impact the number of active stakers, and subsequently, the amount staked with Lido*" [190]. Similarly to other Lido DAO Committees, the RPC has instituted its own processes [191] and technical artefacts [192]. As it essentially addresses third parties it takes care to be transparent about rewards expectations [193] and general terms and conditions [194] when engaging with Lido.

The **Deposit Security Committee** was formed in response to an operational risk event [195] tracked back to a malicious node operator. It was thus considered as "*necessary to prevent the substitution of withdrawal credentials with frontrunning by node operators. Each member of the committee must perform several actions to ensure the security of deposits made by Lido*" [196]. Its tasks include "*monitoring the history of deposits and the set of Lido keys available for the deposit, signing and disseminating messages allowing deposits; signing the special message allowing anyone to pause deposits once the malicious Node Operator pre-deposits are detected*" [197]. It also institutes own processes [198] and implements own artefacts [195]. However, it does not appear to be publishing regular reports. Interestingly, its membership [199] is dominated by NOs, which bears out the point made previously in Sect. 9.6.2 (also schematically in Fig. 9.10) about Lido's idiosyncrasy in according extended governance tasks to a particular agent type.

It is important to add that Lido governance sets, updates, and publicly reports performance against strategic/operational goals through a scorecard [200]. Risk & compliance practitioners in the traditional finance domain will recognize most elements of a corporate risk appetite statement in this scorecard.

We must mention again that Lido DAO is not only a strategy setting body. It relies on human contributors for a broad range of tasks, both strategic and operational. For example, a detailed budget request [201] mentioned 20 (twenty) workstreams funded or managed by the DAO at the time:

1. Node operator management
2. Business development
3. Marketing
4. Design
5. Lido on Ethereum protocol engineering

6. On-chain operations
7. UI
8. Tooling
9. QA testing
10. Integrations
11. DevOps
12. Automation
13. Analytics
14. HR
15. Ecosystem support
16. Information security
17. Finance
18. Legal & operations
19. Product management
20. Advisors

Obviously, these are no tasks that smart contracts can be entrusted with. The request in question mentioned the existence of "*about 75 full-time contributors contributing to the Lido DAO*" but did not specify under which contractual agreements and through which channels/entities.

When it comes to time-critical operational tasks, Lido controls process execution through authorized multi-signature ("multi-sig") crypto wallets [202]. Granular multi-sig processes are also documented[23] [203] and implemented through technical infrastructure. It is essential to correlate this fact with the first stated function [159] of the Lido DAO: "*Build, deploy, update and decide on key parameters of liquid staking protocols, …*". As will be mentioned in the sequel, Lido provides for short-circuit decisioning in critical situations, relying on the afore-mentioned multi-sig setup to defend the ecosystem.

Among the foremost goals of Lido's governance is ensuring the stability[24] of the ecosystem, which entails responsibility for risk management and control. The risks in question are a sum of those endangering the ecosystem as a whole and those affecting its participating agents individually. These two categories obviously overlap, as functional loss of a part of the ecosystem may mean financial losses to affected agents. For example, as per Lido documentation [204], the risks to its stakers are assumed to be:

i. Smart contract security
ii. Technical risks inherited from the Ethereum mainnet infrastructure
iii. Adoption risk

[23] cf. also the discussion on multi-sig wallets in Sect. 10.5.6.

[24] As explicitly stated in [159], "*The DAO members govern Lido to ensure its efficiency and stability*".

iv. Lido DAO key management risk[25]
v. Slashing risk
vi. stETH price risk

which to any traditional finance risk practitioner would be familiar as a combination of operational, strategic, and market risks. Again, these are risks which Lido recognizes as affecting primarily stakers.

However (and this is borne out by Lido Governance records, such as reports and blogs), the actual risk categories managed by Lido across agent types is quite broader and include:

a. Counterparty (node operator non-performance, etc.)
b. Third-party (Oracles, DAO contributors, etc.)
c. Portfolio concentration (staker-related, NO-related, etc.)
d. Liquidity (withdrawal shocks, liquidity pool drainage, etc.)
e. Solvency (treasury operations or funding failure, etc.)
f. Reputational (repeated slashing events, native token exclusion from prominent CEX/DEX, etc.)
g. Business model (token design failure, cooperating third-party failure, DAO inactivity, etc.)
h. Financial crime (money laundering, fraud, market manipulation, etc.)
i. Systemic (cooperating ecosystem failure, etc.)

risks. From a traditional finance viewpoint all of the above are subcategories of established risk typologies (credit, market, liquidity, operational, reputational), considered[26] in the particular business and technical context of this blockchain ecosystem. To manage, resp. control, them, Lido currently implements the following mechanisms:

1. All Lido smart contract (SC) code undergoes internal testing, budget for which is proposed, resp. managed, by the RCC and LEGO Committees. Residual SC technical risk is proactively managed through the funding of SC audits [189] and bug-bounty programs [186, 205], facilitated by the fact that all SC code is open-source and documented [206]. Please note that technical assets in-scope of said programs [207] extend to the entire technical infrastructure of the protocol and not merely its smart contracts. Hence, the incentivization of Lido DAO contributors (and by extension the minimization of workload—and the

[25] Or "key custody risk"—the risk of financial losses to any Lido participant (including its Governance) if private keys used in any internal Lido process are compromised, stolen or lost.

[26] Please note that the question of whether or not the risk typologies currently addressed by Lido Governance are comprehensive enough is not addressed here. This mainly because, as any blockchain token ecosystem governed decentrally, Lido constantly evolves its end-to-end design. Thus, any commentary, however factual and constructive, would fail to capture new Lido mechanisms introduced and/or threats recognized past the time of writing this case study.

opportunity cost of time—needed by members of its task committees) is a fundamental feature of Lido governance.

2. Lido subordinates notifications (state-, rewards-related, etc.) from the Ethereum mainnet under an internally designed and managed Oracle infrastructure [110]. It is governed by comprehensive, documented, processes [208], and its operations managed by known participants [209] approved by Lido governance [210]. Note that the same infrastructure is the basis for rewards aggregation and allocation from/to agents, as well as for stake withdrawal requests. Hence, the operational integrity of the Lido business model (the incentivization of stakers through rewards and their ability to withdraw liquidity at will) hinges on the technical robustness of the internal oracles.
3. The operational setup of Lido governance (through the research forum, and the regular activity reporting imposed on task Committees) has demonstrably enabled Lido to adapt its business model in the past. For example, the realization of the inability of some cooperating protocols to accommodate the rebasing stETH tokens led to the creation of a new native token type (wstETH), and the design and technical implementation of a new transactional pathway (cf. Sect. 9.6.3.2, [216]). Similarly, the withdrawal from some L-2 cooperating ecosystems [82, 83] is also a demonstration of the factual ability of Lido governance to assess emerging business model risks and take corrective action.
4. All Lido DAO multi-signature key addresses are registered centrally [211] and their co-signers are initially thoroughly vetted by governance. Afterwards they are expected to obey strict procedures of usage [202] and continuous communication [212] with other co-signers. It is thus tacitly assumed that any misappropriated keys will soon be discovered (as the prescribed message flow—e.g. *"Communicate once you've checked and signed the transaction" ("checked, signed, X more required")*—will fail to be observed by other co-signers). However, the fact is that prevention of the first-occurrence of malicious usage is not possible in this trust-based setup. Only after-the fact corrective action (e.g. effective decision reversal through a compensating on-chain transaction) is possible, its extent depending on the speed by which said malicious usage will be ascertained by ethical and diligent co-signers. Note that some Lido multi-sig setups (such as the 2/4 "Emergency Brakes Multi-sig" [213]) are critical for the ecosystem's resilience, with only a handful of malicious actors being potentially able to inflict serious harm. Lido addresses this risk at the organizational level, as task committees (and their multi-sig co-signers) are meant to act independently from each other—hence key person risk is reduced—and multi-sig usage can be immediately tracked on the blockchain. The use of multi-sig key addresses is equivalent to multi-signature approval lists (e.g. a 2/4 key in effect implements a "four-eyes" control principle) in traditional finance, and the risks of breach of trust perpetrated by a high authority person are similar. The use of task committees similarly mirrors a usual "separation of concerns" control principle. The committee/multi-sig setup would thus seem to corroborate the observation made previously in this section

that the current Lido DAO is run essentially on consensus by humans, not by algorithms.

5. Vetting and, at the same time assisting, onboarding of new operators is entrusted to the LNOSG task committee (where existing node operators play a critical role, hence *de facto* incentivized to safeguard the long-term viability of the ecosystem). Post-onboarding, Lido prescribes clear node operator performance management rules [214, 215] and documents a related non-performance risk management policy [216, 217]. The latter is technically implemented by a component of the internal Oracle called "Validators Exit Bus" [218] (mechanism ejecting PoS Validators when specific non-performance indicators [219] are ascertained). Addressing the operational risk of more malignant node operator behaviours is the task of the DSC, as already explained in the previous discussion on task committees.
6. Position drawdown risk for stakers is a real possibility, stemming from slashing risk at the level of PoS validators funded by Lido. To reduce drawdown risk, Lido governance creates mechanisms using two approaches in parallel: proactive quality control of node operator practices; and residual risk insurance. The **first approach** considers slashing risk as being fundamentally an operational risk and attempts to minimize it at its source. The entire NO vetting and monitoring framework [109] explained in the previous point is precisely part of this approach. Another part is the expectation that every slashing event undergoes a root-cause analysis, either by the affected node operator or by Lido DAO contributors. The Lido DAO actually solicits "post-mortem" reports by node operators—i.e. explaining the circumstances of PoS validator non-performance events, irrespective of whether or not they led to slashings. All such reports are published [220] in the research forum [221] (and can thus be accessed by trade publications [222]), whereas those of severe occurrences are also published in a bespoke section of Lido governance communication pages [223]. There thus is an apparent emphasis on understanding the root cause of each event, which suggests that propagating best practices is a recurring activity of the Lido DAO. The "post-mortem" historical archive replicates in effect the operational risk event databases known in traditional finance. The whole setup of this approach seems to intend to replicate a self-corrective risk control framework, such as typically encountered in traditional corporate settings, whereby "lessons learned" sessions and audit reports drive business remediation efforts and staff training adjustments. The **second approach** consists in designating part of the Lido DAO treasury as self-insurance covering pool, the peril being losses to the asset-side of the Lido balance sheet from Slashing Events. This pool—termed "Insurance Fund" [224, 225] in Lido documentation—is provisioned by funds sourced from the regular fee levied on staking rewards by Lido (cf. Sect. 9.6.3.1, steps "8" and "10" in Fig. 9.11). The insurance fund is drawn strictly by way of Lido DAO vote [226] and can thus be used to absorb losses that would otherwise translate to staker position drawdowns. Note that opting for self-insurance was not the first choice of Lido governance, as it had previously been paying for loss insurance coverage from a

third party [227, 228]. Both this historical detail and the fact that the optimal depth of this insurance pool is apparently a matter of consideration [229] suggest that Lido DAO keeps re-examining this second slashing risk minimization approach.

7. Lido governance vetoes all value chain third parties, and every decision about engaging with, e.g., external Oracle providers [95, 230, 231] and new DAO contributors [232] is taken by vote and registered transparently in the research forum. The performance of said third parties post-approval is meant to be tracked by Lido governance and relies on the internal Oracle for monitoring purposes and on the diligence of Lido DAO contributors (essentially, on the directly or indirectly responsible task committees) for corrective action purposes.
8. Asset concentration risk is interpreted by Lido governance as signifying the risk of concentrating staking funds (its working assets) to only a few node operators. This risk is controlled through policy [233] (e.g. stating "*No one node operator should have > 1% of total ETH staked via Lido*" and other dispersion requirements of a mixed business and technical nature[27]) and tracked by metrics [234, 235] publicly accessible through dashboards [236]. The approach appears to be one of transparency guiding governance action.
9. Liquidity risk is addressed at both the asset and liability sides. Lido imposes staking rate limits [237] (on ETH amounts that can be deposited) on stakers, and complements them by a controlled process for staking withdrawals [238] involving a waiting period of the order of a few days. Both mechanisms in effect control the volatility of funds in the liquidity pool. Further guarding against withdrawal shocks and liquidity pool drainage, the associated technical process [239] is based on smart contracts and handled by the internal Oracle [240]. This enables rules-based monitoring through algorithmic mechanisms. Furthermore, the Lido governance initiatives around a "Liquidity Observation Lab" [172, 173] (where also incentives through cooperating ecosystems are addressed, hence the liability-side argument) evidence an effort to continuously improve liquidity risk mechanisms. Incidentally, safeguarding the stability of the liquidity pool also indirectly protects the target valuation of stETH as 1:1 to ETH. The reason is that by minimizing frictions for staking/withdrawals there is less potential for deviations from the target price, hence less incentives for actors to engage in arbitrage among stETH and ETH through exchanges. Thus, liquidity risk controls also contribute to stETH price risk reduction.
10. Lido governance appears to accept that solvency risk is ultimately borne by LDO holders [241, 242], as a position in LDO tokens also forms a major part [243] of the Lido DAO treasury. The approach in the "Lido DAO Treasury Management Principles" [244] accepted [245] by Lido governance is: "*Risk of*

[27] Such as "Node operators should be distributed jurisdictionally", "Validators should be distributed geographically", "Validators should be distributed in terms of infrastructure: No overreliance on cloud providers; No overreliance on specific data center providers", etc.

loss to treasury funds should be minimized at every instance", which in effect assumes that liquidity risk—irrespective of the magnitude of a liquidity shock—is always controllable. If that is true, then this approach ignores the probability of tail risks; tellingly, there is also no mention of "tail risk" in the aforementioned principles. Please note that such a linkage between liquidity risk management and solvency risk control is not commensurate with traditional finance risk frameworks, whereby systemic risk is a principal source of tail risk, and wrong-way risk [246] (e.g. when hedging with assets exhibiting valuations strongly positively correlated with those that must be hedged) must be actively minimized. Systemic risk is quite probable in interconnected and independently risk-managed systems, such as Lido and its cooperating ecosystems. It can also be argued that the case of LDO tokens shoring up the asset-size of the Lido balance sheet is precisely a wrong-way risk situation.

11. As a non-custodial token ecosystem, Lido presently relies on anti-financial crime ("AFC",[28] i.e. guarding against money laundering; fraud; market manipulation; sanctions evasion, etc.) controls carried out by issuers of crypto wallets and upstream exchanges. Financial crime risks in a cryptomarket setting are of increasing concern to law enforcement bodies[29] and regulators globally [251, 252]. Please note that some jurisdictions of probable nexus to Lido mandate, or probably will mandate, AFC controls on owners and/or shareholders [253] of Cryptomarket companies, which would seem to include incorporated node operators. This will undoubtedly impact the NO vetting and onboarding processes of Lido. However, Lido already maintains a transparent NO registry, which could in principle be used to fact-base such controls. Also, the NO keys for ETH reward withdrawals are always owned by Lido [162], which is an additional AFC control.
12. It must be mentioned that there are also **potential** AFC aspects related to LDO holders (e.g. if a major LDO holder or delegate skews Lido governance decisions for own monetary benefit, which would qualify as market manipulation). In this respect, please read in the sequel of this section the discussion about voting mechanisms in Lido governance.
13. Systemic risk [254, 255] in a cryptomarket setting can be more difficult to contain than in traditional financial markets, due to the decentralized nature of token ecosystems. Interconnection with cooperating third parties as per market design means that every token ecosystem can be impacted from critical events at cooperating token ecosystems, information providers or exchanges. This has indeed impacted Lido in the past [256–258]—in the circumstances of the LUNA/TerraUSD collapse [259]—whereupon Lido itself became a contagion

[28] Please consult Sect. 10.5.6 for a discussion on Financial Crime aspects of relevance in token design.

[29] For some archival material on relatively recent criminal cases involving token ecosystem stakeholders, please consult the following links of the US Department of Justice (Criminal Division): [247–250].

link which severely affected [260, 261] other ecosystems and physical-world entities behind their economic agents [262]. For the sake of accuracy, it must be noted that at least one root cause—namely, the impossibility of staking withdrawals [263]—of the Lido-specific contagion mechanism in those circumstances is mute in the current generation [264] of the protocol. That said, the facts continue to be that, first, its third-party interconnections through mechanism design are still potential systemic risk propagation vectors and, second, every token ecosystem has its own mechanisms and practical time-scales [265, 266] to react to events. In other words, failed or sub-optimal mechanisms in third parties may still increase the magnitude of a systemic event when it reaches Lido's own mechanisms. Lido—or any token ecosystem for that matter—is not supposed to continuously monitor performance of mechanisms in other ecosystems, information providers, exchanges etc. It can only do three things: first, analyse the repercussions on its own mechanism design before accepting a new third-party dependency; second, adapt both its market and mechanism designs to minimize contagion risk; third, negotiate with the third-party's governance (or principals) on how to align contagion risk monitoring and containment mechanisms. Lido appears to have pursued at least the first two in the past, then applying preventative controls manifested principally through its governance vetting processes (before new third-party dependencies are accepted), and through its internal Oracles setup. The latter appears to act both as fall-back and as near-real time monitoring mechanism, longer-term monitoring/analysis being assigned to the task committees, e.g. the afore-mentioned liquidity observation lab. The existence of this lab appears to parallel mechanisms in traditional finance, whereby idiosyncratic liquidity risk events are assumed to be early warnings of potential systemic risks [267, 268]. By way of restorative controls, the afore-mentioned insurance fund (for immediate compensation of losses) and PoS validator exit penalties/ recovery processes (for internal funds recovery) appear to work in parallel. Please also note that, stETH and wstETH positions being denominated in Lido-native tokens, Lido would in theory be in a position to cancel and re-issue them if that were deemed to be the only way to compensate Stakers having irrecoverably lost them in cooperating ecosystems In that context, note that in the LUNA/TerraUSD circumstances the immediate risk effect for Lido was stETH:ETH depegging [269], which opened arbitrage opportunities, and not an immediate critical drawdown of the liquidity pool. Hence, Lido governance appears to have both preventative and restorative controls in place for external systemic risks. The situation is different when it comes to Lido being a potential *source* of systemic risk. This consideration has actually been raised repeatedly (by the trade press [270], academics [271], and key Ethereum stakeholders [272] alike in the context of Staking power concentration concerns. As of the time of writing, Lido Governance rejected [273] a proposal [274] for self-imposed limitation of Lido's Ethereum staking market share. It voted [275, 276] instead to help address the related (*but not identical*) problem of staking power centralization through the introduction of "Distributed Validator

Technology" (DVT) [277], meaning that staking would become eventually trustless [278] (its mechanisms permissionless [279, 280], controlled only by smart contracts). This in effect means that Lido governance has opted for addressing systemic risk through own mechanism design alone.

We can now begin interpreting the above mechanisms as calibration choices in reference to the design factors put forth in Sect. 8.5. There is an additional piece of information needed for this, which is given directly below.

In order to examine how the need for effective **consensus** building, **executive decision-making** and **conflict resolution** are taken into account in Lido mechanisms, we must first start from Lido's description of its "regular" Governance process [142]. In that context, it is expedient to explain what the "Aragon" token project is, and what being an "Aragon organization" means.

The "Aragon" [281, 282] token project was started in 2016 [283] with the explicit goal to standardize the logical framework and technical artefacts underpinning DAO's on Ethereum L-1. It created governance process templates and smart contracts that could be copied, amended, and deployed by other token projects. It can best be described as a "Blockchain DAO Framework" project, while being itself a blockchain token ecosystem—its governance token called "ANT" [284] (which ended up being sunset in 2024, as part of the project's evolution [285]). A core part of Aragon's documented products revolved around on-chain voting mechanisms. The development of Aragon itself was in course entrusted to a Swiss-based organization ("Aragon Association" [286]), with legal rights to also steer the Aragon Treasury. The project found itself in a volatile situation [287–289] following an attack [290] on its Governance. ANT was the immediate victim [291], being monitored as a precursor to being delisted [292] by major CEXs. However, its delivered process templates and smart contracts already underpin the operational governance of several stable token ecosystems [293]. In industry jargon, a DAO using them is sometimes designated as being an "*Aragon Organization*". As of the time of writing, Aragon was being steered by a new, also Swiss-based, legal entity, called "Aragon Foundation" [294].

Please note that token projects may opt for adopting only specific Aragon artefacts and furthermore may amend them, hence a DAO being such an organization does not completely describe its governance mechanisms. In effect, some projects have adopted only its voting smart contracts and associated configuration, as they are already proven on Ethereum L-1.

As of the time of writing, the Lido DAO is an Aragon organization [295], implementing Aragon smart contracts for the final step of its "regular" Governance voting. Before that, however, it goes through a "voting admittance" step, implemented through yet another third-party technical voting infrastructure ("Snapshot" [141]) which is simply web-, not blockchain-, based [296]. In other words, Lido's "regular" governance voting process is a three-step one. It expects proposals to be first formulated and ideally debated in the research forum (first step), then to be voted on (second step, carried out through Snapshot [297]) for final admittance to a binding vote on the blockchain (third step, through an Aragon smart contract).

In Lido's jargon, the snapshot vote is the "*off-chain*", whereas the Aragon SC vote the "*on-chain*" one. Both off-chain and on-chain votes have their own procedural mechanisms[30] (thresholds, quorum, duration, etc.) which are separately configurable. Note that to calculate voting power thresholds, quorum, etc., LDO token holdings must be made visible also during off-chain voting [301]. The aforementioned process is termed "regular" so as to distinguish it from an additional one, meant to be used only in time-critical situations. The latter is called "emergency track" [302] and provides for skipping the first two steps and going straight to the on-chain voting one. These two processes together cover in effect the **consensus** aspect.

Executive decisions are principally the domain of the task committees and are facilitated through a third voting guardrail called "easy track" [303]. This track is reserved only for proposals initiated by task committees which, as per original intent [304], "*Every day … need to take routine actions only related to their field of expertise. The decisions they make hardly ever spark any debate in the community, and votings on such decisions often struggle to attract wider DAO attention and thus, to pass*". Easy track votings [305] are registered through smart contracts created by Lido [306], not Aragon. To ensure that the short-circuiting track does not violate the consensus principle of the regular process, an easy track proposal is considered "rejected" if holders of as little as 0.5% of the LDO total supply vote against it. This forces the initiating task committee to have first reached near complete internal consensus.

Importantly, Lido governance does not currently seem to provide for a bespoke **conflict resolution** mechanism outside of the regular governance process. Note that Lido had the option to inherit precisely such a mechanism instituted [307–309] by Aragon, called "Aragon Court" [310].

When it comes to mechanisms impacting price discovery and price formation along transactional pathways (the **Market Structure** factor), these are different per Lido agent type.

Bargaining by stakers is impossible, as they are pure price takers along both main transactional pathways available to them. In the purchase of stETH (Sect. 9.6.3.1) their offering price is pegged 1:1 to ETH, whereas in the wrapping of stETH to wstETH (Sect. 9.6.3.2) the conversion rate among the two is specified by the internal share bookkeeping formula. In both cases the Lido dApp quotes a non-negotiable price to the staker, and the transaction is executed through smart contracts. Prospective LDO holders have recourse only to exchanges (CEX/DEX), as Lido offers no primary market for its governance token. Similarly, the terms offered by Lido to node operators accepting stakes (principally the rewards participation fee) are also fixed, set by Lido governance; there exists no documented option for individual node operators to negotiate said terms (there are indeed different incentives scheduled for smaller node operators using the novel DVT module

[30] E.g. for Snapshot: [298–300].

[277], however they are applied uniformly [311]). There are currently also no transactional pathways involving auctions anywhere within Lido proper, although Lido governance does track its own collateral risk in cooperating ecosystems [312, 313].

Price **information exchange** within Lido is completely dependent on the combination of external Oracles and the internal Oracle setup (referred to in mechanisms 5., 7., 9., 13. above), where node operators are also contributing.

Please remember from the previous chapter that the "**taxation**" aspect of the market structure factor refers to transaction fees that the ecosystem itself levies on its participating agents, i.e. it does not refer to corresponding physical-world tax obligations imputed on the principals of said agents (which are of course very much expected, at least in jurisdictions (e.g. [314]) recognizing staking as a distinct cryptomarket activity (e.g. [315]). As explained in several sections already and as depicted on Fig. 9.11 (steps #8 and #10), Lido extracts a commission (a service "fee") on whatever staking rewards flow back to its ETH liquidity pool by node operators, while the rest is credited to the stETH token balance owed to stakers (step #9). This commission is calculated as a percentage (currently 10% [107, 316]) of the rewards delta and is then split between Lido treasury and node operators. Hence, that is the effective tax rate levied by the ecosystem governance on stakers' income.

Please note that the technical funds withdrawal process [239, 317] when the agent "unstakes" (i.e. withdraws funds from the ecosystem, causing stETH and/or wstETH tokens to be burned) may cause a discrepancy between the credited and the withdrawn amounts of the order of at most 2 Gwei [318]. This is due to a known integer division problem [319] when rounding [320] during the internal calculation of Shares (cf. the discussion in Sect. 9.6.3.2 around Fig. 9.14), and is not a hidden fee. Other than that, and apart from standard L-1 gas fees when invoking Lido's smart contracts, there are no other transaction-level charges on stakers.

Regarding **financial/non-financial incentives** for Lido governance **voting**, the last two steps of the "regular" Governance process both implement "quorum voting" (cf. Table 8.4). Off-chain voting requires that more than 5% of the LDO total supply [321] must have voted for the winning proposal. On-chain (i.e. "Aragon") voting requires that both more than 5% of the LDO total supply and 50% of the votes cast must have voted for it.

In terms of voting power, it is proportional to the LDO tokens held. There are no voting rewards, hence also no voting rewards **allocation** policy. Note that the Lido DAO does not allow "delegated voting" (cf. Table 8.4), even though relating proposals have been discussed [322, 323].

This concludes our *exposé* on the current mechanism design of the Lido token ecosystem.

9.8 Summary

Lido, an EVM-compatible blockchain ecosystem that implements on-chain traditional finance notions of:

i. Promissory notes
ii. Financial guarantees
iii. Alternative investment funds

was used as a case study of mechanism design. Based on Lido project documentation and Lido governance records, its mechanisms were identified and interpreted as calibration options in reference to the influencing factors put forth in Sect. 8.5 of the previous chapter.

It was demonstrated that the mechanism design pillar of the proposed token ecosystem design framework does indeed align with current crypto-industry practices.

References

1. [Lido Token ecosystem] https://lido.fi/
2. *Top Liquid Staking Derivatives Tokens by Market Capitalization*. CoinMarketCap. Retrieved March 25, 2025, from https://www.coingecko.com/en/categories/liquid-staking-tokens
3. Barone, A. (2024, February 27). *Promissory Note: What It Is, Different Types, and Pros and Cons*. Retrieved March 25, 2025, from https://www.investopedia.com/terms/p/promissorynote.asp
4. (2018, February). *Research Note - The use of promissory notes in relations with consumers. Research and Documentation Directorate*. Court of Justice of the European Union. Retrieved March 25, 2025, from https://curia.europa.eu/jcms/jcms/p1_3321112/el/
5. Intermediary. (2025, March 27). In *Wikipedia*. Retrieved March 25, 2025, from https://en.wikipedia.org/wiki/Intermediary
6. [U.K.] *Bills of Exchange Act 1882*, part IV. Official U.K. Legislation pages. Retrieved March 25, 2025, from https://www.legislation.gov.uk/ukpga/Vict/45-46/61/part/IV.
7. [For borrowed amounts greater than GBP 30 for personal or GBP 25000 for business purposes, U.K.] Consumer Credit Act 1974 *(as amended)*. Official U.K. Legislation pages. Retrieved March 25, 2025, from https://www.legislation.gov.uk/ukpga/1974/39/contents (https://www.legislation.gov.uk/ukpga/2006/14/contents).
8. *The* [U.K.] *Consumer Credit (Agreements) Regulations 1983, Regulation 2*. Official U.-K. Legislation pages. Retrieved March 25, 2025, from https://www.legislation.gov.uk/uksi/1983/1553/regulation/2/made
9. [U.S.] U.C.C. [(Uniform Commercial Code)] – *Article 3 – Negotiable Instruments (2002)*. Legal Information Institute, Cornell Law School. Retrieved March 25, 2025, from https://www.law.cornell.edu/ucc/3
10. [Singapore Bills of Exchange Act] Part IV – *Promissory Notes*. Singapore Statutes Online. Retrieved March 25, 2025, from https://sso.agc.gov.sg/Act-Rev/23/Published?DocDate=19990801&ProvIds=P1IV-
11. [Hong Kong Cap. 19] *Bills of Exchange Ordinance – Art. 89*. Hong Kong e-Legislation. Retrieved March 25, 2025, from https://www.elegislation.gov.hk/hk/cap19?xpid=ID_1438402813613_003

12. [Switzerland] *Federal Act on the Amendment of the Swiss Civil Code (Part Five: The Code of Obligations), of 30 March 1911. Chapter 4, Part C, Art. 1096-1099* [and all references therein]. Retrieved March 25, 2025, from https://www.fedlex.admin.ch/eli/cc/27/317_321_377/en#part_5/tit_33/chap_4/lvl_C
13. [France] Code de commerce: Chapitre II - Du billet à ordre (Articles L512-1 to L512-8). Retrieved March 25, 2025, from https://www.legifrance.gouv.fr/codes/section_lc/LEGITEXT000005634379/LEGISCTA000006146083/ (available in French only)
14. *Spanish Commercial Code, Title XI - On aquittals, coupons and promissory notes to order and payment orders called cheques*. Retrieved March 25, 2025, from https://www.mjusticia.gob.es/es/AreaTematica/DocumentacionPublicaciones/Documents/Code_of_Comerce_%28Codigo_de_Comercio%29.PDF
15. [South Korea] *2004 Issuance and Distribution of Electronic Bills Act* (last amended by Act No. 15022, Oct. 31, 2017). English translation retrieved March 25, 2025, from https://elaw.klri.re.kr/kor_service/lawView.do?hseq=46760&lang=ENG. To be read together with the *Bills of Exchange and Promissory Notes Act* (Act No. 10198, Mar. 31, 2010); English translation retrieved March 25, 2025, from https://elaw.klri.re.kr/kor_service/lawView.do?hseq=18175&lang=ENG
16. Tank, M. H. K., & Whitaker, R. D. (2021). *Enotes and the MERS® eRegistry - enabled by lenders, embraced by borrowers, enforced by the courts, and now ready for the future: what you need to know about other electronic debt obligations and the MERS® eRegistry*. The Intercontinental Exchange. Retrieved March 25, 2025, from https://www.theice.com/publicdocs/eNote_White_Paper.pdf
17. Kenton, W. (2021, July 5). *IOU: What It Is, How It Works, and Examples*. Retrieved March 25, 2025, from https://www.investopedia.com/terms/i/iou.asp
18. Smyth, C.-M., & Gatto, M. (2018). *Contract law: A comparison of civil law and common law jurisdictions*. Business Expert Press.
19. Dobbyn, J. F., & French, C. C. (2016). *Insurance law in a nutshell* (5th ed.). West Academic Publishing.
20. Kenton, W. (2024, August 29). *Surety: Definition, How It Works With Bonds, and Distinctions*. Retrieved March 25, 2025, from https://www.investopedia.com/terms/s/surety.asp
21. Mann, R. A., & Roberts, B. S. (2019). *Essentials of business law and the legal environment* (13th ed.). Cengage.
22. (2021, August 2). *The difference between suretyship guarantees and demand guarantees*. Allen & Overy Shearman (A&O Shearman). Retrieved March 25, 2025, from https://www.allenovery.com/en-gb/global/blogs/compact-contract/the-difference-between-suretyship-guarantees-and-demand-guarantees
23. Ostendorf, P. (2021, September 4). *Demand Guarantee or Suretyship Guarantee – Have corporate guarantors lost the benefit of the doubt?* Faculty of Law blogs. University of Oxford. Retrieved March 25, 2025, from https://blogs.law.ox.ac.uk/business-law-blog/blog/2021/09/demand-guarantee-or-suretyship-guarantee-have-corporate-guarantors
24. James, H. (1996, June 15). *International Monetary Cooperation Since Bretton Woods*. Oxford University Press. https://doi.org/10.5089/9781475506969.071
25. Hayes, A. (2024, July 11). Black-Scholes Model: What It Is, How It Works, and Options Formula. Retrieved March 25, 2025, from https://www.investopedia.com/terms/b/blackscholes.asp
26. Financialization. (2025, April 18). In *Wikipedia*. Retrieved April 20, 2025, from https://en.wikipedia.org/wiki/Financialization
27. Reduced instruction set computer. (2025, March 25). In *Wikipedia*. Retrieved April 4, 2025, from https://en.wikipedia.org/wiki/Reduced_instruction_set_computer
28. Long-Term Capital Management. (2025, March 15). In *Wikipedia*. Retrieved April 4, 2025, from https://en.wikipedia.org/wiki/Long-Term_Capital_Management

29. Baker, K., & Filbeck, G. (2013). *Alternative investments - instruments, performance, benchmarks, and strategies*. Wiley.
30. [Context: European Union] *Directive 2011/61/EU of the European Parliament and of the Council of 8 June 2011 on Alternative Investment Fund Managers and amending Directives 2003/41/EC and 2009/65/EC and Regulations (EC) No 1060/2009 and (EU) No 1095/2010 Text with EEA relevance*. Retrieved March 25, 2025, from https://eur-lex.europa.eu/eli/dir/2011/61/oj/eng
31. [Context: U.S.A.] *Alternative Investment Funds Laws and Regulations USA 2024-2025*. Retrieved March 25, 2025, from https://iclg.com/practice-areas/alternative-investment-funds-laws-and-regulations/usa
32. [Context: England & Wales] *Alternative Investment Funds Laws and Regulations England & Wales 2024-2025*. Retrieved March 25, 2025, from https://iclg.com/practice-areas/alternative-investment-funds-laws-and-regulations/england-and-wales
33. [Context: Cayman Islands] *Alternative Investment Funds Laws and Regulations Cayman Islands 2024-2025*. Retrieved March 25, 2025, from https://iclg.com/practice-areas/alternative-investment-funds-laws-and-regulations/cayman-islands
34. [Context: Luxembourg] *Alternative Investment Funds Laws and Regulations Luxembourg 2024-2025*. Retrieved March 25, 2025, from https://iclg.com/practice-areas/alternative-investment-funds-laws-and-regulations/luxembourg
35. [Context: Switzerland] *Alternative Investment Funds Laws and Regulations Switzerland 2024-2025*. Retrieved March 25, 2025, from https://iclg.com/practice-areas/alternative-investment-funds-laws-and-regulations/switzerland
36. [Context: Honk Kong SAR] *Alternative Investment Funds Laws and Regulations Hong Kong 2024-2025*. Retrieved March 25, 2025, from https://iclg.com/practice-areas/alternative-investment-funds-laws-and-regulations/hong-kong
37. [Context: Singapore] *Alternative Investment Funds Laws and Regulations Singapore 2024-2025*. Retrieved March 25, 2025, from https://iclg.com/practice-areas/alternative-investment-funds-laws-and-regulations/singapore
38. [Context: United Arab Emirates, and in particular Dubai] *Collective Investment Funds*. Dubai Financial Services Authority. Retrieved March 25, 2025, from https://www.dfsa.ae/what-we-do/collective-investment-funds
39. (2025). *Alternative Investment Features, Methods, and Structures*. CFA Refresher Readings. CFA Institute. Retrieved March 25, 2025, from https://www.cfainstitute.org/en/membership/professional-development/refresher-readings/introduction-alternative-investments
40. Mirabile, K. (2013). *Hedge Fund Investing. A Practical Approach to Understanding Investor Motivation, Manager Profits, and Fund Performance*. Wiley.
41. Gompers, P. A., & Kaplan, S. N. (2022). *Advanced introduction to private equity*. Edward Elgar Publishing.
42. Lin, W. (2023). *The VC Field Guide. Fundamentals of Venture Capital*. Wiley.
43. Nesbitt, S. L. (2023). *Private Debt. yield, safety and the emergence of alternative lending* (2nd ed.). Wiley.
44. Hartzell, D., & Baum, A. E. (2021). *Real estate investment. Strategies, structures, decisions* (2nd ed.). Wiley.
45. James, T. (2016). *Commodity market trading and investment. A practitioners guide to the markets*. Palgrave Macmillan.
46. Gibner, S. (Ed.). (2013). *Commodity investing and trading*. Risk books.
47. Zorloni, A. (2013). *The Economics of Contemporary Art*. Markets, Strategies, and Stardom. Springer.
48. Bainbridge, D., & Howell, C. (2014). *Intellectual Property Asset Management. How to identify, protect, manage and exploit intellectual property within the business environment*. Routledge.

49. (2024, May 7). *The impact of tokenization on alternative assets markets*. Moody's. Retrieved March 25, 2025, from https://www.moodys.com/web/en/us/creditview/blog/the-impact-of-tokenization-on-alternative-assets-markets.html
50. Landry, L. (2021, July 8). *What are alternative investments?* Business Insights. Harvard Business School Online. Retrieved March 25, 2025, from https://online.hbs.edu/blog/post/what-are-alternative-investments
51. [CAIA Association of Chartered Alternative Investment Analysts] https://caia.org/
52. Chambers, D. R., Anson, M. J. P., Black, K. H., & Kazemi, H. B. (2020). *Alternative Investments, CAIA Level I* (4th ed., p. 431). Wiley.
53. Calamos, N. P. (2003). *Convertible arbitrage: Insights and techniques for successful hedging*. Wiley.
54. U.S. Securities and Exchange Commission. (2017, February 3). Investor Bulletin: Alternative Mutual Funds. Retrieved March 25, 2025, from https://www.sec.gov/resources-investors/investor-alerts-bulletins/alternative-mutual-funds
55. Dhir, R. (2025, March 18). *What Is a Prospectus? Example, Uses, and How to Read It*. Retrieved March 25, 2025, from https://www.investopedia.com/terms/p/prospectus.asp
56. European Securities and Markets Authority (ESMA). *CESR's template for the Key Investor Information document*. CESR/10-1321. Retrieved March 25, 2025., from https://www.esma.europa.eu/document/cesr%E2%80%99s-template-key-investor-information-document
57. *EU laws and initiatives relating to collective investment funds*. Retrieved March 25, 2025, from https://finance.ec.europa.eu/capital-markets-union-and-financial-markets/financial-markets/investment-funds_en
58. Hudson, M. (2014). *Funds - private equity, hedge and all core structures*. Wiley
59. [Context: U.K.] *The Perimeter Guidance Manual - Scope of the Alternative Investment Fund Managers Regime*. Chapter 16. FCA Handbook. Retrieved March 25, 2025, from https://www.handbook.fca.org.uk/handbook/PERG/16.pdf [please search within document for "Limited Partnerships Act 1907"]
60. (2024, September 3). *Proof-of-stake (POS)*. Ethereum documentation pages. Retrieved March 22, 2025, from https://ethereum.org/en/developers/docs/consensus-mechanisms/pos/
61. (2024, April 16). *Why do validators need 32 ETH?* Ethereum documentation pages. Retrieved March 22, 2025, from https://ethereum.org/en/developers/docs/consensus-mechanisms/pos/faqs/#why-32-eth
62. (2025, February 25). *The two types of validator keys*. Ethereum documentation pages. Retrieved March 25, 2025, from https://ethereum.org/en/developers/docs/consensus-mechanisms/pos/keys#two-types-of-keys
63. *Validator*. Staking Glossary. EthStaker documentation pages. Retrieved March 25, 2025, from https://docs.ethstaker.cc/ethstaker-knowledge-base/staking-glossary#validator
64. *Finality issues*. Staking Glossary. EthStaker documentation pages. Retrieved March 25, 2025, from https://docs.ethstaker.cc/ethstaker-knowledge-base/staking-glossary#finality-issues
65. *How does my validator earn ETH?* EthStaker documentation pages. Retrieved March 25, 2025, from https://docs.ethstaker.cc/ethstaker-knowledge-base/rewards/chain-rewards
66. (2024, November 23). *Inactivity leak*. Ethereum documentation pages. Retrieved March 25, 2025, from https://ethereum.org/en/developers/docs/consensus-mechanisms/pos/rewards-and-penalties/#inactivity-leak
67. *(2024, November 23). Slashing*. Ethereum documentation pages. Retrieved March 25, 2025, from https://ethereum.org/en/developers/docs/consensus-mechanisms/pos/rewards-and-penalties/#slashing
68. *(2024, November 23). Penalties*. Ethereum documentation pages. Retrieved March 25, 2025, from https://ethereum.org/en/developers/docs/consensus-mechanisms/pos/rewards-and-penalties/#penalties
69. *Slashable offenses*. EthStaker documentation pages. Retrieved March 25, 2025, from https://docs.ethstaker.cc/ethstaker-knowledge-base/staking-glossary#slashable-offenses

70. *(2024, September 3). Crypto-economic security*. Ethereum documentation pages. Retrieved March 25, 2025, from https://ethereum.org/en/developers/docs/consensus-mechanisms/pos/#crypto-economic-security
71. Edgington, B. (2025, March 5). *Upgrading Ethereum - A technical handbook on Ethereum's move to proof of stake and beyond.* Retrieved March 25, 2025, from https://eth2book.info/ [esp. the section on Slashing, https://eth2book.info/capella/part2/incentives/slashing/]
72. Nijkerk, M. (2023, April 17). *Ethereum Unstaking Requests Pile Up After Shanghai Upgrade, Now at 2-Week Wait.* CoinDesk. Retrieved March 25, 2025, from https://www.coindesk.com/tech/2023/04/13/ethereum-unstaking-requests-pile-up-after-shanghai-upgrade-now-at-2-week-wait/
73. *Unstake your Ethereum (ETH).* WealthSimple support pages. Retrieved March 25, 2025, from https://help.wealthsimple.com/hc/en-ca/articles/13470854670619-Unstake-your-Ethereum-ETH- [please search for "How long does it take to exit a validator set?" and "How long does it take to process unstaking requests?"]
74. CoinMarketCap ETH *page.* CoinMarketCap. Retrieved March 25, 2025, from https://coinmarketcap.com/currencies/ethereum/
75. Staking Pool. CoinMarketCap "Academy" pages. Retrieved March 25, 2025, from https://coinmarketcap.com/academy/glossary/staking-pool
76. [U.S.] Securities and Exchange Commission. (2025, May 29). *Statement on Certain Protocol Staking Activities.* Retrieved May 31, 2025, from https://www.sec.gov/newsroom/speeches-statements/statement-certain-protocol-staking-activities-052925
77. *How To Liquid Stake - Step-by-Step Guide to Liquid Stake on PancakeSwap.* PancakeSwap documentation pages. Retrieved March 25, 2025, from https://docs.pancakeswap.finance/archive/legacy-products/archived-liquid-staking-integration/how-to-liquid-stake https://blog.pancakeswap.finance/articles/your-comprehensive-guide-to-liquid-staking
78. Edwards, J. (2023, May 5). *The Biggest Crypto Trend of 2023: Liquid Staking Derivatives (LSDs).* Retrieved March 20, 2025, from https://www.nasdaq.com/articles/the-biggest-crypto-trend-of-2023-liquid-staking-derivatives-lsds
79. Sharnowski, S. & Jahanshahloo, H. (2023). *The economics of liquid staking derivatives: Basis determinants and price discovery.* https://papers.ssrn.com/sol3/papers.cfm?abstract_id=4180341
80. (2025, February 13). *Increase the max effective balance.* Prague-Electra (Pectra). Ethereum Roadmap documentation pages. Retrieved March 25, 2025, from https://ethereum.org/en/roadmap/pectra/#7251
81. (2023, October 16) *Lido On Solana Sunset.* Lido blog pages. Retrieved March 25, 2025, from https://blog.lido.fi/sunset-lido-on-solana/
82. (2023, October) *Sunset Lido on Polygon.* Lido governance discussion pages. Retrieved March 25, 2025, from https://research.lido.fi/t/sunset-lido-on-polygon/5655/3
83. (2023, March) Sunsetting of Lido on Polkadot and Kusama. Lido governance discussion pages. Retrieved March 25, 2025, from https://research.lido.fi/t/sunsetting-of-lido-on-polkadot-and-kusama/4067/13
84. *Collateralized Debt Position (CDP).* CoinMarketCap Glossary pages. Retrieved March 25, 2025, from https://coinmarketcap.com/academy/glossary/collateralized-debt-position-cdp
85. Virtual machine. (2025, May 13). In *Wikipedia.* Retrieved May 18, 2025, from https://en.wikipedia.org/wiki/Virtual_machine
86. Containerization (computing). (2025, April 27). In *Wikipedia.* Retrieved May 18, 2025, from https://en.wikipedia.org/wiki/Containerization_(computing)
87. Lido DAO. Lido documentation pages. Retrieved March 25, 2025, from https://docs.lido.fi/lido-dao/
88. *What is LDO.* Lido documentation pages. Retrieved March 25, 2025, from https://docs.lido.fi/guides/lido-tokens-integration-guide/#what-is-ldo
89. Lido DAO - *Mission-driven decentralized organization.* Lido governance pages. Retrieved March 25, 2025, from https://lido.fi/governance [please search in the page for "Committees"]

90. *Lido Node Operator functionality - onboarding*. Lido [PoS Validator] Node Operator Portal. Retrieved March 25, 2025, from https://operatorportal.lido.fi/apply-to-be-a-lido-node-operator
91. CoinMarketCap LDO *page*. CoinMarketCap. Retrieved March 25, 2025, from https://coinmarketcap.com/currencies/lido-dao/
92. (2021, January 5) *Introducing LDO - The Lido DAO Governance Token*. Lido blog pages. Retrieved March 25, 2025, from https://blog.lido.fi/introducing-ldo/ [please search in the page for "LDO Token Allocation"]
93. *Price feeds*. Lido documentation pages. Retrieved March 25, 2025, from https://docs.lido.fi/deployed-contracts/#price-feeds
94. *Chainlink Data Feed for stETH/USD*. Chainlink operational pages. Retrieved March 25, 2025, from https://data.chain.link/ethereum/mainnet/crypto-usd/steth-usd
95. *Lido tokens integration guide*. Lido documentation pages. Retrieved March 25, 2025, from https://docs.lido.fi/guides/lido-tokens-integration-guide#integration-utilities-chainlink-price-feeds
96. *AccountingOracle*. Lido documentation pages. Retrieved March 25, 2025, from https://docs.lido.fi/contracts/accounting-oracle
97. *The fee* [financing rewards of Node Operators in Lido]. Lido documentation pages. Retrieved March 25, 2025, from https://docs.lido.fi/guides/node-operators/general-overview#the-fee
98. *General Overview* [of Node Operators' rights and responsibilities in Lido]. Lido documentation pages. Retrieved March 25, 2025, from https://docs.lido.fi/guides/node-operators/general-overview
99. *Request withdrawal and mint NFT* [to realize Staking yield in Lido]. Lido documentation pages. Retrieved March 25, 2025, from https://docs.lido.fi/guides/lido-tokens-integration-guide#request-withdrawal-and-mint-nft
100. [Staking functionality of Lido dApp] https://stake.lido.fi/
101. [Withdrawal – realizing Staking yield – functionality of Lido dApp] https://stake.lido.fi/withdrawals/request/
102. [Taking part in Lido governance votings] https://vote.lido.fi/
103. *Deposit* [Smart Contract description]. Lido documentation pages. Retrieved March 25, 2025, from https://docs.lido.fi/contracts/lido/#deposit
104. *Lido* [Smart Contracts description]. Lido documentation pages. Retrieved March 25, 2025, from https://docs.lido.fi/contracts/lido [page also contains links to source code, rsp. Ethereum addresses, operational as of the time of writing: e.g., https://github.com/lidofinance/lido-dao/blob/master/contracts/0.4.24/Lido.sol, rsp. https://etherscan.io/address/0xae7ab96520de3a18e5e111b5eaab095312d7fe84]
105. (2021, February 4) *The Lido DAO Treasury Fund*. Lido blog pages. Retrieved March 25, 2025, from https://blog.lido.fi/lido-dao-treasury-fund/
106. *Lido Monthly Reports*. Lido blog pages. Retrieved March 25, 2025, from https://blog.lido.fi/category/reports/
107. *Protocol fee* [on Staking rewards]. Lido governance pages. Retrieved March 25, 2025, from https://docs.lido.fi/#protocol-fee
108. *NodeOperatorsRegistry* [Smart Contract]. Lido documentation pages. Retrieved March 25, 2025, from https://docs.lido.fi/contracts/node-operators-registry/
109. *Lido Fees Dashboard* [tracking operational performance of PoS Validators financed by Lido]. https://fees-monitoring.lido.fi/
110. *Intro*[duction to the Lido Oracle mechanism]. Lido documentation pages. Retrieved March 25, 2025, from https://docs.lido.fi/guides/oracle-operator-manual#intro
111. [Explanation of the Lido] *Accounting oracle* [mechanism]. Lido documentation pages. Retrieved March 25, 2025, from https://docs.lido.fi/guides/lido-tokens-integration-guide/#accounting-oracle
112. Lielacher, A. (2023, June 26). *Rebase Tokens: What Are They & How Do They Work?* CryptoNews. Retrieved March 25, 2025, from https://cryptonews.com/exclusives/rebase-tokens.htm

113. *Note on ERC-20 compliance* [of the Smart Contract minting the stETH tokens]. Lido documentation pages. Retrieved March 25, 2025, from https://docs.lido.fi/guides/lido-tokens-integration-guide#note-on-erc-20-compliance
114. Vogelsteller, F. & Buterin, V. (2015, November 20). *ERC-20: Token Standard.* Ethereum Improvement Proposals, no.20. Retrieved March 17, 2025, from https://eips.ethereum.org/EIPS/eip-20
115. *Terms of use* [of the Lido dApp's functionality]. Retrieved March 17, 2025, from https://lido.fi/terms-of-use
116. Lido FAQ [around dApp functionality and process steps]. Retrieved March 17, 2025, from https://lido.fi/faq
117. *What is the Insurance fund used for?* Lido support pages. Retrieved March 17, 2025, from https://help.lido.fi/en/articles/5230602-what-is-the-insurance-fund-used-for
118. [Invocation and expected yield of] *Liquid Ethereum Staking*. Retrieved March 17, 2025, from https://lido.fi/ethereum [please search in the page for "Lido APR"]
119. [PoS Validator funds] *Withdrawal credentials* [in Ethereum]. Ethereum documentation pages. Retrieved March 25, 2025, from https://ethereum.org/en/developers/docs/consensus-mechanisms/pos/keys#withdrawal-credentials
120. [Lido] *Target shares*. ADR: Staking Router. Lido documentation pages. Retrieved March 17, 2025, from https://hackmd.io/f1wvHzpjTIq41-GCrdaMjw?view#Target-shares (URL linked into by the official Lido documentation section https://docs.lido.fi/contracts/staking-router/#stake-allocation, retrieved on same date)
121. [PoS Validator] *Withdrawal Credentials* [defined by Lido]. Lido documentation pages. Retrieved March 25, 2025, from https://docs.lido.fi/guides/node-operators/validator-keys#withdrawal-credentials
122. Rebasing Tokens. Uniswap documentation pages. Retrieved March 25, 2025, from https://docs.uniswap.org/contracts/v2/reference/smart-contracts/common-errors#rebasing-tokens
123. *Token Integration Issues*. Uniswap documentation pages. Retrieved March 25, 2025, from https://docs.uniswap.org/concepts/protocol/integration-issues
124. [Wrap/Unwrap stETH/wstETH functionality in Lido dAPP] https://stake.lido.fi/wrap/
125. *wstETH* [specification]. Lido documentation pages. Retrieved March 25, 2025, from https://docs.lido.fi/contracts/wsteth (URL also links to the relevant Smart Contract source code, rsp. Ethereum address, https://github.com/lidofinance/lido-dao/blob/master/contracts/0.6.12/WstETH.sol, rsp. https://etherscan.io/token/0x7f39c581f595b53c5cb19bd0b3f8da6c935e2ca0)
126. *CoinMarketCap wstETH/ETH page*. CoinMarketCap. Retrieved March 25, 2025, from https://coinmarketcap.com/currencies/lido-finance-wsteth/wsteth/eth/
127. *CoinMarketCap wstETH/USD page*. CoinMarketCap. Retrieved March 25, 2025, from https://coinmarketcap.com/currencies/lido-finance-wsteth/
128. *Bookkeeping shares* [used to effect rebasing of stETH]. Lido documentation pages. Retrieved March 25, 2025, from https://docs.lido.fi/guides/lido-tokens-integration-guide/#bookkeeping-shares
129. *stETH internals: share mechanics*. Lido documentation pages. Retrieved March 25, 2025, from https://docs.lido.fi/guides/lido-tokens-integration-guide/#steth-internals-share-mechanics
130. *Rewards accounting*. Lido documentation pages. Retrieved March 25, 2025, from https://docs.lido.fi/guides/lido-tokens-integration-guide/#rewards-accounting
131. [stETH to wstETH] Wrap & Unwrap. Lido documentation pages. Retrieved March 25, 2025, from https://docs.lido.fi/guides/lido-tokens-integration-guide/#wrap%2D%2Dunwrap
132. [wstETH Smart Contract]. Lido GitHub pages. Retrieved March 25, 2025, from https://github.com/lidofinance/lido-dao/blob/master/contracts/0.6.12/WstETH.sol
133. [Shares-related methods]. Lido GitHub pages. Retrieved March 25, 2025, from https://github.com/lidofinance/docs/blob/main/docs/contracts/lido.md#shares-related-methods

134. Chen, J. (2024, April 24). *Open-Ended Fund: Definition, Example, Pros and Cons*. Retrieved March 25, 2025, from https://www.investopedia.com/terms/o/open-endfund.asp
135. Gerber, M. (2008). *How to create and manage a mutual fund or exchange-traded fund: A professional's guide*. Wiley.
136. Gremillion, L. (2005). *Mutual fund industry handbook: A comprehensive guide for investment professionals*. Boston Finance Institute of Finance Series, Wiley.
137. U.S. Securities and Exchange Commission. *Net Asset Value*. Retrieved March 25, 2025, from https://www.investor.gov/introduction-investing/investing-basics/glossary/net-asset-value
138. (2021, January 5). *Introducing LDO - The Lido DAO Governance Token*. Lido blog pages. Retrieved March 25, 2025, from https://blog.lido.fi/introducing-ldo/
139. *What are the use cases for LDO?* Lido support pages. Retrieved March 25, 2025, from https://help.lido.fi/en/articles/5231889-what-are-the-use-cases-for-ldo
140. *Proposal: Introducing $LDO Staking*. Lido governance discussion pages. Retrieved March 25, 2025, from https://research.lido.fi/t/proposal-introducing-ldo-staking/4636
141. [Snapshot voting management platform] https://snapshot.org/
142. [Governance voting] *Regular process*. Lido governance pages. Retrieved March 25, 2025, from https://lido.fi/governance#regular-process
143. [Governance voting] *FAQs*. Lido Snapshot documentation pages. Retrieved March 25, 2025, from https://docs.snapshot.org/faq#how-can-i-vote
144. Why I *can't vote?* Snapshot GitHub pages. Retrieved March 25, 2025, from https://github.com/snapshot-labs/snapshot/discussions/767
145. Lido DAO [Governance]. Lido governance pages. Retrieved March 25, 2025, from https://lido.fi/governance (please search in the page for "Snapshot voting cadence:")
146. E.g., *Lido Montlhy Report for November 2023*. Lido blog pages. Retrieved March 25, 2025, from https://blog.lido.fi/lido-monthly-report-november-2023/ (please search in the page for "Protocol Performance" and for "Additional Notes", under which appears: "The Lido protocol achieved a significant milestone as the number of first-time ETH stakers surpassed the 200,000 mark")
147. Banton, C. (2025, February 8). *Share repurchase: Why do companies do share buybacks?* Retrieved March 25, 2025, from https://www.investopedia.com/terms/s/sharerepurchase.asp
148. (2021, January 27). *Guide: Using Lido's stETH and LDO on SushiSwap*. Lido blog pages. Retrieved March 25, 2025, from https://blog.lido.fi/liquidity-mining-with-sushiswap-onsen/
149. Swapping ETH *for LDO in Uniswap*. Uniswap dApp. Retrieved March 25, 2025, from https://app.uniswap.org/explore/tokens/ethereum/0x5A98FcBEA516Cf06857215779Fd812CA3beF1B32
150. *How to Vote, Override, Delegate with Etherscan*. Lido documentation pages. Retrieved March 25, 2025, from https://docs.lido.fi/guides/etherscan-voting/
151. Hertig, A. (2017, March 30). *What Is a DAO?* CoinDesk. Retrieved March 25, 2025, from https://www.coindesk.com/learn/what-is-a-dao/
152. (2022, March). *Legal Engineering RFC/RFP: Establish Lido Legal Entities*. Lido governance discussion pages. Retrieved March 25, 2025, from https://research.lido.fi/t/legal-engineering-rfc-rfp-establish-lido-legal-entities/1790
153. Unincorporated association. (2025, March 8). In *Wikipedia*. Retrieved March 25, 2025, from https://en.wikipedia.org/wiki/Unincorporated_association
154. Bainbridge, S. (2022). *Agency, partnerships, and limited liability entities: Cases and materials on unincorporated business associations* (5th ed.). Foundation Press.
155. Campbell, N., Baughen, S., & Stewart, N. (2011). *The law of unincorporated associations*. Oxford University Press.
156. *Why DAO?* Lido documentation pages. Retrieved March 25, 2025, from https://docs.lido.fi/lido-dao/#why-dao
157. (2025, March 14). Lido DAO Liquid Staking: A Guide to LDO Token & Rewards. Retrieved March 25, 2025, from https://www.withtap.com/blog/what-is-lido-dao-ldo (please search in

the page for "Who created the Lido DAO platform?". Note that this publication is not officially sanctioned by Lido)

158. *21Shares* Lido DAO ETP, *ISIN: CH1275043318*. Exchanged-Traded Financial Instrument offering exposure to LDO (issued by Swiss-based company). Retrieved March 25, 2025 from https://21shares.com/product/LIDO (also trackable through https://www.bloomberg.com/quote/LIDO:NA)
159. [Lido DAO] *Functions*. Lido documentation pages. Retrieved March 25, 2025, from https://docs.lido.fi/lido-dao/#functions
160. [Overview page]. Lido governance discussion pages. Retrieved March 25, 2025, from https://research.lido.fi/
161. *Landing Page for Node Operators and Open Applications for Terra and Solana*. Lido governance discussion pages. Retrieved March 25, 2025, from https://research.lido.fi/t/landing-page-for-node-operators-and-open-applications-for-terra-and-solana/642
162. [Node Operator related processes] General Overview. Lido documentation pages. Retrieved March 25, 2025, from https://docs.lido.fi/guides/node-operators/general-overview/
163. [Lido-funded PoS] *Validator Exits Protocol, Penalties and Recovering* [entitlements]. Lido documentation pages. Retrieved March 25, 2025, from https://docs.lido.fi/guides/node-operators/general-overview/#validator-exits-policy-penalties-and-recovering
164. *Lido on Ethereum Validator Exits Policy*. Lido GitHub pages. Retrieved March 25, 2025, from https://github.com/lidofinance/documents-and-policies/blob/7595317b8fd2ee60ab25f5cac8eac2cc2cafa149/Lido%20on%20Ethereum%20-%20Validator%20Exits%20Policy.md
165. *Lido Node Operator functionality*. Lido [PoS Validator] Node Operator Portal. Retrieved March 25, 2025, from https://operatorportal.lido.fi/
166. *Lido Operators Database*. Lido [PoS Validator] Node Operator Portal. Retrieved March 25, 2025, from https://operatorportal.lido.fi/lido-operators-database
167. (2023, November) *Post mortem: Downtime of Staking Facilities / Lido validators*. Lido governance discussion pages. Retrieved March 25, 2025, from https://research.lido.fi/t/post-mortem-downtime-of-staking-facilities-lido-validators/6021
168. (2023, December) *Post mortem: Downtime of Lido validators (Gateway.fm AS)*. Lido governance discussion pages. Retrieved March 25, 2025, from https://research.lido.fi/t/post-mortem-downtime-of-lido-validators-gateway-fm-as/6164
169. (2021, December) *Proposal to form reWARDS Committee*. Lido governance discussion pages. Retrieved March 25, 2025, from https://research.lido.fi/t/proposal-to-form-rewards-committee/1447
170. (2023, February) *# [reWARDS] March '23 Budget*. Lido governance discussion pages. Retrieved March 25, 2025, from https://research.lido.fi/t/rewards-march-23-budget/3954
171. [wstETH orderflow metrics]. Retrieved March 23, 2025, from https://dune.com/pipistrella/wsteth-orderflow-metrics
172. (2023, July 8). *Lido v2 Liquidity Program*. Retrieved March 23, 2025, from https://docs.google.com/document/d/1uVTpnfOfddKzmzRq3P6oyPnqUXMEaR7WLd872coZotA/edit
173. (2023, August). *Liquidity Observation Lab (LOL): Liquidity Strategy and application to Curve stETH:ETH Pool*. Lido governance discussion pages. Retrieved March 25, 2025, from https://research.lido.fi/t/liquidity-observation-lab-lol-liquidity-strategy-and-application-to-curve-steth-eth-pool/5335
174. (2023, March). *Objective-based liquidity design for stETH and directions for further research*. Lido governance discussion pages. Retrieved March 25, 2025, from https://research.lido.fi/t/objective-based-liquidity-design-for-steth-and-directions-for-further-research/4156
175. *Committees* [production Smart Contract addresses on Mainnets]. Lido documentation pages. Retrieved March 25, 2025, from https://docs.lido.fi/deployed-contracts/#committees
176. (2022, March) *Proposal to form Resourcing and Compensation Committee (RCC)*. Lido governance discussion pages. Retrieved March 25, 2025, from https://research.lido.fi/t/

proposal-to-form-resourcing-and-compensation-committee-rcc/1767?pk_vid=03ea1c3850 9ffd161704165461e94319
177. (2023, April) *[LIDO-v2] May 1, 2023 - December 31, 2023 | Lido Ongoing Grant Request*. Lido governance discussion pages. Retrieved March 25, 2025, from https://research.lido.fi/t/lido-v2-may-1-2023-december-31-2023-lido-ongoing-grant-request/4476
178. (2023, February) *Lido DAO Token Rewards Plan (TRP). Operations plan*. Lido governance discussion pages. Retrieved March 25, 2025, from https://research.lido.fi/t/lido-dao-token-rewards-plan-trp-operations-plan/3820
179. (2022, December) *Lido DAO Token Rewards Plan (TRP)*. Operations plan. Lido governance discussion pages. Retrieved March 25, 2025, from https://research.lido.fi/t/lidodao-token-rewards-plan-trp/3364
180. *Lido Token Rewards Plan* [functionality of the Lido dApp]. Retrieved March 17, 2025, from https://trp.lido.fi/
181. (2021, March) *Project: Lido Ecosystem Grants Organization*. Lido governance discussion pages. Retrieved March 25, 2025, from https://research.lido.fi/t/project-lido-ecosystem-grants-organization/406
182. *LEGO (Lido Ecosystem Grants Organization)*. Lido governance pages. Retrieved March 25, 2025, from https://lido.fi/lego (please search in the page for "Grant Application Process" and further for "LEGO Nominees")
183. *LEGO Quarterly Reporting*. Lido governance pages. Retrieved March 25, 2025, from https://lego.lido.fi/lego-quarterly-reporting
184. *Successful* [LEGO] *grants*. Lido governance pages. Retrieved March 25, 2025, from https://lego.lido.fi/successful-grants
185. *LEGO – Grant Opportunities*. Lido governance pages. Retrieved March 25, 2025, from https://docs.google.com/spreadsheets/d/1WWYpKbOBR20rZZEuycWYegxAIswSG7LkcvOKpdoPDbw/edit#gid=172089462
186. *Bug Bounty Program*. Lido governance pages. Retrieved March 25, 2025, from https://lido.fi/bug-bounty
187. *Bug Bounties with Immunefi*. Lido documentation pages. Retrieved March 25, 2025, from https://docs.lido.fi/security/bugbounty/
188. *Security*. Lido documentation pages. Retrieved March 25, 2025, from https://docs.lido.fi/#security
189. *Lido Protocol Audits*. Lido GitHub pages. Retrieved March 25, 2025, from https://github.com/lidofinance/audits
190. (2021, June) *Lido Referral Program*. Lido governance discussion pages. Retrieved March 25, 2025, from https://research.lido.fi/t/lido-referral-program/715
191. (2024, March) *Rewards-Share Program 2024*. Lido governance discussion pages. Retrieved March 25, 2025, from https://lido.fi/rewards-share
192. *Lido Referral Program*. Lido GitHub pages. Retrieved March 25, 2025, from https://github.com/lidofinance/referral-program-integration-examples
193. Tiered Rewards Share Program: A Sustainable Approach to stETH Growth. Lido governance discussion pages. Retrieved March 25, 2025, from https://research.lido.fi/t/tiered-rewards-share-program-a-sustainable-approach-to-steth-growth/4851
194. *Terms of use* [of the Lido dApp]. https://lido.fi/terms-of-use
195. (2021, October) *Mitigations for deposit front-running vulnerability*. Lido governance discussion pages. Retrieved March 25, 2025, from https://research.lido.fi/t/mitigations-for-deposit-front-running-vulnerability/1239
196. *Deposit Security Committee manual*. Lido documentation pages. Retrieved March 25, 2025, from https://docs.lido.fi/guides/deposit-security-manual/
197. *The Deposit Security Committee*. Lido documentation pages. Retrieved March 25, 2025, from https://docs.lido.fi/guides/deposit-security-manual/#the-deposit-security-committee
198. *Preparation steps*. Lido documentation pages. Retrieved March 25, 2025, from https://docs.lido.fi/guides/deposit-security-manual/#preparation-steps

199. [Deposit Security] *Committee membership*. Lido documentation pages. Retrieved March 25, 2025, from https://docs.lido.fi/guides/deposit-security-manual/#committee-membership
200. *Lido on Ethereum - Scorecard* [on the Lido dApp] https://lido.fi/scorecard
201. (2022, July) *Lido DAO Core Contributors Provisional Budget*. Lido governance discussion pages. Retrieved March 25, 2025, from https://research.lido.fi/t/lido-dao-core-contributors-provisional-budget/2556
202. *Verifying address ownership for Lido DAO operational multisigs*. Lido documentation pages. Retrieved March 25, 2025, from https://docs.lido.fi/guides/address-ownership-guide/
203. [Preparing and sharing address & signature] *In case of using externally owned account (EOA)*. Lido documentation pages. Retrieved March 25, 2025, from https://docs.lido.fi/guides/address-ownership-guide#in-case-of-using-externally-owned-account-eoa
204. (2020, November) *Welcome to Lido DAO*. Lido governance discussion pages. Retrieved March 25, 2025, from https://research.lido.fi/t/welcome-to-lido-dao/7 (please search in the page for "What are the risks of staking with Lido?")
205. [Immunefi page relating to] Lido. Immunefi. Retrieved March 23, 2025, from https://immunefi.com/bounty/lido/
206. *Introduction* [to Lido documentation. Lido documentation pages. Retrieved March 25, 2025, from https://docs.lido.fi/. Subsequently, please locate all URLs under the "Contracts" left menu root directory (e.g., https://docs.lido.fi/contracts/lido-locator [retrieved March 25, 2025], etc.)
207. [Immunefi page relating to Lido] *Total Assets in Scope*. Immunefi. Retrieved March 25, 2025, from https://immunefi.com/bounty/lido/ (please search in the page for "Assets in Scope")
208. *Intro* [to the Lido Oracle mechanism]. Lido documentation pages. Retrieved March 25, 2025, from https://docs.lido.fi/guides/oracle-operator-manual#intro
209. [Oracle Operator Manual] *Committee membership*. Lido documentation pages. Retrieved March 25, 2025, from https://docs.lido.fi/guides/oracle-operator-manual/#committee-membership
210. (2022, August) *Expansion of Lido's Ethereum Oracle set*. Lido governance discussion pages. Retrieved March 25, 2025, from https://research.lido.fi/t/expansion-of-lidos-ethereum-oracle-set/2836/13
211. Lido DAO *Multisigs*. Lido documentation pages. Retrieved March 25, 2025, from https://docs.lido.fi/deployed-contracts/#lido-dao-multisigs
212. *Guide to being a signer at any Lido DAO multisigs*. Lido documentation pages. Retrieved March 25, 2025, from https://docs.lido.fi/guides/multisig-signer-manual/
213. (2022, July) *Emergency Brakes multi-sig upgrade*. Lido governance discussion pages. Retrieved March 25, 2025, from https://research.lido.fi/t/emergency-brakes-multi-sig-upgrade/2608
214. *Introduction* [to Ethereum Withdrawals for Node Operators]. Lido documentation pages. Retrieved March 25, 2025, from https://docs.lido.fi/guides/node-operators/exits/introduction
215. [Lido-funded PoS] *Validator exits and penalties*. Lido documentation pages. Retrieved March 25, 2025, from https://docs.lido.fi/guides/oracle-spec/penalties
216. *Lido on Ethereum Validator Exits Policy V1.0*. Lido Snapshot pages. Retrieved March 25, 2025, from https://snapshot.org/#/lido-snapshot.eth/proposal/0xa4eb1220a15d46a1825d5a0f44de1b34644d4aa6bb95f910b86b29bb7654e330
217. *Lido on Ethereum Validator Exits Policy*. Retrieved March 25, 2025, from https://hackmd.io/@lido/HJYFjmf6s
218. *Validators Exit Bus*. Lido documentation pages. Retrieved March 25, 2025, from https://docs.lido.fi/guides/oracle-spec/validator-exit-bus
219. (2022, October) *Withdrawals. On validator exiting order*. Lido governance discussion pages. Retrieved March 25, 2025, from https://research.lido.fi/t/withdrawals-on-validator-exiting-order/3048
220. E.g., https://research.lido.fi/t/post-mortem-downtime-of-staking-facilities-lido-validators/6021, https://research.lido.fi/t/post-mortem-downtime-of-lido-validators-gateway-fm-as/6164,

https://research.lido.fi/t/lido-on-ethereum-node-operator-infstones-platform-vulnerability-investigation-november-22-2023/6001, etc.

221. [Node Operators themes]. Lido governance discussion pages. Retrieved March 25, 2025, from https://research.lido.fi/c/node-operators/12 (please search for "post-mortem" through the page's search function)
222. Lindrea, B. (2023, October 12). *Lido Finance discloses 20 slashing events due to validator config issues.* CoinTelegraph. Retrieved March 25, 2025, from https://cointelegraph.com/news/lido-finance-launchnodes-validator-slashed
223. *Post Mortem* [reports]. Lido blog pages. Retrieved March 25, 2025, from https://blog.lido.fi/category/postmortem/
224. *What is the Insurance fund used for?* Lido support pages. Retrieved March 25, 2025, from https://help.lido.fi/en/articles/5230602-what-is-the-insurance-fund-used-for
225. *Lido Insurance Fund.* Lido GitHub pages. Retrieved March 25, 2025, from https://github.com/lidofinance/insurance-fund
226. (2023, July) *Does it take a DAO vote for LIDO insurance fund to cover a slashing event?* Lido governance discussion pages. Retrieved March 25, 2025, from https://research.lido.fi/t/does-it-take-a-dao-vote-for-lido-insurance-fund-to-cover-a-slashing-event/5006
227. Hajji, M. (2021, February 23). Lido and Unslashed create a new standard: insurance as an integrated solution. Medium. Retrieved March 25, 2025, from https://medium.com/unslashed/lido-and-unslashed-create-a-new-standard-insurance-as-an-integrated-solution-e9b3406f3136
228. (2021, October 21). *Offline & Slashing Risks: Are Self-Cover Options Enough?* Lido blog pages. Retrieved March 25, 2025, from https://blog.lido.fi/offline-slashing-risks-are-self-cover-options-enough/ (please also note the actuarial model - complete with modelling assumptions, analysis code and back-testing results - put forth in this blog)
229. (2022, July) *Redirecting incoming revenue stream from insurance fund to DAO treasury.* Lido governance discussion pages. Retrieved March 25, 2025, from https://research.lido.fi/t/redirecting-incoming-revenue-stream-from-insurance-fund-to-dao-treasury/2528
230. (2021, December 20) *Lido Adopts stETH/USD Chainlink Price Feed to Expand stETH Adoption Across DeFi.* Lido blog pages. Retrieved March 25, 2025, fromhttps://blog.lido.fi/lido-adopts-steth-usd-chainlink-price-feed/
231. *Price feeds* [deployed by Lido]. Lido documentation pages. Retrieved March 25, 2025, from https://docs.lido.fi/deployed-contracts/#price-feeds
232. (2022, October). *[REF] Introducing the Lido Contributors Group, including Pool Maintenance Labs and Argo Technology Consulting.* Lido governance discussion pages. Retrieved March 25, 2025, from https://research.lido.fi/t/ref-introducing-the-lido-contributors-group-including-pool-maintenance-labs-and-argo-technology-consulting/3069
233. *Lido Operator Set Strategy.* Retrieved March 25, 2025, from https://hackmd.io/K6udDz1nSZOoX8t-vE98qg
234. (2021, November). *Lido Node Operator & Validator Metrics.* Lido governance discussion pages. Retrieved March 25, 2025, from https://research.lido.fi/t/lido-node-operator-validator-metrics/1431
235. (2022, December 13) *Lido on Ethereum 'VaNOM' - Validator & Node Operator Metrics.* Lido blog pages. Retrieved March 25, 2025, from https://blog.lido.fi/lido-vanom-validator-node-operator-metrics-release/
236. (2025, February 24). *VaNOM: Lido on Ethereum Validator & Node metrics.* Retrieved March 23, 2025, from https://app.hex.tech/8dedcd99-17f4-49d8-944e-4857a355b90a/app/3f7d6967-3ef6-4e69-8f7b-d02d903f045b/latest
237. *Staking rate limits.* Lido documentation pages. Retrieved March 25, 2025, from https://docs.lido.fi/guides/lido-tokens-integration-guide/#staking-rate-limits
238. *FAQ: Ethereum Withdrawals.* Lido support pages. Retrieved March 25, 2025, from https://help.lido.fi/en/articles/7858292-faq-ethereum-withdrawals
239. *Withdrawals (unstETH).* Lido documentation pages. Retrieved March 25, 2025, from https://docs.lido.fi/guides/lido-tokens-integration-guide/#withdrawals-unsteth

240. *Accounting oracle*. Lido documentation pages. Retrieved March 25, 2025, from https://docs.lido.fi/guides/oracle-spec/accounting-oracle
241. (2022, July). *Redirecting incoming revenue stream from insurance fund to DAO treasury*. Lido governance discussion pages. Retrieved March 25, 2025, from https://research.lido.fi/t/redirecting-incoming-revenue-stream-from-insurance-fund-to-dao-treasury/2528/8
242. (2023, September). *Surplus Management Framework: Discussion and Draft Proposal*. Lido governance discussion pages. Retrieved March 25, 2025, from https://research.lido.fi/t/surplus-management-framework-discussion-and-draft-proposal/5454/4
243. [Lido Treasury balances]. Retrieved March 25, 2025, from https://dune.com/giraffa/lido-treasury
244. (2023, April). *Proposal to approve Lido DAO Treasury Management Principles and authorize the formation of a Treasury Management Committee*. Lido governance discussion pages. Retrieved March 25, 2025, from https://research.lido.fi/t/proposal-to-approve-lido-dao-treasury-management-principles-and-authorize-the-formation-of-a-treasury-management-committee/4279
245. *Proposal to approve Lido DAO Treasury Management Principles and authorize the formation of a Treasury Management Committee*. Lido Snapshot pages. Retrieved March 25, 2025, from https://snapshot.org/#/lido-snapshot.eth/proposal/0xac31f800288c68e32d1eb3cea7a525022faae3eb3bf805d1b3d248cda5375a13
246. *Wrong-way risk (WWR)* [definition]. Risk glossary. Risk.net. Retrieved March 25, 2025, from https://www.risk.net/definition/wrong-way-risk-wwr
247. (2023, March 28). *United States v. Samuel Bankman-Fried*. Docket Number 22-CR-00673. Criminal Division. U.S. Department of Justice. Retrieved March 25, 2025, from https://www.justice.gov/criminal/criminal-fraud/case/united-states-v-samuel-bankman-fried
248. (2024, March 28). *Samuel Bankman-Fried Sentenced to 25 Years for His Orchestration of Multiple Fraudulent Schemes*. U.S. Department of Justice. Retrieved March 25, 2025, from https://www.justice.gov/opa/pr/samuel-bankman-fried-sentenced-25-years-his-orchestration-multiple-fraudulent-schemes
249. (2023, November 21). *Binance and CEO Plead Guilty to Federal Charges in $4B Resolution*. U.S. Department of Justice. Retrieved March 25, 2025, from https://www.justice.gov/opa/pr/binance-and-ceo-plead-guilty-federal-charges-4b-resolution
250. (2023, July 13). *Celsius Founder And Former Chief Revenue Officer Charged In Connection With Multibillion-Dollar Fraud And Market Manipulation Schemes*. U.S. Department of Justice. Retrieved March 25, 2025, from https://www.justice.gov/usao-sdny/pr/celsius-founder-and-former-chief-revenue-officer-charged-connection-multibillion
251. Example from the EU: "Anti-money laundering: Council adopts rules which will make crypto-asset transfers traceable", Council of the EU (2023). Text and links to regulation URLs at https://www.consilium.europa.eu/en/press/press-releases/2023/05/16/anti-money-laundering-council-adopts-rules-which-will-make-crypto-asset-transfers-traceable/
252. Further example, from the UK: "Future financial services regulatory regime for cryptoassets; Response to the consultation and call for evidence", HM Treasury (2023). Available at: https://assets.publishing.service.gov.uk/media/653bd1a180884d0013f71cca/Future_financial_services_regulatory_regime_for_cryptoassets_RESPONSE.pdf
253. (2023, October 20). *Crypto Shareholder Requirements Set Out by EU Banking Regulators*. CoinDesk. Retrieved March 25, 2025, from https://www.coindesk.com/policy/2023/10/20/crypto-shareholder-requirements-set-out-by-eu-banking-regulators/
254. Systemic risk. (2024, March 20). In *Wikipedia*. Retrieved March 25, 2025, from https://en.wikipedia.org/wiki/Systemic_risk
255. Chen, J. (2024, August 28). *What Is Systemic Risk? Definition in Banking, Causes and Examples*. Retrieved March 25, 2025, from https://www.investopedia.com/terms/s/systemic-risk.asp

256. Kessler, S. (2022, June 29). *Nansen Report Shows Links Between Terra Collapse and stETH 'De-peg'*. CoinDesk. Retrieved March 25, 2025, from https://www.coindesk.com/business/2022/06/29/nansen-casts-blame-for-steth-de-peg-on-terra/
257. (2022, June 29). *On-Chain Forensics: Demystifying stETH's "De-peg"*. Nansen.ai. Retrieved March 25, 2025, from https://www.nansen.ai/research/on-chain-forensics-demystifying-steth-depeg
258. Badev, A. & Watsky, C. (2023). Interconnected DeFi: Ripple Effects from the Terra Collapse. *Finance and Economics Discussion Series 2023-044*. Federal Reserve Board (Washington, D.C.). Retrieved March 25, 2025, from https://doi.org/10.17016/FEDS.2023.044
259. Treehouse. (2023, February 7). *The Crypto Contagion and Its Looming After-Effects (Part 1)*. Medium. Retrieved April 5, 2025, from https://medium.com/coinmonks/the-crypto-contagion-and-its-looming-after-effects-part-1-367beda6bc
260. McSweeney, M. (2023, May 16). *Celsius moves to unstake hundreds of millions of dollars worth of ETH*. TheBlock. Retrieved March 25, 2025, from https://www.theblock.co/post/231051/celsius-moves-to-unstake-hundreds-of-millions-of-dollars-worth-of-eth
261. Chawla, V. (2024, January 5). *Ethereum validator exit queue spikes as Celsius, Figment withdraw stakes*. TheBlock. Retrieved March 25, 2025, from https://www.theblock.co/post/270578/ethereum-validator-exit-queue-celsius-figment
262. Lido Governance bulletin on X: https://x.com/LidoFinance/status/1525129266689622016
263. [Staking withdrawals] *How did we get here?* Ethereum.org. Retrieved March 25, 2025, from https://ethereum.org/en/staking/withdrawals/#how-did-we-get-here
264. (2023, February 7). [Staking Router] *Overview*. Lido blog pages. Retrieved March 25, 2025, from https://blog.lido.fi/introducing-lido-v2/#overview
265. Nansen.ai. (2023, April 17). *The Truth About Ethereum Withdrawals: How It Works, Key Metrics and Misconceptions*. Retrieved March 25, 2025, from https://www.linkedin.com/pulse/truth-ethereum-withdrawals-how-works-key-metrics-misconceptions (please search in the page for "Why does it take 2-5 days to complete?")
266. [Ethereum Validator Queue] https://www.validatorqueue.com/
267. Van den End, J. W., & Tabbae, M. (2012). When liquidity risk becomes a systemic issue: Empirical evidence of bank behaviour. *Journal of Financial Stability, 8*(2), 107–120. Accessible at. https://doi.org/10.1016/j.jfs.2011.05.003
268. Li, Q. (2019). The Impact of Liquidity Risk of Commercial Banks on Systematic Risk of Banking Industry: Study of 16 Listed Commercial Banks. *Modern Economy, 10*, 645–665. https://doi.org/10.4236/me.2019.103044
269. (2022, June 20). *Analysts urged not to compare the stETH discount and the collapse of Terra*. New day crypto. Retrieved March 25, 2025, from https://newdaycrypto.com/analysts-urged-not-to-compare-the-steth-discount-and-the-collapse-of-terra/
270. Kessler, S., & Young, S.D. (2022, April 20). *Is Ethereum Staking Pool Lido's Growth an Omen of Centralization?* CoinDesk. Retrieved March 25, 2025, from https://www.coindesk.com/layer2/2022/04/20/is-ethereum-staking-pool-lidos-growth-an-omen-of-centralization/
271. Grandjean, D., Heimbach, L. & Wattenhofer, R. (2023). *Ethereum Proof-of-Stake Consensus Layer: Participation and Decentralization*. Retrieved March 25, 2025, from https://doi.org/10.48550/arXiv.2306.10777
272. Buterin, V. (2023, September 30). *Should Ethereum be okay with enshrining more things in the protocol?* Retrieved March 25, 2025, from https://vitalik.eth.limo/general/2023/09/30/enshrinement.html (please search in the page for "Enshrining liquid staking")
273. (2022, June 23). *Should Lido consider self-limiting?* Lido Snapshot pages. Retrieved March 25, 2025, from https://snapshot.org/#/lido-snapshot.eth/proposal/0x10abedcc563b66b1adee60825e78c387105110fa4a1e7354ab57bc9cc1e675c2
274. (2022, May). *Should Lido on Ethereum be limited to some fixed % of stake?* Lido governance discussion pages. Retrieved March 25, 2025, from https://research.lido.fi/t/should-lido-on-ethereum-be-limited-to-some-fixed-of-stake/2225/76

275. (2023, October). *Staking Router Module Proposal: Simple DVT*. Lido governance discussion pages. Retrieved March 25, 2025, from https://research.lido.fi/t/staking-router-module-proposal-simple-dvt/5625/18
276. (2023, October 26). *Staking Router Module Proposal: Simple DVT*. Lido Snapshot pages. Retrieved March 25, 2025, from https://snapshot.org/#/lido-snapshot.eth/proposal/0xf3ac657484444f0b54eba2c251135c47f875e3d1821496247d11bdd7fab0f291
277. (2023, November 15). *Leveraging Distributed Validator Technology (DVT) with Simple DVT*. Lido blog pages. Retrieved March 25, 2025, from https://blog.lido.fi/leveraging-distributed-validator-technology/
278. (2021, July 27). *The Road to Trustless Ethereum Staking*. Lido blog pages. Retrieved March 25, 2025, from https://blog.lido.fi/the-road-to-trustless-ethereum-staking/
279. (2023, November). *Community Staking Module*. Lido governance discussion pages. Retrieved March 25, 2025, from https://research.lido.fi/t/community-staking-module/5917/33
280. (2023, December 7) *Lido Community Staking Module*. Lido Snapshot pages. Retrieved March 25, 2025, from https://snapshot.org/#/lido-snapshot.eth/proposal/0xa39815519107002997769f0b79a9e3957c3bf793166ab948fc6413ce5b3def55
281. [Aragon Governance Framework project] https://aragon.org/
282. [Aragon Whitepaper] Aragon Network. Aragon GitHub pages. Retrieved March 25, 2025, from https://github.com/aragon/whitepaper
283. *About Aragon*. Retrieved March 25, 2025, from https://www.aragon.org/about
284. CoinMarketCap ANT *page*. CoinMarketCap. Retrieved March 25, 2025, from https://coinmarketcap.com/currencies/aragon/
285. (2024, November 3). *ANT Redemption Initiative Report*. Aragon blog pages. Retrieved March 25, 2025, from https://blog.aragon.org/ant-redemption-initiative-report/
286. [Aragon Association record in Crunchbase] Retrieved March 25, 2025, from https://www.crunchbase.com/organization/aragon-association
287. (2023, November 2). *A New Chapter for the Aragon Project*. Aragon blog pages. Retrieved March 25, 2025, from https://blog.aragon.org/a-new-chapter-for-the-aragon-project/
288. Blackstone, T. (2023, November 2). *Aragon Association to dissolve, will disburse $155M in assets to tokenholders*. CoinTelegraph. Retrieved March 25, 2025, from https://cointelegraph.com/news/aragon-association-dissolves-disburse-assets-token-holders
289. Reguerra, E. (2023, November 21). *Aragon DAO votes to fund legal action against its founders*. CoinTelegraph. Retrieved March 25, 2025, from https://cointelegraph.com/news/aragon-dao-lawsuit-founders-patagon-management
290. Mitchelhill, T. (2023, May 10). *Aragon launches defensive measures against Arca's '51% attack'*. CoinTelegraph. Retrieved March 25, 2025, from https://cointelegraph.com/news/aragon-launches-defensive-measures-against-arca-s-51-attack
291. (2025, May 1). *Coinbase suspends trading of Aragon token ANT*. Coinlive. Retrieved March 25, 2025, from https://www.coinlive.com/news-flash/414544
292. (2024, January 4). *Binance Will Extend the Monitoring Tag to Include ANT, FIRO, KP3R, MDX, MOB, REEF, VAI, XMR, ZEC & ZEN, and Remove the Seed Tag for GMX & SUSHI on 2024-01-04*. Binance News. Retrieved March 25, 2025, from https://www.binance.com/en/support/announcement/binance-will-extend-the-monitoring-tag-to-include-ant-firo-kp3r-mdx-mob-reef-vai-xmr-zec-zen-and-remove-the-seed-tag-for-gmx-sushi-on-2024-01-04-fd710b5e647c480ab9fe2d87e3cd4b39
293. [Accessible through the Paragon dApp] *Governed on Aragon - Explore the organizations using our modular governance stack to secure their onchain governance*. Retrieved March 25, 2025, from https://app.aragon.org/
294. (2024, October 31). *The Aragon Foundation: New Council Carrying Forward the Mission*. Aragon Foundation corporate communication. Retrieved March 25, 2025, from https://www.aragonfoundation.org/announcement/the-aragon-foundation-new-council-carrying-forward-the-mission

295. [Lido DAO] *Software*. Lido documentation pages. Retrieved March 25, 2025, from https://docs.lido.fi/lido-dao/#software/ (please search in the page for "Aragon organization")
296. *What is Snapshot?* Snapshot documentation pages. Retrieved March 25, 2025, from https://docs.snapshot.box/#welcome-to-snapshot
297. [Lido DAO page on Snapshot] https://snapshot.org/#/lido-snapshot.eth
298. [FAQs] *How can I vote?* Snapshot support pages. Retrieved March 25, 2025, from https://docs.snapshot.org/faq#how-can-i-vote
299. *Voting strategies*. Snapshot documentation pages. Retrieved March 25, 2025, from https://docs.snapshot.box/user-guides/voting-strategies
300. *Validation strategies*. Snapshot documentation pages. Retrieved March 25, 2025, from https://docs.snapshot.box/user-guides/validation-strategies
301. *Token verification*. Snapshot documentation pages. Retrieved March 25, 2025, from https://docs.snapshot.box/v1-interface/token-verification
302. [Lido DAO governance entry page on the Lido dApp] https://lido.fi/governance (please search in the page for "Emergency track")
303. Ibid. (please search in the page for "Committees")
304. (2021, June). *LIP-3: Easy Track Motions for DAO routine operations*. Lido governance discussion pages. Retrieved March 25, 2025, from https://research.lido.fi/t/lip-3-easy-track-motions-for-dao-routine-operations/680
305. [Governance "Easy track" functionality on the Lido dApp] https://easytrack.lido.fi/
306. *Easy Track* [Smart Contracts]. Lido documentation pages. Retrieved March 25, 2025, from https://docs.lido.fi/deployed-contracts/#easy-track
307. Baker, P. (2020, January 7). *DAO Platform Aragon Begins Recruiting Jurors for Tokenized 'Court'*. CoinDesk. Retrieved March 25, 2025, from https://www.coindesk.com/tech/2020/01/07/dao-platform-aragon-begins-recruiting-jurors-for-tokenized-court/
308. Weidner, D. (2020, February 17). *Aragon Court: The World's First Decentralized Jurisdiction*. CryptoTicker. Retrieved March 25, 2025, from https://cryptoticker.io/en/aragon-court-jurisdiction/
309. Cryptopedia staff. (2021, October 21). *Aragon (ANT): DAOs for Communities and Businesses*. Cryptopedia. Retrieved March 25, 2025, from https://www.gemini.com/cryptopedia/aragon-crypto-dao-ethereum-decentralized-government#section-aragon-court
310. (2021, August 17). *The Optimistic DAO: Aragon Govern + Aragon Voice + Aragon Court*. Aragon blog pages. Retrieved March 25, 2025, from https://blog.aragon.org/the-optimistic-dao-aragon-govern-aragon-voice-aragon-court/
311. *Fee distribution*. Lido documentation pages. Retrieved March 25, 2025, from https://docs.lido.fi/contracts/staking-router/#fee-distribution
312. Katunina, I. (2022, May 10). *Lido stAssets Collateral Risk Monitoring*. Lido blog pages. Retrieved March 25, 2025, from https://blog.lido.fi/lido-stassets-collateral-risk-monitoring/
313. *LDO Liquidations Statistics*. Coinalyze. Retrieved March 25, 2025, from https://coinalyze.net/lido-dao/liquidations/
314. [Context: Switzerland] (2023, October 19). *Swiss Federal Tax Administration Guidance on taxation of Cryptocurrencies*. Retrieved March 25, 2025, from https://www.estv.admin.ch/dam/estv/de/dokumente/estv/steuersystem/dossier-steuerinformationen/b/b-kryptowaehrung.pdf.download.pdf/b-kryptowaehrung.pdf [German], https://www.estv.admin.ch/dam/estv/fr/dokumente/estv/steuersystem/dossier-steuerinformationen/b/b-kryptowaehrung.pdf.download.pdf/b-kryptowaehrung.pdf [French] (please consult chapter "2.3 Staking")
315. [Context: Switzerland] (2023, December 20) *FINMA Guidance 08/2023 - Staking*. Retrieved March 25, 2025, from https://www.finma.ch/en/~/media/finma/dokumente/dokumentencenter/myfinma/4dokumentation/finma-aufsichtsmitteilungen/20231220-finma-aufsichtsmitteilung-08-2023.pdf
316. *Fees* [raised on Staking rewards]. Lido documentation pages. Retrieved March 25, 2025, from https://docs.lido.fi/guides/lido-tokens-integration-guide/#fees

317. WithdrawalQueueERC721 [Smart Contract]. Lido documentation pages. Retrieved March 25, 2025, from https://docs.lido.fi/contracts/withdrawal-queue-erc721/
318. Tardi, C. (2024, May 5). *What Is Gwei? The Cryptocurrency Explained*. Retrieved March 25, 2025, from https://www.investopedia.com/terms/g/gwei-ethereum.asp
319. 1-2 wei corner case. Lido documentation pages. Retrieved March 25, 2025, from https://docs.lido.fi/guides/lido-tokens-integration-guide/#1-2-wei-corner-case
320. *Account's stETH balance getting lower on 1 or 2 wei due to rounding down integer math #442*. Lido GitHub pages. Retrieved March 25, 2025, from https://github.com/lidofinance/lido-dao/issues/442
321. Kozin, S. (2022, June 7). *LDO governance mechanics*. Retrieved March 25, 2025, from https://hackmd.io/@skozin/HkiEBPiO5 (please note that percentages mentioned are calculated on the LDO *total* supply, not on the LDO circulating supply)
322. (2022, February). *Lido Governance Optimisation - Snapshot Delegation*. Lido governance discussion pages. Retrieved March 25, 2025, from https://research.lido.fi/t/lido-governance-optimisation-snapshot-delegation/1707
323. (2022, June). *LDO+stETH dual governance*. Lido governance discussion pages. Retrieved March 25, 2025, from https://research.lido.fi/t/ldo-steth-dual-governance/2382

Token Design 10

We now arrive at the last main pillar of the proposed token-based ecosystem design framework, namely, token design. Without detracting from the role of the other two, market and mechanism, token design is the most important one. The reason is that value and transactional calibrations enabled by the digital token are the crucial characteristics differentiating blockchain-based ecosystems from other physical, or indeed digital, ones.

To a large extent, market and mechanism designs harked back to notions of economic organization also evident in human physical ecosystems. The notions to be explained in this chapter will be more distinctive in nature, as the blockchain has introduced a profoundly disruptive infrastructure paradigm.

The reference token typology discussed near the end of Chap. 4 (Sect. 4.3) will be used here as a basis, upon which to explain the objectives, scope, importance, and material factors of token design.

10.1 Introduction to Token Design

It is assumed that at least first iterations of market and mechanism designs have been created. Hence, there already exist: an economic agent taxonomy; descriptions of the possible transactional pathways among agents; the set of rules and incentives applying on each pathway; and a corresponding high-level description of tokens used. The last point means that there exist first assumptions on:

- How many different tokens will be needed.
- Their basic functional requirements.

It is at this stage that a knowledge of existing token typologies is useful, namely (as laid out in Sect. 4.3) to facilitate **baseline design by association**. In other words, if one is familiar with the salient features of existing tokens, then one can allocate one's own specific use case requirements to "most probable" token types. For

I. Giannakouros, *Cryptocurrencies and Tradable Crypto-Tokens*, Future of Business and Finance, https://doi.org/10.1007/978-3-031-98423-5_10

example, if an asset token can be reasonably assumed to be needed along transaction "A", then knowledge of how other protocols have implemented such tokens enables an own "baseline asset token" design. If a Stablecoin, backed by collateral in the form of another token, is a candidate along transaction "B", then similar knowledge can help create the first token blueprint.

Why "baseline design" and "first blueprint"? If one has already gleaned functional requirements matching those of, e.g. a cryptocurrency, isn't that enough information to start implementing such a token for the target blockchain?

The answer is obviously "no". What the principals behind the economic agents will want to know before buying this cryptocurrency are details such as: How is the token to be bought at issuance, against other tokens or against fiat currencies? Is the buying price fixed or dynamic? Is there a market maker involved, and if yes, is it a human or a smart contract? Is there a secondary market for the cryptocurrency? Which crypto wallets are compatible? Are there any added due-diligence requirements (on top of the ones fulfilled when onboarding onto the ecosystem) for buying the token? Are there any reporting requirements to any authority after buying, and after selling, the token? What are the transaction fees when the token is bought, sold, or used in ecosystem transactions? Is there any limit on how many tokens can be bought at any given time? How soon can a transaction in the token be settled?

Similar but different questions will be asked for a non-fungible asset token or a security token: e.g. what are the underlying property rights? Are there any income inflows accruing, or any outflows expected, during the holding period? How liquid is the token expected to be as an investment? Does the ecosystem provide both issuance and marketplace, or only issuance? What are the due-diligence obligations? What are the due-diligence rights? Can the token be transferred onto any crypto wallet without restrictions?

A relevant set of questions can be expected for Stablecoins, utility tokens, etc. Irrespective of token type, there will also be questions related to minting and burning, transaction security, negotiability, price "slippage", tax-reporting, long-term prospects as store of value, and quite a few more.

So, a "baseline token" suggested by market and mechanism designs is still only a provisional template. There are many features which will have to be defined in much more detail, and parameters calibrated to fit precise use case requirements, including practical token lifecycle events. While defining the more granular features and parameters, it may happen that the "behaviour" of the token may change to such an extent that it will end up resembling another type much closer than what the baseline suggested. It may even need to have a "hybrid" type, otherwise the use case requirements may not be fulfilled. In other cases, it may prove impossible to fulfil all transaction requirements through a single token type, in which case the "baseline token" may have to be split into two tokens of different types.

The detailed specification of functional features, lifecycle events, and operational implementation details for all tokens existing in a blockchain-based ecosystem is the objective of token design.

10.2 Rationale of Token Design for Token-Based Ecosystems

In Chap. 6, we proposed that designing the economics of a token-based ecosystem is akin to designing the economy of a new country. In the fundamental 3-pillar design framework (market, mechanism, token), we postulated time and again that token design is equivalent to a monetary design for the country. In light of Sect. 4.1, where we explained that a token can be designed, but it does not have, to be the currency of the ecosystem, does this postulate still hold true? Have we somehow deceived the reader?

We respectfully suggest that we did not. First, in all the analogies between the framework and a country-economy, we were careful to write "akin to", not "same as". Second, a token was defined as being a digital representation of value that in some circumstances *can* be used as either money, or as an alternative to money, within a particular ecosystem. Hence, a token is at least an alternative to money, and can be (as is the case with *cryptocurrencies*) money itself. Given that the governance functions of the ecosystem may at any time choose to impose this money as its only medium of exchange, then every token is at least potential currency, and maybe ab initio currency by design. This is why we believe that the "token-to-currency" analogy is a valid one. The same aspects (and pathologies) of currency systems apply to tokens, e.g. existence of effective demand-and-supply transfer mechanisms, variations in purchasing power against reference goods and services, hoarding, theft, etc. However, for the sake of logical rigour, we will explain the importance of generic token design for any token-based ecosystem, including both "currency" and "non-currency" token types. The point of departure will be an examination of the objectives, as opposed to functions, of a token.

In Sect. 3.2, when explaining value creation in blockchain-based ecosystems, we identified the following three objectives of tokens: first, to enable price discovery, execution of transactions, and storage of value for later consumption; second, to capture the economic substance of assets represented (values "in being") and services exchanged (values "in action") on the ecosystem; and, third, to incentivize active participation in governance tasks so as to safeguard the value of network effects. Thus, depending on its type, a token will be called upon to fulfil one or more of these objectives. Pure cryptocurrencies will only have the first objective. Asset tokens such as NFTs will have only the second. Utility tokens may have a combination of the second and third, but in some situations may also underpin the first. As we pointed out in Sect. 4.2.6, the blockchain creates many degrees of freedom in terms of asset class and property right combinations that can be bundled in tokens. When taking stock of the existing cryptocurrency and tradable crypto-token universe, we stressed that any taxonomy, however detailed, is still bound to be a non-exhaustive one. New and "hybrid" types will appear in due course, and this is where token design will be called to ensure that the three objectives can still be met through a constellation of ecosystem tokens. Please note that not all blockchain ecosystems need all objectives met through their own tokens, or even—for one or two of them—met through tokens at all; this is where market and mechanism designs need to align as well, hence the reason why the main 3-pillar design framework is necessarily iterative.

In reference, yet again, to the "new country" analogy, a country may decide to either issue its own currency, or to adopt the currency of another country [1], or even that of a supranational jurisdiction [2]. Assets and services exchanged in that country will always need to be denominated in some currency, assuming economic sophistication above barter trade level. Hence, a blockchain-based ecosystem will need to always have either a native token, or another reference rate, through which other types of tokens can be priced. In the former case, token design will incorporate currency design. In the latter, it will also have to provide token features enabling buyers and investors to execute currency overlay strategies (similar to foreign exchange hedging in traditional finance). In both cases, token design will have to be explicit on what the admissible media of exchange and stores of value in the ecosystem will be. In short:

- Token design is the **monetary and financial** design of the ecosystem.

Summarizing the above, token design will generally have to consider both "currency" and "non-currency" token types. The blockchain creates many degrees of freedom for functional features to implement in tokens, covering practically the entire gamut of traditional asset classes, liquidity, and risk profiles; and even allowing to go beyond them. Those degrees of freedom are both a power and a responsibility in the hands of the token designer. All token types are potentially of importance to their underlying ecosystem, by helping to fulfil the three objectives of tokens. Any single token must not be designed in isolation but rather be calibrated in alignment with the market and mechanism designs. Thus, token design is a central component of the end-to-end ecosystem design framework and must be approached accordingly.

10.3 Token Design for Token-Based Ecosystems in Short

Token design combines economic and financial engineering. It is meant to describe all aspects pertaining to how a blockchain protocol creates ("mints") a token; how the latter is used in which kinds of transactions; how is its price arrived at; how are its risks to the ecosystem controlled; and finally, how it is withdrawn from circulation ("burned"). The "how" in the above refers to the economic agents, processes, and technical mechanisms (including algorithm specification and calibration) involved.

Of course, particular aspects will have different importance depending on token type, e.g. on whether the token is a "currency" or a "non-currency" one. However, all pertinent aspects will have to be considered, irrespective of the precise token type.

Token design is meant to provide:

1. Complete alignment with the market and mechanism designs, i.e. it should strictly involve only economic agents or possible interaction pathways that have already been defined in market design, and align with descriptions of

governance, market structure, and incentives that have already been provided for in mechanism design.

2. Clarity on which tokens are allowed in the ecosystem and what are their functional and non-functional features.
3. Anchors to facilitate token valuation logic for price discovery purposes by buyers/investors (human and algorithmic).
4. Anchors to facilitate systemic risk management and control by protocol governance bodies, pertaining to risks influenced by the existence of the token (s) (either risks due primarily to the token, or transformed through the token).
5. Anchors to enable platform fee calculations on transactions involving tokens.

As already mentioned, the main token ecosystem design framework (market, mechanism, token designs) is in principle an iterative process, and ideally a dynamic one as the ecosystem goes through successive generations. Any pathology discovered during implementation or operational use may necessitate re-calibration of one or more of the design pillars. Hence, adequate documentation of both design features and of their rationalization is necessary to avoid blind spots and propagation of pitfalls across time.

10.3.1 Process and Components of Token Design

To design, we first need to analyse.

Token design as a thought process does not necessarily start with the outcomes of market and mechanism designs. The business case of an ecosystem may actually *start* with a rough token idea, around which market and mechanism designs are then created. However, even then the 3-pillar iterative process may soon produce a refined token or suggest a token of a different type. Another possible situation occurs when the new token idea is based upon synergies with pre-existing tokens from the same or different ecosystems. In this case, again, token design actually drives the market and mechanism ones in the iteration.

As a general rule, whenever a new business case is predicated on linkage with features of pre-existing ecosystems, the latter's market and mechanism designs may have to be considered as *constraints* on the ones to be designed for the new protocol. It can also occur that said linkage may be in terms of the respective ecosystem tokens. For instance, minting of tokens in the current protocol may necessitate staking of positions in tokens originating from other protocols. Thus, we will need to introduce two new terms: "native" and "foreign" tokens.

In reference to a target protocol (of ecosystem "A" in Fig. 10.1), a "native" token is one that is introduced in, resp. removed from, circulation ("minted", resp. "burned") exclusively through the protocol. A "foreign" token is one that is used, or referenced, in token lifecycle events or in transactions on the target protocol, while being "native" to a different protocol (of ecosystems "B" and "C" in Fig. 10.1).

The business case of the ecosystem will create a frame of objectives to meet, whereupon functional token design choices will be either clear-cut or subject to optimization. A clear-cut choice could be token fungibility, i.e. in reference to the

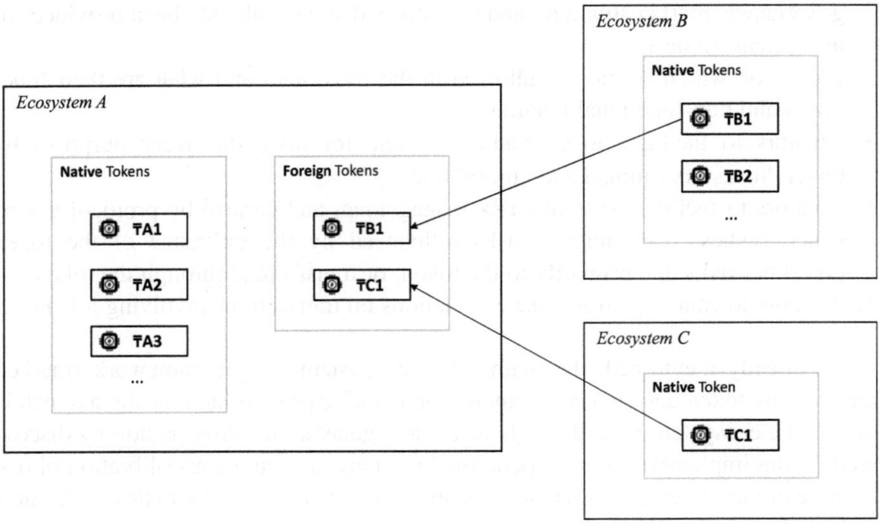

Fig. 10.1 Native and foreign tokens in an ecosystem

Fig. 10.2 The two fundamental token natures

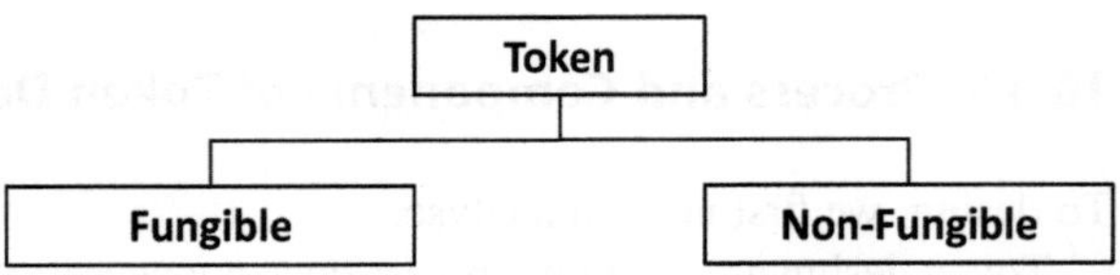

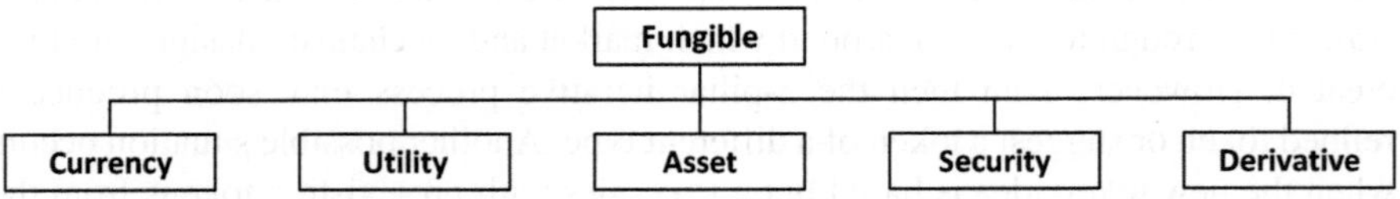

Fig. 10.3 High-level fungible token typology

two fundamental token natures originally mentioned in Sect. 4.2.1, the explanatory figure of which is repeated here for convenience (Fig. 10.2):

Token design *optimization*, on the other hand, will depart from a basic functional envelope, taking market and mechanism designs into account. For example, assume that the specific business case calls for a fungible token. The currently observed crypto-asset typologies allow to break the "fungible token" category into subtypes as per Fig. 10.3 (repeated from Sect. 4.3). Should the business case call for facilitating ecosystem transactions through a medium of exchange, or through investment or risk-management instruments, etc., a rough first-cut mapping to high-level token types could use this figure.

Choosing a candidate token type provides the basic template upon which to then refine functional features (such as lifecycle events, transaction modalities, etc.) and to calibrate parameters. The specific business case will drive this refinement process

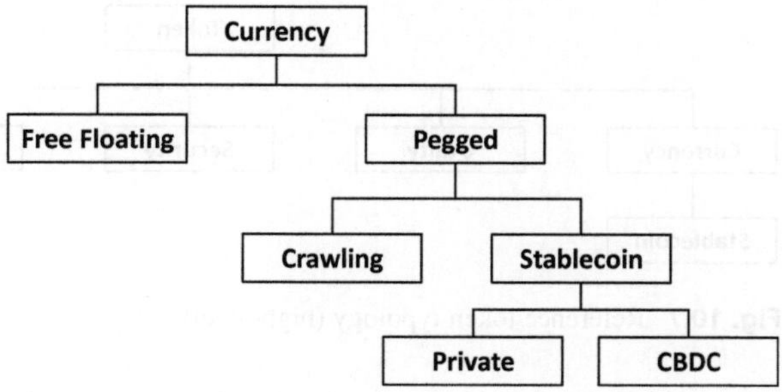

Fig. 10.4 Currency token typology (high-level)

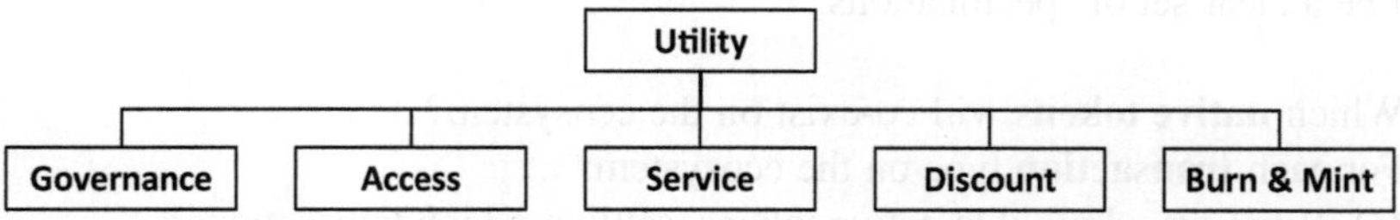

Fig. 10.5 Utility token typology (high-level)

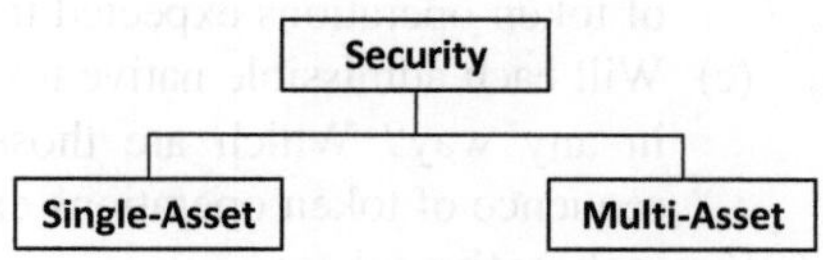

Fig. 10.6 Security token typology (high-level)

and will eventually suggest more granular templates to work on. For instance, choosing a basic "currency" token type will then lead to design decisions translating to currency subtypes as per the typology explained in Sect. 4.2.1 (repeated on Fig. 10.4).

Choosing a subtype will then provide a more granular template, with its own lifecycle events and calibration parameters. The same is true when choosing "utility token" as base type (cf. typology of Sect. 4.2.2, repeated for convenience as Fig. 10.5), which will then lead to an examination of required functional features against those offered by its subtypes. The final token design will specify all such features and also calibrate non-functional ones.

Similarly, a base "security" token will immediately lead to the design choice of whether a single asset or a portfolio of assets will be referenced (cf. Fig. 10.6). Then on to specifying the asset class, the cash flows or value flows, etc.

Please note that for the rest of this chapter, in order to be as specific as possible when describing process steps and factors in token design, we will consider only the highest-level "reference token typology" put forward in Sect. 4.3, repeated here in Fig. 10.7.

Concepts will be the same across various subtypes, hence the emphasis of this chapter will be not on a detailed specification but rather on a *detailed design process* within the context of the wider framework. Thus, the *process* of token design will

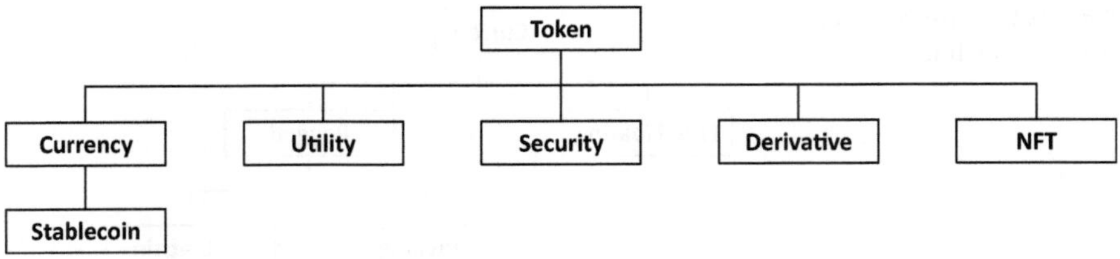

Fig. 10.7 Reference token typology (high-level)

necessarily align with token nature and token type. The *end point* of token design will be a clear set of specifications:

1. Which **native tokens** will co-exist on the ecosystem?
2. For each **transaction** type on the ecosystem:
   (a) What are admissible native tokens, settling which transactions?
   (b) Will each admissible native token need to be supported by other *native* tokens in any way? Which are these other tokens, and what is the sequence of token operations expected to be?
   (c) Will each admissible native token need to be supported by "*foreign*" tokens in any way? Which are those possible foreign tokens, and how is the sequence of token operations expected to be?
3. For each **native** token:
   (a) What is its nature? Is it fungible or non-fungible?
   (b) What is its type? Is it a "currency", "utility", "NFT", "security", "derivative", or "hybrid" token?
4. For each **native** token:
   (a) What is the process of introducing it into circulation ("minting")? Which are the economic actors involved, are there other native or foreign tokens involved in the process, and if yes, which ones and how?
   (b) What is the process of removing it from circulation ("burning")? Which are the economic actors involved, are there other native or foreign tokens involved in the process, and if yes, which ones and how?
5. For each **native** currency token:
   (a) Is its price to fluctuate freely based on supply and demand ("floating token") or is it to be pegged against a reference asset ("pegged token"), or even vary through some formula depending on an underlying asset or basket of assets?
   (b) If it is to be a floating token, is the float "pure" ("clean float") or "banded" ("crawling peg")?
   (c) If it is to be a pegged token, is the reference asset a fiat currency unit ("Stablecoin")? If so, which is the price stabilization mechanism? Does it involve managing a reserve through a "treasury" entity ("Reserve-backed Stablecoin")? If so, what kinds of assets are admissible in this reserve, what are their expected maturity profiles and how is treasury risk managed? Does it involve an algorithm instead ("Algorithmic Stablecoin")? If so, what is the algorithmic specification and how is valuation risk managed?

6. For each **native** currency token:
   (a) Which is the entity authorized to issue it and risk-manage its circulation (including reserve requirements, pegs and floating ranges, inflation/deflation)? Is said entity part of the governance bodies of the ecosystem, or not? Is it an algorithm, implemented, e.g., through smart contracts ("continuous token offering" case)?
   (b) If it is a Stablecoin, is the entity a Central Bank (case: "Central Bank Digital Currency")? If not, what is its precise charter (the rights and responsibilities of the entity), how is it governed and how is it audited?
7. For each **native** token:
   (a) Does holding the token confer any rights (monetary, non-monetary), privileges, or optionalities in its home ecosystem?
   (b) Is there a payoff expected for holders, on top of its face value? If so, what is the nature of the payoff (is it "dividend-like", "derivative-like", or "participation-like") and in which form (token, other blockchain asset, or even fiat currency) is it to be paid out?
   (c) Does the token lose its time-value in any pre-defined manner? Is it expiring after a set cut-off time or time interval? How are these changes in value effected (e.g. through a smart contract)? Are they irrevocable, or not—if not, which is the entity authorized to overrule such changes, and through which process?
   (d) Does the token change in value based upon exogenous events (case: "programmable money")? How are occurrences of said events notified, validated, and transmitted to the value-changing decision-point? Is the latter implemented purely algorithmically (e.g. through smart contracts), or are there humans-in-the-loop (e.g. validators, reviewers, etc.)?
8. For each **native** token:
   (a) Are there any restrictions in exchanging it for other tokens or fiat currencies, on its home ecosystem or on (external) Centralized/Decentralized Exchanges?

Arriving at this *end point* presupposes a careful analysis of pros and cons for each feature specification. To that end, what are the practical analysis tools for token design?

As in mechanism design, that would be any conceptual, technical, or algorithmic tool fitting the particular purpose. Per token type, such purposes would include:

- **Currency tokens**: textual description of issuance/cancellation ("minting"/"burning") processes, textual or mathematical description of price formation at issuance (e.g. bonding curve definition, dynamic scarcity/supply limits, etc.).
- **Pegged tokens/Stablecoins**: textual description of issuance/cancellation processes, textual, and mathematical description of price stabilization algorithm, stochastic simulation tools for treasury risk management (if reserve-backed), stochastic, or game-theoretic tools for model risk management (if algorithmic).

- **Utility tokens**: textual description of issuance/cancellation processes, stochastic simulation, or game-theoretic tools to calibrate value stream parameters and/or rewards policy.
- **Non-Fungible Tokens**: textual description of underlying property rights, issuance/cancellation processes, mathematical description of NAV changes contingent on asset events.
- **Security tokens**: textual description of underlying property rights and cash/value streams, textual description of issuance/cancellation processes, mathematical description of NAV (if applicable).
- **Derivative tokens**: textual or mathematical description of underlying or referenced assets, textual description of issuance/cancellation processes, stochastic or game-theoretic tools for value streams and contingent payoffs (valuation), stochastic tools for risk management sensitivities.

It is important to include only such functional specifications as can be feasibly implemented in accordance with realistic market and mechanism designs. The purpose of a first-cut functional specification is to identify token calibration ranges that will create approximately the same economic end-effects, while leaving more granular degrees of freedom to the discretion of the token designer.

10.4 Characteristics of a Successful Token Design

In reference to the basic analogy of designing a new country-level economy, imagine if all institutions and laws of a country had already been created; its citizens and companies were ready to transact with each other and with citizens and companies abroad; there were as yet no currency in the country, no units of account and no financial products. Also—as this is, again, a special kind of country[1]—that the policy decision has already been taken that transactions must be blockchain compatible. **This is time zero.**

At a later time, the level of economic activity in the country is already high. There are blockchain-based currencies ("currency tokens") circulating, and goods and services are priced and settled in them. All citizens, companies and governing bodies transact with each other, and accounts kept, on the blockchain. Blockchain-based financial instruments ("utility tokens", "non-fungible tokens", "security tokens", "derivative tokens") exist for investment and risk management purposes. **At this time, an expert reviewer is tasked with rating the extent to which the health of the country's economy is indeed being promoted by the currencies and financial instruments available** to its citizens, companies, and governing bodies. What information will that reviewer seek to cull, and how will they evaluate it?

[1] Cf. the relevant comment near the end of Sect. 8.4.

We believe that the reviewer in question will seek to base their judgement on the following list of criteria:

1. Is it clear which native and foreign tokens are allowed to co-exist in the ecosystem? Is the nature (currency, non-currency) of each native token clear, or not? For non-currency ones, is it clear which category (utility, non-fungible, security, derivative) they belong to?

Regarding c**urrency** tokens in particular:

1. For each currency token, are all its lifecycle aspects (when it is minted, when it is burned, what are the processes, transactions, and agents involved, how are token price vs supply at minting/burning determined [e.g. "Bonding Curve" or other mechanism], what ancillary fees are due between which economic agents, etc.) clearly documented in some form (text or code)?
2. How stable are the prices of goods and services, when denominated in the native token(s)?
3. Is there a relative balance in the total value of transactions involving buying vs. selling the native token(s)? If not, are persistent trends in buy-side vs. sell-side dynamics?
4. How is the total supply of the native token(s) been developing? Are there persistent trends in the supply dynamics? Are these trends commensurate with the token design, or not?
5. Are there other token-based ecosystems with the same or similar goods or services as the current one? If yes, how are the parity rates of the respective tokens vs reference fiat currencies been developing? Are there material differences in parity rate dynamics between native and foreign token(s)?
6. How is the parity rate of the native token(s) vs *reference* foreign ones been developing? Are there persistent trends in the parity rate dynamics?
7. How is the parity rate of the native token(s) vs *reference* fiat currencies been developing? Are there persistent trends in the parity rate dynamics?

When it comes to **Stablecoins**:

1. Is it clear which native and foreign Stablecoins are allowed to co-exist in the ecosystem?
2. For each native token, are all its lifecycle aspects (when it is minted, when it is burned, what are the processes, transactions, and agents involved, how are token price vs supply ["bonding curve"] at minting/burning determined, what ancillary fees are due between which economic agents, etc.) clearly documented in some form (text or code)?
3. Has the *design* parity with the target asset always stayed within acceptable ranges in practice? Is there persistent failure to observe said parity?

Examining **utility** tokens:

1. For each utility token, is it clear which functional use case is supported by it?
2. Are all its lifecycle aspects (when it is minted, when it is burned, what are the processes, transactions, and agents involved, what is the price formation mechanism, what ancillary fees are due between which economic agents, etc.) clearly documented in some form (text or code)?
3. Is there a relative balance in the total value of transactions involving buying vs. selling the token? If not, are persistent trends in buy-side vs. sell-side dynamics?
4. How is the total supply of the utility token been developing? Are there persistent trends in the supply dynamics? Are these trends commensurate with the token design, or not?
5. How is the parity rate of the utility token vs *reference* currency tokens been developing? Are there persistent trends in the parity rate dynamics?
6. How is the parity rate of the utility token vs *reference* fiat currencies been developing? Are there persistent trends in the parity rate dynamics?

Relating to **non-fungible tokens (NFTs)**:

1. For each NFT, is it clear which underlying asset class and ownership share is represented by it?
2. Are all its lifecycle aspects (when it is minted, when it is burned, what are the processes, transactions, and agents involved, what is the price formation mechanism, what ancillary fees are due between which economic agents, etc.) clearly documented in some form (text or code)?
3. Is there a relative balance in the total value of transactions involving buying vs. selling the NFT? If not, are persistent trends in buy-side vs. sell-side dynamics?
4. How is the total supply of the NFT been developing? Are there persistent trends in the supply dynamics? Are these trends commensurate with the token design, or not?
5. How is the price of the NFT vs *reference* currency tokens been developing? Are there persistent trends in its valuation?
6. How is the price of the NFT vs *reference* fiat currencies been developing? Are there persistent trends in its valuation?

On **security** tokens:

1. For each security token, is it clear which underlying asset class(es) and ownership share(s) is (are) represented by it?
2. What are the reference asset class allocation limits and what the allowable ranges around them? Have these ranges always been observed in time, or were they violated sporadically or even consistently? How was the reference allocation been implemented in practice, purely by smart contract or also by humans in the loop?

3. Are all its lifecycle aspects (when it is minted, when it is burned, what are the processes, transactions, and agents involved, what is the price formation mechanism, what ancillary fees are due between which economic agents, etc.) clearly documented in some form (text or code)?
4. Is there a relative balance in the total value of transactions involving buying vs. selling the token? If not, are persistent trends in buy-side vs. sell-side dynamics?
5. How is the total supply of the token been developing? Are there persistent trends in the supply dynamics? Are these trends commensurate with the token design, or not?
6. How is the price of the token vs *reference* currency tokens been developing? Are there persistent trends in its valuation?
7. How is the price of the token vs *reference* fiat currencies been developing? Are there persistent trends in its valuation?

Taking stock of **derivative** tokens:

1. For each derivative token, is it clear what is (are) its underlying(s), what is (are) the trigger event(s), and which the event-contingent payoff(s)? How are its sensitivity parameters (to prices of underlying[s], volatility[ies], time, etc.) calculated, and what has been their evolution?
2. Are all its lifecycle aspects (when it is minted, when it is burned, what are the processes, transactions, and agents involved, what is the price formation mechanism, what ancillary fees are due between which economic agents, etc.) clearly documented in some form (text or code)?
3. Is there a relative balance in the total value of transactions involving buying vs. selling the token? If not, are persistent trends in buy-side vs. sell-side dynamics?
4. How is the total supply of the token been developing? Are there persistent trends in the supply dynamics? Are these trends commensurate with the token design, or not?
5. How have the sensitivity parameters of the token vs *reference* currency tokens been developing? Are trends in their evolution commensurate with the token design, or not?
6. How have the sensitivity parameters of the token vs *reference* fiat currencies been developing? Are trends in their evolution commensurate with the token design, or not?

All such legitimate questions map to what we would propose are the essential criteria of good token design, namely, that it should:

(a) Be clear, fully documented, and auditable.
(b) Be completely aligned with the market and mechanism designs.
(c) Facilitate and not hinder price discovery of goods and services offered on the ecosystem.
(d) Promote price stability of goods and services as denominated in the native token(s).

(e) Enable long-term value preservation of assets, when represented in terms of ecosystem token(s).
(f) Facilitate price discovery (intrinsic valuation, observable parity rates) and frictionless trading of native against foreign tokens and/or fiat currencies.
(g) Promote competitiveness of the ecosystem relative to others offering the same or similar goods or services.

The aggregated effect of a good token design should be clarity on all information that economic agents will need to assess before buying the ecosystem token(s). It should be adequate enough to help them justify a token buying decision, either because they need it to transact on the ecosystem or because they regard it as a compelling store of value.

Is it realistic to strive for the "best possible" or only for a "good enough" token design? And what differentiates the latter from the former?

Here again, we will invoke the decentralized nature of decision-making in a blockchain-based ecosystem to posit that only "good enough" is realistic. It would be tempting to disregard the blockchain aspect and confine ourselves to traditional macroeconomic arguments along the lines of "there is no sustainable growth without monetary stability in any economy", "persistent inflationary pressures do not portend well for foreign investments", "asset/liability management is not possible without a view on interest rate evolution", etc. It would also be intellectually questionable. Our "country-level" analogy was precisely that—an analogy. Blockchain-based ecosystems do not have a central bank, nor do they have mechanisms to enforce pricing of goods and services. They represent a new economic paradigm, where transparency and consensus is the cornerstone of economic life, and where tokens (in any one of the six afore-mentioned categories taken as representative of today's token landscape) are meant to capture the business value of ecosystems and to enable informed investment decisions. Avoiding any side-effects that could potentially hinder investor's trust in the token investment, be it lack of lifecycle transparency, unclear liquidity and valuation risks, de facto rent effects, etc., should be the primary consideration of functional and non-functional token design. Exactly how to achieve this (initially and continuously as the ecosystem evolves) under decentralized decision-making is a matter of choosing the correct design attributes of ecosystem token(s).

Not succeeding in producing a token design with said attributes is tantamount to creating an inherently unsustainable value proposition for potential token investors. The causes may vary, but the end-effect will be the same: the ecosystem will ultimately fail to create a long-term market in its token(s).

10.5 Factors of Consideration in Token Design

As already mentioned, token design combines economic and financial engineering. Depending on the high-level target functionality ("currency", "non-currency"), and the particulars of the individual use case, there are many possible degrees of freedom to calibrate, hence as many factors to consider. However, in our experience there are some design factors that will always be present, irrespective of use case idiosyncrasies. These are:

(i) Transaction **velocity**.
(ii) Built-in **scarcity**.
(iii) **Inflation**.
(iv) **Valuation**.
(v) **Minting mode**.
(vi) **Minting optionalities**.
(vii) **Property rights** structure.
(viii) **Token treasury** structure.
(ix) **Composability**.
(x) **Programmability**.
(xi) **Computational complexity**.

In the sequel we will explain each design factor in detail, also providing corresponding factor calibration examples from already circulating tokens.

10.5.1 Transaction Velocity

The first token design factor to consider is transaction velocity.

The notion of "money velocity" is a proxy for the level of economic activity within an economic system, and as such it can be used to both validate its health and understand its pathologies (e.g. price level mismatches, transactional frictions, etc.). In traditional economics, it is intended to capture how fast the average currency amount changes hands when goods or services transactions are carried out within a set time frame. Hence, it relates to a well-defined economic system, with set boundaries and monetary units. It is not directly observable, but can be proxied through models based on variations of the "equation of exchange" (stemming from the quantity theory of money):

$$M \cdot V = P \cdot Q$$

where "M" is the total money supply in circulation, "P" the price level in the economy, "Q" the quantity of goods and services exchanged in the time frame of consideration, and "V" the money velocity.

Of course, let us not forget from traditional economics that the QTM applies at country-level and further assumes that there is only one currency per country. It is legitimate to question its applicability in the token ecosystem case. Satisfying the first precondition comes from the country-level economy analogy, first postulated in Chap. 6. Based on this analogy, the QTM would be strictly relevant for currency tokens only, and then useful at most as a trend analogy in the case of other token types (asset, utility, security, etc.). The second precondition would necessitate some form of effective "legal tender" setting, i.e. either imposed or simply prevailing in practice.

Let us start with the latter case ("prevailing in practice"), present in situations when token buyers and investors *will absolutely want to use* the native token *only*. That is, when there will always be a critical mass of participants in the ecosystem's underlying business use case, using only that particular token which is meant to enable it locally and capture its economic benefits. Token enthusiasts, investors,[2] and even speculators would be obvious examples of participants "sticking" to a token (Bitcoin-BTC would be an example). The first case ("imposed") would apply whenever the ecosystem itself *mandates* the use of only its native token in the localized use case. As a first example, it is not possible to pay for gas on the Ethereum ecosystem using Solana or another foreign Layer-1 currency token. The outcome is that registering transactions on the Ethereum blockchain necessitates an ancillary payment denominated in ETH ("gas"), irrespective of whether or not the block of transactions originated in an EVM-compatible L-2 blockchain. As another example, it is necessary to have NXM so as to participate in Nexus Mutual staking pools. Thus, the second precondition for the applicability of the QTM would be fulfilled if there are reasons (commitment to a token ecosystem) or obligations (necessity to participate in the local business case, whenever the ecosystem in question has a commanding market share or presents a unique value proposition).

Assuming the applicability of the QTM, translating into a blockchain-token setting needs adjusting the notion of "money supply in circulation" [3], but still allows to use our fundamental analogy of a country-level economy when considering token-based ecosystems. Then, even though the notion of velocity in economics has been primarily used to understand *monetary* systems, that is it would seem to be directly applicable only to what we have called "currency tokens" in our context, it is still very useful as a generic token design consideration. This usefulness stems from its ability to help capture cause-and-effect relations in transactionality and investor behaviour [4], hence in effect to substantiate the actual role of a token within its ecosystem in a particular time frame. For example, the incentive to hold tokens as long-term financial assets will translate into lower transaction velocity. This relates first and foremost to NFTs and security tokens, potentially less to derivative and utility tokens, and definitely less to currency tokens (especially Stablecoins). In other words, currency tokens will be generally expected to have higher levels of transaction velocity than non-currency ones.

Transaction velocity is as much a token-design parameter as it is an observed operational metric of the ecosystem. Consider for example, the three tokens Bitcoin (BTC), Bitcoin Cash (BCH), and Bitcoin Satoshi Vision (BSV). All three follow the exact same whitepaper [5–7], have the same "block validation time" design parameter (10 min [8]), the same policy for token rewards per block minted, and the same target—total—token supply (21 million). The only difference in their token design relates to the physical size of the block of transactions that is to be validated by the

[2] Including safety seekers, cf. discussion on token utility in Sect. 10.5.4.

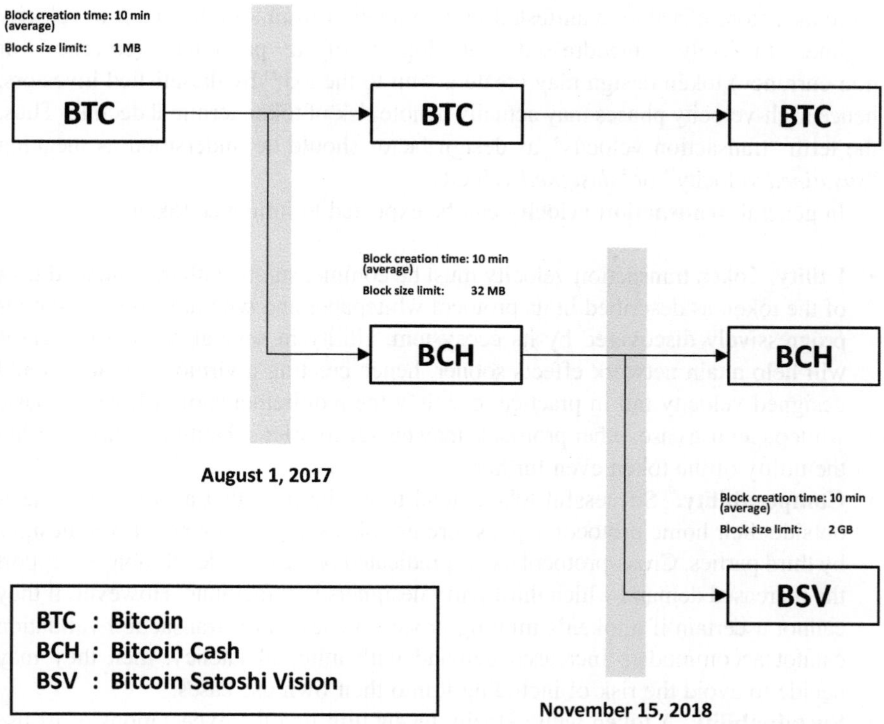

Fig. 10.8 BTC, BCH, BSV same Whitepaper, 2 forking actions, 3 different velocities

protocol miners in order to receive their Bitcoin reward. As depicted in Fig. 10.8 (giving an overview of the original forking actions that led to the BTC-BCH-BSV constellation), block size at their inception was: for BTC 1 MB, for BCH 32 MB, and for BSV 2 GB.[3] As a result, their velocities have always been very different [9].

Expected—i.e. estimated—levels of token transaction velocity should influence design decisions related to minting/burning and transaction fees. It would make no sense to allow inordinate frictions (e.g. elevated price discovery costs and fees) into high-velocity tokens as this would detract from their usefulness to generic ecosystem participants. Long-term investors may be less impacted, but they may have to judge long-term appreciation potential in comparison to that of similar but lower-velocity tokens. However, both ecosystem providers of goods/services and fee-collecting agents will need to have an indication of the optimal level of hidden frictions that consumers and investors can tolerate in order for a market (primary and secondary) in the token to be sustainable. This is precisely what is observed in the BTC/BCH/BSV example [10] above.

It should not be forgotten that an unintended consequence of a successful currency token design may be its usefulness less as a medium of exchange and

[3] Increased since further to 4 GB (current as of the time of writing, early 2025).

more as a store of value, manifested in its transition from a high- to a low-velocity regime. Inversely, unaddressed pathologies of a particular (currency or non-currency) token design may create a "run to the exit" by dissatisfied investors, hence high-velocity phases may actually denote risk of token terminal decline. Thus, the term "transaction velocity" as design factor should be understood as meaning "*sustained* velocity" or "*designed* velocity".

In general, **transaction velocity** can be expected to influence token:

- **Utility**. Token transaction velocity must be commensurate with the intended uses of the token as described in its protocol whitepaper and with any additional ones progressively discovered by its ecosystem. Utility in several parallel use cases will help attain network effects sooner, hence creating a virtuous circle. Should designed velocity fail in practice to satisfy the requirements of at least the basic whitepaper use case, other protocols may decide to offer substitutes; thus, limiting the utility of the token even further.
- **Composability.**[4] Successful tokens tend to be the ones that also find use cases outside their home protocol, e.g. as foreign tokens supporting new token designs by third parties. Cross-protocol use is predicated on velocity levels able to support the increased demand which third-party designers will facilitate. However, if they cannot ascertain if a token's minting process scales and if transaction validation cannot accommodate increased demand with minimal latency, then they may decide to avoid the risk of including it into their own use cases.
- **Sustainability**. A token with velocity levels fulfilling the expectations of its use cases will help reach network effects sooner and also create "stickiness" for the protocol, raising the effective barriers to entry into the same agent ecosystem for alternative tokens. Both outcomes will have the effect of preserving the long-term value proposition of the token for buyers and investors alike.
- **Valuation**. Different design velocities will be "signals" to the ecosystem about the intended utility of different tokens. Buyers and investors will thus adjust their valuation analyses and investment cases accordingly. This fact is explained further in Sect. 10.5.4, where velocity metrics are shown to play the role of explicit parameters within valuation models.

Hence, calibration of target velocity levels should be a fundamental token design factor. Failure to take it into account may negate the value proposition of the token for ecosystem participants, in general, and token investors in particular.

10.5.2 Built-in Scarcity

Another token design factor to consider is built-in scarcity. Scarcity of a good is defined as the deficit in potential supply vis-à-vis potential demand:

[4]Cf. also Sect. 10.5.9, where this term is explained in detail as a design factor.

$$\text{Scarcity} = \text{Potential Demand} - \text{Potential Supply}$$

In general, it is not a directly observable quantity, nor is it constant in time. For instance, a commodity may be at times scarce or plentiful. As the difference [*Actual* Demand—*Actual* Supply] is indeed observable in time, its forecast can be used as a proxy for scarcity.

Based on its primary cause, we need to distinguish between two types of token scarcity:

(a) **Market-induced**.
(b) **Built-in** (or "designed").

Only "built-in scarcity" is a token design factor. Market-induced scarcity results when short-term market dynamics create the potential for token demand to materially overtake supply. This can mean that a token's success as store of value induces investors to hold their tokens long-term, so there is a projected dearth of sellers in the market. Alternatively, it can also mean that net token creation (minting-burning rate) is forecast to be skewed towards burning, i.e. that buyers are moving funds away from the token. So, it can be either a secondary or a primary market effect, totally dependent on the behaviour of market participants.

Built-in scarcity is the outcome of token design choices to induce either "point-in-time" (PIT) or "trend-across-time" (TAT) limitations on the net issuance of tokens. Such design choices include:

1. **Minting rate constraints**
2. **Total-supply limits**

and affect both the primary and secondary markets for a token. The business case of the ecosystem and the token nature will dictate degrees of freedom and guide the optimal design of built-in scarcity mechanisms. Examples:

Non-fungible tokens are created once, and then can be traded in the secondary market. Their "point-in-time" minting rate constraint equals zero at any time after creation, and their "trend-across-time" limit is their initial supply (constant).

Cryptocurrencies are minted constantly, but at different rates and with different total supply limits. For instance, according to the minting rate constraints of the Bitcoin protocol, miners are rewarded with a set number of BTC (currently, 3.125 BTC per valid block mined [11]) roughly every 10 min—this is the BTC minting rate. Ethereum has a different rewards structure [12], with average block time currently close to 12 s [13, 14]. Both BTC and ETH mining rate constraints are designed to be different at different points in time (e.g. BTC rewards are reduced by half once subsequent batches of 210,000 blocks have been mined ["Bitcoin halving" [15], occurring approximately every 4 years]), hence the "point-in-time" designation.

The Bitcoin protocol also prescribes a total supply limit of 21 million BTC, whereas there is no such limit in the Ethereum protocol; however, the latter does induce natural destruction ("burning") of a controlled proportion of ETH tokens in the course of ecosystem transactions. The current ETH supply is significantly above 100 million [16]. Plotting the forecast curves of BTC and ETH token supply in the future results in visualizing the respective trends in net token issuance, hence the "trend-across-time" designation above.

Both BTC and ETH were originally "Proof-of-Work" protocols, ETH having transitioned since to a "Proof-of-Stake" paradigm. Their different designs vis-à-vis minting rate constraints and total supply limits resulted in totally different "point-in-time" and "trend-across-time" net token issuance curves. That is, assuming the same levels of token demand they resulted in different built-in scarcities.

For security tokens, zeroing the minting rate after inception reproduces non-dilutable securities and "closed-end" investment funds. Different combinations of minting rate constraints and total supply limits will produce token scarcities positioned at any wished-for point along the spectrum spanning (by analogy to unit investments) "closed-end" and "open-end" unit funds. Adding burning rate (point-in- and trend-across-time) design choices results in induced scarcities that are not usually found in traditional securities. This demonstrates the power of the token concept and the importance of the built-in scarcity as token design factor.

We will not expand into utility and derivative tokens, as business use cases and risk/payoff calibrations inherent in those token classes are already too diverse by nature. Suffice it to say that induced scarcity adds yet another optionality in their configurations, which can only increase their appeal as investment instruments.

What are the implications of choosing different built-in scarcity levels in token design?

Scarcity has repercussions for token:

- **Valuation**. Effective scarcity is part of a token's value proposition as store of value. In a qualitative sense, the value of a good is a product of its utility and scarcity. Assuming a sustained level of utility, the scarcer a token, the higher its value.
- **Volatility**. Scarcity is by definition associated with less frequent transactions, i.e. with less ability to use historical prices to advise future price discovery. Hence, in general, the scarcer a token, the more volatile its price.
- **Concentration**. The more valuable and volatile a token is expected to become, the higher the incentive for large investors to progressively add to their holdings to either maximize long-term wealth or take advantage of price swings for speculative gains, or both. Hence, it can be expected that the scarcer the token, the more concentrated its ownership allocation will eventually become.

Of course, scarcity by itself will not guarantee token success and may even hinder it, for instance when the primary business case for a token is to be a medium of exchange in an ecosystem. What constitutes "token success" and how to achieve it is precisely what should be constantly in the background of proper token design considerations. Built-in token scarcity is an important factor, but only one of several, to advise such considerations.

10.5.3 Inflation

In traditional economics, price inflation is the increase of the price level in an economy. There are several theories (mostly divided into "quality" and "quantity" schools) about its onset and principal dependencies. However, the broad scientific consensus is that long-run price inflation is materially dependent on a mismatch between the growth rates of money supply and economic activity. The increase in money supply has come to be called "monetary inflation".

The currently prevalent notion of "**inflation**" in token-based ecosystems refers only to "**monetary inflation**", i.e. to the growth rate of the number of tokens in circulation. Similarly, when used in a token-ecosystem context, "deflation"[5] has come to refer to the rate of decline of tokens in circulation (due to retiring them in the course of ecosystem transactions, i.e. "burning") and not to a decrease in the price level of goods and services in the ecosystem. Hence, when considering "inflation" as a token design factor, we confine ourselves to aspects relating to the minting and burning of tokens, generally expected to produce a net positive token creation rate—hence, the name.

As with scarcity, the business case of the ecosystem and the token nature will dictate what needs and degrees of freedom exist to influence token inflation.

New protocols have to contend with the problem that their business cases are as yet unproven, and thus they cannot know which token supply is commensurate with a mature phase of operations. What usually occurs in practice is that said protocols start with a—usually low—circulating supply, minting a first batch of tokens and then letting ecosystem participants drive demand, so to speak. Non-pegged *currency* tokens, in particular, are initially inflationary. The expectation is to have them generate an increasing volume of transactions, both in their original and in derivative business cases. Hence, to ideally reach that critical stage of token activity past which network effects will take the token from being primarily a medium of exchange to becoming a compelling store of value. The task of token design will then be to control the mechanics of token minting and burning in such a way that no token debasement occurs before this critical transition takes place. Cryptocurrency protocols typically control their supply increase either by keeping the minting rate effectively constant or by imposing a cap of new tokens issued at any given period. For example, the BTC protocol dynamically adjusts its "difficulty" parameter [17] in order to keep the time needed to validate a block (thus to reap the constant BTC reward, i.e. to have new BTC tokens emitted) at approximately 10 min. Ethereum used to implement a similar "network difficulty" parameter [18] in its Proof-of-Work instantiation (which was kept active in the run-up to its Eth2 Proof-of-Stake [PoS] "merge" [19]), but at the same time imposed a cap on the number of new ETH per year [20]. Post its PoS go-live implementation, ETH is calculated to be slightly deflationary [21].

---

[5] The industry also uses the term "Disinflation", to mean inflation with declining rate in time (i.e. the time-series of token supply has positive first derivative and negative second derivative).

For Stablecoins specifically, in spite of the fact that fiat-currency-related appreciation is unwanted by definition, it should not be assumed that there is no need to control token supply. First, in the case of privately issued Stablecoins such as USDC or USDT, if the token is backed by fiat-currency reserves then there exists treasury risk that needs to be actively managed, and this will end up imposing limits on token circulation. Second, again for privately issued Stablecoins, should asset management vehicles such as institutional investment funds and hedge funds opt to use them instead of fiat currency as liquidity positions (at the limit, imagine a purely Stablecoin-based money market fund) then all token metrics—including token supply—will fall under the purview of financial law and regulation for several reasons (investor protection, market abuse risk, systemic risk, etc.). Third, in the particular case of Central Bank Digital Currencies, their token supply can be considered as being part of the total fiat-currency money supply metrics (M0 or M1, depending on CBDC use case [22, 23]—retail, wholesale, or general purpose).

Utility tokens may or may not have to control token supply, depending on the individual business case. Similarly, non-fungible tokens may have zero net new token supply post-issuance in some cases (art and collectibles) and non-zero in others (game tokens, etc.). Token design will have to consider the idiosyncrasies of each use case.

As already mentioned in the frame of the scarcity factor, security tokens may or may not have to control token supply depending on the requisite end-effect in terms of investor base. Here again, the power of the token concept and the importance of inflation as token design factor both manifest themselves. Due to the investment vehicle nature of security tokens, all their operational attributes—including aspects of issuance/"minting" and retirement/"burning"—can be expected to fall under the purview of financial law and regulation. The same expectation will carry over to derivative tokens, as risk management instruments can also be used for taking directional views on the market, either on purpose or inadvertently.

In summary, inflation has repercussions for token:

- **Propagation**. Increased token supply will make it available to a broader user population. This will help to validate the economic purpose of the token ecosystem and thus drive a virtuous circle of token ownership.
- **Sustainability**. Increased levels of ownership will help both the token and its ecosystem become economically relevant in the long term. Effective feedback loops from token circulation metrics to ecosystem governance can help re-calibrate the end-to-end ecosystem towards more long-term optimal outcomes.
- **Valuation**. Successful inflation calibration will help a cryptocurrency take advantage of the network effect to break into "store of value" territory. For most other token natures, transparent inflation design and metrics will help manage legal and regulatory risks, hence safeguard the value of the token.

It is therefore essential to ensure that the inflation factor is considered during token design.

10.5.4 Valuation

One of the most important factors to consider in token design is token valuation. To do this properly, the designer needs to step in the shoes of the token buyer or investor and ask: What are the attributes of the token design that help understand the token pricing and long-term value proposition? Why would a buyer decide to purchase this token instead of others covering the same, or a similar, use case? Is the value which the token represents quantifiable in some way? Is the pricing structure of the token clear? What are the costs and fees involved, both at purchase and during the holding period? What are the upside potential and downside risks at any point in time when a purchasing or selling decision needs to be made?

General valuation drivers will be:

- Utility
- Intrinsic value
- Transaction costs
- Opportunity costs

Token **utility** is primarily a function of its use case within the ecosystem. However, it also depends on substitutability and user segment attributes, such as geography. For example, currency tokens that target the payments market (i.e. whose business case is primarily that of a medium of exchange) may end up competing with traditional money transfer businesses. Their value for prospective buyers will depend strongly on the comparison (in terms of usability and transaction costs) with alternative ways of effecting the same money transfers and on their availability in various combinations of source and destination countries. On the other hand, for residents of countries facing high inflation or other macroeconomic instability, a currency token may represent a compelling long-term value store [24], in effect a "flight to safety" value proposition [25, 26]. If a currency token makes for a compelling value proposition for some buyer group, this elevated "topical" utility may end up lifting the average utility of the token across the board. Higher utility will lead to higher demand, hence to higher price.

The same is true for **opportunity costs**. Purchasing and then holding a token will be of different value to users with different perceptions of hurdle rate of return and investment horizon. Specific features of some token types (e.g. volatility drag in reference to some derivative tokens) may also create effective investment horizon cut-offs for buyers. Opportunity cost comparisons will depend strongly on token type and on the existence of any parallel revenue streams (e.g. platform rewards) accruing to holders by design.

Transaction costs will generally be of different importance to primary- vs. secondary-market buyers, but all-in-all they can definitely impact market potential. For some buyers, non-optimal minting/burning costs and buy/sell spreads will fall into the "cost of doing business" part of their investment equation, whereas for others they may be the decisive criterion for opting to invest in a different token. All aspects potentially influencing transaction costs (minting difficulty, primary market fees, price slippage through automated market makers, technical compatibility with secondary market infrastructures, draining of token liquidity by other use cases or by other ecosystems, etc.) should be considered in token design.

Intrinsic value calibration is *the* most important token valuation driver. The word "intrinsic" suggests that something is both inherent and objective. This had been a question mark in early attempts at crypto-token valuation (i.e. whether or not there is any inherent value in them) and still continues to be a bone of contention among some investors, especially in regards to currency tokens [27]. As we explained in Sect. 5.1, each newly minted token is linked to factors of production employed in its creation, so we hope that the reader considers that this point is already settled—at least at issuance. After issuance, the analyst needs to follow the trajectory of how this inherent value evolves, and which factors influence it. This becomes a classical problem of asset valuation, straddling the boundary between crypto and traditional finance.

Asset valuation has always been an activity interpolating the "science-to-art" continuum and the best criterion of its success has been ballpark agreement with the asset's observable market price. Financial analysts know very well that there is no such thing as valuation without assumptions, be it on the asset itself or on its economic environment. Hence, we will offer both "intrinsic valuation guidance" and commentary on necessary assumptions to the token designer, as a way of explaining the usual buy-side expectations on parameters that need to be quantifiable and range-bounded to justify a pricing opinion. Traditional financial valuation follows two paths, namely:

(a) **Comparable-asset** pricing.
(b) **Fundamental analysis**.

The first path seeks to identify asset features or metrics permitting an analogy with similar assets which have already been priced by the market. The second considers the asset in isolation and either makes an assumption about its capturing part of an addressable market; or strives to identify income streams directly or indirectly attributable to holding the asset, and then applies a discounted cash-flow model. The underlying blockchain ecosystem paradigm adds a third potential path, that of:

(c) **Network economics**.

We will give examples of all three paths for each token type in our reference typology separately. It is important to add that analysts typically pursue several methods in parallel, so as to cover as many valuation angles as possible. Hence, one should expect to use each of the three paths separately and then rationalize a final valuation assumption, e.g. by applying appropriate weights on their outcomes and then adding them.

For **currency tokens**, currently prevailing valuation models depart from the "equation of exchange" (cf. also the discussion on the velocity factor in Sect. 10.5.1):

$$M \cdot V = P \cdot Q$$

where "*M*" is the total token money supply, "*P*" the price level in the ecosystem when transactions are settled in the token, "*Q*" the quantity of goods and services exchanged in the time frame of consideration, and "*V*" the token velocity in said transactions and time frame. If n_{T} and P_{T} are the number of tokens in circulation and their unit price, respectively, then:

$$M = n_{\mathsf{T}} \cdot P_{\mathsf{T}}$$

The product $P \cdot Q$ is the total value of transactions in said time frame, which is generally observable on the blockchain. Hence, from the equation of exchange:

$$P_{\mathsf{T}} = \frac{P \cdot Q}{n_{\mathsf{T}} \cdot V}$$

For example, assume that the time frame is 1 year. The total value of transactions measured on the token's blockchain within the year is 100 mil USD. There are a total of 10,000 tokens in circulation and the average token velocity is estimated to equal 5. From the equation, estimated token price is 2K USD. The main assumptions behind this formula are that the total value of transactions is observable (which should be straightforward if a token is used only on a single blockchain, but may be more involved otherwise) and that transaction velocity (which is time-varying) can be reliably estimated. Of course, when the formula is used as a projection, then the numerator is substituted by an assumed addressable market and the velocity similarly by an assumed value. Probable ranges on addressable market and velocity give corresponding ranges on token price. Input ranges can be gleaned either from stochastic simulations or from projections of the token business case. Please note that the first model proposed along these lines (INET model [28]) has since been extended to compensate for difficulties in calculating a reliable on-chain velocity metric (VOLT model [29]) and to account for time-changing velocities ("Rational Market Value" model [30]).

In terms of comparative asset pricing, one indicative metric is the "Network Value to Transactions" [31] (NVT). It is assumed that a cryptocurrency draws its utility primarily from being a "medium of exchange" and only secondarily as a store of value. Based on that, an immediate, short-term, "utility proxy" would be the value of transactions executed daily through the token. The comparison metric then is:

$$NVT = \frac{M}{P \cdot Q}$$

where M, P, and Q have the same meanings as before and the time frame of reference is 1 day. M is actually the "Network Value" (or token market capitalization) behind the concept. Please note that as the daily volume of transaction changes, NVT becomes a function of time. If it can be assumed that cryptocurrencies in their "mature phases" (i.e. long after first issuance, and after network effects have been attained) should have approximately the same utility, then for two different tokens, X and Y:

$$NVT_X \sim NVT_Y$$

Substituting $M = n \cdot P$ for each of the tokens and assuming that $[P \cdot Q]^{\text{daily}}$ is observable on the blockchain:

$$\frac{n_X \cdot P_X}{[P \cdot Q]_X^{\text{daily}}} \sim \frac{n_Y \cdot P_Y}{[P \cdot Q]_Y^{\text{daily}}}$$

which allows to estimate the price of one of the cryptocurrencies, say P_Y, in terms of the other, through metrics that are directly observable. As before, there are several computational fine-tunings which proved useful in the operational application of this metric. For example, the original publication [32] employed a simple point-in-time calculation for $[P \cdot Q]^{\text{daily}}$. Later refinements included using a 90-day moving average [33, 34] instead of point-in-time daily transaction value; accounting for token inflation by normalizing the NVT value through a "dilution factor" [35]; and also for non-active tokens (either kept—"hodled"—as value stores, or simply lost) by postulating a "Realized Value" [36] in place of the network value. Of course, changing the time frame of reference produces still more NVT "views" [37], which can be used to better inform valuation. It goes without saying that, when used as a projection, the NVT formula hinges on *estimated* ranges for its constituent variables which may come from stochastic simulation, expert judgement, or any other admissible source.

Another metric which might seem to qualify as a "comparable-asset" one, but which nevertheless has only been used for BTC so far, is the "Stock-to-Flow" [38] (S2F). It applies a normalizing factor to the current token price, the factor being calculated as the ratio of the current total circulating supply over its yearly increase:

$$S2F = \frac{n_X}{[\Delta n]_X^{\text{yearly}}}$$

As the cryptocurrency is being steadily minted, n_X is changing in time. Also, if the block validating period and the per-block reward are held constant (as is the case of several cryptocurrencies, including BTC), then the yearly token supply increase can be easily calculated. Hence, S2F is also changing in time, depending practically only on n_X. The graph of S2F was shown to follow closely the historically observed BTC price evolution [39] and in that sense would be justified as a means of future price projection. However, theoretical underpinnings of this method are rather shallow, which might explain its applicability only in the BTC case so far. Intuitively, the observation that S2F can follow the "jumps" in BTC price around Bitcoin halving times could be easily attributable to the fact that this token has achieved network effects and is showing almost constant demand. As Bitcoin halving means that the "primary market" token issuance is about to (or has just) become more difficult, one part of this constant demand is being redirected towards the "secondary market". Suddenly increasing demand against slower increasing supply thus helps explain price spikes that are observed in the graphs. Please note that the S2F graphs show undershoots as well. Nevertheless, the S2F graph's general agreement with that of observed BTC price is rather remarkable; which is why we include it in our list of valuation methods.

In Sect. 3.1, it was mentioned that Metcalfe's law has been proved to hold true *empirically* in blockchain-based token ecosystems [40, 41]. With "*M*" being a cryptocurrency's total market capitalization and "*k*" the number of blockchain addresses using it, the formula:

$$M = A \cdot \frac{k \cdot (k-1)}{2}$$

(where "*A*" is a regression scaling coefficient) was shown to fit the BTC protocol's value evolution with R^2 above 80% [42]. This is simply the expression of network effects having been attained, and, as already explained in Sect. 3.1, it is valid only in the limit and under simplifying assumptions. For example, nodes may be once connected but then stay inactive; similarly, a blockchain address with assets worth 1 token and another one with assets worth one million tokens are weighted equally under this correlation; in both cases, the network value is understated. Also, its theoretical basis on an internal, static, network view means that exogenous economic factors are not considered. For example, prolonged market dislocations; cross-ecosystem effects; structural market changes propagating from the physical to the digital world; are all not accounted for in this equation. In short, there are strong uniformity assumptions in the network model behind it, which may or may not hold true in actual ecosystems and thus fail to capture exogenous valuation influences. If the analyst intends to keep using this model, then the "*A*" regression coefficient will have to be re-calibrated in each new market regime. Under these caveats, substituting $M = n \cdot P$ gives:

$$P = A \cdot \frac{k \cdot (k-1)}{2 \cdot n}$$

which can be used for token price projections, based on calculated or estimated ranges for the evolution of "*n*" and "*k*".

Another possible "comparable-asset" valuation metric relates specifically to ecosystems using smart contracts to allocate buyer's funds to cryptocurrency positions. As all smart contract transactions are registered on the blockchain, calculating the current value of all these positions gives an observable first-order estimate of the *capital* locked into the token. The outcome of this calculation is called "Total Value Locked" (TVL [43, 44]) in industry parlance. The metric used in comparative valuations is the ratio:

$$r = \frac{M}{\text{TVL}}$$

The difference between the values in the numerator and the denominator comes from the fact that the funds going into the transactions producing the TVL calculation are in the form of fiat currencies or other tokens (which are swapped for the own token). "*M*", on the other hand, is calculated based on the value of the *own* token. There are two main uses of "*r*" [45]: if it deviates significantly from 1, to estimate if the cryptocurrency is under- or over-valued; and, if it differs among cryptocurrencies having the same or similar use cases, to opine whether one is holding up its value proposition against the other and if/how they would be expected to converge [46]. There are assumptions behind both its calculation and relevance across tokens [47], hence its use for valuation projections must be made carefully.

For private **Stablecoins,** there is an additional, subtle, point around valuation, relating to the difference among investing in:

(a) the token itself,
(b) a liquidity position in the token, or
(c) the token-issuing project.

By definition, a successful Stablecoin should not deviate much from its peg. Hence, a valuation effort around the **token itself** is justified only in a few short-time-horizon cases, for instance, to exploit arbitrage opportunities between the primary and secondary markets should there be systematic deviation between the two because of a mis-calibration of the price stabilization mechanism. Otherwise, the utility of buying the Stablecoin is idiosyncratic to the buyer.

A Stablecoin **liquidity position** is a totally different investment and valuation situation. There are actually two different investment cases, depending on whether the investor is a liquidity *taker* or a liquidity *provider*. As explained in much more detail in the Sects. 10.5.7 and 10.5.8, there are significant variations among Stablecoins relating to which assets are exchanged to acquire this position and through which mechanism. Some protocols (such as MakerDAO [48]) issue their Stablecoins as collateralized loan positions, requiring posting of collateral in some admissible assets; and possibly also acquiring a volatility token (which may also be yield-accruing, through secondary utility as platform-rewards-returning governance token). Figure 10.9, also explained in detail in Sect. 10.5.8, gives the generic constellation of tokens and assets involved in this liquidity *taking* case.

The liquidity *provision* investment case (explained through the example of the Uniswap [49] protocol in Sect. 10.5.7) involves using acquired Stablecoins to fund

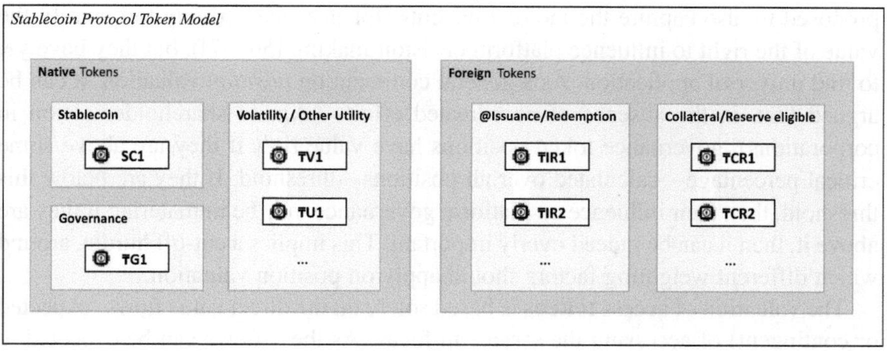

Fig. 10.9 Generic Stablecoin token model

liquidity pools of market makers, which may also *make markets in Stablecoins*. The two cases have very different risk-payoff profiles, which transforms position valuation to, in effect, *portfolio* valuation, where the token is only one of the portfolio assets.

Investment in a **Stablecoin-issuing project** [50, 51] can be either explicit or implicit. For instance, an explicit case would be an outright investment in the underlying volatility token as per Fig. 10.9. An implicit case would be through the corresponding governance token or through the participation in yield on collateral. Both positions imply an expectation of profit through the platform rewards pool and—depending on the particular project—may or may not be contingent on also acquiring the Stablecoin.

Please note that, apart from the metrics mentioned above, there are a plethora of others [52] that are used in valuation tasks, depending on the individual analyst. For example, "Fully Diluted Valuation" (FDV [53, 54]) can be substituted for token market capitalization. Similarly, using a valuation on cryptocurrencies as an intermediate step towards downstream valuation can involve an aggregation across ecosystems (an example would be the "Total Value Secured" [55] (TVS) in the case of Oracle valuation). As already mentioned, analysts typically pursue several methods—and use several metrics—in parallel, to cover as many valuation angles as possible.

The valuation of **utility tokens** has one common theme, with variations depending on their subtype. The common theme is the existence of value flows (direct and predictable cash flows—inflows and outflows—as well as indirect flows of monetizable benefits) associated with the token, which can be used as inputs to discounted cash flow models. The idiosyncratic variations are explained in the sequel, arranged by subtype.

Governance tokens are meant to help preserve the value of their ecosystem as network effects set in. To incentivize acquisition, and active participation in governance processes through staking, of governance tokens, several protocols redistribute funds from their platform rewards pool to token holders and/or stakers. These represent the direct cash flow component of valuation. Some models have been proposed to also capture the indirect benefits (for instance, striving to quantify the value of the right to influence platform decision-making [56, 57]), but they have yet to find universal application. As a general comment on *position* valuation, it can be argued that, in the absence of coordinated efforts (akin to shareholder action in corporations), governance token positions have value *only* if they are above some critical percentage—calculated over all positions—threshold. If they are below this threshold, then their influence on platform governance may be immaterial; if they are above it, then it can be indeed overly important. This implies a cut-off hurdle, around which different weighting factors should apply on position valuation.

The valuation of **access tokens** is based solely on the direct value flows (expected or contingent) of accessing the service in focus. As these flows can be expected to scale with the actual use of resources and with the number of acquired tokens, analysis should more properly be approached as *position*, rather than individual token, valuation. In other words, the benefits of owning such a token may depend on the number of tokens acquired.

Service tokens dictate a similar valuation path, albeit *value* flows now become quite clearly *cash* flows. Prospective buyers must buy, then stake, the token; afterwards they expect an income stream by providing the service; and can be penalized (through receiving reduced income or even forfeiting of part of the staked tokens) if some quality-of-service metric is not met. All these are cash flows, with probabilistic assumptions on the income stream (as it depends on actual demand for services) and quality-of-service outcomes. If the descriptive statistics of both the income stream and the outcomes can be assumed known, then valuation can be standardized across service tokens [58, 59]. If not, then analysis should again proceed as *position* valuation.

Discount tokens come in two variations "on-stake" and "on-use" (cf. Sect. 4.2.2) which create different valuation paths. They both need descriptive statistics on the actual use of the right to a discount and the discount benefit—frequency and value—and also on any holding period limits. If the token limits never expire, then the aforementioned statistics serve to price the token as an annuity. It is useful to add that, since the discount benefit increases with the number of token owners, there is also a linear factor at play. In short, the cumulative benefit of the token scales linearly with the number of buyers. All these factors enter a DCF model [60], with value flows estimated as per the above statistics. This allows to price discount tokens uniformly.

"Burn & Mint" tokens were explained in 4.2.2 as representing in effect a fee for services provided. Purchasing and staking the token (the "burn" leg) entitles the buyer to receive a service. Scaling the service and receiving the reward (the "mint" leg) is income for the service provider. Hence, valuation can be made from three standpoints: those of the service requestor; the service provider; and the issuing project (owning the fees pool, out of which rewards are paid). These are three different valuation cases. All are done through DCF modelling, but the second and third standpoint necessitate descriptive statistics and scenario analysis [61].

Asset tokens minted as **NFT**s can encompass a wide variety of underlying property rights (cf. Sect. 10.5.6), which can be on fixed assets, contingent assets, income streams, and optionalities. Said rights can be also "transformed" through fractionization, which may influence their transferability, hence their liquidity risk profile. The extent and direction of this influence depends on the specific property right. For example, fractionization of an NFT representing an interest in income-producing real estate may confer rights on either a building or on a special-purpose vehicle owning a building. If the ownership structure implies restrictions on transferring the F-NFT, then that will have an impact on its value. In short, every non-fungible token (whole or fractional) will generally have to be approached as a bespoke investment case for valuation purposes. Starting from a careful analysis of the underlying property rights (including restrictions, such as in the case of intellectual property intrinsic to physical or digital artworks), valuation will involve either comparable asset or fundamental analysis. Network economics are typically difficult to justify in NFT cases. Technical token design must create clarity on said rights, either through descriptions included as part of the on-chain token object or by way of off-chain documentation linked to smart contracts minting and/or transferring the token. Conceptual token design must be unambiguously specific on the structure and jurisdictional aspects of the same rights within the off-chain documentation, which must be available to prospective buyers and valuation analysts irrespective of the technical token implementation. Another important valuation angle is the existence and depth of active marketplaces for the NFT. Token design can influence NFT negotiability by including such technical features as are necessary to enable compatibility with technical requirements of the most probable secondary markets for the token (and of the most prominent crypto wallet providers, for that matter).

Interestingly, **security tokens** are the most straightforward to value. As they are by default financial instruments, they have to comply with strict disclosure obligations even before they are offered to the investing public, starting with documentation describing precisely the constellation of asset classes and corresponding positions (or allowable position ranges) allocated to each. Our analysis in Sect. 4.2.4 demonstrated that all currently observable security token subtypes correspond precisely to traditional financial instruments. Hence, valuation of lending tokens can proceed in exactly the same way as traditional lending positions. Fixed income tokens contain the same notions of principal, yield, maturity, duration, etc., as traditional bonds. For equity tokens, the financials of the corresponding physical-world legal entity can be used to evaluate the same dividend discount models, cost of capital formulas, fundamental analysis metrics, etc., as in traditional financial valuation. The rest of security subtypes (money market, repo, investment fund, structured product) inherit the same notions of risk and return as in the off-chain world. Even though they can bundle both on-chain and off-chain positions, their issuers' reporting obligations are very much *off-chain* and are expected to remain so, due to the fundamental obligation to ensure fairness in the treatment of all security token holders. Even if the underlying security is issued only on-chain, there will always have to be a link between on-chain information and off-chain statutory reporting. Thus, all parameters needed for valuation analysis can be expected to be retrievable.

Similar disclosure obligations apply to **derivative tokens**, hence valuation parameters are expected to be retrievable, if they are offered to the general investing public. However, for derivative positions issued on the blockchain as tokens (e.g. for hedging purposes, or directional market views of professional investors), if the issuance is strictly on a bilateral basis, then generally no disclosure requirements apply. In the latter case, token valuation is in effect position valuation and can proceed as per traditional finance methodologies (Black-Scholes, Binomial trees, Heston model, Copulae, etc.) carried out by the counterparties themselves or by their valuation agents.

In summary, all token types have valuation modalities associated with them. Token design can facilitate valuation tasks on the part of buyers and analysts by creating clarity on the underlying property rights and by specifying unequivocally the linkages between on-blockchain objects and off-chain documentation and reporting. Enabling adequate and explainable valuation models has repercussions for token:

- **Investability**. As several token types qualify as financial instruments, their investment suitability per client segment is subject to legal and regulatory obligations mandating clarity of asset class descriptions and adequate explanation of risk/return profiles. Only when valuation models support investment cases can "buy" and/or "hold" recommendations be justified.
- **Tradability**. Both primary and secondary markets need robust price discovery mechanisms to enable negotiation of token transactions. As *technical* indicators depend on market conditions, there need to exist *fundamental* valuation methodologies to support price discovery.
- **Volatility**. The risk profile of token positions must be always clear so that the cost of risk management can be correctly estimated—and adequately funded—by buyers and investors. If robust valuation metrics and sensitivities cannot be produced, then appropriate risk management of token positions cannot be carried out. The result will be unexplainable market price swings of token positions, which may be interpreted as manifestations of deficient design of the token itself.
- **Scalability**. Network effects will be achieved only if prospective buyers and investors feel that the token has a risk/return profile matching their expectations. If valuation fails to support creation of robust and explainable risk/return profiles, then buyers and investors may feel compelled to avoid the token.
- **Sustainability**. Only reliable valuation methodologies will provide the factual basis for a token's long-term value proposition. If they are not available, then the possibility of material downside investment risk may make buyers avoid, or sell, the token at any price point if prevalent crypto-market conditions (i.e. across tokens) suggest de-risking urgency. This way, the token will be constantly volatile, not being able to find price support levels. Its long-term value proposition may suffer as a result.

It is therefore essential for token design to enable valuation tasks by creating clarity on the utility, underlying property rights, income streams, transaction costs, and opportunity costs of the token.

10.5.5 Minting Mode

The token-**minting mode** is also an important factor to consider, as it impacts directly the costs of token creation (hence the fees that the buyer or investor may have to assume) but also indirectly the usability and safety aspects of transacting in the token. The current state of the art consists in three major minting modes, namely:

1. Block minting reward.
2. Platform primitive.
3. Smart contract.

"**Block minting reward**" is typically associated with Layer-1 ("Settlement" layer as per taxonomy proposed in Sect. 1.5) tokens, such as BTC [62], ETH [63, 64], LTC [65], but can also be found in Layer-2 ones, e.g. POL [66], LRC [67]. The tacit intention behind choosing this minting mode is for the token to be the main native token of its platform, through which other, higher-layer tokens, may also be enabled. For example, whenever a new Layer-1 platform is created (e.g. based on a novel cryptographic algorithm or blockchain consensus paradigm), issuing new native tokens to executors of the block consensus mechanism is a way to immediately reward the provision of a service (validation of transactions) on the platform.

"**Platform primitive**" refers to Layer-1 configurable objects which can be called by applications to instantiate tokens based on pre-specified templates. They are offered as part of the platform's basic functionality, hence, the designation "primitive", as in "primitive object". An example would be Algorand [68] Standard Assets (ASA [69]), which template both fungible and non-fungible tokens.

"**Smart Contract**" mode is typically associated with tokens created at higher layers. We find it expedient to explain the "smart contract" (SC for short) notion in some detail, before going into its relevance for token minting.

The term "Smart Contract" was first defined in a 1994 academic publication by Nicholas Szabo [70] and was simply adopted by subsequent blockchain literature to fit a particular purpose. Namely, denoting *pieces of code stored on the blockchain ("on-chain") and executing once specific on-chain conditions have been met ("triggering events")*. For example, imagine that, in the course of an ecosystem transaction, one counterparty has delivered the promised goods (or executed the promised service), and this effect is registered on the blockchain. A piece of code which is monitoring precisely such events then executes the sending of tokens (for direct payment or other reward, such as a discount) to the counterparty on the blockchain. This piece of code is a SC.

Suffice it to say that there is nothing "smart" in a blockchain SC per se, in the sense of an expert-based or inference-based logic that optimizes some decision. It is also not a "contract" in the legal sense (satisfying the validity criteria of Contract Law, resp. Law of Obligations, in common, resp. civil law jurisdictions). Simply, it has come to be accepted as a trade term in blockchain technical implementations in general, and in token-based ecosystems in particular.

The outcome of a SC may not even be of a monetary nature, as it can simply be to write a different piece of information on the blockchain or to trigger a new event for another SC. In short, a SC is simply a piece of code stored on the blockchain, programmed to execute once some pre-specified conditions have been met, as registered in the underlying distributed ledger. It contains deterministic logic, possibly calibrated by off-chain parameters (such as current market prices, provided, e.g., through responses by third-party services, called "Oracles" —another trade-term in blockchain implementations) which may or may not be stochastic.[6] Actually, the concept of having platform-registered code executing upon occurrence of some on-platform conditions has not even originated in the blockchain world. For instance, database professionals have been using so-called "Database Triggers" [72] for precisely the same effect, long before blockchain platforms were invented. And, above "settlement" layer (moving to the equivalent concept outside the blockchain world), the entire software industries of business rules management [73] and complex event processing [74] systems are based on similar "trigger event—automated code execution" concepts.

Why is "[by] Smart Contract" a token-minting mode?

In essence, this term refers to a specific token creation pattern, in which the underlying settlement layer is explicitly asked to create token(s) and then assign them to specific blockchain addresses *by executing a piece of on-chain code.* All "administrative" matters of this action (e.g. "how many tokens"; "which token type"; "to be sent to which address"; "all tokens to the same address, or different addresses by token type and amount"; "which notes to insert as part of the execution record", etc.) are to be specified as part of the code execution sequence—through so-called "input variables", or through other parametrization—mandated as per said pattern. Similarly, for all "technical" matters ("what if an error occurs during execution"; "what kinds of exceptional situations are to be handled automatically", etc.). This piece of code executes only if some pre-specified on-chain conditions are met (e.g. once some "address onboarding" is completed; or some [human or technical] authorizations have been granted successfully; or some fiat-currency amount has been successfully deposited into a pre-specified platform account, etc.). Hence, this is deterministic logic, implemented in on-chain code, which executes only once some on-chain conditions have been met. It is a smart contract.

What degrees of freedom does a token designer have when choosing this minting mode?

The answer depends on the underlying Layer-1 or -2 platform and can be decisive for the success of the token. There are three main questions that need to guide design at this juncture:

[6] But must be observable, i.e. their point-in-time values must be unique and ascertainable. If that is not the case, then they are not blockchain-compatible. This is a well-established antipattern in Smart Contract design, which can have many manifestations and causes. For example, in the context of Oracles, the "Oracle Problem" was identified early enough in token evolution [71].

(a) Does the underlying (Layer-1/-2) platform come with standard ("normalized", i.e. established in some sense) SC templates?
(b) If so, do any of these fit the specific business case and are they commensurate with the creation fees that our target buyers and investors can be reasonably expected to afford?
(c) In they do not, is it justified to design and implement a bespoke SC template for the new token? Or should a new (Layer-1/-2) platform be used?

The answers to these questions will mean the difference between re-using a standardized SC template and having to create one's own. This can be important for token acceptance by buyers and investors, as standardized SC templates:

- Crystallize the operational experience of previous token ecosystems in sidestepping blockchain pathologies.
- Are usually subject to rigorous approval, resp. peer-review, processes at the design, resp. implementation, phases.
- Are more readily accepted by investors, as they can be audited and given "seals of approval" by specialized auditing firms.
- Are progressively better understood by regulators, which will help in any discussion relating to token authorization jurisdiction-wise.
- When backed up by standards, allow for "mix-and-match" aggregation of functionalities to quickly implement new business cases for the token, by the same or different ecosystems which then adopt it as "foreign token".

In short, choosing to create a new, bespoke SC template for a token, instead of adopting one or several of the existing ones, can be a bold decision; by no means unwarranted if the designer stands behind a compelling value proposition, but bold nevertheless. Similarly, being able to make a judgement call on whether or not "mixing-and-matching" is able to produce a new SC template with low acceptance risk is also very important. It is thus imperative to be familiar with the pros and cons of pre-existing SC templates for token minting. By way of example, we propose to go into some detail for some of the currently standardized ones, arranged per Layer-1 platform only.

10.5.5.1 Algorand

Minting is possible on Algorand through smart contracts as well as through platform primitives. Algorand Smart Contracts [75] come in two flavours, stateful [76] and stateless [77], and can in principle be used to mint both fungible and non-fungible tokens [78, 79].

10.5.5.2 Cardano

Minting is possible on Cardano also through both smart contracts [80] and platform primitives since the platform's "Alonzo" fork [81]. As of the time of writing this, Cardano Smart Contracts [82] afford great flexibility through the use of scripting languages, but do not appear to be subject to standardization in terms of API or allocation to functional use cases [83]. They can be used to mint both fungible [84] and non-fungible tokens [85].

10.5.5.3 Ethereum

ERC-20

The ERC-20 standard [86] specifies an application programming interface (API) for smart contracts to transfer a single fungible token on Ethereum and allow it to be approved for transactions among on-chain addresses. Strictly speaking, it does not specify explicit methods to mint a new token, however declaring the source address of a token transfer to "0 × 0" (zero) is precisely the minting case. Concrete implementations of the standard [87] have opted for making this explicit, hence this is an obvious design choice.

ERC-165

The ERC-165 standard [88] specifies a way for the implementing smart contract to declare to calling applications (i.e. applications which need to use it for minting or indeed any other task) that they conform to one of the ERC standards. This way, "mixing-and-matching" pre-existing smart contract implementations should be much safer. It is in effect a way to promote re-useability of smart contracts in new business cases, as long as they are implemented on Ethereum.

ERC-721

Standard [89] specifying an API for smart contracts to track and transfer non-fungible tokens (NFTs) and also other operations (such as to approve and query amounts). Strictly speaking, it does not specify methods specific to minting a new token, rather only ones to be implemented when an NFT is moved from or to any on-chain address. However, the specification of the API's "*Transfer*" event (which is called whenever NFTs are moved) as per standard mentions: "*This event emits when NFTs are created ('from' == 0) and destroyed ('to' == 0)*". This in effect allows for the minting of NFTs, as concrete standard implementations[7] [90] have already demonstrated.

ERC-777

Standard [91] extending and improving ERC-20. Specifies API for smart contracts to transfer, approve, and burn multiple fungible tokens at once (as opposed to a single token as per ERC-20). Transferring tokens may take place among any number of source and destination on-chain addresses, as long as the summed token amounts on each side balance. Each and every individual token transfer is meant to be backwards compatible with ERC-20, hence a token transfer from "0 × 0" (zero) is precisely the minting case. Helpfully, the API does provide for a "*Minted*" event, whose specification explicitly states "*NOTE: This event MUST NOT be emitted outside of a mint*

[7] Search under "NFT Implementations and Other Projects" in the ERC-721 standard URL.

process". A reference implementation currently linked to the standard [92] has opted to extend the API by a bespoke "mint" function.

ERC-1155

Standard [93] specifying an API for smart contracts to transfer, approve, and query balances on any combination of fungible and non-fungible tokens in batch mode. Strictly speaking, it does not specify methods specific to minting new tokens, rather only ones to be implemented when tokens are moved from or to any on-chain address. However, the specification of the API's "*TransferSingle*" and "*TransferBatch*" events (which are called whenever tokens are moved) as per standard mentions: "*When minting/creating Tokens, the 'from' argument MUST be set to '0x0' (i.e., zero address)*". This in effect allows for the batch minting of tokens, as concrete implementations[8] have demonstrated through bespoke minting functions built on the API.

ERC-1363

Standard [94] with API geared towards on-chain payments in terms of ERC-20 tokens (optimizing costs for a "Payable token" use case). Designed for "medium-of-exchange" cryptocurrency operations, such as transaction execution and settlement on Ethereum.

ERC-2309

Standard [95] with API for smart contracts when creating/transferring one or many non-fungible tokens using consecutive token identifiers. It is possible to create, transfer, and burn up to 2^{255} NFTs through a single smart contract execution (i.e. in massively batch mode). Strictly speaking, it does not specify methods specific to minting new tokens, rather only ones to be implemented when tokens moved from or to any on-chain addresses. However, the specification of the API's "*ConsecutiveTransfer*" event (which is called whenever tokens are moved) as per standard mentions: "*When minting/creating Tokens, the 'from' argument MUST be set to '0×0' (i.e., zero address)*".

ERC-3643

Standard [96] with API for smart contracts, aiming to represent all stages of the lifecycle of *security* tokens (from issuance to transfers between eligible investors) in a way that can be audited for compliance to rules set by regulated trading venues. Also used to implement "Real-World Asset" (RWA) tokenization [97] on Ethereum. For an explanation of the RWA use case, please consult Sect. 14.5.3.9.

[8] Search under "Implementations" in the ERC-1155 standard URL.

The above is a small sample of Ethereum SC standards relevant to token-minting design. There exist several more, currently at various stages of approval[9] through the Ethereum improvement proposals (EIP) lifecycle [98].

One of the arguments in favour of following an ERC standard is that the designer will profit from *future* standards specifically building on previous specifications. For example, ERC-3386 allows to wrap ERC-721/ERC-1155 conforming tokens into ERC-20 ones, i.e. to implement business cases where individual NFTs and pools of NFTs can be further tokenized and sold as fungible unit-fund securities. In another example, the final ERC-2981 standard provides for "*a standardized way to retrieve royalty payment information for non-fungible tokens (NFTs) to enable universal support for royalty payments across all NFT marketplaces and ecosystem participants*", provided that said NFTs implement the ERC-721 or ERC-1155 standards.

In the following list, we provide a high-level overview of quite compelling existing and upcoming ERC standards relevant to token design. We do not group them as "Final", "Draft", etc., as their status constantly evolves. The interested reader should check the current approval status of each individual standard (by invoking https://eips.ethereum.org/EIPS/eip-nnnn, where "nnnn" is the numeric specifier) before adopting it for implementation.

ERC-num	Description
20	Token Standard (Note: Fungible Token)
165	Standard Interface Detection
721	Non-Fungible Token Standard
777	Token Standard (Note: Backward compatible with ERC-20)
998	Composable Non-Fungible Token Standard
1132	Extending ERC20 with Token locking capability
1155	Multi-class Token Standard (Note: specifically for NFT's)
1203	Multi-Class Token Standard (ERC-20 Extension)
1363	Payable Token
1450	A compatible Security Token for issuing and trading SEC-compliant securities
1462	Base Security Token (Note: "An extension to ERC-20 standard Token that provides compliance with securities regulations and legal enforceability" [99])
1948	Non-fungible Data Token (Note: NFTs are extended with data that can change during the Token's lifetime)
2309	ERC-721 Consecutive Transfer Extension
2981	NFT Royalty Standard
3135	Exclusive Claimable Token
3386	ERC-721 and ERC-1155 to ERC-20 Wrapper
3589	Assemble assets into NFT's
3643	T-REX—Token for Regulated EXchanges
4519	Non-Fungible Tokens Tied to Physical Assets

(continued)

[9] Stages are "Draft", "Review", "Last Call", "Final". Generally, both the last 2 stages signify standards that are safe to implement.

ERC-num	Description
4910	Royalty Bearing NFT's
5023	Shareable Non-Fungible Token
5528	Refundable Fungible Token
5725	Transferable Vesting NFT
5773	Context-Dependent Multi-Asset Tokens
6059	Parent-Governed Nestable Non-Fungible Tokens
6150	Hierarchical NFT's
6672	Multi-redeemable NFT's
7092	Financial Bonds

10.5.5.4 Tezos

FA1.2

Standard [100, 101] specifying an API for single fungible token transfers and approvals. Strictly speaking, it does not specify methods specific to minting a new token, rather only ones to be implemented when an NFT is moved from or to any on-chain address. Similarly to ERC-20, minting occurs when a token is transferred from source address "0 × 0" (zero). Reference implementations have already applied [102, 103] the minting functionality.

FA2

Standard [104–106] specifying an API for transfers and approvals of multiple tokens. As per specification, "*A particular FA2 implementation may support either a single token type per contract or multiple tokens per contract, including hybrid implementations where multiple token kinds (fungible, non-fungible, non-transferable, etc.) can co-exist (e.g. in a fractionalized NFT contract)*". Strictly speaking, it does not specify methods specific to minting a new token; minting occurs when a token is transferred from source address "0 × 0" (zero). The Tezos tutorials microsite contains examples of such smart contracts minting tokens [107].

The above are only indicative examples of standardized smart contract templates for token minting on Tezos. There exists also a dedicated smart contract programming language [108] and a corresponding visual modelling tool [109].

10.5.5.5 Zilliqa

ZRC-1

ZRC-1 [110] specifies an API for non-fungible token creation, management, trading, and tracking. It provides explicitly for "mint" methods, as is also evident from the reference implementation [111]. Simultaneous ("batch-mode") minting of NFTs is also provided for, as well as extensions to the basic contract to implement ancillary functionalities such as NFT-based royalties [112].

ZRC-2

ZRC-2 [113] is an API template for fungible token creation, management, trading, and tracking. Interestingly, the "mint" functionality is currently defined as "optional", however, one of the reference implementations [114] does extend it out of the box.

In summary, there are standardized templates already for smart contract programming on L-1 blockchains. Token designers and implementors should always familiarize themselves with the SC state of the art.

Choice of **minting mode** has repercussions for tokens:

- **Costs**. Some Layer-1 platforms provide optimized templates for token minting, through either platform primitives or standardized smart contracts. These allow for reduced (in some cases, drastically so) token creation gas fees, when compared to unoptimized paradigms. These can make the difference between a token that is economically viable and one that is good on paper but impossible to sell.
- **Auditability**. Corporate auditors, regulators, and fraud examiners will be much more comfortable giving an unqualified no-objection decision to a token design that follows precedent in all major operational respects, starting from the minting mode. The reason is that previous token ecosystems will have helped them fine-tune their questionnaires regarding features of prevalent industry standards, and focus on salient design characteristics, thus avoiding having to raise issues which they already know are secondary. If a token project creates a token design whose operational aspects were never encountered before, the natural reaction of corporate controllers would be to scrutinize each and every detail starting from first principles—and they will be right to do so.
- **Investability**. De facto industry standards generate trust with buyers and long-term investors. Venture capital scouts, independent crypto-asset advisors, and commentators will gladly recommend a token the lifecycle of which has some features already encountered in the market. Even if a market participant is willing to devote time to understand the value proposition of a new token with bespoke lifecycle mechanisms, this time's opportunity cost is already raising the bar, which will need to be compensated elsewhere.
- **Composability.**[10] The most successful tokens tend to be the ones that find use cases outside their home ecosystem. Cross-platform usage is greatly facilitated when fully documented APIs and cost structures allow third-party implementors to mix-and-match tokens, adopting a foreign token with confidence as part of their own use cases (think, e.g., of reserve token staking). If they cannot know if a token's minting process scales and if the secondary market can accommodate

[10] Cf. also Sect. 10.5.9, where this term is explained as a design factor.

demand spikes, then they may well decide to avoid the risk of admitting a particular foreign token.

- **Scalability**. Scalable minting processes will help a cryptocurrency attain network effects to break into "store of value" territory. If the token cannot satisfy proven economic demand in its early stages (the "Primary Market" focused ones), then it will not make itself known to its broader possible market.
- **Sustainability**. Operational stability and issue transparency breed trust in a token. Major Layer-1 and higher platforms keep investing resources in third-party "bug-bounty programs" around their technical implementations, especially on the ways tokens are minted, transferred, and burned. Achieving this level of trust is the cornerstone of long-term success.

In conclusion, if token creators feel strongly that their technical architecture represents a new Layer-1 platform, then they can opt for the "block minting reward" mode. However, if they feel that their business value proposition is more strongly dependent on interaction with already established token ecosystems, then they can opt for building a higher-layer token through either platform primitives, or smart contracts on an already existing Layer-1 platform. In the latter case, the choice of smart contract type will need careful functional and non-functional requirements analysis. The fundamental design decision then will be between re-using a pre-existing, platform-standard, type; and creating and implementing a new smart contract specification, that may offer compelling comparative advantages to its surrounding use case.

10.5.6 Property Rights Structure

How to define and structure the property rights[11] inherent in a token is a fundamental token design factor. A generic token being simply an on-chain digital representation of value (cf. Sect. 4.1), clarity on what exactly this value represents is a basic expectation by token transaction participants. However, the latter are not the only economic agents interested in a clear property rights specification. Acting on behalf of token buyers and investors, it is inescapable that financial advisors; financial institutions; auditors; lawyers; law enforcement authorities (including financial

[11] Please note that the legally correct terminology would be "*personal and property rights*"; we kindly ask legal professionals reading this book to please accept the abridged designation "property rights", used throught for the sake of brevity. Of course, token analysis and design profiting from the services of legal counsel will immediately distinguish between the two terms.

intelligence units); courts of law; industry bodies; regulators (potentially central banks); will also need to:

1. Categorize the token (understand its functions; its relation to other asset classes and other tokens; its cash or value flows; its risks and payoff optionalities [implying effective valuation and insurability]; its operational lifecycle aspects [minting, custody, burning], etc.).
2. Based on its asset class categorization, identify applicable statutory/case law and regulations per involved jurisdiction (where is the governing organization of the token-issuing project incorporated; where are buyer/investor/advisor type agents domiciled; where do exchanges or custodians operate from, etc.) and assign competent regulatory authority(-ies).
3. Should several jurisdictions be involved, understand potential conflict-of-law situations and legal/regulatory gaps that will need addressing long-term, or at least risk-managing short-term.
4. Specify concrete legal/regulatory obligations accruing to token issuers/buyers/ investors, especially conditions precedent for validity of token transactions, such as:
   (a) Transaction negotiation (CEX/DEX, smart contract, etc.) and perfection (when is the transaction taken to have concluded and when is it still contingent on events) aspects.
   (b) Transaction controls (client suitability, anti-financial-crime[12], Know-Your-Customer [KYC] and Know-Your-Transaction [KYT]) and jurisdictional specificities (extra authorizations and controls needed at the individual or legal entity level, etc.).
   (c) Contractual arrangements (underlying deeds, title to actual rights passed-on in NFTs, other rights and obligations, governing law, seat of arbitration, etc.).
   (d) Rights and responsibilities of transaction participants at the account/address level (multi-signature key holders, hierarchy of signatories, custodians involved, etc.).

[12] Generally, financial crimes are crimes committed in the context of a jurisdiction's banking and financial markets services, and include violations of laws on (in alphabetic order): Anti-Boycott, Anti-Bribery, Anti-Corruption, Anti-Money-Laundering, Banking, Counter-Terrorist-Financing, Capital Controls, Conflict Minerals, Cultural Goods & Antiquities, Customs, Dual-Use Goods and Materials, Endangered Species, Import/ Export Licensing, Investment, Fiduciaries, Financial Market Infrastructures, Financial Services, Fraud, Information Security, International Traffic in Arms, Intellectual Property Protection, Market Abuse (Insider Dealing and Market Manipulation), Payment Services, Property, Protection of the Currency, Receipt/ Possession/ Trafficking of Property obtained by Crime, Sanctions, Securities, Tax, Trade, Trusts & Trustees. Please note: some jurisdictions may not have created or enacted several of these laws; while others may consider some of these violations to not be financial crimes.

5. License the token (authorize its marketing; issuance; custody; post-issuance monitoring; ancillary services; transactions/tax/portfolio/statutory/regulatory reporting by all concerned individuals, legal entities, and legal arrangements, etc.).
6. Define status of token positions and of their holders (possessors or absolute owners) in corporate (borrowing; pledging; lending; securities lending; securitization; re-hypothecation; liens/encumbrances; insolvency; bankruptcy, etc.) and private (lending; pledging; posting collateral; insolvency; probate; estate planning; trusts, etc.) settings.
7. Monitor its market flows and risk indicators (transactions; transaction participants; pricing; risk metrics) for regulatory (potentially including also monetary and systemic risk) oversight purposes.
8. Take appropriate law enforcement or judicial action when wrongs and crimes involve token transactions and holdings. Eventually, trace[13] token-denominated funds, and issue and/or carry out injunctions/freezing orders on token assets.
9. Potentially adjust the legal/regulatory and risk frameworks relevant to the token as market conditions, state policy or case law evolve at the jurisdiction level (hardening privacy and security arrangements; restricting/banning the token type; restricting buyer/investor suitability; adjusting transaction controls; specifying tracing regime of token positions; delineating conditions for injunctions/asset freezes, etc.).
10. Potentially adjust the international legal/regulatory frameworks (accounting; position reporting; taxation; claiming jurisdiction; law enforcement cooperation; judicial cooperation and comity; arbitration; mutual recognition/convertibility [e.g. in the case of CBDCs]; treaties for recognition/enforcement of court decisions and arbitral awards, etc.) relevant to the token.

Hence, the functions of the token (store of value, medium of exchange, representation of other rights and obligations) will need to be translated clearly into property rights both on-chain and off-chain. Said functions will also have to make explicit reference to points from the market and mechanism designs pertaining, e.g. to transactional pathways (as the role of primary and secondary markets will need to be clarified), agent types (as the principals behind agents transacting in, and holding,

[13] At law, in equity, or both.

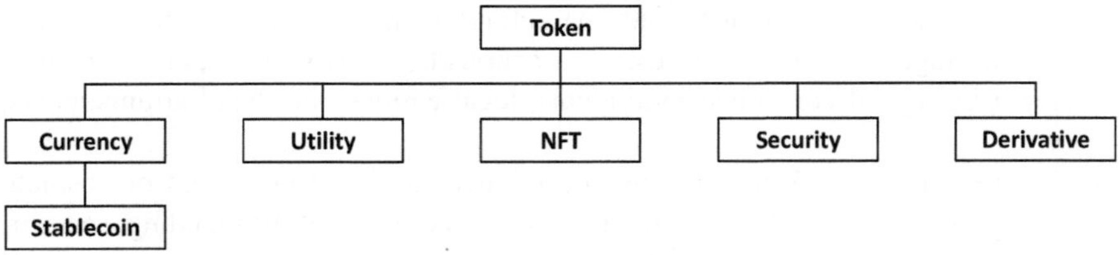

Fig. 10.10 Reference token typology (high-level)

the token will ultimately have to be identified) and individual mechanisms (as they may have to implement transaction controls).

That tokens are indeed property per se is already either settled law or regulatory guidance in major jurisdictions[14,15,16,17,18,19]. Exactly what *kind* of property rights are crystallized in them is precisely the question to be answered by the token designer. We explain some salient legal points in terms of the reference token topology of Sect. 10.3.1, Fig. 10.7, repeated here for the sake of reading convenience (Fig. 10.10):

Cryptocurrencies and Stablecoins represent the simplest property right constructs in the token world. The only complications that might arise around them are due to ancillary income streams accruing to such positions during transaction lifecycle, above and beyond the nominal value of the currencies themselves. For example, if seeding-phase ("pre-mining" or "pre-minting" phase) investors of cryptocurrency project launches acquire these tokens at a discount to their nominal value in terms of fiat currency, then this discount is an asset in excess of the nominal

[14] AA v Persons Unknown & Ors, Re Bitcoin [2019] EWHC 3556 (Comm), reported in [115], whereby the England & Wales High Court held that Cryptocurrency is personal property. Separately, the UK Jurisdiction Task Force published a statement concluding that crypto-assets in general (not only Cryptocurrencies) are indeed "property" under English law, but not "things in possession" (the statement is not legally binding, but it does constitute expert opinion by the UK Law Tech Panel that is usually taken under consideration in cases concerning all commercial law aspects in E&W, including insolvency law [116]).

[15] Already in 2014, the US Internal Revenue Service advised that for federal tax purposes, Cryptocurrencies are treated as property [117].

[16] In B2C2 Ltd. v Quoine Pte Ltd. [2019] SGHC(I) 3, the Singapore International Commercial Court held that Cryptocurrencies met all the requirements of the classic definition of property [118].

[17] On September 25, 2020, the Swiss parliament approved the "DLT-Law" (formally "Federal Act on the adaptation of Federal Legal Law to developments in Distributed Electronic Register Technology", original text under [119], and links contained in [120, 121]), whereby crypto-assets acquire equal status with off-chain assets under Swiss law.

[18] On November 29, 2019, the German Federal Parliament already included the term "crypto-asset" as property falling within the perimeter of Anti-Money-Laundering laws (through the "Act on the transposition of the amendment directive to the 4th EU Anti-Money-Laundering Directive" [122]).

[19] Under a May 28, 2020, amendment to China's Civil Code [123, 124], the PRC National People's Congress legislated that state-approved Cryptocurrencies had the status of property for the purposes of determining inheritances (Fig. 10.10).

value of the position; should the token post-launch be valued above the discounted price, then the difference can be monetized as extra income. In another example, if acquiring and retaining a Stablecoin position creates participation rights to platform rewards, then this is an extra income stream akin to that of a utility token. Irrespective of whether this ancillary income stream is available to buyers or investors pre-launch, or through primary or secondary market acquisitions, the resulting combined property rights (nominal value plus ancillary asset) most probably create a financial security out of the token as it is for all intents and purposes "*an investment in a common venture premised on a reasonable expectation of profits to be derived from the entrepreneurial or managerial efforts of others*". If this ancillary income stream is available only pre-launch, then tokens subsequently acquired in the primary and secondary markets are most probably not securities.[20] Of course, only a thorough legal analysis on a case-by-case basis can advise the proper categorization of cryptocurrencies or Stablecoins in reference to securities law.[21]

Inversely, it should be clear to the cryptocurrency/Stablecoin designer that token property rights structuring should be carried out iteratively with competent legal feedback, the latter meant to also advise the imputed obligations to the token project regarding registration, authorization, transaction controls, and pre-sale notification[22] to regulators (should a token transaction be deemed to be a constructive securities transaction). Legal risks to the issuing project may also arise by failure to anticipate the compliance obligations of *Exchanges* on which the token is offered for sale.[23]

Security and derivative tokens are clearly investment products, hence their entire lifecycle is subject to legal and regulatory obligations relating to registration; authorization; transaction controls; pre-sale notification; investor communications; client suitability; clearing/settlement; custody; tax; and position reporting involving all of token issuers, exchanges, and buyers/investors [129–132]. The precise nature of these obligations will hinge on the involved jurisdictions [133, 134], however the driving considerations from the point of view of the token designer should be about:

- Underlying on-chain and off-chain property rights.
- Availability of pricing mechanisms.

[20] "*And putting aside the fundraising that accompanied the creation of Ether, based on my understanding of the present state of Ether, the Ethereum network and its decentralized structure, current offers and sales of Ether are not securities transactions*" [125].

[21] "*Whether or not a particular transaction involves the offer and sale of a security - regardless of the terminology used - will depend on the facts and circumstances, including the economic realities of the transaction*" [126].

[22] In [127] the SEC charged that failure to disclose the consideration received for promoting a token offering is a violation of the anti-touting provisions of the Securities Act of 1933, Section 17 (b) (https://www.sec.gov/news/press-release/2021-125).

[23] "*Market participants should use caution when promoting or touting the offer and sale of coins without first determining whether the securities laws apply to those actions. Similarly, those who operate systems and platforms that effect or facilitate transactions in these products should be aware that they may be operating unregistered exchanges or broker-dealers that are in violation of the Securities Exchange Act of 1934*" [128].

- Implementation of asset management mechanisms.
- Account and wallet compatibility.

An on-chain security token may be simply a tokenized security (representation of positions in off-chain assets, such as shares or corporate bonds, originally registered outside any blockchain) or it may be a "native" security token[24] (representing rights to assets or income streams registered only on the same or other blockchains[25]), or a mixture of the two. The token design must specify clearly both the assets (in terms of identifiers, especially pre-registered off-chain ones such as ISIN and related LEI numbers) and the mode of its registration on-chain (especially if smart contracts will be involved [137]). Especially for off-chain assets, there are (pre- and post-transaction) legal issues related to their custody [138] that simply cannot be ignored when designing the token. Provision of accurate current *prices* for a security or derivative token may hinge either on the availability of on-chain transaction history through the targeted trading venue type (Centralized or Decentralized Exchange; simply registering last transaction prices, or keeping an order book), or through Oracles [139, 140]. Absent the availability of, or ease of procuring, current prices on account of the token design (say because on- and off-chain assets are mixed in the same underlying portfolio and updates to their individual prices have different latencies) can create resistance to token acceptance by buyers and investors and will probably attract regulatory attention to the whole token project business case, e.g. due to investor protection laws and "best-execution" obligations [141–146]. The problem is even more pronounced in the case of derivative tokens, where pricing time delays may detract from the risk management proposition of the token and may actually introduce legal risks for the issuing project on account of material misrepresentation [147, 148].

Asset management of positions represented by the token refers mainly to portfolio rebalancing and asset servicing. In the most generic case of a security token representing a portfolio of positions, the relative weighting of these positions may be changing from time to time through the intervention of either a human or an algorithm (e.g. smart contract) implementing a particular investment strategy, or restoring asset class allocation limits. This rebalancing must be possible to register on-chain and propagate to accounts and crypto wallets. Token design must provide for such post-transaction registration/event propagation in technically and legally robust ways and specify these in the investor documentation. Failure to do so may create unforeseen tax repercussions for buyers and investors, and also blind spots in reporting views, for trading venues where the token is traded on the one hand, and for on-chain brokers and financial advisors on the other. The asset servicing angle stems from all operational activities relating to fees; allocation of induced income streams (e.g. crediting/reinvesting dividends of equity- or equity-like positions; coupons of fixed-income positions; vesting of other rights); asset conversions;

---

[24] We follow the terminology of [135] in the present context.

[25] For example, generalizations of wrapped tokens [136].

position expirations/rollovers; splits/reverse splits; position valuation, etc. Irrespective of how (by humans, algorithms, or both) and where (off-/on-chain, mixed) these activities are performed, token design must account for them. Tokens with explicit or implicit position optionalities (e.g. derivative tokens and security tokens with embedded convertible assets) have the additional complication that their underlying property rights are meant to be transformed during token lifetime by design, hence they must be able to reliably assign new identifiers and asset class descriptions on-chain (eventually having to include primary off-chain reference data through Oracles, and also synchronize with off-chain datasources such as central securities depositories and registrars of intermediated securities). The lifecycle of derivative tokens, in particular, generally involves significant off-chain documentation requirements, documentation which must be kept-in sync with on-chain events in a technically and legally robust manner [149]. Security tokens are investment products, so they are expected to be as transparent for investors, financial advisors, trading venues, and custodians as traditional asset classes are. Both corporates and privates also reasonably expect a financial instrument to be easy to import into some sort of treasury. In the digital world, it would mean either a custody account with a legal entity that is authorized and able to provide such accounts, or a crypto wallet (hardware- or software based), or both. However, not all accounts and not all crypto wallets have the same functional and technical characteristics. This is why the token designer must be proactive in avoiding building technical features (or make the design dependent on platform or third-party features) such that would make it difficult to use the token with at least the most prevalent account and crypto wallet types used by serious investors. Two functional features are important to mention in this respect:

(a) **Custody-Account accessibility** from both Decentralized and Centralized Exchanges.
(b) **Multi-signature wallet compatibility**.

Multi-signature ("multi-sig") wallets are crypto wallets that require two or more private keys to sign before a transaction can be executed. They are typically used by token exchanges, investment fund managers, brokers, etc., as transaction-level authorization controls to guard against fraud or hacking risk.[26] They are also recommended for private investors and their financial advisors/trustees looking to set up a shared crypto-asset custody account (e.g. crypto-investment account accessible by all named family members[27]); settle a trust with crypto-assets as property; or an escrow account (e.g. for the sale of property, where part of the transaction funds or of the collateral is in crypto-assets). For example, they can be configured for "*m-of-n*" setups.[28] Some multi-sig wallet vendors also allow to "inherit" pre-existing

[26] Similarly to how brick-and-mortar bank safety boxes, or vaults, require more than one key to open. Hence the term "Vault" also in use for multi-sig wallets.

[27] Whenever the intention is for no single person to be able to change the composition of the investment portfolio or to unilaterally transfer funds out of the account.

[28] E.g., "3-of-4", meaning "if any 3 of the 4 authorized addresses sign, then allow the transaction".

single-signature wallets into a new "multi-signature address"[29] [150]. For individual investors, this reduces the risk that a wallet's private key is forgotten or lost after a person's incapacitation or death. They are particularly useful in the context of crypto-assets settled as property of discretionary or testamentary trusts (i.e. private trusts created under a will and taking effect only upon the settlor's death), as they allow better control of when exactly the funds leave the control of the settlor, and also better alignment of several trustees at once[30] with the settlor's wishes. Of course, they are best considered as part of an end-to-end crypto-asset protection or estate planning process [151] as they still can have their own particular risks [152, 153]. The important fact for the token designer is that multi-sig wallets are enabled at the L-1 and L-2 protocol layers. Once activated, then any higher-layer tokens on the same L-1/L-2s are immediately compatible with the wallet. So, if a token is in effect the native cryptocurrency of a new L-1 and/or L-2 platform, then the project must proactively take all necessary steps for multi-sig compatibility of their protocol. Should it turn out, for whatever technical or organizational reasons, that the token does not allow multi-sig wallet functionality, then a whole class of investors may choose to avoid it.

Utility tokens can be broadly classified into five subtypes as per typology shown earlier in the chapter on Fig. 10.5, namely: governance, access, service, discount, and "burn & mint" tokens. Property rights to an asset or a direct income stream are not typically found in governance, access, or "burn & mint",[31] but they are expected when buying **service** or **discount** tokens. These may indeed fall under securities laws and regulatory obligations; thus, the token design and project lifecycle have to take them into account. The business model behind service tokens is actually rather old in the off-chain world[32] and continues to be standard practice, e.g.. in the form of performance bonds in project finance [158]. The terms of offering/accepting to perform the service; and what constitutes service completion; are the main points that need to be somehow captured in the token design. In discount tokens, both the direct asset (benefit in the form of a discount) of acquiring the token and any ancillary income stream have to be well described and represented appropriately in the token, or correctly and robustly referenced through the token. The terms of both transactions (the discount token exchange and the at-discount purchase of the associated object) may have important repercussions for tax, and potentially for

[29] E.g., when bringing individual hardware wallets under a single "multi-sig" setup.

[30] Or of Trustees and Protectors, in particular Trust contexts depending on the governing law jurisdiction.

[31] These in effect replicate the off-chain business model of "Group Buying Schemes" [154]. However, the object of the group buying must specifically exclude investments [155].

[32] Purchasing officer commissions was standard practice in some European armies before the twentieth century (cf. for instance [156]), the deposited sums being forfeited in cases of cowardice or gross misconduct (the "incentive" aspect in the token case)—hence the term "cashiering an officer" [157], meaning reducing him of any rank. The incoming consideration in the contract law sense was, of course, the salary and rewards of the rank (corresponding to the "income stream" in the case of tokens).

AML/CFT, purposes. In both service and discount token cases, the issuing project; trading venue, brokers/intermediaries; and the token purchaser will need expert legal advice on how best to fulfil these obligations. The token designer must be at least cognizant of how specific token features may trigger such obligations.

Assets classes already tokenized through **non-fungible tokens** are as varied [159] as internet memorabilia [160]; online game artefacts [161]; digital art [162, 163]; digital postal stamps [164]; physical collectibles, such as wines and paintings [165]; warehouse stocks [166, 167]; and trade finance receivables [168]. However, what exactly is represented through the NFT itself (what title to which property rights and through which ownership structures), and hence what the intrinsic value of the NFT is can be difficult for the buyer or investor to ascertain. Similarly, as obligations of NFT transaction participants for on-chain fees and off-chain reporting (e.g. for accounting and tax purposes) are dependent on what exactly was exchanged during the transaction and which laws and regulations apply, the NFT property rights specification is of fundamental importance for its value proposition as an investment.

The problem is particularly evident in precisely the "low-hanging" NFT business case, i.e. that of tokenizing digital art. The latter may have been created—or be commissioned as part of the NFT issuance—either on- or off-chain. If off-chain, there is nothing to distinguish it from traditional, physical artwork. It still must be authenticated, stored, preserved, and retrieved for expositions and due diligence. In effect, its off-chain nature is completely distinct from its NFT tokenization. There are two assets involved: the original digital work and the NFT. How are the two linked to each other? Does the legal agreement specify that buying the NFT means buying the exclusive rights to the digital work itself or is it silent on that point?

Copyright law usually provides that the author of a digital work may elect to keep the intellectual property rights to the original, indeed to keep reproducing copies of it. The NFT issuer may offer to the market not a single NFT, but a limited number of NFTs to be issued against the same original; this is also perfectly legal, as long as not validly specified otherwise. In this case, the NFT buyer or investor will end up acquiring in effect simply a "certified digital copy" of an original digital artwork. There may indeed be an investment case to such an acquisition on account of the induced scarcity of the limited number of NFT's, but this much should be clear to the buyer or investor: unless the transaction contract specifies otherwise, the NFT transaction may involve acquiring a certified digital copy of the original and not the original itself.

Even in the case of physical works of art tokenized through NFTs, which property rights on the original the NFT actually confers should by no means be a foregone conclusion. For example, a copyright owner typically[33] retains exclusive rights to reproduce, prepare derivative works of, perform, display, and distribute the copyrighted work. Hence, even in the physical art world, purchasing a work of art does not transfer all copyright in said work to the buyer. Buying a physical painting from an artist gives the buyer the right to possess and display it, but does not transfer

[33] As under section 106 [169] of the US Copyright Act [170].

the rights to reproduce, or even distribute copies of the original painting away from the artist. Only if the artist, by valid contract, explicitly sells away these ancillary rights as part of the transaction, does then the buyer acquire them. Similarly, only legally valid documentation about the actual property rights to a work of art that is being offered for sale by way of tokenization through an NFT can create certainty to the buyer about the object of the transaction. If this documentation is unavailable or in any way deficient, then, in cases related to art—digital or physical—the NFT owner may find that even displaying representations of the underlying object in public (in galleries or on the internet) is prohibited by law.

In general, the holder of the original copyright may also claim royalties on every future income stream that is attributable to the NFT. For example, the documentation of the NFT transaction may provide that monetization through derivative uses (e.g. by allowing the digital image to be printed on postcards, apparel, or memorabilia) is allowed, as long as a fixed percentage of these money flows returns to the copyright owner. Similarly for a percentage of the proceeds of each subsequent sale of the NFT itself; this is indeed legally valid and technically feasible as long as the transactions are on-chain and the requisite updated information is encoded by design, e.g. through a smart contract (cf. for Ethereum NFTs the EIP-2981 smart contract standard [171] for handling royalty payments related to ERC-721 tokens). Hence, in this case the functional and technical aspects of token design must be aligned with the underlying property rights structure (both fixed and contingent) ab initio. Neglecting to do this may create considerable legal risks for future NFT owners as claims may arrive from as yet unknown plaintiffs and jurisdictions. At a minimum, transparency and integrity of the documented links between the NFT itself, the underlying object, and the latter's storage location (physical or electronic) must be assured, and either directly visible on-chain or reconstitutable through on-chain data. However, the optimal situation from the point of view of legal clarity would be if also the underlying, physical, legal contract of the entire NFT transaction were also represented in some on-chain form. This way there would be no ambiguity for the object of the transaction and, should at some point in the future the technical token implementation prove to be in some way non-representative of the contractual intent, then the legal contract itself might at least advise good-faith novation and ultimately arbitration. In some blockchains, there is no good technical reason why the legal contract itself could not be represented independently on-chain.[34]

Fractional-NFTs (F-NFTs) inherit all of the afore-mentioned legal structure issues and also add an additional one: that they may actually be financial securities. Should the original, whole, NFT prove to be in effect a managed investment asset (e.g. if its owner expects regular income streams due to royalty participations or other monetization avenues, and/or it has experienced steady valuation growth in an

[34] For example, as already mentioned in Sect. 10.5.1, the Bitcoin Satoshi Vision (BSV) blockchain already admits block sizes of the order of GBs. The first-blockchain-generation argument that on-chain memory is always expensive may not be totally true in some contexts. In any case, the alternative (not persisting potentially material information and choosing to assume or propagate the resulting risks) may be even more expensive in the long run.

active marketplace), then, irrespective of the nature of the underlying asset to the NFT, the essential features of a financial security[35] are most probably present in the derivative F-NFTs. As in the generic security token case, the implications of characterization as financial security for the token project governance and oversight (e.g. relating to licensing; authorizations; documentation; publicity/roadshows notification; selling, etc.); for the imputed controls framework on the token trading venue[36]; as well as for end-buyer transaction reporting obligations; can be significant.

Please note that token classification as financial security is in principle also possible for a "whole" NFT; it is just more probable for F-NFTs.

There is still another important point that makes clarity of property rights specification a crucial token design success factor. Namely, the all too real prospect of token positions being used as collateral in on-chain, off-chain, and mixed on-/off-chain financial transactions. Such transactions can be as simple as private mortgages and Lombard loans or as sophisticated as OTC structured repos and swaps, the nature of title passing notwithstanding (liens; pledges; mortgages; deeds, etc.). Collateral eligible asset classes need to pass due diligence on two fronts: legal title and valuation. As explained in Sect. 10.5.4, assuming that there exists an observable market price or comparable transactions, valuation should not be a problem for crypto-assets. The legal title and how to corroborate it,[37] however, may indeed become a stumbling block if ambiguities of any sort (especially in the case of NFTs) arise. At a minimum, the clearer and more unambiguous the structure of property rights underlying the token, the higher its acceptability as collateral, hence potentially its entire value proposition in the eyes of buyers and investors. In more sophisticated transactional settings (e.g. bilateral transactions among financial institutions and large professional investors), the governing law of both the token title(s) and the financial transaction, as well as the potentially involved jurisdictions[38] (of counterparties; assets; seat of arbitration) may bring even more legal aspects into focus.

As with any property, there are private law aspects relating to family law; usufruct; trusts; inheritance; bankruptcy; encumbrance; securitization; asset following/tracing; proprietary injunctions; freezing orders, etc., that will make any defect in the legal rights built into a crypto-asset focus of court proceedings sooner or later. In extreme cases, when liability of any sort can be traced back to the project issuing the original token, such defects may (on account of the global nature of blockchain

[35]E.g., in a US context, cf. [172] for the "Howey Test" definition.

[36]For example, the US Anti-Money Laundering (AML) Act of 2020 ([173], part of [174]) expands the definition of a financial institution under the Bank Secrecy Act [175, 176, 177] to include "dealers in art" and companies active in the business of exchanging or transmitting virtual currencies. Thus, it is conceivable that some crypto-exchanges may be caught under this definition.

[37]E.g., where is the title registered? Where are encumbrances to the title registered? On a blockchain or on a blockchain explorer? Does registration through blockchain explorer carry the same legal force as on-chain registration?

[38]In an EU setting, the current consultation document for the 2021 review of the Financial Collateral Directive [178] explicitly refers to Crypto-assets as collateral in item 5.

transactions) result in a cascade of claims from several plaintiff classes, in several jurisdictions, at once.

As per the above, underlying **property rights and their structuring** have repercussions for token:

- **Asset class categorization**. In several cases, the token may be deemed to be a financial security, whereas in others the precise asset acquired may be subject to third-party rights. Subsequently, the associated risk and payoff profiles may determine token eligibility for repackaging into more complex on- and off-chain investments (investment funds; token derivatives; structured products; securitized instruments, etc.).
- **Obligations accruing to issuing project**. Should the token be classified as financial security, in most jurisdictions, there are strict legal and regulatory requirements for issuer authorization, instrument registration, investor communications, etc., as already explained in detail. Failure to satisfy said requirements will expose the token project to significant legal risks. Even if it is not a financial security, correct mapping of property rights (fixed and contingent) into the token's technical design may necessitate repeated iterations which can translate into forced protocol upgrades and associated migration costs.
- **Admissibility in trading venues**. Classification of the token as financial security will impose registration/authorization obligations and imputed pre- and post-transaction controls on the trading venue. This may restrict its visibility to only a subset of all potential buyers, thus delaying its achieving network effects.
- **Acquirer eligibility**. In some jurisdictions, acquiring and owning privately issued cryptocurrencies is prohibited by law. In others, investor suitability regulations ban provision of financial advice related to particular crypto-assets (such as crypto-derivatives) to non-qualified investors. In general, the nature of the token may influence the matrix of buyer categories and jurisdictions which it will be allowed to be offered to.
- **Transaction and holding costs**. Depending on the underlying asset and income stream of the token, there may be associated transaction fees (sales tax, stamp-duty, capital gains tax, etc.) and holding costs (withholding tax, royalties, service fees, asset storage fees, platform fees, etc.). These may influence the investment value proposition of the token for prospective buyers.
- **Reporting obligations to/by the acquirer**. The nature of tax reporting obligations on the buyer/investor per token transaction will depend on the jurisdiction. Should the token be classified as a financial security, then it generally can be expected that there will be at least imputed reporting obligations on the trading venue towards the buyer/investor and towards its regulator; on any involved custodians towards the buyer/investor; on involved investment advisors towards the buyer/investor and towards their regulator; etc. There may also be cross-border reporting obligations depending on the token type and jurisdictions involved.

In conclusion, as with any property, there are legal and regulatory aspects relating to acquiring; holding; protecting; selling; and passing-on tokens that may well make any material defect in their underlying legal rights subject to court proceedings.

In extreme cases, when liability of any sort can be traced back to the project issuing the original token, such defects may (on account of the global nature of blockchain transactions) result in a cascade of parallel claims originating from several plaintiff classes in several jurisdictions. Assigning liability and deciding remedies will unavoidably involve examining aspects of domicile (asset, owner, blockchain platform, project governance, etc.) and of the transaction (parties, contractual arrangements, controls, perfection, reporting) in order to decide what exactly was passed on as property, when, where, and how.

The important duty of the token designer in that respect is to contribute to minimizing the legal risks to the issuing project and to its potential acquirers by proactively building into the token the highest possible transparency and robustness in reference to its underlying property rights.

10.5.7 Minting Optionalities

Deciding how to acquire a newly minted token (e.g. whether to buy it at issuance; or to perform validating work in exchange for it, etc.) is obviously at the acquirer's discretion, but this is not what "minting optionalities" stands for. This token design factor refers to the *built-in configurability* of a token *at issuance*, in a way that leaves detailed specification of its underlying property rights to the discretion of the buyer. In effect, minting optionalities are degrees of freedom relating to property rights structuring, and risk-return profiles. The new token is minted bespoke with these optionalities (usually codified as input parameters to a minting smart contract). A good example of such design are non-fungible tokens (NFTs) issued to liquidity providers for each concentrated liquidity position in Uniswap V3 [179]. To best explain the inherent minting optionality, we need to begin from the concept of the constant product market maker, as implemented in earlier Uniswap versions [180].

In traditional financial markets, buyers and sellers of securities come together in auction-based marketplaces. An order-book is kept by authorized agents, and bids/offers are matched based on its entries. A central role in the orderly execution of trades is played by Market Makers [181] (MMs), marketplace-authorized[39] entities or individuals who have the obligation to be always[40] prepared to take the opposite side of transactions, i.e. to quote both bid and offer price pairs. That is, even when there are no external offers, the market maker must step in and quote an offer price to

[39]For an example of localized market-making terms and conditions, please consult [182].

[40]Typically barring "exceptional circumstances", which are defined by marketplace governance in accordance with local regulations.

any prospective bid—and a bid price to any prospective offer.[41] Market makers assume non-trivial market risk (which needs to be hedged with both securities inventory and derivatives), compensated for by getting unique visibility to the order-book and order-flow—a privilege accorded to them by the marketplace organization, in exchange precisely for their obligation to always provide liquidity to the market. Hence, a market maker needs to be able to predict a "probable" price level for the next trade and a corresponding "fair" level of the bid/ask spread. The business model of market makers rests mainly on an income stream through bid/ask spreads and also on taking the de facto "right" side of transactions at market floors and ceilings. Of course, nowadays "market maker" means in effect "Market Making algorithm behind authorized humans", with sophisticated mathematics[42] [184] to match. For the purposes of the current discussion, please keep in mind that "market maker" means in effect "Obliged Liquidity Provider" in traditional finance.

In a blockchain context, centralized exchanges (CEXs) can and do use order-books for order matching and execution. Decentralized exchanges are a different matter, however, and this is where Uniswap V2 made a difference with its original automated market maker model and implementation—the constant product market maker (CPMM [185, 186]). The concept behind the CPMM is the creation of a pool containing quantities of both the target token (what is bought, similar to the share or bond or other traded asset which the traditional MM makes the market in) and the transaction token (what is it bought with, similar to the fiat currency or other asset that the traditional MM exchanges in return). The, deceptively simple, mathematical formula linking the target and transaction token quantities (Y and X, respectively) in the pool at all times is: $X \cdot Y = C$ (with C being a constant).

That is, a Uniswap V2 investor (a "Liquidity Provider" —LP for short, term which seeks to relate to the function of the traditional MM) can contribute a total sum of X and Y tokens at any given time, and their initial Y-to-X proportion will be dictated by the point on which the curve X-Y finds itself at this time.[43] The investor will be compensated by a proportion of the platform trading fees from then on (similar to the "spread" that a traditional MM makes his money from), but their position composition going forward will be dictated by the evolution of the market prices of X and Y. If their relative market prices move from (X_0, Y_0) to (X_1, Y_1), then the value of the LP's position changes as per the curve (cf. Fig. 10.11).

As per research referenced from the official Uniswap documentation [187], the payoff of a LP position can be replicated with a static combination of futures and options. In effect, what the LPs invest into is what in traditional finance is termed a structured product [188, 189]. The decentralized (blockchain) nature of the CPMM adds a dependency to the payoff profile, as does the compensating fee structure

---

[41] Cf. also the case study introduction in Sect. 13.1 and thereafter in that chapter.

[42] An excellent introduction to the mathematics of Market Making in non-derivative markets can be found in Chap. 11 of [183].

[43] Cf. the detailed *exposé* on the mechanics of such "Bonding Functions" in the subsequent Chap. 12.

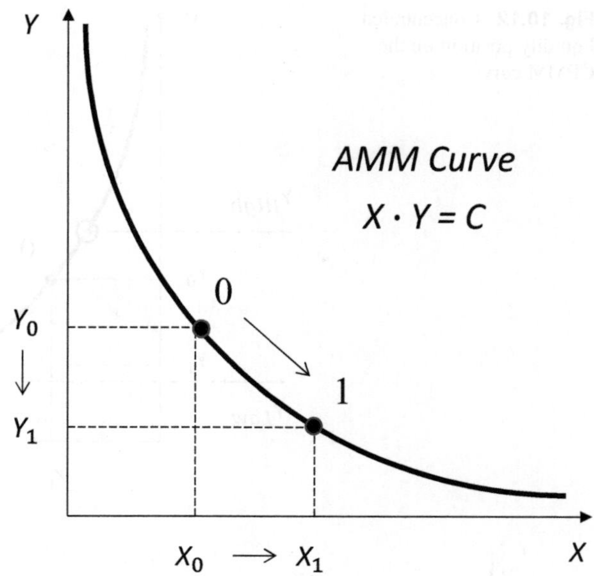

Fig. 10.11 Constant Product Market Maker curve

(yield returns to liquidity providers) of the protocol [190]. Again, as per Uniswap research [191], pool growth (in essence, increasing pool depth caused by the network effect) increases the price range around the target-operating point[44] within which the LP position is "in the money".

Note that a CPMM is only one of closed-form "Automated Market Maker" (AMM) solutions [192, 193].

The third generation of Uniswap ("Uniswap V3") introduced the notion of "Concentrated Liquidity" [194] (Fig. 10.12), which in basic terms gives the option to the LP to specify the exact range of token parities [$\frac{X}{Y}\big|_{\text{Low}}$, $\frac{X}{Y}\big|_{\text{High}}$] within which they are investing. If token prices stay outside this range, then there is no liquidity provision. Once parities move within the range, the LP position is created in the form of a non-fungible token (NFT) which is minted by smart contract and allocated to the LP address. Interestingly, the underlying assets of this NFT (its property rights structure as per Sect. 10.5.6) change as token parities change and end up being single-token positions as the range extremities are crossed. The concept behind issuing a non-fungible, as opposed to a fungible, token is to account for the specificity of each individual range selection, in effect encapsulating the "minting optionality" of V3 tokens.

As explained in the Uniswap v3 whitepaper and further analysed in the trade literature [195], each individual concentrated liquidity position can be interpreted as creating a new automated market maker of constant product type, in transformed coordinates (X′,Y′) (Fig. 10.13).

---

[44]We refrain from using the word "Strike", as it is not currently part of the Uniswap vocabulary.

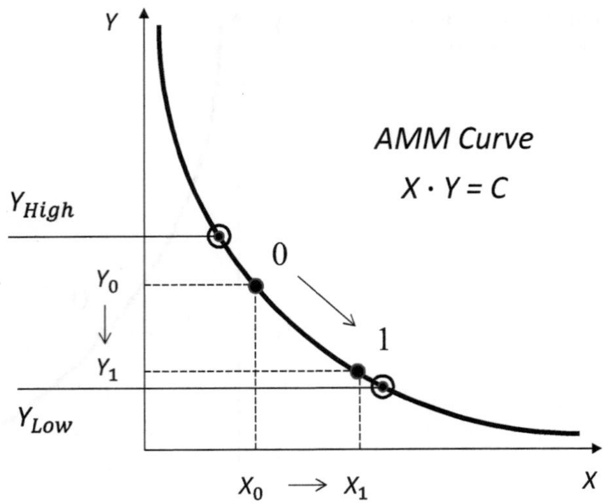

Fig. 10.12 Concentrated liquidity position on the CPMM curve

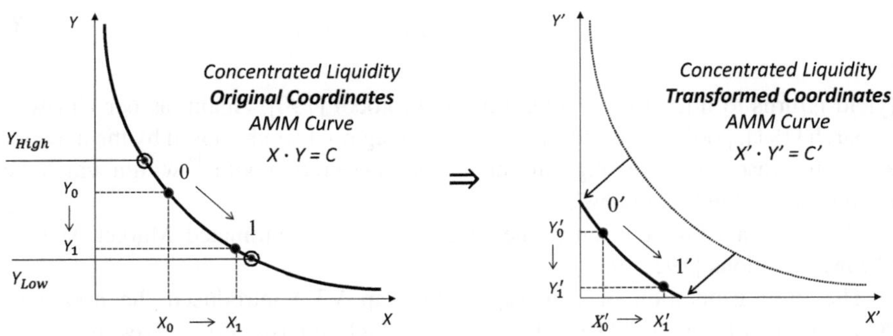

Fig. 10.13 Concentrated liquidity position in transformed (X,Y) coordinates

The reason for enablement of concentrated liquidity on Uniswap was the complexity of representing, then assessing, the risk-return profile of each LP position along the entire AMM curve. This means in practice that a LP investor could be caught in a strongly and persistently trending market in one of the X,Y tokens, whereby the pool fee income could not compensate for the market risk of his initial position in the pool [196]. Simply put, had the investor acquired the exact same X and Y amounts of the two tokens and kept them outside the market making pool, the valuation of his investment in time would turn out to be higher than that of his LP plus market-making fee. By making the investment in the non-concentrated LP, the investor ends up experiencing a deteriorating position valuation ("Impermanent Loss" [197]), which can be reversed only if the two tokens return to a favourable market price range. This is nothing new to seasoned traditional finance investors who simply accept the market risk of investing in the stock and commodity markets—where the exact same position deterioration is termed "Unrealized Loss" [198] (or "paper loss" for the optimists …). Looking at it another way, there are good reasons why traditional financial institutions use both position warehousing *and* derivatives to hedge their market making operations …

As the Uniswap documentation correctly points out [199], the right way to think about a concentrated LP is of it being a range order. Quoting verbatim:

> *Customizable liquidity positions, along with single-sided asset provisioning, allow for a new style of swapping with automated market makers: the range order. ...*
>
> *The nature of AMM design makes some styles of limit orders possible, while others cannot be replicated. The following are four examples of range orders and their traditional counterparts; the first two are possible, the second two are not.*[45]

Some protocols (for example: Curve [200, 201]) chose to minimize market risk by enabling concentrated liquidity only for assets that are expected to trade in close ranges (such as Stablecoins) or that are otherwise strongly correlated [202, 203]. This is yet another indication of the complexity that can be built into a token (in this case, the NFT minted on Uniswap to represent the concentrated LP position) on the basis of minting optionalities.

Based on the above analysis, token-**minting optionalities** have repercussions for token:

- **Asset class categorization**. In several cases, the token may be deemed to be a financial security, on account of the minting optionality alone. Subsequently, the associated risk and payoff profiles may determine token appropriateness for particular investors (investor suitability).
- **Transaction and holding costs**. Depending on the underlying asset and income stream of the token, there may be unclear payoffs (cf. the potential for "Impermanent Loss"). These may influence the investment value proposition of the token to prospective buyers.
- **Sustainability**. The intended beneficial effects of minting optionalities may be reachable only upon attaining a network effect. However, if there are unintended consequences on account of a less-than-robust token design, its ecosystem may never attain this effect.

As with any optionality, it can have both beneficial effects and unintended consequences. The token designer should strive to understand both before proceeding with a robust technical implementation. At the absolute minimum, the business justification; the algorithmic foundation; and the high-level operational implementation; of any minting optionalities must be documented clearly in the issuing project whitepaper.

[45] Our note: first, rsp. second pair, are "Take-profit" and "Buy-Limit", rsp. "Buy-Stop" and "Stop-Loss", orders.

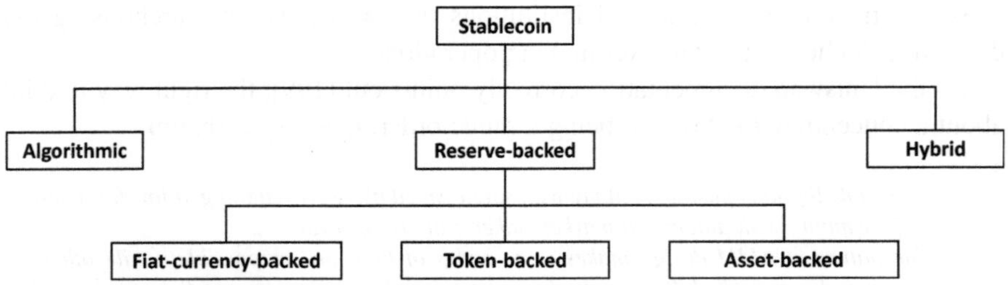

Fig. 10.14 Stablecoin price stabilization mechanisms

10.5.8 Token Treasury Structure

Every token ecosystem has governance structures which need financing in order to keep providing their essential services. As explained in the chapter on mechanism design, orchestrating such financing entails implementing a system of incentives and rewards usually involving the platform tokens, and also a centralized system of accounts for the entire ecosystem—the protocol treasury [204]. However, the discussion in the present context revolves around a different kind of treasury, i.e. the **token treasury**. We define this to be a system of accounts directly supporting the price *of a particular token type*.

In principle, both altcoins and Stablecoins can have a token treasury. In the former case, it can serve as the asset base to both implement an investment policy through, and redistribute platform value by, the token (e.g. the OlympusDAO [205, 206] treasury [207] supporting the OHM [208] token). However, **token treasury structure** as a design factor is most prominent in the case of Stablecoins, as it relates directly to their ability to maintain their target peg. With reference to their price stabilization mechanisms, existing industry terminology categorizes Stablecoins into one of the following types (cf. Fig. 10.14):

- **Algorithmic**
- **Reserve-backed**
- **Hybrid**

This is a rather theoretical categorization as we will explain shortly, but we have to have it in place in order to explain some token treasury fundamentals clearly.

Theoretically, "**Algorithmic**" could be expected to be interpreted as "**purely algorithmic**". Their value proposition is that by monitoring in near real-time the difference between the target reference asset (e.g. 1 USD) and the market price of the tracking Stablecoin, one can in principle intervene in the latter's supply and so mechanically steer towards the peg. In blockchain terms, burning tokens will remove them from circulation, and thus (assuming locally steady demand) will increase their market price. Inversely, minting tokens will increase supply, and thus (ditto for demand) will decrease their price. Thus, if the Stablecoin is trading at a discount (resp. premium) to the USD, burning (resp. minting) some amount of the former will cause it to move towards parity. The technical aspect of estimating the amount to mint or to burn is what makes this paradigm "purely algorithmic".

The concept behind the "**Reserve-backed**" category is the existence of a backing asset pool to manage market risk and liquidity/funding risks. To explain it, one needs to consider the simple Stablecoin issuance and redemption steps. To acquire a Stablecoin, buyers pay the issuing platform in fiat currency or in any admissible crypto-asset. The protocol extracts transaction fees/commissions and then transfers the remaining funds to the supporting asset pool, the "Reserve", against which the Stablecoin is issued *at par*. To sell it back to the issuing platform, they return the Stablecoin and receive the equivalent amount of either fiat currency or admissible crypto-assets *at par*. So, this primary market mechanism acts in effect as a central bank treasury.

The treasurer can change the asset mix (buy and sell fiat currencies or crypto-assets) to best defend the peg. The need for actively managing such a reserve comes from four main facts:

(a) The target peg of the Stablecoin (say 1 USD) may have different price dynamics than the fiat currencies or the crypto-assets exchanged for it. If 6 months ago the buyer exchanged 10 tokens of cryptocurrency A worth 1.05 USD to buy a Stablecoin B with nominal value 1 USD, and today comes back to the platform to sell the Stablecoin in return for crypto-assets, there is no guarantee that the 10 A tokens are still worth around 1 USD. If the price of A decreased in the last 6 months, then, had the treasurer simply kept the original assets in the reserve, the platform would be losing money with this redemption transaction. If enough holders asked to sell their Stablecoins back to the platform at the same time, then there would be not enough assets to return. Then the treasurer would have to make a decision: either to keep redeeming Stablecoin B at par (i.e. 1 USD) and hope that new buyers will progressively replenish the reserve; or start returning the exact same crypto-assets that the old buyers originally paid-in, with the result that the value of Stablecoin A (as redeemed by its issuing platform) would be less than 1 USD, i.e. that it would be losing its peg.

(b) Several major Stablecoins are issued as collateralized debt positions, i.e. the buyer deposits other tokens as collateral and in return is credited the Stablecoins. However, the latter are simply a loan—on which interest is charged. Furthermore, protocols typically reserve the right to adjust parameters calibrating Stablecoin holdings such as requisite overcollateralization thresholds. In effect, the deposited tokens (usually of higher initial value than the at-par Stablecoins returned; hence, the use of the term "overcollateralization") need to be monitored for market risk. Otherwise, the cumulative debt position—Stablecoins at issuance plus accrued interest—might become undercollateralized and have to be called in. Thus, the protocol *has* to keep position-level accounting across all Stablecoin buyers.

(c) If not prohibited by mechanism design, the paid-in assets can in principle be invested in several ways on- and off-chain to generate returns for the platform. What percentage of assets and with which investment horizon to invest is a

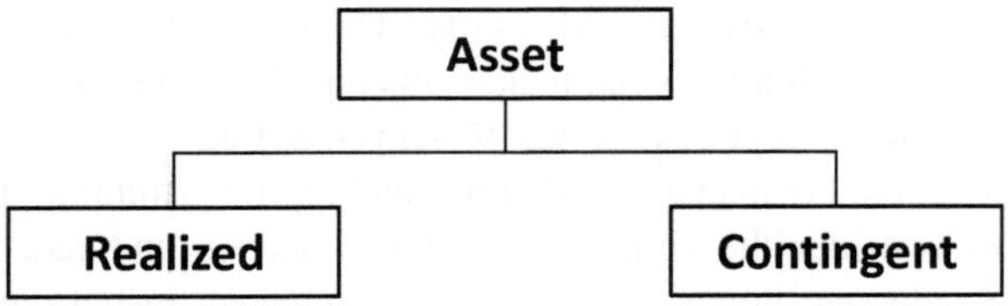

Fig. 10.15 Token reserve asset types

matter of platform policy and treasurer discretion. If the treasurer decides to tie up a part of the assets in mid- to long-term investments, then there may be not be enough assets to satisfy Stablecoin redemption requests in the short-term. This may again threaten the peg effectiveness, and, in adverse scenarios of market evolution, the viability of the token project if some of those investments produce material losses instead of gains.

(d) Paid-in crypto-assets may still be earning profits for the Stablecoin buyer as per purchase terms, or may be linked with governance or utility tokens participating in platform rewards pools (as agreed incentives for buying the Stablecoin in the first place). If these profits/rewards are to be capitalized on-chain (say, through smart contracts), then the reserve balance sheet is a dynamic one by design.

Hence, reserve-backed Stablecoin operations are akin to traditional asset/liability management, now centred around the working assets (the "Reserve") of a token "Treasury".

A **"Hybrid"** Stablecoin would be one combining both "Algorithmic" and "Reserve-backed" features.

In this theoretical worldview, the Stablecoin taxonomy would be indeed as depicted in Fig. 10.14. There are reference examples for coins that were originally intended to be purely fiat-currency-backed (Tether [209], USD coin [210]), token-backed (MakerDAO DAI [211]), or generally asset-backed.

Importantly, said assets can be both realized (or "fixed") and contingent (such as banking guarantees, e.g. CryptoFranc [212]), cf. Fig. 10.15. In both cases, the Stablecoin is considered to be generally "Asset-backed".

However, theoretical classification aside, current industry dynamics suggest that most Stablecoin projects appear to be moving to the "Hybrid" category. Simply put, in spite of the "puristic" views explained in original whitepapers, both established and new Stablecoin projects de facto implement both the algorithmic and reserve-backed paradigms. Thus, it is very important to have an informed view of possible treasury structures for the purposes of token design in general, and Stablecoin design in particular.

We propose the fundamentals of such a view in the Stablecoin case, centred around two diagrams:

(a) **Stablecoin Protocol Token Model** (Fig. 10.16)
(b) **"Treasury" Balance Sheet** (Fig. 10.17)

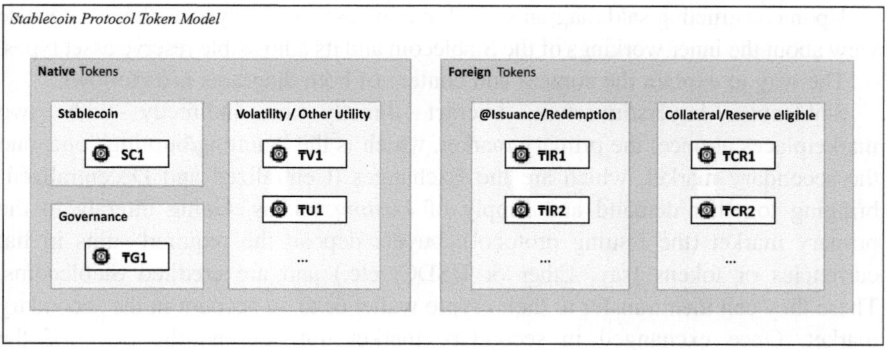

Fig. 10.16 All tokens in a generic Stablecoin's whitepaper: the Stablecoin Protocol Token Model

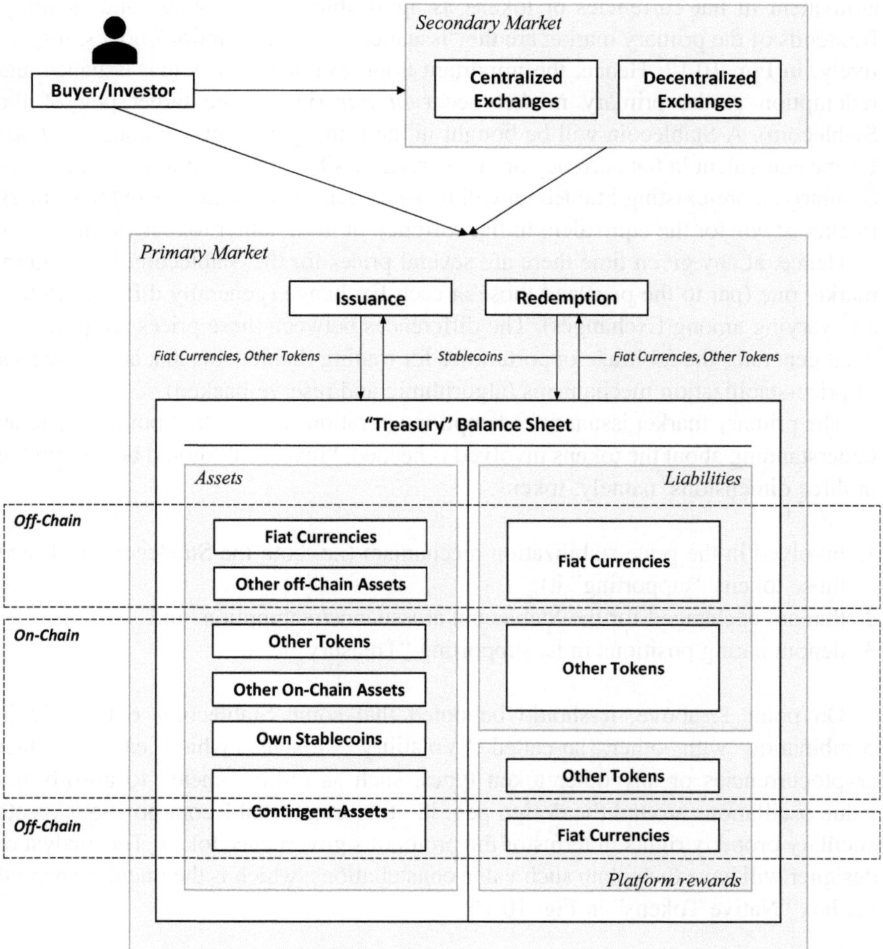

Fig. 10.17 "Treasury" balance sheet for stablecoins. Assets = Liabilities + Platform rewards

Upon constructing said diagrams, the buyer/investor or analyst can have a concise view about the inner workings of the Stablecoin and its admissible reserve asset types.

The way to explain the context and content of both diagrams is as follows:

Stablecoin buyers/investors interact—directly or indirectly—with two marketplaces at once: the primary market, which is the "minting/burning" one, and the secondary market, which are the Exchanges (Centralized and Decentralized) bringing together demand and supply of *existing* tokens. Going directly to the primary market (the issuing protocol), buyers deposit the required sums in fiat currencies or tokens (say, Ether or USDC, etc.) and are credited Stablecoins. These they can then transfer to their crypto wallet or to an account in the secondary market. Once exchanged in secondary market transactions, the price of the Stablecoin is the observed "market" price reported in trading sites. The "market" price dynamics are precisely what causes the deviation of Stablecoins from their peg. Stablecoin owners can sell them back to the primary market, in exchange for the equivalent in fiat currencies or tokens as applicable. The "buying" and "selling" frontends of the primary market are the "issuance" and "redemption" boxes, respectively, in Fig. 10.17. Hence, the important thing to remember is that issuance and redemption at the primary market occur *at par* (i.e. at the target peg of the Stablecoin). A Stablecoin will be bought in the primary market—"issued"—*at par* for the equivalent in fiat currency or in other, admissible, tokens (plus platform fees). Similarly, a pre-existing Stablecoin will be sold back—"redeemed"—in the primary market *at par* for the equivalent in fiat currency or in the other tokens (minus fees).

Hence, at any given time there are several prices for the Stablecoin: the primary market one (par to the peg) and those at each Exchange (generally different to par, and varying among Exchanges). The differences between these prices are precisely what generates the arbitrage opportunities for trading Stablecoins that are at the root of price-stabilization mechanisms (algorithmic and reserve-backed).

The primary market issuance/redemption operations are the first points where an understanding about the tokens involved is needed. "Involved" should be interpreted in three dimensions, namely, tokens:

1. involved in the price stabilization mechanism (i.e. both the Stablecoin itself and those tokens "supporting" it),
2. that are exchanged for the Stablecoin at issuance/redemption, and
3. denominating positions in its supporting "Treasury".

On point 1. above, it should be noted that some Stablecoins exist only in combination with other, so-called "Volatility", tokens—which can be other cryptocurrencies or any other token types, such as utility—meant to absorb any value oscillations around the design peg. In other cases, Stablecoin positions create ancillary property rights in terms of the protocol's governance token. The analyst or designer will have to explain such value constellations, which is the intention behind the box "Native Tokens" in Fig. 10.16.

The need for point 2. is obvious (information reconciled to the box "Foreign Tokens", sub-box "@Issuance/Redemption"). By also explaining what tokens are eligible as collateral/reserve positions supporting the Stablecoin issuance (box "Foreign Tokens", sub-box "Collateral/Reserve eligible"), the static picture of which tokens are involved in the Stablecoin lifecycle is complete. This is the main objective of the **Stablecoin Protocol Token Model** given in Fig. 10.16.

A secondary objective is to begin identifying asset classes (both on- and off-chain [213]) of the supporting Stablecoin "Treasury". This is needed so as to explain the corresponding asset/liability management problem, i.e. to explain the built-in Stablecoin stabilization mechanisms from the point of view of treasury management. The depiction of Fig. 10.17 serves precisely this purpose, by visualizing the whole financial position of the protocol pertaining to its Stablecoin operations. It is a balance sheet, the fundamental equation of which is:

$$\text{Assets} = \text{Liabilities} + \text{Platform rewards}$$

"**Liabilities**" are the amounts which the protocol will need in the future to redeem its already issued Stablecoins. As already mentioned, those will generally be combinations of fiat currencies and of other tokens. "**Platform rewards**" are the amounts which have already been deducted on the basis of fees, commissions, etc., at the issuance and/or redemption points. They are generally owed to the protocol operators and to its governance token holders; they can similarly be in the form of either fiat currencies or tokens; and they are drawable, as per protocol policies. The "**Assets**" side contains all working assets of the protocol supporting its Stablecoin operations. In all generality, Stablecoin projects invest at least a part of incoming funds (i.e. amounts deposited by buyers at issuance and withheld as fees/commissions) to first, manage the market risk of swapped tokens and fiat currencies, and, second, to generate extra yield for the ecosystem. That this is the case will be demonstrated in the sequence through examples of live Stablecoin operations. However, the important information for the time being is precisely this last word: "operations". Stablecoin projects are not one-off token issuers, they expect to keep operating continuously. This is evident for example in the position "Own Stablecoins" under "Assets" in Fig. 10.17. The protocol needs to keep Stablecoins at the ready, so as to avoid having to liquidate other working assets to cover redemptions. In short, the protocol *needs* to have an own view of assets and liabilities similar to that of a "Treasury" balance sheet. This is a fundamental factor of Stablecoin design, as it expresses the combined on-/off-chain mechanisms of its price stabilization. Incidentally, it is also focus of "proof-of-reserves" [214] attestations, which have come to be expected by crypto-market practitioners. For an example of how these attestations can be important, it suffices to refer the reader to the circumstances of the LUNA/TerraUSD collapse [215] (and of the FTX/Alameda [216] case) which ushered in the 2022 crypto-market crash.

In summary of the above, having a target view, along the lines of the Stablecoin protocol token model and the "Treasury" balance sheet diagrams, allows an analyst to understand each and every Stablecoins project by seeking the same basic information, e.g. as per indicative question list below:

1. What rate is the Stablecoin pegged to?
2. What are the types of assets (fiat-currencies, other tokens) exchanged for the Stablecoin in the primary market?
3. What are the allowable asset classes in the balance sheet (both asset- and liability-side, of course) of the primary market's treasury?
4. How are the assets originally provided by buyers transformed to other asset classes within the treasury?
5. What are the monitoring mechanisms to track price deviations between the primary and the secondary markets?
6. What are the responding price stabilization mechanisms (algorithmic and reserve-based)?
7. How effective are said mechanisms? Is there a theoretical proof or heuristic explanation? Are there operational controls built around them?
8. What are the governance aspects of implementing said mechanisms? What is the practical effectiveness of this governance?
9. How is the adequacy of the treasury assets measured? How is it managed?
10. Is there actual market experience of Stablecoin operations? How does this experience align with the whitepaper objectives?

Let us make the process of seeking this information clearer by way of concrete examples.

Imagine that a token analyst wants to understand the workings of DAI [217], which is a Stablecoin pegged to the USD. Research shows that DAI is issued by the Maker protocol [218] of the MakerDAO [219] ecosystem (its primary market) and is actively traded in several Exchanges [220] (its secondary market). Primary market buyers sell to the protocol any Ethereum-based assets that have been declared as eligible [221] by MakerDAO governance [222]. What they receive in return is a sum of DAI tokens that constitute a perpetual loan from the platform to the buyer, secured against the afore-mentioned assets—a "Collateralized Debt Position" (CDP [223]). The terms of issuing this loan are:

- The buyer needs to post-collateral (the afore-mentioned Ethereum-based assets are precisely that collateral).
- In return, he is credited the corresponding DAIs which he can either keep in the protocol or transfer to the secondary market (through account or crypto wallet).
- The market price of collateral over issued DAIs must be always kept above 1 ("position overcollateralization"). The requisite collateralization ratio is defined by MakerDAO governance and depends on the particular assets posted.
- If at any time of holding the DAI position the market price of collateral corresponding to the position falls below this ratio, the protocol automatically (meaning "through smart contracts") puts the collateral in liquidation. An auction [224] is initiated, the winning bidder posting DAI to acquire the collateral assets at a discount. Additionally, the loan position of the original buyer is added a "Liquidation Penalty" [225] charge. In any case, the original buyer gets to keep the DAI.

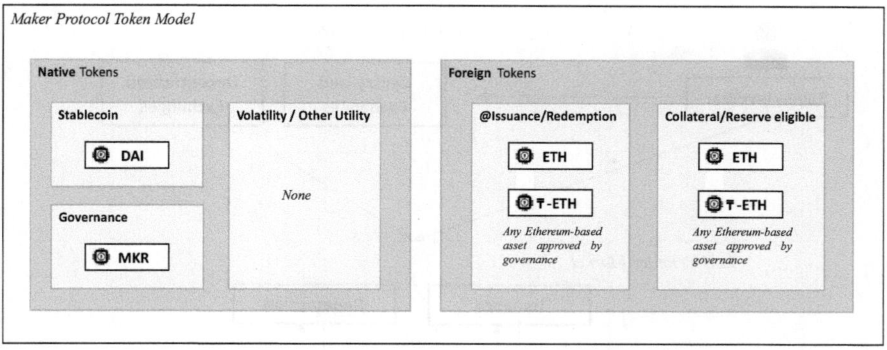

Fig. 10.18 Maker protocol token model underlying the DAI Stablecoin

- The DAI "loan" position is charged a (continuously compounded) lending rate, termed "Stability Fee" [226]. Said charge is denominated in DAI.
- If the buyer has opted to keep their DAI in the protocol, they can also lock them to a "Dai Savings Rate" (DSR) smart contract [227, 228] whereby they earn (continuously compounded) interest [229]. Said interest is paid out in DAI.

Hence, the main feeding mechanism of the DAI treasury "Reserve" is the posting of eligible collateral by primary market buyers. MakerDAO governance continuously updates the eligibility list [230] and does *not* a priori preclude mixing on- and off-chain assets [231, 232]. The current treasury reserve asset mix is available online through third parties [233].

Tracking deviations between primary and secondary market DAI prices is the task of "Key External Actors" [234] (Oracles included), which are compensated through platform rewards and auction participation rights. The operational price stabilization mechanisms of the Stablecoin are:

- Collateralization thresholds.
- Arbitraging between primary and secondary markets.
- Auctions (Surplus, Debt, Collateral).
- Treasury asset appreciation.
- Build-up and draw-down of treasury reserve positions by protocol governance.
- Technical short-circuits [235].

Reserve asset management responsibility of DAI transitioned over time from the hands of an authorized legal entity ("Maker Foundation") to a purely decentralized paradigm [236–238] centred around a DAO, with algorithm and parametrization changes subject to strict governance processes. Expert working committees [239, 240] and functional teams [241] actively contribute to governance tasks. The maker protocol token model is schematically depicted in Fig. 10.18, and the corresponding treasury structure in Fig. 10.19; note that ₸-ETH denotes any EVM-compatible token approved by MakerDAO governance.

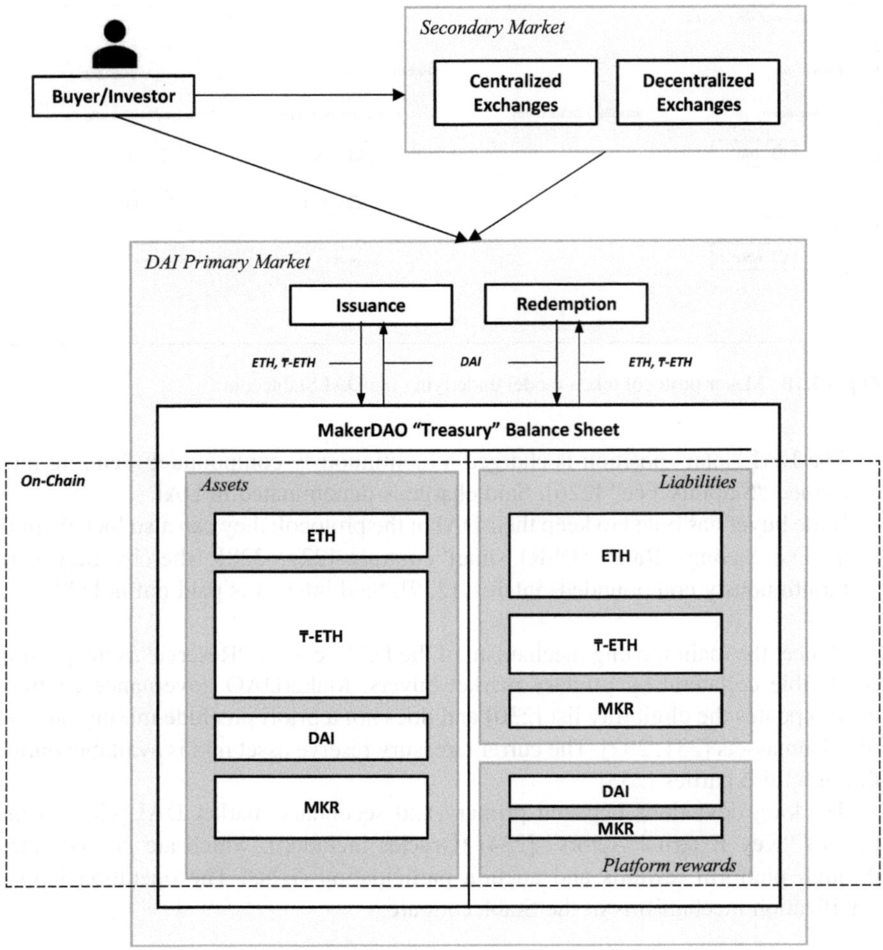

Fig. 10.19 MakerDAO "Treasury" structure supporting the DAI Stablecoin

Thus, using Figs. 10.16 and 10.17 as templates, project documentation and public domain data can advise a succinct picture of the particular Stablecoin stabilization mechanism and current treasury structure.

Let us continue by assuming a token analyst who needs to understand USD Tether (USDT,[46] referred to simply as "Tether" in the sequel[47]), a Stablecoin "soft-pegged" to the USD. Research shows that it is issued and redeemed[48] by two

[46]This is the trading symbol of Tether; for media communication purposes, Tether tokens can be also referred to through the symbol "₮" (Unicode "Tugrik sign"; https://tether.to/en/media).

[47]Note that the Tether ecosystem also issues Stablecoins pegged to other fiat currencies such as EUR, YEN, etc. [242].

[48]Please refer to the current terms of service, as per [243].

affiliated corporations ("Tether Limited" for transactions involving US persons; "Tether International Limited" for non-US persons [243])—its primary market. It is actively traded in several Exchanges [244] (the secondary market). Primary market buyers deposit fiat currency (USD) and get the same amount of USDT minus a transaction fee [245]. This is a payment-vs-payment transaction, and there are no other asset transfers (i.e. no posting of collateral) or intermediaries involved. The buyer can then transfer the USDT to any Centralized or Decentralized Exchange accepting them (through account or crypto wallet).

The issuing legal entity[49] asserts that "*All Tether Tokens are backed 100% by Tether's reserves*" [247]. The tether treasury is actively managed for both liquidity and funding risk and its current asset mix is available to the public [248], also on the legal entity's website [249]. For example, a particular time snapshot[50] shows that apart from around 7% in Bitcoins and "Other Investments" all its other assets were fiat-currency-denominated off-chain ones (T-bills, term and reverse repos, cash & bank deposits, money market funds, secured loans, corporate bonds, and precious metals).

In terms of controlling treasury reserves adequacy (analysis question 9 above), the original protocol whitepaper [251] states:

> *At any given time the balance of fiat currency held in our reserves will be equal to (or greater than) the number of tethers in circulation.*

However, facts seem to have not always corresponded to this assertion [252]. So, an analyst or buyer/investor might want to dig deeper into the actual performance metrics [253, 254] of Tether (analysis question #10 of the list given earlier in this section).

The Tether token model is schematically depicted in Fig. 10.20. It translates the fact that there are no tokens, but only fiat currencies, swapped at issuance/redemption for USDT. As USDT amounts are not collateralized loan positions, there are also no collateralized tokens to declare. Similarly, the existence or not of other tokens in the Stablecoin's reserve is a matter at the absolute discretion of the issuer, both as regards type of token and percentage of funds; there are no stated obligations on either token type or percentage limits. Hence, there can be no more precise indication on the token model depiction. The corresponding tether treasury structure follows in Fig. 10.21.

An analyst wishing to understand FRAX [255], a Stablecoin pegged to the USD, will start from the fact that it is issued by the namesake decentralized finance protocol [256] and is actively traded in several Exchanges (the secondary market).

[49] Please note that "tether.to" is simply a website, not a legal entity. It is operated by "Tether Operations Limited", a company originally incorporated in the British Virgin Islands with the purposes of operating both said website and the entire suite of Tether technical artefacts across blockchains. Incorporation information taken from [246].

[50] For Dec. 31, 2023: [250].

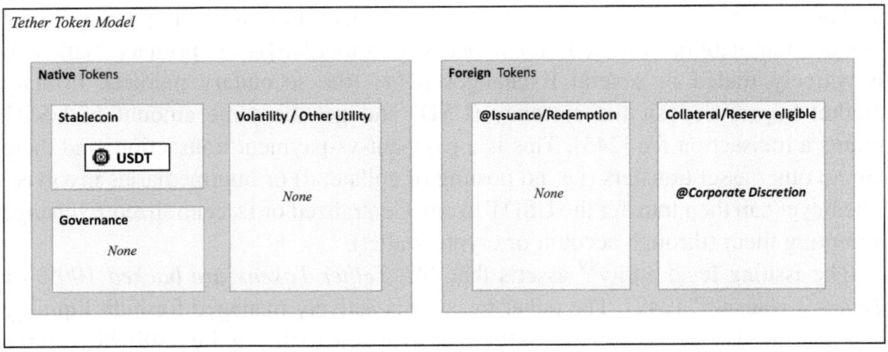

Fig. 10.20 Tether token model

Research shows that said protocol is already in its third generation [257] as of the time of writing, which is reflected in the evolution of features of its FRAX Stablecoin. The current documentation explains that the FRAX ecosystem admits several distinct use cases [258], each with its own ring-fenced technical artefacts, some of which end up forming so-called "subprotocols".[51] There also exists a common business layer of smart contracts; a particular subset of those forms the so-called "Algorithmic Market Operations" (AMO's [259]). Its smart contracts in effect implement issuing; redemption; placement; and rebalancing of financial positions denominated in native and foreign tokens of the FRAX ecosystem.

One of the afore-mentioned "subprotocols" is a money market called "Fraxlend" [260].

As depicted on Fig. 10.22, it enables the creation of liquidity pools ("Vaults") containing pairs of swappable tokens, one of which being the FRAX Stablecoin. Both the ecosystem's own "Fraxlend AMO" SC and third parties can commit FRAX into a vault pairing, e.g. FRAX with USDC, or indeed with any other EVM-compatible ERC-20 token accepted as Fraxlend collateral by governance. Prospective FRAX Stablecoin buyers/investors can deposit collateral into a vault and in return be issued with (interest-charging) FRAX Stablecoins. In short, the Fraxlend subprotocol enables issuance of FRAX as collateralized debt positions (CDPs [261]), of course entailing continuous monitoring of CDPs for credit risk and possible auction-based liquidations [262]. Borrowers can invest their FRAX within the ecosystem or in the secondary market and must ultimately return them (plus interest) in order to retrieve their collateral. Transaction fees and part of the (FRAX-denominated) interest stream accrues to the ecosystem treasury, e.g. to the native governance token FXS (also ERC-20).

Another use case revolves around the issuance and redemption of, in effect, zero-coupon bonds denominated in the FRAX Stablecoin. As depicted on Fig. 10.23, holders of existing FRAX tokens can invoke the "FRAX Bonds AMO" smart contract [263] in order to purchase native "FRAX Bond" (FXB [264]) tokens

[51] note that this term is *not* widely used in the Crypto-markets.

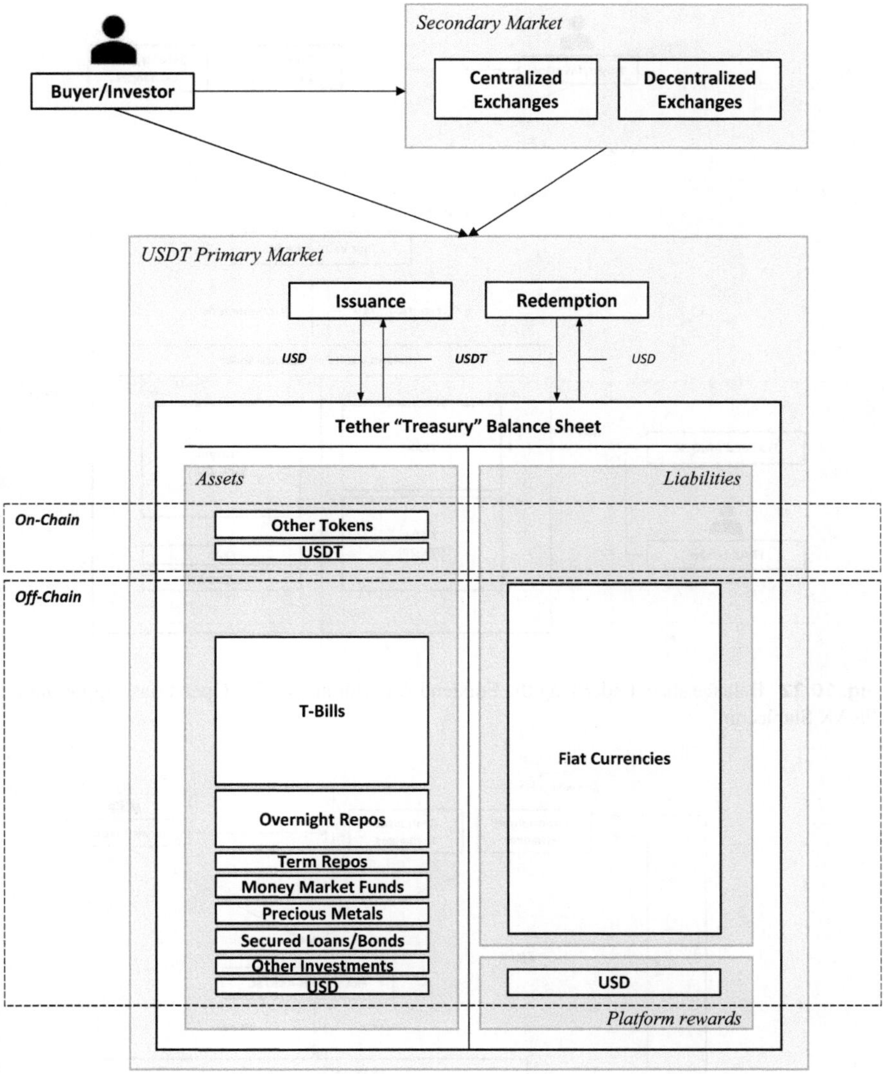

Fig. 10.21 Tether "Treasury" structure supporting the USDT Stablecoin (indicative)

quoting a FRAX amount payable at different maturities [265]. The purchase price is at a discount to par, which expresses the yield of the bond. In order to come up with the difference, FRAX contracts with third parties ("Real-World Asset Partners" [266] or "RWA Partners") the principals of which operate both on- and off-chain. RWA partners can draw the FRAX proceeds of the FXB purchases[52] and invest them off-chain, e.g. in USD-denominated treasury bills and other traditional fixed

[52]Price discovery actually involves a Dutch auction, cf. [267].

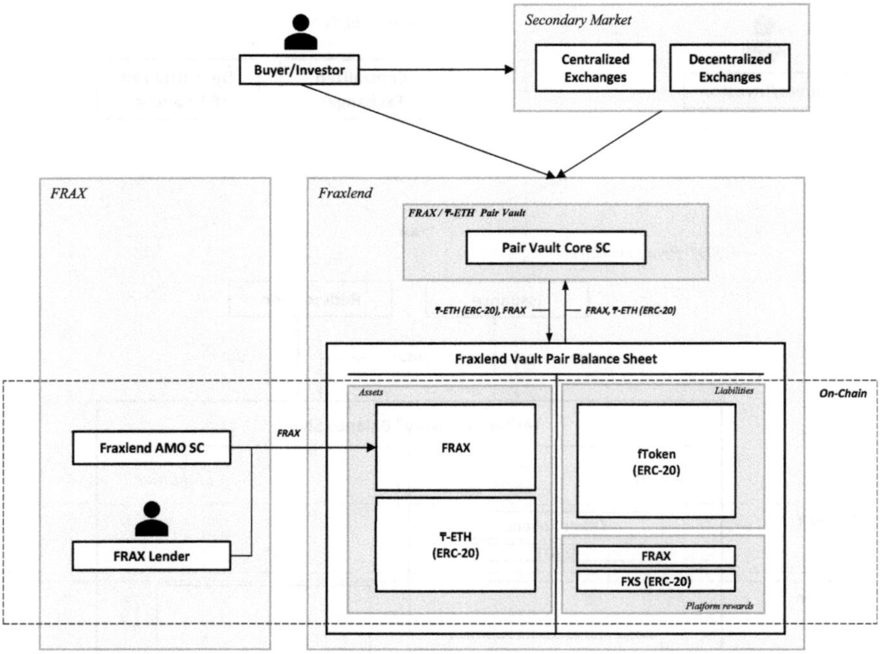

Fig. 10.22 Balance sheet underlying the Fraxlend Algorithmic Market Operations supporting the FRAX Stablecoin

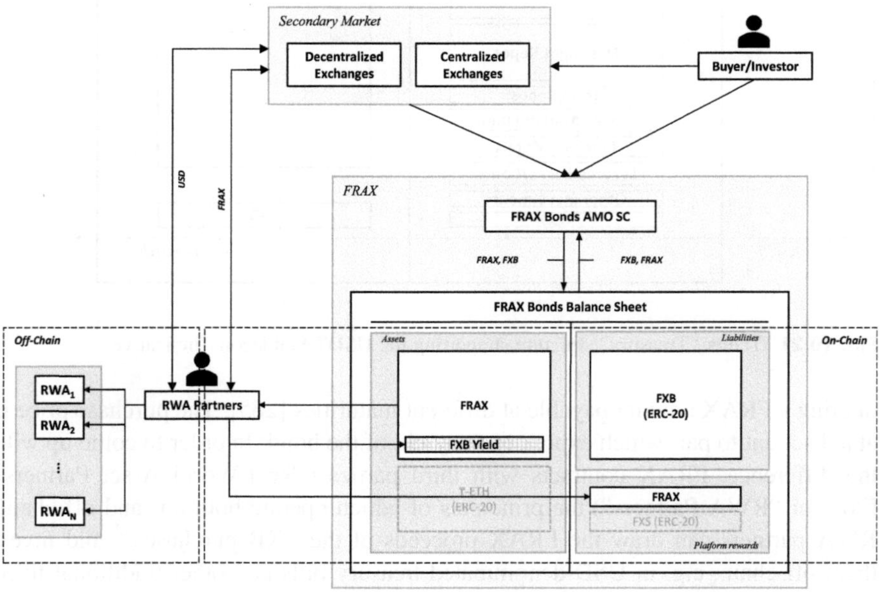

Fig. 10.23 Balance sheet underlying the FRAX Bonds Algorithmic Market Operations supporting the FRAX Stablecoin

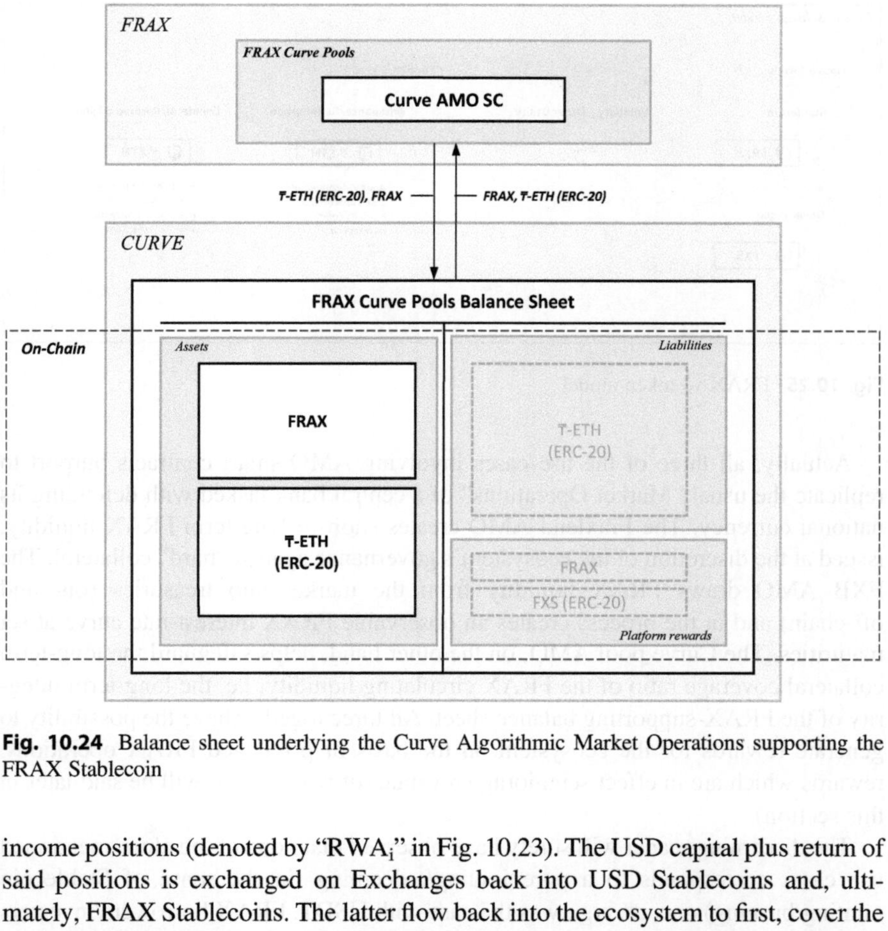

Fig. 10.24 Balance sheet underlying the Curve Algorithmic Market Operations supporting the FRAX Stablecoin

income positions (denoted by "RWA$_i$" in Fig. 10.23). The USD capital plus return of said positions is exchanged on Exchanges back into USD Stablecoins and, ultimately, FRAX Stablecoins. The latter flow back into the ecosystem to first, cover the promised FXB yield, and, second (as excess returns), to increase the discretionary funds of the ecosystem treasury.

Yet another use case involves placing ecosystem FRAX positions to the token pools of the third-party cooperating ecosystem Curve, which is an investment platform. In this case (depicted schematically on Fig. 10.24), the "Curve AMO" smart contract acts as an investment manager for ecosystem liquidity denominated in the FRAX Stablecoin. The intention behind this "Algorithmic Market Operation" is to expand the asset-side of the Frax ecosystem balance sheet, thus achieving two objectives:

(a) Increasing the collateral-coverage ratio (or "Collateral Ratio") of the FRAX Stablecoin, defined as [Market Value of FRAX-supporting Assets] / [Market Value of FRAX in circulation], to bring —and keep—it as close to 100% as possible, and
(b) Generating excess liquidity which can be partially committed to the ecosystem treasury, increasing the value of the governance token FXS.

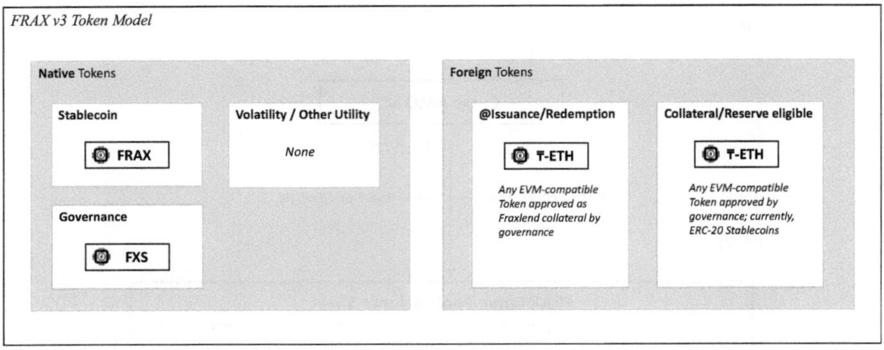

Fig. 10.25 FRAX v3 token model

Actually, all three of the use cases involving AMO smart contracts purport to replicate the usual "Market Operations" of a central bank tasked with defending its national currency. The Fraxlend AMO creates short-to-long-term FRAX liquidity, issued at the discretion of the ecosystem's governance against "hard" collateral. The FXB AMO draws FRAX liquidity from the market into treasuries (on- and off-chain) and in the process creates an observable FRAX interest-rate curve at set maturities. The Curve pool AMO, on the other hand, helps safeguard the long-term collateral coverage ratio of the FRAX circulating liquidity; i.e. the long-term integrity of the FRAX-supporting balance sheet. All three together have the possibility to generate rewards for the ecosystem on the basis of privileged FRAX operations, rewards which are in effect seigniorage revenue (of which more will be said later in this section).

The discerning reader will surely have observed that none of the afore-mentioned use cases corresponds to a pure issuing/redeeming (in the sense of Stablecoin minting/burning) one, as, e.g., was the case with USDT. FRAX borrowers/investors *cannot* cause FRAX to be minted, nor burned. Minting and burning of FRAX tokens is the exclusive prerogative of the FRAX ecosystem governance, and do not occur by request. The closest equivalent to a primary market for FRAX is the Fraxlend money market. However, the underlying Fraxlend balance sheet is coupled to those acted upon also by the FXB and curve AMO smart contracts. There are still more FRAX "sub-protocols" enabling transactional pathways involving the FRAX Stablecoin (e.g. the Fraxswap automated market maker, etc.) but none directly involving the ecosystem's FRAX market operations. On account of the above, to explain the FRAX Stablecoin of the third generation of the FRAX ecosystem (which we will denote as "FRAX v3") the Stablecoin analyst will probably end up creating a FRAX v3 protocol token model as that schematically depicted in Fig. 10.25,whereas the corresponding Stablecoin treasury structure is as depicted in Fig. 10.26.

Note that Ŧ-ETH denotes a generic EVM-compatible token. The current treasury reserve asset mix is available online through the protocol [268]. As already mentioned, the artefacts of the last two figures relate to FRAX protocol v3. The analyst might find added value in tracking the historical evolution of the FRAX Stablecoin.

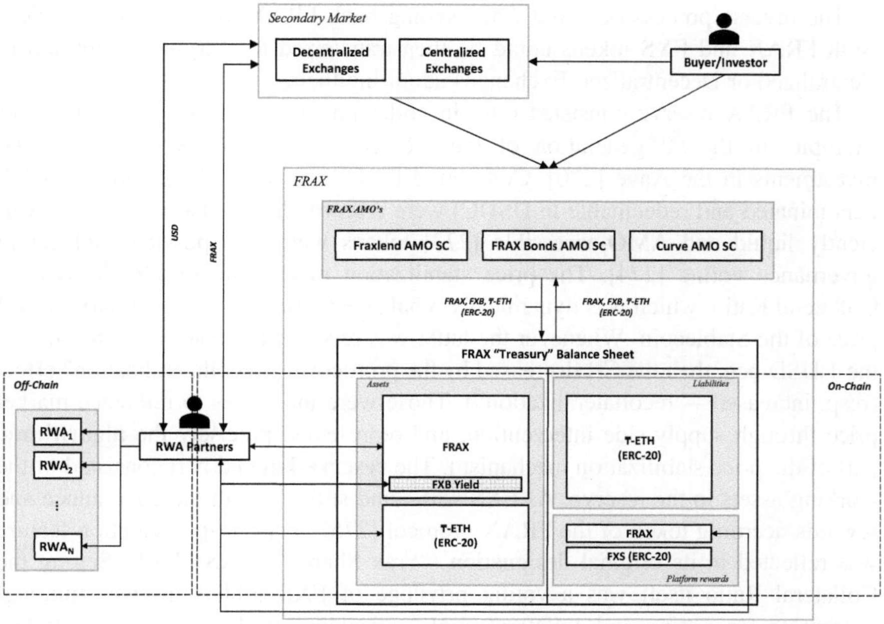

Fig. 10.26 Aggregated FRAX v3 "Treasury" structure and Algorithmic Market Operations supporting the FRAX Stablecoin

We will replicate this research step here, in order to help explain some more facts relating to Stablecoin-supporting treasury structures as a token design factor.

Through project documentation, the analyst will glean that previous versions of FRAX had a different role for the native FXS token. Namely, FXS were also intended to be unpegged (so-called "Volatility") tokens assuming the price risk of FRAX deviations from its peg. Up to and including FRAX v2—i.e. the version before last—primary market buyers needed to deposit tokens in the form of another USD-pegged Stablecoin (USDC [269]) *plus acquire and sell back to the protocol* a number of FXS in set proportion to the Stablecoin. What they got back were newly minted FRAX totalling the USDC+FXS amounts, minus platform fees. The proportion of USDC to FXS needed was controlled by a (time-varying, set by governance) "Collateral Ratio"—CR parameter. The newly minted:

Amount of FRAX = [Value of deposited USDC] + [Value of FXS sold back]or, succinctly ("N_x" denoting the quantity of x and "MP_x" its secondary market price):

$$N_{FRAX} = N_{USDC} \cdot MP_{USDC} + N_{FXS} \cdot MP_{FXS}$$

had to obey the relationship:

$$(1 - CR) \cdot N_{USDC} \cdot MP_{USDC} = CR \cdot N_{FXS} \cdot MP_{FXS}$$

The inverse process occurred when selling back FRAX to the primary market. Both FRAX and FXS tokens could be then transferred to a crypto wallet and to Centralized or Decentralized Exchanges admitting them.

The FRAX reserve consisted only in collateral deposited and reinvested. For example, in the v2 generation of the protocol, only positions in USDC and investments in the Aave [270], Compound [271], and Yearn [272] protocols (all denominated and redeemable in USDC) were reserve-eligible. However, any sufficiently liquid and AMO-accessible [273] tokens were also possible, subject to governance voting [274]. The price stabilization mechanism of FRAX was the Collateral Ratio, which was dynamically rebalanced based on the secondary market price of the Stablecoin. Whenever the latter was reported to be above (resp. below) the 1 USD peg, then the CR decreased by the protocol— "decollateralization" effect (resp. increased—"recollateralization"). Those were incentives to influence market price through supply-side intervention, and represented precisely the **algorithmic** part of the price stabilization mechanism. The **reserve-backed** part consisted of the working assets in the reserve. As FXS was—and still is—both the governance and rewards-accruing token of the FRAX protocol [275], its profit-participation feature was reflected in its original designation ("Frax Shares"—FXS [276]). Setting the Collateral Ratio itself was a voting privilege of FXS-holders, as was minting/redeeming fee setting and collateral pool asset approval. The FRAX project had the discretion of keeping FXS-allocated platform rewards in the Stablecoin reserve; however, this was a "last resort option", and not meant to be activated under normal market conditions.

The constellation of FRAX-USDC-FXS in previous FRAX versions deserves some commentary. With CR > 0, the protocol-issued Stablecoins to the buyer were only partially covered by the "hard" USDC collateral deposited into the reserve. The difference was similar to a commission paid for "services rendered" to the protocol by the buyer. The Frax whitepaper [277] mentioned: "*A … token in the system, Frax Shares (FXS), captures the seigniorage value when minting non-collateralized value*". The current FRAX documentation explicitly states [278]: "*Frax Share (FXS)—The base-layer governance Token for the entire Frax ecosystem of smart contracts. It accrues fees, revenue, and excess collateral value*". The "commission for service rendered" (or "rent") part is precisely the [seigniorage] "revenue" mentioned.

The term "seigniorage" (from the French "*seigneur*"—originally the feudal lord—and meaning "right of the lord to mint money") in practical terms meant the difference between the value of money and the cost to produce and distribute it [279, 280]. If a local potentate had this right, then he could mint money containing, e.g., 95% silver and 5% copper and mandate its value as being the equivalent of 100% silver within his lands. The 5% "debasement" was the "seigniorage", representing in essence the monetization of his privilege to mint coinage. As the minting privilege came to be the prerogative of national (and sometime supranational) governance arrangements, the actual mechanisms of this monetization effect took several forms—each with its own risks of how the missing collateral backing the currency could be managed. In modern times, the history of the "Latin Monetary

Union" [281] used to be *the* textbook example of what could go wrong with seigniorage, at least until the so-called "Nixon shock" [282] provided an even better one. In short, even in physical commodity-backed currencies, seigniorage failures were far from unheard of. Typical benefits accruing to "currency minting" privileges were varied, and in modern times explained [283] in juxtaposition to the corresponding obligations imputed to the body embodying the privilege (in the off-chain world, the jurisdiction's Central Bank). However, there were—and still are—still important but less obvious benefits having to do with the international standing of individual currencies. The economic argument is in essence that currency held as foreign currency abroad is used to buy goods, assets and services from, and at the price dictated by, the economic actors of the originating country—which is in itself a form of "paying for the privilege".[53] Some authors used the term "seigniorage competition" [285], which refers to the strive for currencies to achieve international reserve currency status. This term is not out-of-place in a token ecosystem setting, going back to our basic analogy of a new country-level economy.

Returning to our FRAX analysis, the FXS part of the sums which the FRAX buyer was requested to pay to the protocol is precisely the "seigniorage". If the collateral ratio was >0 (which is the expected state of affairs), then the issued FRAX were only partially, or "fractionally", covered by eligible collateral— hence the name of the token, which is a wordplay around "fractional".[54] It should now be clear why the seminal paper which led to Frax [288] was proposing the notion of "Seigniorage Shares" as a means of Stablecoin price stabilization. The FRAX amounts in circulation were backed only by USDC amounts (originally paid-in and/or invested in other protocols [AAVE, COMP, YFI, etc.]). As explained above, the prospective FRAX buyer/investor had to already hold FXS for the non-USDC part of the transaction at issuance. Also, redemption of FRAX returned both USDC and FXS to the seller. It is legitimate to ask what the opportunity cost of these pre-requisite, resp. resulting FXS holdings, was, and if it detracted from the Stablecoin value proposition. The answer is that the FRAX protocol offered—actually, still offers—the opportunity to keep FXS reinvested in the ecosystem through a platform smart contract [289] (in lieu of FXS-denominated staking) creating a bond-like rolling investment. The platform also offered discretionary buy-back and recollateralization options to FXS holders at preferential rates to those available at issuance/redemption.

[53] "*On the other hand, seigniorage earnings on currency held abroad represent a net transfer of real resources from foreign currency holders to U.S. taxpayers*", from [284].

[54] Any analogy with the Fractional Reserve Banking system [286] beyond the similarity of terms is, in our opinion, misplaced. First, there exists no "central bank policy" allowing controlled money expansion through a multiplier [287]—this intention is simply not present in any of the original "Seigniorage Shares" and FRAX whitepapers. The FRAX Treasury AMO controllers target exclusively defending the USD-peg and not any sort of reserve ratio. FRAX governance is decentralized, not subject to any central authority. The only mechanisms aligning Collateral Ratios and the Stablecoin peg are the profit incentives to buyers/investors through the FRAX subprotocols and, of course, the arbitrage opportunities through the Secondary Market exchanges.

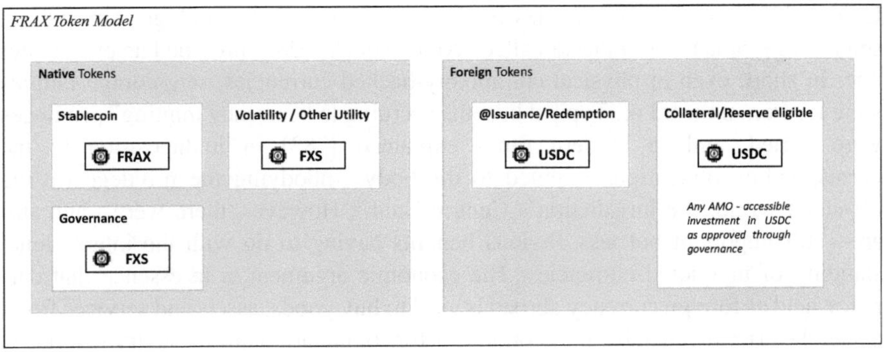

Fig. 10.27 FRAX v1/v2 token model

The FRAX token model of those previous generations is schematically depicted in Fig. 10.27. The corresponding FRAX treasury structure appears in Fig. 10.28.

What information can the FRAX analyst draw from this "historical" view? First, that the role of the FXS token evolved with time—which means that it can still change in the future. Whereas in previous generations it was an integral part of the price-stabilization mechanism, it since evolved into a purely governance and rewards-returning utility token. In effect, the "seigniorage" part of the protocol is now expressed simply in the FXS value accrual. Second, that the Stablecoin "Treasury" structure (the token design factor of consideration) has changed in-between FRAX generations, but the peg appears to be still holding. Hence, it could be argued that the particular Stablecoin could successfully defend its peg across generations, which would seem to speak for the effectiveness of its price-stabilization mechanisms. Third, the inclusion of off-chain "Real-World Assets" into the latter would seem to reduce the risk profile of the FRAX Stablecoin, as RWAs are very conservative traditional finance investments. Taken in the aggregate, the analyst would probably be gaining the impression of a Stablecoin that has steadily gained a more conservative risk profile across generations.

We will not examine any more Stablecoin examples, leaving it to the reader to assess the merit of combining "Protocol Token Model" and "Treasury Balance Sheet" views for token (especially Stablecoin) analysis. We will only mention as a final comment that, in our opinion, the task of reserve management in the token context is the same as the asset/liability management one in traditional finance. The same considerations around structural liquidity gaps and short-/long-term position management; and the same mechanisms of macro-hedges and currency overlays, guided by a combination of market feedback loops and forecasting tools; apply here as well. Once the relevant asset classes have been defined and the "Treasury" balance sheet created, the "on-chain/off-chain" views can be merged. Under the "country-level" analogy of Chap. 6, any token of interest can take the role of a reference currency, and then accounting views for income flows and profitability analyses can be created as well. The only thing that is different to traditional finance is the decentralized governance afforded by the blockchain paradigm, and its

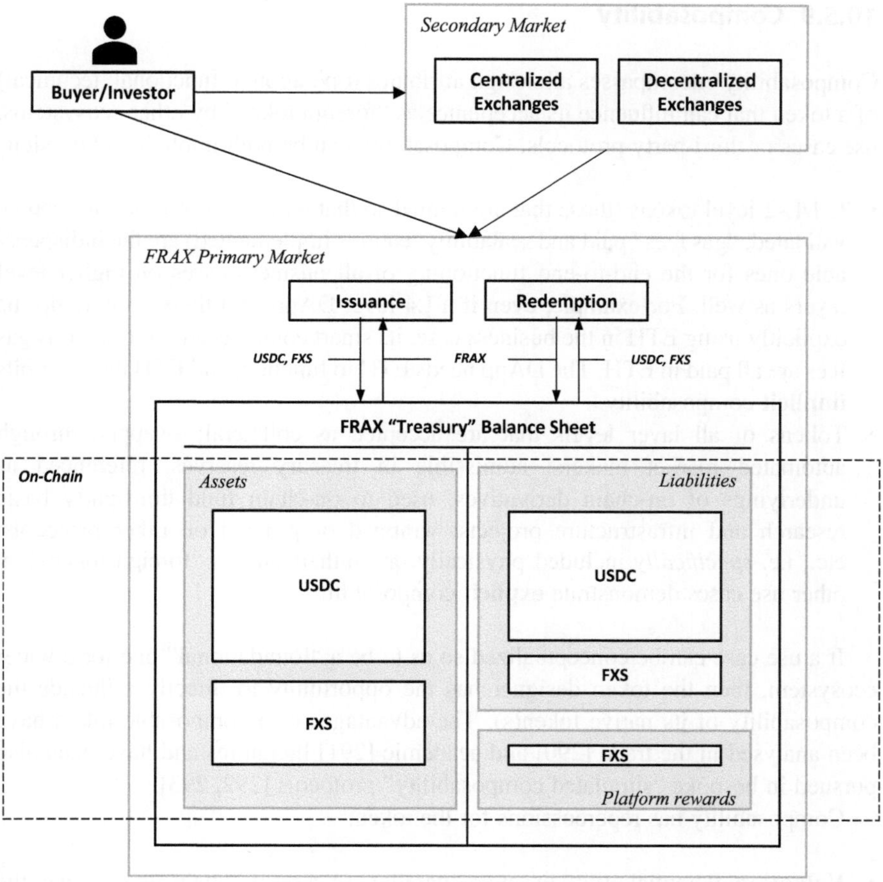

Fig. 10.28 FRAX v1/v2 "Treasury" structure supporting the FRAX Stablecoin

repercussions for time-varying financial parameterization (lending/borrowing interest rates, collateral ratios, margin call levels, etc.).

Of course, our objective here is token design. The intention behind proposing combined "Tokens"/ "Treasury" views and a list of associated "analyst questions" is simply to guide the token designer to proactively address the legitimate questions that rational buyers/investors and token analysts are going to have: namely, what the role of the treasury structure in his token design is; and what ancillary mechanisms are put in place to ensure the adequacy and stability of the end-to-end token (especially Stablecoin) operations. Addressing those questions conclusively will safeguard the value proposition of the token as an investment and as an enabler of its ecosystem's business case.

10.5.9 Composability

Composability encompasses all design attributes (operational, functional, technical) of a token that can influence its acceptance as "foreign token" by other ecosystems, use cases or third-party protocols. Composability can be both implicit and explicit.

- L-1/L-2-level tokens (those that are minted so that base-layer transactions can be validated, "gas fees" paid and scalability features implemented) are the indispensable ones for the end-to-end functioning of all business cases on higher level layers as well. For example, even if a L4-level DApp on Ethereum may not be explicitly using ETH in the business case, its smart contracts and transactions gas fees are all paid in ETH. The DApp needs ETH to function, and ETH thus exhibits **implicit** composability.
- Tokens of all layer levels that are accepted as collateral; swapped through automated market makers; admissible in treasury reserves; referenced as underlyings of on-chain derivatives; used to on-chain fund third-party basic research and infrastructure projects; wrapped or proxied on other protocols; etc., i.e. *specifically* included physically or synthetically as "foreign tokens" in other use cases demonstrate **explicit** composability.

If a use case can be conceptualized so as to be a "foundational" one for a wider ecosystem, then the token designer has the opportunity to directly influence the composability of its native token(s). The advantages of a composable token have been analysed in the trade [290] and academic [291] literatures and have been also pursued in bespoke "simulated composability" protocols [292, 293].

Composability has repercussions for the token:

- **Valuation.** Potential utility in several parallel use cases will help attain sooner the token's intended "network effect". Even after that point, as we saw in Sect. 10.5.4, network economics can be a fundamental driver of a token's increasing valuation. Tokens with implicit composability in particular can be considered as holding the status of international reserve currencies in the "country-level-analogy" of the proposed ecosystem design framework; they are at once "international" media of exchange and stores of value since they are long-term *indispensable* for the delivery of intra-ecosystem services and for the execution of both intra- and inter-ecosystem transactions.
- **Auditability**. The higher the usage of a token, the higher its level of exposure to operational risks. Faster discovery of defects in design and/or implementation discovered as a result will help harden the end-to-end reliability of the token *vis-à-vis* its peer tokens. This is bound to happen by necessity, as not correcting such defects will create "systemic risk" [294, 295] effects across business cases [296] (and even across entire ecosystems, in the case of L-1/L-2 tokens). Corporate auditors, regulators, and fraud examiners will thus be more comfortable giving an unqualified no-objection opinion to a token design that has had its pathologies reviewed and corrected across several productive use cases already.

- **Investability**. Acceptance in already established use cases creates trust with buyers and long-term investors alike. Independent crypto-asset advisors and commentators will probably recommend as an investment a token that has already proved its utility across business ecosystems. Furthermore, should the token prove indispensable for a critical mass of third-party successful use cases, it may eventually create a "too-big-to-fail" [297] effect for its acceptance as a store of value.
- **Sustainability**. Acceptance across use cases may create a virtuous circle for a token, whereby safe long-term income stream to its issuing protocol incentivizes investment into expanding its functional envelope (and of its underlying infrastructure, including smart contract standards), which in return creates acceptance by more use cases, etc. The outcome will be increased long-term utility of the token, contributing also to a "too-big-to-fail" effect as was mentioned above.

Of course, third-party acceptance is not a foregone conclusion. However, the token designer can take the composability factor into account at least as a mid- to late-design *quality control* step. In foundational protocols, however, all design stages should be able to align with this prospect.

10.5.10 Programmability

We have already encountered a notion of "programmability" in token design, namely, when explaining smart contracts (SCs) as a token-minting mode (cf. Sect. 10.5.5). A SC was defined as a piece of on-chain code, programmed to execute once some pre-specified conditions have been met as registered on-chain. It contains deterministic logic, possibly calibrated by off-chain parameters (such as current market prices, provided, e.g. through quote responses by third-party services, called "Oracles").

More generally, programmability as a token design factor encompasses all functional and technical design attributes allowing the **state of the individual token** to change during its lifecycle (i.e. at any time in between "minting" and "burning", including these endpoints).

Actually, underlying property rights can be considered part of this "state". As explained in the preceding sections on property rights structure (Sect. 10.5.6, for example, the discussion about NFTs and future royalty streams allocation between the token owner and intellectual property owner) and minting optionalities (Sect. 10.5.7, especially on liquidity positions in Uniswap V1 to V3), such varying property rights are already featured in existing token designs. However, the scope of possible use cases enabled by token programmability is broad enough that a more detailed explanation of this design factor is warranted.

At first, we need to distinguish between "**Issuer**" and "**Owner**" programmability. In the former paradigm, the functional set and timing of state changes are at the absolute discretion of the governance mechanisms of the issuing protocol. In the latter, the owner (or prospective owner, as a precondition to acquiring the token) is technically enabled to define the same attributes. Thus, from the point of view of the economic agent who is thus empowered, we can distinguish between:

- Issuer,
- Owner, and
- Hybrid.

programmability. All three modes are significant for economically relevant use cases.

The concept of "programmable money" [298] targeted in the design of some Central Bank Digital Currencies (CBDCs) is one example. It addresses the need for government-issued funds that can be targeted to specific user groups (e.g. family assistance funds recipients; residents of designated "natural disaster areas"; documented migrants; other social program beneficiaries, etc.) and can be spent only for approved goods and services, provided by a designated list of suppliers. It is in principle able to reduce moral hazard (misspending for non-approved goods; misappropriating funds; channelling funds abroad through money-service providers, etc.); deliver assistance within the time-scales afforded by modern technologies such as blockchain and mobile networks; reach the "unbanked" segments of the population who are still reasonably expected to use crypto wallets through mobile phone Apps; and provide incentives for the early withdrawal of funds by imposing "token expiration". All these are "**Issuer** programmability" features, the issuer being the Central Bank.

The same target-user-group, defined supply-chain, and time-limitation features can be enabled also in privately issued Stablecoins. For example, if a corporate decides to offer "loyalty-points" denominated in bespoke Stablecoins and redeemable in the same or affiliated enterprises, those tokens would be featuring issuer programmability. Security tokens, derivative tokens, utility tokens, and NFTs are all candidate programmability use cases. The issuer of an on-chain corporate bond may choose to implement all cash flow events (fee loading, coupon distributions, capital redemption, etc.) through token design. The contingent payoff of an on-chain derivative or structured product can be implemented naturally through smart contracts. Projects issuing governance tokens may reserve the option to adjust in time the voting weights of token positions. NFT issuers in the arts market may increase the number of circulating tokens against the same asset, which might dilute the value of existing NFTs. All these are very real and realistic **issuer** programmability implementations [299], serving practical needs of the underlying use case.

It must be pointed out that they are not specific to the blockchain world. Variation of property rights underlying a title of ownership is nothing new in traditional finance. For example, any convertible financial instrument (e.g. convertible bonds [300], contingent convertibles [301], etc.), has a property rights structure that is contingent on future events. Why would anyone choose to implement such an instrument on-chain instead of through traditional channels? First, because both the underlyings and the payoffs may be denominated in terms of crypto-assets (on-chain securities, tokenized intermediated securities, Stablecoins, etc.). Second, because the relative administrative costs of servicing such instruments (e.g. transaction documentation; valuation; lock-up periods; disbursements; reference rate readjustments; maturity profile transformations, etc.) may make for a compelling blockchain value proposition. And third, because of imputed legal and regulatory obligations which may be easier to implement on-chain for particular constellations of issuer and investor jurisdictions.

Importantly, **Issuer** programmability contains "delegation" use cases. That would be the case for example when CBDCs are indeed on the balance sheet of the Central Bank, but the actual token issuance is delegated to commercial, money-centre banks. The latter would be entrusted with the technical on-chain implementation, hence with the activation of the appropriate programmability features. Another case would be a security token which is provided by an issuing protocol, but which is then "configured" (parametrized) by a second corporate before being offered to the end investors. For example, an on-chain ETF that admits dynamic portfolio construction and investment policy calibration by human or algorithmic investment managers. This would be the equivalent of "white-labelling" of traditional financial instruments. In both use cases, the issuing protocol delegates the configuration of programmable token features to third parties before tokens are minted for end-users.

Regarding **Owner** programmability, two prominent use cases reproduce through tokens the off-chain "portfolio reallocation" and "assignment of rights" paradigms. Consider a private investor carrying an on-chain pension-fund portfolio in the form of an NFT. The non-fungibility of the token comes from the particular asset allocation weights, which can be readjusted to exploit market events, or align with recommended portfolio risk profiles as the investor grows older. Any functional features of the NFT allowing this readjustment to happen by explicit user initiative, or at least consent, and to result in user-selected allocations are manifestations of owner programmability. In the same vein, consider a corporate entity having tokenized assets, income streams, or rights to income streams. The entity may wish to cede the usufruct of those assets or rights to a third party for a limited amount of time, or to swap part of those income streams or rights for other on-chain assets regularly at specific swap dates. Such a use case (which may be easily extended to on-chain repurchase agreements, securities lending, and re-hypothecation) is also enabled by owner programmability of tokenized positions.

"Delegation" use cases are included here as well. For example, the private investor may have delegated portfolio reallocation to third-party human or algorithmic investment managers. Similarly, the corporate entity may have implemented multi-signature arrangements for compliance reasons.

"**Hybrid**" use cases cover tokens with *both* issuer and owner programmability built in. For example, consider a security portfolio token that allows readjusting risk class weightings by the end-investor but only up to a specific cut-off date, whereafter weightings remain constant. The "expiry date" of the optionality available to the token owner is the issuer programmability feature.

It can be argued that token programmability is always present in token ecosystems through the mechanisms of governance. That is equivalent to saying that there is no point in having governance (and minting governance tokens) if governance decisions cannot be enforced in all facets of the ecosystem, including its native tokens. If the protocol whitepaper provides that governance has the right to affect the parametrization of native tokens, then that necessarily implies token issuer programmability. However, there are equivalent ways to implement governance processes and decisions through *mechanism* design, not token design. Building programmability (especially owner programmability) into the native token(s) ab initio is a conscious design choice and should be considered in the context of all three main pillars of the end-to-end ecosystem design. The pros and cons must be weighed against the background of the use case and the technical features of the particular blockchain platform the token design will be based on.

For example, smart contract standards are generally expected to differ across platforms and protocols (cf. Sect. 10.5.5). Some technical modalities may simply need to be implemented from first principles by the protocol in order to achieve the desired programmability features. This will impact project costs, both initial and on-going, to cover change management and auditability obligations. Similarly, enabling optionalities through token programmability may alter the *asset class categorization* of a token. If a token suddenly acquires all attributes of a financial instrument, then ancillary issuer and buyer/investor obligations change dramatically. Hence, enabling token programmability is seldom a purely technical decision solely in the purview of the token designer.

In summary, token programmability will generally impact the token:

- **Costs**. If existing smart contract templates do not allow easy implementation of the targeted functional scope, there will be both initial and on-going project costs for token design, operationalization and change management. Also, even if the final token is not categorized as a financial security (cf. below), adequate mapping of property right transitions through the token technical design may necessitate repeated iterations which can translate into forced protocol upgrades and associated migration costs.
- **Auditability**. A token design with programmability features which were never encountered before will face increased auditability duties to satisfy investors, auditors, and regulators that the targeted functional envelope was correctly implemented and that the risk of unforeseen side-effects is contained.
- **Asset class categorization**. The optionality enabled by programmability may cause the token to be characterized as a financial security.
- **Obligations accruing to issuing project**. Should the token be classified as a financial security, then in most jurisdictions there are imputed legal and regulatory requirements for issuer authorization, instrument registration, investor communications, etc. Failure to satisfy said requirements will expose the token project to significant legal risks.
- **Acquirer eligibility**. In some jurisdictions, acquiring and owning privately issued cryptocurrencies and other crypto-tokens is prohibited by law. In others, investor suitability regulations ban provision of financial advice related to particular crypto-assets (such as crypto-derivatives) to non-qualified investors. In general,

the nature of the token may influence the matrix of buyer categories and jurisdictions which it will be allowed to be offered to.

- **Reporting obligations to/by the acquirer**. Should the token be classified as a financial security, then in several jurisdiction it can generally be expected that there will be imputed reporting obligations on the buyer/investors towards tax authorities; on trading venue(s) towards the buyer/investor and competent regulator; on any involved custodian(s) towards the buyer/investor; on any involved investment advisor(s) towards the buyer/investor and competent regulator; etc. There may also be *cross-border* reporting obligations, depending on the jurisdictions involved.
- **Valuation**. Added utility will generally increase the token value proposition as a store of value. Assuming a good fit with the requirements of the particular use case and absence of substitute mechanisms to achieve the same result, the more optionalities enabled though programmability the higher the token value will be.

As with any optionality, token programmability will generally have a positive effect on a token's acceptance in the market. At its base, it represents a technical modality that truly highlights the ability of the blockchain paradigm to both accommodate traditional financial instruments and enable creation of new ones that would be difficult to operationalize off-chain. However, its value proposition will depend strongly on alignment with the concrete business case and on consistency with the end-to-end ecosystem design.

10.5.11 Computational Complexity

The blockchain is an algorithmic as much as it is an information technology architectural paradigm. Different implementations of algorithms and architectures create the universe of L-1/L-2 in evidence today. Choosing combinations of each, e.g. opting for one decentralized consensus mechanism ("Proof-of-Work", "Proof-of-Stake", "Proof-of-History", etc.) over another, and similarly in the context of distributed ledger persistence layers, is not necessarily a decision that token designers have to take—unless they contribute to L-1/L-2 projects. However, all tokens need to live with the consequences of the foundational blockchain platform designs as regards transaction:

(a) Validation **time scales.**
(b) **"Gas fees"**, i.e. costs payable to the platform.

Gas fees can be considered to represent the hidden energy costs of executing transactions on the platform [302–304], which can be non-negligible [305–307] to the point of generating environmental impact concerns [308–310]. All token transactions (including minting/burning operations) are impacted.

From the standpoint of token design, use of smart contracts (either as minting mode—cf. Sect. 10.5.5—or to implement bonding functions—cf. Chap. 12) is one of the salient points where the consequences of the underlying platform features need to be taken into account, and where computational complexity thus enters as a design factor. "Computational complexity" [311] is a term from computer science, denoting the amount of resources (time; processing costs; physical memory; network costs; other platform costs, etc.) needed to execute an algorithm. For example, an algorithm containing a high number of sophisticated mathematical operations on high-dimensional data that need to be culled from memory across several physical data stores, thus taking long times to execute, is said to exhibit high computational complexity. Inversely, another algorithm containing parsimonious operations on low-dimensional data which are fetched from a local data store and executing quickly has low computational complexity. Smart contracts are a salient point where algorithmics and token design intersect. Without going too much into technical detail, there are known pathologies of smart contract design and implementation [312] that bear on the choice of programming languages and optimization modalities in terms of mathematical approximations and data structures used. Token designers need to be aware of the problems that can occur and be ready to address them (ideally proactively) so as to reduce the risk of long transaction times and high token fees.

In short, computational complexity as a token design factor has implications for:

- **Project costs**. Smart contract implementations may necessitate repeated iterations until an acceptable minimization in computational complexity is achieved, which can translate into forced protocol upgrades and associated migrations. Hence, there can result elevated initial and on-going project costs.
- **Transaction fees**. By definition, higher complexities will mean higher use of platform resources for transaction execution/validation. Buyers/investors may be deterred from acquiring the token if transaction fees influence significantly expected payoff profiles, especially for short investment horizons and range-trading tokens.
- **Auditability**. Depending on the use case, complexity minimization solutions may only approximate conditionally the original mathematical models. What-if-scenarios will need to be extensively tested and documented so as to control data quality risks to the entire ecosystem.

It is not among the primary design considerations, but it can have significant repercussions for both token and project economics to the point of impacting the end-to-end value proposition of the token use case.

10.6 Summary

This chapter covered the most important pillar of the token ecosystem design framework, the one that at once exposes and validates the blockchain value proposition: token design.

We began in earlier chapters by postulating the nature of a token as digital store of value and, following the analogy of designing a new country-level economy, we examined attributes that also make it a medium of exchange and unit of account, i.e. *currency* of the new country. However, we then departed from the money paradigm to examine other token usages, as evident from existing token ecosystems. This overview of usages allowed us to create a token typology, and thus to systematize an explanation of token design as a *process* with target objectives aligned to particular token types. In this chapter, we examined several factors that should be considered during the token design thought process and explained each factor both from first principles and through examples of its manifestation in specific token use cases.

The meshing together of all three design pillars (market, mechanism, and token) was in evidence, as notions such as governance, rules, incentives, and economic value—introduced in previous chapters—were found to also drive token design in a cohesive manner. Inversely, several token design factors could be interpreted from the standpoints of the other pillars, by e.g. facilitating ecosystem governance; helping grow the universe of products and services available; enabling price discovery in transactions; and managing risk by individual economic agents (in the case of financial or operational risks) and by the ecosystem as a whole (in the case of systemic risk).

As with previous design pillars, there follows a chapter containing a dedicated token design case study.

References

1. [Case: USD] Adkins, T. (2024, August 23). *Countries using the U.S. Dollar*. Investopedia. Retrieved March 27, 2025, from https://www.investopedia.com/articles/forex/040915/countries-use-us-dollar.asp.
2. [Case: EUR] European Commission. *The Euro*. Retrieved March 27, 2025, from https://economy-finance.ec.europa.eu/euro_en.
3. Pernice, I. G. A., Gentzen, G., & Elendner, H. (2021). Cryptocurrencies and the velocity of money. *Cryptoeconomic Systems, 1*. https://doi.org/10.21428/58320208.f212c00e
4. Durant, R. (2021, May 7). Money velocity: Cryptocurrency valuation and inflation. Retrieved March 27, 2025, from https://seekingalpha.com/article/4425445-money-velocity-Cryptocurrency-valuation-and-inflation.
5. [Bitcoin (BTC) Whitepaper] Nakamoto, S. *Bitcoin: A peer-to-peer electronic cash system*. Retrieved March 27, 2025, from https://bitcoin.org/bitcoin.pdf.
6. [Bitcoin (BCH) Whitepaper] Nakamoto, S. *Bitcoin: A peer-to-peer electronic cash system*. Retrieved March 27, 2025, from https://bch.info/bitcoin.pdf.
7. [Bitcoin Satoshi Vision (BSV) Whitepaper]. Nakamoto, S. *Bitcoin: A peer-to-peer electronic cash system*. Retrieved March 27, from: https://bsvblockchain.org/wp-content/uploads/bitcoin.pdf.
8. *Bitcoin, Bitcoin Cash, Bitcoin SV Block Time historical chart, over the last 3 years—average block time (minutes)*. BitInfoCharts. Retrieved March 27, 2025, from https://bitinfocharts.com/comparison/confirmationtime-btc-bch-bsv.html#3y.
9. *Bitcoin, Bitcoin Cash, Bitcoin SV Transactions historical chart, over the last 3 years—number of transactions in blockchain per day*. BitInfoCharts. Retrieved March 27, 2025, from https://bitinfocharts.com/comparison/transactions-btc-bch-bsv.html#3y.
10. *Bitcoin, Bitcoin Cash, Bitcoin SV Avg. Transaction Fee historical chart, over the last 3 years—average transaction fee, USD*. BitInfoCharts. Retrieved March 27, 2025, from https://bitinfocharts.com/comparison/transactionfees-btc-bch-bsv.html#3y.

11. Conway, L. (2024, August 8). Bitcoin halving: What it is and why it matters for crypto investors. Investopedia. Retrieved March 25, 2025, from https://www.investopedia.com/bitcoin-halving-4843769.
12. (2024, November 23).[Ethereum Proof-of-Stake Validator] *Rewards and Penalties*. Ethereum.org. Retrieved March 25, 2025, from https://ethereum.org/en/developers/docs/consensus-mechanisms/pos/rewards-and-penalties/#rewards.
13. (2024, May 26).[Ethereum proof-of-stake validation] *block time*. Ethereum.org. Retrieved March 25, 2025, from https://ethereum.org/en/developers/docs/blocks/#block-time.
14. *Ethereum Average Block Time Chart, since inception—block time in Secs*. Etherscan. Retrieved March 25, 2025, from https://etherscan.io/chart/blocktime.
15. *What is Bitcoin halving?* Coinbase. Retrieved March 25, 2025, from https://www.coinbase.com/learn/crypto-basics/what-is-a-bitcoin-halving.
16. *Open Source Ethereum Explorer - showing the Ethereum Mainnet*. Retrieved March 25, 2025, from https://beaconcha.in/.
17. [Bitcoin Network] *Difficulty*. Bitcoin Wiki. Retrieved March 25, 2025, from https://en.bitcoin.it/wiki/Difficulty.
18. [Ethereum Proof-of-Work Network] *Difficulty*. 2miners. Retrieved March 26, 2025, from https://2miners.com/eth-network-difficulty.
19. Ethereum GeneSys Foundation. (2021, April 20). *Ethereum GeneSys Foundation has completed a 'Hard Fork' of ethereum to reclaim staked ETH 2.0 coins, and incentivize the PoW mining community on the blockchain network*. PR Newswire. Retrieved March 25, 2026, from https://www.prnewswire.com/news-releases/ethereum-genesys-foundation-has-completed-a-hard-fork-of-ethereum-to-reclaim-staked-eth-2-0-coins-and-incentivize-the-pow-mining-community-on-the-blockchain-network-301272383.html.
20. Rizzo, P. (2018, April 1). *120 Million? Vitalik proposes cap on ether cryptocurrency*. Coindesk. Retrieved March 26, 2025, from https://www.coindesk.com/120-million-vitalik-proposes-cap-ether-Cryptocurrency-creation.
21. (2023, December 8). How the merge impacted ETH supply. Ethereum.org. Retrieved March 26, 2025, from https://ethereum.org/en/roadmap/merge/issuance/.
22. Working Group on E-CNY Research and Development of the People's Bank of China. (2021, July). *Progress of Research & Development of E-CNY in China*. Retrieved March 27, 2025, from http://www.pbc.gov.cn/en/3688110/3688172/4157443/4293696/2021071614584691871.pdf.
23. Kwan, C. H. (2019, December 27). China aiming to issue a Central Bank digital currency—expected macro-level effects. [Japan] Research Institute of Economy, Trade and Industry. Retrieved March 26, 2025, from https://www.rieti.go.jp/en/china/19122701.html.
24. Diwakar, A. *Why are cryptocurrencies booming in Turkey?* TRTWorld. Retrieved March 26, 2025, from https://www.trtworld.com/magazine/why-are-cryptocurrencies-booming-in-turkey-45827.
25. Urquhart, A., & Zhang, H. (2019). Is Bitcoin a hedge or safe haven for currencies? An intraday analysis. *International Review of Financial Analysis, 63*(2) .
26. Baumöhl, E., & Vyrost, T. (2020). Stablecoins as a crypto safe heaven? Not all of them! *ZBW—Leibniz information Centre for Economics*, Kiel, Hamburg. Retrieved April 2, 2025, from https://ideas.repec.org/p/zbw/esprep/215484.html.
27. Coy, P. (2021, March 9). Bitcoin has zero intrinsic value. Some people are OK with that. Bloomberg. Retrieved April 2, 2025, from https://www.bloomberg.com/news/articles/2021-03-09/bitcoin-has-zero-intrinsic-value-some-people-are-ok-with-that.
28. Burniske, C. (2017). *Cryptoasset valuations*. Retrieved March 15, 2025, from https://medium.com/@cburniske/cryptoasset-valuations-ac83479ffca7.
29. Antos, J. (2018, July 2). *Cryptoasset Valuation: Considerations regarding "On Value, Velocity and Monetary Theory"*. Retrieved March 15, 2025, from https://medium.com/blockchain-advisory-group/cryptoasset-valuation-considerations-regarding-on-value-velocity-and-monetary-theory-1b06e659b360.

30. HASH CIB (2018, November 15). *The Next Step in Cryptoasset Valuation*. Retrieved March 15, 2025, from https://medium.com/hash-cib/the-next-step-in-cryptoasset-valuation-34bade0386de.
31. *Bitcoin NVT Ratio* [since inception]. Woobull Charts. Retrieved March 15, 2025, from http://charts.woobull.com/bitcoin-nvt-ratio/.
32. Woo, W. (2017, October 5). Introducing NVT ratio (Bitcoin's PE ratio), use it to detect bubbles. Woobull. Retrieved March 15, 2025, from https://woobull.com/introducing-nvt-ratio-bitcoins-pe-ratio-use-it-to-detect-bubbles/.
33. Kalichkin, D. (2018, February 4). *Rethinking Network Value to Transactions (NVT) Ratio*. Retrieved March 15, 2025, from https://medium.com/cryptolab/https-medium-com-kalichkin-rethinking-nvt-ratio-2cf810df0ab0.
34. *Bitcoin NVT Signal* [since inception]. Woobull Charts. Retrieved March 15, 2025, from http://charts.woobull.com/bitcoin-nvt-signal/.
35. Cryptopoiesis. (2018, September 18). *Bitcoin's Inflation Adjusted NVT Ratio - An UpToDate Assessment*. Retrieved March 15, 2025, from https://blog.goodaudience.com/bitcoins-inflation-adjusted-nvt-ratio-an-uptodate-assessment-f6ee3291d177.
36. Puell, D. (2018, October 2). *Bitcoin Market-Value-to-Realized-Value (MVRV) Ratio*. Retrieved March 15, 2025, from https://medium.com/@kenoshaking/bitcoin-market-value-to-realized-value-mvrv-ratio-3ebc914dbaee.
37. *NVTAdj by CoinMetrics*. CoinMetrics | Coverage. Retrieved March 15, 2025, from https://coverage.coinmetrics.io/asset-metrics-v2/NVTAdj.
38. PlanB. (2019, March 22). *Modeling Bitcoin Value with Scarcity*. Retrieved March 15, 2025, from https://medium.com/@100trillionUSD/modeling-bitcoins-value-with-scarcity-91fa0fc03e25.
39. Ehrlich, S. (2021, June 29). Demystifying Bitcoin's remarkably accurate price prediction model, stock-to-flow. Forbes. Retrieved March 16, 2025, from https://www.forbes.com/sites/stevenehrlich/2021/04/29/demystifying-bitcoins-remarkably-accurate-price-prediction-model-stock-to-flow.
40. Alabi, K. (2017). Digital blockchain networks appear to be following Metcalfe's law. *Electronic Commerce Research and Applications, 24*, 23–29. https://doi.org/10.1016/j.elerap.2017.06.003
41. Alabi, K. (2020). A 2020 perspective on 'digital blockchain networks appear to be following Metcalfe's Law'. *Electronic Commerce Research and Applications, 40*, 100939. https://doi.org/10.1016/j.elerap.2020.100939
42. Peterson, T. F. (2018). Metcalfe's law as a model for Bitcoin's value. Retrieved March 15, 2025, from https://caia.org/sites/default/files/metcalfeslaw_websiteupload_7-5-18.pdf.
43. *Total Value Locked (TVL)*. CoinMarketCap. Retrieved March 16, 2025, from https://coinmarketcap.com/alexandria/glossary/total-value-locked-tvl.
44. Sun, Z. (2021, September 29). *what is total value locked?* Retrieved March 16, 2025, from https://www.nasdaq.com/articles/what-is-total-value-locked-2021-09-29.
45. George, B. (2022, January 26). Why TVL matters in DeFi: Total value locked explained. Coindesk. Retrieved March 16, 2025, from https://www.coindesk.com/learn/why-tvl-matters-in-defi-total-value-locked-explained/.
46. Yap, J. (2021, August 2). Crypto valuation model: Market cap over TVL shows some crypto may be undervalued. Chaindebrief. Retrieved March 16, 2025, from https://pexx.com/chaindebrief/crypto-valuation-market-cap-over-tvl/
47. *Total Value Locked (TVL)*. IQ.wiki. Retrieved March 16, 2025, from https://iq.wiki/wiki/tvl.
48. [MakerDAO Token ecosystem] https://makerdao.world/, currently a subset of the Sky Token ecosystem (https://sky.money/).
49. [Uniswap Token ecosystem]. https://uniswap.org.
50. Larsen, A. (2018, December 6). *The business of stablecoins*. Retrieved March 16, 2025 from https://medium.com/blockchain-capital-blog/business-models-behind-stablecoins-cae801533798.

51. (2021, May 23). How stablecoins make money. Tokenpost. Retrieved March 17, 2025, from https://tokenpost.com/How-Stablecoins-make-money-7641.
52. [*Crypto*] *Asset Metrics by CoinMetrics*. CoinMetrics | Coverage. Retrieved March 17, 2025, from https://coverage.coinmetrics.io/asset-metrics-v2.
53. Philips, D. (2022). *Fully diluted valuation (FDV)—the great dilution Dilemma*. CoinMarketCap. Retrieved March 17, 2025, from https://coinmarketcap.com/alexandria/article/fully-diluted-valuation-fdv-the-great-dilution-dilemma.
54. Yap, J. (2021, August 25). The difference between a market cap and a fully diluted market cap in the crypto world. ChainDebrief. Retrieved March 17, 2025, from https://pexx.com/chaindebrief/difference-between-market-cap-and-fully-diluted-market-cap-crypto/.
55. https://smartcontentpublication.medium.com/defining-total-value-secured-tvs-in-decentralized-oracle-networks-c0a946f1c40.
56. Bonello P. J. (2018, April 12). A framework for valuing governance tokens: 0x. HackerNoon. Retrieved March 17, 2025, from https://hackernoon.com/a-framework-for-valuing-governance-tokens-0x-49d2cf2ef5bc.
57. Brukhman, J. (2019). *A relative value model for governance tokens*. Retrieved March 17, 2025, from https://github.com/coinfund/governance-model.
58. [Token valuation example: REP] Snider, M., Jain, T., & Samani, K. (2017, August 24). *Augur ($REP) analysis and valuation*. Retrieved March 17, 2025, from https://assets.ctfassets.net/qtbqvna1l0yq/1LjeUqRhHBkHvS7rHIQN6S/99d5fa045f79f83684b833cc39147bce/Augur-REP-Analysis-and-Valuation.pdf.
59. HVM Capital (2015, June 1). *Valuing Taxi Medallions: A Simple Framework*. Retrieved March 17, 2025, from http://hvmcapital.com/articles/Valuing Taxi Medallions A Simple Framework.pdf.
60. [Token valuation example: SWC] https://docs.google.com/spreadsheets/d/11TyxD9RPJ0cZDQKELRFyAUdjn7lUAQf4jwcOVz45L7w/edit#gid=1045449269.
61. [Token valuation example: FCT] Snider, M., Jain, T., & Samani, K. *Factom ($FCT) analysis and valuation*. Retrieved March 17, 2025, from https://assets.ctfassets.net/qtbqvna1l0yq/3wytjwPlA72ttczNkVUtHo/61ea8ad474cdc9f54a875d2349677d80/Factom-FCT-Analysis-and-Valuation.pdf.
62. *What is Bitcoin Mining?* Bitcoin.org. Retrieved March 17, 2025, from https://bitcoin.org/en/faq#what-is-bitcoin-mining.
63. [Ethereum Network Validation] *Block Rewards*. Ethereum.org. Retrieved March 17, 2005 from https://ethereum.org/en/developers/docs/consensus-mechanisms/pos/block-proposal/#block-rewards.
64. [Ethereum Proof-of-Stake Validator] *Rewards and Penalties*. Ethereum.org. Retrieved March 17, 2025, from https://ethereum.org/en/developers/docs/consensus-mechanisms/pos/rewards-and-penalties/.
65. [Litecoin Token ecosystem]. https://litecoin.org/.
66. [Polygon Token ecosystem]. *POL Token*. Retrieved March 17, 2025, from https://polygon.technology/pol-token.
67. [Loopring Token ecosystem]. *LRC Token*. Retrieved March 17, 2025, from https://loopring.org/#/lrc.
68. Algorand Technologies. Retrieved March 17, 2025, from https://www.algorandtechnologies.com/.
69. [Algorand Token ecosystem]. Algorand Standard Assets (ASAs). Retrieved March 17, 2025, from https://dev.algorand.co/concepts/assets/overview/.
70. Szabo, N. (1994). *Smart contracts*. Retrieved March 17, 2025, from https://www.fon.hum.uva.nl/rob/Courses/InformationInSpeech/CDROM/Literature/LOTwinterschool2006/szabo.best.vwh.net/smart.contracts.html.
71. Delphi. (2017, July 15). *The Oracle Problem*. Retrieved March 17, 2025, from https://medium.com/@DelphiSystems/the-oracle-problem-856ccbdbd14f.

72. Database trigger. (2025, January 30). In *Wikipedia*. Retrieved March 17, 2025, from https://en.wikipedia.org/wiki/Database_trigger.
73. Business rule management system. (2024, August 31). In *Wikipedia*. Retrieved March 17, 2025, from https://en.wikipedia.org/wiki/Business_rule_management_system.
74. Complex events processing. (2024, October 9). In *Wikipedia*. Retrieved March 17, 2025, from https://en.wikipedia.org/wiki/Complex_event_processing.
75. [Algorand Smart Contracts (ASC1)] *Overview*. Algorand developer portal. Retrieved March 17, 2025, from https://dev.algorand.co/concepts/smart-contracts/overview/.
76. [Algorand Smart Contracts (ASC1)] *Writing Smart Contracts*. Algorand developer portal. Retrieved March 17, 2025, from https://dev.algorand.co/concepts/smart-contracts/overview/#writing-smart-contracts.
77. [Algorand Smart Contracts (ASC1)] *SmartSig details*. Algorand developer portal. Retrieved March 17, 2025, from https://dev.algorand.co/concepts/smart-contracts/logic-sigs/.
78. *Algorand Smart Contract NFT Specification*. Algorand developer portal. Retrieved March 17, 2025, from https://dev.algorand.co/arc-standards/arc-0072/.
79. [Algorand Asset useage example]. Algorand GitHub. Retrieved March 17, 2025, from https://github.com/algorand/pyteal/blob/master/examples/application/asset.py.
80. [Cardano] *Smart Contracts*. Cardano developer portal. Retrieved March 17, 2025, from https://developers.cardano.org/docs/smart-contracts/.
81. [Cardano development updates]. Retrieved March 17, 2025, from https://www.essentialcardano.io/development-update.
82. *Discover Native Tokens*. Cardano developer portal. Retrieved March 17, 2025, from https://developers.cardano.org/docs/native-Tokens/.
83. *How does a* [Cardano] *native token compare to Ada and ERC20?* Retrieved March 17, 2025, from https://cardano-ledger.readthedocs.io/en/latest/explanations/features.html#how-do-native-Tokens-compare-to-erc-20-Tokens.
84. [Cardano] *Minting policy*. Retrieved March 17, 2025, from https://cardano-ledger.readthedocs.io/en/latest/explanations/policies.html #minting-policy.
85. Lacapra, E. (2023, February 22). How to create NFTs on the Cardano blockchain. CoinTelegraph. Retrieved March 17, 2025, from https://cointelegraph.com/news/how-to-create-nfts-on-the-cardano-blockchain.
86. Vogelsteller, F., & Buterin, V. (2015, November 20). ERC-20: Token standard. Ethereum Improvement Proposals, no.20. Retrieved March 17, 2025, from https://eips.ethereum.org/EIPS/eip-20.
87. [OpenZeppelin ERC-20 Smart Contract implementation]. OpenZeppelin GitHub. Retrieved March 17, 2025, from https://github.com/OpenZeppelin/openzeppelin-contracts/blob/master/contracts/token/ERC20/ERC20.sol.
88. Reitwiessner, C., Johnson, N., Vogelsteller, F., Baylina, J., Feldmeier, K. & Entriken, W. (2018, January). ERC-165: Standard Interface detection. *Ethereum Improvement Proposals, 165*. Retrieved March 17, 2025, from https://eips.ethereum.org/EIPS/eip-165
89. Entriken, W., Shirley, D., Evans, J. & Sachs, Nastassia. (2018, January). ERC-721: Non-fungible token standard. *Ethereum Improvement Proposals, 721*. Retrieved March 17, 2025, from https://eips.ethereum.org/EIPS/eip-721
90. [ERC-721 Smart Contract Reference Implementation]. EIP member GitHub. Retrieved March 17, 2025, from https://github.com/0xcert/ethereum-erc721.
91. Dafflon, J., Baylina, J., & Shababi, T. (2017, November). ERC-777: Token standard. *Ethereum Improvement Proposals, 777*. Retrieved March 17, 2025, from https://eips.ethereum.org/EIPS/eip-777.
92. [ERC-777 Smart Contract Implementation]. EIP member GitHub. Retrieved March 17, 2025, from https://github.com/0xjac/ERC777/blob/master/contracts/examples/ReferenceToken.sol.
93. Radomski, W., Cooke., A., Castonguay, P., Therien, J., Binet, E., & Sandford, R. (2018, June). *ERC-1155: Multi Token Standard*. Ethereum Improvement Proposals, no.1155. Retrieved March 17, 2025, from https://eips.ethereum.org/EIPS/eip-1155.

94. Minacori, V. (2018, August). *ERC-1363: Payable Token*. Ethereum Improvement Proposals, no.1363. Retrieved March 17, 2025, from https://eips.ethereum.org/EIPS/eip-1363.
95. Papanikolas, S. (2019, October). ERC-2309: ERC-721 consecutive transfer extension. *Ethereum Improvement Proposals, 2309*. Retrieved March 17, 2025, from https://eips.ethereum.org/EIPS/eip-2309.
96. Lebrun, J., Malghem, T., Thizy, K., Falempin, L. & Boudjemaa, A. (2021, July). ERC-3643: T-REX—token for regulated EXchanges. *Ethereum Improvement Proposals, 3643*. Retrieved March 17, 2025, from https://eips.ethereum.org/EIPS/eip-3643.
97. [ERC-3643 -] *The Token standard for RWA Tokenization*. Retrieved March 17, 2025, from https://www.erc3643.org.
98. *Ethereum Improvement Proposals*. Ethereum.org. Retrieved March 17, 2025, from https://eips.ethereum.org/all.
99. Kupriianov, M. (2018, October). *ERC-1462: Base Security Token [DRAFT]*. Ethereum Improvement Proposals, no.1462. Retrieved March 17, 2025, from https://eips.ethereum.org/EIPS/eip-1462.
100. [Tezos] *FA1.2 tokens*. Tezos documentation pages. Retrieved March 17, 2025, from https://docs.tezos.com/architecture/tokens/FA1.2.
101. [Description of Tezos Smart Contract implementing token transfers and spending approvals]. Tezos GitLab pages. Retrieved March 17, 2025, from https://gitlab.com/tezos/tzip/-/blob/master/proposals/tzip-7/tzip-7.md.
102. *Sample* [Tezos] *Smart Sontracts*. Tezos documentation pages. Retrieved March 17, 2025, from https://docs.tezos.com/smart-contracts/samples.
103. [*Sample* [Tezos] *Smart Contracts, developed in Ligo (high-level language which compliles to optimized Tezos bytecode)*]. Retrieved March 17, 2025, from https://packages.ligolang.org/contracts.
104. [Tezos] *FA2 tokens*. Tezos documentation pages. Retrieved March 17, 2025, from https://docs.tezos.com/architecture/tokens/FA2.
105. [Tezos] *FA2.1 tokens*. Tezos documentation pages. Retrieved March 17, 2025, from https://docs.tezos.com/architecture/tokens/FA2.1.
106. [Description of Tezos TZIP-012 unified Token Smart Contract interface standard]. Tezos GitLab pages. Retrieved March 17, 2025, from https://gitlab.com/tezos/tzip/-/blob/master/proposals/tzip-12/tzip-12.md.
107. [Tezos] *Tutorials*. Tezos documentation pages. Retrieved March 17, 2025, from https://docs.tezos.com/tutorials.
108. *Michelson* [language used for Tezos Smart Contract programming] *Reference Introduction*. Tezos GitLab pages. Retrieved March 17, 2025, from https://tezos.gitlab.io/michelson-reference/.
109. [Visual programming environment for Tezos Smart Contract development] *VisualTez*. Retrieved March 17, 2025, from https://visualtez.com/editor.
110. Lim, E., Chua, H.W. & Vohra, A. [Tezos] *Standard for Non Fungible Tokens* [and implementation - ZRC-1]. Tezos GitHub pages. Retrieved March 17, 2025, from https://github.com/Zilliqa/ZRC/blob/master/zrcs/zrc-1.md.
111. [Reference Tezos NFT Smart Contract]. Tezos GitHub pages. Retrieved March 17, 2025, from https://github.com/Zilliqa/ZRC/blob/main/reference-contracts/nonfungible-token.scilla.
112. Yoo, N. & Tan, J.H. [Reference Tezos NFT Smart Contract Interface - ZRC-6]. *Non-Fungible Token Standard*. Tezos GitHub pages. Retrieved March 17, 2025, from https://github.com/Zilliqa/ZRC/blob/main/zrcs/zrc-6.md.
113. Nagaraj, V. & Wen C.H. [Tezos] *Standard for Non Fungible Tokens* [and implementation - ZRC-2]. Tezos GitHub pages. Retrieved March 17, 2025, from https://github.com/Zilliqa/ZRC/blob/master/zrcs/zrc-2.md.
114. [Reference Tezos Fungible Token Smart Contract]. Tezos GitHub pages. Retrieved March 17, 2025, from https://github.com/Zilliqa/ZRC/blob/main/reference-contracts/FungibleToken-Mintable.scilla.

115. *AA v Persons Unknown & Ors, Re Bitcoin* [2019] EWHC 3556 (Comm). Judgment reported under https://www.bailii.org/ew/cases/EWHC/Comm/2019/3556.html.
116. (2019, December 2019). *What is the legal status of cryptoassets and smart contracts?* Simmons & Simmons LLP. Retrieved March 17, 2025, from https://www.simmons-simmons.com/en/publications/ck400ievr65o00b44el9cfb4p/what-is-the-legal-status-of-cryptoassets-and-smart-contracts-.
117. US Internal Revenue Service (2021). *IRS Notice 2014–21* [describing how existing general tax principles apply to transactions using virtual currency in the U.S. jurisdiction]. Retrieved March 17, 2025, from https://www.irs.gov/pub/irs-drop/n-14-21.pdf.
118. *B2C2 Ltd v Quoine Pte Ltd* [2019] SGHC(I) 3. Judgment reported under https://www.elitigation.sg/gd/gd/2019_SGHCI_12/pdf.
119. [Switzerland] *Federal Act on the adaptation of Federal Legal Law to developments in Distributed Electronic Register Technology* [2020]. Retrieved March 17, 2025, from https://www.fedlex.admin.ch/eli/oc/2021/33/de.
120. [Switzerland] State Secretariat for International Finance. (2023, September 20). *Blockchain / DLT*. Retrieved March 17, 2025, from https://www.sif.admin.ch/en/blockchain-dlt-en.
121. [Switzerland] Federal Department of Finance - FDF (2021, June 18). *Federal Council brings DLT Act fully into force and issues ordinance*. Retrieved March 17, 2025, from https://www.efd.admin.ch/en/nsb?id=84035.
122. [Germany] *Act on the transposition of the amendment directive to the 4th EU Anti-Money-Laundering Directive* [2019]. Retrieved March 17, 2025, from https://www.bundesrat.de/SharedDocs/drucksachen/2019/0501-0600/598-19.pdf.
123. [Announcing PRC Amendment to China's Civil Code, regarding treatment of Cryptoassets in inheritance]. (2020, May 28). *The third session of the 13th National People's Congress closed in Beijing*. Xinhuanet. Retrieved March 17, 2025, from http://www.xinhuanet.com/politics/2020lh/2020-05/28/c_1126046968.htm.
124. Kaaru, S. (2020, May 20). China's new law allows digital currencies inheritance. CoinGeek. Retrieved March 17, 2025, from https://coingeek.com/chinas-new-law-allows-digital-currencies-inheritance/.
125. Hinman, W. (2018, June 14). *Digital asset transactions: When Howey met Gary (plastic)*. Remarks at the Yahoo finance all markets summit: Crypto (San Francisco, CA). Retrieved March 17, 2025, from https://www.sec.gov/news/speech/speech-hinman-061418.
126. [U.S.] Securities & Exchange Commission. (2017, July 25). Report of Investigation Pursuant to Section 21(a) of the Securities Exchange Act of 1934: The DAO. SEC Release No. 81207. Retrieved March 18, 2025, from http://www.sec.gov/litigation/investreport/34-81207.pdf.
127. [U.S.] Securities & Exchange Commission. (2021, July 14). *In the Matter of Blotics Ltd. f/d/b/ a Coinschedule Ltd*. Administrative Proceeding, File No. 3-20398. Retrieved March 18, 2025, from https://www.sec.gov/litigation/admin/2021/33-10956.pdf.
128. [U.S.] Securities & Exchange Commission. (2021, July 14). *ICO "Listing" Website Charged With Unlawfully Touting Digital Asset Securities*. SEC Press Release 2021–125. Retrieved March 18, 2025, from https://www.sec.gov/news/press-release/2021-125.
129. U.S. Securities & Exchange Commission. *Cyber, Crypto Assets and Emerging Technology Enforcements*. Retrieved March 18, 2025, from https://www.sec.gov/about/divisions-offices/division-enforcement/cyber-crypto-assets-emerging-technology.
130. U.S. Financial Industry Regulatory Authority (FINRA). *Investment Products; Crypto Assets*. Retrieved April 3, 2025, from https://www.finra.org/investors/investing/investment-products/crypto-assets.
131. U.S. Securities & Exchange Commission. (2019, July 8). *Joint Staff Statement on Broker-Dealer Custody of Digital Asset Securities*. Retrieved April 3, 2025, from https://www.sec.gov/news/public-statement/joint-staff-statement-broker-dealer-custody-digital-asset-securities.

132. Lambert, T., Liebau, D., & Roosenboom, P. (2021, September 12). Security token offerings. *Small Business Economics, 59*, 299–325. https://link.springer.com/article/10.1007/s11187-021-00539-9 (Open Access).
133. International Organization of Securities Commissions (IOSCO). *Regulators' Statements on Initial Coin Offerings*. Retrieved April 3, 2025, from https://www.iosco.org/publications/?subsection=ico-statements.
134. Security token offering. (2024, June 18). In *Wikipedia*. Retrieved April 3, 2025, from https://en.wikipedia.org/wiki/Security_Token_offering.
135. (2019, November). *Tokenised Securities - A Roadmap for Market Participants and Regulators*. Asia Securities Industry and Financial Markets Association (asifma). Retrieved April 3, 2025, from https://asifma.org/wp-content/uploads/2019/11/tokenised-securities-a-roadmap-for-market-participants-final.pdf.
136. (2021, January 20). *What Are Wrapped Tokens?* Binance Academy. Retrieved April 3, 2025, from https://academy.binance.com/en/articles/what-are-wrapped-Tokens.
137. Mouton, J. (2021). Regulating smart contracts in the domain of financial trading. *California Western Law Review, 57*(2) Article 13. Retrieved April 3, 2025, from https://scholarlycommons.law.cwsl.edu/cwlr/vol57/iss2/13
138. Yates, M., & Montagu, G. (2013). *The law of global custody* (4th ed.). Bloomsbury Professional.
139. Blockchain oracle. (2025, March 13). *In Wikipedia*. Retrieved April 3, 2025, from https://en.wikipedia.org/wiki/Blockchain_oracle
140. (2022, February 4). *Blockchain oracles explained: Decentralized oracles in DeFi*. Gemini Cryptopedia. Retrieved April 3, 2025, from https://www.gemini.com/cryptopedia/crypto-oracle-blockchain-overview#section-blockchain-oracles-explained-why-do-we-need-oracles.
141. [EU MiFId II Directive and implementing/delegated regulations thereof]. *Directive 2014/65/EU of the European Parliament and of the Council of 15 May 2014 on markets in financial instruments and amending Directive 2002/92/EC and Directive 2011/61/EU (recast)*. Basis text retrieved April 3, 2025, from https://eur-lex.europa.eu/legal-content/EN/TXT/?uri=celex%3A32014L0065).
142. U.S. Financial Industry Regulatory Authority (FINRA). *Rule 5310 - Best Execution and Interpositioning*. Retrieved April 3, 2025, from https://www.finra.org/rules-guidance/rulebooks/finra-rules/5310.
143. U.S. Financial Industry Regulatory Authority (FINRA). *Best Execution - Regulatory Obligations and Related Considerations*. Retrieved April 3, 2025, from https://www.finra.org/rules-guidance/guidance/reports/2021-finras-examination-and-risk-monitoring-program/best-execution.
144. [U.K.] Financial Conduct Authority (FCA). *COBS 11.2A Best execution—MiFID provisions*. FCA Handbook. Retrieved April 3, 2025, from https://www.handbook.fca.org.uk/handbook/COBS/11/2A.html.
145. Monetary Authority of Singapore (MAS). *Notice SFA 04-N16 on Execution of Customer's Orders*. Retrieved April 3, 2025, from https://www.mas.gov.sg/regulation/notices/notice-sfa-04-n16.
146. Monetary Authority of Singapore (MAS). *Guidelines to Notice SFA04-N16 on Execution of Customers' Orders*. Retrieved April 3, 2025, from https://www.mas.gov.sg/regulation/guidelines/guidelines-to-notice-sfa04-n16.
147. Bank of International Settlements. (2012, February). *Data requirements for monitoring derivative transactions*. IFC Bulletin, No 35. Retrieved April 3, 2025, from https://www.bis.org/ifc/publ/ifcb35.pdf.
148. U.S. Financial Industry Regulatory Authority (FINRA). *FINRA Disciplinary Actions Online Database*. Retrieved April 3, 2025, from https://www.finra.org/rules-guidance/oversight-enforcement/finra-disciplinary-actions-online.

149. International Swaps and Derivatives Association (ISDA). *ISDA Papers on DLT and Smart Contracts*. Retrieved April 3, 2025, from https://www.isda.org/2019/10/16/isda-smart-contracts/.
150. [Safe Token ecosystem]. https://safe.global/.
151. Neuman, N. (2024). *Introducing casa inheritance: Secure your generational wealth*. Retrieved April 3, 2025, from https://blog.casa.io/introducing-casa-inheritance/
152. Voell, Z., & Pann, D. (2020, October 16). OKEx suspends withdrawals, says key holder not available due to cooperation with investigation. CoinDesk.com. Retrieved April 3, 2025, from https://www.coindesk.com/markets/2020/10/16/okex-suspends-withdrawals-says-key-holder-not-available-due-to-cooperation-with-investigation/.
153. Palmer, D. (2020, October 16). OKEx founder incommunicado while assisting in investigation: Report. Coindesk. Retrieved April 3, 2025, from https://www.coindesk.com/markets/2020/10/16/okex-founder-star-xu-held-in-police-custody-report/.
154. Group buying. (2024, November 11). In *Wikipedia*. Retrieved April 3, 2025, from https://en.wikipedia.org/wiki/Group_buying.
155. U.S. Securities & Exchange Commission (2018, March 20). *Investment Clubs and the SEC*. Retrieved April 3, 2025, from https://www.sec.gov/about/reports-publications/investor-publications/investment-clubs.
156. Purchase of commissions in the British Army. (2025, February 26). In *Wikipedia*. Retrieved April 3, 2025, from https://en.wikipedia.org/wiki/Purchase_of_commissions_in_the_British_Army.
157. Cashiering. (2025, March 12). In *Wikipedia*. Retrieved April 3, 2025, from https://en.wikipedia.org/wiki/Cashiering.
158. Ancheta, A. (June 12, 2024). *What Is a Performance Bond and How Does It Work?* Retrieved April 4, 2025, from https://www.investopedia.com/terms/p/performancebond.asp.
159. *What Are NFTs, Anyway? One Just Sold for $69 Million*. The New York Times. Retrieved April 4, 2025, from https://www.nytimes.com/2021/03/11/arts/design/what-is-an-nft.html.
160. *Jack Dorsey sells his first tweet as an NFT for $2.9 million*. LedgerInsigts. Retrieved April 4, 2025, from https://www.ledgerinsights.com/jack-dorsey-sells-his-first-tweet-as-an-nft-for-2-9-million/.
161. [Flow Token ecosystem]. https://flow.com/.
162. *Visa purchases CryptoPunk NFT for $150,000 as it gets involved in the booming digital-collectibles market*. BusinessInsider. Retrieved April 4, 2025, from https://markets.businessinsider.com/news/currencies/visa-cryptopunks-nft-150000-cryptocurrency-blockchain-fungible-token-digital-asset-2021-8.
163. NFT's on PICTOCLUB Online Art Shop. PICTOCLUB. Retrieved April 4, 2025, from https://www.pictoclub.com/product-category/NFT's/?swoof=1&product_tag=nft&really_curr_tax=1326-product_cat.
164. Crypto stamp art. *Austrian Post (Österreichische Post Aktiengesellschaft)*. Retrieved April 5, 2025, from https://www.post.at/p/c/cryptostampart/.
165. *Wine NFT's collection*. OpenSea. Retrieved April 4, 2025, from https://opensea.io/collection/wiv.
166. Supply Chain NFT's. Ownest. Retrieved April 4, 2025, from https://ownest.io/en/.
167. (July 8, 2024). *Building Connections: NFTs, QR Codes and Social Communities redefining customer engagement*. ApparelResources.com. Retrieved April 4, 2025, from https://apparelresources.com/technology-news/retail-tech/building-connections-nfts-qr-codes-social-communities-redefining-customer-engagement/.
168. TradeTeq (September 27, 2021). *XinFin's XDC Network and Tradeteq Launch World's First Trade Finance-Based NFT Transaction*. Retrieved April 4, 2025, from https://www.tradeteq.com/news/xinfins-xdc-network-and-tradeteq-launch-worlds-first.
169. U.S. Copyright Act, section 106. Retrieved April 4, 2025, from https://www.copyright.gov/title17/92chap1.html.
170. U.S. Copyright Act. Retrieved April 4, 2025, from https://www.copyright.gov/title17/.

171. Burks, Z., Morgan, J., Malone, B., & James, S. J. (2020, September). ERC-2981: NFT royalty standard. *Ethereum Improvement Proposals, 2981*. Retrieved April 4, 2025, from https://eips.ethereum.org/EIPS/eip-2981
172. SEC v. W.J. Howey Co., 328 U.S. 293 (1946). Judgment retrieved April 4, 2025, from https://supreme.justia.com/cases/federal/us/328/293/.
173. U.S. Anti-Money Laundering (AML) Act of 2020. Amended statutes as per AML act and accompanying material made available through the Financial Crimes Enforcement Network (FINCEN). Retrieved April 4, 2025, from https://www.fincen.gov/anti-money-laundering-act-2020.
174. U.S. Nathional Defense Authorization Act of 2021. Text of the Act retrieved April 4, 2025, from https://www.congress.gov/116/plaws/publ283/PLAW-.
175. [U.S.] Office of the Comptroller of the Currency. (June 30, 2021). Bank Secrecy Act/Anti-Money Laundering: Interagency Statement on the Issuance of the Anti-Money Laundering/Countering the Financing of Terrorism National Priorities. OCC Bulletin 2021–29. Retrieved April 4, 2025, from https://www.occ.treas.gov/news-issuances/bulletins/2021/bulletin-2021-29.html.
176. U.S. Bank Secrecy Act (BSA) of 1970. Text of the BSA retrieved April 4, 2025, from http://www.gpo.gov/fdsys/pkg/STATUTE-84/pdf/STATUTE-84-Pg1114-2.pdf.
177. [U.S.] Office of the Comptroller of the Currency, BSA page. Retrieved April 4, 2025, from https://www.occ.treas.gov/topics/supervision-and-examination/bsa/index-bsa.html.
178. EU Commission. (2021). *Targeted consultation on the review of the Directive on financial collateral arrangements*. Retrieved April 4, 2025, from https://finance.ec.europa.eu/system/files/2021-02/2021-financial-collateral-review-consultation-document_en.pdf.
179. Uniswap Labs. (2021, March 23). *Introducing Uniswap v3*. Retrieved April 4, 2025, from https://blog.uniswap.org/uniswap-v3.
180. Angeris, G., Kao, H.-T., Chiang, R., Noyes, C., & Chitra, T. (2019). An analysis of uniswap markets. *Cryptoeconomic Systems Journal*. Retrieved April 4, 2025, from https://ssrn.com/abstract=3602203. Revised and updated versions at https://arxiv.org/abs/1911.03380.
181. Poser, S. W. (2021). Market makers in financial markets: Their role, how they function, why they are important, and the NYSE DMM difference. NYSE. Retrieved April 4, 2025, from https://www.nyse.com/publicdocs/nyse/NYSE_Paper_on_Market_Making_Sept_2021.pdf.
182. Deutsche Börse Cash Markets. (2019). *Market-making programme*. Retrieved April 4, 2025, from https://www.deutsche-boerse-cash-market.com/resource/blob/279694/db2b59f7075f9fa28bb9268b0e1c4dd4/data/market-making-handbook.pdf.
183. Guéant, O. (2016). *The financial mathematics of market liquidity* (Financial mathematics series). Chapman and Hall/CRC.
184. Lu, X., & Abergel, F. (2018). Order-book modelling and market making strategies. *Market Microstructure and Liquidity, 4*(01n02), 1950003. Retrieved April 4, 2025, from https://arxiv.org/abs/1806.05101
185. Zhang, Y., Chen, X., & Park, D. (2018). *Formal specification of constant product ($x \times y = k$) market model and implementation*. Runtime Verification, Inc. Retrieved April 4, 2025, from https://github.com/runtimeverification/verified-smart-contracts/blob/uniswap/uniswap/x-y-k.pdf.
186. Shevchenko, A. (August 29, 2020). Uniswap and automated market makers, explained. CoinTelegraph. Retrieved April 4, 2025, from https://cointelegraph.com/explained/uniswap-and-automated-market-makers-explained.
187. https://docs.uniswap.org/protocol/concepts/advanced/research, please search into the page for "The Replicating Portfolio of a Constant Product Market Maker", which links into: Joseph, C. (2020). *The replicating portfolio of a constant product market*. Retrieved April 4, 2025, from https://ssrn.com/abstract=3550601 (also available at https://doi.org/10.2139/ssrn.3550601).
188. Lamb, K. (June 17, 2024). *An introduction to structured products*. Retrieved April 4, 2025, from https://www.investopedia.com/articles/optioninvestor/07/structured_products.asp.

189. Swiss Structured Products Association. *Swiss Derivative Map ©*. PDF document downloadable from https://sspa.ch/en/products/. E.g., 2025 Version retrieved April 4, 2025, from https://sspa.ch/wp-content/uploads/2025/01/en_sspaswissmap_2025_web.pdf.
190. *Understanding Returns*. Uniswap.org. Retrieved April 4, 2025, from https://docs.uniswap.org/contracts/v2/concepts/advanced-topics/understanding-returns. Please search in the Webpage for "Risks", the text of which links into: Pintail (January 12, 2019). *Uniswap: A good deal for liquidity providers?* Retrieved April 4, 2025, from https://pintail.medium.com/uniswap-a-good-deal-for-liquidity-providers-104c0b6816f2.
191. *Research*. Uniswap.org. Retrieved April 4, 2025, from https://docs.uniswap.org/contracts/v2/concepts/advanced-topics/research. Please search in the page for "Pintail Research", the text of which links into: Pintail (February 14, 2019). *Understanding Uniswap Returns*. Retrieved April 4, 2025, from https://pintail.medium.com/understanding-uniswap-returns-cc593f3499ef.
192. Lau, L. (2021, September 2). A mathematical view of automated market maker (AMM) algorithms and its future. AnchorDAO Lab. Retrieved April 4, 2025, from https://medium.com/anchordao-lab/automated-market-maker-amm-algorithms-and-its-future-f2d5e6cc624a.
193. Robinson, D. (2021). *Uniswap v3: The universal AMM. Paradigm*. Retrieved April 4, 2025, from https://www.paradigm.xyz/2021/06/uniswap-v3-the-universal-amm.
194. [Uniswap v3 Whitepaper] Adams, H., Zinsmeister, N., Salem, M., Keefer, R., & Robinson, D. (2021, March). *Uniswap v3 Core*. Retrieved April 4, 2025, from https://uniswap.org/whitepaper-v3.pdf.
195. Yin, J., & Ren, M. (2021). *On liquidity mining for Uniswap v3*. Retrieved April 4, 2025, from https://arxiv.org/abs/2108.05800.
196. Jackson, R. (2021, November 19). Half of Uniswap liquidity providers are losing money. Nasdaq. Retrieved April 4, 2025, from https://www.nasdaq.com/articles/half-of-uniswap-liquidity-providers-are-losing-money.
197. "*Impermanent Loss*" in: Glossary. Coinmarketcap.com. Retrieved April 5, 2025, from https://coinmarketcap.com/alexandria/glossary/impermanent-loss. "Impermanent Loss" is also termed "Divergence Loss" as per some recent industry blogs, e.g. https://wiki.sovryn.com/en/sovryn-dapp/impermanent-loss.
198. Hays, A. (2022, April 30). Unrealized loss: What it is, how it works, example. Investopedia. Retrieved April 5, 2025, from https://www.investopedia.com/terms/u/unrealizedloss.asp
199. *Range Orders*. Uniswap.org. Retrieved April 4, 2025, from https://docs.uniswap.org/concepts/protocol/range-orders.
200. [Curve Token ecosystem]. https://curve.fi.
201. [Curve Whitepaper - StableSwap] Egorov, M. (2019, November 10). *StableSwap - efficient mechanism for Stablecoin liquidity*. Retrieved April 4, 2025, from https://classic.curve.fi/files/stableswap-paper.pdf, linked into from https://classic.curve.fi/whitepaper.
202. [Curve Whitepaper - Crypto Pools] Egorov, M. (2021, June 9). *Automatic market-making with dynamic peg*. Curve Finance (Swiss Stake GmbH). Retrieved April 4, 2025, from https://classic.curve.fi/files/crypto-pools-paper.pdf, linked into from https://classic.curve.fi/whitepaper.
203. Young, M. (2021, June 10). Curve finance upgrades algorithm for concentrated liquidity. BeInCrypto.com. Retrieved April 5, 2025, from https://beincrypto.com/curve-finance-upgrades-algorithm-for-concentrated-liquidity.
204. Zhang, B., Oliynykov, R., & Balogun, H. (2019). A Treasury system for cryptocurrencies: Enabling better collaborative intelligence. Network and distributed systems security (NDSS) symposium, San Diego. Retrieved April 4, 2025, from https://doi.org/10.14722/ndss.2019.23024.
205. OlympusDAO. *What is olympus*? Retrieved April 4, 2025, from https://docs.olympusdao.finance/main/overview/intro.

206. OlympusDAO. *Why do we need OlympusDAO in the first place?* Retrieved April 4, 2025, from https://docs.olympusdao.finance/main/overview/intro#why-do-we-need-olympus-in-the-first-place.
207. OlympusDAO. (2021, February 2). *Introducing OlympusDAO, An Algorithmic Currency Protocol.* Retrieved April 4, 2025, from https://olympusdao.medium.com/introducing-olympusdao-a-true-digital-currency-protocol-648c00c572d2.
208. *Olympus OHM Price.* Coingecko. Retrieved April 5, 2025 from https://www.coingecko.com/en/coins/olympus.
209. [Original Tether (USDT) Whitepaper] *Tether: Fiat currencies on the Bitcoin blockchain.* Retrieved April 4, 2025, from https://assets.ctfassets.net/vyse88cgwfbl/5UWgHMvz071t2Cq5yTw5vi/c9798ea8db99311bf90ebe0810938b01/TetherWhitePaper.pdf, linked into from https://tether.to/en/whitepaper/.
210. [Circle USDC Whitepaper, conforming to MiCA/EU] *USDC White Paper.* Retrieved April 5, 2025 from https://www.circle.com/legal/mica-usdc-whitepaper, linked into from https://www.circle.com/legal/usdc-terms.
211. [MakerDAO Whitepaper—MCD version preceding migration to Sky.money] *The Maker Protocol: MakerDAO's Multi-Collateral Dai (MCD) System.* Retrieved April 5, 2025 from https://makerdao.com/whitepaper/White%20Paper%20-The%20Maker%20Protocol_%20MakerDAO%E2%80%99s%20Multi-Collateral%20Dai%20(MCD)%20System-FINAL-%20021720.pdf, linked into from https://makerdao.com/en/whitepaper.
212. [XCHF Stablecoin Whitepaper—mentioning the backing Bank Guarantee] *CryptoFranc (XCHF) Introduction & Token Terms 2021-Q4. Version 2.3 - October 15th, 2021.* Bitcoin Suisse. Retrieved on April 5, 2025 from https://files.bitcoinsuisse.com/assets/pdf/2021_Q4_XCHF_TokenTerms.pdf.
213. Moin, A., Gün Sirer E., & Sekniqi, K. (2019). A classification framework for Stablecoin designs. Retrieved April 5, 2025 from https://arxiv.org/abs/1910.10098.
214. *What are proof of reserves?* Chainlink. Retrieved April 5, 2025, from https://chain.link/education-hub/proof-of-reserves.
215. Galati, L., Webb, A., & Webb, R. I. (2024, September). Financial contation in cryptocurrency exchanges: Evidence from the FTT collapse. *Finance Research Letters, 67(A).* Retrieved April 5, 2025, from https://www.sciencedirect.com/science/article/pii/S1544612324007773 (Open Access).
216. Treehouse. (2023, February 7). The crypto contagion and its looming after-effects (part 1). Medium. Retrieved April 5, 2025, from https://medium.com/coinmonks/the-crypto-contagion-and-its-looming-after-effects-part-1-367beda6bc.
217. [MakerDAO Whitepaper—DAI] *The Dai Stablecoin System.* Retrieved April 5, 2025, from https://makerdao.com/whitepaper/DaiDec17WP.pdf, linked into from https://makerdao.com/en/whitepaper/#the-dai-stablecoin. Please note: MakerDAO is currently a subset of the Sky Token ecosystem (https://sky.money/).
218. *An Overview of the Sky Protocol and Its Features.* Retrieved April 4, 2025 from https://makerdao.com/da/whitepaper/#the-sky-protocol.
219. [MakerDAO Token ecosystem] https://makerdao.com/en/. Retrieved April 4, 2025. Please note: MakerDAO is currently a subset of the Sky Token ecosystem (https://sky.money/).
220. *CoinMarketCap DAI page.* CoinMarketCap. Retrieved April 4, 2025 from https://coinmarketcap.com/currencies/multi-collateral-dai/. Please note: exchange information under "Dai Markets".
221. *[Dai] Collateral Assets.* Retrieved April 4, 2025, from https://makerdao.com/en/whitepaper/#collateral-assets. Please note: MakerDAO is currently a subset of the Sky Token ecosystem (https://sky.money/).
222. *Use of the MKR Token in Sky Governance.* Retrieved April 4, 2025, from https://makerdao.com/en/whitepaper/#use-of-the-mkr-token-in-sky-governance. Please note: MakerDAO is currently a subset of the Sky Token ecosystem (https://sky.money/).

223. *Collateralized Debt Position (CDP)*. Retrieved April 4, 2025, from https://coinmarketcap.com/academy/glossary/collateralized-debt-position-cdp. The term was originally introduced by the first generation of Maker protocol (https://docs.makerdao.com/build/dai.js/single-collateral-dai/collateralized-debt-position). Please note: MakerDAO is currently a subset of the Sky Token ecosystem (https://sky.money/).
224. *The Auctions of the Maker Protocol*. Retrieved April 4, 2025, from https://docs.makerdao.com/keepers/the-auctions-of-the-maker-protocol, linked into from https://makerdao.com/da/whitepaper/#sky-protocol-auctions
225. *Risk Parameters Controlled by Sky Governance*. Retrieved April 4, 2025, from https://makerdao.com/en/whitepaper/#risk-parameters-controlled-by-sky-governance, please search in the Webpage for "Liquidation Penalty". Please note: MakerDAO is currently a subset of the Sky Token ecosystem (https://sky.money/).
226. *Risk Parameters Controlled by Sky Governance*. Retrieved April 4, 2025, from https://makerdao.com/en/whitepaper/#risk-parameters-controlled-by-sky-governance, please search in the Webpage for "Stability Fee". Please note: MakerDAO is currently a subset of the Sky Token ecosystem (https://sky.money/).
227. *The Dai Savings Rate*. Retrieved April 4, 2025, from https://makerdao.com/en/whitepaper/#the-dai-savings-rate. Please note: MakerDAO is currently a subset of the Sky Token ecosystem (https://sky.money/).
228. *Rates Module*. Retrieved April 4, 2025, from https://docs.makerdao.com/smart-contract-modules/rates-module. Please note: MakerDAO is currently a subset of the Sky Token ecosystem (https://sky.money/).
229. Bonato, M. (2023, November 9). DAI Savings rate earn strategy—risk report. SwissBorg. Retrieved April 4, 2025, from https://swissborg.com/blog/dai-savings-rate-earn-strategy.
230. (2020, October 1). MakerDAO adds Chainlink, compound, loopring as collateral options. CoinDesk. Retrieved April 4, 2025, from https://www.coindesk.com/tech/2020/09/30/makerdao-adds-chainlink-compound-loopring-as-collateral-options.
231. Liu, B. (2022, July 7). MakerDAO adopts real-world assets as crypto leverage demand wanes. Blockworks. Retrieved April 4, 2025, from https://blockworks.co/news/makerdao-adopts-real-world-assets-as-crypto-leverage-demand-wanes.
232. (2024, January 18). Exploring real-world assets in DeFi. IntoTheBlock. Retrieved April 4, 2025 from https://medium.com/intotheblock/exploring-real-world-assets-in-defi-0f333f3c2eac
233. Nansen Dai page. Retrieved April 3, 2025, from https://app.nansen.ai/, searching for "Dai" through Nansen's "Search" field.
234. *Key External Actors*. Retrieved April 4, 2025, from https://makerdao.com/en/whitepaper/#key-external-actors. Please note: MakerDAO is currently a subset of the Sky Token ecosystem (https://sky.money/).
235. *Price Stability Mechanisms*. Retrieved April 4, 2025, from https://makerdao.com/en/whitepaper/#price-stability-mechanisms. Please note: MakerDAO is currently a subset of the Sky Token ecosystem (https://sky.money/).
236. Dale, B. (2021, July 20). MakerDAO moves to full decentralization; maker foundation to close in 'Months'. CoinDesk. Retrieved April 4, 2025 from https://www.coindesk.com/tech/2021/07/20/makerdao-moves-to-full-decentralization-maker-foundation-to-close-in-months.
237. *MakerDAO Ended Polls*. Retrieved April 4, 2025, from https://vote.makerdao.com/polling. Please note: MakerDAO is currently a subset of the Sky Token ecosystem (https://sky.money/).
238. Das, A. (2023, September 13). Maker's endgame set to revolutionize DeFi protocols. BRAVE NEWCOIN. Retrieved April 4, 2025, from https://bravenewcoin.com/insights/makerdao-news. Please note: MakerDAO is currently a subset of the Sky Token ecosystem (https://sky.money/).
239. *MIPS39: Core Unit Framework*. Retrieved April 4, 2025, from https://mips.makerdao.com/mips/details/MIP39.

240. *MIP102c2-SP1: MIP Amendment Subproposals*. Retrieved April 4, 2025, from https://mips.makerdao.com/mips/details/MIP102c2SP1.
241. *MakerDAO - DAO Teams*. IQ.wiki. Retrieved April 4, 2025, from https://iq.wiki/wiki/makerdao, please search the Webpage for "DAO Teams".
242. *What are Tether tokens and how do they work?* Tether product pages. Retrieved April 4, 2025, from https://tether.to/en/how-it-works/.
243. *Tether Terms of Service*. Retrieved April 4, 2025, from https://tether.to/en/legal/.
244. *CoinMarketCap Tether (USDT) page*. CoinMarketCap. Retrieved April 4, 2025 from https://coinmarketcap.com/currencies/tether/.
245. *[Tether acquisition/redemption] Fees*. Retrieved April 4, 2025 from https://tether.to/fees/.
246. [U.S.] Commodity Futures Trading Commission (CFTC). (2021, October 21). *In the Matter of: Tether Holdings Limited, Tether Operations Limited, Tether Limited, and Tether International Limited, Respondents*. CFTC Docket No. 22–04. Retrieved April 4, 2025, from https://www.cftc.gov/media/6646/enftetherholdingsorder101521/download. Please note: contains incorporation information about Tether entities.
247. Tether "Transparency" page. Retrieved April 4, 2025, from https://tether.to/en/transparency/?tab=usdt. Please note: contains Reserve Audits (Proof-of-Reserves) information.
248. (2021, March 31). *Tether releases breakdown of its reserves*. Retrieved April 4, 2025, from https://tether.io/news/tether-releases-breakdown-of-its-reserves/.
249. [Sample Tether Reserves Audit Report] (2024, December 31). Independent Auditor's Report on the Consolidated Financials Figures and Reserves Report. BDO Italia S.p.A. Retrieved April 4, 2025, from https://assets.ctfassets.net/vyse88cgwfbl/6L2yLNnLltcCP6ZcTxJrll/aea0ec279fea08637445c8be57f63d87/ISAE_3000R_-_Opinion_on_Tether_Consolidated_Financials_Figures_31.12.2024.pdf, linked into from https://tether.to/en/transparency/?tab=reports.
250. [Sample Tether Reserves Audit Report] (2023, December 31). Independent Auditor's Report on the Consolidated Financials Figures and Reserves Report. BDO Italia S.p.A. Retrieved April 4, 2025, from https://assets.ctfassets.net/vyse88cgwfbl/7DZ8nVyr8zTaWhJqTIsMsH/b8e55bc151c9bb74adf20ff840e84088/ESO.03.01_Std_ISAE_3000R_Opinion_31-12-2023_BDO_Tether_CRR_RC134792023BD0684__1_.pdf, linked into from https://tether.to/en/transparency/?tab=reports.
251. [Tether Whitepaper] *Tether: Fiat currencies on the Bitcoin blockchain*. Retrieved April 4, 2025, from https://tether.to/en/whitepaper/.
252. (2019, April 30). Tether lawyer admits Stablecoin now 74% backed by cash and equivalents. CoinDesk. Retrieved April 4, 2025, from https://www.coindesk.com/markets/2019/04/30/tether-lawyer-admits-stablecoin-now-74-backed-by-cash-and-equivalents.
253. [Price, Index and Market data offered by CoinMetrics]. *Welcome & Product Overview - Crypto intelligence for the future of finance*. CoinMetrics. Retrieved April 4, 2025, from https://docs.coinmetrics.io/.
254. *Tether (USDT) Metrics by CoinMetrics*. CoinMetrics | Coverage. Retrieved April 4, 2025, from https://coverage.coinmetrics.io/assets-v2/usdt.
255. *CoinMarketCap FRAX page*. CoinMarketCap. Retrieved April 4, 2025, from https://coinmarketcap.com/currencies/frax/.
256. [Frax Token ecosystem]. https://frax.finance.
257. *Overview—FRAX v3 : The Final Stablecoin*. Frax documentation pages. Retrieved April 4, 2025, from https://docs.frax.finance/frax-v3-100-cr-and-more/overview.
258. *Frax Ecosystem Overview*. Frax documentation pages. Retrieved April 4, 2025, from https://docs.frax.finance/.
259. *AMOs—The Interface Contracts Between FRAX Stablecoins and Subprotocols*. Frax documentation pages. Retrieved April 4, 2025, from https://docs.frax.finance/frax-v3-100-cr-and-more/amos.
260. *Fraxlend overview—an isolated pair lending protocol*. Frax documentation pages. Retrieved April 4, 2025, from https://docs.frax.finance/fraxlend/fraxlend-overview.

261. *Borrowing [business use case in the Frax Ecosystem]*. Frax documentation pages. Retrieved April 4, 2025, from https://docs.frax.finance/fraxlend/borrowing.
262. *Position Health & Liquidations*. Frax documentation pages. Retrieved April 4, 2025, from https://docs.frax.finance/fraxlend/advanced-concepts/position-health-and-liquidations.
263. *FXB AMO* (Frax Bonds AMO). Frax documentation pages. Retrieved April 4, 2025, from https://docs.frax.finance/frax-v3-100-cr-and-more/amos#fxb-amo.
264. *FXBs—Zero-coupon bonds that help stabilize the FRAX peg*. Frax documentation pages. Retrieved April 4, 2025, from https://docs.frax.finance/frax-v3-100-cr-and-more/fxbs.
265. [FXB] *Series Auctions*. Frax documentation pages. Retrieved April 4, 2025, from https://docs.frax.finance/frax-v3-100-cr-and-more/fxbs#series-auctions.
266. *RWAs—real-world assets that yield the IORB rate with minimal maturity risk*. Frax documentation pages. Retrieved April 4, 2025, from https://docs.frax.finance/frax-v3-100-cr-and-more/rwas.
267. *Series Auctions*. Frax documentation pages. Retrieved May 18, 2025 from https://docs.frax.finance/frax-v3-100-cr-and-more/fxbs#series-auctions.
268. *FRAX Stablecoin Balance Sheet*. Retrieved April 4, 2025 from https://facts.frax.finance/frax/balance-sheet.
269. *USDC—fully backed digital dollars*. https://www.circle.com/en/usdc.
270. [Aave Token eosystem]. https://aave.com/.
271. [Compound Token ecosystem.] https://compound.finance/.
272. [Yearn Token ecosystem] https://yearn.fi/.
273. *AMO overview—a framework for composable, autonomous central banking puzzle pieces*. Frax documentation pages. Retrieved April 4, 2025, from https://docs.frax.finance/amo/overview.
274. [Frax Token ecosystem Snapshot (proposals tracking system) pages]. Retrieved April 4, 2025, from https://snapshot.org/#/frax.eth.
275. Frax Shares (FXS). Frax documentation pages. Retrieved April 4, 2025, from https://docs.frax.finance/fxs-and-vefxs/seigniorage.
276. *CoinMarketCap FXS page*. CoinMarketCap. Retrieved April 4, 2025, from https://coinmarketcap.com/currencies/frax-share/.
277. [Frax Whitepaper] Kazemian, S., Iyer, K., & Huan, J. (2020, July). Frax: Fractional-Algorithmic Stablecoin Protocol. Retrieved April 4, 2025, from https://github.com/FraxFinance/frax-solidity/blob/master/frax_whitepaper_v1.pdf.
278. Frax documentation pages. Retrieved April 4, 2025, from https://docs.frax.finance/.
279. Seigniorage. (2025, March 17). In *Wikipedia*. Retrieved April 4, 2025, from https://en.wikipedia.org/wiki/Seigniorage.
280. Majaski, C. (2024, August 5). What Is Seigniorage, and Does It Cause Inflation? Retrieved April 4, 2025, from https://www.investopedia.com/terms/s/seigniorage.asp.
281. Latin Monetary Union. (2025, February 15). In *Wikipedia*. Retrieved April 4, 2025, from https://en.wikipedia.org/wiki/Latin_Monetary_Union.
282. Nixon shock. (2025, Februaly 9). In *Wikipedia*. Retrieved April 4, 2025, from https://en.wikipedia.org/wiki/Nixon_shock.
283. (2022, July 28). *Understanding seigniorage*. Bank of Canada. Retrieved April 12, 2025, from https://www.bankofcanada.ca/2020/05/seigniorage/.
284. Feige, E. (2012). The myth of the Cashless Society: How much of America's currency is overseas? *International Deutsche Bundesbank Cash Conference*. Retrieved April 12, 2025, from https://www.researchgate.net/publication/235942476_The_myth_of_the_Cashless_Society_How_much_of_America's_currency_is_overseas.
285. Yiting, L & Akihiko, M. (2005). A theory of international currency and seigniorage competition. *CARF F-series CARF-F-041*, Center for Advanced Research in Finance, Faculty of Economics, The University of Tokyo. Retrieved April 12, 2025, from https://ideas.repec.org/p/cfi/fseres/cf041.html.

286. Fractional-reserve banking. (2025, March 23). In *Wikipedia*. Retrieved April 12, 2025, from https://en.wikipedia.org/wiki/Fractional-reserve_banking.
287. Money multiplier. (2025, April 12). In *Wikipedia*. Retrieved April 12, 2025, from https://en.wikipedia.org/wiki/Money_multiplier.
288. Sams, R. (2015, April 28). A Note on Cryptocurrency Stabilization: Seigniorage Shares. Retrieved April 12, 2025, from https://github.com/rmsams/stablecoins/blob/master/paper.pdf.
289. *veFXS—locked FXS that provides voting power and other benefits*. Frax documentation pages. Retrieved April 4, 2025, from https://docs.frax.finance/fxs-and-vefxs/vefxs.
290. Von Wachter, V., Rude Jensen, J., & Ross, O. (2020). *Measuring Asset Composability as a Proxy for DeFi Integration*. Retrieved April 12, 2025, from https://arxiv.org/pdf/2102.04227.
291. Tolmach, P., Li, Y., Lin, S. -W., & Liu, Y. (2021). *Formal analysis of composable DeFi protocols*. Retrieved April 12, 2025, from https://arxiv.org/abs/2103.00540.
292. [Vesper Token ecosystem]. https://vesper.finance/.
293. Vesper documentation pages. Retrieved April 12, 2025, from https://docs.vesper.finance/.
294. Wright, T. (2020, November 13). Akropolis DeFi protocol 'paused' as hackers get away with $2M in DAI. Cointelegraph. Retrieved April 12, 2025, from https://cointelegraph.com/news/akropolis-defi-protocol-paused-as-hackers-get-away-with-2m-in-dai.
295. Jones, W. (2023, April 3). *Hackers use sandwich attack to steal over $25.2m from Uniswap*. crypto.news. Retrieved April 12, 2025, from https://crypto.news/hackers-use-sandwich-attack-to-steal-over-25-2m-from-uniswap/.
296. O'Donnell, A. (2025, January 13). BitsLab's ScaleBit flags 'alarming' Uniswap Wallet vulnerability. Cointelegraph. Retrieved April 4, 2025, from https://cointelegraph.com/news/bitslab-flags-uniswap-wallet-vulnerability.
297. Young, J. (2023, November 13). Too big to fail: Definition, history, and reforms. Investopedia. Retrieved April 12, 2025, from https://www.investopedia.com/terms/t/too-big-to-fail.asp.
298. Lee, A. (2021, June 23). What is programmable money? *FEDS notes*. Washington: Board of Governors of the Federal Reserve System. Retrieved April 12, 2025, from https://doi.org/10.17016/2380-7172.2915
299. *Bespoke programmable crypto Token*. United States Patent 10,742,398, Inventors: Rosenoer, et. al. Applicant/Assignee: IBM Corporation, August 11, 2020. Official record at https://pdfpiw.uspto.gov/.piw?Docid=10742398.
300. Chen, J. (2024, June 1). Convertible bond: Definition, example, and benefits. Investopedia. Retrieved April 12, 2025, from https://www.investopedia.com/terms/c/convertiblebond.asp.
301. Chen, J. (2024, October 31). *Contingent convertibles (CoCos): Definition and use in Europe*. Investopedia. Retrieved April 12, 2025, from https://www.investopedia.com/terms/c/contingentconvertible.asp.
302. *Bitcoin's energy consumption*. Bitcoin Suisse. Retrieved April 12, 2025, from https://www.bitcoinsuisse.com/research/decrypt/season-2021/bitcoins-energy-consumption.
303. (2023, October 24). *Ethereum's energy expenditure*. Ethereum.org. Retrieved April 12, 2025, from https://ethereum.org/en/energy-consumption.
304. (2021, November 24). *Solana's energy use report: November 2021*. Solana Foundation. Retrieved April 12, 2025, from https://solana.com/news/solana-energy-usage-report-november-2021.
305. *Bitcoin energy consumption worldwide from February 2017 to February 3, 2025 (in terawatt hours)*. Statista. Retrieved April 12, 2025, from https://www.statista.com/statistics/881472/worldwide-bitcoin-energy-consumption/.
306. *Ethereum average energy consumption per transaction compared to that of VISA as of January 19, 2025*. Statista. Retrieved April 12, 2025, from https://www.statista.com/statistics/1265891/ethereum-energy-consumption-transaction-comparison-visa/.
307. Coinmonks. (2023, June 27). *Proof of Stake Vs Proof of Work: Characteristics, advantages and disadvantages*. Retrieved April 12, 2025, from https://medium.com/coinmonks/proof-of-stake-vs-proof-of-work-characteristics-advantages-and-disadvantages-9dea8af22056.

308. Carter, N. (2021, May 5). *How much energy does bitcoin actually consume?* Harvard Business Review. Retrieved April 12, 2025, from https://hbr.org/2021/05/how-much-energy-does-bitcoin-actually-consume.
309. Martin, K., & Nauman, B. (2021, May 20). *Bitcoin's growing energy problem: 'It's a dirty currency'*. Financial Times. Retrieved April 12, 2025, from https://www.ft.com/content/1aecb2db-8f61-427c-a413-3b929291c8ac.
310. (2021, September 3). *Bitcoin uses more electricity than many countries. How is that possible?* The New York Times. Retrieved April 12, 2025, from https://www.nytimes.com/interactive/2021/09/03/climate/bitcoin-carbon-footprint-electricity.html.
311. Computational complexity. (2025, March 31). In *Wikipedia*. Retrieved April 12, 2025, from https://en.wikipedia.org/wiki/Computational_complexity.
312. Hu, B., Zhang, Z., Liu, J., Liu, Y., Yin, J., Lu, R., & Lin, X. (2021). A comprehensive survey on smart contract construction and execution: paradigms, tools, and systems. *Patterns*, *2*(2): 100179. Retrieved April 12, 2025, from https://doi.org/10.1016/j.patter.2020.100179 (Open Acces).

Case Study in Token Design: Bumper 11

The previous chapter presented theoretical notions of token design in blockchain ecosystems. We now proceed with a case study of how these notions are in evidence in an existing token project. Our analysis will focus on "Bumper" [1], an ehereum-virtual-machine (EVM) compatible project, the business case of which revolves around price-risk hedging of existing token positions.

As in the previous case study (cf. Chap. 9), we begin with an analogue business case from traditional finance in order to demonstrate how blockchain-based token ecosystems can be understood of as translations of established business practices into a new technological context. We then proceed with an examination of the apparent token design calibrations by the protocol designers, based on Bumper's official documentation and on artefacts published under the auspices of its governance body. We thus demonstrate how traditional finance concepts and processes have found direct analogues in the construction of Bumper's crypto-tokens.

11.1 Structured Products

Investment in financial instruments is seldom risk-free. Even acquiring a single asset (say, a particular share or a cash amount in a single foreign currency) can bring with it the risk of at least partial loss, even though it was meant to generate profit—this is the notion of "market risk". Financial derivatives and swaps were created to precisely address the problem of hedging market risk. They are not recent creations; commodity derivatives were first created [2] in the twelfth century to hedge agricultural market risk [3], whereas derivatives and swaps [4] with financial cash-flows as underlyings were created in the last decades of the twentieth century.[1] Their

[1]Trading of FX Futures on the Chicago Mercantile Exchange (CME) began on May 16th, 1972 [5]. The first ever publicly recorded FX Swap was entered into between the World Bank's Treasury and the technology company IBM in 1981 [6]. OTC Equity derivatives had been traded before then,

I. Giannakouros, *Cryptocurrencies and Tradable Crypto-Tokens*, Future of Business and Finance, https://doi.org/10.1007/978-3-031-98423-5_11

taxonomy is quite large [8], and there is a whole body of academic and trade literature devoted to their modelling, pricing, risk management, and operational execution aspects. The interested reader can draw on a vast body of literature on the subject.

We mention here briefly the simplest possible financial derivatives, in order to set the stage for the Bumper business case. A call option contract on the price of a reference asset (called "Underlying") specifies a price point ("Strike") and a future time point ("Expiration"). The contract pays out the difference of the price of the underlying minus the strike, as observed in a specific marketplace at Expiration, multiplied by the "Contract Size" (or "Notional") which is simply a reference number of units of the underlying. So, a call option can be written on a notional of 100 units of the asset, etc.

This is simply a constant multiplying the basic call option "Intrinsic Payoff" formula, which is:

$$Payoff_{Call,\ intrinsic} = \max\left(AP - S, 0\right)$$

where AP stands for the unit "Asset Price" and S for the strike. A put option contract has the same parameters, but at expiration pays out the difference of the strike minus the price of the underlying multiplied by the notional. The put option "Intrinsic Payoff" formula is:

$$Payoff_{Put,\ intrinsic} = \max\left(S - AP, 0\right)$$

Both option types can be bought for a price which is called their "Premium". So, the final payoffs for an option buyer at expiration, per option type, are:

$$Payoff_{Call} = \max\left(AP - S, 0\right) - OP$$

and

$$Payoff_{Put} = \max\left(S - AP, 0\right) - OP$$

where OP stands for "Option Premium". The graphs for the payoff as a function of the asset price of the underlying at expiration appear on Fig. 11.1.

Because of the option premium, an investor in an option will recoup their investment at an asset price point ("$AP_{Breakeven}$") close to, but not coinciding with, the strike. It is important to stress that this is the payoff profile *only at Expiration*. Before that time, there are factors that influence the price of the option, such as its tradability (cf. difference between "European", "American", etc. types); risk-free rates in the capital markets; volatility of the underlying; dividend inflows from the underlying; and time to expiration. Thus, the option premium at the time of purchase is said to consist of three value components, namely:

but there was no standardized contractual framework. Such a framework was first created by the International Swaps and Derivatives Association which was founded in 1985 [7].

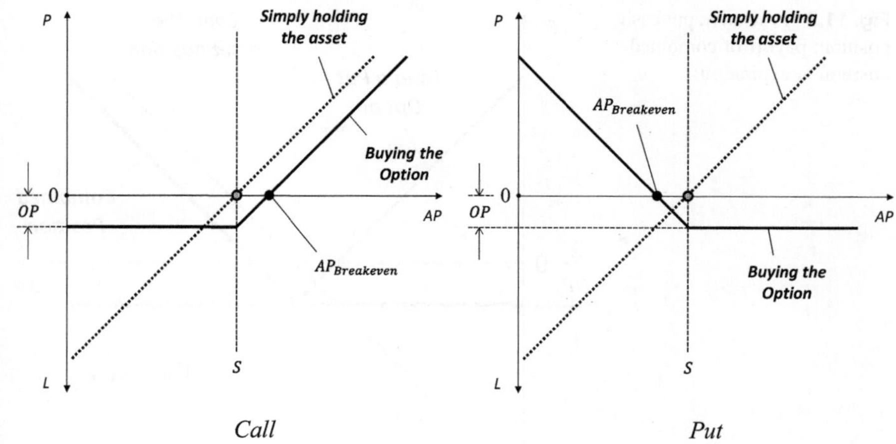

Fig. 11.1 Payoff of options at expiration

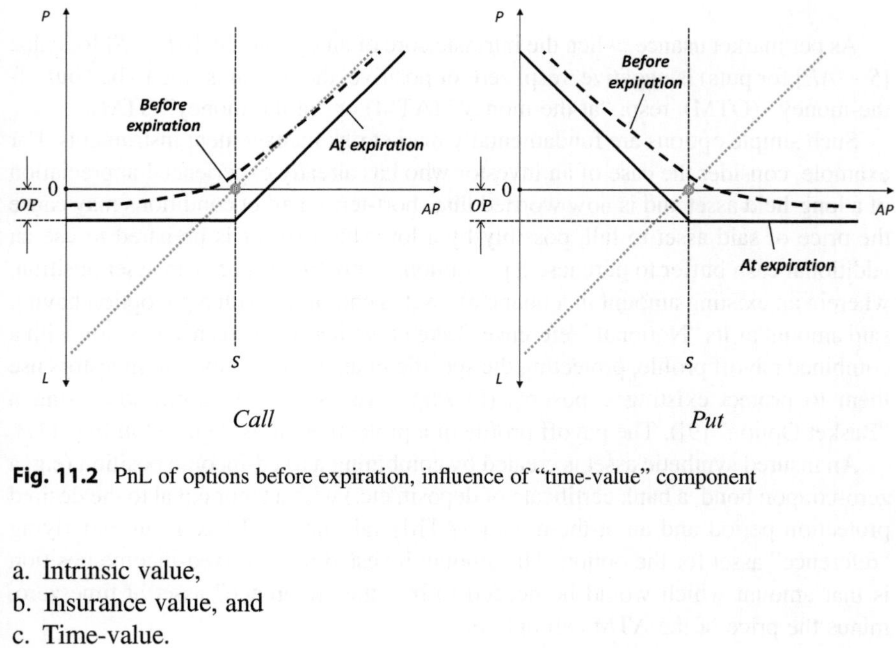

Fig. 11.2 PnL of options before expiration, influence of "time-value" component

a. Intrinsic value,
b. Insurance value, and
c. Time-value.

The *intrinsic* value is given by the intrinsic payoff formula, but with *AP* the asset price as of the time of purchase instead of at expiration. The *insurance* value correlates positively with the volatility of the underlying. The *time value* correlates positively with the time distance to the expiration. Due to these "adding value" components, the graphs for the payoff as a function of the asset price of the underlying at a time *before* Expiration can take the qualitative forms depicted in Fig. 11.2.

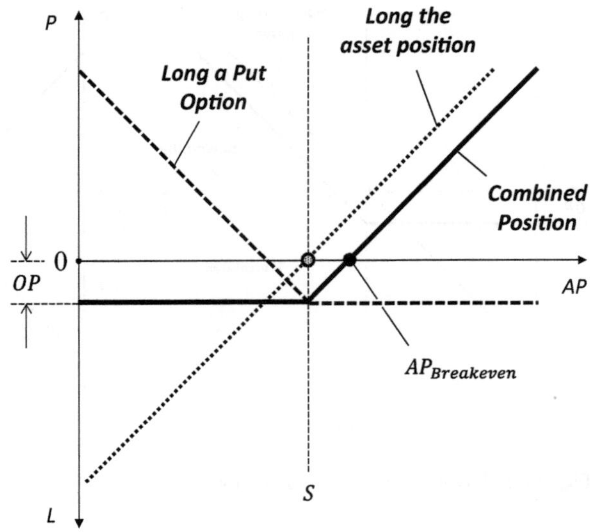

Fig. 11.3 Protective put cash position; payoff of combined position at expiration

As per market usance, when the intrinsic core of an option (i.e. [$AP - S$] for calls; [$S - AP$] for puts) is negative, resp. zero or positive, the option is said to be "out-of-the-money" (OTM), resp. "at-the-money" (ATM) or "in-the-money" (ITM).

Such simple options are fundamentally market risk management instruments. For example, consider the case of an investor who has already experienced appreciation of a long-held asset and is now worried that short-term market conditions may cause the price of said asset to fall, possibly by a lot. The investor is prepared to use an additional cash buffer to purchase a put option. A *protective put* is an asset position, wherein an existing amount in a financial asset is combined with a put option having said amount as its "Notional" reference. Taken together, they create a position with a combined payoff profile, protecting the specific financial asset amount. Investors use them to protect existing exposures (in single assets or even portfolios, using a "Basket Option" [9]). The payoff profile of a protective put is depicted in Fig. 11.3.

An insured synthetic asset is created by combining a fixed-income position (e.g. a zero-coupon bond, a bank certificate of deposit, etc.) with a tenor equal to the desired protection period and an at-the-money (ATM) call option. There is an underlying "reference" asset for the option. The amount invested in said fixed-income position is that amount which would be needed to buy the "reference" asset at time zero, minus the price of the ATM call option.

The payoff profile corresponding to insuring against the price evolution of a particular underlying can be replicated through "synthetic assets". An "Insured Synthetic Asset" is created by combining a fixed-income position (e.g. a zero-coupon bond, a bank certificate of deposit, etc.) with a tenor equal to the desired protection period and an at-the-money (ATM) call option in the underlying "reference" asset. The amount invested in said fixed-income position is that amount which would be needed to buy the "reference" underlying at time zero, minus the price of the ATM call option. The "insured amount" is in effect the sum of the equivalent amount of the "reference" underlying at time zero, plus the yield from the fixed-

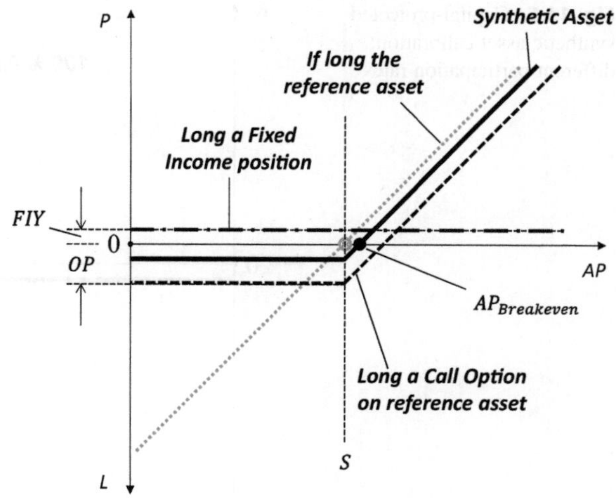

Fig. 11.4 Capital protected synthetic asset construction and payoff at expiration

income position at the time point of option expiration, minus the cost of the call option. The payoff profile (at its option expiration) of such a synthetic asset appears in Fig. 11.4.

Please note the similarity to the protective put payoff profile. Such synthetic assets can be standardized and offered as investment certificates (or "Notes") to investors who want exposure in particular asset classes but have limited, or zero, risk appetite for downside market risk.

A *Capital-Protected Certificate* is a synthetic (unit-based) asset, seeking to replicate a protective put payoff profile, irrespective of the amount of "protected Notional". It can be acquired in units, simply referring to a financial asset's unit-based price and wished-for protection floor. Investors acquire as many units as they wish, thus specifying their own wished-for "protected Notional" equivalent.

A capital-protected certificate belongs to the asset class of *structured products* [8, 10]. The latter are unit-based financial instruments that combine cash assets and/or derivative contracts to offer non-linear risk/reward profiles to investors, that would otherwise have to be created through cash positions at a considerable cost and risk. Such risks (market, counterparty, legal, tax, operational, etc.) can be much better hedged by banks and other sell-side institutions—instead of by individual investors—as they have the appropriate expertise and scale of operations. For instance, banks have large portfolios of assets, derivatives and swaps positions which are "warehoused" so that they can be hedged efficiently across time, taking advantage of negative correlation and/or netting effects.

To address different price sensitivities of individual investors, it is possible to create capital-protected certificates with lower purchase price points by calibrating the constituent option and fixed-income parts. The trade-off is that, while the combined asset is able to essentially keep the wished-for protection floor, it has lower exposure to the upside of the underlying ("lower than 100% *Participation Rate*", in industry parlance). Such "Capital-Protected Participation Certificates" are offered by structure product vendors as a matter of course [11, 12]. An indicative

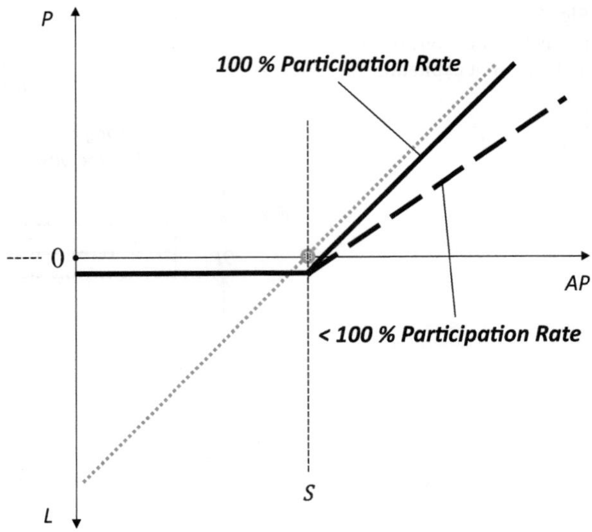

Fig. 11.5 Capital-protected synthetic asset calibration; different participation rates

payoff profile (at Option Expiration) of capital-protected participation structure products is depicted on Fig. 11.5. Please note that there are other possible ways to lower the price of a capital-protected financial instrument, for example, by lowering the protection floor as a percentage of the current price of the underlying.

In summary, a *protective put* is a cash position, wherein an existing amount in a financial asset is combined with a put option having said amount as its "Notional" reference. A *capital-protected certificate* is a synthetic unit-based asset, seeking to replicate a protective put payoff profile, irrespective of the amount of "protected Notional". A capital-protected certificate is a *structured product.*

11.2 Bumper

As per its documentation [13], Bumper is a blockchain-based token project aiming to operate a decentralized non-custodian market-risk hedging marketplace [14]. Bumper participants can:

A. Supply liquidity (denominated in ERC-20 Stablecoins) to be used for underwriting price risk hedging requests.
B. Hedge the downward price risk of existing ETH and general ERC-20 token positions, by purchasing protection on the protocol.
C. Stake liquidity positions (denominated in a Bumper-specific utility token) to generate yield, by assuming liquidity risk on behalf of the protocol.
D. Arbitrage between internal Bumper liquidity pools, making a profit while helping the protocol to manage its balance sheet.
E. Buy Bumper-specific utility tokens at a discount, as bonded tokens to other participants' positions which must be liquidated.

The reason for introducing the fundamentals of structured products in the previous section is that they are the traditional finance equivalents of tokens created in the combined business use cases A.-B. above. In the sequel, we aim to interpret Bumper's token design in reference to its documentation, tracing back to token flows evident in its main transactional pathways.

Even though the focus of the current case study chapter is token design, we will need to first give the basis of the protocol's market design in order to define the base terminology and agent typology needed to explain subsequent notions.

11.3 Bumper Market Design Basics

As per methodology introduced in Sect. 6.4.1, blockchain ecosystem market design must prescribe all possible *economic agent* types, *transactional pathways* joining them, and associated protocol *tokens* created or exchanged in the process. Bumper being a relatively recent token ecosystem, we can only focus on its latest mature protocol as per the time of writing [15]. In the sequel we do not go into Bumper's market design in detail, instead mentioning only those salient points needed to put its token design in context.

Bumper consists of a Layer-3 ("Application"-layer) protocol deployed on the Arbitrum [16] L-2 ("Scalability" layer) blockchain [17]. All its artefacts (tokens, smart contracts, etc.) assume the ethereum-virtual-machine (EVM) as runtime and thus can in principle interoperate with any other EVM-compatible protocol.

Its business processes revolve around the notion of the "Protection Market", meaning a collection of liquidity pools supporting price risk of positions denominated in a single token. For example, currently there exist Bumper "Protection Markets" for ETH, wstETH, wBTC; i.e. serving participants wishing to hedge ETH, wstETH, wBTC, etc., positions. In due course, there may be protection markets for other tokens, eventually even generic EVM compatible (ERC-20, etc.) ones. The basic notions of said business processes are described in the project's "Litepaper" [18].

11.3.1 Economic Agent Typology

The latest version of the Bumper protocol as of the time of writing admits the agent typology depicted in Fig. 11.6.

The non-privileged economic agent types are:

a. Makers
b. Takers
c. Stakers
d. Arbitrageurs
e. Liquidators

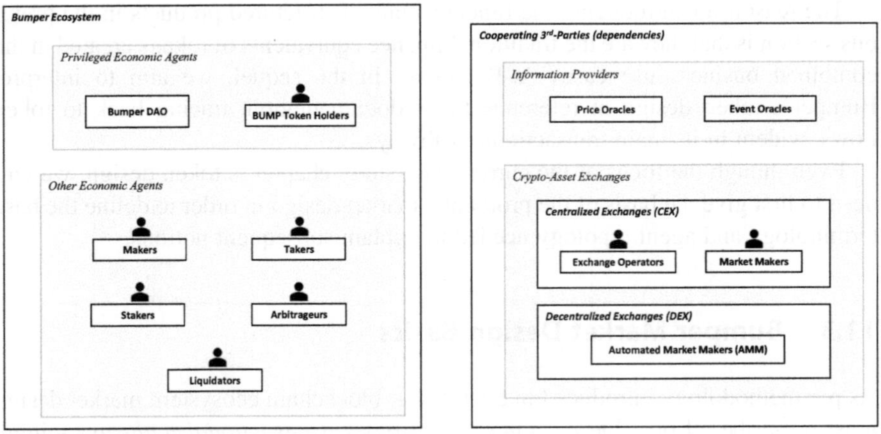

Fig. 11.6 Bumper market economic agent model

The privileged (i.e. governance-related) economic agents are:

f. The Bumper decentralized autonomous organization ("DAO") [19, 20]
g. All holders of the native token (BUMP [21, 22]), as they may take part in governance votings.

There follows an explanation of the salient attributes of said agents in the context of Bumper use cases:

A **Maker** is a Bumper participant who deposits admissible tokens into protection markets' liquidity pools for a specific period of time ("Term"). These pools support the underwriting of Takers' market risk insurance. Profits or losses generated by said pools (through either premia paid by takers or protocol incentives) during the term are allocated to all active makers, thus producing the holding period returns of the Makers' deposits. Makers can roll over their deposits for a new Term ("Renew"), withdraw them at the end of the term ("Discontinue"), or after the term has expired ("Withdraw"); or even exit the protocol at any time ("Abandon")—in which case, they incur a break fee transferred to Bumper's treasury.

A **Taker** is a Bumper participant who seeks to protect an existing position in admissible tokens from downside price risk for a specific period of time (also called "Term"). Takers deposit said tokens into the protocol for the term and pay a hedging premium that is calculated dynamically through smart contracts. Apart from the term length, parameters of the calculation include the protection floor required, observed volatility and liquidity metrics of the tokens in question, etc. At the end of the protection term, Takers either withdraw the same number of original tokens ("Close", if their value is above the floor), or a combination of original tokens and covering liquidity pool tokens that together add up to the value of the protection floor at the time that hedging cover was purchased ("Claim", if below the floor). Takers can roll over their hedged positions for a new term ("Renew"), withdraw them at the end of the term ("Discontinue") or even exit the protocol at any time ("Cancel")—in which case, they incur a break fee transferred to Bumper's treasury.

Importantly, both Makers and Takers need to purchase—from Exchanges—and lock into the protocol a number of native tokens (BUMP) when:

a) Accessing the protocol. This is a one-off fee, which is not reimbursed.
b) Initiating deposits or hedging positions. These are transaction-based fees (called "Bonds"), which are reimbursed at the end of the respective terms.

A **Staker** is a holder of BUMP tokens who stakes them into a Bumper staking smart contract. Staking positions generate a yield (also payable in BUMP) but are in risk of partial liquidation if liquidity or operational risk events create losses not coverable by the balance in protection markets' liquidity pools.

An **Arbitrageur** is a Bumper participant who swaps liquidity across internal liquidity pools, helping to restore an ideal balance ratio, for profit. There are four main types of said liquidity pools—two main (asset pool and capital pool) and two supporting (asset reserve and capital reserve). They come in pairs ("Asset" denotes support of Takers', "Capital" of Makers' positions). Even though they create a balancing mechanism—"Capital" pools underwriting the market risk of the "Asset" ones—all pairs are on the asset side of a protection markets' balance sheet.

A **Liquidator** is an agent who, once notified that another participant's position must be liquidated to protect the protocol from uncovered risk exposures, pays an equivalent amount to the protocol and acquires the corresponding bonded BUMP tokens for free. Maker and Taker positions can be liquidated when counterparty risk is notified, while Staker positions must be partially liquidated when liquidity or operational risk events have manifested themselves (as already mentioned).

The **Bumper DAO** is the highest governance structure deciding on strategy, investment allocations, and operational issues [23]. At the moment it is still an essentially human-driven DAO, using smart contracts to implement some technical steps (voting, staking, etc.) during decision-making.

All **BUMP token holders** have the right to vote for governance decisions by staking their tokens [24].

Bumper implements several transactional pathways whereby the aforementioned agent types cooperate for the use cases mentioned in Sect. 11.3. However, some involve simply swapping of existing tokens, or returning/burning of tokens due to agents' actions ("Abandon", "Cancel", etc.). Only those involving directly issuance of native tokens on the protocol are presented in the sequel, as they serve to explain the rationale behind specific attributes of token design.

Please note that Bumper is a strictly non-custodian protocol, hence all pathways require connecting to the respective agent's crypto wallet from within the Bumper dApp [25].

11.3.2 Main Transactional Pathways

The principal protocol transactions among the aforementioned economic agents are: Makers' liquidity deposits, Takers' hedging protection purchases, stakers' locking of BUMP tokens and liquidators' closing of positions in exchange for bonded BUMP. However, only the first two involve minting of Bumper native tokens (the very first onboarding step, in which agents purchase BUMP to simply access the protocol, is not considered as BUMP are only minted *en masse* by protocol governance decision—cf. Sect. 11.4.1.1). We begin with the Takers' hedging transaction, as this is arguably the main business case of Bumper.

11.3.2.1 Taker Purchases Protection for an ETH/ERC-20 Position

In this transaction, a Bumper participant already possessing ETH or an admissible ERC-20 token—hereafter denoted by ₸—in their crypto wallet become a (protection or hedging) "Taker". As of the time of writing, this is enabled only for positions denominated in ETH, wstETH,[2] and wBTC [26]. The pathway is depicted schematically on Fig. 11.7, with the understanding that it is essentially the same for positions denominated in ETH or in (non-rebasing) ₸ tokens.[3]

Assuming a human agent, the Bumper App will request that the user first connects a crypto wallet [27] and will validate the existence (or suggest the purchase) of BUMP [28] needed to access the protocol. As sufficient BUMP will also need to be bonded to enter the Taker position, the agent may have to purchase more tokens. As Bumper is no Primary Market for BUMP, this is only possible in external—currently only Decentralized [29], in the future possibly also Centralized, Exchanges (depicted by step "1" on Fig. 11.7). The tokens can then be transferred to the agent's Wallet [28] (step "2"), which makes them visible in the Bumper app.

As per Bumper Litepaper, each protection market has its own set of smart contracts managing its liquidity pools. The taker invokes them through the dApp (step "3") as the final step of a process [30] by which the parameters of the protection policy are chosen, and the hedging premium accepted. This causes the ETH or ₸ tokens in question to be moved to a market's asset pool ("4"), and the requisite BUMP tokens (Bond) to its bonding pool ("5"). A first premium instalment and potentially a transaction fee are moved to the market's reserve pool ("6")—please note that (as per Litepaper) premiums are levied against an asset *pool*, and accumulating in an asset *reserve*.

Importantly, the protocol then mints native tokens ("b₸") representing the protected ETH/₸ position, through which the position's future payoff will be credited (through either a "Claim" or a "Close" action by the Taker). These b₸ are

[2]Please cf. the detailed exposé in Sect. 9.6.3.2 on the nature and lifecycle of wstETH.

[3]Please note that the original version of the protocol—deployed on the Ethereum Mainnet—admitted USDC, not USDT, as hedging Stablecoins. Pre-2024 versions of the Litepaper (and its shorter version, called "Flashpaper") reflect that earlier practice.

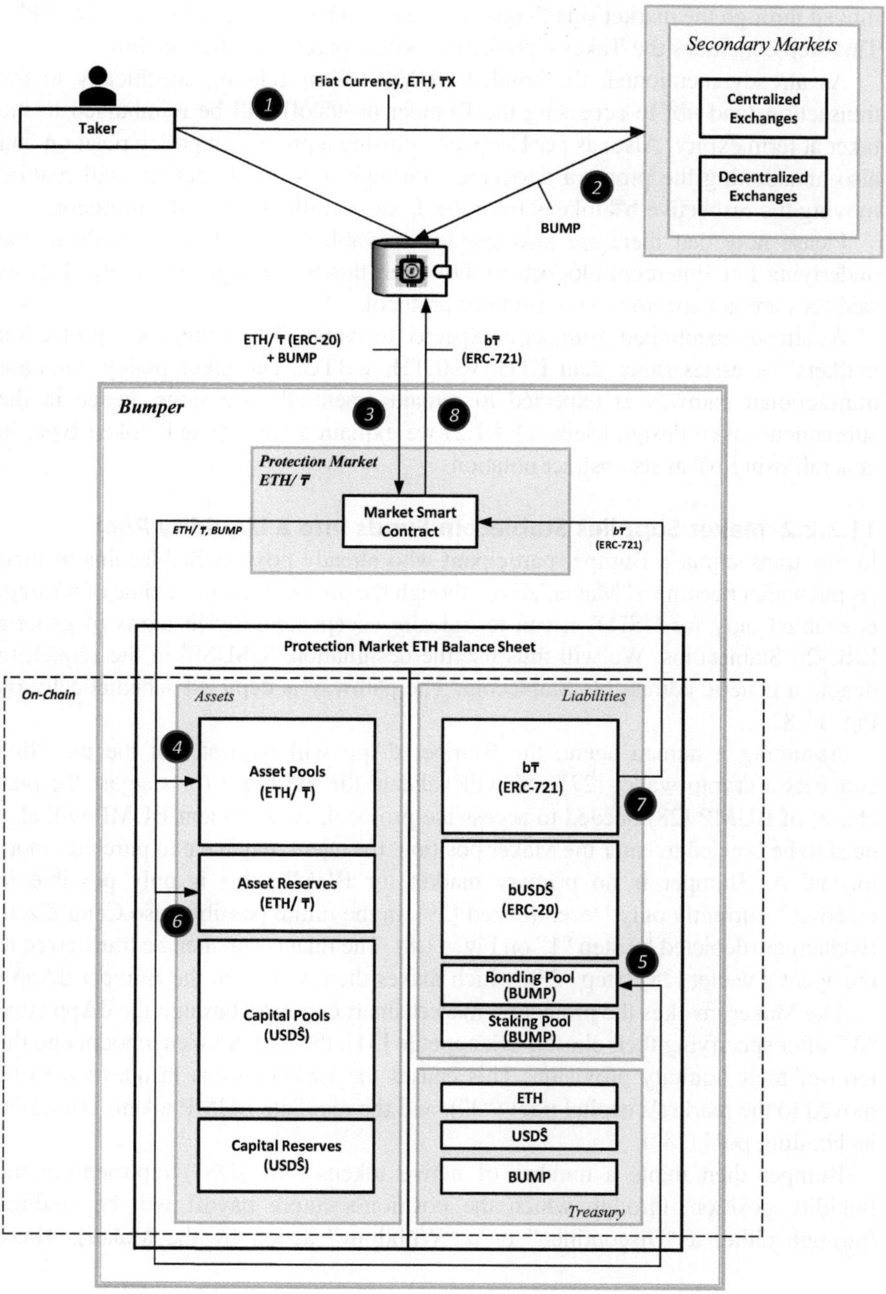

Fig. 11.7 Taker supplies ETH/₸ (ERC-20), receives b₸ tokens

moved through the market smart contract (step "7") back to the Taker's wallet ("8"). This step concludes the Taker's protection policy purchasing transaction.

As already mentioned, the bonded BUMP tokens relating specifically to the transaction (and *not* to accessing the Bumper protocol) will be reimbursed to the taker at term expiry. Also, as per Litepaper, closing a protection policy position and also abandoning the protocol altogether (through a "Cancel" action) will require moving the respective b₸ tokens from the Taker's wallet back to the protocol.

Please note that there are also gas fees payable by the Taker directly to the underlying L-1 Ethereum blockchain; however, this is not depicted on Fig. 11.7 as said fees are not specific to the Bumper protocol.

As already mentioned, Bumper is expected to eventually institute more protection markets for assets other than ETH, wstETH, wBTC. The taker policy purchase transactional pathway is expected to remain essentially the same, hence in the subsequent token design (Sect. 11.4.1.2) we explain a "bProtected" token type, in general, using b₸ as its abstract notation.

11.3.2.2 Maker Supplies Stablecoin Funds into a Liquidity Pool

In this transaction, a Bumper participant who already possess Stablecoins in their crypto wallet become a "Maker". Even though the protocol, as of the time of writing, is enabled only for USDT, it can technically accept liquidity in terms of generic ERC-20 Stablecoins. We will thus use the designation "USDŜ"[4] in the sequel, to denote a generic admissible Stablecoin. The pathway is depicted schematically on Fig. 11.8.

Assuming a human agent, the Bumper dApp will request that the user first connects a crypto wallet [27] and will validate the existence (or suggest the purchase) of BUMP [28] needed to access the protocol. As sufficient BUMP will also need to be bonded to enter the Maker position, the agent may have to purchase more tokens. As Bumper is no primary market for BUMP, this is only possible in external—currently only Decentralized [29], in the future possibly also Centralized, Exchanges (depicted by step "1" on Fig. 11.8). The tokens can then be transferred to the agent's wallet [28] (step "2"), which makes them visible in the Bumper dApp.

The Maker invokes the protection market smart contracts through the dApp (step "3") after specifying their chosen risk appetite [31], the USDŜ token amount and the term of their liquidity provision. This causes the USDŜ tokens in question to be moved to the market's capital pool ("4"), and the requisite BUMP tokens (Bond) to its bonding pool ("5").

Bumper then mints a number of native tokens ("bUSDŜ") representing the liquidity position, through which the position's future payoff will be credited (through either a "Discontinue" or a "Withdraw" action by the Maker). These

[4]Please note that this is not a symbol of the mainstream trade literature and is only used for the first time in this book; a practitioner can substitute USDT or any future Bumper-admissible Stablecoin for the USDŜ symbol in the pathway diagram for the sake of specificity. The projected need to accommodate different Stablecoins in parallel is the reason why the diagram mentions "Capital Pools", resp. "Reserves", using the plural.

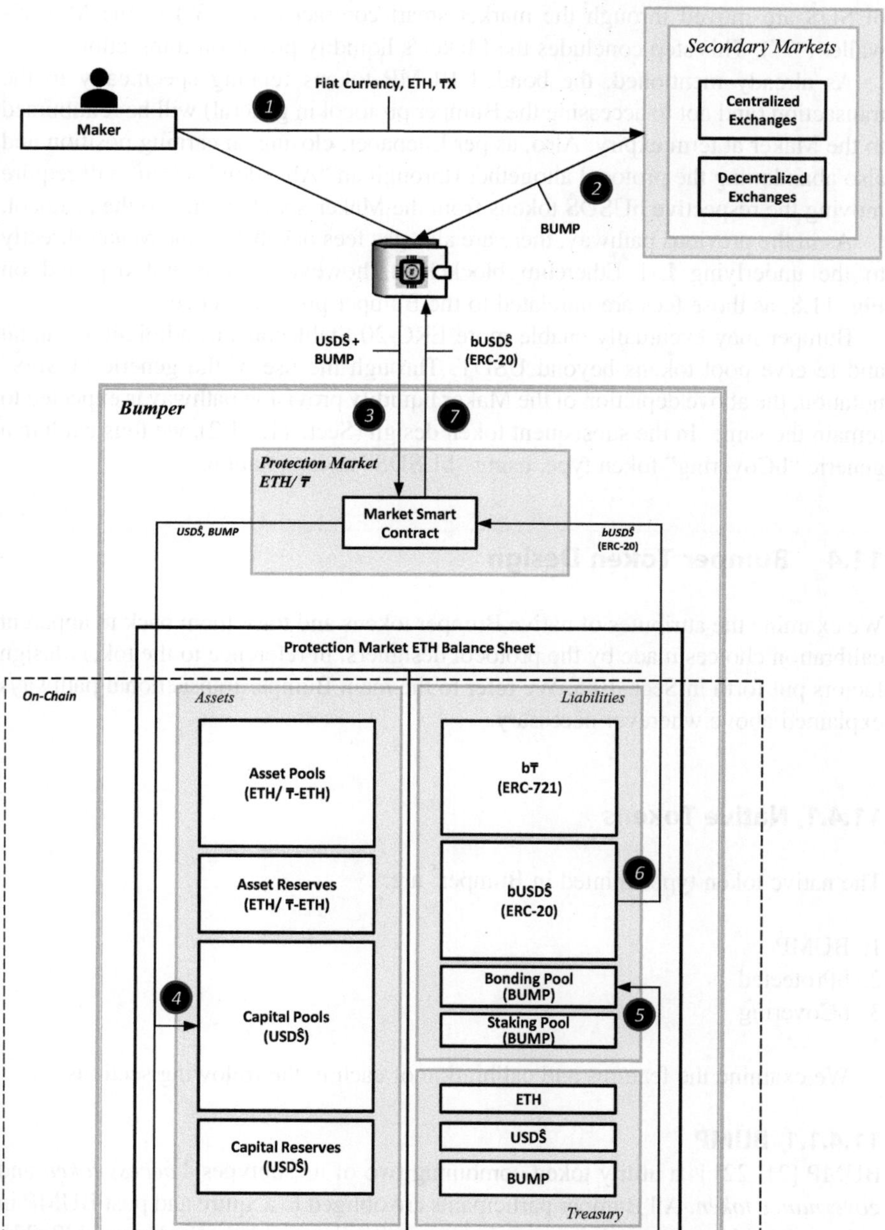

Fig. 11.8 Maker supplies USDŜ Stablecoins, receives bUSDŜ tokens

bUSD$\hat{S}$ are moved through the market smart contract (step "6") to the Maker's wallet ("7"). This step concludes the Maker's liquidity provision transaction.

As already mentioned, the bonded BUMP tokens relating specifically to the transaction (and not to accessing the Bumper protocol in general) will be reimbursed to the Maker at term expiry. Also, as per Litepaper, closing an earning position and also abandoning the protocol altogether (through an "Abandon" action) will require moving the respective bUSD$\hat{S}$ tokens from the Maker's wallet back to the protocol.

As in the previous pathway, there are also gas fees payable by the Maker directly to the underlying L-1 Ethereum blockchain, however this is not depicted on Fig. 11.8, as those fees are unrelated to the Bumper protocol per se.

Bumper may eventually enable more ERC-20 Stablecoins as admissible capital and reserve pool tokens beyond USDT. Through the use of the generic "USD$\hat{S}$" notation, the above depiction of the Maker liquidity provision pathway is expected to remain the same. In the subsequent token design (Sect. 11.4.1.2), we thus explain a generic "bCovering" token type, using "bUSD$\hat{S}$" as its notation.

11.4 Bumper Token Design

We examine the attributes of native Bumper tokens and trace them back to apparent calibration choices made by the protocol designers, in reference to the token design factors put forth in Sect. 10.5. We refer to the main Bumper transactional pathways explained above wherever necessary.

11.4.1 Native Tokens

The native token types minted in Bumper[5] are:

1. BUMP
2. bProtected
3. bCovering

We examine the features and calibration of each in the following sections.

11.4.1.1 BUMP

BUMP [21, 22] is a utility token combining two of its subtypes:[6] *access token* and *governance token*. All Bumper participants are obliged to acquire and post BUMP in order to be able to access the protocol. Acquisition is possible in Exchanges [32, 33], and posting (or "Bonding" [34] in Bumper terminology) is done through the

[5] As of the time of writing, Bumper has yet to abstract the nomenclature "bProtected" or "bCovering". We explain the correspondence with specific tokens in the respective sections below.

[6] Please refer to Sect. 4.2.2.

protocol's dApp [25]. To vote in Bumper DAO, holders must stake [35] BUMP, whereupon they are allocated voting power in terms of 1:1 matching "vBUMP" [36]. The latter, as per Bumper documentation [37], are not separate tokens (i.e. do not constitute a new token type) but rather "accounting" postings allocated through the protocol's staking smart contract. Note that BUMP can also be long-term staked ("locked") into a smart contract, in which case they are allocated extra [38] vBUMP through a formula [39] specified by Bumper governance. Already staked BUMP can be delegated [40] to other blockchain addresses for voting purposes.

Every time an agent opens a Maker [31] or Maker [30] position, additional BUMP may[7] have to be posted. The quantity of all BUMP posted by an agent at any given time is called their "Bond". All posted BUMP are reimbursed—plus earned incentives, minus protocol fees—upon explicitly exiting the protocol (e.g. by closing all Maker and Taker positions [42]).

Technically, BUMP[8] is an ERC-20 compatible token [43], also implementing [44] the ERC-1967 specification [45]. The smart contract code is accessible through the Bumper DAO GitHub [46, 47].

From the standpoint of token design factor calibration:

a. BUMP's design **velocity** is low[9] as it is meant only for the aforementioned use cases: protocol accessing, bonding for Maker and Staker investments, and staking/governance voting.
b. In terms of design **scarcity**: The maximum circulating supply is limited to 250 million BUMP, of which 44 million were minted as part of Bumper's Initial DEX Offering (IDO) [48]. 12.5 million BUMP are currently reserved for the Bumper ecosystem treasury [49]. The current circulating supply [50] can also be ascertained through market trackers.
c. BUMP **inflation** is mainly controlled by Maker and Taker activity on the protocol, as well as vBUMP staking rewards. As long as total market activity on Bumper remains below the current circulating supply there is no new minting of BUMP. However, there it is in principle also controlled by Bumper governance. For example, the Bumper Litepaper [18] (in its s. 4.3.2, "Coordination Stimulus") mentions:

[7] Indicatively, this requirement was provisionally paused after the migration to Arbitrum in order to jump-start liquidity [41].

[8] As the first Bumper implementation was on the Ethereum Mainnet, there still exists a legacy BUMP version tradable on the latter. Thus, at the moment there exist 2 (two) Token Smart Contract addresses, one on Ethereum—https://etherscan.io/token/0x785c34312dfa6b74f6f1829f79ade39042222168—and one on Arbitrum—https://arbiscan.io/token/0xfb930d1a28990820c98144201637c99bea8cb91c.

[9] Actual transactions rate can be ascertained through its Smart Contract scan, available at either https://etherscan.io/dex?q=0x785c34312dfa6b74f6f1829f79ade39042222168#transactions (Ethereum) or https://arbiscan.io/token/0xfb930d1a28990820c98144201637c99bea8cb91c (Arbitrum).

BUMP tokens may be issued to Takers or Makers by the protocol under various conditions in order to support either additional asset or capital liquidity when regular premiums and/or yields are not attracting sufficient new participants quickly enough. This is referred to as the "Boost" incentive.

d. BUMP **valuation** is controlled both through scarcity and through the dynamics between buying and selling on exchanges. So, it is by design only partially controlled by Bumper governance [51]. The evolution of total value locked into Bumper, the sentiment in the general crypto-tokens market, and new Bumper offerings (e.g. new protected/covering token pairs) will influence its price in the secondary market. The token itself is meant to capture the economic value of network effects as protocol transactions increase.
e. **Minting mode**: BUMP is issued at the discretion of its governance. Unless and until the current circulating supply is exceeded, there is no minting/burning at investors' request. Bumper does not function as a primary market for the BUMP token.
f. There are no **minting optionalities** available to acquirers, as it is not minted at their request.
g. BUMP **property rights** are generally claims against the Bumper treasury.
h. BUMP tokens are not Stablecoins, hence there is no underlying notion of managed **treasury**.
i. Regarding **composability**, BUMP tokens are tradable on exchanges and, as ERC-20 tokens, can indeed be transferred across EVM compatible ecosystems. They can be stored in any crypto wallet that supports ERC-20 tokens.
j. BUMP **programmability** is a prerogative of Bumper governance and as such restricted to the methods implemented in its smart contract code [52].
k. The **computational complexity** of BUMP minting is the same as that of base ERC-20 tokens on either the Ethereum or Abritrum blockchains.

11.4.1.2 bProtected (b₸)

As of the time of writing, Bumper offers protection only for positions denominated in ETH, wstETH, and wBTC. In the wBTC case, the original currency tokens are transferred from the Taker's crypto wallet to the protocol and corresponding "bwBTC" tokens ("Bumpered wBTC"—matching in quantity 1:1 the wBTC in question) are minted and returned. Bumper governance is continuously considering new permutations of protected/covering cryptocurrency pairs, and in that sense, it is expedient to consider bwBTC as simply a representative of many possible "bProtected" token types. Please note that "bProtected" is a term coined in this book and not to be found in Bumper's documentation. Other blockchain ecosystems have already used such generic terms for "account-level" tokens (e.g. Aave [53] with its "aTokens" [54] and "DebtTokens" [55] that are also minted 1:1 to their underlying ERC-20 tokens), but Bumper is still evolving its terminology. We thus explain a generic bProtected token, which we have already denoted in Sect. 11.3.2.1 by "b₸" (the symbol "₸" standing for both an ETH and an ERC-20 token).

In reference to Sect. 4.2.4, bŦ would be a security token, of the subtype *Structured Product Token*. Its conceptual design matches that of "Capital-Protected Participation Structured Products" of traditional finance.

bŦ are ERC-721 tokens minted by the action of takers wishing to protect the value of an amount of Ŧ in their possession, with USDŜ (i.e. any specific Stablecoin like USDT) as the numeraire [56]. ERC-721 is a SC standard typically used for non-fungible tokens, and its use aligns with the fact that taker hedging requests are generally bespoke. As already mentioned in Sect. 11.3, takers are asked to specify a coverage tenor (Term) and a protection floor. These contractual terms are coded into bŦ tokens that are returned to their crypto wallet, while the underlying Ŧ are transferred to Bumper. Hence, in effect, takers "buy" bŦ by "selling" Ŧ to Bumper—at 1:1 parity as of the timepoint of the transaction. If subsequently the price of Ŧ falls below the protection floor, then bŦ have a constant value and no longer observe the 1:1 parity. Parity is restored whenever the floor is crossed from below. At term expiry, if Ŧ is above the floor, then takers close their position by "selling back" their bŦ to Bumper for Ŧ. If Ŧ is below the floor, then they claim the contractually agreed protection amount by "selling back" their bŦ for a combination of Ŧ and USDŜ. The bŦ in question are thus transferred from the takers' crypto wallet to Bumper and burned.

As already mentioned in the previous section, BUMP need to be paid to Bumper both to access the protocol and to enter a taker transaction. There are also transaction fees (the protection insurance premia charged to takers, in effect) levied, reducing the effective Ŧ/USDŜ parity of the position amount at transaction inception and at expiry.

In terms of token design factor calibration:

a. Their design **velocity** is low [57], as they can only be minted, transferred, and burned through generally infrequent events (buying protective position, closing or claiming at term expiry, etc.). Please note that Bumper also provides for liquidation events [58], should takers neither close nor claim protective positions at term with the result that expired position penalties and other fees accumulate past a critical level. Velocity gets even lower due to such cases.
b. Their **scarcity** will depend on that of the respective Ŧ (ETH or base ERC-20 tokens) committed to Bumper. E.g., the more Ŧ are transferred consecutively by takers, the more bŦ will be minted. This is of course dependent on the market demand for Ŧ position protection. Currently, there are no direct limits on the amount of mintable bŦ nor are there other protocol risk parameters [59] indirectly influencing this demand.
c. bŦ **inflation** is controlled directly by market demand and indirectly by the respective protocol fees for bETH transactions. There are no other protocol limits imposed through risk parameters on protocol reserves or similar.
d. Their **valuation** at minting is by definition equal to that of the corresponding Ŧ (ETH or base ERC-20 tokens). So, this is not a parameter controlled by Bumper. After minting and until term expiry, bŦ value denominated in USDŜ depends on the market price of Ŧ in relation to the protection floor chosen by the respective taker.

e. **Minting mode**: bT̄ are ERC-721 tokens, minted only through smart contracts [60].
f. bT̄ **minting optionalities** available to takers are setting the protection floor and the term. The latter can be extended before expiry (rolling over with the same conditions, or "renewal" [61] in Bumper terminology [62]).
g. Their **property rights** are claims against the Bumper T̄ ("Asset") and/or USDŜ ("Reserve") pools as per Bumper Litepaper[10] [18]. They are also linked to the right to have the bonded BUMP required to open taker positions returned at term expiry [42, 63]. Please note that said rights may be eroded by cancelling (i.e. when takers choose to exit the protocol before contractual term expiry, thereupon incurring a penalty "break fee"[11]) and in situations conducive to taker liquidation [58].
h. bT̄ are not Stablecoins, hence, there is no underlying notion of managed *treasury*.
i. Regarding **composability**, their use is currently confined to Bumper use cases. There are no cooperating protocols at the moment.
j. bT̄ **programmability** is restricted to the methods available through the Bumper smart contracts specification.
k. The **computational complexity** of bT̄ minting is the same as that of ERC-721 tokens on the Arbitrum blockchain.

We repeat that bT̄ is simply an abstraction for many candidate "bProtected" token types, which can in principle be implemented by Bumper following the same token design. All such "bProtected" will still be formally structured product tokens.

11.4.1.3 bCovering (bUSDŜ)

As of the time of writing, Bumper makers provide liquidity through positions denominated in USDT Stablecoins.[12] The original USDT are transferred from a maker's crypto wallet to the protocol's capital pool and corresponding native tokens then minted and returned. Similarly to the bT̄ case, as new permutations of protected/covering cryptocurrency pairs may be implemented by Bumper, it is expedient to consider the USDT-based covering tokens as only one of many candidate "bCovering" token types. Again, "bCovering" is a term only coined in the book at hand and not to be found in Bumper's documentation. We thus explain a generic

[10] Section "3.2 Liquidity and Liability".

[11] Bumper Litepaper, section "3.1.3 Joint Functions".

[12] Please note that a previous version of Bumper on the Ethereum Mainnet had Makers provide only USDC.

bCovering token, which we have already denoted in Sect. 11.3.2.2 by "bUSDŜ" ("b" standing for "Bumpered" and the symbol "Ŝ" for "Stablecoin").

In reference to Sect. 4.2.4, bUSDŜ would be a security token, of the subtype *investment fund token*. Even though it could be considered as relating to an insurance use case (insuring the taker against the risk that ETH/Ŧ falls below the protection floor—thus making it a candidate insurance policy token, subtype of asset token as per Sect. 4.2.3), it does not represent tradable insurance positions. It is simply a capital-at-risk token, in a pooled investment setting.

bUSDŜ are minted by the action of makers providing liquidity to a Bumper capital pool,[13] the latter used solely to cover capital protection requests by prospective takers. After minting, bUSDŜ tokens are transferred to makers' crypto wallets and start functioning as participation tokens against the capital pool's assets. Those are marked-to-market every epoch taking into account all inflows (new maker positions) and outflows (claims and closings by takers). The outcome is a net asset value calculation adjusting the valuation of individual bUSDŜ positions at epoch's end. When committing USDŜ to a capital pool, makers are asked to declare their personal risk tolerance in terms of risk levels [64] (1–5, from lowest to highest). Thus, the minted bUSDŜ are allocated to a specific virtual sub-pool, used only to cover protection requests of the same risk level. The higher the assumed risk (e.g. the higher the probability that historical ETH/Ŧ volatility will cause crossing of the requested protection floor within the term), the higher the premiums charged to takers. Premiums are calculated based on the actuarial experience at the set risk level, so that the balance between claims and closings ends up increasing the NAV of assets within the corresponding sub-pool. Of course, tail risk events can upset this balance, and this may ultimately cause individual bUSDŜ token positions to become worthless [65]. Makers can request to exit the protocol at any time, by swapping their bUSDŜ tokens for USDŜ as per current NAV calculation. This "Redemption" transaction causes the burning of the makers' bUSDŜ, and also the reimbursement of the BUMP tokens used to open their position in the first place. Protocol fees are also deducted at this point.

In terms of token design factor calibration:

a. The design **velocity** of bUSDŜ is low [57], as they can only be minted, transferred, and burned through generally infrequent events (buying a liquidity position in a capital pool; redeeming when exiting Bumper, etc.). As already mentioned, Bumper also provides for maker liquidation events, causing actual bUSDŜ velocity to drop even further.
b. Their **scarcity** will be dependent on the market demand for liquidity provision to Bumper capital pools. Currently, there are no direct limits on the amount of mintable bUSDŜ nor are there other protocol risk parameters [59] indirectly influencing this demand.

[13] Bumper Litepaper, section "3.2 Liquidity and Liability".

c. bUSDŜ **inflation** is controlled directly by makers' demand for investment premiums and indirectly by the actuarial outcomes of protection coverage sub-pools. There are no other protocol limits imposed through risk parameters on protocol reserves or similar.
d. Their **valuation** at minting is by definition equal to that of the corresponding USDŜ (i.e. USDT or any other ERC-20 Stablecoins eventually admitted by Bumper). So, this is not a parameter controlled by Bumper. After minting and until redemption, bUSDŜ valuation depends on the NAV of the respective capital pool, i.e. on the actual actuarial outcomes of floor protection at the chosen risk level.
e. **Minting mode**: bUSDŜ are minted only through smart contract [66, 67].
f. bUSDŜ **minting optionalities** available to makers [31] are setting the risk tier which the liquidity position will cover and its Tenor of validity (Term). The latter can be closed 70 before expiry and also renewed [68] (rolled over) at expiry.
g. Their **property rights** are claims against the Bumper USDŜ ("Reserve") pool, as per guidane of the Bumper Litepaper.[14] They are also linked to the right to have the bonded BUMP required to open maker positions returned at term expiry [69]. Please note that said rights may be eroded by redeeming (i.e. when makers choose to exit the protocol before contractual term expiry, thereupon incurring a penalty "break fee"[15]) and in situations conducive to maker liquidation [65].
h. bUSDŜ are not Stablecoins, hence there is no underlying notion of managed **treasury**.
i. Regarding **composability**, their use is currently confined to Bumper use cases. There are no cooperating protocols at the moment.
j. bUSDŜ **programmability** is restricted to the methods available through the Bumper smart contracts specification.
k. The **computational complexity** of bUSDŜ minting is the same as that of base ERC-20 tokens on the Arbitrum blockchain.

We repeat that bUSDŜ is simply an abstraction for many candidate "bCovering" token types implementable by Bumper, by following the same token design with different underlying Stablecoins. All such "bCovering" will be still formally investment fund tokens.

11.5 Summary

Bumper, an EVM-compatible blockchain project that replicates on-chain a traditional finance structured products issuance and investment marketplace was used as a case study of token design. Its basic market design and use of native tokens along the main transactional pathways were explained, in reference to the project's

[14] Bumper Litepaper, section "3.2 Liquidity and Liability".

[15] Bumper Litepaper, section "3.1.3 Joint Functions".

documentation. Bumper's token design was then explained by showing how all features of its native token types could be attributed to corresponding calibrations of the influencing factors promulgated in Sect. 10.5.

In summary, it was demonstrated that the token design pillar of the proposed token ecosystem design framework aligns with current crypto-industry market practices.

References

1. [Bumper Token ecosystem]. https://www.bumper.fi/
2. Thales of Miletus. (2025, April 17). In *Wikipedia*. Retrieved April 19, 2025, from https://en.wikipedia.org/wiki/Thales_of_Miletus
3. Chew, H. D. (Ed.). (2008). *Corporate risk management*. Columbia University Press.
4. Derivative (finance). (2025, April 12). In *Wikipedia*. Retrieved April 19, 2025, from https://en.wikipedia.org/wiki/Derivative_(finance)
5. Melamed, L. *The birth of FX futures*. CME Chicago Mercantile Exchange. Retrieved March 26, 2025, from https://www.cmegroup.com/company/files/the-birth-of-fx-futures.pdf
6. (2018). *70 years connecting capital markets to development*. International Bank for Reconstruction and Development / The World Bank. Retrieved March 26, 2025, from https://pubdocs.worldbank.org/en/905031541023749461/70-years-connecting-capital-markets-to-development.pdf
7. *About ISDA*. Retrieved March 26, 2025, from https://www.isda.org/about-isda/
8. Kolb, R. W., & Overdahl, J. A. (2010). *Financial Derivatives Pricing and Risk Management*. Wiley.
9. Mitchell, C. (2022, April 21). *Basket option: Characteristics, considerations and examples*. Retrieved March 26, 2025, from https://www.investopedia.com/terms/b/basketoption.asp
10. Wystup, W. (2017). *FX options and structured products* (2nd ed.). Wiley.
11. *Capital Protection w. Participation*. SIX Structured Product pages. Retrieved March 26, 2025, from https://www.six-structured-products.com/en/know-how/product-know-how/capital-protection-products/capital-protection-with-participation
12. Swiss Structured Products Association (SSPA). (2023, June). *Structured products at a glance v23/2*. Retrieved March 26, 2025, from https://sspa.ch/wp-content/uploads/2023/07/en_sspaswissmap_v.232.pdf (please search in the document for "Capital Protection Note with Participation").
13. *What is Bumper?* Bumper documentation pages. Retrieved March 26, 2025, from https://docs.bumper.org/
14. *Overview - Bumper is a DeFi price protection protocol built on Ethereum*. Bumper documentation pages. Retrieved March 26, 2025, from https://docs.bumper.org/protocol/overview
15. *FAQs*. Bumper documentation pages. Retrieved March 26, 2025, from https://docs.bumper.org/learn/faqs
16. *What network is Bumper on?* Bumper documentation pages. Retrieved March 26, 2025, from https://docs.bumper.org/learn/faqs#what-network-is-bumper-on
17. [Arbitrum Token ecosystem]. https://arbitrum.io/
18. [Bumper Whitepaper, short version]. *Bumper Litepaper Version 1.0*. Retrieved March 26, 2025, from https://drive.google.com/file/d/18mwY6HPlVNT9NNZ1ZE2O1rKDm1GxJDa3/view, linked to from https://www.bumper.fi/resources/litepaper
19. *DAO Overview & Structure*. Bumper documentation pages. Retrieved March 26, 2025, from https://docs.bumper.org/governance/dao-overview-and-structure
20. *DAO Legal*. Bumper documentation pages. Retrieved March 26, 2025, from https://docs.bumper.org/governance/dao-legal
21. *The BUMP Token*. Retrieved March 26, 2025, from https://www.bumper.fi/bump-token

22. *CoinMarketCap BUMP page*. CoinMarketCap. Retrieved March 26, 2025, from https://coinmarketcap.com/currencies/bumper/
23. *Purpose of the DAO*. Bumper documentation pages. Retrieved March 26, 2025, from https://docs.bumper.org/governance/dao-overview-and-structure/purpose-of-the-dao
24. *Voting Power*. Bumper documentation pages. Retrieved March 26, 2025, from https://docs.bumper.org/governance/voting-power
25. [Bumper dApp]. https://app.bumper.fi/
26. [Wrapped Bitcoin (wBTC) Blockchain]. https://wbtc.network/
27. Connect a wallet. Bumper documentation pages. Retrieved March 26, 2025, from https://docs.bumper.org/learn/guides/connect-a-wallet
28. *How do I add my BUMP to Metamask?* Bumper documentation pages. Retrieved March 26, 2025, from https://docs.bumper.org/learn/guides/how-do-i-add-my-bump-to-metamask
29. *How to buy BUMP on Uniswap*. Bumper documentation pages. Retrieved March 26, 2025, from https://docs.bumper.org/learn/guides/how-to-buy-bump-on-uniswap
30. *Hedge - Open a position*. Bumper documentation pages. Retrieved March 26, 2025, from https://docs.bumper.org/learn/guides/open-a-hedging-position
31. *Earn - Open a position*. Bumper documentation pages. Retrieved March 26, 2025, from https://docs.bumper.org/learn/guides/earn-open-a-position
32. *Buy Bumper (BUMP)*. Binance. Retrieved March 26, 2025, from https://www.binance.com/en/how-to-buy/bumper
33. [Swap BUMP for other Tokens at Uniswap]. Retrieved March 26, 2025, from https://app.uniswap.org/swap?inputCurrency=0xa0b86991c6218b36c1d19d4a2e9eb0ce3606eb48&outputCurrency=0x785c34312dfa6b74f6f1829f79ade39042222168
34. (2024, May 10). *Bond Boost*. Bumper announcements. Retrieved March 26, 2025, from https://www.bumper.fi/post/introducing-bond-boost https://docs.bumper.org/learn/bump-token/token-bonding
35. *Staking & Locking*. Bumper documentation pages. Retrieved March 26, 2025, from https://docs.bumper.org/governance/voting-power/staking-and-locking
36. *vBUMP*. Bumper documentation pages. Retrieved March 26, 2025, from https://docs.bumper.org/governance/voting-power/vbump
37. *Staking tokens for vBUMP*. Bumper documentation pages. Retrieved March 26, 2025, from https://docs.bumper.org/governance/dao-overview-and-structure#staking-tokens-for-vbump
38. *How users gain vBUMP*. Bumper documentation pages. Retrieved March 26, 2025, from https://docs.bumper.org/governance/voting-power/vbump#how-users-gain-vbump
39. *Locking BUMP*. Bumper documentation pages. Retrieved March 26, 2025, from https://docs.bumper.org/governance/voting-power/staking-and-locking#locking-bump
40. *Delegating vBUMP*. Bumper documentation pages. Retrieved March 26, 2025, from https://docs.bumper.org/governance/dao-user-guides/delegating-vbump
41. (2023, November 30). *Navigating BUMP Token Expansion on Arbitrum*. Bumper announcements. Retrieved March 26, 2025, from https://www.bumper.fi/post/navigating-bump-token-expansion-on-arbitrum
42. *Hedge - Exit a position*. Bumper documentation pages. Retrieved March 26, 2025, from https://docs.bumper.org/learn/guides/hedge-exit-a-position
43. (2022, August 1). What are BUMP tokens? Retrieved March 26, 2025, from https://www.bumper.fi/post/what-are-bump-tokens
44. [BUMP Token Smart Contract]. Retrieved March 26, 2025, from https://etherscan.io/token/0x785c34312dfa6b74f6f1829f79ade39042222168
45. Palladino, S., Giordano, F., & Croubois, H. (2019, April 24). *ERC-1967: Proxy storage slots*. Ethereum Improvement Proposals, no. 1967. Retrieved March 26, 2025, from https://eips.ethereum.org/EIPS/eip-1967
46. *Bumper DAO*. Bumper GitHub pages. Retrieved March 26, 2025, from https://github.com/bumper-dao

47. [Bumper]. *1a-bootstrap-contracts*. Bumper GitHub pages. Retrieved March 26, 2025, from https://github.com/bumper-dao/1a-bootstrap-contracts
48. *Initial Dex Offering (IDO)*. CoinMarketCap "Academy" pages. Retrieved March 26, 2025, from https://coinmarketcap.com/academy/glossary/initial-dex-offering
49. *Liquidity Mining*. Bumper governance pages. CoinMarketCap "Academy" pages. https://lm.bumper.fi/governance/treasury
50. (2024, April 3). *BUMP Token circulating supply methodology update*. Bumper announcements. Retrieved March 26, 2025, from https://www.bumper.fi/post/bump-token-circulating-supply-methodology-update
51. *CoinMarketCap BUMP page*. CoinMarketCap. Retrieved March 26, 2025, from https://coinmarketcap.com/currencies/bumper/ (please search in the page for both "Self-reported circulating supply" and "Fully diluted market cap").
52. [BUMP Token Smart Contract]. Bumper GitHub pages. Retrieved March 26, 2025, from https://github.com/bumper-dao/1a-bootstrap-contracts/blob/main/BUMPToken.sol
53. [Aave Token ecosystem]. www.aave.com
54. *AToken*. Aave documentation pages. Retrieved March 26, 2025, from https://aave.com/docs/developers/smart-contracts/tokenization#atoken
55. *VariableDebtToken*. Aave documentation pages. Retrieved March 26, 2025, from https://aave.com/docs/developers/smart-contracts/tokenization#variabledebttoken
56. Chen, J. (2022, May 11). *Numeraire: What it is, history, how it works*. Retrieved March 26, 2025, from https://www.investopedia.com/terms/n/numeraire.asp
57. *Doesn't the high number of daily transactions for a user's account incur some kind of additional risk?* Bumper documentation pages. Retrieved March 26, 2025, from https://docs.bumper.org/learn/faqs#doesnt-the-high-number-of-daily-transactions-for-a-users-account-incur-some-kind-of-additional-risk
58. *Taker liquidations*. Bumper documentation pages. Retrieved March 26, 2025, from https://docs.bumper.org/learn/protocol-risks/taker-liquidations
59. *General risks*. Bumper documentation pages. Retrieved March 26, 2025, from https://docs.bumper.org/learn/protocol-risks/general-risks
60. [bwBTC Token minting Smart Contract transactons on Arbitrum]. Retrieved March 26, 2025, from https://arbiscan.io/token/0x39f31e78a81f5cda2fe9516e3fdf5c528db2f828
61. *Hedge - Renew a position*. Bumper documentation pages. Retrieved March 26, 2025, from https://docs.bumper.org/learn/guides/hedge-renew-a-position
62. [Bumper]. *Glossary*. Bumper documentation pages. Retrieved March 26, 2025, from https://docs.bumper.org/additional-information/glossary
63. *Claim below your price floor*. Bumper documentation pages. Retrieved March 26, 2025, from https://docs.bumper.org/learn/guides/hedge-exit-a-position#claim-below-your-price-floor
64. (2023, August 18). *An analysis of Bumper yield potential for liquidity providers*. Retrieved March 26, 2025, from https://www.bumper.fi/post/an-analysis-of-bumper-yield-potential
65. *Maker liquidations*. Bumper documentation pages. Retrieved March 26, 2025, from https://docs.bumper.org/learn/protocol-risks/maker-liquidations
66. How do stablecoins work with the smart contract? Bumper documentation pages. Retrieved March 26, 2025, from https://docs.bumper.org/learn/faqs#how-do-Stablecoins-work-with-the-smart-contract
67. [Smart Contract transactons on Arbitrum for LP-n USDT-WBTC]. Retrieved March 26, 2025, from https://arbiscan.io/token/0xe88c578a58d15f7ba1dca987d13c58f25713e27e#code
68. *Earn - Renew a position*. Bumper documentation pages. Retrieved March 26, 2025, from https://docs.bumper.org/learn/guides/earn-renew-a-position
69. *Earn - Close a position*. Bumper documentation pages. Retrieved March 26, 2025, from https://docs.bumper.org/learn/guides/earn-close-a-position

Bonding Function Design

12

The blockchain paradigm has enabled decentralized transactions and automation, without necessitating the existence of centralized governance. In order to avoid chaos ensuing in token-based ecosystems, crucial process steps must be automated and allowed to execute fast without the need for human intervention. Instabilities can be reduced as long as the rules of this automation are carefully thought through in advance and implemented through robust technical means. Ideally, they should also be sensing and correcting unforeseen side-effects as the economic life of the ecosystem progresses.

The market, mechanism, and token designs are the framework of this thinking-through, akin to the architectural blueprints, if you wish, of a new building. Typically, when progressing to actually constructing the building, more detailed design work is needed. When laying out the floors and rooms, care is needed to see that the doors, the electricity, the heating, and the plumbing, the innards of the infrastructure can actually be joined-up together and operate seamlessly. For example, setting the specifications for the electric circuit powering the motor that opens and closes an automated door; that would be an example of "joining-up" disparate parts of the infrastructure.

Blockchain-based ecosystems where cryptocurrencies and other crypto-assets are minted and transacted have the same need for more detailed "joining-up" design as they progress to technical implementation. Several of them have opted for carrying out this "joining-up" through so-called "Bonding Functions" implemented in smart contracts (please remember the close relationship between the words "joining-up" and "bonding"[1]).

In this chapter, we explain this concept in some detail, progressing from basic definitions to typology, reference implementations, and finally to implementation

[1] This is only a mnemonic which we suggest to the reader. The term actually originated from the industry expression "bonding funds to a smart contract", where "bonding" had the meaning of "tying up, committing".

I. Giannakouros, *Cryptocurrencies and Tradable Crypto-Tokens*, Future of Business and Finance, https://doi.org/10.1007/978-3-031-98423-5_12

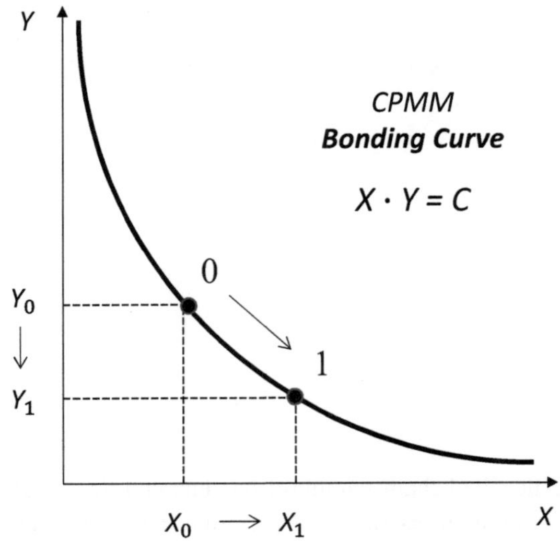

Fig. 12.1 Constant product market maker (CPMM) bonding curve in Uniswap V2

guidelines. The basic notion that needs to be kept in mind is that bonding functions are nothing else but descriptions of how disparate parts of the infrastructure enabling the token lifecycle are to work together; in effect, micro-rules calibrating specific steps along the token lifecycle.

12.1 Bonding Function Definition

Assume that the state of the token ecosystem can be described through a vector of state variables:

$$\vec{S}(t) = [\, s_1(t), s_2(t), \ldots, s_n(t) \,]$$

Further assume that the ecosystem governance postulates a relationship which must hold among several state variables at all times:

$$F(s_i(t)) = 0, \quad i \in A \subseteq \{1,\ 2, \ldots, n\}$$

The mathematical description $F(s_i(t)) = 0$ is a bonding function. In the two-dimensional case ($n = 2$), the function is a bonding curve.

As an example, the mathematical description of the constant product market maker linking quantities X and Y of the two exchangeable tokens in the Uniswap V2 Liquidity Pool [1]:

$$X{\cdot}Y = C \Leftrightarrow X{\cdot}Y - C = 0$$

is a bonding curve (cf. Fig. 12.1).

Fig. 12.2 NXM Price vs. Total Funds bonding curve in Nexus Mutual

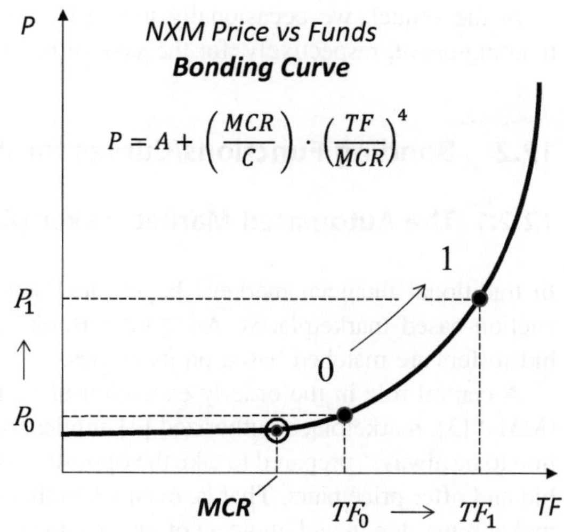

Similarly, the mathematical formulation of the primary-market price P of the NXM token in the Nexus Mutual continuous token model as a function of the total funds TF in the capital pool [2] of the protocol:

$$P = A + \left(\frac{MCR}{C}\right) \cdot \left(\frac{TF}{MCR}\right)^4$$

(where A and C are constants and MCR is the "Minimum Capital Requirement" of the protocol) is another bonding curve (cf. Fig. 12.2).

It is important to not proactively read a fixed "cause-and-effect" relationship in a particular bonding function, i.e. to not assume in advance that one or several of the $s_i(t)$ state variables are the independent ones. Which variables are operational degrees of freedom and which are *de facto* observable outcomes will depend on the particular use case to which the relationship applies. There are no limitations as to which use cases a particular token protocol will decide to implement through a bonding function.

Mathematical descriptions aside, the assumptions, parametrizations, and operational repercussions inherent to the use of bonding functions are of paramount importance for the success of crypto-token use cases and need to be at the forefront of designers' or analysts' considerations.

We will demonstrate the importance of this wider context in reference to two important areas of applicability which were already introduced through the two afore-mentioned protocol examples (Uniswap and Nexus Mutual), namely:

a. *Automated market makers* (AMM)
b. *Continuous token offerings* (CTO)

In the sequel, we occasionally use "BF" and "BC" for bonding function and bonding curve, respectively, for the sake of brevity.

12.2 Bonding Functions/Curves for Automated Market Makers

12.2.1 The Automated Market Maker (AMM) Use Case

In traditional financial markets, buyers and sellers of securities come together in auction-based marketplaces. An "Order Book" is kept by authorized agents, and bids/offers are matched based on its entries.

A central role in the orderly execution of trades is played by "Market Makers" (MMs) [3], marketplace-authorized [4] entities, or individuals who have the obligation to be always[2] prepared to take the opposite side of transactions, i.e. to quote both bid and offer price pairs. That is, even when there are no external offers, the marker maker must step in and quote an offer price to any prospective bid—the opposite for any prospective offer. The MM assumes non-trivial market risk (which needs to be hedged with both inventory and derivatives), compensated for by getting unique visibility to the order book and order-flow—a privilege accorded to it by the marketplace organization, in exchange precisely for its obligation to always provide liquidity to the market. In effect, the MM needs to be able to predict a "probable" price level for the next trade and a corresponding "fair" level of the bid/ask spread. The business model of MMs rests mainly on an income stream through bid/ask spreads and also on taking the *de facto* "right" side of transactions at market floors and ceilings. Of course, nowadays Market Maker means "Market Making algorithm behind the humans" with the mathematics [5, 6] to match.

The important thing to remember is that the MM in traditional finance is an "Obliged Liquidity Provider" who must make informed decisions about which prices to quote at both ends of an exchange transaction. From the market participant's point-of-view, it is a central counterparty of last resort for this particular marketplace, an economic agent with centralized rights and responsibilities.

In a blockchain context, Centralized Exchanges (CEXs) can and do use market making central limit order books (CLOBs) for order matching and execution. Decentralized Exchanges (DEXs), on the other hand, are predicated on the absence of real-time privileged centralized authorities, and this is where the need for automated market makers arose. However, the concept of automated market making is not blockchain-specific.

In traditional finance, academic thinking towards automating the market making function [7] had already created the "prediction-market" analogy [8]. In this analogy, the financial exchange was modelled as a "voting mechanism" whereby the best forecast of future price could be elicited as a scoring outcome similar to voting—the

[2]Typically barring "exceptional circumstances", which are defined by marketplace governance in accordance with local regulations.

voting action of individual market participants being their accepting to buy or sell an asset at a particular price. This model allowed to transpose the market-making logic into a crowdsourced setting (away from presupposing an economic agent with centralized rights and responsibilities), which in turn made it amenable for decentralized decision-making—i.e. for blockchain-based decentralized finance. The logarithmic market scoring rule [9–11] was the earliest automated market maker which bridged the traditional and decentralized finance worlds.

In effect, the use of automated market makers in the crypto-space arose from the need for autonomous execution of token-exchange transactions without intervention of a centralized agent and in a way that would be blockchain-compatible, i.e. always available, non-repudiable, transparent in its implementation through on-chain artefacts such as smart contracts and change-managed through decentralized governance.

The starting notion behind AMMs in the crypto-space is the creation of a "liquidity pool" containing committed quantities of all tokens that are exchangeable through the protocol. That is similar to the inventory of physical positions which the traditional finance MM has access to, however over-dimensionalized in comparison as there are no risk-management overlays. It is reserved liquidity, denominated in whatever tokens the protocol is willing to buy and sell. Liquidity investors are incentivized to invest into "Liquidity Positions", i.e. to fund the liquidity pool in exchange for a protocol-specific income stream on top of the price evolution of their positions.

Building on this notion, the role of the central counterparty is assumed not by a privileged agent or a proprietary algorithm but by a smart contract buying and selling in-pool tokens based on a pre-defined and published algorithm specified by the protocol governance. This smart contract is the AMM (cf. Fig. 12.3, where arrow texts denote asset types transferred), and, as per industry jargon, liquidity investors "bond" their token funds to the SC.

The liquidity pool contains a pre-defined set of admissible tokens ₸Ai, in the respective (time-dependent) quantities Xi(t), $i \in \{1, 2, \ldots, n\}$. A trader can exchange ("swap") any of the tokens ₸Ai with the DEX, either by using own holdings or after buying them in other, Centralized or Decentralized, token Exchanges. What he is getting back in return is determined by the AMM smart contract.

12.2.2 AMM Bonding Function/Curve Design

The mathematical form of the AMM token-swapping algorithm is its bonding function. In the schematic of Fig. 12.3, the token quantities Xi(t) are state variables of the protocol, hence the definition of a BF applies.

What are the main considerations in BF design? Can we say that any mathematical formula that guarantees Xi(t) ≥ 0, $\forall i \in \{1, 2, \ldots, n\}$ is a valid candidate for the AMM use case?

The answer is obviously negative. First, the objective of an automated market maker is to capture the dynamics of an on-chain asset exchange. There are prediction

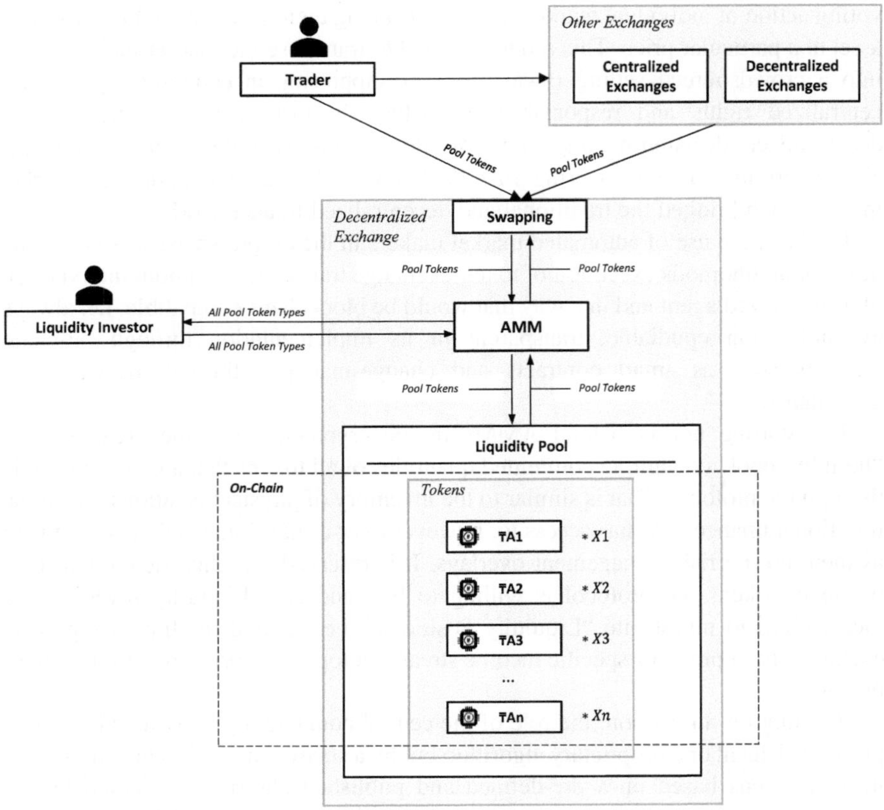

Fig. 12.3 On-chain automated market maker (AMM) use case

(market risk, liquidity risk, etc.) as well as operational aspects (on-chain programmability as smart contract, on-/off-change information exchange, etc.) involved. Second, the targeted decentralized finance paradigm imposes constraints on the parameters that can be considered as state variables of the protocol *per se*, in juxtaposition to extraneous variables which may or may not be trusted at all times. Third, the particular mathematical formula encoded in the BF will have repercussions for the pay-off profile of each investment in a liquidity position.

We will demonstrate these points through the concrete use case of a particular type of AMM, a "Constant Product Market Maker" ("CPMM", as implemented, e.g., in Uniswap V2 [1]). The reference decentralized exchange offers swapping between two tokens, ₸X and ₸Y. It involves a liquidity pool containing time-dependent positions X and Y, wherein liquidity investors bond token funds to the CPMM smart contract (cf. Fig. 12.4).

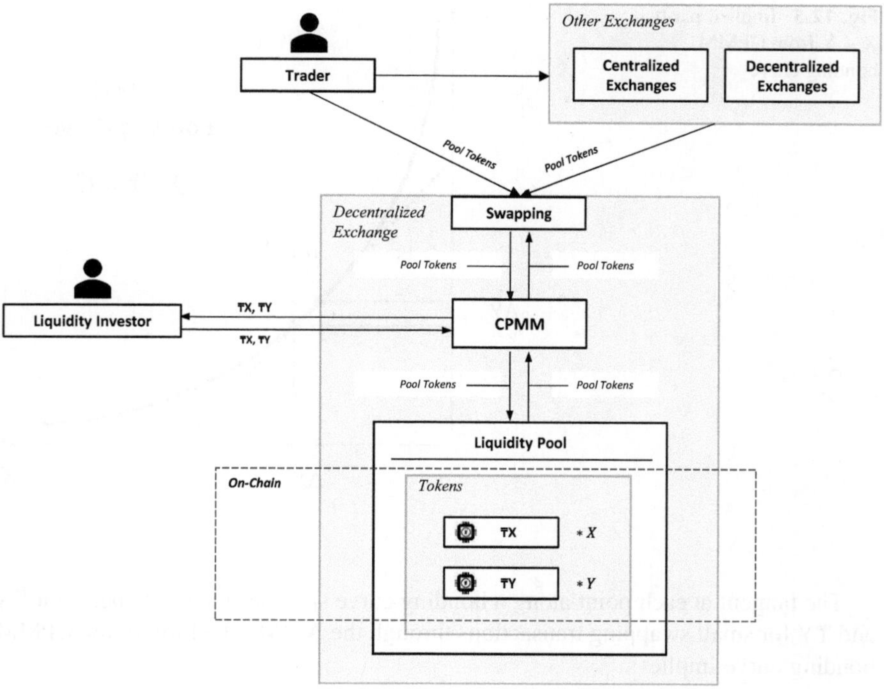

Fig. 12.4 Constant product market maker (CPMM) use case

The bonding curve of the CPMM is:

$$X \cdot Y = C$$

By definition, this is the relationship which the CPMM is programmed to enforce within the liquidity pool at all times. What is the price (market) risk of using this BC?

Let us assume a very small quantity of swapped tokens. A trader comes to the reference DEX and asks to exchange a small quantity of ŦX for ŦY. When the swapping request arrives, the liquidity pool contains X_0 and Y_0 tokens, respectively, satisfying the equation $X_0 \cdot Y_0 = C$; this is the point (X_0, Y_0) in Fig. 12.5. By accepting the request, the liquidity pool has increased its X holding to $X_0 + \Delta X$ and increased its Y to $Y_0 - \Delta Y$.

The price in terms of ŦY which the CPMM offered for ŦX at (X_0, Y_0) was:

$$P_x = -\frac{\Delta Y}{\Delta X}$$

or, at the infinitesimal limit:

$$P_x = -\left.\frac{\mathrm{d}Y}{\mathrm{d}X}\right|_0$$

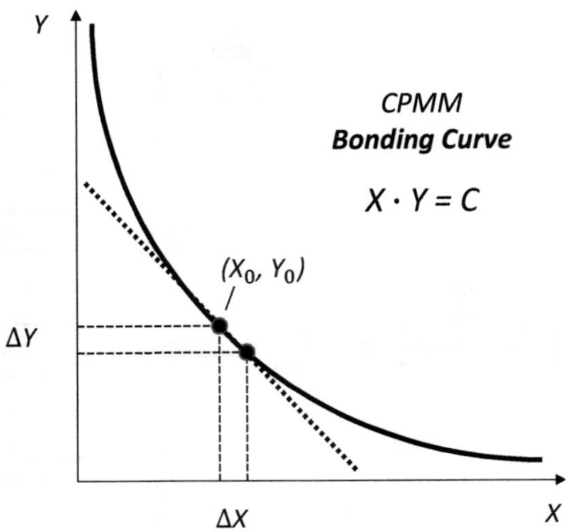

Fig. 12.5 Implied parity X ~ Y from CPMM bonding curve

The tangent at each point along a bonding curve specifies the parity between ŦX and ŦY for small swapping transactions through the AMM. The form of the CPMM bonding curve implies:

$$P_x = -\frac{d\left(\frac{C}{X}\right)}{dX} = -\left(-\frac{C}{X^2}\right) = \frac{X \cdot Y}{X^2} = \frac{Y}{X}$$

There are three agents exposed to price risk: the trader, the DEX itself, and the liquidity investor.

Price risk for the trader comes from the curvature of the bonding curve, which means that for non-deep liquidity pools the average fill price of the swap at transaction completion will be different than the quoted price at transaction inception. To make things concrete, please refer to Fig. 12.6. A trader comes to the DEX to trade ŦX for ŦY. He enters the swap at (X_0, Y_0), where the quoted price P_x is given by the derivative of the curve, hence the implied price is [Y_0/X_0]. As the size of the trade is large relative to the depth of the liquidity pool, the DEX market is actually moved along the CPMM curve and the final ŦX are swapped at the price point (X_1, Y_1). This implies an average fill-price equal to the derivative of the CPMM curve at some intermediate point (X^*, Y^*) between (X_0, Y_0) and (X_1, Y_1), i.e. lower than [Y_0/X_0]. This combined effect of market-making curve and shallow liquidity is also called "slippage" in the trade literature.

Price risk for the DEX comes from having to accept large swapping transactions in volatile markets. Again, in reference to Fig. 12.6, imagine a situation where a trader engages in arbitrage between the reference DEX and another exchange where he has just been able to acquire a large position $\Delta X'$ in ŦX at a lower rate to ŦY than what the CPMM offers around its current operating point (X_0, Y_0). The large incoming swap means that the liquidity pool loses a quantity $Y^* - Y'_1$ of ŦY [due

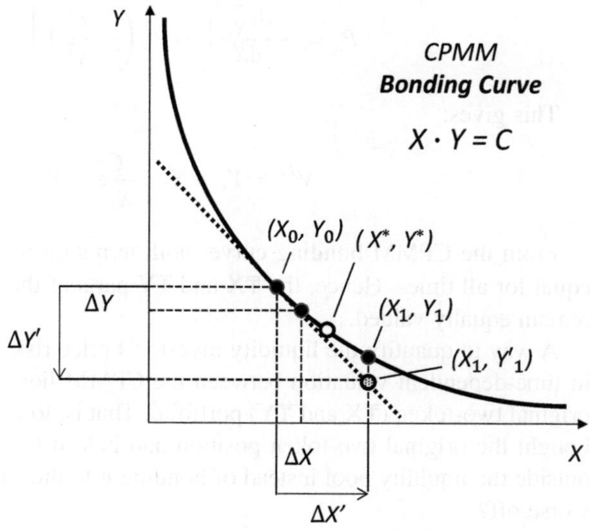

Fig. 12.6 Price impact risk under CPMM

to the average filling point (X^*, Y^*) being in between points 0 and 1 on the curve], which can be substantial if no controls are put around the AMM execution. This is sometimes denoted as "large transaction risk" in trade publications.

The price risk for the liquidity investor is of a different sort. Assuming that (as is usual in some CPMM-based exchanges) the protocol requires the funding of the liquidity position to occur through equally valued ŦX and ŦY positions (i.e. the investor is required to split his funds 50–50 between the ŦX and ŦY tokens), the value of these positions in time will remain equal.

To prove this, we take, without loss of generality, the token ŦY to be the unit of account for both positions.[3] Then the value of the liquidity position at inception is:

$$V_0^{LP} = Y_0 + X_0 \cdot P_x|_0$$

At subsequent times:

$$V_t^{LP} = Y_t + X_t \cdot P_x|_t$$

From

$$P_x = -\left.\frac{\mathrm{d}Y}{\mathrm{d}X}\right|_t$$

and the CPMM bonding curve:

[3] Or, for the more mathematically inclined, we place ourselves in the numeraire on ŦY.

$$P_x = -\frac{\mathrm{d}\left(\frac{C}{X}\right)}{\mathrm{d}X}\bigg|_t = -\left(-\frac{C}{X^2}\right)\bigg|_t = \frac{C}{{X_t}^2}$$

This gives:

$$V_t^{LP} = Y_t + X_t \cdot \frac{C}{{X_t}^2} = Y_t + \frac{C}{X_t}$$

From the CPMM bonding curve, both terms on the right-hand side of V_t^{LP} are equal for all times. Hence, the ₸X and ₸Y parts of the investor's liquidity position remain equally valued.

A way to quantify the liquidity investor's price risk is to calculate the difference in time-dependent valuation between the CPMM liquidity position and that of the original two-token (₸X and ₸Y) portfolio. That is, to ask, if the investor had simply bought the original two-token position and held it ("hodled" it in industry jargon) outside the liquidity pool instead of bonding it to the CPMM, would he be better or worse off?

Without loss of generality, we normalize both positions by dividing it with the value of the ₸Y. Denoting as ξ_t the normalized exchange ratio:

$$\xi_t = \frac{P_x|_t}{P_x|_0}$$

it can be proved [12] that the value of the normalized liquidity position as a function of ξ_t equals:

$$\mathrm{CPMM}\ (\xi_t) = 2\sqrt{\xi_t}$$

That of the bought and hodled portfolio equals:

$$\mathrm{HODL}\ (\xi_t) = 1 + \xi_t$$

And:

$$\frac{\mathrm{CPMM}\ (\xi_t) - \mathrm{HODL}\ (\xi_t)}{\mathrm{HODL}\ (\xi_0)} = \frac{1}{2} \cdot (2\sqrt{\xi_t} - \xi_t - 1)$$

Interestingly, this ratio as a function of $\xi_t > 0$ is always negative, except around parity (cf. Fig. 12.7). This means that the holding period return for the liquidity position is always negative; it is the same outcome that has come to be termed "Divergence Loss"[4] in token industry parlance; hence, we use the initials to denote:

$$\mathrm{DL}\ (\xi) = \frac{\mathrm{CPMM}\ (\xi_t) - \mathrm{HODL}\ (\xi_t)}{\mathrm{HODL}\ (\xi_0)}$$

[4] In earlier industry days also referred to as "Impermanent Loss".

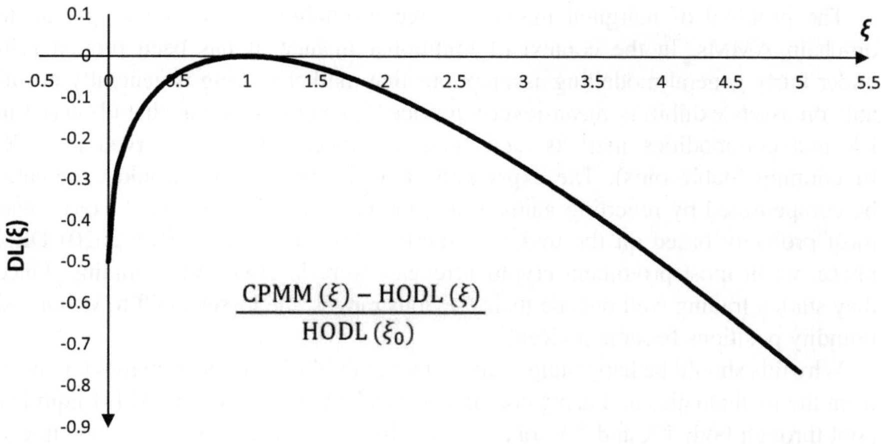

Fig. 12.7 Divergence Loss as a function of parity rate between tokens under CPMM

On account of this result, it would appear that the only way for a CPMM-governed liquidity position to have a payoff above that of simply holding the corresponding ŦX and ŦY parts as an off-liquidity-pool portfolio is if there exists another income stream accruing to the LP. This is precisely what platform fee charging through the CPMM and redistribution to the liquidity investors is trying to achieve [13, 14]. In effect, by adding an expected yield to the payoff, the curve of Fig. 12.7 is moved upwards so as to enter the range of positive values on the vertical axis.

For volatile and not strongly correlated, or not range-trading, token pairs this is not always feasible. As an example, Curve v1 [15], also a CMPP-based[5] exchange and protocol which followed on the steps of Uniswap, initially chose to only allow Stablecoins as admissible tokens in its liquidity pools [16, 17]. The intended effect was minimization of divergence loss probability by having token pairs which would be expected to remain in relatively tight parity ranges around 1, where the upward-moved curve (through the added rewards income) of Fig. 12.7 would enter positive payoff territory.

Newer generations of protocols using CPMMs as central components of DEXs (e.g. Bancor v2+ [18]) have added "Divergence-Loss-Insurance" components by design, whereby a buffer liquidity pool (funded by the protocol and operated in parallel with the investment-eligible one) takes on the market and slippage risks of the liquidity positions and strives to provide them with initial capital protection.

[5] Strictly speaking, Curve v1 implemented an AMM which sums a Constant Product (CPMM) and a Constant Sum Market Maker (CSMM), but the resulting Bonding Curve is still a "flattened" version of the CPMM at its most convex range. Curve v2 then relaxed the mathematical constraints that ensured optimal BC results around parity of 1 and allowed to focus them around any target parity point.

The problem of marginal market-making profitability is not even specific to on-chain AMMs. In the context of traditional finance, it has been proved [19] under fairly general modelling assumptions that market making is generally profitable on assets exhibiting mean-reverting price time-series (such as that observed in FX and commodities markets, and such as expected to be observed in well-functioning Stablecoins). The expectation that divergence loss would eventually be compensated by reverting gains, thus proving to be "Impermanent Loss", was most probably based on the trader's experience of the earlier (2017–2020) DEX phase, when most prominent cryptocurrencies were in effect range-trading. Once they started trading well outside their previous ranges, the losses of CPMM-bonded liquidity positions became noticeable.

Why this should be happening in the context of CPMMs is clear by moving away from the mathematics and using common sense. The funding of the AMM liquidity pool through both ₸X and ₸Y tokens is an obligation of liquidity investors, not of traders. When the price of one of the two, say ₸Y, rises that means that there is excess market demand for it. If this excess demand trend is sustained, traders will increasingly come to the exchange only to buy ₸Y and sell ₸X, not the other way around. Hence, the ₸Y pool will tend towards depletion, which in terms of Fig. 12.5 means that the operating point of the curve will be at the lower right side of the graph. Had the liquidity investors kept their original ₸X and ₸Y they would at least profit from the ₸Y appreciation. By tying their capital to both ₸X and ₸Y positions in the relation dictated by the CPMM bonding curve, they are buying into a pool which is increasingly forced to accumulate more relatively depreciating (₸X) than appreciating (₸Y) tokens, i.e. in effect buying into an equilibrium which the market no longer observes.

This notion of implied "equilibrium"[6] (expressed through a bonding function linking state variables in a deterministic fashion, even though its operating

[6]Several bonding function have been using the term "invariant" as the basis of their mathematical designs. The term "invariant" comes from the natural sciences, means "something unaltered by transformations", and denotes a function whose value stays the same despite any transformation of coordinates. In terms of computation, an invariant function will give the same output even when its input variables are scaled differently or linearly transformed as a whole. The existence of "invariant" functions is either proved mathematically (e.g. the principal invariants of tensors), or based on physical principles which are either self-evident (e.g. preservation of angles in different coordinate frames), or assumed to hold axiomatically (i.e. in lieu of fundamental assumptions about physical phenomena, such as the preservation of total energy in a closed system irrespective of energy form). So as not to confuse things, we respectfully suggest that there is nothing provably "invariant" in a bonding function, aside from artificial constraints on the evolution of its underlying state variables—there is no mathematical proof of statistical stationarity in trading exchanges (except under strict conditions, which is precisely the case of Stablecoin trading pairs—and even then Path Invariance is questionable in real market conditions, as causes of price drops may be operational risk events which translate to reputational risk exposure of a particular token), nor are there any physical concepts such as symmetry or preservation of energy that are *de facto* observed in the crypto-token markets. The only invariants in a bonding function are its constants, and any

environment is stochastic) makes the mathematical form of the bonding curve crucial for understanding the behaviour of AMMs.

We categorize forms of AMM bonding curves into "simple" and "composite". The former tends to be the building blocks of the latter, and their behaviour is much easier to visualize, both as a means to analyse the probable behaviour of existing AMMs and as way to synthesize the design of new ones. Even though any simple mathematical function in several variables will do, prominent examples of operational DEXs involve the use of the following "simple" types:

Constant Product (CPMM)

Governs swapping between two tokens ₸X_1 and ₸X_2. The respective quantities in the liquidity pool must always obey at all times the relationship:

$$X_1 \cdot X_2 = C$$

where C is constant. Already depicted in the figures above. The curve implies the price of ₸X_1 in terms of ₸X_2:

$$P = \frac{X_2}{X_1}$$

Example of DEX using a CPMM: Uniswap v2, and v3 in translated coordinates [20].

Constant Sum (CSMM)

Governs swapping among several tokens ₸Ai, $i \in \{1, 2, \ldots, n\}$. The respective quantities Xi in the pool must obey at all times:

$$\sum_{i=1}^{n} X_i = C$$

where C is constant. For example, in the two-dimensional case (Fig. 12.8):

pre-specified constraints among its parameters—which is also not even the case when it comes to Dynamic Automated Market Makers. These constants and constraints are model parameters (derived through statistical or machine learning algorithms, at best), not implications of any underlying mathematical or physical principle.

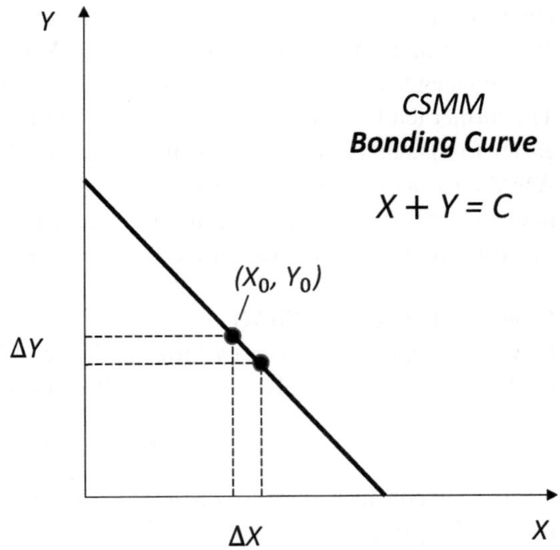

Fig. 12.8 Constant Sum Market Maker (CSMM) bonding curve

which implies a constant price of ₸X_1 in terms of ₸X_2, i.e. practically useful only in the case of Stablecoins exchanges or for tokens trading in very tight ranges. Example of DEX using a CSMM: Shell protocol [21, 22] (Stablecoin exchange) in its "Standard" bonding curve [23] configuration.

Constant Mean (CMMM)

Governs swapping among several tokens ₸Ai, $i \in \{1, 2, \ldots, n\}$. The respective quantities Xi in the liquidity pool must obey at all times:

$$\prod_{i=1}^{n} (X_i)^{W_i} = C$$

where Wi, $i \in \{1, 2, \ldots, n\}$ are weighting factors and C is constant. A graph of the bonding surface whereupon quantities X, Y, Z of a three token pool move, with all weighting factors equal to one-third, is depicted in Fig. 12.9:[7]

The name "Constant Mean Market Maker" comes from the obvious fact that the weighted geometric mean of the Xi (the weights being the Wi) remains constant at all points on the bonding hyper-surface in $\mathbb{R}^n$ space. Example of DEX using a CMMM: Balancer [24].

At the present juncture of cryptocurrency and crypto-token evolution, there is an increasing realization that no single "simple" AMM bonding curve type can accommodate all possible market regimes for tradable crypto-tokens. Consequently, DEX project evolution appears to be pursuing several "composite" directions:

[7] Graph was generated through the "c3d" app of the non-profit educational platform libretexts.org (https://c3d.libretexts.org/CalcPlot3D/index.html).

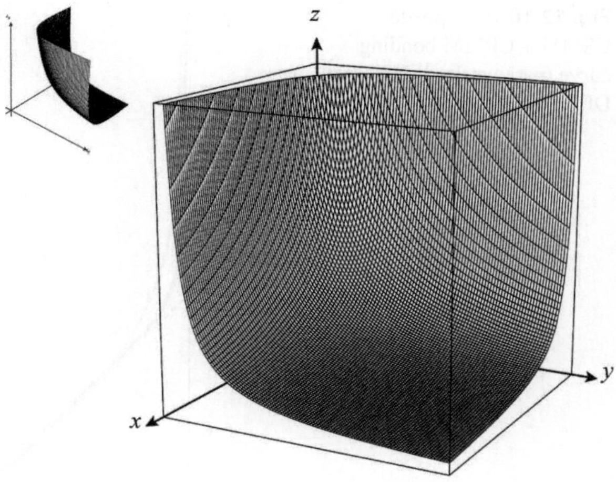

Fig. 12.9 Constant Mean Market Maker (CMMM) bonding surface (view from X-Z plane in inset)

a. *Combining different types of bonding functions* into a single AMM. The general concept revolves around trying to capture the best features of individual "simple" functions, by using each one selectively in particular trading regimes where their use can be justified.
For example, Curve Finance employs[8] a dynamically repegging AMM whose bonding curve is a weighted superposition of a CSMM and a CPMM. The weights are not known *a priori* but re-calculated numerically after each token swap with the liquidity pool. The bonding function is:[9]

$$K(x_i, D) \cdot D^{n-1} \cdot \sum_{i=1}^{n} x_i + \prod_{i=1}^{n} x_i - K(x_i, D) \cdot D^n - \left(\frac{D}{n}\right)^n = 0$$

with

$$K = A \cdot K_o \cdot \frac{\gamma^2}{(\gamma + 1 - K_0)^2}$$

and

$$K_0 = \frac{\prod_{i=1}^{n} x_i}{D^n} \; n^n$$

[8]The first generation of Curve was a Stablecoin-only DEX for token pairs; however the latest protocol whitepaper explains the applicability of its updated AMM re-pegging algorithm to any trading token tuples.

[9]The derivations are contained in the current Curve whitepaper [25].

Fig. 12.10 Composite CSMM + CPMM bonding curve (parametrized) in Curve DEX

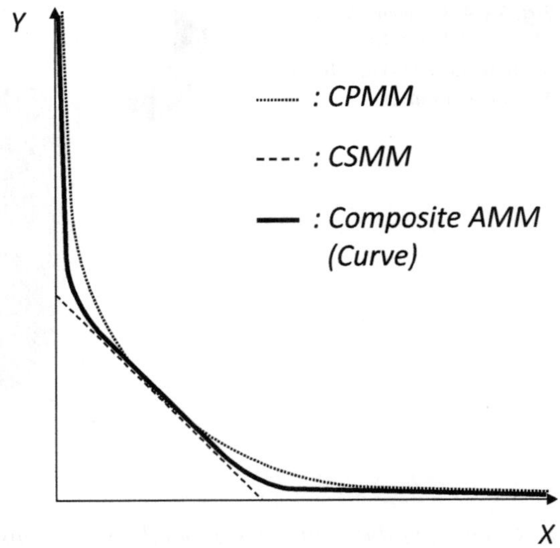

where n is the number of different tokens ŦAi in the pool, A is an amplification coefficient, and γ a parameter proxying as distance measure between curves. In the two-token case, the resulting curve is in between a CSMM and a CPMM, as depicted schematically in Fig. 12.10.

The composite bonding curve is meant to minimize price risk through its being close to a CSMM in the vicinity of the updated peg.

The Balancer "Smart Order Router" (SOR) [26] is also an example, whereby different liquidity pools have their own specific parametrizations of the same underlying Balancer bonding function, and an off-chain algorithm "hops" around, selecting those returning the maximum amount of requested tokens. This in effect creates a composite bonding function, with one part of the swap drawing quotes exclusively from one Balancer pool and then "hoping" to quotes from other pools, to fill the trading order.

As depicted schematically in Fig. 12.11 for a two-token AMM, if there are two Balancer liquidity pools #1 and #2, covering spot price ranges [P_A, P_B] and [P_C, P_D], respectively, then any trader asking to swap a ŦX amount Q when spot prices are less than P_C and more than P_D will be trading with the AMM of #1.

For spot prices between P_C and P_D, the SOR algorithm will be directing trading to both pools #1 and #2 in order to fill the swap at the highest possible average price for the trader. Hence, the trader will be trading in effect with a new AMM, interpolating the quotes of the individual AMMs of the two pools.

Additional flexibility has since been introduced with the later Balance v3 Router Architecture [27].

b. *Combining information from both on-chain AMM and Oracles*. The target design (as also explained in recent academic literature [28]) seeks to minimize exchange

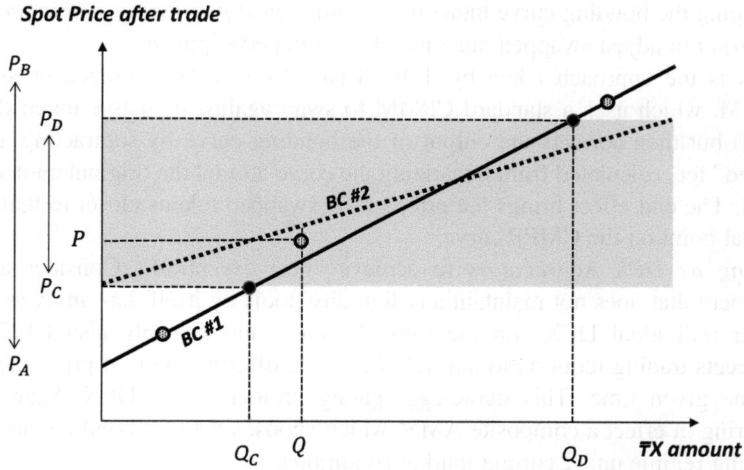

Fig. 12.11 Balancer Smart Order Router

price risk by "fitting" the underlying bonding function to the latest trading regime cross-market.

As an example, Dodo DEX [29, 30] implements a so-called Proactive Market Making algorithm [31], which in its essence quotes prices:

$$P = i \cdot R(X, Y)$$

where "*i*" is an extraneous market price provided by an Oracle and "*R*" is a heuristic [31] of the traded token-pair balances in the liquidity pool. The current Curve Finance whitepaper [32] also mentions the use of an internal Oracle, whose values are used after exponential moving-average filtering.

Even though incorporating off-chain token parity data is an operationally sound concept, for the blockchain purists it does seem to detract from the original value proposition of decentralized finance. Automated market-making based on local-only information is what drove several protocols to use exclusively on-chain bonding functions in the first place, even though the discussions in the first recorded blog about on-chain automated market makers [33] did indeed identify the eventual necessity of linking up AMMs with order-book sourced information—which is precisely what DEX-referencing Oracles provide.

c. *Adjusting in time the parameters defining the bonding curve* ("Dynamic Automated Market Maker", DAMM). Not necessarily feeding back Oracle prices, the concept revolves around keeping the shape of the basis bonding function and re-calibrating its parameters.

Balancer V2 provides [34] for such a DAMM using a weight-changing version of its basic CMMM, to enable community- or third-party-defined algorithmic trading strategies.

d. Keeping the bonding curve intact but *adding a post-processing step in the smart contract* to adjust swapped quantities for estimated slippage.
   This is the approach taken by THORChain [35], a decentralized cross-chain AMM, which uses a standard CPMM to swap against its native token (RUNE [36]) but then corrects the output of the bonding curve by subtracting a "slip-based" fee, calculated from linearizing the curve around the original quoted price [37]. The end effect brings the price of the swapped tokens closer to that of the initial point on the CMPP curve.
e. *Acting as DEX Aggregators* to achieve "best execution". Consider a DEX protocol that does not maintain any liquidity pools by itself, has an overview of other individual DEXs on the same L1-layer and possibly also CEXs, and redirects trading requests to that DEX or CEX offering the best price execution at the given time. This quote-aggregating protocol is a "DEX Aggregator", offering in effect a composite AMM which chooses the best bonding curves per trading regime under current market conditions.
   The OpenOcean Protocol [38] is such a DEX aggregator, purporting to use best price vs. liquidity depth criteria for best execution identification, followed by order-splitting and redirection [39] towards a number of DEXs [40] (and until recently also towards CEX's [41]; there may be workarounds [42], though). Another example would be Matcha [43], similarly using trading venue selection [44] and trade routing [45, 46] strategies among several exchanges [47] at once. Matcha's composite AMM curve is represented by so-called "[trade] fill paths", in effect directed acyclic graphs with each node representing that part of the curve assigned to an individual DEX.
   As a variation of the concept, it is possible for a DEX Aggregator to also add an own liquidity pool as a trading venue. Current examples are Raydium [48, 49] and indeed OpenOcean [50] itself.

What are the ideal attributes of an on-chain automated market maker's bonding function?

As was mentioned in the beginning of this section, there are prediction (market risk, liquidity risk, etc.) as well as operational (on-chain programmability as smart contract, on-/off-change information exchange, etc.) aspects that need to be considered in bonding function design. The target token population will dictate to a large extent the market and liquidity risk parameters of the design; swaps of Stablecoin pairs do not have the same price risk and liquidity depth requirements as tuples of volatile cryptocurrencies, nor is "front-running" risk the same in both cases. Constant re-pegging and refitting of a mathematically sophisticated bonding curve's parameters around prevailing market prices may not be cost-effective in terms of gas fees needed to run the AMM smart contract. Similarly, if improving the stability of a particular AMM strategy practically always necessitates going across the DEX/CEX divide (e.g. through the use of Oracles), then there are two problems that need to be carefully considered:

First, unfiltered third-party information may not necessarily be more robust, especially if the corresponding liquidity pools are not of the same depth, if there are data or network latencies, or if some data sources are becoming stale. For example, as was mentioned above, Curve Finance applies EMA-filtering before using its Oracle data—this is one simple indication of data quality risks.

Second and most importantly, both DEXs and CEXs can be victims of market manipulation by criminal agents. Bringing purposely manipulated data into a consensus-based blockchain paradigm is simply dangerous. Even in traditional finance (in the presence of well-proven Market Making algorithms acting against Central-Limit-Order-Books), such occurrences are not unheard of, for example, gold price manipulation [51] in recent times (e.g. the "London Gold Fix scandal" [52, 53]). As well as gold, several other commodities (silver, platinum, palladium, etc.) have been at times "honoured" by the undivided attention of imaginatively thinking traders [54], to the ultimate benefit and delight of trial lawyers [55] everywhere.

In short, bonding function designs cannot be decoupled from the design of AMM controls.

Considering the above, we believe that fit-for-purpose AMM bonding functions should be:

- *Conformant to realistic trading practices*, not sacrificing reasonableness for mathematical rigour.
- *Mathematically compatible with the pricing dynamics* of the target token types.
- *Adjustable to market conditions* through either parametrization or composition.
- *Adaptable to on-chain quality assurance* through near-real-time quality metrics.
- *Cost-effective in terms of on-chain execution costs* (gas fees).

As the typology of bonding functions is demonstrably complex, more fine-granular features will depend on the particularities of the particular business case.

12.3 Bonding Functions/Curves for Continuous Token Offerings

12.3.1 The Continuous Token Offering (CTO) Use Case

High-risk, high-reward business endeavours are often financed through venture capital, crowdfunding, and other ways that lie outside traditional capital markets. This occurs not by choice but by necessity, as typical credit risk analysis performed by Banks and institutional investors ends up highlighting too many conventional "red flags" (FinTechs in particular get confronted with funding rejection letters that typically cite such decision factors as: totally new target market; unproven market potential; unproven technology; short industry track-record of key individuals; too young average team age; inexistent or too limited borrowing base, etc.).

For startups targeting a product, rather than a service offering, the situation is even more precarious as product development has its own technical and delivery risks that need to be sufficiently contained through investment outlays before productization, supply chain setup and market development can proceed (through still more investment outlays). Typically, only specialized, industry-aware venture capital firms have both the expertise and the risk appetite to accompany all financing stages that startups must go through, from promising idea to business-sustaining cash flows. The patterns and anti-patterns of financing such high-risk, high-reward business cases have been gleaned and validated in countless projects. By the time blockchain and crypto-token FinTechs arrived on the venture capital scene in the early to mid-2010s, best practices had already been scripted into blueprints that captured broad but quite representative stages of how this financing would typically proceed. Thus, there are typically five stages of venture capital[10] financing for crypto-token projects:

1. *Seeding*. At this stage, the project may still only have an idea or at most a simple technology demonstrator. Capital is needed to augment the functional scope, create a minimum viable product, and validate a high-level functional envelope against actual or projected market needs. Potential investors expect to be able to do both due diligence (first-cut technical feasibility and economic risk assessments) and mentoring. Funding needs are modest.
2. *Setting up*. An organizational structure will be created, including management roles with responsibility for product development and alignment with market needs as a pre-cursor to forming a complete, long-term investment case. At the end of this stage, investors expect to see a leadership team presenting a working product, actual market research confirming business case parameters, and technical roadmaps for full functional scope, including delivery risk assessments. Funding needs are higher than in the previous stage.
3. *Early-stage*. The product is placed in the market. Based on market feedback, functional scope needs to be fine-tuned, right-pricing levels discovered, supply chains optimized, sales and marketing activities focused on increasing market share. At the end of this stage, investors must have confirmed the viability of the offering in the marketplace and gauged the additional funding levels required to reach profitability. Funding needs are materially higher in comparison to the setting-up stage.
4. *Expansion*. The product has been established in the market. Focus is now placed on future-proofing the functional envelope, progressing towards profitability, and growing market potential. Investors need to see concrete cashflow outcomes achieved through market development activities and cost structure optimization. The organizational dimension grows in importance, hence financing needs grow proportionally if profitability has not yet been achieved.
5. *Stabilization*. Both the product and the organizational structure managing it are highly visible in the marketplace. The focus now is primarily on managing business risks and on protecting profitability, and secondarily on longer-term strategic initiatives at the product or corporate levels. For the investors, this stage presents the opportunity to introduce concrete steps towards realizing their

[10] Which may be combined with crowdfunding, "angel investing" and Private-Equity financing (post incorporation).

investment payoff. They may choose to capture this payoff in one or several steps, depending on the product's growth prospects and on their own monetization strategy.

Some stages may be skipped in individual cases (spectacular early success, or fast failure of the endeavour), or additional ones introduced as institutional investors also step in. However, these five stages have been typically used to take crypto-projects off-the ground through venture capital.

However, venture capital firms are by definition no long-term investors. Every one of their investments has its own business case, calculated to produce measurable outcomes within a roughly estimated payback period. There is usually a target event taken to delimit this period, for example, a Security Token Offering ("STO", also called Tokenized Initial Public Offering—"Tokenized IPO") when the business case calls for payoff realization through an "exit" event. In effect, the chunks of financing to the startup or project are assumed to be transformed to economic value which is captured in *stores of value* representing realized assets (tangible and intangible), income streams, and growth potential. These stores of value become explicit (e.g. security tokens) through the monetization event. Before and after said event, the owners of these stores of value are the "*Principals*" of the startup or project. As explained in the financing stages above, an organizational structure is formed and legally incorporated to coordinate the activities needed to achieve the target event of the business case. The individuals occupying the critical decision-making roles in this organizational structure are termed "*Agents*" of the principals. There are other roles who are not entrusted with the highest levels of decision-making, but who have a disproportionate influence to the success of the startup or project—these are the "*key employees*".

At all stages of the project evolution, investors and project workers are unknowing participants in a game of sorts, cooperating to solve within their context what is known in economics as the "*Principal-Agent Problem*" [56, 57]. Investors (the "Principals" of the situation) would like to secure as high and early investment payoff as possible, whereas managers and key employees (explicit and implicit "Agents") are sometimes split between the long-term monetary and the short-to-mid-term functional and technical outcomes. Even though this problem is event more prominent in established, mature corporations, the risk-vs-reward profiles of startups, in general, and crypto-startups, in particular, make it more immediate for everyone involved. Mature corporations have a whole list of statutory mechanisms (dual-board structures, risk committees, internal controls systems, internal and external auditors) to discover and surface any manifestations of the problem. Startups have only the experience and track-record of their investors, on the one hand, and the professional diligence and good conscience of their project teams, on the other, to fall back upon during the five initial stages of growth. Simply put, none of these projects could ever afford setting up mature forms of corporate governance at their early stages. Their only "governance" setup consists in those venture capital providers who are willing and able to assume an active role in managing their investment, and in those project managers who are willing and able to follow the former's advice and to consistently execute on their decisions.

Imagine now a situation where the crypto-token project aims for a different form of financing, one that seeks venture capital or angel investors only for the first one or two ("seeding", "setting up") of the five phases. The project is confident that the compelling economic value proposition of their business use case will be made visible in the crypto-investment scene already during early-stage activities, with the result that a critical mass of individual, small-scale investors will be willing to invest continuously from that stage on. The financing model is in effect a mixed "venture capital plus crowdfunding" one, which can be also thought of as "democratized" (or "decentralized" if you wish) venture capital. This financing form is legitimate, as long as it is clear that it democratizes risks as well. Venture capitalists are taking on a more limited risk than before, but at the expense of ceding project governance after the first two stages. The "Principal-Agent Problem" is not going away either, the number of principals having simply increased. This situation is creating two new problems which must be solved for the project to ultimately succeed, namely, of:

a. Achieving *governance* with its two components:
   - Gaining access to clear, expert-level guidance on achieving short and long-term goals, while managing financial and operational (including legal) risks and
   - Prioritizing investment outlays apportioning between short-term technical and longer-term operational/strategic workstreams.
b. Creating an *appropriate store of value* that can:
   - Capture the economic outcomes of the project and
   - Be monetized in some marketplace so as to return measurable investment payoffs.

On governance, there is a marked difference between the traditional venture capital context and the "democratized" venture capital one. The former creates a framework for profiting from individuals who both possess expert market knowledge and have enough "skin in the game" to intervene whenever the project is losing focus or direction. The latter creates the expectation of some sort of collective decision-making for strategic guidance and high-level corrective action. Similarly, whereas venture capitalists can directly or indirectly dictate the type of store of value for their investment returns (by choosing the precise "target" or "exit" event and its venue), the process now calls for aligning interests of co-investors who are not even expected to get to know the project team. Fortunately, token ecosystems do have in-built mechanisms to address both problems. As already explained in previous chapters, ecosystem governance arrangements and store of value capture are the objectives of mechanism and token designs, respectively. Thus, the "*continuous token offering*" (CTO) token use case answers the "democratized venture capital" financing question. The fundamental concept behind CTO is the use of security or access/service (utility) and governance (utility) tokens as stores of value and enablers of governance,

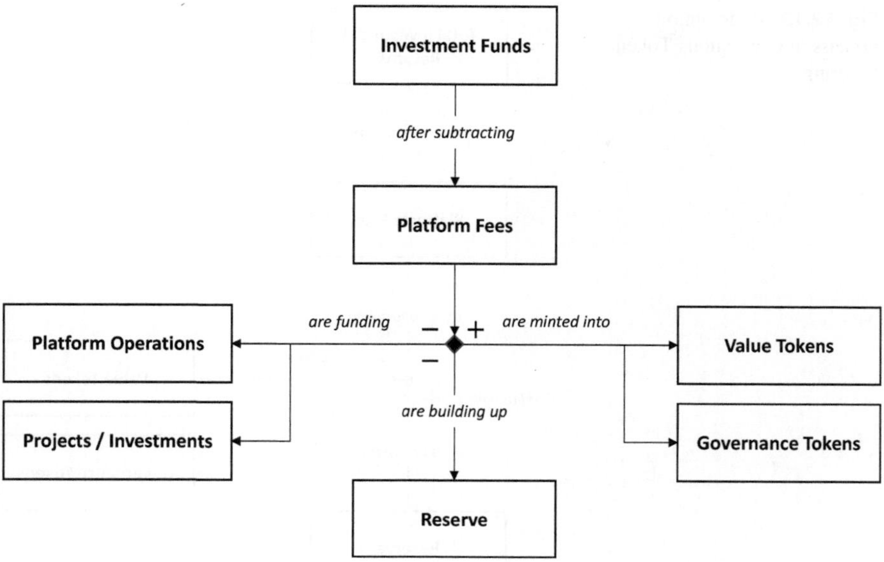

Fig. 12.12 Issuance process in Continuous Token Offering

respectively. The high-level process steps are as depicted in Fig. 12.12, whereby "value tokens" can be of either "Security" or "Access/Service" types.

Investor funds (either in fiat currency or in admissible on-chain tokens, such as Stablecoins) are exchanged for a combination of newly minted value and governance tokens[11] which remain in the protocol. The original funds are used for three purposes, namely to:

a. Cover on-going operational expenses of the platform.
b. Fund strategic and tactical investments.
c. Shore up a financial reserve.

Allocation keys and forms (if the original investor funds are further transformed into tokens that are specifically used for only one or several of the uses) are decided by the protocol governance.

The above is the "Issuance" part of the investment use case, as the newly minted value and governance tokens are *issued* in the name of the investor (credited to the investor's address in blockchain terms). Once the investor requests to recoup the investment, the inverse process is the "Redemption" part. At a high level (cf. Fig. 12.13) upon receiving the request, the protocol removes from circulation ("burns") the corresponding value and governance tokens, and potentially—depending on platform arrangements—also adds on funds drawn from its reserve.

[11] This is the most general case; depending on the implementation the security function may be merged with the governance one.

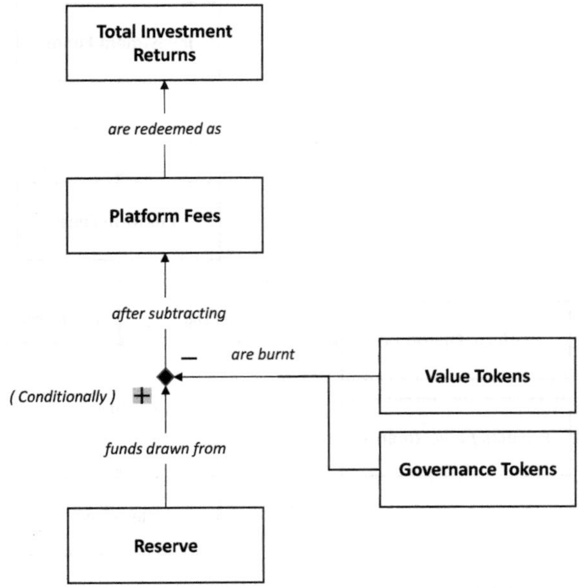

Fig. 12.13 Redemption process in Continuous Token Offering

There are conversion steps involved (from the on-chain tokens into whatever form—fiat currency or particular tokens, such as Stablecoins—the protocol will redeem in).

In all generality, there will be several tokens involved in implementing the use case on the blockchain. Apart from fiat, the investment funds incoming at issuance or returned at redemption will be in the form of several admissible tokens that will pre-exist the protocol. We denote those as (IR for "Issuance/Redemption") ₸IR1 and ₸IR2, to distinguish between L1-tokens (Cryptocurrencies such as ETH) and other tokens such as Stablecoins.

There will be respective constellations denoted as (OI for "Operations/ Investments") ₸OI1 and ₸OI2, and (RC for "Reserve/Collateral") ₸RC1 and ₸RC2. The value (₸V1) and governance (₸G1) tokens will be of course native to the protocol. In terms of tokens, the high level issuance process appears on Fig. 12.14.The corresponding redemption process is depicted schematically in Fig. 12.15.

These diagrams allow us to create the protocol token model for the continuous token offering use case (Fig. 12.16):

Equally useful is the balance sheet view of the notional CTO "Treasury" (Fig. 12.17), which allows to trace both the flow of funds among notional accounts and the tokens involved. Importantly, in a blockchain context all these steps can in principle be automated through smart contracts. If platform governance so allows, this will result in a fully transparent, no-human-in-the-loop decentralized operation of the protocol.

In such a smart contract-driven paradigm, the functional box depicted with "CTO" in Fig. 12.17 will be called upon to execute the minting and burning of

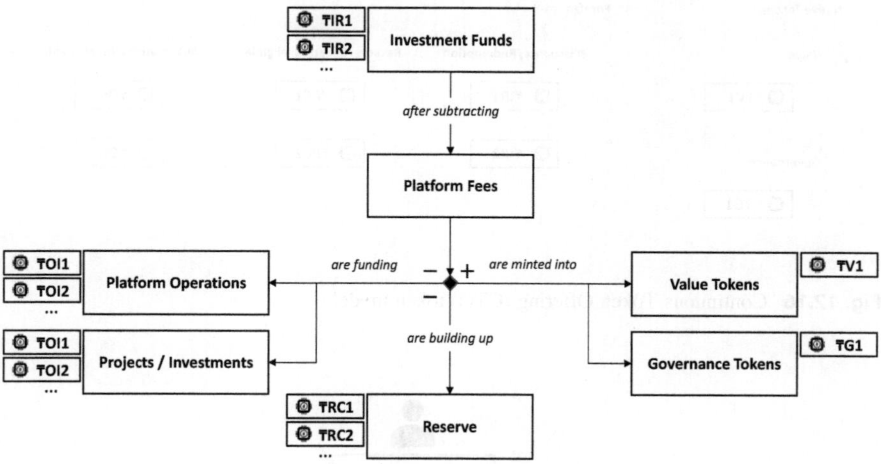

Fig. 12.14 Issuance process in terms of tokens in Continuous Token Offering

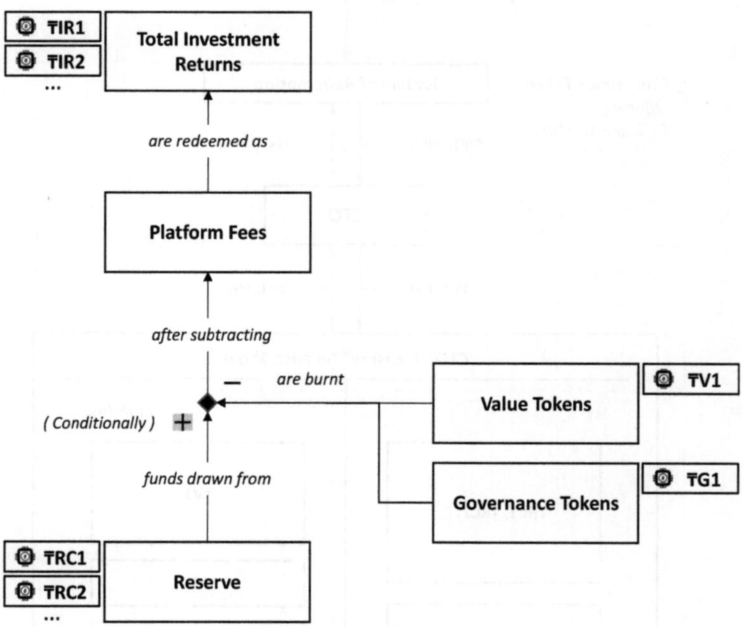

Fig. 12.15 Redemption process in terms of tokens in Continuous Token Offering

value and governance tokens, i.e. the issuance and redemption operations towards investors. The latter will be facing a "Primary Market" in these two token types, i.e. they will interact with an automation similar to that of the "Automated Market Maker" use case.

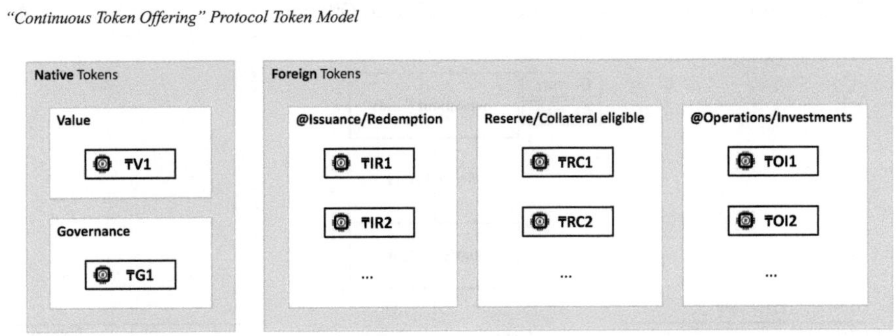

Fig. 12.16 Continuous Token Offering (CTO) token model

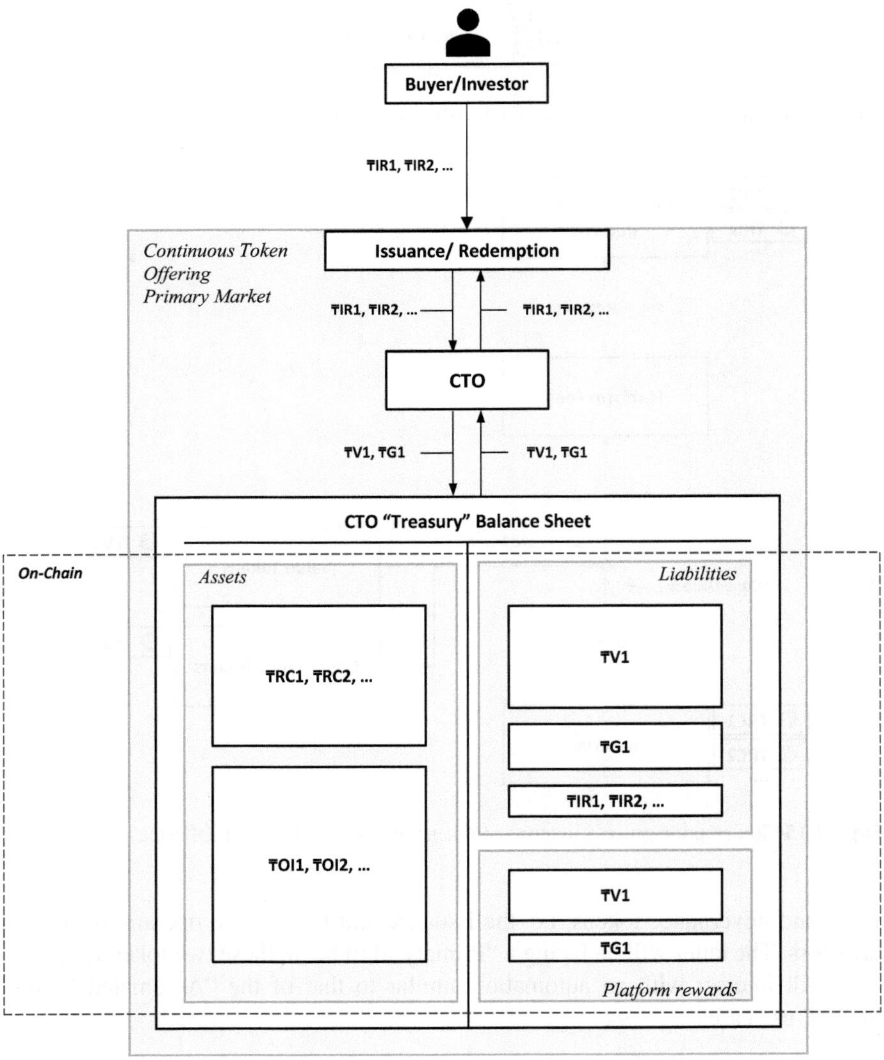

Fig. 12.17 Continuous Token Offering (CTO) use case, balance sheet view

Implementing this functionality through bonding functions is precisely the Continuous Token Offering use case.

12.3.2 CTO Bonding Function/Curve Design

As in the AMM case, the business objectives of the CTO will dictate the mathematical form of the bonding function. Without loss of generality, we will consider only the two-dimensional case, i.e. bonding curves.

The five stages of the generic venture capital case, as explained in Sect. 12.3.1, are useful pointers in bonding curve design because they provide a general estimation of funding needs with increasing time. The ecosystem "state" representing this evolution is taken to be the amount of value tokens in circulation at any given time, (CS for "Circulating Supply") $CS^{₸V1}$ or $CS(t)$ for brevity. As investors naturally expect investment appreciation, whereas they have been issued a fixed number of value tokens, the logical conclusion is that a single bonding function for issuance and redemption must quote prices $P^{₸V1}$ (time – dependent $P(t)$) that capture this appreciation, by linkage to some state variable which proxies for platform economic value. Thus, a generic CTO bonding curve could be of the form depicted on Fig. 12.18, which is a monotonic function of P vs. CS.

The general form of the function does capture both the increasing funding needs along investment stages and the appreciation expected by investors, the state variable capturing economic value being the circulating supply $CS^{₸V1}$. An investor might commit funds at point "0" and redeem the payout at point "1". Implemented in a smart contract, the "Market Maker" aspects of CTO are evident through some of the features (including pathologies) also encountered in the AMM use case. For example, "large transaction risk" is present here as well. An investor wishing to make an investment large enough relative to the present depth of the security token pool may actually "move the market". Keeping the same nomenclature as before, we refer to Fig. 12.19.

If through the new investment the circulating supply CS will increase from CS_0 to CS_1, then the smart contract will return an average token price for the new investment:

$$P_{average} = \frac{1}{CS_1 - CS_0} \cdot \int_{CS_0}^{CS_1} F^{BC}\, dCS$$

That is, away from the initial price P_0. In the same vein, as the number of newly minted value tokens per investment is:

$$N_{₸V1} = \frac{Investment}{P_{average}}$$

then the monotonic form of the bonding curve implies that investing when the circulating supply is lower will cause more value tokens to be issued than when it

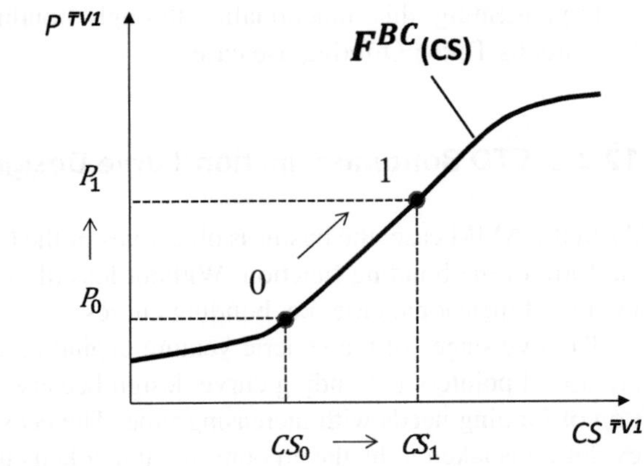

Fig. 12.18 Value token price vs circulating supply bonding curve

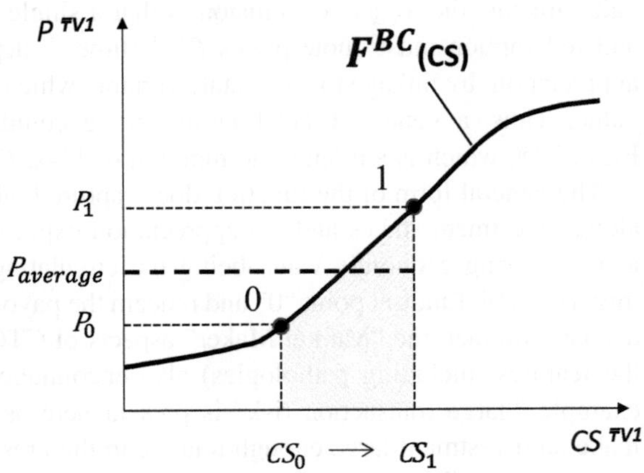

Fig. 12.19 Average token price for new investment

is higher (cf. Fig. 12.20). Thus, if both early and later investors redeem their payouts at the same CS level, the total returns for the former will surpass those for the latter. This is precisely what the design of the bonding curve should strive for, as early investors will be rewarded more for the risk they are undertaking.

At any given time, the area under the curve:

$$TF_{\text{TV1}}(t) = \int_0^{CS(t)} F^{BC}\, dCS$$

is simply the current value of total funds committed to the value token TV1 up to this point, i.e. the current value of all original investments into the protocol minus transaction fees (cf. Fig. 12.21).

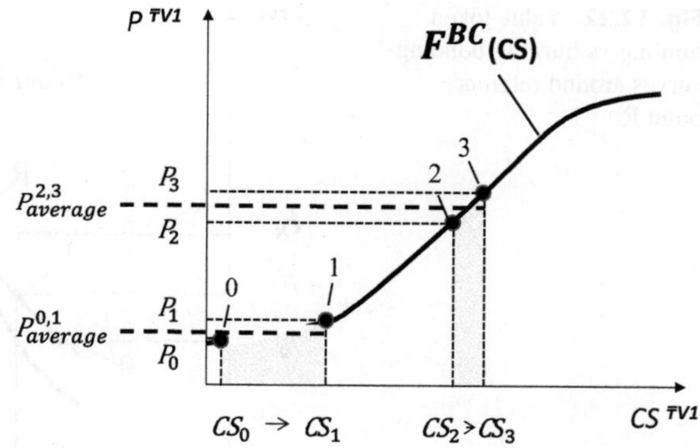

Fig. 12.20 Early investment positions receive more tokens allocated per unit of funds

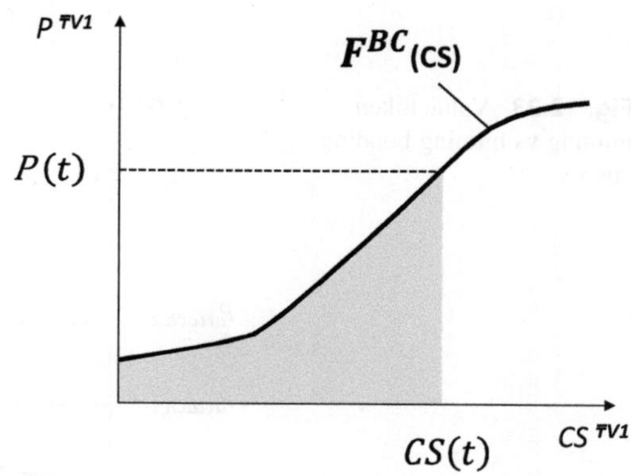

Fig. 12.21 Current total of funds committed in the value token ₸V1

What design considerations should underlie the mathematical form of such a bonding curve?

We already mentioned the need to incentivize early investors and to align expected returns with financing needs of projected investment stages. Another consideration should be the deterrence of so-called "pump-and-dump" actions. This is a speculative pattern whereby the perpetrator enters consecutive investment positions to purposely give the impression of intense upwards pressure on a security's price, and then exits all investment positions short-term as soon as other investors have been deceived into driving the price even higher. One way to guard against such a pattern is to implement two sets of bonding curves around any current (reference) price point. As schematically depicted in Fig. 12.22,

Smart contracts can be used to implement different bonding formulas for burning than for minting security tokens. Around the reference point "R", both "lower" and "upper" burning curves $\boldsymbol{F_{burn}^{BC,l}}$ **(CS)**, $\boldsymbol{F_{burn}^{BC,u}}$ **(CS)** (drawn here at exaggerated scale) penalize near-time withdrawal of funds around the point, i.e. "locally" under normal market conditions. Governance may also decide that exiting the investment at a loss should not be further penalized, in which case only the "upper" burning bonding

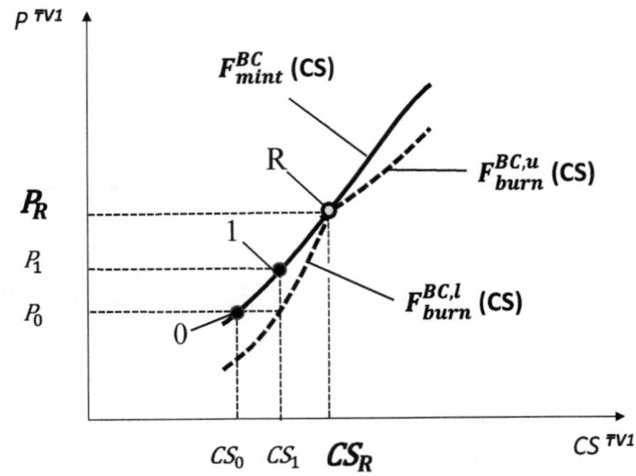

Fig. 12.22 Value token minting vs burning bonding curves around reference point R

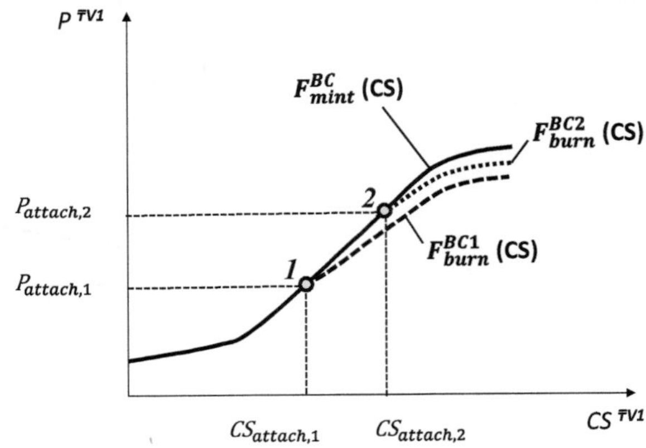

Fig. 12.23 Value token minting vs burning bonding curves

curve should lie under the minting one. In that case, SC parametrization can create separate "local" burning curves as in Fig. 12.23.

Staying with a generic "minting + burning" bonding curve to demonstrate design aspects, another important consideration is cost-effective runtime execution of the implementing smart contract. Smart contract execution can be expensive in some L-1 and L-2 platforms due to "gas fees", i.e. costs that the platform runtime environment imposes on on-chain code execution, payable in cryptocurrency. Depending on the platform and SC programming language, some mathematical operations are much more expensive to implement on-chain than others [58–60].

As in the AMM use case, we can identify some "simple" CTO bonding curves which can be used to analyse design features that can then be implemented into "composite" ones. Some easy to understand (and already implemented in CTO protocols) BCs appear in Fig. 12.24.

All share the desired feature of early investor incentivization, and differ in terms of the degree to which financing "stages" are explicitly considered; and of the effective point at which investment redemption is worth considering. In effect,

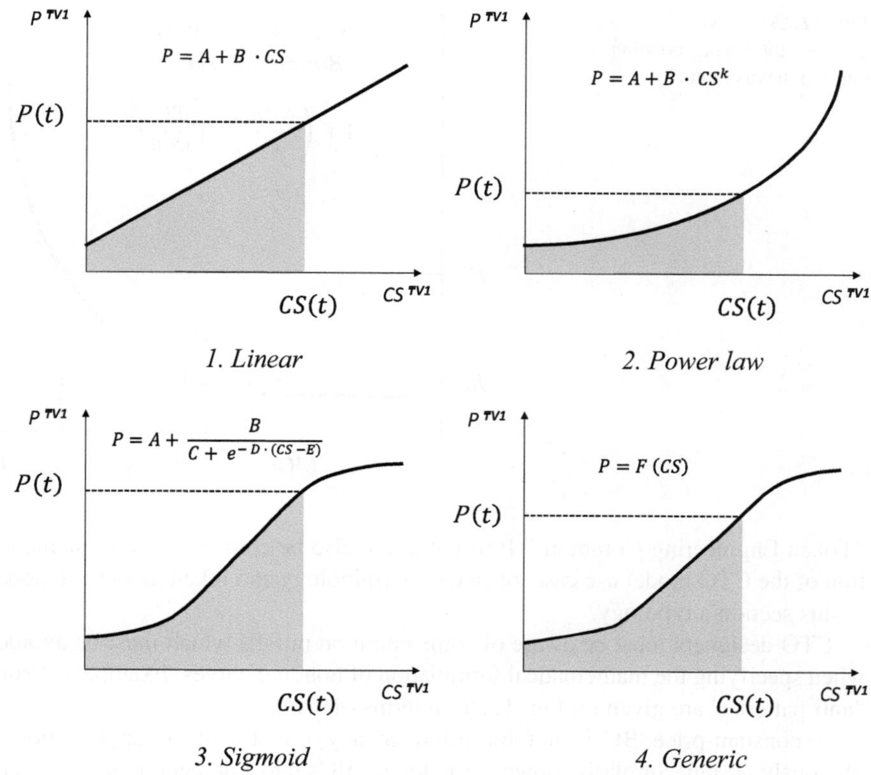

Fig. 12.24 Typology of usual CTO bonding curves

they calibrate differently the balance between investment incentives and withdrawal disincentives and can be made to align to the business risk profile of the individual project. Apart from their mathematical form, their precise parametrization can be made time-dependent (thus producing "composite curves") and subject to protocol governance procedures. It is also worth mentioning that non-mathematical constraints can also be imposed as part of the disincentives structure, such as "lock-down" periods for the withdrawal of funds.

An example of governance-defined parametrization on a "simple" BC form ("Power law" in Fig. 12.24) is the NXM-minting bonding curve of the NexusMutual [61] protocol (Fig. 12.25):

where A and C are constants and MCR is a "Minimum Capital Requirement" on total funds invested, below which the curve is practically horizontal. MCR is a conservative estimate of "core liquidity" needed for the protocol to operate, is slowly increasing monotonically with total funds and has a floor which was set at protocol launch.

The Bumper [62] protocol's is an example of a CTO implementing a Sigmoid minting BC. Its value token, BUMP [63], is of access (utility) type and investment positions in it are locked down for a period specified by protocol governance before they can be redeemed. The "Augmented Bonding Curve" [64, 65] concept by the

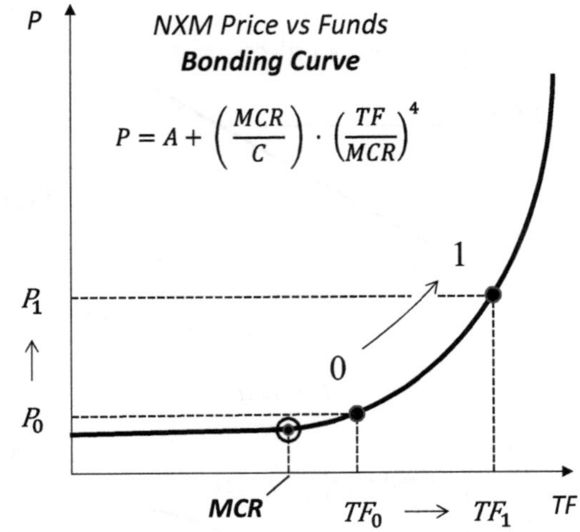

Fig. 12.25 NXM price vs. total funds bonding curve in nexus mutual

"Token Engineering Commons" [66] DAO can also be considered an implementation of the CTO model use case, once their terminology and token model is mapped to this section's typology.

CTO designers must be aware of some common pitfalls which must be avoided when specifying the mathematical formulation of bonding curves. Examples of such "anti-patterns" are given on Fig. 12.26 in terms of "simple" curves.

A constant-price BC is not incentivizing any investment, as appreciation is obviously absent. Similarly, downward-sloping BCs make no economic sense, and abruptly transitioning ones are an invitation for "pump-and-dump" action. All three are theoretically possible as parts of composite BCs, however in practice they should be avoided unless there exists a compelling, economically valid justification. For example, it can be argued that a discontinuously increasing BC may incentivize the attainment of pre-set investment milestones. However, this concept is valid in traditional finance but not necessarily so in a "market-making" algorithmic context. For example, repeated deposit and withdrawal of investment funds around the BC transition points is possible in the CTO use case but not expected in a venture-capital-driven funding case.

There are still other concepts from traditional finance that could find their way to the decentralized, bonding curve on-chain funding paradigm. For example, "share buybacks" could be simulated through enforced "deflation" (in the crypto-sense) of the CTO security tokens. The CTO model is a flexible framework on which designers can bring their own experience and intuition to bear through the design of appropriate bonding curves.

Summarizing the above, successful CTO bonding function designs are those that:

- *Attract* and demonstrably *incentivize investors.*
- Adequately *capture the economic value* of the project.
- Incentivize *active participation* of investors *in project governance.*

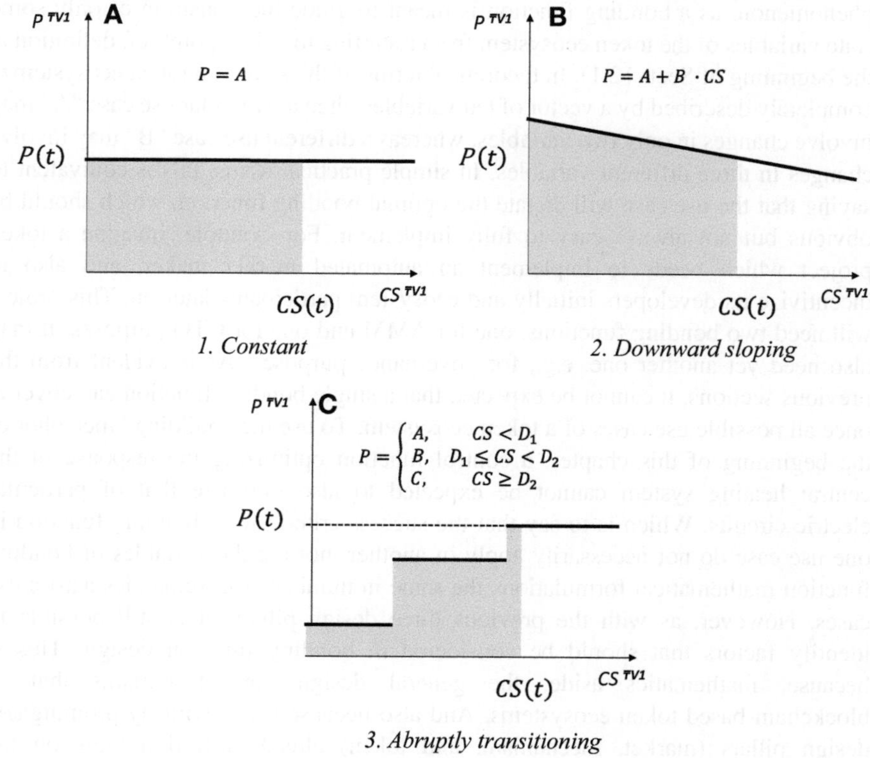

Fig. 12.26 CTO bonding curve anti-patterns

- Incentivize *optimal funding allocation among strategic and operational initiatives.*
- Guide creation of the *right mix of technical, organizational, and business development capabilities* in the project team.
- Guide *product development in alignment with actual market needs.*
- *Discover the actual price point* for the current project offerings.
- Incentivize all employees, *help retain and further incentivize "key" employees.*
- Safeguard *long-term sustainability* of the project.
- Incentivize *gradual repayment of technical and organizational debts.*
- Prove *cost-effective in terms of on-chain execution costs* (gas fees).

Designers must never forget that the mathematical form of a bonding function is simply the vehicle to achieve the above objectives, not a constraint that the use case must align with.

12.4 Factors of Consideration in Bonding Function Design

In the previous sections, the role of bonding functions in two different use cases was explained. Obviously, their general shapes differed enormously and furthermore their success criteria were hardly overlapping across use cases. This is a no isolated phenomenon, as a bonding function is meant to guide the transition of only some state variables of the token ecosystem from a starting to a final point (cf. definition at the beginning of Sect. 12.1). In theoretical terms, if the state of a token ecosystem is completely described by a vector of ten variables, then a particular use case "A" may involve changes in only two variables, whereas a different use case "B" may involve changes in three different variables. In simple practical terms, this is equivalent to saying that the use case will dictate the optimal bonding function, which should be obvious but not always easy to fully implement. For example, imagine a token project which needs to implement an automated market maker, and also to incentivize its developers initially and ecosystem participants later on. This project will need two bonding functions, one for AMM and one for CTO purposes. It may also need yet another one, e.g., for governance purposes. As is evident from the previous sections, it cannot be expected that a single bonding function can cover at once all possible use cases of a token ecosystem. To use the "building" metaphor of the beginning of this chapter, a control function optimizing the response of the central heating system cannot be expected to also optimize that of particular electric circuits. Which is to say that the success criteria for a bonding function in one use case do not necessarily apply in another, nor are the variables of bonding function mathematical formulations the same in number or in semantics across use cases. However, as with the previous three design pillars, it is still possible to identify factors that should be considered in bonding function design. This is because, mathematics aside, the general design context remains that of blockchain-based token ecosystems. And also because the previously promulgated design pillars (market, mechanism, and token) already afford a view on the prominent use cases—and pathologies—specific to cryptocurrencies and tradable crypto-tokens.

Thus, bonding function design should generally:

1. Conform with the **surrounding use case**.
2. Take underlying **token price dynamics** into account.
3. Consider **market depth** effects.
4. Balance **configurability** with **controllability**.
5. Enable **composability**.
6. Display **cost-efficiency**.
7. Minimize **market manipulation risk**.

Each design factor's importance is rationalized with some detail in the following sections.

12.4.1 Surrounding Use Case

Far from repeating the self-evident expectation that a bonding function should serve its use case, this point intends to highlight two risks: first, that the designer of the bonding function may not fully consider (or comprehend) the other three design pillars as they apply to the transactional pathway(s) of the use case—we will call this "*upstream design risk*"; and second, that their mathematical design may have unintended consequences, ultimately frustrating the use case's intended economic outcome—calling this "*downstream design risk*".

For example, some mechanisms (such as Oracles) may be *de facto* imposed on the designer—which should be visible through the market and mechanism designs. If the reasons behind this constraint are not understood, then merging on-chain AMM and Oracle data may not be done appropriately. Similarly, if foreign tokens are part of the transaction, then DEX Aggregators may be necessary for stability. In other cases, a market design amenable to congestion may cause an AMM implementing a native Stablecoin's primary market to be arbitraged through the secondary market, de-pegging it and even seriously depleting its backing reserve—if blocking logic is not built into the swapping AMM's bonding curve. All of these risks have already manifested themselves in various protocols, thus *upstream design risk* is not theoretical.

The best example of *downstream design risk* is, of course, impermanent, or divergence, loss. It was already explained (in Sect. 12.2.2 above) how Uniswap v3 concentrated liquidity positions that were originally understood as capital-efficient yield farming investments [67] were ultimately proven to be structured products [68] (and not even capital-protected [69, 70] at that). Such positions were of course created by liquidity focusing through the "translated" CPMM bonding curve (cf. Sect. 10.5.7). Reactions of ecosystem participants to such unintended consequences of an AMM can range from re-balancing of positions, to closing of positions, all the way to class action suits [71]. The situation is similar in other bonding function use cases, for example the CTO one, where the side-effects of a non-optimal design may range from governance misalignments [72] to difficulty to monetize [73] the network effects of ecosystems.

In summary, both the constraints of the upstream design as well as any probable side-effects must be considered by the bonding function designer, so as to not frustrate the intended economic outcome of the use case. Failure to do so may have significant adverse effects for the growth, and even for the sustainability, of the entire token ecosystem.

12.4.2 Token Price Dynamics

Each tradable token type used in a bonding function will be characterized by an *expected price range*. Consequently, the possible *price movements of different tokens relative to each other* under normal market conditions will also have some expected ranges. Taking those ranges into account helps the designer in two ways: first, to optimize the selection of other parameters (i.e. the other state variables apart from price) to use in the mathematical definition, and second, to design "regime change" logic into—or, at least, telemetry around—the bonding function for when market conditions deviate from normal.

As an example, an AMM used to swap Stablecoins should work differently than one for volatility tokens. In normal market conditions, Stablecoin deviations from their peg should be mean-reverting, or at least range-keeping. If the bonding function is not calibrated accordingly, then it may at best be misallocating liquidity in the underlying pool and at worst ignoring signals of extraordinary market conditions. The latter can become critical for the pool, for example, when one of the Stablecoins has lost its peg completely in other ecosystems and has now become a liquidity risk contagion vector. On the other hand, tail effects in volatility tokens are normal but may still not be commensurate with the current depth of the AMM pool if no external Oracles are used in the market design. In such a case, the designer should create either slippage-compensating logic or "regime-switching" parametrization in the bonding function. There are ways to estimate "normal" ranges and behaviours through stochastic analysis and stress-testing [74] of the bonding function during design.

Obviously, when a bonding function is used in a token minting pathway, there may be also other constraints to observe, such as the interplay between price and supply, current value of any collateral used to issue the token, any price parametrization of the underlying smart contract specification [75], etc.

12.4.3 Market Depth

Depth of a market [76] denotes its price sensitivity to order sizes, correlating positively with its levels of liquidity [77, 78], permanent or temporary. A market experiencing high, resp. low, liquidity is said to be "deep", resp. "shallow". In traditional financial markets, a measure of market depth is the bid-ask spread [79] of orders in the order book. In AMM-based crypto markets, the corresponding measure is essentially slippage [80, 81]. Bid-ask spread and slippage are fundamentally aspects of both liquidity and market risks [82, 83], and their observed levels can thus dissuade traders [84] from entering transactions. In that sense, they are proxy metrics for market frictions [85].

An AMM creates a local market, and can hence facilitate, but not totally control, said market's liquidity. This is obvious for fledgling token ecosystems, which need to "boot-strap" [86] their markets as their tokens are not yet well known, so cannot be expected to immediately attract high liquidity. The bonding function designer should take this fact into account, e.g. through different mathematical shapes, or at least different parameters, per market lifecycle phase. There are still other mechanisms to achieve the initial "boot-strapping" effect, using various combinations of on-chain [87] and off-chain [88] liquidity channels. However, in the absence of such mechanisms, the bonding function will have to compensate for lifecycle effects.

Please note that sophisticated traders in traditional finance typically use market depth metrics to estimate probable hidden transaction costs, especially for large trades. There exists an established methodology, called "*Transaction Cost Analysis*" (TCA [89–91]) used to both estimate such hidden costs and decide among alternative transaction execution modalities (e.g. sequencing orders, or routing orders through several marketplaces in parallel, etc.). In fact, such estimations/decisions may, in some jurisdictions, be necessary on regulatory compliance grounds [92–94]. Note that TCA has already found its way to crypto markets [95–97], a fact which may in due course become an important consideration for bonding function designers, especially (but not only) those designing AMMs.

12.4.4 Configurability vs. Controllability

The interplay between configurability and controllability is an important consideration, influencing, e.g. the selection of degrees of freedom (variables of the mathematical formulation), the creation of telemetry mechanisms around, and finally the programmability features of a bonding function. The more a designer departs from simple mathematical forms and the more sophistication is implemented into the shape and parametrization, the more the potential for unintended consequences if numerical and (especially) operational stability attributes of the final curve are not thoroughly analysed.

There is an *increasing tendency for more sophistication* in the design of bonding functions, especially in the AMM use case (e.g. Uniswap v4 offers the option to implement programmable "hooks" [98]; Bancor Carbon [99] allows two different bonding curves for the "buy" and "sell" sides, while both are parametrizable mathematical functions that depart from the simple forms, etc.). At the same time, there is already considerable experience of token ecosystems with liquidity pools containing more than two token types [100] ("multi-asset" ones in industry jargon, as implemented, e.g., in Balancer [101]). So, design can profit from existing bonding function implementations of quite involved mathematical and computational logic.

The designer must always be able to analyse the repercussions of their choices in bonding function design, under both normal and unusual market conditions.

12.4.5 Composability

Composability was encountered as a term already in token design,[12] where it was defined as encompassing all design attributes (operational, functional, technical) that can influence the acceptance of a token as "foreign token" by other ecosystems, use cases, or third-party protocols. In the context of bonding functions, it should be interpreted as referring to the ability of the resulting use case to be used "as-is" by other use cases within the same ecosystem or across ecosystems (also in the sense of Layer-4 protocols). An example would be the ability of Curve Finance [15] liquidity pool AMMs [102] to be invoked by other protocols (such as Lido [103]) for yield farming.

[12] Cf. Sect. 10.5.9.

The importance of composability in attaining network effects for the token ecosystem (and hence increasing its tokens' valuation) is obvious. It is the task of the designer to avoid building such features into the bonding function as may impede, or even hinder, other use cases from invoking its functionality. There are several aspects in both the mathematical form and the operational (programming) implementation that may need to be considered to that end. Also, other design pillars (especially market and token) may have to be adjusted concurrently. In any case, use case composability should not be assumed as given. For example, MakerDAO [104], Uniswap [105], and SushiSwap [106] AMMs cannot currently use Lido stETH tokens [107], as the latter are rebasing (cf. the discussion in Sect. 9.6.3.1). This is yet another point proving the importance of taking all design pillars into account when seeking to improve ecosystem designs.

12.4.6 Cost-Efficiency

On blockchains where gas fees are comparatively high, the bonding function design should be optimized for cost-efficiency. There are various ways to achieve this, through the mathematical form or through surrounding mechanisms (cf. the case of Uniswap v4 [108]). Please consult the previous discussion on transaction cost analysis for the potential repercussions if such an optimization is not performed.

12.4.7 Market Manipulation Risk

The term "market manipulation" denotes any activity purporting to skew the processes of price discovery and formation in a market in order to gain a direct or indirect advantage. The word "manipulation" implies active and conscious effort to subvert market mechanisms, in particular those relating to market structure (cf. Sect. 8.5.2). In traditional finance, market manipulation [109] is understood as a form of market abuse [110] and its typology (incl. corresponding legal repercussions [111] and imputed regulatory controls [112]) usually refers to specific business domains, e.g. securities trading [113–115]. Consequently, good business practice entails the implementation of "Market Surveillance" [116] mechanisms at the level of market participants. More often than not, this is actually a *de facto* expectation by other market participants, auditors, courts, and regulators alike.

In the context of blockchain-based token ecosystems, the basic definition still applies but the typology is slightly different. This is mainly because the available mechanisms of price discovery and formation are different to those of traditional finance—DEX and AMM being two obvious examples. Some market manipulation vectors are still in essence the same, but the possible agent interaction pathways are different; for example, a delegated voter who uses their voting power in a DAO to skew the valuation of native tokens can be argued to be acting like a delegated shareholder of a public company who misuses block-voting arrangements to skew the valuation of its balance sheet positions.

However, there do exist threat vectors that are unique to blockchain ecosystems, and thus need to be specifically considered in bonding function design.

One prominent example is the technical process of block assembly and validation as per consensus mechanism which registers transactions in the underlying distributed ledger (DL). In several Layer-1 blockchain reference architectures, there is provision for a transient memory buffer ["mempool" [117, 118] in industry jargon] queuing all submitted transactions, each annotated with metadata denoting requested prioritization level. Ecosystem agents (algorithmic, human, or mixed) operating at the technical infrastructure level are tasked with scanning the mempool and proposing the transactions to include in the block to then validate and register into the DL. Said agents also have the right to override the initial prioritization of transactions in the queue, as long as the final proposed block can be validated. Now, if these technical agents have principals controlling economic agents of token ecosystems using the same blockchain (at Layers either 1 or higher), then they can use their visibility into the mempool for own benefit—if unchecked. For example, if a submitted transaction in the mempool buys a number of currency or security tokens, an algorithmic block proposer/validator may be programmed to immediately submit a separate transaction pair: the exact same buy transaction at a lower price point ("buy leg") and an opposite transaction ("sell leg") at a higher one. Said proposer can arrange for the "buy leg", resp. "sell leg", to be included in the block at higher, resp. lower, priority level than the targeted transaction (for example, by paying slightly higher, resp. lower, gas fees). Transaction prioritization defines time sequencing within the same block. Thus, the proposer/validator has just executed a combined "front-running" [119] and "scalping" [120] trade in traditional finance parlance. In crypto industry terms, this is a "sandwich attack" [121], and is a threat vector available not only to block-level agents but also to anyone with the technical means [122] to execute it. Importantly, in permissionless blockchains the mempool is also permissionless—it is open to all; block-level agents simply have a privileged position as they can be validators at the same time.

This is only one action pattern among several through which a block proposer/ validator (or "block miner") can extract value from their—not otherwise incentivized—technical task. Relatively early in token ecosystem evolution, there were published reports and analyses of such parallel activities occurring [123]. After much introspection, the crypto industry accepted these activities as constituting an acceptable level of conduct risk in relation to the important service that block miners provide to blockchain operations. There are of course tolerable risk limits to these activities, which are expressed by the industry term "*Maximum Extractable Value*" (MEV [124], sometimes also "*Miner Extractable Value*" [125–127]. Said limits are potentially enforceable through compensating mechanisms [128, 129] available to blockchain infrastructures, should cost/benefit considerations justify them. Please note that both L-1 [130, 131] and L-2 [132] blockchain ecosystems are susceptible to MEV pathologies, the threat vectors being slightly different in the two cases.

The relevance of the above for the design of bonding functions stems from the possibility that their operational characteristics (e.g. price-volume sensitivity, slip-page, time-to-completion, etc.) may open their surrounding use case to market manipulation. The latter can take the form of, e.g., sustained arbitrage [133–135] attacks threatening short-term liquidity and ultimately long-term solvency of a token pool. Such attacks are currently implemented by bots [136–138] and may in the future be coordinated through Artificial Intelligence, i.e. their logic is already automated and may ultimately become self-adaptive.

If the designer does not build compensating logic into the mathematical model, algorithmic implementation or surrounding technical mechanisms, then the bonding function may prove to be a chokepoint for the integrity not only of its local use case but also of its entire containing ecosystem. Note that even non-automated market manipulation actions—for example "pump-and-dump" [139] schemes in CTOs—can have considerable harmful potential. However, these tend to be "one-off" or "localized" risk events, whereas the combination of automation and AI creates the potential for recurring *systemic* events with dynamic risk profiles.

12.5 Summary

Bonding functions are simply mathematical formulations linking together state variables of token ecosystems. They are needed to "join-up" disparate parts of token infrastructures in an automated, smart contract-enabled paradigm. They open up powerful ways to transplant traditional finance processes into a decentralized, on-chain setting.

The assumptions, mathematical formulation, parametrization, and operational repercussions inherent to bonding functions are of paramount importance for the success of crypto-token use cases and need to be at the forefront of designers' or analysts' considerations. In that sense, their construction is also part of token ecosystem design, supplementing the other design pillars. However, in all cases, they must be understood in the context of the business case which they serve. Reasonableness checks on their effectiveness must be advised by the wider ecosystem dynamics, and especially by mechanism and token designs.

In line with previous design pillars, there follows a chapter with a dedicated bonding function design case study.

References

1. Zhang, Y., Chen, X., & Park, D. (2018). *Formal specification of constant product (x × y = k) market model and implementation.* Runtime Verification. Retrieved April 4, 2025, from https://github.com/runtimeverification/verified-smart-contracts/blob/uniswap/uniswap/x-y-k.pdf
2. [Nexus Mutual]. *Token Model.* Nexus Mutual documentation pages. Retrieved March 23, 2025, from https://docs.nexusmutual.io/protocol/nxm-token/token-model
3. Poser, S. W. (2021). *Market makers in financial markets: Their role, how they function, why they are important, and the NYSE DMM difference.* New York Stock Exchange (NYSE). Retrieved March 26, 2025, from https://www.nyse.com/publicdocs/nyse/NYSE_Paper_on_Market_Making_Sept_2021.pdf

4. Deutsche Börse Cash Markets. (2019). *Market-making programme*. Retrieved April 4, 2025, from https://www.deutsche-boerse-cash-market.com/resource/blob/279694/db2b59f7075f9fa28bb9268b0e1c4dd4/data/market-making-handbook.pdf
5. Guéant, O. (2016). *The financial mathematics of market liquidity*. Financial Mathematics Series, Chapman and Hall/CRC.
6. Lu, X., & Abergel, F. (2018). Order-book modelling and market making strategies. *Market Microstructure and Liquidity, 04*(01n02), 1950003. Retrieved March 26, 2025, from https://arxiv.org/abs/1806.05101
7. Othman, A. (2012). *Automated market making: Theory and practice*. Ph.D. Dissertation, Carnegie Mellon U., Pittsburgh, PA. Retrieved March 26, 2025, from http://reports-archive.adm.cs.cmu.edu/anon/2012/CMU-CS-12-123.pdf
8. Hanson, R. (2002). *Logarithmic market scoring rules for modular combinatorial information aggregation*. Dept. of Economics, George Mason University. Retrieved March 26, 2025, from https://hanson.gmu.edu/mktscore.pdf
9. Scoring rule. (2025, April 19). In *Wikipedia*. Retrieved April 20, 2025, from https://en.wikipedia.org/wiki/Scoring_rule
10. *How does the Logarithmic Market Scoring Rule (LMSR) work? The ultimate guide to crowdsourced forecasting*. Cultivate Labs. Retrieved March 26, 2025, from https://www.cultivatelabs.com/prediction-markets-guide/how-does-logarithmic-market-scoring-rule-lmsr-work
11. De Pablo, N. (2021, June 25). *Introducing Zeitgeist's "Rikiddo Scoring Rule"*. Retrieved March 26, 2025, from https://blog.zeitgeist.pm/introducing-zeitgeists-rikiddo-scoring-rule/
12. Loesch, S., Hindman, N., Welch, N., & Richardson, M. B. (2021, November 17). *Impermanent loss in Uniswap v3*. Retrieved March 26, 2025, from https://arxiv.org/abs/2111.09192
13. Ecosystem Participants. Uniswap documentation pages. Retrieved March 26, 2025, from https://docs.uniswap.org/contracts/v2/concepts/protocol-overview/ecosystem-participants
14. Fan, Z., Marmolejo-Cossio, F., Moroz, D., Neuder, M., Rao, R., & Parkes, D. C. (2024, August 16). *Strategic liquidity provision in Uniswap v3*. Retrieved March 26, 2025, from https://arxiv.org/pdf/2106.12033
15. [Curve Token ecosystem]. https://curve.fi/
16. Egorov, M. (2023, November 1). *Curve (CRV): Optimizing Automated Market Makers (AMMs)*. Retrieved March 26, 2025, from https://www.gemini.com/cryptopedia/curve-crypto-automated-market-maker
17. *Creating a Stableswap pool*. Curve resource pages. Retrieved March 26, 2025, from https://resources.curve.fi/pool-creation/creating-a-stableswap-pool/
18. Loesch, S., & Hindman, N. (2020). Bancor Protocol v2.1; Economic and Quantitative Finance Analysis. Retrieved March 26, 2025, from https://drive.google.com/file/d/1en044m2wchn85aQBcoVx2elmxEYd5kEA/view (linked into from https://docs.bancor.network/about-bancor-network/faqs/resources#papers)
19. Chakraborty, T., & Kearns, M. (2011). Market Making and Mean Reversion. *EC'11 Proceedings of 12th ACM Conference on Electronic Commerce (EC-2011)* (pp. 307–314), San Jose, CA, USA. Retrieved March 26, 2025, from https://dl.acm.org/doi/10.1145/1993574.1993622
20. [Uniswap v3 Whitepaper]. Adams, H., Zinsmeister, N., Salem, M., Keefer, R., & Robinson, D. (2021, March). *Uniswap v3 Core*. Retrieved April 4, 2025, from https://uniswap.org/whitepaper-v3.pdf https://uniswap.org/whitepaper-v3.pdf
21. [Shell Protocol]. https://shellprotocol.io/
22. [Shell Protocol dApp]. https://v1.shellprotocol.io/
23. (2020, October 1). *Shell Protocol White Paper*. Shell Protocol GitHub pages. Retrieved March 26, 2025, from https://github.com/cowri/shell-solidity-v1/blob/master/Shell_White_Paper_v1.0.pdf (please search for the ' "Standard" bonding curve' chapter).

24. *Weighted Math*. Balancer v3 documentation pages. Retrieved March 26, 2025, from https://docs.balancer.fi/concepts/explore-available-balancer-pools/weighted-pool/weighted-math.html
25. [Curve Whitepaper - Crypto Pools]. Egorov, M. (2021, June 9). *Automatic market-making with dynamic peg*. Curve Finance (Swiss Stake GmbH). Retrieved April 4, 2025, from https://classic.curve.fi/files/crypto-pools-paper.pdf, linked into from https://classic.curve.fi/whitepaper
26. *Swapping with the Balancer Smart Order Router and SDK*. Balancer documentation pages. Retrieved March 26, 2025, from https://docs.balancer.fi/integration-guides/swapping/swaps-with-sor-sdk.html
27. *Routers* [in the Balancer v3 architecture]. Balancer documentation pages. Retrieved March 26, 2025, from https://docs.balancer.fi/concepts/router/overview.html
28. Krishnamachari, B., Feng, Q., & Grippo, E. (2021, May). Dynamic Automated Market Makers for Decentralized Cryptocurrency Exchange. In *2021 IEEE International Conference on Blockchain and Cryptocurrency (ICBC)* (pp. 1–2). https://doi.org/10.1109/ICBC51069.2021.9461100
29. [DODO X Cross-chain Aggregator]. https://dodoex.io/
30. [DODO X dApp]. https://app.dodoex.io/
31. [Proactive Market Maker]. *PMM algorithm*. DODO X documentation pages. Retrieved March 26, 2025, from https://docs.dodoex.io/en/product/pmm-algorithm
32. [Proactive Market Maker]. *PMM in details*. DODO X documentation pages. Retrieved March 26, 2025, from https://docs.dodoex.io/en/product/pmm-algorithm/details-about-pmm
33. vbuterin. (2016). *Let's run onchain decentralized exchanges the way we run prediction markets*. Reddit. Retrieved March 26, 2025, from https://www.reddit.com/r/ethereum/comments/55m04x/lets_run_onchain_decentralized_exchanges_the_way/
34. (2021, May 18). *Capital-efficient AMMs with dynamically adjusted weights in balancer V2*. Retrieved March 26, 2025, from https://medium.com/balancer-protocol/capital-efficient-amms-with-dynamically-adjusted-weights-in-balancer-v2-9a7104789cd7
35. [THORChain Token ecosystem]. https://thorchain.org/
36. CoinMarketCap RUNE page. CoinMarketCap. Retrieved March 26, 2025, from https://coinmarketcap.com/currencies/thorchain/
37. [THORChain Whitepaper]. *THORChain: A decentralised liquidity network*. THORChain GitHub pages. Retrieved March 26, 2025, from https://github.com/thorchain/Resources/blob/master/Whitepapers/THORChain-Whitepaper-May2020.pdf
38. [OpenOcean Token ecosystem]. https://openocean.finance/
39. *How it works*. OpenOcean documentation pages. Retrieved March 26, 2025, from https://docs.openocean.finance/protocol/introduction/how-it-works
40. *DEXs integration*. OpenOcean documentation pages. Retrieved March 26, 2025, from https://docs.openocean.finance/products/dex-aggregator/dexs-integration
41. *OpenOcean CEX API*. OpenOcean documentation pages. Retrieved March 26, 2025, from https://docs.openocean.finance/dev/legacy/openocean-cex-api
42. *Swap on Kava*. OpenOcean documentation pages. Retrieved March 26, 2025, from https://docs.openocean.finance/swap/tutorial-swap-token/swap-on-kava#how-to-buy-usdkava
43. [Matcha DEX Aggregator]. https://matcha.xyz/
44. (2020, July 28). *How Matcha finds the best price for DeFi traders*. Retrieved March 26, 2025, from https://blog.matcha.xyz/article/how-matcha-finds-the-best-prices (linked into from https://help.matcha.xyz/en/articles/3981024-how-does-matcha-offer-the-best-prices)
45. Forman, L. (2020, May 19). *0x API's smart order routing*. Retrieved March 26, 2025, from https://medium.com/@merklejerk/0x-apis-smart-order-routing-7af0195515e5
46. [0x v2 Pricing Engine]. https://v2.0x.org/
47. *What decentralized exchanges does Matcha aggregate liquidity from?* March support pages. Retrieved March 26, 2025, from https://help.matcha.xyz/en/articles/4375069-what-decentralized-exchanges-does-matcha-aggregate-liquidity-from

48. [Raydium Automated Market Maker]. https://raydium.io/
49. *Swap FAQ*. Raydium support pages. Retrieved March 26, 2025, from https://docs.raydium.io/raydium/traders/swapping/trade-and-swap
50. *Farms & Vaults; Introducing OpenOcean Liquidity Pools*. OpenOcean documentation pages. Retrieved March 26, 2025, from https://docs.openocean.finance/products/farms-and-vaults#introducing-openocean-liquidity-pools
51. Holmes, F. (2019, May 20). Yes, gold is being manipulated. But to what extent? *Forbes*. Retrieved March 26, 2025, from https://www.forbes.com/sites/greatspeculations/2019/05/20/yes-gold-is-being-manipulated-but-to-what-extent/
52. (2014, July 16). Time called on the London gold fix. *Financial Times*. Retrieved March 26, 2025, from https://www.ft.com/content/f01a1806-0cfd-11e4-bf1e-00144feabdc0
53. Slater, S., & Jones H. (2014, May 23). *Barclays slapped with $44 million fine over gold price fix*. Reuters. Retrieved March 26, 2025, from https://www.reuters.com/article/us-barclays-regulations-gold-idUSBREA4M06620140523
54. Evans, P. (2020, August 19). Scotiabank to pay $127M in fines for traders' price fixing of precious metals. *CBC*. Retrieved March 26, 2025, from https://www.cbc.ca/news/business/scotiabank-spoofing-fine-1.5692117
55. (2018, July 25). *In Re: Commodity Exchange, Inc., Gold futures and options trading litigation*. Case 1:14-md-02548-VEC. U.S. District Court, Southern District of N.Y. Opinion and Order. Retrieved March 26, 2025, from https://www.goldfixsettlement.com/home/100027/DocumentHandler?docPath=/Documents/2018_07_25_Order_granting_UBS_MTD_Gold_.pdf
56. Investopedia Team. (2024, June 15). *Principal-agent problem causes, solutions, and examples explained*. Retrieved March 26, 2025, from https://www.investopedia.com/terms/p/principal-agent-problem.asp
57. Jensen, M., & Meckling, W. (1976). Theory of the firm: Managerial behavior, agency costs and ownership structure. *Journal of Financial Economics, 3*(4), 305–360. Retrieved March 26, 2025, from http://www.sfu.ca/~wainwrig/Econ400/jensen-meckling.pdf
58. (2025, February 25). *Gas and fees*. Ethereum documentation pages. Retrieved March 26, 2025, from https://ethereum.org/en/developers/docs/gas/
59. Correas, J., Gordillo, P., & Roman-Diez, G. (2021, February 5). Static profiling and optimization of ethereum smart contracts using resource analysis. *IEEE Access*. https://doi.org/10.1109/ACCESS.2021.3057565. Retrieved March 26, 2025, from https://ieeexplore.ieee.org/iel7/6287639/9312710/09348894.pdf
60. *Gas in Solidity smart contracts*. Crypto Market Pool. Retrieved March 26, 2025, from https://cryptomarketpool.com/gas-in-solidity-smart-contracts/
61. *Token price formula*. Nexus Mutual documentation pages. Retrieved March 26, 2025, from https://docs.nexusmutual.io/protocol/nxm-token/history-capitalisation-controls#token-price-formula
62. [Bumper Token ecosystem]. https://www.bumper.fi/
63. (2021, December 6). *Bumper Blackpaper v0.1*. Retrieved March 26, 2025, from https://drive.google.com/file/d/16GfUS9cVgsaRf4XvDHmhVptuHlRI8ruW/view
64. Titcomb, A. (2019, April 10). *Deep dive: Augmented bonding curves*. Retrieved March 26, 2025, from https://blog.giveth.io/deep-dive-augmented-bonding-curves-3f1f7c1fa751
65. (2021, July). *Augmented bonding curve – An introduction to the ABC*. Token Engineering Commons forum pages. Retrieved March 26, 2025, from https://forum.tecommons.org/t/augmented-bonding-curve-an-introduction-to-the-abc/497
66. *Token engineering commons*. Retrieved March 26, 2025, from https://tecommons.org/
67. (2021, March 23). Introducing Uniswap v3. Uniswap blog pages. Retrieved March 26, 2025, from https://blog.uniswap.org/uniswap-v3
68. Lambert, G. (2021, June 23). *Uniswap V3 LP Tokens as perpetual put and call options*. Retrieved March 20, 2025, from https://lambert-guillaume.medium.com/uniswap-v3-lp-tokens-as-perpetual-put-and-call-options-5b66219db827

69. Lambert, G. (2021, September 15). *A guide for choosing optimal Uniswap V3 LP positions, Part 2*. Retrieved March 26, 2025, from https://lambert-guillaume.medium.com/a-guide-for-choosing-optimal-uniswap-v3-lp-positions-part-2-4a94b0a12886
70. Newar, B. (2021, November 19). *Half of Uniswap v3 liquidity providers are losing money: New research*. CoinTelegraph. Retrieved March 26, 2025, from https://cointelegraph.com/news/half-of-uniswap-v3-liquidity-providers-are-losing-money-new-research
71. Andersen, D. (2023, May 16). *Bancor DAO hit with class-action suit over impermanent loss protection promises*. CoinTelegraph. Retrieved March 26, 2025, from https://cointelegraph.com/news/bancor-dao-hit-with-class-action-suit-over-impermanent-loss-protection-promises
72. Halabi, K. (2023, March 15). *How can bonding curves help align DAO stakeholders?* Outlier Ventures. Retrieved March 26, 2025, from https://outlierventures.io/article/bonding-curves-and-a-prelude-to-sptokens/
73. (2023, January). *Tokenomics proposal: Replacing the bonding curve*. Nexus Mutual governance discussion pages. Retrieved March 26, 2025, from https://forum.nexusmutual.io/t/tokenomics-proposal-replacing-the-bonding-curve/988
74. Lambert, G. (2021, August 4). *A guide for choosing optimal Uniswap V3 LP positions, Part 1*. Retrieved March 26, 2025, from https://lambert-guillaume.medium.com/a-guide-for-choosing-optimal-uniswap-v3-lp-positions-part-1-842b470d2261
75. Kohlhaas, P. (2019, January 8). *Token bonding curve design parameters*. Retrieved March 26, 2025, from https://medium.com/molecule-blog/token-bonding-curve-design-parameters-95d365cbec4f (please search in the page for "The Token")
76. Twin, A. (2020, October 10). *Depth of market meaning and how to use DOM data*. Retrieved March 26, 2025, from https://www.investopedia.com/terms/d/depth-of-market.asp
77. Muranaga, J., & Ohsawa, M. (1997). *Measurement of liquidity risk in the context of market risk calculation*. Institute for Monetary and Economic Studies, Bank of Japan. Retrieved March 26, 2025, from https://www.bis.org/publ/ecsc07j.pdf
78. Elliott, D. J. (2015, June). *Market liquidity: A primer*. The Brookings Institution. Retrieved March 26, 2025, from https://www.brookings.edu/wp-content/uploads/2016/06/Elliott-Market-Liquidity-A-Primer_06222015.pdf
79. Ganti, A. (2024, June 08). *What is a bid-ask spread, and how does it work in trading?* Retrieved March 26, 2025, from https://www.investopedia.com/terms/b/bid-askspread.asp
80. Aldridge I. (2022, July 27). *Slippage in AMM markets*. Retrieved March 26, 2025, from https://doi.org/10.2139/ssrn.4133897
81. Kaiko. (2020, May 18). *Measuring liquidity: Spread and market depth (and why trade volume is unreliable)*. Kaiko blog pages. Retrieved March 26, 2025, from https://blog.kaiko.com/measuring-liquidity-spread-and-market-depth-56290f2caa0a
82. (2024). *What is price impact vs. price slippage in DeFi?* Retrieved March 26, 2025, from https://help.1inch.io/en/articles/4585109-what-is-price-impact-vs-price-slippage-in-defi
83. Knownsec Blockchain Lab. (2021, April 7). *In-depth analysis of the slippage and impermanence loss of the AMM constant product model*. Retrieved March 26, 2025, from https://medium.com/@Knownsec_Blockchain_Lab/in-depth-analysis-of-the-slippage-and-impermanence-loss-of-the-amm-constant-product-model-fb0a86763a25
84. Chordia, T., Roll, R., & Subrahmanyam, A. (2001). Market liquidity and trading activity. *The Journal of Finance, 56*(2), 501–530. https://www.jstor.org/stable/222572
85. Hayes, A. (2024, December 22). *Implementation shortfall: Meaning, examples, shortfalls*. Retrieved March 26, 2025, from https://www.investopedia.com/terms/i/implementation-shortfall.asp
86. Kenton, W. (2024, June 19). *Bootstrapping definition, strategies, and pros/cons*. Retrieved March 26, 2025, from https://www.investopedia.com/terms/b/bootstrapping.asp
87. *Introduction - What is Arrakis PALM?* Arrakis resource pages. Retrieved March 26, 2025, from https://resources.arrakis.fi/palm/introduction#what-is-arrakis-palm
88. [Flovtec.com]. https://www.flovtec.com/what-is-flovtec

89. *Transaction cost analysis*. (2023, September 21). In Wikipedia. Retrieved March 26, 2025, from https://en.wikipedia.org/wiki/Transaction_cost_analysis
90. D'Hondt, C., & Giraud, J.-R. (2006, September 1). Cash equity transaction cost analysis: State of the art … and beyond. *Journal of Asset Management, 7*, 216–241. https://link.springer.com/article/10.1057/palgrave.jam.2240215
91. (2018, November 13). *TCA: "Is This Good or Bad?"*. GlobalTrading. Retrieved March 26, 2025, from https://www.globaltrading.net/tca-is-this-good-or-bad/
92. D'Hondt, C. & Giraud, J.-R. (2008, November 15). *Transaction cost analysis A-Z: A step towards best execution in the post-MiFID landscape*. EDHEC. Retrieved March 26, 2025, from https://climateimpact.edhec.edu/publications/transaction-cost-analysis-z-step-towards
93. (2023, September 6). *TCA ever more important in compliance, regulatory*. Bloomberg. Retrieved March 26, 2025, from https://www.bloomberg.com/professional/blog/tca-ever-more-important-in-compliance-regulatory/
94. Phillips, A., Stewart, A., & Adams, S. (2020). *TCA and fair execution; The metrics that the FX industry must use*. LMAX Exchange. Retrieved March 26, 2025, from https://www.lmax.com/documents/LMAXExchange-FX-TCA-Transaction-Cost-Analysis-Whitepaper.pdf
95. Lambert, C. (2022, January 28). *BestX to add crypto TCA to service*. The Full FX. Retrieved March 26, 2025, from https://thefullfx.com/bestx-to-add-crypto-tca-to-service/
96. Li, Y. (2021, December). *The future of modern transaction cost analysis*. State Street. Retrieved March 26, 2025, from https://www.statestreet.com/ca/fr/individual/insights/LIVE-RR-nov-2021-yangling-li-transaction-cost-analysis
97. [Coinroutes platform]. https://www.coinroutes.com/
98. (2023, June 13). *Our vision for Uniswap v4*. Uniswap blog pages. Retrieved March 26, 2025, from https://blog.uniswap.org/uniswap-v4
99. [Bancor Carbon Whitepaper]. Richardson, M., & Loesch, S. (2022, November 22). *Carbon; a decentralized protocol for asymmetric liquidity and trading*. Whitepaper v.1.2. Retrieved March 26, 2025, from https://resources.carbondefi.xyz/pages/CarbonWhitepaper.pdf
100. Forgy, E., & Lau, L. (2021, November 15). *A family of multi-asset automated market makers*. Retrieved March 26, 2025, from https://arxiv.org/pdf/2111.08115.pdf
101. Balancer Labs. (2022, September 12). *The benefits of multi-token pools*. Retrieved March 26, 2025, from https://medium.com/balancer-protocol/the-benefits-of-multi-token-pools-653eea3ef03a
102. [ETH-swapping functionality of the Curve dApp]. https://curve.fi/dex/ethereum/swap/
103. *Guide: Stake & provide liquidity on curve*. Lido support pages. Retrieved March 26, 2025, from https://help.lido.fi/en/articles/6213126-guide-stake-provide-liquidity-on-curve
104. [MakerDAO Token ecosystem]. https://makerdao.world/, currently a subset of the Sky Token ecosystem (https://sky.money/).
105. [Uniswap Token ecosystem]. https://uniswap.org
106. [SushiSwap Token ecosystem]. https://www.sushi.com/swap
107. *wstETH* [description and usage]. Lido documentation pages. Retrieved March 26, 2025, from https://docs.lido.fi/guides/lido-tokens-integration-guide/#wsteth
108. [Uniswap v4]. *Improved architecture and gas savings*. Uniswap blog pages. Retrieved March 26, 2025, from https://blog.uniswap.org/uniswap-v4#improved-architecture-and-gas-savings
109. Market manipulation. (2025, April 12). In *Wikipedia*. Retrieved April 19, 2025, from https://en.wikipedia.org/wiki/Market_manipulation
110. Market abuse. (2024, October 18). In *Wikipedia*. Retrieved March 26, 2025, from https://en.wikipedia.org/wiki/Market_abuse
111. [Example context: Singapore]. *Securities and Futures Act 2001* (as amended), especially in its Divisions 1, 2 and 3. Retrieved March 26, 2025, from https://sso.agc.gov.sg/Act/SFA2001
112. [Example context : EU]. *Implementing and delegated acts - MAR* [relating to Regulation (EU) No 596/2014 on market abuse]. Retrieved March 26, 2025, from https://finance.ec.europa.eu/regulation-and-supervision/financial-services-legislation/implementing-and-delegated-acts/market-abuse-regulation_en (and links contained therein).

113. Hayes, A. (2024, July 28). *Manipulation: Definition, methods, types, and example*. Retrieved March 26, 2025, from https://www.investopedia.com/terms/m/manipulation.asp
114. U.S. Securities and Exchange Commission (SEC). *Market manipulation*. Retrieved March 26, 2025, from https://www.investor.gov/introduction-investing/investing-basics/glossary/market-manipulation
115. [Example context : U.S.A.] *15 U.S. Code § 78i - Manipulation of security prices*. Legal Information Institute. Cornell Law School. Retrieved March 26, 2025, from https://www.law.cornell.edu/uscode/text/15/78i
116. Kenton, W. (2022, May 1). *Market surveillance: Meaning, how it works, risks*. Retrieved March 26, 2025, from https://www.investopedia.com/terms/m/marketsurveillence.asp
117. Lepcha, M. (2023, August 28). *Mempool*. Techopedia. Retrieved March 26, 2025, from https://www.techopedia.com/definition/mempool
118. *Mempool*. Binance "Academy" pages. Retrieved March 26, 2025, from https://academy.binance.com/en/glossary/mempool
119. Mitchell, C. (2024, September 16). *Front-running definition, example, and legality*. Retrieved March 26, 2025, from https://www.investopedia.com/terms/f/frontrunning.asp
120. Chen, J. (2025, February 21). *Scalping: Definition in trading, how this strategy is used, and example*. Retrieved March 26, 2025, from https://www.investopedia.com/terms/s/scalping.asp
121. Allen, A. (2023, September 12). *What is a sandwich attack?* Matcha blog pages. Retrieved March 26, 2025, from https://blog.matcha.xyz/article/what-is-a-sandwich-attack
122. Chawla, V. (2024, January 11). *Solana-based MEV bot earns $1.8 million after back-running memecoin trader in seconds*. The Block. Retrieved March 26, 2025, from https://www.theblock.co/post/272079/solana-based-mev-bot-earns-1-8-million-after-back-running-memecoin-trader-in-seconds
123. Daian, Ph., Goldfelder, S., Kell, T., Li, Y., Zhao, X., Bentov, I., Breidenbach, L. & Juels, A. (2019, April 10). *Flash Boys 2.0: Frontrunning, transaction reordering, and consensus instability in decentralized exchanges*. Retrieved March 26, 2025, from https://arxiv.org/abs/1904.05234
124. (2025, February 12). *Maximal Extractable Value (MEV)*. Ethereum documentation pages. Retrieved March 26, 2025, from https://ethereum.org/en/developers/docs/mev/
125. Genç, E. (2022, September 2). *What is MEV, aka Maximal Extractable Value?* CoinDesk. Retrieved March 26, 2025, from https://www.coindesk.com/learn/what-is-mev-aka-maximal-extractable-value/
126. *Intents (MEV Harnessing System) - Shell opens new possibilities for fighting MEV*. Shell Protocol wiki pages. Retrieved March 26, 2025, from https://wiki.shellprotocol.io/how-shell-works/intents-mev-harnessing-system
127. Kulkarni, K., Diamandis, T., & Chitra, T. (2022, July 24). *Towards a theory of maximal extractable value I: Constant function market makers*. Retrieved March 26, 2025, from https://arxiv.org/abs/2207.11835
128. (2023, May 24). *What is Maximal Extractable Value (MEV)?* Chainlink education pages. Retrieved March 26, 2025, from https://chain.link/education-hub/maximal-extractable-value-mev
129. (2020, January). *MEV auction: Auctioning transaction ordering rights as a solution to Miner Extractable Value*. Retrieved March 26, 2025, from https://ethresear.ch/t/mev-auction-auctioning-transaction-ordering-rights-as-a-solution-to-miner-extractable-value/6788
130. [Context: Ethereum]. Kleine, D. (2023, May 19). *Sandwich attacks: Stealing or just playing the DeFi game?* Blockworks. Retrieved March 26, 2025, from https://blockworks.co/news/sandwich-attack-mev-ethereum
131. [Context: Solana]. (2023, May 31). *MEV on Solana*. Umbra Research. Retrieved March 26, 2025, from https://www.umbraresearch.xyz/writings/mev-on-solana
132. (2023, July 10). *Mapping the maze: A deep dive into the future of L2 MEV*. Retrieved March 26, 2025, from https://medium.com/@camelot.022544555/mapping-the-maze-a-deep-dive-into-the-future-of-l2-mev-fa6e152aba70

133. Sylvester, S., McCabe, K. A., Psurek, A., & Bhatt, N. (2022, October 19). *Modeling arbitrage with an automated market maker*. GMU Working Paper in Economics, No. 22-48. Retrieved March 26, 2025, from https://doi.org/10.2139/ssrn.4247283
134. Milionis, J., Moallemi, C. C., & Roughgarden, T. (2023, May 24). *Automated market making and arbitrage profits in the presence of fees*. Retrieved March 26, 2025, from https://arxiv.org/abs/2305.14604
135. Milionis, J., Wan, X., & Adams, A. (2023, June 15). *FLAIR: A metric for liquidity provider competitiveness in automated market makers*. Retrieved March 26, 2025, from https://arxiv.org/abs/2306.09421
136. (2021, March 1). *Polkadex: Optimizing DeFi arbitrage with AMM smart bots*. Retrieved March 26, 2025, from https://polkadex.medium.com/polkadex-optimizing-defi-arbitrage-with-amm-smart-bots-f1af81e0dd09
137. Amajar, E. (2023, June 26). *Building an arbitrage bot: Finding arbitrage opportunities (article 3/n)*. Retrieved March 26, 2025, from https://blog.blockmagnates.com/building-an-arbitrage-bot-finding-arbitrage-opportunities-article-3-n-1ea3c5e0b8ca
138. Amajar, E. (2023, June 2). *Building an arbitrage bot: Automated Market Makers and Uniswap V2 (article 1/n)*. Retrieved March 26, 2025, from https://blog.blockmagnates.com/building-an-arbitrage-bot-automated-market-makers-and-uniswap-article-1-n-2d208215d8c2
139. Ho, B. (2021, February 15). *How to avoid pumps & dumps in your token offering*. The Defiant. Retrieved March 26, 2025, from https://thedefiant.substack.com/p/-how-to-avoid-pumps-and-dumps-in

13 Case Study in Bonding Function Design: Bancor Carbon

The previous chapter presented some theoretical notions of bonding function design in the context of blockchain-based token ecosystems. We thus proceed with a case study of how these notions are in evidence in an existing token project. Our analysis will focus on "Bancor Carbon" [1], a DEX protocol, the business case of which revolves around the trading of crypto-tokens.

Previous case studies have all started with explaining analogue business cases from traditional finance in order to demonstrate how blockchain-based token ecosystems can be understood as translations of established business practices into a new technological context. Even though bonding function design generally has a narrower focus than either of market, mechanism, or token designs (implying that several different bonding functions can in principle co-exist on the same canvas weaved by the wider designs), it is still a design activity targeting a particular business context—that of its implementing use case(s). In that sense, identifying traditional finance processes which a bonding function can be considered as reproducing can indeed add value to a case study like the present one.

On the one hand, traditional finance professionals can relate to patterns and anti-patterns from their own experience and get a better understanding of the actual business problem which protocol designers have had to address, transposed within a blockchain context. On the other, they may be able to appreciate (or at least interpret) the deviations from the traditional finance case which the blockchain ecosystem, with all its constituents—not least of all its token flows—called for in its final design.

As in previous case studies, the onus of the analysis will be on examining whether or not theoretical concepts of the previous chapter can be used to interpret the apparent calibrations of the artefact in focus (i.e. the bonding function). The analysis will be based on Bancor Carbon's official documentation and on third-party archival publications in the public domain. To this end, it will be unavoidable to reconstruct at least those essential points of the other design pillars that will help place the particular bonding function into its proper context, that is, that of its implementing use case(s).

I. Giannakouros, *Cryptocurrencies and Tradable Crypto-Tokens*, Future of Business and Finance, https://doi.org/10.1007/978-3-031-98423-5_13

13.1 Market Making

Economic life depends on the existence of ordered trading venues, where laws and regulations ensure the validity of transactions. Said laws and regulations are typically advised by observed market practices, and in that sense, they evolve together with the latter. For example, new asset classes, new currencies, and new contract types are reasons for changing of market practices, as is also technological evolution. Inversely, new market practices may be imposed by changes in laws and regulations, for example, due to public policy decisions. In short, the functioning of ordered marketplaces follows economic, societal, and technological developments.

The most important marketplaces in modern economic life are arguably those where commodities, currencies, securities, and derivatives are traded. Of course, different countries allow local organizations to create their own distinct local trading venues, governed by their own local rulebooks. Even within the same geography, while one may talk about, for example, "the securities market" in the abstract, there may actually exist several distinct, parallel marketplaces where securities trading takes place. The main reason for this is that sophisticated markets have historically come to accept the need for differentiation in terms of asset lifecycle; transaction cost structures; target trading groups; intermediation modality; latency times; confidentiality features, etc. In short, each of said parallel marketplaces offers optimal conditions for particular combinations of transaction types, target trading groups, intermediation types, etc.

A concise "markets taxonomy" representative of the most sophisticated modern economies would be as depicted in Fig. 13.1.

- A **primary market** is that trading venue where an asset is first issued and sold under a distinct reference, i.e. a distinct tradable title. These markets are strongly regulated regarding the rights and obligations of both asset issuers and first buyers. Primary markets exist for currencies, commodities, securities, and derivatives. The Chicago Mercantile Exchange and the London Metal Exchange would be example primary markets for commodities and derivatives.

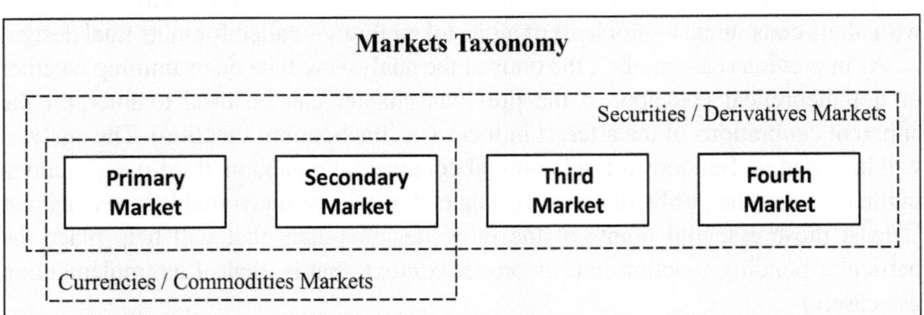

Fig. 13.1 Modern markets taxonomy

- After issuance, assets trade in the **secondary market**. These markets are also strongly regulated, in order to ensure transparency in price discovery and to reduce the risk of market manipulation. Secondary markets exist for all asset classes, while the currency (i.e. foreign exchange) market has been historically the most significant by value. Both private and corporate traders as well as intermediaries are active in the secondary market. All transaction sizes are in principle possible in this market, from small trades by retail investors to large block trades by institutionals. All stock exchanges, such as NYSE [2] and NASDAQ [3] in the United States, Frankfurt Stock Exchange [4] and Euronext Paris [5] in the EU, the Johannesburg Stock Exchange [6] in South Africa, the Dubai Financial Market [7] in the UAE, etc., are secondary markets.
- Securities (and, less frequently, derivatives) are also traded in the **third market**. This market is optimized for large-scale transactions negotiated bilaterally and then settled among qualified market participants (such as broker dealers) and institutionals, including financial institutions. These markets are typically less strongly regulated than the first two types, reflecting the assumed level of professional expertise shared by their participants. However, transaction reporting requirements are still applicable for market monitoring purposes by the regulators. Over-the-counter ("OTC") transactions [8] of exchange-listed securities are third market activities.
- The same asset classes are tradable also in the **fourth market**. It is the most sophisticated one in terms of bespoke technology platforms, latency, and confidentiality attributes. It is also optimized for large-scale transactions, while offering the option to negotiate and settle bilaterally without public visibility of traded assets and transaction sizes. It is typically used by very large institutionals, including financial institutions, wishing to keep transaction costs low and to avoid moving the secondary markets. Electronic communication networks [9], crossing networks [10], dark pools [11], and in general alternative trading systems [12, 13] in the United States and multilateral trading facilities [14, 15] in the EU are all fourth market examples. The degree of regulatory oversight imputed on the fourth market differs per jurisdiction, while transaction reporting requirements are always mandated for market monitoring purposes.

Once admitted to trading, an asset's observable unit price in transactions varies with time and becomes a rate [16]. Plotting this varying rate in time produces a time-series graph, such as that depicted on Fig. 13.2, where "*S*" is the customary symbol for rates of securities, however used here to denote any asset type.[1]

These are recorded rates which can be used for various purposes by traders (e.g. technical analysis [18, 19]) and trading venue operators. However, when it comes to trading decisions, the only available information is that of the past and of the present.

[1]For the sake of completeness, please note that commodities and (to a lesser extent) currency rates are assumed to exhibit mean-reversion [17] for long-enough time-frames. However, their single-trading-session time-series may still exhibit a monotonic trend as in the figure.

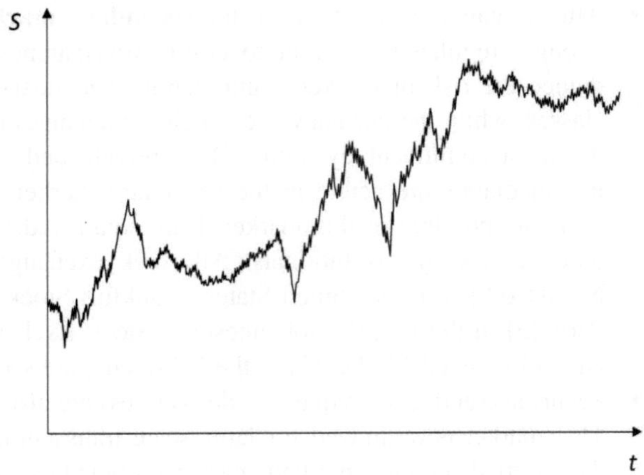

Fig. 13.2 Financial time-series, generic asset type

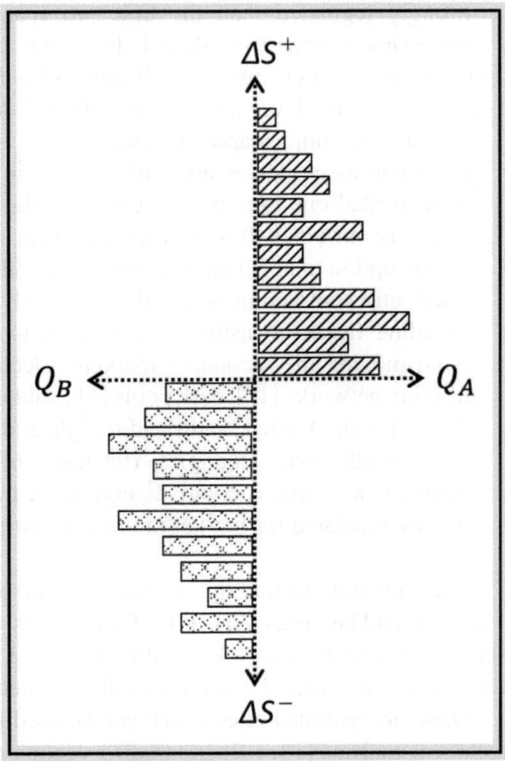

Fig. 13.3 Instantaneous order book around a price point (rate)

That is, at any particular point in time, the only visibility a trader can have in principle is of the last transaction price point (rate) and of the instantaneous orders to either buy or sell the asset. It is customary to refer to "buy" orders as "**bid**", and to "sell" orders as "**ask**" ones (i.e. a trader either "bids to buy" or "asks to sell").

If one were to depict graphically the instantaneous distribution of asset quantities "bid", resp. "asked", at a price distance ΔS from the last transacted rate, one would obtain the graph of Fig. 13.3. In the latter, the subscripts "B" and "A" stand for "bid"

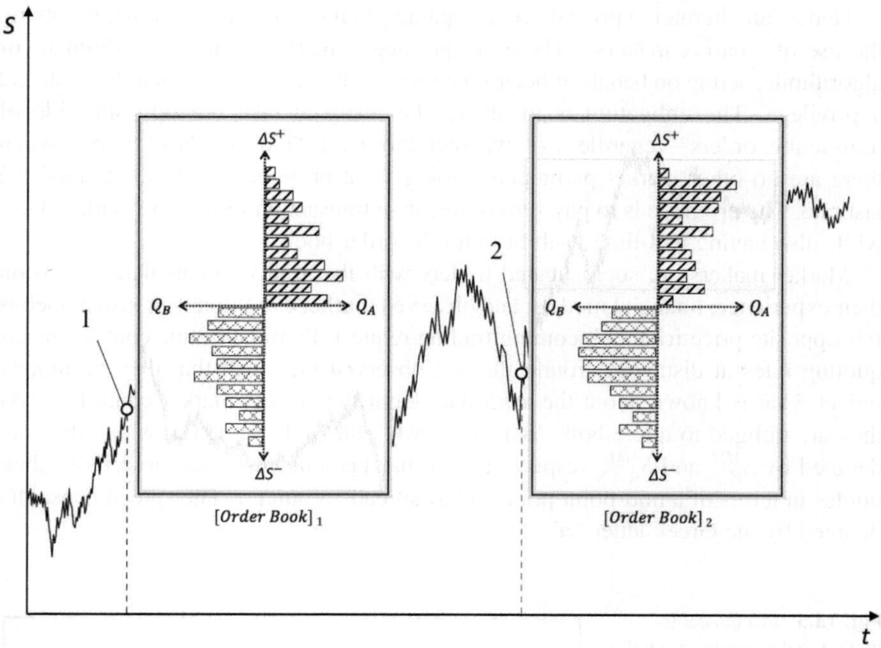

Fig. 13.4 Order-driven market

and "ask", respectively, and the superscript sign denotes the sign of the deviation from the last transacted rate.

This is the instantaneous "order book" at any point (t, S) of the time-series. It is simply the overview of the actual demand and supply in this marketplace for the asset around said point. For example, in reference to the financial time series of Fig. 13.2, at two points "1" and "2" in a trading session, the instantaneous order books observed in this market may look as depicted in Fig. 13.4.

If market participants have only this information at their disposal so as to decide whether to buy or sell at this point, then this market is termed "order-driven". In effect, traders are called upon to interpret the relative balances between requested buy-side and sell-side volumes at close price-points as estimators of the probable direction and strength of the asset's rate movement.

This market structure mechanism is simple but has been shown to not guarantee market liquidity in all circumstances. For example, imagine a situation where, due to market volatility, no counter-offers are available to traders for sizable price ranges near the last transacted rate. That would cause a break in market activity as there is a significant gap in traders' expectations on the "bid" and "ask" sides. Should market conditions remain, or even deteriorate, transaction activity would effectively cease for inordinate periods of time. The market in this asset would provisionally cease to function. As flow of transaction fees from traders to the marketplace is the norm (needed to cover at least part of operational costs of ordered trading venues), that would also mean loss of revenue to marketplace operators. Assets with "shallow" (i.e. low-liquidity) markets tend to exhibit such phenomena systematically; however, even "deep" markets can experience them provisionally due to market conditions.

Hence, an alternative price discovery paradigm has evolved with time, involving the use of "market makers". These are privileged market participants (humans or algorithmic, acting on behalf of licensed entities) who have at once an obligation and a privilege. The obligation is to always be ready to take the opposite side of transaction orders—regardless of whether those are "bid" or "ask" ones—when there are no other market participants doing so at price points "near-enough" the last rate. The privilege is to pay zero or negative transaction fees to the marketplace, while also having real-time visibility into the order book.

Market makers are sophisticated traders with the ability to calculate (based on their experience, financial models, and observed market conditions) an instantaneous fair opposite price for any incoming trading request. Fairness in this context means quoting rates at distances around the last observed rate such that they accurately reflect what is known about the asset and about the current market conditions. As they are obliged to quote both "bid" and "ask" rates (cf. Fig. 13.5, where they are denoted by S_B^{MM} and S_A^{MM}, respectively), it has become customary to refer to their quotes in terms of a mid-point price and a "spread" around it. The spread is usually denoted by the Greek letter "α".

Fig. 13.5 Instantaneous market maker quotes around a price point (α = "spread")

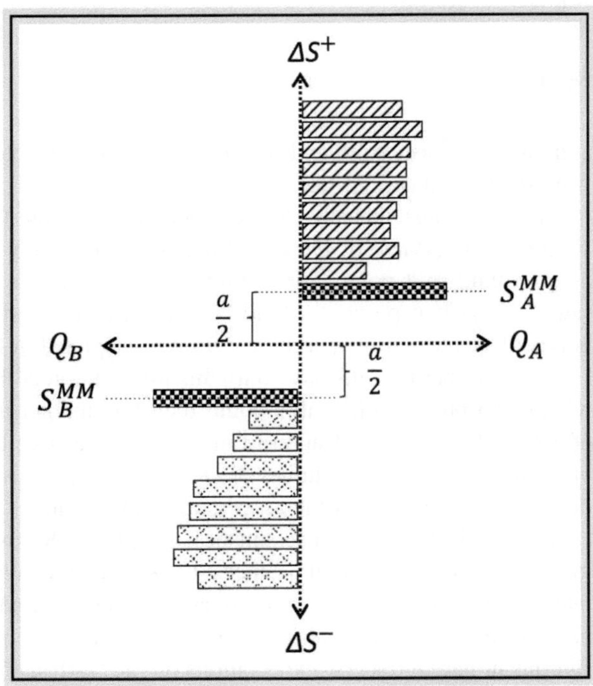

$$a = S_A^{MM} - S_B^{MM}$$

Thus, market makers in effect interject themselves into trading, adopt no "directional view" (market jargon for "offering only to buy, or only to sell, expecting the prices to go only up or down") and, based on whatever means at their disposal, have to always calculate, and quote, a fair spread α around the current trading point (t, S). Subsequently, they must be ready to honour their quotes in whatever trading size (i.e. number of units of the traded asset) their instantaneous counterparties request. This is depicted graphically by the squared bars in Fig. 13.5. The expectation by the marketplace is that market makers will be able to close "gaps" in trading activity by offering spreads around mid-points that are "close enough" to the last transacted rates. It goes without saying that the spread α is time-varying, to reflect current market conditions. Of course, if other traders suddenly offer "bid" or "ask" quotes that are within the spread range, then they will be prioritized by the marketplace. Also, market makers too may cease quoting in exceptional circumstances (e.g. if an asset is removed from trading due to corporate events of the issuer, if the marketplace otherwise bars trading activity in the asset, etc.).

"Market making" as a business activity entails having the financial capacity to, first, always keep a warehouse of sufficient asset units ready to sell against incoming "bid" orders and, second, to be able to buy those offered by "ask" ones. The expectation is that by having sufficient hedges in place, the market maker may generate enough transaction-based income through the spread, at controlled levels of market, liquidity, and issuer risk, to keep providing their service. This presupposes a level of (financial instrument, risk management, market-specific and—nowadays—technical) know-how that is not trivial. For large marketplaces with significant intra-day trading volumes, there are additional requirements relating to solvency, certifications (or equivalent) and corporate governance. Subsequently, only parties that are vetted by the marketplace against stringent criteria are licensed as market makers.

The existence of a market maker creates the price discovery paradigm known as "quote-driven market" (Fig. 13.6). The term means that prospective traders no longer have visibility on the instantaneous order book, but have to base their trading decisions on the "nearest" bid and ask quotes offered by at least the market maker. The implication is that there are always expected to be "near" bid and ask quotes (albeit at a spread, which may be significant). Compared to order-driven markets, quote-driven ones are generally expected to be more liquid with lower odds of exhibiting rate gaps.

In mature trading venues with established asset types, market making has less business risks to deal with. That is why, in the United States for instance, there are market makers active in all secondary markets and in parts of the third and fourth markets as well. Some trading venues may also choose to offer both quote-driven and order-driven markets, not necessarily to the same trader groups. For instance, order book visibility is prized by traders seeking short-term buy-and-sell trades; hence, they are prepared to pay a premium for it even though they could stay within a quote-driven market. NASDAQ is an example of a trading venue activating both paradigms, with quote-driven being offered by default and the order-book made visible for a premium to subscribers of its "Level-2" feed [20, 21].

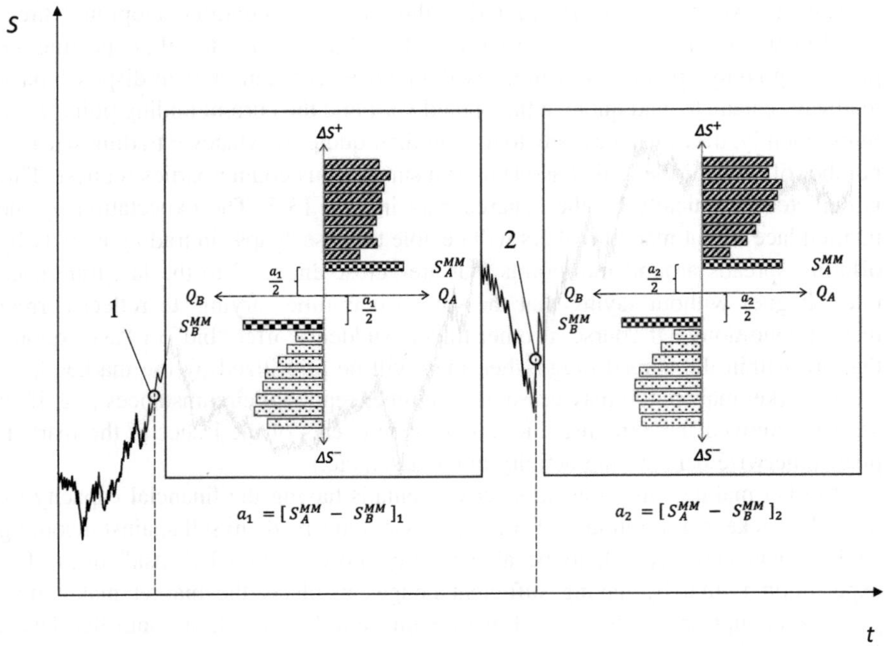

Fig. 13.6 Quote-driven market

13.2 Order Types

It is difficult for a person living in the twenty-first century to imagine that not so long ago (roughly before 1995), computer-based asset trading was the exclusive preserve of large financial institutions. For the non-professional trader, there were limited options of how to estimate the odds of a trading strategy and even how to have it executed through brokers or other direct market participants. It was only through the proliferation of high-bandwidth communication networks and through the competitive pressures unleashed by the internet that trading venue data and near-real-time market access became available to the general public. Nowadays, data-assisted trading (as opposed to purely algorithmic trading [22–24]) is the norm throughout the world. Simple trading strategies can thus be implemented by rules functionality existing in even basic trading packages offered by banks or brokerages. Asset type knowledge notwithstanding (e.g. knowing how to hedge a simple securities position through a derivative), the most basic level of knowledge assumed by marketplaces is how to base market trend expectations and how to use them through order types.

For instance, Fig. 13.7 superimposes generic "price regime" regions on the same financial time series previously depicted in Fig. 13.2. There are regions of high-volatility (typically around large drops in price), regions where asset rates do not exhibit a definite up- or downward trend, and others where some trend is evident.

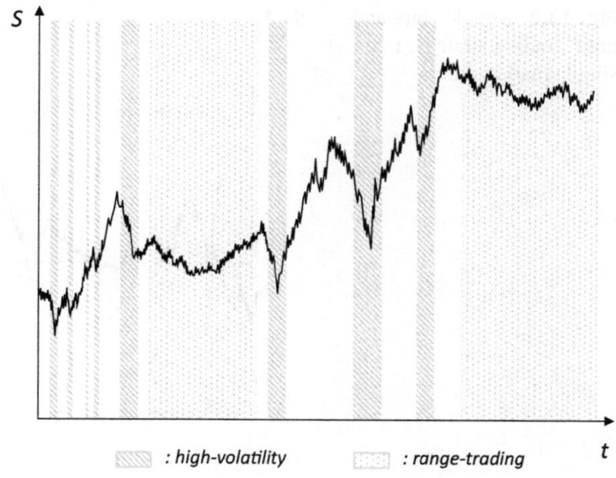

Fig. 13.7 Financial time-series regions

Note that these are "after-the-fact" observations—meaning that they are certain only after the full rate evolution has been recorded. However, the base consideration of traders is that all assets will exhibit such price regions, and that if one could correctly estimate their onset (or progression) in time, then a high-probability trading strategy could be devised.

In short, trading is all about deciding when and how to enter, and then exit, an asset position. The flurry of data (simple price feeds, order books, technical analysis indicators, algorithmic decision-making triggers, etc.) currently available to traders is about the "when". Which financial instruments to use and through which order types is about the "how".

There follows a concise explanation of the most frequently used order types, as offered by major marketplaces and intermediaries:

(a) A **market order** (or "**at best**" order) is the simplest type, signifying that the trader accepts whatever quotes (bid or ask) are offered at this moment in the market. It can be used to implement a simple "buy-and-hold" strategy (cf. Figure 13.8). The risk with this order type is that, first, the quotes may move before the order is executed to the effect that the trade amount may be quite different than what the trader originally estimated; and second, that the price may move significantly in the opposite direction to trader's expectations, negating the strategy outcome.
(b) A **limit order** is one in which the trader specifies an upper, resp. lower, price limit for counter-quotes against which they accept to buy, resp. sell, a quantity in the asset. This way the trade amount stays close to what the trader estimated. The risk with limit orders is that, first, the market may move quickly beyond the limit; thus, the trader may fail to enter the trade; and second, that the counter-quotes may not cover the entire asset quantity stated by the trader, that is, that the trade may be only partially filled.

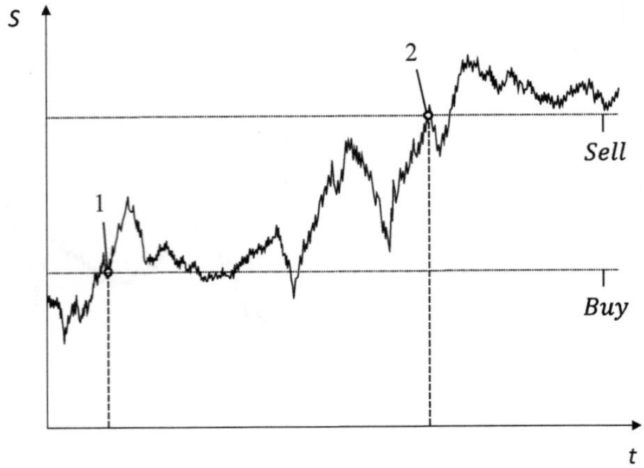

Fig. 13.8 Simple "buy-and-hold" trading strategy, two simple market orders

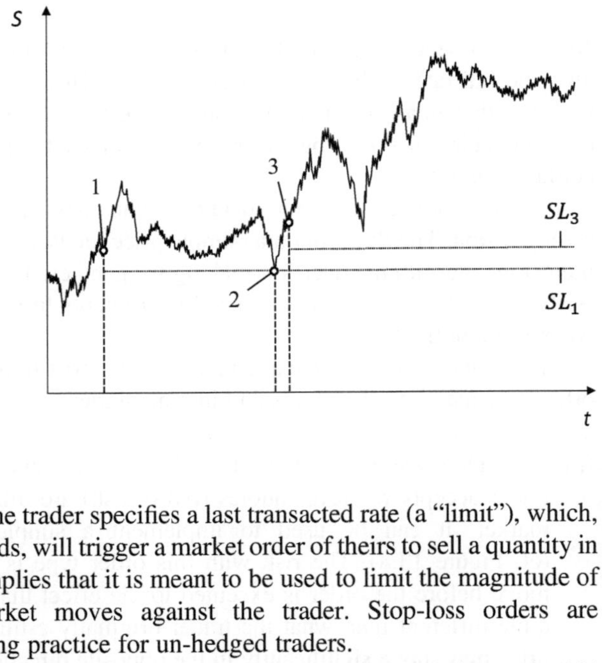

Fig. 13.9 Stop-loss orders

(c) In a **stop-loss order,** the trader specifies a last transacted rate (a "limit"), which, once crossed downwards, will trigger a market order of theirs to sell a quantity in the asset. The name implies that it is meant to be used to limit the magnitude of losses when the market moves against the trader. Stop-loss orders are recommended as trading practice for un-hedged traders.
The risk with stop-loss orders is, first, that—as with market orders—the bid counter-quotes may move fast much below the limit; and second, that if the asset price is systematically volatile by itself, then the limit may fall within its typical variability range, which will cause the trader to miss on the upside. In any case, estimating where to place the limit of a stop-loss order is the key to the success of a strategy using it. Consecutive stop-loss orders are depicted graphically on Fig. 13.9 (where "SL_i" denote the respective limits). Note that rate point "2" in the figure causes the first stop-loss order to execute.

Fig. 13.10 "Sell" trailing-stop orders

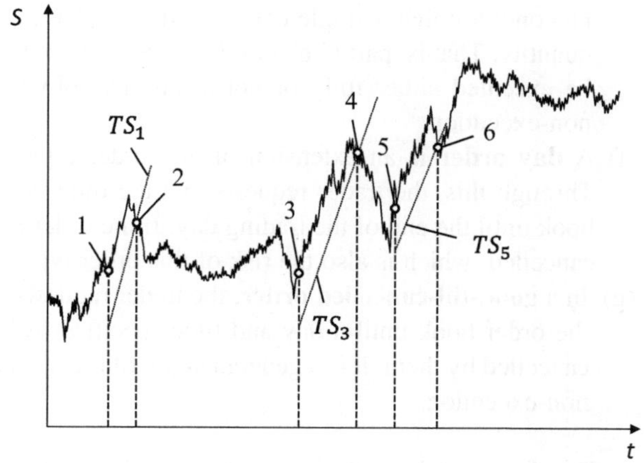

(d) A **trailing-stop order** is one in which the trader specifies a difference to the last "peak-trend" rate (a "trailing limit", expressed either in absolute terms or as a percentage of price), which, once crossed in a specific direction, will trigger a market order of theirs. There are two variations: In a "sell" trailing-stop order, the trader is already long in the asset (i.e. already has bought an asset quantity), which is since increasing in price. This order type is in effect a "moving-limit stop-loss order", where the limit is continuously re-calculated in reference to the last highest transacted rate. As long as the asset rate keeps increasing, or stays above the current moving limit, no sell order is triggered. Once the moving limit is crossed downwards, a selling market order is triggered. In a "buy" trailing stop order, the trader is short in the asset (i.e. has sold an asset quantity which they do not yet own, with the expectation to buy it at a lower price in order to cover their obligation to deliver), which is since decreasing in price. The moving-limit of the trailing stop order is now higher than the last lowest transacted rate. As long as the asset rate keeps decreasing, no buy order is triggered. Once the moving limit is crossed upwards, a buying market order is triggered, allowing the trader to close their short position. The purpose of the trailing-stop order type is to prevent traders from exiting profitable positions too early. The risk with trailing-stop orders is, in essence, the same as with stop-loss ones, namely that the counter-quotes may move fast beyond the moving limit; and that if the typical volatility of the asset is underestimated, then the trader may exit a winning trade too soon. Consecutive "sell" trailing-stop orders are depicted graphically in Fig. 13.10 (where "TS_i" denote the respective limits). Rate points "2", "4", and "6" in the figure cause the preceding trailing-stop orders to execute. Please note that the "trailing lines" are depicted as straight but in reality they are jagged, with step-structures at the levels of the local maximal rates. Bringing this level of detail on a sub-page figure would complicate the picture unduly; hence, we ask the reader to kindly accept the straight-line approximation.

(e) A **fill-or-kill order** is a variation of the limit order, whereby the trader specifies the quantity of the asset that they want bought or sold at their set limits, under the precondition that a single counterparty will have to counter-trade on the *entire* quantity. That is, partial fills of the order will not be accepted, and the order will be executed either fully or not at all. The obvious risk of this order type is non-execution.

(f) A **day order** is an extension of any order type other than the market order. Through this, the trader requests that the order should stay active in the order book until the end of the trading day. If the order is not executed until then, it is cancelled, which is also the risk of this order type.

(g) In a **good-till-cancelled order**, the trader requests that their order stay active in the order book until a day and time specified by them, or until it is explicitly cancelled by them. It is a generalization of the day order and has the same risk of non-execution.

The above are the most frequently offered order types, which can be used to time the entry and exit points of any asset position. As mentioned above, designing a trading strategy presupposes some basic knowledge about the behaviour of an asset class, coupled with an informed estimation about how to take advantage of the current rate evolution. Executing the trading strategy implies choosing the financial instruments to use and the most appropriate order types to enter and exit the respective positions.

13.3 Bancor Carbon

Bancor Carbon[2] [25, 26] is one of the protocols implemented within the Bancor token ecosystem [27]. It offers a decentralized exchange (DEX) functionality to both Bancor participants. Importantly, its proprietary bonding curve technology (for which a patent application has been submitted [28]) is available for licensing to third-party token projects [29]. All Bancor protocols have so far been implemented on the Ethereum L-1 blockchain, and their technical artefacts are addressable from any Ethereum Virtual Machine (EVM) compatible ecosystems.

Bancor Carbon participants can:

A. Supply ERC-20 tokens to the token-pair liquidity pools underlying the DEX, for yield.
B. Supply liquidity within bespoke buy-only and sell-only ranges, thus reproducing a market-making bid-ask spread effect.
C. Define different token swap dynamics (bonding curves) per buy-only and sell-only range.
D. Swap ERC-20 tokens in the spot market.

[2] Attention: Not to be confused with the totally different "Carbon" crypto project, https://carbon.network/

E. Implement directional trading strategies, consisting of linked standing trade (point/range) orders.

The two previous sections (on market making and order types) of the current chapter will be needed in order to glean both similarities and differences of Bancor Carbon use cases with respect to their traditional finance equivalents. The previous chapter (especially Sects. 12.2 and 12.4, including sub-sections) should also be referenced in order to interpret the calibration choices of Bancor Carbon bonding function designers.

There are explanatory formulas and graphs in this chapter, as well as specific references to Bancor Carbon project documentation and third-party archival material, to aid the reader in this quest.

As in previous case studies, even though the focus of the current one is bonding function design, we will need to first review the basis of the protocol's market design in order to set the terminology needed to explain subsequent notions.

13.4 Bancor Market Design Basics

As per the methodology introduced in Chap. 6, blockchain ecosystem market design must prescribe all possible **economic agent** types, **transactional pathways** joining them, and associated protocol **tokens** created or exchanged in the process. However, as our objective is simply to introduce only one protocol in the ecosystem, we will refrain from explaining Bangor's complete market design. We will instead mention only those design elements necessary for positioning Bancor Carbon's agents and transactional pathways in context.

Bancor [27] is a mature token project, the first whitepaper [30] of which appeared in 2017 [31]. Since then, it has already implemented four generations of its main (AMM-based) protocol.

As of the time of writing, it has introduced novel functionalities that deviate [32] from the last (v3 [33]) AMM-based iteration, while retaining backward compatibility of some technical artefacts with that and with still earlier generations [34]. It can be argued that the Bancor ecosystem is on the cusp of a paradigm change, whereby the emphasis is less on a DEX focus and more on directional trading infrastructures. Creation of Bancor Carbon was precisely the first step in that new direction, followed by implementation of an automated arbitrage protocol ("ArbFastLane" [35]) and of an automated liquidation auctions mechanism ("Automatic Auctioneer") [36].

Based on its published documentation [37] (including cross-references to technical artefact repositories in the public domain), the current economic agent model of the Bancor ecosystem is as depicted in Fig. 13.11. This refers to the entirety of protocols currently implemented by Bancor, including the—still active—legacy ones. However, please note that this picture attempts to represent a dynamic domain. For example, external Oracles were introduced by the legacy Bancor AMM v2 iteration [38]; they were then dropped by the later v3, but v2 artefacts are still

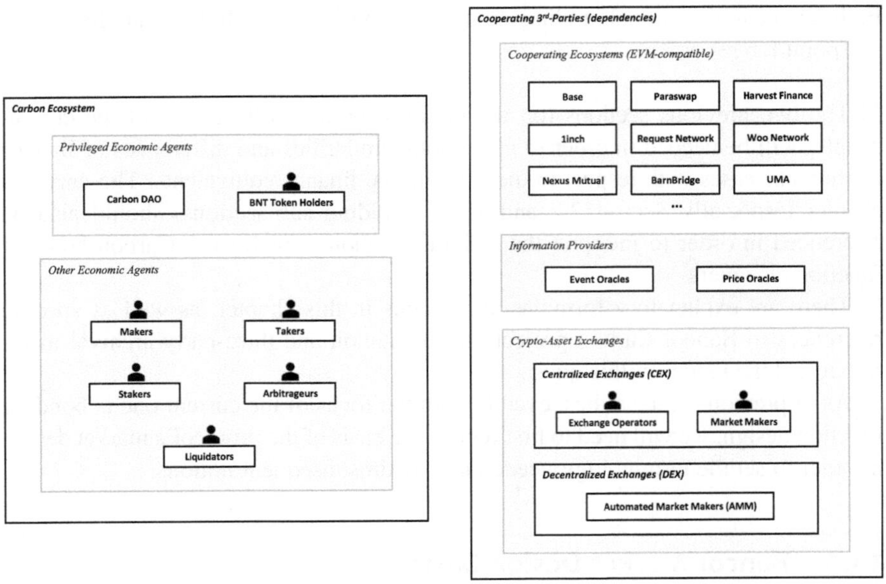

Fig. 13.11 Bancor ecosystem; economic agent model

operational. Also, among cooperating EVM-compatible ecosystems, Base [39] is an Ethereum L-2 ecosystem where apparently only Bancor Carbon and ArbFastLane artefacts are running [40]. On the other hand, 1inch is an EVM-compatible L-4 ("Aggregation") ecosystem, which still lists legacy Bancor protocols as liquidity sources [41] while having subsequently [42] also integrated Bancor Carbon [43]; hence, it will probably keep being part of the Bancor market design.

Bancor governance agents are similarly still evolving. Bancor's current documentation mentions that the ecosystem is "operated" (not governed) by the community as a DAO [44]. However, the main contributors to the evolution of the project until the time of writing appear to have been financed from a non-profit organization based in Switzerland, "Bprotocol Foundation" [45–47], which is also on record as the manager of Bancor's 2017 Initial Coin Offering [48]. That said, the Bancor DAO has an apparently active governance forum [49] with documented processes [50, 51] and voting sessions visible on Snapshot [52]. Voting originally entailed swapping [53] of native BNT [54] tokens against "vBNT" [55] ones (i.e. BNT token holders had the right to vote as long as they were prepared to swap BNT for vBNT); however, the DAO appears to be moving towards a gradual phase-out of vBNT towards BNT [56] used directly as governance token. As of the time of writing, both BNT and vBNT are still admissible as staking tokens for voting [57]. The meaning of the "privileged economic agents" box in Fig. 13.11 is that BNT holders are (directly or indirectly through the intermediate vBNT swapping step) eligible to vote for Bancor governance decisions.

Please note that as of the time of writing this book, it appears that Bancor DAO does not have a DAO Treasury [58]; hence, it is unclear if/how it contributes to the development and operations of the Bancor ecosystem beyond voluntary contributions of its members. Bancor's official "Terms of Use" [59] mention only the Bprotocol Foundation as the owner of the rights to the Bancor website, dApp, and any therein included functionalities. The legal personality and capacity to enter into legal transactions of the Bprotocol Foundation are undisputable. It is debatable if the same is true for the Bancor DAO (even though it has already been named, together with Bprotocol Foundation, as a defendant in court proceedings in the United States [60]).

13.4.1 Bancor Carbon Economic Agent Typology

Bancor Carbon is only one of the protocols implemented within Bancor; hence, it is should not be a surprise that its market design is only a subset of that of the surrounding ecosystem. Its non-privileged agent typology in particular is as depicted in Fig. 13.12. There are only two such economic agent types:

(a) Makers.
(b) Takers.

The salient attributes of said agents in the context of Bancor Carbon use cases are:

A **maker** is a Bancor Carbon participant who deposits admissible tokens into pairwise liquidity pools underlying the DEX functionality. All such pools are aggregated by Bancor Carbon, which then implements a pool matching mechanism to select the most appropriate one(s) for each incoming token swap order. Through the "asymmetric liquidity" option offered by the protocol's bonding function (cf. Sect. 13.5), makers can, in principle, re-produce the traditional finance market making paradigm. However, once the effective spread becomes wide enough, the same option becomes a directional trading strategy on the underlying token pair. Bancor Carbon makers can also define recurring (standing) buy-sell orders, which allow them to in effect play the role of algorithmic traders—albeit in a very basic manner—in a traditional finance sense.

A **taker** is a Bancor Carbon participant who seeks to swap one token kind for another in the spot market. Takers are the counterparties of makers in trades.

Importantly, Bancor Carbon is a non-custodial protocol, which means that both makers and takers need to have connected crypto wallets from within the Bancor Carbon dApp [61] before entering their orders. As the protocol is also permissionless, there are only transaction-based fees for participants. The agent types on which fees are levied and the fee policies/schedules are determined by governance decisions.

There also exists protocol-specific terminology (e.g. on order types, strategies), which will be explained in the following sections on transactional pathways.

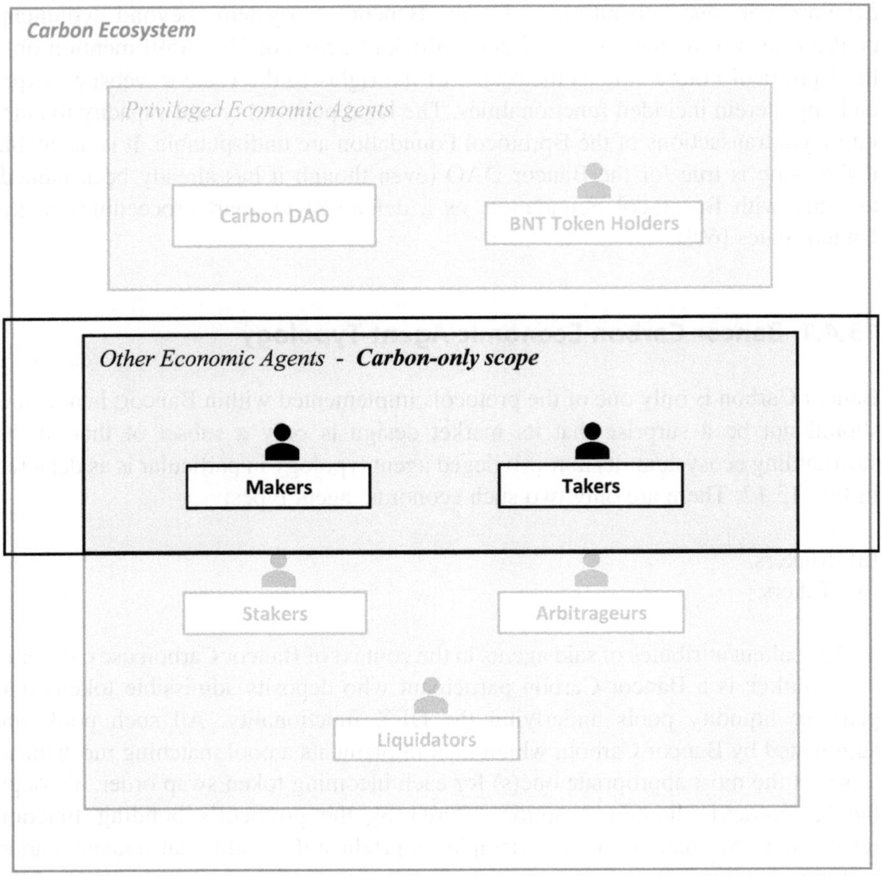

Fig. 13.12 Non-privileged economic agent types, Bancor Carbon protocol only

13.4.2 Main Transactional Pathways

As Bancor Carbon appears to be positioned as a DEX infrastructure protocol by Bancor (in both intra-Bancor and cooperating ecosystem use cases, as well as for L-4 protocol composition), it is not possible to describe all possible transactional pathways. We, thus, confine ourselves to the two most fundamental ones, which will serve as the basis for the bonding function case study. These transactional pathways are: makers' strategy creation and takers' trade execution.

We begin with the makers' strategy creation, which is arguably the main business case of Bancor Carbon.

13.4.2.1 Maker Creates Strategy on Bancor Carbon

In this transaction, a Bancor Carbon participant who already possesses admissible ERC-20 tokens in their wallet becomes a "maker" by defining and implementing a trading strategy. To best explain the various modalities offered by the protocol, it is expedient to begin with some definitions as per its official documentation.

- **Orders** are one-sided (buy-only or sell-only) trading commands that map to traditional finance "limit" (cf. Sect. 13.2, order type b.) and "good-till-cancelled" (ibid., order type g.) orders. They are meant to be executed once (non-recurring or "disposable" as per the dApp label).
- **Strategies** are permutations of orders that are defined to be executed sequentially—"linked" in Bancor Carbon parlance. The latter term is also appropriate in that, for instance, "sell"-legs need the token amounts acquired in the preceding "buy"-legs in order to execute.

Note that the protocol promises "zero slippage" in the order descriptions [62, 63], that is, no "implementation shortfall" [64] in the traditional sense.

As far as the main Bancor Carbon smart contract ("*CarbonController*"; description [65] and GitHub source code [66] both available) and the dApp are concerned, makers always define or change strategies, not orders. That is, even when they want to enter a single buy-only limit order, the latter is expected to be encapsulated within a wrapping "strategy" object. For example, under "strategy type" in the dApp [67], the user will also find individual orders.

Similarly to traditional foreign exchange trading terminology, Bancor Carbon orders must define a token pair in which the first is the "**base**" [68], whereas the second the "**quote**" [69] token—i.e. the numeraire from the trader's point of view.

There are around 5000 different tokens currently available in the drop-down lists of the dApp for the user to select as base or quote tokens. There does not seem to exist an official list of whitelisted tokens; however, a message on the dApp reads "Rebasing and fee-on-transfer tokens are not supported" (cf. the discussion on "rebase" or "rebaseable", tokens in Sect. 9.6.3.1). Once the token pair is selected, the strategy type needs to be defined next. There are four options available to the maker:

1. Limit order.
2. Range order.
3. Recurring order.
4. Concentrated (or "overlapping") liquidity.

The first two create single-order trading instructions, the rest linked-order trading robots ("bots" [70]). We will not explain the **limit order**, as it is the exact equivalent of the traditional finance namesake.

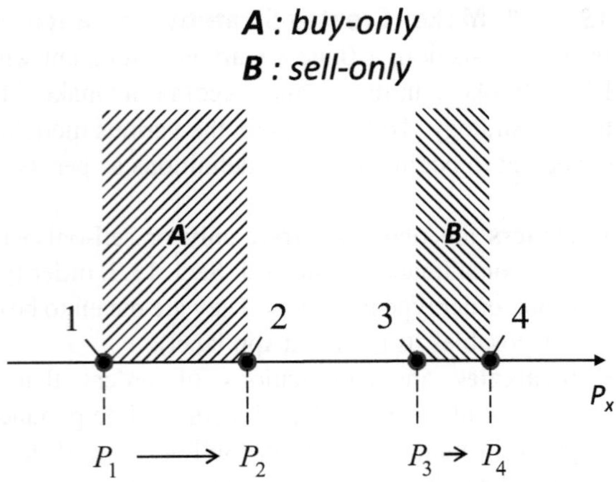

Fig. 13.13 "Recurring order" strategy, two linked range orders

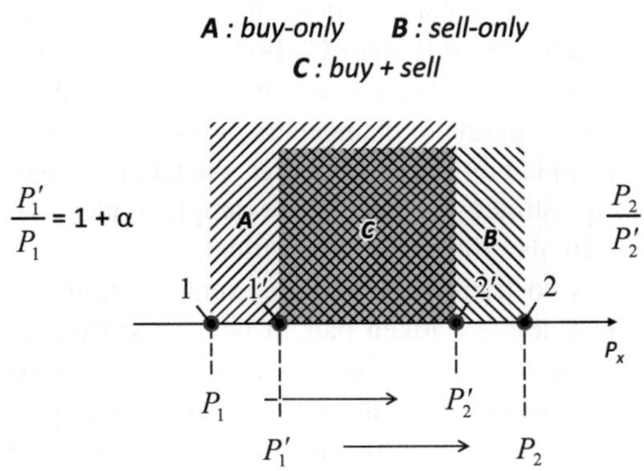

Fig. 13.14 "Concentrated liquidity" (or "overlapping liquidity") strategy; α = effective spread

The **range order** [63] defines simply an upper and lower limit for the quote token price; as long as the price is within this range, the order will execute.

A **recurring order** [71] links a one-sided with an opposite-sided range order; this will cause the two range orders to keep executing sequentially, to take advantage of volatile token pairs, which the maker expects to keep gyrating around the same highs and lows. An indicative recurring order strategy is depicted graphically on Fig. 13.13 (P_x stands for the quote token price).

A **concentrated liquidity** (or **"overlapping liquidity"**) strategy [72] is the closest that Bancor Carbon offers to the traditional market making paradigm. It entails creating two partially overlapping buy-only and sell-only ranges, the inner edges of which are defined by the outer ranges through a single spread-like parameter. An indicative overlapping liquidity strategy is depicted graphically on Fig. 13.14.

A maker needs only to define the lower limit price (P_1 in the figure) of the "buy-only" and the upper limit price (P_2) of the "sell-only" range for the quote token, together with the "α" parameter. These three values also define the inner limits, i.e. lower price point of the "sell-only":

$$P_1' = P_1 \cdot (1 + \alpha)$$

and upper price point of the "buy-only" region:

$$P_2' = \frac{P_2}{1 + \alpha}$$

The rationale behind this construct is apparently that, as traditional market making has no directional view, the user of this strategy assumes that there are equal probabilities of the base token trading below and above the current market price. By defining the inner limits as per the formulas above, the maker ensures that there will be at least an effective spread between the lower-buys and lower-sells on the one side and between the higher-buys and higher-sells on the other. This is precisely the "at-the-margins" profit expectation of traditional finance market makers.

Additionally, a user-configurable concentrated liquidity strategy option in the Bancor Carbon dApp is the starting region for liquidity trading ("below current market price", "above current market price", "around current market price"; leading to trading start in the "A", "B", or "C" regions, respectively). This option is probably meant to increase the odds of profitability, whenever the maker expects a specific directional price move in the short term to be followed by price gyrations.

The makers' strategy creation pathway is depicted schematically on Fig. 13.15. As in all case studies of this book, the protocol's "balance sheet" representation is the author's mapping of token allocations as per its transactional pathways onto an "accounting view". Assuming a human agent, the Bancor Carbon dApp will request that the user first connects a crypto wallet containing admissible ERC-20 tokens.

The maker will have acquired these tokens (denoted by Ŧ-ETH) in either their respective primary market or in Exchanges. In the figure we assume the latter case, whereby the agent purchases them against fiat currency or other tokens as applicable (depicted by step "1"). The tokens can then be transferred to the agent's wallet (step "2"), which makes them visible to the Bancor Carbon dApp. Invoking the "create strategy" functionality in the dApp, the user is asked to select the base/quote token pair, then the strategy type (as per 1. - 4. above) and finally their "Budgets"—that is, the token amounts which they will commit as trading liquidity. For limit and range orders, only one of buy- and sell-side "budgets" will need to be declared, denominated in the quote and base tokens, respectively. For recurring orders and overlapping liquidity strategies both buy- and sell-side "budgets" will need to be declared (again, in the respective tokens). This specifies the depth of the liquidity pool which the maker makes available to traders in all trading regions covered by the strategy.

Accepting the conditions in the dApp (step "3"), the maker causes the *CarbonController* smart contract to execute the following steps: transfer the

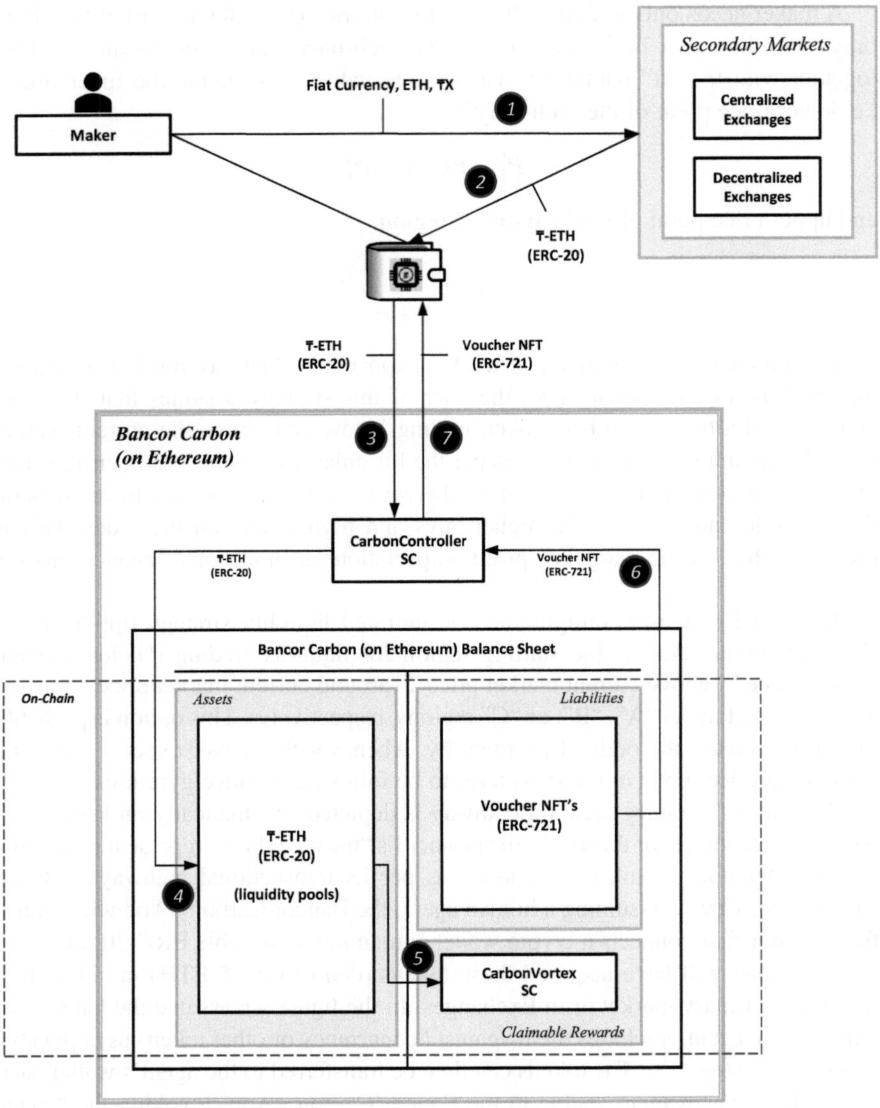

Fig. 13.15 Maker creates strategy on Bancor Carbon, paying in ₮-ETH (ERC-20 tokens)

ERC-20 tokens of the declared budgets to the Bancor Carbon liquidity pools ("4"); deduct any protocol fees by calling the *CarbonVortex* SC (step "5" [65, 73]—please note: as of the time of writing, there are no protocol fees levied on makers [74, 75], but this may change by governance decision [76] in the future); issue a "Voucher" [65, 77] non-fungible token (NFT—ERC-721 compatible) representing the maker's future profit-and-loss under their defined strategy and book it under the protocol's liabilities (step "6"); forward said Voucher to the agent's wallet ("7").

At the end of this pathway, the maker has a live strategy on Bancor Carbon, which is ready to accept countertrades from takers.

13.4.2.2 Taker Executes Trade on Bancor Carbon

In this transaction a Bancor Carbon participant becomes a "taker" by executing a spot trade swapping base for quote tokens. The transactional pathway is depicted schematically on Fig. 13.16. As Bancor Carbon is a non-custodial protocol, the

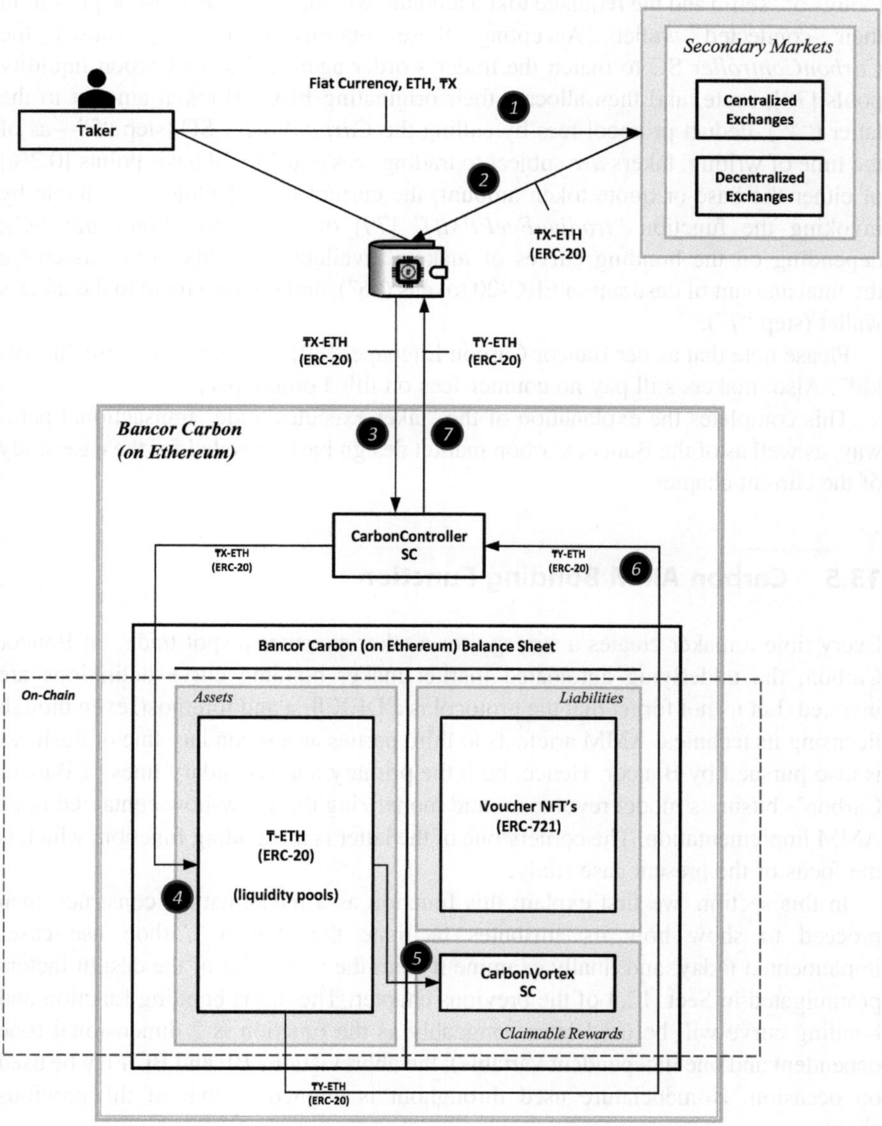

Fig. 13.16 Taker swaps ŦX-ETH for ŦX-ETH (ERC-20 tokens) on Bancor Carbon

dApp will request that the user connects a crypto wallet containing admissible ERC-20 tokens.

The agent will already have acquired such tokens, for example, on Exchanges, paying with fiat currency or with other tokens (step "1" in the figure), and subsequently transferred them to their wallet (step "2"). Invoking the "trade" functionality in the dApp, the agent must specify their base and quote token pair. The latter must be among the ones being represented in liquidity pools already created by makers. After selecting such a pair, the agent is asked to specify the direction of the trade ("buy" or "sell") and the requisite token amount, which, of course, must be present in their connected wallet. Accepting these options (step "3") causes the *CarbonController* SC to match the trader's order against Bancor Carbon liquidity pools [78]; route, and then allocate their originating ERC-20 token amount to the latter ("4"); deduct protocol fees by calling the *CarbonVortex* SC (step "5"—as of the time of writing, takers *are* subject to trading fees equal to 20 basis points [0.2%] of either the base or quote token amount; the current fee schedule is available by invoking the function "*tradingFeePPM()*" [79] of the *CarbonController* SC); depending on the bonding curves of makers' available liquidity pools, assemble the final amount of destination ERC-20 tokens ("6"); and forward them to the taker's wallet (step "7").

Please note that as per Bancor Carbon Litepaper [80], all taker trades are "fill-or-kill". Also, makers still pay no counter-fees on filled orders [81].

This completes the explanation of the "taker executes trade" transactional pathway, as well as of the Bancor Carbon market design basics needed for the case study of the current chapter.

13.5 Carbon AMM Bonding Function

Every time a maker creates a strategy, or a taker executes a spot trade, on Bancor Carbon, the underlying automated market maker bonding curve definitions are invoked. Let us not forget that the protocol is a DEX first and foremost, even though licensing its technical AMM artefacts to third parties as a secondary line of business is also pursued by Bancor. Hence, both the primary and secondary lines of Bancor Carbon's business model revolve around monetizing the know-how contained in its AMM implementation. The cornerstone of the latter is its bonding function, which is the focus of the present case study.

In this section, we first explain this function as a mathematical construct, then proceed to show how its attributes facilitate the Bancor Carbon use cases implemented today, and finally examine it from the viewpoint of the design factors promulgated in Sect. 12.4 of the previous chapter. The terms bonding function and bonding curve will be used interchangeably as the function is 2-dimensional (one dependent and one independent variable); the abbreviations BF and BC may be used on occasion. Nomenclature used throughout is aligned to that of the previous chapter.

Fig. 13.17 Bancor Carbon parametrizable bonding curve

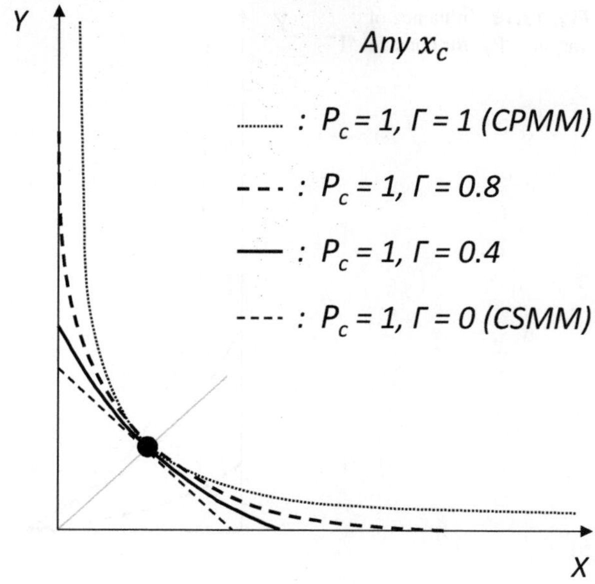

The generic parametrizable BF postulated by Bancor Carbon [25] is[3]:

$$Y = \frac{P_c \cdot X_c \cdot [X \cdot (\Gamma - 1) - X_c \cdot (\Gamma - 2)]}{\Gamma \cdot X - X_c \cdot (\Gamma - 1)}$$

where Y and X denote the instantaneous quantities of the quote (₸Y) and base (₸X) token, respectively,[4] in the "local" liquidity pool created by the maker's liquidity position. In other words, changes ΔY and ΔX in the quantities of said tokens as a result of the pool's utilization are constrained so that points (X, Y) always remain on the BF.

The freely defined constants P_c and X_c can be interpreted as price and pool capacity scalings, respectively, as proved in Bancor Carbon's Whitepaper. The—also freely defined— constant Γ correlates positively with the convexity of the curve. However, P_c and Γ need to be considered together as design parameters, as demonstrated directly below. Keeping P_c and X_c constant and varying only Γ reveals its convexity role. For instance, setting P_c to 1.0 and letting Γ vary from 0.0 to 1.0 produces the curves depicted on Fig. 13.17.

---

[3] Please note that the nomenclature in the Bancor Carbon Whitepaper is different, in that both constants denoted here by P_c and X_c have there the suffix "0" instead of "C". The change in notation is meant to preserve uniformity with the formulas of this book's Chap. 12.

[4] Please note that in the protocol's Whitepaper it is proven that the same general form of the BC is obtained when expressing X in terms of Y. Thus, the role of base and quote token can be reversed; however, then the curve constants have different values. We keep the "one-side" interpretation in the text of this section, so as not to confuse the reader and in order to conform to the nomenclature of the previous chapter.

Fig. 13.18 Influence of varying "P_c" for constant "Γ"

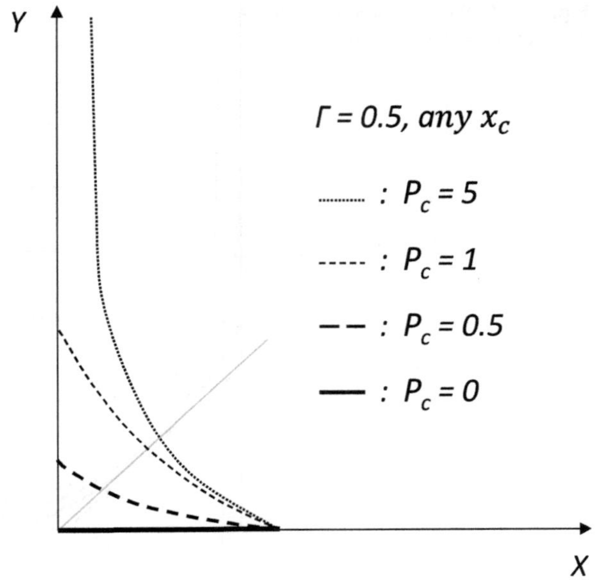

Clearly, $P_c = 1.0$ produces curves that are symmetrical around the $Y = X$ line. For $\Gamma = 0$, the BC becomes a straight line at a 45° angle to the axes, which is typical of a constant-sum market maker. A value of $\Gamma = 1.0$ is shown in the Whitepaper to reproduce the curve of a constant-product market maker, with branches running asymptotically to the axes at infinity. Intermediate Γ values produce curves intersecting the axes symmetrically, with convexities positively correlating with Γ. Keeping Γ constant and varying P_c instead reveals the latter's influence on the BC's deviation from symmetricity around the diagonal.

As shown on Fig. 13.18, setting $\Gamma = 0.5$ will cause the curve to intersect the X axis; while simultaneously increasing P_c from 0 (for which value it is a linear segment of the X axis) will make it "pivot" around the intersection point clockwise. Higher values of P_c will make the other branch of the curve intersect the other axis also at higher Y values, until it becomes practically asymptotic to it.

Thus, by varying its freely chosen parameters P_c, X_c, and Γ, the generic parametrizable Bancor Carbon bonding function can reproduce all basic symmetric AMM curves and can also produce asymmetric ones with features (such as location of points of intersection with the axes, sense, and degree of asymmetricity from the diagonal convexity) that can be totally controlled at design time. The resulting operational flexibility for AMM use cases is proven to be significant.

For example, the quote and/or base token "budget" parameters expected to be declared by makers on the Bancor Carbon dApp (cf. Sect. 13.4.2.1 above) map naturally to the points of intersection of the BF with the Y and/or X axes. Hence, there is no need to translate coordinates as in the case of concentrated liquidity positions, while still being constrained by the symmetric form of a CPMM. The intersecting coordinates Y_{int} and X_{int} can be simply two of the three anchor values needed to completely specify those parameters P_c, X_c, and Γ, that will make the BF match the correct "budget" values. Note that both the Bancor Carbon Whitepaper and its "invention disclosure" document [28] provide quite a few mathematical formulas linking curve parameters with geometrical features of practical meaning.

The repercussions of the BF being able to produce non-diagonally symmetric forms (i.e. when $P_c \neq 1$) are even more far-reaching. For once, this allows to control the effective parity rates offered by a liquidity pool in ways that would be impossible through symmetric AMM forms. To establish this, please recall from the previous chapter that the price in terms of ŦY, which a generic AMM offered for ŦX at a point (X_0, Y_0), was given by the formula:

$$P_x = -\left.\frac{\mathrm{d}Y}{\mathrm{d}X}\right|_0$$

For the Carbon bonding function, by differentiating:

$$\frac{\mathrm{d}Y}{\mathrm{d}X} = \frac{P_c \cdot X_c \cdot (\Gamma - 1)}{\Gamma \cdot X - X_c \cdot (\Gamma - 1)} - \frac{\Gamma \cdot P_c \cdot X_c \cdot [X \cdot (\Gamma - 1) - X_c \cdot (\Gamma - 2)]}{[\Gamma \cdot X - X_c \cdot (\Gamma - 1)]^2} =$$

$$= \frac{P_c \cdot X_c \cdot (\Gamma - 1) \cdot [\Gamma \cdot X - X_c \cdot (\Gamma - 1)] - \Gamma \cdot P_c \cdot X_c \cdot [X \cdot (\Gamma - 1) - X_c \cdot (\Gamma - 2)]}{[\Gamma \cdot X - X_c \cdot (\Gamma - 1)]^2}$$

Evaluating only the denominator:

$$P_c \cdot X_c \cdot (\Gamma - 1) \cdot \Gamma \cdot X - (\Gamma - 1)^2 \cdot P_c \cdot X_c^2 \\ - (\Gamma - 1) \cdot \Gamma \cdot P_c \cdot X_c \cdot X + \Gamma \cdot P_c \cdot X_c^2 \cdot (\Gamma - 2)$$

in which the first and third terms cancel out, leaving:

$$-(\Gamma^2 - 2 \cdot \Gamma + 1) \cdot P_c \cdot X_c^2 + P_c \cdot X_c^2 \cdot (\Gamma^2 - 2 \cdot \Gamma) = -P_c \cdot X_c^2$$

Finally:

$$P_x = -\left.\frac{\mathrm{d}Y}{\mathrm{d}X}\right|_0 = \frac{P_c \cdot X_c^2}{[\Gamma \cdot X - X_c \cdot (\Gamma - 1)]^2}$$

Hence, for constant Γ and X_c the implied price of Y in terms of X depends linearly on P_c, which expresses mathematically the trend visible in Fig. 13.19.

Hence, even declaring the same "budget" and the same desired "end-point" in terms of the quote token (mapping to values Y_o and Y_1, respectively, in Fig. 13.19) still leaves enough flexibility for the maker to define different swap price dynamics (or "exchange rate policy") at each state of the liquidity pool.

Furthermore, the same mathematical feature of the generic Bancor Carbon BF is what enables the creation of "linked" range orders within the same maker liquidity pool. Please recall from the discussion on the "recurring order" strategy (in Sect. 13.4.2.1, also Fig. 13.13) that a "buy-only" range order is used to arrive at a pool

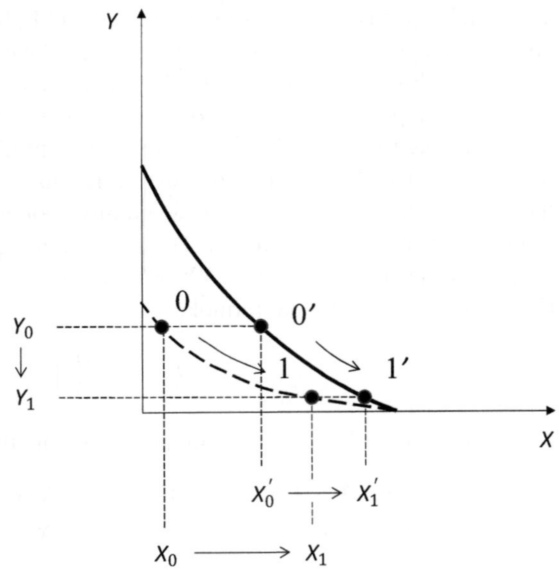

Fig. 13.19 Role of varying "P_c" for maker swap price dynamics

containing only base tokens, which are then swapped back for quote tokens at a higher price in a "sell-only" range order. Thus, a liquidity pool that starts with a set quote token "budget" is first transformed to one containing only base tokens, the last marginal price of which is P_u^A (upper limit of the "buy-only" range A); then the same pool starts selling base tokens, once the first marginal price has reached P_l^B (lower limit of the "sell-only" range B). This is easy to visualize in terms of the intercepts of the Bancor Carbon bonding curve with the coordinate axes, X_{int} and Y_{int}.

To calculate X_{int}, set:

$$Y = 0 \Rightarrow \frac{P_c \cdot X_c \cdot [X_{int} \cdot (\Gamma - 1) - X_c \cdot (\Gamma - 2)]}{\Gamma \cdot X_{int} - X_c \cdot (\Gamma - 1)} = 0 \Rightarrow X_{int} = X_c \cdot \frac{\Gamma - 2}{\Gamma - 1}$$

And with $X = 0$:

$$Y_{int} = \frac{-P_c \cdot X_c^2 \cdot (\Gamma - 2)}{-X_c \cdot (\Gamma - 1)} \Rightarrow Y_{int} = P_c \cdot X_c \cdot \frac{\Gamma - 2}{\Gamma - 1}$$

The Bancor Carbon BC thus implies the corresponding prices:

$$P_{(X_{int},0)} = -\left.\frac{dY}{dX}\right|_{(X_{int},0)} = \frac{P_c \cdot X_c^2}{\left[\Gamma \cdot X_c \cdot \frac{\Gamma-2}{\Gamma-1} - X_c \cdot (\Gamma - 1)\right]^2} \Rightarrow \ldots \Rightarrow P_{(X_{int},0)} = P_c \cdot (\Gamma - 1)^2$$

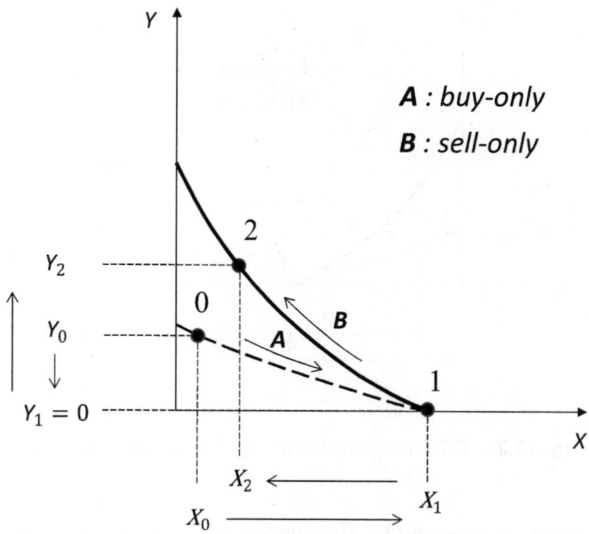

Fig. 13.20 Asymmetric liquidity provision by maker in Bancor Carbon

and

$$P_{(0,Y_{int})} = -\left.\frac{\mathrm{d}Y}{\mathrm{d}X}\right|_{(0,Y_{int})} = \frac{P_c \cdot X_c{}^2}{[\Gamma \cdot X - X_c \cdot (\Gamma - 1)]^2} \Rightarrow \ldots \Rightarrow P_{(0,Y_{int})} = \frac{P_c}{(\Gamma - 1)^2}$$

(Incidentally, please note that for $\Gamma = 0$ one obtains the same implied price for both intercept points—equal to P_c–, which was to be expected as this value reproduces the constant-sum market maker.)

The important information from the equation $P_{(X_{int},0)} = P_c \cdot (\Gamma - 1)^2$ is that one can be at the same intercept (X_{int}, 0) (i.e. a pool containing only base tokens of the same amount) but one may have arrived there through two different marginal price points, depending on the values of the two parameters P_c and Γ. In all generality, different pairs (P_c, Γ) will give different marginal price points. But different pairs (P_c, Γ) mean different parametrization of the Bancor Carbon bonding curve, that is, *different resulting curves*. This is precisely a manifestation of the power which the generic parametrizable Bancor Carbon BF puts in the hands of makers, through its ability to produce non-diagonally-symmetric curves. By creating strategies, makers control the attributes of their liquidity pools; that means both static attributes (e.g. depth or "budget", limits of the "buy-only" and "sell-only" ranges) and dynamic ones (e.g. exchange rate policy). In the particular case of the "recurring order" strategy, the maker controls the initial depth of the liquidity pool in terms of quote tokens and the limits of the two price ranges. Bancor Carbon uses these values to define two (2) bonding curves, corresponding to different triplets (P_c, X_c, Γ). As depicted in Fig. 13.20, the first bonding curve A—starting at point (X_O, Y_O)—will allow the liquidity pool to transition to a state where only X_1 base tokens are contained, the last marginal price P_1^A of which is that implied by the derivative of

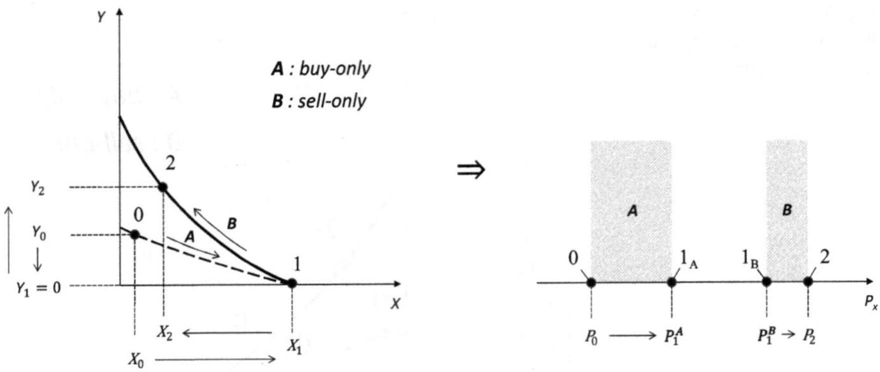

Fig. 13.21 Effective "directional view" by maker in Bancor Carbon

curve A at point (X_1, 0). The second bonding curve B—starting at the (X_1, 0)—will be followed once the first marginal price P_1^B becomes that which is implied by the derivative of curve B at the same point. The liquidity pool will start swapping the acquired base tokens back for quote tokens towards the point (X_2, Y_2) of curve B.

The correspondence between bonding curve paths and implied base token price ranges is shown in Fig. 13.21.

Please note that the right-hand side of Fig. 13.21 is the same as the depiction of a "recurring order" strategy in Fig. 13.13. As a matter of detail, the ability of makers to have each trading direction determined by its own curve and beginning/ending states is termed **"asymmetric liquidity provision"** in the Bancor Carbon documentation.

How can the Bancor Carbon AMM bonding function be interpreted as sum of calibration choices in reference to the design factors promulgated in Sect. 12.4 of the previous chapter? For the sake of convenience, we enumerate them again here:

1. **Surrounding use case.**
2. Underlying **token price dynamics.**
3. **Market depth** effects.
4. Balancing **configurability** and **controllability.**
5. **Composability.**
6. **Cost-efficiency.**
7. **Market manipulation risk.**

Based on our previous analysis and on additional facts gleaned from the protocol's documentation, we can deduce the following:

(a) The bonding function implemented by Bancor Carbon does not rely on external Oracles for either pricing or liquidity pool depth calibration, and its parametrization can be controlled completely through the options offered to makers through the protocol's dApp. The latter attribute is due to the fact that many possible mathematical relationships linking parametres P_c, X_c, and Γ, and observable pool metrics (such as the pool depth, or "budget", the maximum available quantities of either base or quote tokens, the average offered price, etc.) were identified by the BF designers and then implemented in code. The dApp is used in a permissionless manner by makers and takers alike. Hence, the BF design does seem to conform both to the expected attributes of a DEX AMM, as well as to the surrounding market and mechanism designs of the protocol.

(b) The aggregate effect of several individual liquidity pools by makers trading the same token pairs on the same protocol increases the depth of the on-chain market, while the fact that all underlying bonding functions—while behaving differently—are in fact transparent to the protocol facilitates matching logic within Bancor Carbon. Thus, the best prices can be offered to traders (less slippage effects in spot trades), which serves the economic purpose of the underlying use case (DEX). At the same time, compliance with eventual "best execution" obligations can be argued to be materially facilitated by the combination of this bonding function and its surrounding market design.

(c) It was already shown how the different parametrization of the BF along trading directions translates to taking directional views by makers. In general, all maker use cases envisaged in the protocol's Whitepaper (i.e. both symmetric and asymmetric liquidity provision, directional views, limit/range/recurring orders) appear to be covered through appropriate parametrization of combinations of the bonding function. These combinations map clearly to options provided to makers through the protocol's dApp.

(d) Through the same dApp, informed makers can adjust the mathematical form of the BF (through finetuning of the parametres P_c, X_c and Γ) to match the expected "normal" correlation statistics of tokens in the particular traded pair. With the additional option to define range orders, they can also control their exit from the market if said statistics are no longer observed (e.g. due to market dislocations, systemic events, Stablecoin de-pegs, etc.). This means that Bancor Carbon participants have increased odds to control their market entries and exits. The controllability (through configurability) of the BF is intrinsically much higher than that of "symmetric-only" traditional DEX AMMs.

(e) The configurability of the AMM also through the Bancor Carbon SDK implies two things: first, that composability is enabled by default (as long as some documented prerequisites are satisfied, e.g. the use of non-rebasing tokens); second, that matching and routing logic can be implemented by other protocols to increase the effective depth of liquidity available to takers. The last point means both that slippage effects are minimized to the advantage of takers, and that "best execution" obligations can be also complied with by offering protocols, if needed. Both points mean that composability across Bancor and cooperating protocols is in principle materially enabled through this bonding function design.

(f) Regarding cost efficiency of implementation, as per Bancor Carbon documentation, gas fees are incurred only when a strategy is created, changed (structurally, i.e. when it comes to changing its constituent order types) or deleted. That gives makers the ability to change the parameters of an existing strategy without incurring gas fees. Coupled with the fact that makers do not pay protocol fees (as of the time of writing), this is an added incentive for them to keep participating in the protocol's use cases. Thus, they protect its market depth and contribute to its eventual growth. The off-chain configurability of an (already operational) Bancor Carbon AMM bonding function is a result of the combined parametrization and implementation modalities afforded by its mathematical form.

(g) The ability to have different bonding functions per trading direction, hence deviating from a predictable "symmetric" AMM form, can in principle contribute to reduction of losses due to maximum extractable value exploits (cf. discussion in Sect. 12.4.7 of the previous chapter). As also pointed out in the Bancor Carbon whitepaper, provided that the asymmetric liquidity pattern is used (with bonding curves that are non-overlapping), "sandwich" attacks against a single trader have theoretically much lower odds of success. For example, while the "buy" leg (traditional trading "front-running") can still be executed, the "sell" leg (traditional "scalping") is now non-deterministic. This is because either the original trader is not supplying symmetric liquidity (i.e. will not be the one selling along the same curve in the same liquidity pool) or may be executing a linked-range order strategy, which means that they will be selling at a different price range—hence inside a different block of transactions. This "asymmetric liquidity provision" option was shown above (cf. Fig. 13.20) to be attributable to the option of defining different triplets (P_c, X_c, Γ) parametrizing the same underlying mathematical form. An MEV attack is still possible across liquidity pools which are adjacent in price, but it will not involve the same trader. Also, there is no guarantee that different pools will have the exact same mathematical bonding functions as they will have been configured by different makers.

(h) Last but not least, creating an effective DEX bonding function definition and implementation that can be adopted across cooperating ecosystems will increase the odds of DEX arbitrage strategies, which should remove frictions across those ecosystems (less implementation shortfall [64] throughout), thus further increasing market depth.

In summary, based on the above observations, the Bancor Carbon generic parametrizable Bonding Function appears to essentially address all design factors identified in Sect. 12.4 of the previous chapter.

This completes our bonding function design case study.

13.6 Summary

Bancor Carbon, a non-custodial protocol of the EVM-compatible Bancor ecosystem, was used as the context of a case study in bonding function design. Its AMM implementation can be used for two different kinds of use cases:

1. To create DEX liquidity pools wherein makers can provide capital-efficient liquidity for ERC-20 token swaps (totally controlling parameters such as token pairs, parity rate profiles, pool depth, and price limits) and takers can execute spot trades.
2. To allow makers to take directional views on token parity rates; and define, then execute, limit or range order strategies, either one-off or recurring; thus in effect implementing user-configurable trading bots.

It was shown that the protocol in effect replicates on-chain the traditional finance paradigms of:

(i) Market making in quote-driven markets (including own-defined bid-ask spreads).
(ii) Exchange trading through various order types, including limit and range orders.
(iii) Algorithmic trading bots implementing user-configurable trading strategies.

The protocol defines and implements a generic parametrizable bonding function, which was explained both as a mathematical construct and as a foundation of AMM implementations. Its features were analysed through theoretical concepts of the previous Chap. 12 on bonding function design. Its probable design calibration was interpreted against the background of the afore-mentioned use cases and in the context of the specific protocol's market design. Its design was shown to essentially address the calibrating factors promulgated in Sect. 12.4 of the previous chapter.

In summary, the case study demonstrated that the bonding function design principles of the proposed token ecosystem design framework align with current crypto-industry market practices; thus, they can be used for both analysis and design purposes in the context of blockchain-based token ecosystems.

References

1. Bancor Carpon Token protocol. https://www.carbondefi.xyz/
2. New York Stock Exchange (NYSE). https://www.nyse.com/index
3. Nasdaq. https://www.nasdaq.com/
4. Frankfurt Stock Exchange/Börse Frankfurt. https://www.boerse-frankfurt.de/
5. Euronext Paris. https://www.euronext.com/en/markets/paris
6. Johannesburg Stock Exchange (JSE). https://www.jse.co.za/
7. Dubai Financial Market (DFM). https://www.dfm.ae/
8. Liberto, D. (2025, March 6). *Over-the-counter (OTC) Markets: Trading and securities.* Retrieved March 27, 2025, from https://www.investopedia.com/terms/o/otc.asp

9. Hayes, A. (2024, April 30). Electronic Communication Network (ECN): Definition and examples. Retrieved March 27, 2025, from https://www.investopedia.com/terms/e/ecn.asp
10. Crossing network. (2025, April 15). In Wikipedia. Retrieved April 19, 2025, from https://en.wikipedia.org/wiki/Crossing_network
11. Chen, J. (2022, March 22). *What are dark pools? How they work, critiques, and examples.* Retrieved March 27, 2025, from https://www.investopedia.com/terms/d/dark-pool.asp
12. Hayes, A. (2024, April 26). *Alternative trading system (ATS) definition and regulation.* Retrieved March 27, 2025, from https://www.investopedia.com/terms/a/alternative-trading-system.asp
13. U.S. Securities and Exchange Commission (SEC). *Alternative Trading Systems.* Retrieved March 27, 2025, from https://www.sec.gov/tm/tm-alternative-trading-systems
14. Smith, A. (2021, June 6). *What is a multilateral trading facility (MTF) & how does it work?* Retrieved March 27, 2025, from https://www.investopedia.com/terms/m/multilateral_trading_facility.asp
15. MiFID II. *Article 4 Definitions*. European Securities and Markets Authority (ESMA). Retrieved March 27, 2025, from https://www.esma.europa.eu/publications-and-data/interactive-single-rulebook/mifid-ii/article-4-definitions
16. Chen, J. (2024, April 15). Spot rate: What it is, how it works, example. Retrieved March 27, 2025, from https://www.investopedia.com/terms/s/spot_rate.asp
17. Chen, J. (2025, March 11). *What is mean reversion, and how do investors use it?* Retrieved March 27, 2025, from https://www.investopedia.com/terms/m/meanreversion.asp
18. Hayes, A. (2024, July 4). *Technical analysis: What it is and how to use it in investing*. Retrieved March 27, 2025, from https://www.investopedia.com/terms/t/technicalanalysis.asp
19. Pring, M. J. (2014). *Technical analysis explained* (5th ed.). McGraw Hill.
20. *Nasdaq Level 2*. Nasdaq product pages. Retrieved March 27, 2025, from https://www.nasdaqtrader.com/Trader.aspx?id=nqds
21. Chen, J. (2024, August 30). *What is level 2? Definition on Nasdaq, How It Works, and Example.* Retrieved March 27, 2025, from https://www.investopedia.com/terms/l/level2.asp
22. Algorithmic trading. (2025, April 10). In Wikipedia. Retrieved April 19, 2025, from https://en.wikipedia.org/wiki/Algorithmic_trading
23. Chen, J. (2024, March 11). *Algorithmic trading: Definition, how it works, pros & cons.* Retrieved March 27, 2025, from https://www.investopedia.com/terms/a/algorithmictrading.asp
24. Chan, R. P. (2013). *Algorithmic trading; winning strategies and their rationale*. Wiley.
25. Richardson, M. & Loesch, S. (2022, November 22). *Carbon; a decentralized protocol for asymmetric liquidity and trading. Whitepaper v.1.2*. Bancor Carbon Whitepaper. Retrieved March 26, 2025, from https://resources.carbondefi.xyz/pages/CarbonWhitepaper.pdf
26. Bancor Carbon page; entrance to the protocol's dApp. https://www.carbondefi.xyz/
27. Bancor Token ecosystem. https://bancor.network/
28. Richardson, M.B., Levi, Y., Benartzi, G. (2022, October 19). *Invention disclosure*. Retrieved March 27, 2025, from https://resources.carbondefi.xyz/pages/CarbonPatent.pdf
29. Albert, J. (2023, November 8). Bancor's innovative technology licensed to power DeFi protocols across multiple layer 2s. Bancor blog pages. Retrieved March 27, 2025, from https://blog.bancor.network/bancors-innovative-technology-licensed-to-power-defi-protocols-across-multiple-layer-2s-fe67ce9e3aaa
30. Bancor Whitepaper. (2017, April 28). https://bancor.network/whitepaper, linked into from https://bancor.network/about, please search on the Webpage for "DeFi Primitives", "Constant Product". Note: there are 3 (three) links under "DeFi Primitives", each corresponding to a different generation of the ecosystem.
31. *About Bancor* (documentation basics entry page). Bancor documentation pages. Retrieved March 27, 2025, from https://docs.bancor.network/about-bancor-network/faqs/master
32. (2023, August 6). *A primer on Bancor's new trading protocol, Carbon*. Bancor blog pages. Retrieved March 27, 2025, from https://blog.bancor.network/a-primer-on-bancors-new-trading-protocol-carbon-5bc7d6a1a65f

33. *Bancor V3*. Bancor documentation pages. Retrieved March 27, 2025, from https://docs.bancor.network/about-bancor-network/bancor-v3
34. Token pools selection functionality on the Bancor dApp. https://app.bancor.network/earn
35. *ArbFastLane aribtrage framework*. Bancor product pages. Retrieved March 27, 2025, from https://bancor.network/arbfastlane
36. Albert, J. (2024, January 29). *Redefining liquidations in DeFi; Introducing the automatic auctioneer powered by carbon DeFi*. Bancor blog pages. Retrieved March 27, 2025, from https://blog.bancor.network/redefining-liquidations-in-defi-43bb5280626e
37. Bancor documentation. *Resources*. Bancor documentation pages. Retrieved March 27, 2025, from https://docs.bancor.network/about-bancor-network/faqs/resources
38. (2020, June). *Bancor V2 AMM Security Audit*. Consensys diligence. Retrieved March 27, 2025, from https://consensys.io/diligence/audits/2020/06/bancor-v2-amm-security-audit/
39. Base Layer-2 Blockchain. https://www.base.org/
40. Albert, J. (2024, January 22). *Now live on base! Bancor expands beyond Ethereum and onto its first L2!* Bancor blog pages. Retrieved March 27, 2025, from https://blog.bancor.network/now-live-on-base-164d3a78797e
41. 1 inch documentation. *Overview*. 1inch documentation pages. Retrieved March 27, 2025, from https://docs.1inch.io/docs/educational-resources/intermediate/1inch-Liquidity-Sources/ .
42. X post announcing Bancor Carbon's integration with 1inch. Retrieved March 27, 2025, from https://x.com/CarbonDeFixyz/status/1704915319549198618?s=20
43. Albert, J. (2023, October 9). Bancor network update. Bancor blog pages. Retrieved March 27, 2025, from https://blog.bancor.network/bancor-network-update-1da226baf886
44. *What is the Bancor DAO?* Bancor support pages. Retrieved March 27, 2025, from https://support.bancor.network/bancor-dao/what-is-the-bancor-dao
45. *Bprotocol Stiftung (Bprotocol Foundation)* (record in Switzerland's commercial register). Retrieved March 27, 2025, from https://zefix.ch/en/search/entity/list/firm/1301840
46. *Bprotocol Stiftung (Bprotocol Foundation)* (record in the commercial register of the Swiss Canton of Zug). Retrieved March 27, 2025, from https://zg.chregister.ch/cr-portal/auszug/auszug.xhtml?uid=CHE-181.679.849
47. *Bprotocol Stiftung* (record in Switzerland's Foundations register). Retrieved March 27, 2025, from https://stiftungen.stiftungschweiz.ch/organisation/bprotocol-stiftung (registration may be needed to access the page).
48. Kraken Learn Team. (2023, November 14). *What is Bancor?* Kraken CEX support pages. Retrieved March 27, 2025, from https://www.kraken.com/learn/what-is-bancor-bnt (please search in the page for "Bprotocol Foundation").
49. Governance fora overview. Bancor governance discussion pages. Retrieved March 27, 2025, from https://gov.bancor.network/
50. *Bancor Governance Voting Guide*. Bancor support pages. Retrieved March 27, 2025, from https://support.bancor.network/bancor-dao/bancor-governance-voting-guide
51. A Guide to BancorDAO Due Process. Bancor governance discussion pages. Retrieved March 27, 2025, from https://gov.bancor.network/t/a-guide-to-bancordao-due-process/1669
52. *Bancor* (governance votings). Retrieved March 27, 2025, from https://vote.bancor.network/#/
53. *Bancor Vortex Burner* (triggering). Bancor documentation pages. Retrieved March 27, 2025, from https://docs.bancor.network/guides/triggering-the-bancor-vortex-burner
54. *CoinMarketCap BNT page*. CoinMarketCap. Retrieved March 27, 2025, from https://coinmarketcap.com/currencies/bancor/
55. *CoinMarketCap vBNT page*. CoinMarketCap. Retrieved March 27, 2025, from https://coinmarketcap.com/currencies/bancor-governance-token/
56. (2023, September). *Proposal for BNT to become an official governance token*. Bancor governance discussion pages. Retrieved March 27, 2025, from https://gov.bancor.network/t/proposal-for-bnt-to-become-an-official-governance-token/4456/
57. Vote functionality on Bancor's dApp. https://app.bancor.network/vote

58. (2023, January). *A case for a DAO treasury*. Bancor governance discussion pages. Retrieved March 27, 2025, from https://gov.bancor.network/t/a-case-for-a-dao-treasury/4179/
59. (2023, May 11) (Bancor) *Terms of Use*. Retrieved March 27, 2025, from https://restricted.bancor.network/terms-of-use
60. (2023, May 11). *Basic v. BProtocol Foundation (1:23-cv-00533)*. District Court, W.D. Texas. CourtListener. Retrieved March 27, 2025, from https://www.courtlistener.com/docket/67370525/basic-v-bprotocol-foundation/
61. Bancor Carbon dApp. https://app.carbondefi.xyz/
62. *Limit order*. Bancor Carbon support pages. Retrieved March 27, 2025, from https://faq.carbondefi.xyz/strategy-types/limit-order
63. *Range order*. Bancor Carbon support pages. Retrieved March 27, 2025, from https://faq.carbondefi.xyz/strategy-types/range-order
64. Hayes, A. (2023, December 22). *Implementation shortfall: Meaning, examples, shortfalls*. Retrieved March 27, 2025, from https://www.investopedia.com/terms/i/implementation-shortfall.asp
65. Bancor Carbon Smart. *Contracts*. Bancor Carbon documentation pages. Retrieved March 27, 2025, from https://docs.carbondefi.xyz/contracts-and-functions/contracts#carbon-defi-contracts
66. *CarbonController* (Smart Contract implementation). Bancor Carbon GitHub pages. Retrieved March 27, 2025, from https://github.com/bancorprotocol/carbon-contracts/blob/dev/contracts/carbon/CarbonController.sol
67. *Creating a strategy*. Bancor Carbon support pages. Retrieved March 27, 2025, from https://faq.carbondefi.xyz/getting-started/creating-a-strategy#id-2.-select-the-strategy-type
68. Kenton, W. (2024, September 19). *Base currency: Definition, example, vs. quote currency*. Retrieved March 27, 2025, from https://www.investopedia.com/terms/b/basecurrency.asp
69. Hayes, A. (2024, February 14). *What is a quote currency?* Retrieved March 27, 2025, from https://www.investopedia.com/terms/q/quotecurrency.asp
70. Reiff, N. (2024, July 21). *What's the role of bots in crypto trading?* Retrieved March 27, 2025, from https://www.investopedia.com/tech/whats-role-bots-crypto-trading/
71. *Recurring orders*. Bancor Carbon support pages. Retrieved March 27, 2025, from https://faq.carbondefi.xyz/strategy-types/recurring-orders
72. *Concentrated liquidity*. Bancor Carbon support pages. Retrieved March 27, 2025, from https://faq.carbondefi.xyz/strategy-types/concentrated-liquidity
73. *CarbonVortex* (Smart Contract). Bancor Carbon GitHub pages. Retrieved March 27, 2025, from https://github.com/bancorprotocol/carbon-contracts/blob/dev/contracts/vortex/CarbonVortex.sol
74. *Fees & payments*. Bancor Carbon documentation pages. Retrieved March 27, 2025, from https://docs.carbondefi.xyz/carbon-defi/introducing-carbon-defi/fees-and-payments
75. Albert, J. (2023, July 25). *True DEX Limit Orders: Carbon DeFi vs. Existing Solutions.*. Bancor Carbon blog pages. Retrieved March 27, 2025, from https://www.carbondefi.xyz/blog/true-dex-limit-orders-carbon-vs-existing-solutions
76. (2023, April). *Proposing carbon (FINAL)*. Bancor governance discussion pages. Retrieved March 27, 2025, from https://gov.bancor.network/t/proposing-carbon-final/4242
77. *Voucher* (Smart Contract). Bancor Carbon GitHub pages. Retrieved March 27, 2025, from https://github.com/bancorprotocol/carbon-contracts/blob/dev/contracts/voucher/Voucher.sol
78. *Order execution*. Bancor Carbon support pages. Retrieved March 27, 2025, from https://faq.carbondefi.xyz/mechanics/order-execution
79. *tradingFeePPM()* (function returning the network default trading fee, expressed in parts-per-million (PPM)). Bancor Carbon documentation pages. Retrieved March 27, 2025, from https://docs.carbondefi.xyz/contracts-and-functions/read-and-write-functions/read-functions/tradingfeeppm

80. Bancor Carbon Litepaper (shorter version of Whitepaper). (2022, November). *Carbon; a decentralized protocol for asymmetric liquidity and trading*. Working Draft v1.1. Retrieved March 27, 2025, from https://resources.carbondefi.xyz/pages/CarbonLitepaper.pdf
81. Albert, J. (2023, December 20). *New feature: Concentrated liquidity*. Bancor Carbon blog pages. Retrieved March 27, 2025, from https://www.carbondefi.xyz/blog/overlapping-liquidity

14 Case Study in End-to-End Design: Aave

The last case study in the book brings in evidence all token ecosystem considerations across market, mechanism, token, and bonding curve designs at once. We will demonstrate the interplay among all design pillars in a working, mature ecosystem and thus prove the practical usefulness of an end-to-end Design Framework approach, as promulgated in Chap. 4. We will also explain how functional and non-functional requirements evolution (and parallel advances in blockchain and other technology platforms) across protocol generations can be accommodated in a robust, controllable manner by following said approach.

The focus of the end-to-end design case study will be "Aave" [1], which is currently among the top DeFi lending and borrowing ecosystems by token market capitalization [2].

As in previous case studies, we begin with the closest analogues to Aave business cases from traditional finance in order to demonstrate how blockchain-based token ecosystems are simply evolutions in business practices taking advantage of new technological paradigms. We then proceed with a detailed examination of the apparent Aave design calibrations through the lens of the proposed Design Framework pillars. We base our opinions on facts gleaned from Aave's official documentation and from records of its governance decisions. In the process, we demonstrate how traditional finance concepts and processes have found direct analogues in Aave's processes, agent typology, crypto-tokens, and technical artefacts.

We finish the chapter by examining the extent to which the proposed design framework can serve as both an analysis and design tool for blockchain-based token ecosystems, based on the insights which it could afford us into the workings of Aave.

I. Giannakouros, *Cryptocurrencies and Tradable Crypto-Tokens*, Future of Business and Finance, https://doi.org/10.1007/978-3-031-98423-5_14

14.1 Lombard Lending

Lending of money is the fundamental asset-side activity of banking institutions. Within a typical bank there are several distinct lending units, the structure and operating model of each depending mostly[1] on two parameters: the type of counterparty and the financial instruments offered.

- Privates; unincorporated associations; small corporates; large and multinational corporates; special purpose vehicles; institutional investors; financial companies; state institutions; central banks; and supranationals are examples of counterparty types.
- Term loans (fixed- or variable-rate); credit facilities; mortgages; repurchase agreements; etc., are examples of lending financial instruments.

Before lending funds, there are a number of risk management and control activities that banks undertake, the single most important being the counterparty credit risk (CCR) evaluation. The object of this activity is to estimate the capacity of the counterparty (borrower) to actually repay the funds, as per the terms and conditions of the lending transaction—that is, repayment schedule, interest charged, restraining clauses, etc. Supporting this estimation is the inclusion of any credit risk mitigants supplied by the borrower,[2] such as their own collateral and third-party guarantees. There exist different categories of eligible collateral per lending instrument, which also impacts the degree to which they are considered in the CCR valuation methodology of a bank. That said, there are situations where a bank—for its own reasons[3]—may decide to not require posting of collateral by the borrower.

Hence, after estimating the CCR of a borrower, a lending institution may decide to either:

- Request specific collateral or other credit mitigants as a precondition, or
- Lend them money without requiring any specific credit mitigants.

The former situation is termed "**secured lending**", whereas the latter "**unsecured lending**". Secured lending is the norm in financial services. Note that as the CCR is typically monitored during transaction execution, the lending institution may at any time request additional credit risk mitigants, as a precondition for either not forcing repayment acceleration or not increasing the effective interest rate. Such a request is

[1] Syndicated lending is an example of yet another parameter at play; namely the **number of institutions** simultaneously lending funds to a single borrower in a single transaction.

[2] The bank may procure other counterparty risk hedging mechanisms on its own initiative—such as credit default swaps—even after a transaction has been entered into.

[3] For example, in the case of long-standing clients expected to generate fees in parallel transactions predicated on the lending one.

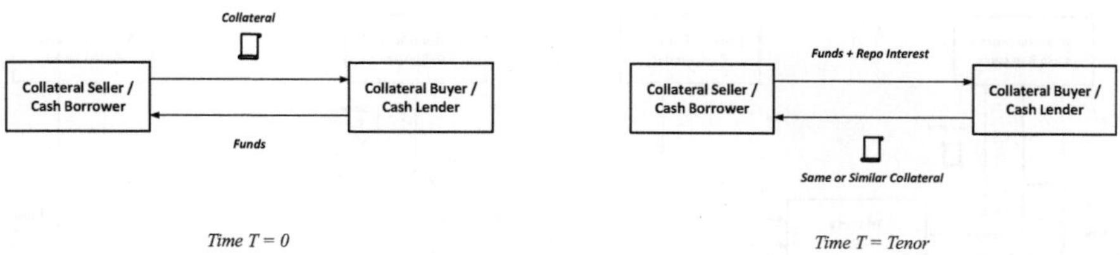

Fig. 14.1 Classic repo

generally termed "credit enhancement call", which may have different variations depending on the terms of the lending agreement.

For the purposes of this chapter, it is expedient to provide some more detail on the distinguishing features of two particular types of lending instruments, namely:

a. Repurchase agreement ("repo")
b. Lombard loan

A **repurchase agreement (repo)** is a transaction in which one party A sells securities to the counterparty B, and simultaneously commits to repurchasing from B the same number of identical securities on a date and at a price which are contractually specified.

Even though the transaction is structured as a sale (i.e. outright transfer of ownership) of securities, its economic purpose is for the seller to borrow cash from the buyer, with said securities being in effect the underlying collateral. Subtracting the price paid for the securities by A at repurchase and that paid by B at purchase gives the return amount on the loaned funds. The return itself is usually referred to as "repo interest" [3], whereas the equivalent annualized rate of return on the loan amount is the "repo rate".

The time duration of the transaction (from collateral sale to repurchase) is called the repo "term" or "tenor".

There are three main types of repurchase agreements [4], namely:

i. Classic repo, or simply repo
ii. Sell/buy-back repo
iii. Tri-party repo

In a **classic repo** (cf. Fig. 14.1), collateral seller and buyer are the only parties to the contractual agreement, and the tenor is finite. In a **sell/buy-back repo**, the transaction is a spot sale and repurchase of assets, executed simultaneously.

In a **tri-party repo** (cf. Fig. 14.2), the contractual agreement involves also a third party, which provides transaction servicing (e.g. transaction documentation; cash and limits monitoring; safekeeping and valuation of securities; corporate actions; collateral substitution; close-of-business reports; and margin calls issuance), acting as an agent to both collateral seller and buyer.

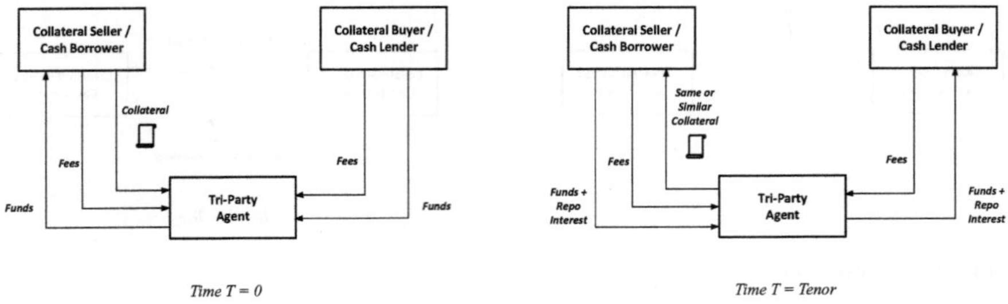

Fig. 14.2 Tri-party repo

In terms of contractual repo rates, there are three types: fixed, floating, and fixed-relative. Floating and fixed-relative rates track a reference rate. In case of non-fixed, how often the repo rate is adjusted is contractually defined by a "repo rate fixing frequency" or "interval".

A repo that does not have a contractually fixed tenor is called an "open repo", or also "on-demand repo" [5]. The borrower (collateral seller) will confirm each morning to the lender that the repo is required for a further overnight term, and negotiate the new repo rate. An open repo can be terminated at one day's notice.

The cash received by the borrower is typically less than the collateral market value by an agreed percentage—called the "haircut" or "initial margin". The size of the initial margin correlates positively with:

- CCR rating of the borrower
- Historical collateral volatility
- Collateral illiquidity
- Tenor of the repo
- Event volatility (e.g. when securities are close to maturity)
- Non-use of market-standard documentation [6]

For example, market-standard documentation typically includes clauses providing for collateral re-evaluation and "variation margin" during the duration of the repo. Variation margin entails posting of extra collateral (if the market value of the original one has dropped below some limit), or extra cash to the borrower, or partial return of collateral (if it has risen above some limit). This limit (in terms of either amount or percentage) is called "margin maintenance limit". Market-standard usance also specifies which securities classes qualify as repo-eligible collateral [7].

Repo transactions involve a broad variety of counterparty types. On one side of the spectrum, Central Banks enter into repos as both sellers and buyers in order to regulate the money supply and commercial bank reserves. On the other side, privates typically use them to finance short-term investments. In the middle of the spectrum, commercial banks and institutional investors use them primarily for treasury management and investment banking operations.

It goes without saying that different counterparty types represent different capabilities in terms of transaction execution. For example, in the Eurozone, the middle market consists of two, fundamentally distinct, segments as per a relevant ECB publication [8]. The first segment, the inter-dealer market, includes large repo dealer banks with access to electronic repo trading platforms. The second segment includes non-dealer banks and non-banks (like mutual funds; money market funds; insurance companies; and pension funds) with no access to such platforms; these trade repos mostly bilaterally with dealer banks over the counter (OTC).

It is important to remember that in a repo, legal title (as opposed to beneficial ownership) to the collateral passes to the buyer (lender of cash). Hence, in the event of the seller's (borrower's) insolvency, the buyer can liquidate it without needing to seek permission from an insolvency court. On the same grounds, the buyer is legally allowed to sell on ("*repo on*") the securities to a third party at any time during the life of the repo transaction. This is referred to as right to "re-use the collateral". The buyer is still obligated to buy the same or similar securities (or, in industry parlance, "to substitute the collateral") so as to return it to the original seller at the end of the repo.

Lombard[4] **lending** is a bilateral lending transaction involving the **pledging** of securities as collateral. It entails posting of collateral which remains under the legal ownership of the borrower (even though it becomes "ring-fenced" in a way controlled by the lender) and thus continues to accumulate income stream and appreciation potential for them.

This setting involves a party A that is in possession of marketable assets or debt claims against third parties. The counterparty B is typically a financial institution (FI) with readily available liquidity. Party A typically seeks liquidity or guarantees in order to finance immediate investment opportunities, or to address pressing funding needs. However, they do not wish to sell their assets. After performing due diligence on the securities in question, B accepts to provide Lombard Loan, which can take several forms, that is:

a. Lombard fixed-term advance
b. Lombard open-ended advance
c. Lombard overdraft facility
d. Lombard guarantee
e. Lombard guarantee facility

In a **Lombard fixed-term advance**, a set cash amount is forwarded immediately to the borrower and begins incurring interest charges, which must be repaid—together with the principal—according to a set repayment schedule. A **Lombard open-ended advance** is similar but involves an indefinite repayment schedule, interruptible at the discretion of any of the two parties, provided that an agreed notice period is observed. The **Lombard overdraft facility** involves setting up a cash account for the borrower, which can be drawn down within set amount and time limits. Interest is charged only on the drawn-down sums and not on the limit amount.

[4]Secured lending has been historically associated with lombard banking [9], but of course was not exclusive to it.

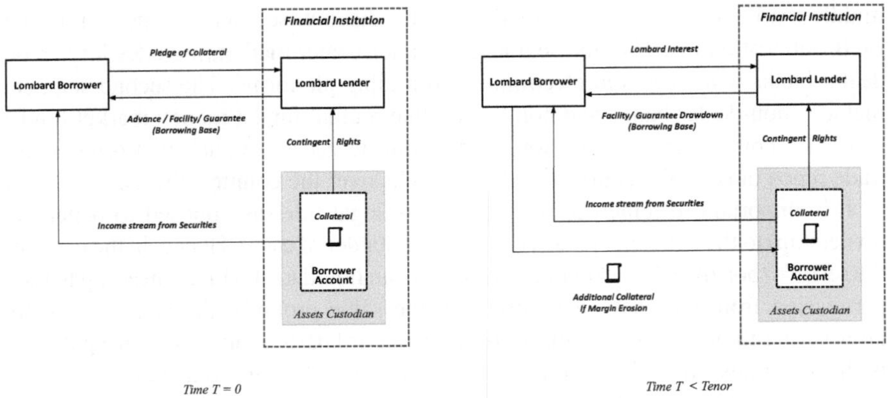

Fig. 14.3 Lombard lending

A **Lombard guarantee** is a credit or performance **limited** guarantee, issued to support trade finance or project finance transactions with fixed notional. Stand-by letters of credit; performance bonds; bid bonds; and other credit guarantees; are all possible types of Lombard guarantees. The **Lombard guarantee facility**, on the other hand, entails extension of credit to cover the market risk of securities and derivatives for speculative trading. The per-case market risk limit is the limit of the facility, and only the actual drawdown is charged interest. The generic Lombard lending setup is depicted graphically in Fig. 14.3.

As in the repo case, the borrowing base (BB) [10] of a Lombard loan is calculated after a discount is applied to the actual market value of the pledged securities portfolio. This discount is again called "haircut" or "margin". Note that Lombard loan haircuts are typically much higher than repo ones. This discounting is meant to cover the volatility, liquidity, and close-out risks of the pledged securities; plus, the expected time risk of margin call non-reaction (cf. below), should the lending financial institution ultimately have to appropriate pledged securities for liquidation.

There is no standard market usance on Lombard-eligible asset classes, admissible securities being at the discretion of each financial institution. For example, when a bank extends Lombard credit to its wealth management clients, all typical asset classes in such clients' portfolios (equities, investment funds, precious metals, fixed-income positions, structured products, life-insurance policies, etc.) can be admitted into the borrowing base calculation—of course, with different haircuts per asset class. Each Lombard lender may also set other constraints on the securities portfolio as a whole, in terms of, for example, asset class diversification, sector concentration, name concentration, etc. The typical first objective of the lender is to receive high-quality collateral with as stable a market value (and/or limited downside risk) as possible. The ultimate objective is to avoid having a partially unsecured credit exposure, as a result of "margin erosion".

To explain this eventuality (and how it relates to "margin calls" or "close-outs" on Lombard loans), we refer the reader to Fig. 14.4. This depicts some collateral market

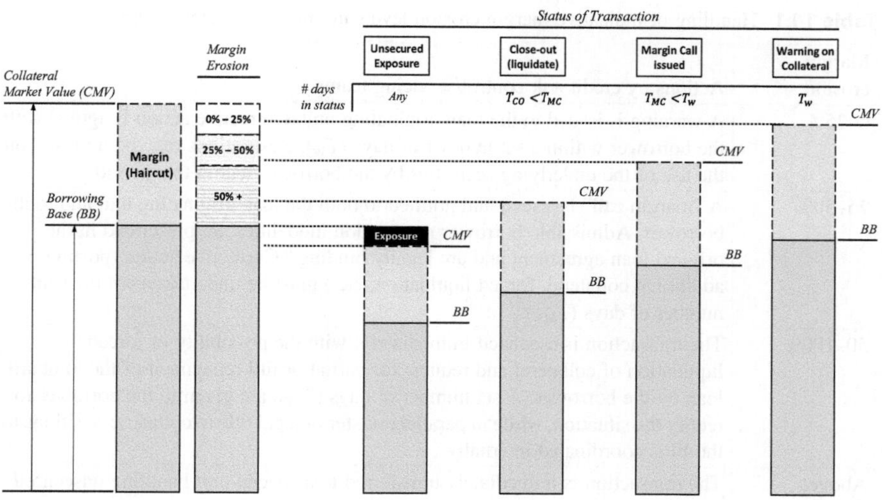

Fig. 14.4 Margin erosion and corresponding Lombard Lending transaction status

value situations that can occur, and the way that a lending institution typically reacts to them.

Ideally, the securities portfolio underlying a Lombard Lending transaction would appreciate while preserving its liquidity risk profile. However, it cannot be precluded that the opposite is true; that is why the lending financial institution initiates credit risk monitoring immediately after the transaction is entered into. Internal policies of the FI typically involve setting some downside market risk limits and mandating corresponding actions by the credit risk control (CRC) and credit servicing teams. Usually, these limits are set within the range [Borrowing Base$_{\text{Initial}}$, Collateral Market Value$_{\text{Initial}}$] and are expressed as percentages of the initial margin. If these downside limits are exceeded, action is taken. As depicted in Fig. 14.4, the FI may mandate downside limits ("margin erosion" levels) at 25%, 50%, and 100% of the original margin. Typical actions are as mentioned in Table 14.1:

Even though this exception-handling logic appears to be well-defined, its operational execution is far from automatic. First of all, it may happen that some securities in the collateral portfolio may exhibit volatility outside their historical ranges, to the effect that the entire portfolio moves to "margin call" status without passing from "warning". Second, within the time allotted for corrective action in a particular state, the portfolio may move to another state—not necessarily more onerous. Third, the time to close out a security position, or indeed the entire transaction, may entail assuming even more risks, which will need to be hedged at own cost.

Hence, it is inescapable that the lending FI will have to calibrate its operational exception handling of margin erosion carefully, also taking market-imposed time delays into account. Its Lombard lending contractual documentation will need to be drafted accordingly, to align risk management principles with operational realities. This is precisely the reason for the haircut on collateral portfolios in the initial

Table 14.1 Handling of indicative margin erosion levels in lombard lending transactions

Margin erosion	Actions by credit risk control/servicing teams
0–25%	A warning is issued to the loan originating unit. Corrective action is agreed with the borrower within a set number of days (T_W). Restrictions may be imposed on the use of the underlying securities by the borrower within this period.
25–50%	A "margin call" is issued and notified to both the loan originating unit and to the borrower. Admissible borrower notification modalities are prescribed in the original loan agreement and are legally binding.[a] Corrective action (posting of additional collateral, forced liquidation, etc.) must be undertaken within a set number of days (T_{MC}).
50–100%	The transaction is escalated immediately, with the possibility of forced liquidation of collateral and request for partial or full repayment of the lombard loan by the borrower. A set number of days (T_{CO}) are given to the borrower to rectify the situation, while in parallel transfer of legal title to collateral positions to the FI is coordinated internally.
Above 100%	The transaction is immediately transferred to a special unit handling unsecured credit exposures.

[a]For a case from the Swiss jurisdiction, whereby a constructive margin call on a Lombard loan was taken to have been notified as per contract even though the borrower was not physically reached, please consult [11]

calculation of borrowing base, and for the need to keep monitoring eventual margin erosion in the sequel.

Finally, in contrast to a repo transaction, the securities of a collateral portfolio supporting a Lombard lending transaction cannot be reused (i.e. they cannot be pledged in a parallel transaction by the borrower, nor can they be offered to a third party—even provisionally—by the lender). Both the legal title and the beneficial interest of said collateral remain with the borrower. Any concomitant income stream (e.g. dividends, interest payments, and rights from corporate actions) is owned exclusively by the borrower.

Viewing it as a cooperative process, Lombard lending involves the following economic agent typology:

a. Borrower
b. Lender/authorized signatory
c. Collateral valuation expert or system
d. Credit risk controller
e. Legal/documentation expert
f. Credit risk operations officer
g. Credit servicer
h. Securities custodian
i. Collateral manager
j. Structurer
k. Collateral broker
l. Securities trader

Please note that pre-onboarding customer due diligence agents are not included in this process view. Also, participation of some of the agent types on the list is contingent on events. For example, a collateral broker will be involved only if collateral transformation is needed (e.g. swapping an asset class for another with lower volatility or with lower correlation to the rest of the securities portfolio). Similarly, a securities trader may be needed if some less-than-liquid securities are to be sold. And a structurer may be needed along the process, if some risk metrics of the collateral portfolio are deemed worthy of improvement.

Summarizing the above, both repurchase agreements (repos) and Lombard loans are secured lending instruments in traditional finance. In contrast to a repo transaction, legal title and beneficial interest of Lombard lending collateral remain with the borrower. Lombard collateral may not be reused.

14.2 Asset-Backed Securitization

Asset-backed securitization is an important risk-transfer activity undertaken by financial institutions. Whenever an FI decides[5] to lend money to a borrower, it does so under a contractually agreed repayment schedule. This creates the right to an income stream flowing back to the FI, consisting of a mix of interest rate and principal (capital) amortization payments. The present value of this income stream is booked on the asset-side of the FI's balance sheet and the yearly repayment amounts on its income statement.

However, depending on the FI's business strategy, it may decide to *not* keep long term this risk exposure on its balance sheet. Reasons behind the decision include the:

a. Contribution to liquidity gap risk, and
b. Imputed regulatory capital requirements

of this particular class of risk exposures (as characterized by, e.g., collateral type, economic sector of the funded activity, and counterparty or collateral location).

For example, **liquidity gap risk** is present in traditional banking by default, stemming from the structural mismatch (in terms of cash-flow profiles) between aggregated liabilities and assets. To explain this term better, consider a typical commercial bank's balance sheet, as depicted schematically in Fig. 14.5. "Off-balance-sheet" items typically include contingent assets and liabilities from derivatives/swaps (and other risk-transfer transactions), explicit or implicit corporate guarantees, etc.

This is of course a simplistic view, as it does not represent banks focused on very specialized products and services; however, it does depict the composition of assets and liabilities found in a typical commercial bank's business model. Based on this

[5] After executing the due diligence steps mentioned in the beginning of this chapter's Sect. 14.1.

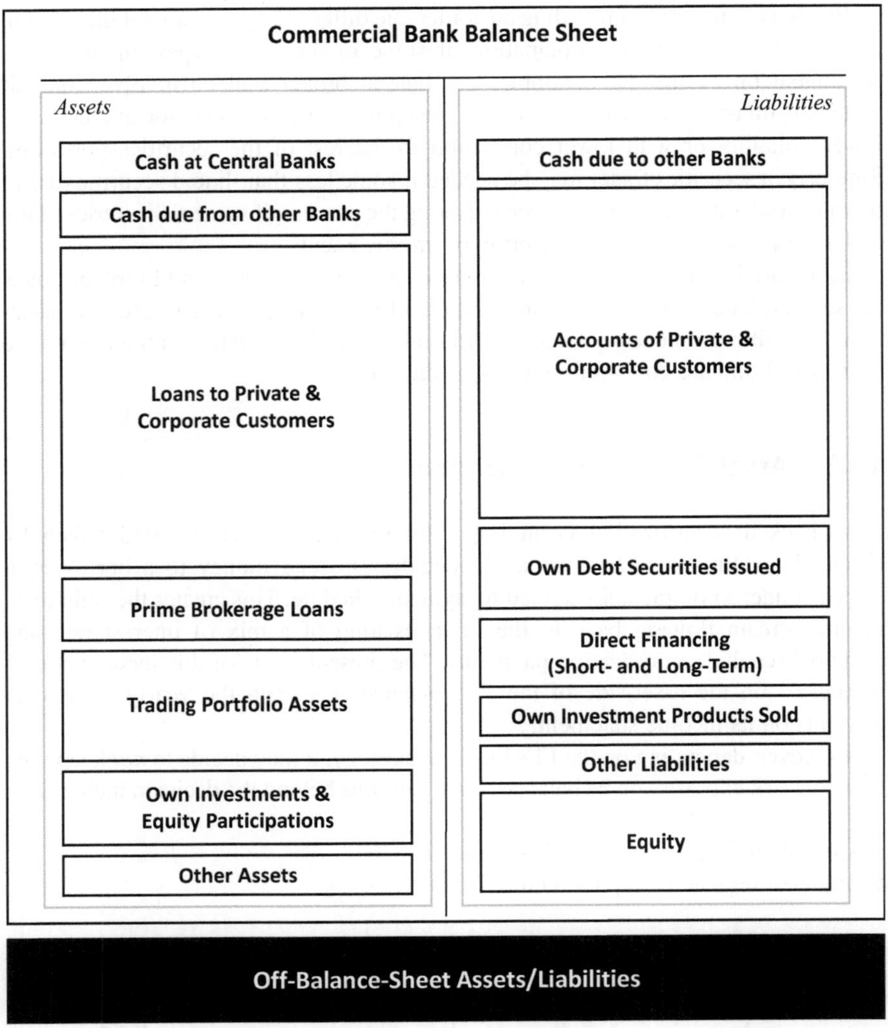

Fig. 14.5 Typical Commercial Bank Assets/Liabilities view

view, there can be gained a useful classification of assets and liabilities in terms of their effective tenors and rates of return (contractually agreed or implicit).

For example, a loan with set maturity date and fixed interest rate can be classified as belonging to a group "fixed tenor & rate asset positions". Any asset-side position with fixed tenor and constant agreed or effective nominal rate of return can be allocated to the same group. A perpetually revolving lending facility with fixed or variable interest rate can be allocated to a different group, "variable tenor or rate asset positions". Any asset having either or both of tenor and effective yearly rate of return variable (or unspecified) can be similarly allocated to that group.

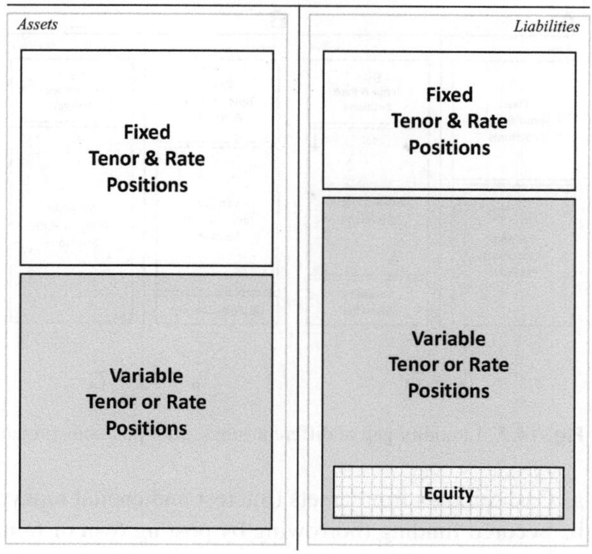

Fig. 14.6 Fixed & Variable Assets/Liabilities view of Commercial Bank

Repeating this exercise on the liability side, a "fixed & variable" view of assets and liabilities as per Fig. 14.6 is obtained.

Please note the relative size of the "fixed vs. variable" groups on both sides. Apart from the obvious "stickiness" of equity, the way to interpret this figure is that large asset groups (e.g. those corresponding to mortgages, corporate loans, and infrastructure loans) tend to have fixed (typically long) tenors and contractually agreed nominal rates. On the other hand, customer deposit and custody accounts (typically a major part of liabilities in banks other than old-type investment banks) have unpredictable tenors.

An assets/liabilities view (including also off-balance-sheet items) is a static one, a snapshot, so to speak, of the financial position of a bank at a given point in time. Changes in this position in between snapshots are, of course, found through the income statement view. However, it is possible to also create another dynamic view of financial position, starting from the balance sheet itself. This can be gleaned at any reference time, by asking "what is the probable evolution of assets and liabilities from now and with a given time horizon, T_h" ?. The answer produces an effective "liquidity position" view, as it involves a projection of **liquidity** flows in and out of assets and liabilities. Projecting these liquidity flows uncovers probable liquidity surpluses or shortfalls, as depicted in Fig. 14.7. The time horizon, T_h is arbitrary—it can be hours, days, months, or longer.

At any given time, the bank will project a liquidity surplus or shortfall—sometimes large. As an example, adverse macroeconomic or political situations may cause an exodus of funds from savings and retirement accounts and also cause long-term bank debt holders to call in their investments. The bank cannot do much to prevent such outflows on the liabilities side. Its possibilities to cover them are through:

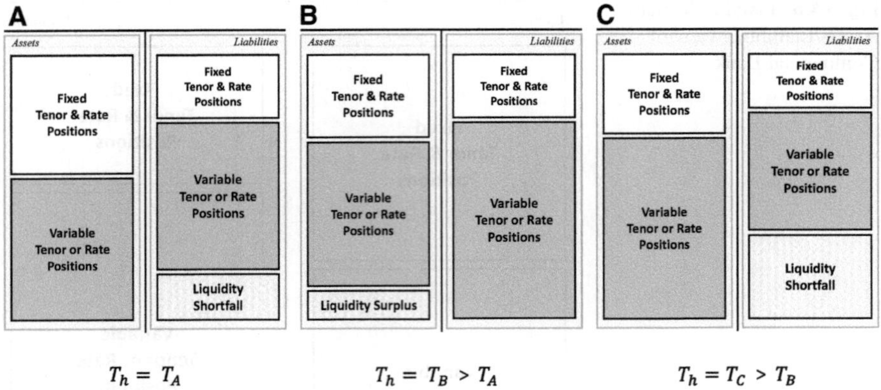

Fig. 14.7 Liquidity gap at different times, with positions projected at horizon T_h

a. Cash inflows from assets (interest and capital repayments)
b. Secured funding (borrowing by posting own or re-usable assets[6] as collateral)
c. Issuing new debt securities or drawing down credit facilities (tapping the money markets)
d. Issuing new equity

However, issuance of new debt or equity is not a near-short-term activity, nor can it be planned long in advance unless it is meant to implement a strategic plan.

Trying to equilibrate liquidity flows on both sides of the balance sheet at different time horizons[7] is a fundamental task of asset/liability management (ALM) [12–14]. The mismatch of liquidity flows in and out of existing assets and liabilities, considering a given time horizon, is termed the "**liquidity gap**"[8] of the bank at said horizon. ALM activities to manage this gap lead to the existence of the "direct financing (short- and long-term)" item in Fig. 14.5, depicted on the liabilities side of the balance sheet to correspond to the more typical case of a liquidity shortfall.

Liquidity gap risk is, as already mentioned, inherent in the banking business. It is primarily due to the longer tenor of (primarily lending-based) asset positions relative to that of liability ones. In the context of our asset-backed securitization discussion, the unpredictability of said liquidity gap may be one reason for a bank to seek to remove some asset classes, especially long-tenor lending positions, from its balance sheet.

[6] Please note that material asset classes, such as mortgages and corporate loans, may be by law ineligible as collateral. Drawing funds against *assignment of receivables* from said asset classes may be possible, though.

[7] Regulators typically use the term "liquidity" for shorter and "funding" for longer time-horizons. The cash inflow and outflow projections follow the same principles in both cases but may differ in algorithmic details.

[8] Also called "structural liquidity gap", when both on- and off-balance-sheet positions are taken into account.

Regulatory capital requirements, on the other hand, are an important obligation imposed through prudential regulation. In effect they oblige all banks to have always available (i.e. not otherwise committed or encumbered) capital of an amount estimated to cover probable adverse developments in their own business or in the financial markets as a whole.

This can be considered as a sort of self-insurance capital, imposed on every bank, as a way of ensuring that it behaves as a "prudent person of business" [15] would. The precise way to calculate said regulatory capital is jurisdiction- and bank-specific.[9] In all generality, it entails multiplying each asset-size position in their balance sheet by a weighting factor, depending on the assumed credit or market risks of similar positions, as prescribed by regulators. For example, each credit exposure CE_i is multiplied by a credit-position-specific "risk weight" W_i. This way, the original asset position gets transformed into a "**risk-weighted-asset**" (RWA_i) amount.

$$\mathrm{RWA}_i = W_i \cdot CE_i$$

Summing all credit RWAs across the asset side of the balance sheet results in the (credit risk) regulatory capital requirement for the bank, through a formula involving yet another set of jurisdiction- and bank-specific parameters[10] K [16, 17]:

$$[\text{Regulatory Capital}]^{\text{Credit Risk}} = K \cdot \sum_i \mathrm{RWA}_i$$

This is capital that the bank must have readily available (i.e. cannot commit it to working assets, hence cannot employ it to generate financial returns) as per regulation. The higher the credit risk of its asset positions, the higher its regulatory capital obligation.

Apart from creating a profitability barrier, regulatory capital is also used by analysts to gauge the "quality" of a bank's financial results. For example, "return on risk-weighted-assets"[11]:

$$\mathrm{RoRWA} = \frac{\text{Profit}}{\sum_i \mathrm{RWA}_i}$$

is one [18] of several profitability metrics regularly tracked by analysts as a way to rank relative performance of banks, cf. Fig. 14.8. Such risk-adjusted performance metrics are meant to answer the question: "How big were the risks that a bank assumed in order to generate its profits?" For the same level of profits, the market generally penalizes the equity of banks that took excessive risks (relative to their

[9] Cf. [16] for banks subject to the Basel Committee of Banking Supervision Framework ("Basel Framework").

[10] E.g., in Switzerland regulatory capital requirements tend to be more onerous that those by application of the Basel Framework—this is referred to euphemistically as "Swiss finish".

[11] Or "Return on Risk Adjusted Capital" (RoRAC [18]).

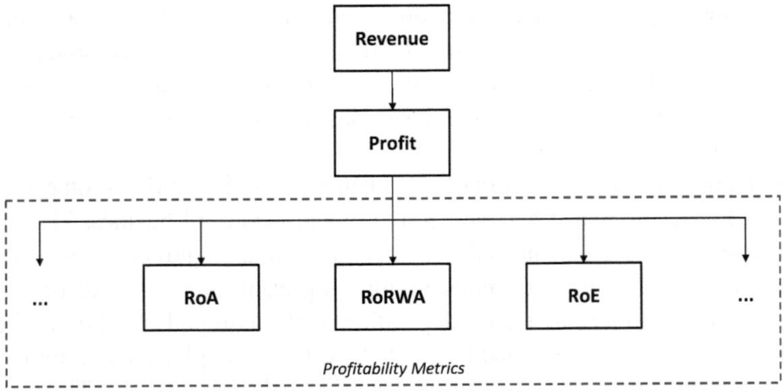

Fig. 14.8 RoRWA is one of the prevailing profitability metrics in Banking

peers) to generate them. Still more risk-adjusted metrics (e.g., "risk-adjusted capital ratio" [19]) involve reference to a bank's RWAs. The logic of regulators and equity analysts alike is the same: The higher a bank's RWAs, the higher the probability that its financial position may be severely impacted if systemic or idiosyncratic risks materialize.

Again, in the context of asset-backed securitization, asset classes contributing relatively high levels of RWAs to a credit institution's regulatory capital calculation may trigger a decision to transfer said assets off its balance sheet. Once the decision has been taken, there are two alternative ways to implement it:

1. Outright sale of assets
2. Asset Securitization

Both have their own merits and risks, but (assuming that the circumstances are not those of a forced sale) Securitization can be the best way as it still allows the FI to keep generating income through these positions in the future. The word "securitization" itself means in effect "transformation into fungible [debt] securities". It is "transformation", in the sense of it being a process creating a new asset class "B" from a pre-existing one "A"[12] and, by doing so, **transforming** the original risk/return profile of A into several distinct ones in B.

The starting point in the process is an analysis of the risk/return profile of the original asset class. In terms of returns, the exact type of assets (mortgages, car loans, corporate real estate loans, shipping or aircraft loans, trade finance positions, etc.) is not of importance; for the purposes of the securitization logic, item "assets" are abstracted by their cash flow schedules. Similarly, only the projected probability distributions of risk statistics are of importance. The only assumption is that the present value of said cash flows, under different scenarios of evolution of business risk metrics and accompanying costs of capital, is positive.

[12]Or several pre-existing classes, cf. subsequent paragraphs.

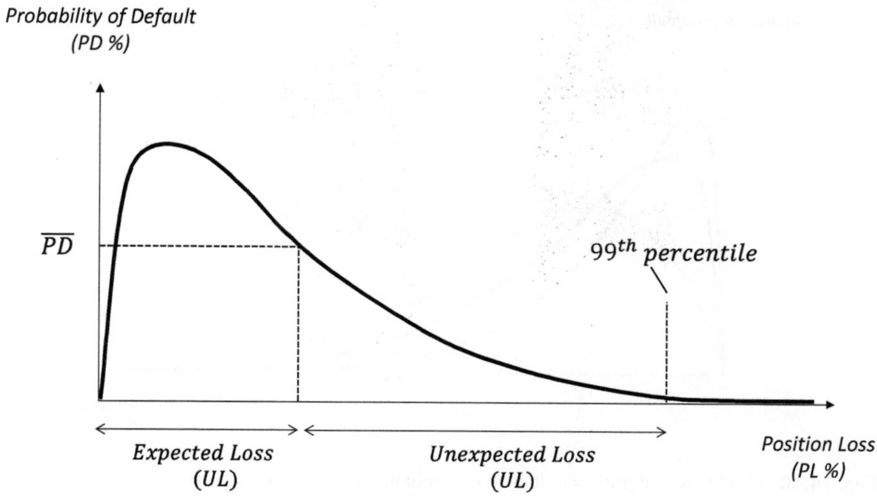

Fig. 14.9 Typical probability of default (PD) distribution for a credit risk position

To be more specific on the securitization logic, please consider the probability of default distribution (PD) of a single credit position, which typically has a form as depicted in Fig. 14.9.

This is qualitatively the statistics that credit risk underwriters must have arrived at before the credit institution (CI) granted the credit to the borrower in the first place. It is based on the underwriting experience (the historical profile of loss statistics) of the CI across many similar credit positions.

Once the credit is granted, the CI immediately starts tracking repayments and updating risk metrics of the borrower. Repayment arrears (indicating potential "non-performing loans" [NPLs]) or significant deterioration in the value of collaterals or of borrowers" general financial condition may affect the projected loss statistics of the entire risk asset class. Changes in the general market environment will cause changes in the actual statistics ("credit risk migrations" in industry parlance), qualitatively shown in Fig. 14.10.

Every single asset is thus represented by its remaining cash flows and actualized risk statistics, which allow to quantify the probability of its returning a positive net present value (NPV) to the CI under different market conditions. Of course, this NPV is realized only in the future (sometimes after decades, as in the case of mortgages)—which creates precisely the credit risk for the CI. The value proposition of asset-backed securitization is that a part of this value can be monetized immediately, while the credit risk is transferred to willing investors. This is achieved by "bundling" many such assets together to create more mathematically predictable risk and return distributions (as per the law of large numbers) and then transforming this portfolio (the "bundle") into fungible securities offered to the public markets. The algorithmic process hinges on identifying "risk tranches" in the portfolio, whereby the average probability of default and the resulting aggregate losses per "tranche"

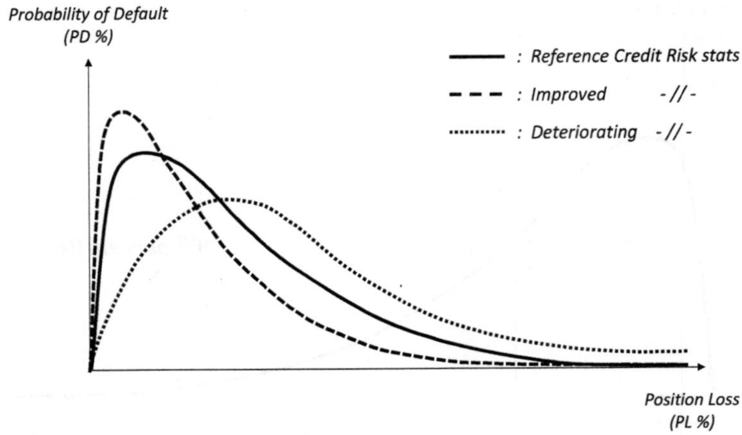

Fig. 14.10 Credit risk migration influence on probability of default statistics

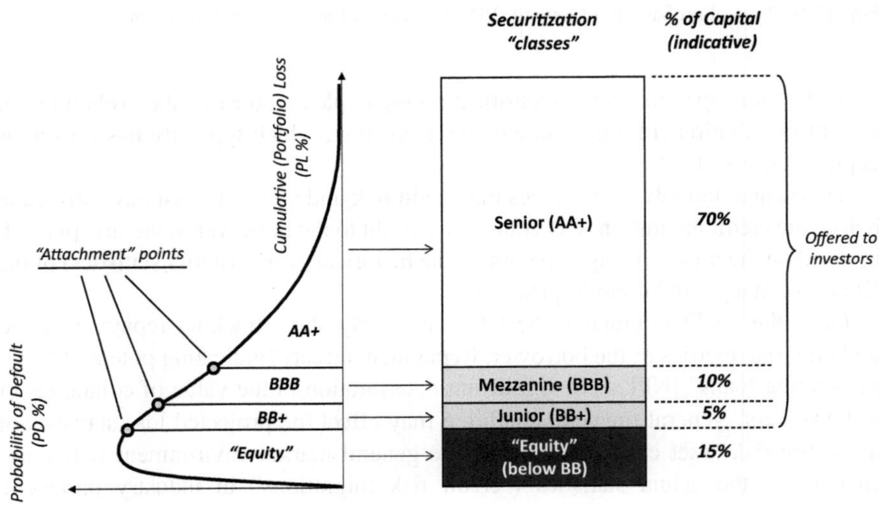

Fig. 14.11 From portfolio PD statistics to securitization structure ("classes" or "tranches", indicative)

can be mapped[13] to a cascading risk-rating "structure", as that in Fig. 14.11. The "risk tranches" thus map[14] onto candidate "risk classes" [21], which can then be issued as distinct classes of interest-bearing securities. The securitization structure of

[13]Following the excellent conceptual mapping put forth in [20], a standard reference on ABS.

[14]The algorithmic logic needs to be advised by expert judgment, reasonableness checks, sensitivity assessments, and eventual need for added credit mitigants (e.g. overcollateralization and credit insurance) to avoid model risk. For a very good discussion on how individual asset risk deterioration can impact the stability of ratings of entire containing tranches (as evidenced by an analysis on the effective credit risk of mortgage-backed securities in the aftermath of the 2008 Global Financial Crisis) consult [21].

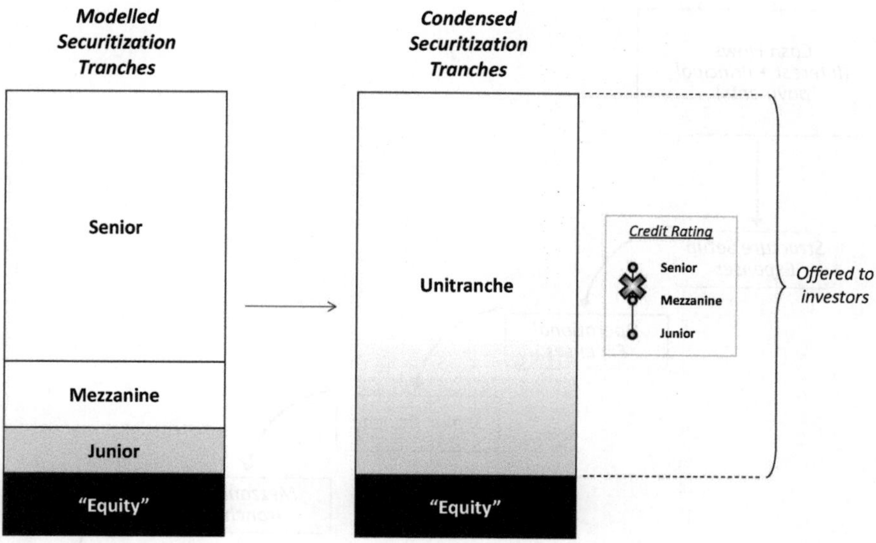

Fig. 14.12 "Unitranche" Securitization Structure

Fig. 14.11 is only indicative, as neither the number of tranches nor their designation is standardized. The word "Mezzanine" (from the Italian "mezzanino", originally used in architecture to mean an intermediate floor in a building [22]—note the "structure" metaphor) is typically used in finance to denote an asset class representing claims on property rights of intermediate priority [23, 24] between the most senior and the most junior levels in a claims hierarchy. A securitization structure above the highest-risk "Equity" class may have more classes (e.g. five; which may be denoted—in decreasing priority of claims—as "Super Senior", "Senior", "Mezzanine", "Subordinated", "Junior") or even only a single one ("Unitranche" [25], cf. Fig. 14.12).

The precise structure (number of tranches, "attachment" points, naming of securitization classes) is at the discretion of economic agents such as the structurer and the underwriter. The seniority level of a tranche in the structure defines, among other things, its sequence in the so-called "securitization waterfall". As depicted in Fig. 14.13, if one were to imagine the periodic cash flows from the assets underlying the asset-backed securities[15] (ABS) as water flows from a higher receptacle into a series of progressively lower terraces, then the sequence of cash allocation into tranches resembles the path of water overflowing terraces—hence the "waterfall" metaphor. First in line are expenses associated with the consistency of the structure (originator fees, valuation agent fees, credit insurance provider premia, legal and

[15]Please note that we are considering only **cash-based** and not **synthetic** asset-backed securitization [26, 27], which involves creating the same risk/return profile tranches using only credit derivatives or guarantees.

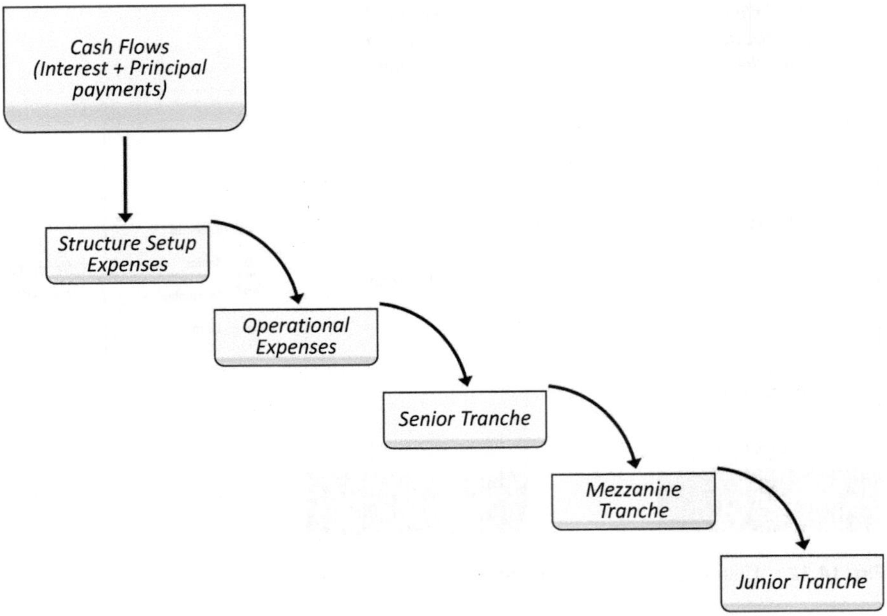

Fig. 14.13 "Securitization waterfall" (indicative)

auditor fees, etc.); once those have been covered, operational expenses (custodian fees, paying agent fees, tax/accounting agents' fees, etc.) follow; the remaining funds go sequentially into the interest/amortization pool of the highest seniority tranche, then into the pool of each lower-seniority tranche one by one.

As already mentioned, the exact type of securitized assets is not of importance. Any asset class with scheduled cash inflows/outflows and associated probabilities of default that can be robustly modelled can be used to issue ABS. The precise kind of obligations behind said inflows/outflows only defines ABS subtypes. Hence, there are ABS with:

i. Credit card receivables [28]
ii. Trade receivables [29]
iii. Mortgages (residential/commercial [30, 31])
iv. Car loans and leases [32]
v. Generic corporate loans [33]
vi. Warehouse loans [34]
vii. Student loans [35]
viii. Shipping loans [36]
ix. Marine container loans [37]
x. Aircraft leases [38]
xi. Intellectual property rights and royalties [39, 40]
xii. Litigation loans [41]

xiii. Arbitration loans [42]
xiv. Structured settlements [43, 44]

as underlyings (the above list is not exhaustive). From a financial modelling perspective, it is also possible to create mixed-asset-class ABS. If the CI can properly manage the operational risks of multi-asset-class ABS construction, then it can indeed create securities with bespoke risk-return characteristics, owing to the diversification of the underlying portfolio. That is, the CI can take advantage of correlation effects (positive or negative) among different asset classes, to create ABS with as close a risk-return profile to what its target ABS investor group may require. However, the inherent complexity of the end-to-end process (cf. Fig. 14.11) means that securitizations tend to be asset-class-specific.

A further note is in order regarding the use of special purpose vehicles (SPVs) [45, 46] in asset-backed securitization. An issue when transferring assets out of a CI's balance sheet to the ownership of another party is whether or not the CI ends up legally retaining effective ownership of the assets. For example, there are situations where the CI transfers assets under a "with recourse" clause. This means that the CI provides a guarantee that if the structured securities fail to return the interest and capital repayment streams promised to investors, then the CI will compensate the difference. This guarantee can be argued to create a continuing nexus with the CI's own balance sheet and can support a finding in court that the transfer of assets was not a "**true sale**". One serious repercussion of continuing effective ownership is that in case of insolvency (or, worst, bankruptcy) of the CI, these assets may be included in the pool of assets available for distribution to creditors—in which case the entire securitization structure fails. There are other potential issues (e.g. failure of the asset-receiving party to properly manage them, with the result that *it*, not the CI, ends up insolvent) that have been recognized early in the evolution of the ABS industry. Thus, an express requirement in securitization is that the CI and the receiving party should be proven to be "**bankruptcy remote**". The typical answer to this requirement has been to create a special purpose vehicle (or a structure of SPVs, cf. below) to transfer the title to the securitization underlyings to. By creating a distinct, purpose-bound, legal entity, with separate ownership structure and decision-making agents, the assets originator can establish the legal preconditions of a "true sale" securitization. It is this SPV that formally buys the assets from the originating CI and then issues the ABS, manages the cashflows of the collateral pool, pays the ongoing structuring and operational expenses, etc. (cf. Fig. 14.14).

In order to further harden the facts helping to establish bankruptcy-remoteness, it is also possible to add a trust[16] in the ownership structure receiving the assets. In such a constellation, the SPV transfers the title to the underlyings onto the trust and

[16] Or any other legal arrangement or legal entity structure that effectively separates the legal and beneficial ownership of, or at least the control and economic interest on, ring-fenced assets. Examples of such legal entities would be foundation types of some jurisdictions, e.g. the Dutch Private Foundation ("*Stichting*"; for a brief overview, please consult [47].

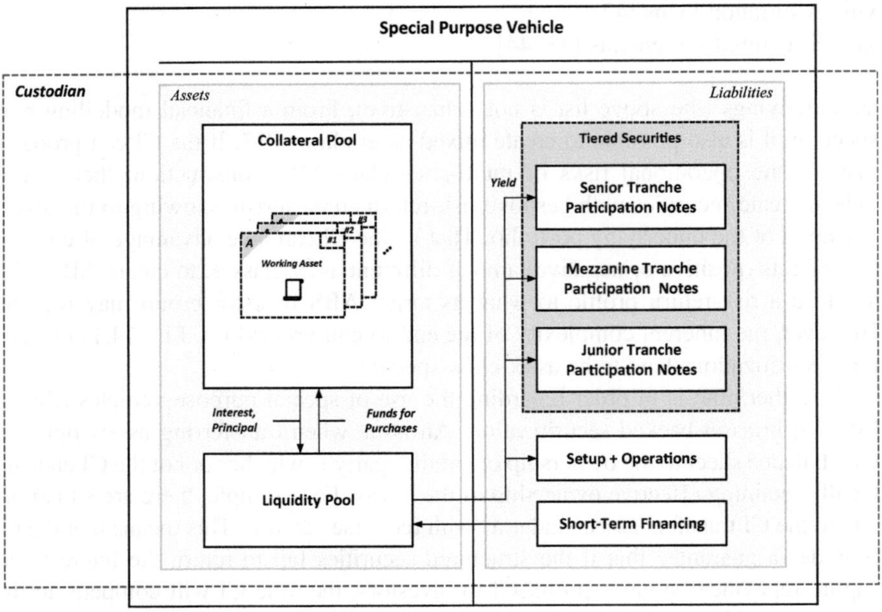

Fig. 14.14 Indicative balance sheet of a single SPV used for securitization

retains only the beneficial ownership. The trustee (typically a trust company) creates a second degree of ownership remoteness,[17] while the economic outcomes of the structure (cashflow and asset management to the benefit of the ABS investors) remain the same. The typical constellation of economic agents in this securitization value chain is as depicted in Fig. 14.15.

Mixing legal entities and trusts is not the only degree of freedom pursued in securitization constellations. For example, using a "protected cell company" as the top-most asset-receiving legal entity, it is possible to create variable-capital investment vehicles containing quite complex securitization structures. A "protected cell company" (PCC [51–53], also "segregated portfolio company" [54] in some jurisdictions) is a legal entity containing many different "cells", each having its own separate balance sheet and (potentially) managing its own cash flows. The precise allocation of powers and liabilities among the "core" (i.e. the PCC) and its "cells" is jurisdiction[18]-specific.

[17] There are still more possible securitization constellations involving a Trust to achieve the same effect, e.g. the trust being the sole or majority shareholder of the SPV, and others. The constellation mentioned in the main text is only indicative of the broad spectrum of roles that trusts and trustees assume in asset-backed securitization. For further references, please consult [48] and industry participants' publications, e.g. [49, 50]

[18] As of the time of writing, jurisdictions offering incorporation of Protected Cell Companies include: Anguilla, Bahrain, Belize, Bermuda, British Virgin Islands, Cayman Islands, Gibraltar, Guernsey, Isle of Man, Jersey, Malaysia (Labuan), Liechtenstein, Malta, Mauritius, Qatar, United Arab Emirates (only Abu Dhabi, Dubai, and Ras al Khaimah), UK, and USA (e.g. Delaware).

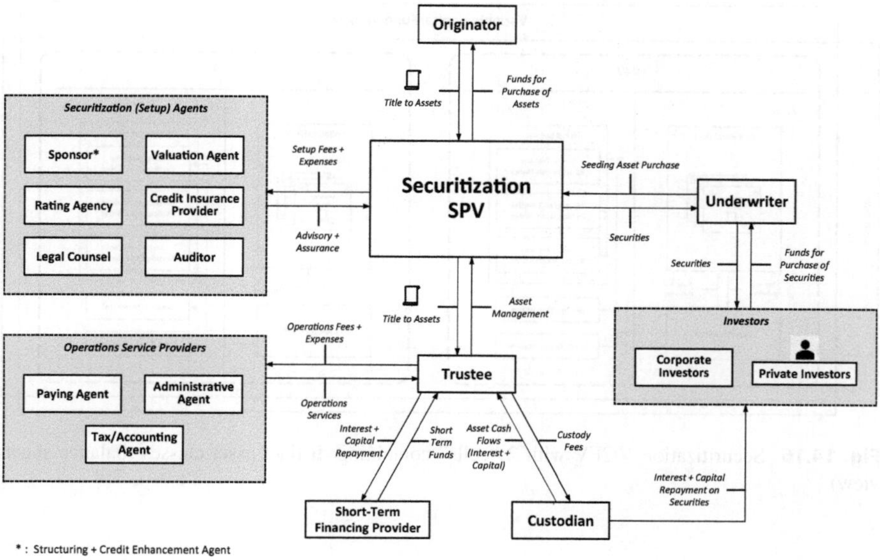

Fig. 14.15 Typical economic agent constellation in securitization (no cascading SPVs)

Using a PCC, different asset classes (or assets of the same class but of different vintages) can be securitized by bundling the underlyings into different cells. This allows reducing the total securitization costs (by setting up a single SPV and by engaging the same structuring and administrative agents across asset classes) while retaining the same level of control over securities issuance and over collateral and cash-flow management. It is also possible to create different trust structures, or at least engage different trustees per cell, as long as the legal repercussions in terms of asset ownership and assumed liabilities are clear and accepted. The "variable capital fund vehicle" depicted in Fig. 14.16 is precisely such a PCC used to issue ABS on different asset classes "A" and "B", each held in the collateral pool of one of two distinct cells, #s 1 and 2. This example assumes a single custodian holding all collateral and liquidity pools, to demonstrate the potential for cost minimization (one custody fee paid by the PCC to cover all asset and liquidity positions, and similarly, one single-agent fee per each type of structure setup or operational service used).

Still another degree of freedom when designing securitizations is afforded by the novel legal entity type of "variable capital company" (VCC [55, 56]). This is still a body corporate acting as an umbrella structure of cells; however, each of the latter may now be a separate SPV itself (cf. Fig. 14.17). Each cell may have different investment objectives, a distinct legal personality to the VCC and to any other cell, and—depending on the jurisdiction—may have to be individually registered (and licensed) separately from the VCC itself. The assets and liabilities of each cell are explicitly owned by no other cell under the VCC. Importantly, there are

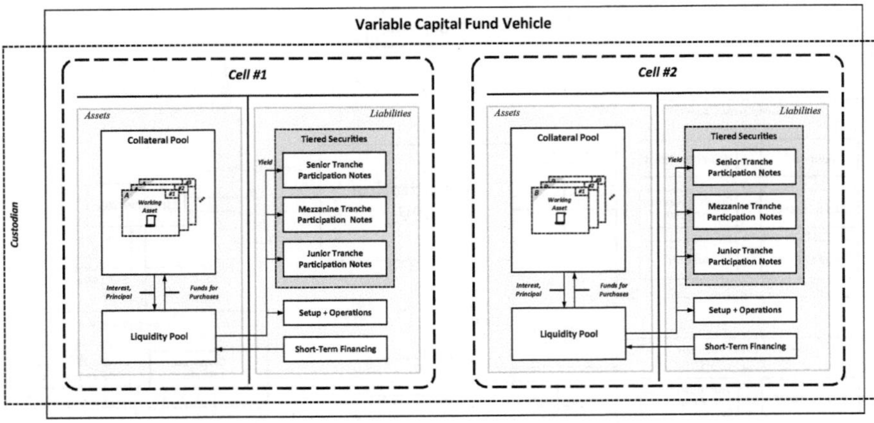

Fig. 14.16 Securitization VCFV with 2 "cells" containing distinct asset classes (balance sheets view)

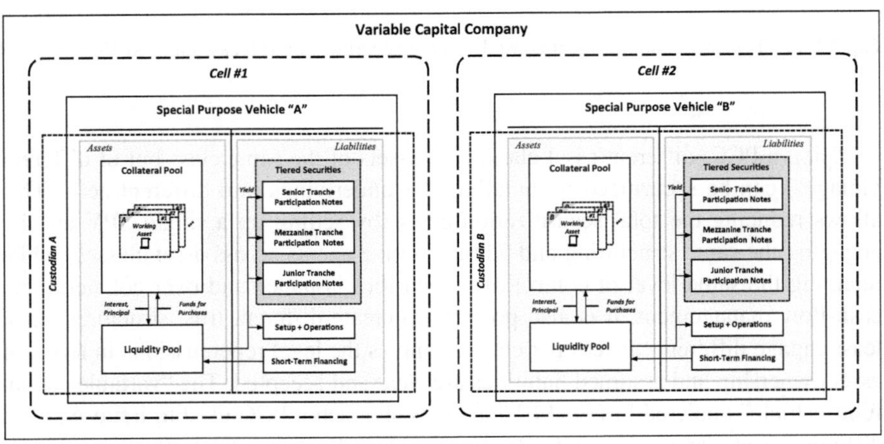

Fig. 14.17 Securitization Variable Capital Company with 2 "cells", each being a separate SPV (balance sheets view)

requirements around the registration and location of corporate directors at the VCC level and concomitant tax and accounting obligations (which may vary per cell). As long as these requirements are met in the aggregate, each constituent cell can pursue its business activities independently from any other.

As in the PCC case, there exists cost optimization potential in terms of having a single VCC-wide executive board and of pooling service providers (even at the cell level, e.g. administrators, fund managers, custodian, auditor, and compliance officer, shared across some cells but not others). However, there may be additional costs in exceptional circumstances (e.g. each cell's SPV may have to be subject to separate

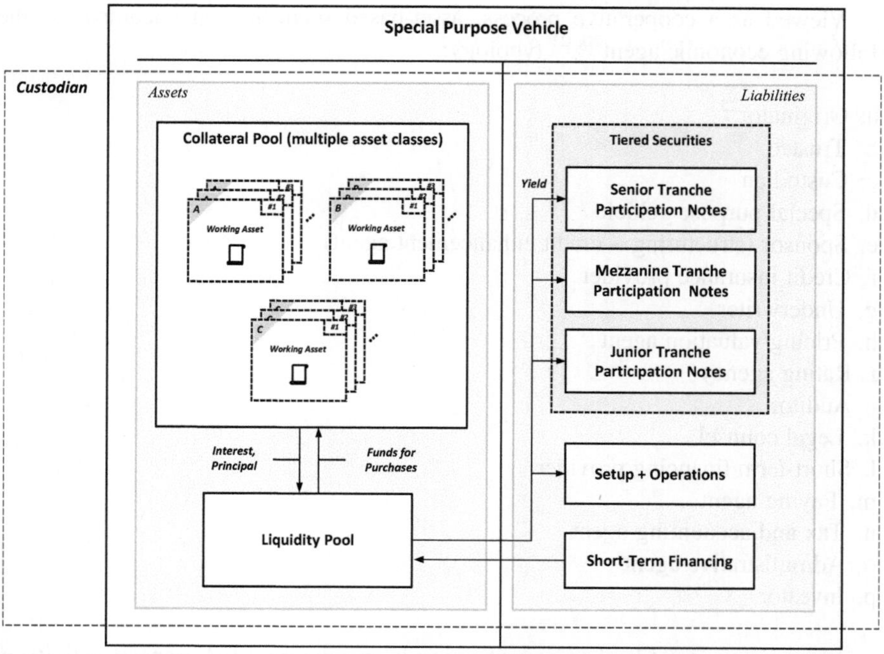

Fig. 14.18 Multiple asset class securitization structure under a single SPV (balance sheet view)

insolvency proceedings, and in any case it will not be able to invoke liquidity support by the balance sheet of any other cell). This legal entity type can reproduce a large number of traditional investment structures (such as the "master-feeder" [57] constellation in the hedge-fund world) and satisfy broad funds administration needs (e.g. effective ring-fencing of assets with distinct legal and beneficial ownership allocations within family offices [58]); however, its relative merits in the ABS case can be asset-type and jurisdiction[19]-dependent.

For the sake of completeness, in the theoretically possible case of a CI being indeed able to manage the operational risks of multi-asset-class ABS construction, a simple constellation of assets and liabilities under an SPV could be as depicted in Fig. 14.18.

[19] As of the time of writing only a few jurisdictions provide for incorporation of variable capital companies. Singapore was first (cf. "Variable Capital Companies Act 2018" [59] and accompanying regulations [60]), followed by Mauritius (cf. "Variable Capital Companies Act 2022" [61]). However, still more recognize the validity of transactions involving VCC's (incorporated elsewhere) in their legal frameworks.

Viewed as a cooperative process, asset-based securitization encompasses the following economic agent[20, 21] typology:

a. Originator[22]
b. Trustee
c. Custodian
d. Special purpose vehicle
e. Sponsor (structuring + credit enhancement agent)
f. Credit insurance provider
g. Underwriter
h. Pricing/valuation agent
i. Rating agency
j. Auditor
k. Legal counsel
l. Short-term financing provider
m. Paying agent
n. Tax and accounting agent
o. Administrative agent
p. Investor

In summary, asset-backed securitization is an important risk-transfer activity in traditional finance. Any asset class representing rights to a predictable income stream can be securitized (i.e. "transformed into fungible [debt] securities" termed asset-backed securities, ABS) and offered in the public securities markets to investors. The latter can purchase ABS of different risk ratings and expect a payback in terms of interest rate and principal (capital) amortization repayments. Issuing ABS involves many different economic agents cooperating to create the necessary legal, organizational, and operational setup.

14.3 Private Debt Markets

Private debt (or private credit [64]) is a relatively recent asset class in traditional finance, denoting the provision of loans directly (i.e. without the intermediation of banks) to either privates or corporates. Types of institutional[23] non-bank lenders include [65, 66]:

[20] Please note that we did not include the public securities registrar (or depository) whereto ABS are notified as this is typically under the auspices of the relevant jurisdiction's regulator (e.g. SEC in the USA [62], ESMA in the EU [63], etc.).

[21] As mentioned before, we are considering only cash-based and not also synthetic ABS.

[22] The "originator of assets", that is, the CI.

[23] Private persons are of course possible as lenders, but the market depth is obviously due to the involvement of institutional investors.

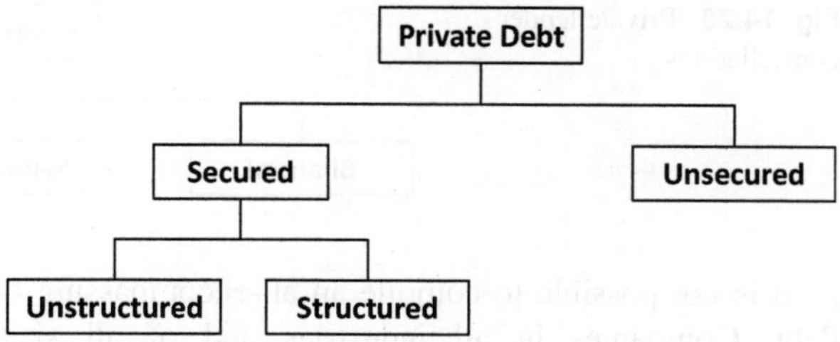

Fig. 14.19 Private Debt and collateral modalities

- Asset managers
- Insurance companies
- Pension funds
- College endowments
- Family offices
- Foundations
- SPVs

There are reasons why this financing activity outside the banking system can be interesting to both lenders and borrowers. On the lender side, first, the economic agent types in the above list do not have to obey the same onerous regulatory capital requirements as banks[24] do (cf. discussion in the previous section); hence, their costs of capital and profitability metrics tend to be more favourable. Second, they tend to have sources of capital with longer average maturities, which allows them to take longer risks if the expected returns justify[25] them. Third, the effective interest rates charged in private debt tend to be relatively high, to compensate for the concentrated counterparty credit risk. On the borrower side, this can be a compelling source of financing in both normal and exceptional situations [65], for example, when they are in distressed circumstances, already have high levels of debt, or need liquidity faster than the expected bank-side credit approval time scales.

As in bank-originated credit, the terms of private debt financings can vary broadly. Despite this being a still-evolving market, one can already discern a typology in terms of collateralization and lender constellations. As depicted in Fig. 14.19, the market effectively replicates the established banking categories.

This is to be expected, as institutional investors already have in-house (or can procure through specialized service providers) many of the same lending-related capabilities—such as counterparty due diligence, collateral due diligence, position risk management, investment structuring, asset portfolio management, etc.—that banks deploy. Similarly, private debt investors can also pool resources (funds and capabilities [67, 68]), thus replicating the "syndicated" and "intermediated" financing categories of the banking world (cf. Fig. 14.20).

[24] Some, such as insurance companies and pension funds, do have relevant regulatory obligations but currently not of the same level as that of the Banking sector.

[25] This feature prompts private debt to be categorized under "alternative investments" in the current trade literature.

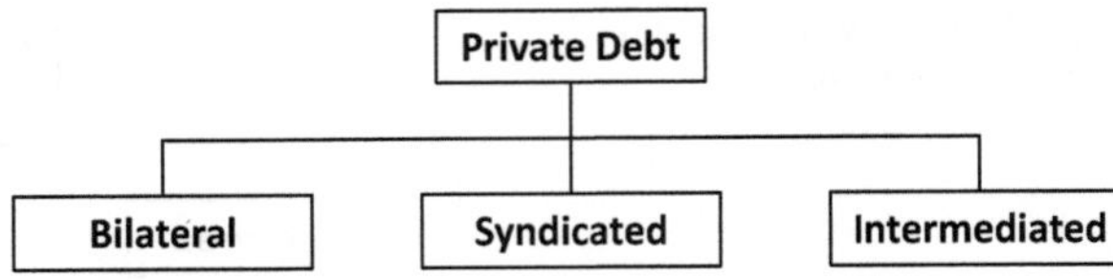

Fig. 14.20 Private lender constellations

It is not possible to compile an all-encompassing borrower typology in private debt. Companies in all industries and of all sizes can find themselves in circumstances where bank-originated lending is either too difficult to arrange or comes with too onerous terms.

Importantly, both sides in private debt transactions are responsible for their own due diligence and contractual arrangements. There are no standardized risk management frameworks, nor recognized (and expected) contractual forms in this business. Apart from commercial law (and possibly investment law and regulation, in the case of "intermediated" private debt), there exist no fine-granular obligations to follow, such as those imposed on banks under the Basel Framework. Simply put, both sides are free to set their own terms and to agree on their own bespoke contractual clauses and covenants, as long as the contract law of their jurisdiction is complied with. How involved this due diligence task can become is perhaps evident by the (non-exhaustive) list of aspects that must ideally be addressed by "prudent people of business", as presented in Table 14.2. Traditional bank-intermediated finance has abstracted most of these aspects, first by codifying terms and industry practices and second by aligning pre-contractual, contractual and post-contractual customer interactions with applicable laws and regulations. An investor in corporate bonds knows a bond's credit risk rating, where to find the credit spread in a bond's term sheet, what the payment schedule will be, whether a bond is callable or not, and which covenants (positive and negative) the issuer accepted. The investor can thus compare among issuers and issues, as this information is published—and made available in the public domain by the intermediating banks themselves. Theirs is an informed investment decision.

Such standardization (and, by extension, transparency) does not exist in private debt markets. All pathologies which traditional finance regulators have historically sought to contain (be it information asymmetries; fraudulent misrepresentation; overleveraging; predatory lending; investment non-suitability; generally deficient internal controls—or simply non-fulfilment of "fit-and-proper" criteria) can, and most probably will, manifest themselves in private markets.

14.4 Aave

Aave [1] is an established blockchain-based token ecosystem functioning as a decentralized non-custodian money market [69]. We will explain the facts underlying each of these aspects in due course; however, for the time being, it is an important task to list the business cases implemented by Aave protocols. In Aave, economic agents can:

Table 14.2 Private debt due diligence checklist (non-exhaustive)

Counterparty credit risk	Investment credit risk	Investment market risk	Investment liquidity risk	Contractual/ legal risk	Expenses/fees structure	Tax obligations
Legal form	Property rights structure	Market fundamentals	Market depth	Property rights robustness	Acquisition expenses/ fees	Withholding tax profile
Corp. structure	Property rights location	Issuer fundamentals	Lockdown period	Source property rights structure	Divestment expenses/ fees	Capital gains tax profile
Key persons/ organization	Underlying value chain transparency	Probable risk/ return profile	Liquidation waiting period	Source property rights location	Performance fees/ commissions	Multiple tax jurisdictions involved
Authorized signatories	Valuation	Market risk sources transparency	Liquidation cooldown period	Transferred property rights structure	Contingent fees/ penalties	Tax reporting obligations/ dependencies
Asset/ services location(s)	Property right encumbrances	Value chain risk	Custodian(s) policies	Transferred property rights location	Tax agent fees/ commissions	Tax payment agent (s) involved
Counterparty financials	Rights/claims seniority	Volatility profile	Payment agent(s)	Conditions/ warranties	3rd party agent fees	Tax records residency
Credit history	Credit enhancements (collateral/risk insurance/ subordination)	Interest rate risk	Investment admissibility as collateral towards third parties	3rd party rights/powers/ duties	Administrative (custodian(s), etc.) Running fee structure	Imputed statutory/ regulatory obligations
Guarantors	Repayment schedule	Currency risk	Convertibility risk	Governing Law	Ad hoc reporting fees	Impact on own cost-of-capital
Other third parties	Maturity profile	Asset/rights convertibility	Jurisdiction risk	Seat of arbitration	Imputed FX fees	Impact on own tax residency
Corporate events risk	Structuring risks	Reinvestment risk	Marketplace risk	Claims enforceability	Collateral variance fees	Deferred tax recognition

(A) Deposit tokens into Aave to gain interest passively, similarly to sight deposits at banks.
(B) Borrow tokens from Aave to either invest them within Aave, swap them in Centralized/Decentralized Exchanges, or simply move them to own wallets. Borrowing incurs interest charges. Borrowers must post collateral (which they either own or "buy"), in the form of already deposited tokens.
(C) Lend tokens to third parties seeking to finance off-chain assets.
(D) Buy tokens at a discount, as collateral of debt positions which must be liquidated.
(E) Buy Aave's own Stablecoin to either invest within Aave, swap for other assets in Centralized/Decentralized Exchanges, or simply move it to own wallets.
(F) Sell Aave's own Stablecoin back to Aave at par.

The reason for having gone, in previous sections, into some detail about Lombard lending and private debt is that those paradigms are in effect the traditional finance equivalents of the combined business use cases (A)–(B) and (E)–(F) above. Similarly, asset-backed securitization and private debt are replicated through (C), whereas (D) is the mechanism enabling execution of traditional credit risk control tasks (such as collateral management and margin calls) in a decentralized finance setting. We will retrace the content of those previous sections in due course, when juxtaposing the details of Aave transactional pathways. This way, established activities of traditional money-markets will be shown to have their direct analogues in this particular token-enabled ecosystem. In the process, some operational differences between the two will also be made clear and will be explained in terms of the technical features of the underlying blockchain technology.

In the sequel, we will examine Aave through the lenses of all three design pillars (plus bonding curve design). We will uncover the granular design decisions which this blockchain project made and how they are implemented operationally in the latest iteration of its protocol, as of the time of writing.

14.5 Aave Market Design

As per the methodology introduced in Chap. 6, blockchain ecosystem market design must prescribe all possible **economic agent** types, **transactional pathways** joining them, and associated protocol **tokens** created or exchanged in the process. Aave being an established token ecosystem and having gone through several generations already, we will need to focus on a particular protocol version; we choose this to be the latest one as per the time of writing, namely Version 3.3.

Aave consists of Layer-3 ("application" layer) protocols built on the Ethereum Layer-1 ("settlement" layer) blockchain. All its artefacts (tokens, smart contracts, etc.) assume the Ethereum Virtual Machine (EVM) as runtime and can, in principle, interoperate with any other EVM-compatible protocol. This has profound implications for the economic cost of Aave transactions and will indeed help explain salient aspects of Aave ecosystem design.

In business terms, Aave is a capital marketplace for short-term liquidity and longer-term funding. As will be shown in the sequel, it is a token ecosystem replicating the Lombard lending paradigm in the traditional finance sense (*not* the repo). Following the fundamental country-level analogy of Sect. 6.1, it can be thought of as a country with citizens active as money/capital buyers and sellers—not only nationally but also internationally. That is, not only do its citizens trade the domestic money/capital market, they are also prepared to trade in international markets. They are prepared to lend, borrow, and invest with counterparties who are citizens of other countries and who want to trade only in their own national marketplaces.

In technical terms, those other marketplaces are third-party blockchain token ecosystems that guarantee compatibility of their own blockchain technical artefacts, and convertibility of their own tokens, with those used in Aave. The mechanism that enables said compatibility and convertibility attributes is the EVM. Thus, by "opening itself up" to blockchain artefacts that are guaranteed to be EVM-compatible, Aave enables its economic agents to be participants in both native and foreign transactions that are then automatically binding across ecosystem boundaries.

In short, Aave adopts the paradigm of country-level capital markets. Now, imagine a physical-world depositor resident in country A and choosing to use their funds as collateral for a loan agreed with a lender resident in another country B. The loan could be denominated in either of the two countries' currencies, or indeed in a third currency, such as USD. In the physical world, it is expected that the lender, while resident in country A, should be legally visible and capable to act also in country B before the lending transaction can be entered into. It is also expected that the terms of the loan contract should have the same meaning for both counterparties. Transferring to a token context, A and B would be Aave and a cooperating ecosystem, respectively. Hence, in order to have valid "international" transactions, Aave and the other ecosystem must have first aligned their "internal" capital markets, starting from own definitions of transaction types and acceptable terms and conditions. For example, each must first have defined the admissible asset types (i.e. crypto-tokens in the role of lending currencies or collateral) for trading locally. Then, they must define those asset types admissible for trading *across* the two markets, the corresponding valuation and convertibility conditions, etc. Such alignment is the precondition of cross-country capital market transactions, and it clearly begins with clarity in the domestic market first. Hence, the fundamental notion at the centre of Aave's use cases is that of the "market", meaning an on-chain capital market that:

a. Follows the business concepts around transaction types, and terms and conditions, as defined in the Aave Whitepaper [70].
b. Follows the exact set of technical prerequisites (e.g. usage of EVM, Oracles) as described in the Aave developer documentation [71].
c. Deploys all smart contracts as specified in the Aave developer documentation and sourced from the official Aave software repositories [72].
d. Synchronizes all software artefacts (infrastructure, smart contracts) with the software lifecycle events decided by Aave's governance [73, 74].

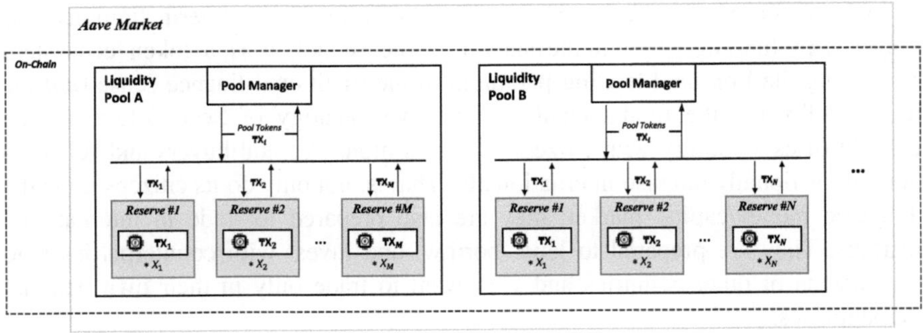

Fig. 14.21 Aave markets, liquidity pools, and reserves

e. Follows all edicts of Aave's governance, including those concerning the usage of the native governance token (AAVE [75]) and the transfer to the Aave treasury [76] of pre-specified rewards (fees, commissions) per transaction execution [77].

Aave defines its own market ("home"—or "domestic"—capital market in a country-level analogy) on the Ethereum Mainnet and accepts several other ecosystems' markets as "equivalent"[26,27] for the purposes of Aave transaction validity. Which other ecosystems to accept as equivalent, and which asset types as admissible in Aave transactions, are decisions involving the project's governance [81]. Please note that, apart from AAVE and the ERC-20 wrapped Ethereum (wETH), it is not obligatory for different markets to have total overlap of admissible token types. This is also a consequence of the fact that each cooperating ecosystem may naturally have its own native ERC-20 currency token.

As of the time of writing, there are 16 Aave markets in operation [82], three on the Ethereum Mainnet and one each on Arbitrum, Avalanche, Metis, Optimism, Polygon, etc. blockchains.

Each Aave market contains several "liquidity pools" [83] (each managed through its own smart contract, albeit all obeying the same SC template specification [84]). Underneath each liquidity pool, there are several "reserves" (each containing positions in a single token) [85]. This enables clean accounting and technical processes around liquidity and collateral management. For example, a liquidity provider may seek yield by providing funds in one token ŦX_1 and at some time in the future may become a borrower in a different token ŦX_2, declaring parts of their original ŦX_1 funds as collateral. The logical structure of market-liquidity pool-reserve immediately enables such transactions, and also facilitates operationally the application of rules and incentives prescribed by Aave governance (explained

[26] Akin to the notion of "stock market equivalence" existing in the regulatory frameworks of several traditional finance jurisdictions, e.g. the EU. Examples of application of said notion: [78, 79].

[27] For a comprehensive analysis of the legal repercussions of market equivalence in traditional financial services transactions, a useful reference is [80].

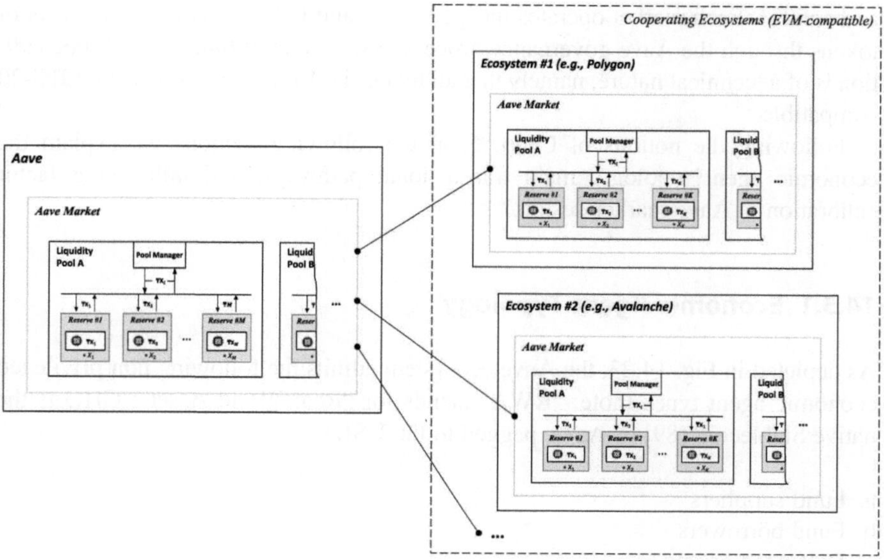

Fig. 14.22 Aave markets in cooperating ecosystems

later in the section on mechanism design). This structure is depicted graphically in Fig. 14.21.

By selecting a market, an underlying liquidity pool, and their preferred transaction token(s), Aave participants interact indirectly (through the Aave software infrastructure) with the corresponding reserve(s), to:

- Supply and withdraw funds drawing interest.
- Declare supplied funds as “collateral ready”.
- Allow other Aave participants to use the same funds as collateral.
- Borrow funds against collateral.
- Change—during the tenor of a lending transaction—the terms of their borrowing.
- Receive and immediately repay “flash loans”.
- Lend funds against collateral.

All these actions (explained in some detail later in the section on “transactional pathways”) follow the exact same rules and are implemented through the exact same smart contracts across Aave markets (cf. Fig. 14.22).

However, as already mentioned, not all token reserves exist across markets. As an example, as of the time of writing, the Polygon Aave Market [86] admits the following 21 tokens for deposits: DAI, LINK, USDC, WBTC, WETH, USDT, AAVE, WPOL, CRV, SUSHI, GHST, BAL, DPI, EURS, jEUR, EURA, MiMATIC, MaticX, wstETH, and USDC. However, the Arbitrum Aave Market [87] admits only the following 18: DAI, LINK, USDC, WBTC, WETH, USD₮0, AAVE, EURS, wstETH, MAI, rETH, LUSD, USDC, FRAX, ARB, weETH, GHO, and ezETH. Each market operates independently and is free to admit its own set of tokens through the Aave governance process [88]. The only fundamental precondition is of a technical nature, namely that all tokens in Aave reserves must be ERC-20 compatible.[28]

Following the notions of Chap. 6, in the following sections we explain the economic agent typology, main transactional pathways, and influencing factor calibration in Aave market design.

14.5.1 Economic Agent Typology

As depicted in Fig. 14.23, the Aave ecosystem admits the following non-privileged economic agent types (note: "RWA" stands for "Real World Asset"; GHO is the native Stablecoin [89] of Aave, pegged to the USD):

a. Fund suppliers
b. Fund borrowers
c. Delegated borrowers
d. Liquidators
e. RWA issuers
f. RWA investors
g. GHO investors

The privileged (i.e. governance-related) economic agents are:

h. The Aave Decentralized Autonomous Organization ("DAO") [73, 90]
i. All holders of the native tokens AAVE, stkAAVE, and aAAVE[29] as they can stake their holdings to vote for governance decisions
j. A committee of "Aave guardians" [91]
k. A set of "Stewards" [92]

There follows an explanation of the salient attributes of said agents in the context of Aave use cases:

A **Funds Supplier** is an Aave participant who deposits admissible tokens into an Aave liquidity pool. Their deposit is rewarded with a continuously compounded interest rate. They have the option to "enable" their token position as collateral for own or delegated borrowing purposes. In the latter case, they can explicitly "delegate" all or part of their borrowing base to a second Aave participant.

A **Funds Borrower** is an Aave participant who takes out a loan denominated in one of the admissible tokens of an Aave liquidity pool, paying a continuously

[28] A repercussion is that, even though Aave is built on top of the Ethereum L-1 blockchain, wrapped ETH (wETH) and not ETH is admissible in Aave reserves.

[29] Explained in detail in Sections 14.7.1.4, 14.5.3.8, and 14.7.1.1, respectively.

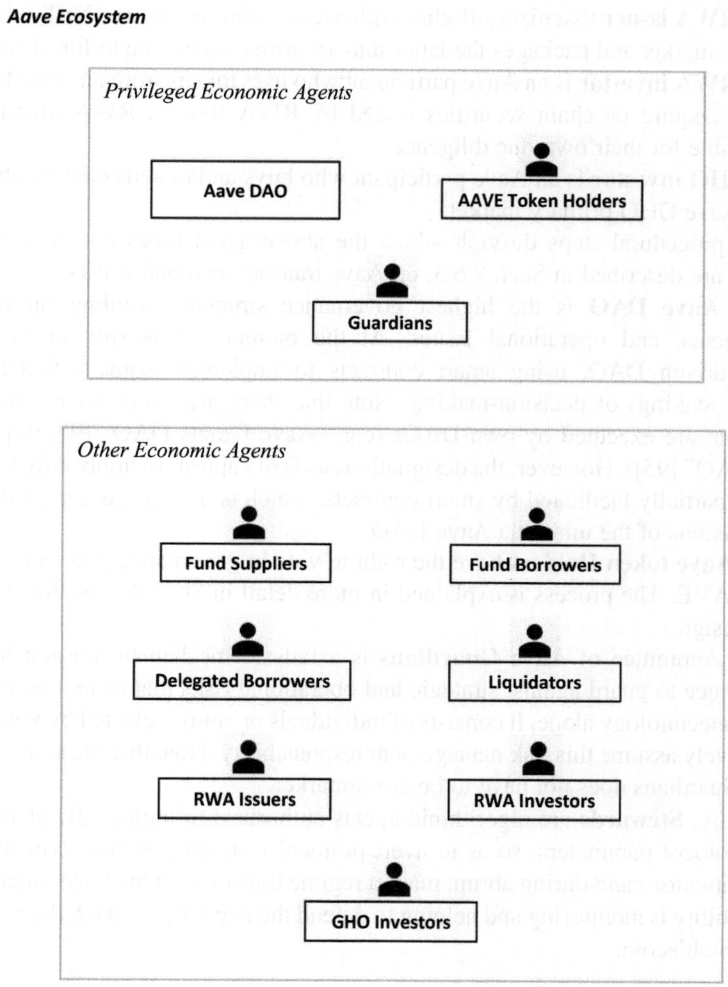

Fig. 14.23 Aave economic agent model

compounded interest rate. Aave loans are always secured by token assets of the participant explicitly declared as eligible collateral. Said collateral keeps accumulating interest yield, and its legal title remains with its original owner as long as no margin call is issued on the combined credit position.

A **delegated borrower** is a funds borrower who reuses the collateral of another funds supplier, by explicit agreement with the latter.

A **liquidator** is an Aave participant who, once notified that a margin call is about to be issued on the combined asset/liability position of a funds borrower, repays the outstanding loan and acquires the covering collateral at a pre-determined discount. A funds borrower may choose to act as their own liquidator.

An **RWA issuer** tokenizes off-chain (physical-world) assets into NFTs visible on an Aave market and packages the latter into securities accessible to funds suppliers.

An **RWA investor** is an Aave participant who uses tokens from an Aave liquidity pool to acquire on-chain securities issued by RWA Issuers. RWA investors are responsible for their own due diligence.

A **GHO investor** is an Aave participant who buys and/or sells GHO Stablecoins in the Aave GHO primary market.

The procedural steps through which the above agent types pursue their main activity are described in Sect. 9.6.3, on Aave transactional pathways.

The **Aave DAO** is the highest governance structure deciding on strategy, investments, and operational issues. At the moment, it is still an essentially human-driven DAO, using smart contracts to implement some technical steps (voting, staking) of decision-making. Note that there are some Aave governance tasks that are executed by own DAOs (e.g. "Aave Grants DAO" [93, 94], "Aave Risk DAO" [95]). However, the designations as DAO appear to imply only a process pattern partially facilitated by smart contracts, which is, in any case, subordinate to the decisions of the umbrella Aave DAO.

All **Aave token Holders** have the right to vote in governance gremia by staking their AAVE. The process is explained in more detail in Sect. 9.7, on Aave mechanism design.

The committee of **Aave Guardians** is a failsafe mechanism created by Aave governance to guard against strategic and operational risks that cannot be managed through technology alone. It consists of individuals or entities elected by vote [91] to collectively assume this risk management responsibility. Note that the assignment of Aave Guardians does not have to be cross-market.

Finally, **Stewards** are algorithmic agents authorized to unilaterally change specific protocol parameters, so as to avert protocol instability in time-critical operational situations and during abrupt market regime transitions. One major area of their applicability is monitoring and helping to defend the peg [96] of GHO, the protocol's native Stablecoin.

14.5.2 Cooperating Ecosystems

Importantly, Aave has achieved cooperation with other EVM-compatible ecosystems in order to establish and extend its business case.

The core concept of "Aave markets" is indeed geared towards this cooperation, the technical details of which are kept up-to-date in the official Aave documentation [97, 98]. At the same time, there are some critical Aave transactional pathways (liquidation, RWA investing) that would be impossible without cooperation with information providers such as price and event Oracles. Similarly, the whole concept of an on-chain money market would be meaningless without the ability to acquire and re-use reserve tokens in Centralized and/or Decentralized Exchanges.

An overview of the Aave core/cooperating economic agents setup is depicted in Fig. 14.24.

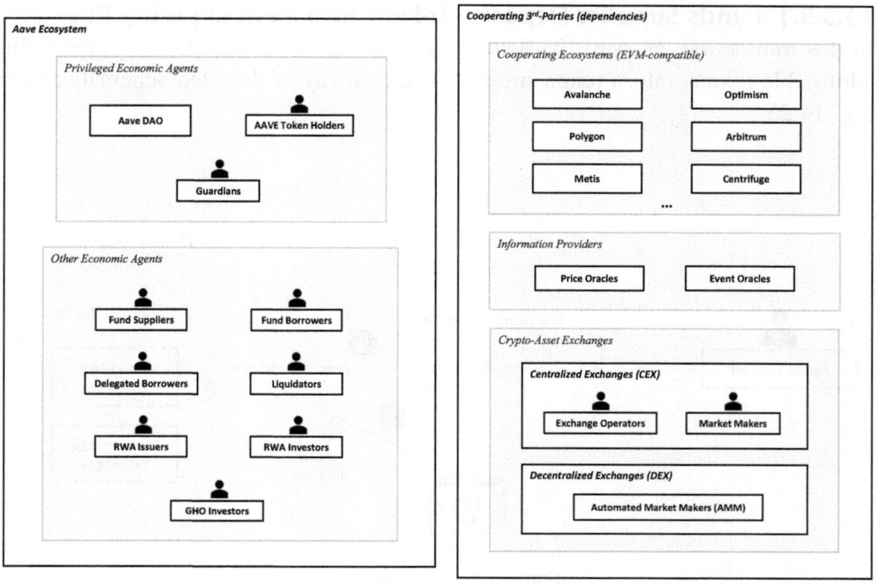

Fig. 14.24 Aave and cooperating third parties

As of the time of writing, Aave uses Chainlink Data Feeds [99, 100] as price Oracle, and Chainlink Automation [101] as event Oracle [102, 103].

14.5.3 Transactional Pathways

In previous case studies, before describing protocol transactional pathways, we were usually explaining the structure of the underlying balance sheet that was recording the respective tokens. However, Aave is somewhat peculiar in that it creates new token types that depend on the transaction type and on the primary reserve token used. Thus, some parts of the protocol balance sheet can be described only as placeholders for templated tokens, and furthermore their precise composition will always be market-dependent. That is, the token types present in the Aave Ethereum market will be different than those of markets in cooperating ecosystems. Taken together with the fact that Aave protocols are strictly non-custodial (i.e. Agents are expected to move tokens immediately to their crypto wallets), this creates a challenge in that the "market balance sheet" (apart from the protocol rewards pool) is only a logical representation of the underlying distributed ledger, filled in through the Aave smart contracts.

The following sections detail the salient transactional pathways, by also indicating the order of execution of each step in the process. This is also different from the notation of previous case studies, as here there exists a sequence of token transfer and issuance steps that is specific to Aave use cases.

14.5.3.1 Funds Supplier Deposits Tokens into Aave Liquidity Pool

In this transaction, an Aave participant becomes a "funds supplier" by depositing admissible tokens into a token reserve. The pathway is depicted schematically in Fig. 14.25.

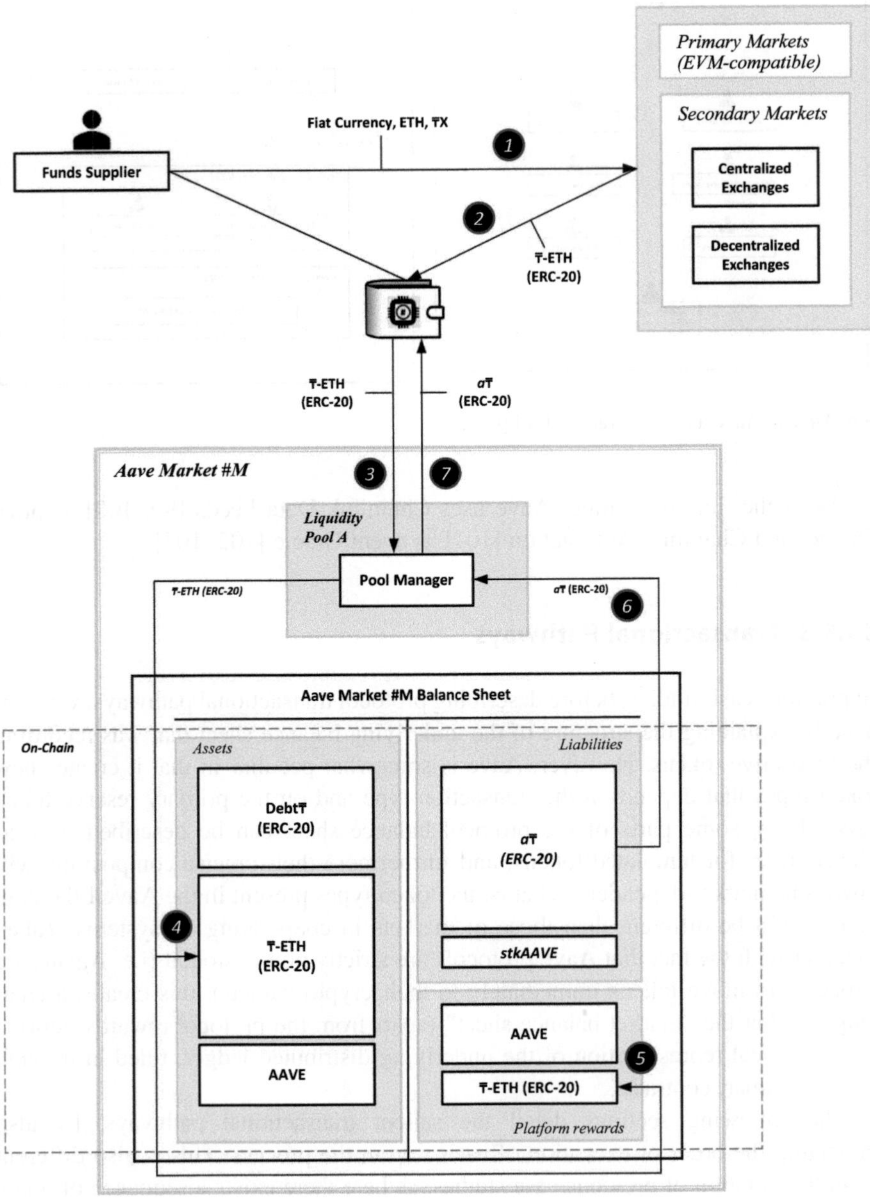

Fig. 14.25 Funds Supplier deposits tokens, receives aTokens

Aave is accessible either programmatically or through the Aave dApp [104]. Assuming a human agent, the dApp will request that the user first connects a crypto wallet (Aave is a non-custodial ecosystem) and second chooses an Aave market. The choice of market will define the accessible liquidity pools and also restrict the universe of admissible ERC-20 tokens. The agent will have purchased the latter (denote them ₸-ETH, as they are EVM-compatible) in their primary markets or in external Centralized or Decentralized Exchanges (depicted by step "1" on Fig. 14.25) and then transferred them to their wallet (step "2"). This will make them visible to Aave.

As already mentioned, each Aave liquidity pool has its own managing smart contract. Before depositing ₸-ETH into the SC ("3"), it is necessary to declare (programmatically or through the dApp) if said funds would be eligible as collateral for future borrowing by the same or other (delegated) agents [105]. This is mandated by Aave's risk framework [106, 107]; however, the declaration can be later reversed at the agent's discretion [108]. The SC will then drive three actions on the Market's balance sheet (referred to as corresponding to the abstract "Market #M" on the schematic): The received ₸-ETH are saved into the correct Reserve ("4"), a transaction fee[30] is transferred to the platform rewards pool ("5"), and supplier position tokens ("aTokens" [109]) are minted. The latter are then added to the market"s liabilities and transferred through the SC ("6") to the agent's wallet ("7"). The aTokens begin immediately accumulating continuous interest.

It is important to note that Aave aTokens are minted to correspond 1:1 to the deposited tokens, also by type. For instance, a deposit in DAI will cause minting of "aDAI", a deposit in USDC corresponding to minting of "aUSDC", etc.

They are created and accounted for as separate token types for various reasons, one of which is that they need to be priced separately and made individually transferrable should they become subject to liquidation. Each Aave market specifies its own distinct minting smart contract address [110] per aToken type[31] (aDAI, aUSDC, etc.).

At the end of the transaction, the funds supplier will have provided a sum of ERC-20 tokens to an Aave reserve and will have acquired assets in terms of equivalent ERC-20 aTokens in their wallet, which begin accruing interest immediately.

14.5.3.2 Funds Supplier Acquires AAVE Tokens and Deposits Them into Aave Liquidity Pool

As already mentioned, AAVE is the (ERC-20 compatible) governance token of the Aave ecosystem [75]. It also has another function (explained later in Sect. 14.5.3.8),

[30] As of the time of writing this book, this fee is set to 0 (zero, i.e. no transaction fee is currently raised for eligible token supplies)

[31] Each Aave market apart from the Ethereum Mainnet one is currently also allocated an own naming scheme for aTokens, by prepending a three-letter short-name for the underlying protocol after the initial "a". For instance, aLINK on Arbitrum becomes aArbLINK, on Polygon aPolLINK, etc.

which entails staking it into a particular Aave smart contract called "safety module", which returns more AAVE tokens in lieu of rewards. Importantly, these tokens cannot be minted upon user request—there is no primary market issuing AAVE. They are distributed by Aave, either as part of ecosystem payouts or as rewards to pre-existing AAVE positions staked in the safety module. AAVE already in circulation can be traded in the secondary market [111], and this is where Aave participants can procure them. Hence, in this transaction, an Aave participant becomes a "Funds Supplier" by acquiring, then depositing AAVE tokens into a token reserve.

The pathway is depicted schematically in Fig. 14.26.

Again, as Aave is accessible either programmatically or through the Aave dApp, a human agent will first have to connect a crypto wallet and choose a market. After purchasing AAVE in external Centralized or Decentralized Exchanges (depicted by step "1" on Fig. 14.26), they transfer them to their crypto wallet ("2"). They then enter the Aave market, select a liquidity pool, and request to deposit AAVE, after choosing "enable as collateral Y/N". The AAVE reserve, whenever present in a liquidity pool, is also managed by the smart contract of the latter. By sending their AAVE to the SC ("3"), they are transferred to the AAVE reserve ("4"), while a transaction fee[32] is transferred to the platform rewards pool ("5"), and supplier position aAAVE tokens are minted.[33] These are then added to the market's liabilities and transferred through the SC ("6") to the agent's wallet ("7"). They start accumulating continuous interest immediately.

As before, aAAVE are minted to correspond 1:1 to the deposited AAVE tokens. They become part of the fund supplier's portfolio of assets on Aave, and as such, they are individually transferrable should they become subject to liquidation. Each Aave market specifies its own aAAVE[34] minting smart contract address [112].

At the end of the transaction, the Funds Supplier will have provided a sum of AAVE tokens to an Aave reserve and will have acquired assets in terms of equivalent aAAVE tokens in their wallet, which begin accruing interest immediately.

14.5.3.3 Funds Borrower Takes Out a Long-Term Loan, Posting Own Collateral

In this transaction, an Aave participant who is already a "Funds Supplier" becomes a "Funds Borrower" by drawing liquidity from a token reserve in exchange for paying interest.[35] The pathway is depicted schematically in Fig. 14.27.

[32] As of the time of writing this book, this fee is set to 0 (zero, i.e. no transaction fee is currently raised for AAVE supplies)

[33] Record of transactions of smart contract minting aAAVE: https://etherscan.io/token/0xFFC97d72E13E01096502Cb8Eb52dEe56f74DAD7B

[34] Each Aave market apart from the Ethereum Mainnet one is currently also allocated an own naming scheme for aAAVE, by prepending a 3-letter short-name for the underlying Protocol after the initial "a". For instance, aAAVE on Arbitrum becomes aArbAAVE, on Polygon aPolAAVE, etc.

[35] It is interesting to note that, up until V3 of the Protocol, the transaction pathway in question had two possible variations, as per the interest rate terms available to the borrower—namely "variable"

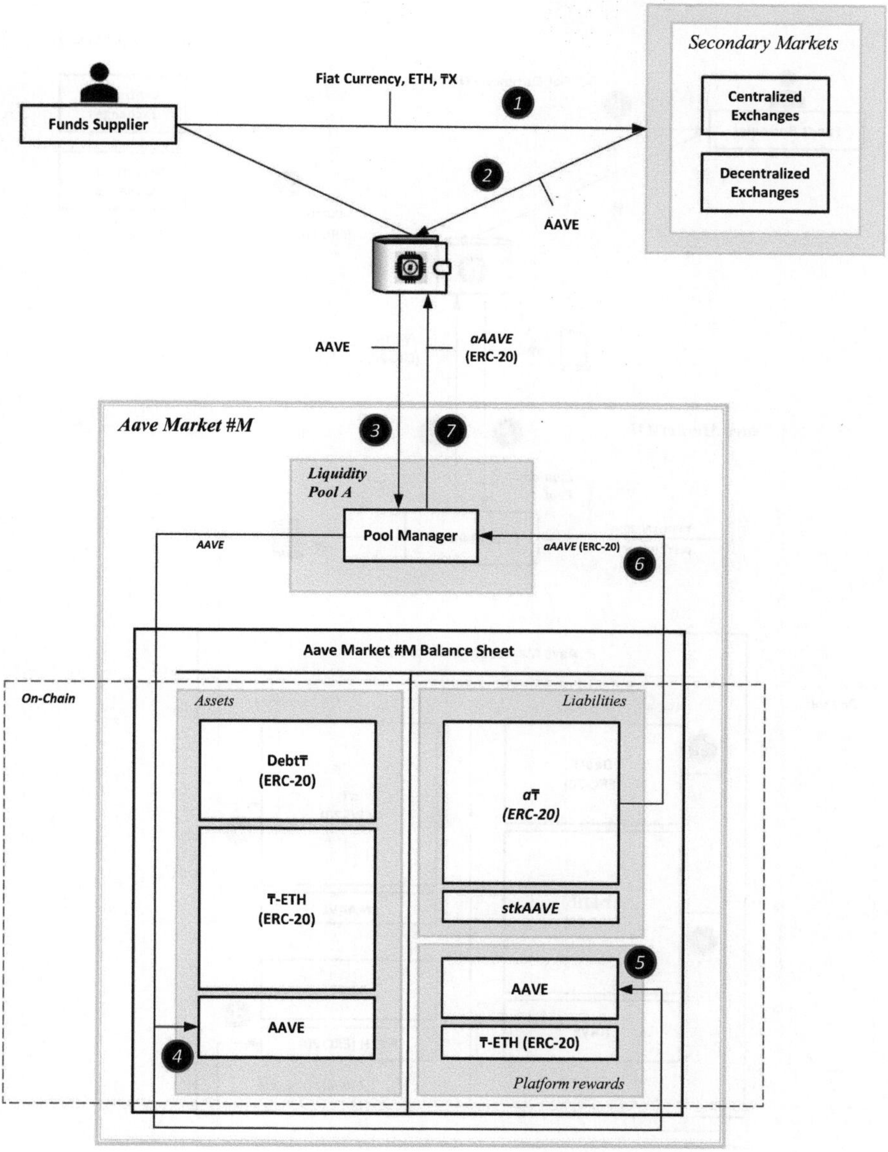

Fig. 14.26 Funds Supplier deposits AAVE, receives aAAVE

and "stable". The **variable** interest rate (also termed "volatile" in Aave documentation) was both token and reserve dependent. It was calibrated based on token liquidity metrics and on the actual drawdown of a reserve (as well as on said drawdown's trend). The latter served as an indication of the demand vs. supply dynamics for the token in question, hence of the near-term cost of funds in the market. Interestingly, the **stable** interest rate was *not a fixed* one; it was still variable but was simply re-setting much less frequently than the variable one. Stable rates were not always quoted,

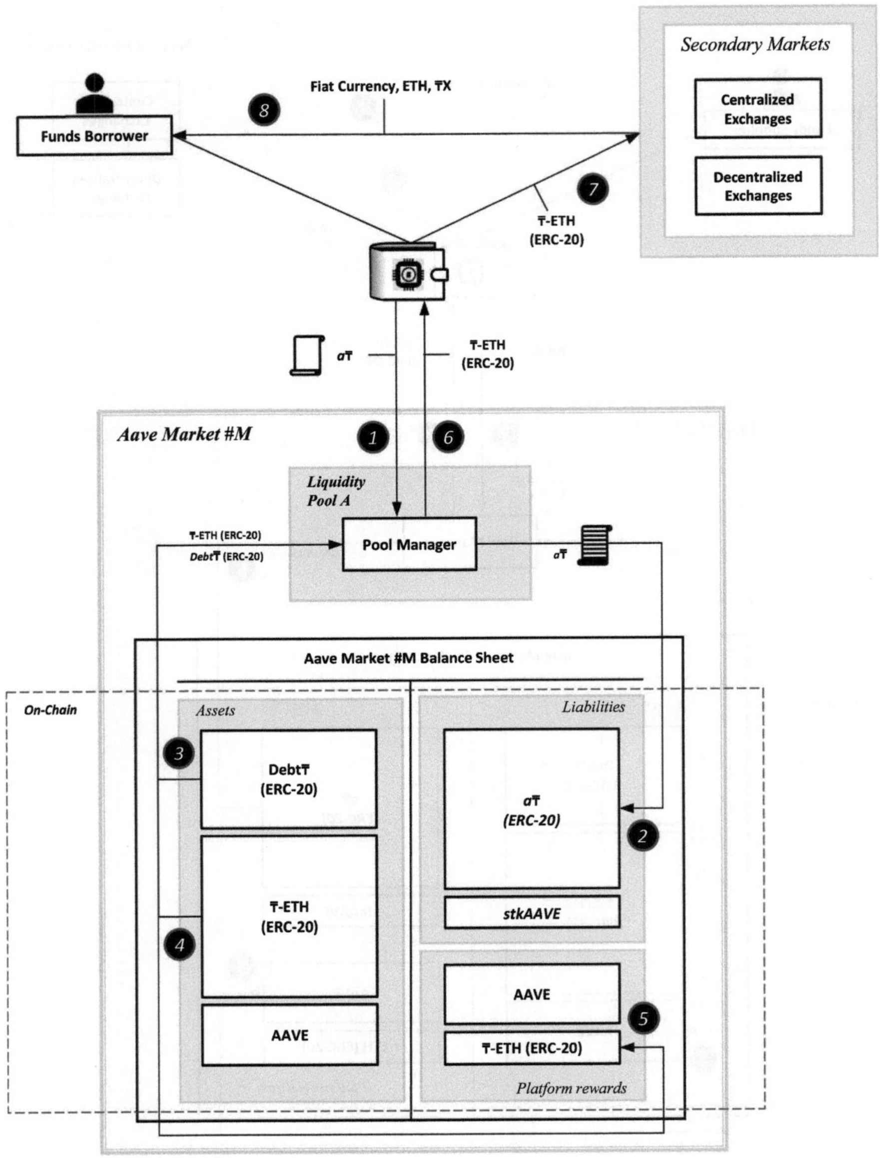

Fig. 14.27 Funds Borrower takes out loan against own collateral

that is, available, for every token in Aave liquidity pools. Also, when quoted, they were under normal market conditions quite higher than the spot variable rates (which was needed to compensate for tenor risk in between resettings). Changes in variable and stable interest rate parameterizations were being decided by Aave governance. Depending on the interest rate terms chosen, Aave minted either a "VariableDebtToken" or a "StableDebtToken"; that is, there existed two different DebtToken Smart Contracts (which are still accessible in the legacy part of the Aave GitHub).

Borrowing in Aave is always secured against assets that already exist in an Aave liquidity pool. The minimum (over) collateralization ratio that needs to be maintained for the entire tenor is token-specific, determined by Aave governance [81], and enforced strictly through smart contracts.

The transaction begins by connecting a crypto wallet containing aTokens, that is, Aave-minted ERC-20 token assets owned by the agent. These already specify indirectly the Aave market (cf. previous section). Assume that the agent owns assets denominated in several aTokens, for example, a₸X_1, a₸X_2, … (these could be aDAI, aUSDC, …, etc.). The agent wishes to borrow a sum either in one of a₸X_i, or in a different ERC-20 ₸-ETH (e.g. aWBTC). The asset tokens must have already been declared as "collateral eligible".

Either programmatically or through the Aave dApp, the agent connects to a liquidity pool, and specifies the assets a₸X_i to post as collateral (step "1" on Fig. 14.27). In the next step, by specifying the borrowing request (borrowing token ₸-ETH and interest rate conditions; all Aave loans are of indefinite tenor), the lending smart contract adjusts the terms by applying Aave risk parameters (LTV, reserve caps, etc. [114]), and is ready to reserve the requested liquidity if the agent agrees with them. Once agreed, the SC does the following: first, it encumbers the specified collateral assets (step "2"); second, mints debt position tokens (of type "DebtToken",[36] and 1:1 to the ₸-ETH in quantity; "3"); third, removes the requested ₸-ETH from the reserve ("4"); fourth, transfers a transaction fee to the platform rewards pool ("5"); and finally, transfers the requested ₸-ETH to the agent's wallet ("6"). The agent is free to transfer the ₸-ETH from their wallet to Centralized or Decentralized Exchanges ("7") and swap them for other assets ("8"). The newly minted DebtTokens begin immediately accruing continuous interest charges, which are added to the debt position.

This is the basic transactional pathway. Interest rate calculation models (including current parametrization) are well described in Aave documentation [117]. Changes in their parameters are decided by Aave governance only, and are generally token and market dependent. DebtTokens issued are recorded against the blockchain address of the Funds Borrower, and in juxtaposition to aTokens allocated to funds suppliers, they are **not transferrable** [118].

However, it was decided by a 2024 Aave governance decision [113] to deprecate the "StableDebtToken" and keep using only the VariableDebtToken smart contract, with concomittant retirement of the stable interest rate option. Hence, there since remains a single debt token smart contract (VariableDebtToken.sol), which in its turn inherits from a DebtTokenBase.sol. As the ultimate evolution of Aave's business model cannot be foreseen, we choose to keep a generic designation in the main text and accompanying illustrations of the borrowing transactional pathway, namely "DebtToken". This is done with the understanding that, as of the time of writing, a DebtToken will be minted through VariableDebtToken.sol; however, should Aave governance reverse its decision at a later time, then it may be minted through additional smart contracts, depending on the prevailing optionality then allowed by the protocol.

[36] We stress again that, as of the time of writing this book, DebtToken is *always* minted through the VariableDebtToken.sol smart contract [115], which in turn inherits from the DebtTokenBase.sol smart contract [116].

Please note that the assets a$\overline{T}X_i$ posted as collateral remain in the ownership of the Funds Borrower and keep accumulating interest (minus a small percentage fee redirected to the platform rewards pool). Hence, the transactional pathway described in this section corresponds to a Lombard loan in the traditional finance sense, and *not* to a repo (cf. Sect. 9.1).

14.5.3.4 Funds Supplier Delegates Own Collateral to a Prospective Borrower

This is a the first stage of an interesting transactional pathway for two reasons: First, it is in general a **combined on-/off-chain transaction** (the participants may choose to negotiate completely off-blockchain and only execute the final step on an Aave market); second, because it allows to extend Aave to **unsecured lending** use cases, if existing Funds Suppliers are willing to underwrite the counterparty credit risk. In short, it is an example of how Aave enables its ecosystem participants to extend its principal business case, as long as the Aave market paradigm (as implemented by existing smart contracts) is respected. Assume that an existing Funds Supplier has collateral-ready assets on Aave, in the form of aTokens in their crypto wallet. Aave then allows for said assets to be "delegated" to [119] (i.e. assigned to, put to the disposal of) another blockchain address should the latter wish to become a Funds Borrower.

The technical basis of this functionality is in the implementation of the smart contracts[37,38] minting aTokens and DebtTokens. The business justification is the need to accommodate various situations known from traditional finance (e.g. unsecured lending, collateral transformation [123]) and others specific to a blockchain setting (e.g. a single human or corporate having more than one blockchain addresses onboarded on Aave—that is, having distinct agent personalities—and needing to redistribute assets and exposures among them without incurring high transaction fees).

The transaction in all generality also has an off-chain part, whereby the right to use the supplied collateral is exchanged for a monetary or other benefit after contractual negotiations. The contractual terms themselves can also be made visible on EVM-compatible blockchains, e.g. by using the templates [124] provided by the "OpenLaw" project [125, 126].

At the end of this assignment of rights (cf. Fig. 14.28), the Delegated Borrower is free to use the delegated assets as collateral.

---

[37] AToken.sol is a contract implementing both ERC-20 and ERC-2612 (EIP-2612—"Permit Extension for EIP-20 Signed Approvals" [120]). The latter's "permit (…)" function allows the caller to authorize usage of funds by another blockchain address. The current version's code for AToken.sol is available at [121].

[38] In [122] please note the methods "approveDelegation(…)" and "delegationWithSig(…)".

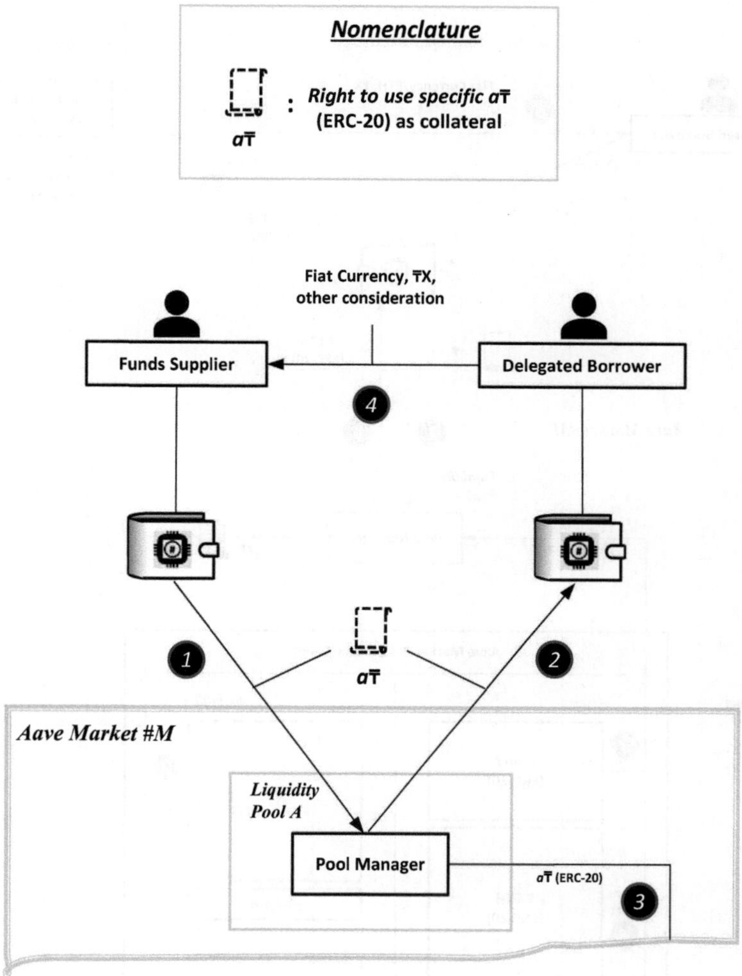

Fig. 14.28 Funds Supplier delegates collateral to borrower

14.5.3.5 Delegated Borrower Takes Out a Long-Term Loan, Posting Delegated Collateral

The distinction between a simple Funds Borrower and a Delegated Borrower is not an academic one. This Aave borrowing transaction [127] is simply the on-chain "leg" of a combined on–/off-chain transaction; hence, the attributes of this agent type in reference to the Aave ecosystem are distinct from those of a simple Funds Borrower. In effect, there are some business risks that the collateral delegator underwrites which are not visible to the rest of the ecosystem. Hence, there exists potential for hidden risk concentration, which may conceivably become systemic. This might be the case, for instance, if a critical mass of on-chain aTokens are delegated to the same collateral borrower by many funds suppliers—unbeknownst to

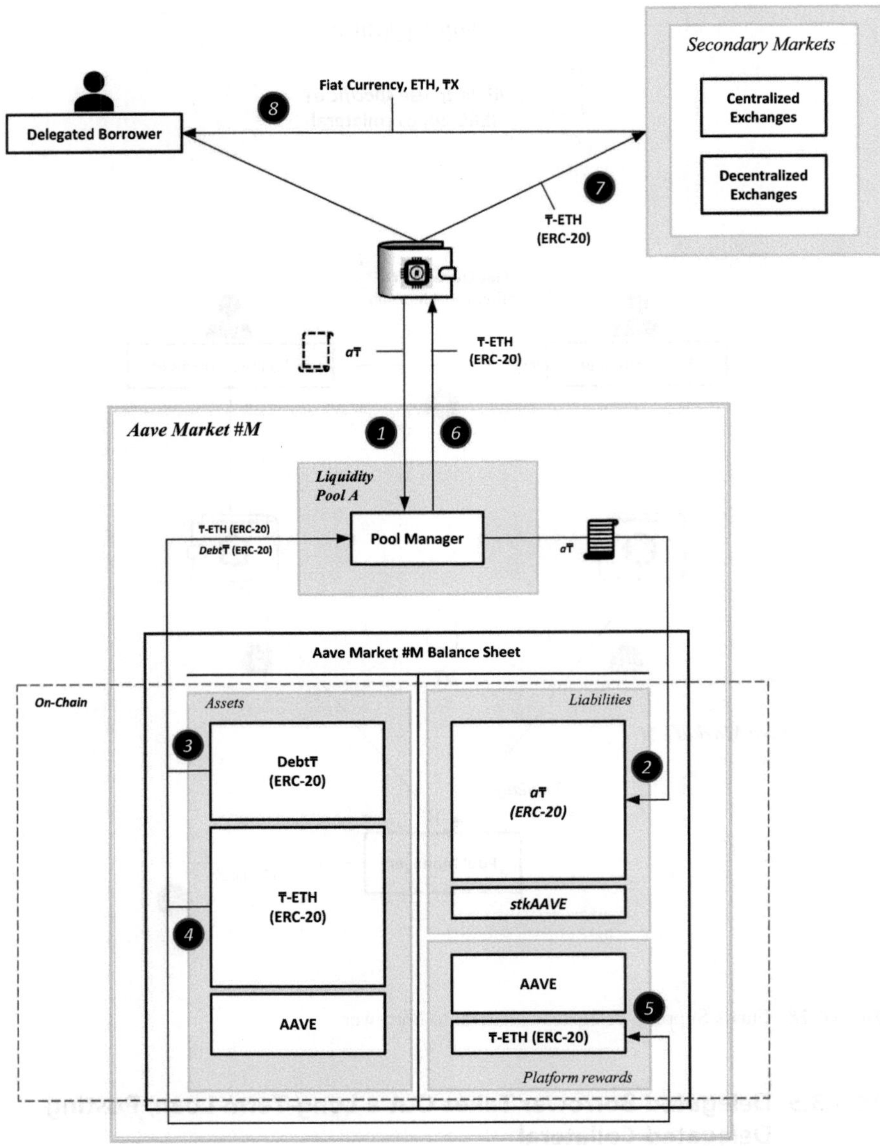

Fig. 14.29 Delegated Borrower takes out loan against delegated collateral

each other—and the collateral borrower then defaults in their off-chain obligations. Thus, this is indeed a new agent type (with new rights and responsibilities), acting along a new transactional pathway.

Once the delegated collateral has been assigned and the action has been confirmed, the Delegated Borrower follows the exact same on-chain steps as a simple Funds Borrower would (cf. Fig. 14.29).

A crypto wallet needs to have been connected, now containing the rights to aTokens in a specific market. Either programmatically or through the Aave dApp, the agent connects to a liquidity pool, and specifies the precise assets a₸X_i (also in value) that they will use as collateral for this transaction (step "1" on Fig. 14.29). In the next step, by specifying the borrowing request (borrowing token ₸-ETH and interest rate conditions—variable or stable), the lending smart contract adjusts the terms by applying Aave risk parameters (LTV, reserve caps, etc.), and is ready to reserve the requested liquidity if the agent agrees with them. Once agreed, the SC proceeds as in the simple funds borrowing case: first, it encumbers the specified collateral assets (step "2"); second, mints debt position tokens (of type "DebtToken", and 1:1 to the ₸-ETH in quantity; "3"); third, removes the requested ₸-ETH from the reserve ("4"); fourth, transfers a transaction fee to the platform rewards pool ("5"); and finally transfers the requested ₸-ETH to the agent's Wallet ("6"). The agent is free to transfer the ₸-ETH from their wallet to Centralized or Decentralized Exchanges ("7") and swap them for other assets ("8"). The newly minted DebtTokens begin immediately accruing continuous interest charges, which are added to the debt position.

Please note that asset encumbrance (step "2") and DebtToken issuance ("3") cause changes in two different crypto wallets (those of the two delegation participants) at once. Should the Delegated Borrower use only part of their delegated collateral, they can proceed with new borrowings until all available collateral has been committed.

14.5.3.6 Liquidator Buys Undercollateralized Exposure

Please recall the discussion on Lombard loan margin calls (explained graphically through Fig. 14.4 of Sect. 9.1) in the context of traditional finance. Aave borrowings in effect replicate this paradigm on-chain, albeit in a private debt setting due to the absence of regulated banking actors. However, it is only logical that there should be a mechanism to avoid uncovered credit exposures that might threaten Funds Suppliers individually and the ecosystem as a whole. This mechanism is [credit positions] liquidation through the action of third parties (i.e., not necessarily one of the original Funds Borrower or Fund Supplier), which are incentivized to play in effect the same role as in-house credit risk and collateral managers in traditional banking. The agent type of said parties is simply "Liquidator".

What is the business process of liquidation, and how is it implemented technically in Aave?

First of all, Aave Liquidation happens not at the item borrowing position but at the blockchain address (across positions) level. In effect, Aave makes the reasonable assumption that any blockchain address owning several assets (and not only those that have been specifically posted as collateral for a loan) can rectify an undercollateralized position by posting additional collateral. Hence, Aave continuously calculates a so-called health factor [128], a numerical ratio formed by continuously valuing the aggregated DebtTokens of all open borrowing positions and all Aave assets (aTokens) corresponding to a blockchain address.[39] Remember that both DebtTokens and aTokens have time-dependent balances, due to the accruing interest. Hence, the health factor (HF) may deteriorate either because the underlying collateral depreciates or because of the accrued debt interest. If this HF ratio falls below a threshold, then all open borrowing positions are declared free for third parties to repay immediately, in exchange for their acquiring part or all[40] assets of said blockchain address at a discount. This discount is the incentive that Aave provides towards liquidators. Of course, there are token- and market-dependent parameters that the profitability of this action depends on [131, 132]; however, the monetary outcome—after platform fees—can be lucrative for agents who are prepared to carry it out as a regular source of income. As already mentioned, Liquidators provide a utility to Aave, assuming the role of credit risk and collateral managers. The discount on liquidated collateral is the way that Aave incentivizes this utility function by otherwise disinterested parties.

Technically, it is important to remember that the blockchain reference architecture per se does not provide for any event-notification mechanism (especially configurable, in the sense of user-defined business rules) outside smart contracts. Even the latter are protocol-specific, meaning that any third-party agent wishing to be notified about specific events would need to create own software to query either the underlying distributed ledger or the execution of specific protocol smart contracts. The basis event of liquidation is: "health factor < threshold, for a particular blockchain address". This is an internal Aave event, which needs to be captured and then utilized by a Liquidator. The latter must have the technical capabilities in place to:

a. Retrieve the blockchain address in question
b. Verify the current value of the borrowing position(s)
c. Verify the token types involved as either DebtTokens or aTokens
d. Decide if the underlying reserve tokens are interesting as prospective assets
e. Decide if it would be preferable to keep the (interest accruing) aTokens or convert to reserve tokens in the event of liquidation
f. Calculate the associated transaction (gas) and platform fees and evaluate the position profitability
g. Call the Aave smart contracts affecting liquidation, by posting their own tokens

That means that a systematic Liquidator must be able to "sense" and exploit liquidation events across all affected blockchain addresses continuously.

Aave has used event Oracles (off-chain software, based on third-party infrastructures [101]) to continuously provide a list of basis events [133]. Liquidators

[39] Of a "user account" as per [129].

[40] As of Aave V3, up to 100% of debt can be liquidated ([130], please search in the page for "MAX_LIQUIDATION_CLOSE_FACTOR").

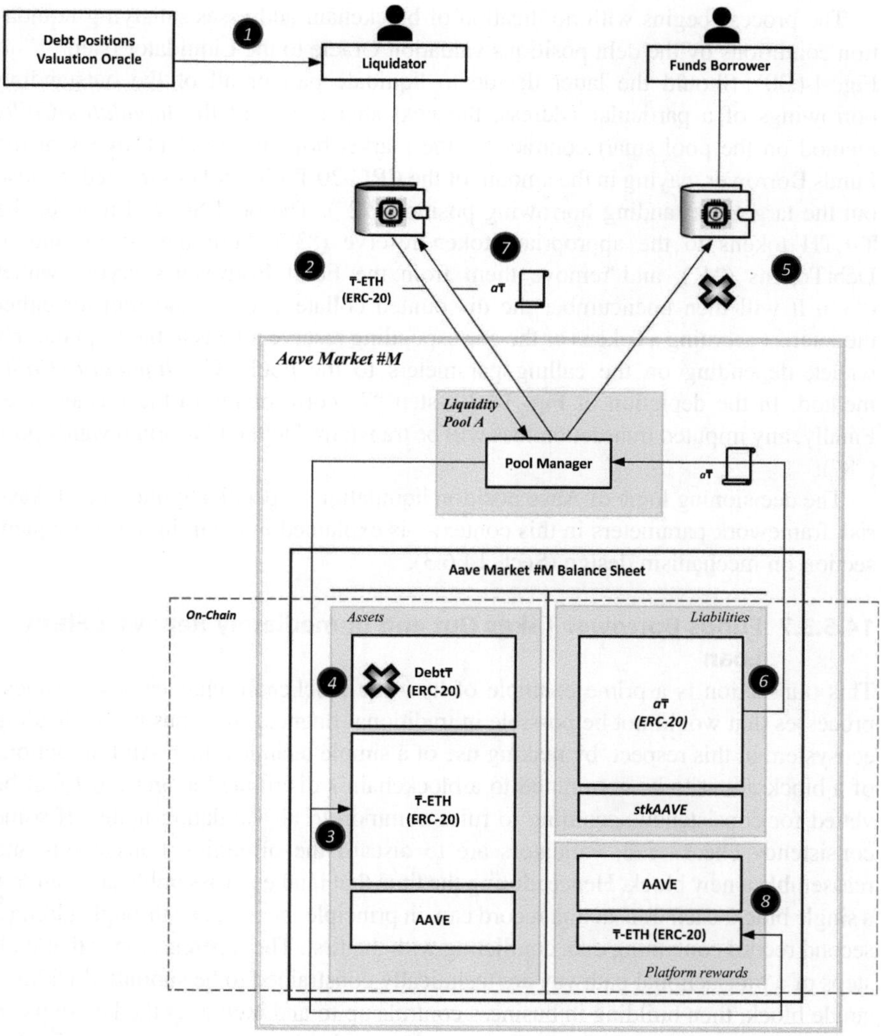

Fig. 14.30 Liquidator buys undercollateralized debt position, acquires discounted collateral

can either implement own sensing and evaluating mechanisms against the Aave distributed ledger (also using accessible Aave platform API's[41]) or use third-party blockchain-compatible notification software [134]. By combining Aave with their own or third-party notification/valuation software, they thus replicate a "debt positions valuation Oracle". The Liquidation transactional pathway is depicted in Fig. 14.30.

---

[41] E.g. "aave-utilities" [379], which provides methods to evaluate data corresponding to individual blockchain addresses.

The process begins with notification of blockchain addresses satisfying liquidation conditions by the debt positions valuation Oracle to the Liquidator (step "1" in Fig. 14.30). Should the latter decide to liquidate part or all of the outstanding borrowings of a particular address, the next step is to call the *liquidationCall()* method on the pool smart contract for the market holding the DebtTokens of the Funds Borrower, paying in the amount of the ERC-20 ₸-ETH tokens needed to close out the target outstanding borrowing position ("2"). The pool SC will transfer the ₸-ETH tokens to the appropriate token reserve ("3"), burn the corresponding DebtTokens ("4"), and remove them from the Fund Borrower's crypto wallet ("5"). It will then unencumber the discounted collateral ("6") and transfer either the interest accruing aTokens or the corresponding reserve tokens to the Liquidator's wallet, depending on the calling parameters to the pool SC's *liquidationCall()* method. In the depiction of Fig. 14.30, step "7" corresponds to the former case. Finally, any imputed transaction fees will be transferred to the Platform rewards pool ("8").

The decisioning logic of Aave position liquidation—specifically the role of Aave risk framework parameters in this context—is explained in detail in the subsequent section on mechanism design (Sect. 14.6.3).

14.5.3.7 Funds Borrower Takes Out and Immediately Repays a Flash Loan

This transaction is a prime example of how the blockchain enables new business processes that would not be possible in traditional finance. Aave has been a leading ecosystem in this respect, by making use of a simple technical fact: All transactions of a block about to be committed to a blockchain's distributed ledger must first be vetted for consistency according to rules common to all validating nodes. If some consistency checks fail, validators are to discard the offending transactions and reassemble a new block. Hence, during the time that it takes to assemble and validate a single block, each transaction record can, in principle, be reversed through adding a second record containing data conflicting with the first. The repercussion is that if all steps of a transactional pathway are technically constrained to be submitted within a single block, then building in business controls up to and including the last step can ensure that either the records of an entire self-contained transaction are committed to the DL, or none at all. This "all-or-none" modality is the technical basis of Aave "flash loans".

A flash loan allows Aave participants to borrow token funds without posting collateral, as long as the entire token amount is repaid (plus a loan fee) within the same block of transactions committed to the distributed ledger.[42] Having the capability to reverse all transaction legs if this condition is not met, Aave avoids incurring

[42] Once the return leg is executed by the smart contract implementing the flash loan, the protocol's infrastructure checks that both the principal and the loan fee have been repaid in full. If not, then, because this sequence happens within a single L-1 validation block of transactions, Aave can technically cause both legs to fail before any data is settled on the distributed ledger.

any counterparty credit risk. For example, the borrower may use the flash funds to immediately buy assets, then sell them on the fly by arbitraging across Exchanges, then return the borrowed funds plus platform fees to Aave and keep the difference.

As far as Aave is concerned, this is a pure pass-through transaction, generating fees[43] for the Aave platform. It is a form of uncollateralized lending, implemented through bespoke smart contracts [136]. EVM smart contracts enabling flash loan functionality must obey the Ethereum ERC-3156 standard [137].

Of course, the onus is on the flash loan borrower to technically orchestrate and execute such a series of transactions and still stay within the time limits of single-block assembly. Accordingly, this is a functionality generally addressed to users who are technically sophisticated at the levels of the EVM, the Aave platform infrastructure, and cross-exchange arbitrage mechanics. However, they are not a new agent type, but remain Funds Borrowers, albeit of a more sophisticated kind. For such borrowers, flash loans are drawable against any token reserves that are enabled for borrowing[44] in liquidity pools.

Three use-cases are mainly targeted with this functionality[45]:

a. Arbitrage between Aave markets and CEX/DEX, or purely outside Aave[46] [141]
b. Collateral transformation [123, 142]
c. Liquidating borrowers' positions[47]

without committing own principal. A depiction of the first one, involving tradable ERC-20 tokens, is provided in Fig. 14.31.

The first step ("1") is invocation of a market pool's smart contract requesting a flash loan. The parameters describe precisely the Ŧ-ETH tokens requested, which then get transferred from the reserve ("2") to the fund borrower's wallet ("3") and then on to other markets outside Aave ("4") where the arbitraging strategy is executed. The outcome is an amount of Ŧ-ETH tokens coming back to the crypto wallet ("5") and then transferred through the Pool SC ("6") to the appropriate Aave

[43] As of the time of writing, equal to between 0.05% and 0.07% of notional [135]. The current value can be queried by calling available methods of the pool smart contract.

[44] There are indeed Aave token reserves that are not enabled for borrowing, either based on market conditions, or following rules of the Aave risk framework, or by decision of Aave governance. An example of the latter would be "frozen reserves". For instance, each market reserve known to Aave comes with a parameter "Frozen", which can be either "True" or "False", as can be verified by scanning the entries of the Market tables at [81].

[45] There are still other possible ones (both internal to Aave—e.g. liquidity swaps; and external—e.g. [138]). Some involve different blockchain addresses (belonging to the same or to different Aave participants, e.g. underwriting each other"s contingent liabilities). For the technical modalities, please consult [139].

[46] Please note that the need for within-block automation may ultimately preclude the usage of arbitrage bots (e.g. [140]).

[47] Including liquidating *one's own* borrowing positions, e.g. [143].

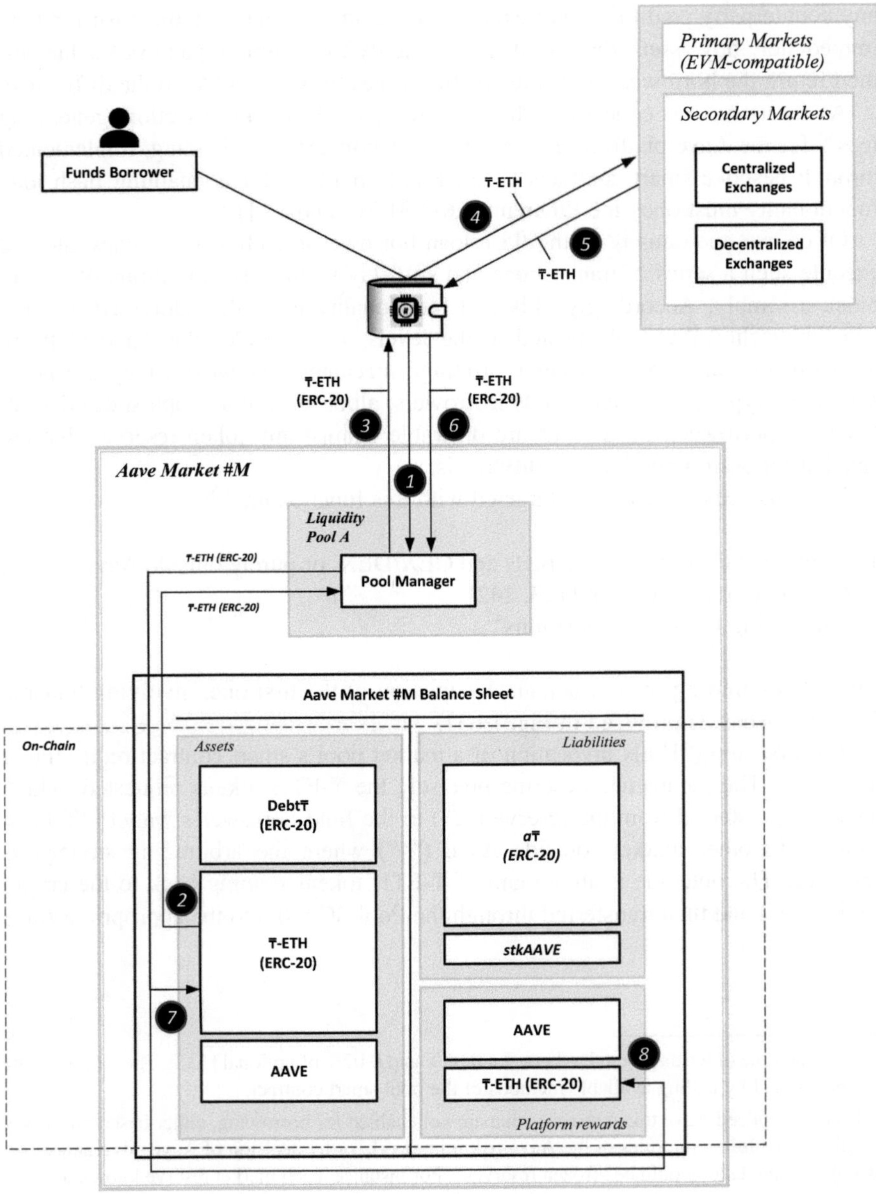

Fig. 14.31 Funds Borrower takes out and immediately repays a flash loan, using it for arbitrage

reserve ("7"). The loan fee is also paid to the platform rewards pool ("8"), completing[48] the flash loan transaction.

Using a flash loan to liquidate a borrower's position is a particularly important transactional pathway (depicted on Fig. 14.32), deserving its own explanation. A liquidator is notified of a "free-to-liquidate" debt position ("1" on Fig. 14.32), whereupon a flash loan request is sent to a market pool's smart contract ("2"). The requested Ŧ-ETH tokens are moved from the reserve to the liquidator's wallet ("3") and then a *liquidationCall()* is invoked against a pool[49] SC, whereby the same tokens are passed ("4") and allocated to a token reserve ("5"), thus provisionally cancelling the DebtTokens in question ("6" in the Aave working assets account, and "7" in the fund borrower's wallet). The underlying collateral (discounted aTokens, as per liquidation rules) passes provisionally to the ownership of the liquidator ("8" in the Aave liabilities account and "9" in the liquidator's wallet). The latter forwards them immediately to markets external to Aave ("10"), where they are exchanged for profit, and the resulting funds return in the form of Aave reserve-admissible ERC-20 Ŧ-ETH tokens to the liquidator's wallet ("11"). The market's pool SC is then called anew, referencing a sufficient amount of the new Ŧ-ETH tokens ("12"), which are transferred to the appropriate token reserve to repay the flash loan ("13") and also to cover the loan fees ("14"), thus completing the flash loan and perfecting all provisional transactions.

The importance of the last pathway lies in the ability to act as Liquidator without committing own funds. Aave, in effect, incentivizes the credit risk and collateral management function, enabling technically savvy agents to gain an income stream by providing this utility service to the ecosystem. They are expected to also make necessary investments (in know-how, opportunity cost of resources, software infrastructure, operational risk management), which they can recoup by means of this combination of flash loan drawing and liquidation.

Interestingly, nothing precludes existing Funds Borrowers to act as their own Liquidator through this pathway. The rationale is that by doing so they can still save their collateral (albeit at the reduced valuation) and also pocket the liquidation discount themselves. The alternative would be for them to lose their collateral completely, thus foregoing any appreciation potential of their aTokens.

14.5.3.8 AAVE Owner Stakes Their AAVE Tokens

As already mentioned, when discussing Aave governance economic agents in 9.6.1, Aave's governance token is also called AAVE (all-uppercase symbol) [75] and is tradable in exchanges. Apart from being used as a store of value, yielding interest to funds suppliers (explained in Sect. 9.6.3.2), it can also be used by Aave agents to

[48] Technically, the smart contract notifies that Ŧ-ETH tokens flagged as covering flash loan funds plus fee are to be found in a particular blockchain address. Aave infrastructure executes the appropriate business controls on said tokens and, if passed, flags the flash loan in the EVM transactions block as completed.

[49] Depicted here as being the same liquidity pool, strictly for the sake of simplicity in explaining the transaction.

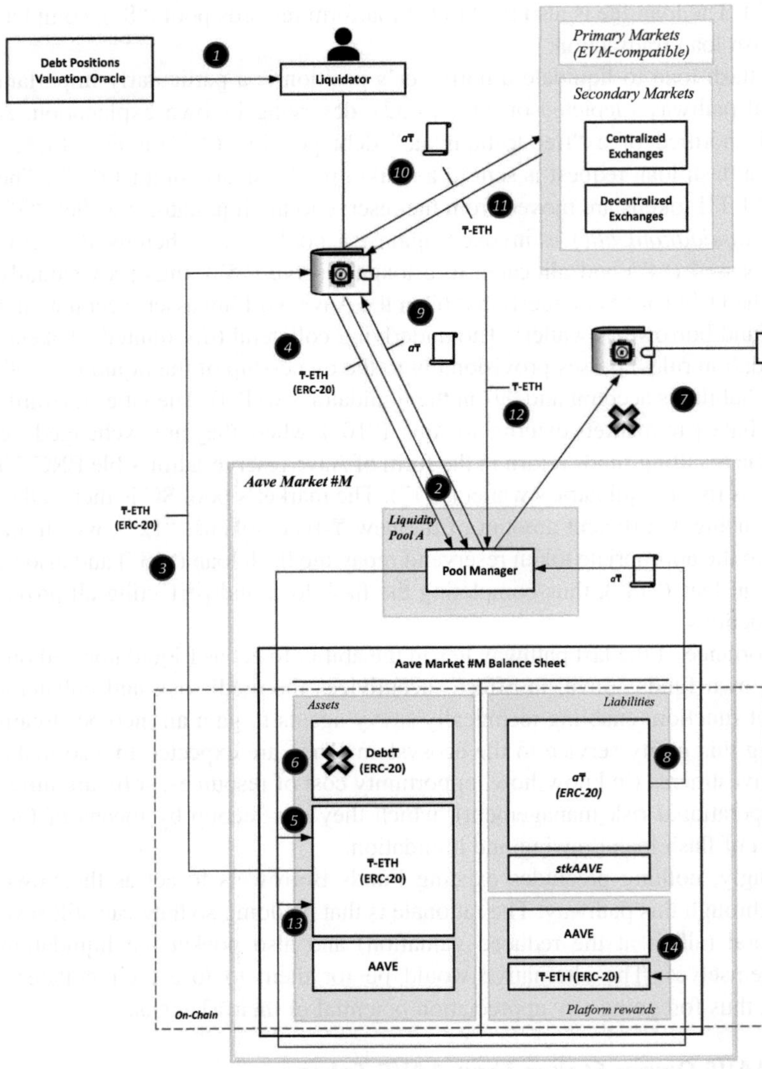

Fig. 14.32 Liquidator buys debt position through flash loan and repays immediately by reselling acquired assets

generate additional income through staking [144]. This transactional pathway entails depositing AAVE tokens into a particular smart contract called "safety module" [145, 146], which returns daily more AAVE tokens in lieu of Platform rewards [147].

However, note that this is no risk-free commitment of funds. The word "staking" itself—in a token ecosystem context—means committing token funds to cover a particular risk. There is always an expectation of rewards but also the possibility of loss should this risk manifest itself. The particular risk in an Aave context is that a market"'s liquidity may become unbalanced, that is, that a shortfall of assets *vis-à-vis* liabilities may cause inability to cover drawdown requests by Funds Suppliers.

How can such an imbalance occur?

Remember that Aave allows only overcollateralized debt positions, and continuously monitors risk parameters (such as reserve concentration risk and individual agent's health factors) [81, 114, 131] so that Aave participants such as Liquidators can rectify credit risk deterioration. However, Aave can only incentivize first-line-of-defence behaviour; it cannot impose it. In other words, Aave does have mechanisms in place enabling notifications of critical exposure threshold crossings and rewarding risk management actions (discount on collateral assets—in effect liquidation bonus—etc.); however, it has no punitive enforcement mechanisms penalizing agents that could have acted as Liquidators but did not. Liquidators are free to act, not compelled. What can happen, especially when crypto-market-wide conditions give rise to general risk-aversion, is that Liquidators may not be willing to take the risk of committing own funds only to then be unable to sell the collateral on because tokens find no buyers on Exchanges. In such situations, individual debt positions may indeed remain undercollateralized on Aave's balance sheet, and should a critical mass of such situations occur, Aave markets may find themselves unable to honour short-term asset withdrawals by Funds Suppliers. This is one situation (among others, collectively called "**Shortfall Events**" [148]), which AAVE staking seeks to rectify. In short, the safety module will redistribute daily AAVE tokens in lieu of rewards (called "Safety Incentives" [149]) to stakers[50] but will also seize and withdraw (in a "slashing" action [150]) up to 30–99% (as per current Aave documentation [148]) of staked tokens—depending on token kind—to cover a shortfall event. This percentage is defined by Aave governance.

In business terms, buying AAVE tokens and staking them (instead of simply depositing them for yield) is an expression of willingness to share in the fortunes of the Aave platform. The Aave owner has already acquired the right to participate in Aave governance; by also staking their tokens, they tie their fortunes even closer to Aave's operational results. In traditional finance terms, Aave stakers are **bail-in** [151] risk-takers. They assume the risk that some of their paid-in funds may be seized to cover platform Shortfall Events. This is a second-line-of-defence liquidity mechanism as far as Aave is concerned (there is also a third-line-of-defence, as explained in the mechanism design analysis in Sect. 9.7). The AAVE staking transactional pathway is depicted in Fig. 14.33.

The Funds Supplier, having purchased AAVE in the secondary market ("1") transfers them into their crypto wallet ("2"). After connecting to the Aave dApp [152], the safety module SC is invoked with the request to approve staking ("3") of the desired AAVE amount. Once approved, the tokens are credited to the AAVE

---

[50] Please note that AAVE stakers also have reduced borrowing interest rates on Aave.

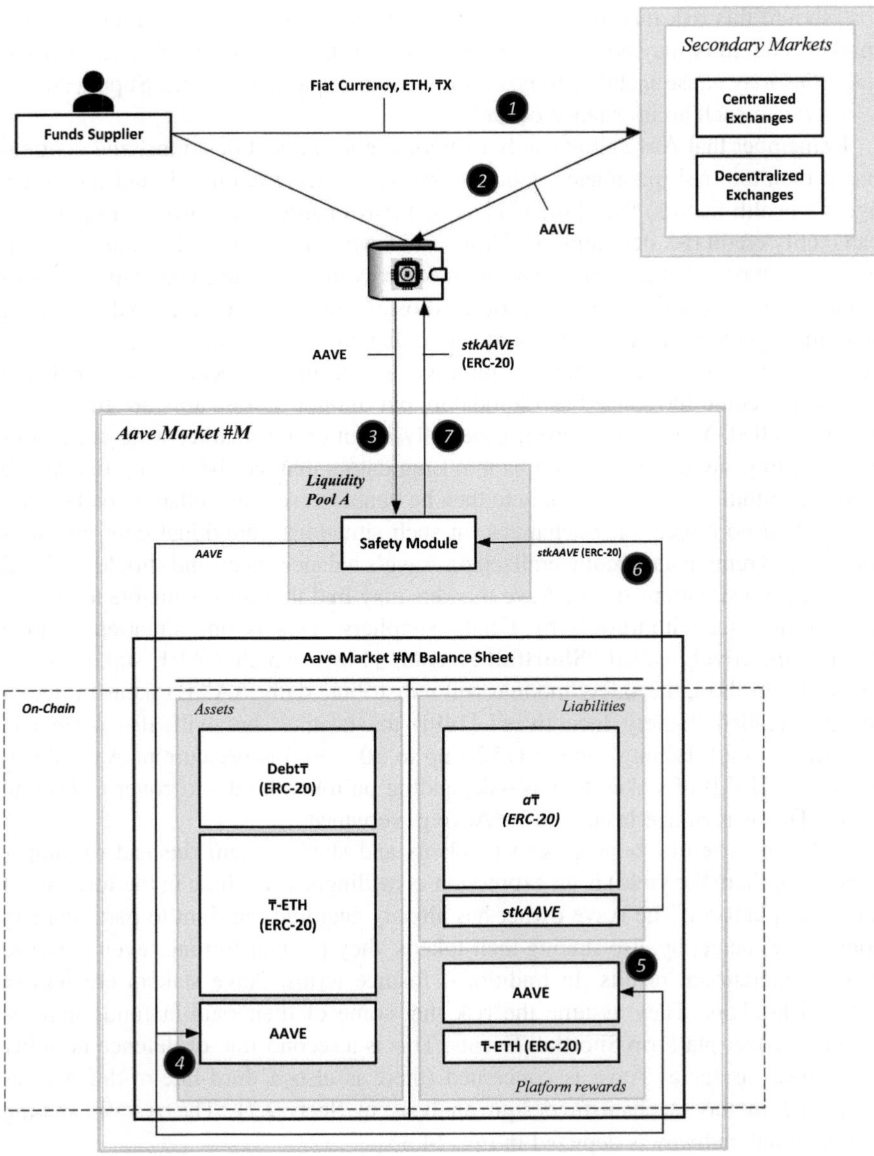

Fig. 14.33 Funds Supplier stakes AAVE tokens, acquires stkAAVE position

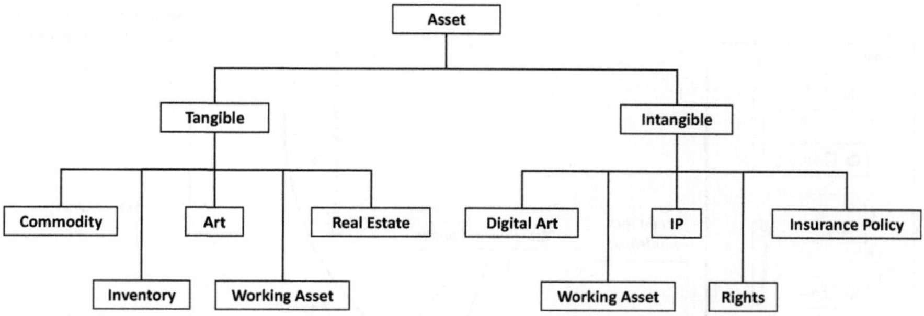

Fig. 14.34 Asset token typology (high-level, non-exhaustive)

reserve of the market ("4"). A transaction fee[51] is paid into the platform rewards pool ("5") and stkAAVE tokens (asset token type, minted in numbers corresponding initially 1:1 [153] to staked AAVE [154, 155]) forwarded, through the SC ("6"), to the agent's wallet ("7"). This completes the Staking transaction.

Please note that not all Aave markets offer AAVE staking smart contracts [156].

14.5.3.9 RWA Investor Buys Tokenized (Physical World) Asset Position

Please recall that in Sect. 4.2.3, we defined an "asset token" to be the blockchain representation of the value of a physical-world property right, when the latter is neither a sum of money nor a financial security or derivative.

Such tokens are meant to accommodate business use cases where the digital asset that is being exchanged is a representation of value that already exists in the physical world. That is, in such cases, asset tokens tokenize a physical-world property right, in whole or in part. We also offered a non-exhaustive asset token typology, repeated in Fig. 14.34 for convenience.

In that same chapter (Sect. 4.2.7), we explained that, even though not strictly correct, the term "non-fungible token" (NFT) has come to be used indiscriminately in the trade literature as being synonymous with "asset token". We opined that several underlying asset types, such as tangible and intangible art (physical paintings, digital art, musical piece, intellectual property, individual real estate, etc.) do indeed have the de facto uniqueness attribute which NFTs can certify on the blockchain. The case of so-called real world assets (RWAs 380) as offered to investors on Aave [157] is precisely such a case of NFT usage and nomenclature.

We are of the opinion that a more correct term would be "physical world assets" (we strongly believe that both physical and digital assets are "real-world" ones); however, this is yet another case of industry usance getting ahead of semantic rigour. In any case, Aave offers precisely such an RWA-market [158] to digital asset investors, by reusing a large part of its existing capital markets infrastructure for EVM-compatible blockchains. The Aave RWA market also incorporates the tokenization policies and parts of the economic agent typology (and of the software infrastructure) of the cooperating Centrifuge [159, 160] ecosystem. The resulting

[51] As of the time of writing this book, this fee is set to 0 (zero—i.e. no transaction fee is currently raised for AAVE stakings).

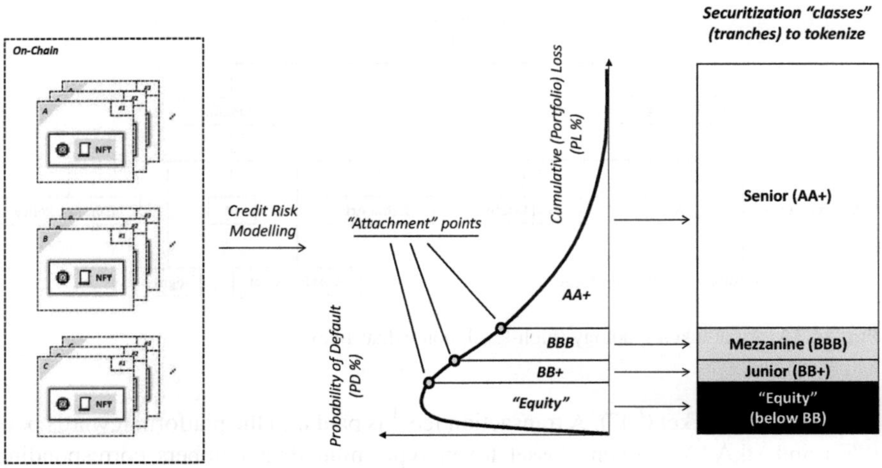

Fig. 14.35 From NFTs (tokenizing physical-world assets) to securitization structure

business use case [161] is asset-backed securitization in a private debt setting (due to the absence of a requirement for regulated banking agents); hence, we will encounter notions and practices already explained in Sects. 14.2 and 14.3.

In the centrifuge RWA paradigm, off-chain assets are tokenized by "RWA originators" and packaged by "RWA Issuers" into securities of different risk/return profiles, available to investors through "investment pools" (smart contract based). Each investment pool has an off-chain special purpose vehicle attached [162] for bankruptcy-remoteness purposes. The combined off- and on-chain rights and responsibilities of said SPV are defined in an "operating agreement" [163], visible on Centrifuge. The ecosystem, in essence, replicates the operating model of traditional ABS (please revisit the agent typology of Fig. 14.15).

The central notion of Centrifuge is the transfer of legal ownership of off-chain assets to the SPV in the form of NFTs. In short, RWA originators expect to finance the acquisition and servicing of off-chain assets by tokenizing them into NFTs and using the latter as collateral for the issuance of investable securities. This happens on an EVM-compatible blockchain (meaning that NFTs are minted through SC conforming to ERC-721, or equivalent). Centrifuge defines a legally robust process for on-chain representation of off-chain property rights [164] (in effect, removing any ambiguity on which property rights are represented by the NFTs). It also includes technical artefacts allowing for on-/off-chain exchange of confidential information [165] needed for bilateral negotiation between transacting parties.

RWA Issuers manage asset pools; they decide which NFTs to include, how to model their income streams and risk/return profiles, and how to package them into a securitization structure (cf. Fig. 14.35). Operationally, they also manage valuation, credit events, cash flows, ABS issuance/redemption, and collateral substitution.

They may decide to involve third parties (including Oracles) for specialized tasks, such as asset marking to market [166], net asset value (NAV) calculation, setting asset credit risk status (e.g., "non-performing", "defaulted", "written-off"), etc.

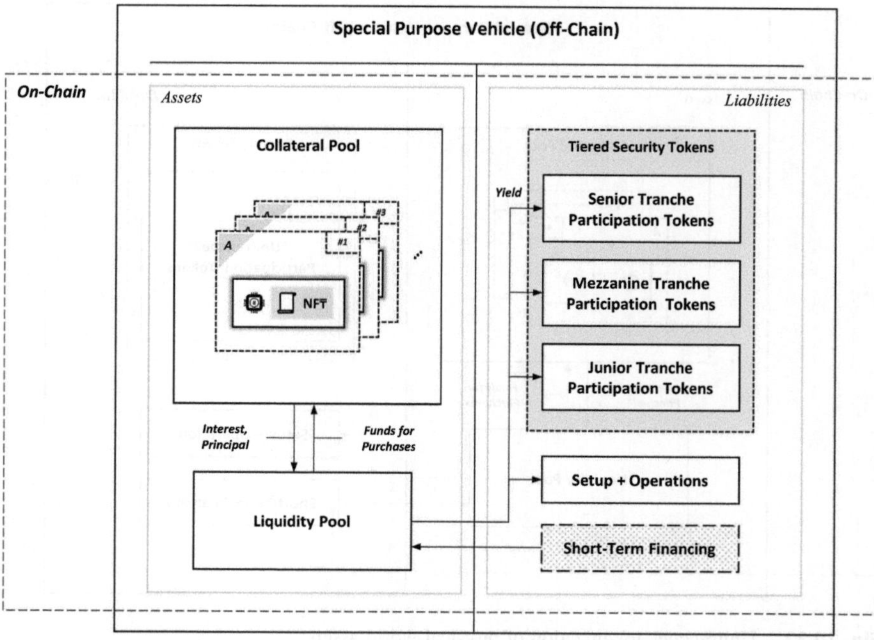

Fig. 14.36 On-chain securitization tokens of physical-world assets through NFTs

Centrifuge already provides the process framework for these tasks around on-chain securitization [164]. The end result is a robust on-chain paradigm allowing exchange of assets and liquidity exclusively in the form of tokens [167]. Centrifuge investment pools [168] typically combine a collateral pool and a cash reserve (liquidity pool), the latter intended to manage cash in–/outflows and to store liquidity not (or, not yet) allocated to assets.

The SPV's balance sheet also manages the liability side through the on-chain issuance and redemption [169] of participation tokens of different seniority tranches [170] (cf. Fig. 14.36).

Centrifuge participation tokens are on-chain fixed-income securities able to span the entire gamut from bullet loans [171] to complex amortization schedules.

Structuring does not have to be complex, so "simple" financings can also be accommodated inside the same process framework through "unitranche" (cf. Fig. 14.12) participation tokens, as depicted in Fig. 14.37.

RWA participation tokens thus offer interest yield on token funds paid into a liquidity pool (based on well-defined on-chain policies [172]), and this is precisely the attachment point to Aave. In short, Aave funds suppliers can also become centrifuge RWA investors by depositing admissible tokens into Centrifuge investment pools. Through its cooperation with Centrifuge, Aave extends its "market" paradigm to include NFT-collateralized participation tokens as interest-yielding mechanism on Aave aTokens. Instead of agents onboarding directly (and incurring transaction fees) in two different ecosystems, Aave and Centrifuge [173], the Aave RWA market allows for investments from within the same non-custodial environment as the typical Aave market.

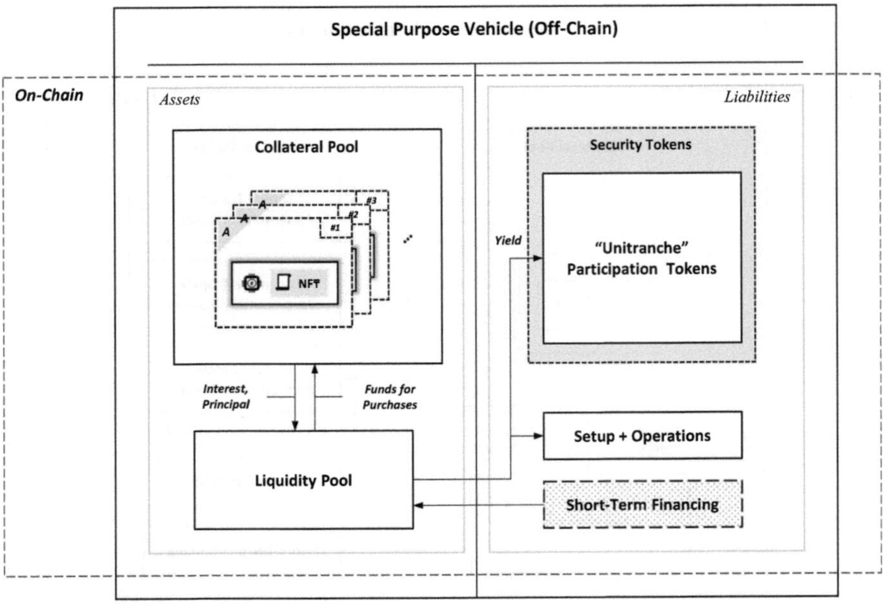

Fig. 14.37 "Unitranche" tokenization of physical-world assets

The transactional pathway in question is depicted in Fig. 14.38. The Aave RWA Investor must first exchange a subscription agreement ("1") with the RWA Issuer of a Centrifuge investment pool. Then by connecting their crypto wallet to the Aave RWA market, they can transfer admissible ERC-20 tokens (currently, Stablecoins) to the investment pool smart contract ("2"), which will become part of the underlying liquidity pool ("3"). When presented with a suitable investment opportunity, they may then use them to purchase participation tokens backed by assets in the corresponding collateral pool, which are ERC-20 aTokens (denoted by a$\bar{\mathrm{T}}$ on Fig. 14.38) in the sense of the Aave operating model. The aTokens are transferred ("4"), through the pool SC, to the agent's crypto wallet ("5"). All incurred transaction fees are moved to the platform rewards pool ("6").

As already mentioned, this is a combined ABS/private debt use case. The calibrating parameters of the RWA market operational model involve both Aave and Centrifuge risk frameworks and are meant to provide controllability and exception handling to the end-to-end transactional pathway.

14.5.3.10 Primary Market Operations of GHO Stablecoin

GHO [89] is the native Stablecoin of the Aave ecosystem, pegged to the USD. It is minted and burned in Aave, in other words, Aave is the GHO primary market where issuance and redemption take place at par. GHO is somewhat unusual in that Aave in effect delegates the definition and execution of price stabilization mechanisms to the issuing market (which is then termed "GHO Facilitator" [174, 175]—note that this is

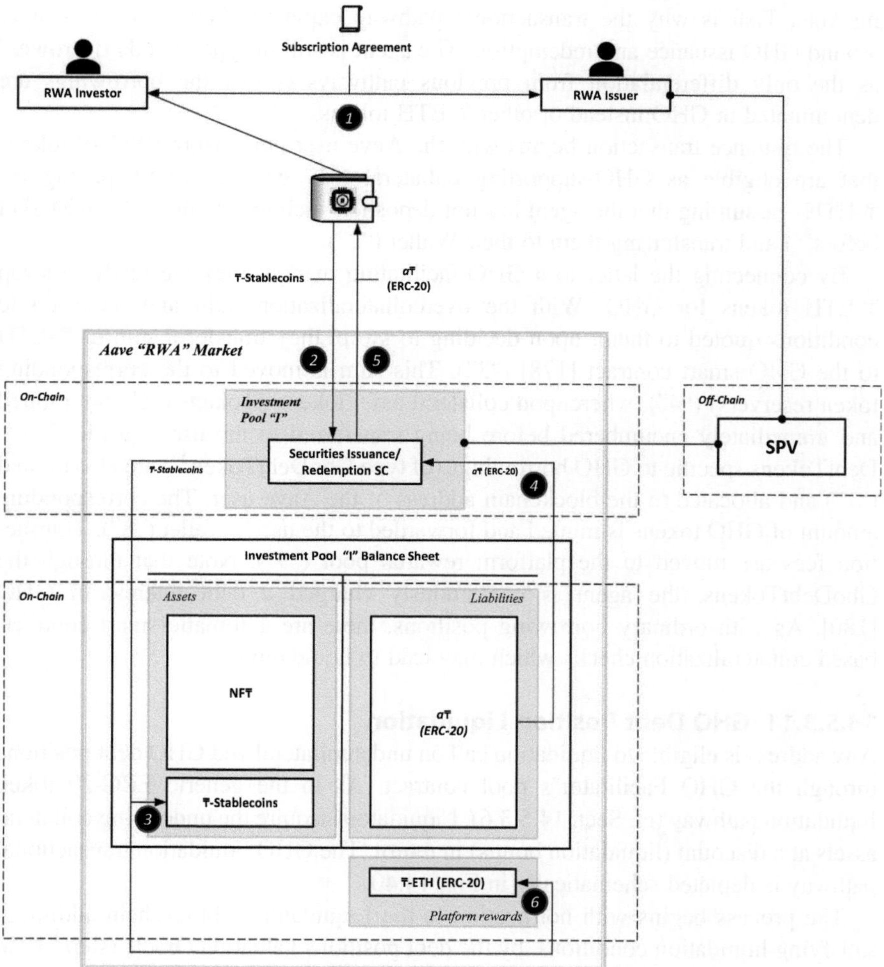

Fig. 14.38 RWA Investor acquires securities

not a new Aave agent type; a more detailed explanation is provided in the subsequent token design Sect. 14.7.1.5).

For the purposes of the current discussion, the issuing market is taken to be that of the Aave Ethereum Mainnet, which implements a reserve-backed stabilization logic using overcollateralization [176]. Both GHO and the backing assets are ERC-20 tokens.

As of the time of writing, GHO are not meant to be used as yield investment tokens (i.e. are not allowed to be deposited[52] by funds suppliers) within Aave

[52] Please note that there are some implementation details about GHO "helper" tokens that may give this impression, but the technical documentation [177] must be read carefully.

markets. That is why the transactional pathway explained here revolves simply around GHO issuance and redemption. The agent is still of type "Funds Borrower" as the only differentiation from previous pathways is that the borrowings are denominated in GHO instead of other Ŧ-ETH tokens.

The issuance transaction begins with the Aave user purchasing ERC-20 tokens that are eligible as GHO-supporting collateral ("1" on Fig. 14.39, paying for Ŧ-ETH—assuming that the agent has not deposited such tokens in an Aave Market before[53]) and transferring them to their Wallet ("2").

By connecting the latter to a GHO-facilitating market, they are ready to swap Ŧ-ETH tokens for GHO. With the overcollateralization ratio and interest rate conditions quoted to them, upon deciding to swap, they transfer a sum of Ŧ-ETH to the GHO smart contract [178] ("3"). This sum is moved to the corresponding token reserve(s) ("4"), whereupon collateral asset tokens aTokens ("5") are minted and immediately encumbered before being transferred to the user's wallet ("6"). DebtTokens specific to GHO borrowings (of type GhoDebtToken[54]) are also minted ("7") and allocated to the blockchain address of the Aave user. The corresponding amount of GHO tokens is minted and forwarded to the user's wallet ("8"). Transaction fees are moved to the platform rewards pool ("9"). Note that through the GhoDebtTokens, the agent is continuously charged a debt interest in GHO [180]. As with ordinary borrowing positions, there are automatic smart contract-based collateralization checks which may lead to liquidation.

14.5.3.11 GHO Debt Position Liquidation

Any address is eligible to liquidation call on undercollateralized GHO debt positions through the GHO Facilitator's pool contract. As in the generic ERC-20 token liquidation pathway (cf. Sect. 14.5.3.6), Liquidators acquire the underlying collateral assets at a discount (liquidation bonus) in return. The GHO liquidation transactional pathway is depicted schematically in Fig. 14.40.

The process begins with notification to the Liquidator of blockchain addresses satisfying liquidation conditions, by the debt positions valuation Oracle (step "1" in Fig. 14.40). Should the agent decide to liquidate part, or all, of the outstanding borrowings of a particular address, the next step is to purchase GHO in external Centralized or Decentralized Exchanges (step "2") and transfer them to the agent's crypto wallet ("3"), which is connected to the Aave market. The agent then calls the *liquidationCall()* method on the GHO primary market smart contract holding the GhoDebtTokens of the Funds Borrower, paying in the amount of GHO tokens needed to close out the target outstanding borrowing position ("4") up to the allowed

[53] If the user already has sufficient eligible collateral, then steps "1" and "2" are obviously redundant.

[54] In the current version of Aave, this is a "GhoVariableDebtToken", even though the interest charged is fixed. This discrepancy between functionality and technical implementation notation is admitted to in the official GHO documentation, e.g. at [179].

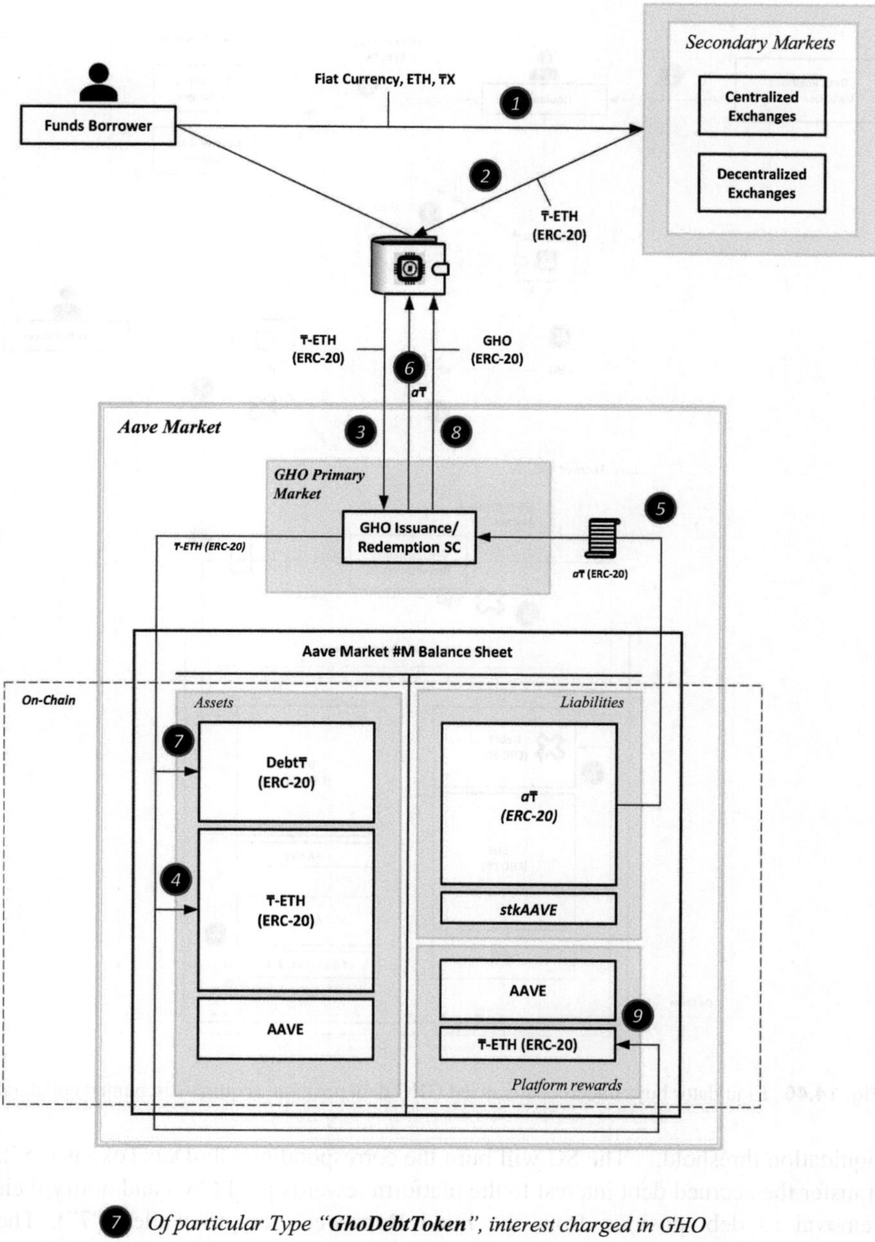

Fig. 14.39 Primary market (Aave) GHO Stablecoin issuance

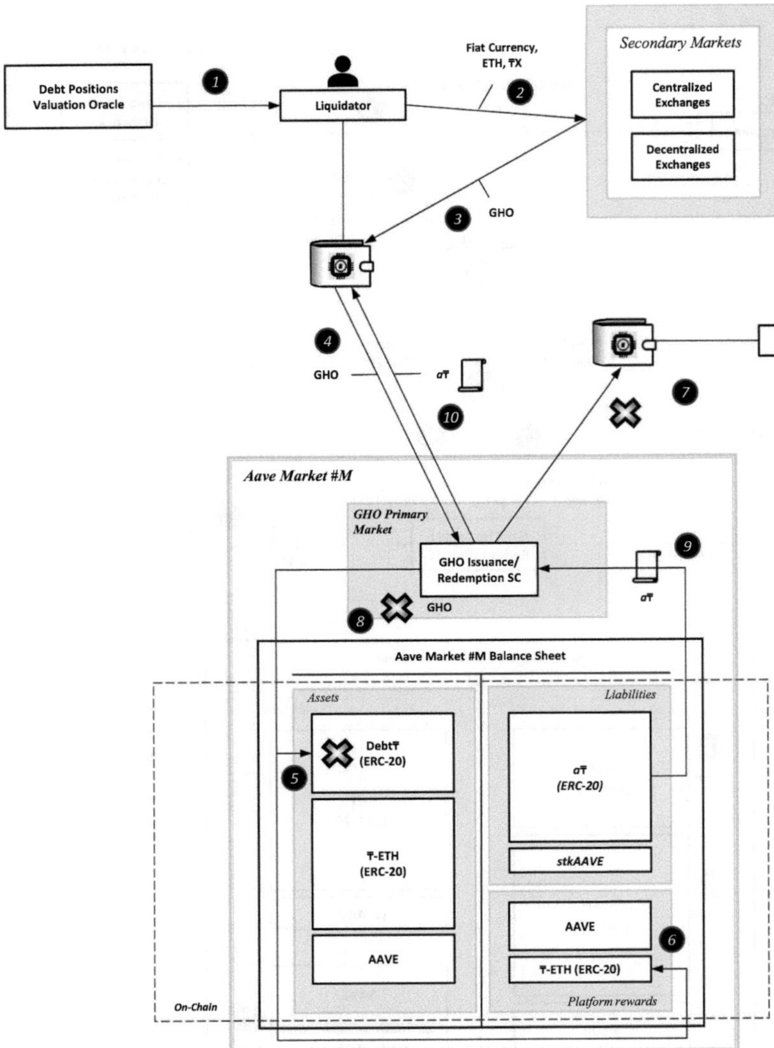

Fig. 14.40 Liquidator buys undercollateralized GHO debt position, acquires discounted collateral

liquidation threshold.[55] The SC will burn the corresponding GhoDebtTokens ("5"), transfer the accrued debt interest to the platform rewards pool ("6") and notify their removal as debt position from the Fund Borrower's crypto wallet ("7"). The redemption SC will then burn the borrowed GHO tokens ("8")—remember that Aave does not have a GHO reserve as it does not allow GHO for deposits.

[55] As of the time of writing, this is 50% of the outstanding borrowing. Please consult [181] for policy updates.

Afterwards, the underlying discounted collateral assets are unencumbered and transferred through the SC ("9") to the Liquidator's wallet ("10").

As in the generic ERC-20 token liquidation, the role of GHO Liquidators is crucial for the health of the Aave ecosystem. In the generic case, they act as de facto credit risk and collateral managers to safeguard the integrity of the underlying Aave market's balance sheet. In a GHO primary market (Facilitator) context, however, their action has a different but equally important effect: namely **to defend the peg of the GHO Stablecoin** to the USD. That is why they are incentivized by Aave through a Liquidation Bonus.

14.5.3.12 GHO Debt Position Liquidation Through a Flash Loan ("FlashMinting")

Aave incentivizes willing Liquidators not wishing to commit own principal through a mechanism equivalent to the flash loan, as explained in Sect. 14.5.3.7, Fig. 14.32. That functionality was explained as based on the ability to technically orchestrate and execute a series of transactions that stay within the time limits of single-block assembly. Either all transactions execute, or they are reversed. The corresponding modality available through GHO Facilitators is called "FlashMinting" [182] and involves platform smart contracts [183] that are different from those of Aave liquidity pools, but still obey the same flash loan standard specification (ERC-3156). The reason for this difference is the fact that flash loans are designed to work on reserve tokens, whereas GHO is not meant to be used within Aave as such.

In other words, as already mentioned, GHO can be minted and burned in the primary market but cannot be supplied for deposits. As per Aave governance decision, FlashMinting is available only through approved GHO Facilitators, called "FlashMinters" [184]. They alone are authorized to provide access to GHO liquidity, as long as the minted GHO tokens plus a FlashMinting fee are returned[56] by the end of the single-block validation.

The FlashMinting transactional pathway is depicted on Fig. 14.41. The trigger to the transaction is notification of a "free-to-liquidate" GHO debt position ("1" on Fig. 14.41) to a Liquidator, whereupon a FlashMinting request is sent to a FlashMinter's smart contract ("2"). The requested GHO tokens are minted and sent by the SC to the liquidator's wallet ("3"). Subsequently, a *liquidationCall()* is invoked against the primary market's SC, whereby the same GHO tokens are passed ("4") and used to provisionally cancel the GhoDebtTokens in question ("5" in the Aave working assets account and "6" in the Fund Borrower's wallet). The originally borrowed GHO tokens are burned ("7"), and the underlying collateral (discounted aTokens, as per liquidation rules) passes provisionally to the ownership of the Liquidator ("8" from the liabilities account to the SC, and "9" to the Liquidator's wallet). The latter forwards them immediately to the secondary market ("10"), where

[56]Or, if a secondary GHO borrowing position is opened, which is no longer a liquidation, but is nevertheless offered as a transaction strategy.

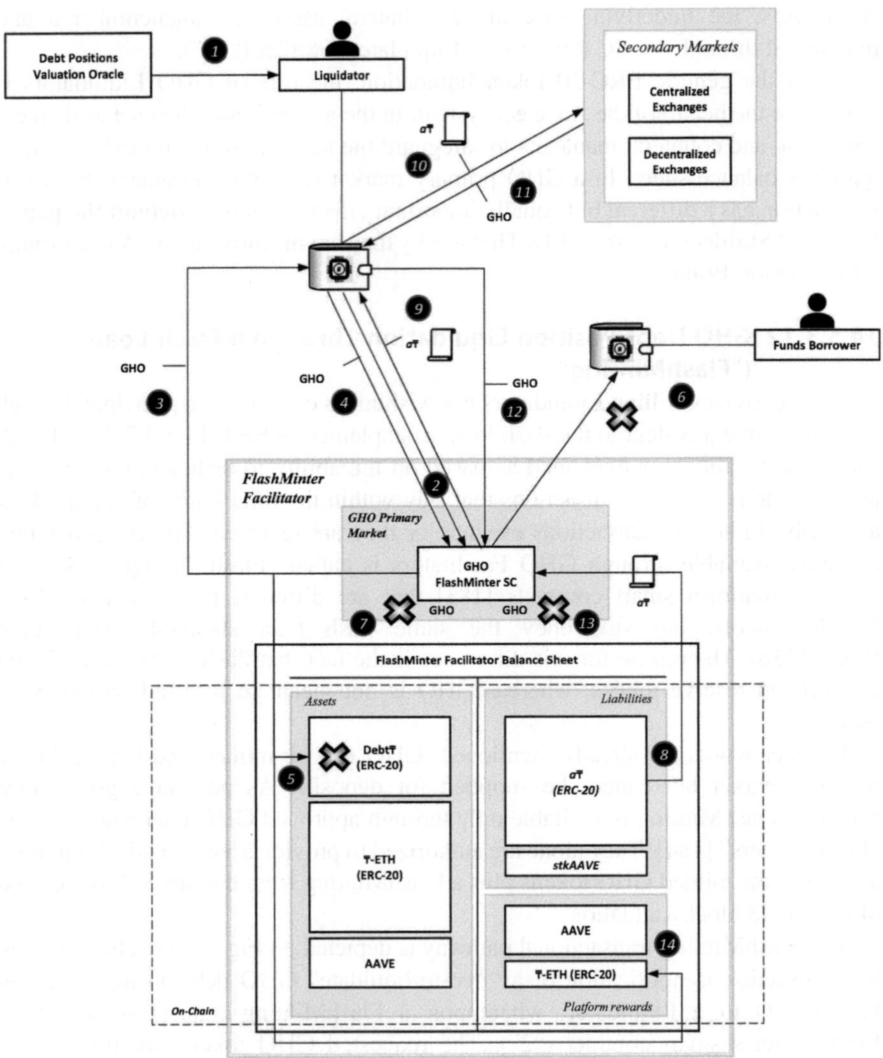

Fig. 14.41 Liquidator buys GHO debt position through FlashMinting and repays immediately by reselling acquired assets

they are exchanged for GHO tokens and the resulting funds return to the Liquidator's wallet ("11"). The FlashMinter's SC is then called anew, referencing a sufficient amount of the new GHO tokens ("12"), which are burned to repay the Flash Loan ("13"). Finally, FlashMinting fees are paid to the Platform rewards pool ("14"), completing the FlashMinting and perfecting all provisional transactions.

As in the generic "liquidation through flash loan" case, the GHO Liquidator acquires the collateral assets at a discount [185], which represents a risk-free income stream. This is the incentive by Aave to technically competent agents to provide the service of (in effect) defending the GHO peg to the USD.

This concludes the overview of the main transactional pathways of the Aave ecosystem. We proceed by analysing how Aave calibrates the major influencing factors of market design, namely thickness, congestion, safety, usability, and conformance to social norms.

14.5.4 Thickness

As was explained in Sect. 6.6.1, thickness—or market depth—is critical for attainment of network effects. To that end, Aave has used EVM-compatibility as a key to deepen its addressable market, in three directions: first, by cooperating with L-2 ecosystems that promise reduced gas fees of L-1 transactions while allowing to adopt all EVM-artefacts (smart contracts, business process software, agent model) of the "market" paradigm. This way, Aave extended its potential user base to the participants of those L-2 ecosystems, and still kept its software stack and ecosystem governance intact. An Aave market on Polygon or Avalanche has different smart contract addresses but is in all other respects the same as that on the Ethereum Mainnet. Second, by cooperating with an ecosystem (Centrifuge) having a complementary business case, that of physical-world asset tokenization. Aave being a capital market, it positioned itself as the on-chain financing layer for securities issued on Centrifuge collateral, thus creating the joint Aave/Centrifuge RWA market. And third, by using the proliferation of ERC-tokens already admissible as Aave collateral to reach Stablecoin investors.

In short, Aave governance sought to increase the thickness of its primary ecosystem by entering partnerships and extending its use case, thus targeting the following advantages for its participating agents:

a. **Reduced gas fees** for transactions
b. Reaching an **extended population of potential counterparties**, that of successful L-2 EVM projects
c. Using **tokens native to those L-2** projects as **collateral or debt positions**
d. Accessing a **new set of transactions** (physical-world asset financing)
e. Having a **"safe harbour" value proposition** through a native **Stablecoin (GHO)**
f. Profiting from **new revenue streams accruing to the Aave rewards pool**[57]

It is worth observing that GHO borrowers have preferential rates if they are also AAVE stakers. This incentivizes existing agents to keep participating in the Aave ecosystem transactions, thus defending the attainment of network effects.

---

[57] Please search for "fees and revenue" (cumulative) in [186].

14.5.5 Congestion

With reference to Sect. 6.6.2, we remind the reader that congestion denotes inherent frictions in the creation or execution of transactions. Aave strives to avoid such frictions by the following market design calibrations:

a. Aave governance maintains a comprehensive and up-to-date documentation [69] of features [187], process steps [188], and feedback channels. The documentation is publicly available, including the developers section [71, 97].
b. Aave supplies its own dApp [104], the features of which align with the documentation. For technology-savvy users, the *developer* documentation explains the features and interaction mode of individual smart contracts [189] (e.g. for liquidations [190]). More detailed technical documentation is also available in the Aave GitHub [72, 191].
c. Market-specific configurations are clearly explained in the documentation and also visible in the Aave dApp. For example, how does fund borrowing accrue interest charges and which tokens come with available Stable rates per Aave Market [82] are made unambiguous so that transactions can be entered into.
d. In terms of transaction costs, Aave market design taps into the L-2 EVM-ecosystems, where gas-fees and "time-to-finality" (TTF [192]) can be lower [193] than on the Ethereum Mainnet. Also, one of the value propositions of funds borrowing is not having to forego interest income by having to swap tokens among primary markets and through Exchanges. Being able to execute this swap on Aave in a risk-controlled manner is a transaction facilitator by itself. Aave uses Oracles [194] to provide up-to-date prices to its market participants; hence, they do not need to query own market feeds or Exchanges.
e. Another example of transaction facilitation is the ability for RWA Investors to read immediately the exact nature of the underlying collateral and of the offered investment terms through the Centrifuge RWA dApp [195]. This affords them a quick and informed investment decision.

In summary, Aave's market design is consciously calibrating its features to manage congestion in its ecosystem.

14.5.6 Safety

As explained in Sect. 6.6.3, an ecosystem is safe if its participants are protected from losses due to factors outside their control. Safety calibration involves both market and mechanism designs, and in Aave market design, it is done along three axes:

1. **Safety of individual transactions** (i.e. protecting mechanisms when entering transactions, during execution)
2. **Safety of supplied funds** (e.g. against theft)
3. **Safety of being a long-term participant** in Aave markets

On the safety of participating in individual transactions, the following observations apply: Aave itself is not a permissioned blockchain ecosystem. However, it does implement blockchain address screening [196] as a matter of course. In cooperation with other ecosystems, it may and does adopt onboarding requirements [197]. To participate in the main Aave markets, users must first connect an external crypto wallet and then rely upon the technical and process infrastructure of Aave to proceed. Aave governance strives for safety at the level of technical infrastructure by having regular smart contract audits [198, 199] and also by funding an actively pursued "bug bounty" program [200]. Process-wise, there is a strict protocol to follow for admittance of ERC-tokens [201] as reserve tokens ("new asset listing"). Price discovery for reserve tokens exchanged in transactions relies on external Oracles [194], which are institutional-grade [202]. Transaction execution relies on Aave smart contracts and on the underlying L-1 or L-2 blockchains, which are by definition EVM-compatible. Hence, there is a risk of "inherited" smart contract events at cooperating ecosystems, which is managed by the fact that governance of both [195] the latter and Aave will be monitoring [196] distributed ledger transactions.

RWA investors have two extra safety mechanisms at their disposal: First, the cooperating ecosystem Centrifuge carries out onboarding due diligence [203], in particular, now-your-client (KYC) checks are mandatory. The onboarding checks were also adopted by the Aave RWA market [204], by explicit proposal of Aave governance [205]. Second, off-chain legal agreements are a prerequisite for RWA investments and are also to be persisted on-chain (thus, they become immutable and immediately available for inspection). Please recall the discussion in Sect. 14.3 on counterparty and transaction due diligence in the context of private debt markets. As already mentioned in Sect. 14.5.3.9, the Aave RWA market is precisely an on-chain private debt market, also offering tokenized asset-backed securities. Hence, due diligence tasks (such are those listed in Table 14.2) are expected to be performed by "prudent people of business"—RWA Issuers and Investors. As also explained in Sect. 14.5.3.9, off-chain legal agreements (operating and subscription-level) are required to be signed and evidenced on the blockchain before any physical-world property rights are tokenized and sold to RWA Investors. This means that the contract law of some physical world jurisdiction will be invoked before tokens are exchanged on the Aave RWA market. Hence, RWA transaction participants have the means to incorporate appropriate conditions and warranties into their contracts to align with the outcomes of bilateral due diligence. Any omission or misrepresentation of facts causing erroneous due diligence outcomes may void RWA transaction contracts, and the injured party may seek legal recourse in the respective physical-world jurisdiction. In summary, onboarding KYC and mandatory off-chain contractual agreements (evidenced on-chain) are two safety mechanisms available specifically to RWA Investors.

Regarding the safety of supplied funds, recall that Aave is strictly a non-custodial ecosystem. To initiate and terminate each and every transaction, participants must connect an external crypto wallet—through the Aave dApp or programmatically. Supplied funds are thus never under the control of Aave, nor of any third-party agent.

The balance of a user's asset or debt position can be deduced by Aave participants through the underlying distributed ledger, but unauthorized transfer of funds is technically impossible as long as the external wallet has not been compromised.

Safety of being a long-term Aave participant follows from mechanisms relating to notions of market integrity, as contained in the regulatory frameworks of several traditional financial jurisdictions [206, 207, 381]. Preservation of market integrity has several aspects in Aave:

a. Management of financial risk assumed by individual funds borrowers (minimization of "self-harm risk")
b. Protection of the token reserves of individual Aave markets
c. Protection of the entire Aave ecosystem against systemic events

Self-harm risk is primarily managed through those aspects of the Aave risk framework controlling individual debt positions (LTV/overcollateralization limits, supply and borrow caps [81], "Health Factor" calculation [130, 208], etc.). Provision for Liquidator agent types and their active incentivization (through both liquidation bonuses and the right to draw flash loans) to act as de facto credit risk and collateral managers combine to create an effective "stop loss" mechanism on individual fund borrower positions. All aspects of the Aave risk framework are documented and publicly available [209], so market participants can be well informed before entering transactions. Asset suitability [131] can also be ascertained by agents through the Aave documentation [210] pages.

The same Liquidators indirectly protect the integrity of token reserves in Aave markets. If uncollateralized credit exposures were allowed to reach a critical mass, then token reserves would be depleted by Funds Borrowers able to draw "good money" in exchange for rapidly depreciating collateral. The Aave risk framework [201] also specifies asset-level limits [211–214]) (supply caps [215, 216] and borrow caps [217, 218]) and other mechanisms (e.g. setting assets to "siloed mode" [219]) to manage the liquidity risk of markets. Individual token proof-of-reserves are monitored through Oracles [220–222]. For the GHO Stablecoin market in particular, the "Facilitator" concept assigns clear responsibility for the management of reserves backing the USD peg [223].

Systemic risk events (of either technical or market provenance) are controlled by policies, and managed by appropriate market and mechanism design calibrations. Aave governance maintains the policies of the Aave risk framework and also commissions regular audits [198] by outside experts on algorithmic consistency [200], response of the Aave protocols' mechanisms under stressed market conditions, etc. All Aave governance initiatives relating to security are also available on Aave's GitHub [224].

Operationally, systemic risks are managed through the existence of an AAVE reserve [76], the smart contracts of the safety module [225], and the incentivization [226] of AAVE suppliers to act as insurance providers through staking [152]. The process [227, 228], and potential risks and returns, of Staking are clearly documented [229] and publicly available for AAVE holders to take informed investment decisions thereupon. Should the Safety Module prove inadequate to cover a systemic shortfall event, Aave governance can trigger AAVE emergency issuance [230] through a "backstop module" [231]. As a measure of last resort, the Aave ecosystem reserve [76, 232] can be drawn down. Aave treasury management is the responsibility of Aave governance [233–235].

14.5.7 Usability

Both the Aave markets and RWA dApps [82, 195] are intuitive, easy to use, and non-verbose, with a clean interface for navigation. The former gives users easy access to all essential information through links to the Aave documentation. The latter is addressed to that section of agents who are prepared to undergo KYC; hence, it presupposes having read the respective documentation and signing the respective off-chain legal agreements.

All in all, the constellation of user and developer documentation pages; the Aave GitHub; the accessible Aave governance pages [236]; and the at-once clear and concise process FAQs [188]; is conducive to a predictable user experience.

14.5.8 Social Norms

The Aave ecosystem business case is capital markets, which is per se a socially accepted activity in traditional finance. Only the Aave RWA market can conceivably be used for socially questionable investments (for instance, by tokenizing and securitizing socially repugnant property rights). However, off-chain legal agreements (operating and subscription-level) are required to be signed and evidenced on the blockchain before any physical-world property rights are tokenized and invested in. This means that the contract law of some physical world jurisdiction will be invoked before tokens are exchanged on the Aave RWA market. Hence, transaction participants have the means to ensure that the underlying property rights involve lawful activities; otherwise, their contracts will be void. As a final recourse, Aave DAO has the means to intervene in individual market activities by voting to terminate unethical behaviours.

In short, the main Aave markets respect social norms by default, while the Aave RWA market provides the mechanisms for individual participants to legally enforce conformance with laws and regulations, and for the Aave governance to correct any intended or unintended deviations therefrom.

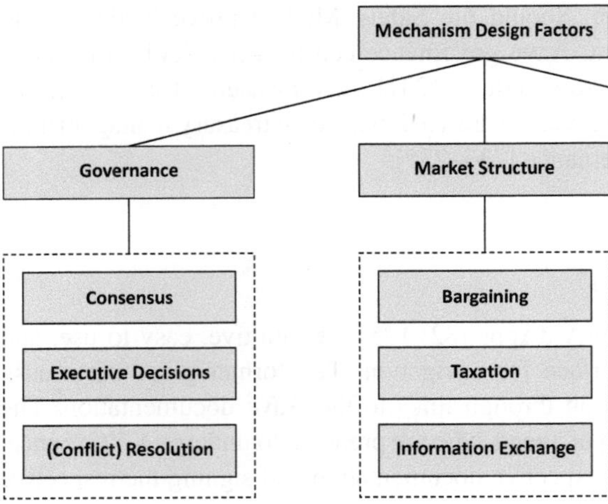

Fig. 14.42 Factors of consideration in mechanism design; more granular aspects thereof

14.6 Aave Mechanism Design

As per Chap. 8, blockchain ecosystem mechanism design must identify all **interaction pathways**[58] among privileged and non-privileged **agent** types and prescribe rules and incentives that are to apply along each. Inherent to this process is an analysis phase, which can be systematized by considering the three design factors:

i. Governance
ii. Market structure
iii. Financial/non-financial incentives

as "lenses" through which to examine pathways. We propose to follow this approach in order to interpret Aave mechanisms as calibration choices. Please recall (cf. Sect. 8.5) that factors of consideration in mechanism design can be broken down into more granular aspects (cf. Fig. 14.42).

As mentioned in Sect. 9.6 on market design, Aave **governance** involves a DAO[59] (driving both "legislative" and "executive" decision-making), deferring to the holders of the ecosystem governance token (AAVE, cf. Sect. 14.7.1.4 below), who can vote for both strategic and tactical decisions. There is also a committee of human "Guardians" [238–241] who have mainly an advisory role, but are also entrusted with time-critical operational decisions (e.g. intervening in the functioning of Aave markets that are at risk from malicious actors). An important piece of information is

[58] Attention: Not only transactional pathways, but all possible hierarchical, horizontal, and constitutive interaction pathways, as explained in Sect. 8.1.

[59] More precisely, a series of DAOs under the auspices of a main Aave DAO. Examples: [93, 237].

that Aave was originally constructed, and was in its early phases operated, under the auspices of a corporate "owner/operator" ("Aave companies", since rebranded [242] to "Avara" [243, 244]) that may still retain a material percentage of the native governance token's (AAVE) circulating supply [245].

Aave relies on its community and participating agents for the stability and evolution of its ecosystem. Its market design, viewed together with its incentivization policies, bears this out [246].

The first step towards governance decisions is a proposal initiated by any community member [247–249]; then being sounded in the Aave community fora [Discord [74, 250], etc.]; ultimately concatenating contributions from several members through consensus, thus reaching a mature stage (status "Aave Request for Final Comments", ARFC [251]); and then formulated into an "Aave Improvement Proposal", AIP [252]. However, only AAVE holders have the power to actually create the AIP record [253] and to submit it (through the "governance module" [254–256]) to a vote. Said vote [257] (the outcome of which is the final decision on the AIP) is taken through smart contract [258], which is again open only to AAVE holders. All holdings, including those tied in AAVE staking smart contracts, are taken into account. The technical description of AIP actually contains a link to the artefacts that are to be implemented. If said artefacts are of purely technical nature, then acceptance of the API schedules them for immediate deployment. Please note that, as Aave is non-custodial, a voting process was originally devised whereby message signing across wallets and a vote "challenging" (in effect, vote verification) mechanism were implemented.

Immediate deployment, however, does not mean immediate execution. In the Aave governance framework, execution is carried out by smart contacts called "executors". Importantly, those are defined to correspond to two criticality levels, #1 [259] and #2 [260], also designated as "short" and "long", executors respectively. Short executors are invoked after a "timelock delay" of shorter duration than long ones. As of the time of writing, the timelock durations were 1 ("short") and 7 days ("long"), counting from the timepoint of scheduling [249]. The intention in both cases is for last-chance reviews to take place by designated experts or interested parties from the Aave community, that is, to avert unintended consequences. Using a long executor generally signifies that a voted outcome has longer-term impact for the Aave ecosystem; hence, that would be a strategic decision, more strongly related to governance **consensus**. Using a short executor is typically associated with decisions of a more operational nature, such as protocol parametrization changes, new asset listings, ecosystem reserve outlays, etc. Those would be more aptly characterized as Aave governance **executive decisions.** Please note that the "Guardian" agent type is meant as a fail-safe mechanism of the last resort, whenever exceptional, time-critical action is called for [261]).

As Aave "installs" markets in other participating ecosystems (i.e. is allowed to have its processes and technical artefacts operating inside them), there had to be a way to "propagate" governance decisions across its main market (on Ethereum Mainnet) and the rest—and also a sense of "decision hierarchy". The way Aave implements this propagation of policies and operating rules is a technical one, called "cross-chain governance bridges" [262, 263]. The current technical setup mandates that voting for Aave governance is allowed only on Ethereum Mainnet, and then said "bridges" execute the technical outcomes of the accepted AIPs into the other Aave Markets.

Regarding **conflict resolution**, there currently does not appear to exist a governance process dedicated to handling of disputes among Aave participants. There do exist Aave contractual terms and conditions [264–266] regulating potential disputes between Aave and outside actors [267], but they would not qualify as relating to a "judiciary" function of the sort promulgated in Chap. 8.

The second "lens" (cf. Fig. 14.42) is **market structure**, a notion expressing all mechanisms impacting price discovery and price formation in transactions among economic agents, both ordinary and privileged.

In all transactional pathways (cf. Sect. 9.6.3), there is a need to have price information, either on directly tradable assets (reserve tokens, including the AAVE token; and aTokens, which again represent value 1:1 to reserve ones); or on RWAs in terms of their mapping NFTs. In the former case (i.e., in all Aave markets aside from the RWA one), Aave always uses price Oracles [194]—the GHO primary market always mints the GHO Stablecoin at 1:1 to USD; however, Oracles are still needed to get the USD/ETH rate and also the rates of those ERC-20 tokens exchanged for GHO against ETH. In the latter case (RWA market) RWA asset valuation happens off-chain and NAV for on-chain security tokens is calculated at the end of each "epoch" [268] through centrifuge's pricing and valuation smart contract ("NAV feed") [269]. Hence, Aave market's **information exchange** mechanisms always rely on Oracles whenever feasible.

Bargaining mechanisms are calibrated both directly and indirectly, the latter through the Aave risk policies. First of all, the main Aave transactional pathways do not involve any kind of auction, not even for debt position liquidation [270] (cf. Sects. 14.5.3.6 and 14.5.3.11/14.5.3.12). The only context where Aave explicitly provides for auctions is in the policies of the safety module [271] as a result of severe shortfall events, which then impact AAVE stakers [272] and the total AAVE circulating supply [273]. The safety module then invokes a smart contract which implements a Dutch auction mechanism (cf. Sect. 8.5.2). The risk management rules of debt positions through liquidation and through assets in the safety module are explained in Sects. 14.6.3 and 14.6.4, respectively.

Aave's **taxation** mechanisms are calibrated around the need to have an ecosystem reserve, fulfilling two roles: first, as an operating capital pool to cover infrastructure/supplier fees and short- to mid-term investment outlays, and second, as a "lender of last resort". The first role is important for ecosystem preservation and growth, as the resulting network effect will increase AAVE token's valuation, thus also its attractiveness to potential investors. This, in return, will promote good governance (more AAVE holders means more potential governance participants), better systemic risk management (more AAVE stakers will support the safety module), and more calculated risk-taking activity (based on research financed by the reserve) to monetize new business use cases. The second role is self-evident, also recalling the discussion in Sect. 14.5.3.8 on the AAVE staking transactional pathway. The first line of defence for shortfall events is the safety module (SM) [225], backed up (second line) by a "backstop module". However, the ecosystem reserve was already considered in the setup of the SM [274] and will conceivably be used to defend the Aave ecosystem in catastrophic crypto-market-wide or idiosyncratic circumstances. The main taxation mechanisms to provision the Aave reserve are:

a. The "reserve factor" on interest paid by borrowers [275]
b. Flash loan (and FlashMinting) fees [276]

The **reserve factor** (RF) is simply a percentage tax levied on interest due, its level depending on market and the specific reserve token borrowed [382]. Each Aave market implements a "collector" smart contract [277] which aggregates all revenues accrued throughout token reserves. All RFs and collector smart contract addresses are indicated in the Aave dApp [278]. **Flash loan** [135, 136] (including FlashMinting) **fees** [276] are levied on flash borrowers as a means to cover the cost of liquidity provisionally supplied by Aave. As per policy, they can be waived for "approved flash borrowers" [279]. All levied taxes flow to the Aave treasury by way of the respective pool smart contract [280].

Aave's financial and non-financial incentives for **voting** participation follow the taxonomy put forth in Sect. 8.5.3. As per said taxonomy, proposals are accepted by Quorum voting [281, 282], under proportional representation (1 AAVE/stkAAVE token equals 1 vote) [283]. Individual voters have the right to delegate their voting powers (in effect "sign over" their AAVE/stkAAVE for voting purposes only—not the associated rewards) to other blockchain addresses, called "delegates" [284–286]. As of the time of writing, there appears to be no institutionalized rewards (in terms of AAVE or other benefits) back to voters, hence also no rewards **allocation** policy.

So far, we explained how the high-level Aave mechanism design considers the influencing factors of Fig. 14.42. We now proceed with an examination of more fine-granular mechanisms underlying specific transactional pathways.

14.6.1 Token Reserve Rules (Aave Markets, non-RWA)

Please revisit the discussion about the constellation of liquidity pools and token reserves in Aave markets (cf. Sect. 9.6), the graphical depiction of which is repeated here as Fig. 14.43 for convenience.

Aave prescribes what is, in effect, a prudential framework to help each market systematically manage capital and liquidity across its own liquidity pools. This framework is defined and parametrized by Aave governance, codified in policies documented as part of the "Aave risk framework" [209] and implemented both by human-owned processes and (for daily market operations) by smart contracts. In traditional finance terms, the Aave so-called market policies [287] are meant to control and manage:

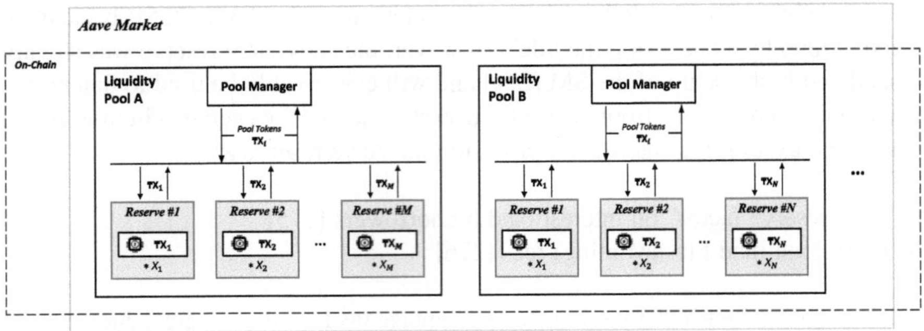

Fig. 14.43 Aave markets, liquidity pools, and reserves

a. Issuer
b. Foreign exchange
c. Volatility
d. Asset correlation
e. Interest rate
f. Counterparty credit
g. Liquidity
h. Concentration

risks. The main rules emanating from these policies are:

1. The case of admitting any new foreign ERC-20 token as reserve token in an Aave market must always undergo a formal due diligence process ("asset listing" [201]), following prescribed steps and a standard risk analysis methodology [288]. The final decision remains a prerogative of Aave governance.
2. A reserve token can be deposited and borrowed but is not automatically admissible as collateral in Aave transactions. There is a whitelisting process, with outcomes specific to token type and market, carried out by Aave governance.
3. Interest rate strategies for collateralized debt positions are also token type and market specific, and currently expressed as curves calibrated with the actual funds-utilization rate [117]. Previous generations of the protocol—before V3, their respective tokens still trading as of the time of writing—offered two high-level strategies ("stable" and "variable" borrowing interest rates [289], the former since deprecated [290]), with calibration defined by Aave governance at token onboarding.
4. Interest rates are, in principle, dynamic, updateable by smart contract depending primarily on individual token supply and demand. The current interest rate *parameters* are listed in Aave documentation [81], while the actual current *rates* per market and reserve token are always quoted in the Aave dApp [291] (and are also available in a synoptic view through a companion "live dashboard" [292]).

5. In some V2/V3 protocol generations (tokens still trading), an Aave market could decide to offer only variable borrowing rates for specific reserve tokens if their volatility risk were deemed too high. A "variable-rate-only" indication was thus always visible in the Aave dApp and in the live dashboard.
6. The borrowing base of a Funds Borrower is calculated initially (loan-to-value [293]) and updated continuously based on smart contracts, considering both the transacted reserve tokens [294] (borrowed and posted as collateral—controlling for issuer risk) and all accessible borrower assets owned across liquidity pools (health factor [209]—controlling for counterparty credit risk).
7. Each and every debt position is continuously tracked for the risk of downwards crossing collateral coverage levels. Once crossing of a critical one is detected, then it is notified immediately to subscribed liquidators (cf. Sect. 14.5.3.6 and also Sect. 14.5.3.7). All risk metrics needed by liquidators (liquidation threshold [295], liquidation bonus [296, 297], etc.) to calibrate their algorithmic logic are described in Aave documentation [128], quoted both through smart contract invocation and through the Aave app (per market and reserve token [298]) and also available in a synoptic view through the same live dashboard [292].
8. Reserve tokens that are highly correlated in price (e.g. Stablecoins with effective pegs) can form higher borrowing bases when borrowed and posted as collateral in the same transactions ("efficiency mode" [299, 300], E-Mode).
9. Inversely, reserve tokens that are proved to have high volatility risk are penalized as borrowing bases ("isolation mode" [301, 302]).
10. Similarly, de facto illiquid reserve tokens are discouraged as borrowing positions due to the risk of contagion to the Aave ecosystem from outside market manipulation (they may still be made available, but only in "siloed mode" [219, 303]).
11. Aave governance imposes both supply [216, 304] and borrow [218, 305] caps at the level of individual reserve tokens as means to control concentration risk. These are applied through privileged agents invoking methods directly on the liquidity pool smart contract [215, 217]; the resulting caps are visible through the live dashboard [292].

Within the afore-mentioned risk framework, Aave allows several variations to its main transactional pathways (cf. Sect. 9.6.3), all controlled by its governance at the token and market levels. For example, Funds Borrowers in approved markets can repay debt positions with assets (aTokens) deposited in liquidity pools other than the one used in the original borrowing ("repay with collateral" [306, 307]) to switch reserve tokens supplied as collateral to other token types ("collateral switch" [308]), etc.

Please note that there currently do not appear to exist macro-hedging mechanisms for asset/liability management (ALM) purposes, for example, covering funding and structural liquidity gap risks, at the level of individual markets. The Aave safety and backstop modules (mentioned in the previous section, in the context of taxation supporting the ecosystem reserve) are meant as ecosystem-level (cross-market) systemic risk defences only. Also, they are in effect credit insurance mechanisms, not active ALM ones.

14.6.2 GHO Stablecoin Primary Market Rules

Aave governance has introduced an own ecosystem Stablecoin [309], called GHO [89, 310], but did not specify a single primary market for it. It instead "delegated" the right to operate a primary market to any entity that would be prepared to act as a "GHO Facilitator" [311]. This term is explained in some detail in the later section on GHO token design (cf. Sect. 14.7.1.5), where it is interpreted as signifying an agent in the sense of a "principal–agent" relationship, with Aave governance as the principal. Aave governance in effect authorizes a Facilitator to issue GHO on its behalf, under the condition that said Facilitator will defend the peg of the Stablecoin through any mechanism which it sees as fit for purpose (and which is acceptable to Aave governance [312]).

The Aave market on Ethereum Mainnet is the first such GHO Facilitator. It creates a GHO primary market by working in a strictly overcollateralized paradigm, in effect adopting the existing Aave risk management framework and considering GHO as yet another borrowing token [313] (but not admissiblein any Aave token reserve). The GHO borrowing and position liquidation transactional pathways on Ethereum Mainnet have been explained in Sects. 14.5.3.10 and 14.5.3.11/14.5.3.12, respectively.

Under the restriction that GHO is not admissible as a supplied token (and consequently, as collateral), all relevant risk control/management mechanisms of the previous Sect. 14.6.1 apply here as well. There is, however, an additional provision in lieu not of a rule but of an incentive. Namely Aave currently incentivizes the acquisition of GHO by existing AAVE/stkAAVE holders through GHO borrowing interest rate discounts available exclusively to them [314]. The rationale is explained in the main Aave documentation [315], and the discount rate strategy is detailed in the GHO-specific one [316]. Please note that this incentivization strategy may be only a provisional one.

14.6.3 Debt Position Risk Management Rules

Aave replicates on-chain a Lombard lending paradigm in the sense of traditional finance, for all markets outside the RWA one in which it extends to asset-backed securitization and private debt. Counterparty credit risk and collateral management is a critical function in those markets, as per practice accumulated over centuries of experience. Aave creates a bespoke agent type ("Liquidator") to execute this function and incentivizes them in kind through a liquidation bonus—the typology and liquidation transactional pathways were explained in detail already in Sects. 9.6.1 and 9.6.3, respectively.

In analogy with the lender-side risk management of Lombard lending positions, please recall (cf. Sect. 9.1, Fig. 14.4) that the established mechanism in traditional finance usance is the "collateral call" or "margin call", and the reference risk metric is the percentage of margin erosion (ME), which can be expressed as:

$$ME_t = \frac{CMV_0 - CMV_t}{\text{Initial Margin}} (\%)$$

where CMV_t is the collateral market value at time t and the Initial Margin (difference between initial collateral market value CMV_0 and initial borrowing base BB_0) is in absolute numbers, not in %. If the haircut (in percent) is denoted as $HC_{\%}$, then one can write:

$$\text{ME} = \frac{\text{CMV}_0 - \text{CMV}_t}{\text{CMV}_0 \cdot \text{HC}_{\%}} \ (\%)$$

The way that this "traditional Lombard" metric relates to the Aave risk parameters is as follows: The current debt position (DP) of the borrower at time t equals the value of the original loan, that is, of BB_0—increased by the continuously charged borrowing interest. Denoting the latter as a constant "i_b" (for demonstration purposes, we consider only the "stable" rate case), then the updated debt position is:

$$\text{DP}_t = \text{BB}_0 \cdot e^{i_b \cdot t} = \text{CMV}_0 \cdot (1 - \text{HC}_{\%}) \cdot e^{i_b \cdot t}$$

We define an "exposure factor" (EF) as the time-varying ratio of the current debt position to the current collateral value:

$$\text{EF}_t = \frac{\text{DP}_t}{\text{CMV}_t} = \frac{\text{CMV}_0 \cdot (1 - \text{HC}_{\%}) \cdot e^{i_b \cdot t}}{\text{CMV}_t}$$

The critical value of the EF when Aave considers the debt position to be essentially undercollateralized is the "liquidation threshold". It is a risk parameter set by Aave governance. Using the abbreviation "LTh":

$$\text{EF}_{\text{critical}} = \text{LTh}$$

The exposure factor being higher than LTh means:

$$\frac{\text{CMV}_0 \cdot (1 - \text{HC}_{\%}) \cdot e^{i_b \cdot t}}{\text{CMV}_t} > \text{LTh}$$

Or equivalently:

$$\text{CMV}_t < \frac{\text{CMV}_0 \cdot (1 - \text{HC}_{\%}) \cdot e^{i_b \cdot t}}{\text{LTh}}$$

This is the collateral market value corresponding to undercollateralized exposure as per Aave definition. It is evident that unsecured lending exposure can result due to adverse market risk, accumulation of debt interest, or re-calibration of the Aave risk framework parameters. The Aave risk framework postulates another parameter called "health factor" (HF, time varying) of collateral positions, defined as:

$$HF_t = \frac{CMV_t \cdot LTh}{BB_0}$$

Assuming, for simplicity, that all assets in the collateral portfolio have the same $HC_{\%}$:

$$HF_t = \frac{CMV_t \cdot LTh}{CMV_0 \cdot (1 - HC_{\%})}$$

Aave requires $HF_t \geq 1$. How does that relate to the margin erosion metrics of traditional Lombard lending practice? Using the definition of ME_t:

$$ME_t = \frac{CMV_0 - CMV_t}{CMV_0 \cdot HC_{\%}} \ (\%) => $$

$$ME_t \ (\%) \cdot CMV_0 \cdot HC_{\%} = CMV_0 - CMV_t => $$

$$CMV_t = CMV_0 \cdot (1 - ME_t \ (\%) \cdot HC_{\%})$$

Substituting into the definition of HF_t:

$$HF_t = \frac{1 - ME_t \ (\%) \cdot HC_{\%}}{1 - HC_{\%}} \cdot LTh$$

Hence, the condition $HF_t \geq 1$ means:

$$\frac{1 - ME_t \ (\%) \cdot HC_{\%}}{1 - HC_{\%}} \cdot LTh \geq 1 => $$

$$(1 - ME_t \ (\%) \cdot HC_{\%}) \cdot LTh \geq 1 - HC_{\%} => $$

$$1 - ME_t \ (\%) \cdot HC_{\%} \geq \frac{1 - HC_{\%}}{LTh} => $$

$$- ME_t \ (\%) \cdot HC_{\%} \geq \frac{1 - HC_{\%}}{LTh} - 1 => $$

$$ME_t \ (\%) \leq \frac{LTh - 1 + HC_{\%}}{LTh \cdot HC_{\%}}$$

Thus, the critical value of equivalent margin erosion for Aave to declare a debt position as essentially undercollateralized is:

$$ME_{critical} \ (\%) = \frac{LTh - 1 + HC_{\%}}{LTh \cdot HC_{\%}}$$

Once this value is reached, Aave sets the status of all assets[60] of the blockchain address owing the debt position as "free for liquidation", and this triggers notification messages to all potential Liquidators (Sects. 14.5.3.6 and 14.5.3.11/ 14.5.3.12).

14.6.4 AAVE Staking Rules

As explained in Sect. 14.5.3.8, AAVE Stakers are in effect bail-in risk takers for the ecosystem. They provide insurance against systemic risk events ("shortfall events") and in return receive an insurance premium (the staking yield) in the form of AAVE tokens ("safety incentives" [149]) regularly allotted specifically to them.

Staked AAVE is deposited into the safety module [145] smart contract and the equivalent in stkAAVE tokens is forwarded to the agent's crypto wallet. The process, potential risks, and returns of acting as staker are clearly documented [228] and publicly available for AAVE holders to take informed investment decisions. In short, should a shortfall event cause significant loss of funds, the safety module has the right to "seize" (i.e. move ownership to itself) up to a set percentage of all funds locked into it. This percentage (30% [148], as of the time of writing) is set by Aave governance [271, 318, 319]. The safety module then invokes a different smart contract ("auction module"[61]), which implements an auction to sell the seized funds. Should the safety module prove inadequate to cover a systemic shortfall event, Aave governance can trigger AAVE emergency issuance [230] through a "backstop module" [231]. As a measure of last resort, the Aave ecosystem reserve [76, 232] can be drawn down. Aave treasury management is a responsibility of Aave governance [233, 235]. Please note that, as per Aave documentation [148]:

> 'The process of identifying … a slashing event is subject to an onchain Aave Governance proposal…'.

Stakers can at any time decide to "unstake", that is, to request their AAVE back from the safety module, thus cancelling their insurance underwriting commitment. There is an operational risk mechanism associated with "unstaking", both for the staker's and the ecosystem's protection. In short, the unstaking process [321] involves a "cooldown" period (enforced also through the Aave dApp) [322], that is, a number of days counting from the time the agent activates "Unstake" in the

---

[60] For the calculation of the health factor [317] mentions explicitly: *"The health factor is calculated from the user"s total collateral, i.e., all reserves for which usageAsCollateral is enabled, balance (in ETH) multiplied by the liquidation threshold percentage for all the user's outstanding assets, divided by the user's total borrow balance across all reserves (in ETH)"*.

[61] At any rate, this was the target architectural design around the safety module; however, it is unclear if the auction module was finally implemented in the end. Cf. the governance forum discussion in [320] (referring to the state of things in Q1'2023).

dApp and during which the protocol still does not allow withdrawal of stkAAVE so that the agent may reconsider. Past the "cooldown" interval, a second time window is defined within which the agent may reverse their stkAAVE into AAVE through the Aave app. The rule is that should the user fail to do so, then their unstaking request is cancelled. These are operational steps that are meant to accommodate Staking situations as they have been observed in practice [323].

As far as the Aave risk framework is concerned, the existence of these enforced time delays is, in effect, meant to protect Aave from both moral hazard and liquidity risk events. The former would involve, for example, lots of stakers being notified that a shortfall event has occurred and immediately trying to cancel their staking positions to avoid part of their funds being seized. The latter would involve a sudden outflow of a critical amount of funds from the safety module, so that it becomes severely undercapitalized in the short term, thus in effect losing effective systemic risk coverage.

The above are the salient mechanisms of AAVE staking. There are still more fine-granular, technical mechanisms underneath (such as the algorithmic calibration of the "cooldown" period and the acceptance/management process of liquidity positions within the safety module); however, those express less mechanism design and more technical implementation decisions, which can change by the protocol governance at shorter time-scales than mechanisms do.

14.6.5 RWA Risk Management

The Aave "RWA market" [158] was already explained in some detail (Sect. 14.5.3.9) as constituting a joint offering with a cooperating ecosystem (centrifuge [159]). The latter contributes the processes and on-/off-chain infrastructure of physical-world asset tokenization into NFTs, whereas Aave provides those of its "market" paradigm. The end result is an on-chain equivalent to the traditional asset-backed securities and private debt markets (also explained previously in this chapter, in Sects. 14.2 and 14.3).

Please recall that, in the Centrifuge RWA paradigm, off-chain assets are tokenized by RWA originators and packaged by RWA Issuers into securities of different risk/return profiles, available to investors through "investment pools" (smart contract based) [168]. Each investment pool has an off-chain special purpose vehicle attached [162] for bankruptcy-remoteness purposes. The central notion of Centrifuge is the transfer of legal ownership of off-chain assets to the SPV in the form of NFTs, which then form the underlying collateral of any financing transaction. Each Centrifuge investment pool combines a collateral pool and a cash reserve (liquidity pool), the latter intended to manage cash in−/outflows and to store liquidity not (or, not yet) allocated to assets. The SPV's balance sheet also manages the liability side, through the on-chain issuance and redemption [169] of participation tokens of different seniority tranches [170]. Aave participants can become

Centrifuge RWA Investors on the Aave RWA market by depositing admissible tokens into Centrifuge Investment Pools.

Hence, Aave extends its "market" paradigm to include NFT-collateralized participation tokens as interest-yielding enhancement for Aave aTokens. Instead of agents onboarding directly (and incurring transaction fees) in two different ecosystems, Aave and Centrifuge [173], the Aave RWA market allows for investments from within the same non-custodial environment of the typical Aave market.

The mechanisms of this market are an amalgam of those instituted by Aave and Centrifuge separately. Those beyond the main Aave context will be precisely the object of our current *exposé*. Thus, in reference to the RWA concepts and processes explained in previous sections:

1. Onboarding and KYC controls are mandatory for RWA Market participants [324].
2. An investment pool will return yield only to capital drawn down to finance assets. Liquidity remaining in the cash reserve does not return yield.
3. The RWA issuer can impose a maximum amount for the cash reserve. This may become an effective limit for new investments.
4. As liquidity available for redemptions back to investors is determined by the case reserve funds, redemption mechanisms may have to be synchronized with the liquidity pools of cooperating ecosystems (Aave in this case).
5. For securitized participation tokens, an investment pool can be defined as admitting tranches (technically unlimited in number, typically up to five deep) with different seniority of claims.
6. The lowest seniority tranche carries the first risk of default losses. Each tranche above the lowest is allocated a mandatory minimum "subordination ratio" [325], defined as the percentage of the asset pool that must be covered by its subordinated tranches. If these subordination ratios are breached, then new investments in the non-conforming tranches are paused until they can be restored.
7. Each tranche in the structure thus notifies an available investment capacity, which is controlled by both cash reserve limits and the minimum subordination ratio.
8. If an investment pool, or any individual participation tranche, is oversubscribed, then no additional RWA Investors can be accepted into it.
9. Credit risk events ("past due", "written off", etc.) are notified based on predefined rules—relating to the amount of the outstanding loan, the time elapsed since day due, etc.—and carry monetary fines for the borrower [326]. The status is also visible on the blockchain.
10. Assets can also be written off manually by a third party [326], authorized by the protocol to that end.

The Aave governance is actively invested in the RWA market [327, 328]; thus, the mechanism design of this joint effort can be expected to evolve further.

14.7 Aave Token Design

In the subsequent sections we examine the attributes of native Aave tokens and trace them back to the apparent choices of calibrating factors made by Aave designers, in reference to the attributes of good token design (as promulgated in Sect. 10.4). We refer to specific Aave transactional paths wherever necessary to better explain token features.

14.7.1 Native Tokens

The native token types minted in Aave money markets are:

1. aToken
2. DelegationAwareAToken
3. DebtToken
4. AAVE.
5. stkAAVE
6. GHO Stablecoin

Aave also "shares" a private debt market with Centrifuge ("RWA Market") where physical world assets are tokenized into:

7. RWA NFTs

We examine the features and calibration of each in the sequel.

14.7.1.1 aToken

"aTokens" [329] are asset tokens minted each time a Funds Supplier deposits reserve tokens into Aave markets (cf. Sect. 14.5.3.1). They are minted in distinct types, to correspond to the precise type of the deposited ERC-20 tokens and to the market where the liquidity pool in question resides. For example, depositing DAI in the Aave Ethereum Mainnet market will cause minting of "aDAI", in the Avalanche market of "aAvaDAI", in the Polygon market of "aPolDAI", etc. They are all aTokens, but they are of distinct types.

Even though they are minted in quantity matching 1:1 the originally deposited ERC-20 tokens, afterwards they act as "account tokens" of sorts, by increasing in number through the interest yield. Aave registers the starting balance of aTokens minted against the blockchain address of the funds supplier and also the value of the sum of tokens in the corresponding reserve at the same time (termed "liquidity index" [330, 331]). The software infrastructure constantly increases the value of the liquidity index by the interest yield offered for the particular reserve tokens in the liquidity pool [332] and thus calculates an updated balance for the aTokens originally allocated to said address. This, in effect, replicates a deposit account in banking terms. In summary, aTokens are "rebasing" (or "rebasable") tokens [333] (cf. the analysis of Sect. 9.6.3.1, which was made in the context of the Lido Protocol stETH tokens).

They are transferrable to other blockchain addresses, so as to enable Aave transactional pathways such as collateral delegation (cf. Sect. 14.5.3.4) and liquidation (cf. Sect. 14.5.3.6). Note that deposits in AAVE and investments in RWA NFTs also generate aTokens.

Redemption requests by funds suppliers (e.g. depositors of aDAI requesting to be reimbursed their original funds plus interest—all denominated in DAI) cause the respective aTokens to be burned and the corresponding number of base ERC-20 tokens to be drawn from the Aave token reserves and transferred to the agents' crypto wallets.

In terms of token design factor calibration:

a. Their **velocity** is low, as they can only be minted; delegated; transferred; and burned, through generally infrequent events (deposit of funds, redemption by depositor, etc.).
b. Their **scarcity** will depend on that of the respective base ERC-20 tokens in the Aave markets. For example, the more USDC are deposited or transferred in a market, the more aUSDC will be minted. However, it will also be limited by the corresponding ERC-20 token "supply cap" [216] specified by Aave governance and implemented by the pool-configuring smart contracts [334]. Please note that Aave governance can also opt for providing alternative sources of liquidity for specific aTokens.
c. aToken **inflation** is controlled by the respective interest yield, as set by Aave governance [117] for the ERC-20 token Reserve of the liquidity pool in question.
d. Their **valuation** is by definition equal to that of the corresponding base ERC-20 tokens. So, this is not a parameter controlled by Aave (even for aTokens issued against AAVE deposits, as AAVE valuation is only partially controlled by Aave events; this ERC-20 token is traded in exchanges).
e. **Minting mode**: aTokens are minted only through smart contracts [329]. The latter implement both ERC-20 and ERC-2612 [120]. Aave minting smart contract *addresses* differ by base ERC-20 token type and by Aave market [383]. The aToken smart contract code is available on GitHub [121].
f. A **minting optionality** available to Funds Suppliers is to opt for enabling aTokens as borrowing collateral. This optionality (i.e. which asset types to be admissible as collateral) is controlled by Aave governance and implemented by the pool-configuring smart contracts [335]. It is provided by the Aave dApp and can be also ascertained through the Aave live dashboard [336].
g. aTokens represent deposited ERC-20 base tokens, or (in the case of the RWA market) bought NFT-based securities. Hence, their **property rights** are generally claims on the deposited principal plus the specified interest yield. Also, all aAAVE tokens (i.e. aTokens representing AAVE deposits) impart to their holders the additional right to participate in Aave Governance votes. Only in the case of RWA aTokens there may be an underlying hierarchy of claims defined by the

contractual agreement between RWA Issuer and RWA Investor (cf. Sect. 14.5.3.9).

h. aTokens are not Stablecoins; hence, there is no underlying notion of managed **treasury**.

i. Regarding **composability**, according to Aave documentation aTokens are tradable [337]. In principle, as ERC-20 tokens, they can indeed be transferred across EVM-compatible ecosystems [338].

j. aToken **programmability** is restricted to the methods available through the Aave smart contracts specification.

k. The **computational complexity** of aToken minting is the same as that of base ERC-20 tokens on the Ethereum Mainnet. Aave also allows aToken transfers among different markets [339] in order to take advantage of the scalability features of the cooperating L-2 ecosystems.

14.7.1.2 DelegationAwareAToken

This is simply an Aave asset token (an aToken) with an extra feature, which technically entails minting through a smart contract [340], which is slightly different from the one minting a usual aToken. It is mentioned here only for the sake of completeness, as the pathway along which it is used is not an asset swapping, but a voting power delegating one.

14.7.1.3 DebtToken

"DebtTokens" [341] are native Aave tokens minted each and every time a Funds Borrower draws funds from a token reserve. Similarly to aTokens, they are also minted in distinct types, corresponding to the precise type of the borrowed ERC-20 token and to the market where they are issued (cf. preceding Sect. 9.6.3.3 on the "borrowing by own collateral" transactional pathway). Thus, borrowing DAI in the Aave Polygon market will cause minting of "variableDebtPolDAI" [342]; borrowing link in the Aave Optimism market will cause minting of "variableDebtOptLink" [343]; borrowing wstETH in the Aave Base market will cause minting of "variableDebtBaswstETH" [344], etc. The important fact is not so much the naming scheme but rather that the tokens are minted by different smart contract *addresses*[62] depending on the ERC-20 token borrowed and the Aave market. They are all DebtTokens, however.

DebtTokens act in effect as "loan account tokens", in the sense that, once minted, they start accruing interest charges through the Aave software infrastructure. Interest rate terms and borrowing caps are explained in the Aave documentation pages [117, 218, 345]. The currently applying borrowing rates per reserve token and per market can be read immediately through the Aave dApp (e.g. for the Aave Ethereum Mainnet [346] and Arbitrum market [347]).

[62] All being accessible from https://aave.com/docs/resources/addresses, by choosing an Aave Market and then the linked URL corresponding to any given reserve token (i.e. following the row having said token as "Symbol" to its intersection with the column "variableDebtToken").

In difference to aTokens, DebtTokens are **not transferrable** to other blockchain addresses.

Repaying the owed amount (i.e. sending from a crypto wallet to a liquidity pool contract a number of base ERC-20 tokens corresponding 1:1 to principal plus accrued interest) causes the respective DebtTokens to be burned.

In terms of token design factor calibration:

a. Their design **velocity** is low, as they can only be minted; delegated; transferred; and burned through generally infrequent events (borrowing of funds, repayment by borrower, etc.).
b. Their **scarcity** will depend on that of the respective base ERC-20 tokens and their availability in the Aave markets. That is, the more wBTC are in circulation, sought after in the Exchanges and also available in a market's liquidity pools, the more wBTC DebtTokens are expected to be minted. Similarly to aTokens, scarcity will also be limited by the corresponding ERC-20 token "borrow cap" [218] specified by Aave governance and implemented by the pool-configuring smart contracts [217, 334]. There are other restricting factors as well, as when the Aave protocol bars a Funds Borrower from borrowing in more than one reserve token type [348].
c. DebtToken **inflation** is controlled by the respective borrowing interest rate strategy and cap, as set by Aave governance [117, 218] for the ERC-20 token reserve of the liquidity pool in question.
d. Their **valuation** is by definition equal to that of the corresponding base ERC-20 tokens. So, this is not a parameter controlled by Aave (even for AAVE DebtTokens; AAVE is traded in Exchanges; hence, its valuation is only partially controlled by Aave events).
e. **Minting mode**: DebtTokens are minted only through smart contracts [115, 341]. The latter implement ERC-20, however omitting the methods relating to transfers to other blockchain addresses. Minting SC addresses differ by base ERC-20 token type and by Aave market.
f. Once an Aave market and the reserve token are chosen, there is no **minting optionality** available to funds borrowers. Aave loans are perpetual; thus, borrowers do not need to choose a tenor. Interest rates offered by market are indicated on the Aave dApp and can be also ascertained through the Aave live dashboard [349].
g. DebtTokens represent obligations, and not **property rights,** of the owning blockchain address.
h. DebtTokens are not Stablecoins; hence, there is no underlying notion of managed **treasury**.
i. Regarding **composability**, as per Aave documentation [341], DebtTokens are not transferrable.
j. DebtToken **programmability** is restricted to the methods available through the Aave smart contracts specification.
k. The **computational complexity** of DebtToken minting is the same as that of base ERC-20 tokens on the Ethereum Mainnet.

14.7.1.4 AAVE

AAVE is the native governance token of the Aave ecosystem [75], hence formally a utility token. It is an ERC-20 compatible token, but also implements the EIP2612 [120] "permit()" function, allowing gas-less transactions and one transaction approval/ transfer. The minting smart contract code, its calling addresses, and audit reports are available through the Aave GitHub [350].

Apart from governance, AAVE has three main uses on Aave markets: yield (interest) investing, use as collateral, and staking [351]. Funds suppliers can purchase AAVE on exchanges and then lend them to an Aave market to generate yield through aAAVE tokens (cf. Sect. 9.6.3.2). After enabling their aAAVE as collateral, they can also use them for borrowing of other reserve tokens (cf. Sect. 9.6.3.3, also Section 14.5.3.4 for delegated lending and Sect. 14.5.3.7 for use in Flash Loans). AAVE staking is done through the Aave safety module (cf. Sect. 14.5.3.8), meant to act as a safety net in case of systemic events. The ecosystem will sell (on Exchanges) AAVE deposited in the safety module to cover capital shortages resulting from redemption requests against its obligations. Please note that AAVE staking is available only in select Aave markets [352].

From the standpoint of token design factor calibration:

a. AAVE's design **velocity** is medium (and transaction statistics bear this out [353]) as it is meant only for the afore-mentioned use cases: yield investing, collateralized borrowing, staking, and governance voting.
b. In terms of design **scarcity**: The maximum circulating supply is limited to 16 million AAVE, of which a maximum of 13 million are to be in free circulation while three million are reserved exclusively for the Aave ecosystem reserve [354]. The latter is also covering AAVE-denominated staking rewards through the safety module.
c. AAVE **inflation** is controlled by Aave policies and is skewed towards **deflationary**. The safety module causes a number of AAVE/day to be split among all stakers [149, 274], which can be reused for any of the main use cases, or sold in Exchanges. Importantly, Aave uses a high percentage of the fees accrued by the markets' reward pool to burn AAVE [355] and remove it from circulation.
d. AAVE **valuation** is controlled both through scarcity and through the dynamics of buying and selling on Exchanges. So, it is by design only partially controlled by Aave governance. The evolution of total value locked into the Aave ecosystem, the sentiment in the general crypto-markets, and news about idiosyncratic Aave project events may also influence its price in the secondary market.
e. **Minting mode**: AAVE is issued at the discretion of its governance. There is no minting/burning at investors' request. Aave markets do not function as primary market for the AAVE token.
f. There are no **minting optionalities** available to acquirers, as it is not minted at their request.
g. AAVE **property rights** are generally claims against the Aave treasury.
h. AAVE tokens are not Stablecoins; hence, there is no underlying notion of managed **treasury**.

i. Regarding **composability**, AAVE tokens are tradable on exchanges and, as ERC-20 tokens, can indeed be transferred across EVM-compatible ecosystems. They can be stored in any crypto wallet that supports ERC-20 tokens.
j. AAVE **programmability** is a prerogative of Aave governance and as such restricted to the methods implemented in the smart contract.
k. The **computational complexity** of AAVE minting is the same as that of base ERC-20 tokens on the Ethereum Mainnet.

14.7.1.5 GHO

GHO is the native Stablecoin of the Aave ecosystem [89], pegged 1:1 to the USD. Its minting (and burning) is carried out and controlled by entities or ecosystems authorized by Aave governance for this specific purpose; said entities or ecosystems being "Facilitators" [356, 357]. The term "Facilitator" was coined by Aave governance [358] and can be interpreted as signifying an agent in the sense of a "principal–agent" relationship [359]. Aave governance (the "principal") in effect appoints[63] another entity (as "agent", i.e. the "Facilitator") to act on its behalf in a particular context, under set conditions and towards an agreed goal. The context in question is GHO primary market operation, and the conditions are: not exceeding a circulating supply limit (called "bucket capacity"—calculated individually for each "Facilitator" [360]) and agreeing to honour set Aave platform fees and interest rate strategies [316]. The goal is to maintain the peg of GHO at 1:1 to the USD.

Aave leaves the "how" of achieving this goal to the discretion of the individual Facilitator. In reference to the discussion of Sect. 10.5.8 (on Stablecoin price stabilization mechanisms and token treasury structures), the Facilitator can opt for any reserve-backed, algorithmic, or hybrid strategy, as long as it accepts the conditions agreed with Aave governance. Aave governance acts as a "sovereign" of the Aave ecosystem (again, the "country-level analogy" of Chap. 6) and delegates the prerogative of issuing a currency in its name (the GHO Stablecoin) to an authorized agent. The platform fee and interest income stream flowing back to the Aave treasury through the actions of the Facilitator is akin to "Seigniorage" [361] (in the same country-level analogy). This concept is explained in more detail in the GHO documentation [357] and in the Aave GHO whitepaper [310]. The Aave V3 Ethereum Mainnet market has been thus authorized [358, 362] to act as GHO Facilitator [363], implementing an overcollateralized borrowing paradigm [364] (GHO being minted in effect as debt position tokens, cf. Sect. 14.5.3.10 and burned upon debt repayment) for maintaining the peg. As already mentioned, any price stabilization paradigm[64] is acceptable to Aave governance as long as it can be reasonably expected to be effective. In reference to the Stablecoin Protocol Token Model proposed in Sect. 10.5.8, the GHO Stablecoin issued by the Aave V3 Ethereum Mainnet market is **not** supported by a volatility token. Its admissible

[63] After due diligence: cf. [312].

[64] E.g., delta-neutral portfolio construction [365], reserve-backed by RWA assets [366], etc.

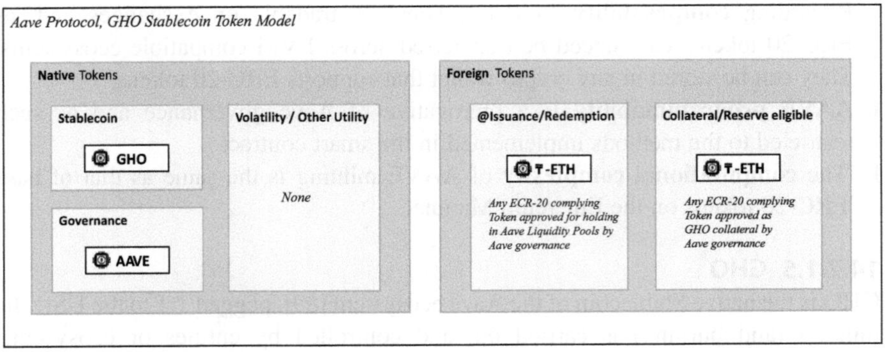

Fig. 14.44 GHO Stablecoin Protocol token model

issuance/redemption and eligible collateral/reserve tokens are the universe of Aave reserve tokens (cf. Fig. 14.44).

In terms of its token design factor calibration:

a. GHO's design **velocity** is medium [367] as it targets a balance between the usual Stablecoin "flight to safety" function (a low-velocity use case) and a medium-of-exchange function (a high-velocity use case, assuming the network effect has been achieved) across EVM-compatible blockchains.
b. Its design **scarcity**: The maximum circulating supply ("bucket capacity") on the Ethereum Mainnet was set at 100 million GHO at launch [362]. Aave governance can change this limit at its discretion by vote.
c. GHO **inflation** is not controlled by Aave as long as the total bucket capacity per facilitator is not exceeded. Under this limit, the amount of GHO in circulation is simply the outcome of minting, resp. burning, activity, for example as a result of fund borrowers' issuance, resp. redemption, requests on Aave Ethereum Mainnet.
d. GHO is pegged at issuance at 1 USD, and this is its design **valuation** midpoint. Of course, as with every Stablecoin, there is the potential for deviations from the target peg when trading GHO on exchanges. As of the time of writing, the only available arbitrage mechanism to restore the peg is liquidation (cf. Sects. 14.5.3.11 and 14.5.3.12), which is not enforced but only incentivized, hence may not always be effective. An alternative mechanism (through a "stability module" smart contract [368, 369]) may provide a better way to defend the peg.
e. **Minting mode**: GHO is minted only through a smart contract ("GhoToken" [370]) which subtypes both the ERC-20 and the OpenZeppelin Library's "AccessControl" specifications [371]. The SC's source code is freely available on GitHub [372], and its implementation is audited [373].
f. There are no **minting optionalities** available to Fund Borrowers triggering GHO minting at issuance.
g. GHO tokens represent obligations, and not **property rights,** of the owning blockchain address on the Aave Ethereum Mainnet market.

h. GHO Facilitators may opt for reserve-backed price stabilization, in which case there is a managed **treasury**. As far as the Aave Ethereum Mainnet Facilitator is concerned, the supporting "token treasury" is simply the particular debt position and its covering collateral. Treasury management is left to Liquidators, using either own funds or flash loans (cf. Sects. 14.5.3.11 and 14.5.3.12, respectively).
i. Regarding **composability**, GHO tokens are tradable on Exchanges and, as ERC-20 tokens, can indeed be transferred across EVM-compatible ecosystems. They can be stored in any crypto wallet that supports ERC-20 tokens.
j. GHO **programmability** is a prerogative of Aave Governance and as such restricted to the methods described in the GHO smart contract specification.
k. The **computational complexity** of GHO minting is the same as that of base ERC-20 tokens on the Ethereum Mainnet.

14.8 Aave Bonding Curves

As of the time of writing, Aave does not appear to define own created bonding curves for any process tied to its smart contracts. There is a single use case where bonding curves are employed by Aave, however involving not an Aave-authored but a foreign-ecosystem automated market maker. The current design of the safety module, namely, prescribes an 80% AAVE/20% ETH liquidity pool which uses Balancer [374] to manage liquidity positions [375, 376].

Aave governance records [375] mention in that regard:

> *The advantage of using Balancer against other AMM solutions is clear when we factor in the possibility of dynamically adjusting the weighting towards AAVE. This allows for the creation of a market and the provision of liquidity whilst maintaining exposure to AAVE. Holding AAVE/ETH liquidity with uneven weights is very close to simply holding AAVE, with the benefits of earning trading fees on top of it. … By also allowing users to simply lock AAVE, we free up less advanced users from the burden of providing two different assets to participate in staking. The SM* [author's note: Safety Module]*will support weighted incentives to attract liquidity in case of AMM imbalance.*

Both Aave [377] and Balancer governance cooperated [378] on this particular mechanism design calibration.

14.9 Summary

Aave, an EVM-compatible blockchain ecosystem that replicates on-chain the traditional finance paradigms of:

i. Lombard lending
ii. Asset-backed securitization
iii. Private debt markets

was used as a case study of the entire token ecosystem design framework. All design pillars (market, mechanism, token, and bonding curve) were explained, with reference to Aave documentation and Aave governance decisions. The influencing factors per design pillar were also explicitly analysed and shown to be in evidence in practically all aspects of Aave strategy and operations.

In summary, it was demonstrated how all pillars of the proposed token ecosystem design framework align with current crypto industry market practices, thus how it can be used as both an analysis and a design tool for blockchain-based token ecosystems.

References

1. [Aave Token ecosystem] https://aave.com/
2. *Top Lending &Borrowing Tokens by Market Capitalization.* CoinMarketCap. Retrieved March 28, 2025, from https://coinmarketcap.com/view/lending-borowing/
3. *What is a repo?* Frequently Asked Questions on Repo. International Capital Market Association (ICMA). Retrieved March 28, 2025, from https://www.icmagroup.org/market-practice-and-regulatory-policy/repo-and-collateral-markets/icma-ercc-publications/frequently-asked-questions-on-repo/1-what-is-a-repo/
4. Choudry, M. (2010). *The Repo handbook* (2nd ed.). Butterworth-Heinemann.
5. Reiff, N. (2024, June 14). *Repurchase agreement (Repo): Definition, examples, and risks.* Retrieved March 28, 2025, from https://www.investopedia.com/terms/r/repurchaseagreement.asp
6. *Global Master Repurchase Agreement (GMRA).* Legal Documentation. International Capital Market Association (ICMA). Retrieved March 28, 2025, from https://www.icmagroup.org/market-practice-and-regulatory-policy/repo-and-collateral-markets/legal-documentation/global-master-repurchase-agreement-gmra/
7. *What types of asset are used as collateral in the repo market?* Frequently Asked Questions on Repo. International Capital Market Association (ICMA). Retrieved March 28, 2025, from https://www.icmagroup.org/market-practice-and-regulatory-policy/repo-and-collateral-markets/icma-ercc-publications/frequently-asked-questions-on-repo/6-what-types-of-asset-are-used-as-collateral-in-the-repo-market/
8. Eisenschmidt, J., Ma, Y. & Zhang, A.L. (2022). Monetary policy transmission in segmented markets. *ECB Working Paper Series*, No 2706. Retrieved March 28, 2025, from https://www.ecb.europa.eu/pub/pdf/scpwps/ecb.wp2706~ba900f49e8.en.pdf
9. Lombard banking. (2025, January 25). In *Wikipedia*. Retrieved March 28, 2025, from https://en.wikipedia.org/wiki/Lombard_banking
10. Bloomenthal, A. (2020, November 7). *Borrowing base: Definition, how it's determined, and example.* Retrieved March 28, 2025, from https://www.investopedia.com/terms/b/borrowing-base.asp
11. *Compulsory realisation of assets to repay a Lombard loan without prior margin call.* Case No. 2020/05. Swiss Banking Ombudsman. Retrieved March 28, 2025, fromhttps://bankingombudsman.ch/en/compulsory-realisation-of-assets-to-repay-a-lombard-loan-without-prior-margin-call/
12. Banton, C. (2024, July 31). *Asset/liability management: Definition, meaning, and strategies.* Retrieved March 28, 2025, from https://www.investopedia.com/terms/a/asset-liabilitymanagement.asp
13. Asset and liability management. (2024, October 29). In *Wikipedia*. Retrieved March 28, 2025, from https://en.wikipedia.org/wiki/Asset_and_liability_management
14. Choudry, M. (2007). *Bank asset and liability management: Strategy, trading, analysis.* Wiley.

15. Chen, J. (2022, April 28). *Prudent-person rule: What it is, how it works*. Retrieved March 28, 2025, from https://www.investopedia.com/terms/p/prudentmanrule.asp
16. *RBC20 – Calculation of minimum risk-based capital requirements*. Basel framework. Basel Committee of Banking Supervision. Retrieved March 28, 2025, from https://www.bis.org/basel_framework/chapter/RBC/20.htm
17. *Switzerland's "too big to fail" regime for banks*. Swiss Financial Market Regulatory Authority (Finanmzmarktaufsicht – FINMA). Retrieved March 28, 2025, from https://www.finma.ch/en/enforcement/recovery-und-resolution-n/das-schweizer-too-big-to-fail-konzept/banken/
18. Hargrave, M. (2021, January 21). *Return on Risk-Adjusted Capital (RORAC) formula & example*. Retrieved March 28, 2025, from https://www.investopedia.com/terms/r/rorac.asp
19. Ganti, A. (2022, June 12). *Risk-adjusted capital ratio: Meaning, overview, calculations*. Retrieved March 28, 2025, from https://www.investopedia.com/terms/a/adjusted-capital-ratio.asp
20. Culp, C. L. (2006). *Structured finance and insurance, the ART of managing capital and risk* (2nd ed.). Wiley.
21. Antoniades, A., & Tarashev, N. (2014). Securitisations: Tranching concentrates uncertainty. *BIS Quarterly Review*. Retrieved March 28, 2025, from https://www.bis.org/publ/qtrpdf/r_qt1412f.htm
22. Mezzanine. (2024, November 2). In *Wikipedia*. Retrieved March 28, 2025, from https://en.wikipedia.org/wiki/Mezzanine
23. Mezzanine capital. (2025, February 11). In *Wikipedia*. Retrieved March 28, 2025, from https://en.wikipedia.org/wiki/Mezzanine_capital
24. Nijs, L. (2014). *Mezzanine financing; Tools, applications and total performance*. Wiley.
25. Kagan, J. (2024, October 8). *Unitranche debt (financing): How these hybrid loans work*. Retrieved March 28, 2025, from https://www.investopedia.com/terms/u/unitranchedebt.asp
26. Chen, J. (2023, December 15). *Synthetic: Definition in finance, types of assets*. Retrieved March 28, 2025, from https://www.investopedia.com/terms/s/synthetic.asp
27. Bank for International Settlements (BIS). (2019, December 19). *Basel III: Securitisation framework – Executive Summary*. Retrieved March 28, 2025, from https://www.bis.org/fsi/fsisummaries/b3
28. (2022, November 29). *Credit card receivables securitizations methodology*. Moody's Investors Service. Retrieved March 28, 2025, from https://ratings.moodys.com/api/rmc-documents/396069
29. (2022, November 8). *Rating European trade receivables securitisation transactions (archived)*. Morningstar – DBRS. Retrieved March 28, 2025, from https://www.dbrsmorningstar.com/research/405112/rating-european-trade-receivables-securitisation-transactions
30. Kagan, J. (2024, June 13). *Mortgage-Backed Securities (MBS): Definition and types of investment*. Retrieved March 28, 2025, from https://www.investopedia.com/terms/m/mbs.asp
31. Fabozzi, F. J., Bhattacharya, A. K., & Berliner, W. S. (2007). *Mortgage-backed securities. Products, structuring, and analytical techniques*. Wiley.
32. (2019). *Auto Asset-Backed Securities (Auto ABS) primer*. Capital Markets Bureau. National Association of [U.S.] Insurance Commissioners (NAIC). Retrieved March 28, 2025, from https://content.naic.org/sites/default/files/capital-markets-primer-auto-abs.pdf
33. (2023, February 7). *Cash flow assumptions for corporate credit securitizations (archived)*. Morningstar – DBRS. Retrieved March 28, 2025, from https://www.dbrsmorningstar.com/research/409499/cash-flow-assumptions-for-corporate-credit-securitizations
34. (2021, October 15). *DBRS morningstar assigns provisional ratings to mello warehouse securitization trust 2021–3*. Morningstar – DBRS. Retrieved March 28, 2025, from https://www.dbrsmorningstar.com/research/386027/dbrs-morningstar-assigns-provisional-ratings-to-mello-warehouse-securitization-trust-2021-3

35. (2022, October 28). *Rating U.S. Private Student Loan Securitizations (Archived)*. Morningstar – DBRS. Retrieved March 28, 2025, from https://www.dbrsmorningstar.com/research/404500/rating-us-private-student-loan-securitizations
36. (2023, May 3). *KBRA assigns preliminary rating to MP 2023 LLC, series 2023-1*. KBRA. Retrieved March 28, 2025, from https://www.kbra.com/publications/ZqZCZsKZ/kbra-assigns-preliminary-rating-to-mp-2023-llc-series-2023-1
37. (2015, February 2). *DBRS publishes methodology for rating securitizations backed by marine container assets*. Morningstar – DBRS. Retrieved March 28, 2025, from https://dbrs.morningstar.com/research/276504/dbrs-publishes-methodology-for-rating-securitizations-backed-by-marine-container-assets
38. (2016, May 3). *DBRS finalizes pooled aircraft lease securitization methodology & related exhibits/appendix*. Morningstar – DBRS. Retrieved March 28, 2025, fromhttps://www.dbrsmorningstar.com/research/294101/dbrs-finalizes-pooled-aircraft-lease-securitization-methodology-related-exhibitsappendix
39. *Royalty Securitizations*. Ocean Tomo. Retrieved March 28, 2025, from https://oceantomo.com/services/royalty-securitizations/
40. Quinn, A., & Burke, D. (2014, June 20). *[Ireland] An ideal location for intellectual property securitisation*. Maples Group. Retrieved March 28, 2025, from https://www.mondaq.com/ireland/securitization-amp-structured-finance/321920/an-ideal-location-for-intellectual-property-securitisation
41. (2022, November 8). *DBRS Morningstar Finalizes U.S. Consumer Litigation Finance Methodology Appendices*. Morningstar – DBRS. Retrieved March 28, 2025, from https://www.dbrsmorningstar.com/research/405085/dbrs-morningstar-finalizes-us-consumer-litigation-finance-methodology-appendices
42. Lieuwveld, L. B., & Sahani, V. S. (2017). *Third-party funding in international arbitration* (2nd ed.). Wolters Kluwer.
43. Structured settlement. (2024, December 1). In *Wikipedia*. Retrieved March 28, 2025, from https://en.wikipedia.org/wiki/Structured_settlement
44. (2022, October 31). *Rating U.S. Structured settlements asset-backed securitizations (archived)*. Morningstar – DBRS. Retrieved March 28, 2025, from https://www.dbrsmorningstar.com/research/404541/rating-us-structured-settlements-asset-backed-securitizations
45. Hayes, A. (2024, June 25). *What Is a Special Purpose Vehicle (SPV), and Why do companies form them?* Retrieved March 28, 2025, from https://www.investopedia.com/terms/s/spv.asp
46. Special-purpose entity. (2025, March 14). In *Wikipedia*. Retrieved March 28, 2025, from https://en.wikipedia.org/wiki/Special-purpose_entity
47. Koele, I. A. (2016). The Dutch private foundation in comparison with trusts: for the same purpose but rather different. *Trust & Trustees, 22*(1), 140–145. https://doi.org/10.1093/tandt/ttv222
48. Orphan structure. (2024, July 18). In *Wikipedia*. Retrieved March 28, 2025, from https://en.wikipedia.org/wiki/Orphan_structure
49. Killourhy, M. (2018, October 1). *Securitisation and the use of Orphan Special Purpose Vehicles*. Ogier. Retrieved March 28, 2025, from https://www.ogier.com/news-and-insights/insights/securitisation-and-the-use-of-orphan-special-purpose-vehicles/https://www.ogier.com/news-and-insights/insights/securitisation-and-the-use-of-orphan-special-purpose-vehicles/
50. *Orphan entities in Securitisation Transactions & Special Purpose Vehicle*. Creatrust Advisory. Retrieved March 28, 2025, from https://www.creatrust.com/investments-funds/securitisation-vehicle-and-security-issuance/securitisation-orphan-entity-special-purpose-vehicle
51. Cell (captive). (2024, January 30). In *Wikipedia*. Retrieved March 28, 2025, from https://en.wikipedia.org/wiki/Cell_captive

52. Kagan, J. (2021, March 31). *Protected cell company: What it is, How it works*. Retrieved March 28, 2025, fromhttps://www.investopedia.com/terms/p/protected-cell-company-pcc.asp
53. Feetham, N., & Jones, G. (2010). *Protected cell companies: A guide to their implementation and use* (2nd ed.). Spiramus Press.
54. Segregated portfolio company. (2024, December 17). In *Wikipedia*. Retrieved March 28, 2025, from https://en.wikipedia.org/wiki/Segregated_portfolio_company
55. Koh, J., & Lee, J. *The many uses and benefits of a variable capital company*. International Bar Association. Retrieved March 28, 2025, from https://www.ibanet.org/article/4D265C70-A7BB-48F8-9C13-0EFF958EAEA9
56. (2023, April 4). *Ten use cases for variable capital companies (VCCs)*. Amicorp. Retrieved March 28, 2025, from https://www.amicorp.com/ami-news/ten-use-cases-for-variable-capital-companies/
57. Hayes, A. (2024, April 10). *Master-Feeder structure: Definition, How it works, pros & cons*. Retrieved March 28, 2025, from https://www.investopedia.com/terms/m/master-feeder-fund.asp
58. Shen, P., & Ho, B. (2022). *When family offices meet funds*. Stephenson Harwood. Retrieved March 28, 2025, from https://www.lexology.com/library/document.ashx?g=be68e713-6178-4de9-8ee1-f696ddce4e94
59. [Singapore] *Variable Capital Companies Act 2018* (as amended). Retrieved March 28, 2025, from https://sso.agc.gov.sg/Act/VCCA2018
60. [Singapore] *Variable Capital Companies regulations*. Retrieved March 28, 2025, from https://www.acra.gov.sg/business-entities/variable-capital-companies
61. [Mauritius] *Variable Capital Companies Act 2022*. Retrieved March 28, 2025, from https://www.fscmauritius.org/media/127896/the-variable-capital-companies-act.pdf
62. U.S. Securities and Exchange Commission (SEC). *Create Asset-Backed Securities (ABS) issuing entities*. SEC "How Do I Guides" pages. Retrieved March 28, 2025, from https://www.sec.gov/page/edgar-how-do-i-create-and-obtain-edgar-access-asset-backed-securities-abs-issuing-entities
63. European Securities and Markets Authority (ESMA). *Securitisation*. Markets and Infrastructure pages. Retrieved March 28, 2025, from https://www.esma.europa.eu/esmas-activities/markets-and-infrastructure/securitisation
64. Private credit. (2024, September 15). In *Wikipedia*. Retrieved March 28, 2025, from https://en.wikipedia.org/wiki/Private_credit
65. Nesbitt, S. L. (2023). *Private debt. Yield, safety and the emergence of alternative lending* (2nd ed.). Wiley.
66. (2019, February 11). *Private debt overview*. Principles for Respsonsible Investment (PRI). Retrieved March 28, 2025, from https://www.unpri.org/private-debt/an-overview-of-private-debt/4057.article
67. Chen, J. (2022, May 21). *Interval fund: What it is, how it works, example*. Retrieved March 28, 2025, from https://www.investopedia.com/terms/i/intervalscheme.asp
68. U.S. Securities and Exchange Commission (SEC). *Interval fund*. SEC Glossary pages. Retrieved March 28, 2025, from https://www.investor.gov/introduction-investing/investing-basics/glossary/interval-fund
69. *Aave Documentation* [pages]. Retrieved March 28, 2025, from https://aave.com/docs/
70. [Aave V3 Whitepaper] Frangella, E., & Herskind, L. (2022, January 27). *Aave V3 Technical Paper*. Retrieved March 28, 2025, from https://github.com/aave/aave-v3-core/blob/master/techpaper/Aave_V3_Technical_Paper.pdf
71. *Aave V3*. Aave documentation pages. Retrieved March 28, 2025, from https://aave.com/docs/developers/aave-v3
72. [Aave GitHub root directory]. Retrieved March 28, 2025, from https://github.com/aave
73. *Governance* [arrangements]. Aave documentation pages. Retrieved March 28, 2025, from https://aave.com/docs/primitives/governance/

74. [Aave governance discussion pages]. Retrieved March 28, 2025, from https://governance.aave.com/
75. *AAVE* [Token]. Aave documentation pages. Retrieved March 28, 2025, from https://aave.com/docs/primitives/aave
76. [Treasury] Aave support pages. Retrieved March 28, 2025, from https://aave.com/faq (please search in the page for "What is the Aave Treasury?")
77. [Member] *Incentives*. Aave documentation pages. Retrieved March 28, 2025, from https://aave.com/docs/primitives/incentives
78. Stock market equivalence. (2024, September 26). In *Wikipedia*. Retrieved March 28, 2025, from https://en.wikipedia.org/wiki/Stock_market_equivalence
79. [Context: EU Financial Markets] *Equivalence of non-EU financial frameworks*. European Commission. Retrieved March 28, 2025, from https://finance.ec.europa.eu/eu-and-world/equivalence-non-eu-financial-frameworks_en
80. Pennesi, F. (2022). *Equivalence in financial services: A legal and policy analysis*. Palgrave Macmillan.
81. *Aave Protocol Parameter Dashboard*. Aave documentation pages. Retrieved March 28, 2025, from https://aave.com/docs/resources/parameters
82. ["Markets" access functionality on the Aave dApp] Retrieved March 28, 2025, from https://app.aave.com/markets/
83. *Liquidity Pool*. Aave documentation pages. Retrieved March 28, 2025, from https://aave.com/docs/primitives/liquidity-pool
84. *Pool* [Smart Contracts]. Aave documentation pages. Retrieved March 28, 2025, from https://aave.com/docs/developers/smart-contracts#pool
85. *Reserve*. Aave documentation pages. Retrieved March 28, 2025, from https://aave.com/docs/primitives/reserve
86. *Polygon Aave Market*. Aave documentation pages. Retrieved March 28, 2025, from https://aave.com/docs/resources/parameters#aave-protocol-parameter-dashboard, by selecting "Polygon V3 Market" in the drop-down menu.
87. *Arbitrum Aave Market*. Aave documentation pages. Retrieved March 28, 2025, from https://aave.com/docs/resources/parameters#aave-protocol-parameter-dashboard, by selecting "Arbitrum V3 Market" in the drop-down menu.
88. *Dynamic Parameters and Governance*. Aave documentation pages. Retrieved March 28, 2025, from https://aave.com/docs/primitives/reserve#dynamic-parameters-and-governance
89. *GHO* [Token]. Aave documentation pages. Retrieved March 28, 2025, from https://aave.com/docs/primitives/gho
90. [Aave DAO GitHub root directory]. Retrieved March 28, 2025, from https://github.com/aave-dao
91. *Guardians*. Aave documentation pages. Retrieved March 28, 2025, from https://aave.com/docs/primitives/governance#community-guardians
92. *Stewards*. Aave documentation pages. Retrieved March 28, 2025, from https://aave.com/docs/primitives/governance#community-stewards
93. [Aave Grants DAO welcome page]. Retrieved March 28, 2025, from https://aavegrants.org/
94. [Aave Grants DAO discussion pages overview]. Retrieved March 28, 2025, from https://governance.aave.com/c/developers/25
95. (2021, July). *Proposal: Aave Risk DAO*. Aave governance discussion pages. Retrieved March 28, 2025, from https://governance.aave.com/t/proposal-aave-risk-dao/4729
96. [Gho-related Smart Contracts]. *Aave GitHub pages*. Retrieved March 28, 2025, from https://github.com/aave/gho-core/tree/main/src/contracts/misc
97. *Smart Contracts*. Aave documentation pages. Retrieved March 28, 2025, from https://aave.com/docs/developers/smart-contracts
98. [Aave V3-origin Smart Contracts]. *Aave GitHub pages*. Retrieved March 28, 2025, from https://github.com/aave-dao/aave-v3-origin/tree/main/src/contracts

99. *Chainlink Data Feeds*. Chainlink product pages. Retrieved March 28, 2025, from https://docs.chain.link/data-feeds
100. *AaveOracle*. Aave documentation pages. Retrieved March 28, 2025, from https://aave.com/docs/developers/smart-contracts/oracles
101. *Chainlink Automation*. Chainlink documentation pages. Retrieved March 28, 2025, from https://docs.chain.link/chainlink-automation/introduction (product was previously called chainlink-keepers and is still mentioned in some URL's, such as https://my.itsa.global/blog/chainlink-keepers).
102. *Oracle Risk*. Aave documentation pages. Retrieved March 28, 2025, from https://aave.com/docs/concepts/risks#oracle-risk
103. *Aave Correlated-assets price oracle (CAPO)*. BGD-Labs GitHub pages. Retrieved March 28, 2025, from https://github.com/bgd-labs/aave-capo
104. [Aave dApp] https://app.aave.com/
105. [Opting out of using a supplied asset as collateral]. Aave support pages. Retrieved March 28, 2025, from https://aave.com/faq (please search under "Supplying & Earning" for "Can I opt-out of my asset being used as a collateral?")
106. *Supply* [of Tokens to the Aave protocol]. Aave documentation pages. Retrieved March 28, 2025, from https://aave.com/docs/concepts/supply#supply
107. [Pool Smart Contract method] *setUserUseReserveAsCollateral()*. Aave documentation pages. Retrieved March 28, 2025, from https://aave.com/docs/developers/smart-contracts/pool#write-methods-setuserusereserveascollateral
108. *Toggle Collateral Status*. Aave support pages. Retrieved March 28, 2025, from https://aave.com/help/supplying/toggle-collateral-status
109. *Introduction To Aave*. Aave support pages. Retrieved March 28, 2025, from https://aave.com/help/aave-101/introduction-to-aave (please search in the page for "Upon supplying, the address receives a corresponding amount of ***aTokens*** *(e.g. aETH, aUSDC) in return.*")
110. [Minting Smart Contract addresses per aToken type on the Ethereum Mainnet Market]. Retrieved March 28, 2025, from https://aave.com/docs/resources/addresses (by selecting "Ethereum V3 Core Market" and "Reserves" as view options; the table column "aToken" contains hyperlinks into the respective operational Smart Contracts).
111. [CEX/DEX trading Aave pairs]. Retrieved March 28, 2025, from https://coinmarketcap.com/currencies/aave/ (please search for the trading pairs tables for CEX and DEX entries under "Aave Markets").
112. [aAAVE minting Smart Contract address on the Ethereum Mainnet Market]. Retrieved March 28, 2025, from https://etherscan.io/address/0xA700b4eB416Be35b2911fd5Dee80678ff64fF6C9 (linked from https://docs.aave.com/developers/deployed-contracts/v3-mainnet/ethereum-mainnet).
113. (2024, January). *BGD. Full deprecation of stable rate*. Aave governance discussion pages. Retrieved March 28, 2025, from https://governance.aave.com/t/bgd-full-deprecation-of-stable-rate/16473/19
114. *Key Reserve Parameters*. Aave documentation pages. Retrieved March 28, 2025, from https://aave.com/docs/primitives/reserve#key-reserve-parameters
115. *VariableDebtToken.sol* [Smart Contract]. Aave GitHub pages. Retrieved March 30, 2025, from https://github.com/aave-dao/aave-v3-origin/blob/main/src/contracts/protocol/tokenization/VariableDebtToken.sol
116. *DebtTokenBase.sol* [Smart Contract]. Aave GitHub pages. Retrieved March 30, 2025, from https://github.com/aave-dao/aave-v3-origin/blob/main/src/contracts/protocol/tokenization/base/DebtTokenBase.sol
117. *Interest Rate Strategy*. Aave documentation pages. Retrieved March 28, 2025, from https://aave.com/docs/developers/smart-contracts/interest-rate-strategy
118. [ERC-20 standard methods NOT implemented by VariableDebtToken]. Aave documentation pages. Retrieved March 28, 2025, from https://aave.com/docs/developers/smart-contracts/tokenization#not-supported-operations

119. *Credit Delegation*. Aave documentation pages. Retrieved March 28, 2025, from https://aave.com/docs/developers/credit-delegation#credit-delegation
120. Lundfall, M. (2020, April). *ERC-2612: Permit Extension for EIP-20 Signed Approvals*. Ethereum Improvement Proposals, no. 2612. Retrieved March 30, 2025, from https://eips.ethereum.org/EIPS/eip-2612
121. [AToken.sol, Smart Contract minting aTokens]. Aave GitHub pages. Retrieved March 30, 2025, from https://github.com/aave-dao/aave-v3-origin/blob/main/src/contracts/protocol/tokenization/AToken.sol
122. *Approving the delegation*. Aave documentation pages. Retrieved March 28, 2025, from https://aave.com/docs/developers/credit-delegation#approving-the-delegation
123. *Collateral transformation*. Treasurers wiki pages. Retrieved March 28, 2025, from https://wiki.treasurers.org/wiki/Collateral_transformation
124. [Aave Master Facility Agreement template]. OpenLaw project. Retrieved March 28, 2025, from https://lib.openlaw.io/web/default/template/Aave%20-%20MASTER%20FACILITY%20AGREEMENT
125. [OpenLaw project] Retrieved March 28, 2025, from https://www.openlaw.io/
126. [OpenLaw documentation pages]. Retrieved March 28, 2025, from https://docs.openlaw.io/
127. *Credit Delegation*. Aave documentation pages. Retrieved March 28, 2025, from https://aave.com/docs/developers/credit-delegation
128. *Liquidations*. Aave documentation pages. Retrieved March 28, 2025, from https://aave.com/docs/concepts/liquidations#liquidations
129. [Liquidation] *Prerequisites*. Aave documentation pages. Retrieved March 28, 2025, from https://aave.com/docs/developers/liquidations#prerequisites
130. *Liquidations* [mechanism]. Aave documentation pages. Retrieved March 28, 2025, from https://aave.com/docs/developers/liquidations#liquidations
131. *Collateral Risk*. Aave documentation pages. Retrieved March 28, 2025, from https://aave.com/docs/concepts/risks#collateral-risk
132. *Tools for Managing Health Factor*. Aave documentation pages. Retrieved March 28, 2025, from https://aave.com/docs/concepts/liquidations#tools-for-managing-health-factor
133. *Smart Contract Use Cases Unlocked by Chainlink Automation*. Chainlink product pages. Retrieved March 28, 2025, from https://chain.link/education-hub/smart-contract-automation-use-cases (in the list, please search for "Aave" and, e.g., "Liquidation").
134. [Example tool: CryptoAPIs]. Retrieved March 28, 2025, from https://cryptoapis.io/products/blockchain-events
135. *Flash Loans*. Aave documentation pages. Retrieved March 30, 2025, from https://aave.com/docs/concepts/flash-loans
136. [Flash Loans] *Overview*. Aave documentation pages. Retrieved March 28, 2025, from https://aave.com/docs/developers/flash-loans#overview
137. Cuesta Cañada, A., Kobayashi, F., fubuloubu & Williams, A. (2020, November). *ERC-3156: Flash Loans*. Ethereum Improvement Proposals, no. 3156. Retrieved March 28, 2025, from https://eips.ethereum.org/EIPS/eip-3156
138. Zeller, M. (2020, February 7). *Sneak peek at Flash Loans*. Medium. Retrieved March 28, 2025, from https://medium.com/aave/sneak-peek-at-flash-loans-f2b28a394d62
139. *Flash Loans*. Aave documentation pages. Retrieved March 28, 2025, from https://aave.com/docs/developers/flash-loans
140. *Crypto Arbitrage Bot*. Wundertrading product pages. Retrieved March 28, 2025, from https://wundertrading.com/en/crypto-arbitrage-bot
141. Nallapaneni, D. *Crypto arbitrage: A comprehensive guide*. CoinLedger. Retrieved March 28, 2025, from https://coinledger.io/learn/crypto-arbitrage
142. *Monetary Mechanics Issue #32: Collateral Transformation*. Maroon Macro. Retrieved March 28, 2025, from https://maroonmacro.substack.com/p/issue-32-collateral-transformation
143. Zeller, M. (2020, February 7). Sneak peek at Flash Loans. Retrieved March 28, 2025, from https://medium.com/aave/sneak-peek-at-flash-loans-f2b28a394d62

144. *Staking* [context: Safety Module]. Aave documentation pages. Retrieved March 28, 2025, from https://aave.com/docs/developers/safety-module#staking
145. *Safety Module*. Aave documentation pages. Retrieved March 28, 2025, from https://aave.com/docs/developers/safety-module#safety-module
146. [Implementation of] *stkAAVE – Delegation compatible*. BGD-Labs GitHub pages. Retrieved March 28, 2025, from https://github.com/bgd-labs/aave-stk-gov-v3
147. [Aave member] *Rewards*. Aave documentation pages. Retrieved March 28, 2025, from https://aave.com/docs/developers/safety-module#rewards
148. *Slashing Risks* [context: Safety Module]. Aave documentation pages. Retrieved March 28, 2025, from https://aave.com/docs/primitives/safety-module#slashing-risks
149. *Safety Incentives*. Aave documentation pages. Retrieved March 28, 2025, from https://aave.com/docs/primitives/safety-module#safety-incentives
150. [Mechanism of] *Slashing*. Aave documentation pages. Retrieved March 28, 2025, from https://aave.com/docs/developers/safety-module#slashing
151. Young, J. (2024, April 26). *Bail-In: Definition and Role in a Financial Crisis*. Retrieved March 28, 2025, from https://www.investopedia.com/terms/b/bailin.asp
152. [Staking functionality of the Aave dApp] https://app.aave.com/staking/
153. *Exchange Rate Mechanism*. Aave documentation pages. Retrieved March 28, 2025, from https://aave.com/docs/developers/safety-module#exchange-rate-mechanism
154. [stkAAVE Smart Contract transactions]. Retrieved March 28, 2025, from https://etherscan.io/token/0x4da27a545c0c5b758a6ba100e3a049001de870f5
155. *CoinMarketCap stkAAVE page*. CoinMarketCap. Retrieved March 28, 2025, from https://coinmarketcap.com/dexscan/ethereum/0x1a76f6b9b3d9c532e0b56990944a31a705933fbd/
156. *Deployed Contracts* [and addresses. Context: Safety Module]. Aave documentation pages. Retrieved March 28, 2025, from https://aave.com/docs/developers/safety-module#deployed-contracts
157. Vogelsang, L. (2021, December 28). *RWA Market: The Aave Market for Real World Assets goes live*. Retrieved March 28, 2025, from https://medium.com/centrifuge/rwa-market-the-aave-market-for-real-world-assets-goes-live-48976b984dde
158. [RWAMarket RWA Tokenization platform and marketplace] https://rwamarket.io/
159. [Centrifuge Tokenization and Fund Management platform] https://centrifuge.io/
160. [Centrifuge documentation pages]. Retrieved March 28, 2025, from https://docs.centrifuge.io/
161. [Centrifuge Whitepaper presentation]. Retrieved March 28, 2025, from https://assets.ctfassets.net/xwo28v1qbyr0/6sW8tiAb96c0o8SKQyCk2O/b470827463c9a1a178f18c4f0f819819/Centrifuge-OS-Whitepaper-1-Pager-English-v20180705.pdf
162. *Legal Structure*. Centrifuge documentation pages. Retrieved March 28, 2025, from https://docs.centrifuge.io/user/centrifuge-pools/legal-offering/
163. [Centrifuge SPV Master Operating Agreement]. Accessible from Centrifuge documentation pages. Retrieved March 28, 2025, from https://drive.google.com/file/d/1tSdZHCT7cqjh0uKCOqgrCvA9yp7XSY4K/view?pli=1
164. *Onchain Securitization*. Centrifuge documentation pages. Retrieved March 28, 2025, from https://docs.centrifuge.io/getting-started/core-concepts/securitization/
165. *Private Data Layer*. Centrifuge documentation pages. Retrieved March 28, 2025, from https://docs.centrifuge.io/getting-started/core-concepts/privacy-first-tokenization/
166. *Pool Valuation (NAV)*. Centrifuge documentation pages. Retrieved March 28, 2025, from https://docs.centrifuge.io/user/centrifuge-pools/pool-valuation/
167. *Integrated with DeFi*. Centrifuge documentation pages. Retrieved March 28, 2025, from https://docs.centrifuge.io/getting-started/core-concepts/integrated-with-defi/
168. *Introduction to Pools*. Centrifuge documentation pages. Retrieved March 28, 2025, from https://docs.centrifuge.io/user/
169. *Epochs and order execution*. Centrifuge documentation pages. Retrieved March 28, 2025, from https://docs.centrifuge.io/user/#epochs-and-order-execution

170. *Tranche tokens*. Centrifuge documentation pages. Retrieved March 28, 2025, from https://docs.centrifuge.io/user/#tranche-tokens
171. Kopp, C. M. (2020, June 27). *Bullet repayment: Definition, examples, vs. amortization*. Retrieved March 28, 2025, from https://www.investopedia.com/terms/b/bulletrepayment.asp
172. *Interest Rate Methodology*. Centrifuge documentation pages. Retrieved March 28, 2025, from https://docs.centrifuge.io/user/centrifuge-pools/interest-rate-methodology/
173. *Investing and Redeeming*. Centrifuge documentation pages. Retrieved March 28, 2025, from https://docs.centrifuge.io/user/using-centrifuge/invest/
174. *Facilitators* [Context: GHO]. Aave documentation pages. Retrieved March 28, 2025, from https://aave.com/docs/primitives/gho#facilitators
175. [Technical implementation of] *Facilitators*. Aave documentation pages. Retrieved March 28, 2025, from https://aave.com/docs/developers/gho#facilitators
176. *How to borrow GHO*. GHO documentation pages. Retrieved March 28, 2025, from https://docs-gho.vercel.app/concepts/faq#how-to-borrow-gho
177. *GhoAToken*. GHO documentation pages. Retrieved March 28, 2025, from https://docs-gho.vercel.app/developer-docs/aave-facilitator/GhoAToken
178. *Ethereum Mainnet Deployment* [of GHO Smart Contracts and addresses]. GHO documentation pages. Retrieved March 28, 2025, from https://docs-gho.vercel.app/developer-docs/contracts-overview#ethereummainnet-gho-deployment
179. *GhoVariableDebtToken*. GHO documentation pages. Retrieved March 28, 2025, from https://docs-gho.vercel.app/developer-docs/aave-facilitator/GhoVariableDebtToken
180. *GhoInterestRateStrategy*. GHO documentation pages. Retrieved March 28, 2025, from https://docs-gho.vercel.app/developer-docs/aave-facilitator/GhoInterestRateStrategy
181. *Liquidations*. GHO documentation pages. Retrieved March 28, 2025, from https://docs-gho.vercel.app/concepts/fundamental-concepts/repay-liquidate-gho#liquidations
182. *FlashMint*. GHO documentation pages. Retrieved March 28, 2025, from https://docs-gho.vercel.app/concepts/fundamental-concepts/flashmint
183. *GhoFlashMinter*. GHO documentation pages. Retrieved March 28, 2025, from https://docs-gho.vercel.app/developer-docs/flashmint-facilitator/GhoFlashMinter
184. *FlashMinter*. GHO documentation pages. Retrieved March 28, 2025, from https://docs.gho.xyz/concepts/how-gho-works/gho-facilitators#flashminter
185. *Repay and Liquidate GHO*. GHO documentation pages. Retrieved March 28, 2025, from https://docs-gho.vercel.app/concepts/fundamental-concepts/repay-liquidate-gho
186. *AAVE (AAVE)*. DefiLlama. Retrieved March 29, 2025, from https://defillama.com/protocol/aave
187. [Aave Protocol] *Concepts*. Aave documentation pages. Retrieved March 28, 2025, from https://aave.com/docs/concepts
188. Aave support pages. Retrieved March 28, 2025, from https://aave.com/faq
189. *ACLManager*. Aave documentation pages. Retrieved March 28, 2025, from https://aave.com/docs/developers/smart-contracts/acl-manager
190. *Executing the liquidation call*. Aave documentation pages. Retrieved March 28, 2025, from https://aave.com/docs/developers/liquidations#executing-the-liquidation-call
191. [Aave V3-Origin root directory]. Aave GitHub pages. Retrieved March 28, 2025, from https://github.com/aave/aave-v3-origin
192. (2023). *What is Time To Finality (TTF)*. CoinMarketCap blog pages. Retrieved March 28, 2025, from https://coinmarketcap.com/community/articles/63dddf7c51387c65b96508e7/
193. (2023, January 30). *Transactions per second(TPS). Why they matter, and why they don't*. Publish0x. Retrieved March 28, 2025, from https://www.publish0x.com/quinto-crypto-news/transactions-per-secondtps-why-they-matter-and-why-they-dont-xnnplln
194. *Oracle*. Aave documentation pages. Retrieved March 28, 2025, from https://aave.com/docs/primitives/oracle
195. ["Pools of real-world assets" functionality in the Centrifuge dApp] https://app.centrifuge.io/#/pools

196. (2022, August). *Address Blocking and TRM Labs*. Aave governance discussion pages. Retrieved March 28, 2025, from https://governance.aave.com/t/address-blocking-and-trm-labs/9301
197. Newar, B. (2022, January 6). *Aave launches its permissioned pool Aave Arc, with 30 institutions set to join*. Retrieved March 28, 2025, from https://cointelegraph.com/news/aave-launches-its-permissioned-pool-aave-arc-with-30-institutions-set-to-join.
198. *Security* [arrangements of Aave Governance]. Retrieved March 28, 2025, from https://aave.com/security
199. [GHO audits]. Aave GitHub pages. Retrieved March 28, 2025, from https://github.com/aave/gho-public/tree/main/audits
200. [Immunefi page relating to] *Aave*. Immunefi. Retrieved March 28, 2025, from https://immunefi.com/bug-bounty/aave/information/
201. (2023, November). *[ARFC] Update the Asset Onboarding Framework*. Retrieved March 28, 2025, from https://governance.aave.com/t/arfc-update-the-asset-onboarding-framework/15629
202. *Chainlink Data*. Chainlink product pages. Retrieved March 28, 2025, from https://data.chain.link/
203. *Onboarding to a Pool*. Centrifuge documentation pages. Retrieved March 28, 2025, from https://docs.centrifuge.io/user/using-centrifuge/onboarding/
204. (2021, December 29). *How to onboard on to the RWA Market – a step-by-step guide*. Retrieved March 28, 2025, from https://medium.com/centrifuge/how-to-onboard-on-to-the-rwa-market-a-step-by-step-guide-7de933e0924a
205. (2021, June). *ARC: Aave Centrifuge Permissioned "RWA" Market Proposal*. Aave governance discussion pages. Retrieved March 28, 2025, from https://governance.aave.com/t/arc-aave-centrifuge-permissioned-rwa-market-proposal/4620
206. [Context: U.S.A.] *Five Steps to Protecting Market Integrity*. [U.S.] Financial Industry Regulatory Authority (FINRA). Retrieved March 28, 2025, from https://www.finra.org/about/what-we-do/five-steps-protecting-market-integrity
207. [Context: UK] *Enhancing market integrity*. [U.K.] Financial Conduct Authority (FCA). Retrieved March 28, 2025, from https://www.fca.org.uk/about/what-we-do/enhancing-market-integrity
208. *How is health factor calculated?* Aave documentation pages. Retrieved March 28, 2025, from https://aave.com/docs/developers/liquidations#appendix-how-is-health-factor-calculated
209. [Aave Protocol] *Risks*. Aave documentation pages. Retrieved March 28, 2025, from https://aave.com/docs/concepts/risks/
210. (2023, January). *Risk parameter recommendations for new asset listings*. Aave governance discussion pages. Retrieved March 28, 2025, from https://governance.aave.com/t/risk-parameter-recommendations-for-new-asset-listings/11479
211. [Mechanism of Supply/Borrow caps]. Aave documentation pages. Retrieved March 28, 2025, from https://aave.com/docs/primitives/reserve#key-reserve-parameters (please search in the page for "Caps").
212. (2022, December). *AAVE V3 Borrow Caps Methodology*. Aave governance discussion pages. Retrieved March 28, 2025, from https://governance.aave.com/t/aave-v3-borrow-caps-methodology/10925
213. (2023, February). *Chaos Labs Updated Supply and Borrow Cap Methodology*. Aave governance discussion pages. Retrieved March 28, 2025, from https://governance.aave.com/t/chaos-labs-updated-supply-and-borrow-cap-methodology/11602
214. *[ARFC] Chaos Labs Risk Parameter Updates – Decrease supply and borrow caps on Aave V3 – 08.28.2024* [Aave DAO voting record]. Aave Snapshot pages. Retrieved March 29, 2025, from https://snapshot.box/#/s:aave.eth/proposal/0x1ea388307b70d30c040f63e8a09d49276c5c8c9ef2fd809809f253654e5f5f06

215. Pool [Smart Contract specification, containing "Supply cap" provision]. Aave documentation pages. Retrieved March 29, 2025, from https://aave.com/docs/developers/smart-contracts/pool (please search in the page for "Supply cap").
216. *Aave Protocol Parameter Dashboard* [containing "Supply cap" parametrization per Market]. Aave documentation pages. Retrieved March 29, 2025, from https://aave.com/docs/resources/parameters (please choose any Aave Market from the dropdown list and then search for "Supply Cap").
217. Pool [Smart Contract specification, containing "Borrow cap" provision]. Aave documentation pages. Retrieved March 29, 2025, from https://aave.com/docs/developers/smart-contracts/pool (please search in the page for "Borrow cap").
218. *Aave Protocol Parameter Dashboard* [containing "Borrow cap" parametrization per Market]. Aave documentation pages. Retrieved March 29, 2025, from https://aave.com/docs/resources/parameters (please choose any Aave Market from the dropdown list and then search for "Borrow Cap").
219. *Siloed Borrowing*. Aave documentation pages. Retrieved March 29, 2025, from https://aave.com/docs/developers/aave-v3#features-siloed-borrowing
220. *Chainlink Proof of Reserve*. Chainlink product pages. Retrieved March 29, 2025, from https://chain.link/proof-of-reserve
221. *What Are Proof of Reserves?* Chainlink education pages. Retrieved March 29, 2025, from https://chain.link/education-hub/proof-of-reserves
222. Licorish, E. (2023, February 7). *Aave integrates chainlink proof of reserve on avalanche to ensure sufficient collateralization of wrapped assets*. Chainlink ecosystem pages. Retrieved March 29, 2025, from https://chainlinktoday.com/aave-integrates-chainlink-proof-of-reserve-on-avalanche-to-ensure-sufficient-collateralization-of-wrapped-assets/
223. *GHO Stability Module*. GHO documentation pages. Retrieved March 29, 2025, from https://docs-gho.vercel.app/developer-docs/gho-stability-module
224. *Aave Governance reports*. Aave DAO GitHub pages. Retrieved March 29, 2025, from https://github.com/aave-dao/aave-proposals-reports
225. *Safety Module*. Aave documentation pages. Retrieved March 29, 2025, from https://aave.com/docs/primitives/safety-module
226. *Safety Incentives* (context: Safety Module). Aave support pages. Retrieved March 29, 2025, from https://aave.com/help/safety-module/safety-incentives
227. *Safety Module*. Aave support pages. Retrieved March 29, 2025, from https://aave.com/help/safety-module
228. [Staking/Unstaking processes and terms] Aave support pages. Retrieved March 29, 2025, from https://aave.com/faq (please search in the page for a. "How do I start staking?", b. "How do I stop staking?", c. "What is the cooldown period?", d."Can I add stkAAVE or stake more AAVE while in cooldown period?").
229. *Aave Docs Glossary*. Aave documentation pages. Retrieved March 29, 2025, from https://aave.com/docs/resources/glossary
230. (2020, July). *Aavenomics Questions*. Aave governance discussion pages. Retrieved March 29, 2025, from https://governance.aave.com/t/aavenomics-questions/172 (please search in the page for "Recovery Issuance")
231. ibid. (please search in the page for "Backstop Module").
232. (2021, August). *The Aave treasury management vision*. Aave governance discussion pages. Retrieved March 29, 2025, from https://governance.aave.com/t/the-aave-treasury-management-vision/5157
233. (2021, September). *Aave – Asset management guidelines*. Aave governance discussion pages. Retrieved March 29, 2025, from https://governance.aave.com/t/aave-asset-management-guidelines/5600
234. *Stewards*. Aave documentation pages. Retrieved March 29, 2025, from https://aave.com/help/governance/aave-community#stewards

235. (2023, August). *[ARFC] Treasury Management – Acquire AURA*. Aave governance discussion pages. Retrieved March 29, 2025, from https://governance.aave.com/t/arfc-treasury-management-acquire-aura/14683
236. [On-chain voting functionality of the Aave dApp] https://app.aave.com/governance/
237. *Aave Risk DAO* [Aave DAO voting record]. Aave Snapshot pages. Retrieved March 29, 2025, from https://snapshot.org/#/aave.eth/proposal/QmZfhgUj3iDhwvopPJJ91RMBhSosqY5ATnWx992fiVXvrT
238. (2021, September). *Aave Guardian Update*. Aave governance discussion pages. Retrieved March 29, 2025, from https://governance.aave.com/t/aave-guardian-update/5693
239. (2022, August). *Community Guardian renewal*. Aave governance discussion pages. Retrieved March 29, 2025, from https://governance.aave.com/t/community-guardian-renewal/9177
240. *Aave Guardian Update* [Aave DAO voting record]. Aave Snapshot pages. Retrieved March 29, 2025, from https://snapshot.org/#/aave.eth/proposal/QmduWeTjh4afJJsbCCvN52u2DAnbm2Hf2RZedga5WGuNhs
241. [List of current] *Guardians*. Aave documentation pages. Retrieved March 29, 2025, from https://aave.com/docs/primitives/governance#community-guardians
242. Liu, B. (2023, November 16). *Aave Companies rebrands to Avara, acquires Ethereum self-custody 'Family Wallet'*. CoinTelegraph. Retrieved March 29, 2025, from https://cointelegraph.com/news/aave-rebrands-to-avara-acquires-ethereum-self-custody-wallet-family
243. [LinkedIn record for] *Avara*. Retrieved March 29, 2025, from https://www.linkedin.com/company/avaraxyz/about/
244. [Avara company Webpage] https://avara.xyz/
245. *AAVE Token Holders* [on-chain report, including addresses]. Retrieved March 29, 2025, from https://etherscan.io/token/tokenholderchart/0x7fc66500c84a76ad7e9c93437bfc5ac33e2ddae9 (please search for "Aave:" entries; it is unclear if such entries, e.g. "Aave: Staked Aave", etc., also include interests effectively owned by Aave Companies or its successor[s]).
246. (2021, December). *Can we introduce some incentives/utility for holding AAVE token?* Aave governance discussion pages. Retrieved March 29, 2025, from https://governance.aave.com/t/can-we-introduce-some-incentives-utility-for-holding-aave-token/6455. Please note (under post https://governance.aave.com/t/can-we-introduce-some-incentives-utility-for-holding-aave-token/6455/29) the assertion that earlier versions of the official Aave documentation mentioned "The goal of the Aave Tokenomics, through its incentives and policies, is to create a Shelling Point where the protocol's growth, sustainability and safety take priority over individual stakeholder objectives."
247. [Governance] *Processes*. Aave documentation pages. Retrieved March 29, 2025, from https://aave.com/docs/primitives/governance#processes
248. [Governance] *Proposals*. Aave support pages. Retrieved March 29, 2025, from https://aave.com/help/governance/proposals
249. [Governance] *Proposal Lifecycle*. Aave documentation pages. Retrieved March 29, 2025, from https://aave.com/docs/primitives/governance#processes-proposal-lifecycle
250. [Governance records overview]. Aave governance discussion pages. Retrieved March 29, 2025, from https://governance.aave.com/c/governance/4
251. [Governance Snapshot records]. Aave Snapshot pages. Retrieved March 29, 2025, from https://snapshot.box/#/s:aave.eth/proposals
252. [Aave Improvement Proposal (AIP)] Contributing. Aave GitHub pages. Retrieved March 29, 2025, from https://github.com/aave/aip
253. Mihajlović, M. (2023, May 8). *AAVE Tokenomics Explained*. Shrimpy "Academy" pages. Retrieved March 29, 2025, from https://academy.shrimpy.io/post/aave-tokenomics-explained
254. *Governance*. Aave documentation pages. Retrieved March 29, 2025, from https://aave.com/docs/developers/governance
255. [Aave Governance v3] *Architecture*. Aave GitHub pages. Retrieved March 29, 2025, from https://github.com/bgd-labs/aave-governance-v3/blob/main/docs/overview.md

256. *Aave Governance V3 Properties.* Aave GitHub pages. Retrieved March 29, 2025, from https://github.com/bgd-labs/aave-governance-v3/blob/main/docs/properties.md
257. *Voting.* Aave support pages. Retrieved March 29, 2025, from https://aave.com/help/governance/voting
258. *Deployed* [Smart] *Contracts.* Aave documentation pages. Retrieved March 29, 2025, from https://aave.com/docs/developers/governance#deployed-contracts-ethereum (please search in the list for "Governance").
259. *Deployed* [Smart] *Contracts.* Aave documentation pages. Retrieved March 29, 2025, from https://aave.com/docs/developers/governance#deployed-contracts-ethereum (please search in the list for "ExecutorLvl1").
260. *Deployed* [Smart] *Contracts.* Aave documentation pages. Retrieved March 29, 2025, from https://aave.com/docs/developers/governance#deployed-contracts-ethereum (please search in the list for "ExecutorLvl2").
261. *Guardians.* Aave support pages. Retrieved March 29, 2025, from https://aave.com/help/governance/aave-community#guardians (please search in the page for "Protocol Emergency Guardian" and then for "Governance Emergency Guardian").
262. (2021, August 26). *Cross-chain governance and open-sourcing the Aave UI.* Aave BlogRetrieved February 15, 2025, from https://medium.com/aave/cross-chain-governance-and-open-sourcing-the-aave-ui-ad9dd632175d
263. *Aave Governance Cross-Chain Bridges.* Aave GitHub pages. Retrieved March 29, 2025, from https://github.com/aave/governance-crosschain-bridges
264. [Aave Protocol] *Terms of Service.* Aave main pages. Retrieved March 29, 2025, from from https://aave.com/terms-of-service
265. [Aave Protocol] *Privacy Policy.* Aave main pages. Retrieved March 29, 2025, from https://aave.com/privacy-policy
266. (2021, December). *Aave V3 Launch strategy: Code licensing.* Aave governance discussion pages. Retrieved March 29, 2025, from https://governance.aave.com/t/aave-v3-launch-strategy-code-licensing/6316/
267. (2022, November). *The risk of WBTC's underlying Bitcoin being claimed in Bankruptcy Proceedings.* Aave governance discussion pages. Retrieved March 29, 2025, from https://governance.aave.com/t/the-risk-of-wbtcs-underlying-bitcoin-being-claimed-in-bankruptcy-proceedings/10768
268. *Epochs and Order Execution.* Centrifuge documentation pages. Retrieved March 29, 2025, from https://docs.centrifuge.io/user/centrifuge-pools/epoch/
269. *Asset value / NAV.* Centrifuge documentation pages. Retrieved March 29, 2025, from https://docs.centrifuge.io/user/#asset-value%2D%2Dnav
270. *Liquidations.* Aave documentation pages. Retrieved March 30, 2025, from https://aave.com/docs/concepts/liquidations
271. (2023, February). *[Discussion] Safety Module.* Aave governance discussion pages. Retrieved March 30, 2025, from https://governance.aave.com/t/discussion-safety-module/12029
272. *Slashing* (mechanism). Aave documentation pages. Retrieved March 30, 2025, from https://aave.com/docs/developers/safety-module#slashing
273. (2020, July). *Aavenomics questions.* Aave governance discussion pages. Retrieved March 30, 2025, from https://governance.aave.com/t/aavenomics-questions/172
274. Safety Module [incentives]. Aave documentation pages. Retrieved March 30, 2025, from https://aave.com/docs/primitives/incentives#safety-module
275. Team RareSkills (2023, December 1). *The interest rate model of AAVE V3 and Compound V2.* RareSkills. Retrieved March 30, 2025, from https://www.rareskills.io/post/aave-interest-rate-model
276. *Flash loan fee.* Aave documentation pages. Retrieved March 30, 2025, from https://aave.com/docs/developers/flash-loans#overview-flash-loan-fee
277. [Aave Collector Smart Contract code] Aave GitHub directory. Retrieved March 30, 2025, from https://github.com/aave/aave-v3-periphery/blob/master/contracts/treasury/Collector.sol

278. [Aave Smart Contracts related to Reserve Factor calculation] Aave dApp. Retrieved March 30, 2025, from https://app.aave.com/reserve-overview/?underlyingAsset=0x7f39c581f595b53c5cb19bd0b3f8da6c935e2ca0&marketName=proto_mainnet_v3 (please search in the page for "Reserve factor" and for "Collector Contract"; on the latter, invoke the link "View contract").
279. *FLASH_BORROWER* [role in Flash Loan Smart Contracts]. Aave documentation pages. Retrieved March 30, 2025, from https://aave.com/docs/developers/smart-contracts/acl-manager#roles-flash-borrower
280. [Pool Smart Contract method] *updateFlashloanPremiums()*. Aave documentation pages. Retrieved March 30, 2025, from https://aave.com/docs/developers/smart-contracts/pool#write-methods-updateflashloanpremiums
281. *Voting and Execution Timeline*. Aave support pages. Retrieved March 30, 2025, from https://aave.com/help/governance/proposals#voting-and-execution-timeline
282. [Voting threshold] Aave support pages. Retrieved March 30, 2025, from https://aave.com/faq (please search in the page for "What is the voting threshold?")
283. [Voting entitlement] Aave support pages. Retrieved March 30, 2025, from https://aave.com/faq (please search in the page for "What do I need to vote?")
284. [Delegates] Aave support pages. Retrieved March 30, 2025, from https://aave.com/help/governance/aave-community (please search in the page for "Delegates" and for "Delegators").
285. (2023, May). *[ARC] Delegate Code Of Conduct*. Aave governance discussion pages. Retrieved March 30, 2025, from https://governance.aave.com/t/arc-delegate-code-of-conduct/12981
286. (2023, May). *[ARC] Framework For Recognized Delegates*. Aave governance discussion pages. Retrieved March 30, 2025, from https://governance.aave.com/t/arc-framework-for-recognized-delegates/12982
287. (2023, January). *Aave Finance Governance Process v0*. Aave governance discussion pages. Retrieved March 30, 2025, from https://governance.aave.com/t/aave-finance-governance-process-v0/11402
288. *Risk Parameters*. Aave GitHub pages. Retrieved March 30, 2025, from https://github.com/aave/risk-v3/blob/main/asset-risk/risk-parameters.md
289. Llamarisk. (2004, August 4). *AAVE interest rate model and the TradFi symbiosis*. Retrieved April 6, 2025, from https://www.llamarisk.com/research/aave-irm
290. BGD. (2024, May). *Full deprecation of stable rate*. Retrieved February 10, 2025, from https://governance.aave.com/t/bgd-full-deprecation-of-stable-rate/16473
291. [APY parameters provided through the] Aave dApp. Retrieved March 30, 2025, from https://app.aave.com/reserve-overview/?underlyingAsset=0xdac17f958d2ee523a2206206994597c13d831ec7&marketName=proto_mainnet_v3 (plase select a Market and a Reserve Token, for example the Aave Ethereum Mainnet Market and USDT; please search for "Borrow info", then for "APY").
292. ["Live Dashboard" of Aave Markets] https://www.config.fyi/
293. *Introduction To Aave* [Borrow process steps]. Aave support pages. Retrieved March 30, 2025, from https://aave.com/help/aave-101/introduction-to-aave (please search int the page for "Collateralisation", "Loan-to-Value (LTV) Ratio" and "Borrowing Process").
294. [Applicable LTV ceiling per Reserve Token]. Aave documentation pages. Retrieved March 30, 2025, from https://aave.com/docs/resources/parameters (please choose an Aave Market, then locate the table cell having "LTV" in the "Parameter" column and the correct Reserve Token as column header).
295. [Liquidation Entry definition in Aave Glossary] Aave documentation pages. Retrieved March 30, 2025, from https://aave.com/docs/resources/glossary (please search for "Liquidation Threshold").
296. [Liquidation Bonus definition in Aave Glossary] Aave documentation pages. Retrieved March 30, 2025, from https://aave.com/docs/resources/glossary (please search for "Liquidation Bonus").

297. *How is liquidation bonus determined?* Aave documentation pages. Retrieved March 30, 2025, from https://aave.com/docs/developers/liquidations#appendix-how-is-liquidation-bonus-determined
298. [Applicable Liquidation Threshold, resp. Liquidation Bonus, per Reserve Token] Aave documentation pages. Retrieved March 30, 2025, from https://aave.com/docs/resources/parameters (please choose an Aave Market, then locate the table cell having "Liquidation Threshold", resp. "Liquidation Bonus", in the "Parameter" column and the correct Reserve Token as column header).
299. [E-Mode definition in Aave Glossary] Aave documentation pages. Retrieved March 30, 2025, from https://aave.com/docs/resources/glossary (please search for "E-Mode").
300. *Efficiency Mode (E-mode).* Aave support pages. Retrieved March 30, 2025, from https://aave.com/help/borrowing/e-mode
301. [Isolation Mode definition in Aave Glossary] Aave documentation pages. Retrieved March 30, 2025, from https://aave.com/docs/resources/glossary (please search for "Isolation Mode").
302. *Isolation Mode.* Aave support pages. Retrieved March 30, 2025, from https://aave.com/help/supplying/isolation-mode
303. [Siloed Borrowing definition in Aave Glossary] Aave documentation pages. Retrieved March 30, 2025, from https://aave.com/docs/resources/glossary (please search for "Siloed Borrowing").
304. [Supply Cap definition in Aave Glossary] Aave documentation pages. Retrieved March 30, 2025, from https://aave.com/docs/resources/glossary (please search for "Supply Cap").
305. [Borrow Cap definition in Aave Glossary] Aave documentation pages. Retrieved March 30, 2025, from https://aave.com/docs/resources/glossary (please search for "Borrow Cap").
306. *Repay.* Aave documentation pages. Retrieved March 30, 2025, from https://aave.com/docs/concepts/repay
307. *Repay With Collateral.* Aave documentation pages. Retrieved March 29, 2025, from https://aave.com/docs/developers/smart-contracts/switch-adapters#repay-with-collateral
308. *Collateral Switch.* Aave documentation pages. Retrieved March 29, 2025, from https://aave.com/docs/developers/smart-contracts/switch-adapters#collateral-switch
309. *Greenlight for GHO* [Aave DAO voting record]. Aave Snapshot pages. Retrieved March 30, 2025, from https://snapshot.org/#/aave.eth/proposal/0xb17b3294dcb08316cb623c717add7f82df54948d558992f886be59d0958e9b24
310. [Aave Whitepaper – GHO] Frangella, E., & Valeri, S. (2022, October). *GHO – A flexible, decentralized stablecoin.* Retrieved March 30, 2025, from https://github.com/aave/gho-core/blob/main/techpaper/GHO_Technical_Paper.pdf
311. *Facilitators.* GHO documentation pages. Retrieved March 30, 2025, from https://docs-gho.vercel.app/concepts/how-gho-works/gho-facilitators
312. (2023, April). *[ARFC] GHO facilitator onboarding process and application.* Aave governance discussion pages. Retrieved March 30, 2025, from https://governance.aave.com/t/arfc-gho-facilitator-onboarding-process-and-application/12929
313. *Interest and Discount Rate Models.* GHO documentation pages. Retrieved March 30, 2025, from https://docs-gho.vercel.app/concepts/how-gho-works/interest-rate-discount-model
314. *Aave Ethereum V3 Market* (context: GHO Facilitators). Aave documentation pages. Retrieved March 30, 2025, from https://aave.com/docs/primitives/gho#facilitators-aave-ethereum-v3-market
315. *Interest Rate Mechanics* (context: GHO Borrowing). Aave support pages. Retrieved March 30, 2025, from https://aave.com/help/gho-stablecoin/interest-rate-mechanics, please search the Webpage for "What is the discount rate?".
316. *Discount Rate Strategy* (context: GHO Borrowing). GHO documentation pages. Retrieved March 30, 2025, from https://docs.gho.xyz/concepts/fundamental-concepts/gho-discount-strategy

317. *How is health factor calculated?* Aave developer documentation pages. Retrieved March 30, 2025, from https://aave.com/docs/developers/liquidations#appendix-how-is-health-factor-calculated
318. *[TEMP CHECK] Raising the Safety Module's Slashing Percentage*. Aave governance discussion pages. Retrieved March 30, 2025, from https://governance.aave.com/t/temp-check-raising-the-safety-module-s-slashing-percentage/14167
319. *[ARFC] Extend Safety Module Coverage to Polygon v3* [Aave DAO voting record]. Aave Snapshot pages. Retrieved March 30, 2025, from https://snapshot.org/#/aave.eth/proposal/0x6045a328e60be9369c4cd87a6b444d88fa1e1e3862d240f244e4190414e8f132
320. (2023, February). *SIZE x Aave | Auction + Safety Module*. Aave governance discussion pages. Retrieved March 30, 2025, from https://governance.aave.com/t/size-x-aave-auction-safety-module/11984
321. [Unstaking]. Aave support pages. Retrieved March 30, 2025, from https://aave.com/faq (please search in the page for "How do I stop staking?")
322. [Cooldown period after Unstaking request]. Aave support pages. Retrieved March 30, 2025, from https://aave.com/faq (please search the page for "What is the cooldown period?")
323. [Allowed Staking actions during Unstaking]. Aave support pages. Retrieved March 30, 2025, from https://aave.com/faq (please search the page for "Can I add stkAAVE or stake more AAVE while in cooldown period?")
324. *Onboarding* [context: RWA Tokenization/Investments]. Centrifuge documentation pages. Retrieved March 30, 2025, from https://docs.centrifuge.io/getting-started/core-concepts/legal-structure/#onboarding
325. *The subordination ratio* [context: RWA Structuring]. Centrifuge documentation pages. Retrieved March 30, 2025, from https://docs.centrifuge.io/user/centrifuge-pools/multi-tranche-system/#the-subordination-ratio
326. *Onchain Securitization* [context: RWA]. Centrifuge documentation pages. Retrieved March 30, 2025, from https://docs.centrifuge.io/getting-started/core-concepts/securitization/#on-chain-nav
327. (2023, September). *[ARFC] Aave Treasury RWA Allocation*. Aave governance discussion pages. Retrieved March 30, 2025, from https://governance.aave.com/t/arfc-aave-treasury-rwa-allocation/14790
328. *[ARFC] Aave Treasury Proposal for RWA Allocation* [Aave DAO voting record]. Aave Snapshot pages. Retrieved March 30, 2025, from https://snapshot.org/#/aave.eth/proposal/0x71db494e4b49e7533c5ccaa566686b2d045b0761cb3296a2d77af4b500566eb0
329. *AToken*. Aave documentation pages. Retrieved March 28, 2025, from https://aave.com/docs/developers/smart-contracts/tokenization#atoken
330. [Liquidity Index definition in Aave Glossary] Aave documentation pages. Retrieved March 30, 2025, from https://aave.com/docs/resources/glossary (please search for "Liquidity Index").
331. [Dune Dashboard for Liquidity Index statistics] Retrieved March 30, 2025, from https://dune.com/sawmon_and_natalie/aave-v3-average-rates-and-indexes (please search for "Average Liquidity Index").
332. Ozoalor, Fr. (2024, April 4). *Understanding DeFi interest rates and on-chain interest accrual: A deep dive into Aave's mechanisms*. Retrieved April 8, 2025, from https://medium.com/@frankozoalor/understanding-defi-interest-rates-and-on-chain-interest-accrual-a-deep-dive-into-aaves-b8fa1b3aaa09
333. Lielacher, A. (2023, June 26). *Rebase tokens: What are they & how do they work?* CryptoNews. Retrieved March 25, 2025, from https://cryptonews.com/exclusives/rebase-tokens.htm
334. *Pool Configurator* [Smart Contract]. Aave documentation pages. Retrieved March 30, 2025, from https://aave.com/docs/developers/smart-contracts/pool-configurator
335. [Aave Smart Contracts when querrying onchain data for assets enabled as collateral]. Aave documentation pages. Retrieved March 30, 2025, from https://aave.com/docs/developers/smart-contracts/view-contracts (please search in the page for "usageAsCollateralEnabled").

336. [Ascertaining enablement of a Reserve Token as potential collateral position through the "Live Dashboard" of Aave Markets] Retrieved March 30, 2025, from https://www.config.fyi/ (please select Protocol version and Market and then consult the "can collateral" column).
337. *AToken* [Smart Contract specification]. Aave documentation pages. Retrieved March 30, 2025, from https://aave.com/docs/developers/smart-contracts/tokenization#atoken (please search in the page for "can be safely stored, transferred or traded").
338. [Tradability of aTokens] (2024, March 1). *Aave Interest-Bearing Tokens: How to Lend Crypto in a Few Taps*. Zerion. Retrieved March 30, 2025, from https://zerion.io/blog/aave-interest-bearing-tokens/
339. [Use of assets across Aave Markets] (2021, November). *Introducing Aave V3*. Aave governance discussion pages. Retrieved March 30, 2025, from https://governance.aave.com/t/introducing-aave-v3/6035 (please search in the page for "allows assets to seamlessly flow between Aave V3 markets over different networks").
340. [DelegationAwareAToken.sol, Smart Contract minting aTokens]. Aave GitHub pages. Retrieved March 30, 2025, from https://github.com/aave/aave-v3-core/blob/master/contracts/protocol/tokenization/DelegationAwareAToken.sol
341. *VariableDebtToken*. Aave documentation pages. Retrieved March 28, 2025, from https://aave.com/docs/developers/smart-contracts/tokenization#variabledebttoken
342. [variableDebtPolDAI: Smart Contract minting of VariableDebtToken with DAI as Reserve Token on Polygon]. Retrieved March 30, 2025, from https://polygonscan.com/token/0x8619d80FB0141ba7F184CbF22fd724116D9f7ffC
343. [variableDebtOptLink: Smart Contract minting of VariableDebtToken with Link as Reserve Token on Optimum]. Retrieved March 30, 2025, from https://optimistic.etherscan.io/token/0x953A573793604aF8d41F306FEb8274190dB4aE0e
344. [variableDebtBaswstETH: Smart Contract minting of VariableDebtToken with stEth as Reserve Token on Base]. Retrieved March 30, 2025, from https://basescan.org/token/0x41A7C3f5904ad176dACbb1D99101F59ef0811DC1
345. *Borrowing*. Aave support pages. Retrieved March 30, 2025, from https://aave.com/faq (please search in the page for "Borrowing").
346. [view of the Aave V3 Core Market on the Aave dApp] https://app.aave.com/markets/?marketName=proto_mainnet_v3 for Aave V3.
347. [view of the Aave V3 Arbitrum Market on the Aave dApp] https://app.aave.com/markets/?marketName=proto_arbitrum_v3 for Aave V3.
348. *Siloed Borrowing*. Aave documentation pages. Retrieved March 30, 2025, from https://aave.com/docs/developers/aave-v3#features-siloed-borrowing
349. [Ascertaining borrow rate of a Reserve Token as potential borrow position through the "Live Dashboard" of Aave Markets] Retrieved March 30, 2025, from https://www.config.fyi/ (please select Protocol version and Market and then consult the "variable borrow rate" column).
350. [AAVE Token code root directory]. Aave GitHub pages. Retrieved March 30, 2025, from https://github.com/bgd-labs/aave-token-v3
351. *Liquidity Pools*. Aave documentation pages. Retrieved March 30, 2025, from https://aave.com/docs/primitives/aave#liquidity-pools
352. *Staking* [functionality on the Aave dApp] https://gho.aave.com/staking/
353. [aAAVE: Smart Contract minting of aToken with AAVE as supplied Token; on Aave's Ethereum (Core) Market]. Retrieved March 30, 2025, from https://etherscan.io/token/0xFFC97d72E13E01096502Cb8Eb52dEe56f74DAD7B
354. *Token Migration* [to AAVE]. Aave GitHub pages. Retrieved March 30, 2025, from https://github.com/aave/aavenomics?tab=readme-ov-file#token-migration
355. (2020, October). *Initial Discussion 2: Origination Fees*. Aave governance discussion pages. Retrieved March 30, 2025, from https://governance.aave.com/t/initial-discussion-2-origination-fees/654
356. *Resources* [incl. Security & Audits]. GHO documentation pages. Retrieved March 30, 2025, from https://docs.gho.xyz/resources

357. *Facilitators*. GHO documentation pages. Retrieved March 30, 2025, from https://docs.gho.xyz/concepts/how-gho-works/gho-facilitators
358. (2023, July). *GHO Mainnet Launch*. Aave governance discussion pages. Retrieved March 30, 2025, from https://governance-v2.aave.com/governance/proposal/268/
359. Gratton, P. (2024, July 23). *Principal-agent relationship: What it is, how it works, and new developments*. Retrieved March 30, 2025, from https://www.investopedia.com/terms/p/principal-agent-relationship.asp
360. (2023, March). *ARFC: GHO Genesis parameters. Aave governance discussion pages*. Retrieved March 30, 2025, from https://governance.aave.com/t/arfc-gho-genesis-parameters/12151
361. Seigniorage. (2025, March 17). In *Wikipedia*. Retrieved March 30, 2025, from https://en.wikipedia.org/wiki/Seigniorage
362. Liu, B. (2023, July 14). *It's GHO time: Aave stablecoin passes community governance vote*. Blockworks. Retrieved March 30, 2025, from https://blockworks.co/news/aave-Stablecoin-gho-mainnet-launch
363. *Aave V3 Ethereum Pool* [context: GHO Facilitators]. GHO documentation pages. Retrieved March 30, 2025, from https://docs.gho.xyz/concepts/how-gho-works/gho-facilitators#aave-v3-ethereum-pool
364. What Is GHO? GHO documentation pages. Retrieved March 30, 2025, from https://docs-gho.vercel.app/concepts/overview
365. Delta neutral. (2024, November 13). In *Wikipedia*. Retrieved March 30, 2025, from https://en.wikipedia.org/wiki/Delta_neutral
366. Liu, J. (2023, February 16). *Centrifuge wants to back Aave's GHO stablecoin with real-world assets*. Blockworks. Retrieved March 30, 2025, from https://blockworks.co/news/centrifuge-wants-to-back-gho-with-rwas
367. [GHO Token Smart Contract on Ethereum Mainnet]. Retrieved March 30, 2025, from https://etherscan.io/token/0x40D16FC0246aD3160Ccc09B8D0D3A2cD28aE6C2f#tokenAnalytics
368. (2023, July) *[TEMP CHECK] GHO Stability Module* [off-chain voting record]. Aave governance discussion pages. Retrieved March 30, 2025, from https://snapshot.org/#/aave.eth/proposal/0x98bdd30f645b2981320f82c671ae9fee31ee771766c13cd2627b66a22f0d438e
369. [GHO] Stability Module. Aave support pages. Retrieved March 30, 2025, from https://aave.com/help/gho-stablecoin/stability-module
370. *GhoToken*. GHO documentation pages. Retrieved March 30, 2025, from https://docs-gho.vercel.app/developer-docs/GHO/gho-token
371. [OpenZeppelin] *AccessControl.sol* [Smart Contract]. OpenZeppelin GitHub pages. Retrieved March 30, 2025, from https://github.com/OpenZeppelin/openzeppelin-contracts/blob/master/contracts/access/AccessControl.sol
372. *GhoToken.sol* [Smart Contract]. Aave GitHub pages. Retrieved March 30, 2025, from https://github.com/aave/gho-core/blob/main/src/contracts/gho/GhoToken.sol
373. [GHO-related] audits. Aave GitHub pages. Retrieved March 30, 2025, from https://github.com/aave/gho-core/tree/main/audits
374. [Balancer Token ecosystem] https://balancer.fi/
375. (2021, February). *Adding BAL on AAVE*. Aave governance discussion pages. Retrieved March 30, 2025, from https://governance-v2.aave.com/governance/proposal/3/?app=x23ai
376. Martinelli, F. (2021, February 23). *Aave & balancer partner to build the first asset manager for balancer V2*. Retrieved March 30, 2025, from https://medium.com/balancer-protocol/balancer-partners-with-aave-to-build-the-first-v2-asset-manager-d9c173330151
377. (2022, March). *ARC – Strategic Partnership with Balancer Part #1*. Aave governance discussion pages. Retrieved March 30, 2025, from https://governance.aave.com/t/arc-strategic-partnership-with-balancer-part-1/7617
378. *Strategic Partnership with Aave DAO* [Balancer governance voting record]. Balancer Snapshot pages. Retrieved March 29, 2025, from https://snapshot.org/#/balancer.eth/proposal/0xcfc6a0a2ecb9bf8a3cb0ed7a2617093b0aba14a4a43f81044dc726ce040cb07f

379. *Aave Utilities*. Aave GitHub pages. Retrieved March 28, 2025, from https://github.com/aave/aave-utilities
380. *Global* [RWA] *Market Overview dashboard*. Retrieved March 28, 2025, from https://app.rwa.xyz/
381. [Context: E.U.] *Market Integrity*. European Securities and Markets Authority (ESMA). Retrieved March 28, 2025, from https://www.esma.europa.eu/esmas-activities/markets-and-infrastructure/market-integrity
382. [Reserve Factor parameter] Aave documentation pages. Retrieved March 30, 2025, from https://aave.com/docs/resources/parameters (please select an Aave Market and search the "Parameter" column for "Reserve Factor").
383. [Minting of aTokens by Smart Contract]. Aave documentation pages. Retrieved March 30, 2025, from https://aave.com/docs/resources/addresses (please select an Aave Market – e.g., "Ethereum V3 Core Market" – and "Reserves" as view options; the table column "aToken" contains hyperlinks into the respective operational Smart Contracts).

Cryptocurrencies and Crypto-Tokens in Short 15

The previous book chapters followed a pedagogical approach, which entailed laying out facts and building up knowledge systematically on topical points of focus. This disciplined approach becomes unavoidable in a book about methodology, and more so in a relatively new field where concepts have been evolving rather chaotically, being discovered and getting accepted together with the field itself.

Having explained concepts in some detail, and hopefully convinced the reader about the importance of a consistent analysis and design methodology in the first place, we now come to a point where it is expedient to place them within a "bigger picture" so to speak. This last chapter could have been named "Why cryptocurrencies? Why crypto-tokens? Why Trading in Them?", but then it would run the risk of being misunderstood for an "exegesis", a legitimation attempt of sorts.

The actual purpose of this chapter is to put the current state of affairs in the crypto-market into a perspective; that is, to help the reader interpret it as an evolutionary stage along appropriate axes. It is not an attempt to justify its existence at all, but rather an explanation of why and how this market appeared and reached the state that it did, why in the general timeframe that it did, and how it could evolve. In short, the intention is to convey a high-level "cause and effect" cum "sense of direction" perspective to the reader, to complement the more fine-granular methodological thinking imparted through the previous chapters in the book.

15.1 Taking a Step Back

The blockchain is a technological development, a new way of doing "old things", and a facilitator of ways to create "new things". It can be debated if it will prove only evolutionary or truly revolutionary in the long run. So far it has proven to be by no means society-changing, at least not to the same extent as, for example, the arrival of the internet was. Even the currently prevailing blockchain architectures depend on infrastructures (such as hosting and communication platforms, etc.) that trace their growth to the internet era. Hence, in contrast to, for example, artificial intelligence,

I. Giannakouros, *Cryptocurrencies and Tradable Crypto-Tokens*, Future of Business and Finance, https://doi.org/10.1007/978-3-031-98423-5_15

the blockchain depends on other technologies that appear to be of even more fundamental importance for our societies. However, blockchain-based ecosystems are now a fact and are still operating healthily. That means that they must truly be addressing some economic needs.

Why did the blockchain appear, and why did the first-ever cryptocurrency use cases gain traction?

The first-ever blockchain architecture (Bitcoin, 2009) and its use cases were monetary and ultimately financial in nature. They were in effect promising to address frictions and instabilities of then-prevailing mechanisms of constructing, preserving, and transmitting financial assets. It is probably not a coincidence that more such use cases arrived on the scene while major global economic events—and their adverse repercussions for ordinary citizens—were unfolding, namely:

- The 2008 global financial crisis (GFC) and the concomitant loss of faith in the resilience of the international, centralized, financial system which harboured it[1].
- A host of sovereign debt crises in the early-to-mid 2010s [2], which made those countries' citizens doubt the ability of centralized decision-making to effectively manage economies.
- Concomitant liquidity injection initiatives by central banks of developed economies ("quantitative easing"), which made citizens everywhere question the ability of established (fiat) reserve currencies to function as long-term stores of value.
- Severe inflationary spirals and balance of payment crises in several emerging economies, which made their citizens look for non-traditional means of asset protection in the face of rapidly devaluating fiat currencies [3].
- Increasing scarcity (sometimes due to political events) of large-scale and readily accessible inventories of long-term assets, such as precious metals and other traditional "safe" stores of value, which unnerved citizens used to investing discretionary funds in them.

In the same general timeframe, large parts of the population in both developed and developing economies started getting acquainted with the fruits of digitalization at scale. Those were propagated everywhere through advances in telecommunication networks coverage and bandwidth, and through the mass availability of reasonably priced high-functionality consumer electronics (such as internet-enabled mobile phones and tablets) running on those networks. This set in motion another set of societal trends which culminated globally to:

[1] And in some cases, even before that. E.g. consider the societal consequences of apparent manipulation of the Greek stock-market in the late 1990s [1], which lasted more than a decade after the fact.

- The familiarization with, and acceptance of, technology as a channel for negotiating transactions and for paying funds—with telecom companies stepping into the role of payment services provider.
- The pervasiveness of global digital business ecosystems (created and operated by major platform companies), which proved that economic agents could indeed be connected directly along truly global value chains.
- The broad digitalization of post-industrial societies—a trend made even more pronounced due to the traumatic experience of the Covid-19 pandemic, which made people fearful of handling physical artefacts such as documents, banknotes, and coins.

Among members of what would usually qualify as the non-corporate clients segment (i.e. retail and SME's) of banks and financial intermediaries, commercial transactions started happening much faster than 15–20 years ago and no longer involving the exchange of physical cash. Even more important than the speed of transactions was the fact that those were *actually* being executed, even though they involved in effect the provision of credit by one of the participants. Suddenly, perfect strangers from different countries started transacting with, and giving credit to, one another as a matter of course, as long as this was happening on established technical platforms and infrastructures. This engendered great faith in technology as the main enabler of a better future in this client segment.

At the same time, the proliferation of technology-centric processing at banks and financial intermediaries—to the point that industry exponents went on record stating [4, 5] half-jokingly their goal to become "technology companies with a banking license"—created a mass of people who were cognizant of operational details in both the financial and the technology domains. Most of those people were young enough to have gained a track record in only specific banking sub-domains (e.g. either in payments processing or in lending origination and execution, etc.). They were technology enthusiasts by upbringing and process optimizers by conviction (and ambition). They were willing to try new ideas but felt stifled by the corporate decision-making processes (and of course the need to avoid business cannibalization) inherent to large organizations.

In the aftermath of the 2008 GFC, the potential of technology to reduce the cost of transactions and to mitigate risks and frictions of economic life had not gone unnoticed by financial regulators. The outcome was that, at their advice, lawgivers of major financial jurisdictions began introducing statutes (and accompanying regulations) intended to facilitate the introduction of new technologies. In the European Union, for example, the 2015 "Second Payment Services Directive" [6, 7] in effect imposed the "Open Banking" paradigm [8–10] on most of their supervised entities. In parallel, starting with the UK Financial Conduct Authority in 2016 [11], major financial regulators sought to practically facilitate this direction through the institution of "Regulatory Sandboxes" [12], that is, innovation-testing environments sponsored by the regulators themselves. The intention was to help both the innovation providers and the regulators preemptively de-risk potential implementations [13], and to identify needed policy changes whenever cost-benefit considerations justified it. Such regulatory initiatives eventually proliferated, to the point that they became regular activities in their books of business. For example, even the Bank for International Settlements has been operating an own (and quite active) "Innovation Hub" [14], spread across several international locations. The direct result was the creation of a totally new part of the financial services industry, bearing the name "FinTech" [15–17] (short for "Financial Technology [Firm(s)]"). The important underlying trend, however, was the emergence of a new generation of regulators who are not shy of technology and are at times willing to implement it themselves [18].

In a parallel development, a side-effect of the afore-mentioned quantitative easing was the ready availability of ultra-low-cost funds (at one point, reference bank rates were negative) for consumption and especially investments. Venture capital firms in particular became a prominent channel of this cheap liquidity towards technological innovation, for two reasons: first, because technology was one of the sectors promising especially high rates of return (especially as most industry experts were predicting a sustained digitalization wave), and second, because the seemingly accelerating rate of technological innovation itself created a "fear of missing out" ("FOMO") effect [19]. In short, investment capital was cheap, technology seemed to be a high-probability-of-success/high-ROI field, and (as it was evolving at break-neck speed) nobody could be sure if a new startup was going to be the next "unicorn" [20] or not.

Hence, for the best part[2] of the period after the 2008 GFC and until early 2022, there was a combination of sustained factors in evidence, namely:

- A critical mass of people with hands-on operational experience (at the intersection of business and technology) in banks and financial intermediaries, lots of ideas, and a willingness to explore them outside a corporate setting.
- An at least lenient, and, on occasion clearly supportive, stance by lawgivers and financial regulators of major financial jurisdictions towards new technologies in banking and financial markets.
- Ready availability of venture capital, seeking high returns in a generally low-interest rate environment, which created an extraordinarily favourable environment for the pursuit of technological innovation in banking and financial markets.

To summarize the above, one way of interpreting the appearance—and then proliferation—of blockchain projects creating cryptocurrencies and crypto-tokens is by considering the global economic and societal context within which they were manifested. In short, after an unavoidable initial "learning curve", blockchain-based tokens seemed to offer to ordinary citizens and investors alike the promise of "new

[2]With a very brief interruption in the initial stages of the Covid-19 pandemic. Please recall that central banks of all major economies had started supplying extra liquidity already by late spring 2020 in order to stave off its societal effects—this lowered the cost of capital again, and led to further increases in the valuation of risk assets. Capital costs started increasing again at the onset of the war in Ukraine.

ways" of responding to perceived societal threats and opportunities. For deeply dissatisfied citizens of developed economies, they represented a practical way to respond to the excesses of centralized capital and financial markets. For young, tech-native citizens of emerging economies, they seemed to offer a way to access new-found stores of long-term value and thus to defend themselves against the hazard of deep and prolonged devaluation of their national currencies. For tech-savvy investors everywhere, they resonated with a conviction in the power of technology to improve lives and correct wrongs while promising extraordinary returns, literally as if a new "internet 2.0" had been created. For regulators, it chimed with their newfound beliefs in reducing frictions and controlling risks better through technology. It can be argued that blockchain-based tokens offered new perspectives to the ideologues; the retail investors; the tech-savvy; and the risk profit-seekers; all at once. They personified intriguing new possibilities that "chimed with the times" as it were.

This was at least the initial impetus. The fact that several of those tokens (especially the first cryptocurrencies) then experienced large appreciations for prolonged periods probably added to the mass appeal of the entire blockchain value proposition. As of the time of writing, there occurred two "crypto-winters" [21] (periods roughly equivalent to "bear markets" in traditional finance jargon) already, namely from early 2018 to late 2020 [22] and from mid-2022 to mid-2023. They both only partially overlapped global systemic events (the first one started one year before the Covid-19 pandemic and progressed while traditional financial markets kept reaching new highs; the second around 3 months after the start of the war in Ukraine and then receded while the war was ongoing). It can actually be argued that they both had causes idiosyncratic to the crypto industry (the first one, technical immaturity across token ecosystems; the second, lack of effective governance—and at times, criminal behaviour at the helm—of critical links in the crypto-token value chain, as exemplified by the LUNA/TerraUSD collapse [23] and the FTX/Alameda [24] case). It may also ultimately be proven that, once put in motion, they were exacerbated by the surrounding systemic events. However, the fact is that a critical mass of the cryptocurrency and crypto-tokens industry is still functioning. None of the major cryptocurrencies has disappeared, and there is manifested interest from the traditional banking [25] and financial markets [26] actors to somehow "attach" to the crypto-market as well. Hence, it can be said the resiliency of this market has already been proven. This may very well make it even more "acceptable" to traditional asset class investors as well.

15.2 The "DeFi" Phenomenon

A note is in order regarding "decentralized finance" and how traditional finance professionals could make better sense of it. The term was mentioned in the very first chapter of this book (Sect. 1.5) as mapping to Layer-3 and Layer-4 protocols. Admittedly, it was not properly defined there nor in subsequent chapters (*mea culpa*), as the focus throughout was on the design of individual token ecosystems. This omission will be rectified in this section; however, we find it expedient to begin with some visual imagery.

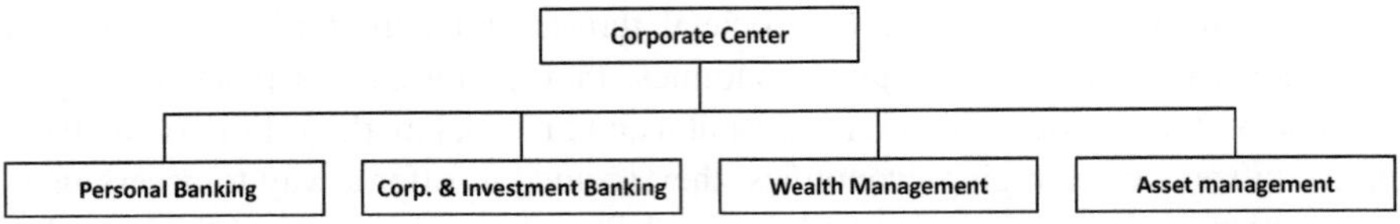

Fig. 15.1 High-level corporate structure of example bank

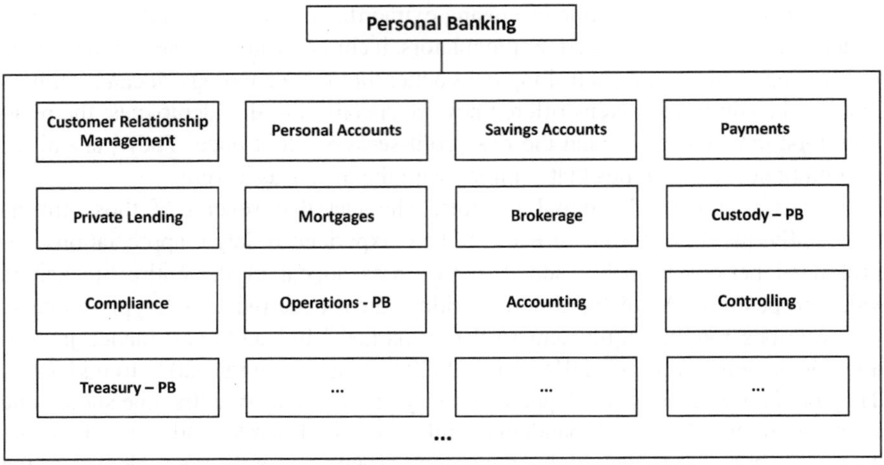

Fig. 15.2 "Personal banking" organizational chart

Imagine a full-fledged bank. Assume that you are an analyst—or a business architect—and must describe the bank as an organizational and operational construct, including its internal flows of funds. To keep things simple, assume that the bank operates in one country only. However, it does offer a full spectrum of banking products and services, across all client segments. It is a "universal bank" [27].

Going through its audited statements, you come to understand its organizational structure and business model. At the highest level, you find business units called "personal banking" (PB), "corporate and investment banking" (CIB), "wealth management" (WM), "asset management" (AM), and "corporate center" (CC) (cf. Fig. 15.1).

Under "personal banking", the organization chart (cf. Fig. 15.2) shows sub-units called "customer relationship management", "personal accounts", "savings accounts", "payments", "private lending", "mortgages", "brokerage", "custody—PB", "compliance", "operations–PB", "accounting", "controlling", "treasury—PB", etc.

Under "corporate and investment banking" (CIB), there are sub-units (cf. Fig. 15.3) called "customer relationship management", "corporate accounts", "corporate lending", "global transaction banking", "treasury products", "trade finance", "working capital solutions", "equities", "fixed income", "foreign exchange", "interest rates", "commodities", "structured products", "syndicated lending", "mergers and acquisitions", "prime brokerage", "custody/corporate actions—CIB", "direct access clients", "correspondent banking", "cash/collateral

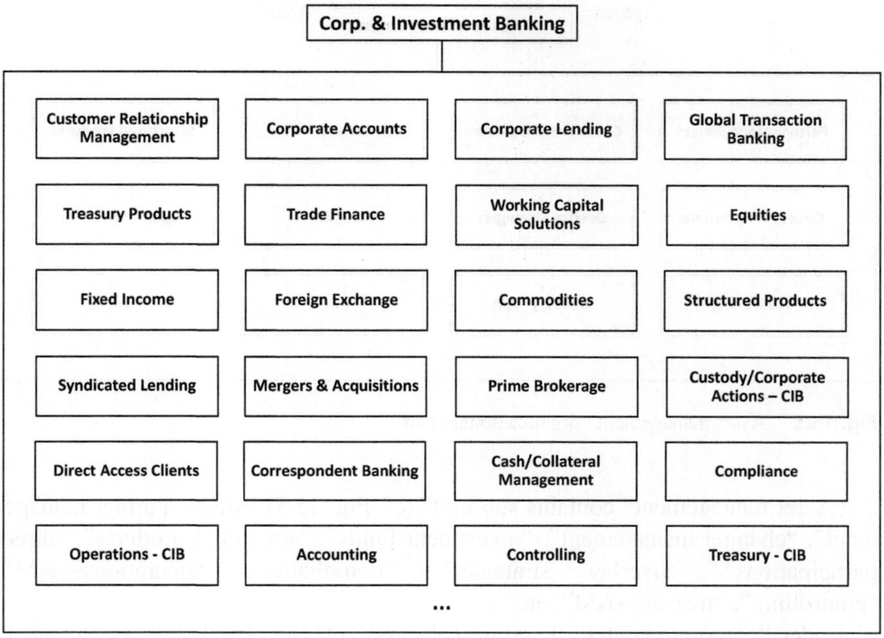

Fig. 15.3 "Corporate and investment banking" organizational chart

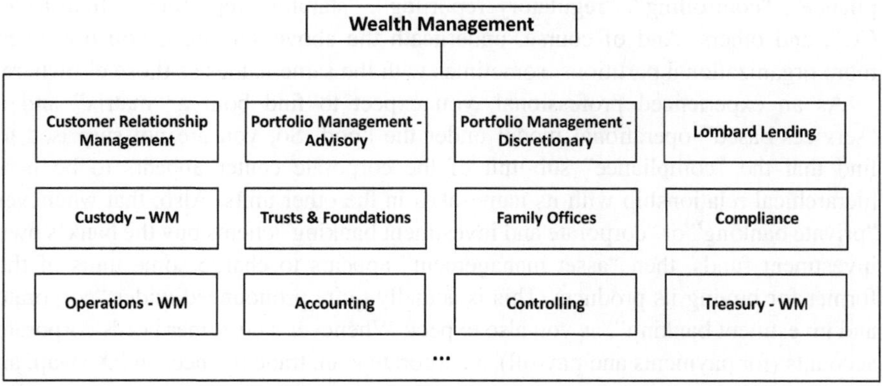

Fig. 15.4 "Wealth management" organizational chart

management", "compliance", "operations—CIB", "accounting", "controlling", "treasury—CIB", and others.

Under "wealth management", you find sub-units with names such as "customer relationship management", "portfolio management—advisory", "portfolio management—discretionary", "lombard lending", "custody–WM", "trusts and foundations", "family offices", "compliance", "operations—WM", "accounting", "controlling", "treasury—WM", etc. With this information, you create an organization chart as depicted in Fig. 15.4.

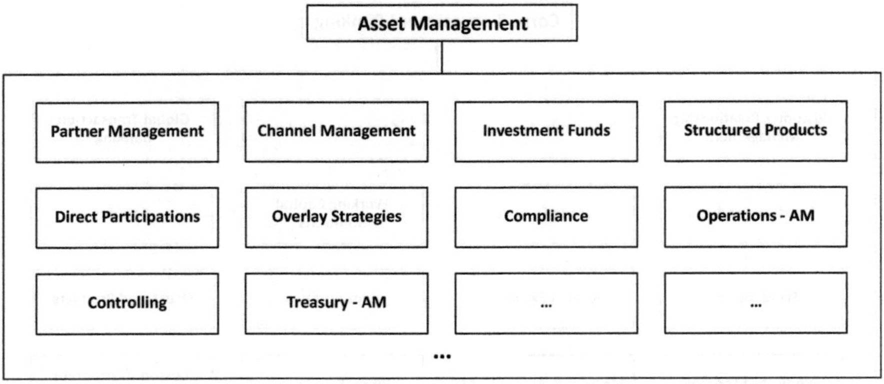

Fig. 15.5 "Asset management" organizational chart

"Asset management" contains sub-units (cf. Fig. 15.5) named "partner management", "channel management", "investment funds", "structured products", "direct participations", "overlay strategies", "compliance", "operations—AM", "controlling", "treasury–AM", etc.

Under "corporate center" there are sub-units (cf. Fig. 15.6) such as "finance", "accounting", "risk management", "legal", "tax", "human resources", "information technology", "operations—CC", "corporate real estate", "investor relations", "compliance", "controlling", "regulatory reporting", "statutory reporting", "treasury—CC", and others. And of course, underneath the above sub-units, you find even more organizational partitions, sometimes with the same names as those elsewhere.

As an experienced professional, you expect to find both a "matrix" and a "services-based" operational model under the hood. So, you are not surprised to find that the "compliance" sub-unit of the corporate center appears to be in a hierarchical relationship with its namesakes in the other units. Also, that whenever "private banking" or "corporate and investment banking" clients buy the bank's own investment funds, then "asset management" appears to charge some units of the former for buying its products. This is actually quite pronounced under "corporate and investment banking", as you also expect: Whenever a customer needs corporate accounts (for payments and payroll), a corporate loan, trade finance, an FX swap, an interest-rate swap, etc. there appears to be a coordinating instance (apparently "customer relationship management"), which then works to fulfil their needs and which is also involved in the rating and final pricing towards the customer. What is more, there appears to be internal revenue sharing and even cross-charging taking place among these sub-units bilaterally. Furthermore, sub-units having "operations" in their name appear to be involved everywhere.

You already know how internal financial flows in such a complex organization work out and how the final profitability measures at the corporate center level are calculated. For instance, you know that all sub-units and their sub-partitions are generally allocated to either "profit centers" or "service centers" in internal

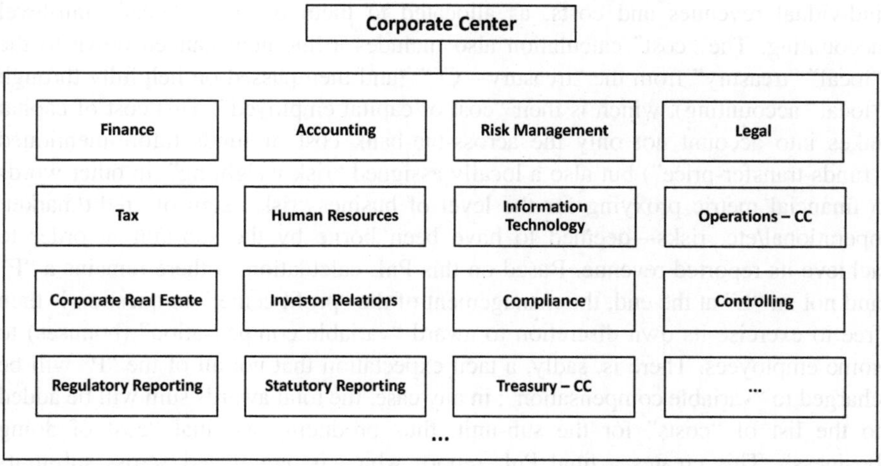

Fig. 15.6 "Corporate center" organizational chart

accounting. Whenever sums of money flow from outside sources into the bank, then one of the "profit centres" is allowed to book these sums as revenue. Some "service center" sub-units which were involved in the value chain are allocated part of this revenue stream directly in internal accounting, whereas others (typically those under the corporate center, but not only) are not.

Another thing which you know is that there are unit-level treasury and accounting teams, which are responsible for aggregating unit revenues/costs and for executing some types of unit-level cash outflows if so authorized by corporate center's treasury (the "treasury—CC" sub-unit). All sub-units with "treasury" in their name have an assets and liabilities management responsibility at the "local" unit level. It is those units that will have to find (short-term) liquidity when it is needed by other "local" sub-units, and they are also the ones tasked with calculating—and advising—(longer-term) funding needs to "treasury—CC". They are expected to do so by having mechanisms in place to estimate the current level of business risks inherent in all other "local" sub-units and to project said risks through financial models to future risk-hedging needs of their entire assigned unit. Said risk hedging needs are first aggregated by "treasury—CC", then netted internally, and finally the net bank-wide "residual risks" are transferred to the financial markets (by issuing bonds, purchasing insurance, entering macro-hedge swaps, etc.). The current and projected residual risk transfer costs are added to the liabilities side of the bank's balance sheet by corporate center accounting. A by-product of the final assets and liabilities management exercise at the level of both corporate center treasury and corporate center accounting is an agreement on the effective "funds transfer price", that is, the bank-internal cost of capital. This all you also know.

Furthermore, you know that before each statutory reporting period is closed (and dividends paid out), there is yet another ritual taking place: each "profit center" sub-unit calculates their own profit and loss ("PnL") for the period, based on their individual revenues and costs, as allocated to them by their “local” unit-level accounting. The “cost” calculation also includes a line-item handed down to the “local” “treasury” from the “treasury—CC” (and then passed on helpfully through “local” accounting), which is their “cost of capital employed”. This cost of capital takes into account not only the across-the-bank cost of funds (afore-mentioned “funds-transfer-price”) but also a locally assigned “risk weighting”, in other words a financial metric proxying for the level of business risk—sum of credit/market/operational/etc. risks—deemed to have been borne by the sub-unit in order to achieve its reported revenue. Based on this PnL calculation, if there remains a “P” and not an “L” at the end, the management of the “profit center” in question is then free to exercise its own discretion to award “variable compensation” (bonuses) to some employees. There is, sadly, a tacit expectation that not all of the “P” will be charged to “variable compensation”; in any case, the total awards sum will be added to the list of “costs” for the sub-unit, thus producing its final “cost of doing business”. This creates a final PnL report, which is aggregated across sub-units and then flows from “local accounting” all the way up to corporate center “accounting”. This is now the “earnings before tax” sum for the entire bank. After corporate taxes are paid, the remaining sum of money should be waiting patiently in the “treasury—CC” sub-unit. Bank management will then decide which part of said sum will be paid out immediately as dividends, while the rest will remain in “treasury—CC” as “retained earnings”. Dividends will profit shareholders (minus personal income tax), while retained earnings can be used for whatever purpose management thinks will help keep the bank as a going concern.

So, you know all the above and are comfortable that you will identify them in the business model of the Bank in question. Now, please stop and do this: **Take the bank apart**.

Please follow this way: Break down the “units” and keep only “sub-units” that do not also have corporate center equivalents. So, there will be no “personal banking”, “corporate and investment banking”, etc. but simply unassorted “customer relationship management”, “personal accounts”, “savings accounts”, “payments”, “private lending”, “mortgages”, “brokerage”, “global transaction banking”, “treasury products”, “trade finance”, “equities”, “fixed income”, “foreign exchange”, “interest rates”, “structured products”, etc. You should have an overview as that depicted in Fig. 15.7.

Now, take all corporate center sub-units, break them into many pieces each and tie dissimilar pieces (i.e. one piece from “accounting”, one from “risk management”, “human resources”, “information technology”, “compliance”, “operations—CC”, “treasury—CC”, etc.) together into bundles, so that each bundle has a piece—and one only—from each and every of the previous whole corporate center sub-units. That should give you a depiction like in Fig. 15.8.

Finally, attach every one of those bundles to a single “sub-unit” above. You should have created a picture like Fig. 15.9, where, for example, “payments” is attached to an own bundle of corporate center pieces, “private lending” to another bundle, “structured products” to yet another, etc.

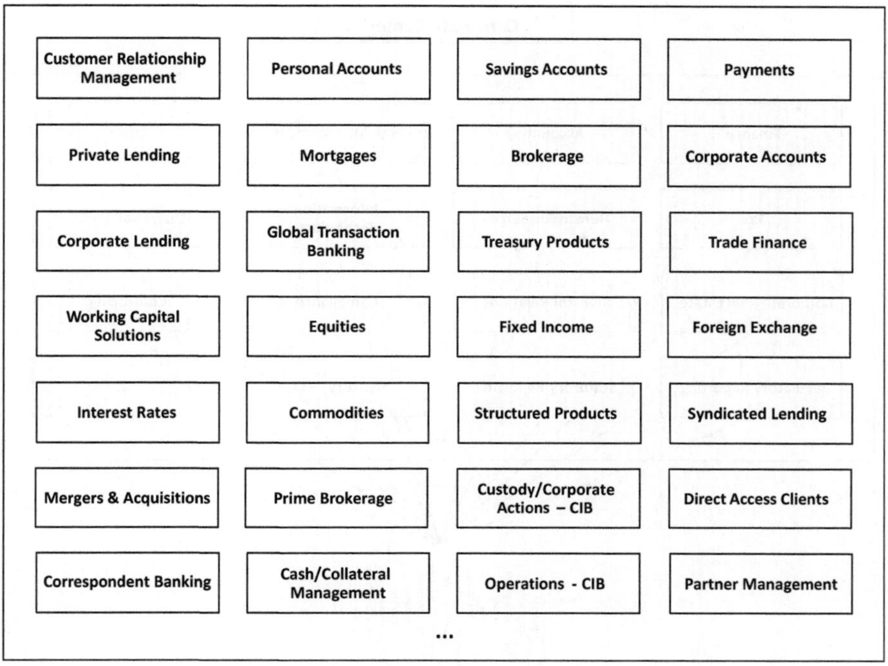

Fig. 15.7 Bank sub-units with no matrix relationship to corporate center ones

Please do not be surprised if the "sub-units" (not the bundled pieces) are now only the previous "profit center" ones. This is precisely what the exclusion of the corporate center duplicates was meant to achieve. You have now broken the bank down into a different organizational construct, in which all "profit centers" have their own HR, risk management, IT, accounting, treasury, etc. Let us denote each one of them—together with their "bundled" corporate center pieces—as being a "profit center cluster". So, you have one profit center cluster focused on payments, one on lending, one on foreign exchange trading, one on structured products, etc. Each cluster must now achieve its own revenue targets, with its own employees, through its own compliance and risk management, own operations and IT, calculate its own cost of capital, find its own liquidity and funding sources, and have its own treasury, whereupon its own management will decide on own staff variable compensation, dividends policy, and allocation of retained earnings.

One more complication, after the breaking-down is complete: **Profit center clusters should keep cooperating, as before.**

So, lending should be able to procure services from savings accounts, global transaction banking from corporate accounts, treasury products from foreign exchange and from structured products, etc. Naturally, they are free to set their own, individual rates, as long as they each cover their own individual costs of capital. Risk management, compliance, IT, operations, and treasury functions of each are under the auspices of their own, independent, executive management.

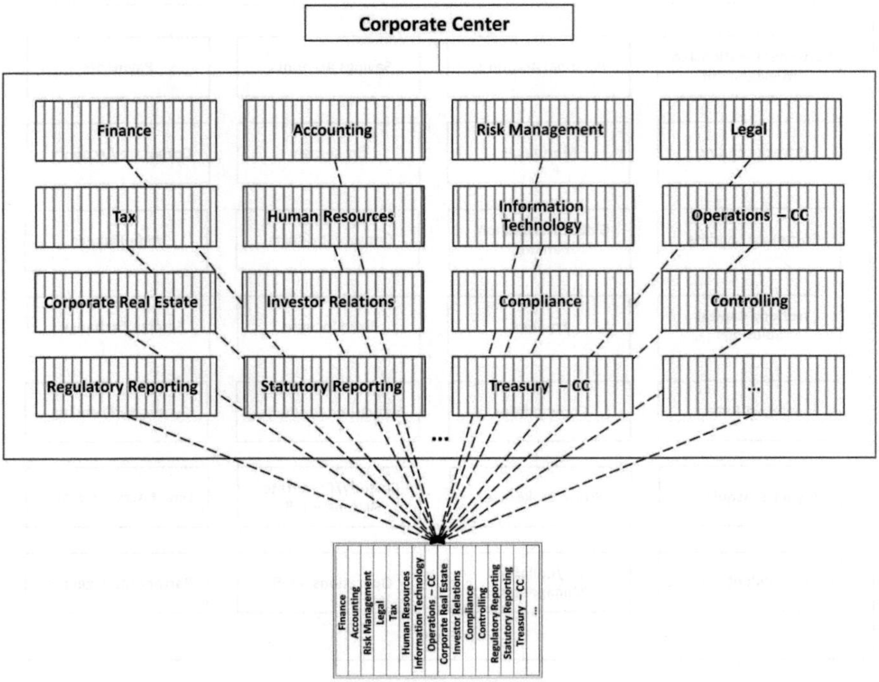

Fig. 15.8 Breaking down "corporate center" sub-units and tying them into service "bundles"

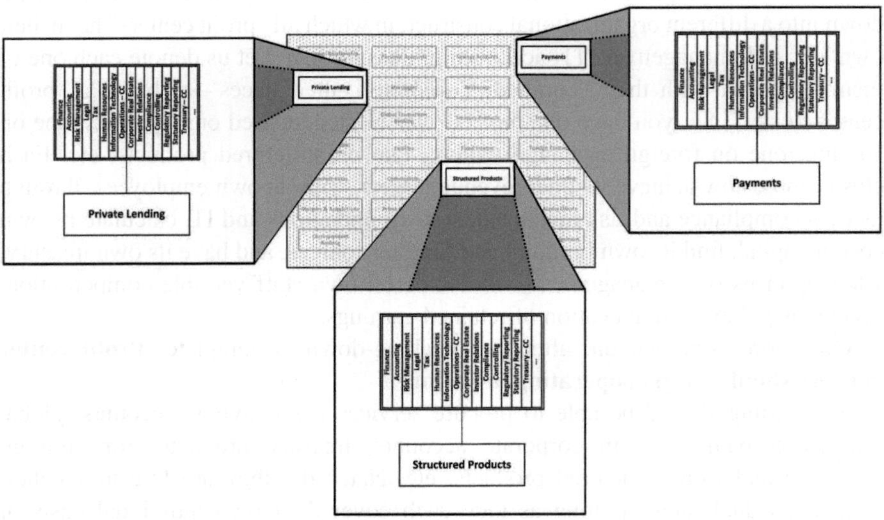

Fig. 15.9 Each profit center sub-unit with an own corporate center "bundle" forms a profit center cluster

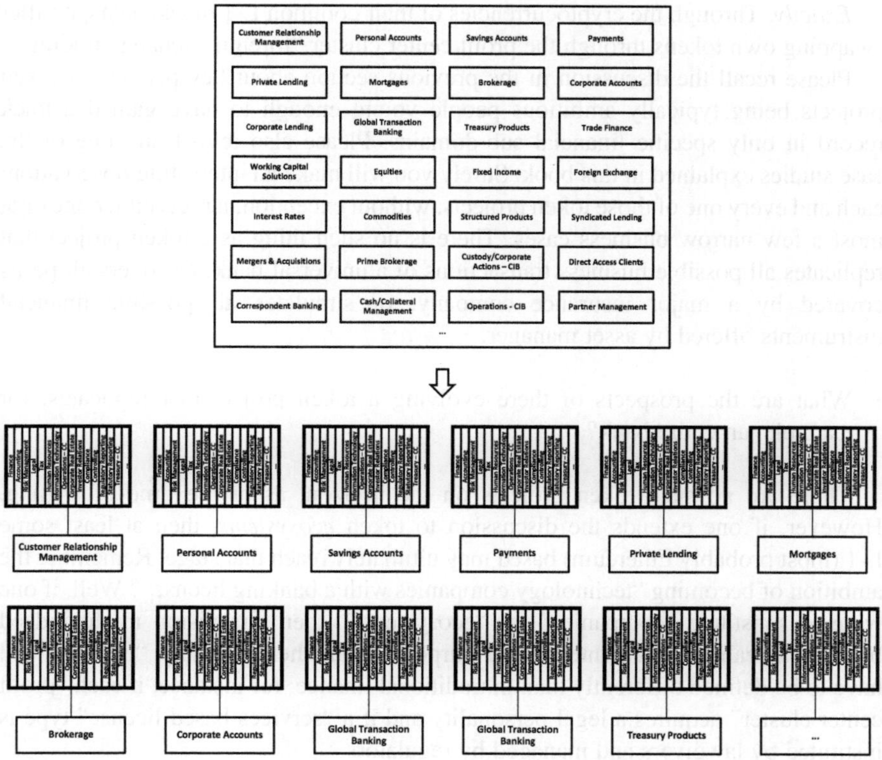

Fig. 15.10 From profit cluster centers to decentralized finance

Congratulations: This picture in front view (Fig. 15.10), with single-purpose profit center clusters all over the place, is **the paradigm of decentralized finance**. For "profit center cluster", please mentally substitute "token project".

Based on this picture, a number of questions may legitimately arise:

- Assuming that you are on a blockchain-based IT infrastructure, how does each profit center cluster know how to calculate its own cost of funds, when it can afford to issue dividends, if it has retained earnings, etc. through its own treasury?

Exactly. Through its crypto-tokens. Be it governance tokens, asset tokens, cryptocurrencies, or whatever type its management (i.e. governance body in token ecosystems parlance) decides to accept as treasury-admissible tokens.

- How can profit center clusters charge one another for services if they do not have the same treasury tokens?

Exactly. Through the cryptocurrencies of their common L-1 blockchains, or after swapping own tokens through the profit center cluster “foreign exchange trading”.

Please recall the discussion in the previous section about key persons of token projects being typically ambitious people young enough to have gained a track record in only specific financial sub-domains. Please also revisit any one of the case studies explained in this book. Surely you will make an interesting observation: each and every one of those token projects, without exception, targets either one or at most a few narrow business cases. There is no such thing as a token project that replicates all possible business transactions of a universal bank; or covers all perils covered by a major insurance company; or simulates all possible financial instruments offered by asset manager.

- What are the prospects of there evolving a token project that replicates, for example, an entire bank?

There are no such token projects on the horizon, as of the time of writing. However, if one extends the discussion to token *ecosystems*, then at least some L-1 (most probably Ethereum) based may ultimately reach that stage. Remember the ambition of becoming “technology companies with a banking license”? Well, if one were to substitute “companies” for “ecosystems”, then this vision might indeed become a reality for all intents and purposes—but then probably “license” will have to be defined differently than in traditional finance; for instance, if each “profit center cluster” acquires a legal personality and if a “services-based license” type is instituted by lawgivers and managed by regulators.

There follows the promised (own) DeFi definition:

> ‘Decentralized Finance’ is a business architectural paradigm based on blockchain infrastructures, whereby individual token projects offer one or at most a few financial services each, and more complex value chains are then built by agents chaining together inflows with outflows of said token projects. Crypto-tokens are used within each token project to: create; represent; and capture the added value of said services; and as stores of transferred or added value. Cryptocurrencies are used both within and across token projects to effect price discovery of said services and stores of value; cross-charging for said services among token projects; and payment of usage fees charged by the blockchain infrastructures. Neither the creation and operation of individual token projects and their artefacts, nor the exception handling of the resulting value chains, are governed by any central authority.

The reader is kindly asked to juxtapose this definition with the metaphor of the broken-apart bank given previously.

Some further comments are in order, based on the author’s own observations regarding the current state of affairs in DeFi.

First, it is true that several token use case creators had pedigrees in traditional financial services companies. However, many “green-field” token use cases were outcomes of purely technological experimentation, much more than they were attempts to recreate or improve traditional procedural or financial paradigms in a blockchain setting. It thus should come as no surprise that unforeseen consequences (e.g. slippage effects, then "divergence losses" through automated market makers, or de-pegging of Stablecoins) occurred; nor that their root causes were understood by creators long after token projects had been deployed in production. Seasoned traditional finance practitioners could have pointed immediately to such market and operational risks (order-driven liquidity only, and wrong-way-risk in the Stablecoin-supporting asset structures) lurking in the original design.

Second, for many a token project, rapid time-to-market (and a quick market exit, through rapid token appreciation, for their backers) was the primary focus—not managing the end-to-end risk profile of the business use case implementation. The fact that a host of tokens seemed to be finding a ready market anyway did nothing to prompt their creators to proactively solicit business and risk advice on their end-to-end designs. At the risk of sounding too simplistic, the fact, for example, that a first version of an Automated Market Maker seemed to do a decent job inside a DEX during stable or rising markets did not help manage the risk that under volatile market conditions it could completely fail to achieve best execution. As noted in Sect. 10.5.7 and explained in more detail in the case study of Chap. 13, there are reasons why Market Maker seats are privileged ones in traditional trading venues after all. What were the odds that a technology-savvy, but financially inexperienced, token project team would be able to predict all probable order-driven market scenarios in the first place?

Third, occurrences such as Stablecoins with uncontrollable amounts of wrong-way risk; token treasury balance sheets with no verifiable positions on either the liability on the asset sides—in spite of their coming from blockchain transactions; crypto Exchanges and market places with no policies in place for separating assets under custody from own assets; smart contracts propagating significant operational risks on account of not being properly tested by their implementors, nor vetted by auditors; non-fungible tokens with no clear description of the underlying asset rights; ecosystems admitting foreign tokens with no real due diligence to avert money laundering and other financial crimes propagation; etc. are all operational risk events that, far from being hypothetical, have already manifested themselves in the crypto industry. So, these risks are very probable in the future as well.

The above comments are only meant to be constructive and are offered as a prelude to the subsequent "main theses of this book" (Sect. 15.4).

15.3 A Not-So-Dystopian Future

One of the main theses of this book is that the true value of the blockchain lies neither in the technology itself, nor in its interplay with other technologies. It lies rather in facilitating new economic cooperation paradigms that would be impossible without it. It is those new paradigms that will ultimately influence our societies, and one way of creating them is what this book set out to explain.

In order to make things more concrete, let us give examples of simple blockchain-based use cases (involving crypto-tokens) that could appear in the not-so-distant future:

- **Wills/testaments**. In most countries, drafting and registering one's last will and testament, then ultimately having it executed, is a process relying on a disjointed network of notaries, executors, and probate courts. Most steps in this process are laden with inherent frictions (last-will discovery, overriding wishes, inheritors' location and notification, assets discovery, encumbrances, competing interests, witness identification, cross-cutting legal arrangements, etc.). Furthermore, there are inescapable privacy and confidentiality aspects involved, usually necessitating that information be disclosed on a strictly need-to-know basis and that decision-making powers are given to only a few people who then need to reach consensus. Whenever multiple nationalities, international residencies, and foreign assets or income streams are also involved (not unusual in our times of increased career and personal mobility), then there are also multi-jurisdictional tax implications to consider. It can be that at least some process frictions and blind spots would be essentially removed if national-level testamentary blockchains could be created and made legally valid as testamentary records. For instance, the testator would be creating a non-fungible token containing all identifying information about themselves, their executors, their letter of wishes, the assets/income streams involved, and potentially also the beneficiaries. This NFT would be accessible by smart contract to executors and court-appointed persons on a need-to-act basis. Multi-signature infrastructures could be used to reach and register consensus, and the decisions would be irrevocable as blockchain records. Last-will discovery, for instance, would be thus accelerated, and all personal notifications could be triggered by smart contract in reference to the information in said NFT and after explicit consensus reached by the authorized persons. Imputed tax obligations could similarly be also notified (including to the concerned jurisdictions) by smart contract. Note that irrespective of token ecosystem design, this case was already identified as a potential blockchain use case before [28, 29] and it has apparently already been implemented in the specific case of crypto-assets as inheritance subject matter [30, 31]. However, the latter is only a private initiative and not a national-level coordinated one.
- **Trusts/foundations**. The common-law trust and the civil-law foundation are related concepts, as far as their economic outcomes are concerned; however, their legal natures as operational constructs are materially different. Whereas the trust is a legal arrangement based on notions of equity [32], but not necessarily of contract law [33], the foundation is always a legal entity based on the latter. Both exhibit wide typologies depending on calibration parameters (beneficiaries or purposes; private or commercial/public; governing laws; decision powers allocation; time of coming into being; imputed registration requirements; etc.). Even their common-/civil-law association is a blurred concept, as there are indeed trust laws provided for in some civil-law jurisdictions [34–37], and similarly foundation provisions exist in common-law ones [38–40]. In spite of this variation, there

are some commonalities across their typologies, which are useful for the purposes of the current discussion; for example, regarding their setup arrangements. In both cases, there are formalities relating to which assets are transferred to the trust/foundation and how they are to be used; formalities which have to be observed, otherwise the trust/foundation may not be recognized as such, and there may be onerous obligations—even legal repercussions—for everyone involved in them. To make matters concrete, let us focus on the trust case. In all generality, a person settles property on trust to another (a fiduciary), either to the benefit of beneficiaries or for a purpose (charitable or non-charitable). This person—the "settlor"—does so through a document evidencing their intention and specifying the assets—the "trust instrument", potentially also accompanying it with the second document expressing their preferences on how said assets should be managed—the "letter of wishes". These documents serve both as guidance to the fiduciary/-ies (at least one "trustee" —which may be a person or an agent of a "trust company") and any person(s) meant to oversee the latter (at least one "protector"); as well as proof that the settlor has made all necessary arrangements before assets become "trust property", that is, that title to them has been robustly transferred to the fiduciary/-ies. If it can be proved that the settlor has kept de facto ownership or control of said assets even after transferring them to the trust, then the latter "fails", meaning that severe tax and potentially legal consequences arise (e.g. if it can be proved that the trust was a sham, as the settlor never intended to actually benefit anyone/anything but themselves). If the trust has been set up correctly, subsequent actions—especially trust property investments and dispositions—*must* always be conformant to the stipulations of the trust instrument and *should* always ideally conform to the letter of wishes. All changes in trust property must be justified and documented, as asset reporting is a legal obligation of the fiduciary/-ies and as there is a legal requirement of avoidance of conflicts of interest on their part. All of the above stipulations—and potentially more, dependent on the actual circumstances and on the governing law jurisdiction—are nowadays observed by human actors (trustees, accountants, lawyers, etc.) and executed mostly manually, or by humans using limited software automation. The fact that, for example, many off-shore jurisdictions explicitly forbid the creation of centralized trust registries means that there may be enhanced confidentiality mechanisms built into a trust by default. However, that does not absolve trust actors from transparency when such is required by law—for example, to protect the interests of beneficiaries or to prove that the intentions of settlors are actually respected. Especially in the case of commercial trusts (e.g. those underlying pension or investment fund structures in several jurisdictions), transparency is indeed an obligation, also from the viewpoint of operating costs optimization. This is where a blockchain-based paradigm could emerge in trust setup and operations. For example, the trustee may be a smart contract. A settlor could transfer either on-chain (i.e. tokens) or off-chain assets (e.g. physical-world property, through real-world-asset tokens, created in a way similar to that explained in Sect. 14.5.3.9) to said SC. Both the trust instrument and the letter of wishes could be enforced algorithmically through the code of the same SC. If that were possible, that is, if the asset transfers, investments, and partial liquidations/disbursements could have actual legal standing—the main obstacle being absence of a legal framework at the moment, then it would address all necessary trust formalities at once. First, there would be no question of the settlor still being in constructive possession of the trust property; second, the classes of beneficiaries or purposes could be described unequivocally; third, property investment/disbursement modalities could be specified completely in the SC; fourth, the blockchain features of transaction finality and non-repudiation would make reporting and accounting of trust property changes completely transparent; fifth, if any logic re-calibration were ever needed for objective reasons, that could be made subject to multi-sig blockchain key arrangements. Importantly, usual cryptographical arrangements on the blockchain would make it possible to have information about trust property composition, ownership, custody, and disbursement recipients made available only to those persons actually entitled to know it. Also, the cost point of setting up and operating a trust could be brought down significantly, in line with the typical experience of other traditional finance use cases implemented on-chain.

- **Education funding**. Tertiary education systems across the world are getting increasingly difficult to fund privately. The financialization phenomenon which influenced several first world economies since the 1990s has meant that fully tax-funded university and post-graduate education is no longer the norm. Means-tested financial help may be available as an option in principle, but the fact of the matter is that most students will emerge from their formative years with some amount of student debt, which their parents may not necessarily be in a position to cover. Scholarships have always been available to the most talented students, but this is typically a very small part of the student population. The problem is fundamentally one of resource optimization: namely, how to channel limited funds to those candidates combining the optimal combination of ability, diligence, character, and societal impact potential. There are fields of study which have undisputed societal impact, but less of an earnings potential. Then there are those fields (mainly the professions) which have a higher earnings potential. The latter could be ultimately funded through a "venture-capital-like" model. Example: a student with top marks in high-school gets admitted in medical school or pre-med studies. Investors could consider funding the student's education, in exchange for a percentage of the student's future income under specific terms and conditions (contingent on continuing good academic performance, capped/uncapped return, number of years of returned income, insured/non-insured, etc.). The student will thus, in effect, be issuing future participation rights on their own income potential, similar to a public company issuing dividend-bearing shares. If such a funding model ever became socially acceptable (please remember the discussion in Sect. 6.6.5 on social norms as a market design factor), then a corresponding blockchain-based token ecosystem could be created. The student would be issuing security tokens in exchange for fiat currency or other media of exchange, and their actualized academic record (including all credentials, degrees, and references) would be also made available on the blockchain—

potentially through an NFT linked to the aforementioned security tokens. If the latter were designed as fungible, then they could be issued to multiple investors at once (similar to shares being sold to several shareholders) and also be tradable. As the income potential of the student's future occupation (or their actual income level post-graduation) changes depending on how societal needs evolve in time, then the value of said tokens will be changing as well. An exchange for such "future income participation" tokens need not be confined to a single country. Investors from developed countries will be able to fund the education of students in developing countries with higher GDP growth potential, thus directly channelling funds to a combination of high-potential country and high-potential individual at once. The blockchain in this case will be the actual record of people's student records, credentials, degrees, references, and education-linked funds.

- **Inheritance in common; tenancy in common**. Whenever property (real estate, intellectual property, entire collections or single collection items, etc.) is inherited jointly by a community of heirs, it is not unusual for such holdings to become effectively illiquid due to differences of opinion among heirs on if/how/when to monetize it. Especially for inherited real estate, it can be that unresolved disputes end up bequeathing the illiquid property to a second generation of heirs in common, who are then confronted with a still bigger problem. With time, agreements become difficult to reach on practical grounds, for example, when heirs have to be tracked in other countries, taxes due change some people's priorities, etc. Even in cases when a forced sale of other heirs' parts could be pursued through the courts, there are considerable coordination and legal costs to weigh against potential proceeds from a fair value sale. A possible mitigation of such problems could be achieved if it became legally possible to bequeath property, including real estate, as non-fungible tokens (full or fractionalized). The blockchain would become the sole source of records about the title to the property itself, the community of heirs (first and succeeding), and ownership changes. Inherited NFTs would become tradable on a token ecosystem, whereby third-parties (i.e. not belonging to the community of heirs) could track prices and bid for NFTs individually. Other heirs' notification requirements could be implemented by smart contracts, and there could also be provision for assigned representatives (e.g. trustees) to be given joint powers of authorization through a multi-signature key. Imputed tax obligations could also be notified by smart contract, while tax burden assumption could be made part of the "sale conditions" within individual NFTs. In any case, an authorized person could deduce immediately the ownership of all NFTs underlying a single piece of property through the blockchain records. For the individual heirs, such an arrangement could facilitate immediate monetization of their inherited share through sale of their NFT(s) to interested parties willing to take on the market risk for their own reasons. For example, institutional investors in such NFTs may feel in better position to elicit forced sale through the courts (especially for high-value property), or they may pursue appreciation opportunities as part of an alternative investments strategy.

- **Trade finance "gap"**. This is a term coined in the trade finance professional literature, denoting the estimated difference between total sums requested by clients and those approved by banks for financing in the credit area generally comprising[3] documentary credits, documentary collections, trade guarantees, pre-export financing, receivables finance, and payables finance. This "gap" is usually expressed in terms of the total value of potential global transactions; for example, it was estimated to be 2.5 trillion USD for 2022 [41]. It has tended to exhibit an increasing trend [42] and is generally assumed to be attributable to the difficulties faced by mostly small and medium enterprises (SMEs), in both developing and developed countries, to fulfil all of the (understandably strict) financing criteria set by banks. In many cases, such enterprises have very good local records, but their borrowing base (especially in the context of international trade transactions) is simply below the cut-off thresholds expected by credit officers. This is nothing unusual, as banks have their own strict risk management obligations to follow (conformance to which is also tracked by auditors and regulators). However, part of this "gap" could potentially be closed by channelling said financing request to capital markets with more risk appetite or lower risk management obligations. Also, as higher risk is generally expected to justify higher reward, that could be a win-win situation for both finance providers and finance requestors for a simple reason: the amounts requested by SMEs are typically smaller than the average trade finance transactions financed by banks. That is, credit risks may be higher percentage-wise, but calculated on smaller notionals. What could be an eventual solution to closing part of the trade finance gap is a "syndicated finance" paradigm, along the lines of that explained in the real-world asset NFT financing transactional pathway (Sect. 14.5.3.9) in the "end-to-end" case study of Chap. 14. In effect, the same party that would request issuance of a trade finance instrument by a bank today could describe the intended transaction and its collateral, embed this description as part of NFTs issued on the blockchain, and sell them to willing investors. Said investors would bear the credit risk of the transaction but would then have the right of refund (plus profit) by the issuer. Financing could be provided in Stablecoins or other cryptocurrencies, as per the agreed terms of the transaction. The completion of the transaction would be tracked on the blockchain (e.g. through smart contracts), which would be a deterrent to moral hazard. Honest counterparties would have the incentive to keep honouring transactions consistently and could also submit to rating on the ecosystem (please recall the discussion on congestion mitigation in

[3] Please note that in many banks, transactions financed under the "trade finance" moniker may exclude those of receivables finance, which are then allocated to a separate "factoring" business area. Similarly, payables finance can be also found under the label "reverse factoring" or "supply chain finance". The list in the main text excludes further categorization of trade finance in terms of transaction type, such as structured trade finance, etc. There are still other categorizations possible, for example, in terms of the transaction collateral (import/export trade finance, commodities trade finance, etc.).

Sect. 6.6.2 of Chap. 6 on market design). Investors could be international,[4] which would allow liquidity from low-growth parts of the globe to profit from trade activity in higher-growth parts. Taxes due could be notified based on blockchain records, acted upon by smart contracts taking into account the domiciles of the investors. Other checks (e.g. export controls) could also be automated through smart contracts acting on the content of transaction documents, the latter having to be submitted by the finance requestors as part of the NFT due diligence step. Irrevocability of blockchain records would enable process auditability, should it come to dispute resolution. In any case, investors might be able to achieve higher yields on funds that could not have financed trade before; and requestors might be able to build enough of a track record (verifiable on the blockchain) and grow their borrowing base to the point that they could start being approved by banks.

The above are just examples of future blockchain-based token ecosystems that might potentially remove frictions evident in today's economies. None of them represents a purely technical use case. Implementing them presupposes an agreement among economic agents about the intended business process, the underlying property rights, the technical artefacts (e.g. tokens and smart contracts) to use, the jurisdictions concerned, the tax implications, the ecosystem governance, etc. They are mentioned here neither in the sense of guidance nor of blueprints. Rather, they are intended to elicit two observations which the reader may share: first, that they are not "exotic" use cases, but actually feasible ones, responding to real—not imagined—societal needs; and second, that they would probably be extremely difficult to implement other than through the blockchain.

15.4 The Main Theses of This Book

The book at hand was consciously structured by building up from a solid foundation of concepts, extended by ideas (such as an original crypto-token taxonomy) proposed by the author. Said concepts and ideas were then used to propose a concrete, detailed token ecosystem analysis and design methodology—albeit in stages. Each individual stage was immediately put to the test of reality by juxtaposition with an actual token ecosystem protocol used as a case study. Care was taken throughout to enable the reader to check facts independently by supplying supporting URLs as text footnotes. The intention from the beginning was to impart a sufficient level of knowledge and familiarity so that the reader would finally be able to judge for themselves the applicability of the main theses of this book. These are as follows:

[4] Today, an import or export letter of credit involves only one bank on the issuing side and at most a few on the advising/confirming/reimbursing side. Those are legal entities operating in a single country (even a branch of the same bank acting on the other side will need to execute its own local-country controls). Hence, SME trade finance requestors today are trying to tap de facto single-country liquidity.

- Cryptocurrencies aside, most other tradable crypto-tokens have direct analogues in traditional banking products and financial instruments. The technological pathway of creating and operationalizing them is simply different from that of traditional finance analogues issued under the auspices of a bank, an insurance company, an asset management company, etc.
- There can indeed exist a systematic methodology used to analyse the economic behaviour of tradable cryptocurrencies and crypto-tokens in terms of use cases, functions, valuation, circulating supply, and other observable metrics. The same methodology would also be capable of guiding the design of new tradable tokens.
- In that sense, cryptocurrencies and crypto-tokens can indeed be made to have predictable behaviours, that is, made to obey an envelope of pre-specified parameters against a set of controllable design factors.
- When seeking to understand the inherent economic value of particular crypto-tokens, it is essential to have:
  1. A basic understanding of blockchain ecosystem value flows and salient artefacts (such as consensus mechanisms, tokens, smart contracts, wallets, Oracles, Exchanges, etc.)
  2. A baseline token taxonomy as a reference, allowing a first-order mapping of major token types to most prominent token features—and the other way around.
  3. Knowledge about the specific token protocol which issues said tokens and of their corresponding business use cases (e.g. through the protocol's Whitepaper and documentation).
  4. A methodology to map concepts from the protocol's documentation—regarding token minting/burning modes, use in business use cases, embedded on-chain property rights, processing along particular value flows, tradability within and outside their generating ecosystem, on-chain custody patterns, etc.—to corresponding (traditional) financial and legal concepts that represent similar circumstances of issuance, constellations of personal/property rights, cash-flow profiles, modes of transfer of ownership, asset lifecycle stages, custody "attachment" points, etc.
  5. Willingness to track said concepts back to token liquidity and effective risk/return profiles, as observed in the crypto-markets (e.g. through use of blockchain explorers and/or dashboards offered by Centralized and Decentralized Exchanges).
- If a personal investment in said tokens is contemplated, know-how (own or through outside experts) will be needed to extrapolate from the above generic information to one's own specific circumstances, in terms of position risk management, portfolio risk management, imputed tax obligations, etc. For example, if some tokens are Stablecoins, they can be assigned to liquidity positions. Other cryptocurrencies, on the other hand, should be treated as generic volatile assets (e.g. currencies or commodities, depending on the jurisdiction). Still other types of crypto-tokens (e.g. liquid-staking tokens, NFT's, etc.) should generally be assumed to be either securities or derivatives, unless your analysis has strongly indicated that they may have a different traditional asset class equivalent.

- Hence, the afore-mentioned methodology (ideally used within workflow steps 1–5. above) can be used to understand the risks inherent in the issuance, trading, investment, and custody of any particular cryptocurrency or crypto-token.
- This understanding can, and should, be used to interpret probable obligations through the intermediary step of mapping to "traditional financial instrument equivalents", or constellations thereof. By the same logic, the **same philosophy can also guide the creation of clear and comprehensive laws and regulations** governing cryptocurrencies and tradable crypto-tokens.
- In that sense, **using the afore-mentioned methodology** (or any similar one for that matter, as long as it is proven to be consistent and complete) **can have far-reaching benefits**, by transposing the regulatory *dictum* "**same business, same risks, same regulation**" [43, 44] to the area of crypto-assets as well. Not only will lawgivers and regulators be able to design new frameworks of obligations using existing ones as baseline (e.g. for regulation: Basel III+/IV [45] in banking, IOSCO [46] in securities, or Solvency II+ [47] in insurance); token industry participants, their legal counsel, auditors, and regulators will also be in a position to interpret and apply said frameworks almost immediately.
- Investment due diligence in traditional finance is expressly required by institutional investors and tacitly assumed by the investing public when such investments are marketed to it by the financial services industry. Were parts of the crypto-token universe to be made broadly accessible to institutional and private investors, then the same due diligence steps will be not only expected but also mandated. As in traditional finance, it is logical to expect that either specialized third parties (rating agencies, research analysts, etc.) or task-specific internal units of sell-side institutions will be called upon to execute crypto-asset due diligence. Thus, they will be required to identify and use all applicable data in systematic risk-return analyses. Our proposed methodology (or a similar one) proves that such systematic analyses are not only feasible but can also be standardized. Imagine if the same breakdown in market, mechanism, token, and bonding function analysis pillars could be used to create definitions and metrics (e.g. ratings) applicable to the whole crypto-token industry.

Finally, it needs to be said that this book was consciously written to address an audience active primarily in traditional finance roles. It is not by coincidence that all case studies start with a brief summary of a particular business instrument from traditional insurance, banking, or investments. The intention throughout was to first make traditional finance experts feel "at ease", so to speak, and then to elicit a direct comparison between the subsequent crypto-token protocol business use case and the traditional finance area that had just been summarized. The starting point was always the traditional area, in reference to which the less familiar crypto-token protocol artefacts were then systematically explained—as the mental thought process of the main audience was expected to be. Similarly, the main rationale behind Chap. 4 was to gain an observable crypto-token taxonomy such that a traditional financial services practitioner could immediately relate to. Furthermore, the depiction of token transactional pathways against the background of an underlying notional balance sheet[5] (from the first case study onwards) was meant to create an accounting view that could be used to "follow" token cash flows through protocol-wide stores of value. By keeping such views throughout, protocol-level crypto-asset pools were ultimately used to address asset-liability management considerations from a traditional finance standpoint. Through several passages in the book there runs an underlying recurrent theme that traditional and blockchain-resident stores of value are not disjoint paradigms; it is rather a failure to identify commonalities in concepts and operational practices—irrespective of technological infrastructure—that can lead analysts and designers to such an erroneous conclusion.

This particular book-writing strategy originated partly from the author's realization (outcome of direct interactions with cryptocurrency and crypto-token creators, that is, token project designers, technical architects, smart contract developers, DEX business developers, etc.) that there exists a knowledge-gap **on both sides** of the notional traditional/crypto dividing line. And also (another realization) that risk awareness—in terms of knowledge about probable risk vectors and proven risk management experience from previous stressed-market conditions—tended to be more prevalent on the *traditional finance* side by comparison. In that sense, if both paradigms ever were to merge, then the vast amount of business and risk management know-how on the *traditional finance* side (along its entire value chain, including legal counsel, financial advisors, consultants, auditors, and regulators) would have a crucial role to play in stabilizing the crypto-market risk landscape—in the author's opinion at least. The reason why the book principally tries to interpret blockchain token ecosystem concepts to traditional finance practitioners, and not the other way around, is the fact that the traditional financial world has had centuries to mature its business practices and make them acceptable within a wider societal context. In other words, that it is the blockchain token ecosystem ("digital") world that stands to profit most from the accumulated experience of the traditional ("physical") one, were the two worlds to merge. And that during a "digital" world maturation process, traditional finance professionals can, and ideally should, act as active mentors.

Technologists and blockchain ecosystem creators, however sophisticated and willing to learn, cannot know how to properly weigh opportunities against risks while living in a crypto-world that tends to evolve quasi-chaotically and under persistent short-term monetization pressure. The odds are simply too high that this world will re-discover the same pathologies that caused major traditional finance crises in the past and will do so by going through essentially the same "valleys of tears". If—again, this is a thesis of the book at hand—cryptocurrencies and crypto-tokens are simply transpositions of traditional financial instruments in a new technological setting, then it is not a matter of *if* major financial and non-financial risks around them will materialize but simply *how soon*. And once

[5] Creating such a "notional balance sheet" view per token protocol is an original idea by the book's author and not yet an established industry practice.

said risks have materialized, both direct effects for their token implementors/investors and indirect ones for their surrounding ecosystems can be devastating—as they have been during the last two "crypto-winters" already. This should come as no surprise, on account of the de-centralized nature of the blockchain architectural pattern—which generates broad threat surfaces, much broader than any centralized ledger could ever present—and also because of the consensus-based governance processes of typical blockchain-based ecosystems. Different (and independently governed) ecosystems existing on the same L-1 and L-2 blockchain layers; interconnectedness of business use cases through enmeshing of native with foreign tokens; and systemic risks caused by de facto "single points of failure" (such as commonly used Stablecoins and high-TVL Exchanges); are all examples of risk-propagating pathways specific to blockchain-based token ecosystems. As was mentioned several times above, blockchains and underlying distributed ledger infrastructures and their artefacts (such as smart contracts) are simply technology architecture paradigms. How they are used and how they are risk-managed in the context of business use cases has nothing to do with the technology itself, but rather with an understanding of the *combined* business and technology risks. That such risks are entirely controllable is tantamount to a call action towards creation of such laws and regulatory frameworks as are needed to properly recognize and manage them.

In that respect, the main theses of this book have been woven upon the canvas of the existing pre-history, as it were, of both traditional finance pathologies and already manifested blockchain-based ones.

15.5 Summary

The intention of this last chapter was to convey a high-level **"cause and effect"** thinking to the reader, to complement the more fine-grained methodological thinking imparted in the previous chapters of the book. **Methodology and technical knowledge** points aside, it is inescapable that the field of cryptocurrencies and crypto-tokens will evolve—either grow or shrink, but definitely change, and quite probably not die.

It would serve the reader well to be able to follow this evolution by using the work at hand as a reference. As was mentioned in the book's introduction, this is a book about *principles*. Principles of methodological analysis and design, originating in economics but transplanted into the context of cryptocurrencies and crypto-tokens. It is highly probable that those principles will remain the same, irrespective of future technological or business developments within said context. By being able to interpret the evolutionary stage which the whole field undergoes at any given time (the *high-level cause and effect* intent) and to understand the ramifications of new business and technical token features implemented by individual blockchain ecosystems (the *methodology and technical knowledge* intent), the reader will have removed blind spots and mitigated confusion risk.

They will be confident in their knowledge that things still "make sense", which was the sole ambition behind this book all along.

References

1. (2017, November 25). *Prosecutor finds 36 guilty for the Stock Exchange Crash in 1999*. Keep Talking Greece. Retrieved March 31, 2025, from https://www.keeptalkinggreece.com/2017/11/25/athens-stock-exchange-crash-1999/
2. [Example: the Greek case] Greek government debt crisis. In *Wikipedia*. Retrieved March 31, 2025, from https://en.m.wikipedia.org/wiki/Greek_government-debt_crisis
3. Kaiko. (2022, December 22). *Developing economies: A proven use case for crypto*. Retrieved March 31, 2025, from https://marketing.kaiko.com/developing-economies-a-proven-use-case-for-crypto
4. (2017, August 8). *'We want to be a tech company with a banking license' – Ralph Hamers*. ING corporate communications. Retrieved March 31, 2025, from https://www.ing.com/Newsroom/News/We-want-to-be-a-tech-company-with-a-banking-license-Ralph-Hamers.htm
5. Skinner, C. (2018, November 1). *Run the bank. Change the bank.* The Banker. Retrieved March 31, 2025, from https://www.thebanker.com/Run-the-bank.-Change-the-bank-1541062824
6. (2025, January 17). *Directive (EU) 2015/2366 of the European Parliament and of the Council of 25 November 2015 on payment services in the internal market, amending Directives 2002/65/EC, 2009/110/EC and 2013/36/EU and Regulation (EU) No 1093/2010, and repealing Directive 2007/64/EC (Text with EEA relevance)*. Retrieved March 31, 2025, from https://eur-lex.europa.eu/legal-content/EN/TXT/?uri=CELEX%3A02015L2366-20250117
7. Payment Services Directive. (2024, July 9). In *Wikipedia*. Retrieved March 31, 2025, from https://en.wikipedia.org/wiki/Payment_Services_Directive
8. Jelicic, N., Braekeveldt, A., Motta Gomes, G. & Haeusler, F. *Open Banking—far more than PSD2*. BankingHub by zeb. Retrieved March 31, 2025, from https://www.bankinghub.eu/topics/open-banking-far-more-than-psd2
9. Urbano, V. (2023, May). *Open banking was born and raised in Europe*. GoCardless. Retrieved March 31, 2025, from https://gocardless.com/guides/posts/open-banking-europe/
10. Simoneschi, F. (2023, January 13). *Europe must lead the way in open banking*. Financial Times. Retrieved March 31, 2025, from https://www.ftadviser.com/investments/2023/01/13/europe-must-lead-the-way-in-open-banking/
11. [U.K.] Financial Conduct Authority (FCA). (2022, March 27). *Regulatory Sandbox*. FCA Innovation Hub. Retrieved March 31, 2025, from https://www.fca.org.uk/firms/innovation/regulatory-sandbox
12. Jeník, I., & Schan, D. (2020, September 1). *How to build a regulatory sandbox : A practical guide for policy makers*. World Bank Group. Retrieved March 31, 2025, from https://documents.worldbank.org/en/publication/documents-reports/documentdetail/126281625136122935/how-to-build-a-regulatory-sandbox-a-practical-guide-for-policy-makers
13. [U.K.] Financial Conduct Authority (FCA). (2022, March 27). *Regulatory Sandbox accepted firms*. FCA Innovation Hub. Retrieved March 31, 2025, from https://www.fca.org.uk/firms/innovation/regulatory-sandbox/accepted-firms
14. https://www.bis.org/about/bisih/about.htm?m=265
15. https://www.forbes.com/advisor/banking/what-is-fintech/
16. https://en.wikipedia.org/wiki/Fintech
17. https://www.investopedia.com/terms/f/fintech.asp
18. https://www.centralbanking.com/fintech/7884981/uks-fca-to-invest-over-150-million-in-move-towards-cloud
19. https://en.wikipedia.org/wiki/Fear_of_missing_out
20. https://en.wikipedia.org/wiki/Unicorn_(finance)

21. https://www.investopedia.com/crypto-winter-5496605
22. https://thedefiant.io/dappradar-winter-is-coming
23. Treehouse. (2023, February 7). *The crypto contagion and its looming after-effects (Part 1)*. Medium. Retrieved April 5, 2025, from https://medium.com/coinmonks/the-crypto-contagion-and-its-looming-after-effects-part-1-367beda6bc
24. Khoo, Y. L., Loew, S., Polk, N., & Chia, D. (2022, November 17). *Blockchain analysis: The collapse of Alameda and FTX*. Nansen.ai . Retrieved March 31, 2025, from https://www.nansen.ai/research/blockchain-analysis-the-collapse-of-alameda-and-ftx
25. Sexton, A. (2023, October 6). *4 Reasons banks are embracing the tokenization of real-world assets*. Forbes . Retrieved March 31, 2025, from https://www.forbes.com/sites/amorsexton/2023/10/06/4-reasons-banks-are-embracing-the-tokenization-of-real-world-assets/
26. Lang, H., & McGee, S. (2024, January 11). *US SEC approves bitcoin ETFs in watershed for crypto market*. Reuters. Retrieved March 31, 2025, from https://www.reuters.com/technology/bitcoin-etf-hopefuls-still-expect-sec-approval-despite-social-media-hack-2024-01-10/
27. Kagan, J. (2023, March 14). *Universal banking: Definition, functions, regulation*. Retrieved March 31, 2025, from https://www.investopedia.com/terms/u/universalbanking.asp
28. Chundi, V. (2018, May 6). *Wills and testaments on the blockchain – Blockchain estate planning*. Retrieved March 31, 2025, from https://vishnuteja-chundi.medium.com/wills-and-testaments-on-the-blockchain-crypto-wills-9d2be9171a7d
29. Crawford, B. J. (2020). Blockchain Wills. *95 Ind. L.J.* 735. Retrieved March 31, 2025, from https://digitalcommons.pace.edu/lawfaculty/1158
30. Sazonov, V. (2023, February 22). *A last will and blockchain testament – Ensuring crypto wealth is passed on to successors*. The Daily Hodl. Retrieved March 31, 2025, from https://dailyhodl.com/2023/02/22/a-last-will-and-blockchain-testament-ensuring-crypto-wealth-is-passed-on-to-successors/
31. [Blockchain Testament Token ecosystem] https://cryptowill.tech/
32. Hudson, A. (2022). *Equity and trusts* (10th ed.). Routledge.
33. Langbein, J. H. (1995). The contractarian basis of the law of trusts. *The Yale Law Journal, 105*(3), 625–675. Accessible at https://www.jstor.org/stable/797196, available at https://law.yale.edu/sites/default/files/documents/pdf/Faculty/Langbein_Contractarian_Basis_Law_of_Trusts.pdf
34. [Context: Liechtenstein] *Persons and Companies Law 1926* (as amended). Retrieved March 31, 2025, from https://www.gesetze.li/chrono/1926004000. (please consult articles 897–932, "Das Salmannenrecht").
35. [Context: Malta] *Trusts and Trustees Act 2024*. Retrieved March 31, 2025, from https://legislation.mt/eli/cap/331/eng/pdf
36. [Context: Hungary] *Civil Code Act V 2013 (as amended)*, Chapter XLIII. Retrieved March 31, 2025, from https://njt.hu/jogszabaly/en/2013-5-00-00
37. [Context: San Marino] *Law No. 42 of March 2010, on Trusts*. Retrieved March 31, 2025, from https://www.bcsm.sm/en/regulations/laws-and-derees/trust-and-trust-laws-and-decrees
38. [Context: United States] 26 U.S. Code § 509 – Private foundation defined. Retrieved March 31, 2025, from https://www.law.cornell.edu/uscode/text/26/509
39. [Context: United States] IRS tax stipulations on private foundations. Retrieved March 31, 2025, from https://www.irs.gov/charities-non-profits/charitable-organizations/private-foundations
40. [Context: Jersey] Foundations (Jersey) Law 2029. Retrieved March 31, 2025, from https://www.jerseylaw.je/laws/current/Pages/13.265.aspx
41. Beck, S., Tayag, M. C., Kim, K., Latoja, M. C., Pandey, A. & Malaket, A. R. (2023, September). 2023 Trade Finance Gaps, Growth, and Jobs Survey. *Asian Development Bank Briefs*, No. 256. Retrieved March 31, 2025, from https://www.adb.org/sites/default/files/publication/906596/adb-brief-256-2023-trade-finance-gaps-growth-jobs-survey.pdf
42. (2024, January 8). The trade finance gap – A new solution? Global Trade Review. Retrieved March 31, 2025, from https://www.gtreview.com/news/global/the-trade-finance-gap-a-new-solution/

43. European Parliament. (2020). *Digital finance strategy for the EU – Q3 2020*. Legislative Train 06.2022. Retrieved March 31, 2025, from https://www.europarl.europa.eu/legislative-train/carriage/fintech-action-plan/report?sid=6001
44. [U.S.] Commodity Futures Trading Commission (CFTC). (2022, October 26). *Financial Stability Risks of Crypto Assets – Remarks of CFTC Commissioner Christy Goldsmith Romero before the International Swaps and Derivatives Association's Crypto Forum 2022, New York*. Retrieved March 31, 2025, from https://www.cftc.gov/PressRoom/SpeechesTestimony/oparomero3
45. Bank for International Settlements (BIS). *The Basel Framework*. Basel Committee on Banking Supervision. Retrieved March 31, 2025, from https://www.bis.org/basel_framework/
46. International Organization of Securities Commissions (IOSCO). *Key Regulatory Standards*. Retrieved March 31, 2025, from https://www.iosco.org/about/?subsection=key_regulatory_standards
47. [E.U.] European Insurance and Occupational Persons Authority (EIOPA). *Solvency II* [links to relevant regulatory texts]. Retrieved March 31, 2025, from https://www.eiopa.europa.eu/browse/regulation-and-policy/solvency-ii_en

Index

I. Giannakouros, *Cryptocurrencies and Tradable Crypto-Tokens*, Future of Business and Finance, https://doi.org/10.1007/978-3-031-98423-5

MIX
Papier aus verantwortungsvollen Quellen
Paper from responsible sources
FSC® C105338

If you have any concerns about our products,
you can contact us on
ProductSafety@springernature.com

In case Publisher is established outside the EU,
the EU authorized representative is:
Springer Nature Customer Service Center GmbH
Europaplatz 3, 69115 Heidelberg, Germany

Printed by Libri Plureos GmbH
in Hamburg, Germany